2008
U.S. Master
Tax Guide®

CCH Editorial Staff Publication

.CCH
a Wolters Kluwer business

This publication is designed to provide accurate and authoritative information in regard to the subject matter covered. It is sold with the understanding that the publisher is not engaged in rendering legal, accounting, or other professional service. If legal advice or other expert assistance is required, the services of a competent professional person should be sought.

ISBN: 978-0-8080-1701-1 (paperback edition)
ISBN: 978-0-8080-1741-7 (hardbound edition)

©2007 CCH. All Rights Reserved.

4025 W. Peterson Ave.
Chicago, IL 60646-6085
1 800 248 3248
www.CCHGroup.com

Printed in the United States of America

Preface

Income taxation in the United States, as we know it on Form 1040, has been around for more than 90 years. From the very beginning, CCH was there and is still setting the standard after all these years. CCH is proud to serve the tax professional community with this new edition of the *U.S. Master Tax Guide* ®. The 91st Edition of this industry standard explains the maze of tax rules, restrictions, and requirements and is designed to provide fast and reliable answers to tax questions affecting individuals and businesses. In all, 29 chapters contain comprehensive, timely, and precise explanation of the ever-changing federal income tax rules for individuals, businesses, and estates and trusts.

The 2008 Edition reflects the Small Business and Work Opportunity Tax Act of 2007 (P.L. 110-28) and other significant developments that took place throughout the year. The Small Business Tax Act, signed on May 25, 2007, by President Bush, targets nearly $5 billion in tax incentives principally for small businesses. In addition, the bill includes provisions to benefit taxpayers recovering from Hurricane Katrina, as well as a package of S corporation reforms. However, unlike past tax bills, the revenue raising provisions will mean higher taxes for certain taxpayers, such as the expansion of the kiddie tax to apply to children who are 18 years old or who are full-time students up to age 24.

As this edition of the *Guide* goes to press, there are legislative proposals in Congress facing uncertain futures. Bills have been introduced that cover a number of tax areas, including the extension of a number of tax incentives that will expire after 2007, alternative minimum tax, energy legislation, technical corrections to the Pension Protection Act of 2006, mortgage cancellation relief and tax incentives for education expenses. However, it is unclear whether any proposals will make it through Congress and reach the President's desk by the end of the year. In an effort to keep users of the *Guide* current on events taking place after we go to press, CCH has established a website at *http://tax.cchgroup.com/mtg* for any late-breaking 2007 year-end tax legislation or for other significant developments that might affect the *Guide's* coverage.

As in previous editions, major legislative provisions are highlighted at ¶ 1 and reflected throughout the *Guide*, while important nonlegislative tax developments are conveniently highlighted at ¶ 2 and concisely explained for quick reference and understanding.

In addition, the *Guide* comes complete with many time-saving features that help users quickly and easily determine how particular tax items and situations should be treated (see the following page for a listing and description of these "Key Features"). The *Guide* also contains a handy Quick Tax Facts card that can be detached for an at-a-glance reference to key tax figures and other often-referenced amounts.

Not only does the *U.S. Master Tax Guide* ® assist in the preparation of 2007 tax returns, it also serves as a reference tool for more comprehensive tax research and tax planning via extensive footnotes and other references to the Internal Revenue Code, Income Tax Regulations, and CCH's STANDARD FEDERAL TAX REPORTS ® and FEDERAL ESTATE AND GIFT TAX REPORTER.

For additional analysis of new and complex tax issues, and as a way to earn valuable continuing education credits, *Top Federal Tax Issues for 2008* is provided along with the *Guide*. This course provides helpful insights for the practitioner to keep abreast of the most significant new rules and changes by explaining the most important new provisions and developments in 2007 specifically applicable to 2008 and the IRS rules and regulations that go into effect in 2008. It also examines current audit and litigation issues that have developed over the past year to create a new environment for tax strategies initiated in 2008.

We also point you to other CCH resources that complement the *Guide* and support your tax season work. *1040 Express Answers* is designed to help you and your staff prepare 1040 tax returns quickly, easily and accurately with line-by-line guidance to common tax preparation questions. *1065 Express Answers* is the ideal quick-answer tool for busy practitioners who prepare partnership returns and the partners' Schedule K-1s. The compliance-oriented *1120S Express Answers* will help you in preparing S corporation tax returns with concise and reliable answers right at your fingertips. The *1041 Express Answers* provides practical, plain-English guidance for practitioners who prepare fiduciary income tax returns. See *http://tax.cchgroup.com/ExpressAnswers* for more details.

Finally, for *Master Guide* type treatment of state tax topics, please refer to CCH's *State Tax Guidebooks* (20 states available–CA, CO, CT, FL, GA, IL, IN, KY, MD, MA, MI, NJ, NY, NC, OH, PA, TN, TX, VA, and WA) and CCH's *State Tax Handbook* covering all 50 states and the District of Columbia.

November 2007

Key Features

In addition to 29 chapters of concise tax law explanations, the *U.S. Master Tax Guide*® provides a wealth of information in the pages that lead up to Chapter 1. Some of these time-saving tools and collections of information are described below, listed by paragraph location:

OVERVIEW (¶ 1-5): The Overview division contains informative features available to facilitate research and dealing with clients. Included are:

- "New Legislation," a highlight of provisions from this year's enacted tax legislation.

- "What to Watch on 2007 Returns," a listing of important nonlegislative tax developments, including key inflation-adjusted amounts.

- "Where to File," a listing of income tax return mailing addresses.

- "Government Agency and Tax/Accounting Directories," a feature comprised of addresses and telephone numbers for numerous federal agencies and tax and accounting organizations.

- "Due Dates in 2008," a tax calendar showing filing dates for 2007 tax returns and tax payments throughout 2008.

TAX RATES (¶ 11-53): This section contains the 2007 and 2008 tax rate schedules for individuals and estates and trusts, the Tax Computation worksheet, the 2007 tax tables for individuals, the corporate tax rate schedule and related rates, and the estate and gift tax rate schedule, as well as a listing of excise and other taxes.

CHECKLISTS (¶ 55-59): A collection of checklists designed to provide tax return preparers with quick answers (and references) to common questions regarding the inclusion of items in income, the deductibility of certain expenses, and the treatment of various medical expenses.

COMPUTATION OF TAXABLE INCOME (¶ 61-64): Provides a summary overview of how taxable income is computed for an individual, a corporation, a partnership, and an estate or trust. References are provided to detailed explanations within the *Guide*.

SPECIAL TAX TABLES (¶ 83-88C): This is a collection of often-used interest rates and percentages including:

- applicable federal rates (AFRs)

- adjusted applicable federal rates

- federal long-term tax-exempt rates

- low-income housing credit percentages

- earned income credit amounts

Also presented are the average itemized deductions for 2005 (the latest year of available figures), broken down by AGI ranges, as well as the AGI thresholds for a number of tax items subject to phaseout restrictions in 2007 and outlines of state conformity with bonus depreciation and the domestic production activities (manufacturer's) deduction.

ADDITIONAL FORMATS: To provide flexibility for users, the *Guide* is available in a loose-leaf edition with quarterly updates, a hardbound edition, and a CD-ROM edition that may be purchased with or without the softbound print edition. The *Guide* is also part of CCH's Federal Tax Guide Library, an electronic tax research library available on the Internet or monthly CDs that combines the quick-reference ease and reliability of the *Guide* with current primary sources including the Internal Revenue Code, Income Tax Regulations, cases, IRS rulings and more.

USER COMMUNITY: CCH has established a website at http://tax.cchgroup.com/mtg for users of the *Guide* to visit periodically in order to stay current with significant post-publication developments.

CCH Tax and Accounting Publishing

EDITORIAL STAFF

Explanation and Analysis

Kimberly Anderle Abma, J.D.

Manish C. Bhatia, J.D.

Louis W. Baker, J.D., M.B.A.

Ginette P. Balleza, J.D.

David Becker, J.D.

Maureen Bornstein, J.D.,
Portfolio Managing Editor

Glenn L. Borst, J.D., LL.M.

Anne E. Bowker, J.D., LL.M.

John O. Buchanan, J.D., LL.M.

Mildred Carter, J.D.

Maurice M. Cashin, J.D.

James A. Chapman, J.D., LL.M.

Tom Cody, J.D., LL.M., M.B.A.

Torie D. Cole, J.D.

Casie Cooper

Eileen Corbett, J.D., LL.M.

Heather Corbin, J.D.

Donna J. Dhein, C.P.A.

Kurt Diefenbach, J.D.,
Managing Editor

Liliana Dimitrova, LL.B., LL.M.

Karen Elsner, C.P.A.

Alicia C. Ernst, J.D.

Shannon Jett Fischer, J.D.

Donna M. Flanagan, J.D.

Mary Jo Gagnon, C.P.A.

Hilary Goehausen, J.D.

Brant Goldwyn, J.D.

Bruno L. Graziano, J.D., M.S.A.

Joy A. Hail, J.D.

Carmela Harnett,
Senior Manager

Kay L. Harris, J.D.

Michael Henaghan, J.D., LL.M.

Karen Heslop, J.D.

Kathleen M. Higgins

Dem A. Hopkins, J.D.

Caroline L. Hosman, J.D., LL.M.

David M. Jaffe, J.D.

George G. Jones, J.D., LL.M.,
Managing Editor

Geralyn A. Jover-Ledesma,
LL.B., C.P.A.

Nicholas J. Kaster, J.D.

Lynn S. Kopon, J.D.

Mary W. Krackenberger, J.D.

Thomas K. Lauletta, J.D.

Ian S. Lesch, J.D., M.B.A., LL.M.

Adam R. Levine, J.D., LL.M.

Jennifer M. Lowe, J.D.,
Portfolio Managing Editor

Laura M. Lowe, J.D.,
Managing Editor

Mark A. Luscombe, J.D., LL.M,
C.P.A.,
Principal Analyst

Michael Menzhuber, J.D., LL.M.

Jela Miladinovich, J.D.

Sheri Wattles Miller, J.D.

Ellen Mitchell, EA

Sherri G. Morris, J.D., LL.M.

Robert A. Morse, J.D.

John J. Mueller, J.D., LL.M.,
Managing Editor

Anita I. Nagelis, J.D.

Jean T. Nakamoto, J.D.

Jerome Nestor, J.D., C.P.A.,
M.B.A

Karen A. Notaro, J.D., LL.M.,
Portfolio Managing Editor

Linda J. O'Brien, J.D., LL.M.,
Managing Editor

John Old, J.D., LL.M.

Lawrence A. Perlman, C.P.A.,
J.D., LL.M.

Deborah M. Petro, J.D., LL.M.

John W. Roth, J.D., LL.M.

Rosanne Schabinger, EA

Linda Scharf, J.D.

Carolyn M. Schiess, J.D.

Michael G. Sem, J.D.

James Solheim, J.D., LL.M.

Raymond G. Suelzer, J.D., LL.M.

Kenneth L. Swanson, J.D., LL.M.

Mary P. Taylor, J.D.

Deanna Tenofsky, J.D., LL.M.

Laura A. Tierney, J.D.

David Trice, J.D., CFP®, EA

Chandra Walker, J.D.

James C. Walschlager, M.A.

Kelley Wolf, J.D.

George L. Yaksick, Jr., J.D.

Ken Zaleski, J.D.

CONTENTS

Filing 2007 Returns

OVERVIEW

¶ 1 New Legislation

2007 Legislation. *Business incentives.* On May 25, 2007, President Bush signed the Small Business and Work Opportunity Tax Act of 2007, which is part of a much larger Act, the U.S. Troop Readiness, Veterans' Care, Katrina Recovery, and Iraq Accountability Appropriations Act of 2007 (P.L. 110-28). The legislation provides incentives primarily for small businesses coupled with an increase in the federal minimum wage. These incentives are designed to help small businesses absorb the cost of the new higher minimum wage. The new law also includes relief for taxpayers recovering from Hurricane Katrina and a package of reforms for S corporations.

The following highlights some of the provisions of the Small Business Tax Act:

(1) The work opportunity credit is extended through August 31, 2011 and expanded to allow a credit to employers who hire disabled veterans and individuals in various counties that have experienced population losses (see ¶ 1342).

(2) The enhanced Code Sec. 179 deduction is extended through 2010 and also indexed for inflation for tax years beginning after 2007 and before 2011. The dollar limitation is increased to $125,000 and the investment limitation is increased to $500,000 for tax years beginning in 2007 (see ¶ 1208).

(3) The Code Sec. 179 deduction is extended to businesses in the Gulf Opportunity Zone (the area devastated by Katrina and other recent hurricanes) through 2008. The dollar limitation is increased to $125,000 and the investment limitation is increased to $500,000 (see ¶ 1208).

(4) For purposes of calculating the credit for employer-paid Social Security taxes on employee cash tips, the federal minimum wage will equal the minimum wage amount as of January 1, 2007, or $5.15 per hour (see ¶ 1341).

(5) A married couple who operate a joint venture and who file a joint return can elect not to be treated as a partnership for federal income tax purposes. The treatment is available for tax years beginning after December 31, 2006 (see ¶ 402).

(6) The sale of qualified subsidiary (QSub) stock that terminates the QSub election and creates a deemed new corporation will be treated as a sale of an undivided interest in the assets of the QSub. The provision is effective for tax years beginning on or after December 31, 2006 (see ¶ 305).

(7) An electing small business trust (ESBT) is allowed to deduct interest paid on money borrowed to acquire S corporation stock. The deduction is effective retroactively, for tax years beginning on or after January 1, 2007 (see ¶ 305).

(8) Any corporation that was an S corporation prior to 1983, but was not an S corporation for its first tax year beginning after December 31, 1996, may reduce its accumulated earnings and profits (E&P) as of the beginning of the first tax year beginning after May 25, 2007, by the amount of any E&P accumulated during the corporation's pre-1983 S corporation years (see ¶ 323).

(9) For tax years beginning after May 25, 2007, gains from the sale or exchange of stock or securities will not be included in an S corporation's passive investment income (see ¶ 341).

The more significant offsets, estimated to raise $5 billion over ten years, include:

(1) The kiddie tax has been expanded to apply to any child who is 18 years old at the end of the tax year or who is a full-time student over the age of 18, but under 24 at the end of the year, effective for tax years beginning after May 25, 2007 (see ¶ 706).

(2) The scope of tax return preparer penalties is expanded to include all types of tax returns, such as employment, excise, exempt organizations, estate and gift tax returns, and the amount of the penalties is increased (see ¶ 2518).

(3) Effective for IRS notices issued after November 25, 2007, the suspension period before the accrual of interest and certain penalties is increased from 18 months to 36 months, after the filing of a tax return if the IRS has not sent the taxpayer a notice specifically stating the taxpayer's liability and the basis for the liability (see ¶ 2813).

For information on further legislative developments in 2007, visit the *U.S. Master Tax Guide's* website at http://tax.cchgroup.com/mtg.

A Decade of Change. A decade of tax cuts began with the Economic Growth and Tax Relief Reconciliation Act of 2001 (P.L. 107-16), which reflected congressional compromises on tax rate reduction, estate tax repeal, marriage penalty relief, education incentives, child tax credit increase, pension reform, and alternative minimum tax relief. However, to meet budgetary constraints, provisions are phased in and out over the next 10 years, with an anticipated sunset in 2011 that would reinstate the Code as it was prior to this enactment.

Subsequent legislation accelerated some of EGTRRA's changes. The following table outlines some of the changes taking place over the next few years, subject to future legislative efforts.

	2007	2008	2009	2010
Tax rate brackets				
Top bracket	35%	35%	35%	35%
Fifth bracket	33%	33%	33%	33%
Fourth bracket	28%	28%	28%	28%
Third bracket	25%	25%	25%	25%
Second bracket	15%	15%	15%	15%
Initial bracket	10%	10%	10%	10%
Child tax credit	$1,000	$1,000	$1,000	$1,000
IRA contributions	$4,000	$5,000	$5,000*	$5,000*
IRA catch-ups	$1,000	$1,000	$1,000	$1,000
SIMPLE contributions	$10,000*	$10,000*	$10,000*	$10,000*
Elective deferrals	$15,000*	$15,000*	$15,000*	$15,000*
Elective catch-ups				
—SIMPLEs	$2,500*	$2,500*	$2,500*	$2,500*
—401(k), 403(b), 457 plans	$5,000*	$5,000*	$5,000*	$5,000*
AMT exemption				
—single	$33,750	$33,750	$33,750	$33,750
—married filing jointly	$45,000	$45,000	$45,000	$45,000
Estate tax				
—top rate	45%	45%	45%	0%
—exemption amount	$2 million	$2 million	$3.5 million	$0
Gift tax				
—exemption amount	$1 million	$1 million	$1 million	$1 million

* subject to inflation adjustments

¶1

¶ 2 What to Watch on 2007 Returns

The *Guide* reflects all of the important administrative and judicial developments of 2007 . . . final regulations, major court decisions, and important rulings of the Internal Revenue Service. Legislative highlights are at ¶ 1. Below are additional highlights of the changes in 2007 with the greatest impact on individuals and businesses.

Individuals

Income levels at which individuals must file income tax returns
have increased for 2007 . . . . ¶ 109

Basic standard deduction amounts have increased for 2007 . . . . ¶ 126

The deduction for each personal exemption has increased to
$3,400 for 2007 . . . . ¶ 133

Inflation-adjusted income amounts that trigger the reduction of
allowable itemized deductions and personal exemptions for
high-income taxpayers have increased for 2007 . . . . ¶ 88A, ¶ 133, ¶ 1014

"Kiddie" tax amount is $1,700 for 2007 . . . . ¶ 706

The standard mileage rate for all business use of a car is 48.5
cents per mile for 2007 . . . . ¶ 947

Per diem rates under the high-low method of substantiating
travel expenses are at $237 for high-cost localities and $152 for
low-cost localities for travel on or after 10/01/07 . . . . ¶ 954A

Student loan interest, up to $2,500 in 2007, may be deducted
"above-the-line" by qualifying taxpayers. . . . . ¶ 1082

Teachers and other education workers can deduct, "above the
line," up to $250 of certain out-of-pocket classroom expenses. . . . . ¶ 1084

The transportation fringe benefit exclusion amount in 2007 for
employer-provided transit passes or vehicles is $110 per month
and $215 per month for employer-provided parking . . . . ¶ 863

Depreciation, Amortization and Depletion

The maximum Code Sec. 179 deduction for 2007 is $125,000 . . . . ¶ 1208

Tax Credits

For 2007, the maximum earned income credit for eligible
taxpayers with no qualifying children is $428, with one
qualifying child is $2,853, and with two or more qualifying
children is $4,716 . . . . ¶ 87, ¶ 1375

The child tax credit is $1,000 for 2007 . . . . ¶ 1302

The education tax credits (Hope and Lifetime Learning) are
$1,650 and $2,000, respectively, for 2007 . . . . ¶ 1303

Withholding

The 2007 OASDI wage base for FICA and self-employment tax
purposes is $97,500 . . . . ¶ 47, ¶ 49, ¶ 2648, ¶ 2670

The 2007 wage threshold for "Nanny Tax" reporting is $1,500 . . . . ¶ 2650

¶ 3 Where to File Returns

Individuals. Listed below are the mailing addresses for filing your own individual income tax return. See ¶ 122. Tax professionals who are filing returns for their clients should use the second set of mailing addresses listed below. See also ¶ 2701 for a discussion of service centers.

Note: The IRS has reorganized its processing of tax returns. As a result of these efforts, many taxpayers *may* have different filing service centers than those used previously.

☐ Per the IRS, if an addressed envelope came with your return, please use it. If you do not have one, or if you moved during the year, mail your return to the Internal Revenue Service Center for the place where you live. No street address is needed. The chart below indicates the address with the ZIP Code and extension for filing Form 1040. To facilitate processing for residents of the 50 states and the District of Columbia, each form (1040, 1040A, 1040EZ) uses a different ZIP+4 ZIP Code extension. Also, different extensions are used if you are making a payment or not. If you are filing Form 1040A and are not making a payment, use the address in the middle column but with the ZIP Code extension, -0015. If you are filing Form 1040A and are making a payment, use the address in the last column but with the ZIP Code extension, -0115. If you are filing Form 1040EZ and are not making a payment, use the address in the middle column but with the ZIP Code extension, -0014. If you are filing Form 1040EZ and are making a payment, use the address in the last column but with the ZIP Code extension, -0114. Be sure to check your particular form's instructions for the proper extension and address.

If you are filing **Form 1040** *and are located in:*	*And are not enclosing a payment, mail your return to:*	*And are enclosing a payment, mail your return to:*
Alabama, Delaware, Florida, Georgia, North Carolina, Rhode Island, South Carolina, Virginia	Atlanta, GA 39901-0002	Atlanta, GA 39901-0102
District of Columbia, Maine, Maryland, Massachusetts, New Hampshire, New York, Vermont	Andover, MA 05501-0002	Andover, MA 05501-0102
Arkansas, Connecticut, Illinois, Indiana, Michigan, Missouri, New Jersey, Ohio, Pennsylvania, West Virginia	Kansas City, MO 64999-0002	Kansas City, MO 64999-0102
Kentucky, Louisiana, Mississippi, Tennessee, Texas, All A.P.O. and F.P.O. addresses	Austin, TX 73301-0002	Austin, TX 73301-0102
Alaska, Arizona, California, Colorado, Hawaii, Idaho, Iowa, Kansas, Minnesota, Montana, Nebraska, Nevada, New Mexico, North Dakota, Oklahoma, Oregon, South Dakota, Utah, Washington, Wisconsin, Wyoming	Fresno, CA 93888-0002	Fresno, CA 93888-0102

¶3

If you are filing **Form 1040** *and are located in:*	*And are not enclosing a payment, mail your return to:*	*And are enclosing a payment, mail your return to:*
American Samoa, non-permanent residents of Guam or the Virgin Islands, Puerto Rico (or if excluding income under Code Sec. 933), dual-status aliens, those filing Form 4563, U.S citizens or tax residents in a foreign country, or those filing Form 2555 or 2555-EZ.	Austin, TX 73301-0215 USA	Austin, TX 73301-0215 USA
Guam: permanent residents	Department of Revenue and Taxation, Government of Guam, P.O. Box 23607, GMF, GU 96921	
Virgin Islands: permanent residents	V.I. Bureau of Internal Revenue, 9601 Estate Thomas, Charlotte Amalie, St. Thomas, VI 00802	

Tax Professionals—Individual Returns. Listed below are the mailing addresses for tax professionals to use when filing individual income tax returns on behalf of a client. See ¶ 122. See also ¶ 2701 for a discussion of service centers.

Note: The IRS has reorganized its processing of tax returns. As a result of these efforts, returns for taxpayers in at least one state *may* have different filing addresses than those used previously.

□ Per the IRS, tax professionals filing Forms 1040 for clients should use the addresses listed below based on the place where the client lives. The first line of the address should be Internal Revenue Service, but no street address is needed. For clients located in the 50 states and the District of Columbia who do not need to enclose a payment with the return, each form (1040, 1040A, 1040EZ) uses a different ZIP+4 ZIP Code extension. If you are filing a client's Form 1040A and are not enclosing a payment, use the address in the middle column with the ZIP Code extension, -0015. If you are filing a client's Form 1040EZ and are not enclosing a payment, use the address in the middle column with the ZIP Code extension, -0014. If a payment is enclosed with the form, each form (1040, 1040A, 1040EZ) uses the same mailing address shown in the last column below.

If you are filing a client's **Form 1040** *and the client is located in:*	*And are not enclosing a payment, mail the client's return to:*	*And are enclosing a payment, mail the client's return to:*
Alabama, Delaware, Florida, Georgia, North Carolina, Rhode Island, South Carolina, Virginia	Atlanta, GA 39901-0002	P.O. Box 105017 Atlanta, GA 30348-5017
District of Columbia, Maine, Maryland, Massachusetts, New Hampshire, New York, Vermont	Andover, MA 05501-0002	P.O. Box 37002 Hartford, CT 06176-0002

If you are filing a client's **Form 1040** and the client is located in:	And are not enclosing a payment, mail the client's return to:	And are enclosing a payment, mail the client's return to:
Arkansas, Connecticut, Illinois, Indiana, Michigan, Missouri, Ohio, West Virginia	Kansas City, MO 64999-0002	P.O. Box 970011 St. Louis, MO 63197-0011
New Jersey, Pennsylvania	Kansas City, MO 64999-0002	P.O. Box 37008 Hartford, CT 06176-0008
Kentucky, Louisiana, Mississippi, Tennessee, Texas, All A.P.O. and F.P.O. addresses	Austin, TX 73301-0002	P.O. Box 660308 Dallas, TX 75266-0308
Alaska, Arizona, California, Hawaii, Nevada, New Mexico, Oregon, Utah	Fresno, CA 93888-0002	P.O. Box 7704 San Francisco, CA 94120-7704
Colorado, Idaho, Iowa, Kansas, Minnesota, Montana, Nebraska, North Dakota, Oklahoma, South Dakota, Washington, Wisconsin, Wyoming	Fresno, CA 93888-0002	P.O. Box 802501 Cincinnati, OH 45280-2501
American Samoa, non-permanent residents of Guam or the Virgin Island, Puerto Rico (or if excluding income under Code Sec. 933), dual-status aliens, those filing Form 4563, U.S. citizens or tax residents in a foreign country, or those filing Form 2555 or 2555-EZ	Austin, TX 73301-0215 USA	P.O. Box 660335 Dallas, TX 75266-0335 USA
Guam: permanent residents	Department of Revenue and Taxation, Government of Guam, P.O. Box 23607, GMF, GU 96921	
Virgin Islands: permanent residents	V.I. Bureau of Internal Revenue, 9601 Estate Thomas, Charlotte Amalie, St. Thomas, VI 00802	

Corporations and Partnerships. A corporation or partnership should file Form 1120 or Form 1065 in accordance with the "Where to File" addresses listed in the instructions to the forms. A corporation or partnership is "located in" the place where it has its principal place of business or principal office or agency. If a corporation or partnership is without a principal office or agency or principal place of business in the United States, returns are to be filed with the Internal Revenue Service Center in Ogden, Utah.

Estates and Trusts. Generally, a fiduciary of an estate or trust, including the fiduciary of a charitable or split interest trust (described in Code Sec. 4947(a)) or of a pooled income fund (described in Code Sec. 642(c)(5), should file Form 1041 in accordance with the instructions to Form 1041. A fiduciary is "located in" the place where he (it) resides or has his (its) principal place of business.

Private Delivery Services. Certain private delivery services designated by the IRS are available to meet the "timely mailed as timely filing/paying" rule for tax returns and payments. The IRS last published this list of the designated private delivery services in December 2004 (Notice 2004-83), removing Airborne Express, Inc. (Airborne) and revising the list of services provided by DHL Express (DHL). The IRS commented in 1999 that a new list will only be published when there is a change to it. Effective January 1, 2005, the designated private delivery services are:

• DHL Express (DHL): DHL Same Day Service, DHL Next Day 10:30 am, DHL Next Day 12:00 pm, DHL Next Day 3:00 pm, and DHL 2nd Day Service.

• Federal Express (FedEx): FedEx Priority Overnight, FedEx Standard Overnight, FedEx 2Day, FedEx International Priority, and FedEx International First.

• United Parcel Service (UPS): UPS Next Day Air, UPS Next Day Air Saver, UPS 2nd Day Air, UPS 2nd Day Air A.M., UPS Worldwide Express Plus, and UPS Worldwide Express.

The private delivery service will provide information for getting written proof of the mailing date.

¶ 4 Government Agency and Tax/Accounting Directories

Listed below are mailing addresses and telephone numbers for key federal government agencies as well as tax and accounting organizations.

FEDERAL GOVERNMENT OFFICES—GENERAL LISTING

Department of Commerce
    1401 Constitution Ave NW Washington DC 20230   202-482-2000
Department of Justice
    950 Pennsylvania Ave NW Washington DC 20530-0001   202-514-2000
Department of The Treasury
    1500 Pennsylvania Ave NW Washington DC 20220   202-622-2000
Executive Office of the President
    Office of Admin.
    725 17th St NW Washington DC 20503   202-395-3000
    Office of the US Trade Representative
    600 Seventeenth St NW Washington DC 20508   202-395-7360
    Office of the Vice President of the US
    1600 Pennsylvania Ave NW Washington DC 20500   202-456-1414
    The White House Office
    1600 Pennsylvania Ave NW Washington DC 20500   202-456-1414
Export-Import Bank of the US
    811 Vermont Ave NW Washington DC 20571   202-565-3946
Federal Deposit Insurance Corporation
    550 Seventeenth St NW Washington DC 20429   202-736-0000
Federal Reserve System Board of Governors
    20th & Constitution Ave NW Washington DC 20551   202-452-3000
National Information Center
    20th & Constitution Ave NW Washington DC 20551   202-452-3301
Government Accountability Office
    441 G St. NW Washington DC 20548   202-512-3000
General Services Administration
    1800 F St NW Washington DC 20405   202-501-0800
Government Printing Office
    732 N Capitol St NW Washington DC 20401   202-512-0000
Library of Congress
    101 Independence Ave SE Washington DC 20540-6001   202-707-5000
National Archives and Records Administration
    8601 Adelphi Rd College Park MD 20740   301-837-0482
Office of Management & Budget
    725 17th St NW Washington DC 20503   202-395-3080
Railroad Retirement Board
    844 N Rush St Chicago Il 60611-2092   312-751-7139
Securities and Exchange Commission
    100 F St NE Washington DC 20549   202-942-8088
Small Business Administration
    409 3rd St SW Washington DC 20416   800-827-5722
Social Security Administration
    6401 Security Blvd Baltimore MD 21235-0001   800-772-1213
United States Tax Court
    400 2nd St. NW Washington DC 20217   202-521-0700

FEDERAL GOVERNMENT OFFICES—SPECIALIZED LISTINGS

MAJOR FEDERAL EXECUTIVE PROCUREMENT AGENCIES

Justice Department
    Justice Management Division
    1331 Pennsylvania Ave NW Ste 1000 Washington DC 20530 .   202-307-2000
Office of Small Business Utilization
    1800 F Street NW Room 6029 Washington DC 20405   202-501-1021
Federal Procurement Data Center
    U.S. General Services Administration
    2011 Crystal Drive Suite 911 Arlington VA 22202   703-872-8621
Treasury Department
    Office of the Procurement Executive
    1500 Pennsylvania Ave Attn: 655 15th St/6183 Washington DC
    20220   202-622-1039

SMALL BUSINESS ADMINISTRATION

SBA Answer Desk
    6302 Fairview Rd Ste 300 Charlotte, NC 28210   800-827-5722

AICPA, NAEA, NATP, NSA AND STATE ACCOUNTING SOCIETIES

AICPA Main Office
    1211 Avenue of the Americas New York NY 10036-8775   212-596-6200
National Association of Enrolled Agents
    1120 Connecticut Ave NW Ste 460 Washington DC 20036 . .   202-822-6232
National Association of Tax Professionals
    720 Association Dr Appleton WI 54914-1483   800-558-3402
National Society of Accountants Main Office
    1010 N Fairfax St Alexandria VA 22314   703-549-6400
National Society of Tax Professionals (NSTP)
    10818 NE Coxley Dr Ste A Vancouver WA 98662   360-695-8309
AL Society of CPAs
    1103 S Perry St PO Box 5000 Montgomery AL 36103   334-834-7650
AK Society of CPAs
    341 W Tudor Rd Ste 105 Anchorage AK 99503   907-562-4334
AZ Society of CPAs
    4801 E Washington St Ste 225-B Phoenix AZ 85034   602-252-4144
AR Society of CPAs
    11300 Executive Center Dr Little Rock AR 72211   501-664-8739
CA Society of CPAs
    1235 Radio Rd Redwood City CA 94065-1217   800-922-5272
CO Society of CPAs
    7979 E Tufts Ave Suite 1000 Denver CO 80237-2847   303-773-2877
CT Society of CPAs
    845 Brook St Bldg 2 Rocky Hill CT 06067-3405   860-258-4800
DE Society of CPAs
    3512 Silverside Rd 8 The Commons Wilmington DE 19810 . .   302-478-7442
DC Institute of CPAs
    1828 L St Ste 900 Washington DC 20036   202-204-8014
FL Institute of CPAs
    325 W College Ave Tallahassee FL 32301   850-224-2727
GA Society of CPAs
    3353 Peachtree Rd NE Ste 400 Atlanta GA 30326-1414   404-231-8676
Greater Washington Society of CPAs
    1828 L St NW Ste 900 Washington DC 20036   202-204-8014
HI Society of CPAs
    900 Fort Street Mall Suite 850 Honolulu HI 96813   808-537-9475

ID Society of CPAs
    250 Bob White Ct Ste 240 Boise ID 83706 208-344-6261
IL CPA Society
    550 W Jackson Ste 900 Chicago IL 60661 312-993-0407
IN Society of CPAs
    8250 Woodfield Crossing Blvd Ste 100 Indianapolis IN
    46240-4348 317-726-5000
IA Society of CPAs
    950 Office Pk Rd West Ste 300 Des Moines IA 50265 515-223-8161
KS Society of CPAs
    1080 SW Wanamaker Rd Ste 200 P O Box 4291Topeka KS
    66604-0291 785-272-4366
KY Society of CPAs
    1735 Alliant Ave Louisville KY 40299 502-266-5272
LA Society of LA CPAs
    2400 Veterans Blvd Ste 500 Kenner LA 70062 504-464-1040
ME Society of CPAs
    153 US Rte 1 Ste 8 Scarborough ME 04074-9053 207-883-6090
MD Association of CPAs
    901 Dulaney Valley Rd Ste 710 Towson MD 21204-2683 . . . 410-296-6250
MA Society of CPAs
    105 Chauncy St 10th Floor Boston MA 02111 617-556-4000
MI Society of CPAs
    5480 Corporate Drive Ste 200 Troy MI 48098 248-267-3700
MN Society of CPAs
    1650 W 82nd St Ste 600 Bloomington MN 55431 952-831-2707
MS Society of CPAs
    306 Southampton Row The Commons Highland Colony Prkwy
    Ridgeland MS 39157 601-856-4244
MO Society of CPAs
    540 Maryville Centre Dr Suite 200 St Louis MO 63141 314-997-7966
MT Society of CPAs
    33 S Last Chance Gulch Ste 2B Helena MT 59601 406-442-7301
NE Society of CPAs
    635 S 14th St Ste 330 Lincoln NE 68508 402-476-8482
NV Society of CPAs
    5250 Neil Rd Ste 205 Reno NV 89502 775-826-6800
NH Society of CPAs
    1750 Elm St Ste 403 Manchester NH 03104 603-622-1999
NJ Society of CPAs
    425 Eagle Rock Ave Ste 100 Roseland NJ 07068-1723 973-226-4494
NM Society of CPAs
    1650 University NE Ste 450 Albuquerque NM 87102 505-246-1699
NY Society of CPAs
    3 Park Ave 18th Flr New York NY 10016-5991 212-719-8300
NC Association of CPAs
    3100 Gateway Centre Boulevard Morrisville NC 27560-9241 . 919-469-1040
ND Society of CPAs
    2701 South Colombia Rd Grand Forks ND 58201-6029 701-775-7100
OH Society of CPAs
    535 Metro Place S PO Box 1810 Dublin OH 43017-7810 614-764-2727
OK Society of CPAs
    1900 NW Expwy Ste 910 Oklahoma City OK 73118 405-841-3800
OR Society of CPAs
    10206 SW Laurel St Beaverton OR 97005-3209 503-641-7200
PA Institute of CPAs
    1650 Arch St 17th Floor Philadelphia PA 19103 215-496-9272
PR Society of CPAs
    Capitol Ctr Bldg 1 239 Ave Arterial Hostos Ste 1401 San Juan
    PR 00918-1477 787-754-1950

RI Society of CPAs
    45 Royal Little Dr Providence RI 02904   401-331-5720
SC Association of CPAs
    570 Chris Dr West Columbia SC 29169   803-791-4181
SD Society of CPAs
    1000 N West Ave Ste 100 Sioux Falls SD 57101   605-334-3848
TN Society of CPAs
    201 Powell Pl Brentwood TN 37027   615-377-3825
TX Society of CPAs
    14651 Dallas Pkwy Suite 700 Dallas TX 75254   972-687-8500
UT Society of CPAs
    220 E Morris Ave Ste 320 Salt Lake City UT 84115   801-466-8022
VT Society of CPAs
    100 State St Ste 500 Montpelier VT 05602   802-229-4939
VA Society of CPAs
    4309 Cox Rd Glen Allen VA 23060   804-270-5344
WA Society of CPAs
    902 140th Ave NE Bellevue WA 98005   425-644-4800
WV Society of CPAs
    900 Lee St East Ste 1201 Charleston WV 25301   304-342-5461
WI Institute of CPAs
    235 N Executive Dr Suite 200 Brookfield WI 53008   262-785-0445
WY Society of CPAs
    504 W 17th St Ste 200 Cheyenne WY 82001   307-634-7039

¶ 5 Due Dates in 2008

Each date shown below is the prescribed last day for filing the return or making the payment of tax indicated. For income tax returns, the due dates apply to calendar-year taxpayers only. Employment tax due dates are determined on a calendar-year basis for all taxpayers. **If any due date falls on a Saturday, Sunday or legal holiday, the due date is the next succeeding day that is not a Saturday, Sunday, or legal holiday (national, District of Columbia, or statewide in the state where the return is to be filed).**

This day 2008	Tax Return Due Dates
Jan. 15th—	**Estimated Taxes.** Final installment of 2007 estimated tax (Form 1040-ES) by individuals unless income tax return is filed with final payment by January 31, 2008. Payment in full of estimated tax by farmers and fishermen unless income tax returns are filed by March 1, 2008.
	Final installment of 2007 estimated tax (Form 1041-ES) by trusts, and by calendar-year estates and certain residuary trusts in existence more than two years, unless Form 1041 is filed and taxes are paid in full by January 31, 2008.
Jan. 31st—	**Employers' Taxes.** Employers of nonagricultural and nonhousehold employees file return on Form 941 for withheld income and FICA taxes in last quarter of 2007.[1]
	Employers of agricultural workers must file the annual Form 943 to report income and FICA taxes withheld on 2007 wages.[1]
	Employers must file Form 940, annual return of federal unemployment (FUTA) taxes for 2007.[1]
	Withholding. Employees' statements (Form W-2 and Form 1099-R) for amounts withheld in 2007 to be furnished by employer to employees. Statements for amounts withheld on certain gambling winnings (Form W-2G) to be furnished by payer to recipients.
	Individuals. Individuals (other than farmers and fishermen) who owed, but did not pay, estimated tax on January 15 must file final 2007 income tax return and pay tax in full to avoid late payment penalty.
	Trusts and Estates. Trusts, as well as estates and certain residuary trusts in existence more than two years, that owed but did not pay estimated tax on January 15 must file final 2007 income tax return and pay tax in full to avoid late payment penalty.
	Information Returns. Annual statements must be furnished to recipients of dividends and liquidating distributions (Form 1099-DIV); interest, including interest on bearer certificates of deposit (Form 1099-INT); patronage dividends (Form 1099-PATR); original issue discount (Form 1099-OID); proceeds from broker and barter exchange transactions (Form 1099-B); proceeds from real estate transactions (Form 1099-S); certain government payments, including unemployment compensation and state and local tax refunds of $10 or more (Form 1099-G); royalty payments of $10 or more, rent or other business payments of $600 or more, prizes and awards of $600 or more, broker payments in lieu of dividends or tax-exempt interest of $10 or more, crop insurance proceeds of $600 or more, fishing boat proceeds, and medical and health care payments of $600 or more (Form 1099-MISC); debt canceled by certain financial entities including financial institutions, credit unions, and Federal Government agencies of $600 or more (Form 1099-C); distributions from retirement or profit-sharing plans, IRAs, SEPs, or insurance contracts (Form 1099-R).
	Business recipients of $600 or more of interest on any mortgage must furnish Form 1098 to payer.

This day 2008	Tax Return Due Dates

Information called for on Form 8300 must be provided to each payer in a transaction of more than $10,000 in cash at any time during 2007. (Form 8300 must have been filed with the IRS by the 15th day after the date of the transaction.)

Partnerships must provide Form 8308 to the transferor and transferee in any exchange of a partnership interest that involved unrealized receivables or substantially appreciated inventory items.

Trustees or issuers of IRAs or SEPs must provide participants with a statement of the account's value.

Feb. 15th—   **Individuals.** Last day for filing Form W-4 by employees who wish to claim exemption from withholding of income tax for 2008.

Feb. 28th—   **Information Returns.** Annual 1099 series returns (together with transmittal Form 1096 for paper filings or Form 4804 for magnetic media filings) must be filed with the IRS to report payments to recipients who received Form 1099 on January 31, as indicated above. If filing electronically (not by magnetic media), the due date is extended to March 31.

Business recipients of $600 or more of interest from an individual on any mortgage must file Form 1098 with the IRS (together with transmittal Form 1096 for paper filings or Form 4804 for magnetic media filings). If filing electronically (not by magnetic media), the due date is extended to March 31.

Withholding. Form W-2 "A" copies for 2007 (together with transmittal Form W-3) must be filed with the Social Security Administration. If filing electronically (not by magnetic media), the due date is extended to March 31.

Form W-2G and Form 1099-R for 2007 "A" copies (together with transmittal Form 1096 for paper filings or Form 4804 for magnetic media filings) must be filed with the IRS. If filing electronically (not by magnetic media), the due date is extended to March 31.

Mar. 1st—   **Individuals.** Last day for farmers and fishermen who owed, but did not pay, estimated tax on January 15 to file 2007 calendar-year income tax return and pay tax in full to avoid late payment penalty.

Mar. 15th—   **Corporations.** Due date of 2007 income tax returns (Form 1120 or Form 1120-A) for calendar-year U.S. corporations or calendar-year foreign corporations with offices in the U.S. Fiscal-year U.S. corporations and foreign corporations with a U.S. office must file by the 15th day of the 3rd month following the close of the tax year.

Due date of 2007 income tax returns for calendar-year S corporations (Form 1120S).

Last date for filing application (Form 7004) by calendar-year corporations for automatic six-month extension to file 2007 income tax return.

Form 5452 for reporting nontaxable corporate distributions made to shareholders during calendar year 2007 should be filed by calendar-year corporations with income tax return. Fiscal-year corporations file Form 5452 with income tax return for first fiscal year ending after calendar year in which distributions were made.

Calendar-year corporations' 2007 information return (Form 5471) with respect to foreign corporations. (Fiscal-year corporations file form with income tax return.)

Last date for a calendar-year corporation to file an amended income tax return (Form 1120X) for the calendar year 2004.[2]

This day 2008   **Tax Return Due Dates**

Withholding. File returns on Form 1042 and Form 1042S to report tax withheld at the source from nonresident aliens, foreign corporations, foreign partnerships and foreign fiduciaries of a trust or estate.

Mar. 31st— **Information Returns—Electronic Filing.** Due date for filing Form 1098 (for reporting receipt of mortgage interest) or Form 1099 (for reporting certain payments) with the IRS electronically (not by magnetic media).

Withholding—Electronic Filing. Last day for filing Form W-2 with the SSA or Form W-2G with the IRS if filing electronically (not by magnetic media).

Apr. 15th— **Individuals.** Income tax and self-employment tax returns of individuals for calendar year 2007 and income tax returns of calendar-year decedents who died in 2007. (Form 1040, Form 1040A, or Form 1040EZ.) Fiscal-year individuals must file returns or requests for extension by the 15th day of the 4th month after the close of the tax year.

Last day for calendar-year individuals to file application (Form 4868) for automatic six-month extension to file 2007 income tax return.

Individuals' information returns (Form 5471) with respect to foreign corporations to be filed with Form 1040.

Last day for individuals to file amended income tax returns (Form 1040X) for the calendar year 2004.

Estimated Tax. Calendar-year corporations pay 25% of estimated tax if requirements are met before April 1, 2008. Fiscal-year corporations are to make payments on the 15th day of the 4th, 6th, 9th and 12th months of the tax year.

Payment of first installment of 2008 estimated income taxes by calendar-year individuals (other than farmers and fishermen) (Form 1040ES). Estimated tax payments for fiscal-year individuals are due on the 15th day of the 4th, 6th and 9th months of the tax year and the 1st month of the following tax year.

Trusts (and calendar-year estates and certain residuary trusts in existence more than two years) must make first payment of estimated taxes for 2008 (Form 1041-ES). Fiscal-year estates must make payments on the 15th day of the 4th, 6th, and 9th months of the fiscal year and the 1st month of the following fiscal year.

Trusts and Estates. Fiduciary income tax return (Form 1041) for calendar year 2007. (Fiscal-year estates must file by the 15th day of the 4th month following close of the tax year.)

Last day for calendar year estates and trusts to file application (Form 7004) for automatic six-month extension of time to file 2007 income tax return.

Last day for estates and trusts to file amended tax returns for calendar year 2004.

Partnerships. Last day for filing income tax return (Form 1065) for calendar year 2007. Returns for fiscal-year partnerships are due on the 15th day of the 4th month after the close of the tax year.

Last day for calendar-year U.S. partnerships to file application (Form 7004) for automatic six-month extension to file 2007 income tax return.

Last day for calendar-year partnerships to file an amended return for 2004.

Information Returns. Annual information return (Form 1041-A) for split-interest trusts and complex trusts claiming charitable deductions under Code Sec. 642(c) and annual information return (Form 5227) for Code Sec. 4947(a)(2) trusts must be filed.

This day 2008	**Tax Return Due Dates**

Apr. 30th—   **Employers' Taxes.** Employers of nonagricultural and nonhousehold employees must file return on Form 941 to report income tax withholding and FICA taxes for the first quarter of 2008.[3]

May 15th—   **Exempt Organizations.** Annual information return (Form 990) for 2007 by calendar-year organizations exempt or claiming exemption from tax under Code Sec. 501 or Code Sec. 4947(a)(1). Fiscal-year organizations must file by 15th day of 5th month after close of the tax year.

Calendar-year private foundations and Code Sec. 4947(a) trusts treated as private foundations must file Form 990-PF, and private foundations must pay the first quarter installment of estimated excise tax on net investment or tax on unrelated business income. Fiscal-year organizations must file by 15th day of 5th month after close of tax year, for both Form 990-PF and estimated taxes referred to above.

Calendar-year Code Sec. 501(a) organizations with unrelated business income must file income tax return on Form 990-T. Fiscal-year organizations must file by 15th day of 5th month following close of tax year.

Exempt organizations requesting an extension of time to file Form 990 may file Form 8868. Certain entities must file Form 2758 in time for it to be processed by the filing deadline to request a nonautomatic extension.

May 31st—   **Information Returns.** Annual statement to IRS regarding 2007 account balances for an IRA or SEP (Form 5498). Participants and IRS must be provided with IRA plan contribution information.

June 15th—   **Individuals.** Last day for nonresident alien individuals not subject to withholding to file income tax return for calendar year 2007.

Estimated Tax. Calendar-year corporations must pay second installment of 2008 estimated tax.

Payment of second installment of 2008 estimated tax by individuals (other than farmers and fishermen), by trusts and by estates and certain residuary trusts in existence more than 2 years. Nonresident aliens who have no wages subject to U.S. withholding must make first payment (Form 1040ES(NR)).

Corporations. Last day for foreign corporations that do not maintain an office or place of business in U.S. to file income tax return (Form 1120F) for calendar year 2007.

July 31st—   **Employers' Taxes.** Employers of nonagricultural and nonhousehold employees must file return on Form 941 to report income tax withholding and FICA taxes for the second quarter of 2007.[4]

Sept. 15th—   **Estimated Tax.** Payment of third installment of 2008 estimated tax by calendar-year corporations.

Payment of third installment of 2008 estimated tax by individuals (other than farmers and fishermen), by trusts and by estates and certain residuary trusts in existence more than 2 years.

Corporations. Last day for filing 2007 income tax return by calendar-year corporations that obtained automatic six-month filing extension.

Exempt Organizations. Last day for exempt calendar-year farmers' cooperatives to file 2007 income tax returns (Form 1120-C). Fiscal-year cooperatives must file by the 15th day of the 9th month following the close of the tax year. An automatic six-month extension of the filing date may be obtained by filing Form 7004.

October 15th—   **Estates and Trusts.** Last day for filing 2007 Form 1041 for calendar-year estates and trusts that obtained an automatic six-month filing extension.

Partnerships. Last day for filing 2007 Form 1065 for calendar-year partnerships that obtained an automatic six-month filing extension.

¶5

This day 2008	**Tax Return Due Dates**
	Individuals. Last day for filing 2007 income tax return by calendar-year individuals who obtained automatic six-month filing extension.
Oct. 31st—	**Employers' Taxes.** Employers of nonagricultural and nonhousehold employees must file return on Form 941 to report income tax withholding and FICA taxes for the third quarter of 2008.[5]
Dec. 15th—	**Estimated Tax.** Payment of last installment of 2008 estimated tax by calendar-year corporations.
This day 2009	
Jan. 15th—	**Estimated Tax.** Final installment of 2008 estimated tax by individuals, trusts and estates and certain residuary trusts in existence more than two years. (Payment of estimated tax in full by individuals, trusts and estates that are first required to pay estimated tax for calendar year 2008.) Payment not necessary if returns filed and tax paid in full by January 31, 2009. Payment of estimated tax in full by farmers and fishermen who are not filing final returns by March 1, 2009.
Jan. 31st—	**Individuals.** Final income tax return for 2008 by calendar-year individuals and by trusts and estates in existence more than two years who owed but did not pay 2008 estimated tax otherwise due January 15th.

[1] If timely deposits in full payment of tax due were made, the due date for Forms 940, 941, and 943 is February 10.

[2] In general, fiscal-year corporations must file within three years of the date the original return was due.

[3] If timely deposits in full payment of taxes due were made, the due date for Form 941 is May 10.

[4] If timely deposits in full payment of taxes due were made, the due date for Form 941 is August 10.

[5] If timely deposits in full payment of taxes due were made, the due date for Form 941 is November 10.

EMPLOYMENT TAX DEPOSITS

Income Tax Withholding, FICA Taxes, Backup Withholding. Employment taxes are withheld income tax, FICA contributions and backup withholding on reportable payments. Generally, an employer must make either MONTHLY or SEMI-WEEKLY deposits during a calendar year based upon the aggregate amount of employment taxes paid during the "lookback" period. The lookback period for each calendar year is the 12-month period that ended the preceding June 30. Thus, an employer's obligation to make deposits in 2008 will be based upon the aggregate employment taxes paid during the period July 1, 2006, through June 30, 2007. (New employers are considered to have an aggregate tax liability of zero for any calendar quarter in which the employer did not exist.) See ¶ 2650.

Monthly Deposits. Monthly deposits are required if the aggregate amount of employment taxes reported by the employer for the lookback period is $50,000 or less. Monthly deposits are due on the 15th day of the following month in which the payments were made.

Semi-Weekly Deposits. An employer is a semi-weekly depositor for the entire calendar year if the aggregate amount of employment taxes during the lookback period exceeds $50,000. Further, a monthly depositor will become a semi-weekly depositor on the first day after the employer becomes subject to the One-Day Rule, discussed below. Semi-weekly deposits are generally due on either Wednesday or Friday—depending upon the timing of the employer's pay period. Employers with payment dates (paydays) that fall on Wednesday, Thursday or Friday must deposit the employment taxes on or before the following Wednesday. Employers with payment dates that fall on Saturday, Sunday, Monday or Tuesday must make their deposit on or before the following Friday. However, an employer will always have

three banking days in which to make the deposit. Thus, if any of the three weekdays following the close of a semi-weekly period is a holiday, then the employer will have an additional banking day in which to make the deposit.

Next-Day Rule. If an employer has accumulated $100,000 or more of undeposited employment taxes, then the taxes must be deposited by the close of the next banking day.

Federal Unemployment Taxes. The calendar year is divided into four quarters for purposes of determining when deposits of federal unemployment tax (FUTA) are necessary. The periods end on March 31, June 30, September 30 and December 31. If the employer's FUTA tax liability is $500 or less, then the employer does not have to deposit the tax, instead the amount may be carried forward and added to the liability for the next quarter to determine if a deposit is required. If the employer owes more than $500 in undeposited federal unemployment tax at the end of a quarter (including any FUTA tax carried forward from an earlier quarter), then the tax owed must be deposited by the end of the next month either by electronic funds transfer (EFTPS) or in an authorized financial institution using Form 8109.

2008

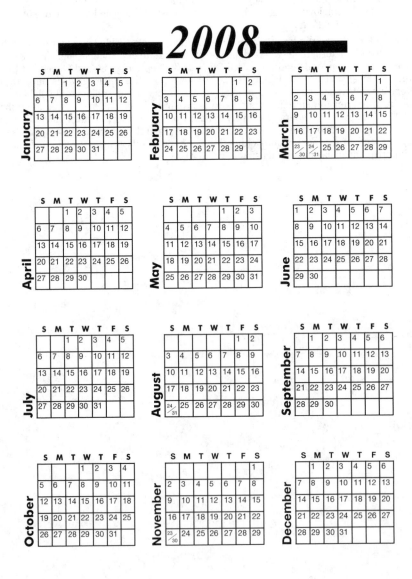

Schedules and Tables

TAX RATES

TAX RATE SCHEDULES FOR 2007 AND 2008

NOTE. The 2007 Tax Rate Schedules reproduced below are based on the Instructions to the 2007 Form 1040. The 2008 Tax Rate Schedules reproduced below are based on the rate changes and inflation adjustments to the tax brackets released by the Internal Revenue Service in Revenue Procedure 2007- 66, I.R.B. 2007-45.

The 2007 and 2008 tax rate schedules reflect changes from the Working Families Tax Relief Act of 2004 (P.L. 108-311) (WFTRA), the Jobs and Growth Tax Relief Reconciliation Act of 2003 (P.L. 108-27) (JGTRRA), and the Economic Growth and Tax Relief Reconciliation Act of 2001 (P.L. 107-16) (EGTRRA). The 2007 and 2008 tax rate schedules for single individuals are at ¶ 11; for married individuals filing jointly and surviving spouses, see ¶ 13; for married individuals filing separately, see ¶ 15; for heads of households, see ¶ 17; and for estates and nongrantor trusts, see ¶ 19.

Besides the current impact on 2007 and 2008 of lower tax rates, EGTRRA, JGTRRA and WFTRA also implemented changes in the sizes of the tax brackets over the next few years. For more details on how the brackets will be structured in future years, see ¶ 21.

¶ 11 SCHEDULE X: Single Individuals

2007

Taxable Income Over	But Not Over	Pay	+	% on Excess	of the amount over—
$0—	$7,825	$0		10 %	$0
7,825—	31,850	782.50		15	7,825
31,850—	77,100	4,386.25		25	31,850
77,100—	160,850	15,698.75		28	77,100
160,850—	349,700	39,148.75		33	160,850
349,700—	. . . . . .	101,469.25		35	349,700

Example: Nancy Gary, a single individual, has gross income of $115,000 in 2007. She has no dependents and claims a standard deduction because she lacks sufficient itemized deductions. Her taxable income is $106,250 ($115,000 – $5,350 standard deduction – $3,400 personal exemption). Her tax is $23,860.75 ($15,698.75 + .28 ($106,250 – $77,100)).

2008

Taxable Income Over	But Not Over	Pay	+	% on Excess	of the amount over—
$0—	$8,025	$0		10 %	$0
8,025—	32,550	802.50		15	8,025
32,550—	78,850	4,481.25		25	32,550
78,850—	164,550	16,056.25		28	78,850
164,550—	357,700	40,052.25		33	164,550
357,700—	. . . . . .	103,791.75		35	357,700

¶ 13 SCHEDULE Y-1: Married Filing Jointly and Surviving Spouses

2007

Taxable Income Over	But Not Over	Pay	+	% on Excess	of the amount over—
$0—	$15,650	$0		10%	$0
15,650—	63,700	1,565.00		15	15,650
63,700—	128,500	8,772.50		25	63,700
128,500—	195,850	24,972.50		28	128,500
195,850—	349,700	43,830.50		33	195,850
349,700—	. . . . . .	94,601.00		35	349,700

Example: Barbara and Ken Doosee have a combined income of $165,000 in 2007. They have two dependent children and allowable itemized deductions (consisting solely of medical expense deductions) totaling $16,000. They file a joint return. Their taxable income is $135,400 ($165,000 – $16,000 itemized deductions – $13,600 (four personal exemptions)). Their tax is $26,904.50 ($24,972.50 + .28 ($135,400 – $128,500)).

2008

Taxable Income Over	But Not Over	Pay	+	% on Excess	of the amount over—
$0—	$16,050	$0		10%	$0
16,050—	65,100	1,605.00		15	16,050
65,100—	131,450	8,962.50		25	65,100
131,450—	200,300	25,550.00		28	131,450
200,300—	357,700	44,828.00		33	200,300
357,700—	. . . . . .	96,770.00		35	357,700

¶ 15 SCHEDULE Y-2: Married Individuals Filing Separately

2007

Taxable Income Over	But Not Over	Pay	+	% on Excess	of the amount over—
$0—	$7,825	$0		10%	$0
7,825—	31,850	782.50		15	7,825
31,850—	64,250	4,386.25		25	31,850
64,250—	97,925	12,486.25		28	64,250
97,925—	174,850	21,915.25		33	97,925
174,850—	. . . . .	47,300.50		35	174,850

2008

Taxable Income Over	But Not Over	Pay	+	% on Excess	of the amount over—
$0—	$8,025	$0		10%	$0
8,025—	32,550	802.50		15	8,025
32,550—	65,725	4,481.25		25	32,550
65,725—	100,150	12,775.00		28	65,725
100,150—	178,850	22,414.00		33	100,150
178,850—	. . . . .	48,385.00		35	178,850

¶ 17 SCHEDULE Z: Heads of Households

2007

Taxable Income Over	But Not Over	Pay	+	% on Excess	of the amount over—
$0—	$11,200	$0		10%	$0
11,200—	42,650	1,120.00		15	11,200
42,650—	110,100	5,837.50		25	42,650
110,100—	178,350	22,700.00		28	110,100
178,350—	349,700	41,810.00		33	178,350
349,700—	. . . . .	98,355.50		35	349,700

2008

Taxable Income Over	But Not Over	Pay	+	% on Excess	of the amount over—
$0—	$11,450	$0		10%	$0
11,450—	43,650	1,145.00		15	11,450
43,650—	112,650	5,975.00		25	43,650
112,650—	182,400	23,225.00		28	112,650
182,400—	357,700	42,755.00		33	182,400
357,700—	. . . . .	100,604.00		35	357,700

¶ 19 INCOME TAX RATE SCHEDULES FOR USE BY ESTATES AND NONGRANTOR TRUSTS

2007

Taxable Income Over	But Not Over	Pay	+	% on Excess	of the amount over—
$0—	$2,150	$0		15%	$0
2,150—	5,000	322.50		25	2,150
5,000—	7,650	1,035.00		28	5,000
7,650—	10,450	1,777.00		33	7,650
10,450—	. . . . . .	2,701.00		35	10,450

2008

Taxable Income Over	But Not Over	Pay	+	% on Excess	of the amount over—
$0—	$2,200	$0		15%	$0
2,200—	5,150	330.00		25	2,200
5,150—	7,850	1,067.50		28	5,150
7,850—	10,700	1,823.50		33	7,850
10,700—	. . . . . .	2,764.00		35	10,700

¶ 20 2007 Tax Computation Worksheet

2007 Tax Computation Worksheet—Line 44

⚠️ CAUTION   *See the instructions for line 44 that begin on page 33 to see if you must use the worksheet below to figure your tax.*

Note. If you are required to use this worksheet to figure the tax on an amount from another form or worksheet, such as the Qualified Dividends and Capital Gain Tax Worksheet, the Schedule D Tax Worksheet, Schedule J, Form 8615, or the Foreign Earned Income Tax Worksheet, enter the amount from that form or worksheet in column (a) of the row that applies to the amount you are looking up. Enter the result on the appropriate line of the form or worksheet that you are completing.

Section A—Use if your filing status is **Single.** Complete the row below that applies to you.

Taxable income. If line 43 is—	(a) Enter the amount from line 43	(b) Multiplication amount	(c) Multiply (a) by (b)	(d) Subtraction amount	Tax. Subtract (d) from (c). Enter the result here and on Form 1040, line 44
At least $100,000 but not over $160,850	$	× 28% (.28)	$	$ 5,889.25	$
Over $160,850 but not over $349,700	$	× 33% (.33)	$	$ 13,931.75	$
Over $349,700	$	× 35% (.35)	$	$ 20,925.75	$

Section B—Use if your filing status is **Married filing jointly** or **Qualifying widow(er).** Complete the row below that applies to you.

Taxable income. If line 43 is—	(a) Enter the amount from line 43	(b) Multiplication amount	(c) Multiply (a) by (b)	(d) Subtraction amount	Tax. Subtract (d) from (c). Enter the result here and on Form 1040, line 44
At least $100,000 but not over $128,500	$	× 25% (.25)	$	$ 7,152.50	$
Over $128,500 but not over $195,850	$	× 28% (.28)	$	$ 11,007.50	$
Over $195,850 but not over $349,700	$	× 33% (.33)	$	$ 20,800.00	$
Over $349,700	$	× 35% (.35)	$	$ 27,794.00	$

Section C—Use if your filing status is **Married filing separately.** Complete the row below that applies to you.

Taxable income. If line 43 is—	(a) Enter the amount from line 43	(b) Multiplication amount	(c) Multiply (a) by (b)	(d) Subtraction amount	Tax. Subtract (d) from (c). Enter the result here and on Form 1040, line 44
At least $100,000 but not over $174,850	$	× 33% (.33)	$	$ 10,400.00	$
Over $174,850	$	× 35% (.35)	$	$ 13,897.00	$

Section D—Use if your filing status is **Head of household.** Complete the row below that applies to you.

Taxable income. If line 43 is—	(a) Enter the amount from line 43	(b) Multiplication amount	(c) Multiply (a) by (b)	(d) Subtraction amount	Tax. Subtract (d) from (c). Enter the result here and on Form 1040, line 44
At least $100,000 but not over $110,100	$	× 25% (.25)	$	$ 4,825.00	$
Over $110,100 but not over $178,350	$	× 28% (.28)	$	$ 8,128.00	$
Over $178,350 but not over $349,700	$	× 33% (.33)	$	$ 17,045.50	$
Over $349,700	$	× 35% (.35)	$	$ 24,039.50	$

¶20

¶ 21 Tax Rate Changes Beyond 2007

The Economic Growth and Tax Relief Reconciliation Act of 2001 (EGTRRA) (P.L. 107-16), implemented a staged decrease in the tax rates that began in 2001 and was accelerated by the Jobs and Growth Tax Relief Reconciliation Act of 2003 (JGTRRA) (P.L. 108-27). EGTRRA also added a 10% tax bracket for individuals and provided marriage penalty relief through expansion of the 15% tax bracket for joint filers which was also accelerated by JGTRRA. Here is how the tax rate brackets will evolve over the next few years.

10% bracket. The Working Families Tax Relief Act of 2004 (WFTRA) (P.L. 108-311) provided that the expanded 10-percent individual tax bracket applies through 2010 and will be adjusted for inflation. However, the expansion of the 10-percent tax bracket had no effect on head-of-household filers. Taxable income subject to the 10-percent bracket for heads of households remains $10,000. Also, it is important to note that the 10% bracket applies to individual rate schedules but not for the estate and trust rate schedule (¶ 19).

Thus, for 2007, the 10% tax bracket applies to single filers (including those married filing separately) on the first $7,825 of taxable income, and to joint filers on the first $15,650 of taxable income. For 2008, the 10-percent bracket will be applicable on the first $8,025 of taxable income for single filers (including those married filing separately) and on the first $16,050 of taxable income for married taxpayers filing joint returns.

Other brackets. EGTRRA and JGTRRA provided a rate reduction for all brackets, except the 10% and the 15% brackets, through 2010, as follows. Without further congressional action, the pre-2001 rates will return in 2011 as indicated.

Tax Years

2007—2010	27% rate reduced to	25%
	30% rate reduced to	28%
	35% rate reduced to	33%
	38.6% rate reduced to	35%
2011 and after	25% rate goes back up to	28%
	28% rate goes back up to	31%
	33% rate goes back up to	36%
	35% rate goes back up to	39.6%

Planning for change. With the reduced tax rates continuing through 2010, tax practitioners will need to keep aware of the effect on their clients' withholding (¶ 2601) and estimated taxes (¶ 2682). To review the rate schedules for 2007 and 2008, see ¶ 11-¶ 17. Also, with the reduced rates on capital gains (¶ 1736) and dividends (¶ 733) and the expansion of the kiddie tax by the Small Business and Work Opportunity Tax Act of 2007 (P.L. 110-28) (¶ 706), some investment decisions will need to be reconsidered as the potential tax impact on certain transactions lessens. Finally, as the income tax rates have declined, the alternative minimum tax (AMT) continues to play a larger role as "regular" tax liability amounts have decreased without a corresponding drop in AMT rates. Although future Congressional action may reduce the AMT impact by the increasing the AMT exemption amounts, for 2007, the AMT exemption amounts have reverted back to the amounts that applied in the 2000 tax year (¶ 1401 and ¶ 1405).

2007 TAX TABLE—INDIVIDUALS

¶ 25 2007 Tax Table for Use with Form 1040

   ☐ The Tax Table that follows is for use with Form 1040. A similar Tax Table applies to Forms 1040A and 1040EZ, except that the table for Form 1040A refers to taxable income on line 27, Form 1040A, and the table for Form 1040EZ refers to taxable income on line 6, Form 1040EZ.

   ☐ **Note:** The Tax Table reproduced in the *Guide* is for use with Form 1040 by taxpayers with taxable income of less than $100,000. Because Forms 1040A and 1040EZ cannot be filed by taxpayers with taxable incomes of $100,000 or more, tax tables for use with those forms end at taxable income of $100,000.

2007 TAX TABLE   Based on Taxable Income. For persons with
taxable incomes of less than $100,000.

Read down the income columns of the tax table until you find the line covering the taxable income shown on line 43 of Form 1040 (line 27 of Form 1040A or line 6 of Form 1040EZ). Then read across that income line until you find the column heading that describes your filing status. Enter the tax found there on line 44, Form 1040 (line 28, Form 1040A or line 10, Form 1040EZ).

2007 Tax Table

CAUTION See the instructions for line 44 that begin on page 33 to see if you must use the Tax Table below to figure your tax.

Example. Mr. and Mrs. Brown are filing a joint return. Their taxable income on Form 1040, line 43, is $25,300. First, they find the $25,300–25,350 taxable income line. Next, they find the column for married filing jointly and read down the column. The amount shown where the taxable income line and filing status column meet is $3,016. This is the tax amount they should enter on Form 1040, line 44.

Sample Table

At least	But less than	Single	Married filing jointly *	Married filing separately	Head of a household
			Your tax is—		
25,200	25,250	3,393	3,001	3,393	3,224
25,250	25,300	3,400	3,009	3,400	3,231
25,300	25,350	3,408	(3,016)	3,408	3,239
25,350	25,400	3,415	3,024	3,415	3,246

At least	But less than	Single	Married filing jointly *	Married filing separately	Head of a household
			Your tax is—		
0	5	0	0	0	0
5	15	1	1	1	1
15	25	2	2	2	2
25	50	4	4	4	4
50	75	6	6	6	6
75	100	9	9	9	9
100	125	11	11	11	11
125	150	14	14	14	14
150	175	16	16	16	16
175	200	19	19	19	19
200	225	21	21	21	21
225	250	24	24	24	24
250	275	26	26	26	26
275	300	29	29	29	29
300	325	31	31	31	31
325	350	34	34	34	34
350	375	36	36	36	36
375	400	39	39	39	39
400	425	41	41	41	41
425	450	44	44	44	44
450	475	46	46	46	46
475	500	49	49	49	49
500	525	51	51	51	51
525	550	54	54	54	54
550	575	56	56	56	56
575	600	59	59	59	59
600	625	61	61	61	61
625	650	64	64	64	64
650	675	66	66	66	66
675	700	69	69	69	69
700	725	71	71	71	71
725	750	74	74	74	74
750	775	76	76	76	76
775	800	79	79	79	79
800	825	81	81	81	81
825	850	84	84	84	84
850	875	86	86	86	86
875	900	89	89	89	89
900	925	91	91	91	91
925	950	94	94	94	94
950	975	96	96	96	96
975	1,000	99	99	99	99

1,000

At least	But less than	Single	Married filing jointly *	Married filing separately	Head of a household
1,000	1,025	101	101	101	101
1,025	1,050	104	104	104	104
1,050	1,075	106	106	106	106
1,075	1,100	109	109	109	109
1,100	1,125	111	111	111	111
1,125	1,150	114	114	114	114
1,150	1,175	116	116	116	116
1,175	1,200	119	119	119	119
1,200	1,225	121	121	121	121
1,225	1,250	124	124	124	124
1,250	1,275	126	126	126	126
1,275	1,300	129	129	129	129

At least	But less than	Single	Married filing jointly *	Married filing separately	Head of a household
			Your tax is—		
1,300	1,325	131	131	131	131
1,325	1,350	134	134	134	134
1,350	1,375	136	136	136	136
1,375	1,400	139	139	139	139
1,400	1,425	141	141	141	141
1,425	1,450	144	144	144	144
1,450	1,475	146	146	146	146
1,475	1,500	149	149	149	149
1,500	1,525	151	151	151	151
1,525	1,550	154	154	154	154
1,550	1,575	156	156	156	156
1,575	1,600	159	159	159	159
1,600	1,625	161	161	161	161
1,625	1,650	164	164	164	164
1,650	1,675	166	166	166	166
1,675	1,700	169	169	169	169
1,700	1,725	171	171	171	171
1,725	1,750	174	174	174	174
1,750	1,775	176	176	176	176
1,775	1,800	179	179	179	179
1,800	1,825	181	181	181	181
1,825	1,850	184	184	184	184
1,850	1,875	186	186	186	186
1,875	1,900	189	189	189	189
1,900	1,925	191	191	191	191
1,925	1,950	194	194	194	194
1,950	1,975	196	196	196	196
1,975	2,000	199	199	199	199

2,000

At least	But less than	Single	Married filing jointly *	Married filing separately	Head of a household
2,000	2,025	201	201	201	201
2,025	2,050	204	204	204	204
2,050	2,075	206	206	206	206
2,075	2,100	209	209	209	209
2,100	2,125	211	211	211	211
2,125	2,150	214	214	214	214
2,150	2,175	216	216	216	216
2,175	2,200	219	219	219	219
2,200	2,225	221	221	221	221
2,225	2,250	224	224	224	224
2,250	2,275	226	226	226	226
2,275	2,300	229	229	229	229
2,300	2,325	231	231	231	231
2,325	2,350	234	234	234	234
2,350	2,375	236	236	236	236
2,375	2,400	239	239	239	239
2,400	2,425	241	241	241	241
2,425	2,450	244	244	244	244
2,450	2,475	246	246	246	246
2,475	2,500	249	249	249	249
2,500	2,525	251	251	251	251
2,525	2,550	254	254	254	254
2,550	2,575	256	256	256	256
2,575	2,600	259	259	259	259
2,600	2,625	261	261	261	261
2,625	2,650	264	264	264	264
2,650	2,675	266	266	266	266
2,675	2,700	269	269	269	269

At least	But less than	Single	Married filing jointly *	Married filing separately	Head of a household
			Your tax is—		
2,700	2,725	271	271	271	271
2,725	2,750	274	274	274	274
2,750	2,775	276	276	276	276
2,775	2,800	279	279	279	279
2,800	2,825	281	281	281	281
2,825	2,850	284	284	284	284
2,850	2,875	286	286	286	286
2,875	2,900	289	289	289	289
2,900	2,925	291	291	291	291
2,925	2,950	294	294	294	294
2,950	2,975	296	296	296	296
2,975	3,000	299	299	299	299

3,000

At least	But less than	Single	Married filing jointly *	Married filing separately	Head of a household
3,000	3,050	303	303	303	303
3,050	3,100	308	308	308	308
3,100	3,150	313	313	313	313
3,150	3,200	318	318	318	318
3,200	3,250	323	323	323	323
3,250	3,300	328	328	328	328
3,300	3,350	333	333	333	333
3,350	3,400	338	338	338	338
3,400	3,450	343	343	343	343
3,450	3,500	348	348	348	348
3,500	3,550	353	353	353	353
3,550	3,600	358	358	358	358
3,600	3,650	363	363	363	363
3,650	3,700	368	368	368	368
3,700	3,750	373	373	373	373
3,750	3,800	378	378	378	378
3,800	3,850	383	383	383	383
3,850	3,900	388	388	388	388
3,900	3,950	393	393	393	393
3,950	4,000	398	398	398	398

4,000

At least	But less than	Single	Married filing jointly *	Married filing separately	Head of a household
4,000	4,050	403	403	403	403
4,050	4,100	408	408	408	408
4,100	4,150	413	413	413	413
4,150	4,200	418	418	418	418
4,200	4,250	423	423	423	423
4,250	4,300	428	428	428	428
4,300	4,350	433	433	433	433
4,350	4,400	438	438	438	438
4,400	4,450	443	443	443	443
4,450	4,500	448	448	448	448
4,500	4,550	453	453	453	453
4,550	4,600	458	458	458	458
4,600	4,650	463	463	463	463
4,650	4,700	468	468	468	468
4,700	4,750	473	473	473	473
4,750	4,800	478	478	478	478
4,800	4,850	483	483	483	483
4,850	4,900	488	488	488	488
4,900	4,950	493	493	493	493
4,950	5,000	498	498	498	498

* This column must also be used by a qualifying widow(er).

(Continued on page 64)

¶25

2007 Tax Table—*Continued*

If line 43 (taxable income) is— At least	But less than	Single	Married filing jointly *	Married filing separately	Head of a household
5,000					
5,000	5,050	503	503	503	503
5,050	5,100	508	508	508	508
5,100	5,150	513	513	513	513
5,150	5,200	518	518	518	518
5,200	5,250	523	523	523	523
5,250	5,300	528	528	528	528
5,300	5,350	533	533	533	533
5,350	5,400	538	538	538	538
5,400	5,450	543	543	543	543
5,450	5,500	548	548	548	548
5,500	5,550	553	553	553	553
5,550	5,600	558	558	558	558
5,600	5,650	563	563	563	563
5,650	5,700	568	568	568	568
5,700	5,750	573	573	573	573
5,750	5,800	578	578	578	578
5,800	5,850	583	583	583	583
5,850	5,900	588	588	588	588
5,900	5,950	593	593	593	593
5,950	6,000	598	598	598	598
6,000					
6,000	6,050	603	603	603	603
6,050	6,100	608	608	608	608
6,100	6,150	613	613	613	613
6,150	6,200	618	618	618	618
6,200	6,250	623	623	623	623
6,250	6,300	628	628	628	628
6,300	6,350	633	633	633	633
6,350	6,400	638	638	638	638
6,400	6,450	643	643	643	643
6,450	6,500	648	648	648	648
6,500	6,550	653	653	653	653
6,550	6,600	658	658	658	658
6,600	6,650	663	663	663	663
6,650	6,700	668	668	668	668
6,700	6,750	673	673	673	673
6,750	6,800	678	678	678	678
6,800	6,850	683	683	683	683
6,850	6,900	688	688	688	688
6,900	6,950	693	693	693	693
6,950	7,000	698	698	698	698
7,000					
7,000	7,050	703	703	703	703
7,050	7,100	708	708	708	708
7,100	7,150	713	713	713	713
7,150	7,200	718	718	718	718
7,200	7,250	723	723	723	723
7,250	7,300	728	728	728	728
7,300	7,350	733	733	733	733
7,350	7,400	738	738	738	738
7,400	7,450	743	743	743	743
7,450	7,500	748	748	748	748
7,500	7,550	753	753	753	753
7,550	7,600	758	758	758	758
7,600	7,650	763	763	763	763
7,650	7,700	768	768	768	768
7,700	7,750	773	773	773	773
7,750	7,800	778	778	778	778
7,800	7,850	783	783	783	783
7,850	7,900	790	788	788	788
7,900	7,950	798	793	798	793
7,950	8,000	805	798	805	798

If line 43 (taxable income) is— At least	But less than	Single	Married filing jointly *	Married filing separately	Head of a household
8,000					
8,000	8,050	813	803	813	803
8,050	8,100	820	808	820	808
8,100	8,150	828	813	828	813
8,150	8,200	835	818	835	818
8,200	8,250	843	823	843	823
8,250	8,300	850	828	850	828
8,300	8,350	858	833	858	833
8,350	8,400	865	838	865	838
8,400	8,450	873	843	873	843
8,450	8,500	880	848	880	848
8,500	8,550	888	853	888	853
8,550	8,600	895	858	895	858
8,600	8,650	903	863	903	863
8,650	8,700	910	868	910	868
8,700	8,750	918	873	918	873
8,750	8,800	925	878	925	878
8,800	8,850	933	883	933	883
8,850	8,900	940	888	940	888
8,900	8,950	948	893	948	893
8,950	9,000	955	898	955	898
9,000					
9,000	9,050	963	903	963	903
9,050	9,100	970	908	970	908
9,100	9,150	978	913	978	913
9,150	9,200	985	918	985	918
9,200	9,250	993	923	993	923
9,250	9,300	1,000	928	1,000	928
9,300	9,350	1,008	933	1,008	933
9,350	9,400	1,015	938	1,015	938
9,400	9,450	1,023	943	1,023	943
9,450	9,500	1,030	948	1,030	948
9,500	9,550	1,038	953	1,038	953
9,550	9,600	1,045	958	1,045	958
9,600	9,650	1,053	963	1,053	963
9,650	9,700	1,060	968	1,060	968
9,700	9,750	1,068	973	1,068	973
9,750	9,800	1,075	978	1,075	978
9,800	9,850	1,083	983	1,083	983
9,850	9,900	1,090	988	1,090	988
9,900	9,950	1,098	993	1,098	993
9,950	10,000	1,105	998	1,105	998
10,000					
10,000	10,050	1,113	1,003	1,113	1,003
10,050	10,100	1,120	1,008	1,120	1,008
10,100	10,150	1,128	1,013	1,128	1,013
10,150	10,200	1,135	1,018	1,135	1,018
10,200	10,250	1,143	1,023	1,143	1,023
10,250	10,300	1,150	1,028	1,150	1,028
10,300	10,350	1,158	1,033	1,158	1,033
10,350	10,400	1,165	1,038	1,165	1,038
10,400	10,450	1,173	1,043	1,173	1,043
10,450	10,500	1,180	1,048	1,180	1,048
10,500	10,550	1,188	1,053	1,188	1,053
10,550	10,600	1,195	1,058	1,195	1,058
10,600	10,650	1,203	1,063	1,203	1,063
10,650	10,700	1,210	1,068	1,210	1,068
10,700	10,750	1,218	1,073	1,218	1,073
10,750	10,800	1,225	1,078	1,225	1,078
10,800	10,850	1,233	1,083	1,233	1,083
10,850	10,900	1,240	1,088	1,240	1,088
10,900	10,950	1,248	1,093	1,248	1,093
10,950	11,000	1,255	1,098	1,255	1,098

If line 43 (taxable income) is— At least	But less than	Single	Married filing jointly *	Married filing separately	Head of a household
11,000					
11,000	11,050	1,263	1,103	1,263	1,103
11,050	11,100	1,270	1,108	1,270	1,108
11,100	11,150	1,278	1,113	1,278	1,113
11,150	11,200	1,285	1,118	1,285	1,118
11,200	11,250	1,293	1,123	1,293	1,124
11,250	11,300	1,300	1,128	1,300	1,131
11,300	11,350	1,308	1,133	1,308	1,139
11,350	11,400	1,315	1,138	1,315	1,146
11,400	11,450	1,323	1,143	1,323	1,154
11,450	11,500	1,330	1,148	1,330	1,161
11,500	11,550	1,338	1,153	1,338	1,169
11,550	11,600	1,345	1,158	1,345	1,176
11,600	11,650	1,353	1,163	1,353	1,184
11,650	11,700	1,360	1,168	1,360	1,191
11,700	11,750	1,368	1,173	1,368	1,199
11,750	11,800	1,375	1,178	1,375	1,206
11,800	11,850	1,383	1,183	1,383	1,214
11,850	11,900	1,390	1,188	1,390	1,221
11,900	11,950	1,398	1,193	1,398	1,229
11,950	12,000	1,405	1,198	1,405	1,236
12,000					
12,000	12,050	1,413	1,203	1,413	1,244
12,050	12,100	1,420	1,208	1,420	1,251
12,100	12,150	1,428	1,213	1,428	1,259
12,150	12,200	1,435	1,218	1,435	1,266
12,200	12,250	1,443	1,223	1,443	1,274
12,250	12,300	1,450	1,228	1,450	1,281
12,300	12,350	1,458	1,233	1,458	1,289
12,350	12,400	1,465	1,238	1,465	1,296
12,400	12,450	1,473	1,243	1,473	1,304
12,450	12,500	1,480	1,248	1,480	1,311
12,500	12,550	1,488	1,253	1,488	1,319
12,550	12,600	1,495	1,258	1,495	1,326
12,600	12,650	1,503	1,263	1,503	1,334
12,650	12,700	1,510	1,268	1,510	1,341
12,700	12,750	1,518	1,273	1,518	1,349
12,750	12,800	1,525	1,278	1,525	1,356
12,800	12,850	1,533	1,283	1,533	1,364
12,850	12,900	1,540	1,288	1,540	1,371
12,900	12,950	1,548	1,293	1,548	1,379
12,950	13,000	1,555	1,298	1,555	1,386
13,000					
13,000	13,050	1,563	1,303	1,563	1,394
13,050	13,100	1,570	1,308	1,570	1,401
13,100	13,150	1,578	1,313	1,578	1,409
13,150	13,200	1,585	1,318	1,585	1,416
13,200	13,250	1,593	1,323	1,593	1,424
13,250	13,300	1,600	1,328	1,600	1,431
13,300	13,350	1,608	1,333	1,608	1,439
13,350	13,400	1,615	1,338	1,615	1,446
13,400	13,450	1,623	1,343	1,623	1,454
13,450	13,500	1,630	1,348	1,630	1,461
13,500	13,550	1,638	1,353	1,638	1,469
13,550	13,600	1,645	1,358	1,645	1,476
13,600	13,650	1,653	1,363	1,653	1,484
13,650	13,700	1,660	1,368	1,660	1,491
13,700	13,750	1,668	1,373	1,668	1,499
13,750	13,800	1,675	1,378	1,675	1,506
13,800	13,850	1,683	1,383	1,683	1,514
13,850	13,900	1,690	1,388	1,690	1,521
13,900	13,950	1,698	1,393	1,698	1,529
13,950	14,000	1,705	1,398	1,705	1,536

* This column must also be used by a qualifying widow(er).

(Continued on page 65)

¶25

2007 Tax Table–Continued

If line 43 (taxable income) is—		And you are—			
At least	But less than	Single	Married filing jointly *	Married filing separately	Head of a household
		Your tax is—			
14,000					
14,000	14,050	1,713	1,403	1,713	1,544
14,050	14,100	1,720	1,408	1,720	1,551
14,100	14,150	1,728	1,413	1,728	1,559
14,150	14,200	1,735	1,418	1,735	1,566
14,200	14,250	1,743	1,423	1,743	1,574
14,250	14,300	1,750	1,428	1,750	1,581
14,300	14,350	1,758	1,433	1,758	1,589
14,350	14,400	1,765	1,438	1,765	1,596
14,400	14,450	1,773	1,443	1,773	1,604
14,450	14,500	1,780	1,448	1,780	1,611
14,500	14,550	1,788	1,453	1,788	1,619
14,550	14,600	1,795	1,458	1,795	1,626
14,600	14,650	1,803	1,463	1,803	1,634
14,650	14,700	1,810	1,468	1,810	1,641
14,700	14,750	1,818	1,473	1,818	1,649
14,750	14,800	1,825	1,478	1,825	1,656
14,800	14,850	1,833	1,483	1,833	1,664
14,850	14,900	1,840	1,488	1,840	1,671
14,900	14,950	1,848	1,493	1,848	1,679
14,950	15,000	1,855	1,498	1,855	1,686
15,000					
15,000	15,050	1,863	1,503	1,863	1,694
15,050	15,100	1,870	1,508	1,870	1,701
15,100	15,150	1,878	1,513	1,878	1,709
15,150	15,200	1,885	1,518	1,885	1,716
15,200	15,250	1,893	1,523	1,893	1,724
15,250	15,300	1,900	1,528	1,900	1,731
15,300	15,350	1,908	1,533	1,908	1,739
15,350	15,400	1,915	1,538	1,915	1,746
15,400	15,450	1,923	1,543	1,923	1,754
15,450	15,500	1,930	1,548	1,930	1,761
15,500	15,550	1,938	1,553	1,938	1,769
15,550	15,600	1,945	1,558	1,945	1,776
15,600	15,650	1,953	1,563	1,953	1,784
15,650	15,700	1,960	1,569	1,960	1,791
15,700	15,750	1,968	1,576	1,968	1,799
15,750	15,800	1,975	1,584	1,975	1,806
15,800	15,850	1,983	1,591	1,983	1,814
15,850	15,900	1,990	1,599	1,990	1,821
15,900	15,950	1,998	1,606	1,998	1,829
15,950	16,000	2,005	1,614	2,005	1,836
16,000					
16,000	16,050	2,013	1,621	2,013	1,844
16,050	16,100	2,020	1,629	2,020	1,851
16,100	16,150	2,028	1,636	2,028	1,859
16,150	16,200	2,035	1,644	2,035	1,866
16,200	16,250	2,043	1,651	2,043	1,874
16,250	16,300	2,050	1,659	2,050	1,881
16,300	16,350	2,058	1,666	2,058	1,889
16,350	16,400	2,065	1,674	2,065	1,896
16,400	16,450	2,073	1,681	2,073	1,904
16,450	16,500	2,080	1,689	2,080	1,911
16,500	16,550	2,088	1,696	2,088	1,919
16,550	16,600	2,095	1,704	2,095	1,926
16,600	16,650	2,103	1,711	2,103	1,934
16,650	16,700	2,110	1,719	2,110	1,941
16,700	16,750	2,118	1,726	2,118	1,949
16,750	16,800	2,125	1,734	2,125	1,956
16,800	16,850	2,133	1,741	2,133	1,964
16,850	16,900	2,140	1,749	2,140	1,971
16,900	16,950	2,148	1,756	2,148	1,979
16,950	17,000	2,155	1,764	2,155	1,986

If line 43 (taxable income) is—		And you are—			
At least	But less than	Single	Married filing jointly *	Married filing separately	Head of a household
		Your tax is—			
17,000					
17,000	17,050	2,163	1,771	2,163	1,994
17,050	17,100	2,170	1,779	2,170	2,001
17,100	17,150	2,178	1,786	2,178	2,009
17,150	17,200	2,185	1,794	2,185	2,016
17,200	17,250	2,193	1,801	2,193	2,024
17,250	17,300	2,200	1,809	2,200	2,031
17,300	17,350	2,208	1,816	2,208	2,039
17,350	17,400	2,215	1,824	2,215	2,046
17,400	17,450	2,223	1,831	2,223	2,054
17,450	17,500	2,230	1,839	2,230	2,061
17,500	17,550	2,238	1,846	2,238	2,069
17,550	17,600	2,245	1,854	2,245	2,076
17,600	17,650	2,253	1,861	2,253	2,084
17,650	17,700	2,260	1,869	2,260	2,091
17,700	17,750	2,268	1,876	2,268	2,099
17,750	17,800	2,275	1,884	2,275	2,106
17,800	17,850	2,283	1,891	2,283	2,114
17,850	17,900	2,290	1,899	2,290	2,121
17,900	17,950	2,298	1,906	2,298	2,129
17,950	18,000	2,305	1,914	2,305	2,136
18,000					
18,000	18,050	2,313	1,921	2,313	2,144
18,050	18,100	2,320	1,929	2,320	2,151
18,100	18,150	2,328	1,936	2,328	2,159
18,150	18,200	2,335	1,944	2,335	2,166
18,200	18,250	2,343	1,951	2,343	2,174
18,250	18,300	2,350	1,959	2,350	2,181
18,300	18,350	2,358	1,966	2,358	2,189
18,350	18,400	2,365	1,974	2,365	2,196
18,400	18,450	2,373	1,981	2,373	2,204
18,450	18,500	2,380	1,989	2,380	2,211
18,500	18,550	2,388	1,996	2,388	2,219
18,550	18,600	2,395	2,004	2,395	2,226
18,600	18,650	2,403	2,011	2,403	2,234
18,650	18,700	2,410	2,019	2,410	2,241
18,700	18,750	2,418	2,026	2,418	2,249
18,750	18,800	2,425	2,034	2,425	2,256
18,800	18,850	2,433	2,041	2,433	2,264
18,850	18,900	2,440	2,049	2,440	2,271
18,900	18,950	2,448	2,056	2,448	2,279
18,950	19,000	2,455	2,064	2,455	2,286
19,000					
19,000	19,050	2,463	2,071	2,463	2,294
19,050	19,100	2,470	2,079	2,470	2,301
19,100	19,150	2,478	2,086	2,478	2,309
19,150	19,200	2,485	2,094	2,485	2,316
19,200	19,250	2,493	2,101	2,493	2,324
19,250	19,300	2,500	2,109	2,500	2,331
19,300	19,350	2,508	2,116	2,508	2,339
19,350	19,400	2,515	2,124	2,515	2,346
19,400	19,450	2,523	2,131	2,523	2,354
19,450	19,500	2,530	2,139	2,530	2,361
19,500	19,550	2,538	2,146	2,538	2,369
19,550	19,600	2,545	2,154	2,545	2,376
19,600	19,650	2,553	2,161	2,553	2,384
19,650	19,700	2,560	2,169	2,560	2,391
19,700	19,750	2,568	2,176	2,568	2,399
19,750	19,800	2,575	2,184	2,575	2,406
19,800	19,850	2,583	2,191	2,583	2,414
19,850	19,900	2,590	2,199	2,590	2,421
19,900	19,950	2,598	2,206	2,598	2,429
19,950	20,000	2,605	2,214	2,605	2,436

If line 43 (taxable income) is—		And you are—			
At least	But less than	Single	Married filing jointly *	Married filing separately	Head of a household
		Your tax is—			
20,000					
20,000	20,050	2,613	2,221	2,613	2,444
20,050	20,100	2,620	2,229	2,620	2,451
20,100	20,150	2,628	2,236	2,628	2,459
20,150	20,200	2,635	2,244	2,635	2,466
20,200	20,250	2,643	2,251	2,643	2,474
20,250	20,300	2,650	2,259	2,650	2,481
20,300	20,350	2,658	2,266	2,658	2,489
20,350	20,400	2,665	2,274	2,665	2,496
20,400	20,450	2,673	2,281	2,673	2,504
20,450	20,500	2,680	2,289	2,680	2,511
20,500	20,550	2,688	2,296	2,688	2,519
20,550	20,600	2,695	2,304	2,695	2,526
20,600	20,650	2,703	2,311	2,703	2,534
20,650	20,700	2,710	2,319	2,710	2,541
20,700	20,750	2,718	2,326	2,718	2,549
20,750	20,800	2,725	2,334	2,725	2,556
20,800	20,850	2,733	2,341	2,733	2,564
20,850	20,900	2,740	2,349	2,740	2,571
20,900	20,950	2,748	2,356	2,748	2,579
20,950	21,000	2,755	2,364	2,755	2,586
21,000					
21,000	21,050	2,763	2,371	2,763	2,594
21,050	21,100	2,770	2,379	2,770	2,601
21,100	21,150	2,778	2,386	2,778	2,609
21,150	21,200	2,785	2,394	2,785	2,616
21,200	21,250	2,793	2,401	2,793	2,624
21,250	21,300	2,800	2,409	2,800	2,631
21,300	21,350	2,808	2,416	2,808	2,639
21,350	21,400	2,815	2,424	2,815	2,646
21,400	21,450	2,823	2,431	2,823	2,654
21,450	21,500	2,830	2,439	2,830	2,661
21,500	21,550	2,838	2,446	2,838	2,669
21,550	21,600	2,845	2,454	2,845	2,676
21,600	21,650	2,853	2,461	2,853	2,684
21,650	21,700	2,860	2,469	2,860	2,691
21,700	21,750	2,868	2,476	2,868	2,699
21,750	21,800	2,875	2,484	2,875	2,706
21,800	21,850	2,883	2,491	2,883	2,714
21,850	21,900	2,890	2,499	2,890	2,721
21,900	21,950	2,898	2,506	2,898	2,729
21,950	22,000	2,905	2,514	2,905	2,736
22,000					
22,000	22,050	2,913	2,521	2,913	2,744
22,050	22,100	2,920	2,529	2,920	2,751
22,100	22,150	2,928	2,536	2,928	2,759
22,150	22,200	2,935	2,544	2,935	2,766
22,200	22,250	2,943	2,551	2,943	2,774
22,250	22,300	2,950	2,559	2,950	2,781
22,300	22,350	2,958	2,566	2,958	2,789
22,350	22,400	2,965	2,574	2,965	2,796
22,400	22,450	2,973	2,581	2,973	2,804
22,450	22,500	2,980	2,589	2,980	2,811
22,500	22,550	2,988	2,596	2,988	2,819
22,550	22,600	2,995	2,604	2,995	2,826
22,600	22,650	3,003	2,611	3,003	2,834
22,650	22,700	3,010	2,619	3,010	2,841
22,700	22,750	3,018	2,626	3,018	2,849
22,750	22,800	3,025	2,634	3,025	2,856
22,800	22,850	3,033	2,641	3,033	2,864
22,850	22,900	3,040	2,649	3,040	2,871
22,900	22,950	3,048	2,656	3,048	2,879
22,950	23,000	3,055	2,664	3,055	2,886

* This column must also be used by a qualifying widow(er).

(Continued on page 66)

¶125

2007 Tax Table—Continued

If line 43 (taxable income) is—		And you are—			
At least	But less than	Single	Married filing jointly*	Married filing separately	Head of a household
		Your tax is—			
23,000					
23,000	23,050	3,063	2,671	3,063	2,894
23,050	23,100	3,070	2,679	3,070	2,901
23,100	23,150	3,078	2,686	3,078	2,909
23,150	23,200	3,085	2,694	3,085	2,916
23,200	23,250	3,093	2,701	3,093	2,924
23,250	23,300	3,100	2,709	3,100	2,931
23,300	23,350	3,108	2,716	3,108	2,939
23,350	23,400	3,115	2,724	3,115	2,946
23,400	23,450	3,123	2,731	3,123	2,954
23,450	23,500	3,130	2,739	3,130	2,961
23,500	23,550	3,138	2,746	3,138	2,969
23,550	23,600	3,145	2,754	3,145	2,976
23,600	23,650	3,153	2,761	3,153	2,984
23,650	23,700	3,160	2,769	3,160	2,991
23,700	23,750	3,168	2,776	3,168	2,999
23,750	23,800	3,175	2,784	3,175	3,006
23,800	23,850	3,183	2,791	3,183	3,014
23,850	23,900	3,190	2,799	3,190	3,021
23,900	23,950	3,198	2,806	3,198	3,029
23,950	24,000	3,205	2,814	3,205	3,036
24,000					
24,000	24,050	3,213	2,821	3,213	3,044
24,050	24,100	3,220	2,829	3,220	3,051
24,100	24,150	3,228	2,836	3,228	3,059
24,150	24,200	3,235	2,844	3,235	3,066
24,200	24,250	3,243	2,851	3,243	3,074
24,250	24,300	3,250	2,859	3,250	3,081
24,300	24,350	3,258	2,866	3,258	3,089
24,350	24,400	3,265	2,874	3,265	3,096
24,400	24,450	3,273	2,881	3,273	3,104
24,450	24,500	3,280	2,889	3,280	3,111
24,500	24,550	3,288	2,896	3,288	3,119
24,550	24,600	3,295	2,904	3,295	3,126
24,600	24,650	3,303	2,911	3,303	3,134
24,650	24,700	3,310	2,919	3,310	3,141
24,700	24,750	3,318	2,926	3,318	3,149
24,750	24,800	3,325	2,934	3,325	3,156
24,800	24,850	3,333	2,941	3,333	3,164
24,850	24,900	3,340	2,949	3,340	3,171
24,900	24,950	3,348	2,956	3,348	3,179
24,950	25,000	3,355	2,964	3,355	3,186
25,000					
25,000	25,050	3,363	2,971	3,363	3,194
25,050	25,100	3,370	2,979	3,370	3,201
25,100	25,150	3,378	2,986	3,378	3,209
25,150	25,200	3,385	2,994	3,385	3,216
25,200	25,250	3,393	3,001	3,393	3,224
25,250	25,300	3,400	3,009	3,400	3,231
25,300	25,350	3,408	3,016	3,408	3,239
25,350	25,400	3,415	3,024	3,415	3,246
25,400	25,450	3,423	3,031	3,423	3,254
25,450	25,500	3,430	3,039	3,430	3,261
25,500	25,550	3,438	3,046	3,438	3,269
25,550	25,600	3,445	3,054	3,445	3,276
25,600	25,650	3,453	3,061	3,453	3,284
25,650	25,700	3,460	3,069	3,460	3,291
25,700	25,750	3,468	3,076	3,468	3,299
25,750	25,800	3,475	3,084	3,475	3,306
25,800	25,850	3,483	3,091	3,483	3,314
25,850	25,900	3,490	3,099	3,490	3,321
25,900	25,950	3,498	3,106	3,498	3,329
25,950	26,000	3,505	3,114	3,505	3,336

If line 43 (taxable income) is—		And you are—			
At least	But less than	Single	Married filing jointly*	Married filing separately	Head of a household
		Your tax is—			
26,000					
26,000	26,050	3,513	3,121	3,513	3,344
26,050	26,100	3,520	3,129	3,520	3,351
26,100	26,150	3,528	3,136	3,528	3,359
26,150	26,200	3,535	3,144	3,535	3,366
26,200	26,250	3,543	3,151	3,543	3,374
26,250	26,300	3,550	3,159	3,550	3,381
26,300	26,350	3,558	3,166	3,558	3,389
26,350	26,400	3,565	3,174	3,565	3,396
26,400	26,450	3,573	3,181	3,573	3,404
26,450	26,500	3,580	3,189	3,580	3,411
26,500	26,550	3,588	3,196	3,588	3,419
26,550	26,600	3,595	3,204	3,595	3,426
26,600	26,650	3,603	3,211	3,603	3,434
26,650	26,700	3,610	3,219	3,610	3,441
26,700	26,750	3,618	3,226	3,618	3,449
26,750	26,800	3,625	3,234	3,625	3,456
26,800	26,850	3,633	3,241	3,633	3,464
26,850	26,900	3,640	3,249	3,640	3,471
26,900	26,950	3,648	3,256	3,648	3,479
26,950	27,000	3,655	3,264	3,655	3,486
27,000					
27,000	27,050	3,663	3,271	3,663	3,494
27,050	27,100	3,670	3,279	3,670	3,501
27,100	27,150	3,678	3,286	3,678	3,509
27,150	27,200	3,685	3,294	3,685	3,516
27,200	27,250	3,693	3,301	3,693	3,524
27,250	27,300	3,700	3,309	3,700	3,531
27,300	27,350	3,708	3,316	3,708	3,539
27,350	27,400	3,715	3,324	3,715	3,546
27,400	27,450	3,723	3,331	3,723	3,554
27,450	27,500	3,730	3,339	3,730	3,561
27,500	27,550	3,738	3,346	3,738	3,569
27,550	27,600	3,745	3,354	3,745	3,576
27,600	27,650	3,753	3,361	3,753	3,584
27,650	27,700	3,760	3,369	3,760	3,591
27,700	27,750	3,768	3,376	3,768	3,599
27,750	27,800	3,775	3,384	3,775	3,606
27,800	27,850	3,783	3,391	3,783	3,614
27,850	27,900	3,790	3,399	3,790	3,621
27,900	27,950	3,798	3,406	3,798	3,629
27,950	28,000	3,805	3,414	3,805	3,636
28,000					
28,000	28,050	3,813	3,421	3,813	3,644
28,050	28,100	3,820	3,429	3,820	3,651
28,100	28,150	3,828	3,436	3,828	3,659
28,150	28,200	3,835	3,444	3,835	3,666
28,200	28,250	3,843	3,451	3,843	3,674
28,250	28,300	3,850	3,459	3,850	3,681
28,300	28,350	3,858	3,466	3,858	3,689
28,350	28,400	3,865	3,474	3,865	3,696
28,400	28,450	3,873	3,481	3,873	3,704
28,450	28,500	3,880	3,489	3,880	3,711
28,500	28,550	3,888	3,496	3,888	3,719
28,550	28,600	3,895	3,504	3,895	3,726
28,600	28,650	3,903	3,511	3,903	3,734
28,650	28,700	3,910	3,519	3,910	3,741
28,700	28,750	3,918	3,526	3,918	3,749
28,750	28,800	3,925	3,534	3,925	3,756
28,800	28,850	3,933	3,541	3,933	3,764
28,850	28,900	3,940	3,549	3,940	3,771
28,900	28,950	3,948	3,556	3,948	3,779
28,950	29,000	3,955	3,564	3,955	3,786

If line 43 (taxable income) is—		And you are—			
At least	But less than	Single	Married filing jointly*	Married filing separately	Head of a household
		Your tax is—			
29,000					
29,000	29,050	3,963	3,571	3,963	3,794
29,050	29,100	3,970	3,579	3,970	3,801
29,100	29,150	3,978	3,586	3,978	3,809
29,150	29,200	3,985	3,594	3,985	3,816
29,200	29,250	3,993	3,601	3,993	3,824
29,250	29,300	4,000	3,609	4,000	3,831
29,300	29,350	4,008	3,616	4,008	3,839
29,350	29,400	4,015	3,624	4,015	3,846
29,400	29,450	4,023	3,631	4,023	3,854
29,450	29,500	4,030	3,639	4,030	3,861
29,500	29,550	4,038	3,646	4,038	3,869
29,550	29,600	4,045	3,654	4,045	3,876
29,600	29,650	4,053	3,661	4,053	3,884
29,650	29,700	4,060	3,669	4,060	3,891
29,700	29,750	4,068	3,676	4,068	3,899
29,750	29,800	4,075	3,684	4,075	3,906
29,800	29,850	4,083	3,691	4,083	3,914
29,850	29,900	4,090	3,699	4,090	3,921
29,900	29,950	4,098	3,706	4,098	3,929
29,950	30,000	4,105	3,714	4,105	3,936
30,000					
30,000	30,050	4,113	3,721	4,113	3,944
30,050	30,100	4,120	3,729	4,120	3,951
30,100	30,150	4,128	3,736	4,128	3,959
30,150	30,200	4,135	3,744	4,135	3,966
30,200	30,250	4,143	3,751	4,143	3,974
30,250	30,300	4,150	3,759	4,150	3,981
30,300	30,350	4,158	3,766	4,158	3,989
30,350	30,400	4,165	3,774	4,165	3,996
30,400	30,450	4,173	3,781	4,173	4,004
30,450	30,500	4,180	3,789	4,180	4,011
30,500	30,550	4,188	3,796	4,188	4,019
30,550	30,600	4,195	3,804	4,195	4,026
30,600	30,650	4,203	3,811	4,203	4,034
30,650	30,700	4,210	3,819	4,210	4,041
30,700	30,750	4,218	3,826	4,218	4,049
30,750	30,800	4,225	3,834	4,225	4,056
30,800	30,850	4,233	3,841	4,233	4,064
30,850	30,900	4,240	3,849	4,240	4,071
30,900	30,950	4,248	3,856	4,248	4,079
30,950	31,000	4,255	3,864	4,255	4,086
31,000					
31,000	31,050	4,263	3,871	4,263	4,094
31,050	31,100	4,270	3,879	4,270	4,101
31,100	31,150	4,278	3,886	4,278	4,109
31,150	31,200	4,285	3,894	4,285	4,116
31,200	31,250	4,293	3,901	4,293	4,124
31,250	31,300	4,300	3,909	4,300	4,131
31,300	31,350	4,308	3,916	4,308	4,139
31,350	31,400	4,315	3,924	4,315	4,146
31,400	31,450	4,323	3,931	4,323	4,154
31,450	31,500	4,330	3,939	4,330	4,161
31,500	31,550	4,338	3,946	4,338	4,169
31,550	31,600	4,345	3,954	4,345	4,176
31,600	31,650	4,353	3,961	4,353	4,184
31,650	31,700	4,360	3,969	4,360	4,191
31,700	31,750	4,368	3,976	4,368	4,199
31,750	31,800	4,375	3,984	4,375	4,206
31,800	31,850	4,383	3,991	4,383	4,214
31,850	31,900	4,393	3,999	4,393	4,221
31,900	31,950	4,405	4,006	4,405	4,229
31,950	32,000	4,418	4,014	4,418	4,236

* This column must also be used by a qualifying widow(er).

(Continued on page 67)

¶25

2007 Tax Table—*Continued*

If line 43 (taxable income) is— At least	But less than	And you are— Single	Married filing jointly *	Married filing sepa-rately	Head of a house-hold
		Your tax is—			
32,000					
32,000	**32,050**	4,430	4,021	4,430	4,244
32,050	**32,100**	4,443	4,029	4,443	4,251
32,100	**32,150**	4,455	4,036	4,455	4,259
32,150	**32,200**	4,468	4,044	4,468	4,266
32,200	**32,250**	4,480	4,051	4,480	4,274
32,250	**32,300**	4,493	4,059	4,493	4,281
32,300	**32,350**	4,505	4,066	4,505	4,289
32,350	**32,400**	4,518	4,074	4,518	4,296
32,400	**32,450**	4,530	4,081	4,530	4,304
32,450	**32,500**	4,543	4,089	4,543	4,311
32,500	**32,550**	4,555	4,096	4,555	4,319
32,550	**32,600**	4,568	4,104	4,568	4,326
32,600	**32,650**	4,580	4,111	4,580	4,334
32,650	**32,700**	4,593	4,119	4,593	4,341
32,700	**32,750**	4,605	4,126	4,605	4,349
32,750	**32,800**	4,618	4,134	4,618	4,356
32,800	**32,850**	4,630	4,141	4,630	4,364
32,850	**32,900**	4,643	4,149	4,643	4,371
32,900	**32,950**	4,655	4,156	4,655	4,379
32,950	**33,000**	4,668	4,164	4,668	4,386
33,000					
33,000	**33,050**	4,680	4,171	4,680	4,394
33,050	**33,100**	4,693	4,179	4,693	4,401
33,100	**33,150**	4,705	4,186	4,705	4,409
33,150	**33,200**	4,718	4,194	4,718	4,416
33,200	**33,250**	4,730	4,201	4,730	4,424
33,250	**33,300**	4,743	4,209	4,743	4,431
33,300	**33,350**	4,755	4,216	4,755	4,439
33,350	**33,400**	4,768	4,224	4,768	4,446
33,400	**33,450**	4,780	4,231	4,780	4,454
33,450	**33,500**	4,793	4,239	4,793	4,461
33,500	**33,550**	4,805	4,246	4,805	4,469
33,550	**33,600**	4,818	4,254	4,818	4,476
33,600	**33,650**	4,830	4,261	4,830	4,484
33,650	**33,700**	4,843	4,269	4,843	4,491
33,700	**33,750**	4,855	4,276	4,855	4,499
33,750	**33,800**	4,868	4,284	4,868	4,506
33,800	**33,850**	4,880	4,291	4,880	4,514
33,850	**33,900**	4,893	4,299	4,893	4,521
33,900	**33,950**	4,905	4,306	4,905	4,529
33,950	**34,000**	4,918	4,314	4,918	4,536
34,000					
34,000	**34,050**	4,930	4,321	4,930	4,544
34,050	**34,100**	4,943	4,329	4,943	4,551
34,100	**34,150**	4,955	4,336	4,955	4,559
34,150	**34,200**	4,968	4,344	4,968	4,566
34,200	**34,250**	4,980	4,351	4,980	4,574
34,250	**34,300**	4,993	4,359	4,993	4,581
34,300	**34,350**	5,005	4,366	5,005	4,589
34,350	**34,400**	5,018	4,374	5,018	4,596
34,400	**34,450**	5,030	4,381	5,030	4,604
34,450	**34,500**	5,043	4,389	5,043	4,611
34,500	**34,550**	5,055	4,396	5,055	4,619
34,550	**34,600**	5,068	4,404	5,068	4,626
34,600	**34,650**	5,080	4,411	5,080	4,634
34,650	**34,700**	5,093	4,419	5,093	4,641
34,700	**34,750**	5,105	4,426	5,105	4,649
34,750	**34,800**	5,118	4,434	5,118	4,656
34,800	**34,850**	5,130	4,441	5,130	4,664
34,850	**34,900**	5,143	4,449	5,143	4,671
34,900	**34,950**	5,155	4,456	5,155	4,679
34,950	**35,000**	5,168	4,464	5,168	4,686

If line 43 (taxable income) is— At least	But less than	And you are— Single	Married filing jointly *	Married filing sepa-rately	Head of a house-hold
		Your tax is—			
35,000					
35,000	**35,050**	5,180	4,471	5,180	4,694
35,050	**35,100**	5,193	4,479	5,193	4,701
35,100	**35,150**	5,205	4,486	5,205	4,709
35,150	**35,200**	5,218	4,494	5,218	4,716
35,200	**35,250**	5,230	4,501	5,230	4,724
35,250	**35,300**	5,243	4,509	5,243	4,731
35,300	**35,350**	5,255	4,516	5,255	4,739
35,350	**35,400**	5,268	4,524	5,268	4,746
35,400	**35,450**	5,280	4,531	5,280	4,754
35,450	**35,500**	5,293	4,539	5,293	4,761
35,500	**35,550**	5,305	4,546	5,305	4,769
35,550	**35,600**	5,318	4,554	5,318	4,776
35,600	**35,650**	5,330	4,561	5,330	4,784
35,650	**35,700**	5,343	4,569	5,343	4,791
35,700	**35,750**	5,355	4,576	5,355	4,799
35,750	**35,800**	5,368	4,584	5,368	4,806
35,800	**35,850**	5,380	4,591	5,380	4,814
35,850	**35,900**	5,393	4,599	5,393	4,821
35,900	**35,950**	5,405	4,606	5,405	4,829
35,950	**36,000**	5,418	4,614	5,418	4,836
36,000					
36,000	**36,050**	5,430	4,621	5,430	4,844
36,050	**36,100**	5,443	4,629	5,443	4,851
36,100	**36,150**	5,455	4,636	5,455	4,859
36,150	**36,200**	5,468	4,644	5,468	4,866
36,200	**36,250**	5,480	4,651	5,480	4,874
36,250	**36,300**	5,493	4,659	5,493	4,881
36,300	**36,350**	5,505	4,666	5,505	4,889
36,350	**36,400**	5,518	4,674	5,518	4,896
36,400	**36,450**	5,530	4,681	5,530	4,904
36,450	**36,500**	5,543	4,689	5,543	4,911
36,500	**36,550**	5,555	4,696	5,555	4,919
36,550	**36,600**	5,568	4,704	5,568	4,926
36,600	**36,650**	5,580	4,711	5,580	4,934
36,650	**36,700**	5,593	4,719	5,593	4,941
36,700	**36,750**	5,605	4,726	5,605	4,949
36,750	**36,800**	5,618	4,734	5,618	4,956
36,800	**36,850**	5,630	4,741	5,630	4,964
36,850	**36,900**	5,643	4,749	5,643	4,971
36,900	**36,950**	5,655	4,756	5,655	4,979
36,950	**37,000**	5,668	4,764	5,668	4,986
37,000					
37,000	**37,050**	5,680	4,771	5,680	4,994
37,050	**37,100**	5,693	4,779	5,693	5,001
37,100	**37,150**	5,705	4,786	5,705	5,009
37,150	**37,200**	5,718	4,794	5,718	5,016
37,200	**37,250**	5,730	4,801	5,730	5,024
37,250	**37,300**	5,743	4,809	5,743	5,031
37,300	**37,350**	5,755	4,816	5,755	5,039
37,350	**37,400**	5,768	4,824	5,768	5,046
37,400	**37,450**	5,780	4,831	5,780	5,054
37,450	**37,500**	5,793	4,839	5,793	5,061
37,500	**37,550**	5,805	4,846	5,805	5,069
37,550	**37,600**	5,818	4,854	5,818	5,076
37,600	**37,650**	5,830	4,861	5,830	5,084
37,650	**37,700**	5,843	4,869	5,843	5,091
37,700	**37,750**	5,855	4,876	5,855	5,099
37,750	**37,800**	5,868	4,884	5,868	5,106
37,800	**37,850**	5,880	4,891	5,880	5,114
37,850	**37,900**	5,893	4,899	5,893	5,121
37,900	**37,950**	5,905	4,906	5,905	5,129
37,950	**38,000**	5,918	4,914	5,918	5,136

If line 43 (taxable income) is— At least	But less than	And you are— Single	Married filing jointly *	Married filing sepa-rately	Head of a house-hold
		Your tax is—			
38,000					
38,000	**38,050**	5,930	4,921	5,930	5,144
38,050	**38,100**	5,943	4,929	5,943	5,151
38,100	**38,150**	5,955	4,936	5,955	5,159
38,150	**38,200**	5,968	4,944	5,968	5,166
38,200	**38,250**	5,980	4,951	5,980	5,174
38,250	**38,300**	5,993	4,959	5,993	5,181
38,300	**38,350**	6,005	4,966	6,005	5,189
38,350	**38,400**	6,018	4,974	6,018	5,196
38,400	**38,450**	6,030	4,981	6,030	5,204
38,450	**38,500**	6,043	4,989	6,043	5,211
38,500	**38,550**	6,055	4,996	6,055	5,219
38,550	**38,600**	6,068	5,004	6,068	5,226
38,600	**38,650**	6,080	5,011	6,080	5,234
38,650	**38,700**	6,093	5,019	6,093	5,241
38,700	**38,750**	6,105	5,026	6,105	5,249
38,750	**38,800**	6,118	5,034	6,118	5,256
38,800	**38,850**	6,130	5,041	6,130	5,264
38,850	**38,900**	6,143	5,049	6,143	5,271
38,900	**38,950**	6,155	5,056	6,155	5,279
38,950	**39,000**	6,168	5,064	6,168	5,286
39,000					
39,000	**39,050**	6,180	5,071	6,180	5,294
39,050	**39,100**	6,193	5,079	6,193	5,301
39,100	**39,150**	6,205	5,086	6,205	5,309
39,150	**39,200**	6,218	5,094	6,218	5,316
39,200	**39,250**	6,230	5,101	6,230	5,324
39,250	**39,300**	6,243	5,109	6,243	5,331
39,300	**39,350**	6,255	5,116	6,255	5,339
39,350	**39,400**	6,268	5,124	6,268	5,346
39,400	**39,450**	6,280	5,131	6,280	5,354
39,450	**39,500**	6,293	5,139	6,293	5,361
39,500	**39,550**	6,305	5,146	6,305	5,369
39,550	**39,600**	6,318	5,154	6,318	5,376
39,600	**39,650**	6,330	5,161	6,330	5,384
39,650	**39,700**	6,343	5,169	6,343	5,391
39,700	**39,750**	6,355	5,176	6,355	5,399
39,750	**39,800**	6,368	5,184	6,368	5,406
39,800	**39,850**	6,380	5,191	6,380	5,414
39,850	**39,900**	6,393	5,199	6,393	5,421
39,900	**39,950**	6,405	5,206	6,405	5,429
39,950	**40,000**	6,418	5,214	6,418	5,436
40,000					
40,000	**40,050**	6,430	5,221	6,430	5,444
40,050	**40,100**	6,443	5,229	6,443	5,451
40,100	**40,150**	6,455	5,236	6,455	5,459
40,150	**40,200**	6,468	5,244	6,468	5,466
40,200	**40,250**	6,480	5,251	6,480	5,474
40,250	**40,300**	6,493	5,259	6,493	5,481
40,300	**40,350**	6,505	5,266	6,505	5,489
40,350	**40,400**	6,518	5,274	6,518	5,496
40,400	**40,450**	6,530	5,281	6,530	5,504
40,450	**40,500**	6,543	5,289	6,543	5,511
40,500	**40,550**	6,555	5,296	6,555	5,519
40,550	**40,600**	6,568	5,304	6,568	5,526
40,600	**40,650**	6,580	5,311	6,580	5,534
40,650	**40,700**	6,593	5,319	6,593	5,541
40,700	**40,750**	6,605	5,326	6,605	5,549
40,750	**40,800**	6,618	5,334	6,618	5,556
40,800	**40,850**	6,630	5,341	6,630	5,564
40,850	**40,900**	6,643	5,349	6,643	5,571
40,900	**40,950**	6,655	5,356	6,655	5,579
40,950	**41,000**	6,668	5,364	6,668	5,586

* This column must also be used by a qualifying widow(er).

(Continued on page 68)

2007 Tax Table—Continued

41,000 – 43,000

At least	But less than	Single	Married filing jointly *	Married filing separately	Head of a household
41,000	41,050	6,680	5,371	6,680	5,594
41,050	41,100	6,693	5,379	6,693	5,601
41,100	41,150	6,705	5,386	6,705	5,609
41,150	41,200	6,718	5,394	6,718	5,616
41,200	41,250	6,730	5,401	6,730	5,624
41,250	41,300	6,743	5,409	6,743	5,631
41,300	41,350	6,755	5,416	6,755	5,639
41,350	41,400	6,768	5,424	6,768	5,646
41,400	41,450	6,780	5,431	6,780	5,654
41,450	41,500	6,793	5,439	6,793	5,661
41,500	41,550	6,805	5,446	6,805	5,669
41,550	41,600	6,818	5,454	6,818	5,676
41,600	41,650	6,830	5,461	6,830	5,684
41,650	41,700	6,843	5,469	6,843	5,691
41,700	41,750	6,855	5,476	6,855	5,699
41,750	41,800	6,868	5,484	6,868	5,706
41,800	41,850	6,880	5,491	6,880	5,714
41,850	41,900	6,893	5,499	6,893	5,721
41,900	41,950	6,905	5,506	6,905	5,729
41,950	42,000	6,918	5,514	6,918	5,736
42,000	42,050	6,930	5,521	6,930	5,744
42,050	42,100	6,943	5,529	6,943	5,751
42,100	42,150	6,955	5,536	6,955	5,759
42,150	42,200	6,968	5,544	6,968	5,766
42,200	42,250	6,980	5,551	6,980	5,774
42,250	42,300	6,993	5,559	6,993	5,781
42,300	42,350	7,005	5,566	7,005	5,789
42,350	42,400	7,018	5,574	7,018	5,796
42,400	42,450	7,030	5,581	7,030	5,804
42,450	42,500	7,043	5,589	7,043	5,811
42,500	42,550	7,055	5,596	7,055	5,819
42,550	42,600	7,068	5,604	7,068	5,826
42,600	42,650	7,080	5,611	7,080	5,834
42,650	42,700	7,093	5,619	7,093	5,844
42,700	42,750	7,105	5,626	7,105	5,856
42,750	42,800	7,118	5,634	7,118	5,869
42,800	42,850	7,130	5,641	7,130	5,881
42,850	42,900	7,143	5,649	7,143	5,894
42,900	42,950	7,155	5,656	7,155	5,906
42,950	43,000	7,168	5,664	7,168	5,919
43,000	43,050	7,180	5,671	7,180	5,931
43,050	43,100	7,193	5,679	7,193	5,944
43,100	43,150	7,205	5,686	7,205	5,956
43,150	43,200	7,218	5,694	7,218	5,969
43,200	43,250	7,230	5,701	7,230	5,981
43,250	43,300	7,243	5,709	7,243	5,994
43,300	43,350	7,255	5,716	7,255	6,006
43,350	43,400	7,268	5,724	7,268	6,019
43,400	43,450	7,280	5,731	7,280	6,031
43,450	43,500	7,293	5,739	7,293	6,044
43,500	43,550	7,305	5,746	7,305	6,056
43,550	43,600	7,318	5,754	7,318	6,069
43,600	43,650	7,330	5,761	7,330	6,081
43,650	43,700	7,343	5,769	7,343	6,094
43,700	43,750	7,355	5,776	7,355	6,106
43,750	43,800	7,368	5,784	7,368	6,119
43,800	43,850	7,380	5,791	7,380	6,131
43,850	43,900	7,393	5,799	7,393	6,144
43,900	43,950	7,405	5,806	7,405	6,156
43,950	44,000	7,418	5,814	7,418	6,169

44,000 – 46,000

At least	But less than	Single	Married filing jointly *	Married filing separately	Head of a household
44,000	44,050	7,430	5,821	7,430	6,181
44,050	44,100	7,443	5,829	7,443	6,194
44,100	44,150	7,455	5,836	7,455	6,206
44,150	44,200	7,468	5,844	7,468	6,219
44,200	44,250	7,480	5,851	7,480	6,231
44,250	44,300	7,493	5,859	7,493	6,244
44,300	44,350	7,505	5,866	7,505	6,256
44,350	44,400	7,518	5,874	7,518	6,269
44,400	44,450	7,530	5,881	7,530	6,281
44,450	44,500	7,543	5,889	7,543	6,294
44,500	44,550	7,555	5,896	7,555	6,306
44,550	44,600	7,568	5,904	7,568	6,319
44,600	44,650	7,580	5,911	7,580	6,331
44,650	44,700	7,593	5,919	7,593	6,344
44,700	44,750	7,605	5,926	7,605	6,356
44,750	44,800	7,618	5,934	7,618	6,369
44,800	44,850	7,630	5,941	7,630	6,381
44,850	44,900	7,643	5,949	7,643	6,394
44,900	44,950	7,655	5,956	7,655	6,406
44,950	45,000	7,668	5,964	7,668	6,419
45,000	45,050	7,680	5,971	7,680	6,431
45,050	45,100	7,693	5,979	7,693	6,444
45,100	45,150	7,705	5,986	7,705	6,456
45,150	45,200	7,718	5,994	7,718	6,469
45,200	45,250	7,730	6,001	7,730	6,481
45,250	45,300	7,743	6,009	7,743	6,494
45,300	45,350	7,755	6,016	7,755	6,506
45,350	45,400	7,768	6,024	7,768	6,519
45,400	45,450	7,780	6,031	7,780	6,531
45,450	45,500	7,793	6,039	7,793	6,544
45,500	45,550	7,805	6,046	7,805	6,556
45,550	45,600	7,818	6,054	7,818	6,569
45,600	45,650	7,830	6,061	7,830	6,581
45,650	45,700	7,843	6,069	7,843	6,594
45,700	45,750	7,855	6,076	7,855	6,606
45,750	45,800	7,868	6,084	7,868	6,619
45,800	45,850	7,880	6,091	7,880	6,631
45,850	45,900	7,893	6,099	7,893	6,644
45,900	45,950	7,905	6,106	7,905	6,656
45,950	46,000	7,918	6,114	7,918	6,669
46,000	46,050	7,930	6,121	7,930	6,681
46,050	46,100	7,943	6,129	7,943	6,694
46,100	46,150	7,955	6,136	7,955	6,706
46,150	46,200	7,968	6,144	7,968	6,719
46,200	46,250	7,980	6,151	7,980	6,731
46,250	46,300	7,993	6,159	7,993	6,744
46,300	46,350	8,005	6,166	8,005	6,756
46,350	46,400	8,018	6,174	8,018	6,769
46,400	46,450	8,030	6,181	8,030	6,781
46,450	46,500	8,043	6,189	8,043	6,794
46,500	46,550	8,055	6,196	8,055	6,806
46,550	46,600	8,068	6,204	8,068	6,819
46,600	46,650	8,080	6,211	8,080	6,831
46,650	46,700	8,093	6,219	8,093	6,844
46,700	46,750	8,105	6,226	8,105	6,856
46,750	46,800	8,118	6,234	8,118	6,869
46,800	46,850	8,130	6,241	8,130	6,881
46,850	46,900	8,143	6,249	8,143	6,894
46,900	46,950	8,155	6,256	8,155	6,906
46,950	47,000	8,168	6,264	8,168	6,919

47,000 – 50,000

At least	But less than	Single	Married filing jointly *	Married filing separately	Head of a household
47,000	47,050	8,180	6,271	8,180	6,931
47,050	47,100	8,193	6,279	8,193	6,944
47,100	47,150	8,205	6,286	8,205	6,956
47,150	47,200	8,218	6,294	8,218	6,969
47,200	47,250	8,230	6,301	8,230	6,981
47,250	47,300	8,243	6,309	8,243	6,994
47,300	47,350	8,255	6,316	8,255	7,006
47,350	47,400	8,268	6,324	8,268	7,019
47,400	47,450	8,280	6,331	8,280	7,031
47,450	47,500	8,293	6,339	8,293	7,044
47,500	47,550	8,305	6,346	8,305	7,056
47,550	47,600	8,318	6,354	8,318	7,069
47,600	47,650	8,330	6,361	8,330	7,081
47,650	47,700	8,343	6,369	8,343	7,094
47,700	47,750	8,355	6,376	8,355	7,106
47,750	47,800	8,368	6,384	8,368	7,119
47,800	47,850	8,380	6,391	8,380	7,131
47,850	47,900	8,393	6,399	8,393	7,144
47,900	47,950	8,405	6,406	8,405	7,156
47,950	48,000	8,418	6,414	8,418	7,169
48,000	48,050	8,430	6,421	8,430	7,181
48,050	48,100	8,443	6,429	8,443	7,194
48,100	48,150	8,455	6,436	8,455	7,206
48,150	48,200	8,468	6,444	8,468	7,219
48,200	48,250	8,480	6,451	8,480	7,231
48,250	48,300	8,493	6,459	8,493	7,244
48,300	48,350	8,505	6,466	8,505	7,256
48,350	48,400	8,518	6,474	8,518	7,269
48,400	48,450	8,530	6,481	8,530	7,281
48,450	48,500	8,543	6,489	8,543	7,294
48,500	48,550	8,555	6,496	8,555	7,306
48,550	48,600	8,568	6,504	8,568	7,319
48,600	48,650	8,580	6,511	8,580	7,331
48,650	48,700	8,593	6,519	8,593	7,344
48,700	48,750	8,605	6,526	8,605	7,356
48,750	48,800	8,618	6,534	8,618	7,369
48,800	48,850	8,630	6,541	8,630	7,381
48,850	48,900	8,643	6,549	8,643	7,394
48,900	48,950	8,655	6,556	8,655	7,406
48,950	49,000	8,668	6,564	8,668	7,419
49,000	49,050	8,680	6,571	8,680	7,431
49,050	49,100	8,693	6,579	8,693	7,444
49,100	49,150	8,705	6,586	8,705	7,456
49,150	49,200	8,718	6,594	8,718	7,469
49,200	49,250	8,730	6,601	8,730	7,481
49,250	49,300	8,743	6,609	8,743	7,494
49,300	49,350	8,755	6,616	8,755	7,506
49,350	49,400	8,768	6,624	8,768	7,519
49,400	49,450	8,780	6,631	8,780	7,531
49,450	49,500	8,793	6,639	8,793	7,544
49,500	49,550	8,805	6,646	8,805	7,556
49,550	49,600	8,818	6,654	8,818	7,569
49,600	49,650	8,830	6,661	8,830	7,581
49,650	49,700	8,843	6,669	8,843	7,594
49,700	49,750	8,855	6,676	8,855	7,606
49,750	49,800	8,868	6,684	8,868	7,619
49,800	49,850	8,880	6,691	8,880	7,631
49,850	49,900	8,893	6,699	8,893	7,644
49,900	49,950	8,905	6,706	8,905	7,656
49,950	50,000	8,918	6,714	8,918	7,669

* This column must also be used by a qualifying widow(er).

(Continued on page 69)

¶25

2007 Tax Table–*Continued*

50,000 – 52,000

At least	But less than	Single	Married filing jointly	Married filing separately	Head of a household
50,000					
50,000	50,050	8,930	6,721	8,930	7,681
50,050	50,100	8,943	6,729	8,943	7,694
50,100	50,150	8,955	6,736	8,955	7,706
50,150	50,200	8,968	6,744	8,968	7,719
50,200	50,250	8,980	6,751	8,980	7,731
50,250	50,300	8,993	6,759	8,993	7,744
50,300	50,350	9,005	6,766	9,005	7,756
50,350	50,400	9,018	6,774	9,018	7,769
50,400	50,450	9,030	6,781	9,030	7,781
50,450	50,500	9,043	6,789	9,043	7,794
50,500	50,550	9,055	6,796	9,055	7,806
50,550	50,600	9,068	6,804	9,068	7,819
50,600	50,650	9,080	6,811	9,080	7,831
50,650	50,700	9,093	6,819	9,093	7,844
50,700	50,750	9,105	6,826	9,105	7,856
50,750	50,800	9,118	6,834	9,118	7,869
50,800	50,850	9,130	6,841	9,130	7,881
50,850	50,900	9,143	6,849	9,143	7,894
50,900	50,950	9,155	6,856	9,155	7,906
50,950	51,000	9,168	6,864	9,168	7,919
51,000					
51,000	51,050	9,180	6,871	9,180	7,931
51,050	51,100	9,193	6,879	9,193	7,944
51,100	51,150	9,205	6,886	9,205	7,956
51,150	51,200	9,218	6,894	9,218	7,969
51,200	51,250	9,230	6,901	9,230	7,981
51,250	51,300	9,243	6,909	9,243	7,994
51,300	51,350	9,255	6,916	9,255	8,006
51,350	51,400	9,268	6,924	9,268	8,019
51,400	51,450	9,280	6,931	9,280	8,031
51,450	51,500	9,293	6,939	9,293	8,044
51,500	51,550	9,305	6,946	9,305	8,056
51,550	51,600	9,318	6,954	9,318	8,069
51,600	51,650	9,330	6,961	9,330	8,081
51,650	51,700	9,343	6,969	9,343	8,094
51,700	51,750	9,355	6,976	9,355	8,106
51,750	51,800	9,368	6,984	9,368	8,119
51,800	51,850	9,380	6,991	9,380	8,131
51,850	51,900	9,393	6,999	9,393	8,144
51,900	51,950	9,405	7,006	9,405	8,156
51,950	52,000	9,418	7,014	9,418	8,169
52,000					
52,000	52,050	9,430	7,021	9,430	8,181
52,050	52,100	9,443	7,029	9,443	8,194
52,100	52,150	9,455	7,036	9,455	8,206
52,150	52,200	9,468	7,044	9,468	8,219
52,200	52,250	9,480	7,051	9,480	8,231
52,250	52,300	9,493	7,059	9,493	8,244
52,300	52,350	9,505	7,066	9,505	8,256
52,350	52,400	9,518	7,074	9,518	8,269
52,400	52,450	9,530	7,081	9,530	8,281
52,450	52,500	9,543	7,089	9,543	8,294
52,500	52,550	9,555	7,096	9,555	8,306
52,550	52,600	9,568	7,104	9,568	8,319
52,600	52,650	9,580	7,111	9,580	8,331
52,650	52,700	9,593	7,119	9,593	8,344
52,700	52,750	9,605	7,126	9,605	8,356
52,750	52,800	9,618	7,134	9,618	8,369
52,800	52,850	9,630	7,141	9,630	8,381
52,850	52,900	9,643	7,149	9,643	8,394
52,900	52,950	9,655	7,156	9,655	8,406
52,950	53,000	9,668	7,164	9,668	8,419

53,000 – 55,000

At least	But less than	Single	Married filing jointly	Married filing separately	Head of a household
53,000					
53,000	53,050	9,680	7,171	9,680	8,431
53,050	53,100	9,693	7,179	9,693	8,444
53,100	53,150	9,705	7,186	9,705	8,456
53,150	53,200	9,718	7,194	9,718	8,469
53,200	53,250	9,730	7,201	9,730	8,481
53,250	53,300	9,743	7,209	9,743	8,494
53,300	53,350	9,755	7,216	9,755	8,506
53,350	53,400	9,768	7,224	9,768	8,519
53,400	53,450	9,780	7,231	9,780	8,531
53,450	53,500	9,793	7,239	9,793	8,544
53,500	53,550	9,805	7,246	9,805	8,556
53,550	53,600	9,818	7,254	9,818	8,569
53,600	53,650	9,830	7,261	9,830	8,581
53,650	53,700	9,843	7,269	9,843	8,594
53,700	53,750	9,855	7,276	9,855	8,606
53,750	53,800	9,868	7,284	9,868	8,619
53,800	53,850	9,880	7,291	9,880	8,631
53,850	53,900	9,893	7,299	9,893	8,644
53,900	53,950	9,905	7,306	9,905	8,656
53,950	54,000	9,918	7,314	9,918	8,669
54,000					
54,000	54,050	9,930	7,321	9,930	8,681
54,050	54,100	9,943	7,329	9,943	8,694
54,100	54,150	9,955	7,336	9,955	8,706
54,150	54,200	9,968	7,344	9,968	8,719
54,200	54,250	9,980	7,351	9,980	8,731
54,250	54,300	9,993	7,359	9,993	8,744
54,300	54,350	10,005	7,366	10,005	8,756
54,350	54,400	10,018	7,374	10,018	8,769
54,400	54,450	10,030	7,381	10,030	8,781
54,450	54,500	10,043	7,389	10,043	8,794
54,500	54,550	10,055	7,396	10,055	8,806
54,550	54,600	10,068	7,404	10,068	8,819
54,600	54,650	10,080	7,411	10,080	8,831
54,650	54,700	10,093	7,419	10,093	8,844
54,700	54,750	10,105	7,426	10,105	8,856
54,750	54,800	10,118	7,434	10,118	8,869
54,800	54,850	10,130	7,441	10,130	8,881
54,850	54,900	10,143	7,449	10,143	8,894
54,900	54,950	10,155	7,456	10,155	8,906
54,950	55,000	10,168	7,464	10,168	8,919
55,000					
55,000	55,050	10,180	7,471	10,180	8,931
55,050	55,100	10,193	7,479	10,193	8,944
55,100	55,150	10,205	7,486	10,205	8,956
55,150	55,200	10,218	7,494	10,218	8,969
55,200	55,250	10,230	7,501	10,230	8,981
55,250	55,300	10,243	7,509	10,243	8,994
55,300	55,350	10,255	7,516	10,255	9,006
55,350	55,400	10,268	7,524	10,268	9,019
55,400	55,450	10,280	7,531	10,280	9,031
55,450	55,500	10,293	7,539	10,293	9,044
55,500	55,550	10,305	7,546	10,305	9,056
55,550	55,600	10,318	7,554	10,318	9,069
55,600	55,650	10,330	7,561	10,330	9,081
55,650	55,700	10,343	7,569	10,343	9,094
55,700	55,750	10,355	7,576	10,355	9,106
55,750	55,800	10,368	7,584	10,368	9,119
55,800	55,850	10,380	7,591	10,380	9,131
55,850	55,900	10,393	7,599	10,393	9,144
55,900	55,950	10,405	7,606	10,405	9,156
55,950	56,000	10,418	7,614	10,418	9,169

56,000 – 58,000

At least	But less than	Single	Married filing jointly	Married filing separately	Head of a household
56,000					
56,000	56,050	10,430	7,621	10,430	9,181
56,050	56,100	10,443	7,629	10,443	9,194
56,100	56,150	10,455	7,636	10,455	9,206
56,150	56,200	10,468	7,644	10,468	9,219
56,200	56,250	10,480	7,651	10,480	9,231
56,250	56,300	10,493	7,659	10,493	9,244
56,300	56,350	10,505	7,666	10,505	9,256
56,350	56,400	10,518	7,674	10,518	9,269
56,400	56,450	10,530	7,681	10,530	9,281
56,450	56,500	10,543	7,689	10,543	9,294
56,500	56,550	10,555	7,696	10,555	9,306
56,550	56,600	10,568	7,704	10,568	9,319
56,600	56,650	10,580	7,711	10,580	9,331
56,650	56,700	10,593	7,719	10,593	9,344
56,700	56,750	10,605	7,726	10,605	9,356
56,750	56,800	10,618	7,734	10,618	9,369
56,800	56,850	10,630	7,741	10,630	9,381
56,850	56,900	10,643	7,749	10,643	9,394
56,900	56,950	10,655	7,756	10,655	9,406
56,950	57,000	10,668	7,764	10,668	9,419
57,000					
57,000	57,050	10,680	7,771	10,680	9,431
57,050	57,100	10,693	7,779	10,693	9,444
57,100	57,150	10,705	7,786	10,705	9,456
57,150	57,200	10,718	7,794	10,718	9,469
57,200	57,250	10,730	7,801	10,730	9,481
57,250	57,300	10,743	7,809	10,743	9,494
57,300	57,350	10,755	7,816	10,755	9,506
57,350	57,400	10,768	7,824	10,768	9,519
57,400	57,450	10,780	7,831	10,780	9,531
57,450	57,500	10,793	7,839	10,793	9,544
57,500	57,550	10,805	7,846	10,805	9,556
57,550	57,600	10,818	7,854	10,818	9,569
57,600	57,650	10,830	7,861	10,830	9,581
57,650	57,700	10,843	7,869	10,843	9,594
57,700	57,750	10,855	7,876	10,855	9,606
57,750	57,800	10,868	7,884	10,868	9,619
57,800	57,850	10,880	7,891	10,880	9,631
57,850	57,900	10,893	7,899	10,893	9,644
57,900	57,950	10,905	7,906	10,905	9,656
57,950	58,000	10,918	7,914	10,918	9,669
58,000					
58,000	58,050	10,930	7,921	10,930	9,681
58,050	58,100	10,943	7,929	10,943	9,694
58,100	58,150	10,955	7,936	10,955	9,706
58,150	58,200	10,968	7,944	10,968	9,719
58,200	58,250	10,980	7,951	10,980	9,731
58,250	58,300	10,993	7,959	10,993	9,744
58,300	58,350	11,005	7,966	11,005	9,756
58,350	58,400	11,018	7,974	11,018	9,769
58,400	58,450	11,030	7,981	11,030	9,781
58,450	58,500	11,043	7,989	11,043	9,794
58,500	58,550	11,055	7,996	11,055	9,806
58,550	58,600	11,068	8,004	11,068	9,819
58,600	58,650	11,080	8,011	11,080	9,831
58,650	58,700	11,093	8,019	11,093	9,844
58,700	58,750	11,105	8,026	11,105	9,856
58,750	58,800	11,118	8,034	11,118	9,869
58,800	58,850	11,130	8,041	11,130	9,881
58,850	58,900	11,143	8,049	11,143	9,894
58,900	58,950	11,155	8,056	11,155	9,906
58,950	59,000	11,168	8,064	11,168	9,919

* This column must also be used by a qualifying widow(er).

(Continued on page 70)

¶25

2007 Tax Table—Continued

If line 43 (taxable income) is— At least	But less than	Single	Married filing jointly*	Married filing separately	Head of a household
59,000					
59,000	59,050	11,180	8,071	11,180	9,931
59,050	59,100	11,193	8,079	11,193	9,944
59,100	59,150	11,205	8,086	11,205	9,956
59,150	59,200	11,218	8,094	11,218	9,969
59,200	59,250	11,230	8,101	11,230	9,981
59,250	59,300	11,243	8,109	11,243	9,994
59,300	59,350	11,255	8,116	11,255	10,006
59,350	59,400	11,268	8,124	11,268	10,019
59,400	59,450	11,280	8,131	11,280	10,031
59,450	59,500	11,293	8,139	11,293	10,044
59,500	59,550	11,305	8,146	11,305	10,056
59,550	59,600	11,318	8,154	11,318	10,069
59,600	59,650	11,330	8,161	11,330	10,081
59,650	59,700	11,343	8,169	11,343	10,094
59,700	59,750	11,355	8,176	11,355	10,106
59,750	59,800	11,368	8,184	11,368	10,119
59,800	59,850	11,380	8,191	11,380	10,131
59,850	59,900	11,393	8,199	11,393	10,144
59,900	59,950	11,405	8,206	11,405	10,156
59,950	60,000	11,418	8,214	11,418	10,169
60,000					
60,000	60,050	11,430	8,221	11,430	10,181
60,050	60,100	11,443	8,229	11,443	10,194
60,100	60,150	11,455	8,236	11,455	10,206
60,150	60,200	11,468	8,244	11,468	10,219
60,200	60,250	11,480	8,251	11,480	10,231
60,250	60,300	11,493	8,259	11,493	10,244
60,300	60,350	11,505	8,266	11,505	10,256
60,350	60,400	11,518	8,274	11,518	10,269
60,400	60,450	11,530	8,281	11,530	10,281
60,450	60,500	11,543	8,289	11,543	10,294
60,500	60,550	11,555	8,296	11,555	10,306
60,550	60,600	11,568	8,304	11,568	10,319
60,600	60,650	11,580	8,311	11,580	10,331
60,650	60,700	11,593	8,319	11,593	10,344
60,700	60,750	11,605	8,326	11,605	10,356
60,750	60,800	11,618	8,334	11,618	10,369
60,800	60,850	11,630	8,341	11,630	10,381
60,850	60,900	11,643	8,349	11,643	10,394
60,900	60,950	11,655	8,356	11,655	10,406
60,950	61,000	11,668	8,364	11,668	10,419
61,000					
61,000	61,050	11,680	8,371	11,680	10,431
61,050	61,100	11,693	8,379	11,693	10,444
61,100	61,150	11,705	8,386	11,705	10,456
61,150	61,200	11,718	8,394	11,718	10,469
61,200	61,250	11,730	8,401	11,730	10,481
61,250	61,300	11,743	8,409	11,743	10,494
61,300	61,350	11,755	8,416	11,755	10,506
61,350	61,400	11,768	8,424	11,768	10,519
61,400	61,450	11,780	8,431	11,780	10,531
61,450	61,500	11,793	8,439	11,793	10,544
61,500	61,550	11,805	8,446	11,805	10,556
61,550	61,600	11,818	8,454	11,818	10,569
61,600	61,650	11,830	8,461	11,830	10,581
61,650	61,700	11,843	8,469	11,843	10,594
61,700	61,750	11,855	8,476	11,855	10,606
61,750	61,800	11,868	8,484	11,868	10,619
61,800	61,850	11,880	8,491	11,880	10,631
61,850	61,900	11,893	8,499	11,893	10,644
61,900	61,950	11,905	8,506	11,905	10,656
61,950	62,000	11,918	8,514	11,918	10,669

If line 43 (taxable income) is— At least	But less than	Single	Married filing jointly*	Married filing separately	Head of a household
62,000					
62,000	62,050	11,930	8,521	11,930	10,681
62,050	62,100	11,943	8,529	11,943	10,694
62,100	62,150	11,955	8,536	11,955	10,706
62,150	62,200	11,968	8,544	11,968	10,719
62,200	62,250	11,980	8,551	11,980	10,731
62,250	62,300	11,993	8,559	11,993	10,744
62,300	62,350	12,005	8,566	12,005	10,756
62,350	62,400	12,018	8,574	12,018	10,769
62,400	62,450	12,030	8,581	12,030	10,781
62,450	62,500	12,043	8,589	12,043	10,794
62,500	62,550	12,055	8,596	12,055	10,806
62,550	62,600	12,068	8,604	12,068	10,819
62,600	62,650	12,080	8,611	12,080	10,831
62,650	62,700	12,093	8,619	12,093	10,844
62,700	62,750	12,105	8,626	12,105	10,856
62,750	62,800	12,118	8,634	12,118	10,869
62,800	62,850	12,130	8,641	12,130	10,881
62,850	62,900	12,143	8,649	12,143	10,894
62,900	62,950	12,155	8,656	12,155	10,906
62,950	63,000	12,168	8,664	12,168	10,919
63,000					
63,000	63,050	12,180	8,671	12,180	10,931
63,050	63,100	12,193	8,679	12,193	10,944
63,100	63,150	12,205	8,686	12,205	10,956
63,150	63,200	12,218	8,694	12,218	10,969
63,200	63,250	12,230	8,701	12,230	10,981
63,250	63,300	12,243	8,709	12,243	10,994
63,300	63,350	12,255	8,716	12,255	11,006
63,350	63,400	12,268	8,724	12,268	11,019
63,400	63,450	12,280	8,731	12,280	11,031
63,450	63,500	12,293	8,739	12,293	11,044
63,500	63,550	12,305	8,746	12,305	11,056
63,550	63,600	12,318	8,754	12,318	11,069
63,600	63,650	12,330	8,761	12,330	11,081
63,650	63,700	12,343	8,769	12,343	11,094
63,700	63,750	12,355	8,779	12,355	11,106
63,750	63,800	12,368	8,791	12,368	11,119
63,800	63,850	12,380	8,804	12,380	11,131
63,850	63,900	12,393	8,816	12,393	11,144
63,900	63,950	12,405	8,829	12,405	11,156
63,950	64,000	12,418	8,841	12,418	11,169
64,000					
64,000	64,050	12,430	8,854	12,430	11,181
64,050	64,100	12,443	8,866	12,443	11,194
64,100	64,150	12,455	8,879	12,455	11,206
64,150	64,200	12,468	8,891	12,468	11,219
64,200	64,250	12,480	8,904	12,480	11,231
64,250	64,300	12,493	8,916	12,493	11,244
64,300	64,350	12,505	8,929	12,507	11,256
64,350	64,400	12,518	8,941	12,521	11,269
64,400	64,450	12,530	8,954	12,535	11,281
64,450	64,500	12,543	8,966	12,549	11,294
64,500	64,550	12,555	8,979	12,563	11,306
64,550	64,600	12,568	8,991	12,577	11,319
64,600	64,650	12,580	9,004	12,591	11,331
64,650	64,700	12,593	9,016	12,605	11,344
64,700	64,750	12,605	9,029	12,619	11,356
64,750	64,800	12,618	9,041	12,633	11,369
64,800	64,850	12,630	9,054	12,647	11,381
64,850	64,900	12,643	9,066	12,661	11,394
64,900	64,950	12,655	9,079	12,675	11,406
64,950	65,000	12,668	9,091	12,689	11,419

If line 43 (taxable income) is— At least	But less than	Single	Married filing jointly*	Married filing separately	Head of a household
65,000					
65,000	65,050	12,680	9,104	12,703	11,431
65,050	65,100	12,693	9,116	12,717	11,444
65,100	65,150	12,705	9,129	12,731	11,456
65,150	65,200	12,718	9,141	12,745	11,469
65,200	65,250	12,730	9,154	12,759	11,481
65,250	65,300	12,743	9,166	12,773	11,494
65,300	65,350	12,755	9,179	12,787	11,506
65,350	65,400	12,768	9,191	12,801	11,519
65,400	65,450	12,780	9,204	12,815	11,531
65,450	65,500	12,793	9,216	12,829	11,544
65,500	65,550	12,805	9,229	12,843	11,556
65,550	65,600	12,818	9,241	12,857	11,569
65,600	65,650	12,830	9,254	12,871	11,581
65,650	65,700	12,843	9,266	12,885	11,594
65,700	65,750	12,855	9,279	12,899	11,606
65,750	65,800	12,868	9,291	12,913	11,619
65,800	65,850	12,880	9,304	12,927	11,631
65,850	65,900	12,893	9,316	12,941	11,644
65,900	65,950	12,905	9,329	12,955	11,656
65,950	66,000	12,918	9,341	12,969	11,669
66,000					
66,000	66,050	12,930	9,354	12,983	11,681
66,050	66,100	12,943	9,366	12,997	11,694
66,100	66,150	12,955	9,379	13,011	11,706
66,150	66,200	12,968	9,391	13,025	11,719
66,200	66,250	12,980	9,404	13,039	11,731
66,250	66,300	12,993	9,416	13,053	11,744
66,300	66,350	13,005	9,429	13,067	11,756
66,350	66,400	13,018	9,441	13,081	11,769
66,400	66,450	13,030	9,454	13,095	11,781
66,450	66,500	13,043	9,466	13,109	11,794
66,500	66,550	13,055	9,479	13,123	11,806
66,550	66,600	13,068	9,491	13,137	11,819
66,600	66,650	13,080	9,504	13,151	11,831
66,650	66,700	13,093	9,516	13,165	11,844
66,700	66,750	13,105	9,529	13,179	11,856
66,750	66,800	13,118	9,541	13,193	11,869
66,800	66,850	13,130	9,554	13,207	11,881
66,850	66,900	13,143	9,566	13,221	11,894
66,900	66,950	13,155	9,579	13,235	11,906
66,950	67,000	13,168	9,591	13,249	11,919
67,000					
67,000	67,050	13,180	9,604	13,263	11,931
67,050	67,100	13,193	9,616	13,277	11,944
67,100	67,150	13,205	9,629	13,291	11,956
67,150	67,200	13,218	9,641	13,305	11,969
67,200	67,250	13,230	9,654	13,319	11,981
67,250	67,300	13,243	9,666	13,333	11,994
67,300	67,350	13,255	9,679	13,347	12,006
67,350	67,400	13,268	9,691	13,361	12,019
67,400	67,450	13,280	9,704	13,375	12,031
67,450	67,500	13,293	9,716	13,389	12,044
67,500	67,550	13,305	9,729	13,403	12,056
67,550	67,600	13,318	9,741	13,417	12,069
67,600	67,650	13,330	9,754	13,431	12,081
67,650	67,700	13,343	9,766	13,445	12,094
67,700	67,750	13,355	9,779	13,459	12,106
67,750	67,800	13,368	9,791	13,473	12,119
67,800	67,850	13,380	9,804	13,487	12,131
67,850	67,900	13,393	9,816	13,501	12,144
67,900	67,950	13,405	9,829	13,515	12,156
67,950	68,000	13,418	9,841	13,529	12,169

* This column must also be used by a qualifying widow(er).

(Continued on page 71)

¶25

2007 Tax Table—*Continued*

68,000

If line 43 (taxable income) is— At least	But less than	Single	Married filing jointly *	Married filing separately	Head of a household
68,000	68,050	13,430	9,854	13,543	12,181
68,050	68,100	13,443	9,866	13,557	12,194
68,100	68,150	13,455	9,879	13,571	12,206
68,150	68,200	13,468	9,891	13,585	12,219
68,200	68,250	13,480	9,904	13,599	12,231
68,250	68,300	13,493	9,916	13,613	12,244
68,300	68,350	13,505	9,929	13,627	12,256
68,350	68,400	13,518	9,941	13,641	12,269
68,400	68,450	13,530	9,954	13,655	12,281
68,450	68,500	13,543	9,966	13,669	12,294
68,500	68,550	13,555	9,979	13,683	12,306
68,550	68,600	13,568	9,991	13,697	12,319
68,600	68,650	13,580	10,004	13,711	12,331
68,650	68,700	13,593	10,016	13,725	12,344
68,700	68,750	13,605	10,029	13,739	12,356
68,750	68,800	13,618	10,041	13,753	12,369
68,800	68,850	13,630	10,054	13,767	12,381
68,850	68,900	13,643	10,066	13,781	12,394
68,900	68,950	13,655	10,079	13,795	12,406
68,950	69,000	13,668	10,091	13,809	12,419

69,000

At least	But less than	Single	Married filing jointly *	Married filing separately	Head of a household
69,000	69,050	13,680	10,104	13,823	12,431
69,050	69,100	13,693	10,116	13,837	12,444
69,100	69,150	13,705	10,129	13,851	12,456
69,150	69,200	13,718	10,141	13,865	12,469
69,200	69,250	13,730	10,154	13,879	12,481
69,250	69,300	13,743	10,166	13,893	12,494
69,300	69,350	13,755	10,179	13,907	12,506
69,350	69,400	13,768	10,191	13,921	12,519
69,400	69,450	13,780	10,204	13,935	12,531
69,450	69,500	13,793	10,216	13,949	12,544
69,500	69,550	13,805	10,229	13,963	12,556
69,550	69,600	13,818	10,241	13,977	12,569
69,600	69,650	13,830	10,254	13,991	12,581
69,650	69,700	13,843	10,266	14,005	12,594
69,700	69,750	13,855	10,279	14,019	12,606
69,750	69,800	13,868	10,291	14,033	12,619
69,800	69,850	13,880	10,304	14,047	12,631
69,850	69,900	13,893	10,316	14,061	12,644
69,900	69,950	13,905	10,329	14,075	12,656
69,950	70,000	13,918	10,341	14,089	12,669

70,000

At least	But less than	Single	Married filing jointly *	Married filing separately	Head of a household
70,000	70,050	13,930	10,354	14,103	12,681
70,050	70,100	13,943	10,366	14,117	12,694
70,100	70,150	13,955	10,379	14,131	12,706
70,150	70,200	13,968	10,391	14,145	12,719
70,200	70,250	13,980	10,404	14,159	12,731
70,250	70,300	13,993	10,416	14,173	12,744
70,300	70,350	14,005	10,429	14,187	12,756
70,350	70,400	14,018	10,441	14,201	12,769
70,400	70,450	14,030	10,454	14,215	12,781
70,450	70,500	14,043	10,466	14,229	12,794
70,500	70,550	14,055	10,479	14,243	12,806
70,550	70,600	14,068	10,491	14,257	12,819
70,600	70,650	14,080	10,504	14,271	12,831
70,650	70,700	14,093	10,516	14,285	12,844
70,700	70,750	14,105	10,529	14,299	12,856
70,750	70,800	14,118	10,541	14,313	12,869
70,800	70,850	14,130	10,554	14,327	12,881
70,850	70,900	14,143	10,566	14,341	12,894
70,900	70,950	14,155	10,579	14,355	12,906
70,950	71,000	14,168	10,591	14,369	12,919

71,000

At least	But less than	Single	Married filing jointly *	Married filing separately	Head of a household
71,000	71,050	14,180	10,604	14,383	12,931
71,050	71,100	14,193	10,616	14,397	12,944
71,100	71,150	14,205	10,629	14,411	12,956
71,150	71,200	14,218	10,641	14,425	12,969
71,200	71,250	14,230	10,654	14,439	12,981
71,250	71,300	14,243	10,666	14,453	12,994
71,300	71,350	14,255	10,679	14,467	13,006
71,350	71,400	14,268	10,691	14,481	13,019
71,400	71,450	14,280	10,704	14,495	13,031
71,450	71,500	14,293	10,716	14,509	13,044
71,500	71,550	14,305	10,729	14,523	13,056
71,550	71,600	14,318	10,741	14,537	13,069
71,600	71,650	14,330	10,754	14,551	13,081
71,650	71,700	14,343	10,766	14,565	13,094
71,700	71,750	14,355	10,779	14,579	13,106
71,750	71,800	14,368	10,791	14,593	13,119
71,800	71,850	14,380	10,804	14,607	13,131
71,850	71,900	14,393	10,816	14,621	13,144
71,900	71,950	14,405	10,829	14,635	13,156
71,950	72,000	14,418	10,841	14,649	13,169

72,000

At least	But less than	Single	Married filing jointly *	Married filing separately	Head of a household
72,000	72,050	14,430	10,854	14,663	13,181
72,050	72,100	14,443	10,866	14,677	13,194
72,100	72,150	14,455	10,879	14,691	13,206
72,150	72,200	14,468	10,891	14,705	13,219
72,200	72,250	14,480	10,904	14,719	13,231
72,250	72,300	14,493	10,916	14,733	13,244
72,300	72,350	14,505	10,929	14,747	13,256
72,350	72,400	14,518	10,941	14,761	13,269
72,400	72,450	14,530	10,954	14,775	13,281
72,450	72,500	14,543	10,966	14,789	13,294
72,500	72,550	14,555	10,979	14,803	13,306
72,550	72,600	14,568	10,991	14,817	13,319
72,600	72,650	14,580	11,004	14,831	13,331
72,650	72,700	14,593	11,016	14,845	13,344
72,700	72,750	14,605	11,029	14,859	13,356
72,750	72,800	14,618	11,041	14,873	13,369
72,800	72,850	14,630	11,054	14,887	13,381
72,850	72,900	14,643	11,066	14,901	13,394
72,900	72,950	14,655	11,079	14,915	13,406
72,950	73,000	14,668	11,091	14,929	13,419

73,000

At least	But less than	Single	Married filing jointly *	Married filing separately	Head of a household
73,000	73,050	14,680	11,104	14,943	13,431
73,050	73,100	14,693	11,116	14,957	13,444
73,100	73,150	14,705	11,129	14,971	13,456
73,150	73,200	14,718	11,141	14,985	13,469
73,200	73,250	14,730	11,154	14,999	13,481
73,250	73,300	14,743	11,166	15,013	13,494
73,300	73,350	14,755	11,179	15,027	13,506
73,350	73,400	14,768	11,191	15,041	13,519
73,400	73,450	14,780	11,204	15,055	13,531
73,450	73,500	14,793	11,216	15,069	13,544
73,500	73,550	14,805	11,229	15,083	13,556
73,550	73,600	14,818	11,241	15,097	13,569
73,600	73,650	14,830	11,254	15,111	13,581
73,650	73,700	14,843	11,266	15,125	13,594
73,700	73,750	14,855	11,279	15,139	13,606
73,750	73,800	14,868	11,291	15,153	13,619
73,800	73,850	14,880	11,304	15,167	13,631
73,850	73,900	14,893	11,316	15,181	13,644
73,900	73,950	14,905	11,329	15,195	13,656
73,950	74,000	14,918	11,341	15,209	13,669

74,000

At least	But less than	Single	Married filing jointly *	Married filing separately	Head of a household
74,000	74,050	14,930	11,354	15,223	13,681
74,050	74,100	14,943	11,366	15,237	13,694
74,100	74,150	14,955	11,379	15,251	13,706
74,150	74,200	14,968	11,391	15,265	13,719
74,200	74,250	14,980	11,404	15,279	13,731
74,250	74,300	14,993	11,416	15,293	13,744
74,300	74,350	15,005	11,429	15,307	13,756
74,350	74,400	15,018	11,441	15,321	13,769
74,400	74,450	15,030	11,454	15,335	13,781
74,450	74,500	15,043	11,466	15,349	13,794
74,500	74,550	15,055	11,479	15,363	13,806
74,550	74,600	15,068	11,491	15,377	13,819
74,600	74,650	15,080	11,504	15,391	13,831
74,650	74,700	15,093	11,516	15,405	13,844
74,700	74,750	15,105	11,529	15,419	13,856
74,750	74,800	15,118	11,541	15,433	13,869
74,800	74,850	15,130	11,554	15,447	13,881
74,850	74,900	15,143	11,566	15,461	13,894
74,900	74,950	15,155	11,579	15,475	13,906
74,950	75,000	15,168	11,591	15,489	13,919

75,000

At least	But less than	Single	Married filing jointly *	Married filing separately	Head of a household
75,000	75,050	15,180	11,604	15,503	13,931
75,050	75,100	15,193	11,616	15,517	13,944
75,100	75,150	15,205	11,629	15,531	13,956
75,150	75,200	15,218	11,641	15,545	13,969
75,200	75,250	15,230	11,654	15,559	13,981
75,250	75,300	15,243	11,666	15,573	13,994
75,300	75,350	15,255	11,679	15,587	14,006
75,350	75,400	15,268	11,691	15,601	14,019
75,400	75,450	15,280	11,704	15,615	14,031
75,450	75,500	15,293	11,716	15,629	14,044
75,500	75,550	15,305	11,729	15,643	14,056
75,550	75,600	15,318	11,741	15,657	14,069
75,600	75,650	15,330	11,754	15,671	14,081
75,650	75,700	15,343	11,766	15,685	14,094
75,700	75,750	15,355	11,779	15,699	14,106
75,750	75,800	15,368	11,791	15,713	14,119
75,800	75,850	15,380	11,804	15,727	14,131
75,850	75,900	15,393	11,816	15,741	14,144
75,900	75,950	15,405	11,829	15,755	14,156
75,950	76,000	15,418	11,841	15,769	14,169

76,000

At least	But less than	Single	Married filing jointly *	Married filing separately	Head of a household
76,000	76,050	15,430	11,854	15,783	14,181
76,050	76,100	15,443	11,866	15,797	14,194
76,100	76,150	15,455	11,879	15,811	14,206
76,150	76,200	15,468	11,891	15,825	14,219
76,200	76,250	15,480	11,904	15,839	14,231
76,250	76,300	15,493	11,916	15,853	14,244
76,300	76,350	15,505	11,929	15,867	14,256
76,350	76,400	15,518	11,941	15,881	14,269
76,400	76,450	15,530	11,954	15,895	14,281
76,450	76,500	15,543	11,966	15,909	14,294
76,500	76,550	15,555	11,979	15,923	14,306
76,550	76,600	15,568	11,991	15,937	14,319
76,600	76,650	15,580	12,004	15,951	14,331
76,650	76,700	15,593	12,016	15,965	14,344
76,700	76,750	15,605	12,029	15,979	14,356
76,750	76,800	15,618	12,041	15,993	14,369
76,800	76,850	15,630	12,054	16,007	14,381
76,850	76,900	15,643	12,066	16,021	14,394
76,900	76,950	15,655	12,079	16,035	14,406
76,950	77,000	15,668	12,091	16,049	14,419

* This column must also be used by a qualifying widow(er).

(Continued on page 72)

¶25

2007 Tax Table–*Continued*

77,000

At least	But less than	Single	Married filing jointly	Married filing separately	Head of a household
77,000	77,050	15,680	12,104	16,063	14,431
77,050	77,100	15,693	12,116	16,077	14,444
77,100	77,150	15,706	12,129	16,091	14,456
77,150	77,200	15,720	12,141	16,105	14,469
77,200	77,250	15,734	12,154	16,119	14,481
77,250	77,300	15,748	12,166	16,133	14,494
77,300	77,350	15,762	12,179	16,147	14,506
77,350	77,400	15,776	12,191	16,161	14,519
77,400	77,450	15,790	12,204	16,175	14,531
77,450	77,500	15,804	12,216	16,189	14,544
77,500	77,550	15,818	12,229	16,203	14,556
77,550	77,600	15,832	12,241	16,217	14,569
77,600	77,650	15,846	12,254	16,231	14,581
77,650	77,700	15,860	12,266	16,245	14,594
77,700	77,750	15,874	12,279	16,259	14,606
77,750	77,800	15,888	12,291	16,273	14,619
77,800	77,850	15,902	12,304	16,287	14,631
77,850	77,900	15,916	12,316	16,301	14,644
77,900	77,950	15,930	12,329	16,315	14,656
77,950	78,000	15,944	12,341	16,329	14,669

78,000

At least	But less than	Single	Married filing jointly	Married filing separately	Head of a household
78,000	78,050	15,958	12,354	16,343	14,681
78,050	78,100	15,972	12,366	16,357	14,694
78,100	78,150	15,986	12,379	16,371	14,706
78,150	78,200	16,000	12,391	16,385	14,719
78,200	78,250	16,014	12,404	16,399	14,731
78,250	78,300	16,028	12,416	16,413	14,744
78,300	78,350	16,042	12,429	16,427	14,756
78,350	78,400	16,056	12,441	16,441	14,769
78,400	78,450	16,070	12,454	16,455	14,781
78,450	78,500	16,084	12,466	16,469	14,794
78,500	78,550	16,098	12,479	16,483	14,806
78,550	78,600	16,112	12,491	16,497	14,819
78,600	78,650	16,126	12,504	16,511	14,831
78,650	78,700	16,140	12,516	16,525	14,844
78,700	78,750	16,154	12,529	16,539	14,856
78,750	78,800	16,168	12,541	16,553	14,869
78,800	78,850	16,182	12,554	16,567	14,881
78,850	78,900	16,196	12,566	16,581	14,894
78,900	78,950	16,210	12,579	16,595	14,906
78,950	79,000	16,224	12,591	16,609	14,919

79,000

At least	But less than	Single	Married filing jointly	Married filing separately	Head of a household
79,000	79,050	16,238	12,604	16,623	14,931
79,050	79,100	16,252	12,616	16,637	14,944
79,100	79,150	16,266	12,629	16,651	14,956
79,150	79,200	16,280	12,641	16,665	14,969
79,200	79,250	16,294	12,654	16,679	14,981
79,250	79,300	16,308	12,666	16,693	14,994
79,300	79,350	16,322	12,679	16,707	15,006
79,350	79,400	16,336	12,691	16,721	15,019
79,400	79,450	16,350	12,704	16,735	15,031
79,450	79,500	16,364	12,716	16,749	15,044
79,500	79,550	16,378	12,729	16,763	15,056
79,550	79,600	16,392	12,741	16,777	15,069
79,600	79,650	16,406	12,754	16,791	15,081
79,650	79,700	16,420	12,766	16,805	15,094
79,700	79,750	16,434	12,779	16,819	15,106
79,750	79,800	16,448	12,791	16,833	15,119
79,800	79,850	16,462	12,804	16,847	15,131
79,850	79,900	16,476	12,816	16,861	15,144
79,900	79,950	16,490	12,829	16,875	15,156
79,950	80,000	16,504	12,841	16,889	15,169

80,000

At least	But less than	Single	Married filing jointly	Married filing separately	Head of a household
80,000	80,050	16,518	12,854	16,903	15,181
80,050	80,100	16,532	12,866	16,917	15,194
80,100	80,150	16,546	12,879	16,931	15,206
80,150	80,200	16,560	12,891	16,945	15,219
80,200	80,250	16,574	12,904	16,959	15,231
80,250	80,300	16,588	12,916	16,973	15,244
80,300	80,350	16,602	12,929	16,987	15,256
80,350	80,400	16,616	12,941	17,001	15,269
80,400	80,450	16,630	12,954	17,015	15,281
80,450	80,500	16,644	12,966	17,029	15,294
80,500	80,550	16,658	12,979	17,043	15,306
80,550	80,600	16,672	12,991	17,057	15,319
80,600	80,650	16,686	13,004	17,071	15,331
80,650	80,700	16,700	13,016	17,085	15,344
80,700	80,750	16,714	13,029	17,099	15,356
80,750	80,800	16,728	13,041	17,113	15,369
80,800	80,850	16,742	13,054	17,127	15,381
80,850	80,900	16,756	13,066	17,141	15,394
80,900	80,950	16,770	13,079	17,155	15,406
80,950	81,000	16,784	13,091	17,169	15,419

81,000

At least	But less than	Single	Married filing jointly	Married filing separately	Head of a household
81,000	81,050	16,798	13,104	17,183	15,431
81,050	81,100	16,812	13,116	17,197	15,444
81,100	81,150	16,826	13,129	17,211	15,456
81,150	81,200	16,840	13,141	17,225	15,469
81,200	81,250	16,854	13,154	17,239	15,481
81,250	81,300	16,868	13,166	17,253	15,494
81,300	81,350	16,882	13,179	17,267	15,506
81,350	81,400	16,896	13,191	17,281	15,519
81,400	81,450	16,910	13,204	17,295	15,531
81,450	81,500	16,924	13,216	17,309	15,544
81,500	81,550	16,938	13,229	17,323	15,556
81,550	81,600	16,952	13,241	17,337	15,569
81,600	81,650	16,966	13,254	17,351	15,581
81,650	81,700	16,980	13,266	17,365	15,594
81,700	81,750	16,994	13,279	17,379	15,606
81,750	81,800	17,008	13,291	17,393	15,619
81,800	81,850	17,022	13,304	17,407	15,631
81,850	81,900	17,036	13,316	17,421	15,644
81,900	81,950	17,050	13,329	17,435	15,656
81,950	82,000	17,064	13,341	17,449	15,669

82,000

At least	But less than	Single	Married filing jointly	Married filing separately	Head of a household
82,000	82,050	17,078	13,354	17,463	15,681
82,050	82,100	17,092	13,366	17,477	15,694
82,100	82,150	17,106	13,379	17,491	15,706
82,150	82,200	17,120	13,391	17,505	15,719
82,200	82,250	17,134	13,404	17,519	15,731
82,250	82,300	17,148	13,416	17,533	15,744
82,300	82,350	17,162	13,429	17,547	15,756
82,350	82,400	17,176	13,441	17,561	15,769
82,400	82,450	17,190	13,454	17,575	15,781
82,450	82,500	17,204	13,466	17,589	15,794
82,500	82,550	17,218	13,479	17,603	15,806
82,550	82,600	17,232	13,491	17,617	15,819
82,600	82,650	17,246	13,504	17,631	15,831
82,650	82,700	17,260	13,516	17,645	15,844
82,700	82,750	17,274	13,529	17,659	15,856
82,750	82,800	17,288	13,541	17,673	15,869
82,800	82,850	17,302	13,554	17,687	15,881
82,850	82,900	17,316	13,566	17,701	15,894
82,900	82,950	17,330	13,579	17,715	15,906
82,950	83,000	17,344	13,591	17,729	15,919

83,000

At least	But less than	Single	Married filing jointly	Married filing separately	Head of a household
83,000	83,050	17,358	13,604	17,743	15,931
83,050	83,100	17,372	13,616	17,757	15,944
83,100	83,150	17,386	13,629	17,771	15,956
83,150	83,200	17,400	13,641	17,785	15,969
83,200	83,250	17,414	13,654	17,799	15,981
83,250	83,300	17,428	13,666	17,813	15,994
83,300	83,350	17,442	13,679	17,827	16,006
83,350	83,400	17,456	13,691	17,841	16,019
83,400	83,450	17,470	13,704	17,855	16,031
83,450	83,500	17,484	13,716	17,869	16,044
83,500	83,550	17,498	13,729	17,883	16,056
83,550	83,600	17,512	13,741	17,897	16,069
83,600	83,650	17,526	13,754	17,911	16,081
83,650	83,700	17,540	13,766	17,925	16,094
83,700	83,750	17,554	13,779	17,939	16,106
83,750	83,800	17,568	13,791	17,953	16,119
83,800	83,850	17,582	13,804	17,967	16,131
83,850	83,900	17,596	13,816	17,981	16,144
83,900	83,950	17,610	13,829	17,995	16,156
83,950	84,000	17,624	13,841	18,009	16,169

84,000

At least	But less than	Single	Married filing jointly	Married filing separately	Head of a household
84,000	84,050	17,638	13,854	18,023	16,181
84,050	84,100	17,652	13,866	18,037	16,194
84,100	84,150	17,666	13,879	18,051	16,206
84,150	84,200	17,680	13,891	18,065	16,219
84,200	84,250	17,694	13,904	18,079	16,231
84,250	84,300	17,708	13,916	18,093	16,244
84,300	84,350	17,722	13,929	18,107	16,256
84,350	84,400	17,736	13,941	18,121	16,269
84,400	84,450	17,750	13,954	18,135	16,281
84,450	84,500	17,764	13,966	18,149	16,294
84,500	84,550	17,778	13,979	18,163	16,306
84,550	84,600	17,792	13,991	18,177	16,319
84,600	84,650	17,806	14,004	18,191	16,331
84,650	84,700	17,820	14,016	18,205	16,344
84,700	84,750	17,834	14,029	18,219	16,356
84,750	84,800	17,848	14,041	18,233	16,369
84,800	84,850	17,862	14,054	18,247	16,381
84,850	84,900	17,876	14,066	18,261	16,394
84,900	84,950	17,890	14,079	18,275	16,406
84,950	85,000	17,904	14,091	18,289	16,419

85,000

At least	But less than	Single	Married filing jointly	Married filing separately	Head of a household
85,000	85,050	17,918	14,104	18,303	16,431
85,050	85,100	17,932	14,116	18,317	16,444
85,100	85,150	17,946	14,129	18,331	16,456
85,150	85,200	17,960	14,141	18,345	16,469
85,200	85,250	17,974	14,154	18,359	16,481
85,250	85,300	17,988	14,166	18,373	16,494
85,300	85,350	18,002	14,179	18,387	16,506
85,350	85,400	18,016	14,191	18,401	16,519
85,400	85,450	18,030	14,204	18,415	16,531
85,450	85,500	18,044	14,216	18,429	16,544
85,500	85,550	18,058	14,229	18,443	16,556
85,550	85,600	18,072	14,241	18,457	16,569
85,600	85,650	18,086	14,254	18,471	16,581
85,650	85,700	18,100	14,266	18,485	16,594
85,700	85,750	18,114	14,279	18,499	16,606
85,750	85,800	18,128	14,291	18,513	16,619
85,800	85,850	18,142	14,304	18,527	16,631
85,850	85,900	18,156	14,316	18,541	16,644
85,900	85,950	18,170	14,329	18,555	16,656
85,950	86,000	18,184	14,341	18,569	16,669

* This column must also be used by a qualifying widow(er).

(Continued on page 73)

¶25

2007 Tax Table – Continued

If line 43 (taxable income) is — And you are — (Single | Married filing jointly* | Married filing separately | Head of a household). *This column must also be used by a qualifying widow(er).

86,000

At least	But less than	Single	Married filing jointly*	Married filing separately	Head of a household
86,000	86,050	18,198	14,354	18,583	16,681
86,050	86,100	18,212	14,366	18,597	16,694
86,100	86,150	18,226	14,379	18,611	16,706
86,150	86,200	18,240	14,391	18,625	16,719
86,200	86,250	18,254	14,404	18,639	16,731
86,250	86,300	18,268	14,416	18,653	16,744
86,300	86,350	18,282	14,429	18,667	16,756
86,350	86,400	18,296	14,441	18,681	16,769
86,400	86,450	18,310	14,454	18,695	16,781
86,450	86,500	18,324	14,466	18,709	16,794
86,500	86,550	18,338	14,479	18,723	16,806
86,550	86,600	18,352	14,491	18,737	16,819
86,600	86,650	18,366	14,504	18,751	16,831
86,650	86,700	18,380	14,516	18,765	16,844
86,700	86,750	18,394	14,529	18,779	16,856
86,750	86,800	18,408	14,541	18,793	16,869
86,800	86,850	18,422	14,554	18,807	16,881
86,850	86,900	18,436	14,566	18,821	16,894
86,900	86,950	18,450	14,579	18,835	16,906
86,950	87,000	18,464	14,591	18,849	16,919

87,000

At least	But less than	Single	Married filing jointly*	Married filing separately	Head of a household
87,000	87,050	18,478	14,604	18,863	16,931
87,050	87,100	18,492	14,616	18,877	16,944
87,100	87,150	18,506	14,629	18,891	16,956
87,150	87,200	18,520	14,641	18,905	16,969
87,200	87,250	18,534	14,654	18,919	16,981
87,250	87,300	18,548	14,666	18,933	16,994
87,300	87,350	18,562	14,679	18,947	17,006
87,350	87,400	18,576	14,691	18,961	17,019
87,400	87,450	18,590	14,704	18,975	17,031
87,450	87,500	18,604	14,716	18,989	17,044
87,500	87,550	18,618	14,729	19,003	17,056
87,550	87,600	18,632	14,741	19,017	17,069
87,600	87,650	18,646	14,754	19,031	17,081
87,650	87,700	18,660	14,766	19,045	17,094
87,700	87,750	18,674	14,779	19,059	17,106
87,750	87,800	18,688	14,791	19,073	17,119
87,800	87,850	18,702	14,804	19,087	17,131
87,850	87,900	18,716	14,816	19,101	17,144
87,900	87,950	18,730	14,829	19,115	17,156
87,950	88,000	18,744	14,841	19,129	17,169

88,000

At least	But less than	Single	Married filing jointly*	Married filing separately	Head of a household
88,000	88,050	18,758	14,854	19,143	17,181
88,050	88,100	18,772	14,866	19,157	17,194
88,100	88,150	18,786	14,879	19,171	17,206
88,150	88,200	18,800	14,891	19,185	17,219
88,200	88,250	18,814	14,904	19,199	17,231
88,250	88,300	18,828	14,916	19,213	17,244
88,300	88,350	18,842	14,929	19,227	17,256
88,350	88,400	18,856	14,941	19,241	17,269
88,400	88,450	18,870	14,954	19,255	17,281
88,450	88,500	18,884	14,966	19,269	17,294
88,500	88,550	18,898	14,979	19,283	17,306
88,550	88,600	18,912	14,991	19,297	17,319
88,600	88,650	18,926	15,004	19,311	17,331
88,650	88,700	18,940	15,016	19,325	17,344
88,700	88,750	18,954	15,029	19,339	17,356
88,750	88,800	18,968	15,041	19,353	17,369
88,800	88,850	18,982	15,054	19,367	17,381
88,850	88,900	18,996	15,066	19,381	17,394
88,900	88,950	19,010	15,079	19,395	17,406
88,950	89,000	19,024	15,091	19,409	17,419

89,000

At least	But less than	Single	Married filing jointly*	Married filing separately	Head of a household
89,000	89,050	19,038	15,104	19,423	17,431
89,050	89,100	19,052	15,116	19,437	17,444
89,100	89,150	19,066	15,129	19,451	17,456
89,150	89,200	19,080	15,141	19,465	17,469
89,200	89,250	19,094	15,154	19,479	17,481
89,250	89,300	19,108	15,166	19,493	17,494
89,300	89,350	19,122	15,179	19,507	17,506
89,350	89,400	19,136	15,191	19,521	17,519
89,400	89,450	19,150	15,204	19,535	17,531
89,450	89,500	19,164	15,216	19,549	17,544
89,500	89,550	19,178	15,229	19,563	17,556
89,550	89,600	19,192	15,241	19,577	17,569
89,600	89,650	19,206	15,254	19,591	17,581
89,650	89,700	19,220	15,266	19,605	17,594
89,700	89,750	19,234	15,279	19,619	17,606
89,750	89,800	19,248	15,291	19,633	17,619
89,800	89,850	19,262	15,304	19,647	17,631
89,850	89,900	19,276	15,316	19,661	17,644
89,900	89,950	19,290	15,329	19,675	17,656
89,950	90,000	19,304	15,341	19,689	17,669

90,000

At least	But less than	Single	Married filing jointly*	Married filing separately	Head of a household
90,000	90,050	19,318	15,354	19,703	17,681
90,050	90,100	19,332	15,366	19,717	17,694
90,100	90,150	19,346	15,379	19,731	17,706
90,150	90,200	19,360	15,391	19,745	17,719
90,200	90,250	19,374	15,404	19,759	17,731
90,250	90,300	19,388	15,416	19,773	17,744
90,300	90,350	19,402	15,429	19,787	17,756
90,350	90,400	19,416	15,441	19,801	17,769
90,400	90,450	19,430	15,454	19,815	17,781
90,450	90,500	19,444	15,466	19,829	17,794
90,500	90,550	19,458	15,479	19,843	17,806
90,550	90,600	19,472	15,491	19,857	17,819
90,600	90,650	19,486	15,504	19,871	17,831
90,650	90,700	19,500	15,516	19,885	17,844
90,700	90,750	19,514	15,529	19,899	17,856
90,750	90,800	19,528	15,541	19,913	17,869
90,800	90,850	19,542	15,554	19,927	17,881
90,850	90,900	19,556	15,566	19,941	17,894
90,900	90,950	19,570	15,579	19,955	17,906
90,950	91,000	19,584	15,591	19,969	17,919

91,000

At least	But less than	Single	Married filing jointly*	Married filing separately	Head of a household
91,000	91,050	19,598	15,604	19,983	17,931
91,050	91,100	19,612	15,616	19,997	17,944
91,100	91,150	19,626	15,629	20,011	17,956
91,150	91,200	19,640	15,641	20,025	17,969
91,200	91,250	19,654	15,654	20,039	17,981
91,250	91,300	19,668	15,666	20,053	17,994
91,300	91,350	19,682	15,679	20,067	18,006
91,350	91,400	19,696	15,691	20,081	18,019
91,400	91,450	19,710	15,704	20,095	18,031
91,450	91,500	19,724	15,716	20,109	18,044
91,500	91,550	19,738	15,729	20,123	18,056
91,550	91,600	19,752	15,741	20,137	18,069
91,600	91,650	19,766	15,754	20,151	18,081
91,650	91,700	19,780	15,766	20,165	18,094
91,700	91,750	19,794	15,779	20,179	18,106
91,750	91,800	19,808	15,791	20,193	18,119
91,800	91,850	19,822	15,804	20,207	18,131
91,850	91,900	19,836	15,816	20,221	18,144
91,900	91,950	19,850	15,829	20,235	18,156
91,950	92,000	19,864	15,841	20,249	18,169

92,000

At least	But less than	Single	Married filing jointly*	Married filing separately	Head of a household
92,000	92,050	19,878	15,854	20,263	18,181
92,050	92,100	19,892	15,866	20,277	18,194
92,100	92,150	19,906	15,879	20,291	18,206
92,150	92,200	19,920	15,891	20,305	18,219
92,200	92,250	19,934	15,904	20,319	18,231
92,250	92,300	19,948	15,916	20,333	18,244
92,300	92,350	19,962	15,929	20,347	18,256
92,350	92,400	19,976	15,941	20,361	18,269
92,400	92,450	19,990	15,954	20,375	18,281
92,450	92,500	20,004	15,966	20,389	18,294
92,500	92,550	20,018	15,979	20,403	18,306
92,550	92,600	20,032	15,991	20,417	18,319
92,600	92,650	20,046	16,004	20,431	18,331
92,650	92,700	20,060	16,016	20,445	18,344
92,700	92,750	20,074	16,029	20,459	18,356
92,750	92,800	20,088	16,041	20,473	18,369
92,800	92,850	20,102	16,054	20,487	18,381
92,850	92,900	20,116	16,066	20,501	18,394
92,900	92,950	20,130	16,079	20,515	18,406
92,950	93,000	20,144	16,091	20,529	18,419

93,000

At least	But less than	Single	Married filing jointly*	Married filing separately	Head of a household
93,000	93,050	20,158	16,104	20,543	18,431
93,050	93,100	20,172	16,116	20,557	18,444
93,100	93,150	20,186	16,129	20,571	18,456
93,150	93,200	20,200	16,141	20,585	18,469
93,200	93,250	20,214	16,154	20,599	18,481
93,250	93,300	20,228	16,166	20,613	18,494
93,300	93,350	20,242	16,179	20,627	18,506
93,350	93,400	20,256	16,191	20,641	18,519
93,400	93,450	20,270	16,204	20,655	18,531
93,450	93,500	20,284	16,216	20,669	18,544
93,500	93,550	20,298	16,229	20,683	18,556
93,550	93,600	20,312	16,241	20,697	18,569
93,600	93,650	20,326	16,254	20,711	18,581
93,650	93,700	20,340	16,266	20,725	18,594
93,700	93,750	20,354	16,279	20,739	18,606
93,750	93,800	20,368	16,291	20,753	18,619
93,800	93,850	20,382	16,304	20,767	18,631
93,850	93,900	20,396	16,316	20,781	18,644
93,900	93,950	20,410	16,329	20,795	18,656
93,950	94,000	20,424	16,341	20,809	18,669

94,000

At least	But less than	Single	Married filing jointly*	Married filing separately	Head of a household
94,000	94,050	20,438	16,354	20,823	18,681
94,050	94,100	20,452	16,366	20,837	18,694
94,100	94,150	20,466	16,379	20,851	18,706
94,150	94,200	20,480	16,391	20,865	18,719
94,200	94,250	20,494	16,404	20,879	18,731
94,250	94,300	20,508	16,416	20,893	18,744
94,300	94,350	20,522	16,429	20,907	18,756
94,350	94,400	20,536	16,441	20,921	18,769
94,400	94,450	20,550	16,454	20,935	18,781
94,450	94,500	20,564	16,466	20,949	18,794
94,500	94,550	20,578	16,479	20,963	18,806
94,550	94,600	20,592	16,491	20,977	18,819
94,600	94,650	20,606	16,504	20,991	18,831
94,650	94,700	20,620	16,516	21,005	18,844
94,700	94,750	20,634	16,529	21,019	18,856
94,750	94,800	20,648	16,541	21,033	18,869
94,800	94,850	20,662	16,554	21,047	18,881
94,850	94,900	20,676	16,566	21,061	18,894
94,900	94,950	20,690	16,579	21,075	18,906
94,950	95,000	20,704	16,591	21,089	18,919

* This column must also be used by a qualifying widow(er).

(Continued on page 74)

¶25

2007 Tax Table–*Continued*

If line 43 (taxable income) is—		Single	Married filing jointly*	Married filing separately	Head of a household
At least	But less than				
		Your tax is—			

95,000

At least	But less than	Single	Married filing jointly*	Married filing separately	Head of a household
95,000	95,050	20,718	16,604	21,103	18,931
95,050	95,100	20,732	16,616	21,117	18,944
95,100	95,150	20,746	16,629	21,131	18,956
95,150	95,200	20,760	16,641	21,145	18,969
95,200	95,250	20,774	16,654	21,159	18,981
95,250	95,300	20,788	16,666	21,173	18,994
95,300	95,350	20,802	16,679	21,187	19,006
95,350	95,400	20,816	16,691	21,201	19,019
95,400	95,450	20,830	16,704	21,215	19,031
95,450	95,500	20,844	16,716	21,229	19,044
95,500	95,550	20,858	16,729	21,243	19,056
95,550	95,600	20,872	16,741	21,257	19,069
95,600	95,650	20,886	16,754	21,271	19,081
95,650	95,700	20,900	16,766	21,285	19,094
95,700	95,750	20,914	16,779	21,299	19,106
95,750	95,800	20,928	16,791	21,313	19,119
95,800	95,850	20,942	16,804	21,327	19,131
95,850	95,900	20,956	16,816	21,341	19,144
95,900	95,950	20,970	16,829	21,355	19,156
95,950	96,000	20,984	16,841	21,369	19,169

96,000

At least	But less than	Single	Married filing jointly*	Married filing separately	Head of a household
96,000	96,050	20,998	16,854	21,383	19,181
96,050	96,100	21,012	16,866	21,397	19,194
96,100	96,150	21,026	16,879	21,411	19,206
96,150	96,200	21,040	16,891	21,425	19,219
96,200	96,250	21,054	16,904	21,439	19,231
96,250	96,300	21,068	16,916	21,453	19,244
96,300	96,350	21,082	16,929	21,467	19,256
96,350	96,400	21,096	16,941	21,481	19,269
96,400	96,450	21,110	16,954	21,495	19,281
96,450	96,500	21,124	16,966	21,509	19,294
96,500	96,550	21,138	16,979	21,523	19,306
96,550	96,600	21,152	16,991	21,537	19,319
96,600	96,650	21,166	17,004	21,551	19,331
96,650	96,700	21,180	17,016	21,565	19,344
96,700	96,750	21,194	17,029	21,579	19,356
96,750	96,800	21,208	17,041	21,593	19,369
96,800	96,850	21,222	17,054	21,607	19,381
96,850	96,900	21,236	17,066	21,621	19,394
96,900	96,950	21,250	17,079	21,635	19,406
96,950	97,000	21,264	17,091	21,649	19,419

97,000

At least	But less than	Single	Married filing jointly*	Married filing separately	Head of a household
97,000	97,050	21,278	17,104	21,663	19,431
97,050	97,100	21,292	17,116	21,677	19,444
97,100	97,150	21,306	17,129	21,691	19,456
97,150	97,200	21,320	17,141	21,705	19,469
97,200	97,250	21,334	17,154	21,719	19,481
97,250	97,300	21,348	17,166	21,733	19,494
97,300	97,350	21,362	17,179	21,747	19,506
97,350	97,400	21,376	17,191	21,761	19,519
97,400	97,450	21,390	17,204	21,775	19,531
97,450	97,500	21,404	17,216	21,789	19,544
97,500	97,550	21,418	17,229	21,803	19,556
97,550	97,600	21,432	17,241	21,817	19,569
97,600	97,650	21,446	17,254	21,831	19,581
97,650	97,700	21,460	17,266	21,845	19,594
97,700	97,750	21,474	17,279	21,859	19,606
97,750	97,800	21,488	17,291	21,873	19,619
97,800	97,850	21,502	17,304	21,887	19,631
97,850	97,900	21,516	17,316	21,901	19,644
97,900	97,950	21,530	17,329	21,915	19,656
97,950	98,000	21,544	17,341	21,929	19,669

98,000

At least	But less than	Single	Married filing jointly*	Married filing separately	Head of a household
98,000	98,050	21,558	17,354	21,948	19,681
98,050	98,100	21,572	17,366	21,965	19,694
98,100	98,150	21,586	17,379	21,981	19,706
98,150	98,200	21,600	17,391	21,998	19,719
98,200	98,250	21,614	17,404	22,014	19,731
98,250	98,300	21,628	17,416	22,031	19,744
98,300	98,350	21,642	17,429	22,047	19,756
98,350	98,400	21,656	17,441	22,064	19,769
98,400	98,450	21,670	17,454	22,080	19,781
98,450	98,500	21,684	17,466	22,097	19,794
98,500	98,550	21,698	17,479	22,113	19,806
98,550	98,600	21,712	17,491	22,130	19,819
98,600	98,650	21,726	17,504	22,146	19,831
98,650	98,700	21,740	17,516	22,163	19,844
98,700	98,750	21,754	17,529	22,179	19,856
98,750	98,800	21,768	17,541	22,196	19,869
98,800	98,850	21,782	17,554	22,212	19,881
98,850	98,900	21,796	17,566	22,229	19,894
98,900	98,950	21,810	17,579	22,245	19,906
98,950	99,000	21,824	17,591	22,262	19,919

99,000

At least	But less than	Single	Married filing jointly*	Married filing separately	Head of a household
99,000	99,050	21,838	17,604	22,278	19,931
99,050	99,100	21,852	17,616	22,295	19,944
99,100	99,150	21,866	17,629	22,311	19,956
99,150	99,200	21,880	17,641	22,328	19,969
99,200	99,250	21,894	17,654	22,344	19,981
99,250	99,300	21,908	17,666	22,361	19,994
99,300	99,350	21,922	17,679	22,377	20,006
99,350	99,400	21,936	17,691	22,394	20,019
99,400	99,450	21,950	17,704	22,410	20,031
99,450	99,500	21,964	17,716	22,427	20,044
99,500	99,550	21,978	17,729	22,443	20,056
99,550	99,600	21,992	17,741	22,460	20,069
99,600	99,650	22,006	17,754	22,476	20,081
99,650	99,700	22,020	17,766	22,493	20,094
99,700	99,750	22,034	17,779	22,509	20,106
99,750	99,800	22,048	17,791	22,526	20,119
99,800	99,850	22,062	17,804	22,542	20,131
99,850	99,900	22,076	17,816	22,559	20,144
99,900	99,950	22,090	17,829	22,575	20,156
99,950	100,000	22,104	17,841	22,592	20,169

$100,000 or over — use the Tax Computation Worksheet on page 75

* This column must also be used by a qualifying widow(er)

¶25

CORPORATION INCOME TAX RATES FOR 2007

¶ 33 Corporations

2007

Taxable Income Over	But Not Over	Pay	+	% on Excess	of the amount over—
$0—	$50,000	$0		15%	$0
50,000—	75,000	7,500		25	50,000
75,000—	100,000	13,750		34	75,000
100,000—	335,000	22,250		39	100,000
335,000—	10,000,000	113,900		34	335,000
10,000,000—	15,000,000	3,400,000		35	10,000,000
15,000,000—	18,333,333	5,150,000		38	15,000,000
18,333,333—	. . . .			35	0

Taxable income of certain personal service corporations is taxed at a flat rate of 35%. See ¶ 219.

¶ 34 Controlled Group of Corporations

A controlled group of corporations is subject to the same rates as those listed above as though the group was one corporation. See ¶ 289.

¶ 35 Personal Holding Companies

In addition to regular corporate income taxes, a special tax is imposed on any corporation which is a personal holding company. For tax years beginning in 2007, the additional tax is 15% of the corporation's undistributed personal holding company income. See ¶ 275.

¶ 36 Insurance Companies and Regulated Investment Companies

The regular corporate tax rates apply to an insurance company's taxable income (see ¶ 2370 and ¶ 2378). In the case of regulated investment companies, the corporate tax rates apply to investment company taxable income. See ¶ 2303.

¶ 37 Accumulated Earnings Tax

In addition to regular corporate income taxes, a corporation may be subject to a special tax on its accumulated taxable income. For tax years beginning in 2007, the tax is 15% of the corporation's accumulated taxable income. A corporation is entitled to a $250,000 accumulated earnings credit ($150,000 for personal service corporations) against the tax. See ¶ 251.

¶ 38 Foreign Corporations

The income of a foreign corporation that is not effectively connected with a U.S. trade or business is taxed at a rate of 30%. Domestic corporate rates apply to the income of a foreign corporation that is effectively connected with a U.S. trade or business. See ¶ 2425.

¶ 39 Real Estate Investment Trusts

A real estate investment trusts will be subject to regular corporate income tax rates on its "real estate investment trust taxable income." See ¶ 2329.

ESTATE AND GIFT TAXES

¶ 40 Computation of Taxes

Estate Taxes. Estate taxes are computed by applying the unified rate schedule (¶ 42) to the aggregate of cumulative lifetime transfers and transfers at death and subtracting the gift taxes payable on the lifetime transfers. The unified rate schedule is effective for gifts made after December 31, 1976, and to estates of decedents dying after that date until the scheduled repeal of the estate tax in 2010 (Economic Growth and Tax Relief Reconciliation Act of 2001 (P.L. 107-16)). See ¶ 2925 and following.

Gift Taxes. Gift taxes are computed by applying the unified rate schedule (¶ 42) to cumulative lifetime taxable transfers and subtracting the taxes payable for prior taxable periods. Although the estate tax is being repealed in 2010, the gift tax will remain in effect. There is an annual exclusion of $12,000 for 2007 and 2008 per donee for gifts, with an annual maximum of $24,000 for 2007 and 2008 per donee applicable to spouses who utilize gift-splitting. Additionally, there is an unlimited exclusion for payments of tuition and medical expenses. See ¶ 2903 and following.

Generation-Skipping Transfer Tax. The tax on generation-skipping transfers (GST) is computed with reference to a flat rate equal to the product of the maximum estate tax rate (45% in 2007 and 2008) and the inclusion ratio with respect to the transfer. The GST tax is also scheduled to be repealed in 2010. See ¶ 2942.

¶ 41 Applicable (Unified) Credit

Amount of Credit. The applicable credit amount (formerly, the unified credit) for estates of decedents dying during 2007 and 2008 is $780,800. The applicable credit amount exempts $2 million (the applicable exclusion amount) from estate tax liability in 2007 and 2008 (see ¶ 2901). The applicable exclusion amount for estate tax purposes will increase to $3.5 million in 2009; however, for gift tax purposes, the applicable exclusion amount will remain at $1 million. It is subtracted from the taxpayer's estate or gift tax liability. Although the credit must be used to offset gift taxes on lifetime transfers, regardless of the amount so used, the full credit is allowed against the tentative estate tax at death.[1]

Footnote references are to paragraphs of the 2008 Standard Federal Tax Reports.

[1] This is so because, under Code Sec. 2001(b)(1), any gifts to which the unified credit was previously applied are added back to the taxable estate to compute the tentative estate tax. After reducing the tentative tax by the amount of gift taxes payable, the full unified credit amount is subtracted to arrive at estate tax payable. Thus, what may at first appear to be a double application of the unified credit is eliminated by way of a calculation that effectively increases the estate tax payable in the amount of the unified gift tax credit used to shelter lifetime gifts.

¶ 42 Unified Transfer Tax Rate Schedule

The unified rate schedule applying to estates of decedents dying and gifts made in 2007 appears below.

Table A—Unified Rate Schedule For 2007

Column A	Column B	Column C	Column D
Taxable amount over	Taxable amount not over	Tax on amount in column A	Rate of tax on excess over amount in column A Percent
$0	$10,000	$0	18
10,000	20,000	1,800	20
20,000	40,000	3,800	22
40,000	60,000	8,200	24
60,000	80,000	13,000	26
80,000	100,000	18,200	28
100,000	150,000	23,800	30
150,000	250,000	38,800	32
250,000	500,000	70,800	34
500,000	750,000	155,800	37
750,000	1,000,000	248,300	39
1,000,000	1,250,000	345,800	41
1,250,000	1,500,000	448,300	43
1,500,000	2,000,000	555,800	45
2,000,000	. . . .	780,800	45

The top estate and gift tax rate incrementally decreased from 2002 to 2007, when it reached 45 percent where it will remain for 2007 through 2009, the year prior to the scheduled repeal of the estate tax (Code Sec. 2001(c), as amended by P.L. 107-16). For estates of decedents dying, and gifts made, in 2008, the top estate and gift tax rate is as follows:

2008

If the amount is: Over (1)	But not over (2)	Tax on (1)	Rate on Excess (1)
2,000,000	. . . .	780,800	45

The gift tax will continue after the repeal of the estate tax; however, the top tax rate will be 35 percent applicable to transfers over $500,000. Although the estate tax is scheduled to be repealed in 2010, without further legislative action, it will be reestablished in 2011 under the 2001 rules because of budgetary constraints. The changes are discussed in Chapter 29.

Benefits phased out for transfers exceeding $10,000,000 before 2002. For estates of decedents dying and gifts made after 1997 and before 2002, the benefits of the graduated rates under the unified transfer tax system were phased out beginning with cumulative transfers rising above $10,000,000. This was accomplished by adding five percent of the excess of any transfer over $10,000,000, but not over $17,184,000, to the tentative tax computed in determining the ultimate transfer tax liability. The surcharge was repealed for estates of decedents dying and gifts made after 2001 (Code Sec. 2001(c)(2), prior to being stricken by P.L. 107-16).

¶ 43 Credit for State Death Taxes

The table below is to be used in calculating the amount of the credit available for state death taxes paid with respect to property included in a decedent's gross estate. However, the state death tax credit was gradually phased-out between 2002 and 2004 (Code Sec. 2011(b), as amended by P.L. 107-16). Beginning in 2005, the state death tax credit is replaced by a deduction for state death taxes paid until the repeal of the federal estate tax in 2010.

State Death Tax Credit Table[1]

| Adjusted Taxable Estate[2] | | | | | Of Excess |
At least	But less than	Credit =	+	%	Over
$0	$40,000	$0		0.0	$0
40,000	90,000	0		.8	40,000
90,000	140,000	400		1.6	90,000
140,000	240,000	1,200		2.4	140,000
240,000	440,000	3,600		3.2	240,000
440,000	640,000	10,000		4.0	440,000
640,000	840,000	18,000		4.8	640,000
840,000	1,040,000	27,600		5.6	840,000
1,040,000	1,540,000	38,800		6.4	1,040,000
1,540,000	2,040,000	70,800		7.2	1,540,000
2,040,000	2,540,000	106,800		8.0	2,040,000
2,540,000	3,040,000	146,800		8.8	2,540,000
3,040,000	3,540,000	190,800		9.6	3,040,000
3,540,000	4,040,000	238,800		10.4	3,540,000
4,040,000	5,040,000	290,800		11.2	4,040,000
5,040,000	6,040,000	402,800		12.0	5,040,000
6,040,000	7,040,000	522,800		12.8	6,040,000
7,040,000	8,040,000	650,800		13.6	7,040,000
8,040,000	9,040,000	786,800		14.4	8,040,000
9,040,000	10,040,000	930,800		15.2	9,040,000
10,040,000	. . . .	1,082,800		16.0	10,040,000

[1] There is a limitation on the credit in estates of nonresident aliens. See Code Sec. 2102.
[2] The adjusted taxable estate is the taxable estate reduced by $60,000.

¶ 45 Nonresident Aliens

The gift and estate tax rates that are applicable to U.S. citizens are also applicable to the estate of a nonresident alien. Where permitted by treaty, the estate of a nonresident alien is allowed a credit equal to the unified credit available to a U.S. citizen multiplied by the proportion of the decedent's entire gross estate situated in the United States. In computing the credit, property is not treated as situated in the United States if such property is exempt from tax under any treaty. In other cases, a unified credit of $13,000 is allowed.

For estates of decedents dying and gifts made after 1997 and before 2002, the additional 5% rate applicable to transfers in excess of $10 million but not exceeding $17,184,000 was adjusted to reflect the fact that in some cases the estate of a nonresident noncitizen does not receive the same unified credit available to U.S. citizens. Accordingly, the additional 5% rate applied to the taxable transfers of nonresident noncitizens prior to 2002 in excess of $10 million only to the extent necessary to phase out the benefit of the graduated rates actually allowed by statute or treaty.

The estate of a resident of a U.S. possession is entitled to a unified credit equal to the greater of (1) $13,000 or (2) $46,800 multiplied by the proportion of the decedent's entire gross estate situated in the United States. See ¶ 2940.

OTHER TAXES

¶ 47 Self-Employment Taxes

A tax of 15.3% is imposed on net earnings from self-employment. The rate consists of a 12.4% component for old-age, survivors, and disability insurance (OASDI) and a 2.9% component for Medicare. The OASDI rate (12.4%) applies to net earnings within the OASDI earnings base, which is $97,500 for 2007 and $102,000 for 2008. The Medicare rate (2.9%) applies to all net earnings since there is no limit on the amount of earnings subject to the Medicare portion of the tax.

¶ 49 Social Security Taxes

Social Security, Hospital Insurance. A combined tax rate of 7.65% (6.2% for old-age, survivors, and disability insurance (OASDI) and 1.45% for hospital insurance (Medicare)) is imposed on both employer and employee. The OASDI rate (6.2%) applies to wages within the OASDI wage base, which is $97,500 for 2007 and $102,000 for 2008. The Medicare rate (1.45%) applies to all wages since there is no limit on the amount of earnings subject to the Medicare portion of the tax. Regarding household employees, any person who paid cash wages of $1,500 or more in 2007 and $1,600 or more in 2008 to any one household employee must withhold and pay social security and Medicare taxes.

Medicare Payments. Medicare Part B premiums ($93.50 per month for 2007 and $96.40 per month in 2008) qualify as deductible medical expenses. See ¶ 1019.

Unemployment Compensation. A tax rate of 6.2% is imposed on the first $7,000 of wages paid to a covered employee by an employer who employs one or more persons in covered employment in each of 20 days in a year, each day being in a different week, or who has a payroll for covered employment of at least $1,500 in a calendar quarter in the current or preceding calendar year. Because employers are allowed credits against the 6.2% FUTA rate through participation in state unemployment insurance laws, the net FUTA rate actually paid by most employers is 0.8% except when credit reductions are in effect in a state. The unemployment tax also applies to any person who paid total cash wages of $1,000 or more to a household employee during any calendar quarter in the current or preceding calendar year. For wages paid in 2007 and 2008, the FUTA rate remains at 6.2%.

Railroad Retirement Tax. Identical tier 1 tax rates apply to both employees and employers, which finance tier 1 benefits. The tier 1 tax rate for 2007 and 2008 is 7.65 percent. The contribution and benefit base is $97,500 for compensation paid in 2007 ($102,000 for compensation paid in 2008). The tier 1 tax rate for Medicare is 2.9%. A separate annual base applies to the tier 2 tax, which finances tier 2 benefits. The contribution and benefit base under the tier 2 tax is $72,600 for compensation paid in 2007 ($75,900 for compensation paid in 2008). The Railroad Retirement and Survivors' Improvement Act of 2001 (P.L. 107-90), set the 2002 and 2003 tier 2 tax rates. The Act provided a means of determining future adjustments in the tier 2 tax rates, depending on railroad retirement fund levels. The change allowed tier 2 tax rates to increase or decrease without congressional action, depending on the level of funds available to pay benefits. Thus, the tier 2 tax rates are be based on an average account benefits ratio, which refers to the average determined by the Secretary of Treasury of the account benefits ratios for the 10 most recent fiscal years ending before such calendar year.

¶ 53 Excise Taxes

Identified below are various excise taxes.

FUELS

Gasoline

Gasoline, including gasohol (per gallon) .... 18.4¢

Special Fuels

Diesel fuel (except if used on a farm for farming purposes) (per gallon) .... 24.4¢
Diesel fuel for use in trains (per gallon) .... 0.1¢
Diesel-water fuel emulsions (per gallon) .... 19.8¢
Alternative fuels (per gallon) .... 18.4¢
Qualified ethanol (per gallon) .... 13.25¢
Qualified methanol (per gallon) .... 12.35¢
Inland waterways fuel use tax (per gallon) .... 20.1¢
Commercial aviation fuel (other than gasoline) (jet fuel) (per gallon) .... 4.4¢
Noncommercial aviation gasoline (per gallon) .... 19.4¢
Noncommercial aviation fuel (other than gasoline) (jet fuel) (per gallon) .... 21.9¢
Compressed natural gas (per energy equivalent of a gallon of gasoline) .... 18.3¢
Any liquid fuel (other than ethanol and methanol) derived from coal (including peat)
   through the Fischer-Tropsch process .... 24.4¢
Liquid hydrocarbons derived from biomass .... 24.4¢
Liquefied natural gas .... 24.3¢
Kerosene (per gallon) .... 24.4¢
Crude oil (after 3/31/2006) .... 5¢ per barrel

HEAVY TRUCKS, TRAILERS

Truck chassis or body (that is suitable for use with a vehicle in excess of 33,000 lbs. gross
   vehicle weight) .... 12% of retail price
Trailer and semitrailer chassis or body (that is suitable for use with a trailer or semitrailer in
   excess of 26,000 lbs. gross vehicle weight) .... 12% of retail price
Parts and accessories installed on taxable vehicles within 6 months after being placed in
   service (when cost of parts or accessories exceeds $1,000) .... 12% of retail price

HIGHWAY-TYPE TIRES

Tires with load capacity of 3,500 lbs. or less .... No tax
Tires with load capacity over 3,500 lbs. ...... 9.45¢ for each 10 lbs. of tire load capacity over
   3,500 lbs.
Biasply tires .... 4.725¢ for each 10 lbs. of tire load capacity over 3,500 lbs.
Super single tires .... 4.725¢ for each 10 lbs. of tire load capacity over 3,500 lbs.

GAS GUZZLER TAX

Mileage ratings per gallon of at least 22.5 .... $ 0
Mileage ratings per gallon of at least 21.5 but less than 22.5 1,000
Mileage ratings per gallon of at least 20.5 but less than 21.5 1,300
Mileage ratings per gallon of at least 19.5 but less than 20.5 1,700
Mileage ratings per gallon of at least 18.5 but less than 19.5 2,100
Mileage ratings per gallon of at least 17.5 but less than 18.5 2,600
Mileage ratings per gallon of at least 16.5 but less than 17.5 3,000
Mileage ratings per gallon of at least 15.5 but less than 16.5 3,700
Mileage ratings per gallon of at least 14.5 but less than 15.5 4,500
Mileage ratings per gallon of at least 13.5 but less than 14.5 5,400
Mileage ratings per gallon of at least 12.5 but less than 13.5 6,400
Mileage ratings per gallon of less than 12.5 7,700

FACILITIES AND SERVICES

Communications

Local telephone service and teletypewriter service 3%

Transportation by air

Domestic passenger tickets: 7.5% plus $3.40 (from 1/1/07-12/31/07) for each flight segment (excepting segments to or from rural airports)

Alaska and Hawaii passenger tickets (per person per departure) (from 1/1/07-12/31/07) .. $7.50

International passenger tickets (per person for each arrival and for each departure) (from 1/1/07-12/31/07) $15.10

Air freight waybill 6.25%

Transportation by water

Persons $3.00

Port use tax on imports (harbor maintenance tax) .... 0.125% of cargo value

ALCOHOL TAXES

Distilled spirits (per gallon) $13.50

Beer (per barrel).. $18.00 (31 gallons or less)

Wines

Not more than 14% alcohol (per gallon) $1.07

More than 14 to 21% alcohol (per gallon) $1.57

More than 21 to 24% alcohol (per gallon) $3.15

Artificially carbonated wines (per gallon) $3.30

More than 24% alcohol (per gallon) $13.50

Champagne and other sparkling wines (per gallon) $3.40

TOBACCO TAXES

Cigarettes (per 1,000) .... $19.50 to $40.95 per 1,000

Cigarette papers (per 50 papers) .... 1.22¢

Cigarette tubes (per 50 tubes).. 2.44¢

Cigars (per 1,000) .... $1.828 to $48.75 per 1,000

Snuff (per pound) .... 58.5¢

Chewing tobacco (per pound) .... 19.5¢

Pipe tobacco (per pound) $1.0969

Roll-your-own tobacco (per pound) $1.0969

WAGERING TAXES

State authorized wagers placed with bookmakers and lottery operators . 0.25% of wager amt.

Unauthorized wagers placed with bookmakers and lottery operators..... 2% of wager amt.

License fee on person accepting wagers authorized under state law (each year) $50

License fee on person accepting wagers (each year) $500

HIGHWAY MOTOR VEHICLE USE TAX

Vehicles of less than 55,000 lbs.. No tax

Vehicles of 55,000 lbs.—75,000 lbs. (per year) ... $100 per year + $22 for each 1,000 lbs. (or fraction thereof) over 55,000 lbs.

Vehicles over 75,000 lbs. (per year) $550

FIREARMS

Transfer taxes (per firearm) .... $5 (concealable weapons) or $200

Occupational taxes (per year) . $1,000 (importers or manufacturers), or $500 (dealers, small importers or manufacturers)

Pistols and revolvers .... 10% of sales price

Firearms other than pistols and revolvers .... 11% of sales price

Ammunition (shells and cartridges) .... 11% of sales price

OTHER TAXES

Electric outboard motors .... 3% of sales price

Sport fishing equipment.. 10% of sales price

Bows with a peak draw weight of at least 30 pounds .... 11% of sales price

Quivers, broadheads, points .... 11% of sales price

Arrow shafts.. 42¢ per shaft

Coal—underground mines .... lower of $1.10 per ton or 4.4% of sales price

Coal—surface mines .... lower of $0.55 per ton or 4.4% of sales price

Vaccines .... 75¢ per dose on taxable vaccines

Preparing Income Tax Returns

CHECKLISTS

¶ 55 Checklist for Items of Income

The determination of whether an item of income is includible in income and, thus, taxable, or whether it is excludable from income is crucial to the determination of tax liability. An item that is includible increases tax liability, depending on the amount, whereas an excludable item decreases tax liability. The following chart, which is arranged alphabetically by income item, indicates whether the item is includible or excludable from income. A reference to further details in the 2008 STANDARD FEDERAL TAX REPORTER is also provided.

Income Item	Includible in Income	Paragraph Reference
Accident and health insurance premiums, employer-paid (except for long-term care benefits provided through flexible spending accounts and subject to limitation as to medical savings accounts)	No	¶ 6803.01
Accident and health plans proceeds (under insurance purchased by taxpayer or under employee supported plans) where premiums did not give taxpayer a previous medical expense deduction	No	¶ 6662.035
Agreement not to compete, payments received for	Yes	¶ 30,422.033
Airline deregulation benefits, special rule, unemployment compensation	Yes	¶ 6412.15
Alimony, support and separate maintenance payments, receipt of	Yes	¶ 6094.01
Allowances received by dependents of members of the Armed Forces	No	¶ 7501.01
Annuities (amounts in excess of cost)	Yes	¶ 6114.022
Annuities, interest on advance premiums	Yes	¶ 5504.023
Annuity contract, death benefit	Yes	¶ 6114.35
Antitrust action, punitive damages recovered	Yes	¶ 5900.03
Armed Forces pay (except "combat zone" or "missing" status pay)	Yes	¶ 5507.037; ¶ 7082.021
Athletic facilities on employer's premises, value of use	No	¶ 7438.057
Attorney's contingent fee, includible in plaintiff's gross income	Yes	¶ 5504.032
Awards, generally	Yes	¶ 6204.01
Awards, if donated by recipient to qualified entity	No	¶ 6204.025
Back pay	Yes	¶ 5507.129
Bad debts, prior taxes and interest on taxes, recovery of, provided no tax benefit in prior year	No	¶ 7062.043; ¶ 7062.047
Bargain purchases from employer to extent discount exceeds gross profit percentage	Yes	¶ 7438.026
Barter income	Yes	¶ 5508.028
Beauty contest winners, receipt of scholarships and amounts for personal appearances	Yes	¶ 7183.305
Bequests and devises, generally	No	¶ 6553.01
Bonds, state, city, etc., interest on, generally	No	¶ 6602.01
Bonuses	Yes	¶ 5507.024

Income Item	Includible in Income	Paragraph Reference
Buried treasure	Yes	¶ 5504.6916
Business interruption insurance proceeds:		
. based on income experience	Yes	¶ 29,650.053
. based on per diem idleness	No	¶ 29,650.053
Business profits	Yes	¶ 5600.01
Business subsidies for construction or contributions by customer or potential customer	Yes	¶ 7202.021
Capital contributions to corporation	No	¶ 7202.01
Car pool receipts by car owner for transportation of other employees	No	¶ 5504.144
Car used for business purposes by full-time car salesperson, value of use	No	¶ 7438.038
Checks, uncashed by payee, for previously deducted items	Yes	¶ 5507.698
Child or dependent care plan benefits, employer-subsidized, limited	No	¶ 7381.01
Child support payments	No	¶ 6094.027
Christmas bonuses from employer, based on percentage of salary (aside from token gifts such as hams, turkeys, etc., given for goodwill)	Yes	¶ 5507.2942
Civil Rights Act violation, back pay recovery	Yes	¶ 5900.021
Clergy fees and contributions received unless earned as agent of religious order	Yes	¶ 5507.04
"Combat zone" pay, military	No	¶ 5507.037; ¶ 7082.021
Commissions	Yes	¶ 5507.022
Commodity credit loans, receipt of (optional)	Yes	¶ 6304.01
Compensation, property received, value of	Yes	¶ 5508.021
Contract cancellation, payments received for	Yes	¶ 21,005.126
Damages:		
. back pay	Yes	¶ 5507.129
. loss of anticipatory benefits (business)	Yes	¶ 5900.14
. personal physical injuries or sickness	No	¶ 5900.021; ¶ 6662.04
. slander or libel of personal reputation	Yes	¶ 5900.025
Death benefits, employer-paid	Yes	¶ 6507.01
Debts, cancellation of, related to Hurricane Katrina	No	¶ 5802.027
Debts, nongratuitous cancellation of	Yes	¶ 5802.021
Defamation damage award, compensating injury to business and professional reputation	Yes	¶ 5900.025
Deferred income under certain nonqualified deferred compensation plans	Yes	¶ 18,956.01
Dependent care assistance program payments, limited	No	¶ 7381.01
Disability payments, other than for loss of wages, all taxpayers, including veterans	No	¶ 6662.01
Disability pensions, Veterans' Administration	No	¶ 6662.01; ¶ 6662.046
Disaster unemployment payments	Yes	¶ 6412.021
Discharge of indebtedness, nongratuitous	Yes	¶ 5802.021
Discharge of indebtedness, related to Hurricane Katrina	No	¶ 5802.027
Dividends, stock distributed in lieu of money	Yes	¶ 15,402.01
Drawing account, excess cancelled by employer	Yes	¶ 5507.154
Educational assistance, employer-provided under a nondiscriminatory plan (including educational assistance for graduate-level courses that begin after December 31, 2001)	No	¶ 7353.01
Embezzlement proceeds	Yes	¶ 5901.021
Employee achievement awards, qualified	No	¶ 5507.024; ¶ 6204.03
Employee discount, qualified	No	¶ 7438.025
Employment contract, amounts received by employee for cancellation	Yes	¶ 21,005.116

Income Item	Includible in Income	Paragraph Reference
Endowment policies, generally as to non-annuity payments until cost is recovered	No	¶ 6114.01; ¶ 6114.0405
Farm income	Yes	¶ 5602.01
Farmers, government payments to offset operating losses or lack of profits	Yes	¶ 5602.03
Fellowships and scholarships, degree programs	No	¶ 7183.01
Financial counseling fees, employer-paid	Yes	¶ 5507.2927
Foreign earned income, limited election	No	¶ 28,049.01
Foster parents, reimbursements for care of a qualified foster child	No	¶ 7402.01
Fringe benefits, if no additional cost service, qualified employee discount, working condition fringe, *de minimis* fringe, qualified transportation fringe, qualified moving expense reimbursement	No	¶ 7438.01
Future services, prepayment for	Yes	¶ 21,005.027
Gain on sale of personal residence:		
. up to $250,000 ($500,000 for joint filers)	No	¶ 7266.024
Gains:		
. condemnation of nonresidential property unless award is used for replacement	Yes	¶ 29,650.01; ¶ 29,650.319
. discount on later sale or redemption of bonds purchased with excess number of interest coupons detached (stripped bonds)	Yes	¶ 31,481.023
. obligations purchased or satisfied for less than face value	Yes	¶ 5804.51
. partner's sale of asset to partnership	Yes	¶ 25,182.01
. sales of depreciable property	Yes	¶ 30,909.01
. sales of goodwill	Yes	¶ 30,422.032
. sales of patents	Yes	¶ 30,653.01
. sales of property, generally	Yes	¶ 5700.01
. sales of stock in foreign corporations	Yes	¶ 30,968.01
. sales of stock of foreign investment company	Yes	¶ 30,921.01
. swap-fund transfers	Yes	¶ 16,405.03
Gambling winnings:		
. illegal	Yes	¶ 5901.01; ¶ 5901.40
. legal	Yes	¶ 5504.22
Gifts	No	¶ 6553.03
Government employees, additional compensation as inducement to accept foreign service employment ("post differentials")	Yes	¶ 28,063.01
Health insurance proceeds, not paid by the insured's employer or financed by the insured's employer through contributions that were not included in the employee's gross income	No	¶ 6662.035
Health Savings Accounts partner's/shareholder's contributions made by partnership/S corporation	Yes	¶ 12,785.25
Hedging transactions, commodity futures transactions . .	Yes	¶ 30,426.03
Hobby income (nonprofit activities, deductions limited) .	Yes	¶ 12,177.01
Illegal transactions, gains from: gambling, betting, lotteries, illegal businesses, embezzlement, protection money, etc.	Yes	¶ 5901.01
Illness, employee's compensation during, except to extent qualifying as insurance benefits	Yes	¶ 6662.0355
Incentive stock options	No	¶ 19,806.021
Income tax refunds:		
. state, to extent of tax benefit from prior deduction . .	Yes	¶ 5504.041
Inheritances	No	¶ 6553.021
Insider's profits	Yes	¶ 5504.2645

Income Item	Includible in Income	Paragraph Reference
Insurance policy dividends:		
. distributed, up to total of all net premiums paid	No	¶ 5707B.01; ¶ 6114.0405
. retained by insurer and applied against premium . . .	No	¶ 5707B.01; ¶ 6114.04
Insurance proceeds:		
. business interruption insurance, based on lost income	Yes	¶ 29,650.053
. use or occupancy, actual loss of net profits	Yes	¶ 29,650.053
Interest-free loans:		
. loans in excess of *de minimis* amount, deemed interest	Yes	¶ 43,960.01
. loans within *de minimis* amount	No	¶ 43,960.066
Interest on:		
. bank deposits or accounts	Yes	¶ 5704.023
. bonds, debentures, or notes	Yes	¶ 5704.044
. claim awarded by judgment	Yes	¶ 5704.279
. condemnation awards	Yes	¶ 30,575.166
. deferred legacies	Yes	¶ 5704.347
. federal obligations	Yes	¶ 6602.03
. insurance contracts	Yes	¶ 6504.045
. refund of federal taxes	Yes	¶ 21,005.922
Involuntary conversions, gain from, if reinvested	No	¶ 29,650.01
Juror's mileage allowance	No	¶ 5504.5006
Jury fees	Yes	¶ 5507.021
Layoff pay benefits:		
. supplemental unemployment benefit plan, company-financed	Yes	¶ 5507.032
Lease cancellation, payments received for	Yes	¶ 5706.031
Leased retail space, cash or rent reductions received for construction or improvements	No	¶ 5706.025
Legal services plan, employer contributions and value of benefits received	Yes	¶ 7244.01
Lessee's improvements, value of to lessor upon termination of lease	No	¶ 7022.01
Libel or slander of personal reputation, exemplary damages	Yes	¶ 5900.03
Life insurance contract, distributed from retirement plan	Yes	¶ 6367.039
Life insurance dividends:		
. distributed, up to total of all net premiums paid	No	¶ 5707B.01; ¶ 6114.0405
. retained by insurer and applied against premium . . .	No	¶ 5707B.01; ¶ 6114.04
Life insurance dividends, veterans	No	¶ 5504.74
Life insurance, group-term premiums paid by employer, to extent of employer's cost of $50,000 or less of insurance	No	¶ 6367.01
Life insurance proceeds, paid on death of the insured . . .	No	¶ 6504.01
Living expenses paid by insurance while damaged home being repaired	No	¶ 7302.01
Lodging and meals, *unless* furnished on employer's premises for employer's convenience and the employee must accept lodging as a condition of employment . . .	Yes	¶ 7222.01; ¶ 7222.021
Lodging, cost of, furnished on employer's premises for employer's convenience and employee must accept lodging as a condition of employment	No	¶ 7222.021
Losses, previously deducted, reimbursement for or expense items	Yes	¶ 7062.01
Meals, cost of, furnished on employer's premises for employer's convenience	No	¶ 7222.01
Medicaid rebates to drug manufacturers	No	¶ 5600.31

Income Item	Includible in Income	Paragraph Reference
Medical care reimbursements, employer-financed accident and health plan	No	¶ 6702.01
Mileage allowance	Yes	¶ 5507.3267
Military personnel, basic pay	Yes	¶ 5507.037
Military service, employer-payments to employees	Yes	¶ 5507.107
Mortgage indebtedness, prepayment at a discount to the extent of the discount	Yes	¶ 5802.295
Moving expenses, qualified, employer-reimbursement (under qualified fringe benefit rules)	No	¶ 12,623.035
Mustering-out pay, military personnel	Yes	¶ 5507.037
National Labor Relations Board, back-pay award	Yes	¶ 5507.129
National Service Life Insurance dividends	No	¶ 5504.74
Nobel prize and similar awards if donated by recipient to qualified entity	No	¶ 6204.025
Nonqualified deferred compensation plan, assets set aside to fund	Yes	¶ 18,960.037
Obligations, federal interest on	Yes	¶ 6602.03
Old age, disability, survivors' benefit payments, Social Security or Railroad Retirement Acts, below base amount	No	¶ 6421.03
Parsonage, rental value of, furnished to a minister or rabbi as part of compensation; rental allowances if used to rent or provide a home	No	¶ 6852.01
Partnership, distributive share of taxable income	Yes	¶ 25,124.01
Patents, sale to controlled foreign corporation	Yes	¶ 30,982.01
Peace Corps volunteers, basic living and travel allowances	No	¶ 28,063.01
Pensions:		
. annuities, etc., for personal injuries or sickness resulting from active service in armed forces of any country, National Oceanic and Atmospheric Administration, or U.S. Public Health Service	No	¶ 6662.045
. distributions attributable to employer contributions	Yes	¶ 5507.033; ¶ 6140.0236; ¶ 6140.03
Personal physical injuries, damages	No	¶ 6662.01
Political campaign contributions, with exceptions	No	¶ 6553.42
Prizes	Yes	¶ 6204.01
Professional fees	Yes	¶ 5507.022
Pulitzer prize and similar awards if donated by recipient to qualified entity	No	¶ 6204.025
Punitive damages	Yes	¶ 5900.03
Purchases, nondiscriminatory employee-discounts	No	¶ 7438.025
Railroad Retirement Act benefits, below base amount	No	¶ 6421.01
Rebates, credits, price reductions received by customers	No	¶ 5504.492
Rent reductions received by retail tenants for construction or improvements	No	¶ 5706.025
Rents	Yes	¶ 5706.01
Retired public safety officer's government pension plan distributions, up to $3,000 used for health insurance premiums	No	¶ 6140.0457
Retirement pay attributable to employer contributions other than veterans' disability retirement pay	Yes	¶ 5507.033
Reward, informer's	Yes	¶ 5504.2642
Roth contributions, designated (elective contributions)	Yes	¶ 18,112.127
Royalties	Yes	¶ 5706.01
Salaries, including those of state and federal employees and amounts employer withholds for income, Social Security, and Railroad Retirement taxes	Yes	¶ 5507.021; ¶ 5507.043; ¶ 5507.044
Scholarships and fellowships, degree programs, qualified	No	¶ 7183.01
Security deposits, when retained by lessor	Yes	¶ 21,005.027

Income Item	Includible in Income	Paragraph Reference
Sickness and injury benefits:		
. employer's plan, subject to limitations	No	¶ 6662.035
. workers' compensation equivalent	No	¶ 6662.025
Social Security old age, disability and survivor's benefits,		
below base amount	No	¶ 6421.01
State contracts, profits on	Yes	¶ 5504.023; ¶ 5511
Stock distributions in general	No	¶ 15,402.01
. convertible preferred stock or debentures	Yes	¶ 15,402.01
. disproportionate distributions	Yes	¶ 15,402.01
. distributions of common and preferred stock	Yes	¶ 15,402.01
. dividends on preferred stock	Yes	¶ 15,402.01
. increasing shareholder's proportionate interest	Yes	¶ 15,402.01
. in lieu of money	Yes	¶ 15,402.01
Stock options incentive	No	¶ 19,806.021
Strike benefits, generally	Yes	¶ 6553.03
Strike benefits, union and non-union employees in need,		
paid in form of food, clothes, etc.	No	¶ 6553.03
Supper money, employer-paid, occasional due to overtime		
work	No	¶ 7438.053
Supplemental security income (SSI) payments	No	¶ 5507.034; ¶ 6421.021
Support payment, received from former spouse	Yes	¶ 6094.01
Surviving spouse, decedent's salary continued, limited		
depending on intent	No	¶ 5507.4741
Survivor annuities, paid to family of public safety officer .	No	¶ 5507.045; ¶ 6507.05
Taxes:		
. employees', employer-paid	Yes	¶ 5508.046
. refunds of, not previously deducted or deducted		
without tax benefit	No	¶ 5504.041; ¶ 7062.043
Tenancy, payments for surrender of	Yes	¶ 30,575.206
Tips	Yes	¶ 5507.023
Treasure trove	Yes	¶ 5504.6916
Treaty-exempt income	No	¶ 26,805.01
Tuition, employer-paid under qualified plans (including		
tuition paid for graduate-level courses that begin after		
December 31, 2001)	No	¶ 7353.01
Unemployment benefit plans, supplemental payments . .	Yes	¶ 6412.021
Unemployment benefits	Yes	¶ 6412.021
U.S. Savings Bonds, earned increase during year, if cash-		
method taxpayer elects	Yes	¶ 6602.04
Use and occupancy insurance proceeds, income		
experience	Yes	¶ 29,650.053
Vacation fund allowance, union agreement	Yes	¶ 5507.47
Veterans Administration payments	No	¶ 5504.027
Veterans' benefits, generally	No	¶ 5504.027
Veterans' bonuses, state	No	¶ 5504.775
Wages	Yes	¶ 5507.021
Workers' Compensation Acts, payments under	No	¶ 6662.01; ¶ 6662.025
"Wrap-around" annuity contracts sold by life insurance		
companies, interest on	Yes	¶ 6114.48

¶ 57 Checklist for Deductions

The Internal Revenue Code permits a number of wide-ranging deductions that may be taken into account in arriving at taxable income. However, the Code contains a number of rules and restrictions concerning the expenses that qualify as deductions and the taxpayers who may claim them. Although deductions generally reduce taxable income, deductions from gross income, available to all qualifying taxpayers, must be distinguished from deductions from adjusted gross income, available only to those taxpayers who itemize. Certain miscellaneous itemized deductions, including un-reimbursed employee business expenses and investment expenses, are deductible by an individual only if the aggregate amount of such deductions exceeds two percent of adjusted gross income (see ¶ 6064.01 of the STANDARD FEDERAL TAX REPORTER). In addition, deductions that can be taken currently must be distinguished from those that can be taken over a number of tax years through depreciation or amortization.

The chart below lists a number of expenses that a taxpayer might incur. The chart indicates for each expense a symbol(s) representing the possible availability of a deduction, its timing, and whether it is deductible from gross income or adjusted gross income. Many deductions have special rules. The chart also provides the 2008 STANDARD FEDERAL TAX REPORTER paragraph number where further information on the deduction may be found.

The following symbols are used:

D/GI = Deductible from gross income

D/AGI = Deductible from adjusted gross income

D/Am = Deductible over a period of time

ND = Nondeductible

Abandonment of business
real property . . . .   D/GI, ¶ 9902.177

Accident and health plans
. employer contributions   D/GI, ¶ 8522.386

Accounting fees
. business . . . .   D/GI, ¶ 8520.315
. capital transactions . . .   D/Am, ¶ 13,709.01
. connected with trade or
business . . . .   D/GI, ¶ 8520.315
. investors . . . .   D/AGI, ¶ 12,523.03
. organization of business
($5,000 deduction and
excess amortizable over
15 years) . . . .   D/GI, D/Am, ¶ 13,352.01
. reorganization of
business . . . .   ND, ¶ 13,709.017, ¶ 13,709.83

Accounting system,
installation . . . .   D/GI, ¶ 13,709.135

Administrative expenses of
estate . . . .   D/AGI, ¶ 24,308.021

Admissions to political
dinners, programs,
inaugural balls, etc. . . . .   ND, ¶ 14,552.025

Advertising expenses
. business cards . . . . .   D/GI, ¶ 8851.133
. catalogs
. . long term . . . .   D/Am, ¶ 21,817.2075
. generally . . . .   D/GI, ¶ 8851.01
. home demonstrations .   D/GI, ¶ 8851.1337
. package design costs .   D/GI, ¶ 8520.028
. political convention
programs and other
political publications .   ND, ¶ 14,552.021
. prizes and contests . . .   D/GI, ¶ 8851.1657
. product launch costs . .   D/GI, ¶ 8520.028
. promotional activities .   D/GI, ¶ 8851.1659

Airline pilot, special clothing .
. . . .   D/AGI, ¶ 8524.265

Airplane, heavy maintenance
expenses . . . .   D/GI, ¶ 8630.45
Alcohol fuels credit, unused   D/Am, ¶ 12,430.01

Alimony payments . . . . . . D/GI, ¶ 12,573.01

Amortization of premium on taxable bonds (optional) . D/AGI, ¶ 11,855.01

Appraisal fees
. acquisition of capital asset . . . . ND, ¶ 13,709.017, ¶ 13,709.121

. connection with trade or business . . . . D/AGI, ¶ 8520.3152

Architect's fees (capital expenditure) . . . . D/Am, ¶ 13,709.149

Architectural services
. domestic production activities . . . . D/GI, ¶ 12,476.01

Attorney's and accountant's fees in contesting tax claims (nonbusiness) . . . D/AGI, ¶ 8526.462

Attorney's fees
. accounting suit by former partner, defense of . . . . D/GI, ¶ 13,603.243

. acquisition of corporate control . . . . ND, ¶ 8526.4213
. business debts, collection of . . . . D/GI, ¶ 8526.429
. civil rights suits . . . . . D/GI, ¶ 6005.07
. condemnation proceeding, defense of ND, ¶ 8526.4198
. disbarment proceedings . . . . D/GI, ¶ 8526.032
. divorce
. . obtaining alimony . . D/GI, ¶ 13,603.223
. . proceedings . . . . . . ND, ¶ 13,603.223
. . property settlement . ND, ¶ 13,603.223
. personal affairs . . . . . ND, ¶ 13,603.01
. slander prosecution (personal) . . . . ND, ¶ 13,603.253
. tax advice on investments . . . . . . D/AGI, ¶ 12,523.346
. title clearance
. . land . . . . ND, ¶ 8526.469
. . stock . . . . ND, ¶ 13,709.93
. will preparation . . . . . ND, ¶ 13,603.259

Automobile expenses
. business use by employee
. . unreimbursed . . . . . D/AGI, ¶ 8590.01

. business use by self-employed person
. . chauffeur's salary . . . D/GI, ¶ 8590.1344
. . cost of car . . . . D/GI, D/Am, ¶ 8590.033
. . garage rentals . . . . . D/GI, ¶ 8590.024
. . gas . . . . D/GI, ¶ 8590.024
. . insurance . . . . . . D/GI, ¶ 8590.252
. . license fees . . . . . . D/GI, ¶ 8590.024
. . loss on sale . . . . . . D/GI, ¶ 8590.037
. . oil and lubrication . . D/GI, ¶ 8590.024
. . parking . . . . D/GI, ¶ 8590.024
. . repairs . . . . D/GI, ¶ 8590.024
. . tires . . . . D/GI, ¶ 8590.024
. . washing . . . . D/GI, ¶ 8590.024
. nonbusiness casualty loss (limited) . . . . . D/AGI, ¶ 10,005.01
. pleasure use . . . . ND, ¶ 13,603.109
. rural mail carriers (limited) . . . . D/AGI, ¶ 8590.022

Bad debts, ¶ 10,650.01
. business . . . . D/GI, ¶ 10,650.021

. nonbusiness . . . . D/GI, ¶ 10,650.021, ¶ 10,700.01, ¶ 10,700.03

Bar admission and examination fees . . . . . . ND, ¶ 8634.1172, ¶ 13,709.016

Baseball player's uniforms . D/AGI, ¶ 8524.265

Baseball team equipment for business publicity . . . . . D/GI, ¶ 8851.184

Black lung benefits trust, employer contributions . D/GI, ¶ 12,291.01

Bookmakers, business
expenses . . . . D/GI,
¶ 8521.1260

Building property, energy
efficient property for
commercial buildings
(2006-2008) . . . . D/GI,
¶ 12,138D.01

Building replacements
(capital expenditure) . . . D/Am,
¶ 8630.51

Burglar alarm system, cost of
installing (business capital
expenditure) . . . . D/Am,
¶ 13,709.119

Burial expenses . . . . ND,
¶ 12,543.047

Business bad debts . . . . . D/GI,
¶ 10,650.021

Business conventions
. cruise ship (limited) . . D/GI,
¶ 14,408A.059

. foreign conventions
(limited) . . . . D/GI,
¶ 14,408A.0591

. political conventions
(must be related to
trade or business) . . . D/GI,
¶ 8550.2835

. travel expenses . . . . . D/GI,
¶ 8550.025,
¶ 8550.275—
¶ 8550.284

Business expenses . . . . . . D/GI, ¶ 8520.01
Business meals . . . . 50% D/GI,
¶ 8523.024,
¶ 8570.021,
¶ 14,408A.027

Business startup expenses
($5,000 deduction and
excess amortizable over 15
years) . . . . D/GI, D/Am,
¶ 12,371.01

Campaign contributions . . ND, ¶ 8952.53
Capital expenditures . . . . . ND, D/Am,
¶ 13,709.01 et
seq.

Capital loss individual
(limited) . . . . D/GI,
¶ 30,392.01

Car expenses (see
"Automobile expenses")
Career counseling costs . . D/AGI,
¶ 8524.25

Caribbean convention
expenses (business) . . . D/GI,
¶ 14,408A.0591

Carrying charges deductible
as interest where
installment sales contract
states carrying charge
separately . . . . D/AGI,
¶ 9200.03

Casualty losses, personal,
deduction limited to
amount of each loss in
excess of $100 and then
only to the extent losses
exceed 10% of adjusted
gross income . . . . D/AGI,
¶ 10,005.041

Charitable contributions
. corporations (limited) . D/GI,
¶ 11,680.021

. . computer technology
equipment to schools
and public libraries
(through 2007) . . . . D/GI,
¶ 11,680.037

. individuals (limited) . . D/AGI,
¶ 11,670.01

. . appreciated property . D/AGI,
¶ 11,660.04—
¶ 11,660.047

. where organization
carries on lobbying
activities . . . . ND,
¶ 11,620.052

Child support payments . . . ND, ¶ 6094.027
Circulation expenditures,
newspapers, magazine
periodicals . . . . D/GI,
¶ 12,032.01

Classroom expenses,
teachers (2002-2007) . . . D/GI,
¶ 6005.029

Clean fuel vehicle property
(limited) (through 2005) . D/GI,
¶ 12,133.01

Clinical testing deduction if
credit is elected . . . . . . ND,
¶ 14,954.025

Club dues (limited) . . . . . D/AGI,
¶ 8853.025

Coal royalty contracts
. expenses related to . . . ND, ¶ 14,311.01
. if there is no production,
or no income, under
contracts . . . . D/AGI,
¶ 14,311.01

Commissions
. paid as compensation . D/GI,
¶ 5507.022,
¶ 8636.169

. sale of real estate or
securities

. . dealers	D/GI, ¶ 8521.046, ¶ 8521.049
. . other taxpayers	ND, ¶ 8521.1357
Commissions on sale of real estate and securities, dealer only (other than taxpayers deduct from selling price)	D/GI, ¶ 8521.046, ¶ 8521.049
Commuting expenses	ND, ¶ 8550.269
Compensation, reasonable .	D/GI, ¶ 8636.01
Computer software (business use)	
. development costs . . .	D/GI, D/Am, ¶ 12,047.057
. leased software	D/GI, ¶ 12,047.115
. purchased software . .	D/Am, ¶ 11,009.027, ¶ 12,047.115, ¶ 13,709.016
Construction . domestic production activities	D/GI, ¶ 12,476.01
Contributions by employer to employer-financed accident and health plans for benefit of employees	D/GI, ¶ 8752.01
Contributions by employer to state unemployment insurance and state disability funds	D/GI, ¶ 8752.025
Contributions by members to a labor union (voluntary)	ND, ¶ 8853.20
Contributions paid (within certain limits) during year to charitable, etc., organizations	D/AGI, ¶ 11,670.01, ¶ 11,620.04
Convention (political) programs, cost of advertising in	ND, ¶ 14,552.021
Conventions (see "Business conventions")	
Cooperative housing corporation, share of taxes or interest paid by	D/AGI, ¶ 12,603.01, ¶ 12,603.15
Copyright costs	D/Am, ¶ 11,016.021
Cost recovery, business property or property held for the production of income	D/Am, ¶ 11,004.01

Cruise ship business conventions (limited) . . .	D/GI, ¶ 14,408A.059
Custodian fees	D/AGI, ¶ 12,523.115, ¶ 13,709.591
Day care providers . standard meal deduction	D/GI, ¶ 8520.5843
Defending title to property (capital expenditure) . . .	ND, ¶ 8526.469
Demolition of structure . . .	ND, ¶ 14,901.01
Dependents	D/AGI, ¶ 8005.03, ¶ 8250.021
Depletion	D/Am, ¶ 23,924.01
Depreciation, business property or property held for production of income .	D/Am, ¶ 11,004.01
. election to expense (limited)	D/GI, ¶ 12,126.01
Diaper service	ND, ¶ 12,543.71
Disbarment proceedings, attorneys' fees and expenses in defending . .	D/GI, ¶ 8526.032
Doctor's staff privilege fees at hospital (capital expenditures)	D/Am, ¶ 13,709.323
Domestic production activities	D/GI, ¶ 12,476.01
Dues . chamber of commerce .	D/GI, ¶ 8853.155
. charitable, religious, educational organizations	D/AGI, ¶ 8853.15— ¶ 8853.175
. clubs organized for business, pleasure, recreation, or any other social purpose	ND, ¶ 14,408A.035
. professional associations	D/GI, ¶ 8634.102— ¶ 8634.1142
. union dues	D/AGI, ¶ 8853.20
Education expenses . higher education expenses (2002-2007)	D/GI, ¶ 12,772.01

Education expenses
(employee)
. maintaining or improving
required skills . . . . . D/AGI,
¶ 8632.01
. minimum requirements
for job . . . . ND, ¶ 8632.3865
. new trade or business . ND, ¶ 8632.3873
Educational assistance plan
payments . . . . D/GI,
¶ 7353.023
Efficiency engineers' fees . . D/GI,
¶ 8520.317
Electricity
. domestic production
activities . . . . D/GI,
¶ 12,476.01
Embezzlement loss . . . . . D/GI,
¶ 10,101.024
Employee's expenses
. entertaining customers
. . reimbursed expenses D/GI,
¶ 8524.025
. . unreimbursed
expenses . . . . 50% D/AGI,
¶ 8523.021
. meals and lodging away
from home
. . reimbursed . . . . . . D/GI,
¶ 8550.021
. . unreimbursed lodging .
. . . . D/AGI,
¶ 8550.075
. . unreimbursed meals . 50% D/AGI,
¶ 14,408A.051
. move to a new work
location . . . . D/GI,
¶ 12,623.021
. transportation expenses
. . unreimbursed (limited)
. . . . D/AGI,
¶ 8550.075
Employees' life insurance,
paid by employer
. employee beneficiary . D/GI,
¶ 8522.386
. employer beneficiary . ND,
¶ 14,008.035
Employees, payments for
injuries to, not
compensated by insurance;
disability benefits . . . . . D/GI,
¶ 8752.2959
Employees, severance
payments to . . . . D/GI,
¶ 8752.676
Employees, training expenses
for . . . . D/GI,
¶ 8752.676

Employment, fees for
obtaining . . . . D/AGI,
¶ 8524.03,
¶ 8524.25
Employment taxes
. employer's payment
under Federal
Unemployment Tax Act
. . employer (but not
deductible if paid on
wages of domestics) . D/GI,
¶ 9502.042,
¶ 9502.30
. employer's taxes under
Federal Insurance
Contributions Act
. . employer (deductible
only as business
expense) . . . . D/GI,
¶ 9502.042
. employer's taxes under
Railroad Retirement Act
. . employer (deductible
only as business
expense) . . . . D/GI, ¶ 9502.28
. Federal Unemployment
Tax Act . . . . D/GI,
¶ 9502.042
. Railroad Retirement Act .
. . . . D/GI, ¶ 9502.28
. Social Security Act . . . D/GI, ¶ 9502.29
Energy efficient property,
commercial building
property (2006-2008) . . . D/GI,
¶ 12,138D.01
Engineering services
. domestic production
activities . . . . D/GI,
¶ 12,476.01
Entertainment expenses
(business, nonemployee)
. athletic club dues . . . . ND,
¶ 14,408A.035
. facilities owned and used
by the taxpayer . . . . ND,
¶ 14,408A.036
. food
. . furnished to employees
on premises . . . . . . D/GI,
¶ 7438.052
. . meals directly related
to business . . . . 50% D/GI,
¶ 8523.024
. . provided for customers
. . . . 50% D/GI,
¶ 8523.024
Environmental cleanup costs
(brownfields) (through
2007) . . . . D/GI,
¶ 12,465.01

Gifts (business), but limited
to $25 per donee per year — D/GI,
¶ 14,408A.038

Gifts to charity
. corporations (limited) . — D/GI,
¶ 11,680.021

. . computer technology
equipment to schools
and public libraries
(through 2007) . . . . — D/GI,
¶ 11,680.037

. individuals (limited) . . — D/AGI,
¶ 11,670.01

. . appreciated property . — D/AGI,
¶ 11,660.04—
¶ 11,660.047

. where organization
carries on lobbying
activities . . . . — ND,
¶ 11,620.052

Gifts to employees
. awards for length of
service (limited) . . . . — D/GI,
¶ 14,408A.045

. gifts valued above $25 . — ND, ¶ 8520.334,
¶ 14,408A.038

. gifts valued at $25 or less
. . . . — D/GI,
¶ 8520.334,
¶ 14,408A.038

Gifts to individuals . . . . . — ND, ¶ 11,620.03

Golden parachutes
. excess parachute
payments . . . . — ND, ¶ 15,152.01,
¶ 34,941.01

. parachute payments . . — D/GI,
¶ 15,152.01—
¶ 15,152.066

Golf course
. land preparation costs,
modern greens . . . . — D/Am,
¶ 11,007.189

. maintenance and
operating costs . . . . — D/GI,
¶ 8521.124,
¶ 8630.1292

. original construction . . — ND,
¶ 8630.1292,
¶ 13,709.237

Hobby losses . . . . — ND, ¶ 12,177.01

Home office (limited) . . . . — D/GI,
¶ 14,854.021

. employee . . . . — D/AGI,
¶ 14,854.021

. principal place of
business . . . . — D/GI,
¶ 14,854.027

. storage of product
samples . . . . — D/GI,
¶ 14,854.021

House rent . . . . — ND, ¶ 13,603.01,
¶ 13,603.295

Husband to wife, allowance
paid as housewife's salary — ND,
¶ 13,603.171

Illegal business, legitimate
expenses . . . . — D/GI, ND,
¶ 8521.1255—
¶ 8521.1269,
¶ 15,051.01

Illegal drugs . . . . — ND, ¶ 15,051.01

Impairment-related work
expenses
. attendant care services at
work . . . . — D/AGI,
¶ 6064.01

. necessary expenses at
work . . . . — D/AGI,
¶ 6064.01

Import duties (unless as a
business expense) . . . . — ND, ¶ 9502.032

Improvements made by
lessee, depreciation and
amortization . . . . — D/Am,
¶ 12,105.42

Income tax (state) . . . . . . — D/AGI,
¶ 9502.031

Income tax liability, cost of
determining . . . . — D/AGI,
¶ 12,523.3844

Income tax returns, cost of
preparing (non-business) — D/AGI,
¶ 8526.462,
¶ 12,523.3844,
¶ 12,523.44

Individual retirement account,
contributions (limited) . . — D/GI,
¶ 18,922.01

Infringement litigation in
course of business . . . . — D/GI,
¶ 8526.449

Inheritance tax . . . . — ND, ¶ 9502.035

Injuries to employees,
payments for, not
compensated by insurance
. . . . — D/GI, ¶ 8752.01

Insurance expenses
. business
. . casualty . . . . — D/GI,
¶ 8522.3815

. . malpractice . . . . . . — D/GI,
¶ 8522.392

. individuals (medical) . — D/AGI,
¶ 12,543.01

. . self-employed
individuals (health
insurance) . . . . — D/GI, ¶ 8522.03

. insured employees
. . employee or other
beneficiary . . . . — D/GI,
¶ 8522.386

. . employer beneficiary	ND, ¶ 14,008.03
. . key employees	D/GI, ¶ 14,008.01
. personal residence . . .	ND, ¶ 13,603.01
. required for credit	
. . premiums paid by creditor	D/GI, ¶ 14,008.035
. . premiums paid by debtor	ND, ¶ 14,008.035
Intangible assets (as defined in Code Sec. 197)	D/Am, ¶ 12,455.01
Interest and carrying charges related to a commodity straddle position in excess of income generated by straddle position	ND, ¶ 13,709.028
Interest (with exceptions and limitations, see below) . .	D/AGI, ¶ 9104.01
. education loans (limited)	D/GI, ¶ 12,695.01
. interest related to tax-exempt income	ND, ¶ 9104.01, ¶ 14,054.01
. interest related to life insurance contracts (limited)	D/AGI, ¶ 9104.048, ¶ 14,008.021
. personal obligations (limited)	ND, ¶ 9104.01, ¶ 9402.01
. points, purchase of residence	D/AGI, ¶ 9402.01
. prepaid	D/Am, D/GI, ¶ 9402.04
. property held for production of rent or royalties	D/GI, ¶ 9104.01
. trade or business debts	D/GI, ¶ 9104.01
Interest forfeiture	
. premature withdrawal from time savings account	D/GI, ¶ 9805.165
Interest on tax deficiencies	
. corporation	D/GI, ¶ 9400A.04
. individual, generally . .	ND, ¶ 9400A.04, ¶ 9400A.50
. . related to trade or business	D/GI, ND, ¶ 9400A.04
. underpayment attributable to nondisclosed reportable transaction	ND, ¶ 9104.05
Investigatory costs	
. acquisition of specific business	ND, ¶ 12,371.25
. . business search	D/GI, D/Am, ¶ 12,371.25
Investor's expenses (except incurred in earning tax-exempt interest)	D/AGI, ¶ 12,523.03
ISO 9000 costs	D/GI, ¶ 8520.028, ¶ 8520.3175
Job hunting expenses	
. new trade or business .	ND, ¶ 8524.03, ¶ 8524.25
. resume preparation costs	D/AGI, ¶ 8524.03, ¶ 8524.25
. same trade or business	D/AGI, ¶ 8524.03, ¶ 8524.25
. travel and transportation to new area	D/AGI, ¶ 8524.03, ¶ 8524.25
Jockey's riding apparel . . .	D/AGI, ¶ 8524.265
Labor union dues	D/AGI, ¶ 8853.20
Laundry, dry cleaning, pressing charges (business travel)	D/AGI, ¶ 8550.021
Legal expenses and fees	
. business	D/GI, ¶ 8526.021— ¶ 8526.05
. investors	D/AGI, ¶ 8526.4394, ¶ 12,523.025
. production of income .	D/AGI, ¶ 12,523.3375
. tax determination	D/AGI, ¶ 12,523.346
Legislators	
. congressional living expenses, away from home	
. . expenses of moving to capital	D/AGI, ¶ 8570.1218, ¶ 12,623.117

. state
. . local transportation   .   D/AGI,
                                      ¶ 8570.1222
. . meals and lodging . .   D/AGI,
                                      ¶ 8570.1222
. . travel expenses . . . .   D/AGI,
                                      ¶ 8570.1222
License fees
. treated as personal
   property tax . . . . . .   D/AGI,
                                      ¶ 9502.398
Life insurance premiums,
   debts incurred to purchase,
   paid by employer . . . . .   D/GI, ¶ 8636.27
. employee or other
   beneficiary . . . .   D/GI,
                                      ¶ 14,008.01
. employer beneficiary .   ND, ¶ 5508.24,
                                      ¶ 14,008.03
Loan cost—stock
   reacquisition . . . .   ND, ¶ 9052.01
Lobbying expense
. appearances before
   legislative bodies . . .   ND, ¶ 8952.021
. expenditures to influence
   voters . . . .   ND, ¶ 8952.021
. professional lobbyist's
   expenses . . . .   D/GI,
                                      ¶ 8952.0664,
                                      ¶ 8952.468
Losses
. gambling (trade or
   business) . . . .   D/AGI,
                                      ¶ 6005.028
. net operating loss . . . .   D/GI,
                                      ¶ 12,014.01
. sale or exchange of
   property
. . business property . .   D/GI, ¶ 9804.03
. . related parties . . . . .   ND, ¶ 14,161.02
. . capital assets (business
   motive) . . . .   D/GI, ¶ 9804.03
. theft or casualty
. . individual property . .   D/AGI,
                                      ¶ 9804.02,
                                      ¶ 9807.01
. . rent- or royalty-
   generating property .   D/GI, ¶ 9808.01
. worthless stock and
   securities . . . .   D/GI,
                                      ¶ 10,001.01
Lump sum distribution-
   ordinary income portion .   D/GI,
                                      ¶ 18,217A.026
Machinery
. incidental repairs . . . .   D/GI,
                                      ¶ 8630.025
Materials and supplies,
   business (incidentals) . .   D/GI, ¶ 8610.01

Maternity clothes . . . .   ND, ¶ 12,543.71
Meals provided for employees
. employer's cost of
   providing meals on
   premises . . . .   D/GI,
                                      ¶ 7438.052
. meals directly related to
   business . . . .   50% D/GI,
                                      ¶ 8523.024
Medical, dental and hospital
   expenses (to the extent
   exceeding 7.5% of adjusted
   gross income) (for a
   detailed list of such
   expenses, see ¶ 59) . . . .   D/AGI,
                                      ¶ 12,543.01
Medical, dental and hospital
   expenses less than 7.5% of
   adjusted gross income . .   ND, ¶ 12,543.01
Medical insurance premiums
   (see ¶ 59)
Medical savings account . .   D/GI,
                                      ¶ 12,675.01
Mine development
   expenditures . . . .   D/GI,
                                      ¶ 24,094.01
Mine exploration
   expenditures . . . .   D/GI,
                                      ¶ 24,115.01
Mortgages
. insurance premiums
   (2007) . . . .   D/AGI,
                                      ¶ 9402.026
. interest . . . .   D/AGI,
                                      ¶ 9402.023,
                                      ¶ 9402.025
Moving expenses
. meals . . . .   ND, ¶ 12,623.50
. other expenses
. . employee, reimbursed
   . . . .   D/GI,
                                      ¶ 12,623.01
. . employee,
   unreimbursed . . . . .   D/GI
                                      ¶ 12,623.021
. . self employed . . . . .   D/GI,
                                      ¶ 12,623.021
Moving machinery . . . . . .   D/GI, ¶ 8520.50
Musician's clothing, used
   exclusively in business . .   D/AGI,
                                      ¶ 8524.265
National Labor Relations
   Board award to employees,
   payment by employer . . .   D/GI,
                                      ¶ 8954.3265
Net operating loss deduction
   . . . .   D/GI,
                                      ¶ 12,014.01

Professional books and journals and information services
. unreimbursed employee expense . . . . D/AGI, ¶ 8634.01, ¶ 8634.1201— ¶ 8634.121

Promotional activities
. coupons . . . . D/GI, ¶ 21,015.01
. prizes and contests . . . D/GI, ¶ 8851.1657

Protective clothing . . . . . . D/AGI, ¶ 8524.05

Raffle tickets, cost of . . . . . ND, ¶ 11,620.511

Railroad retirement tax paid by employers . . . . D/GI, ¶ 9502.28

Railway trainman's uniform D/AGI, ¶ 8524.265

Real estate impact fees . . . ND, ¶ 20,620.2412

Reconditioning and health-restoring expenses of employees paid by employers . . . . D/GI, ¶ 8520.246

Refinery property (limited) . D/GI, ¶ 12,137E.01

Reforestation costs . . . . . . D/GI, D/Am, ¶ 23,929.195

Reimbursed expenses (otherwise deductible) . . D/GI, ¶ 8524.025

Removal of architectural and transportation barriers to the handicapped and elderly (limited) . . . . . . D/AGI, ¶ 12,264.01

Rent, business property . . . D/GI, ¶ 8754.01

Reorganization expenditures .
. . . . ND, ¶ 13,709.017, ¶ 13,709.83

Repairs to business property .
. . . . D/GI, D/Am, ¶ 8630.01

Repairs to personal residence
. . . . ND, ¶ 8630.574

Research and experimental expenditures connected with a trade or business . D/GI, D/Am, ¶ 12,047.01

Restaurant smallwares (limited) . . . . D/GI, ¶ 8610.146

Retirement plans, contributions to
. employer . . . . D/GI, ¶ 18,347.01

. individuals (limited) . . D/GI, ¶ 18,922.0226
. self-employed individuals
. . . . D/GI, ¶ 17,933.01
. simplified employee pension contributions . . . . D/GI, ¶ 18,922.0245

Return, federal or state income tax, gift tax, etc., cost of having prepared (including investor) . . . . D/AGI, ¶ 8520.73, ¶ 12,523.3844

Safe deposit boxes, rental for protection of income producing property
. investor . . . . D/AGI, ¶ 12,523.03

Salaries
. bonuses . . . . D/GI, ¶ 8642.01
. commissions . . . . . D/GI, ¶ 5507.022
. related parties . . . . . D/GI, ¶ 8638.01

Salespersons' expenses
. reimbursed . . . . D/GI, ¶ 8524.01, ¶ 8520.645
. unreimbursed . . . . . . D/AGI ¶ 8524.02, ¶ 8524.2538
. . automobile expenses D/AGI, ¶ 7438.038, ¶ 8590.01
. . entertaining customers, reimbursed . . . . D/GI, ¶ 8523.021
. . entertaining customers, unreimbursed . . . . . 50% D/AGI, ¶ 8523.277
. . gifts to customers (up to $25) . . . . D/AGI, ¶ 14,408A.038
. . membership dues in business or social clubs
. . . . ND, ¶ 14,408A.035
. . subscriptions to business, professional or trade publications, if for business reasons . D/AGI, ¶ 8524.2509
. . transportation expenses, unreimbursed . . . . . D/AGI, ¶ 8550.075
. . travel expenses . . . . D/AGI, ¶ 14,408A.05

Sales tax (state) (2004-2007) D/AGI, ¶ 9502.031

Self-employment tax (limited
to 50%) . . . .   D/GI,
¶ 9502.043

Servants, social security taxes
paid for . . . .   ND, ¶ 9502.30

Severance payments . . . . .   D/GI,
¶ 8752.676

Shareholder's proxy fight
expenses . . . .   D/AGI,
¶ 12,523.3593

Smallwares, restaurant
(limited) . . . .   D/GI,
¶ 8610.146

Social security taxes
. employees . . . .   ND, ¶ 9502.042

. employers . . . .   D/GI (only as
business
expense),
¶ 9502.042

Soil and water conservation
expenditures, farmers . .   D/GI, D/Am,
¶ 8756.026

Stamp taxes
. dealers/investors . . . .   D/GI,
¶ 9502.032

. trade or business . . . .   D/GI,
¶ 9502.032

. transfer of personal
residence . . . .   ND, ¶ 9502.032

Start-up expenditures,
business ($5,000 deduction
and excess amortizable
over 15 years) . . . .   D/GI, D/Am,
¶ 12,371.01

Stock redemption costs . . .   ND, ¶ 9052.01

Subscriptions, professional
journals (self-employed) .   D/GI, ¶ 8634.02

Supplemental unemployment
compensation benefits,
repayments by recipients   D/GI, ¶ 6005.04

Surgeon's uniform
(employee) . . . .   D/AGI,
¶ 8524.265

Tax penalty payments . . . .   ND, ¶ 8954.33

Tax refresher course,
lawyer's . . . .   D/GI,
¶ 8632.645

Tax returns, cost of
preparation
. business . . . .   D/GI,
¶ 12,523.3844

. individual . . . .   D/AGI,
¶ 12,523.132

Taxes (Deductible by
Manufacturer, Producer,
Importer or Corresponding
Person, but Not by
Consumer) . . . .   ¶ 9502.01

. automobile excise taxes .
. . . .   D/Am,
¶ 9502.35

Teachers, classroom
expenses (2002-2007) . . .   D/GI,
¶ 6005.029

Telephone service (as a
business expense) . . . .   D/GI, ¶ 8520.74

Theft loss
. business . . . .   D/GI,
¶ 10,101.136

. nonbusiness . . . .   D/AGI,
¶ 10,101.01

Timber
. reforestation expenses
($10,000 deduction and
excess amortizable over
7 years) . . . .   D/GI, D/Am,
¶ 12,335.01

. post-establishment
fertilization . . . .   D/GI,
¶ 8520.7455

Tires (see "Automobile
expenses" and "Truck
tires")

Title costs (perfecting or
defending title to property,
including costs of
defending condemnation
proceedings) (capital
expenditure) . . . .   D/Am,
¶ 8526.4682—
¶ 8526.471,
¶ 12,523.35

Tools, unreimbursed cost,
useful life of one year or
less . . . .   D/AGI,
¶ 8524.04

Trade association dues,
unreimbursed employee
expenses . . . .   D/AGI,
¶ 8853.50—
¶ 8853.57

Trade or business expenses
(securities dealers and
traders) . . . .   D/GI, ¶ 8521.04

Trademark and trade name
expenditures . . . .   D/Am,
¶ 13,709.016,
¶ 31,044.055

Transfer taxes . . . .   ND, ¶ 9502.032

Travel expenses (employees)
. commuting expenses .   ND, ¶ 8550.269

. reimbursed . . . .   D/GI, ¶ 8550.29,
¶ 8550.48

. unreimbursed . . . . .   D/AGI,
¶ 8550.022,
¶ 8550.075

.. baseball players (including meals and lodging) while away from "club town," also other business expenses at "club town" if tax "home" in a different city . . . . D/AGI, ¶ 8550.25

.. business and pleasure trips . . . . D/AGI, ¶ 8550.25

.. clergymen, church conventions travel, meals and lodging away from home . . . . D/AGI, ¶ 8550.28

.. commercial fishing boat crew members, for travel, meals, and lodging away from home port . . . . D/AGI, ¶ 8570.1165

.. congressmen, up to $3,000 of living expenses . . . . D/AGI, ¶ 8570.032, ¶ 8570.12

.. expenses of traveling from principal place to minor place of business . . . . D/AGI, ¶ 8570.175

.. government employees, expenses in excess of per diem allowances . . . . D/AGI, ¶ 8570.12

.. lawyers . . . . D/AGI, ¶ 8550.281, ¶ 8550.345

.. meals, reimbursed . . D/GI, ¶ 8550.021, ¶ 14,417.421

.. meals, unreimbursed 50% D/AGI, ¶ 8550.075, ¶ 14,417.01

.. National Guard and Military Reserve members (limited) . . D/GI, ¶ 6005.0295, ¶ 8570.03

.. physician, medical conventions . . . . . D/AGI, ¶ 8550.283

.. railroad employees' meals and lodging while away from "home terminal" . . . . D/AGI, ¶ 8550.269, ¶ 8550.475

.. salespersons . . . . . . D/AGI, ¶ 8570.1505

.. teachers, scientific meetings and conventions . . . . . . D/AGI, ¶ 8570.1254

.. truck drivers' (long line) meals and lodging while away from "home terminal" . . . . D/AGI, ¶ 8570.154

Truck tires
. replacement tires (limited) . . . . D/GI, ¶ 8590.1489, ¶ 8590.612

. with life less than a year . . . . D/GI, ¶ 8590.1489, ¶ 8590.612

Truck use tax (unless as business expense) . . . . ND, ¶ 9502.039

Uncollectible notes (see "Bad debts")

Uniform and special clothing costs
. baseball uniforms . . . . D/AGI, ¶ 8524.265

. clothing required for business . . . . D/AGI, ¶ 8524.2658

. employer-reimbursed costs . . . . D/GI, ¶ 8524.05
. jockey's riding apparel . D/AGI, ¶ 8524.265

. nurses' uniforms . . . . D/AGI, ¶ 8524.265

. protective clothing . . . D/AGI, ¶ 8524.05

. work shoes, metal tipped . . . . D/AGI, ¶ 8524.2658

Union payments
. dues . . . . D/AGI, ¶ 8853.20

. fines . . . . D/AGI, ¶ 8853.205

Utilities, personal . . . . . . ND, ¶ 13,603.323

Wages and salaries . . . . . . D/GI, ¶ 8636.01
Waiters, waitresses
. special uniforms . . . . D/AGI, ¶ 8524.265

Water, potable
. domesitc production activities . . . . D/GI, ¶ 12,476.01

Work shoes, metal tipped for protection of worker . . . D/AGI, ¶ 8524.2658

¶ 59 Checklist for Medical Expenses

Generally, a medical expense deduction is allowed for expenses incurred in the diagnosis, cure, mitigation, treatment or prevention of disease, or for the purpose of affecting any structure or function of the body for the individual or for the individual's spouse or dependents. The deduction covers expenses that have not been reimbursed by medical insurance or other sources.

Despite the broad scope of medical expenses, not every expense incurred for medical care is deductible. Also, there is a 7.5-percent floor on the medical expense deduction. The chart, below, lists specific types of expenses and whether or not a deduction for the expense is permitted. The user can easily check whether an official determination has been made as to the deductibility of a particular type of expense.

Medical Expense	Deductible	Authority
Abortion		
. legal	Yes	Rev. Rul. 73-201, 1973-1 CB 140, as clarified by Rev. Rul. 73-603, 1973-2 CB 76, and Rev. Rul. 97-9, 1997-1 CB 77
Accident and health insurance		
. medical care portion separately stated and reasonable in amount	Yes	Code Sec. 213(d)(1)(D) and (d)(6) and Reg. § 1.213-1(e)(4)
. medical care portion not separately stated or, if separately stated, not reasonable in amount	No	Code Sec. 213(d)(6)(A) and Reg. § 1.213-1(e)(4)
Acupuncture	Yes	Rev. Rul. 72-593, 1972-2 CB 180
Adoption		
. medical costs of adopted child	Yes	Rev. Rul. 60-255, 1960-2 CB 105
. medical costs of natural mother	No	B.L. Kilpatrick, 68 TC 469, Dec. 34,493
Air conditioner		
. allergy relief	Yes	Rev. Rul. 55-261, 1955-1 CB 307
. cystic fibrosis relief	Yes	R. Gerard, 37 TC 826, Dec. 25,331 (Acq.)
. permanent improvement to property	No	G.W. Wade, 61-2 USTC ¶ 9709
Alcoholism, treatment of	Yes	Rev. Rul. 73-325, 1973-2 CB 75
Ambulance hire	Yes	Reg. § 1.213-1(e)(1)(ii)
Anticipated medical expenses	No	W.B. Andrews, 37 TCM 744, Dec. 35,144(M), TC Memo. 1978-174
Attendant to accompany blind or deaf student	Yes	Rev. Rul. 64-173, 1964-1 CB (Part 1) 121; R.A. Baer Est., 26 TCM 170, Dec. 28,352(M), TC Memo. 1967-34
Automobile (see Car)		
Baby sitting expenses to enable parent to see doctor	No	Rev. Rul. 78-266, 1978-2 CB 123
Birth control pills	Yes	Rev. Rul. 73-200, 1973-1 CB 140
Blind persons		
. attendant to accompany student	Yes	Rev. Rul. 64-173, 1964-1 (Part I) CB 121
. braille books and magazines, excess cost of regular editions	Yes	Rev. Rul. 75-318, 1975-2 CB 88
. seeing-eye dog	Yes	Rev. Rul. 55-261, 1955-1 CB 307
. special education (see Schools, special)		
. special educational aids to mitigate condition	Yes	Rev. Rul. 58-223, 1958-1 CB 156
Capital expenditures		
. home modifications for handicapped individual	Yes	Rev. Rul. 87-106, 1987-2 CB 67
. permanent improvement to property	No	Reg. § 1.213-1(e)(1)(iii)
. primary purpose medical care	Yes	Reg. § 1.213-1(e)(1)(iii)
Car		
. depreciation on	No	M.S. Gordon, 37 TC 986, CCH Dec. 25,364; R.K. Weary, CA-10, 75-1 USTC ¶ 9173, 510 F.2d 435, cert. denied, 423 U.S. 838

Medical Expense	Deductible	Authority
. equipped to accommodate wheelchair passengers	Yes	Rev. Rul. 70-606, 1970-2 CB 66
. insurance, medical coverage for persons other than taxpayer, spouse and children	No	Rev. Rul. 73-483, 1973-2 CB 75
. special controls for a person with a disability	Yes	*S.H. Weinzimer,* 17 TCM 712, Dec. 23,100(M), TC Memo. 1958-137
Chauffeur, salary of	No	*W.E. Buck,* 47 TC 113, CCH Dec. 28,175
Chemical dependency treatment (see Alcoholism, treatment of, and Drug addiction, recovery from)		
Childbirth preparation classes		
. "coach"	No	IRS Letter Ruling 8919009, 2-6-89, CCH IRS LETTER RULINGS REPORTS
. mother	Yes	IRS Letter Ruling 8919009, 2-6-89, CCH IRS LETTER RULINGS REPORTS
Chiropractors	Yes	Rev. Rul. 63-91, 1963-1 CB 54
Christian Science treatment	Yes	Rev. Rul. 55-261, 1955-1 CB 307, as modified by Rev. Rul. 63-91, 1963-1 CB 54
Clarinet and lessons, alleviation of severe teeth malocclusion	Yes	Rev. Rul. 62-210, 1962-2 CB 89
Clothing, suitable for use other than therapy	No	*M.C. Montgomery,* 51 TC 410, Dec. 29,270, aff'd on other issues, CA-6, 70-2 USTC ¶ 9466, 428 F2d 243
Computer data bank, storage and retrieval of medical records	Yes	Rev. Rul. 71-282, 1971-2 CB 166
Contact lenses	Yes	Reg. § 1.213-1(e)(1)(iii)
. replacement insurance	Yes	Rev. Rul. 74-429, 1974-2 CB 83
Contraceptives, prescription	Yes	Rev. Rul. 73-200, 1973-1 CB 140
Cosmetic surgery		
. necessary to ameliorate a deformity arising from a congenital abnormality, personal injury, or disfiguring disease	Yes	Code Sec. 213(d)(9); Senate Finance Committee Report to P.L. 101-508
. unnecessary	No	Code Sec. 213(d)(9); Senate Finance Committee Report to P.L. 101-508
Crime victims, compensated medical expenses of	No	Rev. Rul. 74-74, 1974-1 CB 18
Crutches	Yes	Reg. § 1.213-1(e)(1)(iii)
Dancing lessons	No	*R.C. France,* CA-6, 82-1 USTC ¶ 9225
Deaf persons		
. hearing aid	Yes	Rev. Rul. 55-261, 1955-1 CB 307
. hearing-aid animal	Yes	Rev. Rul. 68-295, 1968-1 CB 92
. lip reading expenses for the deaf	Yes	Rev. Rul. 55-261, 1955-1 CB 307
. notetaker, deaf student	Yes	*R.A. Baer Est.,* 26 TCM 170, Dec. 28,352(M), TC Memo. 1967-34
. special education (see Schools, special)		
. telephone, specially equipped, including repairs	Yes	Rev. Rul. 71-48, 1971-1 CB 99, as amplified by Rev. Rul. 73-53, 1973-1 CB 139
. television, closed-caption decoder	Yes	Rev. Rul. 80-340, 1980-2 CB 81
. visual alert system	Yes	IRS Letter Ruling 8250040, 9-13-82, CCH IRS LETTER RULINGS REPORTS
Dental fees	Yes	Reg. § 1.213-1(e)(1)(ii)
Dentures (artificial teeth)	Yes	Reg. § 1.213-1(e)(1)(ii)
Deprogramming services	No	IRS Letter Ruling 8021004, February 26, 1980 (estimated), CCH IRS LETTER RULINGS REPORTS
Diagnostic fees	Yes	Reg. § 1.213-1(e)(1)(ii)
Diaper service	No	Rev. Rul. 55-261, 1955-1 CB 307
Diapers, disposable, used due to severe neurological disease	Yes	IRS Letter Ruling 8137085, 6-17-81, CCH IRS LETTER RULINGS REPORTS
Doctors' fees	Yes	Reg. § 1.213-1(e)(1)(i)
Domestic aid, type that would be rendered by nurse	Yes	Rev. Rul. 58-339, 1958-2 CB 106
Drug addiction, recovery from	Yes	Rev. Rul. 72-226, 1972-1 CB 96

Medical Expense	Deductible	Authority
Drugs, illegal/controlled substances, even when prescribed	No	Rev. Rul. 97-9, 1997-1 CB 77
Drugs, prescription	Yes	Code Sec. 213(b)
Dust elimination system	No	*F.S. Delp,* 30 TC 1230, Dec. 23,167
Dyslexia, language training	Yes	Rev. Rul. 69-607, 1969-2 CB 40
Ear piercing	No	Rev. Rul. 82-111, 1982-1 CB 48
Electrolysis	No	Code Sec. 213(d)(9); Senate Finance Committee Report to P.L. 101-508
Elevator, alleviation of cardiac condition	Yes	*J.E. Berry,* DC Okla., 58-2 USTC ¶ 9870, 174 FSupp 748; Rev. Rul. 59-411, 1959-2 CB 100, as modified by Rev. Rul. 83-33, 1983-1 CB 70
Eye examinations and glasses	Yes	Reg. § 1.213-1(e)(1)(ii), (iii)
Fallout shelter, prevention of disease	No	*F.H. Daniels,* 41 TC 324, Dec. 26,414
Fertility enhancement	Yes	IRS Publication No. 502, "Medical and Dental Expenses"
Fluoride device; on advice of dentist	Yes	Rev. Rul. 64-267, 1964-2 CB 69
Funeral expenses	No	*K.P. Carr,* 39 TCM 253, Dec. 36,352(M), TC Memo. 1979-400
Furnace	No	*J.L. Seymour,* 14 TC 1111, Dec. 17,675
Glasses	Yes	Reg. § 1.213-1(e)(1)(ii)
Gravestone	No	*C.W. Libby Est.,* 14 TCM 699, Dec. 21,110(M), TC Memo. 1955-180
Guide animals (see Service animals)		
Hair transplants, surgical	No	Code Sec. 213(d)(9); Senate Finance Committee Report to P.L. 101-508
Halfway house, adjustment to mental hospital	Yes	IRS Letter Ruling 7714016, January 10, 1977, CCH IRS LETTER RULINGS REPORTS
Handicapped persons (see, also, specific handicap or equipment) . home modification (see Capital expenses) . special training or education (see Schools, special)		
Health club dues . not related to a particular medical condition	No	Rev. Rul. 55-261, 1955-1 CB 307
. prescribed by physician for medical condition	Yes	Rev. Rul. 55-261, 1955-1 CB 307
Health Maintenance Organization (HMO)	Yes	IRS Publication No. 502, "Medical and Dental Expenses"
Hearing aids (see Deaf persons)		
Hospital care, in-patient	Yes	Reg. § 1.213-1(e)(1)(v)
Hospital services	Yes	Reg. § 1.213-1(e)(1)(ii)
Hygienic supplies	No	Reg. § 1.213-1(e)(2); *O.G. Russell,* 12 TCM 1276, Dec. 19,973(M)
Indian medicine man	Yes	*R.H. Tso,* 40 TCM 1277, Dec. 37,260(M), TC Memo. 1980-339
Insulin	Yes	Code Sec. 213(b)
Insurance . accident and health insurance (see Accident and health insurance)		
. long term care insurance (within limits)	Yes	Code Sec. 213(d)(1)(D); Code Sec. 7702B
. Medicare A coverage	Yes	Rev. Rul. 79-175, 1979-1 CB 117
. premiums for loss of income	No	Reg. § 1.213-1(e)(4)
. premiums for loss of life, limb or sight	No	Reg. § 1.213-1(e)(4)
. premiums for medical care	Yes	Reg. § 1.213-1(e)(4)
. self-employed	Yes	Code Sec. 162(l)
Iron lung	Yes	Rev. Rul. 55-261, 1955-1 CB 307
Laboratory fees	Yes	Reg. § 1.213-1(e)(1)(ii)
Laetrile, prescribed	No	Rev. Rul. 97-9, 1997-1 CB 77

Medical Expense	Deductible	Authority
Lamaze classes (see Childbirth preparation classes)		
Laser eye surgery	Yes	Rev. Rul. 2003-57, 2003-1 CB 959
Lead paint, removal	Yes	Rev. Rul. 79-66, 1979-1 CB 114
Legal expenses		
. authorization of treatment for mental illness	Yes	Rev. Rul. 71-281, 1971-2 CB 165
. divorce upon medical advice	No	*J.H. Jacobs,* 62 TC 813, Dec. 32,773
Lifetime medical care, prepaid; retirement home	Yes	Rev. Rul. 75-302, 1975-2 CB 86, Rev. Rul. 75-303, 1975-2 CB 87, as clarified by Rev. Rul. 93-72, 1993-2 CB 77
Limbs, artificial	Yes	Reg. § 1.213-1(e)(1)(ii)
Lodging		
. care not provided in hospital or equivalent outpatient facility	No	*A.L. Polyak,* 94 TC 337, CCH Dec. ¶ 46,443
. limited to $50 per night	Yes	Code Sec. 213(d)(2)
Long term care expenses	Yes	Code Sec. 213(d)(1)(C); Code Sec. 7702B
Marriage counseling	No	Rev. Rul. 75-319, 1975-2 CB 88
Maternity clothes	No	Rev. Rul. 55-261, 1955-1 CB 307
Mattress, prescribed for alleviation of arthritis	Yes	Rev. Rul. 55-261, 1955-1 CB 307
Nursing home, medical reasons	Yes	*W.B. Counts,* 42 TC 755, Dec. 26,893 (Acq.)
Nursing services (including board and social security tax if paid by taxpayer)	Yes	Rev. Rul. 57-489, 1957-2 CB 207
Obstetrical expenses	Yes	Reg. § 1.213-1(e)(1)(ii)
Operations		
. illegal	No	Reg. § 1.213-1(e)(1)(ii)
. legal	Yes	Reg. § 1.213-1(e)(1)(ii)
Optometrists	Yes	Rev. Rul. 55-261, 1955-1 CB 307
Orthodontia	Yes	Reg. § 1.213-1(e)(1)(ii)
Orthopedic shoes, excess cost	Yes	IRS Letter Ruling 8221118, 2-26-82, CCH IRS Letter Rulings Reports
Osteopaths	Yes	Rev. Rul. 63-91, 1963-1 CB 54
Oxygen equipment, breathing difficulty	Yes	Rev. Rul. 55-261, 1955-1 CB 307
Patterning exercises, handicapped child	Yes	Rev. Rul. 70-170, 1970-1 CB 51
Plumbing, special fixtures for handicapped	Yes	Rev. Rul. 70-395, 1970-2 CB 65
Prosthesis	Yes	Reg. § 1.213-1(e)(1)(ii)
Psychiatric care	Yes	Rev. Rul. 55-261, 1955-1 CB 307
Psychologists	Yes	Rev. Rul. 63-91, 1963-1 CB 54
Psychotherapists	Yes	Rev. Rul. 63-91, 1963-1 CB 54
Reclining chair for cardiac patient	Yes	Rev. Rul. 58-155, 1958-1 CB 156
Reconstructive surgery, breast	Yes	Rev. Rul. 2003-57, 2003-1 CB 959
Remedial reading for dyslexic child	Yes	Rev. Rul. 69-607, 1969-2 CB 40
Residence, loss on sale, move medically recommended	No	Rev. Rul. 68-319, 1968-1 CB 92
Retirement home, cost of medical care	Yes	*H.W. Smith Est.,* 79 TC 313, Dec. 39,273 (Acq.)
Sanitarium rest home, cost of, medical, educational, or rehabilitative reasons	Yes	Reg. § 1.213-1(e)(1)(v)
Schools, special, relief of handicap	Yes	Rev. Rul. 58-533, 1958-2 CB 108; Rev. Rul. 69-499, 1969-2 CB 39; Rev. Rul. 70-285, 1970-1 CB 52
Scientology "audits" and "processing"	No	*D.H. Brown,* CA-8, 75-2 ustc ¶ 9718, 523 F2d 365, *aff'g* 62 TC 551, Dec. 32,701; Rev. Rul. 78-190, 1978-1 CB 74
Self-help, medical	No	*B. Doody,* 32 TCM 547, Dec. 32,006(M), TC Memo. 1973-126
Service animals		
. hearing-aid animal	Yes	Rev. Rul. 68-295, 1968-1 CB 92
. other	Yes	Senate Finance Committee Report to P.L. 100-647
. seeing-eye dog	Yes	Rev. Rul. 55-261, 1955-1 CB 307
Sexual dysfunction, treatment for	Yes	Rev. Rul. 75-187, 1975-1 CB 92

Medical Expense	Deductible	Authority
Smoking, program to stop	Yes	Rev. Rul. 99-28, 1999-1 CB 1269
Spiritual guidance	No	*M. Miller,* 40 TCM 243, Dec. 36,911(M), TC Memo. 1980-136
Sterilization operation, legal	Yes	Rev. Rul. 73-603, 1973-2 CB 76, clarifying Rev. Rul. 73-201, 1973-1 CB 140
Swimming pool, treatment of polio or arthritis	Yes	*C.B. Mason,* DC Hawaii, 57-2 USTC ¶ 10,012; Rev. Rul. 83-33, 1983-1 CB 70
Tattoos	No	Rev. Rul. 82-111, 1982-1 CB 48
Taxicab to doctor's office	Yes	Rev. Rul. 55-261, 1955-1 CB 307
Teeth, artificial	Yes	Reg. § 1.213-1(e)(1)(ii)
Teeth, whitening	No	Rev. Rul. 2003-57, I.R.B. 2003-22
Telephone, specially equipped		
. deaf persons	Yes	Rev. Rul. 71-48, 1971-1 CB 99, amplified by Rev. Rul. 73-53, 1973-1 CB 139
. modified for person in an iron lung	Yes	Rev. Rul. 55-261, 1955-1 CB 307
Television, closed caption decoder	Yes	Rev. Rul. 80-340, 1980-2 CB 81
Toilet articles	No	*O.G. Russell,* 12 TCM 1276, Dec. 19,973(M)
Transplant, donor's costs of	Yes	Rev. Rul. 68-452, 1968-2 CB 111; Rev. Rul. 73-189, 1973-1 CB 139
Transportation, cost incurred essentially and primarily for medical care	Yes	Code Sec. 213(d)(1)(B) and Reg. § 1.213-1(e)(1)(iv)
Trips, general health improvement	No	Reg. § 1.213-1(e)(1)(iv)
Vacations, health restorative	No	Reg. § 1.213-1(e)(1)(iv) and Rev. Rul. 57-130, 1957-1 CB 108
Vacuum cleaner, alleviation of dust allergy	No	Rev. Rul. 76-80, 1976-1 CB 71
Vasectomy, legal	Yes	Rev. Rul. 73-201, 1973-1 CB 140, clarified by Rev. Rul. 73-603, 1973-2 CB 76, and Rev. Rul. 97-9, 1997-1 CB 77
Visual alert system for hearing impaired	Yes	IRS Letter Ruling 8250040, 9-13-82, CCH IRS LETTER RULINGS REPORTS
Weight loss program for treatment of specific disease	Yes	Rev. Rul. 2002-19, 2002-1 CB 778
Weight loss programs to improve appearance, prescribed	No	Rev. Rul. 79-151, 1979-1 CB 116; IRS Publication 502, "Medical and Dental Expenses"
Wheelchair	Yes	Reg. § 1.213-1(e)(1)(iii)
Wig, alleviation of mental discomfort resulting from disease	Yes	Rev. Rul. 62-189, 1962-2 CB 88
X-rays	Yes	Reg. § 1.213-1(e)(1)(ii)

Return Flow Charts

COMPUTATION OF TAXABLE INCOME

¶ 61 Individuals

The computation of an individual's taxable income involves several steps. Items that constitute income for tax purposes must be sifted from items that do not constitute income. Similarly, expenses that are deductible must be sifted from expenses that are not deductible. In addition, deductible expenses must be divided into expenses that are deductible from gross income and those that are deductible as itemized deductions.

The following outline summarizes the computation of taxable income by an individual and highlights those items that often enter into this computation.

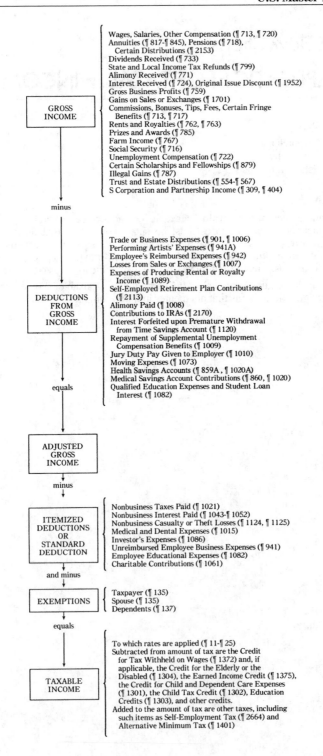

GROSS INCOME

Wages, Salaries, Other Compensation (¶ 713, ¶ 720)
Annuities (¶ 817-¶ 845), Pensions (¶ 718),
    Certain Distributions (¶ 2153)
Dividends Received (¶ 733)
State and Local Income Tax Refunds (¶ 799)
Alimony Received (¶ 771)
Interest Received (¶ 724), Original Issue Discount (¶ 1952)
Gross Business Profits (¶ 759)
Gains on Sales or Exchanges (¶ 1701)
Commissions, Bonuses, Tips, Fees, Certain Fringe
    Benefits (¶ 713, ¶ 717)
Rents and Royalties (¶ 762, ¶ 763)
Prizes and Awards (¶ 785)
Farm Income (¶ 767)
Social Security (¶ 716)
Unemployment Compensation (¶ 722)
Certain Scholarships and Fellowships (¶ 879)
Illegal Gains (¶ 787)
Trust and Estate Distributions (¶ 554-¶ 567)
S Corporation and Partnership Income (¶ 309, ¶ 404)

minus

DEDUCTIONS FROM GROSS INCOME

Trade or Business Expenses (¶ 901, ¶ 1006)
Performing Artists' Expenses (¶ 941A)
Employee's Reimbursed Expenses (¶ 942)
Losses from Sales or Exchanges (¶ 1007)
Expenses of Producing Rental or Royalty
    Income (¶ 1089)
Self-Employed Retirement Plan Contributions
    (¶ 2113)
Alimony Paid (¶ 1008)
Contributions to IRAs (¶ 2170)
Interest Forfeited upon Premature Withdrawal
    from Time Savings Account (¶ 1120)
Repayment of Supplemental Unemployment
    Compensation Benefits (¶ 1009)
Jury Duty Pay Given to Employer (¶ 1010)
Moving Expenses (¶ 1073)
Health Savings Accounts (¶ 859A , ¶ 1020A)
Medical Savings Account Contributions (¶ 860, ¶ 1020)
Qualified Education Expenses and Student Loan
    Interest (¶ 1082)

equals

ADJUSTED GROSS INCOME

minus

ITEMIZED DEDUCTIONS OR STANDARD DEDUCTION

Nonbusiness Taxes Paid (¶ 1021)
Nonbusiness Interest Paid (¶ 1043-¶ 1052)
Nonbusiness Casualty or Theft Losses (¶ 1124, ¶ 1125)
Medical and Dental Expenses (¶ 1015)
Investor's Expenses (¶ 1086)
Unreimbursed Employee Business Expenses (¶ 941)
Employee Educational Expenses (¶ 1082)
Charitable Contributions (¶ 1061)

and minus

EXEMPTIONS

Taxpayer (¶ 135)
Spouse (¶ 135)
Dependents (¶ 137)

equals

TAXABLE INCOME

To which rates are applied (¶ 11-¶ 25)
Subtracted from amount of tax are the Credit
    for Tax Withheld on Wages (¶ 1372) and, if
    applicable, the Credit for the Elderly or the
    Disabled (¶ 1304), the Earned Income Credit (¶ 1375),
    the Credit for Child and Dependent Care Expenses
    (¶ 1301), the Child Tax Credit (¶ 1302), Education
    Credits (¶ 1303), and other credits.
Added to the amount of tax are other taxes, including
    such items as Self-Employment Tax (¶ 2664) and
    Alternative Minimum Tax (¶ 1401)

¶ 62 Corporations

The computation of a corporation's taxable income involves several steps. Items that constitute income for tax purposes must be segregated from items that do not constitute income. Similarly, expenses that are deductible must be segregated from expenses that are not deductible. In addition, deductible expenses must be classified as either ordinary expenses or special deductions.

The following outline summarizes the computation of taxable income by a corporation and highlights those items that often enter into this computation.

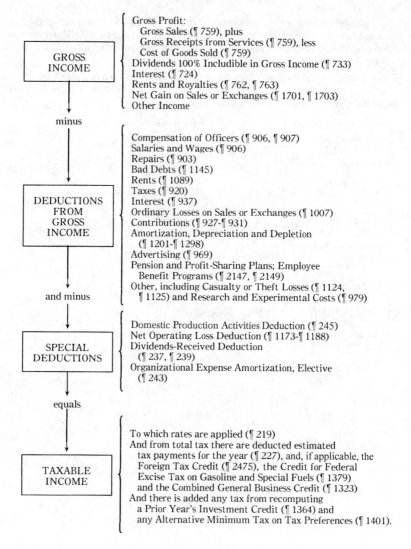

GROSS INCOME

Gross Profit:
Gross Sales (¶ 759), plus
Gross Receipts from Services (¶ 759), less
Cost of Goods Sold (¶ 759)
Dividends 100% Includible in Gross Income (¶ 733)
Interest (¶ 724)
Rents and Royalties (¶ 762, ¶ 763)
Net Gain on Sales or Exchanges (¶ 1701, ¶ 1703)
Other Income

minus

DEDUCTIONS FROM GROSS INCOME

Compensation of Officers (¶ 906, ¶ 907)
Salaries and Wages (¶ 906)
Repairs (¶ 903)
Bad Debts (¶ 1145)
Rents (¶ 1089)
Taxes (¶ 920)
Interest (¶ 937)
Ordinary Losses on Sales or Exchanges (¶ 1007)
Contributions (¶ 927-¶ 931)
Amortization, Depreciation and Depletion
(¶ 1201-¶ 1298)
Advertising (¶ 969)
Pension and Profit-Sharing Plans; Employee
Benefit Programs (¶ 2147, ¶ 2149)
Other, including Casualty or Theft Losses (¶ 1124,
¶ 1125) and Research and Experimental Costs (¶ 979)

and minus

SPECIAL DEDUCTIONS

Domestic Production Activities Deduction (¶ 245)
Net Operating Loss Deduction (¶ 1173-¶ 1188)
Dividends-Received Deduction
(¶ 237, ¶ 239)
Organizational Expense Amortization, Elective
(¶ 243)

equals

TAXABLE INCOME

To which rates are applied (¶ 219)
And from total tax there are deducted estimated
tax payments for the year (¶ 227), and, if applicable, the
Foreign Tax Credit (¶ 2475), the Credit for Federal
Excise Tax on Gasoline and Special Fuels (¶ 1379)
and the Combined General Business Credit (¶ 1323)
And there is added any tax from recomputing
a Prior Year's Investment Credit (¶ 1364) and
any Alternative Minimum Tax on Tax Preferences (¶ 1401).

¶ 63 Partnerships

Although a partnership does not pay tax, it must nevertheless report its income and expenses so that its partners may account for partnership income and expenses on their income tax returns.

Many types of income and expenses are separately stated and flow through to the partners. Similarly, many types of deduction and some types of credit information are separately stated and flow through to the partners. See ¶ 431. The remaining income and deductions that are not separately reported are combined into the partnership's taxable income or loss.

The separately stated income and expense items, information regarding credits, and the partnership's ordinary income or loss are reported on Schedule K. These income, deduction and credit items are allocated to each partner on Schedule K-1, a copy of which is furnished to each partner.

The following outline summarizes the computation of the partnership's income or loss (i.e., its bottom-line income or loss as reflected on page 1, Form 1065) and highlights those items that often enter into this computation.

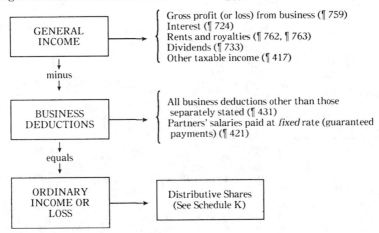

GENERAL INCOME
{ Gross profit (or loss) from business (¶ 759)
Interest (¶ 724)
Rents and royalties (¶ 762, ¶ 763)
Dividends (¶ 733)
Other taxable income (¶ 417)

minus

BUSINESS DEDUCTIONS
{ All business deductions other than those separately stated (¶ 431)
Partners' salaries paid at *fixed* rate (guaranteed payments) (¶ 421)

equals

ORDINARY INCOME OR LOSS → Distributive Shares (See Schedule K)

¶ 64 Estates and Trusts

Estates and trusts are distinct entities for income tax purposes. They are subject to the same income taxes as individuals and are taxed in much the same manner as individuals. However, estates and trusts are not subject to self-employment tax. Although an estate or trust is a taxable entity, it is nevertheless a conduit of income to be distributed. Income is taxed to the estate or trust unless distributed. A deduction is allowed for distributed income, which becomes taxable to the beneficiary distributees.

The following outline summarizes the computation of taxable income by a trust or estate and highlights those items that often enter into this computation.

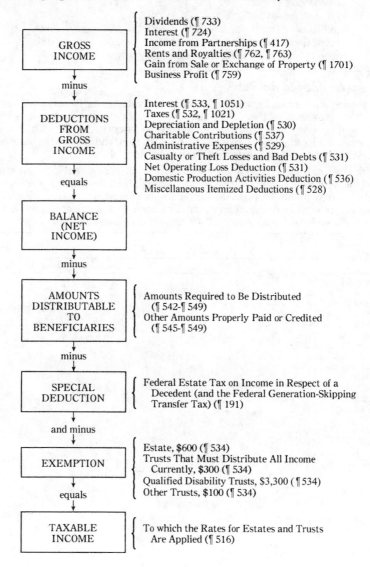

GROSS INCOME
- Dividends (¶ 733)
- Interest (¶ 724)
- Income from Partnerships (¶ 417)
- Rents and Royalties (¶ 762, ¶ 763)
- Gain from Sale or Exchange of Property (¶ 1701)
- Business Profit (¶ 759)

minus

DEDUCTIONS FROM GROSS INCOME
- Interest (¶ 533, ¶ 1051)
- Taxes (¶ 532, ¶ 1021)
- Depreciation and Depletion (¶ 530)
- Charitable Contributions (¶ 537)
- Administrative Expenses (¶ 529)
- Casualty or Theft Losses and Bad Debts (¶ 531)
- Net Operating Loss Deduction (¶ 531)
- Domestic Production Activities Deduction (¶ 536)
- Miscellaneous Itemized Deductions (¶ 528)

equals

BALANCE (NET INCOME)

minus

AMOUNTS DISTRIBUTABLE TO BENEFICIARIES
- Amounts Required to Be Distributed (¶ 542-¶ 549)
- Other Amounts Properly Paid or Credited (¶ 545-¶ 549)

minus

SPECIAL DEDUCTION
- Federal Estate Tax on Income in Respect of a Decedent (and the Federal Generation-Skipping Transfer Tax) (¶ 191)

and minus

EXEMPTION
- Estate, $600 (¶ 534)
- Trusts That Must Distribute All Income Currently, $300 (¶ 534)
- Qualified Disability Trusts, $3,300 (¶ 534)
- Other Trusts, $100 (¶ 534)

equals

TAXABLE INCOME
- To which the Rates for Estates and Trusts Are Applied (¶ 516)

SPECIAL TAX TABLES

¶ 83 Applicable Federal Rates

Following are the monthly applicable federal interest rates for January 2007 through August 2007, published by the IRS for purposes of testing imputed interest in below-market interest loans (¶ 795) and debt-for-property transactions (¶ 1954). The rates are also relevant under the golden parachute rules (¶ 907) and for testing interest in connection with deferred payments for the use of property (¶ 1859).

In the case of below-market interest loans that are demand or gift loans, an amount deemed the "foregone" interest is treated as transferred from the lender to the borrower and retransferred by the borrower to the lender as interest. In order to simplify the computation of such foregone interest, the IRS prescribes a "blended annual rate," which is 4.92% on loans from January 1, 2007, through December 31, 2007.

		Period for Compounding			
		Annual	*Semiannual*	*Quarterly*	*Monthly*
January 2007					
	Short-Term				
	AFR	4.88	4.82	4.79	4.77
110%	AFR	5.37	5.30	5.27	5.24
120%	AFR	5.86	5.78	5.74	5.71
130%	AFR	6.37	6.27	6.22	6.19
	Mid-Term				
	AFR	4.58	4.53	4.50	4.49
110%	AFR	5.04	4.98	4.95	4.93
120%	AFR	5.51	5.44	5.40	5.38
130%	AFR	5.98	5.89	5.85	5.82
150%	AFR	6.92	6.80	6.74	6.71
175%	AFR	8.09	7.93	7.85	7.80
	Long-Term				
	AFR	4.73	4.68	4.65	4.64
110%	AFR	5.22	5.15	5.12	5.10
120%	AFR	5.70	5.62	5.58	5.56
130%	AFR	6.17	6.08	6.03	6.00

Period for Compounding

		Annual	Semiannual	Quarterly	Monthly
February 2007					
	Short-Term				
	AFR	4.93	4.87	4.84	4.82
110%	AFR	5.43	5.36	5.32	5.30
120%	AFR	5.93	5.84	5.80	5.77
130%	AFR	6.43	6.33	6.28	6.25
	Mid-Term				
	AFR	4.69	4.64	4.61	4.60
110%	AFR	5.17	5.10	5.07	5.05
120%	AFR	5.65	5.57	5.53	5.51
130%	AFR	6.12	6.03	5.99	5.96
150%	AFR	7.08	6.96	6.90	6.86
175%	AFR	8.28	8.12	8.04	7.99
	Long-Term				
	AFR	4.86	4.80	4.77	4.75
110%	AFR	5.35	5.28	5.25	5.22
120%	AFR	5.84	5.76	5.72	5.69
130%	AFR	6.34	6.24	6.19	6.16
March 2007					
	Short-Term				
	AFR	5.06	5.00	4.97	4.95
110%	AFR	5.58	5.50	5.46	5.44
120%	AFR	6.09	6.00	5.96	5.93
130%	AFR	6.61	6.50	6.45	6.41
	Mid-Term				
	AFR	4.86	4.80	4.77	4.75
110%	AFR	5.35	5.28	5.25	5.22
120%	AFR	5.84	5.76	5.72	5.69
130%	AFR	6.34	6.24	6.19	6.16
150%	AFR	7.33	7.20	7.14	7.09
175%	AFR	8.58	8.40	8.31	8.26
	Long-Term				
	AFR	5.01	4.95	4.92	4.90
110%	AFR	5.52	5.45	5.41	5.39
120%	AFR	6.03	5.94	5.90	5.87
130%	AFR	6.54	6.44	6.39	6.36
April 2007					
	Short-Term				
	AFR	4.90	4.84	4.81	4.79
110%	AFR	5.39	5.32	5.29	5.26
120%	AFR	5.89	5.81	5.77	5.74
130%	AFR	6.39	6.29	6.24	6.21
	Mid-Term				
	AFR	4.61	4.56	4.53	4.52
110%	AFR	5.08	5.02	4.99	4.97
120%	AFR	5.54	5.47	5.43	5.41
130%	AFR	6.02	5.93	5.89	5.86
150%	AFR	6.96	6.84	6.78	6.74
175%	AFR	8.14	7.98	7.90	7.85
	Long-Term				
	AFR	4.81	4.75	4.72	4.70
110%	AFR	5.30	5.23	5.20	5.17
120%	AFR	5.78	5.70	5.66	5.63
130%	AFR	6.28	6.18	6.13	6.10

Period for Compounding			
	Annual	*Semiannual*	*Quarterly*	*Monthly*

May 2007

Short-Term

	Annual	Semiannual	Quarterly	Monthly
AFR	4.85	4.79	4.76	4.74
110% AFR	5.34	5.27	5.24	5.21
120% AFR	5.83	5.75	5.71	5.68
130% AFR	6.33	6.23	6.18	6.15

Mid-Term

	Annual	Semiannual	Quarterly	Monthly
AFR	4.62	4.57	4.54	4.53
110% AFR	5.09	5.03	5.00	4.98
120% AFR	5.56	5.48	5.44	5.42
130% AFR	6.03	5.94	5.90	5.87
150% AFR	6.98	6.86	6.80	6.76
175% AFR	8.16	8.00	7.92	7.87

Long-Term

	Annual	Semiannual	Quarterly	Monthly
AFR	4.90	4.84	4.81	4.79
110% AFR	5.39	5.32	5.29	5.26
120% AFR	5.89	5.81	5.77	5.74
130% AFR	6.39	6.29	6.24	6.21

June 2007

Short-Term

	Annual	Semiannual	Quarterly	Monthly
AFR	4.84	4.78	4.75	4.73
110% AFR	5.33	5.26	5.23	5.20
120% AFR	5.82	5.74	5.70	5.67
130% AFR	6.31	6.21	6.16	6.13

Mid-Term

	Annual	Semiannual	Quarterly	Monthly
AFR	4.64	4.59	4.56	4.55
110% AFR	5.11	5.05	5.02	5.00
120% AFR	5.59	5.51	5.47	5.45
130% AFR	6.06	5.97	5.93	5.90
150% AFR	7.01	6.89	6.83	6.79
175% AFR	8.19	8.03	7.95	7.90

Long-Term

	Annual	Semiannual	Quarterly	Monthly
AFR	4.91	4.85	4.82	4.80
110% AFR	5.41	5.34	5.30	5.28
120% AFR	5.90	5.82	5.78	5.75
130% AFR	6.41	6.31	6.26	6.23

July 2007

Short-Term

	Annual	Semiannual	Quarterly	Monthly
AFR	4.97	4.91	4.88	4.86
110% AFR	5.47	5.40	5.36	5.34
120% AFR	5.98	5.89	5.85	5.82
130% AFR	6.48	6.38	6.33	6.30

Mid-Term

	Annual	Semiannual	Quarterly	Monthly
AFR	4.95	4.89	4.86	4.84
110% AFR	5.45	5.38	5.34	5.32
120% AFR	5.96	5.87	5.83	5.80
130% AFR	6.46	6.36	6.31	6.28
150% AFR	7.47	7.34	7.27	7.23
175% AFR	8.74	8.56	8.47	8.41

Long-Term

	Annual	Semiannual	Quarterly	Monthly
AFR	5.15	5.09	5.06	5.04
110% AFR	5.68	5.60	5.56	5.54
120% AFR	6.20	6.11	6.06	6.03
130% AFR	6.73	6.62	6.57	6.53

		Period for Compounding			
		Annual	*Semiannual*	*Quarterly*	*Monthly*
August 2007					
	Short-Term				
	AFR	5.00	4.94	4.91	4.89
110%	AFR	5.50	5.43	5.39	5.37
120%	AFR	6.02	5.93	5.89	5.86
130%	AFR	6.52	6.42	6.37	6.34
	Mid-Term				
	AFR	5.09	5.03	5.00	4.98
110%	AFR	5.61	5.53	5.49	5.47
120%	AFR	6.13	6.04	6.00	5.97
130%	AFR	6.65	6.54	6.49	6.45
150%	AFR	7.69	7.55	7.48	7.43
175%	AFR	8.99	8.80	8.71	8.64
	Long-Term				
	AFR	5.31	5.24	5.21	5.18
110%	AFR	5.84	5.76	5.72	5.69
120%	AFR	6.39	6.29	6.24	6.21
130%	AFR	6.93	6.81	6.75	6.72
September 2007					
	Short-Term				
	AFR	4.82	4.76	4.73	4.71
110%	AFR	5.31	5.24	5.21	5.18
120%	AFR	5.79	5.71	5.67	5.64
130%	AFR	6.29	6.19	6.14	6.11
	Mid-Term				
	AFR	4.79	4.73	4.70	4.68
110%	AFR	5.27	5.20	5.17	5.14
120%	AFR	5.76	5.68	5.64	5.61
130%	AFR	6.24	6.15	6.10	6.07
150%	AFR	7.23	7.10	7.04	7.00
175%	AFR	8.45	8.28	8.20	8.14
	Long-Term				
	AFR	5.09	5.03	5.00	4.98
110%	AFR	5.61	5.53	5.49	5.47
120%	AFR	6.13	6.04	6.00	5.97
130%	AFR	6.65	6.54	6.49	6.45
October 2007					
	Short-Term				
	AFR	4.19	4.15	4.13	4.11
110%	AFR	4.62	4.57	4.54	4.53
120%	AFR	5.04	4.98	4.95	4.93
130%	AFR	5.47	5.40	5.36	5.34
	Mid-Term				
	AFR	4.35	4.30	4.28	4.26
110%	AFR	4.79	4.73	4.70	4.68
120%	AFR	5.23	5.16	5.13	5.11
130%	AFR	5.67	5.59	5.55	5.53
150%	AFR	6.55	6.45	6.40	6.36
175%	AFR	7.67	7.53	7.46	7.41
	Long-Term				
	AFR	4.88	4.82	4.79	4.77
110%	AFR	5.37	5.30	5.27	5.24
120%	AFR	5.86	5.78	5.74	5.71
130%	AFR	6.37	6.27	6.22	6.19

Period for Compounding				
	Annual	Semiannual	Quarterly	Monthly
November 2007				
Short-Term				
AFR	4.11	4.07	4.05	4.04
110% AFR	4.53	4.48	4.46	4.44
120% AFR	4.94	4.88	4.85	4.83
130% AFR	5.36	5.29	5.26	5.23
Mid-Term				
AFR	4.39	4.34	4.32	4.30
110% AFR	4.83	4.77	4.74	4.72
120% AFR	5.28	5.21	5.18	5.15
130% AFR	5.72	5.64	5.60	5.57
150% AFR	6.62	6.51	6.46	6.42
175% AFR	7.74	7.60	7.53	7.48
Long-Term				
AFR	4.89	4.83	4.80	4.78
110% AFR	5.38	5.31	5.28	5.25
120% AFR	5.88	5.80	5.76	5.73
130% AFR	6.38	6.28	6.23	6.20

¶ 84 Adjusted Applicable Federal Rates

Code Sec. 1288 provides that, in determining original issue discount on tax-exempt obligations, an adjustment must be made to the applicable federal rates (¶ 83) to take into account the tax exemption for interest on the obligations.

Adjusted Applicable Federal Rates

	Annual Compounding	SemiAnnual Compounding	Quarterly Compounding	Monthly Compounding
January 2007				
Short-term rate	3.39%	3.36%	3.35%	3.34%
Mid-term rate	3.54%	3.51%	3.49%	3.48%
Long-term rate	4.03%	3.99%	3.97%	3.96%
February 2007				
Short-term rate	3.46%	3.43%	3.42%	3.41%
Mid-term rate	3.58%	3.55%	3.53%	3.52%
Long-term rate	4.07%	4.03%	4.01%	4.00%
March 2007				
Short-term rate	3.58%	3.55%	3.53%	3.52%
Mid-term rate	3.71%	3.68%	3.66%	3.65%
Long-term rate	4.18%	4.14%	4.12%	4.10%
April 2007				
Short-term rate	3.50%	3.47%	3.46%	3.45%
Mid-term rate	3.65%	3.62%	3.60%	3.59%
Long-term rate	4.04%	4.00%	3.98%	3.97%
May 2007				
Short-term rate	3.47%	3.44%	3.43%	3.42%
Mid-term rate	3.61%	3.58%	3.56%	3.55%
Long-term rate	4.11%	4.07%	4.05%	4.04%

June 2007

	Annual Compounding	SemiAnnual Compounding	Quarterly Compounding	Monthly Compounding
Short-term rate	3.52%	3.49%	3.47%	3.46%
Mid-term rate	3.68%	3.65%	3.63%	3.62%
Long-term rate	4.15%	4.11%	4.09%	4.08%

July 2007

	Annual Compounding	SemiAnnual Compounding	Quarterly Compounding	Monthly Compounding
Short-term rate	3.66%	3.63%	3.61%	3.60%
Mid-term rate	3.81%	3.77%	3.75%	3.74%
Long-term rate	4.32%	4.27%	4.25%	4.23%

August 2007

	Annual Compounding	SemiAnnual Compounding	Quarterly Compounding	Monthly Compounding
Short-term rate	3.75%	3.72%	3.70%	3.69%
Mid-term rate	3.97%	3.93%	3.91%	3.90%
Long-term rate	4.50%	4.45%	4.43%	4.41%

September 2007

	Annual Compounding	SemiAnnual Compounding	Quarterly Compounding	Monthly Compounding
Short-term rate	3.65%	3.62%	3.60%	3.59%
Mid-term rate	3.92%	3.88%	3.86%	3.85%
Long-term rate	4.44%	4.39%	4.37%	4.35%

October 2007

	Annual Compounding	SemiAnnual Compounding	Quarterly Compounding	Monthly Compounding
Short-term rate	3.60%	3.57%	3.55%	3.54%
Mid-term rate	3.79%	3.75%	3.73%	3.72%
Long-term rate	4.49%	4.44%	4.42%	4.40%

November 2007

	Annual Compounding	SemiAnnual Compounding	Quarterly Compounding	Monthly Compounding
Short-term rate	3.40%	3.37%	3.36%	3.35%
Mid-term rate	3.61%	3.58%	3.56%	3.55%
Long-term rate	4.30%	4.25%	4.23%	4.21%

¶ 85 Federal Long-Term Tax-Exempt Rates

Code Sec. 382 provides that the long-term tax-exempt rate for purposes of net operating loss carryforwards shall be the highest of the adjusted federal long-term rates (¶ 84) for the three months ending with the month in which the particular ownership change occurs. Each rate below is the highest for the 3-month period.

Long-Term Tax-Exempt Rates

Month	Rate
January 2007	4.15%
February 2007	4.14%
March 2007	4.18%
April 2007	4.18%
May 2007	4.18%
June 2007	4.15%
July 2007	4.32%
August 2007	4.50%
September 2007	4.50%
October 2007	4.50%
November 2007	4.49%

¶ 86 Applicable Credit Percentages for Low-Income Housing

Code Sec. 42 provides that applicable credit percentages for low-income housing are to be computed so that the present value of the 10 annual credit amounts at the beginning of the 10-year credit period equals either 70% or 30% of the qualified basis of the low-income units in a project. The discount rate for determining the present value in these computations is a rate equal to 72% of the average of the month's AFR for mid-term and long-term obligations. The applicable credit percentage for new construction or rehabilitation expenditures not federally subsidized is indicated under the 70% rate column. The applicable credit percentage for subsidized construction or rehabilitation expenditures and the acquisition of existing housing is indicated under the 30% rate column. See ¶ 1334.

Applicable Credit Percentages for Low-Income Housing

Month	70% Rate	30% Rate
January 2007	8.08%	3.46%
February 2007	8.11%	3.48%
March 2007	8.15%	3.49%
April 2007	8.10%	3.47%
May 2007	8.11%	3.47%
June 2007	8.11%	3.48%
July 2007	8.18%	3.50%
August 2007	8.21%	3.52%
September 2007	8.15%	3.49%
October 2007	8.07%	3.46%
November 2007	8.08%	3.46%

¶ 87 Earned Income Credit

The earned income credit tables are used in conjunction with the Form 1040or Form 1040A, and Schedule EIC. The appropriate Schedule must be filed with the taxpayer's tax return in order to claim the earned income credit. The credit, as computed on the Schedules, is entered on line 65a, Form 1040, or on line 41a, Form 1040A. Form 1040EZ may be used to claim the earned income credit in limited circumstances.

☐ The tables on the following pages refer to lines on Schedule EIC, which Form 1040 filers must attach to claim the earned income credit. Taxpayers filing Form 1040A should use similar tables appearing in the Form 1040A instructions.

2007 Earned Income Credit (EIC) Table
Caution. This is **not** a tax table.

1. To find your credit, read down the "At least - But less than" columns and find the line that includes the amount you were told to look up from your EIC Worksheet.

2. Then, go to the column that includes your filing status and the number of qualifying children you have. Enter the credit from that column on your EIC Worksheet.

Example. If your filing status is single, you have one qualifying child, and the amount you are looking up from your EIC Worksheet is $2,455, you would enter $842.

If the amount you are looking up from the worksheet is—		And your filing status is— Single, head of household, or qualifying widow(er) and you have—		
At least	But less than	No children	One child	Two children
				Your credit is—
2,400	2,450	186	825	970
2,450	2,500	189	842	990

If the amount you are looking up from the worksheet is—		Single, head of household, or qualifying widow(er) and you have—			Married filing jointly and you have—		
At least	But less than	No children	One child	Two children	No children	One child	Two children
		Your credit is—			Your credit is—		
$1	$50	$2	$9	$10	$2	$9	$10
50	100	6	26	30	6	26	30
100	150	10	43	50	10	43	50
150	200	13	60	70	13	60	70
200	250	17	77	90	17	77	90
250	300	21	94	110	21	94	110
300	350	25	111	130	25	111	130
350	400	29	128	150	29	128	150
400	450	33	145	170	33	145	170
450	500	36	162	190	36	162	190
500	550	40	179	210	40	179	210
550	600	44	196	230	44	196	230
600	650	48	213	250	48	213	250
650	700	52	230	270	52	230	270
700	750	55	247	290	55	247	290
750	800	59	264	310	59	264	310
800	850	63	281	330	63	281	330
850	900	67	298	350	67	298	350
900	950	71	315	370	71	315	370
950	1,000	75	332	390	75	332	390
1,000	1,050	78	349	410	78	349	410
1,050	1,100	82	366	430	82	366	430
1,100	1,150	86	383	450	86	383	450
1,150	1,200	90	400	470	90	400	470
1,200	1,250	94	417	490	94	417	490
1,250	1,300	98	434	510	98	434	510
1,300	1,350	101	451	530	101	451	530
1,350	1,400	105	468	550	105	468	550
1,400	1,450	109	485	570	109	485	570
1,450	1,500	113	502	590	113	502	590
1,500	1,550	117	519	610	117	519	610
1,550	1,600	120	536	630	120	536	630
1,600	1,650	124	553	650	124	553	650
1,650	1,700	128	570	670	128	570	670
1,700	1,750	132	587	690	132	587	690
1,750	1,800	136	604	710	136	604	710
1,800	1,850	140	621	730	140	621	730
1,850	1,900	143	638	750	143	638	750
1,900	1,950	147	655	770	147	655	770
1,950	2,000	151	672	790	151	672	790
2,000	2,050	155	689	810	155	689	810
2,050	2,100	159	706	830	159	706	830
2,100	2,150	163	723	850	163	723	850
2,150	2,200	166	740	870	166	740	870
2,200	2,250	170	757	890	170	757	890
2,250	2,300	174	774	910	174	774	910
2,300	2,350	178	791	930	178	791	930
2,350	2,400	182	808	950	182	808	950
2,400	2,450	186	825	970	186	825	970
2,450	2,500	189	842	990	189	842	990
2,500	2,550	193	859	1,010	193	859	1,010
2,550	2,600	197	876	1,030	197	876	1,030
2,600	2,650	201	893	1,050	201	893	1,050
2,650	2,700	205	910	1,070	205	910	1,070
2,700	2,750	208	927	1,090	208	927	1,090
2,750	2,800	212	944	1,110	212	944	1,110
2,800	2,850	216	961	1,130	216	961	1,130
2,850	2,900	220	978	1,150	220	978	1,150
2,900	2,950	224	995	1,170	224	995	1,170
2,950	3,000	228	1,012	1,190	228	1,012	1,190
3,000	3,050	231	1,029	1,210	231	1,029	1,210
3,050	3,100	235	1,046	1,230	235	1,046	1,230
3,100	3,150	239	1,063	1,250	239	1,063	1,250
3,150	3,200	243	1,080	1,270	243	1,080	1,270
3,200	3,250	247	1,097	1,290	247	1,097	1,290
3,250	3,300	251	1,114	1,310	251	1,114	1,310
3,300	3,350	254	1,131	1,330	254	1,131	1,330
3,350	3,400	258	1,148	1,350	258	1,148	1,350
3,400	3,450	262	1,165	1,370	262	1,165	1,370
3,450	3,500	266	1,182	1,390	266	1,182	1,390
3,500	3,550	270	1,199	1,410	270	1,199	1,410
3,550	3,600	273	1,216	1,430	273	1,216	1,430
3,600	3,650	277	1,233	1,450	277	1,233	1,450
3,650	3,700	281	1,250	1,470	281	1,250	1,470
3,700	3,750	285	1,267	1,490	285	1,267	1,490
3,750	3,800	289	1,284	1,510	289	1,284	1,510
3,800	3,850	293	1,301	1,530	293	1,301	1,530
3,850	3,900	296	1,318	1,550	296	1,318	1,550
3,900	3,950	300	1,335	1,570	300	1,335	1,570
3,950	4,000	304	1,352	1,590	304	1,352	1,590
4,000	4,050	308	1,369	1,610	308	1,369	1,610
4,050	4,100	312	1,386	1,630	312	1,386	1,630
4,100	4,150	316	1,403	1,650	316	1,403	1,650
4,150	4,200	319	1,420	1,670	319	1,420	1,670
4,200	4,250	323	1,437	1,690	323	1,437	1,690
4,250	4,300	327	1,454	1,710	327	1,454	1,710
4,300	4,350	331	1,471	1,730	331	1,471	1,730
4,350	4,400	335	1,488	1,750	335	1,488	1,750
4,400	4,450	339	1,505	1,770	339	1,505	1,770
4,450	4,500	342	1,522	1,790	342	1,522	1,790
4,500	4,550	346	1,539	1,810	346	1,539	1,810
4,550	4,600	350	1,556	1,830	350	1,556	1,830
4,600	4,650	354	1,573	1,850	354	1,573	1,850
4,650	4,700	358	1,590	1,870	358	1,590	1,870
4,700	4,750	361	1,607	1,890	361	1,607	1,890
4,750	4,800	365	1,624	1,910	365	1,624	1,910
4,800	4,850	369	1,641	1,930	369	1,641	1,930
4,850	4,900	373	1,658	1,950	373	1,658	1,950
4,900	4,950	377	1,675	1,970	377	1,675	1,970
4,950	5,000	381	1,692	1,990	381	1,692	1,990

(Continued on page 52)

¶87

2007 Earned Income Credit (EIC) Table—*Continued*   (**Caution**. This is **not** a tax table.)

If the amount you are looking up from the worksheet is—		Single, head of household, or qualifying widow(er) and you have—			Married filing jointly and you have—		
At least	But less than	No children	One child	Two children	No children	One child	Two children
		Your credit is—			**Your credit is—**		
5,000	5,050	384	1,709	2,010	384	1,709	2,010
5,050	5,100	388	1,726	2,030	388	1,726	2,030
5,100	5,150	392	1,743	2,050	392	1,743	2,050
5,150	5,200	396	1,760	2,070	396	1,760	2,070
5,200	5,250	400	1,777	2,090	400	1,777	2,090
5,250	5,300	404	1,794	2,110	404	1,794	2,110
5,300	5,350	407	1,811	2,130	407	1,811	2,130
5,350	5,400	411	1,828	2,150	411	1,828	2,150
5,400	5,450	415	1,845	2,170	415	1,845	2,170
5,450	5,500	419	1,862	2,190	419	1,862	2,190
5,500	5,550	423	1,879	2,210	423	1,879	2,210
5,550	5,600	428	1,896	2,230	428	1,896	2,230
5,600	5,650	428	1,913	2,250	428	1,913	2,250
5,650	5,700	428	1,930	2,270	428	1,930	2,270
5,700	5,750	428	1,947	2,290	428	1,947	2,290
5,750	5,800	428	1,964	2,310	428	1,964	2,310
5,800	5,850	428	1,981	2,330	428	1,981	2,330
5,850	5,900	428	1,998	2,350	428	1,998	2,350
5,900	5,950	428	2,015	2,370	428	2,015	2,370
5,950	6,000	428	2,032	2,390	428	2,032	2,390
6,000	6,050	428	2,049	2,410	428	2,049	2,410
6,050	6,100	428	2,066	2,430	428	2,066	2,430
6,100	6,150	428	2,083	2,450	428	2,083	2,450
6,150	6,200	428	2,100	2,470	428	2,100	2,470
6,200	6,250	428	2,117	2,490	428	2,117	2,490
6,250	6,300	428	2,134	2,510	428	2,134	2,510
6,300	6,350	428	2,151	2,530	428	2,151	2,530
6,350	6,400	428	2,168	2,550	428	2,168	2,550
6,400	6,450	428	2,185	2,570	428	2,185	2,570
6,450	6,500	428	2,202	2,590	428	2,202	2,590
6,500	6,550	428	2,219	2,610	428	2,219	2,610
6,550	6,600	428	2,236	2,630	428	2,236	2,630
6,600	6,650	428	2,253	2,650	428	2,253	2,650
6,650	6,700	428	2,270	2,670	428	2,270	2,670
6,700	6,750	428	2,287	2,690	428	2,287	2,690
6,750	6,800	428	2,304	2,710	428	2,304	2,710
6,800	6,850	428	2,321	2,730	428	2,321	2,730
6,850	6,900	428	2,338	2,750	428	2,338	2,750
6,900	6,950	428	2,355	2,770	428	2,355	2,770
6,950	7,000	428	2,372	2,790	428	2,372	2,790
7,000	7,050	426	2,389	2,810	428	2,389	2,810
7,050	7,100	422	2,406	2,830	428	2,406	2,830
7,100	7,150	418	2,423	2,850	428	2,423	2,850
7,150	7,200	414	2,440	2,870	428	2,440	2,870
7,200	7,250	410	2,457	2,890	428	2,457	2,890
7,250	7,300	407	2,474	2,910	428	2,474	2,910
7,300	7,350	403	2,491	2,930	428	2,491	2,930
7,350	7,400	399	2,508	2,950	428	2,508	2,950
7,400	7,450	395	2,525	2,970	428	2,525	2,970
7,450	7,500	391	2,542	2,990	428	2,542	2,990
7,500	7,550	387	2,559	3,010	428	2,559	3,010
7,550	7,600	384	2,576	3,030	428	2,576	3,030
7,600	7,650	380	2,593	3,050	428	2,593	3,050
7,650	7,700	376	2,610	3,070	428	2,610	3,070
7,700	7,750	372	2,627	3,090	428	2,627	3,090
7,750	7,800	368	2,644	3,110	428	2,644	3,110
7,800	7,850	365	2,661	3,130	428	2,661	3,130
7,850	7,900	361	2,678	3,150	428	2,678	3,150
7,900	7,950	357	2,695	3,170	428	2,695	3,170
7,950	8,000	353	2,712	3,190	428	2,712	3,190
8,000	8,050	349	2,729	3,210	428	2,729	3,210
8,050	8,100	345	2,746	3,230	428	2,746	3,230
8,100	8,150	342	2,763	3,250	428	2,763	3,250
8,150	8,200	338	2,780	3,270	428	2,780	3,270
8,200	8,250	334	2,797	3,290	428	2,797	3,290
8,250	8,300	330	2,814	3,310	428	2,814	3,310
8,300	8,350	326	2,831	3,330	428	2,831	3,330
8,350	8,400	322	2,853	3,350	428	2,853	3,350
8,400	8,450	319	2,853	3,370	428	2,853	3,370
8,450	8,500	315	2,853	3,390	428	2,853	3,390
8,500	8,550	311	2,853	3,410	428	2,853	3,410
8,550	8,600	307	2,853	3,430	428	2,853	3,430
8,600	8,650	303	2,853	3,450	428	2,853	3,450
8,650	8,700	299	2,853	3,470	428	2,853	3,470
8,700	8,750	296	2,853	3,490	428	2,853	3,490
8,750	8,800	292	2,853	3,510	428	2,853	3,510
8,800	8,850	288	2,853	3,530	428	2,853	3,530
8,850	8,900	284	2,853	3,550	428	2,853	3,550
8,900	8,950	280	2,853	3,570	428	2,853	3,570
8,950	9,000	277	2,853	3,590	428	2,853	3,590
9,000	9,050	273	2,853	3,610	426	2,853	3,610
9,050	9,100	269	2,853	3,630	422	2,853	3,630
9,100	9,150	265	2,853	3,650	418	2,853	3,650
9,150	9,200	261	2,853	3,670	414	2,853	3,670
9,200	9,250	257	2,853	3,690	410	2,853	3,690
9,250	9,300	254	2,853	3,710	407	2,853	3,710
9,300	9,350	250	2,853	3,730	403	2,853	3,730
9,350	9,400	246	2,853	3,750	399	2,853	3,750
9,400	9,450	242	2,853	3,770	395	2,853	3,770
9,450	9,500	238	2,853	3,790	391	2,853	3,790
9,500	9,550	234	2,853	3,810	387	2,853	3,810
9,550	9,600	231	2,853	3,830	384	2,853	3,830
9,600	9,650	227	2,853	3,850	380	2,853	3,850
9,650	9,700	223	2,853	3,870	376	2,853	3,870
9,700	9,750	219	2,853	3,890	372	2,853	3,890
9,750	9,800	215	2,853	3,910	368	2,853	3,910
9,800	9,850	212	2,853	3,930	365	2,853	3,930
9,850	9,900	208	2,853	3,950	361	2,853	3,950
9,900	9,950	204	2,853	3,970	357	2,853	3,970
9,950	10,000	200	2,853	3,990	353	2,853	3,990
10,000	10,050	196	2,853	4,010	349	2,853	4,010
10,050	10,100	192	2,853	4,030	345	2,853	4,030
10,100	10,150	189	2,853	4,050	342	2,853	4,050
10,150	10,200	185	2,853	4,070	338	2,853	4,070
10,200	10,250	181	2,853	4,090	334	2,853	4,090
10,250	10,300	177	2,853	4,110	330	2,853	4,110
10,300	10,350	173	2,853	4,130	326	2,853	4,130
10,350	10,400	169	2,853	4,150	322	2,853	4,150
10,400	10,450	166	2,853	4,170	319	2,853	4,170
10,450	10,500	162	2,853	4,190	315	2,853	4,190
10,500	10,550	158	2,853	4,210	311	2,853	4,210
10,550	10,600	154	2,853	4,230	307	2,853	4,230
10,600	10,650	150	2,853	4,250	303	2,853	4,250
10,650	10,700	146	2,853	4,270	299	2,853	4,270
10,700	10,750	143	2,853	4,290	296	2,853	4,290
10,750	10,800	139	2,853	4,310	292	2,853	4,310
10,800	10,850	135	2,853	4,330	288	2,853	4,330
10,850	10,900	131	2,853	4,350	284	2,853	4,350
10,900	10,950	127	2,853	4,370	280	2,853	4,370
10,950	11,000	124	2,853	4,390	277	2,853	4,390

(Continued on page 53)

¶87

2007 Earned Income Credit (EIC) Table—*Continued*   (**Caution.** This is **not** a tax table.)

If the amount you are looking up from the worksheet is—		Single, head of household, or qualifying widow(er) and you have—			Married filing jointly and you have—		
At least	But less than	No children	One child	Two children	No children	One child	Two children
		Your credit is—			Your credit is—		
11,000	11,050	120	2,853	4,410	273	2,853	4,410
11,050	11,100	116	2,853	4,430	269	2,853	4,430
11,100	11,150	112	2,853	4,450	265	2,853	4,450
11,150	11,200	108	2,853	4,470	261	2,853	4,470
11,200	11,250	104	2,853	4,490	257	2,853	4,490
11,250	11,300	101	2,853	4,510	254	2,853	4,510
11,300	11,350	97	2,853	4,530	250	2,853	4,530
11,350	11,400	93	2,853	4,550	246	2,853	4,550
11,400	11,450	89	2,853	4,570	242	2,853	4,570
11,450	11,500	85	2,853	4,590	238	2,853	4,590
11,500	11,550	81	2,853	4,610	234	2,853	4,610
11,550	11,600	78	2,853	4,630	231	2,853	4,630
11,600	11,650	74	2,853	4,650	227	2,853	4,650
11,650	11,700	70	2,853	4,670	223	2,853	4,670
11,700	11,750	66	2,853	4,690	219	2,853	4,690
11,750	11,800	62	2,853	4,716	215	2,853	4,716
11,800	11,850	59	2,853	4,716	212	2,853	4,716
11,850	11,900	55	2,853	4,716	208	2,853	4,716
11,900	11,950	51	2,853	4,716	204	2,853	4,716
11,950	12,000	47	2,853	4,716	200	2,853	4,716
12,000	12,050	43	2,853	4,716	196	2,853	4,716
12,050	12,100	39	2,853	4,716	192	2,853	4,716
12,100	12,150	36	2,853	4,716	189	2,853	4,716
12,150	12,200	32	2,853	4,716	185	2,853	4,716
12,200	12,250	28	2,853	4,716	181	2,853	4,716
12,250	12,300	24	2,853	4,716	177	2,853	4,716
12,300	12,350	20	2,853	4,716	173	2,853	4,716
12,350	12,400	16	2,853	4,716	169	2,853	4,716
12,400	12,450	13	2,853	4,716	166	2,853	4,716
12,450	12,500	9	2,853	4,716	162	2,853	4,716
12,500	12,550	5	2,853	4,716	158	2,853	4,716
12,550	12,600	*	2,853	4,716	154	2,853	4,716
12,600	12,650	0	2,853	4,716	150	2,853	4,716
12,650	12,700	0	2,853	4,716	146	2,853	4,716
12,700	12,750	0	2,853	4,716	143	2,853	4,716
12,750	12,800	0	2,853	4,716	139	2,853	4,716
12,800	12,850	0	2,853	4,716	135	2,853	4,716
12,850	12,900	0	2,853	4,716	131	2,853	4,716
12,900	12,950	0	2,853	4,716	127	2,853	4,716
12,950	13,000	0	2,853	4,716	124	2,853	4,716
13,000	13,050	0	2,853	4,716	120	2,853	4,716
13,050	13,100	0	2,853	4,716	116	2,853	4,716
13,100	13,150	0	2,853	4,716	112	2,853	4,716
13,150	13,200	0	2,853	4,716	108	2,853	4,716
13,200	13,250	0	2,853	4,716	104	2,853	4,716
13,250	13,300	0	2,853	4,716	101	2,853	4,716
13,300	13,350	0	2,853	4,716	97	2,853	4,716
13,350	13,400	0	2,853	4,716	93	2,853	4,716
13,400	13,450	0	2,853	4,716	89	2,853	4,716
13,450	13,500	0	2,853	4,716	85	2,853	4,716
13,500	13,550	0	2,853	4,716	81	2,853	4,716
13,550	13,600	0	2,853	4,716	78	2,853	4,716
13,600	13,650	0	2,853	4,716	74	2,853	4,716
13,650	13,700	0	2,853	4,716	70	2,853	4,716
13,700	13,750	0	2,853	4,716	66	2,853	4,716
13,750	13,800	0	2,853	4,716	62	2,853	4,716
13,800	13,850	0	2,853	4,716	59	2,853	4,716
13,850	13,900	0	2,853	4,716	55	2,853	4,716
13,900	13,950	0	2,853	4,716	51	2,853	4,716
13,950	14,000	0	2,853	4,716	47	2,853	4,716
14,000	14,050	0	2,853	4,716	43	2,853	4,716
14,050	14,100	0	2,853	4,716	39	2,853	4,716
14,100	14,150	0	2,853	4,716	36	2,853	4,716
14,150	14,200	0	2,853	4,716	32	2,853	4,716
14,200	14,250	0	2,853	4,716	28	2,853	4,716
14,250	14,300	0	2,853	4,716	24	2,853	4,716
14,300	14,350	0	2,853	4,716	20	2,853	4,716
14,350	14,400	0	2,853	4,716	16	2,853	4,716
14,400	14,450	0	2,853	4,716	13	2,853	4,716
14,450	14,500	0	2,853	4,716	9	2,853	4,716
14,500	14,550	0	2,853	4,716	5	2,853	4,716
14,550	14,600	0	2,853	4,716	*	2,853	4,716
14,600	14,650	0	2,853	4,716	0	2,853	4,716
14,650	14,700	0	2,853	4,716	0	2,853	4,716
14,700	14,750	0	2,853	4,716	0	2,853	4,716
14,750	14,800	0	2,853	4,716	0	2,853	4,716
14,800	14,850	0	2,853	4,716	0	2,853	4,716
14,850	14,900	0	2,853	4,716	0	2,853	4,716
14,900	14,950	0	2,853	4,716	0	2,853	4,716
14,950	15,000	0	2,853	4,716	0	2,853	4,716
15,000	15,050	0	2,853	4,716	0	2,853	4,716
15,050	15,100	0	2,853	4,716	0	2,853	4,716
15,100	15,150	0	2,853	4,716	0	2,853	4,716
15,150	15,200	0	2,853	4,716	0	2,853	4,716
15,200	15,250	0	2,853	4,716	0	2,853	4,716
15,250	15,300	0	2,853	4,716	0	2,853	4,716
15,300	15,350	0	2,853	4,716	0	2,853	4,716
15,350	15,400	0	2,853	4,716	0	2,853	4,716
15,400	15,450	0	2,847	4,709	0	2,853	4,716
15,450	15,500	0	2,839	4,698	0	2,853	4,716
15,500	15,550	0	2,831	4,688	0	2,853	4,716
15,550	15,600	0	2,823	4,677	0	2,853	4,716
15,600	15,650	0	2,815	4,667	0	2,853	4,716
15,650	15,700	0	2,807	4,656	0	2,853	4,716
15,700	15,750	0	2,799	4,645	0	2,853	4,716
15,750	15,800	0	2,791	4,635	0	2,853	4,716
15,800	15,850	0	2,783	4,624	0	2,853	4,716
15,850	15,900	0	2,775	4,614	0	2,853	4,716
15,900	15,950	0	2,767	4,603	0	2,853	4,716
15,950	16,000	0	2,759	4,593	0	2,853	4,716

(Continued on page 54)

*If the amount you are looking up from the worksheet is at least $12,550 ($14,550 if married filing jointly) but less than $12,590 ($14,590 if married filing jointly), your credit is $2. Otherwise, you cannot take the credit.

¶87

2007 Earned Income Credit (EIC) Table—Continued (Caution. This is not a tax table.)

If the amount you are looking up from the worksheet is— At least	But less than	Single, head of household, or qualifying widow(er) and you have— No children	One child	Two children	Married filing jointly and you have— No children	One child	Two children
16,000	16,050	0	2,751	4,582	0	2,853	4,716
16,050	16,100	0	2,743	4,572	0	2,853	4,716
16,100	16,150	0	2,735	4,561	0	2,853	4,716
16,150	16,200	0	2,727	4,551	0	2,853	4,716
16,200	16,250	0	2,719	4,540	0	2,853	4,716
16,250	16,300	0	2,711	4,530	0	2,853	4,716
16,300	16,350	0	2,703	4,519	0	2,853	4,716
16,350	16,400	0	2,695	4,509	0	2,853	4,716
16,400	16,450	0	2,687	4,498	0	2,853	4,716
16,450	16,500	0	2,679	4,487	0	2,853	4,716
16,500	16,550	0	2,671	4,477	0	2,853	4,716
16,550	16,600	0	2,663	4,466	0	2,853	4,716
16,600	16,650	0	2,655	4,456	0	2,853	4,716
16,650	16,700	0	2,647	4,445	0	2,853	4,716
16,700	16,750	0	2,639	4,435	0	2,853	4,716
16,750	16,800	0	2,631	4,424	0	2,853	4,716
16,800	16,850	0	2,623	4,414	0	2,853	4,716
16,850	16,900	0	2,615	4,403	0	2,853	4,716
16,900	16,950	0	2,607	4,393	0	2,853	4,716
16,950	17,000	0	2,599	4,382	0	2,853	4,716
17,000	17,050	0	2,591	4,372	0	2,853	4,716
17,050	17,100	0	2,583	4,361	0	2,853	4,716
17,100	17,150	0	2,575	4,351	0	2,853	4,716
17,150	17,200	0	2,567	4,340	0	2,853	4,716
17,200	17,250	0	2,559	4,330	0	2,853	4,716
17,250	17,300	0	2,551	4,319	0	2,853	4,716
17,300	17,350	0	2,543	4,308	0	2,853	4,716
17,350	17,400	0	2,535	4,298	0	2,853	4,716
17,400	17,450	0	2,527	4,287	0	2,847	4,709
17,450	17,500	0	2,519	4,277	0	2,839	4,698
17,500	17,550	0	2,511	4,266	0	2,831	4,688
17,550	17,600	0	2,503	4,256	0	2,823	4,677
17,600	17,650	0	2,495	4,245	0	2,815	4,667
17,650	17,700	0	2,487	4,235	0	2,807	4,656
17,700	17,750	0	2,479	4,224	0	2,799	4,645
17,750	17,800	0	2,471	4,214	0	2,791	4,635
17,800	17,850	0	2,463	4,203	0	2,783	4,624
17,850	17,900	0	2,455	4,193	0	2,775	4,614
17,900	17,950	0	2,448	4,182	0	2,767	4,603
17,950	18,000	0	2,440	4,172	0	2,759	4,593
18,000	18,050	0	2,432	4,161	0	2,751	4,582
18,050	18,100	0	2,424	4,151	0	2,743	4,572
18,100	18,150	0	2,416	4,140	0	2,735	4,561
18,150	18,200	0	2,408	4,129	0	2,727	4,551
18,200	18,250	0	2,400	4,119	0	2,719	4,540
18,250	18,300	0	2,392	4,108	0	2,711	4,530
18,300	18,350	0	2,384	4,098	0	2,703	4,519
18,350	18,400	0	2,376	4,087	0	2,695	4,509
18,400	18,450	0	2,368	4,077	0	2,687	4,498
18,450	18,500	0	2,360	4,066	0	2,679	4,487
18,500	18,550	0	2,352	4,056	0	2,671	4,477
18,550	18,600	0	2,344	4,045	0	2,663	4,466
18,600	18,650	0	2,336	4,035	0	2,655	4,456
18,650	18,700	0	2,328	4,024	0	2,647	4,445
18,700	18,750	0	2,320	4,014	0	2,639	4,435
18,750	18,800	0	2,312	4,003	0	2,631	4,424
18,800	18,850	0	2,304	3,993	0	2,623	4,414
18,850	18,900	0	2,296	3,982	0	2,615	4,403
18,900	18,950	0	2,288	3,972	0	2,607	4,393
18,950	19,000	0	2,280	3,961	0	2,599	4,382
19,000	19,050	0	2,272	3,950	0	2,591	4,372
19,050	19,100	0	2,264	3,940	0	2,583	4,361
19,100	19,150	0	2,256	3,929	0	2,575	4,351
19,150	19,200	0	2,248	3,919	0	2,567	4,340
19,200	19,250	0	2,240	3,908	0	2,559	4,330
19,250	19,300	0	2,232	3,898	0	2,551	4,319
19,300	19,350	0	2,224	3,887	0	2,543	4,308
19,350	19,400	0	2,216	3,877	0	2,535	4,298
19,400	19,450	0	2,208	3,866	0	2,527	4,287
19,450	19,500	0	2,200	3,856	0	2,519	4,277
19,500	19,550	0	2,192	3,845	0	2,511	4,266
19,550	19,600	0	2,184	3,835	0	2,503	4,256
19,600	19,650	0	2,176	3,824	0	2,495	4,245
19,650	19,700	0	2,168	3,814	0	2,487	4,235
19,700	19,750	0	2,160	3,803	0	2,479	4,224
19,750	19,800	0	2,152	3,793	0	2,471	4,214
19,800	19,850	0	2,144	3,782	0	2,463	4,203
19,850	19,900	0	2,136	3,771	0	2,455	4,193
19,900	19,950	0	2,128	3,761	0	2,448	4,182
19,950	20,000	0	2,120	3,750	0	2,440	4,172
20,000	20,050	0	2,112	3,740	0	2,432	4,161
20,050	20,100	0	2,104	3,729	0	2,424	4,151
20,100	20,150	0	2,096	3,719	0	2,416	4,140
20,150	20,200	0	2,088	3,708	0	2,408	4,129
20,200	20,250	0	2,080	3,698	0	2,400	4,119
20,250	20,300	0	2,072	3,687	0	2,392	4,108
20,300	20,350	0	2,064	3,677	0	2,384	4,098
20,350	20,400	0	2,056	3,666	0	2,376	4,087
20,400	20,450	0	2,048	3,656	0	2,368	4,077
20,450	20,500	0	2,040	3,645	0	2,360	4,066
20,500	20,550	0	2,032	3,635	0	2,352	4,056
20,550	20,600	0	2,024	3,624	0	2,344	4,045
20,600	20,650	0	2,016	3,614	0	2,336	4,035
20,650	20,700	0	2,008	3,603	0	2,328	4,024
20,700	20,750	0	2,000	3,592	0	2,320	4,014
20,750	20,800	0	1,992	3,582	0	2,312	4,003
20,800	20,850	0	1,984	3,571	0	2,304	3,993
20,850	20,900	0	1,976	3,561	0	2,296	3,982
20,900	20,950	0	1,968	3,550	0	2,288	3,972
20,950	21,000	0	1,960	3,540	0	2,280	3,961
21,000	21,050	0	1,952	3,529	0	2,272	3,950
21,050	21,100	0	1,944	3,519	0	2,264	3,940
21,100	21,150	0	1,936	3,508	0	2,256	3,929
21,150	21,200	0	1,928	3,498	0	2,248	3,919
21,200	21,250	0	1,920	3,487	0	2,240	3,908
21,250	21,300	0	1,912	3,477	0	2,232	3,898
21,300	21,350	0	1,904	3,466	0	2,224	3,887
21,350	21,400	0	1,896	3,456	0	2,216	3,877
21,400	21,450	0	1,888	3,445	0	2,208	3,866
21,450	21,500	0	1,880	3,434	0	2,200	3,856
21,500	21,550	0	1,872	3,424	0	2,192	3,845
21,550	21,600	0	1,864	3,413	0	2,184	3,835
21,600	21,650	0	1,856	3,403	0	2,176	3,824
21,650	21,700	0	1,848	3,392	0	2,168	3,814
21,700	21,750	0	1,840	3,382	0	2,160	3,803
21,750	21,800	0	1,832	3,371	0	2,152	3,793
21,800	21,850	0	1,824	3,361	0	2,144	3,782
21,850	21,900	0	1,816	3,350	0	2,136	3,771
21,900	21,950	0	1,808	3,340	0	2,128	3,761
21,950	22,000	0	1,800	3,329	0	2,120	3,750

(Continued on page 55)

¶87

2007 Earned Income Credit (EIC) Table—Continued   (Caution. This is not a tax table.)

If the amount you are looking up from the worksheet is— At least	But less than	Single, head of household, or qualifying widow(er) and you have— No children	One child	Two children	Married filing jointly and you have— No children	One child	Two children
22,000	22,050	0	1,792	3,319	0	2,112	3,740
22,050	22,100	0	1,784	3,308	0	2,104	3,729
22,100	22,150	0	1,776	3,298	0	2,096	3,719
22,150	22,200	0	1,768	3,287	0	2,088	3,708
22,200	22,250	0	1,760	3,277	0	2,080	3,698
22,250	22,300	0	1,752	3,266	0	2,072	3,687
22,300	22,350	0	1,744	3,255	0	2,064	3,677
22,350	22,400	0	1,736	3,245	0	2,056	3,666
22,400	22,450	0	1,728	3,234	0	2,048	3,656
22,450	22,500	0	1,720	3,224	0	2,040	3,645
22,500	22,550	0	1,712	3,213	0	2,032	3,635
22,550	22,600	0	1,704	3,203	0	2,024	3,624
22,600	22,650	0	1,696	3,192	0	2,016	3,614
22,650	22,700	0	1,688	3,182	0	2,008	3,603
22,700	22,750	0	1,680	3,171	0	2,000	3,592
22,750	22,800	0	1,672	3,161	0	1,992	3,582
22,800	22,850	0	1,664	3,150	0	1,984	3,571
22,850	22,900	0	1,656	3,140	0	1,976	3,561
22,900	22,950	0	1,649	3,129	0	1,968	3,550
22,950	23,000	0	1,641	3,119	0	1,960	3,540
23,000	23,050	0	1,633	3,108	0	1,952	3,529
23,050	23,100	0	1,625	3,098	0	1,944	3,519
23,100	23,150	0	1,617	3,087	0	1,936	3,508
23,150	23,200	0	1,609	3,076	0	1,928	3,498
23,200	23,250	0	1,601	3,066	0	1,920	3,487
23,250	23,300	0	1,593	3,055	0	1,912	3,477
23,300	23,350	0	1,585	3,045	0	1,904	3,466
23,350	23,400	0	1,577	3,034	0	1,896	3,456
23,400	23,450	0	1,569	3,024	0	1,888	3,445
23,450	23,500	0	1,561	3,013	0	1,880	3,434
23,500	23,550	0	1,553	3,003	0	1,872	3,424
23,550	23,600	0	1,545	2,992	0	1,864	3,413
23,600	23,650	0	1,537	2,982	0	1,856	3,403
23,650	23,700	0	1,529	2,971	0	1,848	3,392
23,700	23,750	0	1,521	2,961	0	1,840	3,382
23,750	23,800	0	1,513	2,950	0	1,832	3,371
23,800	23,850	0	1,505	2,940	0	1,824	3,361
23,850	23,900	0	1,497	2,929	0	1,816	3,350
23,900	23,950	0	1,489	2,919	0	1,808	3,340
23,950	24,000	0	1,481	2,908	0	1,800	3,329
24,000	24,050	0	1,473	2,897	0	1,792	3,319
24,050	24,100	0	1,465	2,887	0	1,784	3,308
24,100	24,150	0	1,457	2,876	0	1,776	3,298
24,150	24,200	0	1,449	2,866	0	1,768	3,287
24,200	24,250	0	1,441	2,855	0	1,760	3,277
24,250	24,300	0	1,433	2,845	0	1,752	3,266
24,300	24,350	0	1,425	2,834	0	1,744	3,255
24,350	24,400	0	1,417	2,824	0	1,736	3,245
24,400	24,450	0	1,409	2,813	0	1,728	3,234
24,450	24,500	0	1,401	2,803	0	1,720	3,224
24,500	24,550	0	1,393	2,792	0	1,712	3,213
24,550	24,600	0	1,385	2,782	0	1,704	3,203
24,600	24,650	0	1,377	2,771	0	1,696	3,192
24,650	24,700	0	1,369	2,761	0	1,688	3,182
24,700	24,750	0	1,361	2,750	0	1,680	3,171
24,750	24,800	0	1,353	2,740	0	1,672	3,161
24,800	24,850	0	1,345	2,729	0	1,664	3,150
24,850	24,900	0	1,337	2,718	0	1,656	3,140
24,900	24,950	0	1,329	2,708	0	1,649	3,129
24,950	25,000	0	1,321	2,697	0	1,641	3,119
25,000	25,050	0	1,313	2,687	0	1,633	3,108
25,050	25,100	0	1,305	2,676	0	1,625	3,098
25,100	25,150	0	1,297	2,666	0	1,617	3,087
25,150	25,200	0	1,289	2,655	0	1,609	3,076
25,200	25,250	0	1,281	2,645	0	1,601	3,066
25,250	25,300	0	1,273	2,634	0	1,593	3,055
25,300	25,350	0	1,265	2,624	0	1,585	3,045
25,350	25,400	0	1,257	2,613	0	1,577	3,034
25,400	25,450	0	1,249	2,603	0	1,569	3,024
25,450	25,500	0	1,241	2,592	0	1,561	3,013
25,500	25,550	0	1,233	2,582	0	1,553	3,003
25,550	25,600	0	1,225	2,571	0	1,545	2,992
25,600	25,650	0	1,217	2,561	0	1,537	2,982
25,650	25,700	0	1,209	2,550	0	1,529	2,971
25,700	25,750	0	1,201	2,539	0	1,521	2,961
25,750	25,800	0	1,193	2,529	0	1,513	2,950
25,800	25,850	0	1,185	2,518	0	1,505	2,940
25,850	25,900	0	1,177	2,508	0	1,497	2,929
25,900	25,950	0	1,169	2,497	0	1,489	2,919
25,950	26,000	0	1,161	2,487	0	1,481	2,908
26,000	26,050	0	1,153	2,476	0	1,473	2,897
26,050	26,100	0	1,145	2,466	0	1,465	2,887
26,100	26,150	0	1,137	2,455	0	1,457	2,876
26,150	26,200	0	1,129	2,445	0	1,449	2,866
26,200	26,250	0	1,121	2,434	0	1,441	2,855
26,250	26,300	0	1,113	2,424	0	1,433	2,845
26,300	26,350	0	1,105	2,413	0	1,425	2,834
26,350	26,400	0	1,097	2,403	0	1,417	2,824
26,400	26,450	0	1,089	2,392	0	1,409	2,813
26,450	26,500	0	1,081	2,381	0	1,401	2,803
26,500	26,550	0	1,073	2,371	0	1,393	2,792
26,550	26,600	0	1,065	2,360	0	1,385	2,782
26,600	26,650	0	1,057	2,350	0	1,377	2,771
26,650	26,700	0	1,049	2,339	0	1,369	2,761
26,700	26,750	0	1,041	2,329	0	1,361	2,750
26,750	26,800	0	1,033	2,318	0	1,353	2,740
26,800	26,850	0	1,025	2,308	0	1,345	2,729
26,850	26,900	0	1,017	2,297	0	1,337	2,718
26,900	26,950	0	1,009	2,287	0	1,329	2,708
26,950	27,000	0	1,001	2,276	0	1,321	2,697
27,000	27,050	0	993	2,266	0	1,313	2,687
27,050	27,100	0	985	2,255	0	1,305	2,676
27,100	27,150	0	977	2,245	0	1,297	2,666
27,150	27,200	0	969	2,234	0	1,289	2,655
27,200	27,250	0	961	2,224	0	1,281	2,645
27,250	27,300	0	953	2,213	0	1,273	2,634
27,300	27,350	0	945	2,202	0	1,265	2,624
27,350	27,400	0	937	2,192	0	1,257	2,613
27,400	27,450	0	929	2,181	0	1,249	2,603
27,450	27,500	0	921	2,171	0	1,241	2,592
27,500	27,550	0	913	2,160	0	1,233	2,582
27,550	27,600	0	905	2,150	0	1,225	2,571
27,600	27,650	0	897	2,139	0	1,217	2,561
27,650	27,700	0	889	2,129	0	1,209	2,550
27,700	27,750	0	881	2,118	0	1,201	2,539
27,750	27,800	0	873	2,108	0	1,193	2,529
27,800	27,850	0	865	2,097	0	1,185	2,518
27,850	27,900	0	857	2,087	0	1,177	2,508
27,900	27,950	0	850	2,076	0	1,169	2,497
27,950	28,000	0	842	2,066	0	1,161	2,487

(Continued on page 56)

¶87

2007 Earned Income Credit (EIC) Table—*Continued*   (**Caution.** This is **not** a tax table.)

If the amount you are looking up from the worksheet is—		Single, head of household, or qualifying widow(er) and you have—			Married filing jointly and you have—		
At least	But less than	No children	One child	Two children	No children	One child	Two children
		Your credit is—			Your credit is—		
28,000	28,050	0	834	2,055	0	1,153	2,476
28,050	28,100	0	826	2,045	0	1,145	2,466
28,100	28,150	0	818	2,034	0	1,137	2,455
28,150	28,200	0	810	2,023	0	1,129	2,445
28,200	28,250	0	802	2,013	0	1,121	2,434
28,250	28,300	0	794	2,002	0	1,113	2,424
28,300	28,350	0	786	1,992	0	1,105	2,413
28,350	28,400	0	778	1,981	0	1,097	2,403
28,400	28,450	0	770	1,971	0	1,089	2,392
28,450	28,500	0	762	1,960	0	1,081	2,381
28,500	28,550	0	754	1,950	0	1,073	2,371
28,550	28,600	0	746	1,939	0	1,065	2,360
28,600	28,650	0	738	1,929	0	1,057	2,350
28,650	28,700	0	730	1,918	0	1,049	2,339
28,700	28,750	0	722	1,908	0	1,041	2,329
28,750	28,800	0	714	1,897	0	1,033	2,318
28,800	28,850	0	706	1,887	0	1,025	2,308
28,850	28,900	0	698	1,876	0	1,017	2,297
28,900	28,950	0	690	1,866	0	1,009	2,287
28,950	29,000	0	682	1,855	0	1,001	2,276
29,000	29,050	0	674	1,844	0	993	2,266
29,050	29,100	0	666	1,834	0	985	2,255
29,100	29,150	0	658	1,823	0	977	2,245
29,150	29,200	0	650	1,813	0	969	2,234
29,200	29,250	0	642	1,802	0	961	2,224
29,250	29,300	0	634	1,792	0	953	2,213
29,300	29,350	0	626	1,781	0	945	2,202
29,350	29,400	0	618	1,771	0	937	2,192
29,400	29,450	0	610	1,760	0	929	2,181
29,450	29,500	0	602	1,750	0	921	2,171
29,500	29,550	0	594	1,739	0	913	2,160
29,550	29,600	0	586	1,729	0	905	2,150
29,600	29,650	0	578	1,718	0	897	2,139
29,650	29,700	0	570	1,708	0	889	2,129
29,700	29,750	0	562	1,697	0	881	2,118
29,750	29,800	0	554	1,687	0	873	2,108
29,800	29,850	0	546	1,676	0	865	2,097
29,850	29,900	0	538	1,665	0	857	2,087
29,900	29,950	0	530	1,655	0	850	2,076
29,950	30,000	0	522	1,644	0	842	2,066
30,000	30,050	0	514	1,634	0	834	2,055
30,050	30,100	0	506	1,623	0	826	2,045
30,100	30,150	0	498	1,613	0	818	2,034
30,150	30,200	0	490	1,602	0	810	2,023
30,200	30,250	0	482	1,592	0	802	2,013
30,250	30,300	0	474	1,581	0	794	2,002
30,300	30,350	0	466	1,571	0	786	1,992
30,350	30,400	0	458	1,560	0	778	1,981
30,400	30,450	0	450	1,550	0	770	1,971
30,450	30,500	0	442	1,539	0	762	1,960
30,500	30,550	0	434	1,529	0	754	1,950
30,550	30,600	0	426	1,518	0	746	1,939
30,600	30,650	0	418	1,508	0	738	1,929
30,650	30,700	0	410	1,497	0	730	1,918
30,700	30,750	0	402	1,486	0	722	1,908
30,750	30,800	0	394	1,476	0	714	1,897
30,800	30,850	0	386	1,465	0	706	1,887
30,850	30,900	0	378	1,455	0	698	1,876
30,900	30,950	0	370	1,444	0	690	1,866
30,950	31,000	0	362	1,434	0	682	1,855
31,000	31,050	0	354	1,423	0	674	1,844
31,050	31,100	0	346	1,413	0	666	1,834
31,100	31,150	0	338	1,402	0	658	1,823
31,150	31,200	0	330	1,392	0	650	1,813
31,200	31,250	0	322	1,381	0	642	1,802
31,250	31,300	0	314	1,371	0	634	1,792
31,300	31,350	0	306	1,360	0	626	1,781
31,350	31,400	0	298	1,350	0	618	1,771
31,400	31,450	0	290	1,339	0	610	1,760
31,450	31,500	0	282	1,328	0	602	1,750
31,500	31,550	0	274	1,318	0	594	1,739
31,550	31,600	0	266	1,307	0	586	1,729
31,600	31,650	0	258	1,297	0	578	1,718
31,650	31,700	0	250	1,286	0	570	1,708
31,700	31,750	0	242	1,276	0	562	1,697
31,750	31,800	0	234	1,265	0	554	1,687
31,800	31,850	0	226	1,255	0	546	1,676
31,850	31,900	0	218	1,244	0	538	1,665
31,900	31,950	0	210	1,234	0	530	1,655
31,950	32,000	0	202	1,223	0	522	1,644
32,000	32,050	0	194	1,213	0	514	1,634
32,050	32,100	0	186	1,202	0	506	1,623
32,100	32,150	0	178	1,192	0	498	1,613
32,150	32,200	0	170	1,181	0	490	1,602
32,200	32,250	0	162	1,171	0	482	1,592
32,250	32,300	0	154	1,160	0	474	1,581
32,300	32,350	0	146	1,149	0	466	1,571
32,350	32,400	0	138	1,139	0	458	1,560
32,400	32,450	0	130	1,128	0	450	1,550
32,450	32,500	0	122	1,118	0	442	1,539
32,500	32,550	0	114	1,107	0	434	1,529
32,550	32,600	0	106	1,097	0	426	1,518
32,600	32,650	0	98	1,086	0	418	1,508
32,650	32,700	0	90	1,076	0	410	1,497
32,700	32,750	0	82	1,065	0	402	1,486
32,750	32,800	0	74	1,055	0	394	1,476
32,800	32,850	0	66	1,044	0	386	1,465
32,850	32,900	0	58	1,034	0	378	1,455
32,900	32,950	0	51	1,023	0	370	1,444
32,950	33,000	0	43	1,013	0	362	1,434

(Continued on page 57)

¶87

2007 Earned Income Credit (EIC) Table—*Continued* (**Caution.** This is **not** a tax table.)

If the amount you are looking up from the worksheet is—		Single, head of household, or qualifying widow(er) and you have—			Married filing jointly and you have—		
At least	But less than	No children	One child	Two children	No children	One child	Two children
		Your credit is—			Your credit is—		
33,000	33,050	0	35	1,002	0	354	1,423
33,050	33,100	0	27	992	0	346	1,413
33,100	33,150	0	19	981	0	338	1,402
33,150	33,200	0	11	970	0	330	1,392
33,200	33,250	0	*	960	0	322	1,381
33,250	33,300	0	0	949	0	314	1,371
33,300	33,350	0	0	939	0	306	1,360
33,350	33,400	0	0	928	0	298	1,350
33,400	33,450	0	0	918	0	290	1,339
33,450	33,500	0	0	907	0	282	1,328
33,500	33,550	0	0	897	0	274	1,318
33,550	33,600	0	0	886	0	266	1,307
33,600	33,650	0	0	876	0	258	1,297
33,650	33,700	0	0	865	0	250	1,286
33,700	33,750	0	0	855	0	242	1,276
33,750	33,800	0	0	844	0	234	1,265
33,800	33,850	0	0	834	0	226	1,255
33,850	33,900	0	0	823	0	218	1,244
33,900	33,950	0	0	813	0	210	1,234
33,950	34,000	0	0	802	0	202	1,223
34,000	34,050	0	0	791	0	194	1,213
34,050	34,100	0	0	781	0	186	1,202
34,100	34,150	0	0	770	0	178	1,192
34,150	34,200	0	0	760	0	170	1,181
34,200	34,250	0	0	749	0	162	1,171
34,250	34,300	0	0	739	0	154	1,160
34,300	34,350	0	0	728	0	146	1,149
34,350	34,400	0	0	718	0	138	1,139
34,400	34,450	0	0	707	0	130	1,128
34,450	34,500	0	0	697	0	122	1,118
34,500	34,550	0	0	686	0	114	1,107
34,550	34,600	0	0	676	0	106	1,097
34,600	34,650	0	0	665	0	98	1,086
34,650	34,700	0	0	655	0	90	1,076
34,700	34,750	0	0	644	0	82	1,065
34,750	34,800	0	0	634	0	74	1,055
34,800	34,850	0	0	623	0	66	1,044
34,850	34,900	0	0	612	0	58	1,034
34,900	34,950	0	0	602	0	51	1,023
34,950	35,000	0	0	591	0	43	1,013
35,000	35,050	0	0	581	0	35	1,002
35,050	35,100	0	0	570	0	27	992
35,100	35,150	0	0	560	0	19	981
35,150	35,200	0	0	549	0	11	970
35,200	35,250	0	0	539	0	*	960
35,250	35,300	0	0	528	0	0	949
35,300	35,350	0	0	518	0	0	939
35,350	35,400	0	0	507	0	0	928
35,400	35,450	0	0	497	0	0	918
35,450	35,500	0	0	486	0	0	907
35,500	35,550	0	0	476	0	0	897
35,550	35,600	0	0	465	0	0	886
35,600	35,650	0	0	455	0	0	876
35,650	35,700	0	0	444	0	0	865
35,700	35,750	0	0	433	0	0	855
35,750	35,800	0	0	423	0	0	844
35,800	35,850	0	0	412	0	0	834
35,850	35,900	0	0	402	0	0	823
35,900	35,950	0	0	391	0	0	813
35,950	36,000	0	0	381	0	0	802
36,000	36,050	0	0	370	0	0	791
36,050	36,100	0	0	360	0	0	781
36,100	36,150	0	0	349	0	0	770
36,150	36,200	0	0	339	0	0	760
36,200	36,250	0	0	328	0	0	749
36,250	36,300	0	0	318	0	0	739
36,300	36,350	0	0	307	0	0	728
36,350	36,400	0	0	297	0	0	718
36,400	36,450	0	0	286	0	0	707
36,450	36,500	0	0	275	0	0	697
36,500	36,550	0	0	265	0	0	686
36,550	36,600	0	0	254	0	0	676
36,600	36,650	0	0	244	0	0	665
36,650	36,700	0	0	233	0	0	655
36,700	36,750	0	0	223	0	0	644
36,750	36,800	0	0	212	0	0	634
36,800	36,850	0	0	202	0	0	623
36,850	36,900	0	0	191	0	0	612
36,900	36,950	0	0	181	0	0	602
36,950	37,000	0	0	170	0	0	591
37,000	37,050	0	0	160	0	0	581
37,050	37,100	0	0	149	0	0	570
37,100	37,150	0	0	139	0	0	560
37,150	37,200	0	0	128	0	0	549
37,200	37,250	0	0	118	0	0	539
37,250	37,300	0	0	107	0	0	528
37,300	37,350	0	0	96	0	0	518
37,350	37,400	0	0	86	0	0	507
37,400	37,450	0	0	75	0	0	497
37,450	37,500	0	0	65	0	0	486
37,500	37,550	0	0	54	0	0	476
37,550	37,600	0	0	44	0	0	465
37,600	37,650	0	0	33	0	0	455
37,650	37,700	0	0	23	0	0	444
37,700	37,750	0	0	12	0	0	433
37,750	37,800	0	0	**	0	0	423
37,800	37,850	0	0	0	0	0	412
37,850	37,900	0	0	0	0	0	402
37,900	37,950	0	0	0	0	0	391
37,950	38,000	0	0	0	0	0	381

(Continued on page 58)

*If the amount you are looking up from the worksheet is at least $33,200 ($35,200 if married filing jointly) but less than $33,241 ($35,241 if married filing jointly), your credit is $3. Otherwise, you cannot take the credit.

**If the amount you are looking up from the worksheet is at least $37,750 but less than $37,783, your credit is $4. Otherwise, you cannot take the credit.

¶87

2007 Earned Income Credit (EIC) Table—*Continued* (**Caution.** This is **not** a tax table.)

If the amount you are looking up from the worksheet is—		Single, head of household, or qualifying widow(er) and you have—			Married filing jointly and you have—			If the amount you are looking up from the worksheet is—		Single, head of household, or qualifying widow(er) and you have—			Married filing jointly and you have—		
At least	But less than	No children	One child	Two children	No children	One child	Two children	At least	But less than	No children	One child	Two children	No children	One child	Two children
		Your credit is—			Your credit is—					Your credit is—			Your credit is—		
38,000	38,050	0	0	0	0	0	370	39,000	39,050	0	0	0	0	0	160
38,050	38,100	0	0	0	0	0	360	39,050	39,100	0	0	0	0	0	149
38,100	38,150	0	0	0	0	0	349	39,100	39,150	0	0	0	0	0	139
38,150	38,200	0	0	0	0	0	339	39,150	39,200	0	0	0	0	0	128
38,200	38,250	0	0	0	0	0	328	39,200	39,250	0	0	0	0	0	118
38,250	38,300	0	0	0	0	0	318	39,250	39,300	0	0	0	0	0	107
38,300	38,350	0	0	0	0	0	307	39,300	39,350	0	0	0	0	0	96
38,350	38,400	0	0	0	0	0	297	39,350	39,400	0	0	0	0	0	86
38,400	38,450	0	0	0	0	0	286	39,400	39,450	0	0	0	0	0	75
38,450	38,500	0	0	0	0	0	275	39,450	39,500	0	0	0	0	0	65
38,500	38,550	0	0	0	0	0	265	39,500	39,550	0	0	0	0	0	54
38,550	38,600	0	0	0	0	0	254	39,550	39,600	0	0	0	0	0	44
38,600	38,650	0	0	0	0	0	244	39,600	39,650	0	0	0	0	0	33
38,650	38,700	0	0	0	0	0	233	39,650	39,700	0	0	0	0	0	23
38,700	38,750	0	0	0	0	0	223	39,700	39,750	0	0	0	0	0	12
38,750	38,800	0	0	0	0	0	212	39,750	39,783	0	0	0	0	0	4
38,800	38,850	0	0	0	0	0	202								
38,850	38,900	0	0	0	0	0	191								
38,900	38,950	0	0	0	0	0	181								
38,950	39,000	0	0	0	0	0	170								

- 58 -

¶ 88 Average Itemized Deductions

For those taxpayers who itemize their deductions on Schedule A of Form 1040, the following chart should be of special interest. This chart (based on preliminary statistics for 2005 returns) shows the average deductions of taxpayers for tax year *2005* for interest (¶ 1043), taxes (¶ 1021), medical and dental expenses (¶ 1015), and charitable contributions (¶ 1058). While it may be interesting for those who itemize their deductions to compare them with these average figures, the chart should not be considered as indicating amounts that would be allowed by the IRS. In any case, taxpayers must be able to substantiate claimed itemized deductions.

Preliminary Average Itemized Deductions for Tax Year 2005 by AGI Ranges (Source: *Winter 2006-2007 Statistics of Income (SOI) Bulletin*).

PRELIMINARY AVERAGE ITEMIZED DEDUCTIONS FOR TAX YEAR 2005 BY ADJUSTED GROSS INCOME RANGES

Adjusted Gross Income Ranges	Medical Expenses	Taxes	Interest	Contributions
Under $ 15,000	$7,529	$2,532	$7,393	$1,403
$ 15,000 to $ 30,000	6,515	2,783	7,293	1,916
$ 30,000 to $ 50,000	5,625	3,623	7,582	2,158
$ 50,000 to $ 100,000	6,144	5,812	8,946	2,703
$ 100,000 to $ 200,000	9,727	10,504	11,927	4,056
$ 200,000 or more	30,952	39,321	21,165	20,434

¶ 88A AGI Phaseout Thresholds for 2007

Adjusted gross income (AGI) levels in excess of certain phaseout thresholds limit the following deductions, credits and other tax benefits. This chart provides the beginning point for the *2007* thresholds and the ending point of the phaseout (where applicable).

Tax Item	Taxpayers Affected	Phaseout—Begin	Phaseout—End
Itemized Deductions (Overall Limit)	single, head of household, joint filers	$156,400	phaseout varies by taxpayer
	married filing separate	$78,200	phaseout varies by taxpayer
7.5% Floor on Medical Deductions	those itemizing medical expenses	7.5% of AGI	N/A
2% Floor on Misc. Itemized Deductions	those itemizing misc. expenses	2% of AGI	N/A
10% Floor on Casualty Loss	those itemizing casualty loss	10% of AGI	N/A
Personal Exemption	single	$156,400	$278,900
	head of household	$195,500	$318,000
	joint filers	$234,600	$357,100
	married filing separate	$117,300	$178,550
Child Tax Credit*	single, head of household	$75,000	phaseout varies by taxpayer
	married filing separate	$55,000	phaseout varies by taxpayer
	joint filers	$110,000	phaseout varies by taxpayer
Dependent Care Credit*	joint filers, head of household, single	35% credit if AGI not over $15,000	20% credit if AGI over $43,000

Tax Item	Taxpayers Affected	Phaseout—Begin	Phaseout—End
Elderly and Disabled Credit	single, head of household	$7,500	$17,500
	joint filers	$10,000	$20,000 if one qualifying spouse; $25,000 if two qualifying spouses
	married filing separate	$5,000	$12,500
Adoption Credit*	all filers	$170,820	$210,820
Adoption Assistance Programs*	all filers	$170,820	$210,820
Earned Income Credit*	single, head of household, no child	$7,000	$12,590
	single, head of household, one child	$15,390	$33,241
	single, head of household, two or more children	$15,390	$37,783
	joint filers, no child	$9,000	$14,590
	joint filers, one child	$17,390	$35,241
	joint filers, two or more children	$17,390	$39,783
Hope Credit*	single, head of household	$47,000	$57,000
	joint filers	$94,000	$114,000
Lifetime Learning Credit*	single, head of household	$47,000	$57,000
	joint filers	$94,000	$114,000
Student Loan Interest Deduction*	single, head of household	$55,000	$70,000
	joint filers	$110,000	$140,000
Savings Bonds Interest Exclusion	single, head of household	$65,600	$80,600
	joint filers	$98,400	$128,400
Coverdell Education Accounts (formerly Education IRAs)	single, head of household, married filing separate	$95,000	$110,000
	joint filers	$190,000	$220,000
IRA Deduction	single, head of household	$52,000	$62,000
	joint filers	$83,000	$103,000
	married filing separate	$0	$10,000
Roth IRA Eligibility	single, head of household	$99,000	$114,000
	joint filers	$156,000	$166,000
	married filing separate	$0	$10,000
First-time DC Homebuyer*	single, head of household, married filing separate	$70,000	$90,000
	joint filers	$110,000	$130,000
Rental Real Estate Passive Losses	single, head of household, joint filers	$100,000	$150,000
	married filing separate	$50,000	$75,000
Mortgage Bond Subsidy Recapture	all filers	AGI relative to area median income	N/A

* Modified AGI, as defined by the relevant Code Sections, is used instead of AGI.

¶ 88B Federal Bonus Depreciation Conformity

The Working Families Tax Relief Act of 2004 (P.L. 108-311) and the American Jobs Creation Act of 2004 (P.L. 108-357) made numerous changes to Code Sec. 167 and Code Sec. 168, concerning depreciation. Some of the most significant changes include: bonus depreciation for noncommercial aircraft placed in service after September 10, 2001; a 15-year recovery period for qualified leasehold improvements and qualified restaurant property placed in service after October 22, 2004 and before January 1, 2006; increased recovery periods for land-clearing costs and electric utility property; and the extension of shortened recovery periods for Indian reservation property through December 31, 2005. The American Jobs Act also made changes that affect the film and television industry. State conformity to the federal provisions varied across the country and the chart below reflects the states' corporate income tax treatment of depreciation under the federal depreciation rules.

Conforming states.—The following states allow bonus depreciation for state corporate income tax purposes.

Alabama	Kansas	North Dakota
Alaska	Louisiana	Oregon
Colorado	Montana	Utah
Delaware	New Mexico	West Virginia
Florida		

Nonconforming states.—The following states do not allow bonus depreciation for state corporate income tax purposes.

Arizona	Kentucky	Ohio
Arkansas	Maine	Pennsylvania
California	Maryland	Rhode Island
Connecticut	Massachusetts	South Carolina
District of Columbia	Mississippi	Tennessee
Georgia	Nebraska	Texas
Hawaii	New Hampshire	Vermont
Idaho	New Jersey	Virginia
Illinois	North Carolina	Wisconsin
Indiana		

States with special situations.—The following states have special rules for how the bonus depreciation deduction is handled:

Nevada, South Dakota, Washington, and **Wyoming** do not impose a general corporate income tax.

Iowa disallows 30% bonus depreciation on property placed in service between September 11, 2001, and September 11, 2004, but allows 50% bonus depreciation for qualified property acquired after May 5, 2003, and before 2005.

Michigan requires an add-back in computing the federal taxable income amount that is the tax base for the Single Business Tax and for the Michigan Business Tax, effective for tax years after 2007.

Minnesota will allow the bonus depreciation subject to modifications.

Missouri does not allow 30% bonus depreciation for assets purchased between July 1, 2002, and June 30, 2003, but allows 50% bonus depreciation to the same extent as the federal law.

New York does not allow bonus depreciation for tax years beginning after 2002, except with respect to qualified Resurgence Zone property or qualified New York Liberty Zone property.

Oklahoma does not allow the 30% bonus depreciation, but the 50% bonus depreciation is allowed.

¶ 88C Federal Manufacturer's Deduction Conformity

The American Jobs Creation Act of 2004 (P.L. 108-357) created the domestic production activities deduction for manufacturers (Code Sec. 199), that effectively reduces the federal corporate income tax rate for domestic manufacturing by 3 percent, from a top rate of 35 percent down to 32 percent. When fully phased in by 2010, the deduction will be equal to 9 percent of the lesser of qualified production activities income for the year, or taxable income for the year. The state response to the federal provision has varied and the chart below reflects the states' positions regarding this deduction.

Conforming states.—The following states allow the deduction for state corporate income tax purposes.

Alabama	Iowa	Ohio
Alaska	Kansas	Oklahoma
Arizona	Lousiana	Pennsylvania
Colorado	Missouri	Rhode Island
Connecticut	Montana	Utah
District of Columbia	Nebraska	Vermont
Florida	New Mexico	Virginia
Idaho	New York	Wisconsin
Illinois		

Nonconforming states.—The following states do not allow the deduction for state corporate income tax purposes.

Arkansas	Maryland	North Dakota
California	Massachusetts	South Carolina
Georgia	Mississippi	Tennessee
Hawaii	New Hampshire	Texas
Indiana	New Jersey	West Virginia
Maine	North Carolina	

States with special situations.—The following states have special rules for how the manufacturer's deduction is handled:

Nevada, South Dakota, Washington, and **Wyoming** do not impose a general corporate income tax.

Delaware does not incorporate Code Sec. 199 by reference, however, provides that the starting point for computing taxable income is federal taxable income as currently defined by the Internal Revenue Code.

Kentucky requires an addition for the amount of the federal deduction.

Michigan conforms for taxpayers who elect to use the Internal Revenue Code as in effect for the tax year in computing the Single Business Tax. However, it does not conform for taxpayers who use the 1999 incorporation date for single business tax purposes or for purposes of computing the Michigan Business Tax.

Minnesota requires an addition to federal taxable income for the deduction allowed under Code Sec. 199 for qualified production activity income.

Oregon requires an add-back for the amount of the federal deduction.

Chapter 1

INDIVIDUALS

January Payments of Estimated Tax

101. Final Adjustments to the 2007 Estimated Tax. As 2007 ends, the first responsibility of the calendar-year taxpayer is to review payments of estimated tax for 2007 to make sure that these tax payments and the income tax withheld from wages during the year are at least sufficient to avoid penalties (¶ 2875) on the last installment, which is due January 15, 2008.

The 2007 estimated tax payments (plus income tax withheld from wages) are credited against tax due for 2007 (¶ 124). Any underpayment of tax must be made up by a payment with the final return, and any overpayment is either refunded or credited against the estimated tax for the next year, whichever the taxpayer elects on the return (see ¶ 2679 and following).

105. Overpayment. An individual who has been making payments of estimated tax for 2007, and who finds that by paying the installment scheduled for January 15, 2008, he or she will overpay the 2007 tax, may:

(1) make the payment as scheduled on or before January 15, 2008, file the return on or before April 15, 2008, and direct whether the overpayment should be refunded or credited toward the 2008 estimated tax;

(2) reduce the payment due on or before January 15, 2008, so that the estimated tax payments plus withholding will meet the tax liability that will be shown on the return to be filed on or before April 15, 2008;

(3) pay enough estimated tax to cover the minimum requirement as described at ¶ 2875 in order to avoid a penalty on the January 15, 2008, payment and then pay any difference on the final return, filed on or before April 15, 2008; or

(4) file the final return on or before January 31, 2008, add up all payments of estimated tax plus any withholding, and use this return for a final accounting of 2007 tax liability.

107. Underpayment. The law provides a penalty for underpayment of estimated tax. However, a taxpayer can avoid this penalty by paying the minimum installment authorized under one of the exceptions described at ¶ 2682.[1]

The taxpayer may file the tax return for calendar year 2007 on or before January 31, 2008, and pay any balance of tax that may still be due for 2007. Under this method, no penalty will apply for failure to make the last quarterly installment and any penalty for

---

Footnote references are to paragraphs of the 2008 Standard Federal Tax Reports.

[1] ¶ 39,560.01, ¶ 39,560.021, ¶ 39,560.048

underpayment of any of the three earlier installments will not be increased any further (see ¶ 2688). See also ¶ 2691 for special rules on 2007 payments of estimated tax for farmers and fishermen.

Who Must File a Return

109. Citizens and Residents. For each tax year, a return must be filed by a U.S. citizen or a resident alien who has at least a specified minimum amount of gross income. See ¶ 124 for which form to file. The income levels at which individuals must file income tax returns for 2007 (even though no tax is owed) are generally as follows (Code Sec. 6012):[2]

Single individual (also individuals treated as unmarried for tax purposes; see ¶ 173)	$8,750
Single individual, 65 or older	10,050
Married individual, separate return	3,400
Married couple, joint return	17,500
Married couple, joint return, one spouse 65 or older	18,550
Married couple, joint return, both spouses 65 or older	19,600
Head of household	11,250
Head of household, 65 or older	12,550
Qualifying widow(er) (surviving spouse)	14,100
Qualifying widow(er) (surviving spouse), 65 or older	15,150

The above income levels for a married couple filing a joint return are not applicable if, at the close of their tax year, the couple does not share the same household or if some other taxpayer is entitled to a dependency exemption for either spouse (e.g., a married student who is supported by a parent). In such a case, a return for 2007 must be filed if gross income equals $3,400 or more (to increase to $3,500 in 2008) (Code Sec. 6012(a)(1)(A)(iv)).[3]

With respect to a dependent child or other individual who is neither blind nor age 65 or older for whom a dependency exemption is allowed to another taxpayer, a return must be filed for the 2007 tax year if the individual:

(1) has over $850 of unearned income (to increase to $900 in 2008),

(2) has over $5,350 of earned income (to increase to $5,450 in 2008), or

(3) has a total of unearned and earned income which exceeds the larger of (a) $850 or (b) earned income (up to $5,050) plus $300 (respectively, to increase to $5,150 and the $300 will remain the same in 2008) (see ¶ 126).

All married dependents under age 65 with gross income of at least $5 whose spouse files a separate return on Form 1040 and itemizes deductions on Schedule A must file a return.

If a child under age 18, but see ¶ 114 for exceptions, had no earned income, received unearned income (interest and dividends, including Alaska Permanent Fund dividends) in an amount less than $8,500 as indexed for inflation (to increase to $9,000 for 2008) that was not subject to backup withholding, and made no estimated tax payments, the parents may elect to report the income on their return. If the parents make this election, the child need not file a return (see ¶ 114).

Dependents who are blind and/or age 65 or older must file returns if:

(1) their earned income exceeds their maximum standard deduction amount,

(2) they have unearned income in excess of the sum of $850 plus additional standard deduction amounts to which they are entitled, or

(3) their gross income exceeds the total of earned income up to the regular standard deduction amount or $850, whichever is larger, plus the applicable additional standard deduction amounts (see ¶ 126).

Even if the income levels noted above are not reached, an individual is required to file a return if:

Footnote references are to paragraphs of the 2008 Standard Federal Tax Reports.

[2] ¶ 35,142, ¶ 35,150.21   [3] ¶ 35,142, ¶ 35,150.21

(1) net earnings from self-employment in 2007 are at least $400,

(2) advance earned income credit payments were received during 2007,

(3) FICA and/or Medicare taxes are due on 2007 tip income not reported to the employer or if uncollected FICA, Medicare, and/or RRTA taxes are due on tips reported to the employer or on group-term life insurance,

(4) liability for alternative minimum tax is incurred,

(5) tax on an IRA or a qualified retirement plan is due,

(6) tax is due from the recapture of an investment credit, a low-income housing credit, or recapture tax on the disposition of a home purchased with a federally subsidized mortgage, or

(7) wages of $108.28 or more were earned from a church or qualified church-controlled organization that is exempt from employer FICA and Medicare taxes.

The income-level test applies to *gross* income and not to *adjusted* gross income. Also, the amount includes foreign earned income excludable under Code Sec. 911 (see ¶ 2401) (Reg. § 1.6012-1(a)(3)).[4]

Any person who is required to file an income tax return must report on that return the amount of tax-exempt interest received or accrued during the tax year (see ¶ 724 and following) (Code Sec. 6012(d)).[5]

If the applicable gross income test is met, a return must be filed even though the individual's exemptions and deductions are such that no tax will be due. Even if the gross income test is *not* met, a return should be filed whenever a refund of tax or the earned income credit is available.

> **Example:** John, a 66-year-old retired single person, worked at a part-time job in 2007 and earned wages of $9,000 from which his employer withheld a total of $900 in income taxes for the year. Although John is not required to file a return because he did not meet the $10,050-or-more gross income test for a single person 65 or older, he should file a return to receive a refund of the $900 in withheld income tax. Certain taxpayers may be exempt from withholding if they had no income tax liability for their preceding tax year and expect none for the current year (see ¶ 2634).

112. Resident Alien. Generally, a resident alien is taxable on income from all sources, including sources outside the United States, at the same rates and in the same manner as a U.S. citizen.[6]

An alien individual is treated as a U.S. resident for any calendar year in which the individual:

(1) is a lawful permanent resident of the U.S. at any time during such year,

(2) elects to be treated as a U.S. resident (this election is revocable only with IRS consent), or

(3) satisfies the substantial presence test requiring presence in the U.S. for at least 31 days during the current calendar year and at least 183 days during the three-year period that includes the current calendar year and the preceding two calendar years. In computing the 183-day test, the individual may include all the days present during the current calendar year, one-third of the days present during the preceding calendar year, and one-sixth of the days present during the second preceding calendar year. However, exceptions to this rule apply (see ¶ 2409) (Code Sec. 7701(b)).[7]

114. Child or Dependent. A child or dependent is taxed on income, including wages, income from property, and trust income (see ¶ 554 and following). No personal exemption will be allowed to an individual eligible to be claimed as a dependent on another taxpayer's return. The basic standard deduction for dependents is limited to the greater of $850 (to increase to $900 for 2008) or the sum of $300 (to remain the same for

---

Footnote references are to paragraphs of the 2008 Standard Federal Tax Reports.

[4] ¶ 35,143, ¶ 35,150.022   [6] ¶ 3290.01   [7] ¶ 43,080, ¶ 43,116A—
[5] ¶ 35,142   ¶ 43,125A

2008) plus earned income (up to the regular standard deduction for a single filer) (see ¶ 126). Therefore, a dependent who has gross income of $850 or less will not be taxed on that amount and does not have to file an income tax return.[8]

For 2007, investment income of a child under age 18 at the close of the tax year (Code Sec. 1(g)(2)(A)) is generally taxed at the parents' top marginal rate if such income exceeds the sum of the $850 standard deduction (to increase to $900 in 2008) and the greater of $850 or the itemized deductions directly connected to the production of that investment income. This rule applies to a child's investment income regardless of its source and requires a calculation of the parents' "allocable parental tax" (see ¶ 126 and ¶ 706) (Code Sec. 1(g)).[9] For tax years beginning after May 25, 2007, the "kiddie" tax will apply to unearned (investment) income of a child under age 18 at the close of the tax year or to a child that has attained the age of 18 at the close of the tax year that meets the age requirements under Code Sec. 152(c)(3) for claiming a dependency exemption and their earned income does not exceed one half of the amount of the child's support (Code Sec. 1(g)(2)(A)(ii)(II), as amended by the Small Business and Work Opportunity Act of 2007 (P.L. 110-28)).

There are three exceptions to the general rule that a child's unearned income is taxed at the parental rate beginning with tax years after December 31, 2005, but before tax years beginning after May 25, 2007. The first exception is that neither parent is alive at the close of the tax year (Code Sec. 1(g)(2)(B)). The second exception is if the child files a joint return with their spouse for the tax year (Code Sec. 1(g)(2)(C)). The third exception is for funds distributed from a qualified disability trust as defined under Code Sec. 642(b)(2)(c)(ii). These distributions are to be treated as earned income for purposes of the kiddie tax rules (Code Sec. 1(g)(4)(C)). A fourth exception will apply in tax years beginning after May 25, 2007. The exception is that the kiddie tax will not apply to individuals that attain age 18 by the close of the tax year if they are able to substantiate that over one half of the amount of their support comes from their earned income. Form 8615, Tax for Children Under Age 18 With Investment Income of More Than $1,700, is used to figure the child's tax for 2007.

Even though, under state law, compensation for a child's personal services may be treated as belonging to the parent, and even though the money is not retained by the child, for federal income tax purposes, it is considered gross income of the child (Reg. § 1.73-1).[10] If a child's income tax is not paid, an assessment made against the child will be treated as if it were also made against the child's parent, to the extent that the tax is attributable to amounts received for the child's services (Code Sec. 6201(c)).[11]

A parent may elect on Form 8814, Parents' Election To Report Child's Interest and Dividends, to include on his or her return the unearned income of a child who is under the age of 18 on January 1, 2008, whose income is less than $8,500 (to increase to $9,000 for 2008) and consists solely of interest, dividends, capital gain distributions, or Alaska Permanent Fund dividends. This election is not available if estimated tax payments were made for the tax year in the child's name and social security number or if the child is subject to backup withholding. Electing parents are taxed on their child's income in excess of $1,700 for the 2007 tax year (to increase to $1,800 for 2008). Also, they must report an additional tax liability of either $85 in 2007 if the child's taxable income is less than $850 or 10 percent of the child's income exceeding $850 in 2007 (to increase to $90 and $900, respectively, for 2008) (Code Sec. 1(g)(7)(A)(ii) and Code Sec. 1(g)(7)(B)(ii)).[12]

If a guardian or other person is charged with the care of a minor (or a person under a disability) or the minor's property, the return for the minor should be filed by the responsible person, unless already filed by the minor or some other person (see ¶ 504).

Prior law. For tax years beginning before January 1, 2006, the unearned or investment income of a child under the age of 14 at the close of the tax year was to be taxed at the "allocable" parental rate.

Footnote references are to paragraphs of the 2008 Standard Federal Tax Reports.

[8] ¶ 3270.035   [10] ¶ 6151   [12] ¶ 3260, ¶ 3280
[9] ¶ 3260   [11] ¶ 37,502, ¶ 37,504.025

116. Identifying Number. Every taxpayer must record his taxpayer identification number (TIN) on his return. Generally, this is either the taxpayer's social security number, individual taxpayer identification number (ITIN) (for use by resident or nonresident aliens who do not qualify for a social security number) or adoption taxpayer identification number (ATIN) (a temporary taxpayer identification number for use by adoptive parents adopting a child for whom they are unable to obtain either a social security number or an individual taxpayer identification number). If a taxpayer does not have a TIN, he should apply for either a social security number using Form SS-5, an ITIN using Form W-7 or an ATIN using Form W-7A. Taxpayers must provide TINs for dependents and qualifying children for the purpose of claiming a dependency exemption, the earned income tax credit (EIC or EITC), the child care credit, the adoption credit and the child tax credit (Code Secs. 21(e)(10), 23(f), 24(e), 32(c) and 151).[13] However, an ATIN cannot be used for purposes of claiming the earned income tax credit. Individuals claiming the earned income tax credit must also include TINs for themselves and their spouses (if married) (Code Sec. 32(c)(1)(F)). Failure to include a correct TIN will be treated as a mathematical or clerical error under Code Sec. 6213(g)(2), as will instances when the information provided differs from the information on file with the IRS.

The parent of any child to whom the rules governing taxation of unearned income of minor children apply must provide his or her taxpayer identification number to the child for inclusion on the child's tax return (see ¶ 114) (Code Sec. 1(g)(6)).[14]

When and Where Return Is Filed

118. Due Date. The individual income tax return is due on or before the 15th day of the 4th month following the close of the tax year (April 15 in the case of a calendar-year taxpayer) (Reg. § 1.6072-1(a)).[15] If the due date falls on a Saturday, Sunday, or legal holiday, the return may be filed on the next succeeding day that is not a Saturday, Sunday, or legal holiday (Reg. § 301.7503-1).[16]

A nonresident alien who has wages *not* subject to withholding generally may file a return as late as the 15th day of the 6th month after the close of the tax year (June 15 in the case of a calendar-year taxpayer). A nonresident alien who has wages subject to withholding must file a return by the 15th day of the 4th month following the close of the tax year (Reg. § 1.6072-1(c)).[17]

120. Extension for Filing. An individual may obtain an automatic extension of six months for filing Forms 1040, 1040A or 1040EZ if the individual files, on or before the due date of the return, an application (Form 4868, Application for Automatic Extension of Time To File U.S. Individual Income Tax Return) accompanied by a proper estimate of tax due for the year (¶ 2509).[18] A U.S. citizen or resident who, on April 15, 2008, lives and has a main place of business or post of duty outside the U.S. and Puerto Rico, or who is in military or naval service on duty outside the U.S. and Puerto Rico, is given an automatic two-month extension. An automatic additional four-month extension for filing the of correct income tax return may obtained by filing Form 4868 and including a reasonable estimate of tax due for the year (Reg. § 1.6081-5).[19] Finally, interest will be charged on any unpaid tax from the original due date of the return. For further details, see ¶ 2509.

122. Where to File Returns. The individual's return is filed by mail with the Internal Revenue Service Center for the region in which the individual's residence or principal place of business is located (Reg. § 1.6091-2).[20] It must be noted that returns completed by a professional tax preparer which include a payment are mailed to a different address than the one given in the instructions to the form. Also, payment vouchers for electronically filed returns are to be sent to a third address (see IRS Pub. 1045). In addition, nonresident aliens are to file Form 1040NR at the Philadelphia Service Center. For filing locations, see ¶ 3.

Footnote references are to paragraphs of the 2008 Standard Federal Tax Reports.

[13] ¶ 36,960, ¶ 36,964　　[16] ¶ 42,631　　[19] ¶ 36,795, ¶ 36,796.01
[14] ¶ 3260　　[17] ¶ 36,721　　[20] ¶ 36,808
[15] ¶ 36,721　　[18] ¶ 36,793

The Return Form

124. Forms in Use for 2007. Three principal forms are available for use by the majority of individuals for 2007. These forms include Form 1040, a shorter return form, Form 1040A, and for certain taxpayers with no dependents, Form 1040EZ. If the applicable filing conditions are met, any of the forms in the 1040 series may serve as a separate return or as a joint return. However, if a married person's filing status is married filing separately and the taxpayer uses Form 1040 and itemizes deductions, a spouse can file Form 1040 and either itemize deductions or claim a standard deduction of zero. If they decide to claim a standard deduction of zero, they may choose to file Form 1040A. These rules do not apply to a spouse who is eligible to file as unmarried or as head of household (see ¶ 173).

Form 1040EZ. For the 2007 tax year, the simplified income tax return, Form 1040EZ, may be used by taxpayers who:

(1) have single or joint filing status (if you are a nonresident alien at any time in 2007, your filing status can only be married filing jointly);

(2) claim no dependents;

(3) do not claim any adjustments to income (i.e., student loan interest, educator's expenses, or tuition and fees deduction);

(4) only claim the earned income tax credit;

(5) are under age 65 on January 1, 2008, and are not blind at the end of 2007;

(6) have taxable income of less than $100,000;

(7) have income from *only* wages, salaries, tips, unemployment compensation, taxable scholarships and fellowship grants, Alaska Permanent Fund dividends, and taxable interest income not exceeding $1,500;

(8) have received no advance earned income credit payments;

(9) owe no household employment taxes on wages paid to a household employee; and

(10) are not a debtor in a chapter 11 bankruptcy case filed after October 16, 2005.

If the taxpayer does *not* meet *all* the requirements, the taxpayer must use either Form 1040 or Form 1040A. If social security tax is owing on tip income, the taxpayer must use Forms 1040 and 4137, Social Security and Medicare Tax on Unreported Tip Income. The "Single" or "Married Filing Jointly" column of the Tax Table (¶ 25) must be used to find the correct amount of income tax, which is entered on the appropriate line of Form 1040EZ.

An individual who has no qualifying children and who received less than a total of $12,590 ($14,590 for joint filers) in taxable earned income may be able to take the earned income credit (EIC) on Form 1040EZ if the taxpayer or his spouse was at least age 25 at the end of 2007. The IRS will calculate the EIC for taxpayers who indicate that they desire such a computation on the appropriate line of the form.

Form 1040A. Form 1040A is a two-page form accompanied by four schedules. It is to be used by an individual, a married couple filing jointly or separately, a head of household (¶ 171), or a qualifying widow(er) with a dependent child (a surviving spouse) (¶ 175) who does not itemize personal deductions; whose gross income consists only of wages, salaries, tips, taxable scholarship and fellowship grants, IRA distributions, pensions or annuities, taxable social security or railroad retirement benefits, unemployment compensation, ordinary and qualified dividends, interest, Alaska Permanent Fund dividends, capital gains distributions and jury duty pay; whose only adjustments to gross income are the penalty for early withdrawal of savings, an individual retirement (IRA) deduction, a student loan interest deduction, and surrendered jury duty pay; whose tax credits are limited to the child tax credit, the educational credits, earned income credit, child and dependent care credit, the elderly and disabled credit, and the retirement saving contributions credit; and whose taxable income is less than $100,000.

The respective parts of Schedules 1 through 3 or Schedule EIC for Form 1040A must be completed if the taxpayer:

(1) receives more than $1,500 of either taxable interest income or ordinary dividend income,

(2) claims the exclusion of interest from series EE U.S. savings bonds issued after 1989 (¶ 730),

(3) receives interest or ordinary dividends as a nominee,

(4) receives interest from a seller-financed mortgage where the buyer used the property as a personal residence (¶ 726),

(5) claims the credit for child and dependent care expenses (¶ 1301),

(6) receives employer-provided dependent care benefits (¶ 869),

(7) claims the credit for the elderly or the disabled (¶ 1304), or

(8) is eligible for the earned income credit (¶ 1375).

For taxpayers to claim either or both of the education credits (¶ 1303), and/or the retirement savings contributions credit (¶ 1307), Form 8863, Education Credits (Hope and Lifetime Learning Credits), and/or Form 8880, Credit for Qualified Retirement Savings Contributions, must be completed and attached. The child tax credit (¶ 1302) is figured on the child tax credit worksheet and is entered on the appropriate line of Form 1040A. To claim the additional child tax credit, Form 8812, Additional Child Tax Credit, must be attached. The IRA deduction (¶ 2170), nondeductible IRA contributions (¶ 2173), educator expenses deduction (¶ 1084), the tuition and fees deduction (¶ 1082), student loan interest deduction (¶ 1082), alternative minimum tax liability (¶ 1401 and following) and advance EIC payments may also be reported on Form 1040A.

A taxpayer who made estimated tax payments (¶ 2679 and following) and wishes to apply any part of the refund to 2008 estimated tax, or who is subject to an underpayment of estimated tax penalty determined on Form 2210, Underpayment of Estimated Tax by Individuals, Estates, and Trusts, can reflect these items on Form 1040A.

However, Form 1040A may *not* be used by an individual who is required to file any of the schedules necessary to support Form 1040 (other than the information contained in the Schedules to Form 1040A), has taxable income of $100,000 or more, or if any of the following applies to the taxpayer:

(1) itemizes deductions;

(2) claims any credit against tax (see the discussion of *Form 1040*, following) other than the credits allowable for:

(a) the child and dependent care credit (¶ 1301),

(b) earned income credit (¶ 1375),

(c) the elderly or the disabled credit (¶ 1304),

(d) the education credits (¶ 1303),

(e) the retirement savings contributions credit (¶ 1307),

(f) the child tax credit (¶ 1302), or

(3) realizes taxable gain on the sale of a personal residence (¶ 1705 and following);

(4) claims any adjustments to income (other than the deduction for certain contributions made to an IRA (¶ 2168), for student loan interest (¶ 1082), for tuition and fees (¶ 1082), or for educator expenses (¶ 1084));

(5) receives in any month tips of $20 or more that are not reported fully to the employer, has a Form W-2 that shows allocated tips that must be reported in income, owes social security and Medicare tax on tips not reported to the employer, or has a Form W-2 that shows any uncollected social security, Medicare, or RRTA tax on tips or on group-term life insurance;

(6) is a nonresident alien at any time during the year and does not file a joint return with a U.S. citizen or resident spouse, or is married at the end of the year to a nonresident alien or dual-status alien who has U.S.-source income and who has not elected to be treated as a resident alien (however, such a married taxpayer may

¶124

be able to use Form 1040A if considered unmarried and eligible to use the head of household tax rate);

(7) owes or claims any of the items set out as *Other Taxes* in the discussion of *Form 1040*, following, with the exception of advance earned income credit payments and the alternative minimum tax;

(8) receives income from:

    (a) self-employment (net earnings of at least $400) (¶ 2667),

    (b) rents and royalties (¶ 762 and ¶ 763),

    (c) taxable state and local income tax refunds,

    (d) alimony received (¶ 771),

    (e) capital gains (¶ 1735),

    (f) business income (¶ 759), or

    (g) farm income (¶ 767);

(9) is the grantor of, or transferor to, a foreign trust (¶ 588);

(10) can exclude either (a) foreign earned income received as a U.S. citizen (¶ 2402) or resident alien or (b) certain income received from sources in a U.S. possession while a resident of American Samoa for all of 2007 (¶ 2410);

(11) receives or pays accrued interest on securities transferred between interest payment dates;

(12) earns wages of $108.28 or more from a church or church-controlled organization that is exempt from employer social security taxes;

(13) receives any nontaxable dividends or capital gain distributions;

(14) is reporting original issue discount in an amount more or less than that shown on Form 1099-OID (¶ 1859 and following);

(15) receives income as a partner (¶ 415, ¶ 431), an S corporation shareholder (¶ 309), or a beneficiary of an estate or trust (¶ 554—¶ 556); or

(16) has financial accounts in foreign countries (exceptions apply if the combined value of the accounts was $10,000 or less during all of 2007 or if the accounts were with a U.S. military banking facility operated by a U.S. financial institution).

An individual otherwise eligible to use Form 1040A should use Form 1040 if allowable itemized deductions exceed the appropriate standard deduction amount (see ¶ 126).

Form 1040. The basic Form 1040 is a single-sheet, two-page form. To it are added any necessary supporting schedules, depending upon the particular circumstances of the individual taxpayer. The chart that appears at ¶ 61 illustrates an individual's computation of taxable income on Form 1040. Items listed on the chart are explained at the paragraphs indicated.

The Tax Table (¶ 25) is used to determine the amount of tax if taxable income is less than $100,000 (see ¶ 128). If taxable income is $100,000 or more, taxpayers must use the 2007 Tax Computation Worksheet—Line 44 (¶ 20) or, alternatively, the appropriate Tax Rate Schedule (¶ 11—¶ 17), to compute the tax (see ¶ 130). Further, taxpayers who realized a net capital gain may owe less tax if they calculate their liability using either the "Schedule D Tax Worksheet" in the instruction to Schedule D of Form 1040 or the "Qualified Dividends and Capital Gain Tax Worksheet" in the Instruction to Form 1040 (see ¶ 126).

Generally, investment income of a child who is under age 18 on January 1, 2008, and who has investment income totaling more than $1,700 (to increase to $1,800 for 2008) is taxed at the parent's top marginal tax rate. Form 8615, Tax for Children Under Age 18 With Investment Income of More Than $1,700, is used to calculate the child's tax for 2007 (see ¶ 126). However, taxpayers may elect to be taxed on the unearned income of their children who are under age 18 at the close of the tax year (see ¶ 114). These taxpayers will use Form 8814, Parent's Election to Report Child's Interest and Dividends, to determine the additional amount of tax to be added to the taxpayer's Form 1040 tax liability. If this election is made, then the child will not have to file a return or Form 8615.

The Form 8814 amount must be entered in the space provided on Form 1040. Also included in the total tax liability is any tax from Form 4972, Tax on Lump-Sum Distributions (see ¶ 2153); Form 5329, Additional Taxes on Qualified Plans (Including IRAs) and Other Tax-Favored Accounts (see ¶ 2157); and Schedule J, Farm Income Averaging (see ¶ 767).

Beginning in 2008, the unearned (investment) income of a child will be taxed at the parent's marginal tax rate if the child is under age 18 or the child has attained age 18 by the end of the year, meets the age requirements of Code Sec. 152(c)(3) and whose earned income does not exceed one half of the amount of their support for the year. Thus, a full-time student up to the age up of 24 will have any unearned income taxed at the parent's marginal tax rate unless they can demonstrate that their earned income exceeds one half of their support amount.

Adjustments to Income. Adjustments to income (on page 1 of Form 1040) are principally those deductions that may be taken whether or not the standard deduction is employed. They include the deductions for:

(1) educator expenses (¶ 1084);

(2) employee business expenses of certain fee-basis state or local government officials (Code Sec. 62(a)(2)(C)) (¶ 941), performing artists (¶ 941A) and reservist's business expenses (¶ 941E);

(3) health savings accounts (including Archer Medical Saving Accounts (MSAs) and Health Savings Accounts (HSAs) (¶ 860, ¶ 1020, ¶ 1020A);

(4) moving expenses (¶ 1073);

(5) one-half of self-employment tax (¶ 2664);

(6) contributions to self-employed retirement plans (¶ 2113);

(7) health insurance premiums paid by self-employed individuals (¶ 908);

(8) the forfeited interest penalty for premature withdrawals from a time savings account (¶ 1120);

(9) alimony paid (¶ 771);

(10) contributions to individual retirement arrangements (IRAs) (¶ 2168);

(11) student loan interest (¶ 1005, ¶ 1082);

(12) tuition and fees (¶ 1082);

(13) the domestic production activities deduction (¶ 245);

(14) jury duty pay given to an employer (¶ 941, ¶ 1010);

(15) forestation or reforestation amortization (¶ 1287);

(16) repayment of supplemental unemployment benefits (¶ 1009);

(17) contributions to Code Sec. 501(c)(18) pension plans (¶ 602);

(18) expenses incurred with respect to the rental of personal property (¶ 1085); and

(19) attorney's fees and court cost for certain federal claims (¶ 1093).

Credits. A number of credits whose excess over tax liability is not refundable in the current year are subtracted from the resulting tax *in the following order:*

(1) credit for child and dependent care expenses (¶ 1301);

(2) credit for the elderly or for the permanently and totally disabled (¶ 1304);

(3) education credits (¶ 1301);

(4) residential energy credits (¶ 1313—¶ 1314);

(5) foreign tax credit (¶ 2475);

(6) child tax credit (¶ 1302);

(7) retirement savings contributions credit (¶ 1307);

(8) mortgage interest credit (¶ 1308);

(9) first-time homebuyers credit for District of Columbia (¶ 1310);

(10) adoption credit (¶ 1306);

¶124

(11) alternative motor vehicle credit (personal use) (¶ 1315–¶ 1315D);

(12) alternative fuel vehicle refueling property credit (personal use) (¶ 1316);

(13) general business credit (¶ 1323), which consists of the (a) investment tax credit (which is composed of the rehabilitation credit, the energy credit, the qualifying advanced coal project credit and the qualifying gasification project credit) (¶ 1345 and following), (b) work opportunity credit (¶ 1342), (c) research credit (¶ 1330), (d) low-income housing credit (¶ 1334), (e) disabled access credit (¶ 1338), (f) renewable electricity production credit (¶ 1339), (g) Indian employment credit (¶ 1340), (h) orphan drug credit (¶ 1344), (i) new markets credit (¶ 1335), (j) small employer pension plan startup costs credit (¶ 1344B), (k) employer-provided child care credit (¶ 1344C), (l) railroad track maintenance credit (¶ 1344D), (m) biodiesel and renewable diesel fuels credit (¶ 1329A), (n) low sulfur diesel fuel production credit (¶ 1344E), (o) distilled spirits credit (¶ 1344K), (p) nonconventional source fuel credit (¶ 1319), (q) energy efficient home credit (¶ 1344H), (r) energy efficient appliance credit (¶ 1344I), (s) alternative motor vehicle credit (business use) (¶ 1315—¶ 1315D), (t) alternative fuel vehicle refueling property credit (business use) (¶ 1316), (u) Hurricane Katrina housing credit (only from S corporations, partnerships, estates, and cooperatives) (¶ 1322A), (v) mine rescue team training credit (¶ 1344L), (w) credit for contributions to selected community development corporations (¶ 1325), and (x) general credits for electing large partnerships.

The following credits, although part of the general business credit, are separate from the general business credit and not subject to the general limiation rule are:

(a) the alcohol fuels credit for tax years beginning after December 31, 2004 (¶ 1326);

(b) the electricity produced from certain renewable sources credit including refined coal for facilities placed into service in tax years after October 22, 2004 (¶ 1339);

(c) the employer-paid Social Security taxes on employee tips credit and such carry backs for tax years beginning after December 31, 2006 (¶ 1341);

(d) the amended work opportunity credit, which inlcudes the welfare-to-work credit, and such carrybacks for tax years beginning after December 31, 2006 (¶ 1342); and

(e) the trans-Alaska pipeline credit.

(14) empowerment zone and renewal community employment credit (¶ 1339A);

(15) credit for prior year alternative minimum tax (¶ 1370);

(16) the clean renewable energy bond credit (¶ 1344J).

The enhanced oil recovery credit (Code Sec. 43) is not available since the price of a barrel of oil exceeded the phaseout threshold amount times the inflation adjustment for 2007. The credit may still be available to calendar-year taxpayers because of it having been passed through from a fiscal year pass-through entity. The credit for producing oil and gas from marginal wells (Code Sec. 45I) is also unavailable since the credit completely phased out when the price of a barrel of oil reached $18 per barrel.

Other Taxes. The following taxes are then added:

(1) self-employment tax (¶ 2664);

(2) alternative minimum tax (¶ 1401);

(3) recapture of any investment tax credit (¶ 1364), low-income housing credit (¶ 1334), federal mortgage subsidy (¶ 1308), qualified electric vehicle credit (¶ 1321), Indian employment credit (¶ 1340), or new markets credit (¶ 1335);

(4) FICA, Medicare, and/or RRTA tax owing on tip income not reported to the employer (computed on Form 4137, Social Security and Medicare Tax on Unreported Tip Income) and employee FICA, Medicare, and/or RRTA tax on tips where the employer did not withhold proper amounts (¶ 2639);

(5) excess contribution, excess distribution, and premature distribution taxes for IRAs and qualified pension or annuity plans, excess accumulations in qualified pension plans (including IRAs), Archer MSAs and HSAs, or early distribution tax for a modified endowment contract entered into after June 20, 1988 (computed on Form 5329, Additional Taxes on Qualified Plans (Including IRAs) and Other Tax-Favored Accounts) (¶ 1020, ¶ 1020A, ¶ 2157, ¶ 2174, ¶ 2179);

(6) advance earned income credit payments received (¶ 1375);

(7) household employment taxes (¶ 2650);

(8) the "Section 72(m)(5) excess benefits tax" imposed on a 5-percent owner of a business who receives a distribution of excess benefits from a qualified pension or annuity plan;

(9) uncollected FICA, Medicare, and/or RRTA tax on tips with respect to employees who received wages that were insufficient to cover the FICA, Medicare, and RRTA tax due on tips reported to their employers;

(10) uncollected FICA, Medicare, and/or RRTA tax on group-term life insurance (¶ 721);

(11) any excise tax due on "golden parachute" payments (¶ 2609); and

(12) tax on accumulated distribution of trusts (¶ 907).

Payments. To arrive at final tax due or refund owed, the taxpayer subtracts from the above balance the following:

(1) federal income tax withheld (¶ 2601 and following);

(2) 2007 estimated tax payments and amounts applied from 2006 returns (¶ 2679 and following);

(3) earned income credit (¶ 1375);

(4) amounts paid with applications for automatic filing extensions (¶ 2509);

(5) excess social security tax and/or Tier I railroad retirement (RRTA) tax withheld from individuals paid more than a total of $94,200 in wages by two or more employers and/or excess Tier II RRTA tax withheld from individuals paid more than a total of $69,900 by two or more employers (¶ 2648);

(6) health insurance costs credit (¶ 1377);

(7) credit for excise tax on gasoline and special fuels used in business and credit on certain diesel-powered vehicles (¶ 1379); and

(8) a shareholder's share of capital gains tax paid by a regulated investment company (¶ 2305).

The following schedules and forms are filed with the basic Form 1040 as needed:

(1) Schedule A for itemizing deductions;

(2) Schedule B for reporting (a) more than $1,500 of ordinary dividend income and/or other stock distributions, (b) more than $1,500 of taxable interest income or claiming the exclusion of interest from series EE U.S. savings bonds issued after 1989 used for higher educational expenses, and (c) declaring any interests in foreign accounts and trusts;

(3) Schedule C or Schedule C-EZ for claiming profit or loss from a sole proprietorship;

(4) Schedule D for reporting capital gains and losses;

(5) Schedule E for reporting income or loss from (a) rents and royalties, (b) partnerships and S corporations, (c) estates and trusts, and (d) real estate mortgage investment conduits (REMICs);

(6) Schedule EIC for providing information regarding the earned income credit;

(7) Schedule F for computing income and expenses from farming;

(8) Schedule H for reporting employment taxes for domestic workers paid $1,500 or more during 2007;

(9) Schedule J for reporting farm income averaging;

(10) Schedule R for claiming the tax credit for the elderly or the disabled;

(11) Schedule SE for computing the tax due on income from self-employment;

(12) Form 4797 for reporting gains and losses from sales of business assets or from involuntary conversions other than casualty or theft losses (casualty and theft losses are reported on Form 4684);

(13) Form 6251 for computing the alternative minimum tax;

(14) Form 4562 for reporting depreciation and amortization;

(15) Form 2106 or 2106-EZ for computing employee business expenses;

(16) Form 8582 for computing the amount of passive activity loss;

(17) Form 3903 for calculating moving expenses;

(18) Form 4835 for reporting farm rental income and expenses;

(19) Form 8283 for claiming a deduction for a noncash charitable contribution where the total claimed value of the contributed property exceeds $500;

(20) Form 8606 for reporting nondeductible IRA contributions, for figuring the basis of an IRA, and for calculating nontaxable distributions;

(21) Form 8615 for computing the tax for children under age 18 who have investment income in excess of $1,700 in 2007;

(22) Form 8829 for figuring allowable expenses for business use of a home;

(23) Form 8853 for figuring the allowable deduction for contributions to a Archer Medical Savings Account (Archer MSA) (for accounts established prior to January 1, 2008);

(24) Form 8889 for figuring the allowable deduction for contributions to a Health Savings Account (HSA);

(25) Form 8903 for figuring the allowable domestic production activities deduction;

(26) Form 8888 for direct deposit of income tax refunds into more than one account including but not limited to individual retirement accounts; and

(27) Form 8824 to report like-kind exchanges.

The following forms are for computing and claiming credits:

(1) Form 4136 to claim the credit for federal tax on gasoline and special fuels;

(2) Form 3468 to claim the investment credit, to the extent available;

(3) Form 5884 to calculate the work opportunity credit;

(4) Form 2441 to figure the child and dependent care credit;

(5) Form 8859 to claim the District of Columbia first-time homebuyers credit;

(6) Form 1116 to compute the foreign tax credit for individuals, estates or trusts;

(7) Form 6478 to compute the alcohol fuels credit;

(8) Form 6765 to claim the credit for increased research activities;

(9) Form 3800 if more than one of the components of the general business credit are claimed;

(10) Form 4255 to compute the recapture of investment credits;

(11) Form 8396 to figure the mortgage interest credit and any carryforwards;

(12) Forms 8586 and 8609 and 8609-A to compute the low-income housing credit available for buildings placed in service during 2007;

(13) Form 8611 to compute the recapture of the low-income housing credit;

(14) Form 8801 to compute the credit for prior year alternative minimum tax including the refundable portion;

(15) Form 8812 to claim the additional child tax credit;

(16) Form 8826 to claim the disabled access credit;

(17) Form 8828 to compute the recapture of a federal mortgage subsidy;

(18) Form 8835 to claim the renewable electricity production, refined coal or Indian coal production credit;

(19) Form 8834 to determine eligibility for the qualified electric vehicle credit;

(20) Form 8845 to claim the Indian employment credit;

(21) Form 8846 to claim the credit for employer-paid FICA and Medicare taxes on employee cash tips;

(22) Form 8847 to claim the credit for contributions to selected community development corporations;

(23) Form 8844 to claim the empowerment zone and renewal community employment credit;

(24) Form 8839 to claim the adoption credit;

(25) Form 8863 to claim the education credits;

(26) Form 8820 to claim the orphan drug credit;

(27) Form 8874 to claim the new markets credit;

(28) Form 8860 to claim the qualified zone academy bond credit;

(29) Form 8880 to claim the credit for qualified retirement savings contributions;

(30) Form 8882 to claim the credit for employer-provided child care facilities and services;

(31) Form 8881 to claim the credit for small employer pension plan startup costs;

(32) Form 8885 to claim the health insurance costs credit;

(33) Form 8864 to claim the biodiesel and renewable diesel fuels credit;

(34) Form 8896 to claim the sulfur diesel fuel production credit;

(35) Form 5695 to claim the residential energy credits;

(36) Form 8906 to claim the distilled spirits credit;

(37) Form 8910 to claim the alternative motor vehicle credit;

(38) Form 8911 to claim the alternative fuel vehicle refueling property credit; and

(39) Form 8912 to claim the credit for renewable energy and Gulf tax credit bonds.

IRS Computation of Tax. Any taxpayer who files an individual tax return by the due date, April 15, 2008 (April 16, 2008, for taxpayers living in Maine, Maryland, Massachusetts, New Hampshire, New York, Vermont and the District of Columbia that file in Massachusetts due to the state Patriot's Day holiday) can have the IRS compute the tax under certain conditions. These returns must have all applicable lines completed and be signed and dated. The inclusion of a daytime telephone number will speed processing should any questions arise. If you have overpaid your tax liability, a refund will be sent to you. You will be billed for any balance due on your tax liability. You must pay the amount due to avoid interest or the penalty for late payment by the later of 30 days from the billing date or the due date of your return.

Form 1040EZ. Lines 1 through 9 of Form 1040EZ that are applicable to the taxpayer should be completed. If the filing status is married, filing jointly, then in the left margin next to Line 6 each spouse must separately list their total income. The IRS will also calculate the earned income credit if you print "EIC" in the margin to the left of Line 8a and enter, if any, the nontaxable combat pay elected to be include in earned income on line 8b.

Form 1040A. To enable the IRS to compute the tax using Form 1040A, complete Lines 1 through 27, 29 through 33, 36, and 38 through 42 that are applicable to the taxpayer and include any schedules and forms asked for on those lines.

If the taxpayer wishes the IRS to calculate the credit for the elderly and disabled and/or earned income credit, Lines 30 and 40a should be left blank. For calculation of the credit for the elderly and disabled, write "CFE" in the space to the left of Line 30 and attach a completed Schedule 3 to the return. The box on Schedule 3 for filing status and age should be checked, and Part II and Part III, Lines 11 and 13, should be completed if necessary. To have the earned income credit calculated, print "EIC" directly to the right of Line 40a and enter, if any, the nontaxable combat pay elected to be included in earned income on line 40b and, if there is a qualifying child(ren), Schedule EIC must be completed and attached to Form 1040A.

When filing a joint return, the taxable income of each spouse must be separately listed in the margin to the left of Line 27. However, the IRS will not figure the tax for taxpayers who are claiming the credit for child and dependent care expenses (Line 29) or the adoption credit or who are required to file Form 8615 for computing the tax on investment income of a child under 18 years of age (see ¶ 126).

Form 1040. The IRS will figure the tax for a taxpayer using Form 1040 who:

(1) files a signed and dated return by April 15, 2008,

(2) does not itemize deductions,

(3) does not receive foreign earned income or claim a deduction or exclusion in connection with working abroad (Form 2555 or 2555-EZ),

(4) does not request application of a refund to next year's tax,

(5) has taxable income that (a) is less than $100,000 and (b) consists only of wages, salaries, tips, dividends, interest, taxable social security benefits, unemployment compensation, IRA distributions, pensions and/or annuities,

(6) does not elect to report a child's interest and dividends (Form 8814),

(7) owes no social security or Medicare tax on unreported tip income (Form 4137),

(8) did not receive an accumulation distribution made by a trust (Form 4970),

(9) did not receive a lump-sum distribution from a qualified retirement plan (Form 4972),

(10) did not realize profit or loss from an at-risk activity (Form 6198),

(11) is not liable for alternative minimum tax (Form 6251),

(12) is not required to file Form 8615 regarding the tax due on investment income of a child under age 18 (see ¶ 126),

(13) does not claim a credit for adoption expenses (Form 8839), and

(14) does not claim a deduction for contributions to an Archer MSA or long-term care insurance contract (Form 8853).

A taxpayer who wants the IRS to figure the tax on Form 1040 should complete Lines 1-43 and 45-72 if applicable (the "Total" lines should not be computed), along with any related forms or schedules. Line 64, indicating income tax withheld, and Line 65, indicating the amount of estimated tax paid, must be filled in. If a joint return is being filed, the taxable income of each spouse must be separately listed under the words "Adjusted Gross Income" on the front of Form 1040. All necessary forms and schedules must be attached in sequential order to the return.

If eligible for the tax credit for the elderly or for the permanently and totally disabled, the taxpayer should write "CFE" on the dotted line next to Line 48 and attach Schedule R with the necessary information completed. The box on Schedule R for filing status and age must be checked, and Part II and Lines 11 and 13 of Part III, if applicable, must be filled in.

If eligible for the earned income credit, the taxpayer, should write "EIC" directly to the right of Line 66a and enter, if any, nontaxable combat pay elected to be included in

¶124

earned income on line 66b. A taxpayer who has a qualifying child(ren) should fill in Schedule EIC and attach it to the return.

Rounding Off Amounts. Dollar amounts on the return and accompanying schedules and forms may be rounded off to the nearest whole dollar.

Computing the Tax

126. Taxable Income and Rates. Certain taxpayers must use the Tax Table (¶ 128) to compute their tax; other taxpayers must use the Tax Computation Worksheet (based on the Tax Rate Schedules) in the Form 1040 instructions (¶ 130). Under either method, taxable income must first be computed. Taxable income is equal to adjusted gross income (¶ 1005) minus allowances for deductions and exemptions (¶ 133). See the chart at ¶ 61. Thus, taxable income for a taxpayer who does not itemize deductions is equal to adjusted gross income minus the applicable standard deduction and allowable exemptions. Taxable income for a taxpayer who itemizes is equal to adjusted gross income minus total itemized deductions and allowable exemptions.

Standard Deduction. Taxpayers who do not itemize their deductions are entitled to a standard deduction (Code Sec. 63(c)).[21] Taxpayers have the choice of itemizing deductions or taking the applicable standard deduction amount, whichever figure will result in a higher deduction (for exceptions, see *Taxpayers Ineligible for Standard Deduction,* following). An individual whose AGI exceeds a specified threshold amount must reduce the amount of otherwise allowable itemized deductions (¶ 1014).

The amount of the standard deduction varies according to the taxpayer's filing status. This deduction, together with the taxpayer's personal and dependency exemptions, applies to reduce adjusted gross income in arriving at taxable income. Listed below are the standard deduction amounts available in 2007 to individuals other than those who are age 65 or older or who are blind (Code Sec. 63(c)(7); Rev. Proc. 2006-53):

Filing status	2007 standard deduction amount
Married filing jointly and surviving spouses	$10,700
Married filing separately	5,350
Head of household filers	7,850
Single filers	5,350

A special rule applies to an individual for whom a dependency exemption is allowable to another taxpayer. Such individual's basic standard deduction may not exceed the greater of $850 (to increase to $900 in 2008) or the sum of $300 (to remain the same in 2008) and the individual's earned income, up to the applicable standard deduction amount ($5,350 for single taxpayers) (Code Sec. 63(c)(5)).[22] Thus, a child who may be claimed as a dependent by his parents and who has no earned income and $850 of interest or dividend income in 2007 will have a $850 standard deduction. A scholarship or fellowship grant that is *not* excludable from the dependent's income (see ¶ 879) is considered earned income for standard deduction purposes.[23]

Note that the standard deduction for dependents other than those age 65 or older or blind cannot exceed the basic standard deduction amount shown above. If the taxpayer is age 65 or older or blind, the standard deduction is increased by the additional amount allowed to such taxpayers (see *Elderly and/or Blind Taxpayers,* following).

Standard Deduction Amounts for 2008. The standard deduction amounts for 2008 are as follows:

Filing status	2008 standard deduction amount
Married filing jointly and surviving spouses	$10,900
Married filing separately	5,450
Head of household filers	8,000
Single filers	5,450

Standard Deduction Marriage Penalty Relief. The standard deduction amount for taxpayers filing jointly (and surviving spouses) will equal twice the amount (200 percent)

Footnote references are to paragraphs of the 2008 Standard Federal Tax Reports.

[21] ¶ 6020   [22] ¶ 6020   [23] ¶ 7170.06

of the inflation-adjusted standard deduction amount of a single filer (Code Sec. 63(c)(7)). Additionally, the basic standard deduction for a married taxpayer filing separately is equal to one-half of the inflation-adjusted standard deduction of a joint filer (Code Sec. 63(c)(2)). These provisions are subject to the sunset provision of the Economic Growth and Tax Relief Reconciliation Act of 2001 (EGTRRA) (P.L. 108-27) and, barring further Congressional action, will terminate for tax years beginning after December 31, 2010.

Elderly and/or Blind Taxpayers. Taxpayers who are age 65 or older or who are blind receive an additional standard deduction amount that is added to the basic standard deduction shown in the above table. The additional amount for married individuals (whether filing jointly or separately) and surviving spouses in 2007 is $1,050 (to remain the same for 2008), while the additional amount in 2007 for unmarried individuals (whether filing as single or as head of household) is $1,300 (to increase to $1,350 in 2008) (Code Sec. 63(f)).[24] Two additional standard deduction amounts are allowed to an individual who is both over 65 and blind. Thus, married taxpayers filing jointly, both of whom are over 65 and blind, would claim four of the additional standard deduction amounts.

Generally, to qualify for the additional standard deduction amount, a taxpayer must be age 65 (or blind) before the close of the tax year. However, an individual who reaches age 65 on January 1st of any year is deemed to have reached that age on the preceding December 31st.[25] A taxpayer claiming the additional amount for blindness must obtain a certified statement from a doctor or registered optometrist. The statement, which should be kept with the taxpayer's records, must state either that:

(1) the individual cannot see better than 20/200 in the better eye with glasses or contact lenses, or

(2) the individual's field of vision is 20 degrees or less.

A married taxpayer filing separately may claim the additional amounts for a spouse who had no gross income and was not claimed as a dependent by another taxpayer. A taxpayer who claims a dependency exemption for an individual who is blind or age 65 or older may not claim the additional standard deduction amounts for that individual.

Taxpayers Ineligible for Standard Deduction. When married taxpayers file separate returns, both spouses should either itemize their deductions or claim the standard deduction. If one spouse itemizes and the other does not, the non-itemizing spouse's standard deduction amount will be zero, even if such spouse is age 65 or older or blind. However, the IRS has determined that this rule may not apply if one spouse qualifies to file as "head-of-household" (Service Center Advice 200030023). A zero standard deduction amount also applies to nonresident aliens, estates or trusts, common trust funds, or partnerships, and to individuals with short tax years due to a change in their annual accounting period (Code Sec. 63(c)(6)).[26] Taxpayers who itemize even though their itemized deductions are less than the standard deduction must enter "IE" (itemized elected) next to the line 40 of Form 1040.

> **Example:** A husband and a wife who are eligible to file a joint return elect to file separate returns. The husband itemizes. The wife, whose adjusted gross income is $12,100, has itemized deductions of $1,070. The wife should itemize since her standard deduction would otherwise be zero. Her taxable income is $7,630—adjusted gross income of $12,100 less $1,070 in itemized deductions less the $3,400 personal exemption.

Tax Rates in 2007. The six tax rates applicable to individual taxpayers for 2007 are: 10%, 15%, 25%, 28%, 33%, and 35% (see ¶ 133) (Code Sec. 1(a)-(e)).[27] See ¶ 11—¶ 17 for the 2007 tax rate schedules.

For 2007, the 10-percent bracket applies to the first $7,825 of taxable income for single filers and married taxpayers filing separately, the first $11,200 for head-of-household filers, and $15,650 for married taxpayers filing jointly and surviving spouses (Code Sec. 1(i)(1); Rev. Proc. 2006-53). The upper limit of the 15-percent tax bracket for

---

Footnote references are to paragraphs of the 2008 Standard Federal Tax Reports.

[24] ¶ 6020, ¶ 6023.034   [26] ¶ 6020
[25] ¶ 6023.034   [27] ¶ 3260

joint filers will be 200 percent of the upper limit of the 15-percent tax bracket for single filers (Code Sec. 1(f)(8)).

Tax Rates until 2011. For tax years through 2010, the tax rates for individuals will remain the same. However, under the sunset provision of EGTRRA, the individual tax rates will return to their pre-2001 levels in 2011. Thus, without further Congressional action, there will be only five tax brackets effective in 2011 and thereafter; the 10-percent tax bracket will be eliminated. The five tax brackets will be the 15-, 28-, 31-, 36-, and 39.6-percent tax brackets. The following chart indicates the applicable rates under the new law:

Tax years beginning 2011:	*Rate brackets*					
pre-2011	10%	15%	25%	28%	33%	35%
2011 and after	—	15%	28%	31%	36%	39.6%

Tax Calculation on Form 8615. Generally, Form 8615 must be used to calculate the tax for any child who was under age 18 on January 1, 2008, and who had more than $1,700 of investment income (to increase to $1,800 for 2008). However, if neither of the child's parents was alive on December 31, 2007, Form 8615 cannot be used to figure the tax (see ¶ 706). Taxpayers required to calculate their tax on Form 8615 may compute taxable income using Form 1040, 1040A, or 1040EZ. Form 8615 is not filed if the child's parent elects to include the child's unearned income on the parent's return (see ¶ 114).

Capital Gain Tax Calculation. Taxpayers who had a net capital gain from a sale or exchange use Schedule D, Part III, to determine which, if either, of the capital gains tax worksheet to use to calculate the amount of tax on the capital gains. For taxpayers with sales or exchanges of assets taxed at the 28% rate or with unrecaptured Sec. 1250 gains or both complete the "Schedule D Tax Worksheet" in the instruction to Schedule D of Form 1040. All other taxpayers, including those with only qualified dividends and net capital gains from a distribution of a regulated investment company (i.e., a mutual fund), complete the "Qualified Dividends and Capital Gain Tax Worksheet" in the Form 1040 or 1040A instructions.

128. Tax Table Simplifies Computation. A table prepared by the IRS (reproduced at ¶ 25) simplifies determination of the tax. The table is based on taxable income and applies to taxpayers who file Form 1040, 1040A and 1040EZ.

Taxpayers may *not* use the table if they have taxable income of $100,000 or more or if they file short-period returns because of a change in their annual accounting periods (¶ 1507—¶ 1509). Also, estates and nongrantor trusts may not use the table; instead, they must use the Tax Rate Schedule at ¶ 19.

> **Example:** An unmarried individual has adjusted gross income of $28,240 for 2007. He has itemized deductions of $5,500. Since his itemized deductions exceed the allowable standard deduction ($5,350), he elects to itemize. His taxable income is $19,340—adjusted gross income of $28,240 less $5,500 in itemized deductions less the $3,400 personal exemption amount. His tax is $2,508 using the Tax Table.

130. Tax Rate Schedules. A taxpayer with taxable income of $100,000 or more must use the Tax Computation Worksheet (¶ 20), which is based on the tax rate schedules (¶ 11—¶ 17) in order to compute his tax (unless he is required to compute his tax on Form 8615, uses the "Schedule D Tax Worksheet" or the "Qualified Dividends and Capital Gain Worksheet" (see ¶ 126)).

> **Example 1:** Married taxpayers who file a joint return for 2007 have adjusted gross income of $155,950, four exemptions, and no itemized deductions. Their taxable income is $131,650 ($155,950 less $10,700 for the standard deduction less $13,600 for four exemptions). Their tax is $25,854.50 ($24,972.50 + 28% of $3,150 ($131,650 – $128,500)) and is computed by using the Tax Rate Schedule Y-1 at ¶ 13.

> **Example 2:** Same facts as **Example 1**, except the calculation to determine the tax liability follows the Tax Computation Worksheet. The tax liability is determined by multiplying their taxable income found on line 43 of the Form 1040 ($131,650) by 28 percent ($36,862) and then subtracting $11,007.50 to give these married taxpayers a tax liability of $25,854.50.

Exemption Amount

133. Exemption Amount. The amount of a personal exemption (for taxpayer and his spouse) and of a dependency exemption (for taxpayer's dependents) is $3,400 for 2007. This amount is adjusted annually to reflect the inflation rate (Code Sec. 151(d); Rev. Proc. 2006-53).[28] For 2008, the exemption amount will increase to $3,500. The dependency exemption amount is denied to claimants who fail to provide the dependent's correct taxpayer identification number on the return claiming the dependency exemption (Code Sec. 151(e)).

The deduction for personal and dependency exemptions may be reduced or eliminated for higher-income taxpayers (Code Sec. 151(d)).[29] The total exemption amount for a taxpayer whose adjusted gross income exceeds the set threshold amount, based on filing status, is reduced by 2 percent for each $2,500 ($1,250 for a married person filing separately) or fraction thereof by which AGI exceeds the threshold amount. The 2007 threshold amounts are:

    (1) $234,600 for joint returns or a surviving spouse;

    (2) $195,500 for a head of household;

    (3) $156,400 for single taxpayers; and

    (4) $117,300 for married persons filing separately.

Phaseout thresholds for 2008 are $239,950 for joint filers or a surviving spouse, $199,950 for a head of household, $159,950 for single taxpayers, and $119,975 for married persons filing separately.

Exemptions Phaseout Repealed. In tax years beginning in 2006 and 2007, the amount of the exemption phaseout reduction that would otherwise apply is reduced by one-third and for tax years beginning in 2008 and 2009 by two-thirds. For tax years beginning after 2009, the exemption phaseout is repealed (Code Sec. 151(d)(3)(E) and (F)).

135. Exemptions. Generally, the exemptions allowed to a taxpayer are a "personal" exemption of $3,400 (to increase to $3,500 in 2008) and an exemption of $3,400 (to increase to $3,500 in 2008) for each dependent.

A husband and wife filing a joint return are allowed at least two "personal" exemptions of $3,400 in 2007 since each spouse is regarded as a taxpayer, plus any exemptions for dependents (¶ 137 and following). If a husband and wife file separate returns, each must take his or her own exemptions on their respective return. If, however, a husband or wife files a separate return and the other spouse has no gross income and is *not* the dependent of another taxpayer, the combined personal exemptions of the spouses may be claimed on the separate return (Reg. § 1.151-1(b)).[30] Additionally, a taxpayer who files a separate return may *not* claim two exemptions for his spouse—one as a spouse and one as a dependent (Code Sec. 152(a)(9)).[31]

If the husband and wife file a joint return, neither can be claimed as a "dependent" on the return of any other person (Reg. § 1.151-1(b)).[32]

Also, *no* exemption will be allowed to an individual who is eligible to be claimed as a dependent on another taxpayer's return. Thus, students who work part-time during the year or for the summer may *not* claim a personal exemption on their own return if their parents (or other taxpayers) are *entitled* to claim them on their return. However, if dependents who are not allowed their own exemptions have gross income in an amount not exceeding $850 (to increase to $900 for 2008), they will *not* be taxed on that amount and need *not* file income tax returns (see ¶ 109).

A resident alien may claim his own personal exemption and, if he files a joint return, may claim a similar exemption for his spouse. However, unless one of the elections noted at ¶ 152 applies, the filing of a joint return is not permissible if either he or his spouse was a nonresident alien at any time during the tax year (Code Sec. 6013(a)(1); Reg. § 1.6013-1(b)).[33] For a detailed discussion regarding nonresident aliens, see ¶ 2444.

Footnote references are to paragraphs of the 2008 Standard Federal Tax Reports.

[28] ¶ 8000, ¶ 8005.12   [30] ¶ 8001   [32] ¶ 8001
[29] ¶ 8000   [31] ¶ 8007   [33] ¶ 35,160, ¶ 35,161

137. Exemption for Dependent. Code Sec. 150(c) allows a taxpayer to claim an exemption amount for each individual that may be claimed as a dependent as defined under Code Sec. 152. Under Code Sec. 152(a) an individual will be considered a dependent if they satisfy either the "qualifying child" or the "qualifying relative" requirements. An individual cannot be claimed as a dependent if they file a joint return with their spouse for the same tax year (Code Sec. 152(b)(2)) (see ¶ 138 for the exception). The individual to be claimed as a dependent must also be a U.S. citizen, national, or resident of the United States or a contiguous country (Code Sec. 152(b)(3); Reg. § 1.152-2(a)(2)).[34] Anyone claimed as a dependent is barred from claiming another individual as a dependent (Code Sec. 152(b)(1)). Additionally, the IRS may adjust the application of the tax laws for tax years beginning in 2005 and 2006 to ensure that taxpayers do not lose any credit or experience a change in filing status by reason of relocations caused by Hurricanes Katrina, Rita and Wilma (see ¶ 140) (Code Sec. 1400S(e)).

137A. "Qualifying Child" Definition. An individual must satisfy four tests to be considered a "qualifying child" for purposes of the dependency exemption: relationship, age, principal place of abode and support.

(1) *Relationship.* The child must bear one of the following relationships to the taxpayer:

(a) a son, daughter, stepson, stepdaughter or a descendant of such child; or

(b) a brother, sister, stepbrother, stepsister or a descendant of such relative (Code Sec. 152(c)(2)).

The relationship test includes foster and adopted children. An eligible foster child is a child who is placed with the taxpayer by an authorized placement agency or by a decree issued by the courts. An eligible adopted child includes both a legally adopted child and a child legally placed for adoption (Code Sec. 152(f)(1)).

(2) *Age.* The child must not have attained the age of 19 by the end of the calendar year or must be a student that has not attained the age of 24 by the end of the calendar year. A student is defined as an individual attending, on a full-time basis for at least five calendar months in a year, a qualified educational institution or a qualified on-farm training program (Code Sec. 152(c)(3) and (f)(2)). This requirement is suspended for any individual who is totally and permanently disabled at any time during the year.

(3) *Principal Place of Abode.* The child must have the same principal place of abode of the taxpayer for more than one-half of the year (Code Sec. 152(c)(1)(B)).

(4) *Support.* The child must *not* provide more than one-half of their own support for the year (Code Sec. 152(c)(1)(D)).

In the event that a child can be claimed as the qualifying child by two or more individuals, the child is considered the qualifying child of their parents first and, if neither is the parent of the child, then the taxpayer with the highest adjusted gross income. For a discussion of the tie-breaking rules for divorced or separated parents, see ¶ 139.

A full exemption may be claimed for a child born at any time during the tax year, so long as the child lives momentarily and the birth is recognized under state or local law as a "live" birth.[35]

If the child or individual fails to meet all the requirement to be considered a qualifying child, the individual may still be claimed as a dependent if they meet all the requirements for a "qualifying relative."

137B. "Qualifying Relative" Definition. For individuals who fail to satisfy all the requirements to be considered a "qualifying child," they may still qualify to be claimed as a dependent if they satisfy four similar tests, which are similar to the tests used prior to 2005 to determine whether a taxpayer was entitled to claim an individual as a

---

Footnote references are to paragraphs of the 2008 Standard Federal Tax Reports.

[34] ¶ 8007, ¶ 8050   [35] ¶ 8250.36

dependent. The four tests are: relationship, gross income, support and dependency (Code Sec. 152(d)).[36]

(1) *Relationship.* The individual must fall within one of the following relationships:

(a) a child or a descendant of such child;

(b) brother, sister, stepbrother or stepsister;

(c) father, mother or an ancestor of either (i.e., grandmother and /or grandfather);

(d) stepfather or stepmother;

(e) son or daughter of a brother or sister of the taxpayer (i.e., nieces and/or nephews);

(f) brother or sister of the father or mother of the taxpayer (i.e., aunts and/or uncles);

(g) son-in-law, daughter-in-law, father-in-law, mother-in-law, brother-in-law or sister-in-law; or

(h) an individual that for the tax year has the same principal place of abode as the taxpayer and is a member of the taxpayer's household (Code Sec. 152(d)(2)).[37]

(2) *Gross Income.* The individual in 2007 must have *less* than $3,400 (to increase to $3,500 in 2008) of gross income for the calendar year (Code Sec. 152(d)(1)(B)).

(3) *Support.* Over half of the dependent's total support for that calendar year must have been furnished by the taxpayer (with exceptions relating to multiple support agreements (¶ 147) and children of divorced parents (¶ 139)) (Code Sec. 152(d)(1)(C)).

(4) *Dependency.* The individual must not be the qualifying child of the taxpayer or of any other taxpayer for the tax year (Code Sec. 152(d)(1)(D)).

Example 1: Margaret, age 25, and her infant son from another relationship, Billy, move in and live with Jeff in his home in December of 2006. Margaret does not work at all in 2007 but stays at home to care for Billy while Jeff supports them both. Since Billy is a qualifying child of Margaret's, Jeff is barred from claiming him as a dependent. Because Jeff cannot claim Billy as a dependent, he cannot file as head-of-household and must file as single. He can only claim one additional dependent, Margaret. Since Margaret does not have to file a return, the dependent exemption for Billy goes unclaimed.

The definition of a child for qualifying relative purposes is the same as for a qualifying child. Thus, a legally adopted child or a child lawfully placed for adoption is treated as a child or individual related by blood to the taxpayer. If a foster child is lawfully placed with the taxpayer by an authorized agency or decree of the courts, the child may also be treated as related to the taxpayer (Code Sec. 152(f)(1)).[38]

The relationship of affinity, once existing, is not destroyed for income tax purposes by divorce or by the death of a spouse.

Example 2: Mr. Golden contributes more than half the support of his wife's mother. Mrs. Golden divorces Mr. Golden, but he continues to contribute more than half the support of his former mother-in-law. Mr. Golden may continue to claim his former mother-in-law as a dependent on his separate return.

138. Married Dependents. A married individual cannot be claimed as a dependent if such individual joins with their spouse to file a joint return under Code Sec. 6013 (Code Sec. 152(b)(2)). The exception to this rule that would allow a married individual to be claimed as a dependent if the sole purpose for filing the joint return was to obtain a refund and neither individual would have a tax liability if they had filed separately (Rev. Rul. 65-34, affirming Rev. Rul. 54-567). In this situation, the IRS views the return as only a claim for refund.

Footnote references are to paragraphs of the 2008 Standard Federal Tax Reports.

[36] ¶ 8005.85   [37] ¶ 8007, ¶ 8250.48   [38] ¶ 8007

139. Two or More Taxpayers Claiming the Same Qualifying Child. Code Sec. 152(c)(4) addresses the tie-breaking procedure when two or more taxpayers are trying to claim the same qualifying child. If one of the individuals is a parent of the child, then they are entitled to claim the child. If none of the taxpayers are a parent, then the taxpayer with the highest adjust gross income is entitled to claim the child. In the event both parents are claiming the child and are not filing a joint return, then the parent with whom the child resided for the longest period of time during the tax year is entitled to claim the child. If the child resided with both parents for an equal amount of time, then the parent with the highest adjust gross income is entitled to claim the child. See ¶ 139A for the tie-breaking rules for separated or divorced parents. When applying the tie-breaking rules under Code Sec. 152(c)(4), the individual that is allowed to claim the child is the only individual that may claim any tax benefits that employ the uniform definition of a qualifying child (Notice 2006-86).

139A. Exemptions for Children of Divorced Parents. Generally, the dependency exemption for children of divorced taxpayers will go to the parent who has custody of the child for the greater part of the calendar year. When the child spends an equal amount of time with each parent, the parent with the higher adjusted gross income is allowed to claim the dependency exemption. This rule applies only if the child receives over one-half of his or her support from parents who are divorced, legally separated, or have lived apart for the last six months of the calendar year. In addition, the child must have been in the custody of one or both parents for more than one-half of the calendar year (Code Sec. 152(e)).[39]

There are three exceptions to the rule that a custodial parent is entitled to the dependency exemption.[40] The first exception arises when there is a multiple support agreement that allows the qualifying child to be claimed as a dependent by a taxpayer other than the custodial parent. The second exception is when the custodial parent of a dependent child transfers the right to claim the dependency exemption to the noncustodial parent by signing a written waiver (Form 8332). The waiver must be attached to the noncustodial parent's tax return. The parents do not need a written divorce decree or separation agreement containing the noncustodial parent's right to the exemption and the waiver does not need to be permanent. The waiver may only be used by the noncustodial parent for purposes of claiming the child tax credit and the dependency exemption (Notice 2006-86). The final exception is when a pre-1985 divorce decree or separation agreement between the parents grants the exemption to the noncustodial parent and the noncustodial parent provides at least $600 for the support of the child for the year in question.

When a parent has remarried, support received from the parent's spouse is treated as received from the parent (Code Sec. 152(d)(5)(B)).[41]

140. Additional Exemption for Hurricane Katrina Evacuees (Expired). An additional exemption amount may be claimed by individuals who house evacuees for a period of more than 60 days during either 2005 or 2006. The additional amount is $500 per evacuee limited to a maximum additional amount of $2,000 for both years. The evacuee must have had their principal residence located in the core disaster area or, if outside the core disaster area, forced to evacuate the area due to Hurricane Katrina or their principal place of residence was destroyed by Hurricane Katrina. The taxpayer claiming the extra exemption for housing the evacuee(s) must *not* receive any compensation from any source. Finally, a spouse or dependent may not be claimed by the taxpayer as an evacuee (Act Sec. 302 of the Katrina Emergency Tax Relief Act of 2005 (P.L. 109-73)).

141. How the "Dependency" Exemption Is Claimed. On a joint return, the dependency exemption is allowed if the prescribed relationship (¶ 137—¶ 137B) exists between one of the spouses and the claimed dependent (all other conditions being satisfied) (Reg. § 1.152-2(d)).[42]

Footnote references are to paragraphs of the 2008 Standard Federal Tax Reports.

[39] ¶ 8007
[40] ¶ 8007, ¶ 8200

[41] ¶ 8007
[42] ¶ 8050

On a separate return, however, only a person who meets the requirements outlined at ¶ 137—¶ 137B can be claimed as a dependent by the taxpayer.

> **Example:** Mr. and Mrs. Parker file a joint tax return. If Mr. Parker provides more than one-half of the support for Mrs. Parker's uncle, the exemption may be claimed on their joint return, even though the uncle does not live with them. If Mr. and Mrs. Parker file separate returns, Mr. Parker may claim the exemption for the uncle only if the uncle is a member of Mr. Parker's household and lives with him for the entire tax year.

In a community property state (¶ 710), if a child's support is derived from community income, some or all of the exemptions may, by agreement, be taken by either the husband or wife on a separate return. A single $3,400 exemption amount (to increase to $3,500 for 2008) may *not* be divided between them.[43]

143. "Qualifying Relative" Dependent's Income. Generally, in order to claim a "qualifying relative" as a dependent, that individual may *not* have gross income of $3,400 (to increase to $3,500 for 2008) or more for the year. This is an important differentiation from a taxpayer's qualifying child (¶ 137A) who has not attained age 19 or who was under age 24 and was a full-time student at a regular educational institution or was pursuing a full-time, accredited, on-farm training course during each of five calendar months in 2007 and who may be claimed as a dependent (if the taxpayer satisfies the support test), regardless of the amount of the child's income. The five calendar months need not be consecutive.

In fixing the $3,400 income ceiling, any income excludable from the claimed dependent's gross income (such as exempt interest, disability, or social security) is disregarded. This income, however, if used to any extent for support of the dependent, must be taken into account (to the extent that it was so used) to determine whether the taxpayer has furnished more than one-half of the claimed dependent's support (Reg. § 1.151-3(b), Reg. § 1.152-1).[44]

> **Example:** Paul's mother, who lived in his home, earned $500 in 2007 from baby-sitting. She was injured in an accident and received $2,650 in damages. Paul contributed $2,000 for her support in 2007. The damages award is not taxable income and is not counted for purposes of the $3,400 gross income test, but, if the mother spent at least $1,500 of this amount (plus the $500 she received for baby-sitting) in 2007 for her own support, Paul could *not* claim her as a dependent, because he would not have furnished more than one-half of her support. If less than $2,000 was spent by the mother for her own support, Paul would be entitled to the exemption for a dependent.

If the taxpayer is on a fiscal-year basis, the determinations as to whether the dependent had gross income and whether the taxpayer furnished more than one-half of the dependent's support are made on the basis of the calendar year in which the fiscal year begins (Reg. § 1.151-2(a), Reg. § 1.152-1(a)).[45]

If a parent is barred from claiming an exemption for a child who was a student age 24 or over during 2007 or whose gross income was $3,400 or more, the child may claim an exemption on his own return.[46]

A dependent, whether a "qualifying child" or a "qualifying relative," who has earned wages in 2007 on which income tax has been withheld should file a return even though claimed as a dependent by another. The return will serve as a claim for refund of the tax withheld where the dependent incurs no tax liability. If a dependent child of the taxpayer has only earned income in excess of $5,350, $1 or more of unearned income and gross income in excess of $850, or self-employment income of $400 or more, a return must be filed whether or not the child is claimed as a dependent (see ¶ 109 and ¶ 2670).

Footnote references are to paragraphs of the 2008 Standard Federal Tax Reports.

[43] ¶ 8005.23
[44] ¶ 8000, ¶ 8003, ¶ 8008
[45] ¶ 8002, ¶ 8008
[46] ¶ 8000

Income received by a permanently and totally disabled individual at a sheltered workshop school is disregarded in determining that individual's status as a dependent.[47]

145. Exemption for Married Child. A parent cannot claim a married child as a dependent if the child joins their spouse in filing a joint return under Code Sec. 6013 (Code Sec. 152(b)(2)). The sole exception that allows the claiming of a married child as a dependent is if the married child joined in filing the joint return for the sole purpose of claiming a refund and neither the child nor the spouse would have a tax liability if they filed individually (see ¶ 138).

147. Support of a "Qualifying Relative" Dependent. A taxpayer must furnish more than one-half of the *total* support provided for a "qualifying relative" dependent during the calendar year before claiming an exemption for that individual (but see the special rule for children of divorced parents at ¶ 139) (Reg. § 1.152-1).[48] If more than half of the support is provided by two or more people, the dependency exemption is not necessarily lost. A person can be treated, for purposes of the exemption, as having provided more than half of an individual's support if:

(1) no one person provided over half of the support;

(2) over half of the support was received from persons who each would have been entitled to claim the exemption had they contributed more than half of the support;

(3) over 10 percent of the support was provided by the person claiming the exemption; and

(4) each person who contributed more than 10 percent of the support signs a written declaration (Form 2120, Multiple Support Declaration) stating that they will not claim the exemption. These statements must be retained with the taxpayer's records in the event the taxpayer is called upon to justify claiming the dependency exemption (Reg. § 1.152-3).[49]

"Total" support is determined on a yearly basis and is the sum of:

(1) the fair rental value of lodging furnished to a "qualifying relative" dependent,

(2) the costs of all items of expense paid out directly by or for the benefit of the "qualifying relative" dependent, such as clothing, education, medical and dental care, gifts, transportation, church contributions, and entertainment and recreation, and

(3) a proportionate share of the expenses incurred in supporting the whole household that cannot be directly attributed to each individual, such as food.[50]

Item (3) does not include items that represent the cost of maintaining a house, such as heat, electricity, repairs, taxes, etc., because these costs are accounted for in the fair rental value of the lodging furnished the dependent. Medical care includes the premiums paid on a medical care policy, but not the benefits provided by the policy. Medicare benefits, both basic and supplementary, as well as Medicaid,[51] are also disregarded in determining support.[52]

Some capital expenditures qualify as items of support, such as the cost of an automobile purchased for a "qualifying relative" dependent and the cost of furniture and appliances provided to the "qualifying relative" dependent.[53] However, the following have been held or ruled not to be items of support:

(1) income and social security taxes paid by a dependent child from his own income,

(2) funeral expenses of a "qualifying relative" dependent,

(3) costs incurred by a parent in exercising visitation rights, and

(4) life insurance premium costs.[54]

Footnote references are to paragraphs of the 2008 Standard Federal Tax Reports.

[47] ¶ 8000
[48] ¶ 8008
[49] ¶ 8100
[50] ¶ 8005.54, ¶ 8005.80
[51] ¶ 8005.80
[52] ¶ 8005.80
[53] ¶ 8005.80
[54] ¶ 8005.38, ¶ 8005.80

In determining whether a taxpayer furnished more than one-half of a "qualifying relative" dependent's total support, the support provided by the taxpayer, by the dependent, and by third parties must be taken into account.[55] In addition, only the amount of the cash actually expended for items of support is taken into account. However, the source and tax status of money used to provide support is, generally, not controlling. It may come from taxable income, tax-exempt receipts, and loans. Furthermore, the year in which the support is received, and not the year of payment of the indebtedness incurred, is controlling in determining whether over one-half of the support is furnished by the taxpayer, regardless of his method of tax accounting.[56]

In the case of the taxpayer's child (as defined at ¶ 137) or stepchild who is a student, any amounts received as scholarships (including the value of accommodations furnished to a student nurse)[57] do not have to be taken into account (Reg. § 1.152-1(c)).[58] Educational benefits received under the U.S. Navy's educational assistance program are not considered to be scholarships.[59]

Survivor and old-age insurance benefits received under the Social Security Act and used for support are considered as having been contributed by the recipient to his own support.[60] Benefit payments made to an individual under state public assistance laws and measured solely by the needs of the recipient are considered as having been used entirely by that individual for his own support unless it is shown otherwise.[61] Amounts expended by a state for the training and education of handicapped children (including mentally retarded children who qualify as "students" and are in a state institution that qualifies as an "educational institution") are not considered to constitute support, except where the state assumes custody of the child involved.[62] Aid to Families with Dependent Children (AFDC) payments are considered support by the state and not by the parent.[63]

"Qualifying Child" Support. The issue of support shifts from whether the taxpayer contributed more than one-half of the support of the child to the child contributing more than one-half of his or her own support (Code Sec. 152(c)(1)) (see ¶ 143).

149. Effect of Death on Exemption. The $3,400 exemption amount for 2007 (to increase to $3,500 in 2008) is not reduced because of the death of a taxpayer, his spouse, or a dependent during the tax year.[64]

> **Example 1:** A child is born on December 31, 2007, and dies in January 2008. A full exemption is allowed for the child in both years.

The death of one spouse will *not* deprive the survivor of the right to claim the exemptions of the deceased. The crucial date for determining marital status is the last day of the tax year; however, where a spouse dies during the tax year, such determination is made as of the date of death (Code Sec. 7703(a)).[65]

On the final separate return of a decedent, in addition to the deceased's own exemptions, the exemptions for the surviving spouse may be taken if the survivor had no gross income and was not a dependent of anyone else. Further, since the dependency exemption is based upon furnishing over half the support during the calendar year in which the tax year of the taxpayer begins, a decedent who furnished over half the support to a person otherwise qualifying as a dependent would be entitled to the full exemption for such dependent, without proration.

> **Example 2:** Allen furnishes the full support for his aged father up to the date of Allen's death on September 1, 2007, and over one-half of the total support for the year. A $3,400 exemption is allowed for the father on Allen's final return. But if Allen died on April 1 and his brother, Bob, supported the father for the balance of the year, incurring a larger expense than Allen did during the first part of the year, Bob alone would be entitled to the exemption. If the support in the latter case was

---

Footnote references are to paragraphs of the 2008 Standard Federal Tax Reports.

[55] ¶ 8005.045
[56] ¶ 8005.81
[57] ¶ 8005.62
[58] ¶ 8008

[59] ¶ 8005.62
[60] ¶ 8005.71
[61] ¶ 8005.60
[62] ¶ 8005.72

[63] ¶ 8005.60
[64] ¶ 8005.055, ¶ 8008
[65] ¶ 43,170

furnished equally by Bob and another brother, Carl, from April 1 on, and if none of the three brothers furnished over half of the father's support for the calendar year, any one of them (including the executor of Allen's estate, on Allen's final return) could take the exemption if the other two renounced their right to the exemption for that year (¶ 147). Regardless of the amount of support, no exemption is allowed to any of the three brothers for their father if the father has gross income of $3,400 or more during calendar year 2007.

150. Missing and/or Kidnapped Children. A dependency exemption may be claimed for any child of the taxpayer, regardless of whether they qualify as a "qualifying child" or "qualifying relative," if the child is presumed by a law enforcement agency to have been kidnapped by someone other than a member of the family and had resided at the taxpayer's principal place of abode for more than one-half of the year before the kidnapping (Code Sec. 152(f)(6)).

Joint Return

152. Who May File. A husband and wife may file a joint return even though one spouse has no income or deductions (Reg. § 1.6013-1),[66] but only if:

>   (1) their tax years begin on the same date,

>   (2) they are not legally separated under a decree of divorce or separate maintenance on the last day of the tax year, and

>   (3) neither is a nonresident alien at any time during the year.

However, a U.S. citizen or resident and his or her nonresident alien spouse can elect to file a joint return if they agree to be taxed on their worldwide income and supply all necessary books and records and other information pertinent to the determination of tax liability (Code Sec. 6013(g)).[67] Further, a one-time election to file a joint return is available in the year in which a nonresident alien spouse becomes a resident (Code Sec. 6013(h)).[68]

If a husband and wife are on a calendar-year basis or have fiscal years that begin on the same date, they can file a joint return. If, however, they have different tax years, for some reason other than the intervention of death (see ¶ 164), then they cannot file a joint return. If newly married spouses with different tax years want to change the year of one spouse to coincide with that of the other so as to be able to file jointly, they may do so by following the rules described at ¶ 1513.

A husband and wife may file a joint return even though they have different accounting methods (e.g., where one is on the cash basis and the other is on the accrual basis) if such methods clearly reflect their income.

Even though a husband and wife are not living together on the last day of the tax year, they may still file a joint return if they are *not* legally separated under a decree of divorce or separate maintenance on that date (Reg. § 1.6013-4).[69] Spouses who are separated under an interlocutory decree of divorce are considered husband and wife and are entitled to file a joint return until the decree becomes final.[70] But certain married individuals living apart may file separate returns as heads of households (see ¶ 173) (Code Sec. 2(c) and Code Sec. 7703(b)).[71]

Spouses of military personnel serving in a combat zone and missing in action may file a joint return for any tax year beginning before the date that is two years after the termination of combat activities in that zone (Code Sec. 6013(f)).

154. Election to File Joint Return. There can be a change of election from a separate return or returns to a joint return. Generally, this change of election is achieved by the filing of a Form 1040X within three years of the last date prescribed by law for the filing of the separate return or returns, without taking into account any extension of time

---

Footnote references are to paragraphs of the 2008 Standard Federal Tax Reports.

[66] ¶ 35,161
[67] ¶ 35,160
[68] ¶ 35,160
[69] ¶ 35,165
[70] ¶ 35,165, ¶ 35,171.39
[71] ¶ 3310, ¶ 43,170

granted to either spouse (Code Sec. 6013(b)(2)).[72] Additionally, the change to a joint return cannot be made:

(1) after either spouse timely files a petition with the Tax Court pursuant to a notice of deficiency which was mailed to either spouse for the tax year;

(2) after either spouse commences a suit in any court for the recovery of any part of the tax for such tax year;

(3) after either spouse enters into a closing agreement with respect to such tax year; or

(4) after either spouse has compromised any civil or criminal case arising with respect to such tax year.

Once a joint return has been filed for a tax year, the spouses may not thereafter file separate returns after the time for filing the return of either spouse has expired (Reg. § 1.6013-1(a)).[73] The exception being if either spouse dies during the tax year, then only the executor or administrator of the estate of the deceased spouse may elect to change from a separate to a joint return (see also ¶ 168).

However, the Tax Court has ruled that a couple could elect to file a joint return even though the IRS had previously prepared and filed returns for the husband with a status of married filing separately (*J.V. Millsap*, 91 TC 926 (1988)).[74] The IRS's filing of substitute returns did not bar the taxpayer from contesting either the deficiency or the IRS's choice of his filing status. The former standard, i.e., that the IRS's choice precludes taxpayers from selecting a different filing status (*R.E. Smalldridge*, 86-2 USTC ¶ 9764 (1986)),[75] will be applied only when the issue is appealable to the U.S. Court of Appeals for the Tenth Circuit.

156. Joint v. Separate Return. The gross income and deductions of a husband and wife are aggregated on a joint return. Deductions that are limited to a percentage of the adjusted gross income (e.g., medical expenses) are computed on combined adjusted gross income. Similarly, losses of a husband and wife from sales or exchanges of capital assets are combined. The "taxable income" (¶ 126) on a joint return, for this purpose, is the entire taxable income. Although there are two taxpayers on a joint return, there is only one taxable income and only one adjusted gross income amount (Reg. § 1.6013-4).[76] The total exemptions of a husband and wife are subtracted in determining taxable income.

The filing of a joint return will result in a savings of tax in those instances in which differences in the tax rate brackets for joint and separate returns result in higher tax rates for married individuals filing separately.

> **Example:** For 2007, Joe has taxable income in the amount of $14,500, and his wife, Trisha, has taxable income in the amount of $32,000. If they elect to file a joint return, they will not be subject to the 25% tax rate because their combined taxable income of $46,500 does not exceed $63,700 (see ¶ 13). However, if they opt to file separate returns, $150, which represents the portion of Trisha's income that exceeds $31,850, falls within the 25% tax bracket (see ¶ 15).

Similarly, it might be advantageous to file jointly if a couple's tax situation triggers alternative minimum tax liability. Both the greater exemption amount available to joint filers ($45,000 as opposed to $22,500) and the higher phaseout of exemption amount ($150,000 compared to $75,000) allow couples filing jointly to shelter a larger amount of preference income from the tax (see ¶ 1405).[77]

Also, if only one spouse has income, it would be impractical for the income earner to use married filing separately status. This filing status carries a basic standard deduction of $5,350, whereas joint filers have a basic standard deduction of $10,700 in 2007 (see ¶ 126). It should be noted that a married person generally may *not* claim the credit for:

Footnote references are to paragraphs of the 2008 Standard Federal Tax Reports.

[72] ¶ 35,160	[74] ¶ 35,171.026, ¶ 35,171.687	[76] ¶ 35,165
[73] ¶ 35,161	[75] ¶ 35,171.026, ¶ 35,171.687	[77] ¶ 5100

(1) the elderly or permanently disabled (¶ 1304),

(2) the child and dependent care credit (

(3) the earned income credit (¶ 1375), or

(4) the educational credits (¶ 1303)

unless he/she and his/her spouse file a joint return.

There are circumstances under which married taxpayers might reduce their tax liability by filing separate returns. For example, a spouse whose medical expenses are high, but not high enough to exceed 7.5 percent of the adjusted gross income reported on a joint return, may exceed the AGI threshold on a separate return (see ¶ 1015). In light of the 2-percent-of-AGI floor on miscellaneous itemized deductions (see ¶ 1011), a spouse who incurs substantial unreimbursed employee business or investment expenses might be better off filing separately. The same rationale holds true for casualty and disaster loss deductions, which are subject to a 10-percent-of-AGI floor (see ¶ 1137).

Actual tax comparisons should be made using both joint and separate returns if there is doubt as to which method produces more favorable results. Considerations other than tax savings might enter into the decision to file a separate, rather than a joint, return. For example, one spouse may wish to avoid a deficiency liability assessed against the other spouse (see ¶ 162).

Marriage Penalty Relief. The size of the 15-percent rate bracket for joint returns has been increased to twice the size of the corresponding rate bracket for single returns (Code Sec. 1(f)(8)). The upper limit of the 15-percent tax bracket for married taxpayers filing separately is 50 percent of the upper limit of the 15-percent tax bracket of a joint filer and mirrors the 15-percent bracket for single filers during this same period (see ¶ 126). This marriage penalty relief is subject to the sunset provisions of the Economic Growth and Tax Relief Reconciliation Act of 2001 (EGTRRA) (P.L. 108-27) and, barring Congressional action, will expire for tax years after December 31, 2011.

162. Liability on Joint Return. A husband and wife are generally liable jointly and individually for the entire tax on a joint return. However, relief from this general rule is available under certain circumstances, commonly referred to as "innocent spouse relief." One must elect the form of relief being sought on Form 8857, Request for Innocent Spouse Relief (and Separation of Liability and Equitable Relief), within two years of the IRS beginning collection of a tax deficiency or assessment.

The types of relief available to the electing spouse are:

(1) innocent spouse,

(2) separation of liability, or

(3) equitable relief.

Any determination by the IRS is reviewable in Tax Court.[78] Notice of the election for relief is required to be given to the non-electing spouse who may participate in any hearings on the relief requested.[79] The Tax Court has held that the non-electing spouse has the right to a "stand-alone" hearing regarding the appropriateness of granting relief to the electing spouse (*T. Corson*, 114 TC 354 (2000) and *K.A. King*, 115 TC 118 (2000)).[80] Recently the appellate courts have limited the jurisdiction of the Tax Court with regard to innocent spouse relief. The Tax Court has no jurisdiction to make a innocent spouse relief determination unless the IRS has issued a deficiency notice to the taxpayer (*G.A. Ewing*, CA-9, 2006-1 USTC ¶ 50,191; *T.E. Bartman*, CA-8, 2006-1 USTC ¶ 50,298). There are additional requirements for jurisdictions located in community property states.[81]

To qualify for the innocent spouse relief election, the taxpayer must meet *all* the following requirements:

Footnote references are to paragraphs of the 2008 Standard Federal Tax Reports.

[78] ¶ 35,192.028
[79] ¶ 35,192.027
[80] ¶ 35,192.77
[81] ¶ 35,192.021, ¶ 35,192.024

(1) have filed a joint return which has an *understatement of tax* due to *erroneous items* of the spouse,

(2) establish that at the time of signing the tax return the taxpayer did not know, or have reason to know, there was an understatement of tax, and

(3) taking into account all the facts and circumstances, show that it would be unfair to hold the innocent spouse liable for the understatement of tax.[82]

A key element for the IRS will be whether the electing spouse received any substantial benefits or later was divorced or separated from, or deserted by, the other spouse.

The "innocent spouse" may elect to obtain relief by separation of liabilities.[83] To qualify, an individual must have:

(1) filed a joint return and

(2) either (a) be no longer married to, or be legally separated from, the spouse with whom the joint return was filed or (b) must *not* have been a member of the same household with the spouse for a 12-month period ending on the date of the filing of Form 8857.

The burden of proof on income and deductions is on the taxpayer who elects relief under separation of liability.

Finally, should one fail to qualify for either of the first two types of relief, one may still obtain relief from the tax liabilities, interest and penalties by electing equitable relief.[84] The taxpayer must show that, under *all* facts and circumstances, it would be unfair to be held liable for the understatement or underpayment of taxes. One should note that under equitable relief, the "innocent spouse" can receive relief from tax liabilities caused by underpayment of taxes (Code Sec. 6015; IRS Pubs. 555 and 971).

163. Injured Spouse Claim. When married taxpayers file a joint return and one spouse has not paid child or spousal support or certain federal debts, such as student loans, all or part of the tax overpayment shown on the delinquent spouse's return may be used to satisfy the past-due debt. However, the nonobligated spouse may be entitled to a refund of his or her part of the overpayment if that individual:

(1) is not required to pay the past-due amount,

(2) received and reported income, such as wages, taxable interest, etc., on the joint return, and

(3) made and reported payments, such as withheld federal income taxes or estimated taxes, on the joint return.

To make this type of claim, the nonobligated spouse must write "Injured Spouse" in the upper left corner of Form 1040 and attach Form 8379, Injured Spouse Claim and Allocation. If the joint return has already been filed for 2007 or prior years, the nonobligated spouse should file Form 8379 by itself to claim the refund.

164. Effect of Death on Joint Return. A joint return may be filed when one or both spouses died during the year, and the tax year of both began on the same day, whether such year is a fiscal or calendar year. When a joint return is filed, it is treated as if the tax years of both spouses ended on the closing date of the surviving spouse's tax year (Reg. § 1.6013-3).[85]

166. When Surviving Spouse May Not File Joint Return. A joint return may not be filed in the year a spouse dies if the surviving spouse has remarried before the close of the tax year. However, the survivor may file a joint return with the new spouse if all other requirements are met. Also, the survivor may not file a joint return with the deceased spouse if the tax year of either spouse is a fractional part of a year resulting from a change of accounting period (Reg. § 1.6013-1(d)).[86]

Footnote references are to paragraphs of the 2008 Standard Federal Tax Reports.

[82] ¶ 35,192.073
[83] ¶ 35,192.35
[84] ¶ 35,192.023
[85] ¶ 35,164
[86] ¶ 35,161

Example: Stan and Tracy file joint returns on a calendar-year basis. Tracy dies on March 1, 2007. Thereafter, Stan receives permission to change his accounting period to a fiscal year beginning July 1, 2007. A joint return cannot be filed for the short tax year ending June 30, 2007.

168. Who Files the Return for a Deceased Spouse. Generally, where one spouse dies, a joint return can be filed only by the executor/administrator and the survivor. The surviving spouse, alone, however, may file a joint return if:

(1) no return was filed by the decedent for the tax year at issue;

(2) no executor or administrator was appointed; and

(3) no executor or administrator was appointed before the last day for filing the return of the surviving spouse, including any extensions of time for filing.

Even if all of the above tests are met, an administrator or executor, subsequently appointed, may disaffirm a joint return made by the surviving spouse by filing a separate return for the decedent. This disaffirmance must be made within one year after the last day allowed for filing the return of the surviving spouse (including extensions). If a disaffirmance is made, then the already filed joint return will be considered the survivor's separate return. The survivor's tax will be figured on the basis of this joint return, with all of the items properly includible in the return of the deceased spouse deleted from the joint return (Reg. § 1.6013-1(d)).[87]

Head of a Household

171. Special Tax Table. A portion of the benefits that the more favorable tax rates bestow upon a married couple filing a joint return are given to an unmarried individual who qualifies as the "head of a household." See Tax Rate Schedule Z (¶ 17) or the Tax Computation Worksheet (¶ 20) and the "Head of a Household" column in the Tax Table (¶ 25). See ¶ 128 and ¶ 130 for determining whether the schedule/worksheet or the table is used.

173. Who Is a Head of Household. In order to qualify for head of household status, a taxpayer must not be married or a surviving spouse (¶ 175) at the close of the tax year. In addition, the taxpayer must maintain as his home a household which, for more than one-half of the tax year, is the principal place of abode of one of the following who is a member of such household:

(1) a qualifying child of the taxpayer as defined in Code Sec. 152(c), determined without regard to the rules for divorced parents under Code Sec. 152(e). However, if the child is married at the close of the taxpayer's tax year, files a joint return with their spouse, or is not a citizen or national of the United States or a resident of the United States or a contiguous country, the taxpayer may not claim head of household filing status. For purposes of this requirement, an adopted child or a foster child, as defined in Code Sec. 152(f), shall be treated as the taxpayer's child by blood; or

(2) any other person who is a dependent of the taxpayer if, under Code Sec. 151, they are entitled to claim that person as a dependency deduction.[88] However, a taxpayer cannot claim head-of-household if the only reason for being able to claim an individual as a dependent is based on either Code Sec. 152(d)(2)(H), living as a member of the taxpayer's household for the full year, or Code Sec. 152(d)(3), claiming the dependency exemption under a multiple support agreement (Code Sec. 2(b)(3)).

Additionally, an individual qualifies for head of household status if a *separate* household is maintained, for the tax year, for a parent. The separate household must be the parent's principal place of abode, and the parent must qualify as the child's dependent (see ¶ 137—¶ 137B). A parent's principal place of abode can include residence in a rest home or home for the aged. An institutionalized or hospitalized

---

Footnote references are to paragraphs of the 2008 Standard Federal Tax Reports.

[87] ¶ 35,161   [88] ¶ 3340.12

dependent, other than a parent, may also qualify a taxpayer as head of a household if the taxpayer can prove that the taxpayer's home was the "principal" place of abode of the dependent, even though the dependent may never return home because of the nature of the infirmity.[89]

The marital status of an individual for the purpose of applying the "head of household" rates is determined at the end of a tax year. A taxpayer is considered to be unmarried at the end of a tax year if his spouse was a nonresident alien at any time during the tax year or if he is legally separated from his spouse under a decree of divorce or separate maintenance at the close of the tax year. A taxpayer under an interlocutory decree of divorce is not legally separated.[90] A widow or widower may not use the "head of household" rates in those tax years in which he or she is eligible to use the joint tax rates under the "surviving spouse" rules discussed at ¶ 175.

A married taxpayer will be considered unmarried and eligible for head of household status if the taxpayer's spouse was not a member of the household for the last six months of the year and if the household is the principal place of abode of a child for whom the taxpayer is entitled to a dependency exemption under Code Sec. 151.[91] However, the taxpayer will still be eligible for head-of-household status even if no dependency exemption is available for a child because the taxpayer waived the exemption or because of the existence of a pre-1985 divorce decree or separation agreement (¶ 139).[92]

An individual "maintains a household" only if the individual furnishes (with funds the source of which are attributable to the taxpayer) more than one-half the cost of maintaining the home during the tax year and if at least one of the persons described in (1) and (2) above (with an exception for institutionalized or hospitalized dependents) lives there for more than one-half of the year (except for temporary absence, such as time spent at school). Birth or death of such a person during the year will not disqualify the taxpayer as the head of a household if the person lived in the household for the part of the year during which he was alive (Reg. § 1.2-2(c)).[93]

The cost of maintaining a household includes the expenses incurred for the mutual benefit of the occupants by reason of its use as the principal place of abode. These expenses include property taxes, mortgage interest, rent, utility charges, upkeep and repairs, property insurance, food consumed on the premises, and other household expenses. They do not include the cost of clothing, education, medical treatment, vacations, life insurance, transportation, food consumed off the premises, or the value of services rendered by the taxpayer or by any person who qualifies the taxpayer as head of a household (Reg. § 1.2-2(d)).[94]

Qualifying Widow(er) (Surviving Spouse)

175. Surviving Spouse. A surviving spouse may use the joint return tax rates for two tax years following the year of death of the husband or wife, but *only* if the survivor remains unmarried and maintains as a home a household (see ¶ 173) that, for the entire tax year, is the principal place of abode of a son or daughter, adopted child, foster child, or stepchild who is a member of the surviving spouse's household and for whom the taxpayer is entitled to the dependency exemption (¶ 137) (Code Sec. 2(a)).[95] As to joint returns for the year of death, see ¶ 164.

A widow or widower who qualifies as a "surviving spouse" uses the joint return rate schedule (Schedule Y-1) at ¶ 13, the Tax Computation Worksheet at ¶ 20 or the Tax Table at ¶ 25 and must use either Form 1040 or Form 1040A. This benefit is afforded a surviving spouse only if he or she was entitled to file a joint return with the deceased spouse during the latter's lifetime.

Footnote references are to paragraphs of the 2008 Standard Federal Tax Reports.

[89] ¶ 3340.16
[90] ¶ 3340.03, ¶ 3340.17
[91] ¶ 3335.01, ¶ 8007

[92] ¶ 3335.01, ¶ 8007
[93] ¶ 3325
[94] ¶ 3325

[95] ¶ 3310

It should be emphasized that the benefit entitles the survivor only to the joint return *tax rates;* it does not authorize him or her to file a joint return or claim any personal exemptions other than his or her own and those of the dependent or dependents for whom the household is maintained.

For 2007, a qualifying widow(er) (surviving spouse) with dependent children is generally entitled to joint return rate benefits if the spouse died at any time during 2005 or 2006.

In determining eligibility for filing as a surviving spouse (qualifying widow(er)), the date of death of a person serving in a combat zone and missing in action is considered to be two years after the termination of combat activities in that zone (Code Sec. 2(a)(3)), unless death has been established at an earlier time.

Tax Treatment of Decedent's Final Return

178. Who Must File for a Decedent. A taxpayer's tax year ends on the date of his or her death.[96] The final return of a decedent for the part of the year up to and including the date of death[97] is filed on Form 1040, 1040A, or 1040EZ. A return is required if the decedent met the gross income filing test (¶ 109) for the short period. A return must also be made for the decedent if earnings from self-employment amounted to $400 or more or if the decedent is owed a refund. See ¶ 2664—¶ 2676.

The return for the decedent must be filed by his administrator, executor, or any other person charged with responsibility for the decedent's affairs (see ¶ 168). Whoever files the return for the decedent may file a separate return or a joint return (¶ 164— ¶ 168). All personal exemptions to which the decedent was entitled while he was alive may be claimed. If a refund is due, Form 1310, Statement of Person Claiming Refund Due a Deceased Taxpayer, is to be attached to the return.

180. Due Date. The final return of a decedent is due by the date on which the return would have been due had death not occurred (see ¶ 118). Thus, for a calendar-year taxpayer who died in 2007, the final return is due by April 15, 2008 (Reg. § 1.6072-1(a)).[98]

182. How Income Is Treated. When a cash-basis taxpayer dies, only income actually or constructively received up to the date of death is included in the final return. If the decedent was on the accrual basis, income accrued up to the date of death is included in the final return. However, income that accrues *only because of death* is not included (Code Sec. 451; Reg. § 1.451-1(b)).[99] These rules also apply to successive decedents as to rights to receive "income in respect of a prior decedent" (Reg. § 1.691(a)-1(c)).[100]

Any amount of gross income not reported on the return of the decedent is, when received, includible in the income of the person receiving such amounts by inheritance or survivorship. This may be the decedent's estate. Or, if the estate does not collect an item of income but distributes the right to receive it to a testamentary trust or to the heir, next of kin, legatee, or devisee, it is included in the income of such trust, heir, next of kin, legatee, or devisee (Code Sec. 691(a); Reg. § 1.691(a)-2).[101]

The depreciation recapture rules under Code Sec. 1245 and Code Sec. 1250 (see ¶ 1779—¶ 1795) apply to sales or other dispositions of property subject to those rules where the income therefrom is treated as income on the decedent's final return or as income in respect of a decedent under Code Sec. 691. But these rules do not apply to transfers of depreciable property at death (Code Sec. 1245(b)(2) and Code Sec. 1250(d)(2)).[102]

184. Installment Obligation. Collections on an installment obligation acquired from a decedent are treated as items of income in respect of a decedent if the decedent

---

Footnote references are to paragraphs of the 2008 Standard Federal Tax Reports.

[96] ¶ 21,817.03	[99] ¶ 21,002, ¶ 21,003	[102] ¶ 30,902, ¶ 31,000
[97] ¶ 20,501	[100] ¶ 24,901	
[98] ¶ 36,721	[101] ¶ 24,900, ¶ 24,902	

¶184

had been reporting the profit on the installment basis (Code Sec. 691(a)(4); Reg. § 1.691(a)-5).[103]

If, however, the obligor of the installment obligation acquires the uncollected obligation, then the decedent's estate is considered to have made a taxable disposition of the installment obligation. Thus, any previously unreported gain will be recognized by the estate. This rule also applies if the obligation is canceled because of the death of the payee or if the estate allows the obligation to become unenforceable because it is canceled by the executor.[104]

187. Deductions. Deductible expenses and other items are not accrued on the final return of a decedent (unless his accounting method requires it) but are deductible instead by the estate or person who pays them or is liable for their payment (Code Sec. 461; Reg. § 1.461-1(b)).[105] Similar treatment is given the foreign tax credit (Code Sec. 691(b); Reg. § 1.691(b)-1).[106]

Expenses for medical care of the decedent, paid out of his estate within one year from the date of his death, are deductible on the decedent's final return (Reg. § 1.213-1(d)). However, the estate must attach a statement (in duplicate) to the decedent's return waiving the right to claim the deduction on the estate tax return.[107]

Business expenses, income-producing expenses, interest, and taxes for which the decedent was liable but which were not properly allowable as a deduction on his last return will be allowed when paid (a) as a deduction by the estate or (b) if the estate was not liable, then as a deduction by the person who by reason of the decedent's death acquires—subject to such obligation—an interest in property of the decedent (Reg. § 1.691(b)-1(a)).[108]

The percentage depletion deduction is allowed only to the person who receives the income in respect of the decedent to which the deduction relates (Reg. § 1.691(b)-1(b)).[109]

189. How Recipient Treats Decedent's Income. A decedent's income that is to be accounted for by the recipient retains the same character it would have had in the hands of the decedent (Code Sec. 691(a)(3); Reg. § 1.691(a)-3).[110] Thus, if the income would have been earned income, exempt income, or interest to the decedent, it is the same kind of income to the recipient.

191. Deduction of Death Taxes. If a person includes in gross income an item of income that had accrued as of the date of death of a decedent or prior successive decedents, so that it was included in the valuation of the estate for estate tax purposes, that person may take a corresponding deduction based on the estate tax attributable to the net value of the income item (Code Sec. 691(c); Reg. § 1.691(c)-1).[111] This deduction is taken by individuals on Form 1040 and by estates and trusts on Form 1041. In the case of individuals, it may be taken only if deductions are itemized on Schedule A.[112] For individuals, as well as for estates and trusts, the deduction is not subject to the two-percent-of-AGI floor on miscellaneous deductions (Code Sec. 67(b)(7)).[113]

In the case of any generation-skipping transfer tax imposed on a taxable termination or a direct skip as a result of the death of the transferor, a deduction is available for the portion of such tax attributable to items of gross income that were not properly includible in the gross income of the trust before the date of such termination (Code Sec. 691(c)(3)).[114]

Footnote references are to paragraphs of the 2008 Standard Federal Tax Reports.

[103] ¶ 24,900, ¶ 24,905
[104] ¶ 24,900, ¶ 24,906.29
[105] ¶ 21,802, ¶ 21,805
[106] ¶ 24,900, ¶ 24,907
[107] ¶ 12,541
[108] ¶ 24,907
[109] ¶ 24,907
[110] ¶ 24,900, ¶ 24,903
[111] ¶ 24,900, ¶ 24,909
[112] ¶ 24,911.11
[113] ¶ 6060, ¶ 24,911.025
[114] ¶ 24,900

Chapter 2

CORPORATIONS

Organizations Taxed as Corporations

201. How Organizations Are Taxed. A corporation, like any business entity, is formed by one or more persons to conduct a business venture and divide profits among investors (Reg. § 301.7701-2).[1] A corporation files a charter or articles of incorporation in a state, in a U.S. possession, with a foreign government or (in certain cases) with the U.S. government. It prepares by-laws, has its business affairs overseen by a board of directors, and issues stock. Under the "check-the-box" regulations, entities formed under a corporation statute are automatically classified as corporations and may not elect to be treated as any other kind of entity (Reg. § 301.7701-2, Reg. § 301.7701-3(a)).[2] Further, other entities are allowed to elect corporate status on Form 8832, Entity Classification Election. Thus, an entity that is a partnership or limited liability company under the laws of the state in which it is formed may elect to be taxed as a C corporation or an S corporation under the Code (Reg. § 301.7701-3).[3] However, an entity organized under a state's corporation statute cannot elect to be taxed as a partnership. Partnerships that are publicly traded are taxed as corporations unless 90 percent or more of the gross income consists of qualifying passive-type income (Code Sec. 7704; Reg. §§ 1.7704-1 and 1.7704-3).[4]

For tax purposes, the predominant forms of business enterprises are C corporations, S corporations, partnerships, limited liability companies (LLCs), and sole proprietorships. To choose among these is to choose among significant differences in federal income tax treatment. Although many of the Code's provisions apply to all of these entities, some areas of the law are specially tailored for each type. The classification of an entity will have a lingering tax impact throughout the entity's existence.

Of the types of business organization, C corporations are subject to the toughest tax bite. Their earnings are taxed twice. First, a *corporate* income tax is imposed on its net earnings and then, after the earnings are distributed to shareholders as dividends, each shareholder must pay taxes separately on his or her share of the dividends (Code Secs. 11 and 301(c)).[5] Fortunately, there is some relief available for individual shareholders. Qualified dividend income received by an individual is taxed at the same rate as net long-term capital gain (Code Sec. 1(h)(11)).[6] A corporation can reduce, or even eliminate, its federal income tax liability by distributing its income as salary to shareholder-employees

Footnote references are to paragraphs of the 2008 Standard Federal Tax Reports.

[1] ¶ 43,082
[2] ¶ 43,082
[3] ¶ 43,083
[4] ¶ 43,180, ¶ 43,180B, ¶ 43,181D
[5] ¶ 3365, ¶ 15,302
[6] ¶ 3285.051

who actually perform valuable services for the corporation. Although this can reduce taxation at the corporate level, employees who receive payments from a corporation in exchange for services must nevertheless pay tax on the amount received, which is treated as salary (Code Sec. 162(a)(1)).[7]

This scheme of taxation differs radically from that applied to S corporations, partnerships, limited liability companies and sole proprietorships. These entities do not pay an entity-level tax on their earnings. There is no income tax on partnerships, or on limited liability companies treated as partnerships for federal tax purposes (Code Sec. 701).[8] Nor (in most cases) is there an S corporation income tax or sole proprietorship income tax (Code Sec. 1363; Reg. § 301.7701-2(a)).[9] Rather, the owners or members of these entities are taxed on their share of the entity's earnings.

For more on S corporations, see ¶ 301. Partnerships are discussed at ¶ 401, while LLCs are discussed at ¶ 402B. Foreign corporations are discussed at ¶ 2425. Sole proprietorships are discussed throughout this book as part of the material on individual income taxation. For the tax treatment of corporate distributions to the shareholders, see ¶ 733–¶ 757.

203. Tax-Free Contributions in Exchange for Stock. A corporation is formed by the transfer of money or property from shareholders to the corporate entity in return for corporate stock. If one or more shareholders transfer money or property to a corporation solely in exchange for stock of that corporation, and if the shareholders control the corporation immediately after the exchange, neither the shareholders nor the corporation recognizes any gain or loss (Code Secs. 351(a) and 1032).[10] To be considered in "control," the shareholders as a group must own, immediately after the exchange, (1) at least 80 percent of the total combined voting power of all classes of stock entitled to vote and (2) at least 80 percent of the total number of shares of all other classes of stock (Code Sec. 368(c)).[11] The exchanges need not actually be simultaneous to avoid the imputation of gain. Rather, the statute describes a situation where the rights of the parties have been previously defined and the execution of the agreement proceeds in an orderly manner (Reg. § 1.351-1(a)(1)).

Money or property transferred to a controlled corporation generally includes all property, tangible or intangible, with certain limitations. Stock issued for services, indebtedness of the corporation which is not evidenced by a security, or interest on indebtedness of the corporation which accrued on or after the beginning of the transferor's holding period for the debt are not considered as issued in return for property (Code Sec. 351(d)).[12]

Corporate shareholders can be individuals, estates, trusts, partnerships or other corporations (Reg. § 1.351-1(a)(1)).[13] However, the rules permitting tax-free transfers to a corporation in exchange for corporate stock do not apply if the transferee corporation is an investment company (Code Sec. 351(e)(1)).[14]

Generally, the tax-free organization of a business is not wholly negated if the transferor owners receive additional property along with the stock when they transfer property to the corporation. However, the owners are taxed on any additional property received ("boot"). Thus, gain is recognized, but only to the extent of the cash received, plus the fair market value of the other property received. No loss is recognized on the transfer (Code Sec. 351(b); Reg. § 1.351-2(a)).[15]

Assumption of Liabilities. If property transferred in what would otherwise be a Code Sec. 351 tax-free transaction is subject to liabilities, the acceptance of the transfer or the assumption of the liabilities does not prevent the transaction from being tax free.[16] This rule does not apply if the principal purpose of the transfer is tax avoidance or if liabilities assumed by the transferee exceed the transferor's basis in the property (Code Sec. 357).[17]

Footnote references are to paragraphs of the 2008 Standard Federal Tax Reports.

[7] ¶ 16,403	[11] ¶ 16,750	[15] ¶ 16,402, ¶ 16,404B
[8] ¶ 25,060	[12] ¶ 16,402	[16] ¶ 16,402
[9] ¶ 32,060	[13] ¶ 16,402	[17] ¶ 16,520
[10] ¶ 16,402, ¶ 29,622	[14] ¶ 16,402	

Bankruptcy. A debtor must recognize gain or loss upon its transfer of assets to a controlled corporation pursuant to a plan approved by a bankruptcy court (other than a reorganization plan) in which the stock is exchanged (Code Sec. 351(e)(2)).[18] Essentially, the transaction is treated as if the property had first been transferred to the creditors and then transferred by them to the controlled corporation. If less than all the stock is transferred to creditors, only a proportionate share of the gain or loss must be recognized. Both the basis of the stock and of the assets are adjusted for the gain or loss recognized on the transfer to the corporation. Note that this rule does not apply to a transfer by one corporation to another corporation in a bankruptcy case. Instead, such a transfer is considered a Code Sec. 368(a)(1)(G) reorganization and its tax consequences are determined accordingly.

Reporting Requirements. If a person receives stock of a corporation in exchange for property and no gain or loss is recognized, the person and the corporation must each attach to their tax returns a complete statement of all the facts pertinent to the exchange, including (Reg. § 1.351-3):[19]

(1) The name and employer identification number (if any) of the transferee corporation, or of every significant transferor, as applicable;

(2) The date(s) of the transfer(s) of assets;

(3) The aggregate fair market value and basis, determined immediately before the exchange, of the property transferred by such transferor, or received by the transferee, in the exchange; and

(4) The date and control number of any private letter ruling(s) issued by the Internal Revenue Service in connection with the section 351 exchange.

Return of Corporation and Payment of Taxes

211. Annual and Short-Period Returns. A corporation must file an income tax return even if it has no income or if no tax is due (Code Sec. 6012(a)(2)).[20] Form 1120, U.S. Corporation Income Tax Return, must be filed on or before the 15th day of the third month that follows the close of its tax year (Code Secs. 6012(a)(2) and 6072(b); Reg. §§ 1.6012-2 and 1.6072-2).[21] If the last day of a corporation's tax year does not end on the last day of a month (as in the case of a dissolved corporation whose tax year ends on the date of dissolution), the return is due on or before the 15th day of the third full month following the date of dissolution.

A shorter version of the form, Form 1120-A, U.S. Corporation Short-Form Income Tax Return, may be filed by a corporation that has gross receipts of less than $500,000, if all the following amounts are under $500,000: (1) gross receipts, (2) total income (includes dividends received, interest, rent, royalties, capital gains and certain other income), and (3) total assets from Form 1120, Schedule L, line 15. Further, all dividend income must come from domestic corporations, and the dividends must qualify for the 70-percent deduction and must not be from debt-financed securities (see ¶ 237). Also, the corporation must not be a member of a controlled group, a member of a personal holding company, filing a consolidated return, filing its final return, or dissolving or liquidating, and the corporation must not owe alternative minimum tax. The corporation must have no nonrefundable credits other than the general business credit. Finally, the corporation must not have any ownership in a foreign corporation or partnership, foreign shareholders owning more than 25 percent of the stock, or ownership in a foreign trust.

If the due date for filing a return falls on a Saturday, Sunday, or legal holiday, the return must be filed by the first following business day (Code Sec. 7503; see ¶ 2549).[22] Timely mailing generally is regarded as timely filing (Code Sec. 7502; see ¶ 2553).[23]

A corporation's tax year may be a calendar year or a fiscal year (Code Sec. 441(b)(1), (d), and (e)).[24] Its return may not cover a period of more than a year. In a

---

Footnote references are to paragraphs of the 2008 Standard Federal Tax Reports.

[18] ¶ 16,402
[19] ¶ 16,404C
[20] ¶ 35,142

[21] ¶ 35,142, ¶ 35,145, ¶ 36,720, ¶ 36,724
[22] ¶ 42,630

[23] ¶ 42,620
[24] ¶ 20,302

slight exception to this rule, a corporation may elect to use an annual filing period that fluctuates between 52 and 53 weeks (Code Sec. 441(f); see ¶ 1505).[25] A return may cover less than a year if a corporation was formed during the year or dissolved during the year (Code Sec. 443(a)(2); Reg. § 1.443-1(a)(2)).[26] For example, if a corporation elects the calendar year method but starts operations on August 1, it must report income from August 1 to December 31. If it dissolves on June 30, it must file a short-period return covering the period from January 1 to June 30. In addition to filing its regular income tax return, a corporation that has adopted a resolution to dissolve itself or liquidate all or part of its stock must file Form 966, Corporate Dissolution or Liquidation (Code Sec. 6043; Reg. § 1.6043-1).[27]

213. Accounting Methods. Generally, a corporation (other than a personal service corporation) must use the accrual method of accounting if its average annual gross receipts exceed an average of $5 million for the three tax years preceding the current tax year (Code Sec. 448(c)).[28] A corporation engaged in farming operations also must use the accrual method (Code Sec. 447) unless it has gross receipts of $1 million or less ($25 million for a family farming corporation).[29] Securities dealers must use the "mark-to-market" method of accounting (Code Sec. 475).[30]

214. Corporate Taxable Income. A corporation pays tax on its "taxable income" (Code Sec. 11).[31] Taxable income is the corporation's total income for the year (such as gross receipts, interest, rents and royalties) minus the corporation's deductions for the year (such as compensation and salaries paid, repairs, maintenance, rents paid, interest paid, depreciation, advertising and deductible amounts paid into pension and profit-sharing plans and other employee benefit programs). See the flowchart at ¶ 62 that outlines the determination of a corporation's taxable income.

215. Due Date for Taxes. The due date for the payment of a corporation's taxes is the same as the due date for the filing of a return (Code Sec. 6151).[32] However, corporations that anticipate a tax liability of $500 or more must estimate their taxes and make quarterly estimated tax payments (including estimated payments of the minimum tax) using Form 8109 (Code Sec. 6655(f) and (g)(1)(A)(ii); Reg. § 1.6302-1).[33] If the liability exceeds the total estimated payments, the corporation must pay the remaining amount by the due date of its return. Failure to pay estimated taxes may be penalized (see ¶ 225). For a discussion of an extension of time to file returns or to pay taxes, see ¶ 2509 and ¶ 2537.

Rate of Taxation

219. Graduated Tax Rates. Corporations are subject to the following tax rates on their taxable income (Code Secs. 11 and 1201):[34]

If taxable income is:						
Over—	But not over—	Tax is—				Of the amt. over—
$0	$50,000			15%		$0
50,000	75,000	$7,500	+	25%		50,000
75,000	100,000	13,750	+	34%		75,000
100,000	335,000	22,250	+	39%		100,000
335,000	10,000,000	113,900	+	34%		335,000
10,000,000	15,000,000	3,400,000	+	35%		10,000,000
15,000,000	18,333,333	5,150,000	+	38%		15,000,000
18,333,333	—			35%		0

Qualified Personal Service Corporations. The corporate graduated rates do not apply to qualified personal service corporations. Such corporations are instead taxed at a flat rate of 35 percent of taxable income. Qualified personal service corporations perform services in the fields of health, law, engineering, architecture, accounting (including the

---

Footnote references are to paragraphs of the 2008 Standard Federal Tax Reports.

[25] ¶ 20,302	[29] ¶ 20,700	[33] ¶ 38,061, ¶ 39,565
[26] ¶ 20,500, ¶ 20,501	[30] ¶ 22,265	[34] ¶ 3365, ¶ 30,352
[27] ¶ 35,880, ¶ 35,881	[31] ¶ 3365	
[28] ¶ 20,800	[32] ¶ 37,080	

¶213

preparation of tax returns), actuarial science, the performing arts, or consulting. Substantially all of the stock of a personal service corporation is held by employees, retired employees, or their estates (Code Secs. 11(b)(2) and 448(d)(2)).[35] See also ¶ 1575. For information on personal service corporations, see ¶ 273.

Foreign Corporations. Foreign corporations are taxed at regular U.S. corporate rates on most income that is effectively connected with a U.S. trade or business and at a flat 30-percent rate on U.S.-source fixed or determinable income that is not effectively connected (see ¶ 2425–¶ 2460). Tax treaties between the U.S. and foreign countries may provide for lower rates or exemptions from taxation.

220. Additional Taxes. In addition to the regular corporate income tax, the alternative minimum tax (AMT) may be imposed on a corporation having tax preference items. See ¶ 1401. Also, certain corporations used by their shareholders for the purpose of avoiding taxes might be subject to the accumulated earnings tax (¶ 251–¶ 271) or the personal holding company tax (¶ 275–¶ 287).

A corporation is treated as a "small corporation" exempt from the AMT if it is the corporation's first year or its average annual gross receipts for the three-tax-year period (or portion thereof) ending before its current tax year did not exceed $7.5 million (see ¶ 1401). The $7.5 million amount is reduced to $5 million for the corporation's first three-tax-year period (Code Sec. 55(e)).[36]

Estimated Tax

225. Penalty for Underpayment of Estimated Tax. A corporation that anticipates a tax bill of $500 or more must estimate its income tax liability for the current tax year and pay four quarterly estimated tax installments (with Form 8109) during that year (Code Sec. 6655).[37] Any underpayment of a required installment results in an addition to tax on the amount of the underpayment for the period of underpayment (Code Sec. 6655). The addition to tax is based on current interest rates (see ¶ 2838 and ¶ 2890).

The period of underpayment begins with the due date of the underpaid installment and ends with the earlier of (1) the date that the underpayment is satisfied or (2) the 15th day of the third month after the close of the tax year (Code Sec. 6655(b)).[38] Each estimated tax payment is credited against unpaid installments in the order in which they are required to be paid.

In determining the required amount of any installment (¶ 227), a corporation must take into account its regular corporate (or insurance company) income tax, the corporate alternative minimum tax (¶ 1401 and following), and the four-percent tax on gross transportation income of a foreign corporation (Code Sec. 887).[39] No addition to tax applies if the tax shown on the return (or the actual tax if no return is filed) is less than $500 (Code Sec. 6655).[40] If there is an underpayment, Form 2220 should be attached to the return to show whether the addition to tax applies and, if so, the amount of the penalty.

What is the Tax? The tax liabilities to which corporate estimated tax applies are the corporate income tax imposed by Code Sec. 11[41] or by the alternative minimum tax (Code Sec. 55(b)),[42] the environmental tax (Code Sec. 59A),[43] and the gross transportation income tax (Code Sec. 887).[44] For this purpose, the 30-percent tax on foreign corporations not connected with a U.S. business is considered a Code Sec. 11 tax (Code Sec. 6655(g)(1)).[45] The total expected tax liability is reduced by the sum of the credits against tax. Special rules apply for estimating the book income adjustment by corporations that use the annualization method to calculate estimated tax liability.

227. Time and Amount of Installment Payments. For calendar-year corporations, estimated tax installments are due on April 15, June 15, September 15, and December 15. Installments of fiscal-year corporations are due on the 15th day of the fourth, sixth,

---

Footnote references are to paragraphs of the 2008 Standard Federal Tax Reports.

[35] ¶ 3365
[36] ¶ 5100
[37] ¶ 39,565
[38] ¶ 39,565

[39] ¶ 27,580
[40] ¶ 39,565
[41] ¶ 3365
[42] ¶ 5100

[43] ¶ 5450
[44] ¶ 27,580
[45] ¶ 39,565

ninth, and twelfth months of the tax year (Code Sec. 6655).[46] If any due date falls on a Saturday, Sunday or legal holiday, the payment is due on the first following business day.

Corporations required to deposit taxes in excess of $200,000 must transfer their tax deposits electronically from their accounts to the IRS's general account (Reg. § 31.6302-1(h)(2)(ii)).[47] To avoid a penalty, each installment must equal at least 25 percent of the lesser of:

(1) 100 percent of the tax shown on the current year's tax return (or of the actual tax if no return is filed) or

(2) 100 percent of the tax shown on the corporation's return for the preceding tax year, provided a positive tax liability was shown and the preceding tax year consisted of 12 months (Code Sec. 6655(d))[48] (but see special limitation on "*Large Corporations,*" below).

A lower installment amount may be paid if it is shown that use of an annualized income method or, for corporations with seasonal incomes, an adjusted seasonal method would result in a lower required installment (see ¶ 229).

> **Example:** The X Corporation, a calendar-year taxpayer, estimates at the end of March 2007 that its federal income tax for 2007 would be $800,000. Accordingly, it pays $200,000 [25% of ($800,000 × 100%)] of estimated tax by April 17, 2007, and another $200,000 by June 15, 2007. At the end of August 2007, a recalculation shows that its 2007 tax is expected to be $1,000,000. Assuming that there is no later change in the estimated tax, the estimated tax installments for September and December are computed as follows:

Estimated tax required to be paid by 9/15/2007 [75% of ($1,000,000 × 100%)]	$750,000
Less payments made in April and June	400,000
Payment due in September	$350,000
Payment due in December [25% of ($1,000,000 × 100%)]	$250,000
Total estimated tax payments	$1,000,000

For all corporations, a certain percentage of estimated tax payments due in September of 2010 and 2011 is deferred. Specifically, 20.5 percent of the payment due in September, 2010, is deferred until October 1, 2010, while 27.5 percent of the payment due in September, 2011, is deferred until October 1, 2011 (Act Sec. 401 of the Tax Increase Prevention and Reconciliation Act of 2005 (P.L. 109-222)).

Large Corporations. A "large corporation"—one with taxable income of at least $1 million in any one of the three immediately preceding tax years—is prohibited from using its prior year's tax liability (method (2), above), *except* in determining the first installment of its tax year (Code Sec. 6655(d)(2) and (g)(2)).[49] Any reduction in a large corporation's first installment as a result of using the prior year's tax must be recaptured in the corporation's second installment. In applying the $1 million test, taxable income is computed without regard to net operating loss carryovers or capital loss carrybacks. Also, a controlled group of corporations (¶ 291) must divide a single $1 million amount among its members.

Corporations with $1 Billion in Assets. Corporations with more than $1 billion in assets are required to make larger (or smaller) estimated tax payments in certain months in 2006, 2012, and 2013. Specifically, such corporations must make payments that are 105 percent of the amount otherwise due in July, August, or September of 2006; 114.75 percent of the amount otherwise due in July, August, or September of 2012; and 100.75 percent of the amount otherwise due in July, August, or September of 2013. These payments are balanced out, in that the payments due in October, November, or December of 2006 are 95 percent of the amount otherwise due; those due in October, November, or December of 2012 are 85.25 percent of the amount otherwise due; and

---

Footnote references are to paragraphs of the 2008 Standard Federal Tax Reports.

[46] ¶ 39,565
[47] ¶ 38,055B
[48] ¶ 39,565
[49] ¶ 39,565

¶227

those due in October, November, or December of 2013 are 99.25 percent of the amount otherwise due (Act Sec. 401 of the Tax Increase Prevention and Reconciliation Act of 2005 (P.L. 109-222); Act Sec. 8248 of the Small Business and Work Opportunity Tax Act of 2007 (P.L. 110-28); Act Sec. 4 of the Andean Trade Preferences Act of 2007 (P.L. 110-42); Act Sec. 3 of the Burmese Freedom and Democracy Act of 2007 (P.L. 110-52)).

229. Annualization and Seasonal Income Methods. A corporation may compute any annualized income installment by computing its taxable income (including alternative minimum taxable income and modified alternative minimum taxable income) for the corresponding portion of the tax year on an annualized basis, computing the tax, and paying the following percentages of the tax after deducting all prior required installments for the tax year (Code Sec. 6655(e)(1)).[50] A corporation can choose between using the standard monthly periods or either of two optional monthly periods.

Installment	Standard Monthly Periods	Optional Monthly Periods #1	Optional Monthly Periods #2
1st	first 3 months	first 2 months	first 3 months
2nd	first 3 months	first 4 months	first 5 months
3rd	first 6 months	first 7 months	first 8 months
4th	first 9 months	first 10 months	first 11 months

An election to use either of the two optional monthly periods is effective only for the year of election. The election must be made on or before the date required for the first installment payment (Code Sec. 6655(e)(2)(C)(iii)).[51]

To annualize income, multiply the income for the applicable period by 12 and divide by the number of months in the period (Reg. §1.6655-3).[52] A corporation that uses the annualization method and switches to another method during the same tax year must, in its first installment under the new method, recapture 100 percent of any reduction achieved in the earlier installments (Code Sec. 6655(e)(1)).

Adjusted Seasonal Installments. Adjusted seasonal installments may be used only if, in each of the three preceding tax years, taxable income for the same six-month period averaged 70 percent or more of annual taxable income. An adjusted seasonal installment is the excess (if any) of (a) 100 percent of the amount determined by following the four steps set forth below over (b) the aggregate amount of all prior required installments for the tax year. The steps are as follows:

(1) take the taxable income for the portion of the tax year up to the month in which the installment is due (filing month);

(2) divide this amount by the "base period percentage" for such months;

(3) determine the tax on the result; and

(4) multiply the tax by the base period percentage for the filing month and all preceding months during the tax year.

For any period of months, the "base period percentage" is the average percentage that the taxable income for the corresponding months in each of the three preceding tax years bears to the taxable income for those years (Code Sec. 6655(e)(3)).[53]

231. Quick Refund for Estimated Tax Overpayment. A corporation may apply for an adjustment (i.e., a refund of an overpayment of estimated tax) immediately after the close of its tax year if its overpayment is at least 10 percent of the expected tax liability and amounts to at least $500. "Overpayment," for this purpose, is the excess of the estimated tax paid over what the corporation expects its final income tax liability to be at the time the application is filed. The application must be filed by the 15th day of the 3rd month after the close of the tax year and before the day on which the corporation files its income tax return for the tax year for which a quick refund is requested (Code Secs. 6425 and 6655(h); Reg. §§1.6425-1—1.6425-3).[54] Application must be made on Form 4466, Corporation Application for Quick Refund of Overpayment of Estimated Tax. An extension of time to file Form 1120 will not extend the time for filing Form 4466.

Footnote references are to paragraphs of the 2008 Standard Federal Tax Reports.

[50] ¶ 39,565
[51] ¶ 39,565
[52] ¶ 39,570
[53] ¶ 39,565
[54] ¶ 38,840—¶ 38,843, ¶ 39,565

Special Deductions for Corporations

235. Base to Which Rates Apply. The tax rates described in ¶ 219 are applied to taxable income. The term "taxable income" means the gross income of the corporation, minus deductions allowed by Code Sec. 1 through Code Sec. 1400T (Reg. § 1.11-1).[55] The principal items of corporation income include gross sales receipts, dividends and interest received, rent and royalty income, and capital gains. The common deductions for a corporation in computing its taxable income include compensation paid to officers and workers, expenses for repairs and maintenance of corporation property, taxes, licenses, interest paid, depreciation and depletion, advertising, and deductible amounts paid to pension and profit-sharing plans and employee benefit programs. In addition, a corporation may be entitled to the special deductions described below. See the flowchart at ¶ 62, which outlines the determination of a corporation's taxable income.

237. Dividends Received from Other Corporations. A corporation is entitled to a special deduction from gross income for dividends received from a domestic corporation that is subject to income tax (Code Sec. 243).[56] This deduction is: (1) 70 percent of dividends received from corporations owned less than 20 percent (by stock vote and value) by the recipient corporation; (2) 80 percent of dividends received from a "20-percent owned corporation," i.e., a corporation having at least 20 percent (but generally less than 80 percent) of its stock owned by the recipient corporation; (3) 100 percent of qualifying dividends received from members of the same affiliated group (generally, 80 percent or more common ownership) to which the recipient corporation belongs (¶ 239); and (4) 100 percent of dividends received by a small business investment company (¶ 2392). These rules also apply to dividends received from a foreign corporation that are paid out of the earnings and profits of a taxable domestic predecessor corporation (see ¶ 241).

The aggregate amount of dividends-received deductions that may be taken by a corporation is limited to 70 percent (80 percent in the case of 20-percent owned corporations) of its taxable income, computed without regard to any net operating loss deduction, dividends-received deduction, dividends-paid deduction in the case of public utilities, the deduction for the U.S.-source portion of dividends from 10-percent owned foreign corporations, the deduction for certain dividends received from wholly owned foreign subsidiaries, capital loss carryback, or adjustment for nontaxed portions of extraordinary dividends received. This limitation is applied first with respect to any 80 percent deductible dividends and then separately for 70 percent deductible dividends (after reducing taxable income by the 80 percent deductible dividends), but it does not apply for the year if the full deduction results in a net operating loss (Code Sec. 246(b)(2)).[57] Further, it does not apply in the case of small business investment companies.

The dividends-received deduction cannot be taken in computing the accumulated earnings tax (¶ 251) or the tax on personal holding companies (¶ 275). The deduction is allowed to a resident foreign corporation as well as to a domestic corporation. No deduction is allowed for dividends received from a corporation exempt from income tax (including an exempt farmers' cooperative) during the tax year or the preceding year (Code Sec. 246(a)).[58]

Holding Period. The dividends-received deduction is only allowed if the underlying stock is held for at least 46 days during the 91-day period beginning on the date 45 days before the ex-dividend date of the stock. If the stock is cumulative preferred stock with an arrearage of dividends, it must be held at least 91 days during the 181-day period beginning on the date 90 days before the ex-dividend date (Code Sec. 246(c)).[59]

The holding period is reduced for any period during which the taxpayer's risk of loss with respect to the stock is diminished because the taxpayer has (1) an option to sell, is under an obligation to sell, or has made (and not closed) a short sale of substantially identical stock or securities; (2) granted an option to purchase substantially

---

Footnote references are to paragraphs of the 2008 Standard Federal Tax Reports.

[55] ¶ 3370
[56] ¶ 13,051
[57] ¶ 13,200
[58] ¶ 13,200
[59] ¶ 13,200

¶235

identical stock or securities; or (3) reduced the risk by virtue of holding one or more other positions with respect to substantially similar or related property.

Debt-Financed Portfolio Stock. The dividends-received deduction is reduced for dividends received from debt-financed portfolio stock by a percentage related to the amount of debt incurred to purchase such stock. The deduction is calculated by multiplying the difference between 100 percent and the average portfolio indebtedness by 70 percent (80 percent in the case of 20-percent-owned corporations) (Code Sec. 246A).[60] However, any required reduction is limited to the amount of the interest deduction allocable to the related dividend (Code Sec. 246A(e)). This deduction does not apply to dividends that are eligible for 100-percent dividends-received deduction for (1) qualifying dividends received from a member of an affiliated group and (2) dividends received from a small business investment company.

Other Limitations. Capital gain dividends from a regulated investment company (mutual fund) or a real estate investment trust, and distributions that are a return of capital, do not qualify for the dividends-received deduction. Additionally, the dividends-received deduction is not allowed to the extent that the taxpayer is under an obligation (pursuant to a short sale or otherwise) to make related payments with respect to positions in substantially similar or related property (Code Sec. 246(c)(1)(B)).[61]

A corporation may take the dividends-received deduction for dividends on preferred stock of a public utility, unless the utility is entitled to a dividends-paid deduction under Code Sec. 247 (Reg. §1.243-2(d)).[62] In the latter event, the deduction is limited under Code Sec. 244.[63] No deduction is allowed with respect to a dividend received pursuant to distributions under Code Sec. 936(h)(4) (¶ 2419) made to qualify for the possessions tax credit (Code Sec. 246(e)).[64] See also ¶ 2487.

Extraordinary Dividends. If a dividend is deemed to be "extraordinary," a corporate taxpayer may be required to reduce its basis in the stock by the nontaxed portion of the dividend, i.e., the amount offset by the dividends-received deduction. This rule generally applies if the dividend exceeds 10 percent (5 percent in the case of preferred dividends) of (1) the taxpayer's adjusted basis in the stock or (2) the fair market value of the stock just before the ex-dividend date, and if the taxpayer has not held the stock for more than two years before the day the dividend is declared, agreed to, or announced. Generally, if the nontaxed portion of the dividend exceeds basis, gain must be recognized in the tax year in which the dividend is received instead of recognized upon the later sale or disposition of the stock. The Conference Committee Report to the IRS Restructuring and Reform Act of 1998 clarifies that, except as the IRS may provide in regulations, Code Sec. 1059 does not cause current gain recognition to the extent that the consolidated return regulations require the creation or increase of an excess loss account with respect to a distribution. Thus, Reg. §1.1059(e)-1(a)[65] does not result in gain recognition with respect to distributions within a consolidated group to the extent such distribution results in the creation or increase of an excess loss account under the consolidated return regulations.

238. Debt-Equity Rule. For instruments issued by corporations and advances made to corporations, a question can arise as to whether such instruments and advances are treated as a bona fide debt of the corporation or as an equity-stock interest in the corporation. If they are treated as a bona fide debt of the corporation, the corporation can deduct interest payments as a business expense, and the shareholders can receive principal payments as a tax-free return of capital. However, if they are treated as stock, the corporation cannot deduct distributions of the corporation's earnings and profits made with respect to such instruments (Code Sec. 385).[66]

The Code lists five factors that may be considered in making the debt-equity determination:

Footnote references are to paragraphs of the 2008 Standard Federal Tax Reports.

[60] ¶ 13,250	[63] ¶ 13,100	[66] ¶ 17,340
[61] ¶ 13,200	[64] ¶ 13,200	
[62] ¶ 13,053	[65] ¶ 30,020B	

(1) whether there is a written, unconditional promise to pay on demand or on a specified date a sum certain in money in return for an adequate consideration in money or money's worth, and to pay a fixed rate of interest,

(2) whether there is subordination to or preference over any indebtedness of the corporation,

(3) the ratio of debt to equity of the corporation,

(4) whether there is convertibility into the stock of the corporation, and

(5) the relationship between holdings of stock in the corporation and holdings of the interest in question.

The courts have developed other guidelines to be used in making a debt-equity determination.[67]

239. 100-Percent Dividends-Received Deduction for Affiliates. Affiliated corporations are allowed a 100-percent dividends-received deduction for "qualifying dividends" received from members of the affiliated group (Code Sec. 243(a)(3)).[68] A qualifying dividend is any dividend received by a corporation that is a member of the same affiliated group as the corporation distributing it. The term also includes a dividend paid by an affiliated corporation that has made an election pertaining to the Puerto Rico and possessions tax credit.

If the affiliated group includes at least one life insurance company, no dividend by any member of the group will be treated as qualified unless a special election is in effect for the tax year in which the dividend is received (Code Sec. 243(b)).[69] If any member of an affiliated group elects the foreign tax credit, then all members of the group that pay or accrue foreign taxes must elect the credit in order for any dividend paid by a member of the group to qualify for the 100-percent dividends-received deduction (Code Sec. 243(b)(2)).[70]

241. Dividends from Foreign Corporations. A domestic corporation is entitled to a 70-percent (80-percent in the case of 20-percent-owned corporations—see ¶ 237) deduction of the U.S.-source portion of dividends received from a foreign corporation that is at least 10-percent owned, by vote and value, by the domestic corporation. The U.S.-source portion of a dividend is the amount that bears the same ratio to the dividend as undistributed U.S. earnings bear to total undistributed earnings (Code Sec. 245(a)).[71]

A 100-percent dividends-received deduction is allowed to a domestic corporation for dividends paid by a wholly owned foreign subsidiary out of its earnings and profits for the tax year. All of the foreign subsidiary's gross income must be effectively connected with a U.S. trade or business (Code Sec. 245(b)).[72] A temporary dividend deduction is available for repatriated earnings of a controlled foreign corporation (¶ 2487).

Debt-Financed Portfolio Stock. Any reduction in the dividends-received deduction resulting from the rules concerning debt-financed portfolio stock (¶ 237) must be computed before applying the above ratios.

243. Organizational and Start-Up Expenditures. A corporation may elect to deduct up to $5,000 of any organizational expenses (in addition to $5,000 of any startup costs; see ¶ 904) it incurs in the tax year in which it begins business (Code Sec. 248(a)).[73] (This is a change from the law applicable to organizational expenses paid or incurred before October 22, 2004, which a corporation could elect to amortize over a 60-month period.) Like the deduction for startup costs, the $5,000 deducted for organizational expenses must be reduced by the amount by which the expenses exceed $50,000. Any remaining balance of organizational expenditures which are not immediately deductible must be amortized over a 180-month period. Form 4562 is used by a corporation to make the election.

Organizational expenditures are those which are (1) connected directly with the creation of the corporation, (2) chargeable to capital account, and (3) of a character that

---

Footnote references are to paragraphs of the 2008 Standard Federal Tax Reports.

[67] ¶ 15,704.264
[68] ¶ 13,051
[69] ¶ 13,051
[70] ¶ 13,051
[71] ¶ 13,150
[72] ¶ 13,150
[73] ¶ 13,350

would be amortizable over the life of the corporation if its life were limited by its charter. They include expenses of temporary directors and organizational meetings, state fees for incorporation privileges, accounting service costs incident to organization, and legal service expenditures, such as for drafting of documents, minutes of organizational meetings, and terms of the original stock certificates.

Expenditures connected with issuing or selling stock or with the transfer of assets to a corporation are not amortizable (Reg. § 1.248-1(b)(3)); instead, such costs must be netted against the proceeds of the stock sale.[74] Preopening or startup expenses, such as employee training, advertising, and expenses of lining up suppliers or potential customers, are not organizational expenses. However, a new business may be eligible to amortize startup expenditures under Code Sec. 195.[75] Corporate expenditures that are incurred in investigating the creation or acquisition of an active trade or business or in creating such a trade or business do not qualify for amortization as organizational expenses. However, such expenses may qualify as startup expenses (¶ 904) (Rev. Rul. 99-23).[76]

245. Domestic Production Activities. Effective for tax years beginning after December 31, 2004, a corporation may claim a deduction against gross income equal to the applicable percentage of its qualified production activities income (QPAI) or its taxable income (whichever is less) (i.e., manufacturer's deduction) (Code Sec. 199).[77] The amount of the deduction for any tax year, however, may not exceed 50 percent of the W-2 wages the taxpayer deducts in calculating its QPAI (Code Sec. 199(b)(2)(B)). For a more detailed discussion, see ¶ 980A and following.

Accumulated Earnings Tax

251. Rate and Nature of Tax. In addition to being liable for regular income taxes, every corporation (other than personal holding companies (¶ 277), tax-exempt organizations (¶ 601), or passive foreign investment companies (¶ 2490)) may be liable for the accumulated earnings tax. The tax is in the form of a penalty and applies if a corporation is formed or used for the purpose of avoiding the imposition of income tax upon its shareholders by permitting its earnings or profits to accumulate instead of being distributed (Code Secs. 531—537).[78]

The accumulated earnings tax is 15 percent of the corporation's accumulated taxable income (for tax years beginning prior to 2003, the tax rate was equal to the highest income tax rate applicable to individuals) (Code Sec. 531). There is no particular form which a corporation files to compute the tax. Instead, the IRS enforces the tax by reaching a conclusion whether enough dividends were paid during the tax year based on the corporation's filed income tax return. A penalty may apply for any underpayment of the accumulated earnings tax due to negligence (¶ 2856) (Rev. Rul. 75-330).[79] Interest on any underpayment is computed from the date the corporation's tax return is due without regard to extensions (Code Sec. 6601(b)(4)).[80]

253. Income on Which Tax Is Levied. The accumulated earnings tax is imposed on a corporation's "accumulated taxable income" for the tax year. "Accumulated taxable income" means taxable income with certain adjustments, and minus the sum of the dividends-paid deduction (¶ 259) and the accumulated earnings credit (¶ 261). The adjustments to taxable income include (Code Sec. 535; Reg. § 1.535-2):[81]

(1) A deduction is allowed for federal income taxes, as well as for income, war, and excess profits taxes of foreign countries and U.S. possessions (to the extent not allowed as deductions in computing taxable income) accrued during the tax year, regardless of the accounting method used. The deduction will not include any accumulated earnings tax or personal holding company tax paid.

(2) Charitable contributions for the tax year are deductible without regard to the 10 percent of taxable income limitation.

Footnote references are to paragraphs of the 2008 Standard Federal Tax Reports.

[74] ¶ 13,351
[75] ¶ 12,370
[76] ¶ 12,371.25
[77] ¶ 12,468
[78] ¶ 23,001—¶ 23,070
[79] ¶ 39,651G
[80] ¶ 39,410
[81] ¶ 23,040, ¶ 23,042

(3) No deduction is allowed for dividends received or for dividends paid by public utilities on certain preferred stock.

(4) The net operating loss deduction is not allowed.

(5) A corporation (other than a mere holding company or investment company) is allowed a deduction for net capital losses incurred for the tax year. However, the amount of the reduction is reduced by the lesser of the capital gains deducted in earlier years that have not already been used in a previous year to reduce the capital loss reduction or the corporation's accumulated earnings and profits at the close of the preceding year. A corporation that has net capital gains for the year reduces its taxable income by those gains, reduced by the taxes attributable to them. The amount of net capital gain for this purpose is computed by treating the net capital loss for the previous year as a short-term capital loss for the year. In the case of a foreign corporation, only net capital gains that are effectively connected with the conduct of a trade or business within the United States that are not exempt under treaty are taken into account.

(6) No capital loss carryback or carryover is allowed.

(7) A controlled foreign corporation (CFC) is allowed to deduct the amount of its subpart F income which is required to be included in the income of its U.S. shareholders (see ¶ 2487). However, if the corporation would otherwise calculate its accumulated taxable income on a gross basis, then the corporation's deduction must be reduced by any deduction which may have reduced a U.S. shareholder's income inclusion.

Although exempt interest income is excludable from accumulated taxable income for purposes of determining the accumulated earnings tax base, it is considered for purposes of determining whether earnings and profits have been accumulated beyond the reasonable needs of the business (see ¶ 265).[82]

Holding or Investment Companies. If a corporation is a mere holding or investment company, special rules apply in determining its accumulated taxable income: (1) current capital losses may not be deducted, (2) current net short-term capital gains are deductible only to the extent of any capital loss carryovers, and (3) accumulated earnings and profits cannot be less than they would have been had the rules in (1) and (2) been applied in computing earnings and profits (Code Sec. 535(b)(8)).[83]

257. Re-sourcing Income of U.S.-Owned Foreign Corporations. For purposes of the accumulated earnings tax, if 10 percent or more of the earnings and profits of any foreign corporation is derived from sources within the United States or is effectively connected with the conduct of a trade or business in the United States, then any distribution out of such earnings and profits (and any interest payment) retains its character as U.S.-source income upon receipt by a U.S.-owned foreign corporation (Code Sec. 535(d)(1)).[84] "United States-owned foreign corporation" means any foreign corporation in which 50 percent or more of voting power or total value is held directly or indirectly by U.S. persons (Code Sec. 535(d)(2)).[85]

259. Dividends-Paid Deduction. The "dividends-paid deduction" (Code Secs. 561—565)[86] does not enter into the computation of ordinary corporate income taxes. It is a consideration only in determining the taxation of a regulated investment company (Code Sec. 851),[87] a real estate investment trust (Code Sec. 856),[88] the personal holding company tax (Code Sec. 541),[89] and the accumulated earnings tax (Code Sec. 531).[90]

261. Accumulated Earnings Credit. For a corporation other than a mere holding or investment company, the accumulated earnings credit allowed in computing accumulated taxable income (¶ 253) is an amount equal to the part of the earnings and profits of the tax year retained for the reasonable needs of the business, reduced by the net capital gain (which is itself reduced by the amount of income tax attributable to it).

Footnote references are to paragraphs of the 2008 Standard Federal Tax Reports.

[82] ¶ 23,018.897
[83] ¶ 23,040
[84] ¶ 23,040
[85] ¶ 23,040
[86] ¶ 23,450—¶ 23,530
[87] ¶ 26,400
[88] ¶ 26,500
[89] ¶ 23,152
[90] ¶ 23,001

A minimum amount of $250,000 ($150,000 for personal service corporations (¶ 219)) may be accumulated from past and present earnings combined by all corporations, including holding or investment companies. This minimum amount is the only credit allowable to a holding or investment company (Code Sec. 535(c)).[91] Only one $250,000 accumulated earnings credit is allowed to a controlled group of corporations (¶ 291) (Code Sec. 1561(a)(2)).[92] The single credit is to be divided equally among the corporations.

263. Basis of Liability. Although the accumulated earnings tax is computed as a percentage of the corporation's accumulated taxable income (see ¶ 251, above), liability for the tax hinges on whether the corporation was formed or availed of to avoid the income tax on income otherwise receivable by its shareholders. A corporation can be subject to the accumulated earnings tax for a year in which it has accumulated taxable income on hand even though, because of a stock redemption, no earnings and profits were accumulated for the tax year.[93]

The courts have shifted the focus of attention from earnings and profits to liquidity.[94] The reason for this change in emphasis is that the earnings-and-profits figure often is no indication of the funds available to the corporation to meet its business needs and pay dividends to its shareholders. Whether a corporation can be subjected to the accumulated earnings tax is therefore determined by comparing the reasonable needs of its business (see ¶ 265) to its total liquid assets at the end of the year. Liquid assets include the corporation's cash and marketable securities.

265. Reasonable Needs of the Business. In order to justify an accumulation of income, there must be a reasonable business need for it and a definite plan for its use. Since a corporation is given a credit (¶ 261) for its reasonable business needs (including reasonably anticipated needs) in figuring the accumulated earnings tax, the resolution of most disputes hinges on this issue.

The Code does not contain a comprehensive definition of reasonable business needs. However, a number of acceptable and unacceptable grounds for accumulating income are listed in the regulations (Reg. § 1.537-2).[95] Acceptable grounds include: (1) business expansion and plant replacement; (2) acquisition of a business through purchase of stock or assets; (3) debt retirement; (4) working capital; and (5) investments or loans to suppliers or customers necessary to the maintenance of the corporation's business.

The self-insurance of product liability risks is a business need for which earnings and profits may be accumulated to a reasonable extent without incurring liability for the accumulated earnings tax (Code Sec. 537(b)(4) and Reg. § 1.537-2(b)(6)).[96]

Unacceptable grounds include: (1) loans to shareholders and expenditures for their personal benefit; (2) loans to relatives or friends of shareholders or to others who have no reasonable connection with the business; (3) loans to a sister (commonly controlled) corporation; (4) investments that are not related to the business; and (5) accumulations to provide against unrealistic hazards (Reg. § 1.537-2(c)).[97]

Courts have used an operating-cycle approach to determine the amount of working capital a corporation needs. An operating cycle consists of (1) an inventory cycle (conversion of cash and raw materials into inventory), (2) a receivables cycle (conversion of inventory into accounts receivable and cash), and possibly (3) a credit cycle (accounts payable turnover).[98]

A stock redemption under Code Sec. 303 to pay death taxes and expenses (¶ 745) and a redemption of stock in order to bring a private foundation within the 20 percent excess business holdings limit (¶ 640) are good cause for an accumulation of income (Code Sec. 537(a)).[99] Although other types of stock redemptions are not accorded this certainty, accumulations to redeem a minority interest (or the interest of one of two 50 percent stockholders) have been approved where they would eliminate dissent, would

---

Footnote references are to paragraphs of the 2008 Standard Federal Tax Reports.

[91] ¶ 23,040
[92] ¶ 33,340
[93] ¶ 23,045.37
[94] ¶ 23,045.65, ¶ 23,074.36
[95] ¶ 23,072
[96] ¶ 23,070
[97] ¶ 23,070
[98] ¶ 23,074.625
[99] ¶ 23,070

prevent the minority interest from falling into hostile hands, or were an essential ingredient of an employee incentive plan. Court decisions in this area show that except in rare circumstances, the redemption of a majority interest is not good cause for accumulating income.[100]

267. Burden of Proof. On the issue of whether a corporation has accumulated income in excess of the reasonable needs of its business, the burden of proof in the Tax Court is on the government in two instances. First, the burden is on the government if, in advance of a formal deficiency notice, it does not notify the corporation by certified or registered mail of its intention to assess a deficiency based in whole or in part on the accumulated earnings tax or fails to state the tax years at issue. Second, in the event of such notification, the burden falls on the government if the corporation responds within 60 days with a statement of the grounds on which it relies to establish the reasonableness of all or any part of its accumulation of income (Code Sec. 534; Reg. § 1.534-2).[101] In other courts, the burden of proof is wholly on the corporation.

269. Tax Avoidance Intent. One of the conditions that must exist before a corporation can be subject to the accumulated earnings tax is an intent to avoid the income tax on its shareholders (Code Sec. 533).[102] If the corporation accumulates income beyond the reasonable needs of its business (or if it is a mere holding or investment company), a presumption of tax avoidance intent arises. This presumption can be overcome by showing that tax avoidance was not one of the purposes of the accumulation of income (*Donruss Co.*, 69-1 USTC ¶ 9167, and *Shaw-Walker*, 69-1 USTC ¶ 9198).[103]

271. Publicly Held Corporations. The accumulated earnings tax may be imposed on a corporation without regard to the number of shareholders, meaning that widely held corporations are subject to the tax (Code Sec. 532(c)).[104]

Personal Service Corporations

273. Personal Service Corporations. A personal service corporation is one that furnishes personal services performed by employee-owners (Code Secs. 269A and 280H).[105] An "employee-owner" is an employee who owns, directly or indirectly, more than 10 percent of the outstanding stock of the corporation on any day during the company's tax year. If a corporation meets these requirements and also has as its principal purpose the avoidance or evasion of federal income tax by reducing the income of any employee- owner or securing tax benefits for any employee-owner that would not otherwise be available, the IRS may reallocate income, deductions and other tax attributes between the personal service corporation and the employee-owner. The purpose of evading or avoiding income tax can be shown by a reduction in the tax liability of, or the increase of tax benefits to, an employee-owner or by any other increase in tax benefits. Code Sec. 280H restricts the amount that can be deducted by a personal service corporation for amounts paid to owners if the corporation has elected a non-calendar tax year.

Personal Holding Companies

275. Tax on Personal Holding Companies. In addition to being liable for regular income taxes, a corporation that is classified as a personal holding company will be liable for a separate tax on its "undistributed personal holding company income." The personal holding company tax was enacted when the highest corporate income tax rate was well below the highest individual income tax rate. It was designed to prevent individuals from establishing a corporation to receive and hold investment income or compensation so that it would be taxed at a lower rate (i.e., "incorporated pocketbooks"). Even though the corporate and individual income tax rates have somewhat equalized, the personal holding company tax still applies.

The personal holding company tax is 15 percent of a corporation's undistributed personal holding company income (Code Sec. 541; Reg. § 1.541-1).[106] Undistributed

---

Footnote references are to paragraphs of the 2008 Standard Federal Tax Reports.

[100] ¶ 23,018.895
[101] ¶ 23,020, ¶ 23,022, ¶ 23,025
[102] ¶ 23,015
[103] ¶ 23,018.26
[104] ¶ 23,010
[105] ¶ 14,300, ¶ 15,160
[106] ¶ 23,152, ¶ 23,153

personal holding company income is computed by making certain adjustments to the corporation's taxable income, not just its personal holding company income (Code Sec. 545).[107] After these adjustments are made, the dividends paid deduction is deducted from the adjusted taxable income (Code Sec. 562; Reg. § 1.562-1(a)).[108] Any remaining balance is the corporation's undistributed personal holding company income.

Personal holding company taxes are computed and reported on Schedule PH (U.S. Personal Holding Company (PHC) Tax), which is attached to the corporation's Form 1120, U.S. Corporation Income Tax Return.

277. Personal Holding Company Defined. A "personal holding company" (Code Sec. 542; Reg. § § 1.542-1— 1.542-3)[109] is any corporation (other than those mentioned in ¶ 279) in which at least 60 percent of adjusted ordinary gross income for the tax year is personal holding company income (¶ 281) and at any time during the last half of the tax year more than 50 percent in value of its outstanding stock is owned, directly or indirectly, by or for not more than five individuals (¶ 285). For this purpose, the following are considered individuals: (1) a qualified pension, profit-sharing, and stock bonus plan (Code Sec. 401(a));[110] (2) a trust that provides for the payment of supplemental unemployment compensation under certain conditions (Code Sec. 501(c)(17));[111] (3) a private foundation (Code Sec. 509(a));[112] and (4) a part of a trust permanently set aside or used exclusively for the purposes described in Code Sec. 642(c).[113] For foreign personal holding companies, see ¶ 2488.

279. Exceptions. The term "personal holding company" does not include:

(1) a corporation exempt from tax under Code Sec. 501 et seq.;

(2) a bank as defined in Code Sec. 581 or a domestic building and loan association;

(3) a life insurance company;

(4) a surety company;

(5) a foreign corporation;

(6) some lending and finance companies if they meet prescribed tests as to the source or amount of their interest income and the amount of loans to stockholders;

(7) a small business investment company (unless a shareholder, directly or indirectly, owns 5 percent or more of a concern to which the company supplies funds); or

(8) a corporation subject to the jurisdiction of a court in a bankruptcy or similar proceeding unless the case was started to avoid the tax.[114]

281. Personal Holding Company Income. The term "personal holding company income" (Code Sec. 543)[115] means the portion of the adjusted ordinary gross income that consists of:

(1) Dividends, interest, royalties (other than mineral, oil and gas, copyright, or computer software royalties), and annuities. However, such income does not include interest received by a broker or dealer in connection with any securities or money market instruments held as property under Code Sec. 1221(a)(1),[116] margin accounts, or any financing for a customer secured by securities or money market instruments.

(2) Rents, unless they constitute 50 percent or more of the adjusted ordinary gross income and unless the sum of:

Footnote references are to paragraphs of the 2008 Standard Federal Tax Reports.

[107] ¶ 23,250
[108] ¶ 23,470—¶ 23,471
[109] ¶ 23,190—¶ 23,193
[110] ¶ 17,502

[111] ¶ 22,602
[112] ¶ 22,800
[113] ¶ 24,280
[114] ¶ 23,190

[115] ¶ 23,210
[116] ¶ 30,420

(a) dividends paid during the tax year,

(b) dividends paid after the close of the tax year but, nevertheless, considered to be paid on the last day of the tax year under Code Sec. 563(d) as limited by Code Sec. 563(b), and

(c) consent dividends for the tax year

equals or exceeds the amount by which personal holding company income exceeds 10 percent of the ordinary gross income.[117]

(3) Mineral, oil, and gas royalties, unless (a) they constitute 50 percent or more of the adjusted ordinary gross income, (b) the other personal holding company income for the tax year is not more than 10 percent of the ordinary gross income, and (c) the ordinary and necessary business expense deductions, other than compensation for personal services rendered by shareholders, and apart from deductions otherwise specifically allowable under Code sections other than Code Sec. 162,[118] are 15 percent or more of adjusted ordinary gross income.

(4) Copyright royalties, unless (a) apart from royalties derived from the works of shareholders, they make up 50 percent or more of the ordinary gross income, (b) personal holding company income for the tax year (not taking into account copyright royalties and dividends in any corporation in which the taxpayer owns at least 50 percent of all classes of voting stock and at least 50 percent of the value of all classes of stock) is 10 percent or less of the ordinary gross income, and (c) business deductions (other than deductions for compensation for services rendered by shareholders, deductions for royalties, and deductions specifically allowable under sections other than Code Sec. 162)[119] equal or exceed 25 percent of the amount by which the ordinary gross income exceeds the sum of royalties paid or accrued and depreciation allowed.

(5) Rents from the distribution and exhibition of produced films (that is, rents from a film interest acquired before the film production was substantially complete) unless such rents are 50 percent or more of the ordinary gross income.

(6) Amounts received as compensation for the use of, or right to use, tangible property of the corporation where, at any time during the tax year, 25 percent or more in value of the outstanding stock of the corporation is owned, directly or indirectly, by or for an individual entitled to the use of the property, whether such right is obtained directly from the corporation or by means of a sublease or other arrangement. This paragraph applies only if the corporation's other personal holding company income (computed with certain adjustments) for the tax year is more than 10 percent of its ordinary gross income.

(7) Amounts received by a corporation from contracts for personal services, including gain from the sale or other disposition thereof, if (a) some person other than the corporation has the right to designate (by name or by description) the individual who is to perform the services or if the individual who is to perform the services is designated (by name or by description) in the contract and (b) at some time during the tax year 25 percent or more in value of the outstanding stock of the corporation is owned, directly or indirectly, by or for the individual who has performed, is to perform, or may be designated (by name or by description) as the one to perform such services.

(8) Income required to be reported by a corporate beneficiary under the income tax provisions relating to estates and trusts.

Active Business Computer Software Royalties. "Active business computer software royalties" received in connection with the licensing of computer software are excluded from personal holding company income (Code Sec. 543(d)).[120] To qualify for the exclusion: (1) the royalties must be derived by a corporation actively engaged in the trade or business of developing, manufacturing or producing computer software; (2) the royalties must make up at least 50 percent of the corporation's gross income; (3)

Footnote references are to paragraphs of the 2008 Standard Federal Tax Reports.

[117] ¶ 23,490
[118] ¶ 8500
[119] ¶ 8500
[120] ¶ 23,210

business and research expenses relating to the royalties must equal or exceed 25 percent of ordinary gross income; and (4) dividends must equal or exceed the excess of personal holding company income over 10 percent of ordinary gross income. If one member of an affiliated group receives software royalties, it will be treated as having met the above requirements if another member meets the requirements (Code Sec. 543(d)).[121]

283. Adjusted Ordinary Gross Income. In determining whether 60 percent or more of a corporation's "adjusted ordinary gross income" is personal holding company income, the following adjustments must be made (Code Sec. 543(b)(2)):[122]

(1) Rental income must be reduced by deductions for depreciation and amortization, property taxes, interest, and rents paid that are attributable to such income.

(2) Income from mineral, oil, and gas royalties and from working interests in oil and gas wells must be reduced by deductions for depreciation, amortization and depletion, property and severance taxes, interest, and rents paid which are attributable to such income.

(3) Interest on U.S. bonds held for sale by a dealer who is making a primary market for these obligations and interest on condemnation awards, judgments and tax refunds must be excluded.

(4) Rent received from the lease of tangible personal property manufactured by a taxpayer engaged in substantial manufacturing or production of property of the same type must be reduced by deductions for depreciation and amortization, taxes, rent and interest paid that are attributable to such income.

All capital gains are excluded in determining whether the 60-percent test has been met because it is based on *adjusted ordinary gross income* (Code Sec. 543(b)(2)).[123]

285. Stock Ownership. Constructive ownership rules apply in determining whether (1) a corporation is a personal holding company (¶ 277), (2) amounts received under a personal service contract are personal holding company income (¶ 281), (3) copyright royalties are personal holding company income, or (4) compensation for the use of property is personal holding company income (¶ 281) (Code Sec. 544; Reg. § § 1.544-1—1.544-7).[124] Under the constructive ownership rules:

(1) Stock owned, directly or indirectly, by or for a corporation, partnership, estate, or trust is considered as being owned proportionately by its shareholders, partners, or beneficiaries.

(2) An individual is considered as owning the stock owned, directly or indirectly, by or for his family (brothers and sisters (whole or half blood), spouse, ancestors, and lineal descendants), or by or for his partner.

(3) If any person has an option to acquire stock, such stock is considered as owned by such person. An option to acquire an option, and each one of a series of such options, is regarded as an option to acquire stock. This rule is applied in preference to rule (2), above, when both rules apply (Code Sec. 544(a)(6)).[125]

(4) Stock constructively owned by a corporation, partnership, estate, or trust will be reattributed to its owners or beneficiaries so that they are treated as constructive owners of the stock. However, stock constructively and not actually owned by an individual will not be reattributed.

(5) Outstanding securities convertible into stock (whether or not during the tax year) are considered as outstanding stock, but only if the effect of the inclusion of all such securities is to make the corporation a personal holding company (Code Sec. 544(b)).[126]

287. Deficiency Dividend Deduction. If a deficiency is determined in the personal holding company tax, the corporation may then distribute dividends and, in redetermining the undistributed personal holding company income, reduce or eliminate the

---

Footnote references are to paragraphs of the 2008 Standard Federal Tax Reports.

[121] ¶ 23,210
[122] ¶ 23,210

[123] ¶ 23,210
[124] ¶ 23,230—¶ 23,237

[125] ¶ 23,230
[126] ¶ 23,230

deficiency by means of a deduction for "deficiency dividends" in the amount of the dividends so paid. The distribution must be made within 90 days after the deficiency determination. Claim for the deduction must be filed within 120 days of the determination (Code Sec. 547; Reg. §§ 1.547-1—1.547-7).[127]

Controlled Corporate Group

289. Allocation of Tax Benefits. A controlled group of corporations is allowed only one set of graduated income tax brackets (¶ 219) and one $250,000 accumulated earnings credit (¶ 261). Controlled groups are also allowed one $40,000 exemption amount for alternative minimum tax purposes (¶ 1405). Each of these items is to be allocated equally among the members of the group unless they all consent to a different apportionment (Code Sec. 1561).[128]

Dividends-Received Deduction. Since a parent-subsidiary controlled group (see ¶ 291) is also an affiliated group, a 100-percent dividends-received deduction may be taken with respect to dividends paid from one member to another (¶ 239). A 70-percent deduction is allowed for distributions between members of a brother-sister controlled group (¶ 291).

291. What Is a Controlled Group. There are two types of controlled corporate groups—parent-subsidiary and brother-sister. A parent-subsidiary controlled group exists if: (1) one or more chains of corporations are connected through stock ownership with a common parent corporation; (2) 80 percent or more of the voting power or value of the stock of each corporation in the group other than the parent is owned by one or more corporations in the group; and (3) the common parent owns at least 80 percent of the voting power or value of the stock of one of the other corporations in the group (not counting stock owned directly by other members) (Code Sec. 1563(a)(1)).[129]

A brother-sister controlled group exists if five or fewer persons (individuals, estates, or trusts) own stock possessing more than 50 percent of the total combined voting power of all classes of stock entitled to vote, or more than 50 percent of the total value of all stock, taking into account the stock ownership of each person only to the extent the person owns stock in each corporation. (Code Sec. 1563(a)(2)).[130]

293. Controlled Corporations—Expenses, Interest and Losses. Controlled groups of corporations are subject to the related parties' transaction rules of Code Sec. 267,[131] under which controlled members must use a matching rule that defers the deductibility of an expense or interest by a payor until the payment is included in the payee's income (Code Sec. 267(a)(2)).[132] Also, losses on sales between members of a controlled group must be deferred until the property is sold to an unrelated person (Code Sec. 267(f)(2)).[133] The loss deferral rule does not apply, however, to sales to a domestic international sales corporation (DISC) (see ¶ 2468), to sales of inventory in the ordinary course of business if one of the parties is a foreign corporation, or to loan repayment losses attributable to foreign currency value reductions (Code Sec. 267(f)(3)).[134]

Consolidated Return

295. Consolidated Return. The privilege of filing a consolidated return is extended to an affiliated group of corporations under Code Secs. 1501 and 1504(b).[135] An "affiliated group" is defined as one or more chains of includible corporations connected through stock ownership with a common parent that is an includible corporation if (1) the common parent must directly own stock possessing at least 80 percent of the total voting power of at least one of the other includible corporations and having a value equal to at least 80 percent of the total value of the stock of the corporation, and (2) stock meeting the 80-percent test in each includible corporation other than the common parent must be owned directly by one or more of the other includible corporations (Code Sec. 1504(a)).[136]

Footnote references are to paragraphs of the 2008 Standard Federal Tax Reports.

[127] ¶ 23,290—¶ 23,297
[128] ¶ 33,340
[129] ¶ 33,360
[130] ¶ 33,360, ¶ 33,382.85
[131] ¶ 14,150
[132] ¶ 14,150
[133] ¶ 14,150
[134] ¶ 14,150
[135] ¶ 33,121, ¶ 33,260
[136] ¶ 33,260

¶289

A consolidated return may be filed only if all corporations that were members of the affiliated group *at any time* during the tax year consent to all the consolidated return regulations prior to the last day for filing the return. The making of a consolidated return is such consent. The common parent corporation, when filing a consolidated return, must attach Form 851 (Affiliations Schedule). In addition, for the first year a consolidated return is filed, each subsidiary must attach a Form 1122 (consent to be included in the consolidated return).

The following corporations may not file consolidated returns (Code Sec. 1504(b)):[137]

(1) corporations that are exempt under Code Sec. 501 (except that such organizations may be affiliated with other such organizations at least one of which is organized only to hold title for exempt organizations and from which the others derive income);

(2) insurance companies subject to tax under Code Sec. 801 (see, however, Code Sec. 1504(c));[138]

(3) foreign corporations;

(4) corporations electing the Sec. 936 possessions tax credit (¶ 2419);

(5) regulated investment companies and real estate investment trusts (but see ¶ 2340 for circumstances in which a REIT may treat income and deductions of a qualified subsidiary as its own);

(6) DISCs (Code Sec. 992(a));[139] and

(7) S corporations.

297. Advantages and Disadvantages. The advantages in filing consolidated returns include: (1) offsetting operating losses of one company against the profits of another (but see the rule for dual resident companies below); (2) offsetting capital losses of one company against the capital gains of another (but see ¶ 2285 on newly acquired corporations); (3) avoidance of tax on intercompany distributions; (4) deferral of income on intercompany transactions; (5) use by the corporate group of the excess of one member's foreign tax credit over its limitation; and (6) designation of the parent company as agent of the group for all tax purposes.

The disadvantages include: (1) the effect on later years' returns; (2) deferral of losses on intercompany transactions; (3) additional bookkeeping required to keep track of deferred intercompany transactions; (4) intercompany profit in inventories still within the group must be reflected in annual inventory adjustments; (5) possible elimination of foreign tax credits when the limiting fraction is diminished because of lack of foreign income on the part of some members; and (6) possible accumulated earnings tax liability when the consolidated accumulated earnings and profits of the group exceed the minimum credit amount.

Dual Resident Companies. If a U.S. corporation is subject to foreign tax on its worldwide income, or on a residence basis as opposed to a source basis, any net operating loss it incurs in a year cannot reduce the taxable income of any other member of a U.S. affiliated group for any tax year (Reg. § 1.1503-2(c)).[140]

The IRS has issued regulations addressing the losses of dual resident companies filing consolidated returns (T.D. 9315, adding Reg. §§ 1.1503(d)-1 through 1.1503(d)-8).[141]

Preferred Dividends. Income out of which a member of an affiliated group, other than a common parent, distributes preferred dividends to a nonmember may not be offset by the group's net operating losses or capital losses (Code Sec. 1503(f)).[142] Taxes on that income may not be offset by most group tax credits.

Golden Parachutes. All members of an affiliated group are treated as a single corporation when determining excessive payments that are contingent on a change in corporate control (Code Sec. 280G(d)(5) and ¶ 907).[143]

Footnote references are to paragraphs of the 2008 Standard Federal Tax Reports.

[137] ¶ 33,260
[138] ¶ 33,260
[139] ¶ 28,960
[140] ¶ 33,242
[141] ¶ 33,240
[142] ¶ 33,240
[143] ¶ 15,150

Chapter 3
S CORPORATIONS

S Corporation Status

301. Corporate Income Taxed to Shareholders. An S corporation is a corporation that elects and is eligible to choose S corporation status (¶ 305) and whose shareholders have all consented to the corporation's choice (¶ 306). In general, an S corporation does not pay any income tax. Instead, the corporation's income and deductions are passed through to its shareholders. The shareholders then must report the income and deductions on their own income tax returns.

To the extent the special S corporation rules (found in Subchapter S of the Code) do not apply, S corporations are governed by the "regular" (C corporation) rules. Thus, the taxation of income earned by, and the allocation of losses incurred by, S corporations closely parallel the taxation of partnerships with respect to items of partnership income and loss. However, S corporations generally continue to be treated as regular corporations for purposes of the rules (found in subchapter C of the Code) relating to corporate distributions, redemptions, liquidations and reorganizations (Code Sec. 1371).[1]

An S corporation must file an annual return on Form 1120S, U.S. Income Tax Return for an S Corporation, which is due on or before the 15th day of the 3rd month following the close of the corporation's tax year (Code Sec. 6072(b)).[2]

The tax year of an S corporation must be a "permitted year." Permitted years include the calendar year, a tax year elected under Code Sec. 444,[3] a 52-53 week tax year ending with reference to the calendar year or a taxable year elected under Code Sec. 444, or any other tax year for which the corporation establishes a business purpose to the satisfaction of the IRS under Code Sec. 442 (Reg. § 1.1378-1(a)).[4]

305. Corporations Eligible to Elect S Corporation Status. To become an S corporation, an organization must be a "small business corporation" (Code Sec. 1361(a)).[5] All the following requirements must be met (Code Sec. 1361(b); Reg. § 1.1361-1(b)):[6]

(1) The entity must be a domestic corporation that is organized under the laws of any state or U.S. territory or an unincorporated association that is taxed as a corporation for Code purposes[7] (Reg. § 1.1361-1(c)).[8]

(2) The corporation may have as shareholders only individuals, estates, certain trusts, banks, and certain exempt organizations. Partnerships and corporations cannot be shareholders.

(3) Only citizens or residents of the United States can be shareholders.

(4) The corporation can have only one class of stock.

A few limited types of corporations are ineligible to be "small business corporations:" a financial institution that uses the reserve method of accounting, an insurance company taxed under subchapter L of the Code, a corporation that has elected to take the Puerto Rico and possessions tax credit under Code Sec. 936, or a DISC or former DISC (Code Sec. 1361(b)(2)).[9]

Footnote references are to paragraphs of the 2008 Standard Federal Tax Reports.

[1] ¶ 32,140
[2] ¶ 36,720
[3] ¶ 20,600
[4] ¶ 20,400
[5] ¶ 32,021
[6] ¶ 32,021, ¶ 32,024A
[7] ¶ 43,080
[8] ¶ 32,024A
[9] ¶ 32,021

Shareholder Limitations. All shareholders of an S corporation must be individuals, estates, certain defined trusts, or certain tax-exempt organizations. A qualifying S corporation can have no more than 100 shareholders (Code Sec. 1361(b)(1)(A)).

For purposes of applying the 100-shareholder limit, in certain cases two or more shareholders can be counted as only one shareholder if they have one of several relationships to one another. A husband and wife (and their estates) are counted as a single shareholder under the limit. In addition, all qualifying members of a family who hold corporation stock are treated as one shareholder of the S corporation (Code Sec. 1361(c)(1)). A family is defined as a common ancestor, the lineal descendants of the common ancestor, and the spouses (or former spouses) of the common ancestor and the descendants. The common ancestor can be no more than six generations removed from the youngest shareholder who is treated as a member of the family on the latest of (1) the date the S Corporation election under Code Sec. 1362(a) is made; (2) the earliest date that a family member first holds stock in the corporation; or (3) October 22, 2004 (Code Sec. 1361(c)(1)(B)). Additionally, in determining whether certain children are lineal descendants and members of a family, any legally adopted child, any child lawfully placed with the individual for legal adoption, and any eligible foster child are treated as a child by blood (Code Sec. 1361(c)(1)(C)). The estate of a family member is treated as a member of the family for purposes of determining the number of shareholders (Code Sec. 1361(c)(1)(A)).

The term "eligible shareholders" includes a grantor trust (where the grantor is regarded as the shareholder), a voting trust (where each beneficiary is treated as a shareholder), and any testamentary trust that receives S corporation stock. However, the testamentary trust is treated as an eligible shareholder only for two years after the deemed owner's death (Code Sec. 1361(c)(2)(A); Reg. §1.1361-1(h)).[10] The IRS may extend the two-year limit under an extension for estate tax payments.[11]

Stock Ownership Through Single-Member LLCs. The prohibition on partnerships holding stock in an S corporation does not extend to single-member LLCs that are disregarded for federal tax purposes if the member is eligible to own S corporation stock. The stock is considered held directly by the owner for purposes of applying the rules of Code Sec. 1361(b) (IRS Letter Ruling 200107025). In the situation discussed in the private letter ruling, none of the single-member LLCs formed by the shareholders elected treatment as an association taxable as a corporation under the " check-the-box" rules (see ¶ 402A). Instead, they were disregarded entities in accordance with their default classification under Reg. §301.7701-3.[12] As a result, each shareholder was treated as the direct owner of the S corporation stock.

Restricted Bank Director Stock. Restricted bank director stock is not taken into account as outstanding stock in applying the provisions of subchapter S. Accordingly, an individual will not be treated as a shareholder in an S corporation solely on account of owning restricted bank director stock in the S corporation. "Restricted bank director stock" is stock in a bank or depositary institution holding company, if the stock is required to be held by an individual under applicable federal or state law in order to permit the individual to serve on the board of directors of the bank or holding company and where there is an agreement under which the individual is required to sell the stock back to the bank or holding company when he or she leaves the board at the same price at which it was purchased (Code Sec. 1361(f)(2), as added by the Small Business and Work Opportunity Tax Act of 2007 (P.L. 110-28)).[13]

ESBTs. An electing small business trust (ESBT) can be an S corporation shareholder (Code Sec. 1361(e)).[14] An ESBT is a trust that does not have as a beneficiary any person other than (1) an individual, (2) an estate, or (3) an organization eligible to accept charitable contributions under Code Sec. 170 (other than political entities).[15]

Any portion of an ESBT that consists of S corporation stock is treated as a separate trust and will be taxed at the highest rate of tax for estates and trusts with limited deductions and credits and no exemption amount for alternative minimum tax purposes.

Footnote references are to paragraphs of the 2008 Standard Federal Tax Reports.

[10] ¶ 32,021, ¶ 32,024A [12] ¶ 43,083 [14] ¶ 32,021
[11] ¶ 32,026.024 [13] ¶ 32,021 [15] ¶ 11,600

Also, an ESBT cannot have any interest acquired by purchase, and a specific election to be treated as an electing trust must have been filed by the trustee. This election is irrevocable without the consent of the IRS. This type of trust does not include a qualified subchapter S trust (see below) or a trust that is exempt from income tax.

In the case of an ESBT, each potential current beneficiary of the trust is treated as a shareholder, except that for any period if there is no potential current beneficiary of the trust, the trust itself is treated as the shareholder during this period (Code Sec. 1361(c)(6)).[16] A potential current beneficiary is a person who is entitled to a distribution from the trust or who may receive a distribution at the discretion of any person. Any person who may benefit from a power of appointment is not a potential current beneficiary if the power has not been exercised (Code Sec. 1361(e)(2)).

If the potential current beneficiaries of an ESBT would disqualify an S corporation, the ESBT has a grace period of one year to dispose of its stock in the S corporation, thereby avoiding disqualification (Code Sec. 1361(e)(2)).

A charitable remainder trust is not an eligible S corporation shareholder (Rev. Rul. 92-48). A trust that qualifies as an individual retirement account cannot hold stock in a nonbank S corporation (Rev. Rul. 92-73).[17]

Exempt Organizations as Shareholders. Certain tax-exempt organizations can be S corporation shareholders. These are qualified pension, profit-sharing and stock bonus plans, charitable organizations and any other organization exempt from taxation under Code Sec. 501.[18] An IRA or a Roth IRA may hold stock in a bank S corporation if the IRA held the stock on October 22, 2004 (Code Sec. 1361(c)(2)). If the IRA decides to sell bank stock held on October 22, 2004, it can sell the stock to the IRA beneficiary within 120 days after the corporation made the S corporation election without violating the prohibited transaction rules in Code Sec. 4975.

QSSTs. A qualified subchapter S trust (QSST) whose beneficiary chooses to be treated as owner of the S corporation stock held by the trust also may hold stock in an S corporation (Code Sec. 1361(d)).[19] A QSST must own stock in at least one S corporation and must distribute all of its income to one individual who is a citizen or resident of the United States. The QSST beneficiary is taxed on all items of income, loss, deduction and credit attributable to the S corporation stock held by the QSST. However, Reg. § 1.1361-1(j)(7) treats the QSST, not the beneficiary, as the owner of the S corporation stock for purposes of determining the tax consequences of the trust's disposition of the S corporation stock. In addition, under Code Sec. 1361(d)(3),[20] the terms of the QSST must provide:

(1) there may be only one income beneficiary at any time;

(2) trust corpus may be distributed only to the income beneficiary;

(3) each income interest must end no later than the death of the income beneficiary; and

(4) if the trust ends at any time during the life of the income beneficiary, it must distribute all of its assets to the beneficiary.

However, successive income beneficiaries are permitted. The income beneficiary's election to treat the trust as a QSST may be revoked only with the consent of the IRS. The election is effective for up to two months and 15 days before the election date. A separate election must be made with respect to each corporation the stock of which is held by the trust and must be made by each successive income beneficiary.[21]

C Corporation or S Corporation Subsidiaries. An S corporation can have a C corporation or an S corporation subsidiary. An S corporation can hold qualifying wholly owned subsidiaries (Code Sec. 1361(b)(3))[22] and can own 80 percent or more of the stock of a C corporation. The C corporation subsidiary can elect to join in the filing of a consolidated return with its affiliated C corporations, but the S corporation cannot join in

---

Footnote references are to paragraphs of the 2008 Standard Federal Tax Reports.

[16] ¶ 32,021   [19] ¶ 32,021   [22] ¶ 32,021
[17] ¶ 32,026.40   [20] ¶ 32,021
[18] ¶ 22,602   [21] ¶ 32,021

¶305

the election. Dividends received by an S corporation from a subsidiary C corporation of which the S corporation owns 80 percent or more of the stock are not treated as passive investment income from stock ownership. Instead, the classification of the income is determined by whether the subsidiary C corporation generated the income through the active conduct of a trade or business (Code Sec. 1362(d)(3)(E)).[23]

QSSS. An S corporation is permitted to own a qualified subchapter S subsidiary (QSSS or QSub). This includes any domestic corporation that qualifies as an S corporation and is 100 percent owned by an S corporation parent which elects to treat it as a QSSS. A QSSS is not taxed as a separate corporation, and all its tax items are treated as belonging to the parent (Code Sec. 1361(b)(3)).[24]

Form 8869, Qualified Subchapter S Subsidiary Election, should be used by all S corporations to elect QSub treatment for wholly owned corporate subsidiaries.

Single Class of Stock. A qualifying S corporation may have only one class of stock outstanding. These shares must confer identical rights to distribution and liquidation proceeds (Reg. § 1.1361-1(l)(1)).[25] Differences in voting rights, however, are permitted. A corporate obligation that qualifies as "straight debt" is not considered a second class of stock (Code Sec. 1361(c)(5); Reg. § 1.1361-1(l)(5)).[26] Buy-sell and redemption agreements restricting transferability of the stock are generally disregarded in determining whether the corporation has a single class of stock (Reg. § 1.1361-1(l)(2)(iii)).[27]

Stock of an S corporation does not include stock received for the performance of services that is substantially nonvested, unless the holder has made a Code Sec. 83(b)[28] election to include the value of the stock in income (Reg. § 1.1361-1(b)(3)).[29] However, stock warrants, call options, or other similar stock rights to purchase stock (collectively, "options") generally are treated as stock of the corporation if the options are substantially certain to be exercised at a strike price substantially below fair market value. This rule does not apply if the option was issued:

    (1) to a commercial lender,

    (2) in connection with the performance of services, provided the option is nontransferable and does not have a readily ascertainable fair market value when issued, or

    (3) at a strike price that is at least 90 percent of the stock's fair market value (Reg. § 1.1361-1(l)(4)(iii)).[30]

In addition, restricted bank director stock is not taken into account as outstanding stock in applying the provisions of subchapter S (Code Sec. 1361(f)(1) , as added by the Small Business and Work Opportunity Tax Act of 2007 (P.L. 110-28)). Accordingly, it is not treated as a second class of stock in the S corporation.

306. How to Make An S Election. The election of S corporation status must be made by a qualified corporation, with the unanimous consent of the shareholders, on or before the 15th day of the 3rd month of its tax year in order for the election to be effective beginning with the year when made. The election is made on Form 2553, Election by a Small Business Corporation. The corporation must meet all of the eligibility requirements for the pre-election portion of the tax year, and all persons who were shareholders during the pre-election portion also must consent to the election. If these requirements are not met during the pre-election period, the election becomes effective the following year (Code Sec. 1362(a) and (b); Reg. § 1.1362-6).[31]

A simplified method for shareholders to request relief for late filing of S corporation elections, electing small business trust elections, qualified subchapter S trust (QSST) elections and qualified subchapter S subsidiary (QSub) elections has been provided. Under this procedure, certain eligible entities may be granted relief for failing to timely file these elections if the request for relief is filed within 24 months of the due date of the election. The procedure is to be followed in lieu of the letter ruling process previously

---

Footnote references are to paragraphs of the 2008 Standard Federal Tax Reports.

[23] ¶ 32,040
[24] ¶ 32,021
[25] ¶ 32,021, ¶ 32,024A

[26] ¶ 32,021, ¶ 32,026.03
[27] ¶ 32,024A
[28] ¶ 6383

[29] ¶ 32,024A
[30] ¶ 32,024A
[31] ¶ 32,040, ¶ 32,047

used to obtain relief for a late election under subchapter S. Therefore, user fees do not apply to corrective actions under the procedure (Rev. Proc. 2003-43).[32]

If an entity has failed to timely file both its S corporation election and its election to be treated as a corporation, a separate relief procedure applies (Rev. Proc. 2004-48).[33] An entity seeking to obtain this relief must file Form 2553 within six months after the due date of the tax return for the first year of the intended S corporation election, excluding extensions. The form must state at the top that it is "FILED PURSUANT TO REV. PROC. 2004-48" and include a statement explaining the entity's failure to timely file the S corporation and entity classification elections; among the eligibility requirements is reasonable cause for that failure. An entity that obtains relief under the revenue procedure is treated as having made both an election to be classified as an association taxable as a corporation under Reg. § 301.7701-3(c) and an S corporation election as of the same date.

Shareholders in community property states are eligible for automatic relief for late S elections if their spouses did not file timely shareholder consents. To qualify for relief, the S corporation election must be invalid solely because the spouse's signature is missing from the election form. Shareholders must alert the IRS that they are seeking relief under Rev. Proc. 2004-35 and identify the number of shares they own as of the date of the election. Each spouse must sign a separate statement indicating his or her consent to the election.

307. Termination of S Election. S corporation status is automatically terminated if any event occurs that would prohibit the corporation from making the election in the first place. The election is ended as of the date on which the disqualifying event occurs. Also, if a corporation has accumulated earnings and profits as of the end of three consecutive years, and the corporation's passive investment income exceeds 25 percent of its gross receipts in each of those three years, its election is ended beginning with the following tax year (Code Sec. 1362(d)(3); Reg. § 1.1362-2(b)).[34]

An S corporation election may be revoked with the consent of shareholders holding more than 50 percent of the outstanding shares of stock (voting and nonvoting) on the day the revocation is made. A revocation may designate a prospective effective date (Code Sec. 1362(d)(1); Reg. § 1.1362-2(a)).[35] If no date is specified, a revocation made on or before the 15th day of the 3rd month of a corporation's tax year is retroactively effective on the first day of the tax year. A revocation made after this date is effective on the first day of the following tax year (Code Sec. 1362(d)(1)(C); Reg. § 1.1362-2(a)(2)).[36]

If an election is ended or revoked, the corporation may not reelect S corporation status without IRS consent until the 5th year after the year in which the termination or revocation became effective (Code Sec. 1362(g); Reg. § 1.1362-5).[37] An S corporation whose status as a qualified subchapter S subsidiary (QSub or QSSS) has ended also cannot elect to be treated as a qualified subchapter S subsidiary until the 5th year after the year in which the termination was effective (Code Sec. 1361(b)(3)(D)).[38]

In addition to formally filing an election to end S corporation status, an S corporation can simply create a situation that bars it from being an S corporation. For example, an election to revoke S corporation status relates back to the beginning of the tax year only if the election is made before the 16th day of the third month of the corporation's tax year. Elections made after that date apply to the next tax year. However, if an S corporation wants to end S status immediately and it is too late for a election to end S status for the current year, an S corporation can create a situation where S status will immediately be ended. For example, the S corporation's shareholders can create another corporation and transfer one share of S corporation stock to the new corporation. Because corporations cannot be S corporation shareholders, the S corporation status ends on the date the share of stock is transferred to a disqualified shareholder and it is

---

Footnote references are to paragraphs of the 2008 Standard Federal Tax Reports.

[32] ¶ 32,053.41
[33] ¶ 46,676
[34] ¶ 32,040, ¶ 32,043

[35] ¶ 32,040, ¶ 32,043
[36] ¶ 32,040, ¶ 32,043
[37] ¶ 32,040, ¶ 32,046

[38] ¶ 32,021

¶307

not necessary to wait until the next tax year for the revocation of the S corporation election to become effective.

Correction of Inadvertent Terminations. If a corporation's S election is inadvertently terminated or invalid when made, and the corporation makes a timely correction, the IRS can waive the termination or can permit the election (Code Sec. 1362(f); Reg. § 1.1362-4(a)).[39] The IRS is also authorized to provide a waiver where an election to treat family members as one shareholder or to treat a corporation as a qualified subchapter S subsidiary is invalid when made or inadvertently terminated (Code Sec. 1362(f)). To obtain a waiver, the corporation must correct any condition that barred it from qualifying as a small business corporation, or otherwise made an election invalid, and must obtain any required shareholder consents. All shareholders must agree to make such adjustments as may be required by the IRS (Code Sec. 1362(f)).[40]

Election to End Tax Year. Further, if a shareholder disposes of his interest in the S corporation and all " affected" shareholders consent to the termination, the tax year can be treated as two tax years, the first of which ends on the date of termination. For this purpose, affected shareholders include the shareholder whose interest is terminated and all shareholders to whom such shareholder has transferred shares during the tax year (Code Sec. 1377(a)(2)).[41]

Taxation of Shareholders

309. Tax Treatment of Shareholders—In General. Each shareholder of an S corporation separately accounts for his pro rata share of corporate items of income, deduction, loss, and credit in his tax year in which the corporation's tax year ends (Code Sec. 1366(a)).[42] All items must be separately stated whenever they could affect the shareholder's individual tax liability (Reg. § 1.1366-1(a)).[43] A shareholder's share of each item generally is computed based on the number of shares he held on each day of the corporation's tax year (Reg. §§ 1.1366-1 and 1.1377-1).[44] However, a shareholder's currently deductible share of the corporation's losses and deductions is limited to the total of his adjusted basis in the corporation's stock and any debt the corporation may owe him. Disallowed losses and deductions may be carried forward to any subsequent year in which he has a restored basis in the stock or debt (Code Sec. 1366(d)).[45] Disallowed losses and deductions may be transferred to a current or former spouse when S corporation stock is transferred between spouses or incident to divorce in a nontaxable transaction under Code Sec. 1041(a) (Code Sec. 1366(d)(2)). Following the termination of an S corporation election, any disallowed loss or deduction is allowed if the shareholder's basis in his stock is restored (1) within one year after the effective date of the termination or by the due date for the last subchapter S return, whichever is later, or (2) within 120 days after a determination that the corporation's S election had terminated for a previous year (Code Sec. 1366(d) and Code Sec. 1377(b)).[46]

At-Risk and Passive Activity Rules. The at-risk rules disallow losses that exceed an investor's amount at risk. Generally, the amount at risk is the amount of investment that an investor could lose. The at-risk rules apply to all individuals, including S corporation shareholders and are applied at the shareholder level (Code Sec. 465(a)(1)).[47] The at-risk amount is determined at the close of the S corporation's tax year. Thus, an S corporation shareholder who realizes that his or her at-risk amount is low, and wishes to deduct an anticipated S corporation net loss, can make additional contributions to the entity. See ¶ 2045.

Likewise, passive activity loss (PAL) rules generally are applied at the shareholder level (Code Sec. 469).[48] However, several determinations that affect the application of the PAL rules must be made at the corporate level. For example, the determination of whether an activity constitutes a trade or business as opposed to a rental activity is made at the corporate level. The distinction between portfolio and non-portfolio income is also

---

Footnote references are to paragraphs of the 2008 Standard Federal Tax Reports.

[39] ¶ 32,045
[40] ¶ 32,040
[41] ¶ 32,240
[42] ¶ 32,080

[43] ¶ 32,081
[44] ¶ 32,081, ¶ 32,240C
[45] ¶ 32,080
[46] ¶ 32,080, ¶ 32,240

[47] ¶ 21,850
[48] ¶ 21,960

made at the corporate level. This information is conveyed via the Schedule K-1 that is provided to the shareholder by the corporation. The shareholder then uses the information to apply the PAL and at-risk limitations when preparing his individual tax return. See ¶ 2053.

Since a QSST is treated as the shareholder when it disposes of S corporation stock, the application of the at-risk and PAL rules would normally be determined at the trust level, not the beneficiary level. To ensure that the beneficiary can take disallowed losses on the QSST's disposition of the stock, the at-risk and passive activity loss rules apply as if the beneficiary disposed of the stock (Code Sec. 1361(d)(1)).

312. Tax Treatment of Shareholders—Domestic Production Activities. An S corporation cannot claim the deduction for qualified production activities (i.e., manufacturer's deduction) (see ¶ 980A and following). Instead, the deduction is determined at the shareholder level (Code Sec. 199(d)(1); Temporary Reg. § 1.199-5T(b); Notice 2005-14, Section 4.06).[49] Generally, each shareholder computes its deduction separately on Form 8903 by aggregating its pro rata share of qualified production activity (QPA) items of the S corporation (i.e., income, expenses) with its share of QPA items from other sources. The shareholder does not have to be directly engaged in the S corporation's trade or business to claim the deduction on the basis of its share of QPA items.

However, for purposes of determining the deduction, the activities of an S corporation are not attributed to its shareholders (or vice-versa) (Temporary Reg. § 1.199-5T(g)). For example, if the S corporation manufactures qualified production property within the United States and then distributes the property to the shareholder who subsequently sells, licenses, leases or otherwise disposes the property, then the income derived by the shareholder will not qualify as domestic production gross receipts (DPGR). A limited exception is provided for expanded affiliated groups.

Allocation of Items. A shareholder's pro rata share of expenses allocable to the S corporation's QPA must be taken into account even if the corporation has no taxable income. If the shareholder is unable to claim a loss or deduction of the corporation for regular tax purposes (i.e., at-risk, passive loss, or basis limitations), then such loss or deduction cannot be used when computing the Code Sec. 199 deduction. The amount of any loss or deduction is subject to proportionate reduction if it is only partially allowed for regular tax purposes. Also, a loss or deduction that is temporarily disallowed for regular tax purposes may be taken into account in computing the Code Sec. 199 deduction in the tax year that it is allowed for regular tax purposes.

Instead of taking into account its pro rata share of each QPA item of the S corporation, a shareholder may compute its deduction by combining its pro rata share of the S corporation's qualified productions activities income (QPAI) and W-2 wages with its QPAI and W-2 wages from other sources. However, this option only applies if the S corporation has elected to use the small business overall method for allocating costs, expenses and other deductions to its DPGR (see ¶ 980A and following).

Sale of Stock. Gain or loss recognized on the sale of S corporation stock will not be taken into account by a shareholder in computing its QPAI (Temporary Reg. § 1.199-5T(e)). This is because the sale of an interest in the corporation does not reflect the realization of DPGR by the entity.

W-2 Wage Limitation (Tax years beginning prior to May 18, 2006). Prior to enactment of the Tax Increase Prevention and Reconciliation Act of 2005 (TIPRA) (P.L. 109-222), a shareholder of an S corporation computed the W-2 wage limitation for the Code Sec. 199 deduction by aggregating its share of all W-2 wages allocated to it by the S corporation with all its W-2 wages from other sources. For this purpose, a shareholder's share of the W-2 wages from an S corporation was limited to the *lesser of:* (1) the shareholder's allocable share of W-2 wages of the corporation or (2) two times the applicable percentage (three percent in tax years beginning in 2005 and 2006) of the shareholder's share of the S corporation's QPAI. Generally, W-2 wages of the S corporation were allocated in the same manner as wage expenses. If the S corporation used the

---

Footnote references are to paragraphs of the 2008 Standard Federal Tax Reports.

[49] ¶ 12,468, ¶ 12,476.15

small business simplified method to allocate costs, expenses and other deductions to its DPGR, then the QPAI used by the shareholder was the same as its allocated share of QPAI. In either case, if the shareholder's share of QPAI was not greater than zero, then the shareholder could not take into account any W-2 wages of the S corporation in computing its Code Sec. 199 deduction.

W-2 Wage Limitation (Tax years beginning on or after May 18, 2006). For all tax years that begin after May 17, 2006, TIPRA's enactment date, a shareholder of an S corporation computes the W-2 wage limitation for the Code Sec. 199 deduction by aggregating its share of W-2 wages from the S corporation allocable to DPGR with W-2 wages allocable to DPGR from other sources. TIPRA changed the W-2 wage limitation by limiting the amount of W-2 wages taken into account for purposes of the W-2 wage limitation to wages allocable to DPGR. It also eliminated the limitation (based on QPAI and discussed in the previous paragraph) on the shareholder's share of W-2 wages allocated to it by the S corporation.

315. Shareholder's Original Basis in Stock. An S corporation shareholder's basis in his stock is determined under the same rules as apply to C corporation shareholders. Thus, the original basis of the shareholder's stock is the purchase price for the stock (money or the fair market value of any property given in exchange for the stock) (Code Sec. 1012).[50] Stock acquired by gift normally carries over the donor's basis (Code Sec. 1015(a)).[51] The basis of stock acquired from a decedent is its fair market value on the date of the decedent's death or on the alternate valuation date, if elected (Code Sec. 1014(a)).[52]

317. Adjustments to Shareholder's Stock Basis. The stock basis of each S corporation shareholder is *increased* by the shareholder's portion of:

(1) all income items of the corporation (including tax-exempt income) that are separately computed and passed through to shareholders,

(2) the income of the corporation that is not separately computed, and

(3) the excess of the corporation's deductions for depletion over the basis of the property subject to depletion (Code Sec. 1367(a)(1); Reg. § 1.1367-1(b)).[53]

A shareholder's basis is *decreased* by the portion of:

(1) distributions that are not includible in the shareholder's income due to the provisions of Code Sec. 1368 (¶ 309),

(2) all loss and deduction items of the corporation that are separately stated and passed through to shareholders (but see the caution note below with respect to charitable contributions of appreciated property),

(3) the nonseparately computed loss of the corporation,

(4) any expense of the corporation not deductible in computing its taxable income and not properly chargeable to the capital account, and

(5) the amount of the shareholder's deduction for depletion with respect to oil and gas wells to the extent that it does not exceed his proportionate share of the adjusted basis of such property (Code Sec. 1367(a)(2); Reg. § 1.1367-2(e)).[54]

Caution Note: Code Sec. 1367(a)(2), as amended by the Pension Protection Act of 2006 (P.L.109-280), provides that for tax years beginning in 2006 and 2007 the amount of a shareholder's basis reduction in the stock of an S corporation by reason of a charitable contribution made by the corporation equals the shareholder's pro rata share of the adjusted basis of the contributed property.

If a shareholder's stock basis is reduced to zero, the remaining net decrease attributable to losses and deductions is applied to reduce any basis in debt owed to the shareholder by the corporation. Distributions may not be applied against basis in debt. Any net increase in basis in a subsequent year is applied to restore the basis of indebtedness

---

Footnote references are to paragraphs of the 2008 Standard Federal Tax Reports.

[50] ¶ 29,330
[51] ¶ 29,390
[52] ¶ 29,370
[53] ¶ 32,100, ¶ 32,100B
[54] ¶ 32,100, ¶ 32,100C

before it may be applied to increase the shareholder's stock basis (Code Sec. 1367(b)(2); Reg. § 1.1367-2(e)).[55]

Adjustment to Basis in Indebtedness. Detailed rules on the adjustments in the basis of a shareholder's basis in corporate indebtedness are found at Reg. § 1.1367-2.[56]

Cancellation of Indebtedness. Discharge of indebtedness income of an S corporation that is excluded from the corporation's income under Code Sec. 108(a)[57] is not taken into account as an item of income that flows through to any shareholder under Code Sec. 1366(a) and so does not increase a shareholder's basis in S corporation stock.

321. Taxable Income. Income and loss realized by an S corporation are passed through to the shareholders. Computation of an S corporation's taxable income parallels the computation of the taxable income of an individual, except that organizational expenditures may be amortized under Code Sec. 248,[58] and the reduction in certain corporate tax benefits provided in Code Sec. 291[59] must be made if the S corporation was a C corporation for any of the three immediately preceding tax years. Furthermore, items that a shareholder must report separately must be computed separately, and certain deductions, such as those for personal exemptions, charitable contributions, medical expenses, alimony and net operating losses, are not allowed the corporation (Code Sec. 1363(b)).[60]

322. Fringe Benefits. The tax treatment of fringe benefits paid to employees of an S corporation is different for owner-employees than for other employees. Fringe benefits paid to S corporation employees who are not shareholders, or who own two percent or less of the outstanding S corporation stock, are tax free. They can be excluded from the employees' taxable wages and are deductible as fringe benefits by the corporation. Employee-owners owning more than two percent of the S corporation stock, on the other hand, are not treated as employees for fringe benefit purposes, and their fringe benefits may not be tax free. More-than-two-percent owners are treated in the same manner as partners in a partnership (Code Sec. 1372(b)).[61]

Payments to a partner for services are considered guaranteed payments to the extent the payments are made without regard to the income of the partnership (Code Sec. 707(c)).[62] Guaranteed payments are treated as made to a person who is not a member of the partnership, but only for certain purposes. This generally means that the payment is includible in income to the partner (Code Sec. 61(a)).[63]

Health Insurance Expenses. An owner-employee who owns more than two percent of the S corporation stock can deduct 100 percent of the amount paid for medical insurance for himself, his spouse and dependents (Code Sec. 162(l)(1) and (5)).[64]

For purposes of the deduction, a more-than-two-percent shareholder's wages from the S corporation are treated as the shareholder's earned income. No deduction is allowed in excess of an individual's earned income within the meaning of Code Sec. 401(c)[65] derived from the trade or business with respect to which the plan providing the health insurance is established.

Tax Treatment of Distributions

323. S Corporation Distributions. Distributions of cash or property are taxed according to a priority system that depends upon whether the S corporation has earnings and profits. An S corporation has no earnings and profits unless these are attributable to tax years when the corporation was not an S corporation. An S corporation may also succeed to the earnings and profits of an acquired or merged corporation (IRS Letter Ruling 9046036).[66] For an S corporation without earnings and profits, distributions are treated first as a nontaxable return of capital to the extent of the shareholder's stock basis and then as a gain from the sale or exchange of property

---

Footnote references are to paragraphs of the 2008 Standard Federal Tax Reports.

[55] ¶ 32,100, ¶ 32,100C
[56] ¶ 32,100C
[57] ¶ 7002
[58] ¶ 13,350

[59] ¶ 15,190
[60] ¶ 32,060
[61] ¶ 32,160
[62] ¶ 25,180

[63] ¶ 5502
[64] ¶ 8500
[65] ¶ 17,502
[66] ¶ 32,121.20

(Code Sec. 1368(b); Reg. § 1.1368-1(c)).[67] For an S corporation with earnings and profits, unless an election is made (see ¶ 333), distributions are treated as follows:

> (1) a nontaxable return of capital, to the extent of the corporation's "accumulated adjustments account" (AAA) (see ¶ 325),

> (2) dividends, to the extent of the S corporation's accumulated earnings and profits,

> (3) a nontaxable return of capital, to the extent of the shareholder's remaining stock basis, and

> (4) gain from the sale or exchange of property (Code Sec. 1368(c); Reg. § 1.1368-1(d)).[68]

Before applying these rules, the shareholder's stock basis and the AAA are adjusted for the corporate items passed through from the corporate tax year during which the distribution is made.

If an employee stock ownership plan holds S corporation shares that are employer securities, and the ESOP took out a loan to purchase the employer securities, the prohibited transaction rules will not apply to distributions by the S corporation that are used to repay the loan, and the plan's status as an ESOP will not be jeopardized (Code Sec. 4975(f)(7)).

325. Accumulated Adjustments Account. The accumulated adjustments account (AAA) is used to compute the tax effect of distributions made by an S corporation with accumulated earnings and profits. The AAA is generally a measure of the corporation's accumulated gross income, less expenses, that has not been distributed. The AAA is zero on the first day of an S corporation's first tax year. It is *increased* by:

> (1) all corporate income items (excluding tax-exempt income items) that are separately stated and passed through,

> (2) nonseparately computed corporate income, and

> (3) the excess of deductions for depletion over the basis of the property subject to depletion (Reg. § 1.1368-2).

Tax-exempt income is income that is permanently excludable in all circumstances from the gross income of an S corporation and its shareholders (Reg. § 1.1366-1(a)(2)(viii)).[69]

The AAA is *decreased* by:

> (1) certain nontaxable corporate distributions,

> (2) all loss and deduction items of the corporation that are separately stated and passed through (other than items that are not deductible in computing taxable income and not properly chargeable to the capital account),

> (3) the nonseparately computed loss of the corporation,

> (4) the nondeductible amounts that are unrelated to the production of tax-exempt income, and

> (5) the amount of the shareholder's deduction for oil and gas depletion.

No adjustment is made for federal taxes arising when the corporation was a C corporation. Because the AAA may become negative, the account becomes positive only after the negative balance is restored by later income (Code Sec. 1368(e)(1)(A); Reg. § 1.1368-2).[70] The amount in the accumulated adjustments account as of the close of a tax year is determined without regard to any net negative adjustment for the tax year. A negative adjustment occurs in any tax year in which negative adjustments to the account exceed increases to the account.

Distributions received by an S corporation shareholder in a stock redemption that is treated as a Code Sec. 301 distribution are treated as distributions that reduce the S corporation's AAA (Rev. Rul. 95-14).[71] For a distribution in redemption of an S corporation's stock, if the redemption is treated as an exchange under Code Sec. 302 or Code

---

Footnote references are to paragraphs of the 2008 Standard Federal Tax Reports.

[67] ¶ 32,120, ¶ 32,120B
[68] ¶ 32,120, ¶ 32,120B
[69] ¶ 32,081
[70] ¶ 32,120, ¶ 32,120C
[71] ¶ 32,121.20

Sec. 303, the AAA is decreased by an amount determined by multiplying the account balance by the number of shares redeemed and dividing the product by the total number of shares outstanding. This adjustment is made before the distribution rules are applied (Code Sec. 1368(e)(1)(B)).[72]

The AAA relates only to the most recent continuous period in which the corporation has been an S corporation. However, the period does not include tax years beginning before January 1, 1983 (Code Sec. 1368(e)(2); Reg. § 1.1368-2(a)).[73] If corporate distributions during a tax year exceed the amount in the AAA at the end of that year, the balance of the account is allocated among distributions in proportion to their respective sizes (Code Sec. 1368(c))[74] (see ¶ 329).

329. Post-Termination Distributions. If an S corporation ends its election, the corporation has the opportunity for a limited period of time to unfreeze the income that was previously taxed to shareholders under the pass-through rules but that was not actually distributed by the corporation. Specifically, any cash distribution by the corporation with respect to its stock during the post-termination transition period (Code Sec. 1377(b)(1))[75] is applied against and reduces stock basis to the extent that the amount of the distribution does not exceed the AAA (Code Sec. 1371(e)(1)).[76]

The term "post-termination transition period" means:

(1) the period beginning on the day after the last day of the corporation's last tax year as an S corporation and ending on the later of: (a) the day which is one year after such last day or (b) the due date for filing the return for the last tax year as an S corporation (including extensions);

(2) the 120-day period beginning on the date of any determination pursuant to an audit of the taxpayer which follows the termination of the corporation's election and which adjusts a subchapter S item of income, loss, or deduction of the corporation arising during the S period (Code Sec. 1368(e)(2));[77] or

(3) the 120-day period beginning on the date of a determination that the corporation's election had ended for a previous tax year (Code Sec. 1362(a)).[78]

If the AAA is not exhausted by the end of the post-termination transition period, it disappears. Any distributions made thereafter are taxed under the usual subchapter C rules (that is to say, first, as a distribution of current earnings and profits; second, as a distribution of accumulated earnings and profits; third, as a return of capital to the extent of the shareholder's basis; and, finally, as a capital gain). Because the AAA is always reflected in the basis of the shareholder's stock, failure to exhaust it during the transition period moves it, in effect, below current and accumulated earnings and profits in the priority system for distributions. The grace period for post-termination distributions applies only to cash distributions. It does not apply to noncash distributions. A noncash distribution is taxed under the usual subchapter C rules.[79]

333. Election to Distribute Earnings First. An S corporation can avoid the priority system (¶ 323) for treatment of distributions by electing to treat distributions as dividends. An S corporation might elect to treat a distribution as taxable dividends if it wants to avoid S-status termination for excess passive investment income.[80] However, all shareholders who receive a distribution during the tax year must consent to such treatment (Code Sec. 1368(e)(3)).[81] If such an election is made, the corporation is not required to distribute its entire AAA at the end of its tax year before it can pay a dividend.

Taxation of Corporation

335. Tax Treatment of the Corporation. Since an S corporation is a pass-through entity, it is generally not subject to federal income taxes. However, an S corporation may be liable for:

Footnote references are to paragraphs of the 2008 Standard Federal Tax Reports.

[72] ¶ 32,120
[73] ¶ 32,120, ¶ 32,120C
[74] ¶ 32,120
[75] ¶ 32,240
[76] ¶ 32,140
[77] ¶ 32,120
[78] ¶ 32,040
[79] ¶ 32,240E
[80] ¶ 32,120B
[81] ¶ 32,120

(1) the tax imposed on built-in gains or capital gains (Code Sec. 1374) (¶ 337),[82]

(2) the tax on excess net passive income (Code Sec. 1375) (¶ 341),[83]

(3) the tax from the recapture of a prior year's investment credit,[84] and

(4) the LIFO recapture tax (Code Sec. 1363(d)) (¶ 339).[85]

If the S corporation was incorporated after 1982, immediately became an S corporation and has no earnings or profits, only the capital gains tax applies. If the S corporation was incorporated and elected S corporation status before 1987, the tax on built-in gains does not apply. S corporations are required to make estimated tax payments (¶ 2679) attributable to the corporate-level tax liabilities listed above (Code Sec. 6655(g)(4)).[86]

337. Tax on Built-In Gains. The tax on built-in gains (imposed by Code Sec. 1374) is a corporate-level tax on S corporations that dispose of assets that appreciated in value during years when the corporation was a C corporation. Code Sec. 1374[87] applies only to corporations that made S corporation elections after 1986. Former Code Sec. 1374 continues to apply to corporations that made S elections before 1987.

Under Code Sec. 1374, an S corporation may be liable for tax on its built-in gains if:

(1) it was a C corporation prior to making its S corporation election,

(2) the S corporation election was made after 1986,

(3) it has a net recognized built-in gain within the recognition period, and

(4) the net recognized built-in gain for the tax year does not exceed the net unrealized built-in gain minus the net recognized built-in gain for prior years in the recognition period, to the extent that such gains were subject to tax (Code Sec. 1374(c)).[88]

A recognized built-in loss is any loss recognized during the recognition period on the disposition of any asset to the extent that the S corporation establishes that: (1) the asset was held by the S corporation at the beginning of its first tax year as an S corporation and (2) the loss is not greater than the excess of (a) the adjusted basis of the asset at the beginning of the corporation's first tax year as an S corporation over (b) the fair market value of the asset at that time (Code Sec. 1374(d)(4)).[89]

Recognition Period. The recognition period is the ten-year period beginning on the first day on which the corporation is an S corporation or acquires C corporation assets in a carryover basis transaction (Code Sec. 1374(d)(7); Reg. § 1374-1(d)).[90] For example, if the first day of the recognition period is July 12, 2005, the last day of the recognition period will be July 11, 2015.

The tax is computed by applying the highest corporate income tax rate to the S corporation's net recognized built-in gain for the tax year. The amount of the net recognized built-in gain is taxable income. However, any net operating loss carryforward arising in a tax year in which the corporation was a C corporation is allowed as a deduction against the net recognized built-in gain of the S corporation. Capital loss carryforwards may also be used to offset recognized built-in gains (Code Sec. 1374(b) and (d); Reg. § 1.1374-5).[91]

Furthermore, business tax credit carryovers of an S corporation, arising in a tax year in which the corporation was a C corporation, can offset the built-in gains tax of the S corporation (Code Sec. 1374(b)(3)(B); Reg. § 1.1374-6).[92]

The term "net recognized built-in gain" means the lesser of (1) the amount that would be the taxable income of the S corporation if only recognized built-in gains and recognized built-in losses were taken into account or (2) the corporation's taxable income. In the case of a corporation that made its S corporation election on or after March 31, 1988, any net recognized built-in gain that is not subject to the built-in gains

---

Footnote references are to paragraphs of the 2008 Standard Federal Tax Reports.

[82] ¶ 32,201
[83] ¶ 32,201
[84] ¶ 32,140.80
[85] ¶ 32,060

[86] ¶ 39,565
[87] ¶ 32,201
[88] ¶ 32,201
[89] ¶ 32,201

[90] ¶ 32,201, ¶ 32,201C
[91] ¶ 32,201, ¶ 32,202H
[92] ¶ 32,201, ¶ 32,202J

tax due to the net income limitation is carried forward (Code Sec. 1374(d)(2); Reg. § 1.1374-2).[93]

The amount of recognized built-in gain passed through and taxed to shareholders is reduced by the tax imposed on the built-in gain and paid by the S corporation (Code Sec. 1366(f)(2)).[94]

339. LIFO Recapture. A C corporation that maintains its inventory using the last-in, first-out (LIFO) method for its last tax year before an S corporation election becomes effective must include in gross income a LIFO recapture amount when it converts to S corporation status. LIFO recapture is also required for transfers of inventory from a C corporation to an S corporation in a tax-free reorganization (Code Sec. 1363(d); Reg. § 1.1363-2).[95] The LIFO recapture amount is the amount, if any, by which the amount of the inventory assets using the first-in, first-out (FIFO) method exceeds the inventory amount of such assets under the LIFO method (¶ 1559).

The tax attributable to the inclusion in income of any LIFO recapture amount is payable by the corporation in four equal installments. The first payment is due on or before the due date of the corporate tax return for the electing corporation's last tax year as a C corporation. The three subsequent installments are due on or before the respective due dates of the S corporation's returns for the three succeeding tax years. No interest is payable on these installments if they are paid by the respective due dates.

The Tax Court has taken the position that an existing corporation must include its pro rata share of LIFO recapture when it makes an S corporation election (*Coggin Automotive Corporation*, 115 TC 349, CCH Dec. 54,087). In *Coggin*, the corporation, upon a reorganization, obtained its subsidiaries' limited partnership interests. The existing corporation did not have any inventory itself, but rather its subsidiaries held inventory. The Tax Court determined that in light of the aggregate approach to partnerships, a pro-rata share of the pre-S-election LIFO reserves were attributable to the corporation. However, the U.S. Court of Appeals for the 11th Circuit reversed the Tax Court on this issue (*Coggin Automotive Corporation*, CA-11, 2002-1 USTC ¶ 50,448). The Court of Appeals found that because the corporation did not hold inventory and because the restructuring did not occur for tax avoidance purposes, that there was no LIFO recapture attributable to the corporation.[96] Thus, the Tax Court's decision is the law for all states except those in the 11th Circuit (Alabama, Georgia and Florida).

341. Excess Net Passive Income. S corporations with subchapter C earnings and profits and with total net passive investment income totaling more than 25 percent of gross receipts are subject to an income tax computed by multiplying the corporation's excess net passive income by the highest corporate income tax rate (Code Sec. 1375(a); Reg. § 1.1375-1).[97] "Passive investment income" means gross receipts derived from royalties, rents, dividends, interest (excluding interest on installment sales of inventory to customers and income of certain lending and financing businesses) and annuities (Code Sec. 1362(d)(3)(C), as amended by the Small Business and Work Opportunity Tax Act of 2007).[98] However, such income derived by an S corporation in the ordinary course of its trade or business is generally excluded from the definition of passive investment income (Reg. § 1.1362-2(c)(5)).[99] In the case of a bank S corporation (including a bank holding company and a depository institution holding company), passive investment income does not include interest earned by the bank and any dividends received on assets that the bank is required to hold. The exception for assets applies to stock in the Federal Reserve Bank, Federal Home Loan Bank, or Federal Agriculture Mortgage Bank, and participation certificates issued by a Federal Intermediate Credit Bank (Code Sec. 1362(d)(3)(F)).

Capital gains. For S corporation tax years beginning before May 25, 2007, passive investment income also includes gains (but not losses) from the sale or exchange of stock or securities. However, for tax years ending after that date, gains from the sale or

---

Footnote references are to paragraphs of the 2008 Standard Federal Tax Reports.

[93] ¶ 32,201, ¶ 32,202B	[96] ¶ 32,062.15, ¶ 32,061B	[99] ¶ 32,043
[94] ¶ 32,080	[97] ¶ 32,220, ¶ 32,221	
[95] ¶ 32,060, ¶ 32,061B	[98] ¶ 32,040	

exchange are no longer included in an S corporation's passive investment income (Code Sec. 1362(d)(3)(C), as amended by the 2007 Small Business and Work Opportunity Tax Act of 2007 (P.L. 110-28)).

"Net passive income" means passive investment income reduced by any allowable deduction directly connected with the production of such income except for the net operating loss deduction under Code Sec. 172[100] (¶ 1182) and the special deductions allowed to corporations by Code Sec. 241–Code Sec. 249[101] (¶ 235–¶ 243).

"Excess net passive income" is the amount that bears the same ratio to net passive income as the amount of passive investment income that exceeds 25 percent of gross receipts bears to passive investment income. "Excess net passive income" cannot exceed the corporation's taxable income for the year computed without regard to any net operating loss deduction (Code Sec. 172)[102] and without regard to the special deductions allowed by Code Sec. 241–Code Sec. 249,[103] other than the deduction for organizational expenditures allowed by Code Sec. 248[104] (Code Sec. 1375(b)(1)(B); Reg. § 1.1375-1(b)(1)(ii)).[105] Passive investment income is determined without taking into account any recognized built-in gain or loss during the recognition period (Code Sec. 1375(b)(4)).[106] This means that S corporations without earnings and profits cannot be taxed on excess net passive income if they have no taxable income. This can happen if the corporation has net operating losses and income from passive investments. The tax is not merely carried over; there is no tax due if during the year the corporation did not have taxable income.

The tax on excess net passive income reduces each item of passive income by the amount of tax attributable to it and thereby reduces the amount of passive investment income that each shareholder must take into account in computing gross income (Code Sec. 1366(f)(3)).[107]

The only credits allowable against the passive investment income tax are those for certain uses of gasoline and special fuels under Code Sec. 34 (Code Sec. 1375(c); Reg. § 1.1375-1(c)).[108]

The IRS may waive the tax on excess net passive income if the S corporation establishes that it made a good-faith determination at the close of the tax year that it had no C corporation earnings and profits and that it distributed such earnings and profits within a reasonable time after determining that they existed (Code Sec. 1375(d); Reg. § 1.1375-1(d)).[109]

345. Fringe Benefits. As noted at ¶ 322, for fringe benefit purposes, an S corporation is treated as a partnership, and a more-than-two-percent shareholder is treated as a partner. Amounts paid for fringe benefits of a partner, or benefits provided in kind, generally constitute guaranteed payments that are deductible by the partnership (¶ 421). Accordingly, the cost of fringe benefits provided by an S corporation to a more-than-two-percent shareholder, including the payment of accident and health insurance premiums, is deductible by the corporation (Code Sec. 1372; Rev. Rul. 91-26).[110]

349. Foreign Income. Foreign taxes paid by an S corporation pass through as such to the shareholders, who can elect to treat them as deductions or credits on their individual returns (Code Sec. 1373(a)).[111] Since an S corporation is treated as a partnership (rather than a corporation) for purposes of the foreign tax credit provisions of the Code (Code Sec. 1373(a)), neither it nor its shareholders may claim the indirect foreign tax credit (Code Sec. 902) for taxes paid by a foreign corporation in which the S corporation is a shareholder.[112] The foreign loss recapture rules apply to an S corporation that previously passed foreign losses through to the shareholders and subsequently terminates its S corporation status. For the purpose of computing the amount of foreign losses that must be recaptured, the making or termination of an S corporation election is treated as the disposition of a business (Code Sec. 1373(b)).[113]

Footnote references are to paragraphs of the 2008 Standard Federal Tax Reports.

[100] ¶ 12,002	[105] ¶ 32,220, ¶ 32,221	[110] ¶ 32,160
[101] ¶ 13,002, ¶ 13,400	[106] ¶ 32,220	[111] ¶ 32,180, ¶ 32,181.01
[102] ¶ 12,002	[107] ¶ 32,080	[112] ¶ 27,843.02
[103] ¶ 13,002, ¶ 13,400	[108] ¶ 4150, ¶ 32,220, ¶ 32,221	[113] ¶ 32,180
[104] ¶ 13,350	[109] ¶ 32,220, ¶ 32,221	

Chapter 4
PARTNERSHIPS

Association v. Partnership

401. Partnership Distinguished. A "partnership" includes a syndicate, group, pool, joint venture, or other unincorporated organization that carries on any business, financial operation, or venture, and that is not, within the meaning of the Code, a trust, estate, or corporation (Code Sec. 761).[1] A noncorporate entity with at least two members can be classified under the "check-the-box" rules (¶ 402A) either as a partnership or as an association taxable as a corporation. A noncorporate entity with one member can be taxed either as a corporation or as a sole proprietorship (Reg. § 301.7701-3).[2]

401A. Limited Partnerships. A limited partnership has one or more general partners and one or more limited partners. Limited partnerships are formed under the limited partnership laws of each state. Unlike general partnerships in which all the partners are responsible for partnership liabilities, limited partners are not responsible for partnership liabilities beyond the amount of their investments. In addition, under state law, limited partners cannot participate in partnership management.

401B. Limited Liability Partnerships. Limited liability partnerships (LLPs) are generally used by professionals such as accountants or attorneys. An LLP is a general partnership in which each individual partner remains liable for his or her own malpractice as well as the liabilities arising out of the wrongful acts or omissions of those over whom the partner has supervisory duties. The increasing use of LLPs reflects changed perceptions as to the traditional concepts of joint and several liability for large professional partnerships with hundreds of partners scattered over the country or even on different continents.

Each state and the District of Columbia have LLP-enabling legislation. Some states offer members of LLPs limited protection from partnership liabilities, such as limiting the protection to malpractice claims against other partners. Other states offer full protection from liabilities, including the partnership's contractual liabilities. These are called "full shield" states.

As a practical matter, LLPs are most likely to be used to give liability protection to partners in an existing partnership. This conversion does not create a new partnership, as the IRS has ruled that the registration of a general partnership as a registered limited

---

Footnote references are to paragraphs of the 2008 Standard Federal Tax Reports.

[1] ¶ 25,600   [2] ¶ 43,082

¶401

liability partnership does not cause a termination of the partnership for purposes of Code Sec. 708(b) (Rev. Rul. 95-55).[3] In such a case, the partnership is required to continue to use the same method of accounting used before its registration. Each partner's total percentage interest in the partnership's profits, losses and capital remains the same after the registration as an LLP.

Limited Liability Limited Partnerships. Some states have passed legislation allowing limited liability limited partnerships (LLLPs). These entities operate like a traditional limited partnership, but the "general partner" also has the limitations on personal liability of a partner in a limited liability partnership.

402. Exclusion from Partnership Provisions. In two different sets of circumstances, entities that would otherwise be considered partnerships may elect to not have all or part of Subchapter K apply or to not be treated as partnerships for federal income tax purposes. Application of the partnership tax rules can be avoided in certain cases where the income of the partners can be adequately determined without partnership-level computation and in the case of certain husband-wife partnerships.

Unincorporated organizations may elect not to be taxed as partnerships if they are used either for investment purposes only or for the joint production, extraction, or use—but not the sale—of property under an operating agreement. The exclusion also can be used by securities dealers for a short period for the purpose of underwriting, selling, or distributing a particular issue of securities. The exclusion can be elected only if the partners' incomes can be determined without computing the entity's income first (Code Sec. 761(a)).[4]

An unincorporated organization may choose to be completely or only partially excluded from the partnership provisions. However, the IRS does not allow an organization making the partial election to be excluded from the tax-year conformity rules of Code Sec. 706 or from the limitations on the allowance of losses (Rev. Rul. 57-215)[5] (see ¶ 416 and ¶ 425).[6] This election removes the entity from all or a portion of the subchapter K partnership provisions.

Effective for tax years beginning after December 31, 2006, a limited liability company or state-law partnership whose only members are a husband and wife filing a joint return may elect not to be treated as a partnership for federal tax purposes. Code Sec. 761(f) provides that a "qualified joint venture" will not be treated as a partnership for federal tax purposes. A qualified joint venture is a joint venture involving the conduct of a trade or business if (1) the only members of the joint venture are a husband and wife, (2) both spouses materially participate in the trade or business, and (3) both spouses elect to have the provision apply.

A qualified joint venture conducted by a husband and wife who file a joint return is not treated as a partnership for federal tax purposes. All items of income, gain, loss, deduction and credit are divided between the spouses in accordance with their respective interests in the venture. Each spouse takes into account his or her respective share of these items as a sole proprietor. Each spouse should account for his or her respective share on the appropriate form, such as Schedule C (Code Sec. 761(f), as amended by the Small Business and Work Opportunity Tax Act of 2007 (P.L. 110-28)).[7]

402A. Check-the-Box Regulations. Most entities that qualify for partnership treatment also qualify for electing out of partnership treatment under the "check-the-box" regulations. Any business entity not required to be treated as a corporation for federal tax purposes may choose its own classification (Reg. § 301.7701-3).[8] An entity with two or more members can be classified either as a partnership or as an association taxed as a corporation. An entity with only one member can choose to be taxed as a corporation or can be disregarded as an entity separate from its owner. A single-member limited liability company cannot elect partnership status because a partnership, by definition, has two or more partners.

The default classification for entities existing before January 1, 1997, is the classification the entity claimed immediately prior to that date. For new domestic entities that

---

Footnote references are to paragraphs of the 2008 Standard Federal Tax Reports.

[3] ¶ 25,200, ¶ 25,202.27   [5] ¶ 25,602.11   [7] ¶ 25,602.027, ¶ 25,602.045
[4] ¶ 25,600   [6] ¶ 25,602.11   [8] ¶ 43,083

do not file an election, an entity with two or more members is classified as a partnership. A domestic entity with one member is ignored and the taxpayer is treated as a sole proprietorship. Thus, a domestic LLC will be taxed as a partnership or disregarded entity unless it files an election to be taxed as a corporation.

The check-the-box rules apply somewhat differently to foreign business organizations. Entities listed in Reg. § 301.7701-2(b)(8) are considered corporations and are not eligible to be partnerships under the check-the-box rules. Any other foreign entity may be taxed as either a corporation or partnership (or a disregarded entity if it has one owner). A foreign business entity where all owners have limited liability will generally be treated as a corporation unless it elects to be taxed as a partnership. A foreign business entity where one or more owners has unlimited liability will generally be taxed as a partnership unless it elects to be taxed as a corporation. Thus, the foreign equivalent of an LLC (such as a German GmbH), where all members have limited liability, will be taxed as a corporation unless it elects to be taxed as a partnership.

Note that the term "limited liability" is not precisely defined by the regulations and it may be uncertain whether the IRS would consider a given foreign law to provide for limited liability for all members of an entity. It will usually be easier and safer for practitioners to file an election under the check-the-box rules for a foreign entity rather than to determine what its default classification would be.

An election not to be taxed as a partnership under the check-the-box regulations is filed on Form 8832 and applies to all Code provisions. This is different from an election under Code Sec. 761 (see ¶ 402), which removes a partnership only from the provisions of Code Sec. 701—Code Sec. 777.

Limited Liability Companies

402B. Limited Liability Companies. A state-registered limited liability company (LLC) can be taxed as a partnership for federal income tax purposes. However, its members, like corporate shareholders, are not personally liable for the entity's debts or liabilities. Under the check-the-box rules, an LLC can choose partnership status to avoid taxation at the entity level as an "association taxed as a corporation."

Unlike limited partners, LLC members may participate in management without risking personal liability for company debts. No limitations are placed on the number of owners (compare, a maximum of 100 shareholders for S corporations) or different types of owners of an LLC (S corporations may generally only have U.S. resident individuals or certain types of trusts as shareholders). Additional advantages over S corporations include the ability to make disproportionate allocations and distributions (Code Sec. 704) and to distribute appreciated property to members without the recognition of gain (Code Sec. 731(b)). Members may also exchange appreciated property for membership interests without the recognition of gain or loss (Code Sec. 721).

Conversion from Partnership to LLC. A conversion of a partnership into an LLC that is taxed as a partnership for federal income tax purposes is treated as a nontaxable partnership-to-partnership conversion. The conversion is treated as a contribution of assets to the new partnership under Code Sec. 721 and does not result in gain or loss to the partners. The tax results are the same whether the LLC is formed in the same state as the former partnership or in a different state. Upon such a conversion, the tax year of the converting partnership does not close with respect to any of the partners, and the resulting LLC does not need to obtain a new taxpayer identification number (Rev. Rul. 95-37).[9]

Publicly Traded Partnerships

403. Special Tax Rules. A publicly traded partnership (PTP) is taxed as a corporation unless 90 percent or more of its gross income is derived from qualifying passive income sources (such as interest, dividends, real property rents, gain from the disposition of real property, mining and natural resource income, and gain from the disposition of capital assets or Code Sec. 1231(b) property held for the production of such income) (Code Sec. 7704).[10] A PTP is a partnership with interests traded on an established

---

Footnote references are to paragraphs of the 2008 Standard Federal Tax Reports.

[9] ¶ 25,243.13   [10] ¶ 43,180

¶402B

securities market or readily tradable on a secondary market (or its substantial equivalent), including master limited partnerships. A partnership that was publicly traded on December 17, 1987, continues to be treated as a partnership rather than a corporation if it meets certain conditions (Code Sec. 7704(g); Reg. § 1.7704-2(a)(1)).[11]

When the PTP rules were enacted in 1987, a 10-year grandfather rule exempted certain existing partnerships from corporate treatment. The exception provided that a PTP would not be taxed as a corporation in tax years beginning before 1998 if the partnership existed as a PTP or was treated as having existed as a PTP on December 17, 1987, and did not add a substantial new line of business during that 10-year window. A grandfathered PTP electing to continue its partnership status must pay an annual 3.5 percent tax on any income from the conduct of an active business.

The grandfather provision originally applied only until tax years beginning after December 31, 1997. However, the Taxpayer Relief Act of 1997 (P.L. 105-34) extended the exemption, allowing PTPs covered by the grandfather rule to elect to extend grandfather treatment as an "electing 1987 partnership" beyond the original 10-year period if they agree to pay a tax equal to 3.5 percent of the partnership's gross income (Code Sec. 7704(g)).[12]

Return and Payment of Tax

404. Partners, Not Partnership, Subject to Tax. A partnership does not pay federal income tax; rather, income or loss "flows through" to the partners who are taxed in their individual capacities on their distributive shares of partnership taxable income. However, a partnership is a tax-reporting entity that must file an annual partnership return (see ¶ 406). In determining federal income tax, a partner must take into account his distributive share of partnership income or loss for the year, as well as his distributive share of certain separately stated items (listed at ¶ 431) of partnership income, gain, loss, deduction or credit. A partner's distributive share of partnership items is includible on his individual income tax return (or corporate income tax return for corporate partners) for his tax year in which the partnership tax year ends (Code Sec. 706(a)).[13] See the flowchart at ¶ 63 that outlines the determination of a partner's distributive share.

A partner is generally not taxed on distributions of cash (including marketable securities) or property received from the partnership, except to the extent that any money (including marketable securities) distributed exceeds the partner's adjusted basis in his partnership interest immediately before the distribution (see ¶ 453). Taxable gain can also result from distributions of property that was contributed to a partnership with a "built-in gain" (if property has a fair market value in excess of its adjusted basis) and from property distributions that are characterized as sales and exchanges (see ¶ 432).

406. Return Used by Partnership. Annual information reporting on Form 1065 is required regardless of whether the partnership has taxable income for the tax year. Although Code Sec. 6063[14] states that the return may be signed by any one of the partners, the draft version of 2007 Form 1065 available at the time this publication went to print indicated that the return is to be signed by the partnership's tax matters partner (see ¶ 415). A U.S. partnership's return on Form 1065 is due on or before the 15th day of the fourth month following the close of the tax year. A foreign partnership that does not have U.S.-source income is not required to file a partnership return if the partnership has no effectively connected income and no U.S. partners at any time during the partnership's tax year (Reg. § 1.6031(a)-1(b)(3)(ii)).[15]

For partnerships with an original due date for filing Form 1065 after 2005, Form 7004 should be used to apply for an automatic six-month filing extension. If the original due date is before 2006, then the partnership should use Form 8736 to obtain an automatic three-month filing extension, and then Form 8800 to request an additional three-month extension if reasonable cause can be shown (Temporary Reg. § 1.6081-2T).[16] A partnership that fails to timely file Form 1065 or files an incomplete

---

Footnote references are to paragraphs of the 2008 Standard Federal Tax Reports.

[11] ¶ 43,181	[13] ¶ 25,160	[15] ¶ 35,383
[12] ¶ 43,180	[14] ¶ 36,640	[16] ¶ 36,788

return is liable for a penalty of $50 per partner per month for a maximum of five months unless reasonable cause is shown. A partnership may not contest the penalty assessment in the Tax Court but must pay the entire penalty and then sue for a refund (Code Sec. 6698).[17] Certain domestic partnerships with 10 or fewer partners do not have to pay the penalty if all partners have fully reported their distributive shares on timely filed income tax returns (Rev. Proc. 84-35).[18]

410. Reorganization, Dissolution, or Changes in Membership. The tax year of a partnership closes with respect to a partner whose entire interest in the partnership ends, whether by a sale of the entire interest or otherwise (Code Sec. 706(c)(2)(A)).[19] The sale of a portion of a partnership interest does not result in the closing of the partnership's tax year with respect to the selling partner.

In the case of a sale, exchange or liquidation of a partner's entire interest in a partnership, the partnership "closes the books" as to that partner. In this case, the date of the disposition of the partnership interest is treated *as to the withdrawing partner* as if it is the close of the tax year. That partner's share of the partnership tax items is then determined as of that date, and the partner must include his share of partnership tax items in his income for the tax year in which his partnership interest ends. However, a partnership does not have to make an interim closing of the books. Instead, a retiring partner's share of income may, by agreement among the partners, be estimated by taking a pro rata portion of the amount of such items the partner would have included in his income had he remained a partner until the end of the partnership tax year. The prorated amount may be based on the portion of the tax year that has elapsed prior to the sale, exchange or liquidation, or may be determined under any other method that is reasonable (Reg. § 1.706-1(c)(2)(ii)).[20]

The transfer of a partnership interest by gift closes the partnership tax year with respect to the donor. The share of the partnership income up to the date of the gift is taxed to the donor (Code Sec. 706(c)(2)(A)).[21]

Changes in Partnership Interests During Tax Year. If there is a change in any partner's interest in the partnership (for instance, because of the retirement of a partner, entry of a new partner or simply a change in the allocations of partnership items), each remaining partner's distributive share must take into account the varying interests during the partnership tax year. Generally, this rule may be satisfied either by using an interim closing of the books or by prorating income, losses, etc., for the entire year. However, special rules apply with respect to cash-basis items and tiered partnerships (Code Sec. 706(d)(2); Reg. § 1.706-1(c)(2)(ii)).[22]

If there is a change in any partner's interest in the partnership, the distributive shares of certain cash-method items are determined by assigning the appropriate portion of each item to each day to which it is attributable and then by allocating the daily portions among the partners in proportion to their interests in the partnership at the close of each day (Code Sec. 706(d); Reg. § 1.706-1(c)).[23] For this purpose, cash-method items are (1) interest, (2) taxes, (3) payments for services or for the use of property, and (4) any other item specified in the regulations. Cash-method items deductible or includible within the tax year but attributable to a time period before the beginning of the tax year (for example, payment during the tax year for services performed in the prior tax year) are assigned by Code Sec. 706(d)(2)(C) to the first day of the tax year. If persons to whom such items are allocable are no longer partners on the first day of the tax year, then their portion of the items must be capitalized by the partnership and allocated to the basis of partnership assets pursuant to Code Sec. 755.[24] Cash-method items attributable to periods following the close of the tax year (for example, properly deductible prepaid expenses) are assigned to the last day of the tax year.

In the case of changes in a partner's interest in an upper-tier partnership that has an ownership interest in a lower-tier partnership, each partner's distributive share of any

---

Footnote references are to paragraphs of the 2008 Standard Federal Tax Reports.

[17] ¶ 39,995	[20] ¶ 25,161	[23] ¶ 25,160
[18] ¶ 40,000.10	[21] ¶ 25,161	[24] ¶ 25,580
[19] ¶ 25,160	[22] ¶ 25,160, ¶ 25,161	

items of the upper-tier partnership attributable to the lower-tier partnership is determined by (1) assigning the appropriate portion of each such item to the appropriate days of the upper-tier partnership's tax year on which the upper-tier partnership is a partner in the lower-tier partnership and (2) allocating the assigned portion among the partners in proportion to their interests in the upper-tier partnership as of the close of each day (Code Sec. 706(d)(3)).[25]

Partnership Audits

415. Administrative and Judicial Proceedings at Partnership Level. The determination of the tax treatment of partnership items is generally made at the partnership level in a single administrative partnership proceeding rather than in separate proceedings with each partner. Rules from the Tax Equity and Fiscal Responsibility Act of 1982 (or "TEFRA audit rules") govern proceedings that must be conducted at the partnership level for the assessment and collection of tax deficiencies or for tax refunds arising out of the partners' distributive shares of income, deductions, credits and other partnership items. (Code Secs. 6221– 6233).[26] (See also ¶ 482 and following for special rules applying to electing large partnerships.)

Notice of the beginning of administrative proceedings and the resulting final partnership administrative adjustment (FPAA) must be given to all partners whose names and addresses are furnished to the IRS, except those with less than a one-percent interest in partnerships that have more than 100 partners. However, a group of partners having an aggregate profits interest of five percent or more may request notice to be mailed to a designated partner (Code Sec. 6223).[27] Each partnership has a "tax matters partner", who is to receive notice on behalf of small partners not entitled to notice and to keep all of the partners informed of all administrative and judicial proceedings at the partnership level. The tax matters partner is either the general partner designated as such by the partnership or, in the absence of a designation, the general partner with the largest interest in partnership profits for the relevant tax year (Code Sec. 6231).[28] Settlement agreements may be entered into between the tax matters partner and the IRS that bind the parties to the agreement and may extend to other partners who request to enter into consistent settlement agreements (Code Sec. 6224).[29] This rule has been applied even in cases where the designated tax matters partner had resigned from the partnership but had not formally resigned as tax matters partner (*Monetary II Ltd. Partnership*, CCH Dec. 48,528(M) (1992), *aff'd* 95-1 USTC ¶ 50,073 (1995)).[30]

Consistency Requirement. Each partner is required to treat partnership items on his return in a manner consistent with the treatment of such items on the partnership return. A partner may be penalized for intentional disregard of this requirement (Code Sec. 6222).[31] The consistency requirement may be waived if the partner files a statement (Form 8082) identifying the inconsistency or shows that it resulted from an incorrect schedule furnished by the partnership.

The IRS may apply entity-level audit procedures when it appears from the return that such procedures should apply. The IRS's determination will stand even if it later proves to be erroneous (Code Sec. 6231(g)).[32]

Innocent Spouse Relief. Innocent spouse relief is available with respect to partnership-level proceedings (Code Sec. 6230).[33]

If the spouse of a partner in a partnership subject to the TEFRA audit rules asserts that the innocent spouse rules apply with respect to a liability attributable to any adjustment to a partnership item, the spouse may file a request for an abatement of the assessment with the IRS. The spouse must file the request within 60 days after the notice of a computational adjustment has been mailed by the IRS. Upon receipt of the request, the IRS must abate the assessment. If the IRS chooses to reassess the abated tax, it then has 60 days after the date of the abatement in which to make any

---

Footnote references are to paragraphs of the 2008 Standard Federal Tax Reports.

[25] ¶ 25,160	[28] ¶ 37,770	[31] ¶ 37,570
[26] ¶ 37,565—¶ 37,910	[29] ¶ 37,640	[32] ¶ 37,770
[27] ¶ 37,590	[30] ¶ 37,749.10	[33] ¶ 37,750

reassessment. In such a scenario, the regular deficiency procedures apply (Code Sec. 6230(a)(3)(A); Temp. Reg. § 301.6231(a)(12)-1T).[34]

If the taxpayer claiming innocent spouse relief files a Tax Court petition under Code Sec. 6213[35] with respect to the request for abatement, the Tax Court can determine only whether the innocent spouse requirements have in fact been satisfied. For purposes of this determination, the treatment of the TEFRA partnership items under the settlement, the final partnership administrative adjustment (FPAA) or the court decision that gave rise to the liability in question is conclusive (Code Sec. 6230(a)(3)(B)).[36]

Small Partnership Exception. The TEFRA audit rules do not apply to partnerships with 10 or fewer partners if each partner is an individual U.S. resident, a C corporation or an estate, and each partner's share of any partnership item is the same as his distributive share of every other partnership item. However, these small partnerships may elect to have the TEFRA audit rules apply (Code Sec. 6231(a)(1)(B)).[37] The partnership also can specially allocate items without jeopardizing its exception from the TEFRA audit rules. Once a small partnership elects to have the TEFRA rules apply, the election cannot be revoked without IRS consent (Code Sec. 6231(a)(1)(B)(ii)).[38]

Partnership Tax Year

416. Required Tax Year. Generally, a partnership cannot have a tax year other than its "majority-interest taxable year" (Code Sec. 706(b)).[39] This is the tax year that, on each "testing day," constitutes the tax year of one or more partners having an aggregate interest in partnership profits and capital of more than 50 percent. The testing day is the first day of the partnership's tax year (determined without regard to the majority interest rule). In general, a partnership that changes to a majority-interest tax year is not required to change to another tax year for the two tax years following the year of change.

If the partnership has no majority-interest tax year, then its tax year must be the same as the tax year of all of the partnership's principal partners (partners who individually own five percent or more of the partnership's profits or capital). Partnerships that are unable to determine a tax year under either of the foregoing methods must adopt a tax year that results in the least aggregate deferral of income to the partners (Reg. § 1.706-1).[40] A partnership may avoid the tax year rules set out above if it can establish a business purpose for selecting a different tax year (Code Sec. 706(b)(1)(C); Reg. § 1.706-1(b)(2)).[41]

Code Sec. 444 Election. Certain partnerships are permitted to make an election under Code Sec. 444(a)[42] to have a tax year other than the normally required tax year (Code Sec. 444).[43] For any tax year for which an election is made, a partnership generally must make a "required payment" that is intended to represent the tax on the income deferred through the use of a tax year other than a required year. The payment is due on May 15 of the calendar year following the calendar year in which the Code Sec. 444 election year begins (Code Sec. 7519; Temp. Reg. § 1.7519-2T(a)(4)(ii)) (see ¶ 1501).[44]

Partnership Taxable Income

417. Partnership as Pass-Through Entity. While a partnership is not subject to tax, its "taxable income" is the key feature by which the partnership passes through its income or loss to its partners (Code Sec. 701).[45] Each partner generally must account for his distributive share of partnership taxable income in computing his income tax. The partner's share of partnership tax items is reported to him by the partnership on Schedule K-1 of Form 1065. A partner's basis in his partnership interest is increased by his distributive share of partnership taxable income, while the partner's basis generally decreases by the amount distributed to him by the partnership. Thus, if a partnership distributes all of its taxable income by the end of the partnership tax year, the basis of

---

Footnote references are to paragraphs of the 2008 Standard Federal Tax Reports.

[34] ¶ 37,750
[35] ¶ 37,545
[36] ¶ 37,750
[37] ¶ 37,770
[38] ¶ 37,770
[39] ¶ 25,160
[40] ¶ 25,161
[41] ¶ 25,160, ¶ 25,161
[42] ¶ 20,600
[43] ¶ 20,600
[44] ¶ 42,770, ¶ 42,773
[45] ¶ 25,060

each partner's interest in the partnership does not change (Code Sec. 705 and Code Sec. 731(a)).[46]

The taxable income of a partnership is computed in the same manner as that of an individual except that the following deductions and carryovers are not allowed to a partnership:

(1) the deduction for personal exemptions,

(2) the deduction for foreign taxes (note that the taxes are allocated to the partners as separately stated items),

(3) the net operating loss deduction (which is determined at the partner level, not the partnership level),

(4) the deduction for charitable contributions (which is allocated to the partners as a separately stated item),

(5) individuals' itemized deductions (medical expenses, etc.) set out in Code Sec. 211–Code Sec. 219,[47]

(6) the capital loss carryover (which is determined at the partner level, not the partnership level),

(7) the domestic production activities deduction (which is determined at the partner level, not the partnership level), and

(8) depletion deductions under Code Sec. 611 with respect to oil and gas wells (which are allocated to the partners as separately stated items) (Code Sec. 703(a); Reg. § 1.703-1).[48]

In addition, certain items of gain, loss, etc. (listed at ¶ 431) must be separately stated.

418. Anti-Abuse Regulations. Regulations give the IRS the power to recast transactions that attempt to use the partnership provisions for tax-avoidance purposes (Reg. § 1.701-2).[49] Under the rules, a partnership must be *bona fide* and each partnership transaction must be entered into for a substantial business purpose. The form of each transaction must be respected under substance-over-form rules. Finally, the tax consequences to each partner of partnership operations and transactions must accurately reflect the partners' economic agreement and clearly reflect each partner's income.

Whether there is a "principal purpose" of "substantially" reducing the present value of the partners' aggregate tax liability is determined at the partnership level.

In abusive situations, the IRS can treat a partnership as the aggregate of its partners, in whole or in part, as appropriate to carry out the purpose of any Code or regulation provision. However, to the extent that a Code or regulation provision prescribes treatment of the partnership as an entity and the treatment and ultimate tax results are clearly contemplated by the provision, the IRS will not recast a transaction.

419. Elections by Partnerships. Most elections affecting the computation of income derived from a partnership must be made by the partnership. Thus, elections as to methods of accounting, methods of computing depreciation, the Code Sec. 179 expensing election, the election not to use the installment sales provision, the option to expense intangible drilling and development costs, and similar elections must be made by the partnership and must apply to all partners, insofar as the partnership transactions are concerned (Reg. § 1.703-1(b)).[50] In the case of an involuntary conversion of partnership property, the partnership also must purchase replacement property and elect nonrecognition of gain treatment (Rev. Rul. 66-191).[51]

Individual partners must make the elections to (1) use as a credit or as a deduction their distributive shares of foreign taxes of the partnership, (2) deduct or capitalize their shares of the partnership's mining exploration expenditures, and (3) reduce basis in connection with discharge of indebtedness under Code Sec. 108 (Code Sec. 703(b)).[52]

Footnote references are to paragraphs of the 2008 Standard Federal Tax Reports.

[46] ¶ 25,140, ¶ 25,320
[47] ¶ 12,502, ¶ 12,650
[48] ¶ 25,100, ¶ 25,101
[49] ¶ 25,061B
[50] ¶ 23,950.218, ¶ 25,101
[51] ¶ 29,650.704
[52] ¶ 25,100

Regulations provide for an automatic six-month extension for making elections if the time for making the election also is the due date of the return for which the election is made (Reg. § § 301.9100-1, 301.9100-2, and 301.9100-3).

421. Guaranteed Payments to Partners. Any fixed payments to partners for services or for the use of capital made without regard to partnership income are treated as though paid to a nonpartner for purposes of computing partnership gross income and business expense deductions (see ¶ 432). Thus, guaranteed payments are regarded as ordinary income to the recipient and are deductible by the partnership as ordinary and necessary business expenses (assuming they are, in fact, "ordinary and necessary") (see ¶ 902) (Code Sec. 707(c); Reg. § 1.707-1(c)).[53] This rule applies only to the extent that the amounts paid are in fact "guaranteed payments" determined without regard to the income of the partnership (Code Sec. 707(c); Reg. § 1.707-4).[54] The partner must report the payments on his return for the tax year within or with which ends the partnership year in which the partnership deducted the payments as paid or accrued under its method of accounting.

> **Example 1:** In the AB partnership, Ann is the managing partner and is entitled to receive a fixed annual payment of $100,000 for her services, without regard to the income of the partnership. Her distributive share of partnership profit and loss is 10%. After deducting her guaranteed payment, the partnership has $300,000 ordinary income. Ann must include $130,000 ($100,000 guaranteed payment plus $30,000 distributive share) as ordinary income for her tax year within or with which the partnership tax year ends. If the partnership had shown a $100,000 loss after deduction of Ann's guaranteed payment, her guaranteed payment ($100,000) would be reported as income and her $10,000 distributive share of the loss, subject to the loss limitations of Code Sec. 704(d) (see ¶ 425), would be taken into account by her on her return.

If a partner is entitled to a minimum payment and the percentage of profits is less than the minimum payment, the guaranteed payment is the difference between the minimum payment and the distributive share of the profits determined before the deduction of the minimum payment (Reg. § 1.707-1(c)).[55] Only the amount of the guaranteed payment may qualify as a deductible business expense of the partnership.

> **Example 2:** The AB partnership agreement provides that Ann is to receive 30% of partnership income before taking into account any guaranteed payments, but not less than $100,000. The income of the partnership is $600,000, and Ann is entitled to $180,000 (30% of $600,000) as her distributive share. Because her distributive share exceeds the minimum amount that was guaranteed, no part of the $180,000 is a guaranteed payment. If the partnership had income of only $200,000, Ann's distributive share would have been $60,000 (30% of $200,000), and the remaining $40,000 payable to Ann would have been a guaranteed payment.

A partner who receives a guaranteed salary payment is not regarded as an employee of the partnership for the purpose of withholding of income or Social Security taxes or for pension plans. The guaranteed salary is includible in self-employment income for the purpose of the self-employment tax along with the partner's share of ordinary income or loss of the partnership (Reg. § 1.707-1(c); Rev. Rul. 56-675).[56]

Fringe Benefits. The value of fringe benefits provided to a partner for services rendered in the capacity as a partner is generally treated as a guaranteed payment (Rev. Rul. 91-26).[57] As such, the value of the benefit is generally deductible by the partnership as an ordinary and necessary business expense; the value of the benefit is included in the partner's gross income, unless a Code provision allowing exclusion of the benefit specifically provides that the exclusion applies to partners.

Thus, a payment of premiums by a partnership for a partner's health or accident insurance is generally deductible by the partnership and included in the partner's gross income. As an alternative, a partnership may choose to account for premiums paid for a partner's insurance by reducing that partner's distributions; in this case the premiums are not deductible by the partnership and all partners' distributive shares are unaffected

---

Footnote references are to paragraphs of the 2008 Standard Federal Tax Reports.

[53] ¶ 25,180, ¶ 25,181   [55] ¶ 25,181   [57] ¶ 25,183.16
[54] ¶ 25,180, ¶ 25,181C   [56] ¶ 25,181, ¶ 25,183.30

by payment of the premiums. (Rev. Rul. 91-26).[58] A partner can deduct 100 percent of the cost of the health insurance premiums paid on his behalf (Code Sec. 162(l)).[59]

423. Net Operating Loss Deduction of Partners. The benefit of the net operating loss deduction (¶ 1173) is not allowed to the partnership but instead to its partners. For purposes of determining his individual net operating loss, each partner takes into account his distributive share of income, gain, loss, deduction, or credit of the partnership as if each item were realized directly from the source from which it was realized by the partnership or incurred in the same manner as it was incurred by the partnership (Reg. § 1.702-2).[60]

Limitations on Partnership Loss Deductions

425. Loss Limited to Partner's Basis. The amount of partnership loss (including capital loss) that may be recognized by a partner is limited to the amount of the adjusted basis (before reduction by the current year's loss) of his interest in the partnership at the end of the partnership tax year in which the loss occurred. Any disallowed loss is carried forward to and may be deducted by the partner in subsequent partnership tax years (to the extent that his basis exceeds zero before deducting the loss) (Reg. § 1.704-1(d)).[61] Techniques that have been used to increase a partner's basis so that he can deduct losses that otherwise would be unavailable are making additional contributions to the capital of the partnership (¶ 443) and increasing the partner's share of partnership liabilities, if this is permitted under the "substantial economic effect" rules (¶ 428).

426. Partners and the At-Risk Rules. The rules limiting a partner's deduction for any tax year to the amount he is at risk in the partnership for that year (¶ 2045) apply at the partner level, not the partnership level. A partner is not at risk for any portion of a partnership liability for which he has no personal liability. The at-risk loss limitation rules are applied before taking into account the basis limitation for partners' losses or computing any passive activity loss for the year (Code Sec. 465).[62]

Real Estate Exception. The at-risk rules generally apply to the holding of property in the same manner as they apply to other activities. However, an exception applies to the holding of real estate. A taxpayer is "at risk" with respect to qualified nonrecourse financing that is secured by the real property used in the activity of holding real estate. Thus, lending provided by any person actively and regularly engaged in the business of lending money is qualified nonrecourse financing. Such lenders generally include banks, savings and loan associations, credit unions, insurance companies regulated under federal, state or local law, or pension trusts. Further, qualified nonrecourse financing includes a loan made by any federal, state, or local government or a governmental entity or a loan that is guaranteed by any federal, state or local government. Convertible debt cannot be treated as qualified nonrecourse financing (Code Sec. 465(b)(6)).[63]

In addition, qualified nonrecourse financing can be provided by a related person (generally, family members, fiduciaries, and corporations or partnerships in which a person has at least a 10-percent interest) if the financing from the related person is commercially reasonable and on substantially the same terms as loans involving unrelated persons.[64]

427. Partnerships and the Passive Activity Loss Rules. The passive activity loss limitations (see ¶ 2053) apply at the partner level to each partner's share of any loss or credit attributable to a passive activity of the partnership (Code Sec. 469).[65] A partnership may engage in both passive and nonpassive activities. For example, a partnership may engage in business that is a passive activity of its limited partners (who normally do not participate in the management of a limited partnership), and it may also have investment assets that produce portfolio income (not a passive activity). Thus, a partner who disposes of his interest in a partnership must allocate any gain or loss among the various activities of the partnership in order to determine the amount that is passive gain

---

Footnote references are to paragraphs of the 2008 Standard Federal Tax Reports.

[58] ¶ 25,183.16
[59] ¶ 8500, ¶ 25,183.16
[60] ¶ 25,084

[61] ¶ 25,121
[62] ¶ 21,850
[63] ¶ 21,850

[64] ¶ 21,850
[65] ¶ 21,960

or loss and the amount that is nonpassive gain or loss. In general, the allocation is made in accordance with the relative value of the partnership's assets.

To allow a partner to make these calculations, a partnership must report separately a partner's share of income or losses and credits from each of its : (1) trade or business activity, (2) rental real estate activity, and (3) rental activity other than rental real estate. A partnership's portfolio income, which is excluded from passive income, must also be separately reported (Code Sec. 703).[66]

Generally, a passive activity of a partner is: (1) a trade or business activity in which the partner does not materially participate or (2) any rental activity. Except as otherwise provided (Temp. Reg. § 1.469-5T(e)(2)),[67] an interest in an activity as a limited partner in a limited partnership is not one in which the partner materially participates. If a partnership reports amounts from more than one activity on a partner's Schedule K-1 and one or more of the activities is passive to the partner, the partnership must attach a statement detailing the income, losses, deductions, and credits from each passive activity and the line of Schedule K-1 on which that amount is included.

Partner's Distributive Share of Partnership Items

428. Allocations Under Partnership Agreement Must Have Substantial Economic Effect. A partner's distributive share of income, gain, loss, deduction or credit is generally determined by the partnership agreement. Allocations of any partnership item under the partnership agreement must have substantial economic effect if they are to be recognized for Code purposes. If a partnership agreement does not provide for the allocation of partnership items or if partnership allocations lack substantial economic effect, the partner's distributive share is determined according to his interest in the partnership (Code Sec. 704; Reg. § 1.704-1(b)).[68]

Economic Effect. Allocations have economic effect if they are consistent with the underlying economic arrangement of the partners. For instance, a limited partner who has no risk under the partnership agreement other than his initial capital contribution ordinarily may not be allocated losses attributable to a partnership recourse liability to the extent such losses exceed his capital contribution. These "recourse" losses ordinarily must be allocated to the partners (usually the general partners) who bear the ultimate burden of discharging the partnership's liability. A partnership's "nonrecourse deductions"—those attributable to those liabilities of the partnership for which no partner bears personal liability (for example, a mortgage secured only by a building and the land on which it is located)—are deemed to lack economic effect and, consequently, must be allocated according to the partners' interests in the partnership (Reg. § 1.704-2).[69] See ¶ 448 for a discussion of the allocation of tax basis with respect to recourse and nonrecourse liabilities.

Partnership allocations may be deemed to have substantial economic effect if a set of complicated *optional* safe harbor provisions are met. Generally, to satisfy the safe harbor, a partnership must maintain its "book" capital accounts as set out by Reg. § 1.704-1 and make tax allocations consistent with the capital accounts. A second safe harbor in Reg. § 1.704-2 applies to the allocation of nonrecourse deductions.

Substantiality. The economic effect of an allocation generally is substantial if there is a reasonable possibility that the allocation will substantially affect the dollar amounts to be received by the partners from the partnership, independent of tax consequences (Reg. § 1.704-1(b)(2)(iii)).[70]

Contributed Property. Income, gain, loss, and deductions attributable to property contributed to a partnership by a partner must be allocated among the partners to take into account the variation between the property's fair market value and its basis to the partnership at the time of contribution. (The partnership's basis in the contributed property at the time of contribution in exchange for a partnership interest is the basis of the property in the hands of the contributing partner.) The potential gain or loss ("built-in gain or loss") with respect to the contributed property must be allocated to the

---

Footnote references are to paragraphs of the 2008 Standard Federal Tax Reports.

[66] ¶ 25,100   [68] ¶ 25,120, ¶ 25,121   [70] ¶ 25,121
[67] ¶ 21,965   [69] ¶ 25,130

contributing partner. A similar rule applies to contributions by cash-method partners of accounts payable and other accrued but unpaid items (Code Sec. 704(c)).[71] The distribution of built-in gain or loss property to partners other than the contributing partner within seven years of its contribution to the partnership may result in the recognition of gain or loss to the contributing partner if distributed to the other partners (see ¶ 453).

430. Disproportionate Distributions. The disproportionate distribution rules apply if an actual or constructive distribution to a partner changes his proportionate interest in the partnership's unrealized receivables or inventory. The purpose of these rules is to prevent conversion of ordinary income to capital gain on the distribution or a change in share of unrealized receivables or substantially appreciated inventory.

A disproportionate distribution is treated as a sale or exchange of the receivables or inventory items from the partnership to the partner (Code Sec. 751(b)).[72] This results in ordinary income rather than capital gain. Under Code Sec. 751(f), these rules cannot be avoided through the use of tiered partnerships. Sale or exchange treatment does not apply to a distribution of property that the distributee contributed to the partnership or to payments to a retiring partner or a successor in interest of a deceased partner.

Although the "substantially appreciated inventory" test was dropped for most appreciated inventory in the case of a sale or exchange of a partnership interest (see ¶ 434), it remains in effect for disproportionate distributions from a partnership to its partners. Inventory is considered to be "substantially appreciated" if its fair market value exceeds the partnership's basis in the property by 120 percent or more. The inventory need not appreciate in value after the partnership acquired it to satisfy the 120-percent test.

431. Separate Reporting of Partnership Items. In determining tax, each partner must account separately for his distributive share of the following partnership items (Code Sec. 702):[73]

(1) short-term capital gains and losses,

(2) long-term capital gains and losses,

(3) gains and losses from sales or exchanges of property used in a trade or business or subject to involuntary conversion (¶ 1747),

(4) charitable contributions (¶ 1061),

(5) dividends for which there is a dividends-received deduction (¶ 237),

(6) taxes paid or accrued to foreign countries and to U.S. possessions (¶ 2475),

(7) taxable income or loss, exclusive of items requiring separate computation, and

(8) other items required to be stated separately either by Reg. § 1.702-1[74] or because separate statement could affect the income tax liability of any partner, including:

- recovery of bad debts, prior taxes, and delinquency amounts,
- gains and losses from wagering transactions (¶ 787),
- soil and water conservation expenditures (¶ 982),
- deductible investment expenses (¶ 1085),
- medical and dental expenses (¶ 1015),
- alimony payments (¶ 771),
- amounts paid to cooperative housing corporations (¶ 1040),
- intangible drilling and development costs (¶ 989),
- alternative minimum tax adjustments and tax preference items (¶ 1425, ¶ 1430),
- investment tax credit recapture (¶ 1364),

Footnote references are to paragraphs of the 2008 Standard Federal Tax Reports.

[71] ¶ 25,120
[72] ¶ 25,500
[73] ¶ 25,080
[74] ¶ 25,081

- recapture of mining exploration expenditures (¶ 987),
- information necessary for partners to compute oil and gas depletion allowances (¶ 1289),
- cost of recovery property being currently expensed (¶ 1208),
- work opportunity tax credit (¶ 1342),
- alcohol fuels credit (¶ 1326),
- net earnings from self-employment (¶ 2670),
- investment interest (¶ 1094),
- income or loss to the partnership on certain distributions of unrealized receivables and inventory items to a partner (¶ 453),
- any items subject to a special allocation under the partnership agreement (¶ 428),
- contributions (and the deductions for contributions) made on a partner's behalf to qualified retirement plans (¶ 2113), and
- domestic production activities income and expenses (¶ 431A).

In general, the need for a separate statement of various partnership items gives rise to the separate reporting of these items on Form 1065 and Schedules K and K-1.

Partnerships that regularly carry on a trade or business are required to furnish to tax-exempt partners a separate statement of items of unrelated business taxable income (Code Sec. 6031(d)).[75]

431A. Domestic Production Activities by Partnerships. A partnership cannot claim the deduction for qualified production activities (i.e., manufacturer's deduction) (see ¶ 980A and following). Instead, the deduction is determined at the partner level (Code Sec. 199(d)(1); Temporary Reg. § 1.199-5T(a); Notice 2005-14).[76] Generally, each partner computes its deduction separately on Form 8903 by aggregating its proportionate share of qualified production activity (QPA) items of the partnership (i.e., income, expenses) with its share of QPA items from other sources. The partner does not have to be directly engaged in the partnership's trade or business to claim the deduction on the basis of its share of QPA items.

However, a partner will not be treated as directly conducting the QPA of the partnership (and vice versa) with respect to property transferred between the parties (Temporary Reg. § 1.199-5T(g)). For example, if a partner manufactures qualified production property within the United States and then contributes the property to the partnership which subsequently sells, licenses, leases or otherwise disposes of the property, then the income derived by the partnership will not qualify as domestic production gross receipts (DPGR). A limited exception is provided for certain qualifying oil and gas partnerships and expanded affiliated groups.

Allocation of Items. QPA items of a partnership are allocated to each partner as any other tax item (see ¶ 428). This includes special allocations of QPA items, subject to the rules of Reg. § 1.704-1(b), including the rules for determining substantial economic effect. A partner's distributive share of expenses allocable to the partnership's QPA must be taken into account even if the partnership has no taxable income. If a partner is unable to claim a loss or deduction for regular tax purposes (i.e., at-risk, passive loss, or basis limitations), then such loss or deduction cannot be taken into account in computing the Code Sec. 199 deduction. The amount of any loss or deduction is subject to proportionate reduction if it is only partially allowed for regular tax purposes. Also, a loss or deduction that is temporarily disallowed for regular tax purposes may be used in computing the Code Sec. 199 deduction in the tax year that it is allowed for regular tax purposes.

Instead of taking into account its distributive share of each QPA item of the partnership, a partner may compute its deduction by combining its distributive share of the partnership's qualified productions activities income (QPAI) and W-2 wages with its QPAI and W-2 wages from other sources. However, this option only applies if the

---

Footnote references are to paragraphs of the 2008 Standard Federal Tax Reports.

[75] ¶ 35,381　　　　　　　　[76] ¶ 12,468, ¶ 12,476.15

¶431A

partnership has elected to use the small business overall method for allocating costs, expenses and other deductions to its DPGR (see ¶ 980A and following). A partner's share of QPAI from a partnership may be less than zero under this method.

Sale of Partnership Interest. Gain or loss recognized on the sale of a partnership interest will not be taken into account by a partner in computing its QPAI (Temporary Reg. § 1.199-5T(e)). This is because the sale of the partnership interest does not reflect the realization of DPGR by the entity. However, if the taxpayer receives a distribution of unrealized receivables or partnership inventory for its entire partnership interest (Code Sec. 751 property, see ¶ 434 and ¶ 436), then any gain or loss which would be attributable to the sale or other disposition of such assets which would give rise to QPAI may be taken into account by the partner.

W-2 Wage Limitation (Tax years beginning prior to May 18, 2006). Prior to enactment of the Tax Increase Prevention and Reconciliation Act of 2005 (TIPRA) (P.L. 109-222), a partner computed the W-2 wage limitation for the Code Sec. 199 deduction by aggregating its share of all W-2 wages allocated to it by the partnership with all its W-2 wages from other sources. For this purpose, a partner's share of the W-2 wages from partnership was limited to the *lesser of:* (1) the partner's allocable share of W-2 wages of the partnership or (2) two times the applicable percentage (three percent in tax years beginning in 2005 and 2006) of the partner's share of the partnership's QPAI. Generally, wages of the partnership were allocated among the partners in the same manner as wage expenses. If the partnership used the small business simplified method to allocate costs, expenses and other deductions to its DPGR, then the QPAI used by the partner was the same as its allocated share of QPAI. In either case, if the partner's share of QPAI was not greater than zero, then the partner could not take into account any W-2 wages of the partnership in computing its Code Sec. 199 deduction.

W-2 Wage Limitation (Tax years beginning on or after May 18, 2006). For all tax years that begin after May 17, 2006, a partner computes the W-2 wage limitation for the Code Sec. 199 deduction by aggregating its share of W-2 wages from the partnership allocable to DPGR with its W-2 wages allocable to DPGR from other sources. TIPRA changed the W-2 wage limitation by limiting the amount of W-2 wages taken into account for purposes of the W-2 wage limitation to wages allocable to DPGR. It also eliminated the limitation (based on QPAI and discussed in the previous paragraph) on the partner's share of W-2 wages allocated to it by the partnership.

432. Members' Dealings with Own Partnership. Transactions may be deemed to be between the partnership and a nonpartner if direct or indirect allocations and distributions to a partner are related to the partner's performance of services for, or to the transfer of property to, the partnership and, when viewed together, are properly characterized as a payment to the partner acting other than in his capacity as a member of the partnership (Code Sec. 707(a)).[77] This rule prevents the use of disguised payments to circumvent the requirement that a partnership capitalize certain expenses (such as syndication and organization expenses).

Disguised Sales. While recognizing the fact that a taxpayer may enter into transactions with a partnership both as a partner and as a nonpartner, the Code also recognizes that such transactions are sometimes structured to bypass the requirement that certain partnership payments be capitalized. In order to prevent such manipulation, the Code provides that if:

> (1) a partner performs services for a partnership or transfers property to a partnership,

> (2) there is a related direct or indirect allocation and distribution to the partner, and

> (3) the performance of the partner's service (or the partner's transfer of property) and the allocation and distribution, when viewed together, are properly characterized as a transaction that occurred between the partnership and the partner acting as a nonpartner,

---

Footnote references are to paragraphs of the 2008 Standard Federal Tax Reports.

[77] ¶ 25,180

then the transaction is treated as if it occurred between the partnership and a nonpartner for income tax purposes.[78]

If this provision applies to a transaction, then the "allocation and distribution" made by the partnership to the partner is recharacterized as a payment for services or property and, where required, the payment must be capitalized or otherwise treated in a manner consistent with its recharacterization, and the partners' shares of taxable income or loss must be redetermined (Code Sec. 707).[79]

Whether a transfer constitutes a disguised sale is based on facts and circumstances. However, contributions and distributions made within a two-year period are presumed to be a sale, while such transactions occurring more than two years apart are presumed not to be a sale (Reg. § 1.707-3(c) and (d)).[80] Certain key exceptions to these presumptions are listed for guaranteed payments for capital, reasonable preferred returns, and operating cash flow distributions (Reg. § 1.707-4).[81]

Transactions Between Controlled Partnerships. Special rules also apply to controlled partnerships. Loss is not allowed from a sale or exchange of property (other than an interest in the partnership) between a partnership and a person whose interest in the partnership's capital *or* profits is more than 50 percent. Loss is also not allowed if the sale or exchange is between two partnerships in which the same persons own more than 50 percent of the capital or profits interests (Code Sec. 707(b)(1)).[82] In either case, if one of the purchasers or transferees realizes gain on a later sale, the gain is taxable only to the extent it exceeds the amount of the disallowed loss attributable to the property sold. Gain recognized on transactions involving controlled partnerships are treated as ordinary income if the property sold or exchanged is not a capital asset in the hands of the transferee (Code Sec. 707(b)(2)).[83]

Code Sec. 267(a)(1) disallows deductions for losses from the sale or exchange of property between persons who are in one of the twelve relationships ("related taxpayers") described in Code Sec. 267(b), including a partnership and a corporation controlled by the same persons. See ¶ 1717. Although this loss-denial rule does not apply to a transaction between a partnership and a partner, it does apply to a transaction between a partnership and a person who has a relationship with a partner that is otherwise specified in Code Sec. 267(b) (Reg. § 1.267(b)-1(b)).[84] Under Code Sec. 267(a)(2), accrued interest and expense deductions are not deductible until paid if the amount giving rise to the deduction is owed to a related cash-method taxpayer. For purposes of this rule, a partnership and persons holding interests in the partnership (actually or constructively) or persons related (under Code Secs. 267(b) or 707(b)(1)) to actual or constructive partners are treated as related persons (Code Sec. 267(e)(1)).[85] See ¶ 905 and ¶ 1527.

Sale and Liquidation of Partner's Interest

434. Purchase or Sale of a Partnership Interest. The sale or exchange of a partnership interest generally is treated as the sale of a single capital asset rather than a sale of each of the underlying partnership properties (Code Sec. 741).[86] The amount of gain or loss is based on the partner's basis in his partnership interest and the amount realized on the sale (Code Sec. 721).[87] (The sale of a partnership interest to a partner or to a nonpartner should be distinguished from the redemption of a partner's interest by the partnership. Redemptions are discussed at ¶ 435.)

Despite the general rule that the gain or loss on the sale of a partnership interest is a capital gain or loss, a partner may recognize ordinary income or loss under the constructive sale rules if he receives a disproportionate distribution of partnership unrealized receivables or inventory (see ¶ 430).

If a partner abandons or forfeits his partnership interest, he recognizes a loss equal to his basis in his partnership interest. If the partnership has liabilities, the abandoning

---

Footnote references are to paragraphs of the 2008 Standard Federal Tax Reports.

[78] ¶ 25,180
[79] ¶ 25,180
[80] ¶ 25,181B
[81] ¶ 25,181C

[82] ¶ 25,180
[83] ¶ 25,180
[84] ¶ 14,153
[85] ¶ 14,150

[86] ¶ 25,440
[87] ¶ 25,240

partner is deemed to have received a distribution from the partnership when he is relieved of the liabilities. In such a case, the partner's loss is his basis in his interest less any liabilities of which he is relieved. An abandonment of a partnership interest, if there are no partnership liabilities from which the partner is relieved, results in an ordinary loss because no sale or exchange has taken place (*P.B. Citron*, CCH Dec. 47,513 (1991); *G.G. Gannon*, CCH Dec. 18,304 (1951)).[88] If there are partnership liabilities of which the abandoning partner is relieved, the resulting gain or loss is a capital gain or loss (*A.O. Stilwell*, CCH Dec. 27,950 (1966)).[89] Even a *de minimis* actual or deemed distribution generally results in a capital loss treatment to the partner. Capital loss is also mandated if the transaction is, in substance, a sale or exchange (Rev. Rul. 93-80).[90]

Unrealized Receivables and Inventory. A partner recognizes ordinary income or loss on any portion of a sale of a partnership interest that is attributable to his share of the partnership's unrealized receivables and inventory (Code Sec. 751(a)).[91] The gain is measured by the portion of the selling price attributable to unrealized receivables and inventory and the partner's basis in these assets. The partner's basis is the basis the partner's share of partnership unrealized receivables and inventory would have if these assets were distributed to him in a current distribution (Reg. § 1.751-1(a)(2)).[92] Capital gain or loss is determined by subtracting his remaining basis from the rest of the amount realized (Reg. § 1.741-1(a)).[93]

435. Partnership Interest Redeemed by Partnership. If a partner's interest is liquidated solely through a distribution of partnership property other than money (including marketable securities), no gain is recognized. The partner's basis in his partnership interest is transferred to the distributed assets, and any gain is recognized when the assets are disposed of (Code Sec. 731(a)).[94]

If a partner receives money or marketable securities as all or part of his liquidating distribution, he recognizes gain to the extent that the value of the cash or marketable securities exceeds his basis in the partnership interest (Code Sec. 731(c);[95] Code Sec. 732(b)).[96] A partner recognizes loss if no property other than money, unrealized receivables and inventory items are distributed to him, and his basis in his partnership interest exceeds the amount of money plus the basis of the distributed receivables and inventory (Code Sec. 731(a)).[97] However, if the partner is relieved of any or all of his share of partnership liabilities, the relief from liability is treated the same as a cash distribution (Reg. § 1.731-1(a)(1)).[98]

If a partner receives cash and unrealized receivables and inventory for his partnership interest, loss can be recognized in the amount by which the basis in the partnership interest exceeds the amount of money, plus the basis of the distributed receivables and inventory (Code Sec. 731(a)(2)).[99]

> **Example:** Martin has an adjusted basis in his partnership interest of $100,000. He retires from the partnership and receives as a distribution in liquidation of his interest his share of partnership property. This share is $50,000 cash and inventory with a basis to him of $30,000. Martin can recognize a loss of $20,000, his basis minus the money received and his basis in the inventory distributed to him ($100,000 − ($50,000 + $30,000) = $20,000).

If a partner receives money or property in exchange for any part of his partnership interest, the amount attributable to the partner's share of the partnership's unrealized receivables or inventory items results in ordinary income or loss. This treatment applies to the unrealized receivables portion of the payments to a retiring partner or successor in interest of a deceased partner only if that part is not treated as paid in exchange for partnership property. The rationale behind this rule is that the inventory or the accounts receivable would give rise to ordinary income had the partnership interest not been sold. However, if the partner does not sell the distributed inventory items within five years

---

Footnote references are to paragraphs of the 2008 Standard Federal Tax Reports.

[88] ¶ 25,442.12, ¶ 25,422.545, ¶ 25,422.545
[89] ¶ 25,422.545
[90] ¶ 25,442.12
[91] ¶ 25,500
[92] ¶ 25,501
[93] ¶ 25,441
[94] ¶ 25,320
[95] ¶ 25,320
[96] ¶ 25,340
[97] ¶ 25,320
[98] ¶ 25,321
[99] ¶ 25,320

from the date of distribution, the gain can be recognized as a capital gain (Code Sec. 735(a)(2)).[100] For purposes of this rule, the term "inventory" does not include real estate or depreciable trade or business property (Code Sec. 735(c)(1)).[101] (Compare the general definition of "inventory" at ¶ 436, below.)

For exchanges of partnership interests involving unrealized receivables or inventory, the partnership must file an information return describing the exchange and furnish statements to each party (Reg. § 1.6050K-1).[102] See also ¶ 453.

436. "Unrealized Receivables" and "Inventory Items" Defined. The term "unrealized receivables" includes any rights to income for services or goods that are not capital assets that have not been included in gross income under the method of accounting employed by the partnership (Code Sec. 751(c); Reg. § 1.751-1(c)).[103] For the most part, this classification relates to cash-method partnerships that have acquired a contractual or legal right to income for goods or services. In the usual case, the term does not apply to an accrual-method partnership because it has already included unrealized receivables in gross income.

The term "unrealized receivables" also includes certain property to the extent of the amount of gain that would have been realized and recharacterized or recaptured as ordinary income by the partnership if it had sold the property at its fair market value at the time of the sale or exchange of the partnership interest being considered. The types of property covered, which include depreciable personal property and real property, are listed in the flush language of Code Sec. 751(c) (Reg. § 1.751-1(c)(4)). This property is not treated as an unrealized receivable for purposes of Code Sec. 736, relating to payments in liquidation of a retiring or deceased partner's interest.

The term "inventory items" is broader than the term itself might suggest (Code Sec. 751(d)). It includes not only inventory, but also any other assets that would not be treated either as capital assets or Sec. 1231 assets (generally, depreciable property and land used in a trade or business) if they were sold by the partnership (or by the partner, if he had held them). Thus, the term might include a copyright or artistic work, accounts receivable for services and inventory, or any unrealized receivables (Reg. § 1.751-1(d)(2)).

Distributions of inventory made in exchange for all or a part of a partner's interest in other partnership property, including money, are governed by the "substantially appreciated" rule (Code Sec. 751(b)). Thus, gain from such distributions is taxed as ordinary income if the fair market value of the partnership's inventory exceeds 120 percent of its adjusted basis (Reg. § 1.751-1(d)).[104]

438. Retiring Partner's or Successor's Shares. Payments made in liquidation of the interest of a retiring or deceased partner are considered distributions by the partnership to the extent that the payments are in exchange for the partner's interest in partnership property (Code Sec. 736(b) and Code Sec. 761(d)).[105] This provision does not apply if the estate or other successor in interest of a deceased partner continues as a partner in its own right under local law. In addition, it applies only to payments made by the partnership and not to transactions, such as the sale of a partnership interest, between the partners (Reg. § 1.736-1(a)(1)).[106]

Under Code Sec. 731, distributions are generally nontaxable except to the extent that money distributed exceeds the partner's adjusted basis for his partnership interest (see ¶ 453); the excess is treated as capital gain. However, all gain relating to inventory is treated as being from the sale of a noncapital asset (Code Sec. 751(b)).[107] The partners' valuation in an arm's-length agreement of a retiring or deceased partner's interest in partnership property is presumptively correct, but that presumption may be rebutted (Reg. § 1.736-1(b)(1)).[108]

Payments for unrealized receivables and goodwill are treated as distributive shares of partnership income or as guaranteed payments if capital is not a material income-

---

Footnote references are to paragraphs of the 2008 Standard Federal Tax Reports.

[100] ¶ 25,400	[103] ¶ 25,500, ¶ 25,501	[106] ¶ 25,421
[101] ¶ 25,400	[104] ¶ 25,501	[107] ¶ 25,500
[102] ¶ 36,241	[105] ¶ 25,420, ¶ 25,600	[108] ¶ 25,421

¶436

producing factor and the retiring or deceased partner was a general partner.[109] Such payments are deductible by the partnership. If these two requirements are not met, payments for goodwill are treated as payments for partnership property and do not create a deduction for the partnership. However, payments for goodwill can be treated as payments for property if:[110]

(1) goodwill was originally purchased by the partnership or otherwise acquired in a transaction resulting in a cash basis to the partnership, *or*

(2) the partnership agreement calls for a reasonable payment for goodwill.

Such payments result in capital gain or loss to the extent of the partnership's basis in the goodwill. In fixing the amount attributable to goodwill, an amount arrived at under an arm's-length agreement generally is accepted by the IRS. A formula approach involving the capitalization or earnings in excess of a fair market rate or return on the partnership's net tangible assets may be used, but only where there is no better basis for making such a determination (Rev. Rul. 68-609).[111]

These excluded amounts and other payments made for an interest in the partnership property are treated as either distributive shares of partnership income or as guaranteed payments (Code Sec. 736(a)).[112] If the payments are determined by reference to partnership income, they are taxed as a distributive share to the recipient; if not, they are treated as "guaranteed payments" (¶ 421). Accordingly, if the payments consist of a percentage of partnership profits, they reduce the distributive shares of income of the remaining partners. If they are guaranteed payments, the effect is the same because they are deductible as business expenses in determining partnership taxable income. In either event, the payments are treated as ordinary income in the hands of the recipient partner.

Example 1: Partnership ABC is a personal service partnership and its balance sheet is as follows:

Assets			Liabilities and Capital		
	Adjusted basis	Market value		Adjusted basis	Market value
Cash	$130,000	$130,000	Liabilities .	$30,000	$30,000
Accounts			Capital:		
receivable . .	0	300,000	A	100,000	210,000
Capital and Sec.			B	100,000	210,000
1231 assets .	200,000	230,000	C	100,000	210,000
Total	$330,000	$660,000	Total .	$330,000	$660,000

General Partner A retires from the partnership in accordance with an agreement whereby his share of liabilities (⅓ of $30,000) is assumed. In addition, he is to receive $90,000 in the year of retirement plus $100,000 in each of the two succeeding years, a total of $300,000 (including his $10,000 share of liabilities), for his partnership interest. The value of A's interest in the partnership's section 736(b) property is $120,000 (⅓ of $360,000, the sum of $130,000 cash and $230,000, the fair market value of Code Sec. 1231 assets). The accounts receivable are not included in A's interest in partnership property because A is a general partner in a partnership in which capital is not a material income-producing factor. Assuming that the basis of A's interest is $110,000 ($100,000, the basis of his capital investment, plus $10,000, his share of partnership liabilities), he realizes a capital gain of $10,000 on the sale of his interest in partnership property. The $180,000 balance to be received by him is treated as guaranteed payments taxable to A as ordinary income.

The $100,000 that A receives in each of the three years would ordinarily be allocated as follows: $40,000 as payments for A's interest in section 736(b) property ($120,000/$300,000 × $100,000) and the balance of $60,000 as guaranteed payments. While the $10,000 capital gain is normally recognized in the first year, A may elect to prorate the gain over the three-year period.

Footnote references are to paragraphs of the 2008 Standard Federal Tax Reports.

[109] ¶ 25,420
[110] ¶ 25,422.04
[111] ¶ 25,422.04
[112] ¶ 25,420

Example 2: Assume the same facts as in Example 1, above, except that the agreement provides for payments to A for three years of a percentage of annual income instead of a fixed amount. In such case, all payments received by A are treated as payments for A's interest in partnership property until he has received $120,000. Thereafter, the payments are treated as a distributive share of partnership income to A (Reg. § 1.736-1(b)(7)).[113]

For income tax purposes, a retired partner or a deceased partner's successor is treated as a partner until his interest has been completely liquidated (Reg. § 1.736-1(a)(6)).[114]

440. Partner Receiving Income "In Respect of a Decedent". All payments to the successor of a deceased partner under Code Sec. 736(a), relating to payments made in liquidation of a deceased partner's interest and considered as a distributive share or guaranteed payment (see ¶ 438), are income "in respect of a decedent" (Code Sec. 753).[115] Under Code Sec. 691 the payments are taxed to the recipient when received to the extent that they are not properly includible in the short tax year ending with the decedent's death.

The estate or heir of a deceased partner is also treated as receiving income in respect of a decedent to the extent that amounts are received from an outsider in exchange for rights to future payments by the partnership representing distributive shares or guaranteed payments (Reg. § 1.753-1(a)).[116]

Partnership Contributions and Basis

443. Contribution to Partnership. No gain or loss is recognized, either by the partnership or by any of its partners, upon a contribution of property to the partnership in exchange for a partnership interest (Code Sec. 721(a)).[117] This is true whether the contribution is made to an existing partnership or to a newly formed partnership (Reg. § 1.721-1).[118] However, a partner must recognize any gain realized on the transfer of appreciated property to a partnership that would be treated as an investment company if the partnership were incorporated (Code Sec. 707(c) and Code Sec. 721(b)).[119] Further, the value of a capital interest in a partnership that is transferred to a partner in exchange for his services is taxable to him as ordinary income, provided that the interest is not subject to a substantial risk of forfeiture (Reg. § 1.721-1(b)) (see ¶ 1933).

The receipt of a profits interest (as opposed to a capital interest) in exchange for services rendered is not taxable as ordinary income (Rev. Proc. 93-27).[120]

The basis of a partner's interest acquired in exchange for his contribution to the partnership is the amount of the money contributed plus the adjusted basis to the contributing partner of any property contributed (Code Sec. 722).[121] If a partner receives a partnership interest as compensation for services rendered or to be rendered, resulting in taxable income to the incoming partner, that income is added to the basis of his interest (Reg. § 1.722-1).[122] If the contributed property is subject to debt or if liabilities of the partner are assumed by the partnership, the basis of the contributing partner's interest is reduced by the portion of the indebtedness assumed by the other partners. Such assumption of the partner's debt by others is treated as a distribution of money to him and as a contribution of money by those assuming the debt (Code Sec. 752).[123] See ¶ 447.

The basis to the partnership of property contributed by a partner is the adjusted basis of such property in the hands of the contributing partner at the time of the contribution and any gain he recognized on the transfer to the partnership under Code Sec. 721(b) (Code Sec. 723).[124] However, it has been held that the basis of a nonbusiness asset (for example, a personal automobile) converted to a business asset upon contribution to a partnership was its fair market value at the time of contribution (*L.Y.S.*

Footnote references are to paragraphs of the 2008 Standard Federal Tax Reports.

[113] ¶ 25,421	[117] ¶ 25,240	[121] ¶ 25,260
[114] ¶ 25,421	[118] ¶ 25,241	[122] ¶ 25,261
[115] ¶ 25,540	[119] ¶ 25,180, ¶ 25,240	[123] ¶ 25,520
[116] ¶ 25,541	[120] ¶ 25,243.12	[124] ¶ 25,280

¶440

Au, 64-1 USTC ¶ 9447).[125] The holding period of a contributed asset includes the period during which it was held by the contributing partner (Reg. § 1.723-1).[126]

Only the contributing partner may take into account any built-in loss. In determining items allocated to the other (noncontributing) partners, the basis of the contributed property is the property's fair market value at the time of contribution. This rule applies to contributions made after October 22, 2004 (Code Sec. 704(c)(1)(C)).

Under Code Sec. 724,[127] unrealized receivables and inventory items contributed by the partner to the partnership retain their ordinary income character in the hands of the partnership. That is to say, unrealized receivables remain ordinary income property up to the time of disposal by the partnership and inventory items remain ordinary income property for the five-year period beginning on the date of contribution (Code Sec. 735(a)).[128] In addition, a partner's contribution of property with a built-in capital loss (when the fair market value of the property is less than its adjusted basis) results in retention of the property's capital loss status in the hands of the partnership to the extent of built-in loss for the five-year period beginning on the date of contribution.

To prevent avoidance of these rules through the partnership's exchange of contributed unrealized receivables, inventory items, or capital loss property in a nonrecognition transaction (or series of transactions), the rule applies to any substituted basis property resulting from the exchange. It does not apply, however, to any stock in a C corporation received in an exchange of property for stock if the contributor is in control following the exchange (Code Secs. 351 and 735(c)(2)).[129] For this purpose, control is at least 80 percent of the total combined voting power of all classes of stock entitled to vote and at least 80 percent of the total number of shares of all other classes of stock of the corporation (Code Sec. 368(c)).[130]

445. Increases and Decreases in Basis of Partner's Interest. The basis of a partner's interest is *increased* by his distributive share of partnership taxable income, the partnership's tax-exempt income, and the excess of the partnership deductions for depletion over the basis to the partnership of the depletable property. The basis of the partner's interest is *decreased* (but not below zero) by distributions to him from the partnership (applying the rules at ¶ 453) and by the sum of his share of partnership losses, his share of partnership expenditures not deductible in computing its taxable income and not chargeable to capital account, and his depletion deduction for oil and gas wells (Code Sec. 705(a)).[131] Distributions are to be taken into account before losses in adjusting the partner's interest basis (Rev. Rul. 66-94).[132]

Example: Partner A of ABC partnership has an $80,000 basis for her partnership interest. During the tax year, she receives cash distributions of $50,000, and her share of the partnership's losses is $40,000. Her interest is adjusted as follows:

Basis at beginning of year	$80,000	
Less cash distributions	50,000	$30,000
Less share of losses ($40,000) but only to the extent that the basis is not reduced below zero		30,000
Adjusted basis for interest		0

Because basis is decreased by distributions received before reduction by A's share of partnership losses, no gain is recognized under Code Sec. 731 on the cash distribution. However, $10,000 of A's share of partnership loss is disallowed and carried forward to subsequent tax years (see ¶ 425).[133]

Bases of partnership interests may also be determined by reference to proportionate shares of the adjusted basis of partnership property that would be distributable if the partnership were to be ended. This alternative rule is available only in limited circumstances if a partner cannot practicably apply the general rule or when the IRS approves (Code Sec. 705(b); Reg. § 1.705-1(b)).[134]

Footnote references are to paragraphs of the 2008 Standard Federal Tax Reports.

[125] ¶ 25,282.02
[126] ¶ 25,281
[127] ¶ 25,300
[128] ¶ 25,400
[129] ¶ 16,402, ¶ 25,400
[130] ¶ 16,750
[131] ¶ 25,140
[132] ¶ 25,144.12
[133] ¶ 25,320
[134] ¶ 25,140, ¶ 25,141

For purposes of determining a partner's basis in his partnership interest or for figuring gain or loss on a distribution, advances or drawings of money or property against a partner's distributive share of income are treated as current distributions made on the last day of the partnership's tax year (Reg. § 1.731-1(a)(1)(ii)).[135] Money received by a partner under an obligation to repay the partnership is not a distribution but is a loan that is treated as a transaction between the partnership and a nonpartner (Reg. § 1.707-1(a) and Reg. § 1.731-1(c)(2)).[136]

447. Liabilities Treated as Distributions or Contributions. Any increase in a partner's share of partnership liabilities, including a partner's assumption of partnership liabilities or receipt of partnership property subject to a liability (limited to the fair market value of the encumbered property), is treated as a contribution of money that increases a partner's basis in his interest (Code Sec. 722 and Code Sec. 752(a)).[137] A decrease in a partner's share of partnership liabilities is treated as a distribution of money by the partnership, which decreases the distributee partner's basis in his partnership interest (but not below zero) (Code Sec. 733 and Code Sec. 752(b)).[138] When a partner's basis has been reduced to zero, such "deemed distributions" can result in a taxable gain. See ¶ 453.

448. Allocation of Liabilities Among Partners. Partners' shares of partnership liabilities (and corresponding allocations of basis) depend upon whether the liability is "recourse" or "nonrecourse." In addition, separate rules apply in the case of nonrecourse debts of the partnership if a partner is the lender or has guaranteed repayment of the debt.

Recourse Liabilities. Liabilities are recourse to the extent that a partner bears the economic risk of loss if the liability is not satisfied by the partnership. Recourse liabilities are allocated in accordance with the partners' economic risk of loss (Reg. § 1.752-2(a)).[139] As a general matter, economic risk of loss is borne by a partner to the extent that he must make a contribution to the partnership (including the obligation to restore a deficit capital account) or pay a creditor if all partnership assets, including money, were deemed worthless and all partnership liabilities were due and payable (Reg. § 1.752-2(b)(1)).[140] Accordingly, a limited partner cannot be allocated recourse liabilities in excess of his capital contribution and future contribution obligations unless he has agreed to restore any deficit in his capital account or to indemnify other partners for their debts with respect to a liability. A partner does not bear the economic risk of loss if he is entitled to reimbursement (for example, through an indemnification agreement or a state law right to subrogation) from other partners or the partnership (Reg. § 1.752-2(b)(5)).[141] Recourse liabilities must be allocated to a partner if a related person bears the risk of loss for the liability (Reg. § 1.752-4(b)).[142]

Nonrecourse Liabilities. Nonrecourse liabilities are those for which no partner bears the economic risk of loss—for example, a mortgage on an office building that is secured only by a lien on the building and on the rents, but with no personal obligation to repay the loan on the part of any of the owners. Such liabilities are generally shared by the partners in a manner that correlates with their allocations of deductions attributable to these liabilities under Code Sec. 704(b).[143] (See ¶ 428.) A partner's share of nonrecourse liabilities of a partnership equals the sum of: (1) the partner's share of partnership minimum gain, (2) the amount of any taxable gain under Code Sec. 704(c)[144] that would be allocated to the partner if the partnership disposed of all partnership property subject to one or more nonrecourse liabilities of the partnership in full satisfaction of the liabilities and no other consideration, and (3) the partner's share of the excess nonrecourse liabilities as determined in accordance with the partner's share of partnership profits (Reg. § 1.752-3(a)).[145]

Although excess nonrecourse liabilities are allocated in accordance with the partners' respective profits interests, the partnership agreement may state their profits

---

Footnote references are to paragraphs of the 2008 Standard Federal Tax Reports.

[135] ¶ 25,321	[139] ¶ 25,523	[143] ¶ 25,120
[136] ¶ 25,181, ¶ 25,321	[140] ¶ 25,523	[144] ¶ 25,120
[137] ¶ 25,260, ¶ 25,520	[141] ¶ 25,523	[145] ¶ 25,524
[138] ¶ 25,360, ¶ 25,520	[142] ¶ 25,525	

interests for purposes of sharing nonrecourse liabilities, provided that the stated sharing ratios are reasonably consistent with the allocation of some significant item of partnership income or gain among the partners (Reg. § 1.752-3(a)(3)).[146] Because no partner bears the economic risk of loss for nonrecourse liabilities, limited partners may be allocated shares of such liabilities (and the basis in such liabilities) in amounts exceeding their total capital contribution obligations.

Partner Nonrecourse Loans and Guarantees. A partner who lends money to the partnership on a nonrecourse basis bears the economic risk of loss for the liability. Likewise, a partner who guarantees an otherwise nonrecourse liability bears the risk of loss to the extent of his guarantee (Reg. § 1.752-2(d)(2)).[147]

A loss incurred on the abandonment or worthlessness of a partnership interest is an ordinary loss if sale or exchange treatment does not apply. If there is an actual or deemed distribution to the partner, or if the transaction is otherwise in substance a sale or exchange, the partner's loss is capital except as provided in Code Sec. 751(b).[148] A "deemed distribution" includes the relief from partnership debts in which the abandoning partner shares. As with other losses, the partners must establish the finality and uncollectability of the loss (Reg. § 1.165-1(d)).[149]

Distributions of Partnership Assets

453. Gain or Loss on Distribution. The income of a partnership is taxable to the partners in accordance with their distributive shares (see ¶ 428). It does not matter when or if the income is actually distributed to the partners. However, distributions to partners decrease the partners' bases for their partnership interests (see ¶ 445).

> **Example 1:** A partner contributes $100,000 to the capital of a partnership. During the first year, his share of the partnership taxable income is $25,000, but only $10,000 of this amount is actually distributed to him. The $25,000 taxable income increases his basis to $125,000, and the $10,000 distribution decreases it to $115,000.

No gain or loss is recognized by a partnership on a distribution of property to a partner, including money, except to the extent that any money distributed exceeds the adjusted basis of the partner's interest in the partnership immediately before the distribution (Code Sec. 731(b)(1)).[150] Loss is not recognized by the partner, except upon a distribution in liquidation of a partner's interest in a partnership. If no property other than money and certain securities is distributed to such partner, loss is recognized to the extent of the excess of the adjusted basis of the partner's interest in the partnership over the sum of any money distributed and the basis to the partner of any unrealized receivables (Code Sec. 751(c)) and inventory (Code Sec. 751(d)).[151]

If a distribution of money exceeds a partner's basis for his interest, gain is recognized by the partner as though he had sold or exchanged his partnership interest (Code Sec. 731(a)).[152] This applies both to current distributions (that is, those not in liquidation of an entire interest) and to distributions in liquidation of a partner's entire interest in a partnership (Reg. § 1.731-1(a)).[153]

> **Example 2:** A purchases a partnership interest for $100,000. During the first year, A receives a cash distribution of $100,000 and a distribution of property with a fair market value of $30,000. He recognizes no gain on the distributions since the amount of money distributed does not exceed A's basis for his partnership interest ($100,000). If he had received a cash distribution of $130,000, a $30,000 gain would have been recognized.

Distribution of marketable securities generally is treated the same as a distribution of money. The securities are valued at their fair market value on the date of the distribution (Code Sec. 731(c); Reg. § 1.731-2).[154]

Gain is determined only by reference to *money* (including marketable securities) distributed. Generally, a partner recognizes no gain on a distribution of property until he

---

Footnote references are to paragraphs of the 2008 Standard Federal Tax Reports.

[146] ¶ 25,524
[147] ¶ 25,523
[148] ¶ 25,500
[149] ¶ 9804.33
[150] ¶ 25,320
[151] ¶ 25,321
[152] ¶ 25,320
[153] ¶ 25,321
[154] ¶ 25,320, ¶ 25,321B

sells or otherwise disposes of the distributed property. Thus, if the taxpayer in Example 2 had received property in kind rather than cash or marketable securities, no gain would have been realized (Reg. § 1.731-1(a)).[155]

However, a distribution of property encumbered by a liability may cause a partner's share of partnership liabilities to decrease, resulting in a "deemed distribution" of money to that partner (see ¶ 447). For instance, if a partner receives a distribution of property subject to a secured liability, the liability becomes a personal liability of the distributee partner, and there is a decrease in the liabilities of all other partners who had been allocated a share of the liability (Code Sec. 752(b)).[156] These partners must decrease the bases in their partnership interests in the amount of their "deemed distributions" (but not below zero), and any amounts deemed distributed in excess of their respective bases are taxable as capital gain.

The nonrecognition rules of Code Sec. 731 may not apply if, within "a short period" before or after property is contributed to a partnership, there is a distribution of either (1) other partnership property to the contributing partner or (2) the contributed property to another partner. If the distribution is made in order to effect an exchange of property between the partnership and a partner or between two or more partners, then the transaction is treated as an exchange, and the "disguised sale" rules (¶ 432) may apply (Code Sec. 707(a)(2)(B); Reg. § 1.731-1(c)(3)).[157] Under Reg. § 1.707-3(c),[158] there is a presumption that distributions made within two years of a contribution are made as part of a sale arrangement. However, the presumption can be rebutted if the facts and circumstances clearly establish that there is no sale (Reg. § 1.707-4).[159]

Loss is recognized only if the distribution terminates the partner's interest—and then only if the distribution is limited to money, unrealized receivables, or inventory items (¶ 436). The amount of the recognized loss is the excess of the adjusted basis of the partner's interest over the sum of any money distributed and the basis to him (which is ordinarily the same as the basis to the partnership (see ¶ 456) of any unrealized receivables or inventory items (Code Sec. 731(a)(2))).[160]

> **Example 3:** A partner whose basis for his partnership interest is $100,000 retires from the partnership, receiving $50,000 in cash and inventory items having a basis to the partnership of $30,000. The taxpayer has a capital loss of $20,000.

These provisions do not apply to the extent that payments are made in liquidation to a retiring or deceased partner and are treated as a distributive share or guaranteed payment (¶ 438), to a distribution for unrealized receivables or appreciated inventory items (¶ 436) (Code Sec. 731(d)),[161] or if the rules governing precontribution gain (¶ 454) are called into play.[162]

454. Property Distribution Within Certain Periods of Contribution. A partner who contributes property may have to recognize gain or loss if the contributed property is distributed to another partner within five years of the contribution (for property contributed before June 9, 1997) or within seven years (for property contributed after June 8, 1997) (Code Sec. 704(c)).[163] The gain or loss recognized under this rule is limited to the difference between the property's tax basis and its fair market value at the time of contribution. Upon distribution of the property within the five-year (or seven-year) period, the "precontribution" gain or loss recognized is equal to the amount that would have been allocated to the contributing partner had the partnership sold, rather than distributed, the property. Appropriate adjustments must be made to the basis of the contributing partner's partnership interest and to the basis of the distributed property to reflect any gain or loss recognized (see ¶ 445 and ¶ 456).

The recognition rule does not apply if the property is distributed to the contributing partner (or its successor). Also, the rule does not apply with respect to certain distributions made as part of an exchange of like-kind property.

A similar rule may cause a partner contributing appreciated property to recognize precontribution gain if he receives a distribution of other partnership property (except

---

Footnote references are to paragraphs of the 2008 Standard Federal Tax Reports.

[155] ¶ 25,321
[156] ¶ 25,520
[157] ¶ 25,180, ¶ 25,321

[158] ¶ 25,181B
[159] ¶ 25,181B
[160] ¶ 25,320

[161] ¶ 25,320
[162] ¶ 25,120
[163] ¶ 25,120

¶454

money or marketable securities) within a seven-year period (Code Sec. 737(b)).[164] Precontribution gain must be recognized to the extent that it exceeds the partner's basis for his partnership interest at the time the distribution is received.

456. Basis of Property Distributed to Partner. The basis of property received in a distribution, other than in liquidation of a partner's interest, is ordinarily the same as the basis in the hands of the partnership immediately prior to distribution. In no case may the basis of property in the hands of the distributee exceed the basis of his partnership interest reduced by the amount of money distributed to him in the same transaction (Code Sec. 732(a)).[165]

> **Example 1:** Taxpayer has a basis of $100,000 for his partnership interest. He receives a nonliquidating distribution of $40,000 in cash and property with a basis to the partnership of $80,000. The basis to the partner of the distributed property is $60,000 ($100,000 minus $40,000). (The partnership can "recover" the $20,000 difference by making the election described at ¶ 459.)

The basis of property distributed *in liquidation* of a partner's interest is the basis of the distributee's partnership interest less any money received in the same transaction (Code Sec. 732(b)).[166]

A distributee partner's basis adjustment is allocated among distributed assets, first to unrealized receivables and inventory items in an amount equal to the partnership's basis in each such property (Code Sec. 732(c)).[167] Under these rules, the term "unrealized receivables" includes any property the sale of which would create ordinary income. This would include, for example, depreciation-recapture property. However, the amount of unrealized receivables is limited to that amount that would be treated as ordinary income if the property were sold at fair market value (Code Sec. 751(c)).[168]

Basis is allocated first to the extent of each distributed property's adjusted basis to the partnership. Any remaining basis adjustment that is an increase is allocated among properties with unrealized appreciation in proportion to their respective amounts of unrealized appreciation (to the extent of each property's appreciation) and then in proportion to their respective fair market values.

> **Example 2:** A partnership has two assets, a tractor and a steam shovel. Both assets are distributed to a partner whose adjusted basis in his partnership interest is $550,000. The tractor has a basis to the partnership of $50,000 and a fair market value of $400,000. The steam shovel has a basis to the partnership of $100,000 and a fair market value of $100,000. Basis is first allocated to the tractor in the amount of $50,000 and to the steam shovel in the amount of $100,000 (their adjusted bases to the partnership). The remaining basis adjustment is an increase of $400,000 (the partner's $550,000 basis minus the partnership's total basis of $150,000 in the distributed assets). Basis is then allocated to the tractor in the amount of $350,000, its unrealized appreciation, with no allocation to the steam shovel attributable to unrealized appreciation because its fair market value equals the partnership's adjusted basis. The remaining basis adjustment of $50,000 is allocated in the ratio of the assets' fair market values, which is $40,000 to the tractor (for a total basis of $440,000) and $10,000 to the steam shovel (for a total basis of $110,000).

If the remaining basis adjustment is a decrease, it is allocated among properties with unrealized depreciation in proportion to their respective amounts of unrealized depreciation (to the extent of each property's depreciation), and then in proportion to their respective adjusted bases, taking into account the adjustments already made.

The result of these changes is that a partner's substituted basis in distributed partnership property is allocated among multiple properties based on the fair market value of the distributed properties. Under the prior rules, allocations were based on the partnership's proportionate basis in the distributed properties.

Optional Basis Adjustments. If a partner has acquired his partnership interest (1) by purchase from a former partner or another partner or (2) from a deceased partner, he can elect to have a special basis adjustment for property other than money received in a

---

Footnote references are to paragraphs of the 2008 Standard Federal Tax Reports.

[164] ¶ 25,425
[165] ¶ 25,340

[166] ¶ 25,340
[167] ¶ 25,340

[168] ¶ 25,200

distribution from the partnership within two years after the partnership interest was acquired. This can be done if the partnership has not made an election to have the special basis adjustment apply to its assets. The partner's election accomplishes substantially the same result as if the partnership had made the election (Code Sec. 732(d)).[169] This special basis adjustment is the difference between the amount paid for his interest, that is, his basis for his partnership interest and his share of the adjusted basis of the partnership assets.

The special basis adjustment applies to property received in current distributions as well as to distributions in complete liquidation of the partner's interest. Reg. § 1.732-1(d)(1)(iv)[170] provides that if the partner makes the election when a distribution of depreciable or depletable property is received, the special basis adjustment is not diminished by any depletion or depreciation on that portion of the basis of partnership property which arises from the special basis adjustment. Depletion or depreciation on that portion for the period before distribution is allowed or allowable only if the partnership made the election.

If a transferee-partner wishes to make the election, it must be made on his tax return for the year of the distribution if the distribution includes any property subject to depreciation, depletion, or amortization. If it does not include any such property, the election may be made with the return for any tax year not later than the first tax year in which the basis of the distributed property is pertinent in determining income tax.

459. Optional Adjustment to Basis of Partnership Assets. If the basis of distributed assets in the hands of the distributee partner is less than the basis of the assets in the hands of the partnership, there may be an "unused" basis. The partnership may elect to adjust the basis of its remaining assets to take up this unused basis (Code Secs. 734, 754 and 755).[171] See ¶ 470.

If gain is recognized by a partner because of a distribution of money, as described in ¶ 453, a similar increase in the partnership's basis of its remaining assets may be made. If an election is made, the partnership may have to decrease the basis of its remaining assets. The decrease would be required for the excess of the basis of distributed assets to the partner over the basis that the partnership had for those assets, in the event of a distribution in liquidation of a partner's interest. Decrease would also be required to the extent that any distribution to a partner resulted in loss to the partner (Code Sec. 734(b)(2)).[172] As explained at ¶ 453, loss results to the partner only if the distribution terminates the partner's interest and generally consists only of money, unrealized receivables, and inventories.

Example: An equal three-person partnership has the following assets:

	Partnership's Basis	Fair Market Value
Cash	$120,000	$120,000
Land	60,000	120,000
Securities	90,000	120,000
Total	$270,000	$360,000

If a partner retires and the partnership pays him $120,000 for the fair market value of his partnership interest, the partnership is really distributing $40,000 as his pro rata share of the partnership's cash and paying him $80,000 for his ⅓ interest in the land and in the securities. However, the retiring partner's share of the partnership's basis for these properties totals only $50,000. Therefore, the partnership, if it wishes to reflect the $30,000 excess cost, may elect to adjust the basis of the land and securities.

A partnership is barred from increasing the adjusted basis of remaining property following a distribution of an interest in another partnership if such other partnership has not made a consistent Code Sec. 754 election. In other words, tiered partnerships must make consistent elections (Code Sec. 734(b)).[173]

Footnote references are to paragraphs of the 2008 Standard Federal Tax Reports.

[169] ¶ 25,340
[170] ¶ 25,340
[171] ¶ 25,380, ¶ 25,560, ¶ 25,580
[172] ¶ 25,380
[173] ¶ 25,380

¶459

The allocation of any increase or decrease in basis is made among the various partnership assets or categories of assets. These rules contemplate generally that the allocation will be made first to "like-kind" assets and will reduce the difference between fair market value and basis of each asset adjusted (Code Sec. 755).[174]

No allocation of basis decrease may be made to stock of a corporate partner. Such basis decrease must be allocated to other partnership property. The partnership recognizes gain to the extent the decrease in basis exceeds the basis of the other partnership assets (Code Sec. 755(c)).

462. Character of Gain or Loss on Disposition of Distributed Property. A partner recognizes ordinary gain or loss on the disposition of unrealized receivables or inventory items distributed by the partnership (¶ 436), regardless of whether the inventory has substantially appreciated in value (Code Sec. 735).[175] In the case of inventory items, this rule applies only if the sale takes place within five years of the date of distribution. If the sale takes place after this period, gain may be treated as capital gain if the assets are capital assets in the hands of the partner at that time (Reg. § 1.735-1).[176]

If a partner disposes of distributed unrealized receivables or inventory items in a nonrecognition transaction (or series of transactions), these rules apply to treat gain or loss on the substituted basis property as ordinary income or loss, except in the case of stock in a C corporation received in a Code Sec. 351 exchange (Code Sec. 735(c)).[177] The House Committee Report to the Deficit Reduction Act of 1984 (P.L. 98-369) states that it is intended that the basis tainting rules regarding distributed property apply only for the period during which the underlying rules as to character of gain or loss under Code Sec. 735 would apply if the property were not disposed of in a nonrecognition transaction. For example, if an inventory item was distributed by the partnership, and the partner subsequently disposed of it in a nonrecognition transaction, ordinary income treatment would apply to any substitute basis property only for the duration of the five-year period beginning on the date of the original distribution.

467. Adjustment of Basis on Sale of Partnership Interest. Generally, the transfer of a partnership interest does not affect the basis of partnership assets. However, the partnership may elect to adjust the basis of partnership assets to reflect the difference between the transferee's basis for his partnership interest (generally, the purchase price) and his proportionate share of the adjusted basis of all partnership property (his share of the partnership's adjusted basis in the partnership property). This election applies only to the transferee partner and applies where there is a "transfer of an interest in a partnership by sale or exchange or upon the death of a partner" and not upon the contribution of property (including money) to the partnership (Code Sec. 743; Reg. § 1.743-1(a)).[178]

Basis adjustments must be made to undistributed partnership property any time there is a distribution of property to a partner with respect to which there is a substantial basis reduction (more than $250,000), whether or not the partnership has a Code Sec. 754 (Code Sec. 734(b)).

The amount of the increase or decrease is an adjustment affecting the transferee partner only. In addition, a partner's proportionate share of the adjusted basis of partnership property is determined in accordance with his interest in partnership capital. Where, however, an agreement on contributed property is in effect, the agreement must be taken into account in determining a partner's proportionate share (Reg. § 1.743-1(b)).[179]

A Code Sec. 743 basis adjustment is mandatory in the case of a transferred partnership interest with a substantial built-in loss. A substantial built-in loss exists if the partnership's adjusted basis in the property is more than $250,000 of the fair market value. An electing investment partnership is excepted from this rule. It will not be treated as having a substantial built-in loss, and therefore it is not required to make basis adjustments to partnership property (Code Sec. 743(e)(1)).

Footnote references are to paragraphs of the 2008 Standard Federal Tax Reports.

[174] ¶ 25,580
[175] ¶ 25,400

[176] ¶ 25,401
[177] ¶ 25,400

[178] ¶ 25,480, ¶ 25,481
[179] ¶ 25,481

The basis adjustment must be allocated among the partnership assets in accordance with the rules set out in Code Sec. 755.[180] See ¶ 459.

470. Election for Basis Adjustment. An election to make the basis adjustments described at ¶ 459 and ¶ 467 is made in a written statement filed with the partnership return for the first year to be covered by the election. The election applies to all property distributions and transfers of partnership interests taking place in the year of the election and in all later partnership tax years until revoked (Reg. § 1.754-1(a)).[181]

Family Partnerships

474. Income-Splitting Device. The family partnership is a common device for splitting income among family members and having more income taxed in the lower tax brackets. A family member is recognized as a partner for income tax purposes if he owns a capital interest in a partnership in which capital is a material income-producing factor, whether or not he purchased the interest. If capital is *not* a material income-producing factor, a partnership resulting from a gift of an interest might be disregarded as an invalid attempt to assign income. In any event, if all the income is attributable to the personal efforts of the donor, the donor is taxed on the entire income. In addition, the donee's distributive share of income must be proportionate to his capital interest, and his control over the partnership must be consistent with his status as partner (Code Sec. 704(e); Reg. § 1.704-1(e)).[182]

Organization, Syndication, Start-Up Costs

477. Syndication and Organization Fees. Generally, no deduction is allowed a partnership or a partner for the costs of organizing a partnership (organization fees) or of selling partnership interests (syndication fees). Guaranteed payments (¶ 421) made to partners for their services in organizing a partnership are capital expenditures and are not deductible by the partnership.

Different rules apply to the deduction of organization fees, depending upon when the expenses are incurred:

• For costs incurred on or before October 22, 2004, the partnership may elect to amortize organization fees (but not syndication fees) over a period of not less than 60 months beginning with the month it begins business (Code Sec. 709).[183]

• For costs incurred after October 22, 2004, the taxpayer may elect to deduct up to $5,000 in organizational expenses in the same manner as start-up expenditures. The remainder of the start-up organizational expenditures may be amortized ratably over a 180-month period, beginning with the month the active trade or business begins (Code Secs. 195(b) and 709(b)). See ¶ 481.

481. Start-Up Expenditures. Different rules apply to the deduction of start-up expenditures, depending upon when the expenses are incurred:

• For costs incurred on or before October 22, 2004, expenditures that do not qualify for 60-month amortization as organization fees but that are incurred in investigating the creation or acquisition of an active trade or business, in creating such a trade or business or in any activity engaged in for profit and for the production of income before, and in anticipation of, the start of the business may qualify for similar amortization under Code Sec. 195.[184]

• For costs incurred after October 22, 2004, for the tax year in which the active trade or business begins, the taxpayer may elect to deduct up to $5,000 in start-up and organizational expenditures. Each $5,000 amount is reduced (but not below zero) by the amount by which the start-up or organizational expenditures exceeds $50,000, respectively. The remainder of the start-up and organizational expenditures may be amortized ratably over a 180-month period, beginning with the month the active trade or business begins (Code Sec. 195(b)).

In the case of start-up expenses incurred by the partnership itself and for which an election is made, the amortization deduction is taken into account in computing partner-

---

Footnote references are to paragraphs of the 2008 Standard Federal Tax Reports.

[180] ¶ 25,580
[181] ¶ 25,561

[182] ¶ 25,120, ¶ 25,121
[183] ¶ 25,220

[184] ¶ 12,370

¶470

ship income. In the case of qualifying investigatory expenses incurred in connection with acquiring a partnership interest, the deduction is taken by the partner who has incurred the expenses. See ¶ 904.

Electing Large Partnerships

482. Simplified Reporting for Electing Large Partnerships. Large partnerships with 100 or more members in the preceding tax year may elect "large partnership" status. An electing large partnership combines most items of partnership income, deduction, credit and loss at the partnership level and passes through net amounts to the partners. Special rules apply to partnerships engaging in oil and gas activities and to partnerships with residual interests in real estate mortgage investment conduits (REMICs). Service partnerships and commodity pools generally are unable to elect large partnership treatment (Code Sec. 772).[185]

A partnership may lose its large partnership status if the number of partners falls below 100 during any partnership tax year. Rules for determining the treatment of a partnership whose membership falls below 100 will be provided by regulations.

An electing large partnership does not terminate for tax purposes solely because 50 percent or more if its interests are sold or exchanged within a 12-month period.

484. Deductions and Credits Generally Combined at Partnership Level. Miscellaneous itemized deductions are not separately reported to the partners. In place of applying the two-percent floor for itemized deductions, 70 percent of the itemized deductions are disallowed at the partnership level (Code Sec. 773(b)(3)).[186] The 70-percent cut is designed to approximate the amount of the deduction that would be lost to the individual partners under the two-percent floor. The remaining 30 percent is allowed at the partnership level in determining the large partnership's taxable income and is not subject to the two-percent floor at the partner level.

Tax credits other than the low-income housing credit, the rehabilitation credit and the credit for producing fuel from nonconventional sources are reported as a single item. Credit recapture also is recognized at the partnership level.

485. Gains and Losses of Electing Large Partnerships. For electing large partnerships, the netting of capital gains and losses occurs at the partnership level. Passive activity items are separated from capital gains stemming from partnership portfolio income. Each partner separately takes into account the partner's distributive shares of net capital gain or net capital loss for passive activity and portfolio items (Code Sec. 773).[187]

Any partnership gains and losses under Code Sec. 1231 (¶ 1747) are netted at the partnership level. Net gain is treated as long-term capital gain and is subject to the rules described above, and any net loss is treated as ordinary loss and consolidated with the partnership's other taxable income.

488. Audit Procedures for Electing Large Partnerships. The TEFRA partnership audit rules normally applicable to partnerships do not apply to electing large partnerships. An electing large partnership, like other partnerships, appoints a representative to handle IRS matters. Unlike under the TEFRA rules, the representative does not have to be a partner (Code Sec. 6255(b)).[188] Only the partnership, and not the individual partners, receive notice of partnership adjustments (Code Sec. 6245(b)).[189] Only the partnership has the right to appeal the adjustment (Code Sec. 6247(a)).[190] After a partnership-level adjustment, prior-year partners and prior tax years generally are not affected. However, prior years can be affected if there has been a partnership dissolution or a finding that the shares of a distribution to partners were erroneous. Instead, the adjustments generally are passed through to current partners.

Footnote references are to paragraphs of the 2008 Standard Federal Tax Reports.

[185] ¶ 25,608
[186] ¶ 25,612
[187] ¶ 25,612
[188] ¶ 37,949Q
[189] ¶ 37,937
[190] ¶ 37,949D

Chapter 5
TRUSTS □ ESTATES

Trust or Corporation

501. Trust, Estate and Fiduciary Defined. A trust is a separate taxable entity for federal income tax purposes. A "trust" usually involves an arrangement created either by a will upon the creator's death or by a trust instrument that may take effect during the creator's life. Under either arrangement, a trustee takes title to the property in order to protect or conserve it for the beneficiaries (see also ¶ 502). Usually, the beneficiaries merely accept the trust's benefits. However, even if the beneficiaries are the persons who planned or created it, the trust will still be recognized as a separate taxable entity if its purpose was to vest responsibility in the trustee for protecting and preserving property for beneficiaries who cannot share in the discharge of this responsibility (Reg. § 301.7701-4(a)).[1] See ¶ 571 and following for rules governing special types of trusts, such as grantor trusts and charitable trusts.

Decedents' estates are also considered separate taxable entities for income tax purposes during the period of administration (see ¶ 507). See also ¶ 504–¶ 506 for the tax treatment of other types of "estates."

Trustees, executors, or certain receivers are considered fiduciaries. A "fiduciary" is a person who occupies a position of special confidence toward another, who holds in trust property in which another person has the beneficial title or interest, or who receives and controls income of another. However, a person who is an "agent" of another person is not necessarily a "fiduciary" for federal income tax purposes, even though a "fiduciary relationship" may be said to exist for state law purposes. For example, when a person receives income as an agent, intermediary debtor or conduit, and the income is paid over to another, the agent is not considered a fiduciary for tax purposes (Reg. § 301.7701-6).[2]

Small Business Trusts. A special kind of trust called an electing small business trust (ESBT) is permitted to be a shareholder in an S corporation. An ESBT is a trust that does not have any beneficiaries other than individuals or estates eligible to be S corporation shareholders, except that charitable organizations may hold contingent remainder interests. The portion of any ESBT that consists of stock in one or more S corporations is treated as a separate trust (Code Sec. 641(c)). See ¶ 305 and ¶ 516.

Qualified Domestic Trusts. A qualified domestic trust (QDOT) is a trust that meets certain requirements and that is subject to a special estate tax (Code Sec. 2056A).

Footnote references are to paragraphs of the 2008 Standard Federal Tax Reports.

[1] ¶ 43,090   [2] ¶ 43,094

Property that is transferred from a citizen decedent to a nonresident alien spouse will not qualify for the usual marital deduction, for purposes of the gift and estate taxes, unless it is transferred from the decedent to a QDOT. See ¶ 2926 and ¶ 2940.

502. Business and Investment Trusts. A "business" or commercial trust is a type of trust created as a means of carrying on a profit-making business, usually using capital or property supplied by the beneficiaries. The trustees or other designated persons are, in effect, managers of the undertaking, whether appointed or controlled by the beneficiaries. This arrangement more closely resembles an association, which may be taxed as a corporation or a partnership and is distinguishable from the type of trust discussed at ¶ 501. The fact that the trust property is not supplied by the beneficiaries is not sufficient in itself to avoid the trust being classified and taxed as a business entity (Reg. § 301.7701-4(b)).[3]

An "investment" trust may also be taxed as an association, rather than a trust, if there is a power under the trust agreement to vary the investment of the certificate holders (Reg. § 301.7701-4(c)).[4] However, if this power is lacking, the arrangement is taxed as a trust. Unit investment trusts, as defined in the Investment Company Act of 1940, that are set up to hold mutual fund shares for investors are also not taxed as trusts. Instead, their income is taxed directly to the investors (Reg. § 1.851-7).[5]

503. Liquidating Trust. A liquidating trust formed for the primary purpose of liquidating and distributing the assets transferred to it is taxed as a trust, and not as an association, despite the possibility of profit. All the activities of the trust must be reasonably necessary to, and consistent with, the accomplishment of the primary purpose of liquidation and distribution. If the liquidation is unreasonably prolonged, or if the liquidation purpose becomes so obscured by business activities that the declared purpose of liquidation can be said to have been lost or abandoned, the arrangement is no longer a liquidating trust (Reg. § 301.7701-4(d)).[6]

504. Return for Persons Under a Disability. Generally, a guardian is required to file a tax return as an agent for a minor or legally disabled person if the individual would otherwise be required to file a return. However, a minor can file a return for himself or herself or have someone else file it, relieving the guardian of this obligation (Code Sec. 6012(b)(2); Reg. § 1.6012-3(b)(3)).[7] For the tax year during which an incompetent person is declared competent and the fiduciary is discharged, the former incompetent person must file the tax return. The estate of an incompetent person is not a separate taxable entity from the incompetent person. Thus, no fiduciary return on Form 1041, U.S. Income Tax Return for Estates and Trusts, is required (Reg. § 1.641(b)-2(b)).[8] However, an agent filing a return for another person should file Form 2848, Power of Attorney and Declaration of Representative, with the taxpayer's return. Both the agent and the taxpayer for whom the return is made may be liable for penalties (Reg. § 1.6012-1(a)(5)).[9] One spouse may execute a valid return on behalf of his or her mentally incompetent or disabled spouse prior to appointment of a legal guardian, even without formal power of attorney (Rev. Rul. 56-22).[10]

505. Trustees in Bankruptcy of Individual Debtors. The property held by a trustee in bankruptcy for an individual under Chapter 7 (liquidation) or Chapter 11 (business reorganization) of the Bankruptcy Code is considered the estate of the debtor. Such an estate is treated as a separate taxable entity (Code Sec. 1398).[11]

A separate taxable entity is not created when the case is brought under Chapter 13 of the Bankruptcy Code, which involves adjustment of debts of an individual with regular income. Further, no separate taxable entity is considered to have been created if a Chapter 7 or Chapter 11 case is dismissed (Code Sec. 1398(b)(1)). A separate taxable entity also is not created when an individual is in receivership (Reg. § 1.641(b)-2(b)).[12]

The fiduciary of a Chapter 7 or Chapter 11 bankruptcy estate is obligated to file the estate's return, or if the bankruptcy plan creates a liquidating trust, the fiduciary must

---

Footnote references are to paragraphs of the 2008 Standard Federal Tax Reports.

[3] ¶ 43,090	[7] ¶ 35,142, ¶ 35,146	[11] ¶ 32,410
[4] ¶ 43,090	[8] ¶ 24,265	[12] ¶ 24,265
[5] ¶ 26,407	[9] ¶ 35,143	
[6] ¶ 43,090	[10] ¶ 35,150.734	

file the trust's return (Code Sec. 6012(b)(4)).[13] The bankruptcy trustee must file a Form 1041 for the bankruptcy estate for any tax year in which the estate in bankruptcy has gross income that equals or exceeds the sum of the personal exemption amount plus the basic standard deduction for married persons filing separately (Code Sec. 6012(a)(9)). For 2007, that sum is $8,750; for 2008, that sum will be $8,950. The tax year for which the fiduciary files a return begins on the date of the filing of the petition in bankruptcy. The return may be for a calendar year or a fiscal year. A trustee in bankruptcy has no authority to file a return on Form 1040 for a bankrupt individual. The individual must file an individual return.

506. Receiver, Trustee in Bankruptcy of Corporate Debtors. The commencement of bankruptcy proceedings for a partnership or corporation does not create a separate taxable entity (Code Sec. 1399).[14] Thus, there is no obligation imposed upon the bankruptcy trustee to file a Form 1041 on behalf of the estate.

However, a receiver, trustee in dissolution, trustee in bankruptcy, or assignee who, by order of a court, has possession of or holds title to all or substantially all the property or business of a corporation must file the income tax return for such corporation on Form 1120, U.S. Corporation Income Tax Return. The receiver, trustee, or assignee must file the return whether or not it is operating the property or business of the corporation. A receiver in charge of only *a small part* of the property of a corporation, such as a receiver in mortgage foreclosure proceedings, need not file the return (Reg. § 1.6012-3(b)(4)).[15] Bankrupt partnerships must file their returns on Form 1065, U.S. Return of Partnership Income.

507. Termination of Estates and Trusts. An estate is recognized as a taxable entity only during the period of administration or settlement (i.e., the period actually required by the executor or administrator to perform the ordinary duties of administration, such as collection of assets, payment of debts and legacies, etc.). This is true whether the period is longer or shorter than that specified under local law for the settlement of estates. However, the administration of an estate may not be unduly prolonged. For federal tax purposes, the estate will be considered terminated after the expiration of a reasonable period for the performance of the duties of administration, or when all the assets of the estate have been distributed except for a reasonable amount set aside in good faith for the payment of contingent liabilities and expenses. If the estate has joined in making a valid election to treat a qualified revocable trust as part of the estate (see ¶ 516), then it does not terminate prior to the termination of the election period (Reg. § 1.641(b)-3(a)).[16]

A trust is recognized as a taxable entity until trust property has been distributed to successors, plus a reasonable time after this event necessary for the trustee to complete the administration of the trust. Further, like an estate, a trust is considered terminated when all the assets have been distributed except for a reasonable amount set aside in good faith to pay contingent liabilities and expenses (other than a claim by a beneficiary in that capacity) (Reg. § 1.641(b)-3(b)).[17]

Once an estate or trust is considered terminated for tax purposes, its gross income, credits, and deductions subsequent to termination are considered to be the gross income, credits, or deductions of the person or persons who succeed to the property (Reg. § 1.641(b)-3(d)).[18]

Fiduciary Return

510. Return of Estate or Trust by Fiduciary. A fiduciary must file a return on Form 1041 for a trust or estate if: (1) the estate has gross income of $600 or more for the tax year; (2) the trust (other than a trust exempt under Code Sec. 501(a)) for the tax year has any taxable income or has gross income of $600 or more, regardless of the amount of taxable income; (3) any beneficiary of the estate or trust is a nonresident alien (unless the trust is exempt under Code Sec. 501(a)); or (4) an individual's bankruptcy estate under Chapter 7 or Chapter 11 of the Bankruptcy Code has gross income equal to or greater than the sum of the personal exemption amount plus the basic standard

---

Footnote references are to paragraphs of the 2008 Standard Federal Tax Reports.

[13] ¶ 35,142	[15] ¶ 35,146	[17] ¶ 24,266
[14] ¶ 32,420	[16] ¶ 24,266	[18] ¶ 24,266

deduction amount for married individuals filing separately (Code Sec. 6012(a); Reg. § 1.6012-3).[19] For 2007, that sum is $8,750; for 2008, that sum will be $8,950.

When there is more than one fiduciary, the return can be filed by any one of them. However, when an estate has both domiciliary and ancillary representatives, each representative must file a return (Reg. § 1.6012-3(a)(1) and (3)).[20] A trustee of two or more trusts must file a separate return for each trust, even though the trusts were created by the same grantor for the same beneficiaries (Reg. § 1.6012-3(a)(4)).[21] However, see ¶ 515 for when two or more trusts may be treated as one trust.

The return must be filed on or before the 15th day of the fourth month following the close of the tax year (Code Sec. 6072(a)).[22] In filing its first return, an estate may choose the same accounting period as the decedent, or it may choose a calendar tax year or any fiscal year it wishes. If it chooses the decedent's accounting period, its first return will be for a short period to cover the unexpired term of the decedent's regular tax year (Code Secs. 441 and 443).[23] An exemption of $600 is allowed on a short-period return, without proration (see ¶ 534) (Reg. § 1.443-1(a)(2)).[24] However, if the estate gets approval from the IRS to change the accounting period, the exemption on the short-period return may be prorated (Reg. § 1.443-1(b)(1)(v)).[25]

Trusts (other than trusts exempt from tax under Code Sec. 501 and wholly charitable trusts under Code Sec. 4947(a)) must adopt a calendar tax year (Code Sec. 644).[26] Thus, a trust must generally file Form 1041 on or before April 15 following the close of the tax year. An existing trust that is required to change its tax year must annualize any income earned in the short year. In addition, the trust must obtain IRS approval to change its annual accounting period to a calendar year (see ¶ 1513).

An estate or trust can apply for an automatic six-month extension of time for filing the fiduciary return by submitting Form 7004, Application for Automatic 6-Month Extension of Time to File Certain Business Income Tax, Information, and Other Returns. The application must be filed on or before the due date for Form 1041 and must show the properly estimated income tax amount for the tax year. The automatic extension does not extend the time for payment of any tax due on the return (Temporary Reg. § 1.6081-6T).[27]

The fiduciary of an estate or trust need not file a copy of the will or trust instrument with the estate or trust income tax return unless the IRS requests it. If the IRS does request a copy, the fiduciary should file it (including any amendments), accompanied by a written declaration of truth and completeness and a statement indicating the provisions of the will or trust instrument that determine the extent to which the income of the estate or trust is taxable to the estate or trust, the beneficiaries, or the grantor (Reg. § 1.6012-3(a)(2)).[28]

An estate or trust that is obligated to file an income tax return must furnish a copy of Schedule K-1 (Form 1041) to each beneficiary: (1) who receives a distribution from the trust or estate for the year or (2) to whom any item with respect to the tax year is allocated. This statement must contain the information required to be shown on the return and be furnished on or before the date on which the return is to be filed (Code Sec. 6034A).[29] In addition, a copy must be attached to Form 1041. For each failure to file a correct information return or payee statement, a $50 penalty may be assessed (Code Secs. 6721 and 6722).[30]

Payment of Tax and Estimated Tax. The entire income tax liability of an estate or trust must be paid on or before the due date for its return (Code Sec. 6151).[31] In addition, estates that have been in existence for more than two years and both new and existing trusts must pay estimated tax in the same manner as individuals. See ¶ 518.

512. Personal Liability of Fiduciary. Any fiduciary (other than a trustee acting under Chapter 11 of the Bankruptcy Code) who pays any debt due by the decedent or

---

Footnote references are to paragraphs of the 2008 Standard Federal Tax Reports.

[19] ¶ 35,142, ¶ 35,146	[24] ¶ 20,501	[29] ¶ 35,460
[20] ¶ 35,146	[25] ¶ 20,501	[30] ¶ 40,210, ¶ 40,230
[21] ¶ 35,146	[26] ¶ 24,350	[31] ¶ 37,080
[22] ¶ 36,720	[27] ¶ 36,797	
[23] ¶ 20,302, ¶ 20,500	[28] ¶ 35,146	

the estate, in whole or in part, before federal tax obligations are satisfied becomes personally liable for the tax of the estate to the extent of such payments. However, the fiduciary is not liable for amounts paid out for debts that have priority over the federal taxes due and owing on the estate, such as a decedent's funeral expenses or probate administration costs (Reg. § 1.641(b)-2; 31 U.S.C. § 3713).[32] Further, an executor or administrator who pays other debts is not personally liable unless the executor or administrator has either personal knowledge of a tax due the United States or knowledge that would put a reasonably prudent person on inquiry that such tax debts exist.[33] Discharge of the fiduciary does not terminate the fiduciary's personal liability for the payment of other debts of the estate without satisfying prior tax claims.

Method of Taxing Estate or Trust

514. Estate or Trust as Separate Entity. An estate or trust is a separate taxable entity (see ¶ 501). In general, its entire income must be reported on a calendar year basis on Form 1041, which must be filed by the fiduciary (see ¶ 510). If income is required to be distributed currently or is properly distributed to a beneficiary, the estate or trust is regarded as a conduit with respect to that income. It is allowed a deduction for the portion of gross income that is currently distributable to the beneficiaries or is properly paid or credited to them (see ¶ 545). Generally, the beneficiaries are taxed on the part of the income currently distributed, and the estate or trust is taxed on the portion that it has accumulated. The income allocated to a beneficiary retains the same character in the beneficiary's hands that it had in the hands of the estate or trust (Reg. § § 1.652(b)-1; 1.662(b)-1).[34]

515. Multiple Trusts. One grantor may create several trusts, and the income may be taxed separately for each trust. When there is intent to create separate trusts for multiple beneficiaries, the fact that the corpus of each trust is kept in one fund will not necessarily defeat the grantor's intent. Although it is not necessary to divide the corpus physically in order to carry out the intent of the parties, it is necessary to comply literally with the terms of the trust instrument in other respects.[35]

However, two or more trusts will be treated as one trust if: (1) the trusts have substantially the same grantor or grantors and substantially the same primary beneficiary or beneficiaries and (2) a principal purpose of the trusts is the avoidance of income tax (Code Sec. 643(f)).[36] A special safe-harbor provision applies to any trust that was irrevocable on March 1, 1984, except to the extent that corpus is contributed to the trust after that date.

516. Tax Rates. An estate or trust computes its tax liability for 2007 by using the separate estate and trust income tax rate schedule at ¶ 19. The taxable income of an estate or trust for purposes of the regular income tax is determined by subtracting from its gross income (¶ 520) allowable deductions (¶ 528 and following), amounts distributable to beneficiaries (to the extent of distributable net income) (¶ 543), and the proper exemption (¶ 534) (Code Sec. 641; Reg. § § 1.641(a)-1 and 1.641(b)-1).[37] See ¶ 64.

The alternative minimum tax (AMT) of an estate or trust is computed by determining distributable net income under the general rules contained in ¶ 543, subject to further adjustments under the minimum tax rules. The AMT is computed on Part III of Schedule I, Form 1041. See ¶ 1401 and following.

Grantor and employees' trusts are subject to special tax treatment. See ¶ 571 and following, and ¶ 2101 and following.

Qualified Revocable Trusts. A trustee of a qualified revocable trust and the executor of a decedent's estate may join in an election to treat the revocable trust as part of the decedent's estate (Code Sec. 645).[38] Such an election allows the revocable trust to enjoy certain income tax treatment that would otherwise be accorded only to the decedent's estate.

Electing Small Business Trust. An electing small business trust (ESBT) (see ¶ 501) is taxed in a different manner than other trusts. First, the portion of the ESBT that

---

Footnote references are to paragraphs of the 2008 Standard Federal Tax Reports.

[32] ¶ 24,265, ¶ 40,730
[33] ¶ 40,735.25
[34] ¶ 24,383, ¶ 24,425
[35] ¶ 24,267.67
[36] ¶ 24,320
[37] ¶ 24,260, ¶ 24,262, ¶ 24,264
[38] ¶ 24,355

consists of stock in one or more S corporations is treated as a separate trust for purposes of computing the income tax attributable to the S corporation stock held by the trust. This portion of the trust's income is taxed at the highest rate imposed on estates and trusts, and includes:

(1) the items of income, loss, deduction or credit allocated to the trust as an S corporation shareholder;

(2) gain or loss from the sale of the S corporation stock;

(3) any state or local income taxes and administrative expenses of the trust properly allocable to the S corporation stock; and

(4) for tax years beginning after 2006, any interest expense paid or accrued on debt incurred to acquire S corporation stock.

Capital losses are allowed in computing an ESBT's income only to the extent of capital gains. Moreover, no deduction is allowed for amounts distributed to beneficiaries, and, except as described above, no additional deductions or credits are allowed. Also, the ESBT's income is not included in the distributable net income of the trust and, therefore, is not included in the beneficiaries' income. Furthermore, no item relating to the S corporation stock is apportioned to any beneficiary. The trust's AMT exemption amount is zero. Special rules apply upon termination of all or a part of the ESBT (Code Sec. 641(c), as amended by the Small Business and Work Opportunity Tax Act of 2007 (P.L. 110-28)).[39] See ¶ 305.

518. Estimated Tax. In general, trusts and estates are required to make quarterly estimated tax payments in the same manner as individuals (see ¶ 2682). However, estates and grantor trusts that receive the residue of a probate estate under the grantor's will are only required to make estimated tax payments beginning with tax years ending two or more years after the decedent's death.

Trusts or estates with a short tax year must pay installments of tax on or before the 15th day of the fourth, sixth and ninth months of the tax year and the 15th day of the first month of the following tax year. The amount of each installment in a short tax year is determined by dividing the required annual payment by the number of payments required for that year (Code Sec. 6654(l)).[40]

Trusts and estates generally have 45 days (rather than the 15 days allowed individuals) to compute the payments under the estimated tax annualization rules. The payment due dates are unchanged (Code Sec. 6654(l)).[41] First-time filers must file Form 1041-ES, Estimated Income Tax for Estates and Trusts, which includes vouchers to be included with quarterly payments. After the first payment, the IRS will provide pre-printed vouchers. A fiduciary paying estimated tax for more than one trust should submit a separate Form 1041-ES and a separate check for each trust. However, a fiduciary may submit a single check for multiple trusts provided that a separate estimated tax voucher is submitted for each trust (Announcement 87-32).

The trustee of a trust, or the fiduciary of an estate whose tax year is reasonably expected to be its last tax year, may elect to treat any or all of an estimated tax payment as a payment made by the beneficiary and credited toward the beneficiary's tax liability. If so elected, the payment is not treated as an estimated tax payment made by the trust or estate. The election is made on Form 1041-T, Allocation of Estimated Tax Payments to Beneficiaries, and must be filed on or before the 65th day after the close of the tax year (March 5, 2008, for calendar tax year 2007) (Code Sec. 643(g)).[42]

Gross Income of Estate or Trust

520. Gross Income of Estate or Trust. The gross income of an estate or trust is generally determined in the same manner as that of an individual (Code Sec. 641(b); Reg. § 1.641(a)-2).[43] The gross income of an estate or trust includes all items of gross income received during the tax year, including:

(1) income accumulated in trust for the benefit of unborn or unascertained persons or persons with contingent interests;

Footnote references are to paragraphs of the 2008 Standard Federal Tax Reports.

[39] ¶ 24,260
[40] ¶ 39,550, ¶ 39,560.82
[41] ¶ 39,550
[42] ¶ 24,320
[43] ¶ 24,260, ¶ 24,263

(2) income accumulated or held for future distribution under the terms of the will or trust;

(3) income that is to be distributed currently by the fiduciary to the beneficiaries, and income collected by the guardian of an infant that is to be held or distributed as the court may direct;

(4) income received by the estate of a deceased person during the period of administration or settlement of the estate; and

(5) income that, at the discretion of the fiduciary, may be either distributed to the beneficiaries or accumulated

Although all the items above are includible in the gross income of the estate or trust, the liability for tax on the income may rest on either the beneficiary or the estate or trust as a separate entity. See ¶ 542 and following for tax consequences of distributions to beneficiaries.

The allocation of income and deductions between a decedent's estate and the surviving spouse in community property states depends on state community property laws. In most states, the surviving spouse is taxable on one-half of the income flowing from the community property of the estate.[44]

522. Income from Real Estate. State law determines whether income from real estate during the period of administration is taxable to the decedent's estate or to the heirs or devisees. The IRS has ruled that, where state law provides that real property is subject to administration, income derived from the property is taxable to the estate even though legal title may pass directly to the heirs or devisees. However, where the administrator is not entitled to possession or control of real property, income from the property is taxable to the heirs or devisees and not to the estate. Even if the property is not subject to the administrator's control, all or a part of the gain from a sale of property is taxable to the estate to the extent that the property was sold, under state law, to raise funds for its administration (Rev. Ruls. 57-133 and 59-375).[45]

523. Income from Personal Property. Income from personal property, including a gain from the sale or exchange of such property, is taxable to the estate. This is because title to personal property vests in the administrator or executor immediately upon appointment and does not pass to the heirs or legatees until the estate is fully administered and distribution is ordered or approved by the courts, and notwithstanding the fact that the basis of the property distributed relates back to the date of the decedent's death.[46]

524. Sale of Property by Estate or Trust. The computation of the gain or loss realized upon the sale of property acquired by an estate, trust or beneficiary is made under special basis rules, the applicability of which is dependent upon the method of acquisition and the nature of the property sold. See ¶ 1601 and following.

526. Gain on Transfer to Beneficiary. Generally, for tax years ending after January 2, 2004, gain or loss is realized by the trust or estate, or by the other beneficiaries, by reason of a distribution of property in kind if the distribution satisfies a beneficiary's right to receive: (1) a specific dollar amount; (2) specific property other than that which is distributed; or (3) other income if the income is required to be distributed currently (Reg. § 1.661(a)-2(f)).[47] For estates of decedents dying on or before December 31, 2009, a special rule limits gain on transfers to qualified heirs of property for which a special use valuation election under Code Sec. 2032A was made (Code Sec. 1040).[48]

For this purpose, a marital deduction trust (established for a spouse to take advantage of the estate tax marital deduction, see ¶ 2926) comprising a portion of the residuary estate and measured by a percentage of the value of the adjusted gross estate is considered as being for a fixed dollar amount. Upon a distribution of property to such a trust, the estate realizes gain or loss measured by the difference between the fair market value at the date of distribution and the federal estate tax value of the property (Rev. Rul. 60-87).[49]

Footnote references are to paragraphs of the 2008 Standard Federal Tax Reports.

[44] ¶ 2350.2473
[45] ¶ 24,267.5204
[46] ¶ 24,267.515
[47] ¶ 24,402
[48] ¶ 29,779
[49] ¶ 24,267.5281

Distribution of a stated percentage of trust corpus to the beneficiary before termination of the trust is not considered a satisfaction of an obligation of the trust for a definite amount of cash or equivalent value in property. Instead, it is treated as a partial distribution of a share of the trust principal. Thus, there is no sale or exchange, and neither the trustee nor the beneficiary realizes taxable income (Rev. Rul. 55-117).[50] However, a trustee or executor may elect to recognize gain or loss on the distribution of noncash property to a beneficiary as if the property had been sold to the beneficiary at its fair market value (Code Sec. 643(e)(3)).[51] The election is made on the return for the year of distribution and applies to all distributions made by the estate or trust during its entire tax year. Thus, an election to recognize gain or loss cannot be made separately for each distribution.

In the event the election is made, the beneficiary's basis in the distributed property is the estate's or trust's adjusted basis just prior to the distribution, adjusted by the gain or loss recognized by the estate or trust. If the election is not made, the beneficiary's basis will be the same as the trust's or estate's, and any gain or loss will be recognized by the beneficiary when the beneficiary disposes of the property.

527. Foreign Estates. The estate of a nonresident alien is taxed on its income received from U.S. sources, including capital gains and dividends (see ¶ 2409 and ¶ 2940). However, the estate is allowed a deduction for distributions to both nonresident aliens and U.S. beneficiaries to the extent that these distributions are not in excess of its distributable net income. The portion of the distribution allocated to capital gains is not includible in the gross income of nonresident alien beneficiaries if they have not resided in the United States for a period of at least 183 days (see ¶ 2435). The portion of a distribution that represents dividends is, however, includible in the gross income of nonresident alien beneficiaries. The fiduciary must withhold U.S. taxes from these dividend distributions at the statutory rate or at the applicable treaty rate (Rev. Rul. 68-621).[52]

Ordinary Deductions of Estate or Trust

528. Deductions Generally. In general, trusts and estates are allowed the same deductions as individuals. However, special rules govern the computation of certain deductions and the allocation of deductions between the beneficiaries and the estate or trust (¶ 529 and following). Further, the estate or trust is permitted to claim a deduction for certain distributions to beneficiaries (¶ 544 and ¶ 545) (Code Sec. 641(b); Reg. § 1.641(b)-1).[53]

Two-Percent Floor on Itemized Deductions. In general, an estate or trust is subject to the two-percent-of-adjusted-gross-income (AGI) floor on miscellaneous itemized deductions. The AGI of an estate or trust is computed in the same manner as it is for an individual, except that the following deductions are allowed from gross income: (1) deductions for expenses paid or incurred in connection with the administration of the estate or trust that would not have been incurred had the property not been so held; (2) the personal exemption deduction allowed to estates and trusts (¶ 534); and (3) the deduction for distribution to beneficiaries (¶ 542 and following). The IRS has the regulatory authority to apply the two-percent floor at the beneficiary level, rather than the entity level, with respect to simple trusts (Code Sec. 67(e)).[54]

Although there is authority suggesting that investment services fees are fully deductible, the IRS and most courts deciding the issue have concluded that such fees are not unique to the administration of a trust and hence they are subject to the two-percent floor.[55] Expenses incurred in administering a bankruptcy estate are fully allowed as a deduction from gross income (IRS Chief Counsel Advice 200630016).[56]

Proposed regulations provide that the two-percent floor applies to administration expenses incurred by an estate or non-grantor trust unless they are unique to estates and trusts. For this purpose, a cost is unique if an individual could not have incurred that cost in connection with property not held in an estate or trust (Proposed Reg. § 1.67-4).

Footnote references are to paragraphs of the 2008 Standard Federal Tax Reports.

[50] ¶ 24,267.5281
[51] ¶ 24,320
[52] ¶ 24,267.4985
[53] ¶ 24,260, ¶ 24,264
[54] ¶ 6060
[55] ¶ 6064.75
[56] ¶ 6064.75

529. Expenses. In general, an estate or trust is allowed deductions for those ordinary and necessary expenses incurred in carrying on a trade or business, those incurred in the production of income or the management or conservation of income-producing property, and those incurred in connection with the determination, collection, or refund of any tax (see ¶ 901, ¶ 1085 and ¶ 1092). Reasonable amounts paid or incurred by a fiduciary on account of administration, including fiduciary fees and litigation expenses, are deductible as well. Such expenses are deductible even if the estate or trust is not engaged in a trade or business, unless the expenses were for the production or collection of tax-exempt income (Reg. § 1.212-1(i)).[57]

No deductions are allowable for: (a) expenses that are allocable to one or more classes of income exempt from tax (other than interest income) or (b) any amount relating to expenses for the production of income that is allocable to tax-exempt interest income. See also ¶ 970. The IRS allows a deduction for an executor's or administrator's commissions, as paid or accrued, except the portion allocable to tax-exempt income.[58]

Alimony Payments. An estate can deduct the value of periodic alimony payments it makes under the rules regarding deductions for distributions to beneficiaries.[59]

Double Deductions Prohibited. Amounts deductible as administration expenses or losses for estate tax (or generation-skipping transfer tax) purposes may not also be deducted by the estate for income tax purposes. However, the estate can deduct such items for income tax purposes if it files a statement (in duplicate) that the items have not been allowed as deductions for estate tax purposes and that all rights to deduct them for such purposes are waived (Code Sec. 642(g); Reg. § 1.642(g)-1).[60]

The prohibition against double deductions by estates extends to trusts and other persons for expenses or losses incurred.[61] Expenses incurred by an estate in selling property to raise funds to pay administration expenses and taxes are also subject to the prohibition against double deductions. Such expenses cannot be claimed as a deduction (or offset against the selling price of the property) in computing the taxable income of the estate unless the estate waives the right to take such deduction for estate tax purposes (Code Sec. 642(g)). However, deductions for taxes, interest, business expenses, and other items accrued *at the date of the decedent's death* are allowed, for both estate and income tax purposes, as claims against the estate and deductions in respect of a decedent, respectively (Reg. § 1.642(g)-2).[62]

530. Depreciation and Depletion. Depreciation and depletion deductions must be apportioned between a trust and its beneficiaries and between an estate and its beneficiaries (Code Secs. 167(d), 611(b), and 642(e)), except for certain term interests created or acquired after July 27, 1989, where the remainder interest is held by a related party.[63]

In the case of a trust, the allowable deduction for depreciation or depletion is apportioned between the income beneficiaries and the trustee on the basis of the trust income allocable to each. However, if the trust instrument or local law requires or permits the trustee to maintain a reserve for depreciation or depletion, the deduction is first allocated to the trustee to the extent that income is set aside for such a reserve. Any part of the deduction in excess of the income set aside for the reserve is then apportioned between the income beneficiaries and the trust on the basis of the trust income (in excess of the income set aside for the reserve) allocable to each. No effect is given to any allocation of the depreciation or depletion deduction that gives any beneficiary or the trustee a share of the deduction greater than a pro rata share of the trust income. The allocation is disregarded despite any provisions in the trust instrument, unless the trust instrument or local law requires or permits the trustee to maintain a reserve for depreciation or depletion (Reg. § § 1.167(h)-1 and 1.611-1(c)).[64]

In the case of an estate, the depreciation or depletion allowance is apportioned between the estate and the heirs, legatees and devisees on the basis of the income from the property allocable to each.[65]

Footnote references are to paragraphs of the 2008 Standard Federal Tax Reports.

[57] ¶ 12,521	[60] ¶ 24,280, ¶ 24,299	[63] ¶ 11,002, ¶ 23,920, ¶ 24,280
[58] ¶ 12,523.51, ¶ 24,686.80	[61] ¶ 24,280	[64] ¶ 11,048, ¶ 23,922
[59] ¶ 6094.31, ¶ 24,267.403,	[62] ¶ 24,300	[65] ¶ 11,048, ¶ 23,922
¶ 24,407.56		

Section 179 Election. Although an estate or trust is entitled to take ACRS or MACRS depreciation on qualified assets, neither can make a Code Sec. 179 election to expense depreciable business assets (¶ 1208) (Code Sec. 179(d)(4)).[66]

Reforestation Expenditures. Estates can elect to expense reforestation expenditures and to amortize any excess expenditures (see ¶ 1287). Trusts cannot elect the expense deduction but can elect to amortize such expenditures. Total reforestation expenditures incurred must be apportioned between the income beneficiaries and the fiduciary. Amounts apportioned to a beneficiary must be taken into account in determining the dollar limit on the reforestation expenditures that the beneficiary can expense (Code Sec. 194).[67]

531. Losses and Bad Debts. An estate or trust can deduct losses from a trade or business or from transactions entered into for profit (see ¶ 1101). Similarly, the rules governing nonbusiness casualty and theft losses discussed at ¶ 1124 apply to an estate or trust. Thus, after the $100-per-occurrence floor has been satisfied, losses in excess of nonbusiness casualty and theft gains are deductible to the extent that they exceed 10 percent of the adjusted gross income (AGI) of the estate or trust. For this purpose, an estate's or trust's administration expenses are allowable as a deduction in computing its AGI (Code Sec. 165(h)(4)(C)).[68]

A nonbusiness casualty or theft loss sustained or discovered during the settlement of an estate is deductible on the estate's income tax return only if it has not been allowed for estate tax purposes. A statement to this effect should be filed with the return for the year for which the deduction is claimed (Code Sec. 165(h)(4)(D); Reg. §§1.165-7(c) and 1.165-8(b)).[69]

Net Operating Losses. An estate or trust is allowed a deduction for net operating loss carryovers and carrybacks (¶ 1173 and following) (Reg. §1.642(d)-1).[70] However, an estate cannot deduct a capital loss or NOL sustained by a decedent during the decedent's last tax year. These losses must be deducted on the decedent's final return.[71] In addition, in computing gross income and deductions for the NOL calculation, a trust must not take into account income and deductions attributable to the grantor or any substantial owner (see ¶ 571and following). Also, in calculating NOLs, an estate or trust cannot claim the deductions for charitable contributions (¶ 537) and distributions to beneficiaries (¶ 544 and ¶ 545).

Bad Debts. An estate or trust is entitled to claim bad debt deductions under the rules governing individuals (see ¶ 1145 and following). The distinction is maintained between business debts, which may be deducted in the year in which they become partially or totally worthless, and nonbusiness debts, which may be deducted as short-term capital losses only if they become totally worthless (Code Sec. 166; Reg. §1.166-5).[72]

532. Taxes. An estate or trust is entitled to the same deductions for taxes as individuals (see ¶ 1021). In addition, an estate or trust is permitted an offset of the allocable federal estate tax against income in respect of a decedent (¶ 191). The portion of state income taxes allocable to exempt income, other than exempt interest income, is nondeductible (¶ 970). The portion of state income taxes attributable to exempt interest income and to income subject to federal income tax is deductible under Code Sec. 164.[73]

533. Interest. Paid or accrued interest is deductible by an estate or trust (Code Sec. 163).[74] However, there are a number of limitations on the deductibility of interest. Interest is not deductible on a debt incurred, or continued, to purchase or carry obligations the interest on which is wholly exempt from federal income taxes (see ¶ 970). Personal interest of an estate or trust is also nondeductible (see ¶ 1045). Further, the deduction for investment interest may not exceed net investment income for the tax year (Code Sec. 163(d)).[75] Net capital gain attributable to the disposition of property held for investment is generally excluded from investment income for purposes

---

Footnote references are to paragraphs of the 2008 Standard Federal Tax Reports.

[66] ¶ 12,120
[67] ¶ 12,330
[68] ¶ 9802
[69] ¶ 9802, ¶ 10,004, ¶ 10,100

[70] ¶ 24,296
[71] ¶ 24,267.451
[72] ¶ 10,602, ¶ 10,691
[73] ¶ 9500, ¶ 9502.453

[74] ¶ 9102
[75] ¶ 9102

of computing this limitation. However, a special election is available to increase net capital gain includible in investment income by reducing the amount eligible for the maximum rate on capital gains (see ¶ 1094).

534. Exemption. An estate can claim a personal exemption of $600. A "simple" trust (¶ 542)—one that is required to distribute all of its income currently—is allowed an exemption of $300. All other trusts ("complex" trusts) are entitled to a $100 exemption (Code Sec. 642(b); Reg. § 1.642(b)-1).[76] A "qualified disability trust," whether taxed as a simple or complex trust, can claim, in lieu of the $100 or $300 exemption, an exemption in the amount that a single individual taxpayer can claim (Code Sec. 642(b)(2)(C)). For 2007, the exemption amount is $3,400, and for 2008, that amount will be $3,500; these amounts are subject to phase-out (see ¶ 133). If a final distribution of assets has been made during the year, all income of the estate or trust must be reported as distributed to the beneficiaries, without reduction for the amount claimed for the exemption (see ¶ 543).

535. Unused Loss Carryovers and Excess Deductions on Termination. A net operating loss, a capital loss carryover (see ¶ 562), and deductions in excess of gross income for the year in which an estate or trust terminates can be deducted by a beneficiary succeeding to the property of the trust or estate. Excess deductions on termination of an estate or trust are allowed only in computing taxable income and must be taken into account in computing the beneficiary's tax preference items. Such deductions may not be used in computing adjusted gross income. In computing excess deductions, the deductions for personal exemptions and amounts set aside for charitable purposes are disregarded. The deduction is claimed as an itemized deduction or capital loss (depending on its nature) on the beneficiary's tax return filed for the year in which the trust or estate terminates (Code Sec. 642(h); Reg. § § 1.642(h)-1–1.642(h)-5).[77]

The bankruptcy estate of an individual debtor in a liquidation (Chapter 7) or reorganization (Chapter 11) proceeding succeeds to certain tax attributes of the debtor, including any net operating loss (NOL) carryover (Code Sec. 1398(g)).[78] The tax attributes that become part of the estate are determined as of the first day of the debtor's tax year in which the bankruptcy case commences. If any carryback year of the estate is a tax year before the estate's first tax year, the carryback is taken into account in the tax year of the debtor that corresponds to such carryback year and, accordingly, may offset the pre-bankruptcy income of the debtor (Code Sec. 1398(j)(2)(A)). When the estate closes upon the issuance of a final decree, any unused NOL carryover is returned to the debtor (Code Sec. 1398(i)). The debtor, however, cannot carry an unused NOL carryback from a tax year that ended after commencement of the bankruptcy case to a tax year that precedes the tax year in which the bankruptcy case was commenced (Code Sec. 1398(j)(2)(B)).

536. Domestic Production Activities by Trusts or Estates. A nongrantor trust or estate, and the beneficiaries of the trust or estate, may claim the deduction for qualified production activities (i.e., manufacturer's deduction) (see ¶ 980A and following) (Code Sec. 199(d)(1)(B); Temporary Reg. § 1.199-5T(e)).[79] In computing the deduction, a trust or estate apportions W-2 wages, domestic production gross receipts (DPGR), cost of goods sold allocable to DPGR, and expenses, losses and deductions properly allocable to DPGR between the beneficiaries and the fiduciary, and among the beneficiaries. The applicable percentage limitation (six percent for tax years beginning in 2007, 2008 and 2009) on the deduction is applied to the lesser of the trust's or estate's qualified production activities income (QPAI) or its adjusted gross income (AGI), as determined under the AGI computation rules for trusts and estates (see ¶ 528).

The trust or estate calculates each beneficiary's share (as well as the trust's or estate's own share, if any) of the trust's or estate's QPAI and W-2 wages at the trust or estate level. The QPAI and W-2 wages are allocated to each beneficiary and to the trust or estate based on the relative proportion of the trust's or estate's distributable net income for the tax year that is distributed or required to be distributed to the beneficiary or is retained by the trust or estate (see ¶ 542 and ¶ 543). If the trust or estate has no

---

Footnote references are to paragraphs of the 2008 Standard Federal Tax Reports.

[76] ¶ 24,280, ¶ 24,286   [78] ¶ 32,410
[77] ¶ 24,280, ¶ 24,301, ¶ 24,305   [79] ¶ 12,468, ¶ 12,472DC

distributable net income for the tax year, QPAI and W-2 wages are allocated entirely to the trust or estate.

Each beneficiary computes its Code Sec. 199 deduction by aggregating its share of QPAI and W-2 wages from the trust or estate with its share of QPAI and W-2 wages from other sources. When determining its total QPAI and W-2 wages from such other sources, the beneficiary does not take into account the items allocated from the trust or estate.

For tax years beginning on or before May 17, 2006, a beneficiary's share of W-2 wages of a trust or estate is limited to the lesser of: (1) the beneficiary's allocable share of the W-2 wages of the trust or estate; or (2) two times the applicable percentage of the beneficiary's share of the trust's or estate's QPAI (Code Sec. 199(d)(1)(A)(iii), prior to amendment by the Tax Increase Prevention and Reconciliation Act of 2005 (P.L. 109-222); Reg. § 1.199-9(e)(3)). If the beneficiary's share of QPAI is not greater than zero, then the beneficiary may not take into account any W-2 wages of the trust or estate in computing its deduction. For tax years beginning after May 17, 2006, this limitation does not apply to a beneficiary's share of W-2 wages from a trust or estate. Instead, the beneficiary's share of W-2 wages is determined under the law applicable to pass-thru entities based on the beginning date of the trust's or estate's tax year, not that of the beneficiary's tax year (Temporary Reg. § 1.199-5T(e)(3)).

Grantor Trust. For a grantor trust (see ¶ 571 and following), the owner computes its QPAI with respect to the owned portion of the trust as if that QPAI had been generated by activities performed directly by the owner (Reg. § 1.199-9(d)).[80] Similarly, for purposes of the wage limitation (see ¶ 980C), the owner takes into account its share of the trust's W-2 wages that are attributable to the owned portion of the trust. The provisions that apply to nongrantor trusts (discussed above) do not apply to the owned portion of the trust.

Charitable Contribution Deductions

537. Charitable Deduction Rules. Estates and complex trusts are allowed an unlimited charitable deduction for amounts that are *paid* to recognized charities out of gross income (other than unrelated business income of a trust) under the terms of the governing instrument during the tax year (Code Sec. 642(c)).[81] For example, amounts bequeathed to charity that are paid out of corpus under state law are not deductible from income as charitable contributions or as distributions to beneficiaries.[82] However, payments in compromise of bequests to charity are deductible.[83] See ¶ 538 for discussion of limitations on the charitable deduction for trusts and estates.

The trustee or administrator may elect to treat payments made during the year following the close of a tax year as having been paid in the earlier year for deduction purposes. This election must be made no later than the time, including extensions, prescribed by law for filing the income tax return for the tax year in which payment is made (Code Sec. 642(c)(1)).[84] The election for any tax year is binding for the year for which it is made and may not be revoked after the time for making the election has expired (Reg. § 1.642(c)-1(b)).[85]

Estates may also claim an unlimited deduction for amounts of gross income permanently set aside for charitable purposes. The income must be permanently set aside for a purpose specified in Code Sec. 170(c) or it must be used exclusively for: (i) religious, charitable, scientific, literary or educational purposes; (ii) the prevention of cruelty to children or animals; or (iii) the establishment, acquisition, maintenance or operation of a nonprofit public cemetery (Reg. § 1.642(c)-2(a)).[86] For most complex trusts, the unlimited deduction does not apply for gross income that is permanently set aside for charitable purposes under the governing instrument (but not actually paid) (Reg. § 1.642(c)-2(b)).[87]

Pooled income funds (¶ 593) may claim a set-aside deduction only for gross income attributable to gain from the sale of a long-term capital asset that is permanently set

---

Footnote references are to paragraphs of the 2008 Standard Federal Tax Reports.

[80] ¶ 12,472H
[81] ¶ 24,280, ¶ 24,308.1135
[82] ¶ 24,308.115
[83] ¶ 24,308.105
[84] ¶ 24,280
[85] ¶ 24,288
[86] ¶ 24,290
[87] ¶ 24,290

aside for the benefit of the charity. No deduction is allowed with respect to gross income of the fund that is: (1) attributable to income other than net long-term capital gains or (2) earned with respect to amounts transferred to the fund before August 1, 1969. The investment and accounting requirements applicable to trusts are also applicable to pooled income funds (Reg. § 1.642(c)-2(c)).[88]

The charitable deduction is normally computed on Form 1041, Schedule A. When unrelated business income is involved, a separate schedule, rather than Schedule A, can be filed showing the computation of the deduction. Pooled income funds claiming the set-aside deduction for long-term capital gain are required to compute their deduction on a separate schedule, which is attached to the return.

Every trust claiming a charitable deduction under Code Sec. 642(c) (and every Code Sec. 4947(a)(2) split-interest trust, including a pooled income fund) is required to file an information return (Code Sec. 6034).[89] The information return is usually filed on Form 1041-A, U.S. Information Return Trust Accumulation of Charitable Amounts, due on or before April 15, 2008, for the 2007 calendar tax year. A nonexempt charitable trust, described in Code Sec. 4947(a)(1) and not treated as a private foundation, must also file a Form 990, Return of Organization Exempt From Income Tax, if its gross receipts are normally more than $25,000. Such a trust may file a Form 990 to satisfy its Form 1041 filing requirement if the trust has zero taxable income (see ¶ 625). Both the trust and the trustee can be liable for a penalty of $10 per day up to a maximum of $5,000 for failure to timely file Form 1041-A. For tax years beginning after 2006, a split-interest trust that fails to file or to provide the required information can be liable for a penalty of $20 per day, up to a maximum of $10,000; if the split-interest trust's gross income exceeds $250,000, the penalty is $100 per day, up to a $50,000 maximum. An additional penalty may be assessed against the person required to file the return if he or she knowingly fails to file or provide the information (Code Sec. 6652(c)(2)(A) and (C)).[90] Penalties also apply for filing a false or fraudulent return (Code Sec. 6663).[91] When all trust net income must be distributed currently each year to the beneficiaries, the trust is relieved of filing Form 1041-A; for tax years beginning after 2006, this filing exception does not apply to split-interest trusts that distribute all current income to the beneficiaries. For Code Sec. 664 charitable remainder trusts, see ¶ 590.

538. Disallowance of and Limitations on Deduction. A trust is not entitled to an unlimited charitable deduction under Code Sec. 642(c) for income that is allocable to its unrelated business income for the tax year (Code Sec. 681(a); Reg. §§ 1.681(a)-1 and 1.681(a)-2).[92] The "unrelated business income" of a trust is computed in much the same manner as the unrelated business taxable income (UBTI) of a tax-exempt organization (see ¶ 655 and ¶ 687). However, in computing its UBTI, a trust can claim deductions for *payments* to charities, subject to the percentage limitations applicable to individuals' charitable deductions. See ¶ 1058 and following.

Charitable deductions are not allowed for otherwise deductible gifts to an organization upon which a tax has been imposed for termination of private foundation status (¶ 649). General contributors will be denied deductions after the organization is notified of the loss of its private foundation status. Substantial contributors (see ¶ 635) will be denied deductions in the year in which action is taken to terminate the organization's private foundation status (Code Sec. 508(d)(1)).[93]

Gain on qualified small business stock held for more than five years that is eligible for the 50-percent exclusion under Code Sec. 1202(a) (¶ 1736) cannot also be taken as a charitable deduction (Code Sec. 642(c)(4)).[94]

Deductions are also denied for contributions to any private foundation, charitable trust, or split-interest trust, as defined in Code Sec. 4947, that fails to meet the governing-instrument requirements for private foundations (Code Sec. 508(d)(2)).[95] Deductions for gifts and bequests to any organization are disallowed during the period that the organization fails to notify the IRS that it is claiming exempt status as a charitable organization (¶ 616). A church, an organization with gross receipts of $5,000

Footnote references are to paragraphs of the 2008 Standard Federal Tax Reports.

[88] ¶ 24,290
[89] ¶ 35,440
[90] ¶ 39,480
[91] ¶ 39,656
[92] ¶ 24,840, ¶ 24,841, ¶ 24,842
[93] ¶ 22,790
[94] ¶ 24,280
[95] ¶ 22,790

or less, and certain other organizations designated by the IRS are exempt from the notification requirements. Charitable deductions are also disallowed for bequests and gifts to a foreign private foundation after the IRS notifies it that it has engaged in a prohibited transaction or for a year in which such an organization loses its exempt status for engaging in such a transaction (Code Sec. 4948(c)(4)).[96]

Credits of Estate or Trust

540. Tax Credits. Generally, the tax credits allowed to individuals are allowed to estates and trusts (see ¶ 1301 and following). The credits typically must be apportioned between the estate or trust and the beneficiaries on the basis of the income allocable to each. However, the foreign tax credit is allocated according to the proportionate share of the foreign taxes (Code Sec. 642(a); Reg. § 1.641(b)-1).[97]

The general business tax credit is a limited nonrefundable credit against income tax that is claimed after all other nonrefundable credits are claimed (see ¶ 1323). The amount of the general business tax credit may not exceed the "net income tax" minus the greater of the tentative minimum tax or 25 percent of the net regular tax liability over $25,000. For estates and trusts, the $25,000 amount must be reduced to an amount that bears the same ratio to $25,000 as the portion of the income of the estate or trust that is not allocated to the beneficiaries bears to the total income of the estate or trust (Code Sec. 38(c)(5)(D)).[98] Any unused credit can be carried back one year and forward 20 years for credits that arose in tax years beginning after 1997, and back three years and forward 15 years for credits that arose in tax years before 1998 (Code Sec. 39).[99]

Estates and trusts are also entitled to claim various refundable tax credits, including the credit for federal income tax withheld on wages and backup withholding (¶ 1372, ¶ 2645), the regulated investment company credit (¶ 1384), and the credit for federal excise taxes paid on fuels (¶ 1379).

Deduction for Distribution to Beneficiary

542. Simple v. Complex Trust. A "simple" trust is a trust that: (1) is required to distribute all of its income currently whether or not distributions of current income are in fact made; and (2) does not allow any amount to be paid or set-aside for charitable contributions (Code Sec. 651; Reg. § 1.651(a)-1).[100] A trust may be a simple trust even though under local law or under the trust instrument capital gains must be allocated to corpus. The "income" required to be distributed in order to qualify for classification as a simple trust is the income under local law and the governing instrument (Code Sec. 643(b)).[101] Generally, this will include only ordinary income, because capital gains, under most trust instruments and state laws, are considered corpus. A trust will lose its classification as a simple trust (but not its $300 exemption) for any year during which it distributes corpus. Thus, a trust can never be a simple trust during the year of termination or in a year of partial liquidation (Reg. § 1.651(a)-3).[102] See ¶ 544. A foreign trust will not be treated as a simple trust if it makes a loan of cash, cash equivalents or marketable securities to a grantor, or beneficiary who is a U.S. person, or a party related to such taxpayers (Code Sec. 643(i)(2)(D)).

The term "complex trust" applies to all trusts other than those described above (Reg. § 1.661(a)-1)[103]. Generally, the same rules that apply to complex trusts also apply to estates. For simple and complex trusts and for estates, the deduction for distributions to beneficiaries is determined by reference to distributable net income (see ¶ 543).

543. Distributable Net Income. The deductions allowable to an estate or trust for amounts paid or credited to beneficiaries (¶ 544 and following) are limited to the entity's "distributable net income" (DNI). It may also limit the amount of the distribution taxable to the beneficiary (¶ 554 and following), and it is a factor in applying the conduit rule (see ¶ 559).

The DNI of a domestic estate or trust generally consists of the same items of gross income and deductions that make up the taxable income of the estate or trust. However, there are important modifications: (1) no deduction is allowed for distributions to

---

Footnote references are to paragraphs of the 2008 Standard Federal Tax Reports.

[96] ¶ 34,160	[99] ¶ 4300	[102] ¶ 24,363
[97] ¶ 24,264, ¶ 24,280	[100] ¶ 24,360, ¶ 24,361	[103] ¶ 24,401
[98] ¶ 4250	[101] ¶ 24,320	

beneficiaries; (2) the deduction for the personal exemption is disallowed; (3) tax-exempt interest on state and local bonds is included, reduced by amounts which would be deductible but for the disallowance of deductions on expenses and interest related to tax-exempt income; (4) for a foreign trust, gross income from outside the United States (reduced by amounts which would be deductible but for the disallowance of deductions on expenses related to tax-exempt income) and within the United States is included; (5) capital gains allocable to corpus that are not paid, credited, or required to be distributed to any beneficiary during the tax year or paid, permanently set aside, or to be used for a charitable purpose are excluded (¶ 537); (6) capital losses are excluded except to the extent of their use in determining the amount of capital gains paid, credited, or required to be distributed to any beneficiary during the tax year; and (7) in the case of a simple trust, extraordinary dividends or taxable stock dividends that the fiduciary, acting in good faith, allocates to corpus are excluded (Code Sec. 643(a); Reg. § § 1.643(a)-0–1.643(a)-7).[104] The DNI of the estate or trust is determined by taking into account a net operating loss deduction.[105] See ¶ 531 and ¶ 556. However, the 50-percent exclusion under Code Sec. 1202(a) for gain on qualified small business stock held for more than five years (¶ 1736) is not taken into account in determining DNI (Code Sec. 643(a)(3)).[106]

For this purpose, the term "income" (without specifying "gross income," "taxable income," or "distributable net income") refers to income of the estate or trust for the tax year determined under the terms of its governing instrument and applicable local law—that is, income as it would be computed in an accounting to the court having jurisdiction over the estate or trust (Code Sec. 643(b); Reg. § 1.643(b)-1).[107] Trust provisions that depart fundamentally from concepts of income and principal are not recognized for tax purposes. However, an allocation of amounts between income and principal pursuant to applicable local law will be respected if local law provides for a reasonable apportionment between the income and remainder beneficiaries of the total return of the trust for the year, including ordinary and tax-exempt income, capital gains and appreciation.

544. Deduction for Distributions to Beneficiaries of a Simple Trust. A simple trust (¶ 542) may deduct the amount of income that the trustee is under a duty to distribute currently to beneficiaries, even if the trustee makes the actual distribution after the close of the tax year (Code Sec. 651; Reg. § § 1.651(a)-2, 1.651(b)-1).[108] If other amounts are distributed—such as a payment from corpus to meet the terms of an annuity payable from income or corpus—the complex trust rules apply for that year, except that the $300 exemption (¶ 534) is still allowed (Reg. § 1.642(b)-1)[109]. If the income required to be distributed exceeds the distributable net income (DNI), the distribution deduction is limited to the DNI (¶ 543), computed without including exempt income (and related deductions).

545. Deduction for Distributions to Beneficiaries of Estate or Complex Trust. A complex trust (¶ 542) or an estate may deduct any amount of income for the tax year that is required to be distributed currently to beneficiaries. This includes any amount required to be distributed that may be paid out of income or corpus, to the extent that it is in fact paid out of income. A complex trust or estate may also deduct any other amounts properly paid or credited or required to be distributed in the tax year, including amounts distributable at the discretion of the fiduciary and a distribution in kind. The amount to be taken into account in determining the deduction depends on whether the estate or trust elected to recognize gain on a noncash distribution of property in kind (see ¶ 526). In no case may the deduction exceed the distributable net income (DNI) of the estate or trust (¶ 543) (Code Sec. 661(a); Reg. § 1.661(a)-2).[110]

The IRS has ruled that where a will is silent, state law determines whether income or gain during the period of estate administration is "properly paid or credited" to a legatee (Rev. Rul. 71-335).[111] Also, a testamentary trustee can be a legatee or beneficiary for the purpose of a taxable distribution.[112]

Footnote references are to paragraphs of the 2008 Standard Federal Tax Reports.

[104] ¶ 24,320, ¶ 24,321—
¶ 24,328
[105] ¶ 24,296
[106] ¶ 24,320

[107] ¶ 24,320, ¶ 24,329
[108] ¶ 24,360, ¶ 24,362,
¶ 24,366
[109] ¶ 24,286

[110] ¶ 24,400, ¶ 24,402
[111] ¶ 24,407.78
[112] ¶ 24,407.7951

When estate or trust income is of varying types, the distribution deduction is treated as consisting of the same proportion as the total of each class of items has in calculating DNI. However, items will be allocated in accordance with a trust instrument or local law providing for a different method of allocation (Code Sec. 661(b); Reg. § 1.661(b)-1).[113] No deduction is allowed to the estate or trust for that part of a beneficiary's distribution that consists of DNI that is not included in the gross income of the estate or trust, such as tax-exempt interest income (Code Sec. 661(c); Reg. § 1.661(c)-1).[114]

In applying the above rule, all deductions entering into the computation of DNI (including charitable contributions) are allocated among the different types of income that make up the DNI in the following manner (Reg. §§ 1.652(b)-3; 1.661(b)-2):[115]

(1) The deductions *directly* attributable to an item of gross income will be allocated to that income. (Thus, real estate taxes, repairs, the trustee's share of depreciation, fire insurance premiums, etc., would be allocated to rental income.)

(2) The deductions *not directly* attributable to a specific item of gross income may be allocated to any item of gross income (including capital gains) included in computing DNI. However, a trust with nontaxable income must allocate a portion of these deductions to nontaxable income. The amount allocated to any one item of gross income may not exceed the amount of that item of gross income after its reduction for expenses directly attributable to it under step (1), above.

(3) The amounts determined under (1) and (2), above, will be deducted from the separate items of gross income. Any excess of deductions may be assigned to any other class of income. However, excess deductions attributable to tax-exempt income may not be offset against any other class of income.

There is no prohibition against allocating the deduction under step (2) to every item of gross income distributed in the ratio that the amount of a particular type of income bears to the entire amount of income distributed. Additionally, for purposes of the computation, the "unlimited" charitable deduction (see ¶ 537) is allocated ratably among all classes of income entering into DNI before any other expenses, unless a different allocation is specified by the governing instrument or local law. The charitable deduction is allocated by multiplying it by a ratio: the numerator is the amount of each single class of income, and the denominator is the total of all income classes (Reg. §§ 1.643(a)-5, 1.661(b)-2).[116]

For an illustration of the allocations, see the examples at ¶ 559.

546. 65-Day Election. The fiduciary of an estate or a complex trust can elect annually to treat any distribution or any portion of any distribution to a beneficiary made within the first 65 days following the end of a tax year as having been distributed in the prior year (Code Sec. 663(b)). The election, which is to be made on Form 1041, is irrevocable for the year involved and is binding for that year only. The amount to which the election can apply is the greater of: (1) the estate or trust's income or (2) distributable net income (¶ 543) for the tax year, reduced by any amounts paid, credited, or required to be distributed during the tax year other than those amounts that are subject to the 65-day election (Code Sec. 663(b); Reg. §§ 1.663(b)-1 and 1.663(b)-2).[117] There is no 65-day election for distributions of accumulated income (¶ 567).

548. Annuities Distributable from Income or Corpus. In the case of recurring distributions, payments by a trust or estate (where the amounts to be distributed, paid, or credited are a charge upon the corpus *or* the income) are usually taxable to the beneficiary and deductible by the trust or estate, to the extent that they are made from income (Code Sec. 661(a)(1); Reg. § 1.661(a)-2(b)).[118]

549. Widow(er)'s Allowance. A widow(er)'s (or dependent's) statutory allowance or award for support during administration of the estate is deductible by an estate if it is paid pursuant to a court order or decree or under local law. The allowance can be paid from either income or principal, but the deduction is limited to the estate's distributable

---

Footnote references are to paragraphs of the 2008 Standard Federal Tax Reports.

[113] ¶ 24,400, ¶ 24,403
[114] ¶ 24,400, ¶ 24,405
[115] ¶ 24,386, ¶ 24,404
[116] ¶ 24,326, ¶ 24,404
[117] ¶ 24,440, ¶ 24,444, ¶ 24,445
[118] ¶ 24,400, ¶ 24,402

net income (DNI) for the year (Reg. § 1.661(a)-2(e)).[119] Such payments are includible in the recipient's income to the extent of his or her share of the estate's DNI (Reg. §§ 1.662(a)-2(c) and 1.662(a)-3(b)).[120] In addition, the IRS will treat such allowances as distributions to beneficiaries, even though the allowances are treated as debts of the estate under local law (Rev. Rul. 75-124).[121]

How the Beneficiary Is Taxed

554. Taxation of Simple Trust Beneficiary. The income (as defined at ¶ 543) required to be distributed currently to a beneficiary of a simple trust is taxable to the beneficiary, whether or not distributed during the tax year, up to the amount of distributable net income (DNI). If the income required to be distributed exceeds DNI, only a proportionate share of each item is includible in the beneficiary's income. In making this apportionment, each item retains the same character (such as rent, dividends, etc.) that it had in the hands of the trust, unless the trust instrument specifically allocates a particular type of income to a particular beneficiary, and deductions reflected in the computation of DNI are to be allocated among the various types of income (see ¶ 545) (Code Sec. 652; Reg. §§ 1.652(a)-1–1.652(b)-3).[122] The amounts reported on the beneficiary's return must be consistent with the amounts reported on the trust return (Code Sec. 6034A(c)).

556. Taxation of Beneficiary of Estate or Complex Trust. A beneficiary of a complex trust or of a decedent's estate must include in taxable income the income (as defined at ¶ 543) that is required to be distributed currently, whether or not it is actually distributed during the tax year, plus any other amounts that are properly paid, credited, or required to be distributed for that year (Code Sec. 662; Reg. § 1.662(a)-1).[123] For example, income of a trust is taxable to the beneficiaries even where there is no direction as to distribution or accumulation and state law requires distribution.[124] If a fiduciary elects to treat a distribution to a beneficiary made in the year as an amount paid in a prior year (¶ 546), the amount covered by the election is included in the beneficiary's income for the year for which the trust takes the deduction. Special rules also apply to distributions by certain trusts out of accumulated income (¶ 567).

If the amount of income required to be distributed currently to all beneficiaries exceeds distributable net income (DNI) (computed without the "unlimited" charitable deduction at ¶ 537), then each beneficiary includes in income an amount that bears the same ratio to DNI as the amount of income required to be distributed currently to the beneficiary bears to the amount required to be distributed currently to all beneficiaries (Code Sec. 662(a)(1); Reg. § 1.662(a)-2(b)).[125]

If the income required to be distributed currently to all beneficiaries, plus any other amounts properly paid, credited, or required to be distributed to all beneficiaries for the tax year, exceeds the DNI for that year, then each beneficiary's share of such other amounts is a proportionate part of DNI (after subtracting the amounts required to be distributed currently) equal to the proportion that the beneficiary's share of these other amounts bears to the total other amounts for all beneficiaries (Code Sec. 662(a)(2); Reg. § 1.662(a)-3(c)).[126] The amount to be used in determining the beneficiary's share of estate or trust income depends on whether the estate or trust elected to recognize gain on the distribution (see ¶ 526).

Any amount which, under a will or trust instrument, is used in full or partial discharge or satisfaction of a legal obligation of any person is included in that person's gross income as though the amount was directly distributed to him or her as a beneficiary. "Legal obligation" includes a legal obligation to support another person only if the obligation is not affected by the adequacy of the dependent's own resources. The amount of trust income included in the gross income of a person obligated to support a dependent is limited by the extent of the person's legal obligation under local law. For example, in the case of a parent's obligation to support his or her child, to the extent that the support obligation (including education) is determined under local law by the family's station in life and the means of the parent, it is determined without considera-

Footnote references are to paragraphs of the 2008 Standard Federal Tax Reports.

[119] ¶ 24,402
[120] ¶ 24,422, ¶ 24,423
[121] ¶ 24,431.84
[122] ¶ 24,380—¶ 24,386
[123] ¶ 24,420, ¶ 24,421
[124] ¶ 24,431.65
[125] ¶ 24,420, ¶ 24,422
[126] ¶ 24,420, ¶ 24,423

¶554

tion of the trust income in question. This rule does not pertain to alimony payments or income of an alimony trust (see ¶ 771 and following) (Reg. § 1.662(a)-4).[127]

If a net operating loss (NOL) carryback of the estate or trust reduces the DNI of the estate or trust for the prior tax year to which the NOL is carried, the beneficiary's tax liability for such prior year may be recomputed based upon the revised DNI of the estate or trust (Rev. Rul. 61-20).[128]

In allocating the various types of income to the beneficiaries so as to give effect to all these rules, the amount reflected in the trust's or estate's DNI is determined first. It is charged with directly related expenses and a proportionate part of other expenses, including the "unlimited" charitable deduction (¶ 537) to the extent it is chargeable to income of the current year. Then, each beneficiary's share of income paid, credited, or required to be distributed to the beneficiary is multiplied by fractions, for each class of income, in which the numerator is the amount of such income included in DNI (whether the aggregate is more or less than the DNI) and the denominator is the DNI. However, if the governing instrument specifies or local law requires a different allocation, such allocation is to be followed (Reg. § § 1.662(b)-1; 1.662(b)-2).[129] These computations are illustrated at ¶ 559.

Special provisions exclude from the beneficiary's gross income any "unlimited" charitable contribution (¶ 537) or a gift or bequest of a specific sum of money or specific property (other than an amount that can be paid or credited only from income of an estate or trust) if it is paid or distributed all at once or in not more than three installments. In determining the number of installments, gifts or bequests of articles of personal use (e.g., personal and household effects, cars, etc.) are to be disregarded. Also disregarded are transfers of specific real estate, title to which passes directly from the decedent to the devisee under local law (Code Sec. 663(a); Reg. § § 1.663(a)-1; 1.663(a)-2).[130]

The amounts reported on the beneficiary's return must be consistent with the amounts reported on the trust or estate return (Code Sec. 6034A(c)).

557. Separate Shares as Separate Trusts or Estates. Where a trust or an estate has two or more beneficiaries and is to be administered in well-defined and separate shares, these shares are to be treated as separate trusts or estates in determining the amount of distributable net income (DNI) allocable to the beneficiaries (¶ 554 and ¶ 556). This rule limits the tax liability of a beneficiary on a distribution of income and corpus where the income is being accumulated for the benefit of another beneficiary. The separate-share treatment is mandatory and not elective. A trustee or an executor will be required to apply it even though separate and independent accounts are not maintained for each share and even though there is no physical segregation of assets.

The separate-share rule does not affect situations in which a single trust instrument creates not one but several separate trusts, as opposed to separate shares in the same trust. It also does not apply to trusts that provide for successive interests (e.g., a trust that provides a life estate to A and a remainder to B).

The treatment of separate shares as separate trusts and estates applies *only* for determining DNI in computing the distribution deduction allowable to the trust or estate and the amount includible in the income of the beneficiary. It cannot be applied to obtain more than one deduction for the personal exemption or to split the income of the trust or estate into several shares so as to be taxed at a lower-bracket rate (Code Sec. 663(c); Reg. § § 1.663(c)-1–1.663(c)-5).[131]

559. How the Complex Trust Rules Operate. The examples below illustrate computations of distributable net income (DNI), the distributive share of a beneficiary, and the taxable income of a complex trust. No "throwback" distributions (¶ 567) are involved.

Footnote references are to paragraphs of the 2008 Standard Federal Tax Reports.

[127] ¶ 24,424
[128] ¶ 24,431.493

[129] ¶ 24,425, ¶ 24,426
[130] ¶ 24,440, ¶ 24,441, ¶ 24,442

[131] ¶ 24,440, ¶ 24,446— ¶ 24,449

Example 1: Trust income: A complex trust has the following items of income in 2007:

Dividends	$16,000
Taxable interest	10,000
Exempt interest	10,000
Rent	4,000
Long-term capital gain allocable to corpus	6,000

The trust has expenses as follows:

Expenses directly allocable to rent	$2,000
Commissions allocable to income	3,000
Commissions allocable to corpus	1,500

On these facts, the trust would have "income" of $40,000 (see ¶ 543). The income items consist of dividends, taxable interest, exempt interest and rent. No expenses or charges against income or corpus are subtracted; only "receipts" treated as income under local law and the governing instrument are counted (e.g., rent). Also, the long-term capital gain is excluded from this income in order to apply the conduit rule (as illustrated in Example 3) because it is not income under local law. It is, however, included in the taxable income computation.

Example 2: Distributable net income: In computing the trust's DNI, the "net" amount of tax-exempt interest is added to the net income of the trust (after subtracting any charitable contribution). The "net" amount of tax-exempt interest is the full amount of such interest minus any expenses directly allocable to it and a proportionate part of all "general" expenses such as commissions. As noted in Example 1, there are $4,500 in general expenses (i.e., expenses not directly allocable to rental income), so $10,000/$40,000 of $4,500, or $1,125, is allocated to the exempt interest ($10,000), leaving a net of $8,875. This $1,125 must also be excluded from the deductions claimed by the trust as an expense "indirectly" related to the production of exempt interest income and therefore disallowed by Code Sec. 265. Accordingly, DNI is $33,500, computed as follows:

Dividends		$16,000
Taxable interest		10,000
Exempt interest ($10,000 less expenses allocable to exempt		
interest of $1,125)		8,875
Rent		4,000
Total		$38,875
Deductions:		
Rent expense	$2,000	
Commissions ($4,500 less $1,125 allocable to exempt		
interest)	3,375	5,375
Distributable net income		$33,500

Example 3: Taxable income of beneficiary: There is one beneficiary to whom the trustee must distribute $20,000 under the terms of the trust instrument. The first step in computing the amount taxable to the beneficiary is to determine the extent to which each income item is reflected in DNI, allocating expenses to the various items. Those allocable to exempt interest have already been reflected in the $8,875 figure carried into DNI in Example 2, so no further allocation of that item is needed. Allocation is needed for dividends, rent, and taxable interest income, but this allocation does not have to be proportionate. Expenses directly related to any source or type of income must be allocated directly to that income, but *general* expenses can be allocated to any taxable income the taxpayer wishes when computing DNI as long as no deficit is created for any item. In this example, it is assumed the trustee allocates all general expenses to taxable interest. Accordingly, the trustee charges the entire $3,375 of general expenses to the taxable interest ($10,000) so that the $33,500 DNI, for the purpose of applying the "conduit" rule, is deemed to have been derived from:

Rent	$2,000
Taxable interest	6,625
Dividends	16,000
Tax-exempt interest	8,875
	$33,500

The total corresponds to the DNI and is only an intermediate or "identification" step. Because the amounts actually distributable are less than the amount of

DNI, the next step is to multiply each of the above amounts by $20,000/$33,500 to determine what part of each is taxable to the beneficiary and deductible by the trust. Using these figures (the same result could be obtained by determining $2,000/$33,500 of $20,000, $6,625/$33,500 of $20,000, and so on), the apportionment is as follows:

Rent.	$1,194.03
Taxable interest	3,955.22
Dividends	9,552.24
Tax-exempt interest	5,298.51
	$20,000.00

The beneficiary's share of income and deductions is reported on Schedule K-1 of Form 1041. The beneficiary will omit the $5,298.51 tax-exempt interest in reporting income from the trust. The $9,552.24 dividend and $3,955.22 taxable interest income should be reported on the beneficiary's Form 1040.

Example 4: Taxable income of the trust: The trust is allowed a deduction for the amount required to be distributed currently up to the amount of its DNI, but not for any portion that consists of tax-exempt income. The deduction for distributions, therefore, is $14,701.49 ($20,000 minus $5,298.51). Taxable income of the trust is then computed as follows:

Dividends	$16,000.00	
Taxable Interest	10,000.00	
Rent	4,000.00	
Long-term capital gain	6,000.00	$36,000.00
Less:		
Expenses allocable to rent	$2,000.00	
Commissions allocable to income ($3,000 minus the $750 [$10,000/$40,000] allocable to exempt interest)	2,250.00	
Commissions allocable to corpus ($1,500 minus the $375 [$10,000/$40,000] allocable to exempt interest)	1,125.00	
Distribution to beneficiary	14,701.49	
Exemption	100.00	20,176.49
Taxable income		$15,823.51

562. Capital Gain or Loss of Estate or Trust. Capital gains are taxed to an estate or trust where the gains must be or are added to principal (corpus), and are not (1) paid, credited, or required to be distributed to any beneficiary during the taxable year; or (2) paid, permanently set aside, or to be used for a charitable purpose. Capital gains are included in distributable net income to the extent they are (1) allocated to income; (2) allocated to corpus but consistently treated by the fiduciary as part of a distribution to a beneficiary; or (3) allocated to corpus but actually distributed to a beneficiary or used by the fiduciary in determining the amount that is distributed or required to be distributed to a beneficiary (Code Sec. 643(a)(3); Reg. § 1.643(a)-3).[132] See ¶ 543.

A net capital loss of an estate or trust will reduce the taxable income of the estate or trust, but no part of the loss is deductible by the beneficiaries. If the estate or trust distributes all of its income, the capital loss will not result in a tax benefit for the year of the loss. Losses from the sale or exchange of capital assets are first netted at the trust level against any capital gains, except for capital gains utilized by the fiduciary in determining the amount to be distributed to a particular beneficiary (Reg. § 1.643(a)-3(d)).[133] On termination of an estate or trust, any unused capital loss carryover of the estate or trust is available to the beneficiaries (see ¶ 535).

564. Gift or Bequest. A trust or estate may not deduct as a distribution to a beneficiary, and a beneficiary does not include in income, a gift or bequest of a specific sum that is paid or credited in not more than three installments. However, an amount will not be treated as an excluded gift or bequest if the governing instrument provides that the specific sum is payable only from the income of the estate or trust (Code Sec. 663(a); Reg. § 1.663(a)-1).[134]

Footnote references are to paragraphs of the 2008 Standard Federal Tax Reports.

[132] ¶ 24,320, ¶ 24,324   [133] ¶ 24,324   [134] ¶ 24,440, ¶ 24,441

565. Different Tax Year. If the tax year of a beneficiary is different from that of the estate or trust, the amount to be included in the gross income of the beneficiary must be based on the distributable net income of the estate or trust and the amounts paid, credited, or required to be distributed to the beneficiary for any tax year or years of the estate or trust ending with or within his tax year (Code Secs. 652(c) and 662(c); Reg. § § 1.652(c)-1 and 1.662(c)-1).[135]

The Throwback Rules

567. "Throwback" of Accumulated Income. Special "throwback rules" generally apply to trust distributions made in tax years beginning before August 6, 1997. Although the throwback rules have been repealed for most trusts, they continue to apply to trusts created before March 1, 1984 that would be treated as multiple trusts under Code Sec. 643(f) and to foreign trusts and domestic trusts that were once treated as foreign trusts.

The throwback rules are designed to prevent the accumulation of trust income by a complex or accumulation trust over a period of years with a distribution to a beneficiary only in low-income years. The rules have the effect of carrying back to preceding years any distributions in excess of distributable net income (ordinary income) for the distribution year and taxing them to the beneficiaries as if they were distributed in the year the income was accumulated by the trust. This additional income is taxed to the beneficiary in the year that the beneficiary receives the accumulation distribution, but the beneficiary's tax liability is computed on Form 4970, Tax on Accumulation Distribution of Trusts, under special rules. Schedule J of Form 1041, Accumulation Distribution for Certain Complex Trusts, is used to determine the amount, the year, and the character of the additional distributions taxable to beneficiaries under the throwback rules. The beneficiary is allowed an offset or credit against the partial tax for the proportionate part of the trust's tax for the prior year, thus eliminating any double tax on the income. Beneficiaries of estates are not subject to the throwback rules (Code Secs. 665–668).[136]

Grantor Trust

571. Overview of Grantor Trust Rules. Under the grantor trust rules, a person (i.e., the grantor) who transfers property to a trust and retains certain powers or interests is treated as the owner of the trust property for income tax purposes. As a result, the income and deductions attributable to the trust are included in the grantor's income to the extent of the owned portion of the trust, including the deduction for domestic production activities (see ¶ 980A and following) (Code Sec. 671).[137]

573. Family Trusts Generally. Income-producing property is often conveyed in trust for the benefit of a family member in an effort to split any income generated by the property or to otherwise lessen the original owner's tax liability. However, there must be an actual transfer of property to accomplish the desired tax savings. It is not enough to transfer income generated by the property.

Limitations in the law (¶ 574 and following) prevent a taxpayer from escaping tax on the income from property where the taxpayer in effect remains the owner of the property by retaining control over the trust. In addition, intrafamily transfers of income-producing property can no longer be used to reduce income tax liability by shifting income from the parents' high marginal rate to their child's generally lower tax bracket if the child is under age 18 (under age 19 (or if a full time student, under age 24) for tax years beginning after May 25, 2007). Instead, if the net unearned income of the child exceeds an annual inflation-adjusted amount, it is taxed at the parents' top marginal rate (see ¶ 706).

574. Family Estate Trusts. A "family estate trust" (i.e., a trust to which an individual transfers personal assets and the right to income in exchange for the beneficial enjoyment of such assets and compensation) will be taxed as a grantor trust. The grantor's assignment of lifetime services or salary to the trust is not recognized for income tax purposes. Such trusts are deemed a "nullity" for income tax purposes and their income is taxable to the persons who created them. Acceptance of this broad

---

Footnote references are to paragraphs of the 2008 Standard Federal Tax Reports.

[135] ¶ 24,380, ¶ 24,387, ¶ 24,420, ¶ 24,427   [136] ¶ 24,480, ¶ 24,500, ¶ 24,520, ¶ 24,540   [137] ¶ 24,680

economic principle deprives a grantor of any possible refuge in the technicalities of the grantor trust provisions (Code Sec. 677).[138] Expenses incurred in setting up these family estate trusts are also not deductible under Code Sec. 212.[139]

575. Funeral Trusts. A qualified funeral trust (QFT) is a non-foreign funeral trust that elects not to be treated as a grantor trust, so that the income tax on the annual earnings of the trust is payable by the trustee (Code Sec. 685).[140] Generally, a QFT is an arrangement that would otherwise be treated as a grantor trust, under which an individual purchases funeral services or property necessary to provide such services for himself or for another individual from a funeral home prior to death and funds the purchase via contributions that do not exceed $8,800 for 2007, $9,000 for 2008 (Rev. Proc. 2006-53; Rev. Proc. 2007-66). The contributions must be held, invested and reinvested by the trust solely to make payments for such services or property upon the individual's or the other trust beneficiaries' death. If the election is made, the income tax rate schedule generally applicable to estates and trusts is applied to the trust by treating each beneficiary's interest as a separate trust. However, the trust is not entitled to a personal exemption in calculating the tax. The trustee's election must be made separately for each such "separate" trust. No gain or loss is recognized to a purchaser of a funeral trust contract as a result of any payment from the trust to the purchaser due to the cancellation of the contract.

The trustee elects QFT status by filing Form 1041-QFT, U.S. Income Tax Return for Qualified Funeral Trusts. The election must be filed no later than the due date (with extensions) for filing the trust income tax return for the year of election. The election applies to each trust reported in the QFT return. The trustee can use the form to file for a single QFT or multiple QFTs having the same trustee. The election may be made for the trust's first eligible year or for any subsequent year. Once made, the election cannot be revoked without IRS consent.

576. Reversionary Interest in Grantor. A grantor is considered to be the owner of any portion of a trust in which the grantor (or the grantor's spouse, see ¶ 578) has a reversionary interest in either the trust corpus or the income if the value of the reversionary interest exceeds five percent of the value of that portion of the trust. The value of the reversionary interest is measured as of the inception of the portion of the trust in which the grantor holds an interest. In determining whether the grantor's reversionary interest exceeds the five-percent threshhold, it is assumed that any discretionary powers will be exercised to maximize the value of the reversionary interest. Any postponement of the reacquisition or enjoyment of the reversionary interest is considered to be a new transfer in trust. However, no trust income is to be included in the grantor's income that would not have been included in the absence of the postponement. In addition, a grantor is exempt from the reversionary interest rule if the grantor retains a reversionary interest that takes effect only upon the death of a beneficiary who is a minor lineal descendant of the grantor (under age 21) and if the beneficiary has the entire present interest in the trust or a trust portion (Code Sec. 673).[141]

578. Powers Held by Grantor's Spouse. A grantor is treated as holding any power or interest in a trust that is held by a person who was the grantor's spouse at the time the power or interest was created, or who became the grantor's spouse subsequent to the creation of the power or interest (but only with respect to periods that the individual was the grantor's spouse). Thus, the grantor trust provisions cannot be avoided by having the spouse of the grantor possess prohibited powers or interests (e.g., spousal remainder trusts). Individuals who are legally separated under a decree of divorce or separate maintenance are not considered to be married for this purpose (Code Sec. 672(e)).[142]

579. Power to Control Beneficial Enjoyment. A grantor is taxed on trust income if the grantor or the grantor's spouse (see ¶ 578) retains the power to control the beneficial enjoyment of trust property or income (Code Sec. 674; Reg. § 1.674(a)-1).[143] However, there are a number of exceptions including, but not limited to: (1) an unexercised power to apply income to support a dependent; (2) power to allocate income

---

Footnote references are to paragraphs of the 2008 Standard Federal Tax Reports.

[138] ¶ 24,780, ¶ 24,783.1973   [140] ¶ 24,895   [142] ¶ 24,700
[139] ¶ 12,523.50   [141] ¶ 24,710   [143] ¶ 24,720, ¶ 24,721

among charitable beneficiaries; (3) power to distribute corpus limited by a reasonably definite standard; and (4) power to withhold income temporarily (Code Sec. 674(b); Reg. §§ 1.674(b)-1–1.674(d)-2).[144]

581. Retention of Administrative Powers. The grantor is taxed on trust income if the grantor or the grantor's spouse (see ¶ 578) retains administrative powers enabling the grantor to obtain, by dealings with the trust, financial benefits that would not be available in an arm's-length transaction (Code Sec. 675; Reg. § 1.675-1).[145] For example, the borrowing of trust corpus or income by the grantor or the grantor's spouse at any time during a tax year results in the grantor's being taxed on the trust income for that entire year, even if the grantor repays the loan with interest during the same year.[146]

582. Power to Revoke Trust. If a grantor creates a trust and reserves a right to revoke it, the income of the trust is treated as the grantor's income. However, the trust income will not be taxed to the grantor if the power can only affect the beneficial enjoyment of the income after the occurrence of an event such that the grantor would not be treated as the owner if the power were a reversionary interest. But the grantor may be treated as the owner after the occurrence of the event unless the power to revoke is then relinquished (Code Sec. 676).[147]

584. Income for Grantor's Benefit. The grantor is taxed on trust income that is or may be accumulated or distributed to the grantor or to the grantor's spouse, or used to pay life insurance premiums on either the grantor's or the spouse's life, except for policies irrevocably payable to charities (Code Sec. 677(a)).[148] To the extent that trust income may be used in satisfaction of the grantor's legal obligation to support a beneficiary (such as a child, but not a spouse), it is regarded as distributable to the grantor. But if the discretion to so use the income is not in the grantor, acting as such, but in another person (for example, the trustee or the grantor acting as trustee or co-trustee), then that income is includible in the grantor's gross income only to the extent that it is actually used for the beneficiary's support or maintenance (Code Sec. 677(b); Reg. § 1.677(b)-1).[149] In addition, any capital gain that, under state law, is added to trust corpus is taxable to the grantor if the corpus reverts to the grantor upon termination of the trust (Reg. §§ 1.671-3(b)(2) and 1.677(a)-1(f); see Rev. Ruls. 58-242 and 75-267).[150]

585. Income Taxable to Person Other Than Grantor. A person other than the grantor of a trust may be taxed on the trust's income if that person has a power, exercisable alone, to vest the corpus or income of the trust in that person (Code Sec. 678(a); Reg. § 1.678(a)-1).[151] For example, in the case of a trust that is established by a father for the benefit of his children, but under which the grantor's brother may at any time take the trust property, the brother is treated as the owner and the income is taxed to him. This rule does not apply if the power is renounced or disclaimed within a reasonable period of time (Code Sec. 678(d); Reg. § 1.678(d)-1).[152]

A U.S. person who is a beneficiary of a trust is treated as the grantor to the extent that the beneficiary transferred property, directly or indirectly, to a foreign person who otherwise would have been treated as the owner under the grantor trust rules (Code Sec. 672(f)(5)).[153]

586. Return for Grantor Trust. Generally, items of income, deduction, or credit that are treated as belonging to a trust grantor or another person are not reported by the trust on Form 1041. Instead, these items are reflected on the income tax return of the grantor (or other person who is taxable on the trust income). A separate statement should be attached to Form 1041 stating the name, taxpayer identification number and address of the person to whom the income is taxable, and setting forth the income, deductions and credits (Reg. § 1.671-4).[154] Alternative reporting methods may be available for certain grantor trusts.

Footnote references are to paragraphs of the 2008 Standard Federal Tax Reports.

[144] ¶ 24,720, ¶ 24,722— ¶ 24,725
[145] ¶ 24,740, ¶ 24,741
[146] ¶ 24,742.10
[147] ¶ 24,760
[148] ¶ 24,780
[149] ¶ 24,780, ¶ 24,782
[150] ¶ 24,684, ¶ 24,781, ¶ 24,783.101, ¶ 24,783.34
[151] ¶ 24,800, ¶ 24,801
[152] ¶ 24,800, ¶ 24,804
[153] ¶ 24,700
[154] ¶ 24,685

588. Foreign Grantor Trust Rules. Any U.S. person transferring property to a foreign trust (other than an employee's trust) that has a U.S. beneficiary will be treated as the owner of that portion of the trust attributable to the property transferred (Code Secs. 678(b) and 679).[155] The transferor is required to file an annual information return (Code Secs. 6048(c) and 6677(a)).[156] Also, the U.S. grantor trust rules generally will not apply to any portion of a trust that would otherwise be deemed to be owned by a foreign person (Code Sec. 672(f)).

Charitable Trust

590. Charitable Remainder Trusts. Whenever there is a noncharitable income beneficiary of a trust, gifts of remainder interests will qualify for a charitable contribution deduction only if the trust is a charitable remainder *annuity trust* (CRAT) or a charitable remainder *unitrust* (CRUT) (Code Sec. 664; Reg. §§1.664-1, 1.664-2and 1.664-3).[157] Charitable contribution deductions are denied for gifts of remainder interests in all other types of trusts. (However, if the grantor gives *all* the interests in a trust to charity, the above rules are not applicable, and a deduction is allowable.)

Qualification. An *annuity trust* is a trust from which a sum certain or a specified amount is to be paid to the income beneficiary or beneficiaries (Code Sec. 664(d)(1); Reg. §§1.664-1 and 1.664-2). The specified amount may not be less than five percent, and cannot be more than 50 percent, of the initial net fair market value of all property placed in trust, and it must be paid at least annually to the income beneficiary. Furthermore, the value of the remainder interest must usually be at least 10 percent of the initial net fair market value of all of the property placed in trust. There are several provisions designed to provide relief to trusts that do not meet the "10-percent" test. No contributions can be made to a CRAT after the initial contribution, and the governing instrument must contain a prohibition against future contributions.

A *unitrust* is a trust that specifies that the income beneficiary or beneficiaries are to receive annual payments based on a fixed percentage of the net fair market value of the trust's assets as determined each year (Code Sec. 664(d)(2); Reg. §§1.664-1 and 1.664-3). The fixed percentage cannot be less than five percent, and cannot be more than 50 percent, of the net fair market value. In the alternative, however, a qualified CRUT can provide for the distribution each year of five percent of the net fair market value of its assets or the amount of the trust income, whichever is lower. For this purpose, trust income excludes capital gains, and trust assets must be valued annually. This payment requirement may not be discretionary with the trustee. Unitrusts may have additional contributions made to them. For most transfers in trust, the value of the remainder interest with respect to each contribution to the unitrust must be at least 10 percent of the net fair market value of such contributed property as of the date the property is contributed to the trust. If an additional contribution would cause the trust to fail the "10-percent" remainder test, then the contribution will be treated as a transfer to a separate trust under regulations. Other provisions may provide relief to trusts that fail to meet the "10-percent" test.

CRATs and CRUTs cannot have noncharitable remainder interests. Generally, the remainder interests must pass to a charity upon the termination of the last income interest and the trust instrument must contain a provision that determines how the final payment of a specified distribution is to be made. However, a charitable trust may make certain limited "qualified gratuitous" transfers of qualified employer securities to an employee stock ownership plan (ESOP) without adversely affecting the status of the charitable remainder trust.

To avoid the possible disqualification of a charitable remainder trust due to a surviving spouse's right of election against the grantor spouse's estate under state law, the IRS created a safe harbor requiring the surviving spouse to irrevocably waive the right (Rev. Proc. 2005-24). However, until further guidance is published, the IRS will disregard the existence of a right of election *without* requiring a waiver, but only if the surviving spouse does not exercise the right (Notice 2006-15).[158]

Footnote references are to paragraphs of the 2008 Standard Federal Tax Reports.

[155] ¶24,800, ¶24,820
[156] ¶36,000, ¶39,815

[157] ¶24,460, ¶24,461, ¶24,464, ¶24,465

[158] ¶24,468.18

There may be more than one noncharitable income beneficiary, either concurrently or successively, and the income interest may be a life estate or for a term of years not in excess of 20 years. However, a contingency clause may be placed in the trust instrument providing that the noncharitable interest is to terminate and the charitable interest is to be accelerated upon the happening of an event such as the remarriage of the noncharitable beneficiary (Code Sec. 664(f)).[159] The income beneficiary can receive only a specified or fixed amount from the trust, and the trustee cannot have additional power to invade corpus or to alter, amend, or revoke the trust for the benefit of the noncharitable income beneficiary. The trustee cannot be restricted from investing in income-producing assets (Reg. § 1.664-1(a)(3)).[160]

Taxation of Trust. A CRAT or a CRUT is exempt from income tax. However, if a CRAT or CRUT has unrelated business taxable income (UBTI), it is subject to a 100-percent excise tax on its UBTI, but will retain its tax-exempt status. The excise tax is treated as if it is imposed under the excise tax rules that apply to private foundations and other tax-exempt organizations (see ¶ 591), other than the rules for abatement of first- and second-tier taxes. The rule preventing the IRS from filing an additional deficiency notice once a taxpayer files a Tax Court petition challenging the deficiency also applies to this tax (Code Sec. 664(c)).[161] (Before 2007, a CRAT or CRUT with UBTI was taxed as a complex trust.)

Treatment of Beneficiaries. Under either an annuity trust or a unitrust, the amount paid to a beneficiary is considered as having the following characteristics in the beneficiary's hands: (1) it will be ordinary income to the extent of the trust's ordinary income for the tax year and its undistributed ordinary income from prior years; (2) it will be capital gain to the extent of the trust's capital gains for the tax year and its undistributed capital gains, determined on a cumulative net basis, for prior years; (3) it will be considered other income to the extent of the trust's other income for the tax year and its undistributed other income from prior years; and (4) any remaining amount will be considered a distribution of principal (Code Sec. 664(b); Reg. §§ 1.664-1–1.664-4).[162] Items within the ordinary income and capital gains categories are assigned to different subcategories based on the federal income tax rate applicable to each type of income within the category. Categories of income that are taxed at the same rate can be combined into a single class if the tax rate will not change in the future. If the tax rate is temporary, then the categories must be maintained as separate groups (Reg. § 1.664-1(d)(1)(i)).[163]

The characterizations of income items distributed or deemed distributed at any time during the tax year of the charitable remainder trust are determined as of the end of the tax year. Distributions are subject to the tax rate applicable to the income class from which the distribution is derived, not the tax rate applicable when the income was received by the trust (Reg. § 1.664-1(d)(1)(ii)(a)). Gains and losses of long-term capital gain classes are netted *prior* to netting short-term capital loss against any class of long-term capital gain (Reg. § 1.664-1(d)(1)(iv)). Special transition rules also apply for classifying long-term capital gains and losses (Reg. § 1.664-1(d)(1)(vi)).[164]

The fiduciary of a CRAT or CRUT must file Form 5227, Split-Interest Trust Information Return. The fiduciary must also file Form 1041-A unless all net income is required to be distributed currently to the beneficiaries. Such returns must be filed on or before the 15th day of the fourth month following the close of the tax year of the trust (Rev. Proc. 83-32).[165]

591. Private Foundation Rules Applicable to Trusts. The income and excise taxes imposed on private exempt foundations extend to all nonexempt charitable trusts with certain modifications (Code Sec. 4947).[166] First, a nonexempt trust that devotes *all* of its "unexpired interests" to charitable, religious, educational, and other purposes that enable contributors to obtain a charitable deduction will be treated as a private foundation. Thus, it will be subject to the excise taxes on: investment income (¶ 633), self-dealing (¶ 635), failure to distribute income (¶ 637), excess business holdings (¶ 640),

---

Footnote references are to paragraphs of the 2008 Standard Federal Tax Reports.

[159] ¶ 24,460	[162] ¶ 24,460—¶ 24,466	[165] ¶ 24,468.20
[160] ¶ 24,461	[163] ¶ 24,461	[166] ¶ 34,140
[161] ¶ 24,460	[164] ¶ 24,461	

investments that jeopardize charitable purposes (¶ 642) and certain taxable expenditures (lobbying , electioneering, etc., ¶ 644). For this purpose, "unexpired interests" include life or term income interests, interests in trust corpus, and remainder interests.

Second, a nonexempt, split-interest trust that *does not* devote *all* of its unexpired interests to charitable purposes (split-interest trust) is subject to the excise taxes on self-dealing, excess business holdings, investments that jeopardize charitable purposes, and certain taxable expenditures (lobbying, electioneering, etc.) as it were a private foundation. However, the taxes apply to income to be paid to trust beneficiaries under the terms of the trust instrument only if the trust was a "charitable remainder annuity trust" or a "charitable remainder unitrust" (¶ 590 and ¶ 631). The taxes do not, in any event, apply to amounts in trust for which a deduction is not allowable if segregated from deductible amounts.

In addition, the taxes on excess business holdings and investments that jeopardize charitable purposes do not apply to a split-interest trust if: (1) the charity is only an income beneficiary and its beneficial interest is no more than 60 percent of the value of the trust property; or (2) the charity's only interest in the trust is as a remainderman. Split-interest trusts are treated like private foundations with regard to the rules on governing instruments and the tax on involuntary termination of status for repeated or willful violations (see ¶ 631 and ¶ 649).

The excise tax on investment income and failure to distribute income do not apply to a split-interest trusts under any circumstances.

593. Pooled Fund Arrangements. Generally, a pooled income fund is a trust to which a person transfers an irrevocable remainder interest in property for the benefit of a public charity while retaining an income interest in the property for the life of one or more beneficiaries living at the time of the transfer (Code Sec. 642(c)(5); Reg. § 1.642(c)-5).[167] Income, estate, and gift tax charitable contribution deductions are allowed for the value of remainder interests in property transferred to a pooled income fund (Code Sec. 642(c)(3)).[168] To protect the value of depreciable property that will pass to the charitable remainderman, the governing instrument of the pooled income fund must provide for the creation of a depreciation reserve.[169] In addition, the fund: (1) must commingle all property contributed to it, (2) cannot invest in tax-exempt securities, and (3) must be maintained by the recipient charity with no donor or income beneficiary acting as a trustee. However, the charity does not have to act as trustee of the fund.

Each person who has an income interest resulting from a transfer of property to the fund must be paid an annual income based on the fund's yearly rate of return (i.e., the trust cannot accumulate income for any beneficiary). A pooled income fund's method of calculating its yearly rate of return must be supported by a full statement attached to the fund's annual income tax return. A pooled income fund cannot include contributions of property from sources other than pooled income funds and general endowment funds. Such a fund and its beneficiaries are taxable under the rules applicable to trusts, except that the substantial owner rules do not apply.

595. Common Trust Fund. Each participant in a common trust fund—maintained by a bank—must report its share of the taxable income of the fund, whether or not distributed or distributable. The taxable income of a common trust fund is computed in much the same manner as an individual's taxable income, except for the exclusion of capital gains and losses and the deduction for charitable contributions (Code Sec. 584).[170]

Footnote references are to paragraphs of the 2008 Standard Federal Tax Reports.

[167] ¶ 24,280, ¶ 24,293   [169] ¶ 24,308.1877,   [170] ¶ 23,630
[168] ¶ 24,280   ¶ 24,308.1880

Chapter 6

EXEMPT ORGANIZATIONS

Overview

601. Overview. A variety of organizations may qualify for exemption from federal income taxation. The most common basis for exempt status is as a charitable organization under Code Sec. 501(c)(3) (¶ 602). Generally, charitable organizations can be either publicly supported or private foundations. While all charitable organizations are subject to limitations on how they operate (¶ 613 and following), private foundations may be subject to certain excise taxes for engaging in prohibited activities (¶ 631). In addition to charitable organizations under Code Sec. 501(c)(3), there are also a number of organizations that may qualify for exempt status if they have a socially beneficial purpose (¶ 696). Regardless of how an entity qualifies as a tax-exempt organization, it may nonetheless still be subject to income tax on any business income not related to its exempt purpose (¶ 655) and any income arising from debt-financed property (¶ 687).

Code Sec. 501(c)(3) Organizations

602. Charitable Organizations Under Code Sec. 501(c)(3). Code Sec. 501 provides that various classes of non-profit organizations are exempt from federal income tax unless they are deemed to be feeder organizations (¶ 694).[1] The most common basis for invoking tax-exempt status falls under Code Sec. 501(c)(3)'s broad category of exemptions for religious, charitable, scientific, literary and educational organizations (commonly referred to as charitable organizations). Among other benefits, exempt status conferred by Code Sec. 501(c)(3) allows an organization to receive tax-deductible contributions from its donors (¶ 1061). In general, charitable organizations under Code Sec. 501(c)(3) are either public charities or private foundations (¶ 631). Application for recognition of Code Sec. 501(c)(3) federal tax-exempt status is made on Form 1023 (¶ 616).

Charitable organizations eligible for tax-exempt status under Code Sec. 501(c)(3) include: Any corporation and any community chest, fund or foundation, organized and operated exclusively for religious (¶ 604), charitable, scientific, testing for public safety, literary, or educational purposes, or to foster national or international amateur sports competition (but only if no part of its activities involve the provision of athletic facilities or equipment), or for the prevention of cruelty to children or animals. A charitable purpose is interpreted broadly and may include purposes beyond those stated in Code Sec. 501(c)(3). For example, a charitable purpose can include: providing relief to the poor or disadvantaged; the advancement of education, religion, or science; or lessening the burdens of government through the promotion of social welfare or other community development (Reg. § 1.501(c)(3)-1(d)).[2] An educational organization can include a child-care center whose services are available to the general public and whose purpose is to enable individuals to be gainfully employed (Code Sec. 501(k)).[3] Regardless of an entity's charitable purpose, however, it must meet organizational, operational and private benefit tests in order to qualify as a charitable organization (Reg. § 1.501(c)(3)-1).[4]

Footnote references are to paragraphs of the 2008 Standard Federal Tax Reports.

[1] ¶ 22,602
[2] ¶ 22,608
[3] ¶ 22,602
[4] ¶ 22,608

Organizational Test. The organizational test requires that the entity's "articles of organization" specifically limit its purpose to one or more exempt purposes, including that its assets are dedicated to an exempt purpose. The articles of organization also must not expressly permit the organization to carry on activities which do not further the organization's exempt purpose, except where these nonexempt activities are an insubstantial part of the organization's activities. For example, the article of organization must not devote more than an insubstantial part of its activities to influencing legislation by propaganda or otherwise (¶ 613); or authorize the organization to directly or indirectly participate or intervene in any political campaign on behalf of or in opposition to any candidate for public office (¶ 614). Whether an organization meets the organizational requirement is determined exclusively from the language of the articles of organization and not from the activities conducted by the organization. For this purpose, "articles of organization" include trust instruments, corporate charters, articles of association or any other written instrument by which an organization is created.

Operational Test. The operational test requires that an entity must be operated exclusively for one or more exempt purposes. An organization is "operated exclusively" for an exempt purpose only if it engages primarily in activities that accomplish one or more of its exempt purposes (Reg. § 1.501(c)(3)-1(c)).[5] No more than an insubstantial part of the entity's activities may be in the furtherance of nonexempt purposes. Whether an organization has a substantial nonexempt purpose is determined by taking into account all facts and circumstances, including the size and extent of all of the organization's activities. For example, if the entity is an "action" organization, then it will *not* be considered as operated exclusively for an exempt purpose. For this purpose, an entity is an "action" organization if it devotes a substantial part of its activities to attempting to influence legislation or if it participates in political campaigns. However, if an organization fails the operational test because it is an "action" organization, it may still qualify for tax-exempt status as a social welfare organization under Code Sec. 501(c)(4) (¶ 692). A charitable organization may also provide commercial-type insurance unless it is an insubstantial part of the organization's activities, in which case the activity will be treated as an unrelated trade or business (¶ 655) (Code Sec. 501(m) and (n)).[6]

An entity will also not be considered as operating exclusively for exempt purpose if any of its net earnings inure in whole or in part to the benefit of private shareholders or individuals. A "private shareholder or individual" is any person having a personal and private interest in the activities of the organization, such as founders of the organization, employees, board members, or family members of officers, employees, etc. The inurement prohibition does not prohibit payments to stockholders or individual but instead is directed at payments that are made for purposes other than as reasonable compensation for goods or services (however, see ¶ 617).

Private Benefit Test. An organization is not organized or operated exclusively for charitable purposes unless it serves a public rather than a private interest (outside interests, as opposed to inside interests addressed by the inurement prohibition above). The question of private benefit often arises in situations in which a charitable organization enters into partnerships and other joint ventures with for-profit entities. The charitable organization can form such ventures and still satisfy the operational test only if it is permitted to act exclusively in furtherance of its exempt purpose and only incidentally for the benefit of the for-profit partners (Rev. Rul. 98-15).[7] In addition, the for-profit party cannot be allowed to control or use the charitable organization's activities or assets for its own benefit unless such control or use is incidental.

604. Churches and Religious Organizations. A church or religious organization will be exempt from federal income tax and eligible to receive tax-deductible contributions if it meets the requirements to be a Code Sec. 501(c)(3) organization (¶ 602). The term "church" is not specifically defined in the Code but generally is used in its generic sense as a place of worship including, for example, mosques and synagogues. It also includes conventions or associations of churches, as well as integrated auxiliaries of a church. For this purpose, a convention or association of churches is a cooperative

---

Footnote references are to paragraphs of the 2008 Standard Federal Tax Reports.

[5] ¶ 22,608   [6] ¶ 22,602   [7] ¶ 22,609.411

undertaking by churches of the same or differing denominations (Rev. Rul. 74-224).[8] However, the fact that such an organization has individuals as members and these members have voting rights will not cause it to lose exempt status (Code Sec. 7701(o)).[9]

Because special tax rules apply to churches, it is important to distinguish churches from other religious organizations. For example, because of the need for the IRS to combat efforts on the part of some individuals and organizations to utilize a church to avoid taxes, and the equally important need to protect legitimate churches from undue IRS interference in their activities, the Code contains detailed rules governing when the IRS may inquire into or examine the activities of a church (Code Sec. 7611; Reg. § 301.7611-1).[10] Thus, "religious organizations" that are not churches but that may still be eligible for tax-exempt status include nondenominational ministries, interdenominational and ecumenical organizations, and other entities whose principal purpose is the study or advancement of religion (IRS Pub. 1828). Unlike churches, religious organizations that wish to be tax exempt generally must apply to the IRS for tax-exempt status by filing Form 1023 (¶ 616).

A religious or apostolic association that does not meet the requirements to be a Code Sec. 501(c)(3) organization may nonetheless qualify as exempt from federal income taxation if it has a common or community treasury. The exemption applies even if the association engages in business for the common good of its members, provided that the members, at the time of filing their returns, include in their gross income their pro rata share of the association's taxable income, whether distributed or not. These amounts are treated as dividends received (Code Sec. 501(d); Reg. § 1.501(d)-1).[11] There is no official exemption application form for this purpose. However, the association must file Form 1065, U.S. Return of Partnership Income, each tax year for information purposes (Reg. § 1.6033-2(e)).[12]

607. Supporting Organizations. A charitable organization under Code Sec. 501(c)(3) that provides support to other public charities will itself be considered to be a public charity rather than a private foundation (¶ 631). As such, the "supporting organization" must file an annual information return on Form 990, regardless of the organization's gross receipts (¶ 625). To qualify as a supporting organization, a Code Sec. 501(c)(3) organization must be:

- organized and operated at all times exclusively for the benefit of, to perform the functions of, or to carry out the purposes of a public charity (organizational and operational test, ¶ 602);

- operated or controlled by a public charity (relationship test); and

- not controlled either directly or indirectly by a disqualified person (¶ 635), other than a foundation manager or publicly supported charity (lack of control test) (Code Sec. 509(a)(3)).[13]

To satisfy the relationship test, a supporting organization must hold one of three close relationships with the supported organization (Reg. § 1.509(a)-4).[14] In a Type I relationship, the supported organization must exercise a substantial degree of control over the programs, activities and policies of the supporting organization (comparable to a parent-subsidiary relationship). In a Type II relationship, there must be common control or supervision by persons controlling or supervising both the supporting organization and the supported organization (comparable to brother-sister corporations). In a Type III relationship, the supporting organization must be operated in connection with the supported organization by being responsive to its needs and demands, and by being significantly involved in its operations to the point that the supported organization is dependent upon the supporting organization for the type of support it provides. Regardless of whether these relationship requirements are met, if a Type I or Type III organization supports an organization that is controlled by a donor, then the supporting organization will be treated as a private foundation rather than as a public charity (Code Sec. 509(f)(2)).

Footnote references are to paragraphs of the 2008 Standard Federal Tax Reports.

[8] ¶ 11,620.205
[9] ¶ 43,080
[10] ¶ 42,910, ¶ 42,912

[11] ¶ 22,602, ¶ 22,659
[12] ¶ 35,422
[13] ¶ 22,800

[14] ¶ 22,804

A number of special rules also apply to Type III supporting organizations. For example, each tax year, a Type III organization must provide each supported organization with any information that may be required by the IRS to ensure that the relationship requirements of being a Type III organization are met (Code Sec. 509(f)(1)). This may include the Type III organization's annual information return (Form 990), any tax return filed (Form 990-T), and any annual report. In addition, a Type III organization may not be operated in connection with any public charity that is organized outside the United States. Similarly, a trust will not be considered to be a Type III organization *solely* based on the facts that it is a charitable trust under state law, the public charity is a beneficiary of the trust, and the public charity has the power to enforce the trust terms (Act Sec. 1241 of the Pension Protection Act of 2006 (P.L. 109-280)).

613. Lobbying by Code Sec. 501(c)(3) Organizations. An organization that otherwise qualifies as a charitable organization under Code Sec. 501(c)(3) will lose its exempt status if: (1) a *substantial* part of its activities consists of carrying on propaganda or attempting to influence legislation or (2) it participates or intervenes in any political campaign on behalf of, or in opposition to, any candidate for public office (Code Sec. 501(h); Reg. § 1.501(h)-1).[15] If a charitable organization engages in substantial legislative activity or participates in any political campaign, then it is an "action" organization (Reg. § 1.501(c)(3)-1).[16] There are no specific guidelines as to what constitutes *substantial* or *unsubstantial* lobbying activities for this purpose. Instead, the substantial part test is determined on the facts and circumstances. On the other hand, the IRS has issued guidance with regard to the facts and circumstances to be evaluated in determining whether or not a Code Sec. 501(c)(3) organization has participated or intervened in a political campaign for public office (Rev. Rul. 2007-41). If the organization has made a political expenditure, it will be subject to an excise tax (¶ 614).[17]

As an alternative to the substantial part test, many public charities may elect on Form 5768 a sliding scale limitation on expenditures to objectively determine their permissible level of lobbying activities (Code Sec. 501(h); Reg. § 1.501(h)-2).[18] Organizations that may not make this election include: churches or a convention or association of churches (¶ 604), private foundations (¶ 631), and supporting organizations (¶ 607) for social welfare organizations, labor unions, trade associations and organizations that test for public safety (¶ 692).

The basic permitted level for lobbying expenditures (but not grass roots lobbying) is 20 percent of the first $500,000 of the electing organization's exempt-purpose expenditures for the year, plus 15 percent of the second $500,000, plus 10 percent of the third $500,000, plus five percent of any additional expenditures (Code Sec. 4911).[19] This amount, however, is subject to an overall maximum limit of $1 million for any one year. In addition, in the case of so-called grass roots lobbying—attempts to influence the general public on legislative matters—the basic permitted level is limited to 25 percent of the general lobbying level described above. An excise tax of 25 percent is imposed on any excess lobbying expenditures above these limits. In addition, if an organization's lobbying expenditures normally—on an average over a four-year period—exceed 150 percent of these limits (computed on Schedule A of Form 990), the organization will lose its tax-exempt status (Reg. § 1.501(h)-3).[20]

614. Political Expenditures by Code Sec. 501(c)(3) Organizations. A 10-percent excise tax is imposed on a Code Sec. 501(c)(3) organization for each political expenditure made during the tax year (Code Sec. 4955).[21] For this purpose, a political expenditure is generally defined as any amount paid or incurred by the organization in connection with any participation or intervention in any political campaign on behalf of (or in opposition to) any candidate for public office (see also ¶ 613). A separate 2.5-percent excise tax (up to $5,000) is imposed on any organization manager who agrees to the making of the expenditure if the manager knows that it is a political expenditure, unless the agreement is not willful and due to reasonable cause. An

---

Footnote references are to paragraphs of the 2008 Standard Federal Tax Reports.

[15] ¶ 22,602, ¶ 22,663
[16] ¶ 22,608
[17] ¶ 22,609.103

[18] ¶ 22,602, ¶ 22,664
[19] ¶ 33,960
[20] ¶ 22,665

[21] ¶ 34,240

organization manager includes a director, officer, trustee, or any individual with comparable responsibilities.

If the political expenditure is not corrected within a "taxable period," then a second-tier excise tax is imposed on the organization equal to 100 percent of the amount of the expenditure. Organization managers who refuse to agree to all or part of the correction are also subject to a second-tier tax of 50 percent of the amount of the expenditure (up to $10,000). If more than one manager is liable for either the first- or second-tier taxes, then each manager will be jointly and severally liable. The "taxable period" is the period beginning on the date on which the taxable expenditure is made and ending on the earlier of: (1) the date on which a deficiency notice for the first-tier tax is mailed; or (2) the date on which the first-tier tax is assessed. A correction of a political expenditure means the foundation takes all reasonable means to recover the expenditure to the extent possible and establish safeguards to prevent future political expenditures. If full recovery is not possible, then the foundation must take whatever corrective action prescribed by the IRS. Both the first and second levels of taxes may be abated under certain circumstances (¶ 647). The organization's taxes are reported on Form 4720.

616. Application and Modification of Exempt Status. Charitable organizations seeking exempt status under Code Sec. 501(c)(3) must file an application for exemption on Form 1023 within 15 months (or 27 months with an automatic 12-month extension) from the end of the month in which they are organized (Code Sec. 508; Reg. § 1.508-1).[22] An organization that fails to file a timely notice will not qualify for exempt status for any period prior to the date actual notice is given. A second notification is required to be included on the application if the organization wants to claim public charity status. An organization that fails to notify the IRS of public charity status will be presumed to be a private foundation subject to the various restrictions on such groups (¶ 631).

Organizations which are exempt from both notification requirements above, include: (1) any organization (other than a private foundation) whose annual gross receipts normally do not exceed $5,000; (2) churches and their affiliates; (3) any subordinate organization (other than a private foundation) covered by a group exemption of a parent; and (4) certain nonexempt charitable trusts (¶ 591). However, in order for such an organization to establish its exemption with the IRS and receive an advance ruling or determination letter, it should file the appropriate information return as proof of its exemption (¶ 625) (Reg. § 1.508-1(a)(4)).

The IRS will issue a favorable determination letter or exemption ruling if the organization's application and supporting documents establish that it meets the particular requirements under which it is claiming tax-exempt status (Rev. Proc. 2007-52).[23] The ruling may be issued in advance of the organization's operations if the organization describes its proposed activities in sufficient detail in its application for exemption. A ruling may also be modified or revoked by the IRS at any time (Reg. § 601.201(n)(6)).[24] Generally, revocations occur prospectively, however, a retroactive revocation may occur where: (1) the IRS was not been fully or correctly informed as to the material facts on which the exemption ruling was based, or (2) there have been material changes in law or fact subsequent to the time the original ruling was issued.

If an organization receives an unfavorable exemption ruling, or its exempt status is revoked, it may seek judicial review only after it has exhausted all administrative remedies with the IRS. If an adverse ruling is issued (or if the IRS fails to issue a ruling), the organization can seek a declaratory judgment that it qualifies for exempt status (Code Sec. 7428).[25] If the organization has actually begun operations before it receives an adverse ruling (or its exempt status is revoked retroactively), it may either pay the taxes on its activities it thought were exempt and file for a refund or it can protest the assessment of any taxes in the Tax Court.

617. Excess Benefit Transactions. An excise tax is imposed on any "excess benefit transaction" involving a public charity under Code Sec. 501(c)(3) (which is not a private foundation) or social welfare organization under 501(c)(4) (Code Sec. 4958).[26] The tax may be applied instead of, or in addition to, the organization being disqualified as an

---

Footnote references are to paragraphs of the 2008 Standard Federal Tax Reports.

[22] ¶ 22,790, ¶ 22,791   [24] ¶ 22,609.4825, ¶ 43,356   [26] ¶ 34,250
[23] ¶ 22,604.10   [25] ¶ 41,720

exempt organization due to the prohibition on private inurement (¶ 602). An excess benefit transaction is any transaction in which an economic benefit is provided to a "disqualified person" by the organization that exceeds any consideration given. It also includes any grant, loan, or other payment from a donor advised fund (¶ 1061) to a disqualified person, or from a qualified supporting organization (¶ 607) to a substantial contributor (¶ 635), family member of a substantial contributor or a 35-percent controlled entity.

The tax is imposed on the disqualified person and is 25 percent of the amount of the excess benefit or the amount of the grant, loan or other compensation received from a donor advised fund or qualified supporting organization. A manager of the exempt organization who knowingly participates in the transaction is subject to a separate excise tax of 10 percent, up to $10,000 per act ($20,000 per act for tax years beginning after August 17, 2006). If more than one manager knowingly participates in the transaction, then all those managers will be jointly and severally liable. However, a manager will not be liable if participation is not willful and due to reasonable cause. An organization manager includes a director, officer, trustee, and any other individual of the exempt organization with comparable responsibilities.

If the excess benefit is not corrected within the "taxable period" (¶ 614), then a second-tier excise tax is imposed on the disqualified person equal to 200 percent of the amount of the excess benefit, grant, loan or other compensation. If more than one person is liable for either the first- or second-tier taxes on disqualified persons, then such persons will be jointly and severally liable. The taxes on disqualified persons and organization managers are reported on Form 4720. However, both levels of taxes may be abated under certain circumstances (¶ 647). In addition, private foundations are subject to different sanctions (¶ 635).

Disqualified persons. For this purpose, a disqualified person is generally a person who is in a position to exercise substantial influence over the affairs of the exempt organization (including a qualified supporting organization), regardless of the individual's title. Certain family members and entities in which a disqualified person holds at least a 35-percent ownership interest are also treated as disqualified persons (Code Sec. 4958(f)). In the case of any donor advised fund, a disqualified person also includes any donor, donor advisor and investment advisor to the fund, as well as any family member or any entity controlled by such persons.

619. Involvement of Exempt Organization in Tax Shelters. Generally, effective for tax years ending after May 17, 2006, a tax-exempt entity that is a party to a prohibited tax shelter transaction (see ¶ 2001 and following) or which becomes a party to a subsequently listed transaction at any time during the tax year is subject to an excise tax (Code Sec. 4965).[27] If the tax-exempt entity is a party to a prohibited tax shelter transaction at any time during the tax year and *knew or had reason to know* the transaction was a prohibited tax shelter transaction, then the amount of the excise tax is increased. In addition, any manager of a tax-exempt entity who approves or otherwise causes the entity to be a party to a prohibited tax shelter transaction at any time during the tax year, and knew or had reason to know that the transaction was a prohibited tax shelter transaction must pay a separate excise tax for each approval. For this purpose, a tax-exempt entity includes any tax-exempt organization under Code Sec. 501(c) or (d), including any charitable organization and any qualified retirement plan, as well as individual retirement accounts (IRA), health savings accounts (HSA), Archer medical savings accounts (MSA), and qualified tuition plans. The tax-exempt entity must file a disclosure of its being a party to a prohibited tax shelter transaction on Form 8886-T and the identity of any other party (including both taxable and tax-exempt parties) to the transaction which is known by the entity (Code Sec. 6033(a)(2); Temporary Reg. § 1.6033-5T(a)).[28]

620. Disclosure Requirements for Contributions. Tax-exempt organizations that are not eligible to receive deductible charitable contributions (¶ 1061) must disclose this fact in a conspicuous and easily recognizable format in their fund-raising solicitations (Code Sec. 6113).[29] Violation of this requirement without reasonable cause will subject

---

Footnote references are to paragraphs of the 2008 Standard Federal Tax Reports.

[27] ¶ 34,305   [28] ¶ 35,420, ¶ 35,424E   [29] ¶ 37,040

an organization to a penalty of $1,000 per day of solicitation (up to $10,000 for any calendar year) (Code Sec. 6710).[30] A higher penalty applies if the failure to comply was due to intentional disregard (not subject to a maximum).

Quid pro quo contributions. Charitable organizations are required to inform donors in a written statement that quid pro quo contributions in excess of $75 are deductible only to the extent that the contributions exceed the value of goods or services provided by the organization (Code Sec. 6115).[31] Failure to make the required disclosure subjects the organization to a penalty of $10 per contribution (Code Sec. 6714).[32] A quid pro quo contribution is any payment made partly as a contribution to the organization and partly in consideration for goods or services provided by the organization (fundraising dinners, benefit auctions).

Donation of vehicles. For donations of motor vehicles, boats and airplanes, a charitable organization must provide the donor a contemporaneous written acknowledgment of the donation including a certification of the organization's use or sale of the vehicle (¶ 1070A). Form 1098-C may be used for this purpose. A donee organization that fails to provide the acknowledgement or that provides a fraudulent acknowledgement will be subject to a penalty (Code Sec. 6720).[33]

625. Annual Information Return. All tax-exempt organizations are required to file an annual information return with the IRS, including organizations whose application for exemption is pending, as well as nonexempt charitable trusts (¶ 591). (Code Sec. 6033; Reg. § 1.6033-2).[34] Generally, an exempt organization must file its information return on Form 990 (or Form 990-EZ) on or before the 15th day of the fifth month following the close of its tax year. The form may satisfy certain state or local filing requirements. Other forms may be required in lieu of Form 990 for certain organizations (private foundations file Form 990-PF (¶ 631), farmers' cooperatives file Form 1120-C (¶ 698), religious and apostolic organizations file Form 1065 (¶ 604), and black lung benefits trusts file Form 990-BL). Organizations that exclude exempt function income from their gross income may be required to file a variation of Form 1120 in lieu of, or in addition to, Form 990 (political organizations file Form 1120-POL (¶ 696) and certain homeowner associations file Form 1120-H (¶ 699)).

Exempt organizations which are not required to file an annual information return include: any organization (other than a private foundation or supporting organization) that has annual gross receipts of $25,000 or less; any church (including its integrated auxiliary) and convention or association of churches (¶ 604); an exclusively religious activity of a religious order; church-sponsored mission societies; governmental units exempt from taxation; corporations organized under an act of Congress; certain schools affiliated with a church or religious order; and certain U.S. possession organizations (Code Sec. 6033(a)(3); Rev. Proc. 2003-21; Rev. Proc. 83-23).[35] However, effective for annual periods beginning after 2006, any exempt organization which is not required to file Form 990 because its gross receipts for the tax year do not exceed $25,000 will be required electronically Form 990-N (Code Sec. 6033(i)).

Information required. An exempt organization must provide on Form 990 information on its programs and activities including: gross income, expenses, disbursements, and balance sheets; total contributions; names and addresses of persons contributing $5,000 or more during the tax year (or substantial contributors in the case of private foundations); and the names, addresses and compensation of its officers, directors, trustees and managers. A Code Sec. 501(c)(3) organization (as well as certain nonexempt charitable trusts under Code Sec. 4947) must include additional information with its return including: its lobbying, grass roots and exempt purpose expenditures; its lobbying and grass roots nontaxable amounts; the compensation paid to its five highest paid employees other than officers, directors and trustees; the compensation paid to its five highest professional service providers; information regarding transfers with (and transactions and relationships with) other noncharitable exempt organizations; and any excise taxes paid by the organization. For tax years ending after August 17, 2006,

---

Footnote references are to paragraphs of the 2008 Standard Federal Tax Reports.

[30] ¶ 40,115
[31] ¶ 37,065
[32] ¶ 40,180
[33] ¶ 40,207
[34] ¶ 35,420, ¶ 35,422
[35] ¶ 35,420, ¶ 35,425.24

additional information is also required on the returns of sponsoring organizations of donor advised funds and supporting organizations (Code Sec. 6033(k)).

Disclosure. Tax-exempt organizations, including private foundations, must make available for public inspection, at the organization's principal, regional, and district offices (having three or more employees) during regular business hours, its three most recent annual information returns, as well as a copy of its application for exemption (Code Sec. 6104).[36] Charitable organizations must also make available for public inspection any returns filed after August 17, 2006, related to the organization's unrelated business taxable income (UBTI). Organizations do not have to honor requests if they reasonably believe that the request is part of a harassment campaign (Reg. § 301.6104(d)-3).[37] Requests may be made either in person or in writing. Copies of an organization's Form 990 must be furnished immediately for requests made in person and within 30 days for written requests. Organizations are permitted to charge a reasonable fee for reproduction and mailing costs. An exempt organization can comply with these disclosure requirements by posting information on the internet.

Penalties. A penalty of $20 per day (up to a maximum for any return of $10,000 or five percent of the organization's gross receipts, whichever is less) is imposed on each exempt organization that fails to file an annual information return, files a late return without reasonable cause, or fails to file the special information return on dissolution or substantial contraction (¶ 628) (Code Sec. 6652(c)).[38] For organizations with gross receipts in excess of $1 million for any year, the penalty increases to $100 per day (up to a maximum for any return of $50,000 or five percent of gross receipts). An additional penalty of $10 a day (up to a maximum $5,000 on any return) is imposed on any officer, trustee, employee, etc., who fails to file the return without reasonable cause after requested by the IRS. Failure to comply with the public disclosure requirements results in a penalty of $20 per day, with a maximum of $10,000 for any annual return. There is no maximum penalty for failure to disclose the organization's exemption application. The penalty for a willful failure to comply with the public disclosure requirements is increased to $5,000 for each return or application (Code Sec. 6685).[39]

628. Information on Dissolution. Generally, an organization that for any of its last five tax years preceding its dissolution, liquidation, termination or substantial contraction was tax-exempt, must include on its annual information return (Form 990) information relating to that event (Code Sec. 6043(b)).[40] Organizations exempt from this requirement include churches, organizations other than private foundations with $5,000 or less in annual gross receipts, and other organizations specified in Reg. § 1.6043-3(b).[41] The penalty for failure to comply is $10 a day (up to $5,000 for any one return), absent reasonable cause (Code Sec. 6652(c)(2)).[42]

Private Foundations

631. Private Foundation Defined. Charitable organizations under Code Sec. 501(c)(3) are either public charities or private foundations. Public charities generally are organizations that have broad public support or that actively function in a supporting relationship to such organizations. On the other hand, a private foundation typically is funded by one individual, family, or corporation. Thus, a "private foundation" is any Code Sec. 501(c)(3) organization *other than*:

(1) a charitable deduction donee listed in Code Sec. 170(b)(1)(A) (¶ 1059);

(2) a publicly supported organization receiving more than ⅓ of its annual support from members and the public and not more than ⅓ of its support from investment income and unrelated business income;

(3) a qualified supporting organization (¶ 607); and

(4) an organization operated for public safety testing (Code Sec. 509).[43]

Like all Code Sec. 501(c)(3) organizations, a private foundation must provide notice to the IRS in order for it to be exempt from taxation (¶ 616). However, even if notice is provided, a private foundation will be denied tax-exempt status unless its governing

---

Footnote references are to paragraphs of the 2008 Standard Federal Tax Reports.

[36] ¶ 36,900	[39] ¶ 39,871	[42] ¶ 39,480
[37] ¶ 36,910E	[40] ¶ 35,880	[43] ¶ 22,800
[38] ¶ 39,480	[41] ¶ 35,885	

instrument specifically prohibits it from accumulating income (¶ 637), engaging in certain prohibited activities including acts of self-dealing (¶ 635), retaining excess business holdings (¶ 640), making investments which jeopardize its charitable purpose (¶ 642), or making certain taxable expenditures (¶ 644) (Code Sec. 508(e))[44] (see also ¶ 1068).

All private foundations must file an annual information return on Form 990-PF reporting gross income, receipts, disbursements, etc. (¶ 625). If at any time during the tax year the foundation has at least $5,000 of assets, it must also include information on its assets, managers, and grants or contributions made during the year (Code Sec. 6033(c); Reg. § 1.6033-3).[45]

633. Investment Income Taxed. A two-percent excise tax is imposed on the "net investment income" of a private foundation for each tax year (Code Sec. 4940).[46] The tax is reduced to one percent if the foundation satisfies certain requirements as to the amount of charitable distributions it made during the tax year and if it was not liable for the excise tax imposed on undistributed income (¶ 637) in any of the preceding five tax years. For this purpose, the net investment income of a private foundation generally includes of the foundation's gross investment income and capital gain net income less the ordinary and necessary business expenses incurred for the production of that income. Gross investment income includes interest, dividends, rents, royalties, and payments with respect to securities loans, as well as any similar source of income such as income from annuities and notional principal contracts. Capital gain net income includes the gain and losses from the disposition of property used for production of any gross investment income. The excise tax is reported on the foundation's annual return, Form 990-PF.

The tax will not apply to an "exempt operating foundation." An operating foundation is a foundation that spends at least 85 percent of the lesser of its adjusted net income or its minimum investment return in carrying on its exempt activities (Code Sec. 4942(j)(3); Reg. § 53.4942(b)-1).[47] An operating foundation is exempt if it has been publicly supported for at least 10 years, at all times during the tax year it is governed by representatives at least 75 percent of whom represent the general public and at no time during the tax year does it have an officer who is a disqualified individual. For this purpose, a disqualified individual is a substantial contributor to the foundation, an owner of more than 20 percent of a business or trust which is a substantial contributor, or a member of the family of any of the preceding. Thus, a nonoperating private foundation is generally a grant-making organization that does not operate its own charitable program.

635. Prohibitions on Self-Dealing. The Code contains a comprehensive list of financial transactions (acts of self-dealing) that are prohibited between a "disqualified person" and a private foundation (Code Sec. 4941).[48] This includes the sale or exchange of property, loans or other extensions of credit, the furnishing goods or services, payments of compensation, or the transfer of income or assets to the disqualified person. For this purpose, a disqualified person includes:

- substantial contributor (any person who contributes more than $5,000 if that amount is more than two percent of the total contributions received by the foundation before the end of its tax year);
- a foundation manager, including an officer, director, or trustee;
- the owner of more than 20 percent of a business or trust which is a substantial contributor;
- a member of the family of any of the preceding (including spouse, ancestor, child, grandchild, great grandchild, or spouse of any of these descendants);
- a corporation, trust, estate, or partnership more than 35 percent of which is owned or held by any of the preceding; or
- a government official (Code Sec. 4946).[49]

The disqualified person is subject to a 10 percent excise tax (five-percent for tax years beginning before August 18, 2006) on the amount involved in any act of self-

Footnote references are to paragraphs of the 2008 Standard Federal Tax Reports.

[44] ¶ 22,790
[45] ¶ 35,420, ¶ 35,423
[46] ¶ 34,000
[47] ¶ 34,040, ¶ 34,044
[48] ¶ 34,020
[49] ¶ 34,120

dealing for each year in the "taxable period." Any foundation manager who knowingly participates in the transaction is subject to a five percent excise tax (2.5-percent for tax years beginning before August 18, 2006) on the amount involved. A second-level tax of 200 percent (50 percent on the manager) applies if the prohibited act is not corrected within the "taxable period." For this purpose, the "taxable period" begins on the date on which the self-dealing act occurs and ends on the earliest of: (1) the date on which the deficiency notice for the first-level tax is mailed; (2) the date on which the first-level tax is assessed; or (3) the date on which the act of self-dealing is completely corrected (Code Sec. 4941(e)).[50] The maximum tax imposed on a foundation manager is $20,000 per act for each level of tax ($10,000 per act for tax years beginning before August 18, 2006). The IRS has discretionary authority to abate both levels of tax for the manager and the disqualified person (¶ 647). However, a third-level tax may be imposed if there are repeated or flagrant acts of self-dealing (Code Sec. 6684).[51] The initial excise tax on an act of self-dealing is reported on Form 4720.

637. Failure to Distribute Income. A private foundation that is a nonoperating foundation (¶ 633) is required to distribute annually its minimum investment return for the tax year, which generally equals five percent of the foundation's net investment assets (adjusted for certain taxes and loan repayments). Failure to do so will cause the foundation to be subject to an excise tax of 30 percent of any undistributed income (15 percent for tax years beginning before August 18, 2006) (Code Sec. 4942).[52] Undistributed income is the amount by which the minimum investment return of the foundation exceeds the amount of qualifying distributions made during the tax year. Qualifying distributions include distributions to public charities and private operating foundations, and payments for expenses and assets to be used for charitable purposes. It does not generally include payments made by the nonoperating private foundation to a supporting organization (¶ 607).

If the foundation fails to make the necessary distributions within the " taxable period," then a second-level tax will be imposed equal to 100 percent of the undistributed income. For this purpose, the "taxable period" is the period that begins on the first day of the tax year and ends on the earlier of: (1) the date on which the deficiency notice for the initial tax is mailed or (2) the date on which the initial tax is assessed. The IRS has discretionary authority to abate both levels of tax (¶ 647). However, a third-level tax may be imposed if there are repeated or flagrant acts of failure to distribute income (Code Sec. 6684).[53] The initial excise tax on undistributed income is reported on Form 4720.

640. Involvement in Unrelated Businesses. A private foundation is allowed to own a certain amount of business enterprises jointly with disqualified persons (¶ 635). However, to curb any abuses, the foundation is subject to an excise tax of 10 percent of any "excess business holdings" during the tax year (five percent for tax years beginning before August 18, 2006) (Code Sec. 4943).[54] If such business holdings are not divested within the "taxable period" (¶ 637), then a second-level tax of 200 percent is imposed. In general, the permitted amount of business ownership that a private foundation and disqualified person may have in any enterprise that is not substantially related to the exempt purposes of the foundation is 20 percent. If third parties have effective control of the business enterprise, then the limit is 35 percent. Special rules apply to certain grandfathered holdings. The IRS has discretionary authority to abate both levels of tax (¶ 647). However, a third-level tax may be imposed if there are repeated or flagrant acts of excess business holdings (Code Sec. 6684).[55]

Effective for tax years beginning after August 17, 2006, the excise tax on excess business holdings will apply to donor advised funds (¶ 1061) and certain qualified supporting organizations (¶ 607). In applying the tax to donor advised funds, a disqualified person is defined as any donor, a member of the donor's family, or a 35-percent controlled entity (Code Sec. 4943(e)). A qualified supporting organization will be subject to the excess business holdings tax only if it is a Type III supporting organization, or a Code Sec. 501(c)(3) organization that meets the organizational and operational test of a qualified supporting organization and it is not controlled by a disqualified person (Code

---

Footnote references are to paragraphs of the 2008 Standard Federal Tax Reports.

[50] ¶ 34,020
[51] ¶ 39,865
[52] ¶ 34,040
[53] ¶ 39,865
[54] ¶ 34,060
[55] ¶ 39,865

Sec. 4943(f)). For this purpose, a disqualified person with respect to the supporting organization is any person with substantial influence over the organization (or any family member of such a person), as well as any substantial contributor, family member of a substantial contributor, or 35-percent controlled entity.

642. Investments Jeopardizing Exempt Purpose. A 10-percent excise tax (five percent for tax years beginning before August 18, 2006) is imposed on any investment of a private foundation that jeopardizes the foundation's exempt status (Code Sec. 4944; Reg. § 53.4944-1).[56] A "jeopardizing" investment is generally one that shows a lack of reasonable business care and prudence in providing for the foundation's short- and long-term financial needs. In addition to the tax on the foundation, a 10-percent excise tax (five percent for tax years beginning before August 18, 2006) is also imposed on any foundation manager who knowingly participates in such an investment. A second-level tax of 25 percent (five percent on the manager, up to a maximum of $10,000) is imposed if the jeopardy situation is not corrected within the "taxable period" (¶ 637). The IRS has discretionary authority to abate both levels of tax (¶ 647). The maximum amount of the first-tier tax imposed on a manager is limited to $10,000 per investment ($5,000 for tax years beginning before August 18, 2006). The maximum amount of the second-tier tax imposed on a manager is limited to $20,000 per investment ($10,000 for tax years beginning before August 18, 2006). A third-level tax may be imposed on either the foundation or a manager if there are repeated or flagrant acts of jeopardizing investments (Code Sec. 6684).[57]

644. Lobbying and Other Prohibited Expenditures. A private foundation is subject to a 20-percent excise tax (10 percent for tax years beginning before August 18, 2006) on the amount of any "taxable expenditure" made during the tax year. Any foundation manager who, without reasonable cause, agrees to the expenditure knowing it is improper, is subject to a five-percent excise tax (2.5 percent for tax years beginning before August 18, 2006) on the expenditure (Code Sec. 4945).[58] A taxable expenditure generally includes any amount paid by the foundation for legislative or political purposes, or any grant to an individual for travel, study, or other similar purpose (unless made under objective standards). It also includes any grant to any organization unless the grantee organization is a public charity, qualified supporting organization (¶ 607) or exempt operating foundation (¶ 633), or the nonoperating private foundation exercises responsibility for the expenditure of the grant. A second-level tax of 100 percent is imposed on the foundation (50 percent on the manager) if the taxable expenditure is not corrected within the "taxable period" (¶ 637). The maximum amount of the first-tier tax imposed on a manager is limited to $10,000 per taxable expenditure ($5,000 for tax years beginning before August 18, 2006). The maximum amount of the second-tier tax imposed on a manager is limited to $20,000 per taxable expenditure ($10,000 for tax years beginning before August 18, 2006). The IRS has discretionary authority to abate both levels of tax for the foundation or the manager (¶ 647). However, a third-level tax may be imposed if there are repeated or flagrant acts of taxable expenditures (Code Sec. 6684).[59]

647. Abatement of Taxes. The IRS has discretionary authority not to assess certain first-tier excise taxes, or to abate such taxes if already assessed, or to provide a credit or refund if the tax is already collected. Abatement will occur only if the violation giving rise to the imposition of the excise tax was due to reasonable cause and is corrected within the "correction period" (Code Sec. 4962).[60] This relief applies to excise taxes imposed on private foundations and disqualified persons (¶ 631 and following), as well as the excise tax on the lobbying and political activities of public charities (¶ 613). However, the excise taxes on acts of self-dealing between a private foundation and a disqualified person (¶ 635) may not be abated. The IRS may withhold or abate an assessment of any second-tier excise taxes if the taxable event in question is corrected voluntarily during the correction period (Code Sec. 4961).[61] For this purpose, the

---

Footnote references are to paragraphs of the 2008 Standard Federal Tax Reports.

[56] ¶ 34,080, ¶ 34,081   [58] ¶ 34,100   [60] ¶ 34,280
[57] ¶ 39,865   [59] ¶ 39,865   [61] ¶ 34,260

correction period is the period beginning on the date of the taxable event and ending 90 days after the deficiency notice for the second-tier tax is mailed (Code Sec. 4963).[62]

649. Termination of Private Foundation Status. The status of any organization as a private foundation may be terminated voluntarily or involuntarily (Code Sec. 507).[63] A voluntary termination requires the foundation to notify the IRS of its plan to terminate. An involuntary termination occurs when the IRS notifies the foundation of the intent to terminate its status because of willful repeated violations, or a willful and flagrant violation, giving rise to excise taxes on the foundation (¶ 631). In either case, the private foundation must pay a termination tax equal to the lesser of: the aggregate amount of tax benefits received by the foundation and any of its substantial contributors (¶ 635) resulting from its exempt status under Code Sec. 501(c)(3); or the value of its net assets.

The IRS may abate a portion or all of the termination tax under certain conditions. First, the tax may be abated if, prior to providing notice to the IRS of its voluntary termination, the foundation distributes all of its net assets to another private foundation or public charity described in Code Sec. 170(b)(1)(A) (¶ 1059) that has been in existence for at least five years immediately before the distribution. Under these circumstances, the transfer of assets is not a termination of the foundation's status. Instead, the foundation retains its status until it gives actual notice of its termination to the IRS. When notice is provided after all net assets are transferred, then the termination tax will be zero (but the distributions may give rise to certain excise taxes). Second, the termination tax may be abated if the foundation becomes a public charity within 12 months or it actually operates as a public charity for at least five years. However, notice of termination must be provided to the IRS prior to the beginning of the 12-month or five-year termination period.

650. Estimated Tax Payments. A private foundation is required to make estimated installment payments for its tax liability on any unrelated business income (¶ 655) and the excise tax imposed on its investment income (¶ 633). The first-quarter payment is due by the 15th day of the fifth month of the foundation's tax year (May 15 for calendar-year taxpayers) (Code Sec. 6655(g)(3)).[64]

Unrelated Business Taxable Income

655. Organizations Subject to Tax. Although a variety of nonprofit organizations with charitable or socially beneficial purposes may be granted tax-exempt status under Code Sec. 501, they may still be subject to taxation on any unrelated business income (Code Sec. 511).[65] Unrelated business taxable income (UBTI) is income from a trade or business regularly carried on by an exempt organization (¶ 664) that is not substantially related (¶ 667) to the organization's exempt purposes (Code Sec. 512).[66] All types of exempt organizations are subject to the tax on UBTI except for government instrumentalities (other than colleges or universities) and federally licensed businesses or educational institutions sponsored by a religious order (Reg. § 1.511-2).[67] Additionally, title-holding companies may be exempt from the tax if the holding corporation and the payee organization file a consolidated return.

658. Rates and Payment. Unless an exempt organization is taxable as a trust, its unrelated business taxable income (UBTI) is subject to regular corporate taxes (¶ 219) (Code Sec. 511(a)).[68] Trusts are taxed at the rates applicable to estates and trusts (¶ 19). Returns are made on Form 990-T , to be filed at the same time as the organization's annual information return (¶ 625) (Reg. § 1.6012-2(e)).[69] Form 990-W should be used by a tax-exempt organization to compute its estimated tax payments on UBTI (¶ 650).

664. Business Must Be "Regularly" Carried On. Unrelated business taxable income (UBTI) is the gross income from any unrelated trade or business *regularly* carried on by an exempt organization, minus any deductions for expenses related to the trade or business (Code Sec. 512(a); Reg. §§ 1.512(a)-1 and 1.513-1(c)).[70] In determining whether a trade or business is regularly carried on, the frequency and continuity with which an activity is pursued is judged with comparable commercial activities of nonex-

---

Footnote references are to paragraphs of the 2008 Standard Federal Tax Reports.

[62] ¶ 34,300	[65] ¶ 22,820	[68] ¶ 22,820
[63] ¶ 22,771	[66] ¶ 22,830	[69] ¶ 35,145
[64] ¶ 39,565	[67] ¶ 22,822	[70] ¶ 22,830, ¶ 22,831, ¶ 22,841

empt organizations. In the case of a social club, voluntary employees' beneficiary association (VEBA), group legal services plan or an organization for the payment of supplemental unemployment benefits (SUB) (¶ 692), UBTI is subject to tax only to the extent that it is not set aside for the purposes that constitute the basis for the organization's exemption (Code Sec. 512(a)(3); Temp. Reg. § 1.512(a)-5T).[71]

667. Business Must Be Unrelated to Exempt Functions. Unrelated business taxable income (UBTI) of a tax-exempt organization includes any income from a business *not substantially related* to the organization's exempt purpose (Code Sec. 513; Reg. § 1.513-1).[72] To determine whether an organization's trade or business activities are substantially related to its exempt function, an analysis must be made of the organization's exempt function and its relationship to the activities in question. However, a number of activities will *not* be considered an unrelated trade or business, including any trade or business which:

- has substantially all the work in carrying on the business performed for the organization without compensation;
- is carried on by a Code Sec. 501(c)(3) organization or governmental college or university primarily for the convenience of its members, students, etc.;
- consists of selling merchandise, substantially all of which has been received by the organization as gifts or contributions;
- is a qualified entertainment activity or a qualified convention and trade show activity (Code Sec. 513(d)) (¶ 685);
- in the case of a public charity hospital, performs services that a tax-exempt cooperative hospital organization may perform (¶ 699) (Code Sec. 513(e));
- consists of conducting any bingo games if the games are conducted in accordance with local law and do not compete with profit-making businesses (Code Sec. 513(f));
- in the case of a mutual or cooperative telephone or electric company, engages in qualified pole rentals (Code Sec. 513(g));
- includes the exchanging or renting of member donor lists between exempt organizations or the distribution of low-cost articles ($8.90 for 2007; $9.10 for 2008) incidental to the solicitation of charitable contributions (Code Sec. 513(h)); or
- involves the soliciting and receiving of qualified sponsorship payment (Code Sec. 513(i)) (¶ 685).

670. Unrelated Business Taxable Income Defined. The unrelated business taxable income (UBTI) of an exempt organization is its gross income derived from any unrelated trade or business regularly carried on (¶ 664 and ¶ 667), generally less the deductions directly connected with such trade or business (¶ 682) (Code Sec. 512).[73] The following income items (and any related deductions) are generally excluded from the calculation of UBTI: dividends, interest, and royalties (¶ 673); rents from real property or incidental rents from personal property leased with real property (¶ 676); all gains or losses from the disposition of property, subject to certain exceptions (¶ 679); certain research income; certain amounts received from controlled entities and foreign corporations; income of a mutual or cooperative electric company derived from the sale of electricity from its members; and gains or losses on the disposition of qualified brownfield sites. Annual dues not exceeding $136 for 2007 ($139 for 2008) that are paid to an exempt agricultural or horticultural organization will also be excluded from UBTI (Code Sec. 512(d)).

An exempt organization's calculation of UBTI must include its share of income and deductions from an unrelated trade or business conducted by a partnership (including a publicly traded partnership) or S corporation in which it is a partner or shareholder (Code Sec. 512(c) and (e)). However, if the tax year of the organization differs from the partnership's, then the amounts used to calculate UBTI will be based on the income and deductions of the partnership in the tax year that ends within the tax year of the exempt organization. In addition, the organization's share of S corporation income and deduc-

---

Footnote references are to paragraphs of the 2008 Standard Federal Tax Reports.

[71] ¶ 22,830, ¶ 22,834   [72] ¶ 22,840, ¶ 22,841   [73] ¶ 22,830

tions must be included regardless of whether they would normally be excluded from UBTI (dividends, interest, royalties).

673. Dividends, Interest, Annuities and Royalties (Investment Income). Generally, the unrelated business taxable income (UBTI) of an exempt organization will *not* include investment income unless derived from debt-financed property (¶ 687) (Code Sec. 512(b); Reg. § 1.512(b)-1(a)).[74] Investment income includes dividends, interest, annuities, royalties, payments with respect to securities loans, amounts received or accrued as consideration for entering into agreements to make loans, and income derived from notional principal contracts (as well as income from ordinary investments that are substantially similar). Royalties for this purpose include amounts paid to an exempt organization for use of its name, trademarks, and other intellectual property rights in connection with the sale of merchandise or services.[75] However, where an exempt organization provides active services in relation to the marketing of products or services associated with its name or other rights, the income may not come within the royalty exclusion.

Membership Organizations. Special rules apply to certain exempt membership organizations including a social and recreational club, voluntary employees' beneficiary association (VEBA), a supplemental unemployment compensation benefit trust (SUB), or an organization or trust forming part of a qualified group legal services plan (¶ 692) which is taxable on its investment income. Generally, such organizations are taxable on gross income less deductions relating to production of that income. However, the gross income for this purpose does not include "exempt function income"—which is income from dues, fees, and charges for providing facilities and services for members, dependents, guests, and income set aside for charitable purposes or by a VEBA to provide insurance benefits (Code Sec. 512(a)(3)).[76] A special exclusion also applies for gain such organizations realize on the sale of assets used in pursuing their exempt function to the extent the proceeds are reinvested (within a four-year period) in other assets for such purposes. However, exempt social clubs may not offset net losses derived from a nonprofit activity against income derived from for-profit unrelated business income. For this purpose, a title-holding corporation whose income is payable to one of the above membership organizations will be treated as the exempt organization.

To eliminate a possible bypass for the club or other membership organization through termination of tax-exempt status, a *nonexempt* social club or other membership organization operated primarily to furnish goods or services to members may deduct the cost of furnishing these goods, services, insurance, etc., *only to the extent of membership-related income* (Code Sec. 277).[77] A nonexempt social club or VEBA is also not allowed to claim the corporate dividends-received deduction (see ¶ 235 and following).

Look-Through Rules. If an exempt organization receives or accrues a payment of interest, annuity, royalty or rent (but not a dividend) from an entity that it controls, then the payment is includible in the exempt organization's UBTI to the extent it either reduces the net unrelated business income of the controlled entity or increases its net unrelated losses (Code Sec. 512(b)(13)).[78] However, effective for tax years 2006 and 2007, any payment received or accrued under a binding written contract in effect on August 17, 2006, is included in the exempt organization's UBTI only to the extent it exceeds the amount that would have been paid if the payment met the requirements for related parties under the transfer pricing rules of Code Sec. 482. A valuation misstatement penalty applies to excess payments that are included in UBTI. In addition, the exempt organization must report the payments from a controlled entity on its annual return (Code Sec. 6033(h)).[79] For this purpose, the threshold of control of a subsidiary which triggers UBTI is having more than 50-percent ownership (more than 50 percent of stock by vote or value in a corporation, or more than 50 percent of a profits, capital, or beneficial interest of a partnership or other entity). The constructive ownership rules of Code Sec. 318 apply in these circumstances (¶ 743).

676. Rents. Excludable from the unrelated business taxable income (UBTI) of an exempt organization are amounts received from the rental of real property, including

---

Footnote references are to paragraphs of the 2008 Standard Federal Tax Reports.

[74] ¶ 22,830, ¶ 22,835
[75] ¶ 22,837.83
[76] ¶ 22,830
[77] ¶ 14,600
[78] ¶ 22,830
[79] ¶ 35,420

those rents from personal property leased with real property so long as they are incidental in relation to the total amount of rents under the lease (10 percent or less of total rents from all leased property) (Code Sec. 512(b)(3); Reg. § 1.512(b)-1(c)).[80] However, all rents are taxable if they are: (1) rents from real property leased with personal property where more than 50 percent of the rent is attributable to the personal property; (2) rents from both the real and the personal property where the rentals are based on a percentage of the net income from the property; and (3) unrelated income from debt-financed property (¶ 687).

679. Gains and Losses from Sales or Exchanges. Excluded from the unrelated business taxable income (UBTI) of an exempt organization are all gains or losses from the sale, exchange or other disposition of property *other than*: (1) stock in trade or other property of a kind properly includible in inventory, or (2) property held primarily for sale to customers in the ordinary course of a trade or business (Code Sec. 512(b)(5); Reg. § 1.512(b)-1(d)).[81] The exclusion also applies to all gains or losses recognized in connection with the organization's investment activities from the lapse or termination of options to buy and sell securities (whether or not written by the organization), as well as options to buy or sell real property. The exclusion does not apply to gains derived from the sale or other disposition of debt-financed property (¶ 687). Gains from certain pension plan investments in the property of troubled financial institutions acquired after 1993 are also excluded (Code Sec. 512(b)(16)).

682. Deductions. In computing unrelated business taxable income (UBTI), an exempt organization is entitled to deduct all ordinary and necessary business *directly connected* with carrying on the unrelated trade or business (¶ 667). Expenses are treated as directly connected with the conduct of an unrelated business if: (1) the business exploits a tax-exempt activity of the organization; (2) the business is of a type normally carried on for profit by a taxable organization; and (3) the exempt activity is of a type normally carried on by a taxable organization in carrying on its business. When facilities or personnel are used for both exempt functions and the conduct of an unrelated business, it is necessary to allocate expenses on a reasonable basis (Code Sec. 512(a) and (b)(12); Reg. § 1.512(a)-1(c)).[82]

In addition to deduction of ordinary and necessary business expenses, an exempt organization is allowed a specific deduction of $1,000, as well as a deduction for charitable contributions, net operating losses (NOLs), and domestic production activities (equal to the appropriate percentage of the lesser of qualified production activities income or unrelated business taxable income, rather than taxable income, see ¶ 980A and following). The charitable contribution deduction is limited to 10 percent of the organization's UBTI, computed without regard to the contributions deduction (Code Sec. 512(b)(10)). With respect to the NOL deduction, carryovers and items attributable to exempt income and expenses are disregarded (Code Sec. 512(b)(6)).

685. Advertising, Sponsorship, and Trade Shows. The profits derived by an exempt organization from the sale of advertising in a periodical, journal, or magazine it publishes is taxable as unrelated business taxable income (UBTI) unless the advertising contributes significantly to the accomplishment of the organization's exempt purposes (Code Sec. 513(c)).[83] An activity such as advertising does not lose its identity as a trade or business merely because it is carried on within a larger complex of other activities which may or may not be related to the organization's exempt purpose (for example, a tour group that promotes itself in the guise of education).

For this purpose, income realized by an exempt organization from the sponsorship of a public event will generally constitute advertising services. However, certain qualified sponsorship payments solicited or received by the organization will not be subject to tax (Code Sec. 513(i)). A qualified sponsorship payment is any payment by a payor engaged in a trade or business that does not expect any substantial return from the exempt organization other than the use or acknowledgment of the payor's name, logo or product lines in connection with the activities of the tax-exempt organization (Reg. § 1.513-4).[84] A qualified sponsorship payment does not include any payment for advertising of the

---

Footnote references are to paragraphs of the 2008 Standard Federal Tax Reports.

[80] ¶ 22,830, ¶ 22,835   [82] ¶ 22,830, ¶ 22,831   [84] ¶ 22,843G
[81] ¶ 22,830, ¶ 22,835   [83] ¶ 22,840

payor's product or services, including messages that contain qualitative or comparative language, price information, an endorsement, or an inducement to purchase, sell or use the payor's products and services. It also does not include any payment which is contingent upon factors indicating the degree of public exposure at one or more events (attendance, broadcast ratings).

A qualified sponsorship payment also does not include any payment made in connection with a qualified convention or trade show activity (Reg. § 1.513-3).[85] A convention or trade show is qualified if it is conducted by a charitable organization (¶ 602), social welfare program, labor organization or business league (¶ 692) that have as one of their purposes the promotion of interest in the products and services of the industry in general, or to educate the attendees regarding new developments or products and services related to the exempt activities of the organizations.

Taxable Income from Debt-Financed Property

687. Unrelated Debt-Financed Income. A percentage of income from debt-financed property must be included in an exempt organization's unrelated business taxable income (UBTI) (¶ 670) regardless of whether the organization is engaged in a trade or business (Code Sec. 514(a); Reg. § 1.514(a)-1).[86] The percentage included in UBTI is the same percentage (not to exceed 100 percent) as the "average acquisition indebtedness" (¶ 689) for the tax year divided by the "average amount of the adjusted basis" of the property. Deductions with respect to each debt-financed property are allowed by the applying the same percentage to expenses related to the property, except for the deduction of capital losses resulting from the carryover of net capital losses. For this purpose, debt-financed property generally means any income-producing property (for example, rental real estate, corporate stock, etc.) on which there is an acquisition indebtedness at any time during the tax year (or preceding 12 months if the property is disposed of during the tax year) (Code Sec. 514(b); Reg. § 1.514(b)-1(a)).[87] Certain property, however, is excepted even if it is held to produce income (¶ 691).

This rule was enacted to prevent a "bootstrap" sale and leaseback transaction, resulting in the conversion of ordinary income into capital gain, and to achieve acquisition of a business by a tax-exempt organization entirely from the earnings of the business. In a typical "bootstrap" sale and leaseback: (1) shareholders of a closely-held corporation sell their stock to an exempt organization with little or no down payment and a promissory note for the balance of the purchase price; (2) the corporation is immediately liquidated and its assets leased by the exempt organization to a new company; (3) the new company pays the exempt organization a percentage of its operating profit as rent; and (4) the exempt organization pays a percentage of the rents received to the selling shareholders to be applied on the promissory note.

689. Acquisition Indebtedness. For any debt-financed property of an exempt organization (¶ 687), "acquisition indebtedness" is the outstanding amount of principal debt: (1) incurred to acquire or improve property; (2) incurred before the acquisition or improvement if it would not have been incurred but for the acquisition or improvement; and (3) incurred after acquisition or improvement if it would not have been incurred but for the acquisition or improvement and was reasonably foreseeable at the time (Code Sec. 514(c); Reg. § 1.514(c)-1).[88]

If property is acquired subject to a mortgage, the amount of the mortgage (or similar lien) is considered acquisition indebtedness, even if the organization does not assume or agree to pay the debt (Code Sec. 514(c)(2)). However, when mortgaged property is received by bequest or devise (or by gift under certain circumstances), the debt will not be treated as an acquisition indebtedness for a period of 10 years from the date of acquisition. A lien for taxes or assessments under State law will be treated similar to a mortgage to the extent the amount becomes due and the organization has an opportunity to pay it.

Acquisition indebtedness does not include a debt which was incurred by an exempt organization in the exercise of its exempt purpose. Generally, it also does not include

---

Footnote references are to paragraphs of the 2008 Standard Federal Tax Reports.

[85] ¶ 22,843
[86] ¶ 22,850, ¶ 22,851

[87] ¶ 22,850, ¶ 22,853
[88] ¶ 22,850, ¶ 22,854

debt incurred by certain qualified organizations (qualified employee benefits trust; an exempt school; exempt title-holding company; retirement income account of church plan) in acquiring or improving real property. Annuities may be excluded from the definition of acquisition indebtedness, as well as certain obligations insured by the Federal Housing Administration or incurred by a small business investment company (¶ 2392) (Code Sec. 514(c)(6)).

691. Exempt Properties. The following types of property are excluded from the definition of debt-financed property (¶ 687):

(1) property substantially all the use of which (85 percent or more) is related to the exercise or performance of an organization's tax-exempt function (special rules apply to real property used as a medical clinic);

(2) property to the extent that its income is subject to tax as income from the carrying on of an unrelated trade or business (¶ 655);

(3) property to the extent that its income is derived from research activities and is excluded from gross income of an unrelated trade or business;

(4) property to the extent it is used in a business where (a) substantially all of the work of carrying on the business is performed without compensation, (b) the Code Sec. 501(c)(3) organization carrying on the business does so primarily for the convenience of members, students, patients, etc., or (c) the business consists of selling merchandise substantially all of which has been received as contributions; and

(5) certain brownfield site property to the extent the gain or loss from its sale or exchange would be excluded from gross income of an unrelated trade or business (Code Sec. 514(b); Reg. § 1.514(b)-1).[89]

For purposes of (1), (3) and (4) above, use of property by a related organization is taken into account in determining use of an exempt organization. In addition, special rules apply to property put to related exempt uses, to life income contracts, and to real property located in the neighborhood of other property owned and used for exempt purposes by the exempt organization.

Other Tax-Exempt Organizations

692. Other Tax-Exemption Organizations under Code Sec. 501(c). In addition to charitable organizations (¶ 602), Code Sec. 501 exempts other types of non-profit organizations from federal income tax unless they are deemed to be feeder organizations (¶ 694). Among the most common are civic leagues and social welfare organizations, business leagues, social and recreation clubs, and fraternal beneficiary societies. Contributions to these organizations are generally *not* deductible as charitable contributions. An organization described in this section generally files an application for exemption on Form 1024.

Civic Leagues. A civic league or organization is exempt from federal income taxes if it is not organized or operated for profit and it is operated exclusively for the promotion of social welfare (Code Sec. 501(c)(4)).[90] This includes any local association of employees, the membership of which is limited to the employees of a designated employer in a particular municipality and whose net earnings are devoted exclusively to charitable, educational or recreational purposes. No exemption is allowed, however, if any part of the net earnings of the civic league or organization inures to the benefit of any private shareholder or individual (see ¶ 602 and ¶ 617).

A civic league or organization will be considered to be operated exclusively for the promotion of social welfare if it primarily engaged in promoting the common good and general welfare of the community (for example, volunteer fire departments or community association) (see also ¶ 699). Promoting social welfare does not include participation or intervention in the political campaign of any candidate for office. In addition, the promotion of social welfare does not include the operation of a social club for the benefit of its members or carrying on a business similar to for-profit organizations (Reg. § 1.501(c)(4)-1).[91] This includes providing commercial-type insurance unless it is an

---

Footnote references are to paragraphs of the 2008 Standard Federal Tax Reports.

[89] ¶ 22,850, ¶ 22,853   [90] ¶ 22,602   [91] ¶ 22,610

¶691

unsubstantial part of the organization's activities, in which case the activity will be treated as an unrelated trade or business (¶ 655) (Code Sec. 501(m) and (n)).[92]

Labor, Agricultural, and Horticultural Organizations. A qualifying labor, agricultural or horticultural organization is tax-exempt if: (1) no net earnings of the organization inure to the benefit of any member, and (2) it has as its objective the betterment of the conditions of those engaged in such pursuits, the improvement of the grade of their products, and the development of a higher degree of efficiency in their respective occupations (Code Sec. 501(c)(5); Reg. § 1-501(c)(5)-1)).[93] This does not include administration of any type of retirement plan. Generally, a qualifying labor organization is an association of workers such as a labor union. An agricultural and horticultural organization is involved with raising livestock, forestry, harvesting crops or aquatic resources, the cultivation of useful or ornamental plants, and similar pursuits (Code Sec. 501(g); IRS Pub. 557).

Business Leagues. A business league, chamber of commerce, real estate board, board of trade or professional football league is tax-exempt if it is not organized for profit and no part of its net earnings inures to the benefit of any private shareholder or individual (Code Sec. 501(c)(6); Reg. § 1.501(c)(6)-1).[94] A business league is an association of persons having some common business interest, the purpose of which is to promote such common interest and not to engage in a regular business of a kind ordinarily carried on for profit. For example, an association engaged in furnishing information to prospective investors, is not a business league, since its activities do not further any common business interest.

Social Clubs. A social club or similar organization is exempt from federal income taxes if it is organized and operated exclusively for pleasure, recreation and other nonprofitable purposes and no part of its net earnings inures to the benefit of any private shareholder (Code Sec. 501(c)(7); Reg. § 1.105(c)(7)-10; IRS Pub. 557).[95] Membership in the club must be limited, but personal contact, commingling and fellowship must exist between the members. In addition, the club's charter, bylaws, or other governing instrument, or any written policy statement must not provide for discrimination against any person on the basis of race, color, or religion (Code Sec. 501(i)). However, a club that in good faith limits its membership to the members of a particular religion to further the teachings or principles of that religion will not be considered as discriminating on the basis of religion. Also, the restriction on religious discrimination does not apply to a club that is an auxiliary of a fraternal beneficiary society if that society limits its membership to the members of a particular religion.

A social club is generally only exempt if it is supported solely by membership fees, dues and assessments. Thus, the club cannot be engaged in any business activities, such as making its facilities available to the general public or by selling real estate, timber or other products. However, a club may receive up to 35 percent of its gross income, including investment income, from sources outside of its membership without losing tax-exempt status. Up to 15 percent of the gross receipts may be derived from the use of the club's facilities or services by the general public or from other activities not furthering social or recreational purposes for members. If an organization has outside income that is more than these limits, all the facts and circumstances will be taken into account in determining whether the organization qualifies for exempt status (IRS Pub. 557).

Fraternal Beneficiary Societies. A fraternal beneficiary society, order or association is exempt from federal income taxes if: (1) it operates under the lodge system for the exclusive benefit of the members of a fraternity itself operating under the lodge system; and (2) it provides for the payment of life, sick, accident, or other benefits to the members of such society, order, or association or their dependents (Code Sec. 501(c)(8)). Contributions by an individual to such societies are deductible as charitable contributions if the gift is to be used exclusively for religious, charitable, scientific, literary or educational purposes, or for the prevention of cruelty to children or animals (¶ 1061). A domestic fraternal society, order, or association that operates under the

---

Footnote references are to paragraphs of the 2008 Standard Federal Tax Reports.

[92] ¶ 22,602
[93] ¶ 22,602, ¶ 22,612

[94] ¶ 22,602, ¶ 22,614
[95] ¶ 22,602, ¶ 22,616

lodge system but does not provide for the payment of life, sickness, accident, or other benefits may nonetheless qualify for exemption if its net earnings are devoted exclusively to religious, charitable, scientific, literary, educational, and fraternal purposes (Code Sec. 501(c)(10)).

Other Non-Profit Organizations. Other non-profit organizations that are may be exempt from federal income taxes include:

- corporations organized as a U.S. instrumentality (Code Sec. 501(c)(1));
- certain title holding corporations (Code Sec. 501(c)(2) and 501(c)(25));
- qualified voluntary employees' beneficiary associations (VEBA) that meet certain participation and discrimination requirements (Code Secs. 501(c)(9) and 505);
- local teachers' retirement fund associations (Code Sec. 501(c)(11));
- local benevolent life insurance associations (Code Sec. 501(c)(12));
- certain cemetery companies (Code Sec. 501(c)(13));
- credit unions and mutual financial organizations (Code Sec. 501(c)(14));
- small insurance companies or associations (other than life insurance) (Code Sec. 501(c)(15));
- corporations organized by a farmer's cooperative marketing or purchasing association or their members (see also ¶ 698) (Code Sec. 501(c)(16));
- supplemental unemployment benefit (SUB) trusts established and maintained under local law (Code Sec. 501(c)(17));
- employee pension trusts created before June 25, 1959 (Code Sec. 501(c)(18));
- organizations for veterans, members of the armed services, and their families (Code Sec. 501(c)(19));
- black lung benefit trusts (Code Sec. 501(c)(21));
- domestic trusts set up to pay for withdrawal liability from multiemployer pension plans under ERISA (Code Sec. 501(c)(22));
- associations organized before 1880 to provide insurance and other benefits to veterans or their dependents (Code Sec. 501(c)(23));
- trusts set up by a corporation in connection with the termination of its pension, profit sharing, or stock bonus plan (Code Sec. 501(c)(24));
- state-sponsored high-risk health coverage organizations (Code Sec. 501(c)(26));
- state-sponsored workers' compensation reinsurance organizations (Code Sec. 501(c)(27)); and
- railroad retirement trusts (Code Sec. 501(c)(28)).

694. Feeder Organizations. An organization whose primary purpose is to operate a trade or business, all the profits of which are paid to one or more tax-exempt entities, is known as a feeder organization (Code Sec. 502; Reg. § 1.502-1).[96] A feeder organization is taxable unless its activities are an integral part of the exempt parent organization's activities. For this purpose, the definition of a trade or business does *not* include: (1) the deriving of rents if the rents received would not be subject to the unrelated business income tax (¶ 655); (2) any trade or business in which substantially all the work of carrying on such trade or business is performed by unpaid individuals or volunteers; or (3) any trade or business that sells merchandise, substantially all of which has been donated or contributed.

696. Political Organizations. A political organization is generally considered a tax-exempt organization only to the extent that it is organized and operated to accept contributions and make expenditures in order to influence the selection, nomination, election or appointment of any individual to public office (Code Sec. 527).[97] Examples of political organizations include political parties, Federal, State or local candidate commit-

---

Footnote references are to paragraphs of the 2008 Standard Federal Tax Reports.

[96] ¶ 22,670, ¶ 22,671   [97] ¶ 22,900

¶694

tees, other political action committees (PACs), as well as certain newsletters and segregated funds. The exempt function income of a political organization consists solely of: (1) contributions of money or property; (2) membership dues or fees; or (3) proceeds from a political fundraising event or the sale of political campaign materials. Any other income received (less deductions not related to exempt functions) will be taxed at the highest income tax rate for corporations. For purposes of calculating its taxable income, a political organization is permitted a specific $100 deduction, but it will not be allowed a net operating loss (NOL) deduction, the dividends received deduction, and other special deductions allowed to corporations (see ¶ 235 and following).

Political organizations with any taxable income must figure and report their tax on Form 1120-POL. Political organizations with $25,000 or more ($100,000 for certain state or local organizations) of gross receipts must also file an annual information return on Form 990 or 990-EZ (Code Sec. 6033(g)).[98] All political organizations must notify the IRS (electronically on Form 8871) of their existence within 24 hours of establishment (Code Sec. 527(i)). They must also provide periodic reports on Form 8872 of the contributions they receive and their expenditures (Code Sec. 527(j)). Organizations do not have to meet these two requirements if they have gross receipts of less than $25,000, are already required to file similar reports with the Federal Election Commission, or are certain state or local political organizations. Failure to provide notification will result in all income (including exempt function income) being taxed. In addition, failure to provide periodic reports will result in all undisclosed contributions and expenditures being taxed. The IRS has set forth a safe harbor that waives the amounts due for failing to comply with the reporting requirements due to reasonable cause but not willful neglect (Rev. Proc. 2007-27).[99] The public disclosure of all returns and forms filed by a political organization is required (Code Sec. 6104).[100]

698. Farmers' Cooperatives. A cooperative (or federation of cooperatives) of farmers, fruit growers, and persons engaged in similar pursuits may qualify for tax-exempt status if the cooperative is organized and operated for the purpose of marketing the products of members and returning to them net proceeds, or purchasing supplies and equipment for the use of members at cost plus expenses (Code Sec. 521; Reg. § 1.521-1).[101] The cooperative can deal with nonmembers, so long as such business does not account for more than 15 percent of all of its business. Application for exemption is filed on Form 1028. A farmers' association which has capital stock will not be denied exemption so long as: (1) the dividend rate is fixed at the legal rate of interest for the state of incorporation or eight percent (whichever is greater), and (2) substantially all of the stock is owned by producers who market their products or purchase their supplies through the association. A farmers' cooperative will also not be denied exemption if it computes its net earnings by offsetting certain earnings and losses in determining any amount available for distribution to patrons (Code Sec. 1388(j)(1)).[102] For these purposes, the marketing of member products includes the feeding of such products to livestock and then the sale of the animals or animal products (Code Sec. 1388(k)).

All cooperatives, including corporations operated on a cooperative basis (unless it is exempt from tax under Code Sec. 501(c)(16)), are subject to regular corporate income taxes and must file Form 1120-C to report its taxable income (Code Secs. 1381 and 1382; Reg. § 1.1382-3).[103] However, in computing taxable income, a cooperative is allowed certain deductions from gross income in addition to other deductions allowed to corporations (see ¶ 235 and following). For example, an exempt farmers' cooperative is permitted a deduction for any dividends paid on capital stock, for amounts paid on a patronage basis arising from certain nonpatronage earnings, and for amounts paid in redemption of certain nonqualified written notices of allocation. In addition, all cooperatives are allowed a deduction for any "patronage dividend" paid or allocated to its members during the tax year. For this purpose, a patronage dividend is an amount paid to a member:

- on the basis of quantity or value of business done with the cooperative;

Footnote references are to paragraphs of the 2008 Standard Federal Tax Reports.

[98] ¶ 35,420
[99] ¶ 22,911.75

[100] ¶ 36,900
[101] ¶ 22,880, ¶ 22,881

[102] ¶ 32,380
[103] ¶ 32,300, ¶ 32,320, ¶ 32,323

    • under an obligation of the cooperative to pay such amount, where the obligation existed before the cooperative received the amount paid; and

    • which is determined by reference to the net earnings of the cooperative from business done with or for its members (however, net earnings will not be reduced by amounts paid as dividends on capital stock to the extent that such dividends are in addition to amounts otherwise payable to patrons) (Code Sec. 1388(a)).[104]

Per-unit retain certificates and per-unit retain allocations paid in cash or other property may be treated as patronage dividends.

    699. Additional Exempt Organizations. There are a number of other organizations that may be eligible to be exempt from federal income taxes, including homeowner's associations, credit counseling organizations, and cooperative service organizations.

    Homeowner's Association. A homeowners' association formed to own and maintain common areas and enforce covenants to preserve the appearance of a development may qualify as a tax-exempt social welfare organization under Code Sec. 501(c)(4) (¶ 692). A homeowners' association that is not exempt under (Code Sec. 501(c)(4)) and that is either a condominium management, real estate management, or timeshare association, may nonetheless elect to exclude certain exempt function income from its gross income (membership dues, fees, and assessments from member-owners). Electing associations are taxed at a flat rate of 30 percent (32 percent for timeshare associations) on both ordinary income and capital gains which are nonexempt. Form 1120-H, U.S. Income Tax Return for Homeowners Associations, is used by the association both to make the election for each tax year and to report annual taxable income (Code Sec. 528).[105]

    Credit Counseling Organizations. An organization for which the providing of credit counseling services is a substantial purpose may not qualify as a tax-exempt organization unless it qualifies as a Code Sec. 501(c)(3) charitable or educational organization (¶ 602), or as a Code Sec. 501(c)(4) social welfare organization (¶ 692) (Code Sec. 501(q)).[106] In addition, the organization must be organized and operated according to a number of requirements, including: (1) it must provide services tailored to customers' specific needs; (2) it must not refuse to provide services to customers due to inability to pay or ineligibility for debt management plan enrollment; (3) it makes no loans to customers; (4) it has a reasonable fee policy and must not pay or receive referral fees; (5) it has limited ownership of related service providers; and (6) it has independent board members with public interests.

    Cooperative Service Organizations. A cooperative hospital service organization is exempt from federal income taxation if it performs specifically enumerated services for two or more patron hospitals that are tax exempt under Code Sec. 501(c)(3) or if it is owned and operated by the federal government or by a state or local government (Code Sec. 501(e)).[107] Services which may be performed include data processing, purchasing (which includes purchasing insurance on a group basis, such as malpractice and general liability insurance), laboratory, billing and collection (including the purchase of patron accounts receivable on a recourse basis), food, personnel, and clinical services. It does not include laundry services.[108] A cooperative arrangement formed and controlled by a group of exempt educational organizations for the collective investment of their funds may also qualify for tax-exempt status (Code Sec. 501(f)).[109] Such organizations qualify for exemption only if all of the relevant requirements of Code Sec. 501(c)(3) are also satisfied.

Footnote references are to paragraphs of the 2008 Standard Federal Tax Reports.

[104] ¶ 32,380	[106] ¶ 22,602	[108] ¶ 22,662.30
[105] ¶ 22,920	[107] ¶ 22,602	[109] ¶ 22,602

Chapter 7

INCOME

What Is "Income"

701. Gross Income Defined. For federal income tax purposes, "gross income" means all income from whatever source, except for those items specifically excluded by the Code (Code Sec. 61).[1]

Fifteen of the more common types of "gross income" are enumerated by Code Sec. 61. They are: (1) compensation for services, including fees, commissions, fringe benefits, and similar items; (2) gross income from business; (3) gains from dealings in property; (4) interest; (5) rents; (6) royalties; (7) dividends; (8) alimony and separate maintenance payments; (9) annuities; (10) income from life insurance and endowment contracts; (11) pensions; (12) income from discharge of debt; (13) partner's share of partnership income; (14) income "in respect of a decedent"; and (15) income from an interest in an estate or trust.

Although nearly every type of accession to wealth (except gifts and inheritances) appears to fall within this comprehensive definition, income items should be checked against the specific exclusions in Code Sec. 101–Code Sec. 139A (see ¶ 801 and following). For special rules relating to foreign income, see ¶ 2401 and following. For a detailed list of income items and exclusions, see the Checklist for Items of Income at ¶ 55.

702. Income from Capital or Labor. Court decisions have developed a concept of the term "income" that is quite different from the layman's concept. The Supreme Court has approved this definition: "Income may be defined as the gain derived from capital, from labor, or from both combined, provided it be understood to include profit gained through a sale or conversion of capital assets." In addition, the Supreme Court has repeatedly held that Congress's broad definition of what constitutes gross income was intended to tax all gain unless specifically exempted.[2]

Footnote references are to paragraphs of the 2008 Standard Federal Tax Reports.

[1] ¶ 5502 [2] ¶ 5504.021

In addition to those items specifically excluded from gross income by law (see ¶ 801 and following), certain other items are not considered income.

Return of Capital. A return of capital, such as repayment of a loan, is not income unless the loan had been previously deducted as a bad debt, resulting in a tax benefit.[3] Similarly, car pool reimbursements are not income even if only one person provides the car and does the driving.[4]

Damages. Damages (other than punitive damages) that compensate an injured person for personal physical injuries or physical sickness are excludable from gross income (Code Sec. 104(a)(2)). Damages received for personal nonphysical injuries, such as employment discrimination or injury to reputation, are generally taxable. See ¶ 852.

Interest on a judgment, including mandatory prejudgment interest, is generally includible in income.[5]

See ¶ 759 for treatment of damages awarded for business claims.

Attorney Fees and Court Costs. Court costs and attorney fees paid on or after October 22, 2004, in connection with an action based on unlawful discrimination under federal law (as well as certain other claims, such as whistleblower actions) are deductible from the determination of adjusted gross income (Code Sec. 62(a)(20)).[6] See ¶ 1010A.

Housing Assistance. Rental assistance payments made by the Department of Housing and Urban Development under the National Housing Act and relocation payments made under the Housing and Community Development Act of 1974 are nontaxable. However, payments made by individuals or other nongovernmental entities are not considered payments for the general welfare and are taxable.[7]

Gift v. Income. The characterization of a payment or transfer as either a gift or as taxable income must be made on a case-by-case basis.[8] The Supreme Court has held that the value of a "gift" transferred to a business friend for furnishing the names of potential customers is taxable compensation.[9] See also ¶ 849.

Strike and Lockout Benefits. Strike benefits received from a labor union may be treated as nontaxable gifts when the benefits paid in the form of food, clothing, and rent are (1) given to both member and nonmember strikers, (2) dependent upon individual need, (3) dependent on the unavailability of unemployment compensation or local public assistance, and (4) given without condition. The fact that benefits are paid only to union members will not, of itself, be determinative as to taxability.[10]

Unrealized Appreciation. Unrealized appreciation in the value of property is not income.[11]

Ownership of Income

704. Tax Liability. In the vast majority of cases, the identity of the taxpayer is clear. The taxpayer is simply the person who is legally entitled to receive income. Thus, an individual who receives wages for services is obviously the person who must pay income tax on the wages. However, under some circumstances (see ¶ 705), a person may be taxed on income even though, at the time of payment, another receives it because of an anticipatory assignment of income.

705. Assignment of Income. The U.S. Supreme Court has held in *G.C. Earl* (2 USTC ¶ 496) that an individual who gave his wife the legally enforceable right to receive the future income generated by his law practice was still taxable on that income.[12] In another case, *P.R.G. Horst* (40-2 USTC ¶ 9787), the Court ruled that an individual who gave his son interest coupons, which were detached from bonds that he owned, was liable for the tax on the interest accrued before the gift and later paid to his son.[13] Generally, an individual can escape tax on income from property only if the individual makes a valid gift or assignment of the income-producing property itself as distinguished

Footnote references are to paragraphs of the 2008 Standard Federal Tax Reports.

[3] ¶ 5504.035, ¶ 5504.103
[4] ¶ 5504.144
[5] ¶ 6662.043
[6] ¶ 6002
[7] ¶ 5504.184
[8] ¶ 6553.03
[9] ¶ 5507.036, ¶ 5507.294
[10] ¶ 6553.46
[11] ¶ 5504.119
[12] ¶ 2200.01, ¶ 5504.031, ¶ 6553.74
[13] ¶ 2150.64

from an assignment of the income (however, see ¶ 706 for the taxation of the unearned income of children under the age of 18, below).

706. Unearned Income of Minor Child. The amount of net unearned income of a child under age 18 that exceeds an annual inflation-adjusted amount generally is taxed at the parents' highest marginal rate. This is referred to as the "kiddie tax." It is designed to lessen the effectiveness of intra-family transfers of income-producing property that would shift income from the parents' high marginal tax rate to the child's generally lower tax bracket, thereby reducing a family's overall income tax liability. The kiddie tax applies to a child's unearned income regardless of source and requires a calculation of the parents' allocable tax, which is the increase in the parents' tax liability that results from adding to the parents' taxable income the net unearned income of all of the parents' children under age 18. The age of a child whose unearned income is taxed at the parents' rate was 14 prior to 2006, but was increased to 18 for the 2006 and subsequent tax years (Code Sec. 1(g), as amended by the Tax Increase Prevention and Reconciliation Act of 2005 (P.L. 109-222)).[14] See ¶ 143 for dependents with earned income.

For tax years beginning after May 25, 2007, the kiddie tax applies to children who are under age 19 or, if a full time student whose earned income does not exceed half of his or her own support for the year, under age 24 (Code Sec. 1(g)(2)(A), as amended by the Small Business and Work Opportunity Tax Act of 2007 (P.L. 110-28)).

Net unearned income of a child is the portion of adjusted gross income for the year that is not attributable to earned income, reduced by $850 in 2007 (to increase to $900 for 2008), and by either (1) the standard deduction amount, which is $850 for 2007 ($900 in 2008), or (2) the child's itemized deductions relating to the production of the unearned income.

In 2007, the combination of the $850 standard deduction for a child without earned income and the $850 used to calculate the net unearned income reported on the "kiddie tax" return usually shields $1,700 of a child's unearned income from taxation at the parents' rate. These amounts are adjusted annually for inflation.

The marginal tax rate of the parent with the greater amount of taxable income applies in the case of married individuals filing separately. In the case of divorced parents, the custodial parent's taxable income is taken into account in determining the child's tax liability.

The parent of a child under the age of 18 (or, if the tax year begins after May 25, 2007, the age of 19, or the age of 24 if a full-time student whose earned income does not exceed half of his or her own support) may elect to include the interest and dividend income of the child in excess of $1,700 in his or her gross income for the 2007 tax year by filing Form 8814. See ¶ 114 for the filing requirements of Form 8814.

709. Joint Tenancy and Tenancy in Common. When property is held in joint tenancy with a right of survivorship, income from the property (and gain or loss upon its sale) is divided between the owners insofar as each is entitled, under state law, to share in the income. There must be evidence that the joint ownership was bona fide and not used merely as a tax-avoidance scheme. These rules also apply to tenants in common.[15]

710. Community Property Income. In community property states (Arizona, California, Idaho, Louisiana, Nevada, New Mexico, Texas, Washington and Wisconsin),[16] property acquired by a husband and wife during their marriage is generally regarded as owned by them together, each owning an undivided interest in the whole property. Similarly, income from the property is divided equally between them. Although each state has exceptions in classifying income as separate or community property, the general rule is that salaries, wages, and other compensation for the services of either or both the husband and wife are community income. But it does not follow in every state that income from separate property is separate income. The states also differ in their treatment of property acquired by inheritance or intestate succession. However, the IRS can disallow the benefits of any community property law to a spouse for any income that

---

Footnote references are to paragraphs of the 2008 Standard Federal Tax Reports.

[14] ¶ 3260   [15] ¶ 2250.021   [16] ¶ 2350.01

the spouse treats as his or hers alone if that spouse fails to notify the other spouse of the nature and amount of income (Code Sec. 66(b)).[17]

711. Joint v. Separate Return in Community Property States. If separate returns are filed by a married couple residing in a community property state, one-half of the community income must be reported by each spouse. In Idaho, Louisiana, Texas and Wisconsin, income from the separate property of a spouse is community income, with one-half being allocable to each spouse. In the other community property states, income from separate property is separate income.[18]

Regardless of which rule is applied, it is usually more beneficial to file a joint return. For those taxpayers living in states where income from separate property remains separate income, separate returns may be beneficial if one spouse has: (1) a nonbusiness casualty loss attributable to separate property that is not deductible on a joint return because it must be reduced by the $100 floor plus 10 percent of the taxpayer's adjusted gross income or (2) medical expenses that are not deductible on a joint return because of the 7.5 percent of adjusted gross income floor on medical expense deductions.

A U.S. citizen or resident who is married to a nonresident alien may elect to file a joint return if both agree to be taxed on their worldwide income (Code Sec. 6013(g)).[19] If the couple does not make this election and has community property income, certain community property laws will be inapplicable for income tax purposes (Code Sec. 879).[20] Further, there is a special one-time election that permits a nonresident alien spouse to file a joint return with his or her resident spouse for the year in which the alien becomes a U.S. resident (Code Sec. 6013(g) and (h)).[21] Moreover, if both spouses are nonresident aliens, one spouse's income that is connected with a U.S. trade or business is treated as income of that spouse only, regardless of foreign community property law (Code Sec. 879(a)).[22]

Separated Spouses and Innocent Spouse Relief in Community Property States. The usual community property rules do not apply to spouse living apart from each other if: (1) they are separated for the entire year, (2) they file separate returns, and (3) they do not transfer to each other more than a *de minimis* amount of earned income (Code Sec. 66(a)).[23] Also, a spouse who files a separate return may be relieved of liability for tax on his or her share of community income earned by the other spouse if he or she did not know (or have reason to know) of community income items attributable to the other spouse. Further, the IRS may provide relief from a tax liability or deficiency arising from community property where failure to do so would be inequitable (Code Sec. 66(c); Reg. § 1.6015-1(h); Rev. Proc. 2003-61).[24]

Salaries, Wages and Benefits

713. Compensation for Personal Services. All compensation for personal services, no matter what the form of payment, must be included in gross income.[25] Wages, salaries, commissions, bonuses, fringe benefits that do not qualify for statutory exclusions, tips, payments based on a percentage of profits, directors' fees, jury fees, election officials' fees, retirement pay and pensions, and other forms of compensation are income in the year received, and not in the year earned, unless the taxpayer reports income on the accrual basis.

Example: A cash-method salesperson who receives commissions in January 2008 for sales made in 2007 must include those amounts in the 2008 return.

Under the claim-of-right doctrine (see ¶ 1543), a taxpayer receiving income under a claim of right and without restrictions on its use or disposition is taxed on that income in the year received even though the right to retain the income is not yet fixed or the taxpayer may later be required to return it.[26]

Footnote references are to paragraphs of the 2008 Standard Federal Tax Reports.

[17] ¶ 6050, ¶ 6051.04
[18] ¶ 2350.023
[19] ¶ 35,160, ¶ 35,171.031
[20] ¶ 27,460, ¶ 27,462.021
[21] ¶ 27,462.01, ¶ 35,160
[22] ¶ 27,460, ¶ 27,462.021
[23] ¶ 6050, ¶ 6051.021
[24] ¶ 6050, ¶ 6051.035
[25] ¶ 5507.01
[26] ¶ 21,005.122

Compensation is income even though the amount is not fixed in advance, as in the case of marriage fees, baptismal offerings, and similar sums received by a member of the clergy.[27] A year-end bonus is usually taxable, particularly if based on salary or length of service. The value of a turkey, ham, or other nominally valued item distributed to an employee on holidays need not be reported as income even though the employer is entitled to deduct the cost as a business expense. However, a distribution of cash, a gift certificate, or a similar item of value readily convertible to cash must be included in the employee's income.[28] Severance pay and vacation pay are taxable as compensation.

The amount of compensation reported on the return is the gross amount before any reductions for withheld income tax or social security taxes, union dues, insurance, or other deductions by the employer.

Restricted Property Transfers. The value of stock or other property provided to employees subject to certain restrictions is includible in income when the restrictions are removed, unless the recipient elects to recognize income on receipt (Code Sec. 83). See ¶ 1681.

Fringe Benefits. Certain fringe benefits may be excluded from an employee's gross income. See ¶ 863. Benefits such as air flights, cars, computers, educational benefits, entertainment (see ¶ 910), or travel (see ¶ 949) may be excludable as working condition fringe benefits. However, these benefits may be includible in income to the extent the employee uses them for personal purposes. In general, an employee is required to include in income the amount by which the fair market value of a fringe benefit exceeds the sum of (1) the amount, if any, paid for the benefit and (2) the amount, if any, specifically excluded by some other provision of the law (Reg. § 1.61-21(b)(1)).

Employer-provided vehicle. The value of the personal use of an employer-provided car may be computed under annual lease value tables. The annual lease value of an automobile is computed by first determining the fair market value (FMV) of the automobile on the first date it was made available to any employee for personal use. Under a safe-harbor provision, the employer's cost can be substituted for FMV, provided certain conditions are met. Once the FMV is established, the Annual Lease Value Table, prepared by the IRS, is consulted to determine the annual lease value that corresponds to the FMV (Reg. § 1.61-21(d)(2)(iii)).[29] The table is reproduced below. The annual lease values include the FMV of maintenance and insurance for the automobile but do not include the cost of gasoline provided by the employer. The fuel provided can be valued either at its FMV or at 5.5 cents per mile for all miles driven within the United States, Canada, or Mexico by the employee (Reg. § 1.61-21(d)(3)).

Automobile fair market value (1)	Annual Lease Value (2)
$ 0 to 999	$600
1,000 to 1,999	850
2,000 to 2,999	1,100
3,000 to 3,999	1,350
4,000 to 4,999	1,600
5,000 to 5,999	1,850
6,000 to 6,999	2,100
7,000 to 7,999	2,350
8,000 to 8,999	2,600
9,000 to 9,999	2,850
10,000 to 10,999	3,100
11,000 to 11,999	3,350
12,000 to 12,999	3,600
13,000 to 13,999	3,850
14,000 to 14,999	4,100
15,000 to 15,999	4,350
16,000 to 16,999	4,600
17,000 to 17,999	4,850
18,000 to 18,999	5,100
19,000 to 19,999	5,350

Footnote references are to paragraphs of the 2008 Standard Federal Tax Reports.

[27] ¶ 5507.04   [28] ¶ 5507.036   [29] ¶ 5906, ¶ 5907.03

Automobile fair market value (1)	Annual Lease Value (2)
20,000 to 20,999	5,600
21,000 to 21,999	5,850
22,000 to 22,999	6,100
23,000 to 23,999	6,350
24,000 to 24,999	6,600
25,000 to 25,999	6,850
26,000 to 27,999	7,250
28,000 to 29,999	7,750
30,000 to 31,999	8,250
32,000 to 33,999	8,750
34,000 to 35,999	9,250
36,000 to 37,999	9,750
38,000 to 39,999	10,250
40,000 to 41,999	10,750
42,000 to 43,999	11,250
44,000 to 45,999	11,750
48,000 to 49,999	12,750
50,000 to 51,999	13,250
52,000 to 53,999	13,750
54,000 to 55,999	14,250
56,000 to 57,999	14,750
58,000 to 59,999	15,250

For vehicles having a fair market value in excess of $59,999, the Annual Lease Value is equal to: (.25 x the fair market value of the automobile) + $500.

Cents-per-mile valuation. The value of the personal use of an employer-provided vehicle may be determined by multiplying personal use mileage (if at least 10,000 miles) by the standard mileage rate (48.5 cents per mile for 2007) if certain requirements are satisfied (Reg. § 1.61-21(e)). For a passenger automobile first made available to an employee in calendar year 2007, the fair market value of the vehicle cannot exceed $15,100 and for a truck or van the fair market value cannot exceed $16,100 (Rev. Proc. 2007-11). Fuel provided by the employer must be valued separately, at either its fair market value or at 5.5 cents per mile for miles driven in North America (Reg. § 1.61-21(d)(3)(ii)(B)).[30]

Employer-provided commuting vehicle. If certain requirements are met, the use of an employer-provided commuting vehicle is valued at $1.50 each way (to and from work) per employee (Reg. § 1.61-21(f)).[31] Even if two or more employees commute in the vehicle (for example, a car pool), each employee includes $1.50 each way in income. To qualify, personal use of the vehicle must be *de minimis* and the employer must require the employee or employees to commute to and/or from work in the vehicle for bona-fide noncompensatory business reasons.

Employer-provided transportation due to unsafe conditions. If it is unsafe for an employee, who would normally do so, to walk or use public transportation to get to work and certain other requirements are met, the employee includes only $1.50 per one-way commute in income with respect to cab fare or an employer-provided vehicle (Reg. § 1.61-21(k)).[32]

Frequent flyer miles. IRS will not try to tax the personal use of airline frequent flyer miles or other in-kind promotional benefits attributable to the taxpayer's business or official travel. Any future guidance on the taxability of these benefits will be applied prospectively. This relief does not apply to travel or other promotional benefits that are converted to cash, to compensation that is paid in the form of travel or other promotional benefits, or in other circumstances where these benefits are used for tax-avoidance purposes (Announcement 2002-18).[33]

Noncommercial aircraft flights. The value of personal flights (domestic or international) on employer-provided noncommercial aircraft is determined under an IRS

Footnote references are to paragraphs of the 2008 Standard Federal Tax Reports.

[30] ¶ 5906, ¶ 5907.03
[31] ¶ 5906, ¶ 5907.032
[32] ¶ 5907.035
[33] ¶ 5907.046

formula (Reg. § 1.61-21(g)) that is based on Standard Industry Fare Level (SIFL) flight mileage rates, a terminal charge and the weight of the aircraft.[34] If a trip made primarily for business purposes includes business and personal flights, the excess of the value of all the actual flights over the value of the flights that would have been taken if there had been no personal flights is included in income. If the trip is primarily personal, the value of the personal flights that would have been taken if there had been no business flights is included in income (Reg. § 1.61-21(g)(4)).

No amount is included in income if the employee takes a personal trip on a noncommercial aircraft and at least one-half of the aircraft's seating capacity is occupied by employees whose flights are primarily business related and excludable from income (Reg. § 1.61-21(g)(12)).

Golden parachute payments. Golden parachute payments are includible benefits (see ¶ 907).

Moving expense reimbursement. Moving expense reimbursements are excludable as a qualified fringe benefit (see ¶ 1076).

Vacation and club expenses. That portion of an employee's vacation, athletic club, or health resort expenses that is paid by the employer is also taxable to the employee.[35]

Cafeteria Plans. Employer contributions under written "cafeteria" plans are excludable from the income of participants to the extent that they choose qualified benefits. See ¶ 861.

Occupational Disability or Insurance Benefit. Compensation received under a workers' compensation act for personal injuries or sickness and amounts received by a taxpayer under a policy of accident and health insurance are excluded from gross income (Code Sec. 104(a)(1); Reg. § 1.104-1). See ¶ 851.

714. Compensation of Federal or State Employee. The salaries of all employees or officials of the United States government are taxed the same as those of other individuals (Code Sec. 3401(c)). This is also true for state and local government employees.[36]

715. Treatment of Excessive Salaries. Although an employer is denied a deduction for compensation paid to the extent that the payment is unreasonable, the full amount of the payment is included in the recipient's income. In the case of an employee-shareholder, excessive compensation may be treated as dividend income. Excessive salaries are taxed only to the extent of the gain if the excess amounts are determined to be payments to the recipient for property rather than compensation (Reg. § 1.162-8).[37]

716. Social Security and Equivalent Railroad Retirement Benefits. A portion of a taxpayer's social security benefits or an equivalent portion of tier 1 railroad retirement benefits may be taxable (Code Sec. 86). The includible amount is the lesser of one-half of the annual benefits received or one-half of the excess of the taxpayer's provisional income over a specified base amount, at lower provisional income levels. However, at higher provisional income levels, up to 85% of the social security benefits may be included (see *"85-Percent Inclusion,"* below). The Form 1040 instructions contain a worksheet for computing the taxable amount.

Provisional income is the taxpayer's modified adjusted gross income plus one-half of the social security or tier 1 railroad retirement benefits. Modified adjusted gross income is the taxpayer's adjusted gross income plus (a) any tax-exempt interest, including interest earned on savings bonds used to finance higher education, and (b) amounts excluded under an employer's adoption assistance program (¶ 1306), deducted for interest on education loans (¶ 1082) or as a qualified tuition expense (¶ 1082), or earned in a foreign country, a U.S. possession, or Puerto Rico and excluded from gross income (¶ 2401–¶ 2415). The base amount is: (a) $32,000 for joint filers, (b) $0 if married filing separately and the taxpayer lived with his or her spouse at any time during the year, and (c) $25,000 married individuals filing separately who live apart from their

---

Footnote references are to paragraphs of the 2008 Standard Federal Tax Reports.

[34] ¶ 5906, ¶ 5907.042
[35] ¶ 5507.47
[36] ¶ 5507.043, ¶ 5507.044
[37] ¶ 8639, ¶ 8640.01

spouse for the entire year and individuals filing as single or head-of-household (Code Sec. 86(c)).[38]

Example 1: John and Jane Mapes have an adjusted gross income of $24,000 for 2007. John, who is retired, receives social security benefits of $7,200 per year. The couple also receives $6,000 a year from a mutual fund that invests solely in tax-exempt municipal bonds. On their joint return for 2007, the Mapes would make the following computation to determine how much (if any) of John's social security benefits must be included in their gross income:

(1) Adjusted gross income	$24,000
(2) Plus: All tax-exempt interest	6,000
(3) Modified adjusted gross income	$30,000
(4) Plus: One-half of social security benefits	3,600
(5) "Provisional income"	$33,600
(6) Less: Base amount	32,000
(7) Excess above base amount	$1,600
(8) One-half of excess above base amount	$800
(9) One-half of social security benefits	3,600
(10) Amount includible in gross income (lesser of (8) or (9))	$800

Although tier 2 railroad retirement benefits are not taken into account under the above rules, such benefits are taxed in the same manner as benefits paid under private employer retirement plans (Code Sec. 72(r)).[39]

85-Percent Inclusion. Up to 85 percent of an individual's social security benefits may be included in gross income. The rules affect married taxpayers filing jointly with provisional income in excess of $44,000, married taxpayers filing separately and not living apart the entire year with provisional income in excess of $0, and all other taxpayers with provisional income in excess of $34,000 (Code Sec. 86).[40]

Those who exceed the higher threshold "adjusted base" amounts must include in income the lesser of: (a) 85 percent of social security benefits or (b) 85 percent of the excess of provisional income over the threshold amount, plus the smaller of (i) the amount that would otherwise be includible if the second threshold did not apply (i.e., the amount calculated under the 50-percent rules discussed above) or (ii) $4,500 ($6,000 for joint filers).

Example 2: Assume the same facts as above, except that the Mapes' provisional income is increased from $33,600 to $53,600. The includible amount is determined as follows:

(1) Provisional income	$53,600
(2) Adjusted base amount	44,000
(3) Excess of (1) over (2)	$9,600
(4) 85% of amount in (3)	$8,160
(5) Amount otherwise includible (½ of benefits in the Mapes' case)	$3,600
(6) Base amount for joint filers	$6,000
(7) Lesser of (5) or (6)	$3,600
(8) Sum of amounts in (4) and (7)	$11,760
(9) 85% of social security benefits	6,120
(10) Amount includible in gross income (lesser of (8) or (9))	$6,120

Supplemental security income (SSI) payments are *not* treated as social security benefits that may be partially includible in gross income.[41]

Footnote references are to paragraphs of the 2008 Standard Federal Tax Reports.

[38] ¶ 6420, ¶ 6421.03
[39] ¶ 6102, ¶ 6140.046
[40] ¶ 6420, ¶ 6421.03
[41] ¶ 5507.034

IRA Contributions. Employed individuals who are covered by a retirement plan and who are receiving social security benefits must make a special computation to determine the amount of an allowable IRA deduction. See ¶ 2170.

717. Tips. Tips received by cab drivers, waiters, barbers, hotel, railroad and cruise ship employees, etc., are taxable.[42] In the absence of proof of the actual amount of tips received, tip income may be reconstructed on the basis of average tips in a given locality for a given type of service.[43]

Tipped employees may use Form 4070A, Employee's Daily Record of Tips (to be retained with the individual's tax records), to maintain a daily record of their tips. Cash, check, and credit card tips in excess of $20 per month are reported to the employer on Form 4070, Employee's Report of Tips to Employer, or a similar statement by the 10th day of the following month (see ¶ 2601). An employer may also allow tips to be reported electronically. Form 4137, Social Security and Medicare Tax on Unreported Tip Income, is used to compute an employee's liability for social security and Medicare taxes on monthly tips in excess of $20 that were not reported to the employer or on tips allocated by a large food and beverage establishment (see ¶ 2601). If an employer was unable to withhold social security and Medicare taxes on reported tip income, the uncollected taxes are shown on Form W-2 and reported as an additional tax on the tipped employee's income tax return. Noncash tips and tips of less than $20 per month are not subject to social security and Medicare tax. These amounts, however, are subject to income tax and must be reported on the employee's return.

Starting in 2007, the IRS began offering a new tip reporting procedure, the Attributed Tip Income Program (ATIP) (Rev. Proc. 2006-30).[44] This program is available to certain employers in the food and beverage industry. The amount of tips a participating employer reports as wages will not be challenged on audit, and tip reporting requirements for the employer will be reduced. An employer may participate in ATIP if, in the year preceding enrollment, at least 20 percent of the employer's gross receipts from food and beverage sales are charge receipts and at least 75 percent of the employer's tip-earning employees agree to participate.

See ¶ 2601 regarding duty to report tips monthly to employer on Form 4070, ¶ 2639 regarding employer's withholding requirements, and ¶ 1341 regarding an employer credit for social security taxes on employee cash tips.

718. Pension. A pension paid to a retired employee is usually taxable compensation (Reg. § 1.61-11).[45] See ¶ 2101 and following.

719. Salary Payments to Employee's Survivor. The IRS and the Tax Court have generally taken the position that salary payments made to the surviving spouse of a deceased employee are taxable income, while several U.S. Courts of Appeal have viewed the payments as tax-free gifts.[46]

720. Compensation Other Than in Cash. When services are paid for in property, the fair market value at the time of receipt must be included in gross income (Reg. § 1.61-2(d)).[47] A note received in payment for services, and not merely as security for such payment, comes within this rule and its fair market value must be included in income. A portion of each payment received under the note is excludable from income as a recovery of capital.[48]

721. Group-Term and Split-Dollar Life Insurance. An employee must include in income the cost (based on the IRS uniform premium cost tables, reproduced below) of more than $50,000 of group-term life insurance provided by the employer (Code Sec. 79; Reg. § 1.79-1—Reg. § 1.79-3).[49] An employee's age is determined as of the last day of the employee's tax year.

Footnote references are to paragraphs of the 2008 Standard Federal Tax Reports.

[42] ¶ 5507.023

[43] ¶ 5507.023, ¶ 5507.4651 and following

[44] ¶ 36,465.11, ¶ 46,527

[45] ¶ 5710

[46] ¶ 5507.030

[47] ¶ 5506, ¶ 5508

[48] ¶ 5508.026

[49] ¶ 6360, ¶ 6362, ¶ 6364, ¶ 6367

Example 1: X Corp. pays the premiums on a $70,000 group-term insurance policy on the life of its president, Dan Fox, with Fox's wife as beneficiary. Fox is 51 years old at the end of 2007. The IRS-established uniform cost for $1,000 of group-term coverage for twelve months is $2.76 ($0.23 × 12) (Reg. § 1.79-3(d)(2)).[50] The cost of the policy includible in Fox's gross income is computed as follows:

Total insurance coverage	$70,000.00
"Tax-free" insurance	50,000.00
Insurance coverage subject to tax	$20,000.00
Taxable cost of policy includible in Fox's gross income ($2.76 × 20)	$55.20

The $50,000 limit relates to the group-term life insurance coverage which the employee receives during any part of the tax year.

Example 2: An employee's group-term life insurance noncontributory coverage for the first six months of the tax year is $50,000 and for the remainder of the tax year is $95,000. The cost of $45,000 of such insurance for the second six months of the tax year is includible in her gross income.

Any amount paid by the employee toward the purchase of group-term life insurance coverage on the employee's life during the tax year reduces the amount includible in gross income. If a discriminatory group-term insurance plan exists, the cost of the life insurance paid by the employer for the tax year is includible in the gross income of key employees and certain former key employees (Code Sec. 79(d)).[51]

Table 1—For Post-June 30, 1999 Coverage

Cost Per $1,000 of Protection for One-Month Period

Age	Cost
Under 25	5 cents
25 through 29	6 cents
30 through 34	8 cents
35 through 39	9 cents
40 through 44	10 cents
45 through 49	15 cents
50 through 54	23 cents
55 through 59	43 cents
60 through 64	66 cents
65 through 69	$1.27
70 and above	$2.06

Split-Dollar Life Insurance Policies Entered into Before September 18, 2003. Under a split-dollar plan, the employer and employee join in purchasing an insurance contract on the employee's life in which there is a substantial investment element (Code Sec. 61(a)(10)).[52] The employer pays that part of the annual premium that represents the increase in the cash surrender value each year, and the employee pays the balance of the annual premium. The employer is entitled to receive, out of the proceeds of the policy, an amount equal to the cash surrender value, or at least a sufficient part of the cash surrender value equal to the funds it has provided for premium payments. The employee's beneficiary as named by the employee is entitled to the rest of the proceeds.

The practical effect of this type of arrangement is that although the employee must pay a substantial part of the first premium, after the first year his share of the premium decreases rapidly, and the employee obtains valuable insurance protection with a relatively small outlay for premiums in the early years and at little or no cost in later years.

Prior to the release of final regulations in September 2003, split-dollar arrangements were classified into two groups. Under the "endorsement system" the employer owns the policy and is responsible for the payment of the annual premiums. The employee is required to reimburse the employer for the employee's share of the premiums.

Footnote references are to paragraphs of the 2008 Standard Federal Tax Reports.

[50] ¶ 6364   [51] ¶ 6360   [52] ¶ 5502

¶721

Under the "collateral assignment system" the employee owns the policy in form and pays the entire premium. The employer makes annual loans without interest (or below the fair rate of interest) to the employee of amounts equal to the yearly increases in the cash surrender value, but not exceeding the annual premiums. Under this system, the employee assigns the policy to the employer as collateral security for the loans, which generally are payable at the termination of employment or at the employee's death.

Valuation of current life insurance protection must be computed under Table 2001 (see below) or the insurer's lower published premium rates only for the purpose of valuing current life insurance protection for Code purposes.

Split-Dollar Life Insurance Plans Entered Into After September 17, 2003. The final regulations provide two new mutually exclusive regimes for taxing split-dollar life insurance arrangements: an economic benefit regime and a loan regime (Reg. §§ 1.61-22, 1.7872-15). Ownership of the life insurance contract determines which regime applies. If the executive is the owner, the employer's premium payments are treated as loans to the executive. If the employer is the owner, the employer's premium payments are treated as providing taxable economic benefits to the executive. Such benefits include the executive's interest in the policy cash value and current life insurance protection.

The regulations also provide similar rules for split-dollar arrangement between family members, and other parties such as corporation and their shareholders.

Valuing term insurance benefit. In the past, the IRS allowed the value of the insurance component to be determined using either the P.S. 58 rate table contained in Rev. Rul. 55-747[53] *or* the insurance company's *lower* published term rates if certain conditions were satisfied. The P.S. 58 rates were generally revoked, effective for tax years ending after December 31, 2001 (or, at the taxpayer's option, for tax years ending after January 9, 2001) and replaced with Table 2001 rates[54] that reflected the lower cost of term insurance protection (Notice 2001-10). For split-dollar arrangements entered into before the effective date of future guidance, taxpayers should continue to use Table 2001 (Notice 2002-8). However, for split-dollar arrangements entered into before January 28, 2002, the P.S. 58 rates may be used to determine the value of current life insurance protection that is provided to an employee if the arrangement requires use of the P.S. 58 rates.

Taxpayers also may continue to determine the value of current life insurance protection by using the insurer's lower published premium rates that are available for all standard risks for initial-issue one-year term insurance. However, for arrangements entered into after January 28, 2002, and before the effective date of future guidance, for periods after 2003, the IRS will not consider an insurer's lower published premium rates to be available to all standard risks who apply for term insurance unless:

(1) the insurer generally makes the availability of such rates known to persons who apply for term insurance coverage from the insurer, and

(2) the insurer regularly sells term insurance at such rates to individuals who apply for term insurance coverage through the insurer's normal distribution channels.

Neither lower published premium rates nor Table 2001 rates may be relied upon to value current life insurance protection for the purpose of establishing the value of any policy benefits to which another party may be entitled (Notice 2002-59).

Arrangements entered into before publication of final regulations. For split-dollar arrangements entered into before publication of the final regulations, the IRS will not tax the growth of the cash value during the term of the arrangement solely because the growth component is not payable to the employer. Before the publication of Notice 2002-8, it was unclear whether the growth in the cash value of existing arrangements would be taxed annually to the employee under Code Sec. 83, which taxes the exchange of property in return for services (see ¶ 1681).

Footnote references are to paragraphs of the 2008 Standard Federal Tax Reports.

[53] ¶ 5508.24   [54] ¶ 5907.052

Further, the IRS will not treat such an arrangement as having been terminated, thus resulting in a taxable transfer of property for so long as the economic benefit of the term insurance is being properly reported as income by the employee.

The IRS will also allow employer premium payments under a split-dollar arrangement entered into before the effective date of the regulations to be treated as loans to the employee. Loan treatment can be chosen even for an existing arrangement. However, if this is done, all previous employer premium payments must be treated as loans entered into at the beginning of the first tax year in which loan recharacterization is chosen.

Finally, for arrangements entered into before January 28, 2002, in which an employer has or is entitled to recoup all of its payments, the IRS will not assert that there has been a taxable transfer of property upon termination of the arrangement if (1) the arrangement is terminated before January 1, 2004, or (2) for all periods beginning after December 31, 2003, employer payments are treated as loans. All prior payments are recharacterized as loans entered into at the beginning of the year that option (2) is chosen.

Table 2001
Interim Table of One-Year Term Premiums for $1,000
Life Insurance Protection

Age	Premium	Age	Premium
0	$0.70	39	1.07
1	0.41	40	1.10
2	0.27	41	1.13
3	0.19	42	1.20
4	0.13	43	1.29
5	0.13	44	1.40
6	0.14	45	1.53
7	0.15	46	1.67
8	0.16	47	1.83
9	0.16	48	1.98
10	0.16	49	2.13
11	0.19	50	2.30
12	0.24	51	2.52
13	0.28	52	2.81
14	0.33	53	3.20
15	0.38	54	3.65
16	0.52	55	4.15
17	0.57	56	4.68
18	0.59	57	5.20
19	0.61	58	5.66
20	0.62	59	6.06
21	0.62	60	6.51
22	0.64	61	7.11
23	0.66	62	7.96
24	0.68	63	9.08
25	0.71	64	10.41
26	0.73	65	11.90
27	0.76	66	13.51
28	0.80	67	15.20
29	0.83	68	16.92
30	0.87	69	18.70
31	0.90	70	20.62
32	0.93	71	22.72
33	0.96	72	25.07
34	0.98	73	27.57
35	0.99	74	30.18
36	1.01	75	33.05
37	1.04	76	36.33
38	1.06	77	40.17

Age	Premium	Age	Premium
78	44.33	89	133.40
79	49.23	90	144.30
80	54.56	91	155.80
81	60.51	92	168.75
82	66.74	93	186.44
83	73.07	94	206.70
84	80.35	95	228.35
85	88.76	96	250.01
86	99.16	97	265.09
87	110.40	98	270.11
88	121.85	99	281.05

PS-58 Uniform One-Year Term Premiums for $1,000
Life Insurance Protection

Age	Premium	Age	Premium
15	$1.27	48	7.89
16	1.38	49	8.53
17	1.48	50	9.22
18	1.52	51	9.97
19	1.56	52	10.79
20	1.61	53	11.69
21	1.67	54	12.67
22	1.73	55	13.74
23	1.79	56	14.91
24	1.86	57	16.18
25	1.93	58	17.56
26	2.02	59	19.08
27	2.11	60	20.73
28	2.20	61	22.53
29	2.31	62	24.50
30	2.43	63	26.63
31	2.57	64	28.98
32	2.70	65	31.51
33	2.86	66	34.28
34	3.02	67	37.31
35	3.21	68	40.59
36	3.41	69	44.17
37	3.63	70	48.06
38	3.87	71	52.29
39	4.14	72	56.89
40	4.42	73	61.89
41	4.73	74	67.33
42	5.07	75	73.23
43	5.44	76	79.63
44	5.85	77	86.57
45	6.30	78	94.09
46	6.78	79	102.23
47	7.32	80	111.04
		81	120.57

722. Unemployment Compensation. Recipients of unemployment compensation benefits must include in income the entire annual amount of benefits received (Code Sec. 85).[55] Payments to laid-off employees from company-financed supplemental unemployment benefit plans (also referred to as "guaranteed annual wage" plans) constitute taxable income to the employees in the year received.[56] Payors report unemployment compensation on Form 1099-G.

Footnote references are to paragraphs of the 2008 Standard Federal Tax Reports.

[55] ¶ 6410, ¶ 6412   [56] ¶ 5507.032, ¶ 5507.60

723. Deferred Compensation. Not all compensation is paid in the year when services are rendered. Some may be deferred to a later year. There are two types of deferred compensation arrangements—funded and unfunded.

Funded Arrangements. If deferred compensation is contributed to a trust or is used to purchase an annuity or other insurance contract, the arrangement is funded and is governed by the rules discussed in Chapter 21, Retirement Plans.

Unfunded Arrangements. If the deferral takes the form of an employer's unsecured promise (not represented by a note) to pay compensation for current services at some time in the future, and if the employee uses the cash method of accounting (as is virtually always the case), the amount promised is not includible in the employee's gross income until it is received or made available (Rev. Rul. 60-31).[57] This rule is not altered merely because the employee agrees with the employer in advance to receive compensation on a deferred basis, so long as the agreement is made before the taxpayer obtains an unqualified and unconditional right to the compensation (*J.F. Oates*,[58] Section 132 of the Revenue Act of 1978).[59]

Unfunded Plans of State and Local Governments and Other Tax-Exempt Organizations. The above-described treatment of unfunded deferred compensation plans is modified for participants in plans maintained by state and local governments and other tax-exempt organizations, except for churches and qualified church-controlled organizations (Code Sec. 457).[60] If the rules discussed below are satisfied by such plans or arrangements, the deferred compensation is includible in income only when received by, or unconditionally made available to, a participant. For distributions from a government plan, the deferred compensation is included in income only when actually paid (Code Sec. 457(a)). If the rules are not satisfied, the present value of the deferred compensation is includible in gross income for the first tax year in which there is no substantial risk of forfeiture. Any interest or other earnings credited to the deferred compensation are taxable (under the annuity rules) only when made available.

For tax years beginning in 2007, the deferral limit is the lesser of $15,000 or 100% of the participant's compensation (Code Sec. 457(b)(2) and (e)(15)(A)). The maximum amount that can be deferred under the normal and special deferral provision for 2007 is $30,000 (Code Sec. 457(b)(3)).[61] Individuals who are age 50 or older by the end of the plan year may make additional "catch-up" contributions, as explained at ¶ 2197B.

Code Sec. 457 does not apply to a bona fide vacation leave, sick leave, compensatory time, severance pay, disability pay, or death benefit plan (Code Sec. 457(e)(11)). Also, Code Sec. 457 does not apply to nonelective deferred compensation attributable to services not performed as an employee (Code Sec. 457(e)(12)).

A Code Sec. 457 plan must also provide: (1) that compensation may be deferred for any month only if an agreement for such deferral has been entered into before the first day of that month; (2) that, except as may be required by (3), deferrals may not be distributed earlier than the calendar year in which the participant attains age 70½ or the date of the participant's separation from service ("severance from employment" for distributions after 2001) except in the case of unforeseeable emergency; and (3) minimum distribution rules as described in Code Sec. 401(a)(9) and discussed at ¶ 2133 and ¶ 2135 (Code Sec. 457(b)(4) and (b)(5)). Code Sec. 457 plans are also discussed at ¶ 2197B.

Unfunded Plans of Taxable Employers. An unfunded plan of a taxable employer is not subject to limitations similar to those that apply to a governmental or other tax-exempt employer. As a practical matter, however, such a plan is limited to providing benefits in excess of those permitted under qualified plans or benefits for highly compensated and managerial employees. This is because any other unfunded deferred compensation plan of a taxable employer would be subject to ERISA participation, vesting, funding, and fiduciary standards (ERISA Sec. 4(b)(5), ERISA Sec. 201(2), ERISA Sec. 301(a)(3), and

---

Footnote references are to paragraphs of the 2008 Standard Federal Tax Reports.

[57] ¶ 18,352.029   [59] ¶ 5905.01   [61] ¶ 21,536.038, ¶ 21,536.039
[58] ¶ 21,009.135   [60] ¶ 21,531

¶723

ERISA Sec. 401(a)(1)). For discussion of nonqualified deferred compensation plans, see ¶ 2197A.

Interest

724. Interest. All interest received or accrued is fully taxable (Reg. § 1.61-7),[62] except interest on (1) tax-exempt state or municipal bonds, (2) certain ESOP loans (¶ 725), and (3) interest on U.S. savings bonds used to pay qualified educational expenses (¶ 730A). A cash-basis taxpayer is taxed on interest when received. Interest on bank deposits, coupons payable on bonds, etc., is considered available and taxed to a cash-basis taxpayer under the doctrine of constructive receipt and is taxed when credited or due.

Interest earned on corporate obligations is generally taxed when actually received by, or credited to, a cash-basis taxpayer (Reg. § 1.61-7(a)). The same rule applies to interest on certificates of deposit, time obligations, and similar deposit arrangements on which interest is credited periodically and can be withdrawn without penalty even though the principal cannot be withdrawn without penalty prior to maturity. However, interest on a six-month certificate that is not credited or made available to the holder without penalty before maturity is not includible in the holder's income until the certificate is redeemed or matures (Rev. Rul. 80-157).[63]

Increments in value on growth savings certificates are taxable in the year that the increase occurs.[64] Any increment in the value of life insurance or annuity prepaid premiums or premium deposits is income when made available to the policyholder for withdrawal or when credited against premiums payable.[65] Interest on a judgment is taxable, even if the underlying award is nontaxable.[66]

When a bond with defaulted interest coupons is bought "flat" (that is, the price covers both principal and unpaid interest), any interest received that was in default on the date of purchase is not taxable but is a return of capital. If the bond is sold, this amount must be applied to reduce the basis, in turn increasing the gain or reducing the loss. If interest is received for a period which *follows* the date of purchase, it is taxable in full.[67]

Under the accrual method, interest is taxable as it accrues even though it is payable later. An exception to this rule is where it is discovered before the close of the tax year that the interest owed to the taxpayer will not be collected.[68]

State and Local Bonds; Tax-Credit Bonds. The federal government provides financial assistance to state and local governmental agencies by excluding from the gross income of the recipient the interest on certain tax-exempt state and local bonds (Code Sec. 103).[69] The federal government also authorizes the issuers of such bonds to issue tax-credit bonds. A tax-credit bond essentially provides the issuer with a tax-free loan. The bond holders receive a tax credit on their federal income tax at the specified credit rate, instead of interest payments, and the issuer only has to repay the principal. The bond holders must include the credit amount in income, then claim the credit against tax on their return. In effect, the holders will usually receive the same net amount from the credit as they would receive in interest from a conventional state or local bond.

The federal government has authorized the states of Louisiana, Alabama, and Mississippi to issue Gulf tax-credit bonds (Code Sec. 1400N(l), as added by the Gulf Opportunity Zone Act of 2005 (P.L. 109-135)).[70] These bonds have a maximum maturity of two years, and, as with other tax-credit bonds, the holders will receive a tax credit against their income tax instead of interest.

726. Mortgage Interest. The Supreme Court (*Midland Mutual Life Ins. Co.*, 37-1 USTC ¶ 9114) has held that when a taxpayer forecloses on a mortgage and purchases the property at a foreclosure sale by bidding the full amount of the mortgage plus accrued unpaid interest, taxable income is realized in the amount of the accrued interest, even

---

Footnote references are to paragraphs of the 2008 Standard Federal Tax Reports.

[62] ¶ 5704	[65] ¶ 5504.023	[68] ¶ 5704.033
[63] ¶ 21,009.3247	[66] ¶ 6662.043	[69] ¶ 6602.01
[64] ¶ 5704.023	[67] ¶ 5704.046, ¶ 5704.3062	[70] ¶ 32,487.023

though the fair market value was less than the bid price. Other courts have applied the same rule to *voluntary* conveyances by the mortgagor in consideration for the cancellation of the principal and interest of the mortgage. But there is no interest income in the case of such a conveyance if the property is worth less than the principal of the loan.[71] Nor is any income realized if only the principal of the mortgage is bid.[72] For repossessions of real property, see ¶ 1841.

If a creditor bids in property for a debt, a loss may be deductible if the property bid in is worth less than the debt.[73] The First Circuit has held that the *Midland Mutual Life Ins. Co.* decision as to interest income does not prevent deduction of a loss in such a case, even though the creditor bid in the property for more than the debt (*Hadley Falls Trust Co.*, 40-1 USTC ¶ 9352).[74] The Tax Court has ruled that the Reg. § 1.166-6 presumption that the fair market value is the bid price applies in the absence of clear and convincing proof to the contrary.[75] See ¶ 1145 for a discussion of the bad debt deduction.

Seller-Provided Financing. A taxpayer who receives or accrues interest from seller-provided financing must include on his or her income tax return the name, address and taxpayer identification number of the person from whom the interest was received or accrued (Code Sec. 6109(h)).[76] Failure to provide this required information will expose the taxpayer to information reporting penalties (¶ 2833).

727. Imputed Interest. Holders of bonds or other obligations issued at a discount may be required to include in income a portion of the discount as "imputed interest" in each year the obligation is held even though no interest corresponding to this amount is paid or accrued during the period (see ¶ 1952). Holders of notes or other debt instruments that were issued in exchange for property or services may be required to include in income "imputed interest" where no interest is provided in the debt instrument or the rate of interest is less than the applicable federal rate (see ¶ 1954). Other loans bearing interest at less than the applicable federal rate may also result in "imputed interest" income to the lender (see ¶ 795).

728. Bond Transaction Between Interest Dates. When a bond is sold between interest dates and an amount representing the interest earned up to the date of sale is added to the selling price, the buyer, upon later receiving the full interest payment, reports as income only the portion representing interest that accrued from the date of sale.[77] The seller must include in income in the year of the sale the portion of the selling price representing interest accrued to the date of sale. This interest adjustment has no effect on the cost of the bond and apparently has no connection with the adjustment for amortizable bond premium (¶ 1967). It is a purchase of accrued interest.

729. Private Activity Bonds. Although interest on obligations of a state or local government is generally excludable from gross income (Code Sec. 103(a)),[78] bond interest is not tax free when it is derived from nonexempt private activity bonds, state or local bonds that have not been issued in registered form, or arbitrage bonds (Code Sec. 103(b)).[79] Private activity bonds that qualify for tax exemption include exempt facility bonds (a category which includes enterprise zone facility bonds (Code Sec. 1394)), qualified veterans' mortgage bonds, qualified student loan bonds, qualified redevelopment bonds, qualified Code Sec. 501(c)(3) bonds, and qualified mortgage and small-issue bonds.[80] Qualified private activity bonds must meet the applicable volume cap requirements of Code Sec. 146[81] and the applicable requirements of Code Sec. 147[82] (Code Sec. 141(e)).[83] Capital expenditures of public schools, except schools owned or operated by private, for-profit businesses, may be financed with private activity bonds. However, bonds issued after 2001 that are used to provide qualified public educational facilities can be treated as exempt facility bonds (Code Sec. 142(a)(13)). A qualified

Footnote references are to paragraphs of the 2008 Standard Federal Tax Reports.

[71] ¶ 5704.043, ¶ 5704.338
[72] ¶ 5704.338
[73] ¶ 10,670.01
[74] ¶ 10,670.123
[75] ¶ 10,750.10

[76] ¶ 36,960, ¶ 36,965.034
[77] ¶ 5704.047
[78] ¶ 6600, ¶ 6602
[79] ¶ 6600, ¶ 6602

[80] ¶ 7702, ¶ 7740, ¶ 7780, ¶ 7810, ¶ 7830.01
[81] ¶ 7850, ¶ 7854
[82] ¶ 7860, ¶ 7861
[83] ¶ 7702

public educational facility is defined as a public school facility owned by a private, for-profit corporation pursuant to a public-private partnership agreement with a state or local educational agency (Code Sec. 142(k)(1)). In addition, facilities that can be financed with exempt facility bonds include qualified green building and sustainable design projects with bonds issued after December 31, 2004, but before October 1, 2009, and qualified highway or surface freight transfer facilities with bonds issued after August 10, 2005 (Code Sec. 142(a)(14) and (15)).[84]

A special exception allows qualified scholarship funding bonds to be treated as state and local bonds (Code Sec. 150(d)).[85] Such bonds must be issued by a not-for-profit corporation that is established and operated exclusively for the purpose of acquiring student loan notes incurred under the Higher Education Act of 1965 and is organized at the request of a state or political subdivision. Also, a qualified volunteer fire department may issue bonds that will be treated as issued by a political subdivision if it is operated under a written agreement with a political subdivision to provide fire-fighting or emergency medical services (Code Sec. 150(e)).[86]

Bonds issued by a governmental unit to fund the acquisition of existing electric and gas generating and transmission systems are generally treated as private activity bonds subject to the state-volume limitations in order to limit their issuance for this purpose (Code Sec. 141(d)).[87]

Generally, income of state and local governments that is derived from the exercise of an essential governmental function is tax exempt. However, arbitrage restrictions limit the ability of governmental units to profit from the investment of tax-exempt bond proceeds (Code Sec. 148).

Prior to 2011, specific tax-exempt private activity bonds, called Gulf Opportunity Zone bonds or GO Zone bonds, may be authorized for the purpose of financing construction or repair of real estate and infrastructure in the Gulf Opportunity Zone (Code Sec. 1400N(a)).[88] The amount of GO Zone bonds that can be issued is in addition to the amount of qualified private activity bonds that are otherwise authorized under the volume cap of the relevant state. These bonds can be issued by Alabama, Louisiana, Mississippi, or any political subdivision of those states, and must meet the relevant state law bond issue requirements. GO Zone bonds can be issued after December 21, 2005 and prior to January 1, 2011. GO Zone bonds can be treated as exempt facility bonds or as qualified mortgage bonds. A GO Zone repair or reconstruction loan will be treated as a qualified rehabilitation loan for purposes of the qualified mortgage bond rules (Code Sec. 1400N(a)(7), as added by the Small Business and Work Opportunity Tax Act of 2007 (P.L. 110-28)).

730. United States Savings Bonds. A taxpayer on the *accrual* basis must include each year the increase in value of a United States savings bond (issued at a discount and payable at par on maturity) in an amount equal to the increase in redemption value as indicated in the table of redemption values shown on the bond, even if the interest will not be received until the bond is surrendered.[89]

Using the *cash* method, none of the increase in value of the bonds issued at a discount (Series E and EE) or interest on Series I bonds is taxable until the earlier of (1) the year the bonds are cashed in or disposed of or (2) the year in which they mature.[90] A taxpayer on the cash basis *may,* however, elect to treat the annual increase in value of Series EE (former Series E) and Series I bonds as income in each year.

Taxable income is not recognized when Series EE or E bonds on which interest reporting was postponed are traded for Series HH or H bonds unless cash is received in the trade. Any cash received is taxed to the extent of interest earned on the Series EE or E bonds. When the Series HH or H bonds mature (or, if earlier, when they are disposed of) the difference between their redemption value and cost is reported as interest income. Cost is the amount paid for the Series EE or E bonds plus any additional

---

Footnote references are to paragraphs of the 2008 Standard Federal Tax Reports.

[84] ¶ 46,506
[85] ¶ 7930, ¶ 7935.021
[86] ¶ 7930, ¶ 7935.03

[87] ¶ 7702, ¶ 7707.043
[88] ¶ 32,487.021
[89] ¶ 6602.035

[90] ¶ 6602.04

amount paid for the Series HH or H bonds. A taxpayer may elect to treat all previously unreported accrued interest on Series EE or E bonds traded for Series HH bonds as income in the year of the trade.

730A. Exclusion for U.S. Savings Bond Income Used for Higher Education. An individual who redeems any qualified U.S. savings bond in a year in which qualified higher education expenses are paid may exclude from income amounts received, provided certain requirements are met (Code Sec. 135).[91] A qualified U.S. savings bond is any such bond issued after 1989 to an individual who has reached age 24 before the date of issuance and which was issued at a discount under 31 U.S.C. § 3105 (Series I or EE bonds). Qualified higher education expenses include tuition and fees required for enrollment or attendance at an eligible educational institution of either a taxpayer, the taxpayer's spouse, or any dependent of the taxpayer for whom the taxpayer is allowed a deduction under Code Sec. 151 (Code Sec. 135(c)(2)). Also, taxpayers are entitled to the exclusion if the redemption proceeds are contributed to a qualified tuition program.

A taxpayer must be able to verify the amount of interest excluded. Therefore, the following records should be kept:

(1) A written record of each post-1989 Series EE U.S. savings bond that is cashed in. It must include the serial number, issue date, face value, and total redemption proceeds (principal and interest) of each bond. Form 8818, Optional Form To Record Redemption of Series EE U.S. Savings Bonds Issued After 1989, may be used for this purpose.

(2) Some form of documentation to show that qualified higher education expenses were paid during the year. This could include canceled checks, credit card receipts or bills from the educational institution.

The amount that may be excluded is limited when the aggregate proceeds of qualified U.S. savings bonds redeemed by a taxpayer during a tax year exceed the qualified higher education expenses paid during that year (Code Sec. 135(b)(1)). Qualified higher education expenses must be reduced by the sum of the amounts received with respect to an individual for a tax year as a qualified scholarship that is not includible in gross income under Code Sec. 117, as an educational assistance allowance under certain chapters of title 38 of the United States Code, as a payment (other than a gift or inheritance) that is exempt from tax (such as employer-provided educational assistance), or as a payment, waiver, or reimbursement under a qualified tuition program (Code Sec. 135(d)(1)). The amount must be further reduced by expenses taken into account for the Hope Scholarship or Lifetime Learning credits as well as amounts taken into account in determining the exclusion for distributions from a qualified tuition program or the exclusion for distributions from an education savings account (Code Sec. 135(d)(2)).

The exclusion is subject to a phaseout in the years in which the bonds are cashed and the tuition is paid (Code Sec. 135(b)(2)(B)).[92] For 2007, the phaseout range is $98,400–$128,400 for joint filers and $65,600–$80,600 for all other filers (Rev. Proc. 2006-53). For 2008, the phaseout range will be $100,650-$130,650 for joint filers and $67,100-$82,100 for all other filers (Rev. Proc. 2007-66).

Below the phaseout ranges, taxpayers may exclude bond interest up to the amount of qualified higher education expenses. Above these ranges, no exclusion is allowed. For those falling within the ranges, the amount of interest excludable from income is reduced, depending on the taxpayer's modified AGI. Modified AGI is adjusted gross income *after* applying (1) the partial exclusion for social security and tier 1 railroad retirement benefits (Code Sec. 86), (2) amounts deducted for contributions to individual retirement arrangements (Code Sec. 219), and (3) adjustments for limitations on passive activity losses and credits (Code Sec. 469), and *before* taking into account (1) the interest exclusion under discussion, (2) the exclusion for qualified adoption expenses (Code Sec. 137), (3) the deduction for domestic production activities (Code Sec. 199), (4) the deduction for interest paid on qualified education loans (Code Sec. 221), (5) the

Footnote references are to paragraphs of the 2008 Standard Federal Tax Reports.

[91] ¶ 7550, ¶ 7551   [92] ¶ 7551.021

¶730A

deduction for qualified tuition and education expenses (Code Sec. 222), (6) the foreign income exclusion (Code Sec. 911), and (7) the exclusion for income from sources within Guam, American Samoa, the Northern Mariana Islands, and Puerto Rico (Code Secs. 931 and 933) (Code Sec. 135(c)(4)).

Form 8815. This exclusion is not available to married individuals who file separate returns. The amount of excludable savings bond interest is determined using Form 8815, which is then filed with the taxpayer's Form 1040 or Form 1040A.

731. Issues of U.S. Obligations. Except for a minor exception, interest on all obligations of the United States and its agencies and instrumentalities issued after February 28, 1941, is subject to federal taxes to the same extent as private obligations (Reg. § 1.103-4).[93]

732. Sale of Federal or State Obligations. The taxing of gain derived from the sale of tax-exempt county or municipal bonds is not in violation of the Constitution.[94] Losses so sustained are deductible, subject to capital loss limitations.

Dividends

733. Dividends. Ordinary dividends are fully includible in gross income. For income tax purposes, the term "dividend" or "ordinary dividend" means any distribution made by a corporation to its shareholders, whether in money or other property, out of its earnings and profits accumulated after February 28, 1913, or out of earnings and profits of the tax year (Code Sec. 316(a); Reg. § 1.316-1).[95] See ¶ 747.

Generally, dividends are taxed as ordinary income. However, qualified dividend income received by an individual between January 1, 2003, and December 31, 2010, is taxed at rates lower than those applicable to ordinary income. "Qualified dividend income" is defined as dividends received during the tax year from (1) a domestic corporation or (2) a qualified foreign corporation.[96]

If a dividend is in cash, the amount of the dividend is the amount of the cash. If the dividend is in both cash and noncash property, the amount of the dividend is the amount of the cash plus the fair market value of the property distributed. See ¶ 735. Special rules apply to distributions received by 20% corporate shareholders (Code Sec. 301(e)).[97]

Qualified dividends paid to shareholders by a domestic corporation or a qualified foreign corporation between January 1, 2003, and December 31, 2010, are taxed at capital gains rates (Code Sec. 1(h)(11); Act Sec. 102 of the Tax Increase Prevention and Reconciliation Act of 2005 (P.L. 109-222), modifying Act Sec. 303 of the Jobs and Growth Tax Relief Reconciliation Act of 2003 (P.L. 108-27)).[98] At the same time, capital gains rates are reduced to 5 percent for taxpayers in the 10- or 15-percent brackets and 15 percent for those in the higher tax brackets. However, a zero-percent rate applies for taxpayers in the 10- or 15-percent brackets for 2008 through 2010.

Corporate stock dividends passed through to investors by a mutual fund or other regulated investment company, partnership, real estate investment trust, or held by a common trust fund are also eligible for the reduced rate assuming the distribution would otherwise be classified as qualified dividend income.

Investments in tax-deferred retirement vehicles such as regular IRAs, 401(k)s and deferred annuities receive no benefit from the rate reduction. Distributions from these accounts are taxed at ordinary income tax rates even if the funds represent dividends paid on the stocks held in the account.

The reduced tax rates also do not apply to dividends paid by corporations such as (among others) credit unions, mutual insurance companies, farmers' cooperatives, nonprofit voluntary employee benefit associations (VEBAs), mutual savings banks, building and loan associations, and certain stock owned for short terms (Code Sec. 1(h)(11)(B)(ii)).[99] Special rules apply to Code Sec. 306 stock, which includes (1) stock other than common stock received as a tax-free stock dividend, (2) stock other than

---

Footnote references are to paragraphs of the 2008 Standard Federal Tax Reports.

[93] ¶ 6606
[94] ¶ 6602.36
[95] ¶ 15,702, ¶ 15,703

[96] ¶ 3285.051
[97] ¶ 15,302, ¶ 15,305.031
[98] ¶ 3260

[99] ¶ 3260

common stock received in certain tax-free divisions or reorganizations, and (3) stock (including common stock) with a substituted or carryover basis determined by reference to other Code Sec. 306 stock.[100] Special rules also apply to dividends received from foreign corporations (Code Sec. 1(h)(11)(C)).[101]

Holding Period of Stocks for Purposes of Claiming a Qualified Dividend. To qualify for the lower rates, investors are required to hold the stock from which the dividend is paid for more than 60 days in the 121-day period beginning 60 days before the ex-dividend date. The ex-dividend date is the date following the record date on which the corporation finalizes the list of shareholders who will receive the dividend (Code Sec. 1(h)(11)).[102]

733A. Corporate Debt v. Equity. The determination of whether an instrument issued by a corporation is to be treated as stock or as evidence of indebtedness for federal income tax purposes is resolved by weighing various factors, such as the source of the payments made to the holder and whether there is an unconditional promise to pay a sum certain together with a fixed rate of interest. For instruments issued after October 24, 1992, the corporate issuer's characterization of the nature of the instrument, made at the time of issuance, is binding upon the corporation and all the holders, but not the IRS. However, interest holders are not bound by the issuer's characterization if they disclose any inconsistent treatment on their tax returns (Code Sec. 385(c)).[103]

The IRS closely scrutinizes instruments containing a combination of debt and equity characteristics which are designed to be treated as debt for federal income tax purposes (Notice 94-47). Of particular interest are instruments that contain such equity features as an unreasonably long maturity or an ability to repay principal with the issuer's stock. No deduction is allowed for any interest paid or accrued on a "disqualified debt instrument" issued after June 8, 1997 (Code Sec. 163(l)). The term means any debt that is payable in equity of the issuer or a related party or equity held by the issuer (or any related party) in any other person, specifically if: (1) a substantial portion of the principal or interest is required to be paid or converted, or at the issuer's or related party's option is payable in, or convertible into, equity of the issuer or a related party; (2) a substantial portion of the principal or interest is required to be determined, or may be determined at the option of the issuer or related party, by reference to the value of equity of the issuer or related party; or (3) the debt is part of an arrangement designed to result in payment of the instrument with or by reference to the equity.

In addition, the IRS examines corporate transactions designed to produce interest deductions with respect to a related issuance of stock and to provide companies with significant tax advantages in satisfying their equity capital requirements (Notice 94-48). The overall substance of an arrangement whereby a corporation creates a partnership that issues notes to investors and uses most of its capital to buy stock of the corporation is viewed by the IRS as merely an issuance of preferred stock by the corporation. Thus, such a corporation could not deduct an allocable portion of interest expense on the note without an offsetting inclusion of dividend income.

734. When Is a Dividend Received. A dividend on corporate stock is taxable when, in an unqualified manner, it is made subject to the demand of the shareholder (Reg. § 1.301-1(b)).[104] For both cash-method and accrual-method shareholders, this generally occurs when the dividend is received. Time of payment, rather than time of declaration, governs taxability. A dividend is taxable when the check is actually received, even though it may be dated and mailed in an earlier tax year, unless the recipient requested delivery by mail in order to delay recognition of income.[105]

Voluntary repayment of a dividend legally declared and distributed does not negate the receipt of dividend income by a shareholder.[106]

Dividends paid by regulated investment companies (a mutual fund) are not always taxable when received. See ¶ 2323.

Footnote references are to paragraphs of the 2008 Standard Federal Tax Reports.

[100] ¶ 15,450
[101] ¶ 3260
[102] ¶ 3285.055

[103] ¶ 17,340, ¶ 17,351.01
[104] ¶ 15,303, ¶ 15,305.034
[105] ¶ 21,009.1235

[106] ¶ 15,704.46, ¶ 15,704.473

735. Dividend Paid in Property. If any part of a dividend is paid in a form other than cash, the property received must be included in gross income at its fair market value at the date of distribution (regardless of whether this date is the same as that on which the distribution is includible in gross income) (Code Sec. 301(b)(1) and (3)).[107] When property is distributed to a corporate shareholder, the adjusted basis of the property in the hands of the distributing corporation at the time of the distribution (plus any gain recognized by the distributing corporation) is substituted for the fair market value of the property if the adjusted basis is less than the fair market value. See also ¶ 733.

The amount of income realized on a distribution is reduced (but not below zero) by the amount of any liability to which property is subject or which is assumed (Code Sec. 301(b)(2); Reg. § 1.301-1).[108] The basis of property received in a distribution is the fair market value of such property (Code Sec. 301(d)).

If a distribution is paid in property having a fair market value in excess of the corporation's earnings and profits (¶ 747), the dividend is limited to earnings and profits (accumulated and current). The portion of the distribution that is not a dividend is applied to reduce the basis of the stock. If the amount of the nondividend distribution exceeds the basis of the stock, the excess is treated as a gain from the sale or exchange of the stock (Code Sec. 301(c)).

736. Gain or Loss to Corporation on Nonliquidating Distributions. No gain or loss is recognized by a corporation on the distribution of its stock, or rights to its stock, to shareholders. Similarly, a corporation generally does not recognize gain or loss on the distribution to its shareholders of corporate property (Code Sec. 311(a)).[109] A corporation generally must recognize gain, however, when it distributes appreciated property to its shareholders in any ordinary, nonliquidating distribution to the extent that the fair market value of the property exceeds its adjusted basis (Code Sec. 311(b)).[110] If property is distributed subject to a liability, or if the distributee assumes a liability upon distribution, the fair market value of the property cannot be less, for purposes of determining gain, than the amount of the liability (Code Secs. 311(b)(2) and 336(b)). Gain or loss rules applicable to corporations on liquidating distributions are discussed at ¶ 2257.

738. Stock Dividends and Stock Rights. As a general rule, a stockholder need not include in gross income the value of stock received as a stock dividend (Code Sec. 305(a); Reg. § 1.305-1—Reg. § 1.305-8).[111] Cash that is paid in lieu of fractional shares may be taxable even though fractional shares themselves would not be taxable (Reg. § 1.305-3(c)).[112] For example, the purpose of the distribution in cash for fractional shares was to give a certain group of shareholders an increased interest in the assets or earnings and profits of the corporation. However, contrary to the general rule, the following distributions by a corporation of its stock (or stock rights) are taxed as a dividend under the rules discussed at ¶ 733.

Distribution in Lieu of Money. If a corporate distribution is, at the election of any of the shareholders (whether exercised before or after the declaration), payable in either the distributing corporation's stock or other property, the distribution is treated as a taxable dividend (Reg. § 1.305-2).

Disproportionate Distribution. If a distribution (or series of distributions) results in the receipt of cash or other property by some shareholders, and in an increase in the proportionate interest of other shareholders in the corporation's assets or earnings and profits, then stock or stock rights distributed to a shareholder on the common stock of the corporation must be treated as a taxable distribution (Reg. § 1.305-3).

Convertible Preferred Stock. A shareholder receiving a distribution from a corporation of convertible preferred stock on common stock must pay tax on the value of the stock received, unless it is proven that the distribution will not result in a disproportionate distribution (Reg. § 1.305-6).

Footnote references are to paragraphs of the 2008 Standard Federal Tax Reports.

[107] ¶ 15,302, ¶ 15,305.024
[108] ¶ 15,302, ¶ 15,303, ¶ 15,305.028
[109] ¶ 15,550
[110] ¶ 15,550, ¶ 15,554.03
[111] ¶ 15,400, ¶ 15,401—¶ 15,401H, ¶ 15,402
[112] ¶ 15,401C

Distribution of Common and Preferred Stock. If, in a distribution or series of distributions, some common stockholders receive preferred stock while other common stockholders receive common stock, all of the stockholders involved in the distribution must pay a dividend tax on the stock they receive. An increase in the stockholders' proportionate interest in the corporation results (Reg. § 1.305-4).[113]

Transaction Increasing Shareholder's Proportionate Interest. Under Code Sec. 305(c), various transactions may be treated as a distribution with respect to any shareholder whose proportionate interest in the earnings and profits or assets of the corporation is increased by such transactions (Reg. § 1.305-7).[114] A taxable distribution may result in these cases.

Dividend on Preferred Stock. Any distribution of stock or stock rights made on preferred stock is taxed as a dividend, with one limited exception (Reg. § 1.305-5). An increase in the conversion ratio of convertible preferred stock made solely to take account of stock dividends or stock splits on the stock into which the convertible stock can be converted is tax free.

The basis of the stock, stock rights, or fractional shares acquired in a nontaxable distribution is an allocable portion of the basis of the stock on which the distribution was made. The basis is allocated in proportion to the fair market value of each on the date of the distribution (not the record date) (Reg. § 1.307-1).[115] An exception is provided in the case of the issuance of rights having a fair market value of less than 15% of the fair market value of the stock on which they are issued. The basis of such rights is zero unless the taxpayer elects to allocate a portion of the basis of the old stock in a timely filed return for the year in which the rights were received. An election, once made, is irrevocable (Reg. § 1.307-2).[116]

Extraordinary Dividends. Any corporation that receives an extraordinary dividend with respect to any share of stock that it has not held for more than two years before the dividend announcement date must reduce its basis in such stock (but not below zero) by the untaxed portion of the extraordinary dividend received. A dividend is extraordinary under the two-year rule if it equals or exceeds 10% (5% in the case of stock preferred as to dividends) of the shareholder's adjusted basis in the stock (Code Sec. 1059).[117]

Subscription Rights. Rights on common stock to subscribe to stock of another corporation may be taxable (Reg. § 1.1081-5).[118]

739. Disposition of Section 306 Stock. A special provision (Code Sec. 306) is designed to prevent a stockholder from receiving a nontaxable stock dividend (other than common on common) or from receiving a stock distribution (other than common stock) in connection with a reorganization and disposing of it to avoid reporting dividend income (Code Sec. 306).[119]

If Code Sec. 306 stock is redeemed by a corporation, the amount realized is treated as a distribution of property to which Code Sec. 301 applies and, therefore, will be treated as ordinary income or as a taxable distribution to the extent that it is made out of earnings and profits (see ¶ 733, ¶ 742, and ¶ 747). If the stock is disposed of otherwise than by a redemption, the amount realized is treated as ordinary income to the extent that the amount realized is not more than the amount that would have been realized as a dividend if, instead of the stock, the corporation had distributed cash in an amount equal to the fair market value of the stock. Therefore, it would be ordinary income up to the stockholder's share of the amount of earnings and profits of the corporation available for distribution.

A shareholder who received a preferred stock dividend on common stock and who donated the dividend to a tax-exempt charitable foundation realized no income on the stock transfer. In addition, the donor would not realize any income from the later sale of the Code Sec. 306 stock by the foundation.[120]

Footnote references are to paragraphs of the 2008 Standard Federal Tax Reports.

[113] ¶ 15,401H, ¶ 15,402
[114] ¶ 15,401G, ¶ 15,402
[115] ¶ 15,501
[116] ¶ 15,501B
[117] ¶ 30,020, ¶ 30,021
[118] ¶ 30,125, ¶ 30,182
[119] ¶ 15,450, ¶ 15,452
[120] ¶ 15,452.19

740. Special Rules and Exceptions for Code Sec. 306 Stock. The rules governing gain realized on Code Sec. 306 stock do not apply to a disposition:[121] (1) if it is not a redemption, is not made, directly or indirectly, to a related person under the constructive ownership rules, and terminates the entire stock interest of the shareholder in the corporation (including stock constructively owned); (2) if it is a complete redemption of all the stock held in the corporation by the shareholder or in redemption of stock held by a shareholder who is not a corporation and in partial liquidation of the distributing corporation; (3) if it is redeemed in a complete liquidation of the corporation; (4) to the extent that gain or loss is not recognized with respect to the disposition; or (5) if the IRS is satisfied that the distribution of the stock and the disposition or redemption (simultaneously or previously) of the stock on which the distribution was made were not in pursuance of a plan having as one of its principal purposes the avoidance of income tax. The sale of Code Sec. 306 stock to an employees' trust was held not to be part of a tax-avoidance plan.[122]

Distribution in Redemption

742. Redemption of Stock as a Dividend. If a corporation cancels or redeems its stock in such a manner as to make the distribution "equivalent" to a dividend distribution, the amount received by the shareholder, to the extent that it is paid out of earnings and profits, is a taxable dividend (Reg. § 1.302-1).[123]

Whether a distribution in connection with a cancellation or redemption of stock is equivalent to a taxable dividend depends on the facts in each case. A cancellation or redemption of a part of the stock, pro rata among all the shareholders, will generally be considered as resulting in a dividend distribution (Reg. § 1.302-2).[124] A redemption can be treated as an exchange of stock, rather than as a dividend, if one of the following four tests is met (Code Sec. 302(b)):[125] (1) the redemption is substantially disproportionate with respect to the shareholder; (2) the redemption terminates the shareholder's entire interest in the corporation; (3) the redemption is not substantially equivalent to a dividend; or (4) the redemption is of stock held by a noncorporate shareholder and is made in partial liquidation of the redeeming corporation. Amounts received by a shareholder in a distribution in complete liquidation of a corporation are not equivalent to the distribution of a taxable dividend (Code Sec. 331).[126]

A distribution is substantially disproportionate as to a shareholder if, after the redemption, the shareholder owns less than 50% of the combined voting power of all classes of voting stock and there is an exchange of stock but not of a dividend. Further, the ratio of the shareholder's holdings of voting stock after the redemption to all the voting stock must be less than 80% of the ratio of the voting stock the shareholder owned immediately before the redemption to the entire voting stock in the corporation. In addition, a distribution is not substantially disproportionate unless the stockholder's ownership of common stock (whether voting or nonvoting) after and before redemption also meets the 80% test (Reg. § 1.302-3).[127]

If a shareholder is entirely bought out, the transaction is treated as an exchange of the stock, and no part of the distribution is taxed as a dividend (Reg. § 1.302-4).[128]

A distribution that is in redemption of stock held by a noncorporate shareholder in partial liquidation of the distributing corporation is a distribution in exchange for the stock and is not taxed as a dividend (Code Sec. 302(b)(4)).[129]

Stock Redemption Expenses. A corporation is not allowed a deduction for any amount paid or incurred in connection with any redemption of its stock or the stock of any related person. This restriction does not apply to deductions for interest paid or accrued within the tax year on indebtedness, deductions for dividends paid in connection with the redemption of stock in a regulated investment company, or deductions for

---

Footnote references are to paragraphs of the 2008 Standard Federal Tax Reports.

[121] ¶ 15,450, ¶ 15,452.03
[122] ¶ 15,452.21
[123] ¶ 15,326, ¶ 15,330

[124] ¶ 15,327
[125] ¶ 15,325, ¶ 15,330.023
[126] ¶ 16,002, ¶ 16,004.01

[127] ¶ 15,328
[128] ¶ 15,329
[129] ¶ 15,325, ¶ 15,330.027

amounts properly allocable to indebtedness and amortized over the term of the debt (Code Sec. 162(k)).[130]

743. Constructive Ownership of Stock. Certain provisions relating to corporate distributions and adjustments (such as distributions in redemption of stock noted at ¶ 742) treat an individual as constructively owning stock held by a "related person." Under these constructive ownership rules an individual is treated as owning stock owned, directly or indirectly, by a spouse (if not legally separated under a decree of divorce or separate maintenance), children (including adopted children), grandchildren, and parents (Code Sec. 318(a)(1)).

Stock constructively owned by an individual under the family attribution rule is not treated as owned by that individual for the purpose of again applying the constructive stock ownership rule to make another the owner of such stock (Reg. § 1.318-4).[131]

Stock owned, directly or indirectly, by or for a partnership, S corporation, or estate is considered as being owned proportionately by the partners, S corporation shareholders, or beneficiaries. Stock owned, directly or indirectly, by or for a partner, S corporation shareholder, or beneficiary is treated as being owned by the partnership, S corporation, or estate.

Stock owned, directly or indirectly, by or for a trust is considered as being owned by its beneficiaries in proportion to their actuarial interests in the trust. Stock owned, directly or indirectly, by or for a beneficiary of a trust is considered as being owned by the trust. However, a contingent beneficial interest of not more than 5% of the value of the trust property is not to be taken into account (Code Sec. 318(a)(2) and (3); Reg. § 1.318-2).[132]

If 50% or more in value of the stock in a corporation is owned, directly or indirectly, by or for any person, that person is considered as owning the stock owned, directly or indirectly, by or for the corporation in the proportion that the value of the stock the person owns bears to the value of all the stock in the corporation. The corporation, on the other hand, is considered as owning the stock owned, directly or indirectly, by or for any person holding 50% or more in value of its stock, directly or indirectly (Code Sec. 318(a)(2)(C) and (a)(3)(C)).[133]

744. Redemption of Stock Through Use of Related Corporations. If stock of an issuing corporation is acquired by a corporation that is controlled by the issuing corporation, the amount paid for the stock will be a dividend by the issuing corporation, provided that, under the rules outlined at ¶ 742, this amount would be considered a taxable dividend. Also, when the stock of one corporation is sold to a related corporation ("brother-sister" corporations), the sale proceeds are considered as distributed in redemption of the stock of the corporation which bought it, governed by the rules at ¶ 742. If the sales are related, it is immaterial whether they are made simultaneously (Reg. § 1.304-2).[134] Whether the sales are related is determined upon the facts and circumstances surrounding all the sales. To the extent that a redemption involving related corporations is treated as a distribution under Code Sec. 301, the transferor and the acquiring corporation are treated as if the transferor had transferred the stock involved to the acquiring corporation in exchange for stock of the acquiring corporation, in a Code Sec. 351(a) nontaxable contribution of capital, and then the acquiring corporation had redeemed the stock it was deemed to have issued (Code Sec. 304(a)(1)).

745. Redemption of Stock to Pay Estate Taxes and Expenses. A distribution of property by a corporation in redemption of its stock that has been included in the gross estate of a decedent for estate tax purposes can qualify as an exchange to the extent that the amount of the distribution does not exceed the sum of the estate, generation-skipping transfer, inheritance, legacy, and succession taxes (including interest) on the estate, plus the funeral and administration expenses allowable as deductions from the gross estate for federal estate tax purposes (Code Sec. 303(a)).[135]

Footnote references are to paragraphs of the 2008 Standard Federal Tax Reports.

[130] ¶ 8500, ¶ 9052.01
[131] ¶ 15,905, ¶ 15,906.052
[132] ¶ 15,900, ¶ 15,902, ¶ 15,906.05
[133] ¶ 15,900, ¶ 15,906.046
[134] ¶ 15,377, ¶ 15,378.01
[135] ¶ 15,350, ¶ 15,353

To qualify for this treatment, the redemption must have been made not later than 90 days after the period of limitations on assessment of the federal estate tax (three years after the return is filed) (Code Sec. 302(b)(1)). When a petition for redetermination of an estate tax deficiency has been filed with the Tax Court, the redemption period is extended to any time before the expiration of 60 days after the decision of the Tax Court becomes final. A distribution made more than 60 days after the decision of the Tax Court becomes final can be timely, providing it is made within 90 days after expiration of the three-year period.[136]

In order for the redemption not to be treated as a taxable dividend, the value of the decedent's stock in a closely held company must exceed 35% of the gross estate, after the deductions for allowable funeral and administration expenses and losses (Code Sec. 302(b)(2)). The shares must be redeemed from a person whose interest in the estate is reduced by payment of estate, generation-skipping transfer, inheritance, and succession taxes or funeral and administration expenses. The value of these redeemed shares is limited to the sum of these deductible expenses.[137]

If stock in a corporation is the subject of a generation-skipping transfer occurring at the same time and as a result of the death of an individual, the tax imposed is treated as an estate tax for purposes of the redemption rules. The period of distribution is measured from the date of the generation-skipping transfer, and the relationship of stock to the decedent's estate is measured with reference solely to the amount of the generation-skipping transfer (Code Sec. 303(d)).[138]

Earnings and Profits

747. Sources of Distributions. To be subject to income tax as a dividend, a distribution received by a shareholder must be paid out of *earnings and profits* of the distributing corporation. A "dividend" is any distribution made by a corporation to its shareholders (1) out of its earnings and profits accumulated after February 28, 1913, or (2) out of the earnings and profits of the tax year (computed as of the close of the tax year without diminution by reason of any distributions made during the tax year), without regard to the amount of the earnings and profits at the time the distribution was made (Code Sec. 316; Reg. § 1.316-1).[139]

In order to determine the source of a distribution, consideration should be given: first, to the earnings and profits of the tax year; second, to the earnings and profits accumulated since February 28, 1913, but only in the case when, and to the extent that, the distributions made during the tax year are not regarded as out of the earnings and profits of that year; third, to the earnings and profits accumulated before March 1, 1913, only after all of the earnings and profits of the tax year and all the earnings and profits accumulated since February 28, 1913, have been distributed; and fourth, to sources other than earnings and profits only after the earnings and profits have been distributed (Reg. § 1.316-2).[140]

If the current year's earnings and profits are sufficient to cover all distributions made during the year, each distribution is a taxable dividend. However, if the year's cash distributions exceed current earnings and profits, a part of the earnings and profits must be allocated proportionately to each distribution, on the basis of the following formula: distribution × (current earnings and profits ÷ total distributions). The remaining portion of each distribution not covered by current earnings and profits is then treated as a taxable dividend to the extent of accumulated earnings and profits. If these are not sufficient to cover the remaining portion of any distribution, they are to be applied against each distribution in chronological order until exhausted.

748. How to Compute Earnings and Profits. In computing earnings and profits, all income that is exempt from tax must be included, as well as all items includible in gross income under Code Sec. 61 (Reg. § 1.312-6).[141] Thus, exempt income such as life insurance proceeds and fully tax-exempt interest on state or municipal obligations is

---

Footnote references are to paragraphs of the 2008 Standard Federal Tax Reports.

[136] ¶ 15,353.021
[137] ¶ 15,353.01

[138] ¶ 15,350
[139] ¶ 15,702, ¶ 15,703, ¶ 15,704.021

[140] ¶ 15,703B, ¶ 15,704.021
[141] ¶ 15,611

included. Similarly, cancellation of indebtedness income and intercorporate dividends are included. The starting point for the computation of earnings and profits is the corporation's taxable income, which is then adjusted to more accurately reflect true economic income available for distribution. This involves the different treatment of certain items from their treatment for tax purposes, including depreciation, depletion, certain reserves, and other items. In many cases, gain or loss from a sale or other disposition will be included in earnings and profits at the time and to the extent that it is recognized for tax purposes (Reg. § 1.312-6).[142] However, there are exceptions to this general rule, and the corporation's earnings and profits are very unlikely to be the same as the corporation's taxable income. As one example, income from installment sales is treated differently than earnings and profits (see ¶ 756). As another example, some items that are required to be capitalized for income tax purposes are deducted in the computation of earnings and profits (Rev. Rul. 60-123).

The general rule on the distribution of property (including cash) by a corporation is that the earnings and profits for future distributions are reduced by the amount of money distributed, the principal amount of any obligations of the corporation distributed, and the adjusted basis of any other property distributed (Reg. § 1.312-1).[143] If appreciated property is distributed with respect to stock, earnings and profits must be increased by the amount of the gain realized upon the distribution even if the gain is not recognized for purposes of computing taxable income. There are special rules for distributions to 20% corporate shareholders.

749. Effect of Deficit on Earnings and Profits. Even if there is an operating deficit at the beginning of the year, total dividends paid are taxable to the extent of profits for the *entire* year (Reg. § 1.316-1(e)).[144] See ¶ 747.

750. Effect of Loss on Earnings. A loss for a preceding year cannot be used to decrease the earnings and profits of the tax year (Reg. § 1.312-6(d)).[145]

751. Redemptions. A corporation that distributes amounts in redemption of its stock can reduce its post-February 28, 1913, accumulated earnings and profits only by the ratable share of those earnings and profits attributable to the redeemed stock (Code Sec. 312(n)(7)).[146]

752. Effect of Reorganization on Earnings. When a corporate reorganization results in no recognized gain or loss, the company's life as a continuing venture does not stop, so that what were earnings and profits of the original company remain, for purposes of distribution, earnings and profits of the continuing corporation.[147]

753. Effect of Nontaxable Distribution on Earnings. Nontaxable stock dividends or stock rights are not a distribution of earnings and profits. The same rule applies to distributions of the stock or securities (or rights to acquire stock or securities) of other corporations and distributions of property or money when they were nontaxable to the recipient when made (Code Sec. 312(d)).[148]

754. Distribution Other Than a Dividend. Any distribution that is a dividend is included in gross income. The portion of a distribution that is not a dividend reduces the basis of the stock. Any excess of distributions over the basis is treated as a gain from the sale or exchange of property (Code Sec. 301(c)).[149]

755. Effect of Depreciation on Earnings and Profits. Depreciation claimed on the corporation's income tax return that is in excess of the straight-line method increases the corporation's current earnings and profits (Code Sec. 312(k)).[150] For tangible property placed in service in tax years beginning after 1986, the alternative MACRS method is used to compute depreciation in order to determine the corporation's earnings and profits (see ¶ 1247). For depreciable assets first placed in service after 1980, but before 1987, the adjustment to earnings and profits for depreciation is determined

---

Footnote references are to paragraphs of the 2008 Standard Federal Tax Reports.

[142] ¶ 15,611
[143] ¶ 15,601, ¶ 15,612.031
[144] ¶ 15,703
[145] ¶ 15,611, ¶ 15,612.45
[146] ¶ 15,600, ¶ 15,612.0364
[147] ¶ 15,612.0327
[148] ¶ 15,600, ¶ 23,045.053
[149] ¶ 15,302, ¶ 15,305.021
[150] ¶ 15,600, ¶ 15,612.032, ¶ 15,612.05

under the straight-line ACRS, using extended recovery periods (see ¶ 1252).[151] For assets placed in service before 1981, the amount of the depreciation deduction for the purpose of computing earnings and profits is generally the amount allowable under the traditional straight-line method, although a corporation that uses the permissible nonaccelerated depreciation method (such as the machine-hour method) can use that method for earnings and profits purposes.

Also, in computing the earnings and profits of a corporation, any amount that can be deducted currently under Code Sec. 179, or Code Sec. 179A for property placed into service after December 31, 2001, or Code Sec. 179B for expenses paid or incurred after December 31, 2002, or Code Sec. 179C (as added by the Energy Tax Incentives Act of 2005 (P.L. 109-58)) for property placed in service after August 8, 2005, or Code Sec. 179D (as added by the Energy Tax Incentives Act of 2005 (P.L. 109-58)) for property placed into service after December 31, 2005, but before January 1, 2008, or Code Sec. 179E (as added by the Tax Relief and Health Care Act of 2006 (P.L. 109-432)) for 50% of the cost of advanced mine safety equipment placed in service after December 20, 2006, and before January 1, 2009,[152] can be deducted ratably over a period of five years (beginning with the year the amount is deductible under Code Sec. 179) (Code Sec. 312(k)(3)(B), as amended by the Energy Tax Incentives Act of 2005 (P.L. 109-58) and the Tax Relief and Health Care Act of 2006 (P.L. 109-432)).[153]

756. Effect of Installment Sales. A corporation that sells property on the installment basis is treated for earnings and profits purposes as if it had not used the installment method (Code Sec. 312(n)(5)).[154]

757. Effect of LIFO Reserve Changes. A corporation's earnings and profits generally must be increased or decreased by the amount of any change in the corporation's LIFO recapture amount at the end of each tax year (Code Sec. 312(n)(4)).[155] The term "LIFO recapture amount" means the amount (if any) by which the inventory amount of the inventory assets under the first-in, first-out (FIFO) method exceeds the inventory amount of the assets under the last-in, first-out (LIFO) method.

Business Income

759. Business Profit. The definition of gross income in Code Sec. 61[156] includes "gross income derived from business." As to a business, however, gross *income* is usually the same as gross *profit,* not gross *receipts.* Gross profit is the total receipts from sales minus the cost of the goods sold. In the case of most mercantile businesses, cost of goods sold includes the purchase price of the article sold plus delivery costs, warehousing, etc. In a manufacturing firm it includes the entire factory cost—materials, direct labor, and factory overhead, including depreciation attributable to manufacturing processes—applicable to goods manufactured and sold. Again, "cost of goods sold" should be distinguished from deductions allowed by law. Thus, salaries, rent, etc., are deductions and not "cost of goods sold."[157]

Damages for Lost Profit or Capital. Damage awards and amounts received in settlement of claims for business injury that represent compensation for lost profits are taxable as ordinary income. This rule applies to proceeds from business interruption insurance, liquidated damages, and awards for breach of contract. Damages for injury to goodwill are a nontaxable return of capital to the extent that the amounts received do not exceed the taxpayer's basis in goodwill. Similarly, injury to or loss of capital is treated as a nontaxable return of capital to the extent of basis; any excess is treated as a capital gain if received for damage to a capital asset.[158] Punitive damages, such as treble damages under antitrust laws, constitute taxable ordinary income (Reg. § 1.61-14(a)).[159]

See ¶ 852 for damages arising out of employment discrimination claims.

Footnote references are to paragraphs of the 2008 Standard Federal Tax Reports.

[151] ¶ 15,612.051
[152] ¶ 12,120, ¶ 12,130
[153] ¶ 15,600, ¶ 15,612.05
[154] ¶ 15,600, ¶ 15,612.036
[155] ¶ 15,600, ¶ 15,612.0358
[156] ¶ 5502
[157] ¶ 5511, ¶ 5600.01, ¶ 5600.03
[158] ¶ 5900.14, ¶ 5900.15, ¶ 5900.26
[159] ¶ 5815

760. Credits Included in Income. If the taxpayer claims a credit for gasoline and special fuels on Form 4136, Credit for Federal Tax Paid on Fuels (see ¶ 1379), the amount of the credit must be included in gross income to the extent that a business deduction for the products was taken.[160] A cash-basis taxpayer must claim the credit and include the amount in gross income in the same tax year. An accrual-basis taxpayer should include the credit in the gross income for the tax year in which the fuel was actually used.

A taxpayer who is eligible for the alcohol fuels credit (see ¶ 1326) must include the allowable credit in gross income for the tax year in which the credit is earned.[161] The total credit allowable is included even though the taxpayer cannot use the credit currently because of the credit limitation based on tax liability.

Rents and Royalties

762. Rents. Amounts received or accrued as rents in payment for the use of property must be included in gross income. As a general rule, the payment by a lessee of any expenses of a lessor is additional rental income of the lessor (Reg. § 1.61-8(c)).[162] Consideration received by the lessor for cancellation of a lease is in substitution for rental payments and, thus, not a return of capital. Any reduction in the value of property due to cancellation of a lease is a deductible loss only when fixed by a closed transaction.[163]

Expenses attributable to property held for the production of rents or royalties are deductible in computing adjusted gross income. See ¶ 1089.

763. Royalties. Royalties from copyrights on literary, musical, or artistic works and similar property or from a patent on an invention are includible in gross income (Code Sec. 61).[164] Royalties received from oil, gas, or other mineral properties are also includible in gross income.[165] For the treatment of timber, coal and iron ore royalties, see ¶ 1772. For the depletion allowance for royalties, see ¶ 1289.

Forms. Royalties are generally reported on Part I of Schedule E of Form 1040. However, Schedule C or Schedule C-EZ (Form 1040) is used to report royalties received by the holder of an operating oil, gas, or mineral interest and self-employed writers, inventors, artists, etc.

764. Improvements by Lessee. Ordinarily, no income is derived by a lessor by reason of acquisition, upon termination of a lease, of improvements made by the lessee (Reg. § 1.109-1).[166] This exclusion applies to improvements that revert to the lessor upon expiration of a lease as well as to those acquired by the lessor upon forfeiture of a lease prior to the end of the full term. But when improvements are made in lieu of rent, the lessor has gross income to the extent of the fair market value of the improvements in the year they were made.[167]

Construction Allowances. A retail tenant that receives cash or rent reductions from the retail lessor with respect to a lease of 15 years or less entered into after August 5, 1997, does not include that amount in gross income if the amounts are used for qualified construction or improvement to the retail space. The lessor must depreciate the improvement as MACRS nonresidential real property. If the improvement is disposed of or abandoned at the termination of the lease, the lessor claims a gain or loss by reference to the remaining adjusted basis of the improvement (Code Sec. 110).

765. Lessor's Obligations Paid by Lessee. Property taxes paid by a tenant on behalf of a landlord are additional rent.[168] When the taxes paid are income to the lessor, they may be treated as if paid by the lessor in determining their deductibility. If a lessee agrees to pay, in lieu of rental, a dividend on the lessor's stock, or interest on its mortgages, the payments will result in rental income to the lessor.[169]

Footnote references are to paragraphs of the 2008 Standard Federal Tax Reports.

[160] ¶ 4150, ¶ 4151, ¶ 5602.35
[161] ¶ 6431.01
[162] ¶ 5705, ¶ 5706.021
[163] ¶ 5706.031
[164] ¶ 5502
[165] ¶ 5502, ¶ 5706.04
[166] ¶ 7021, ¶ 7022.01
[167] ¶ 7020, ¶ 7022.01
[168] ¶ 5706.021
[169] ¶ 5706.021

Farming Income

767. Farming As a Business. Income from farming is treated in the same way as income from any other business. Every individual, partnership or corporation which cultivates, operates, or manages a farm for gain or profit, either as owner or tenant, is designated as a farmer. A person who cultivates or operates a farm for recreation or pleasure, and who experiences a continual net loss from year to year, generally lacks a profit motive and may not deduct the losses. See ¶ 1195.

In addition to filing Form 1040, an individual engaged in farming must file a Schedule F (Form 1040), Farm Income and Expenses. Partnerships engaged in farming must file Form 1065, and corporations engaged in farming must file the appropriate Form 1120. The general rules for all cash-basis taxpayers also apply to a farmer on the cash basis. See ¶ 1515. A farmer must also file Schedule SE (Form 1040) for computing earnings from self-employment. See ¶ 2676.

Cash Basis. A farmer on the cash basis does not use inventories and must include in gross income all cash or the value of merchandise or other property received from the sale of livestock and produce that have been raised, profits from the sale of livestock or other items that have been bought, and gross income received from all other sources.[170] A cash-basis farmer may defer recognition of gain from the sale of a crop delivered in one year until the following year if a valid contract with the purchaser or the purchaser's agent prohibits payment until the following year, but not if the payment is deferred merely at the seller's request.[171]

Profit from the sale of livestock or other items bought by a farmer is computed by deducting the cost from the sales price. For the sale of animals that originally were bought as draft or work animals, or for breeding or dairy purposes and not for resale, the profit is the difference between the sale price and the depreciated basis of the animal sold.

A cash-basis farmer who receives insurance proceeds as a result of destruction or damage to crops may elect to include the proceeds in income in the year after the year of damage if the farmer can show that the income from the crops would normally have been reported in the following year. This includes payments received under the Agricultural Act of 1949, Title II of the Disaster Assistance Act or Title I of the Disaster Assistance Act of 1989 as a result of damage to crops caused by drought, flood, or other natural disaster, or the inability to plant crops because of such a natural disaster (Code Sec. 451(d); Reg. § 1.451-6; Rev. Rul. 91-55).[172]

A cash-method farmer who is forced to sell livestock due to drought, flood, or other weather-related conditions in an area designated as eligible for assistance by the federal government may elect to be taxed on the forced sale income (gain that normally would not have been realized in the year of the forced sale) in the following year if the farmer can show that the income from the sale of livestock would normally have been reported in such following year (Code Sec. 451(e)).[173]

Accrual Method. A farmer on the accrual method must use inventories taken at the start and the end of the tax year (Reg. § 1.61-4(b)).[174]

Although most farmers may use the cash method, the accrual method of accounting is required for certain farming corporations and partnerships and for all farming tax shelters (including farming syndicates) (Code Sec. 447).[175] See ¶ 2028 and ¶ 2032.

Gross profit of a farmer on the accrual basis is calculated by (1) adding the inventory value of livestock and products on hand at the end of the year with the amount received from the sale of livestock and products during the year (including miscellaneous receipts such as for the hire of machinery) and (2) deducting from that total the sum of the inventory value of livestock and products on hand at the beginning of the year and the cost of livestock and products bought during the year (Reg. § 1.61-4(b)).

Footnote references are to paragraphs of the 2008 Standard Federal Tax Reports.

[170] ¶ 5601, ¶ 5602.041
[171] ¶ 21,009.453

[172] ¶ 21,002, ¶ 21,018, ¶ 21,021.28
[173] ¶ 21,002, ¶ 21,021.01

[174] ¶ 5601, ¶ 5602.042
[175] ¶ 20,700

Livestock raised or bought for sale must be inventoried. See ¶ 1569. Livestock bought for draft, breeding or dairy purposes and not for sale may be inventoried or, instead, be treated as capital assets subject to depreciation, if the method used is consistently followed from year to year. If inventoried livestock is sold, its cost must not be taken as an additional deduction in the return of income since the cost is reflected in the inventory.

Aside from ordinary methods, two other inventory methods are available to the farmer—the "farm-price" method or the "unit-livestock-price" method (see ¶ 1569).

Income Averaging. An individual engaged in a farming business or fishing business may elect to average farm income over three years (Code Sec. 1301).[176] The tax imposed in any tax year will equal the sum of the tax computed on taxable income reduced by the amount of farm income elected for averaging plus the increase in tax that would result if taxable income for each of the three prior tax years were increased by an amount equal to one-third of the elected farm income. Schedule J of Form 1040 is to be used to report the income averaging.

For income from the sale of farm property other than inventory, see Chapter 17. For "tax shelter" farming operations, see ¶ 2032.

For expenses of a farmer, see ¶ 982–¶ 985. For the application of the uniform capitalization rules, see ¶ 999.

768. Patronage Dividend. A cooperative and its patrons are taxed in such a way that the business earnings of the cooperative are taxable currently either to the cooperative or to the patrons. See ¶ 698.

769. Commodity Credit Corporation Loan. Normally, income from the sale of a crop is reported in the year of the sale. However, if the farmer has pledged all or part of the crop production to secure a Commodity Credit Corporation (CCC) loan, the farmer may elect to report the loan proceeds as income in the year received rather than reporting the income in the year of the sale. IRS permission is not required to begin reporting CCC loans in this manner, but once a loan has been reported in income in the year received, all succeeding loans must be reported in the same way unless the IRS grants permission to change the method of reporting. The election is made on Schedule F. The amount reported as income becomes the farmer's basis in the commodity and is used to determine gain or loss upon the ultimate disposition of the commodity (Code Sec. 77; Reg. §§ 1.77-1 and 1.77-2).[177] The IRS has adopted procedures for automatic approval in changing accounting methods for reporting CCC loans as loans rather than income (Rev. Proc. 2002-9).[178]

Alimony Payments

771. Classification. Alimony and separate maintenance payments are income to the recipient and are deductible by the payor if certain requirements are met (Code Secs. 62(a)(10), 71 and 215).[179]

Alimony payments are taken as a deduction from gross income in arriving at adjusted gross income and thus may be claimed by taxpayers who do not itemize.

772. Divorce and Separation Instruments. Payments made under a divorce or separation instrument are includible in the gross income of the recipient and deductible by the payor if the following requirements are met: (1) the payment is in cash or its equivalent, (2) the payment is received by or on behalf of a spouse under a divorce or separation instrument, (3) the instrument does not designate the payment as not includible in gross income and not allowable as a deduction under Code Sec. 215, (4) spouses who are legally separated under a decree of divorce or separate maintenance cannot be members of the same household at the time the payment is made, (5) there is no liability to make any payment for any period after the death of the payee spouse or to

---

Footnote references are to paragraphs of the 2008 Standard Federal Tax Reports.

[176] ¶ 31,787
[177] ¶ 6300, ¶ 6301, ¶ 6302, ¶ 6304
[178] ¶ 20,620.285
[179] ¶ 6002, ¶ 6090, ¶ 6094, ¶ 12,570

make any payment (either in cash or property) as a substitute for such payments after the death of the payee spouse, and (6) the spouses must not file joint returns with each other (Code Sec. 71(a), (b) and (e)).[180]

A divorce or separation instrument is defined as (1) a divorce or separate maintenance decree or a written instrument incident to such a decree, (2) a written separation agreement, or (3) a decree that is not a divorce decree or separate maintenance decree but that requires a spouse to make payments for the support or maintenance of the other spouse (Code Sec. 71(b)(2)).[181]

773. Year of Taxability or Deductibility. Alimony payments are generally includible in income in the year received (Code Sec. 71(a); Reg. § 1.71-1)[182] and are deductible in the year paid (Code Sec. 215; Reg. § 1.215-1),[183] regardless of whether the taxpayer employs the cash or the accrual method of accounting. A recapture rule prevents "front-loading" of alimony payments; see ¶ 774.

774. Three-Year Recapture of Excess Alimony Payments. A special recapture rule applies to "excess" alimony payments (Code Sec. 71(f)).[184] Its purpose is to prevent property settlement payments from qualifying for alimony treatment. The rule requires the recapture of excess amounts that have been treated as alimony either during the calendar year in which payments began (the "first post-separation year") or in the next succeeding calendar year (the "second post-separation year"). Excess alimony is recaptured in the payor spouse's tax year beginning in the second calendar year following the calendar year in which payments began (the "third post-separation year") by requiring the payor to include the excess in income. The payee, who previously included the payments in income as alimony, is entitled to deduct the amount recaptured from gross income in his or her tax year beginning in the third post-separation year.

Excess alimony, the amount that must be recaptured in the third post-separation year, is the sum of the excess payments made in the first post-separation year plus the excess payments made in the second post-separation year.

The amount of excess payments in the first and second post-separation years is determined under a statutory formula. For the first recapture year, the excess payment amount is the excess (if any) of the total alimony paid in the first post-separation year over the sum of $15,000 and the average of the amount of alimony paid in the second post-separation year (minus excess payments for that year) and the amount of alimony paid in the third post-separation year. Thus, for the first post-separation year, the following formula would be used:

$$
\text{excess payments} = \text{alimony paid in 1st year} - \left(\$15,000 + \frac{\left[\left(\begin{array}{c} \text{alimony paid in 2nd year} \end{array} - \begin{array}{c} \text{excess payments in 2nd year} \end{array} \right) + \begin{array}{c} \text{alimony paid in 3rd year} \end{array} \right]}{2} \right)
$$

To determine the excess payments in the first year it is necessary to determine the excess payments in the second year. The amount of excess payments in the second year is the excess (if any) of the amount of alimony paid during the second year over the sum of the amount of alimony paid in the third year plus $15,000.

$$
\text{excess payments} = \text{alimony paid in 2nd year} - \left(\text{alimony paid in 3rd year} + \$15,000 \right)
$$

Once the excess payments for both the first and second post-separation years have been determined, the results are added together to determine the amount that must be recaptured in the third post-separation year.

Footnote references are to paragraphs of the 2008 Standard Federal Tax Reports.

[180] ¶ 6090, ¶ 6094
[181] ¶ 6090, ¶ 6094.023

[182] ¶ 6090, ¶ 6091
[183] ¶ 12,570, ¶ 12,571

[184] ¶ 6090, ¶ 6094.03

Example 1: In 2007, Mr. Black makes payments totalling $50,000 to his ex-wife. He makes no payments in either 2008 or 2009. Assuming none of the exceptions set forth below apply, $35,000 will be recaptured in 2009. Mr. Black will have to report an additional $35,000 in income, while his ex-wife will be entitled to a $35,000 reduction in income.

Example 2: In 2007, Ms. Gold makes payments totalling $50,000 to her ex-husband. In 2008, she makes $20,000 in payments, but in 2009 she makes no payments. Assuming that none of the exceptions apply, the total amount that must be recaptured in the third year is $32,500. This represents $5,000 from the second year ($20,000 minus $15,000) and $27,500 from the first year. The amount recaptured from the first year equals the excess of $50,000 (the payments made) over the sum of $15,000 plus $7,500. The $7,500 is the average of the payments for years two and three after reducing the payments by the $5,000 recaptured for year two ($15,000 ($20,000 payment in year two plus $0 payment in year three minus the $5,000 that was required to be recaptured) divided by two equals $7,500).

IRS Publication 504, Divorced or Separated Individuals, contains a worksheet for computing alimony recapture.

Exceptions to Recapture Rule. The recapture of excess payments is not required if the alimony payments terminate because either party dies or the payee-spouse remarries before the end of the third post-separation year. The rules also do not apply to temporary support payments received under an instrument described in Code Sec. 71(b)(2)(C). In addition, they do not apply where the payments fluctuate because of a continuing liability to pay—for at least three years—a fixed portion of income from the earnings of a business or property or from compensation from employment or self-employment (Code Sec. 71(f)(5)(C)).[185]

775. Indirect Alimony Payments. Unlike the rules for pre-1985 instruments, only one type of trust, the Code Sec. 682 trust, is contemplated in connection with divorce or separate maintenance under instruments executed (or modified) after 1984. When a beneficial interest in a trust is transferred or created incident to a divorce or separation, the beneficiary-spouse is entitled to the same treatment as the beneficiary of a regular trust, notwithstanding that the payments by the trust qualify as alimony or otherwise discharge a support obligation (Code Sec. 682).[186]

776. Child Support. Payments made under post-1984 instruments that fix an amount or a portion of the payment as child support qualify as child support for tax purposes and are not deductible by the payor or taxable to the payee (Code Sec. 71(c)).[187] If any amount specified in the instrument is to be reduced based on a contingency set out in the instrument relating to a child—such as attaining a specified age, dying, leaving school, or marrying—the amount of the specified reduction is treated as child support from the outset. The same rule applies if the reduction called for by the instrument is to occur at a time that can clearly be associated with such contingency. Thus, payments that vary with the status of a child are not deductible.

Example: A post-1984 divorce instrument provides that alimony payments will be reduced by $500 per month when a child reaches age 18. Under these circumstances, $500 of each payment is treated as child support.

778. Property Transfers Between Spouses or Former Spouses Incident to Divorce. No gain or loss is recognized to the transferor on a transfer of property (outright or in trust) between spouses or between former spouses incident to divorce (Code Sec. 1041(a)),[188] nor is the value of the property included in the gross income of the transferee (Code Sec. 1041(b)(1)).[189] The transferee's basis is equal to the transferor's basis immediately before the transfer (Code Sec. 1041(b)(2)).[190] A transfer between former spouses is incident to divorce if it occurs within one year after the marriage ceases or is related to the cessation of the marriage (Code Sec. 1041(c)).[191]

Footnote references are to paragraphs of the 2008 Standard Federal Tax Reports.

[185] ¶ 6090
[186] ¶ 24,860, ¶ 24,864
[187] ¶ 6094.027

[188] ¶ 29,802.01
[189] ¶ 29,802.01
[190] ¶ 29,802.01

[191] ¶ 29,802.031

¶775

Nonrecognition is not available to the transferor if the transferee is a nonresident alien (Code Sec. 1041(d))[192] or if there is a transfer in trust to the extent that liabilities assumed by the transferee (including liabilities to which the property is subject) exceed the transferor's adjusted basis in the property (Code Sec. 1041(e)).[193] The transferee's basis is increased for any such gain recognized by the transferor.

Prizes and Awards

785. Taxation of Prizes and Awards. Prizes and awards, other than certain types of fellowship grants and scholarships (see ¶ 879) and limited employee achievement awards, are includible in gross income (Code Sec. 74(a)). Awards for religious, charitable, scientific, educational, artistic, literary, or civic achievement are excluded from the recipient's income only if the award is transferred unused by the payor to a governmental unit or a tax-exempt charitable, religious, or educational organization designated by the recipient. In addition, the recipient must be selected without any action on his or her part to enter the contest or proceeding and cannot be required to render substantial future services as a condition to receiving the prize or award (Code Sec. 74).[194] Thus, Nobel and Pulitzer prize recipients may not exclude from income the value of their awards unless these conditions are met.

Employee achievement awards (items of tangible personal property) are excludable from gross income only to the extent that the cost of the award is deductible by the employer. The awards cannot represent disguised compensation, and the excludable amount can total no more than $400 for nonqualified awards or $1,600 for qualified awards (Code Sec. 74(c) and Code Sec. 274(j)(2)).[195] See ¶ 919.

Gambling Income

787. Gambling and Other Gains. Gain arising from gambling, betting and lotteries is includible in gross income. A gain from an illegal transaction, such as bootlegging, extortion, embezzlement or fraud, is also includible.[196]

788. Gambling Losses. Wagering losses are deductible only to the extent of the taxpayer's gains from similar transactions (Code Sec. 165(d); Reg. § 1.165-10).[197] Non-business gambling losses are deductible only as deductions itemized on Schedule A of Form 1040. If gambling is conducted as a business, the losses are deductible as business losses, but only to the extent of gains.[198]

Shareholder's or Employee's Bargain Purchase

789. Bargain Purchase. If a corporation transfers property to a shareholder, or an employer transfers property to an employee, at less than its fair market value, whether or not the transfer is in the form of a sale or exchange, the difference may be income to the purchaser—as dividends in the case of the shareholder and as compensation for personal services in the case of the employee (Reg. § 1.61-2).[199] However, qualified employee discounts are excluded from income (see ¶ 863).

In the case of a purchase at less than fair market value by a stockholder, the shareholder is treated as having received a distribution from the transferor-corporation and is subject to the general tax rules for including it in income (Reg. § 1.301-1).[200] If there is a later sale of the property, the gain or loss is measured by starting with a basis that is the amount paid for the property, increased by the amount previously included in income.

For treatment of securities transactions as potential income, see ¶ 1901 and following.

Footnote references are to paragraphs of the 2008 Standard Federal Tax Reports.

[192] ¶ 29,802.01
[193] ¶ 29,802.021
[194] ¶ 6200, ¶ 6204
[195] ¶ 14,402
[196] ¶ 5815, ¶ 5901.01, ¶ 5901.021
[197] ¶ 9802, ¶ 10,104
[198] ¶ 10,105.01
[199] ¶ 5506, ¶ 15,704.4803
[200] ¶ 15,303

¶789

Discharge of Debt

791. Debt Canceled. Income from the discharge of indebtedness is includible in gross income unless it is excludable under Code Sec. 108 (or some other applicable legislative provision). Four types of exclusions are provided in the following priority order:[201] (1) a debt discharge in a bankruptcy action under Title 11 of the U.S. Code in which the taxpayer is under the jurisdiction of the court and the discharge is either granted by or is under a plan approved by the court; (2) a discharge when the taxpayer is insolvent outside bankruptcy; (3) a discharge of qualified farm indebtedness; and (4) a discharge of qualified real property business indebtedness. Form 982, Reduction of Tax Attributes Due to Discharge of Indebtedness (and Section 1082 Basis Adjustment), is filed with a debtor's income tax return to report excluded income from the discharge of indebtedness.

The term "insolvent" refers to an excess of liabilities over the fair market value of assets immediately prior to discharge. This exclusion is limited to the amount by which the taxpayer is insolvent. The taxpayer's insolvent amount includes the amount by which a nonrecourse debt exceeds the fair market value of the property securing the debt, but only to the extent that the excess nonrecourse debt is discharged.[202]

When an amount is excluded from gross income as the result of a discharge of indebtedness in a Title 11 case, a discharge of indebtedness during insolvency, or a discharge of qualified farm indebtedness, a taxpayer is required to reduce its tax attributes. The reduction in the foreign tax credit, minimum tax credit, passive activity credit, and general business credit carryovers is to be made at a rate of 33⅓ cents per dollar of excluded income (Code Sec. 108(b)(3)(B)).[203]

A corporation that satisfies a debt by transferring corporate stock to its creditor, or a partnership that transfers a capital or profits interest in the partnership to a creditor, is treated as if it has paid the creditor with money equal to the fair market value of the stock or interest. The corporation or partnership will thus have income from discharge of indebtedness to the extent that the principal of the debt exceeds the value of the stock or partnership interest (and any other property transferred) (Code Sec. 108(e)(8)).[204] A similar rule applies to debtors (corporate or noncorporate) issuing debt instruments in satisfaction of indebtedness (Code Sec. 108(e)(10)).

Nonrecourse Debt. Discharge of indebtedness can result even if the canceled debt is nonrecourse (i.e., no person is personally liable for repayment of the debt). Thus, where property securing a nonrecourse debt is transferred in exchange for cancellation of the debt (such as a foreclosure sale), the amount realized from the sale or exchange includes the principal amount of the debt discharged.[205] The IRS has ruled that the "writedown" of the principal amount of a nonrecourse note by a holder who was not the seller of the property results in the realization of discharge of indebtedness income, even if there is no disposition of the property (Rev. Rul. 91-31).[206]

Farmers. Income arising from the discharge of qualified farm indebtedness owed to an unrelated lender, including a federal, state, or local government or agency, or instrumentality of such an agency, may be excluded from a taxpayer's income if certain requirements are met. The debt must be incurred directly in connection with the operation by the taxpayer of the trade or business of farming. Also, at least 50% of the taxpayer's aggregate gross receipts for the three tax years preceding the tax year in which the discharge of indebtedness occurs must be attributable to the trade or business of farming. The discharge of indebtedness income is excluded only to the extent absorbed by tax attributes (credits are reduced at a rate of 33⅓ cents per dollar of excluded income) and the adjusted bases of qualified property (any property held or used in a trade or business or for the production of income) (Code Sec. 108(g)). Basis reduction occurs first with respect to depreciable property, then with respect to land

---

Footnote references are to paragraphs of the 2008 Standard Federal Tax Reports.

[201] ¶ 7002, ¶ 7010.021   [203] ¶ 7002, ¶ 7010.03   [205] ¶ 5802.34
[202] ¶ 7010.38   [204] ¶ 7002, ¶ 7010.051   [206] ¶ 5802.34

¶791

used in the business of farming, and finally with respect to other qualified property (Code Sec. 1017(b)(4)).[207]

Qualified Real Property Business Indebtedness. A taxpayer other than a C corporation may elect to exclude from gross income amounts realized from the discharge of debt incurred or assumed in connection with real property used in a trade or business and secured by that property (Code Sec. 108(a)(1)(D) and (c)).[208] If the debt is incurred or assumed after 1992, it must be incurred or assumed to acquire, construct, reconstruct, or substantially improve the real property. The excludable amount is limited to the excess of the outstanding principal amount of the debt over the fair market value of the business real property (reduced by the outstanding principal amount of any other qualified business indebtedness secured by the property). Also, the exclusion may not exceed the aggregate adjusted bases of depreciable real property held by the taxpayer immediately before discharge. The excluded amount reduces the basis of depreciable real property.

The election to treat debt as qualified real property business indebtedness must be filed with the taxpayer's timely income tax return (including extensions) for the tax year in which the discharge occurs (Reg. § 1.108-5(b)). The election, which is revocable with the consent of the IRS Commissioner, is made on Form 982. A taxpayer who fails to make a timely election must request consent to file a late election under Reg. § 301.9100-3.

Student Loans. A special income exclusion applies to the discharge of all or part of a student loan if, pursuant to the loan agreement, the discharge is made because the individual works for a specified period of time in certain professions for any of a broad class of employers (e.g., as a doctor or nurse in a rural area) (Code Sec. 108(f)).[209] The loan must be made by (1) a federal, state, or local government (or instrumentality, agency, or subdivision of that government); (2) a tax-exempt public benefit corporation that has assumed control of a public hospital with public employees; or (3) an educational institution if (a) it received funds to loan from an entity described in (1) or (2), above, or (b) the student serves, pursuant to a program of the institution, in an occupation or area with unmet needs under the direction of a governmental unit or a tax-exempt section 501(c)(3) organization (e.g., charitable, religious, educational, scientific organization). Loans refinanced through such a program by the institution (or certain tax-exempt organizations) also qualify for the exclusion.

793. Creditor's Financial Income. An accrual-basis creditor reports interest on loans or obligations as the interest is earned (over the term of the loan, as installment payments are due, etc.) or when it is received if payment is received earlier than when due. A cash-basis creditor reports such interest as it is received.

Rule of 78's. The IRS will not give any tax effect to a provision in a loan agreement that interest shall be allocated in accordance with the Rule of 78's because that method of allocating interest does not accurately reflect the true cost of borrowing.[210] A limited exception permits the Rule of 78's method for purposes of determining a lender's interest income where (1) the loan is a consumer loan, (2) the terms of the loan require the use of the Rule of 78's for allocating interest to the different periods over the term of the loan, and (3) the loan is self-amortizing, requires level payments at regular intervals at least annually over a period of no more than five years, and has no balloon payment at the end of the loan term.[211]

Loan Commission. A loan commission is taxed to an accrual-basis lender in the year the loan is made. A commission deducted from the face amount of the loan is taxed to a cash-basis lender only when received upon payment of the loan or sale of the obligation.[212]

"Points." When "points" (an adjustment of the stated interest rate earned at the commencement of the loan) are paid by the borrower out of funds not originating with

---

Footnote references are to paragraphs of the 2008 Standard Federal Tax Reports.

[207] ¶ 7002, ¶ 7010.04
[208] ¶ 7002, ¶ 7010.045
[209] ¶ 7002, ¶ 7010.049
[210] ¶ 9104.0442
[211] ¶ 9104.0442
[212] ¶ 20,620.03

the lender, they are taxed to a cash-basis lender in the year received and to an accrual-basis creditor when the right to receive arises, or when received, if earlier.[213]

Below-Market Interest Loans

795. Imputed Interest on Below-Market Interest Loans. Under Code Sec. 7872,[214] loans that carry little or no interest are generally recharacterized as arm's-length transactions in which the lender is treated as having made a loan to the borrower bearing the statutory federal rate of interest. Concurrently, there is deemed to be a transfer in the form of gift, dividend, contribution to capital, compensation, or other manner of payment (depending upon the nature of the loan) from the lender to the borrower which, in turn, is retransferred by the borrower to the lender to satisfy the accruing interest (Code Sec. 7872(a)(1)). This rule applies to (1) gift loans, (2) corporation-shareholder loans, (3) compensation loans between employer and employee or between independent contractor and client, (4) tax-avoidance loans, (5) any below-market interest loans in which the interest arrangement has a significant effect on either the lender's or borrower's tax liability, and (6) loans to any qualified continuing care facility not exempt under Code Sec. 7872(g).

In the case of a demand loan or a gift loan, the imputed interest amount is deemed to be transferred from the lender to the borrower on the last day of the calendar year of the loan. As for a term loan (other than a gift loan), there is an imputed transfer from the lender to the borrower, in an amount equal to the excess of the amount loaned over the present value of all payments required under the loan, which is deemed to have taken place on the date the loan was made.

Exceptions. A *de minimis* exception applies to gift loans totalling $10,000 or less between individuals if the loan is not directly attributable to the purchase or carrying of income-producing assets (Code Sec. 7872(c)(2)). There is also a $10,000 *de minimis* exception for compensation-related or corporation-shareholder loans that do not have tax avoidance as a principal purpose (Code Sec. 7872(c)(1)). Further, in the case of gift loans between individuals where the total amount outstanding does not exceed $100,000, the amount deemed transferred from the borrower to the lender at the end of the year will be imputed to the lender only to the extent of the borrower's annual net investment income (Code Sec. 7872(d)). If such income is less than $1,000, no imputed interest is deemed transferred to the lender.

The rule does not apply to below-market loans owed by a facility which, on the last day of the year in which the loan is made, is a qualified continuing care facility, if the loan was made pursuant to a continuing care contract, and if the lender (or the lender's spouse) reaches the age of 62 before the close of the tax year. This exception originally applied through 2010, but has since been made permanent (Code Sec. 7872(h), as added by the Tax Increase Prevention and Reconciliation Act of 2005 (P.L. 109-222) and amended by the Tax Relief and Health Care Act of 2006 (P.L. 109-432)).

Rules exempt certain below-market interest loans by individuals to continuing care facilities made pursuant to a continuing care contract (Code Sec. 7872(g)).[215] Also, in the case of an employer loan to an employee made in connection with the purchase of a principal residence at a new place of work, the applicable statutory federal rate for testing the loan is the rate as of the date the written contract to purchase the residence was entered into (Code Sec. 7872(f)(11)).[216]

Bartered Services

797. Value of Bartered Services. The value of bartered services must be included in gross income, usually on Schedule C or C-EZ of Form 1040. For example, if the owner of an apartment building permitted an artist to use an apartment in exchange for works of art, the building owner's income included the value of the art, and the artist's income included the fair rental value of the apartment.[217]

Footnote references are to paragraphs of the 2008 Standard Federal Tax Reports.

[213] ¶ 20,620.0314
[214] ¶ 43,956, ¶ 43,960
[215] ¶ 43,956, ¶ 43,960.04
[216] ¶ 43,956, ¶ 43,960.038
[217] ¶ 5508.028, ¶ 5508.15

If two individuals are members of a barter club and each agrees to exchange services, the value of the services received by each must be included in gross income. Barter clubs must report exchanges on Form 1099-B in accordance with the rules under Code Sec. 6045.[218] Trade or credit units used by a barter club to account for transactions are also includible in gross income when credited to the taxpayer's account.[219]

Recoveries

799. Tax Treatment of Recoveries. The receipt of an amount that was part of an earlier deduction or credit is considered a recovery and generally must be included, partially or totally, in income in the year of receipt (Code Sec. 111).[220] Common types of recoveries are refunds, reimbursements or rebates. Interest on amounts recovered is income in the year of the recovery.

When the refund or other recovery is for amounts that were paid in separate years, the recovery must be allocated between these years.

> **Example 1:** Marcia VanNauker paid her 2007 estimated state income tax liability of $4,000 in four equal installments in April, June, and September of 2007 and in January of 2008. In May of 2008, she received a $400 refund based on her 2007 state income tax return. Because the tax liability was paid in two years, the amount recovered must be allocated pro rata between the years in which the liability was paid. Since 75% of the liability was paid in 2007, 75% of the $400 refund (or $300) is for amounts paid in 2007 and is a recovery item in 2008 when received. The remaining $100 is offset against the otherwise deductible state tax payments made in 2008. (Refunds of federal income taxes are not included in income because the taxes are not allowed as a deduction from income.)

Itemized Deduction Recoveries. Recoveries of amounts claimed only as itemized deductions are not includible if the taxpayer did not itemize in the year for which the recovery was received. If a deduction is taken, the includible amount is limited to the amount of the deduction. Thus, the amount included is the lesser of the amount deducted or the amount recovered.

> **Example 2:** Brent Martin receives a $1,500 medical expense reimbursement in 2007 for expenses incurred in 2006. However, due to the threshold on medical expenses, he was able to claim only a $450 deduction in 2006. The amount that he must include in income in 2007 is $450.

For situations in which a high-income individual's itemized deductions are reduced by the smaller of three percent of AGI in excess of the threshold phaseout amount (in 2007, $156,400 ($78,200 for married filing separately); in 2008, $159,950 ($79,975 for married filing separately)) or 80 percent of allowable deductions (see ¶ 1014), and, later, all or a portion of the previously deducted amount is recovered, the amount includible in income in the year of receipt is the difference between (1) the amount of the prior year's itemized deductions (after reduction) and (2) the deductions that would have been claimed (the greater of (a) itemized deductions (after reduction) or (b) the standard deduction) had the individual paid the proper amount in the prior year and not received a recovery or refund in a subsequent year (Rev. Rul. 93-75).

> **Example 3:** In 2007, Brian Cummings, a single individual, claimed $9,000 in itemized deductions that were reduced from $12,000 (a $3,000 reduction) because of the 3 percent itemized deduction phaseout. If $2,000 of state income tax is refunded in 2008, his itemized deductions for 2007, prior to reduction, would have been $10,000 ($12,000 minus $2,000). His itemized deductions after reduction would have been limited to $7,000 (a $3,000 reduction) as a result of the 3 percent phaseout. He derives a tax benefit to the extent of the difference between his total allowable itemized deductions for 2007 ($9,000) and the total itemized deductions he would have claimed had he paid the exact amount of his state tax liability ($7,000). Thus, the $2,000 refund is includible in his gross income in 2008.

Footnote references are to paragraphs of the 2008 Standard Federal Tax Reports.

[218] ¶ 35,920, ¶ 35,930.022   [219] ¶ 5508.028, ¶ 5508.15   [220] ¶ 7060, ¶ 7061, ¶ 7062.01

The total amount of all recoveries in a tax year must be included in the taxpayer's income if they are equal to, or less than, the amount by which the taxpayer's itemized deductions exceeded the standard deduction for his or her filing status in the prior year, and the taxpayer had any taxable income in the prior year. Recoveries of state or local income taxes are reported on a different line of Form 1040 than other recoveries; therefore, after the total amount that must be included has been determined, a further allocation may be necessary for reporting purposes.

IRS Publication 525, Taxable and Nontaxable Income, contains a worksheet for computing the amount of a taxable itemized deduction recovery.

Special Rules for Recovery of State Tax Refunds. The American Jobs Creation Act of 2004 (P.L. 108-357) amended Code Sec. 164 to allow taxpayers that itemize their deductions to elect to deduct either state and local income tax or state and local general sales tax beginning with tax year 2004. See ¶ 1021 for discussion of deductible taxes. This changed the method for determining the amount of a state tax refund to be included in gross income for tax year 2005. The 2005 Form 1040 Instructions included a worksheet to calculate this amount (the deduction had not been extended to include 2006 at the time the 2006 instructions were printed, so no equivalent worksheet was included in the 2006 instructions). There are nine exceptions preventing the use of the worksheet. One exception is if the state tax refund is more than the amount of the state and local income tax deduction reduced by the amount of the state and local general sales tax deduction that could have been deducted. The amount of the state tax refund that must be included in gross income is the excess of the amount of tax actually deducted over the amount of tax you could have deducted.

The election has been extended to apply to the 2006 and 2007 tax years (Code Sec. 164(b)(5), as amended by the Tax Relief and Health Care Act of 2006 (P.L. 109-432)).

Example 4: Fred Hayek had a choice of either deducting the amount of state income tax he paid of $2,210 or the amount of state and local general sales tax, which he determined to be $1,310 from the optional sales tax tables, as an itemized deduction on Schedule A. He elected to deduct the state income tax amount of $2,210. After completing and filing his state income tax return, he received a state tax refund of $1,000 in 2007. He needs to include only $900 of the state tax refund in his gross income on his 2007 federal income tax return. This represents the excess of the amount of tax deducted ($2,210) over the amount of tax he could have deducted ($1,310).

Example 5: Fred's cousin, Velma Hayek, who lives in a different state, elected on her 2006 income tax return to deduct as an itemized deduction the amount of state and local general sales tax she paid of $5,750 (based on actual receipts), rather than the amount of state income tax she paid of $5,600. After completing and filing her state income tax return, she received a state refund of $750 in 2007. Later, Velma returns a 72" plasma screen HDTV she purchased because she was unable to get upstairs into her bedroom. The refund she received included $250 of sales tax that she paid when she purchased the TV as a Christmas present to herself. She must include in her gross income for 2007 the entire amount of the sales tax refund of $250, since this amount is less than the excess of the amount of tax she deducted ($5,760) minus the amount of tax she could have deducted ($5,600 - $750 = $4,850). However, none of the state refund of $750 needs to be included in gross income since she chose not to deduct the amount of state income tax she paid on her 2006 return.

Nonitemized Deductions and Amounts Recovered for Credits. Recoveries of amounts for which a nonitemized deduction or a tax credit (other than the foreign tax credit or investment tax credit) was claimed in prior tax years must be included in income to the extent that the deduction or credit reduced the taxpayer's tax liability in the year of the deduction (Code Sec. 111(b)). Special rules apply when a deduction reduced taxable income but the taxpayer's actual tax liability was not reduced because of the application of the AMT rules or because tax credits were claimed that reduced the tax liability to zero. If the taxpayer has both itemized and nonitemized recoveries, the amount includible in income is determined by first figuring the nonitemized recoveries, then adding the nonitemized recoveries to taxable income, and, finally, figuring the itemized recoveries.

¶799

Chapter 8
EXCLUSIONS FROM INCOME

Nontaxable Income

801. What the Law Excludes. Gross income includes all income that is not specifically excluded by statute or administrative and judicial decisions. In addition to the items listed in Code Secs. 101—140, the following are exempt from gross income:

(1) items of income that, under the Constitution, are not taxable by the federal government;

(2) items of income that are exempt from tax under the provisions of any act of Congress not inconsistent with, or repealed by, the revenue acts; and

(3) items that are nontaxable under the provisions of foreign tax treaties designed to prevent double taxation.

These exclusions (and exemptions) should not be confused with *deductions* from gross income (losses, expenses, bad debts, etc.), which must be shown on a tax return. An exclusion generally does *not* have to be shown on a return.

Holocaust Reparation Payments

802. Special Non-Code Exclusion. Restitution or reparation payments received by persons who suffered Nazi persecution and survived the Holocaust are excludable from gross income (Act Sec. 803 of the Economic Growth and Tax Relief Reconciliation Act of 2001 (P.L. 107-16), made permanent by Act Sec. 2 of the Holocaust Restitution Tax Fairness Act of 2002 (P.L. 107-358)).[1] The exclusion extends to any interest earned on these payments. These excludable payments are also *not* to be included in any tax provision that takes into account excluded income in computing modified adjusted gross income, such as the taxation of Social Security benefits. This special non-Code exclusion applies to any payments received on or after January 1, 2000.

Life Insurance

803. General Rule. Life insurance contract proceeds paid by reason of the death of the insured are generally excluded from gross income. Generally, all amounts payable

---

Footnote references are to paragraphs of the 2008 Standard Federal Tax Reports.

[1] ¶ 5504.0285

on the death of the insured are excluded, whether these amounts represent the return of premiums paid, the increased value of the policy due to investment, or the death benefit feature (that is, the policy proceeds exceeding the value of the contract immediately prior to the death of the insured).

It is immaterial whether the proceeds are received in a single sum or otherwise. However, if the proceeds are left with the insurer under an agreement to pay interest, any interest earned and paid is income to the recipient (Code Sec. 101; Reg. §§ 1.101-1(a) and 1.101-3).[2]

A contract must qualify as a life insurance contract under applicable state or foreign law and meet either a cash value accumulation test or a guideline premium/cash value corridor test (Code Sec. 7702).[3] If a contract does not satisfy at least one of these tests, it will be treated as a combination of term insurance and a currently taxable deposit fund, and the policyholder must treat income on the contract as ordinary income in any year paid or accrued (Code Sec. 7702(g)).[4]

Amounts received under a life insurance contract on the life of an insured, terminally or chronically ill individual may be excluded from gross income. Similarly, if a portion of a life insurance contract benefit is assigned or sold to a viatical settlement provider, any amount received from the sale or assignment is also excludable (Code Sec. 101(g)).

804. Company-Owned Life Insurance (COLI). The Pension Protection Act of 2006 (P.L. 109-280) imposed a limit on the amount of company-owned life insurance proceeds that can be excluded from income (Code Sec. 101(j), as added by the Pension Protection Act of 2006 (P.L. 109-280)). For life insurance contracts issued after August 17, 2006, the applicable policyholder (the employer or a related person) with respect to an employer-owned life insurance contract generally may exclude from gross income only an amount not exceeding the total of the premiums and other amount paid by the policyholder. Thus, excess death benefits are included in gross income.

Exceptions. The income inclusion rule does not apply to an amount received by reason of the death of certain insured individuals if certain notice and consent requirements are satisfied. This exception applies if the insured was an employee of the applicable policyholder at any time during the 12-month period before the insured's death, or at the time the contract was issued, was, with respect to the policyholder, a director; a highly compensated employee under Code Sec. 414(q) (determined without regard to the election regarding the top-paid 20 percent of the employees); or a highly compensated individual as defined by the rules relating to self-insured medical reimbursement plans, under Code Sec. 105(h)(5), who is in a group of the highest paid 35 percent of employees.

The inclusion rule also does not apply, if the notice and consent requirements are satisfied, to proceeds that are paid to a member of the insured's family, as defined in Code Sec. 267(c)(4), to any individual who is the designated beneficiary of the insured under the contract (other than the applicable policyholder), to a trust established for the benefit of the insured's family or a designated beneficiary, or to the estate of the insured. In addition, the rule does not apply to proceeds that are used to buy an equity (or capital or profits) interest in the policyholder from the insured's heir.

An officer, director, or highly compensated employee (within the meaning of Code Sec. 414(q)) is an employee. The exceptions to the inclusion rule apply only if the insured is a United States citizen or resident.

Notice and consent. To keep excess benefits from being included in income, the policyholder must satisfy the following notice and consent requirements before the issuance of the insurance contract:

> • the employee must be notified in writing that the policyholder intends to insure the life of the employee and the maximum face amount for which the employee can be insured,

---

Footnote references are to paragraphs of the 2008 Standard Federal Tax Reports.

[2] ¶ 6502, ¶ 6503, ¶ 6508   [3] ¶ 43,150   [4] ¶ 43,150

- the employee must provide written consent to being insured under the contract and acknowledge that such coverage may continue after the insured terminates employment, and

- the employee must be informed in writing that an applicable policyholder will be a beneficiary of any proceeds payable upon death of the employee.

Finally, the policyholder of the contract has additional annual reporting and record retention requirements (Code Sec. 6039I, as added by the Pension Protection Act of 2006 (P.L. 109-280)).

805. Installment Options. If the beneficiary of a life insurance policy receives the proceeds in installments, any interest element in the life insurance proceeds accruing after the date of the insured's death is included in the income of the beneficiary (Code Sec. 101(d); Reg. § 1.101-4).[5]

807. Transfer for Value. If a life insurance policy is transferred for valuable consideration, payments on account of the death of the insured are income to the transferee to the extent that they exceed the premiums and other consideration given for the life insurance policy (see ¶ 845). However, if the policy was transferred as a tax-free exchange or gift, the donor's investment basis in the contract is carried over to the donee, and the death benefits are fully excludable. Also, the benefits are fully excludable if such a transfer of the contract was to the insured, a partner of the insured, a partnership including the insured, or a corporation of which the insured was a share-holder or officer (Code Sec. 101(a)(2); Reg. § 1.101-1(b)).[6]

809. Dividends. Amounts received from an annuity policy prior to the "annuity starting date" in the nature of dividends, or return of premiums or other consideration, are not taxable until the amounts received exceed the aggregate of premiums or other consideration paid or deemed to have been paid for the annuity. However, amounts received in the nature of dividends after the start date of the annuity may be fully taxable (see ¶ 823) (Code Sec. 72(e); Reg. § 1.72-11(b)).[7]

Excludable Death Benefit

813. Incidental Death Benefits. Gross income does not include amounts paid by an employer by reason of the death of an employee who is a " specified terrorist victim," as defined by Code Sec. 692(d)(4) (see ¶ 2533). The exclusion applies to death benefits from a qualified plan that satisfy the incidental death benefit rule (see ¶ 2135) (Code Sec. 101(i)(a)).

Public Safety Officer. The amount paid as a survivor annuity to the spouse, former spouse or child of a public safety officer killed in the line of duty is excludable from the recipient's gross income if the annuity is provided under a governmental plan (Code Sec. 101(h)).

Annuity

817. Exclusion Ratio. Under special rules for the taxation of amounts received as an annuity under any annuity, endowment, or life insurance contract and paid out for reasons other than death of the insured, the tax-free portion of annuity income is spread evenly over the annuitant's life expectancy. However, for contracts with an annuity starting date before 1987, the exclusion remains the same no matter how long the annuitant lives. These annuity rules also apply to contracts whose payments are made over a prescribed number of years (Code Sec. 72; Reg. § § 1.72-1—1.72-11).[8] For Armed Forces personnel annuities, see ¶ 891.

Contracts, with some exceptions, will not be treated as annuity contracts unless they provide that (1) if the contract holder dies on or after the annuity starting date, but before the entire interest in the contract is distributed, the remainder must be distributed at least as rapidly as under the method used as of the day the holder died, and (2) the entire interest in the contract must be distributed within five years of the holder's death (Code Sec. 72(s)).[9]

Footnote references are to paragraphs of the 2008 Standard Federal Tax Reports.

[5] ¶ 6502, ¶ 6510   [7] ¶ 6102, ¶ 6113   [9] ¶ 6102
[6] ¶ 6502, ¶ 6503   [8] ¶ 6102—¶ 6113

To determine the portion of the annuity that is excludable from the recipient's gross income, an exclusion ratio is to be determined for each contract. In general, this ratio is determined by dividing the investment in the contract by the expected return (Reg. § 1.72-2). The exclusion ratio is then applied to the total amount received as an annuity during the tax year. Any excess amount over the portion determined by the application of the exclusion ratio is includible in the recipient's gross income (Reg. § 1.72-4). In the case of distributions from an individual retirement arrangement (IRA), the exclusion ratio is determined by dividing the employee's total nondeductible contributions by the balance of the account. All of an individual's IRAs and distributions during a year must be aggregated (see ¶ 2178). A nontaxable distribution of IRA assets is reported on Form 8606 (see Instructions to Form 8606; IRS Pub. 590).

For annuities with a starting date after 1986, the exclusion of a portion of each annuity payment cannot be continued indefinitely. The annuitant is still required to compute the exclusion ratio as before, but, once the total of all exclusions taken for payments under the annuity contract equals the investment in the contract, all subsequent payments are fully taxed (Code Sec. 72(b)(2)).[10] On the other hand, if the annuitant dies before the investment in the contract is fully recovered tax free through the annuity exclusion, a deduction is provided for the annuitant's last year in an amount equal to the unrecovered portion of the investment (Code Sec. 72(b)(3)).[11]

819. The "Exclusion Ratio" Formula. The excludable portion of an annuity payment is the annuity payment multiplied by the exclusion ratio. The remainder is taxable to the recipient, whether it be the primary annuitant or a secondary annuitant under a joint or joint and survivor annuity. The exclusion ratio is the "investment in the contract" (¶ 821) divided by the "expected return" (¶ 825) under the contract as of the "annuity starting date" (¶ 823). For example, if, as of the annuity starting date, a taxpayer's investment in an annuity contract is $6,000 and his expected return is $10,000, his exclusion ratio is $6,000/$10,000, or 60%. If the taxpayer receives a monthly annuity payment of $200, the monthly exclusion is $120 ($200 × 60%).

821. "Investment in the Contract" Defined. The "investment in the contract" generally is the total amount of premiums or other consideration paid for the contract (other than contributions on behalf of self-employed individuals) less amounts, if any, received before the "annuity starting date" and not included in gross income (Code Sec. 72(c)(1); Reg. § 1.72-6).[12] A special adjustment is provided for a refund annuity (see ¶ 837).

Special rules for computing an employee's investment in an annuity received through an employer are explained at ¶ 2155.

Nonresident Aliens. Effective for distributions on or after October 22, 2004, certain employer or employee contributions made by or on behalf of nonresident aliens will not be considered part of the individual's investment in the contract. The excluded contributions are those: (1) made with respect to compensation for labor or services by an employee who was a nonresident alien at the time the labor or services were performed and treated as from sources outside the United States and (2) that were not subject to tax by the United States or a foreign country (but would have been subject to tax if paid in cash). Thus, contributions to a foreign pension plan are included in the calculation of the participant's basis only if the participant has been subject to tax on the contribution by the United States or a foreign country (Code Sec. 72(w)).[13]

823. "Annuity Starting Date" Defined. The "annuity starting date" is the first day of the first period for which an amount is received as an annuity under the contract. The first day of the first period for which an amount is received as an annuity is the later of: (1) the date upon which the obligations of the contract become fixed or (2) the first day of the period (year, half-year, quarter, or month, depending on whether the payments are made annually, semi-annually, quarterly, or monthly) that ends on the date of the first annuity payment (Code Sec. 72(c)(4); Reg. § 1.72-4(b)).[14]

Footnote references are to paragraphs of the 2008 Standard Federal Tax Reports.

[10] ¶ 6102   [12] ¶ 6102, ¶ 6107   [14] ¶ 6102, ¶ 6104
[11] ¶ 6102   [13] ¶ 6102

EXCLUSIONS FROM INCOME □ Annuity 283

825. "Expected Return" Computation. The "expected return" under the contract is limited to amounts receivable as an annuity or as annuities. If no life expectancy is involved (as in the case of installment payments for a fixed number of years), the expected return is found by totaling the amounts to be received (Code Sec. 72(c)(3); Reg. § 1.72-5(c)).[15]

To determine the expected return under contracts involving life expectancy, actuarial tables prescribed by the IRS must be used (Code Sec. 72(c)(3); Reg. § 1.72-5(a)).[16] The tables provide a multiplier (based on life expectancy) that is applied to the annual payment to obtain the expected return under the contract. The annuity tables are reproduced at ¶ 165 of CCH STANDARD FEDERAL TAX REPORTS.

The expected return will vary, depending on when contributions were made and when amounts were received as an annuity. Gender-neutral tables must be used if the total investment in the contract is made after June 30, 1986. If there was an investment in the contract as of June 30, 1986, and there has been a further investment in the contract after that date, an individual may, instead of using the gender-neutral tables, elect to calculate the exclusion under a special rule. Under this rule, an exclusion amount is calculated using the gender-based tables—as if the investment in the contract as of June 30, 1986, were the only investment in the contract. Then a second exclusion is calculated, using the gender-neutral tables, as if the post-June 30, 1986, investment were the only investment. The two exclusion amounts are then added together to produce the final exclusion. Although, generally, the gender-based annuity tables formerly in effect must still be used if all contributions were made prior to June 30, 1986, an election may be made to use the updated tables if the annuity payments are received after June 30, 1986 (Reg. § 1.72-5 and Reg. § 1.72-6).[17]

For use in the following examples, a portion of Table V (gender-neutral for post-June 30, 1986, investment in the contract (Reg. § 1.72-9))[18] for ordinary life annuities for one life is reproduced below:

TABLE V.—ORDINARY LIFE ANNUITIES—ONE LIFE—EXPECTED RETURN MULTIPLES

Age	Multiple	Age	Multiple
55	28.6	64	20.8
56	27.7	65	20.0
57	26.8	66	19.2
58	25.9	67	18.4
59	25.0	68	17.6
60	24.2	69	16.8
61	23.3	70	16.0
62	22.5	71	15.3
63	21.6	72	14.6

Example 1: In 2007, X purchases for $8,000 an annuity that provides for payments to him of $50 per month for life. At the annuity starting date, his age at his nearest birthday is 64 years. Table V (gender-neutral) must be used since all investment in the contract is post-June 1986 and it shows that for an individual of X's age, the multiple to be used in computing the expected return is 20.8. X's expected return and annual exclusion, therefore, are computed as follows:

Annual payment ($50 per month × 12 months)	$600
Table V multiple	20.8
Expected return ($600 × 20.8)	$12,480
Exclusion ratio .... 8,000 , or 64.1%	
12,480	
Annual exclusion (64.1% of $600)	$385

If payments under the contract are made quarterly, semiannually or annually, or if the interval between the annuity starting date and the date of the first payment is less than the interval between future payments, an adjustment of the multiple found in the actuarial tables may be required (Reg. § 1.72-5).[19] The amount of the adjustment is found in the following table:

Footnote references are to paragraphs of the 2008 Standard Federal Tax Reports.

[15] ¶ 6102, ¶ 6106
[16] ¶ 6102, ¶ 6106
[17] ¶ 6106, ¶ 6107
[18] ¶ 165
[19] ¶ 6106

¶825

If the number of whole months from the annuity starting date to the first payment date is	0-1	2	3	4	5	6	7	8	9	10	11	12
And payments under the contract are to be made:												
Annually	+.5	+.4	+.3	+.2	+.1	0	0	-.1	-.2	-.3	-.4	-.5
Semiannually	+.2	+.1	0	0	-.1	-.2	..	..	..	..	..	..
Quarterly	+.1	0	-.1	..	..	..	..	..	..	..	..	..

Example 2: Assume the same facts as in **Example 1** except that the payments under the contract are to be made semiannually in the amount of $300, the first payment being made six full months from the annuity starting date. The table shows the adjustment to be "-.2". Therefore, X's multiple from Table V, 20.8, is adjusted by subtracting .2. His adjusted multiple then is 20.6, and his expected return and semiannual exclusion are computed as follows:

Annual payment ($300 × 2)		$600
Table V adjusted multiple		20.6
Expected return ($600 × 20.6)		$12,360
Exclusion ratio	$\frac{8,000}{12,360}$, or 64.7%	
Semiannual exclusion (64.7% of $300)		$194.10

There is a simpler computation, illustrated in **Example 3**, following, but it may be used only if the annuity amount does not vary from year to year. The simple computation determines the annual exclusion by dividing the taxpayer's investment in the contract (cost) by the appropriate multiple from the actuarial tables.

Example 3: Assume the same facts as in **Example 1**. X's annual exclusion is computed as follows:

Cost of annuity		$8,000
Annual payment ($50 per month × 12 months) . . .		$600
Table V multiple		20.8
Annual exclusion $\frac{8,000}{20.8}$		$385
Annual taxable income ($600 less $385)		$215

827. Joint and Survivor Annuities and Joint Annuities. In the case of a joint and survivor annuity contract that provides the first annuitant with a fixed monthly income for life and, after his death, provides an identical monthly income for life to the second annuitant, the multiple used in computing expected return is found in Table II (gender-based) or Table VI (gender-neutral) under the ages of the living annuitants as of the annuity starting date (Reg. § 1.72-5(b)(1)).[20]

For use in the following example, a portion of Table VI (gender-neutral for post-June 30, 1986, investment in the contract) providing expected return multiples for ordinary joint life and last survivor annuities for two lives is reproduced below.

TABLE VI.—ORDINARY JOINT LIFE AND LAST SURVIVOR ANNUITIES—TWO LIVES— EXPECTED RETURN MULTIPLES

Ages	65	66	67	68	69	70	71	72
65	25.0	24.6	24.2	23.8	23.4	23.1	22.8	22.5
66	24.6	24.1	23.7	23.3	22.9	22.5	22.2	21.9
67	24.2	23.7	23.2	22.8	22.4	22.0	21.7	21.3
68	23.8	23.3	22.8	22.3	21.9	21.5	21.2	20.8
69	23.4	22.9	22.4	21.9	21.5	21.1	20.7	20.3

Footnote references are to paragraphs of the 2008 Standard Federal Tax Reports.

[20] ¶ 6106

¶827

Ages	65	66	67	68	69	70	71	72
70	23.1	22.5	22.0	21.5	21.1	20.6	20.2	19.8
71	22.8	22.2	21.7	21.2	20.7	20.2	19.8	19.4
72	22.5	21.9	21.3	20.8	20.3	19.8	19.4	18.9

Example: In 2007, Y purchased a joint and survivor annuity providing for payments of $200 a month to be made to Y for life and, upon his death, to his wife, Z, during her lifetime. At the annuity starting date Y's age at his nearest birthday is 68 and Z's is 66. The annuity cost $44,710. The expected return is as follows:

Annual payment ($200 × 12)	$2,400
Table VI multiple (age 68; age 66)	23.3
Expected return ($2,400 × 23.3)	$55,920

The annual exclusion for both Y and Z is computed as follows:

Exclusion ratio . . . . $\frac{44,710}{55,920}$, or 80%

Annual exclusion (80% of $2,400) $1,920.00

If a joint and survivor annuity provides for a different monthly income, rather than an identical monthly income, payable to the second annuitant, the regulations call for a special computation of expected return that involves the use of both Table I and Table II or Table V and Table VI, whichever are applicable.[21]

If a contract involving two annuitants provides for fixed monthly payments to be made as a joint life annuity until the death of the first annuitant (in other words, only as long as both remain alive), the expected return for such a contract is determined under Table IIA or VIA (Reg. § 1.72-5(b)(4)).[22]

Adjustment of the multiple obtained from the annuity tables, as explained at ¶ 825 for single life annuities, may also be necessary for joint and survivor annuities and joint annuities if payments are made less often than monthly or if the first payment is accelerated.

829. Special Types of Annuities. To compute the exclusion ratio for a contract that is acquired for a single consideration and that provides for the payment of two or more annuity obligations or elements, the investment in the contract is divided by the aggregate of the expected returns under all the annuity elements (Reg. §§ 1.72-4(e), 1.72-5(e), and 1.72-6(b)).[23] In the case of variable annuities, a special rule is provided for determining the portion of each payment to be "an amount received as an annuity" and excludable from gross income each year (Reg. § 1.72-2(b)(3)).[24] The computation of the expected return for temporary life annuities is determined by multiplying the total of the annuity payments to be received annually by the multiple shown in Table I or V (whichever is applicable) under the age (as of the annuity starting date) and, if applicable, the gender of the annuitant's life (Reg. § 1.72-5(a)(3)—(5)).[25]

833. Annuity Tables. Actuarial tables are used in computing the expected return under commercial annuity contracts involving life expectancy. Tables I, II, IIA, III, and IV of Reg. § 1.72-9 are used if the investment in the contract does not include a post-June 1986 investment in the contract (as defined in Reg. § 1.72-6(d)(5)).[26] Tables V, VI, VIA, VII, and VIII of Reg. § 1.72-9 are used if the investment in the contract includes a post-June 1986 investment in the contract (as defined in Reg. § 1.72-6(d)(5)). These tables are reproduced at ¶ 165 of the CCH STANDARD FEDERAL TAX REPORTS.

In the case of a contract under which amounts are received as an annuity after June 30, 1986, a taxpayer receiving such amounts may elect to treat the entire investment in the contract as a post-June 1986 investment in the contract and thus apply Tables V through VIII (Reg. § 1.72-9). A taxpayer may make the election in any tax year in which such amounts are received by attaching to the return for such tax year a statement of election to treat the entire investment in the contract as post-June 1986 investment in the

---

Footnote references are to paragraphs of the 2008 Standard Federal Tax Reports.

[21] ¶ 6106   [23] ¶ 6104, ¶ 6106, ¶ 6107   [25] ¶ 6106
[22] ¶ 6106   [24] ¶ 6102D   [26] ¶ 6107

contract. The statement must contain the taxpayer's name, address, and taxpayer identification number.

The election is irrevocable and applies to all amounts that the taxpayer receives as an annuity under the contract in the tax year for which the election is made and in any subsequent tax year. Reg. § 1.72-6(d)(6) contains rules for treating the entire investment in the contract as post-June 1986 investment in the contract if the annuity starting date of the contract is after June 30, 1986, and the contract provides for a disqualifying form of payment or settlement, such as an option to receive a lump sum in full discharge of the obligation under the contract. Reg. § 1.72-6(d) contains special rules concerning the tables to be used and the separate computations required if the investment in the contract includes both a pre-July 1986 investment in the contract and a post-June 1986 investment in the contract.

835. Exclusion for Year Annuity Begins. If the first payment an annuitant receives is for a fractional part of a year, the annuitant need only determine the exclusion ratio, as a percentage, and apply it to the payment received for the fractional part of the payment period, resulting in the amount of the annuitant's exclusion for the tax year (Reg. § 1.72-4(a)).

> **Example:** John purchased an annuity that provides for semiannual payments of $3,000. The annuity starting date is November 1, and on December 31, John received $1,000 as his first payment under the contract. John's exclusion percentage is 70%. He may exclude 70% of $1,000, or $700, from his calendar-year income.

837. Refund Annuity. Generally, a contract contains a refund feature if: (1) the annuity payments depend, in whole or in part, upon the continuing life of one or more persons; (2) there are payments on or after the death of the annuitant if a specified amount or a stated number of payments has not been made prior to death; and (3) the payments are in the nature of a refund of the consideration paid (Code Sec. 72(c)(2); Reg. § 1.72-7).[27] If a refund annuity contract is involved, including a contract for a life annuity with a minimum period of payments certain, an adjustment must be made to the original investment in the contract when determining the exclusion. The original investment in the contract must be reduced by the value of the refund payment or payment certain as of the annuity starting date (Code Sec. 72(b)(4) and (c); Reg. § 1.72-7).[28] The computation of the adjustment, which is explained in the Regulations, is detailed and involves the use of Table III (gender-based) or Table VII (gender-neutral) of Reg. § 1.72-9.[29] If an annuity has a refund feature, the investment in the contract must be reduced by the present value of the refund feature (Code Sec. 72(b)(4)).

839. Employee's Annuity. Subject to the exception noted below, a distribution from a qualified retirement plan (see ¶ 2101 and following) that takes the form of a periodic pension is taxable under the annuity rules described at ¶ 817 and following (Code Sec. 402(a) and Code Sec. 403(a)(1)). For purposes of those rules, the participant's investment in the contract (see ¶ 821) is the total amount of the participant's nondeductible contributions to the plan less any amounts withdrawn by the employee before commencement of the annuity that were not included in income (Reg. §§ 1.72-6, 1.72-8, 1.72-13 and 1.402(a)-1(a)(5)).[30]

Post-November 18, 1996, Annuities.—The Small Business Job Protection Act of 1996 provided a simplified method similar to the IRS safe-harbor method used for pre-November 19, 1996, annuities (see *"Pre-November 19, 1996, Annuities,"* following) for determining the portion of an annuity distribution from a qualified retirement plan, qualified annuity, or tax-sheltered annuity that represents nontaxable return of basis (Code Sec. 72(d)). The simplified method must be used for distributions from a qualified plan when the starting date is after November 18, 1996.

Under the simplified method, the portion of each annuity payment that represents nontaxable return of basis is generally equal to the employee's total investment in the contract as of the annuity starting date, divided by the number of anticipated payments,

---

Footnote references are to paragraphs of the 2008 Standard Federal Tax Reports.

[27] ¶ 6102, ¶ 6108   [29] ¶ 165   [30] ¶ 6107, ¶ 6109, ¶ 6119,
[28] ¶ 6102, ¶ 6108   ¶ 18,203

which are determined by reference to the age of the participant as listed in the table below (Code Sec. 72(d)(1)(B)):

Age of Primary Annuitant on the Annuity Starting Date	Number of Anticipated Payments
55 and under	360
56-60	310
61-65	260
66-70	210
71 and over	160

For annuity starting dates after December 31, 1997, annuities paid over the life of a single individual have anticipated payments as listed in the table above. If, however, the annuity is payable over the lives of more than one individual, the number of anticipated payments is listed in the table below:

Combined Age of Annuitants	Number of Anticipated Payments
110 and under	410
More than 110 but not more than 120	360
More than 120 but not more than 130	310
More than 130 but not more than 140	260
More than 140	210

The investment in the contract is the amount of premiums and other consideration paid (generally, the after-tax contributions to the plan) minus the amount received before the annuity starting date that was excluded from gross income. The number of anticipated payments listed in the table above is based on the employee's age on the annuity starting date. If the number of payments is fixed under the terms of the annuity, that number is to be used rather than the number of anticipated payments listed in the table.

> **Example 1:** At retirement, Jeff Anderson, age 65, begins receiving retirement benefits in the form of a joint and 50% survivor annuity to be paid for the joint lives of Jeff and his wife, Jan, age 59. Jeff's annuity starting date is January 1, 2007. Jeff contributed $24,000 to the plan and has received no distributions prior to the annuity starting date. He will receive a monthly retirement benefit of $1,000, and his wife Jan will receive a monthly survivor benefit of $500 upon his death. Under the safe-harbor method, Jeff's investment in the contract is $24,000 (the after-tax contributions to the plan). The set number of monthly payments per the chart above will be 310 (Jeff's age, 65, plus Jan's age, 59, at the starting date of the annuity equals 124). The tax-free portion of each $1,000 monthly annuity payment to Jeff is now $77.42, determined by dividing Jeff's investment ($24,000) by the number of monthly payments (310). If Jeff has not recovered the full $24,000 investment at his death, Jan will exclude $77.42 from each $500 monthly annuity payment. Any annuity payments received after 310 payments have been made will be fully includible in gross income. If Jeff and his wife die before 310 payments have been made, a deduction is allowed on the survivor's last income tax return in the amount of the unrecovered investment.

The simplified method does not apply if the primary annuitant has attained age 75 on the annuity starting date unless there are fewer than five years of guaranteed payments under the annuity (Code Sec. 72(d)(1)(E)).

If, in connection with commencement of annuity payments, the recipient receives a lump-sum payment that is not part of the annuity stream, the payment is taxed under the annuity rules of Code Sec. 72(e) as if received before the annuity starting date and the investment in the contract used to calculate the simplified exclusion ratio for the annuity payments is reduced by the amount of the payment (Code Sec. 72(d)(1)(D)).

Pre-November 19, 1996, Annuities. The IRS provided an elective alternative to application of the usual annuity rules for distributions from qualified plans when the annuity starting date was before November 19, 1996. This is a simplified safe-harbor method for determining the tax-free and taxable portions of certain annuity payments made from qualified employee plans, employee annuities, and annuity contracts (Notice

98-2).[31] Distributees who elected to use this method are considered to have complied with Code Sec. 72(b). Payors may also use this method to report the taxable portion of the annuity payments on Form 1099-R. This safe-harbor method may be used *only* if the following three conditions are met: (1) the annuity payments depend upon the life of the distributee or the joint lives of the distributee and beneficiary; (2) the annuity payments are made from an employee plan qualified under Code Sec. 401(a), an employee annuity under Code Sec. 403(a), or an annuity contract under Code Sec. 403(b); and (3) the distributee is less than age 75 when annuity payments commence or, if the distributee is age 75 or older, there are fewer than five years of guaranteed payments.

Under the safe-harbor method, the total number of monthly annuity payments expected to be received is based on the distributee's age at the annuity starting date rather than on the life expectancy tables in Reg. § 1.72-9. The same expected number of payments applies to a distributee whether the individual is receiving a single life annuity or a joint and survivor annuity. These payments are set forth in the following table:

Age of Distributee	*Number of Payments*
55 and under	300
56-60	260
61-65	240
66-70	170
71 and over	120

The investment in the contract is the aggregate amount of premiums and other consideration paid by the employee (generally the after-tax contributions to the plan) minus the aggregate amount received before the annuity starting date that was excluded from gross income. No refund feature adjustment (see ¶ 837) is required in computing the employee's investment in the contract.

Under the safe-harbor method, the distributee recovers the investment in the contract in level amounts over the number of monthly payments determined from the above table. The portion of each monthly annuity payment that is excluded from gross income by a distributee who uses the safe-harbor method for income tax purposes is a level dollar amount determined by dividing the investment in the contract, including any applicable death benefit exclusion, by the set number of annuity payments from the above table as follows:

$$\frac{\text{Investment}}{\text{Number of monthly payments}} = \begin{array}{c} \text{Tax-free} \\ \text{portion of} \\ \text{monthly annuity} \end{array}$$

For distributees with annuity starting dates after 1986, annuity payments received after the investment is recovered (generally, after the set number of payments has been received) are fully includible in gross income.

> **Example 2:** Assume the facts as in **Example 1**, except Jeff's annuity start date is January 1, 1996. Under the safe-harbor method, Jeff's investment in the contract is $24,000 (the after-tax contributions to the plan). The set number of monthly payments for a distributee who is age 65 is 240. The tax-free portion of each $1,000 monthly annuity payment to Jeff is $100, determined by dividing Jeff's investment ($24,000) by the number of monthly payments (240). If Jeff has not recovered the full $24,000 investment at his death, Jan will also exclude $100 from each $500 monthly annuity payment. Any annuity payments received after 240 payments have been made will be fully includible in gross income. If Jeff and his wife die before 240 payments have been made, a deduction is allowed on the survivor's last income tax return in the amount of the unrecovered investment.

The dollar amount is excluded from each monthly payment even if the annuity payment amount changes. If the amount excluded is greater than the amount of the monthly annuity, because of decreased survivor payments, each monthly annuity payment is excluded completely until the entire investment is recovered. If annuity payments cease before the set number of payments has been made, a deduction for the unrecovered investment is allowed on the distributee's last tax return. Where payments

---

Footnote references are to paragraphs of the 2008 Standard Federal Tax Reports.

[31] ¶ 6140.0316

are made to multiple beneficiaries, the excludable amount is based on the oldest beneficiary's age. A pro rata portion is excluded by each beneficiary.

For purposes of these rules, the investment in the contract is determined without regard to the adjustment made for a refund feature (Code Sec. 72(d)(1)(C)).

In any case where the annuity payments are not made on a monthly basis, appropriate adjustments will be made to take into account the period on which the payments are actually made (Code Sec. 72(d)(1)(F)).

Employee contributions under a defined contribution plan may be treated as a separate contract for purposes of these rules (Code Sec. 72(d)(2)).

Tier 2 benefits received by retired railroad workers and their survivors under the Railroad Retirement Act are subject to federal income tax in the same manner as pension plan benefits paid by private employers (Code Sec. 72(r)).[32]

841. Discharge of Annuity Obligation. Any amount received, whether in a single sum or otherwise, under an annuity, endowment or life insurance contract in full discharge of the obligation under the contract as a refund of the consideration paid for the contract or any amount received under such contract on its complete surrender, redemption or maturity is includible in gross income to the extent the amounts exceed the investment in the contract (Code Sec. 72(e); Reg. § 1.72-11).[33] The remainder is taxable to the recipient, whether the recipient is the primary annuitant or a secondary annuitant under a joint or joint and survivor annuity.

A penalty is imposed on a policyholder who receives a premature distribution (e.g., before age 59½) unless one of a number of exceptions (e.g., death, disability) applies (Code Sec. 72(q)).[34]

843. Installment Option. If an insured elects under an option in an insurance contract to receive the proceeds as an annuity, instead of a lump sum, and the election is made within 60 days after the day on which the lump sum first became payable, no part of it is taxable under the doctrine of constructive receipt (Code Sec. 72(h); Reg. § 1.72-12).[35] The installment payments are taxed in accordance with the annuity rules.

845. Transfer for Value. If a life insurance, endowment, or annuity contract is transferred for a valuable consideration, and the proceeds of the contract are paid to the transferee for reasons other than the death of the insured (for example, on surrender, redemption or maturity of the contract), the transferee (including a beneficiary of, or the estate of, a transferee) is taxed as follows: (1) if the proceeds are received as an annuity or in installments for a fixed period, the transferee computes the tax under the exclusion ratio formula; or (2) if the proceeds are received in a lump sum, the transferee includes in income only that portion of the proceeds in excess of the consideration paid. Regardless of how the proceeds are received and taxed, the transferee's consideration paid consists of the actual value of the consideration paid for the transfer, plus the amount of premiums or other consideration paid after the transfer. This transferee rule, however, does not apply if the transferred contract has a basis for gain or loss in the hands of the transferee determined by reference to the transferor's basis, as in the case of a gift or tax-free exchange (Code Sec. 72(g); Reg. § 1.72-10).[36]

A loss realized upon the surrender or forfeiture of an annuity contract by the original purchaser is deductible as an ordinary loss under Code Sec. 165, the basis of the contract being its cost less the amounts previously excluded from gross income (Rev. Rul. 61-201).[37] The IRS maintains the loss is deducted on Form 1040, Schedule A as miscellaneous itemized deduction subject to the two-percent of adjusted gross income floor.

Bequest or Gift

847. Bequest. The value of property acquired by bequest, devise, or inheritance is excluded from gross income (Code Sec. 102; Reg. § 1.102-1).[38] But the *income* flowing

---

Footnote references are to paragraphs of the 2008 Standard Federal Tax Reports.

[32] ¶ 6102	[35] ¶ 6102, ¶ 6117	[38] ¶ 6550, ¶ 6551
[33] ¶ 6102, ¶ 6113	[36] ¶ 6102, ¶ 6112	
[34] ¶ 6102	[37] ¶ 9900.111	

from the property is not exempt, as, for example, that received as investment income from the property or as profit from a sale of the property. For the basis of inherited property, see ¶ 1633—¶ 1639.

The exclusion also does not apply if the bequest consists of income from property. Thus, a bequest of annual rent from the testator's property for 10 years is taxable income to the beneficiary. The beneficiary is required to include in gross income each year the amount of the annual rent.

A bequest of a specific sum or of specific property from an estate or trust may be exempt from tax if it is paid or credited all at once or in not more than three installments (Code Sec. 663(a)(1); Reg. § 1.663(a)-1).[39] An amount which is paid from the estate or trust income may qualify as a bequest for this purpose if the amount could have been paid from either income or principal; however, an amount that can only be paid from the estate or trust income will not be treated as bequest and, thus, will not be exempt even when paid in less than four installments.

849. Gift. The value of a gift is excludable from gross income, but *any income* from the gift, including profit upon sale, is taxable (Code Sec. 102(b)). A gift of income from the property of an estate or trust is not exempt except in the case of a gift of a specific sum or of specific property paid or credited all at once or in not more than three installments (see ¶ 847). For a donee's basis for gift property, see ¶ 1630.

Tips are not gifts and are therefore taxable (see ¶ 717).[40] Food, clothing and rent payments furnished as strike benefits by a labor union to a needy worker participating in a strike may be considered gifts;[41] in determining whether a gift was made, the fact that benefits are paid only to union members is not controlling.[42]

The exclusion from gross income applicable to the value of property acquired by gift does not apply to any amount transferred by or for an employer to, or for the benefit of, an employee (Code Sec. 102(c)).[43] Certain employee achievement awards are excludable, however (see ¶ 785), and certain fringe benefits provided by employers are also excludable (see ¶ 863).

Employee Benefits

851. Occupational Disability or Insurance Benefit. Compensation received under a workers' compensation act for personal injuries or sickness and amounts received by a taxpayer under a policy of accident and health insurance are exempt from tax (Code Sec. 104(a)(1); Reg. § 1.104-1).[44] Code Sec. 104(a)(1) also applies to benefits having the characteristics of life insurance proceeds paid under a workers' compensation act to the survivor or survivors of a deceased employee (Reg. § 1.101-1(a)).[45]

Amounts received as a pension, annuity, or similar allowance for personal injuries or sickness resulting from active service in the armed forces of any country or in the Coast and Geodetic Survey or the Public Health Service, or as a disability annuity payable under section 808 of the Foreign Service Act of 1980, are also exempt (Code Sec. 104(a)(4); Reg. § 1.104-1).[46] The exclusion generally is limited to amounts received for combat-related injury or illness. However, the exclusion will not be less than the maximum amount of disability compensation from the Veterans Administration to which the individual is, or would be, entitled upon application (see ¶ 702) (Code Sec. 104(b)).[47]

Benefits that are payable under state law for occupational injury or illness arising out of employment are nontaxable if the benefits are in the nature of workers' compensation payments (Reg. § 1.104-1(b)).[48]

Benefits received under an insurance contract indemnifying an individual against income lost by reason of loss of the use of his body or a portion of his body are tax exempt, as are payments under an income replacement policy in the event of illness.[49] However, amounts received under a policy designed to pay business overhead costs in the case of prolonged disability are taxable.[50] A lump-sum payment received under an

---

Footnote references are to paragraphs of the 2008 Standard Federal Tax Reports.

[39] ¶ 24,440, ¶ 24,441   [43] ¶ 6550   [47] ¶ 6660
[40] ¶ 5507.4651   [44] ¶ 6660, ¶ 6661   [48] ¶ 6661
[41] ¶ 6553.46   [45] ¶ 6503   [49] ¶ 6662.0355
[42] ¶ 6553.46   [46] ¶ 6660, ¶ 6661   [50] ¶ 6662.295

employer-employee contributory disability insurance policy and paid with reference to a permanently disabling illness is excludable to the extent that it is attributable to the employee's contributions.[51] As to excludability of amounts attributable to employer's contributions, see ¶ 853. "No fault" insurance disability benefits received by a passenger injured in an automobile accident under the automobile owner's policy as compensation for loss of income or earning capacity are also excludable from gross income.[52]

If an otherwise excludable amount is for reimbursement of medical expenses previously deducted for tax purposes, the portion must be included in gross income to the extent of the prior deduction. If a portion of an award is specifically allocated to future injury-related medical expenses, the future expenses must be offset by the awarded portion and are not deductible to that extent.[53]

Terrorist Attacks. Disability income received by an individual for injuries received in a terrorist attack while the individual was performing services as a U.S. employee outside the United States is also excludable from gross income (Code Sec. 104(a)(5)).[54]

852. Personal Injuries. Amounts received as damages (other than punitive damages) on account of *personal physical injuries* or *physical sickness* are excludable from income (Code Sec. 104(a)(2)). Damages for emotional distress (including the physical symptoms of emotional distress) may not be treated as damages on account of a personal physical injury or sickness, except to the extent of an amount paid for medical care attributable to emotional distress. Accordingly, back pay received in satisfaction of a claim for denial of a promotion due to employment discrimination is not excludable because it is "completely independent of," and thus is not "damages received on account of," personal physical injuries or sickness (Rev. Rul. 96-65). Damages received for emotional distress in satisfaction of such a claim are also not excludable except to the extent paid for medical care attributable to emotional distress.

The U.S Court of Appeals for the District of Columbia Circuit abandoned its controversial 2005 decision that held that Code Sec. 104(a)(2) unconstitutionally taxed compensatory damages for non-physical injuries. In *Murphy* (2007-2 USTC ¶ 50,531), the court avoided addressing the issue of whether such compensation is includible in gross income. Instead, the court held that a tax on awards for non-physical injuries falls within Congress' power to tax under Article I, Sections 8 and 9 of the U.S. Constitution. The court likened the tax on Murphy's award to an excise tax, which is an indirect tax not subject to the requirement of apportionment, but which operates with the same force and effect throughout the U.S. and thus satisfies the requirement of uniformity.

Interest and Punitive Damage Awards. Interest included in an award of damages for personal injury is includible in gross income.[55] Also, punitive damages arising out of personal physical injury action are includible in gross income (Code Sec. 104(a)).[56] However, punitive damages may be excluded from income *if* received in a civil action for wrongful death and the applicable state law, in effect on September 13, 1995, provides that only punitive damages may be awarded (Code Sec. 104(c)).

Attorney's Fees. The issue of whether the contingent attorney fees paid by the taxpayer/plaintiff are excludable created a split in the appellate courts. The United States Supreme Court ruled that a litigant's award that included the attorney's contingent fee, regardless of whether paid directly to the attorney or to the individual, is includible in the litigant's gross income under the anticipatory assignment of income theory (*J.W. Banks II* and *S.J. Banaitis*, 2005-1 USTC ¶ 50,155). However, effective after October 22, 2004, attorneys fees and court costs paid in prosecuting claims based on unlawful discrimination and certain other federal claims, including but not limited to whistleblower actions, are deductible from gross income as an above-the-line deduction (see ¶ 1010A) (Code Sec. 62(a)(20)).

853. Accident and Health Plans. Amounts received by employees under employer-financed accident and health plans may qualify for exclusion from income (Code Sec. 105; Reg. § 1.105-1).[57] A self-employed person is not an employee for purposes of

---

Footnote references are to paragraphs of the 2008 Standard Federal Tax Reports.

[51] ¶ 6662.26
[52] ¶ 6662.0355
[53] ¶ 6662.41

[54] ¶ 6660
[55] ¶ 6662.513
[56] ¶ 6660

[57] ¶ 6700, ¶ 6701

this exclusion. The exclusion applies to a state government plan (including the District of Columbia) (Code Sec. 105(e)(2); Reg. § 1.105-5),[58] as well as to a plan of a private employer. Amounts received by employees as reimbursement for medical care and payments (computed without regard to the period of absence from work) for permanent injury or loss of bodily function under an employer-financed accident or health plan are excludable. Money, other than reimbursements for medical expenses, received by an employee from accident or health insurance because of personal injuries or sickness generally is includible in income if the amounts: (1) are attributable to contributions from the employer to an insurance plan and were not included in the employee's income or (2) are paid directly by the employer (Code Sec. 105(a)).[59] Payments from an accident and health plan are also excludable from an employee's income to the extent that the plan providing the benefits is funded by the employee (Reg. § 1.105-1(c)).[60]

The exclusion also applies to medical care payments that are made to reimburse the taxpayer, not only for the taxpayer's own medical expenses, but also for the medical expenses of a spouse or any dependents. The reimbursement is excludable in full in the year of receipt without limitation as to amount, even though the taxpayer does not actually pay the medical expenses until a later year. The exclusion does not apply to amounts deductible as medical expenses in any prior tax year (Reg. § 1.105-2).[61] Reimbursement of nondeductible expenses for cosmetic surgery is not excludable from gross income (see ¶ 1016).

Payments for permanent injury include payments for permanent loss of use of a member or function of the body, or the permanent disfigurement of the employee, a spouse, or a dependent. The payments must be based on the nature of the injury rather than on the length of time that the employee is absent from work (Code Sec. 105(c); Reg. § 1.105-3).[62]

Excess reimbursements paid to a highly compensated individual under an employer's self-insured medical reimbursement plan that fails to meet certain nondiscrimination requirements are includible in the individual's gross income (Code Sec. 105(h); Reg. § 1.105-11).[63] A highly compensated employee is an employee who is one of the five highest paid officers, who is among the highest paid 25% of all employees, or who is a shareholder owning more than 10% of the company's stock. The plan must not discriminate in terms of eligibility for coverage or in terms of benefits offered under the plan.

The entire amount of a reimbursement with respect to a benefit that is available only to highly compensated individuals is treated as an excess reimbursement includible in income. In the case of a plan that discriminates in terms of eligibility, the includible excess reimbursement is equal to all the medical expenses for which the highly compensated individual was reimbursed times a fraction, the numerator of which is the total amount reimbursed to all participants who are highly compensated individuals and the denominator of which is the total amount reimbursed to all employees under the plan for such plan year. If the plan discriminates in terms of eligibility *and* benefits, any amount which is included in income by reason of the benefits not being available to all other participants is not to be taken into account in determining the excess reimbursements that result from the plan being discriminatory in terms of eligibility.

There is no eligibility discrimination if the plan benefits: (1) at least 70% of all employees or 80% of all eligible employees if at least 70% of all employees are eligible or (2) a class of employees found by the IRS not to be discriminatory in favor of highly compensated individuals. Certain employees, such as part-time workers, employees with less than three years of service, employees under age 25, and employees excluded as a result of a collective bargaining agreement, may be excluded from coverage. There is no benefits discrimination if the self-insured medical expense plan provides the same benefits for non-highly compensated employees as it does for highly compensated employees.

Footnote references are to paragraphs of the 2008 Standard Federal Tax Reports.

[58] ¶ 6700, ¶ 6708   [60] ¶ 6701   [62] ¶ 6700, ¶ 6705
[59] ¶ 6700   [61] ¶ 6703   [63] ¶ 6700, ¶ 6711

¶853

Railroad Unemployment Insurance. Benefits paid to an employee under the Railroad Unemployment Insurance Act for sick days are included in the employee's gross income unless an illness is due to an on-the-job injury (Code Sec. 105(i)).[64]

Health Reimbursement Arrangements. Health reimbursement arrangements (HRAs) are plans through which employers reimburse employees for medical expenses. Medical benefits paid by HRAs that meet certain requirements are not taxable and HRAs generally are not subject to the complex design requirements for flexible spending arrangements (FSAs) (¶ 861) funded through salary reductions under a cafeteria plan (Rev. Rul. 2002-41).[65]

857. Application of Annuity Rules to Accident or Health Benefits. Amounts received as accident or health benefits are not taxable under the annuity rules at ¶ 817 (Reg. § 1.72-15(b)).[66] However, some employer-established plans pay participants both amounts taxable under the annuity rules (¶ 817—¶ 845, ¶ 2153) and amounts excludable from gross income as payments under an accident or health plan. Reg. § 1.72-15 provides specific rules for determining which amounts are excludable.[67] Benefits attributable to the employee's contributions are excludable from gross income under the rules at ¶ 851. Benefits attributable to the employer's contributions are taxable except to the extent that they are excludable under the rules at ¶ 853.

859. Employer Contribution to Accident or Health Plans. Contributions by an employer to provide (through insurance or otherwise) the accident and health benefits described in ¶ 853 are not taxable to the employees (Code Sec. 106; Reg. § 1.106-1).[68] This rule also covers contributions made by a church to purchase health and accident insurance for its minister.[69] The employer's contributions are deductible expenses (Reg. § 1.162-10; Temp. Reg. § 1.162-10T).[70] A group health plan that fails to satisfy continuation coverage requirements or pediatric vaccine health care coverage requirements may be subject to an excise tax (Code Sec. 4980B).[71]

See ¶ 322 and ¶ 421 for treatment of an S corporation shareholder or partner whose accident or health insurance premiums are paid by the S corporation or partnership.

Government Prescription Drug Plans Subsidy. Employers are allowed to deduct fully all payments for retiree prescription drug plans. To encourage employers to offer retiree prescription drug plans, the federal government, under section 1860D-22 of the Social Security Act, provides an additional subsidy payment. To insure the continuation of these retiree prescription drug plans during the implementation of improvements to Medicare supplemental insurance for prescription drugs, the subsidy payments received under section 1860D-22 of the Social Security Act are fully excludable from gross income and not taken into account when determining the appropriate deduction for maintaining a retiree prescription drug plan. This exclusion is effective for tax years beginning after December 8, 2003 (Code Sec. 139A).

859A. Health Savings Accounts. Workers with high-deductible health insurance coverage can deduct up to $2,850 (for self-only coverage) or $5,650 (for family coverage) for 2007 contributions to their Health Savings Accounts (HSAs) (¶ 1020A) (Code Sec. 223). Any amount paid or distributed out of a HSA which is used exclusively to pay the qualified medical expenses of any account beneficiary is not includible in gross income. However, distributions not used to pay qualified medical expenses are includible in gross income and subject to a 10-percent penalty. Individual eligibility for an HSA is determined on a monthly basis. On the first day of any month an individual must be covered by a high-deductible health plan and not covered under a non-high-deductible health plan.

A high-deductible health plan is defined as a plan with a minimum annual deductible of at least $1,100 for self-only coverage ($2,200 for family coverage) for 2007. In addition, the annual out-of-pocket expenses cannot exceed $5,500 for self-only coverage ($11,000 for family coverage) for 2007. Out-of-pocket expenses include deductibles, co-

---

Footnote references are to paragraphs of the 2008 Standard Federal Tax Reports.

[64] ¶ 6700
[65] ¶ 6702.052
[66] ¶ 6124

[67] ¶ 6124
[68] ¶ 6800, ¶ 6801
[69] ¶ 6803.20

[70] ¶ 8750, ¶ 8751
[71] ¶ 34,600

payments and other amounts (other than premiums) that must be paid for plan benefits (Rev. Proc. 2006-53, as modified and superseded by Rev. Proc. 2007-36).

The minimum deductible and maximum out-of-pocket amounts for defining a high-deductible health plan are adjusted for inflation. The minimum annual deductible for 2008 will remain $1,100 for self-only coverage ($2,200 for family coverage). The annual limit on out-of-pocket expenses will increase to $5,600 for self-only coverage ($11,200 for family coverage) for 2008 (Rev. Proc. 2007-36).

Contributions to HSAs are deductible in determining adjusted gross income. The maximum annual aggregate contributions to an HSA are the lesser of (1) 100 percent of the annual deductible for the high deductible health plan or (2) the statutory maximum, as adjusted for inflation. Excess contributions are includible in gross income and subject to a six percent excise tax.

Individuals who reach age 55 by the end of the tax year can increase their annual contributions by $800 for 2007, $900 for 2008 and $1,000 for 2009 and thereafter. Contributions cannot be made after the participant attains age 65, but withdrawals for qualified medical expenses continue to be excluded from gross income (see ¶ 1020A).

860. Medical Savings Accounts. Employees of small businesses and self-employed individuals can take advantage of Archer medical savings accounts (MSAs) to pay health care expenses, provided that accounts are used in conjunction with "high deductible" health insurance (Code Sec. 220). Archer MSAs are like IRAs created for the purpose of defraying unreimbursed health care expenses on a tax-favored basis. Contribution are made with pre-tax dollars and distributions are not included in gross income if used to pay for qualified medical expenses. The MSA concept originally was to be tested over a four-year period or until the number of accounts reach a specific threshold level (generally 750,000 accounts). Since the number of established MSAs is still significantly less than the 750,000 numerical limit, Congress has extended the ability to establish a MSA through 2007 or the time when the numerical limit is achieved, whichever comes first (Code Sec. 220, as amended by the Tax Relief and Health Care Act of 2006 (P.L. 109-432)). Another pilot program was established to assist seniors and allow for the conversion of Archer MSAs upon reaching 65 years old. This program was initially entitled MedicarePlus Choice MSAs. The Working Families Tax Relief Act of 2004 (P.L. 108-311) changed the name to Medicare Advantage MSAs to reflect the new Medicare prescription drug plan (Code Sec. 138). For additional information, see ¶ 1020.

861. Cafeteria Plans. Cafeteria plans are employer-sponsored benefit packages that offer employees a choice between taking cash and receiving qualified benefits, such as accident and health coverage, group-term life insurance coverage, or coverage under a dependent care program (Code Sec. 125; Proposed Reg. § 1.125-1).[72] No amount is included in the income of a cafeteria plan participant who chooses among the benefits of the plan; however, if a participant chooses cash, it is includible in gross income as compensation. If qualified benefits are chosen, they are excludable to the extent allowed by law.

A cafeteria plan cannot offer anything other than cash or qualified benefits. Qualified benefits are benefits which, with the application of Code Sec. 125(a), are specifically excluded from gross income under a statutory provision. The term "qualified benefits" includes any group-term life insurance includible in gross income because the cost exceeds the dollar limitations of Code Sec. 79. A "qualified benefit" does *not* include benefits under Code Sec. 106(b) (Archer medical savings accounts), Code Sec. 117 (scholarships and fellowship grants), Code Sec. 127 (educational assistance benefits provided by an employer), and Code Sec. 132 (excludable fringe benefits). Also, "qualified benefits" do not include products that are advertised, marketed, or offered as long-term care insurance.

Highly compensated employees are not entitled to exclude any benefit attributable to a plan year in which the plan discriminates in favor of the highly compensated employees with respect to participation, contributions, and benefits. Key employees are not entitled to exclude any benefit attributable to a plan year in which the statutory

---

Footnote references are to paragraphs of the 2008 Standard Federal Tax Reports.

[72] ¶ 7320, ¶ 7321

¶860

qualified benefits provided to key employees exceed 25% of the total of such benefits provided to all employees under the plan. In such cases, the benefits must be included in the gross income of the highly compensated employee or key employee for the tax year in which the plan year ends (Code Sec. 125(b)). Reports on cafeteria plans are required (Code Sec. 6039D).[73]

Generally, a plan that provides deferred compensation is not included in the definition of a cafeteria plan. However, a qualified cash or deferred arrangement (401(k) plan) or a plan of an educational institution (to the extent of amounts that a covered employee may elect to have the employer pay as contributions for post-retirement group life insurance if all contributions for such insurance have to be made before retirement and such life insurance does not have a cash surrender value at any time) may be classified as a cafeteria plan.

Flexible Spending Arrangements. A flexible spending arrangement (FSA) is a benefit that provides employees with coverage under which specified, incurred expenses may be reimbursed (subject to reimbursement maximums and other reasonable conditions). Flexible spending arrangements are sometimes referred to as "flexible spending accounts." These arrangements allow employees to make pre-tax contributions to FSA accounts for reimbursement of health and/or dependent care expenses. However, the employee runs the risk of forfeiture of any unused contributions. Traditionally any amounts not spent before the end of the year were forfeited. However, the "use or lose rule" has been eased somewhat in Notice 2005-42. Cafeteria plans may allow the use of a prior year's contributions to a flexible spending account to reimburse expenses incurred during a grace period (of not more than two months and 15 days). Thus, if a cafeteria plan provides for a grace period, funds contributed during one year can be used to reimburse medical expenses incurred through March 15 of the next year.

Amounts contributed to a health care FSA may be used to reimburse employees for purchases of over-the-counter medications, in addition to other medical expenses. The purchases must be adequately substantiated (Rev. Rul. 2003-102).

Family Medical Leave Act. The Family and Medical Leave Act (P.L. 103-3) (FMLA) imposes certain requirements on employers regarding coverage, including family coverage, under group health plans for employees taking FMLA leave and regarding the restoration of benefits to employees who return from FMLA leave. Reg. § 1.125-3 provides guidance on the effect of the Family Medical Leave Act on the operation of cafeteria plans for tax years beginning on or after January 1, 2002.

863. Fringe Benefits. The following noncash benefits qualify for exclusion from an employee's gross income:

> (1) no-additional-cost services (e.g., free stand-by flights by airlines to their employees);

> (2) qualified employee discounts (e.g., reduced sales prices of products and services sold by the employer);

> (3) working condition fringe benefits (e.g., use of company car for business purposes);

> (4) *de minimis* fringe benefits (e.g., use of copying machine for personal purposes);

> (5) qualified transportation fringe benefits (e.g., transportation in a "commuter highway vehicle," transit passes, and qualified parking);

> (6) qualified moving expense reimbursements;

> (7) qualified retirement planning services; and

> (8) qualified military base realignment and closure fringe benefits (Code Sec. 132(a); Reg. § 1.132-1).

Also, the value of any on-premises athletic facilities provided and operated by the employer is a nontaxable fringe benefit (Code Sec. 132(j)(4)).[74]

Footnote references are to paragraphs of the 2008 Standard Federal Tax Reports.

[73] ¶ 35,660   [74] ¶ 7420

The above benefits may be extended to retired and disabled former employees, to widows and widowers of deceased employees, and to spouses and dependent children of employees. Applicable nondiscrimination conditions must be met (Code Sec. 132(h)).[75]

Denial of a deduction to an employer for its payment of travel expenses of a spouse, dependent, or other individual accompanying an employee on business travel does not preclude those items from qualifying as working condition fringe benefits (Reg. § 1.132-5).

The above benefits that are excluded from an employee's gross income also are excludable from the wage base for purposes of income tax, FICA, FUTA, and RRTA withholding purposes. In the case of taxable noncash fringe benefits in the form of the personal use of an employer-provided vehicle, income tax withholding may be avoided if the employer elects not to withhold and notifies the employee of such election (social security and railroad retirement taxes must be withheld). However, the value of the benefit must be included on the employee's Form W-2 (Code Sec. 3402(s)).[76] The IRS has issued detailed regulations governing the exclusion of fringe benefits from an employee's income.[77]

Qualified Moving Expense Reimbursement. A qualified moving expense reimbursement is an excludable fringe benefit. This is an amount received (directly or indirectly) by an individual from an employer as a payment for (or a reimbursement of) expenses that would be deductible as moving expenses under Code Sec. 217 if directly paid or incurred by the individual. The term does not include a payment for (or a reimbursement of) an expense actually deducted by an individual in a prior tax year (see ¶ 1073) (Code Sec. 132(g)).

Transportation Fringe Benefits. In 2007, employees may exclude a maximum of $110 per month (to increase to $115 for 2008) for the value of employer-provided transit passes or vanpooling in an employer-provided "commuter highway vehicle" (Code Sec. 132(f)).[78] A qualifying vehicle must seat at least six adults (excluding the driver), and at least 80% of its mileage use must be reasonably expected to be for employees' commuting purposes and for trips when the vehicle is at least one-half full (excluding the driver).

Employees may exclude up to $215 per month from gross income for the value of employer-provided qualified parking in 2007 (to increase to $220 for 2008) (Code Sec. 132(f)(2)(B)). The parking must be provided on or near the business premises of the employer or on or near a location from which the employee commutes to work by mass transit, in a commuter highway vehicle, or by carpool. The exclusion does not apply to parking on or near property used by the employee for residential purposes.

The exclusion for these types of transportation fringes also applies if an employer reimburses an employee's expenses for mass transit passes, vanpooling, or qualified parking. Also, employers may offer the employee a choice of one or more qualified transportation benefits or the cash equivalent without loss of the exclusion (Code Sec. 132(f)(4)). The amount is includible if the cash option is chosen. With respect to mass transit passes, employers must provide vouchers and not make cash reimbursements unless vouchers are not readily available for direct distribution by the employer to its employees (Code Sec. 132(f)(4); Reg. § 1.132-9(b)).

Military Base Realignment and Closure Fringe Benefits. The Department of Defense Homeowners Assistance Program (HAP) was established to offset the losses suffered by military and certain civilian employees when closure or realignment of Department of Defense or Coast Guard bases or installations caused a reduction in the fair market value of their homes. These payments are excluded from gross income if made after November 11, 2003 (Code Sec. 132(a)(8)).

Adoption Assistance Programs. Qualified adoption expenses paid to a third party or reimbursed to an employee by an employer under a written adoption assistance program is excludable from the employee's gross income (Code Sec. 137). An adoption assistance program is a written plan that: (1) benefits employees who qualify under rules set up by the employer which do not favor highly compensated employees or their dependents;

Footnote references are to paragraphs of the 2008 Standard Federal Tax Reports.

[75] ¶ 7420
[76] ¶ 33,542, ¶ 33,591
[77] ¶ 7422
[78] ¶ 7420

¶863

(2) does not pay more than five percent of its payments each year to shareholders or owners of more than five percent of the stock; (3) provides for adequate notice to employees of their eligibility; and (4) requires employees to provide reasonable substantiation of qualified expenses that are to be paid or reimbursed. The dollar amounts for the exclusion and the phase out for higher income taxpayers are the same as for the adoption credit; for 2007 the amount that may be excluded is $11,390 (to increase to $11,650 for 2008) and the phaseout range for upper income taxpayers is $170,820 to $210,820 (to increase to $174,730 to $214,730 for 2008). For a child who is a U.S. citizen or resident, the exclusion is taken in the year the payments were made regardless if the adoption became final. However, for the adoption of a foreign child, a taxpayer cannot exclude the payments until the adoption becomes final. Although the excluded amount under an adoption assistance program is not subject to income tax withholding, the payment remains subject to social security, Medicare and federal unemployment taxes. Other requirements and the definition of qualifying adoption expenses are the same as found under the adoption credit (see ¶ 1306) (Code Sec. 23).

869. Employer-Provided Child or Dependent Care Services. Up to $5,000 of child or dependent care assistance services that are paid by an employer and furnished pursuant to a written plan generally are not includible in the employee's gross income (Code Sec. 129).[79] The individual being cared for must be either:

(1) a dependent of the taxpayer (under Code Sec. 152(a)(1)) that has not yet attained the age of 13,

(2) a dependent of the taxpayer who is physically or mentally incapable of caring for themselves and who resides with the taxpayer in their principal place of abode for more than six months of the year, or

(3) the spouse of the taxpayer who is physically or mentally incapable of caring for themselves and who resides with the taxpayer in their principal place of abode for more than six months of the year (Code Sec. 21(b)(1)).

A dependent care assistance plan generally must not discriminate in favor of employees who are highly compensated. However, if a plan would qualify as a dependent care assistance program except for the fact that it fails to meet discrimination, eligibility, or other requirements of Code Sec. 129(d), then despite the failure the plan may still be treated as a dependent care assistance program in the case of employees who are not highly compensated. The amount excludable from gross income cannot exceed $5,000 ($2,500 in the case of a separate return by a married individual). The amount of any payment exceeding these limits is includible in gross income for the tax year in which the dependent care services were provided, even if payment for the services is received in a subsequent tax year (Code Sec. 129(a)(2)(B)).[80]

The exclusion cannot exceed the earned income of an unmarried employee or the earned income of the lower-earning spouse of married employees. The exclusion does not apply unless the name, address, and taxpayer identification number of the person performing the child or dependent care services are included on the return of the employee benefiting from the exclusion (Code Sec. 129(e)(9)). However, the exclusion may be claimed even though the information is not provided if it can be shown that the taxpayer exercised due diligence in attempting to provide this information. See also ¶ 1301, regarding the child and dependent care credits.

871. Employer Payment of Employee's Educational Expenses. Up to $5,250 of payments received by an employee for tuition, fees, books, supplies, etc., under an employer's educational assistance program may be excluded from gross income (Code Sec. 127; Reg. § 1.127-1).[81] Excludable assistance payments may not cover tools or supplies that the employee retains after completion of the course or the cost of meals, lodging, or transportation. Although the courses covered by the plan need not be job related, an exception applies to courses involving sports, games, or hobbies. These courses may only be covered if they involve the employer's business or are required as part of a degree program (Reg. § 1.127-2(c)).[82]

Footnote references are to paragraphs of the 2008 Standard Federal Tax Reports.

[79] ¶ 7380
[80] ¶ 7380
[81] ¶ 7350, ¶ 7351
[82] ¶ 7352

Reports and Records. An employer who maintains an educational assistance plan must maintain records and file an information return (Form 5500, Annual Return/Report of Employee Benefit Plan) for the plan (Code Sec. 6039D). However, the reporting requirement for educational assistance plans has been *suspended* effective on April 22, 2002 (Notice 2002-24).[83]

873. Food and Lodging Provided by Employer. Meals that are excludable from an employee's income under Code Sec. 119 are considered a *de minimis* fringe benefit under Code Sec. 132.[84] If more than one-half of the employees are furnished meals for the convenience of the employer, all meals provided on the premises are treated as furnished for the convenience of the employer (Code Sec. 119(b)(4)). Therefore, the meals are fully deductible by the employer, instead of possibly being subject to the 50-percent limit on business meal deductions, and excludable by the employees.

The value of meals and lodging furnished by an employer to an employee, a spouse, or dependents for the employer's convenience is not includible in the employee's gross income if, in the case of meals, they are furnished on the employer's business premises and if, in the case of lodging, the employee is required to accept the lodging on the employer's business premises as a condition of employment (Code Sec. 119; Reg. § 1.119-1).[85] The fact that the employer imposes a partial charge for meals or that the employee may accept or decline meals does not affect the exclusion if all other conditions are met, but cash reimbursements of the employee's meal expenses are included in gross income (Code Sec. 119(b)).[86] If meals are furnished for the convenience of the employer, they must be furnished for substantial noncompensatory business reasons (such as having the employee on call) (*Boyd Gaming Inc.,* 99-1 USTC ¶ 50,530)[87] rather than as additional compensation (Reg. § 1.119-1(a)(2)).[88]

The term "business premises of the employer" generally means the place of employment of the employee. It can include a camp located in a foreign country if an employee is furnished lodging.

For tax year 2006, qualified employees in the Gulf Opportunity (GO) Zone affected by Hurricane Katrina may exclude the value of in-kind lodging provided to them and their families by or on behalf of a qualified employer (Code Sec. 1400P(a)(2)). The amount of the exclusion cannot exceed $600 for any month lodging is provided. A qualified employee is an individual who, on August 28, 2005, had a principal residence in the GO Zone and who performed substantially all of his or her employment services in the GO Zone for the qualified employer furnishing the lodging (Code Sec. 1400P(c)). A qualified employer is any employer with a trade or business located in the GO Zone (Code Sec. 1400P(d)). The exclusion of housing costs of up to $600 per month is only available from January 1, 2006, through June 30, 2006.

Faculty Housing. The value of campus lodging furnished to employees by educational or medical research institutions is excludable from the employee's gross income if an adequate rental is charged. A rental is considered inadequate and thus the exclusion will not apply to the extent of the excess of: (a) the lesser of (1) 5% of the appraised value of the lodging or (2) an amount equal to the average of the rentals paid by nonemployees or nonstudents during the year for comparable lodging provided by the institution over (b) the rent paid by the employee for the calendar year (Code Sec. 119(d)).[89] The appraised value under (1), above, will be determined as of the close of the calendar year in which the tax year begins or, in the case of a rental period not greater than one year, at any time during the calendar year in which such period begins.

875. Minister's Home or Rental Allowance. Ministers of the gospel may exclude the rental value of homes furnished by churches as part of their compensation (Code Sec. 107(2)).[90] This includes the portion of a retired minister's pension designated as a rental allowance by the national governing body of a religious denomination having

---

Footnote references are to paragraphs of the 2008 Standard Federal Tax Reports.

[83] ¶ 35,660
[84] ¶ 7420
[85] ¶ 7220, ¶ 7221
[86] ¶ 7220, ¶ 7222.59
[87] ¶ 7222.29
[88] ¶ 7221
[89] ¶ 7220
[90] ¶ 6850, ¶ 6851

complete control over the retirement fund.[91] The exemption also applies to the rental value of a residence furnished to a retired minister (but not a widow).[92]

A minister is entitled to deduct mortgage interest and real property taxes paid on a personal residence even if the amounts expended are derived from a rental allowance that is excludable from the minister's gross income (Code Sec. 265(a)(6)).[93]

Reimbursed Living Expenses

877. Exclusion for Reimbursement. A taxpayer whose residence is damaged or destroyed by fire, storm, or other casualty and who must temporarily occupy another residence during the repair can exclude from gross income any insurance payments received as reimbursement for living expenses during such period. This also applies to a person who is denied access to his principal residence by governmental authorities because of the occurrence or threat of occurrence of a casualty (Code Sec. 123; Reg. § 1.123-1).[94]

This exclusion is limited to the excess of actual living expenses incurred by the taxpayer and members of the household over the normal living expenses they would have incurred during the period. The exclusion covers additional costs incurred in renting suitable housing and any extraordinary expenses for transportation, food, utilities, and miscellaneous items.

Scholarship or Fellowship Grant

879. Scholarship or Fellowship Grant Is Not Income. Any amount received as a qualified scholarship by an individual who is a candidate for a degree at a qualified educational organization, which normally maintains a regular faculty and curriculum and normally has a regularly enrolled body of students in attendance where its educational activities are regularly carried on, is excluded from that individual's gross income (Code Sec. 117; Reg. § 1.117-1).[95] A qualified scholarship includes any amount received by an individual as a scholarship or fellowship grant so long as the amount was used for qualified tuition and related expenses such as fees, books, supplies, and equipment required for courses of instruction at a qualified educational organization.

Tuition Reduction. The amount of any qualified tuition reduction to employees of educational institutions is, similarly, excluded from gross income (Code Sec. 117(d)).[96] The tuition reduction must be provided to an employee of a qualified educational organization as defined under Code Sec. 170(b)(1)(A)(ii). The reduction can be for education provided by the employer or by another qualified educational organization. Moreover, it can be for education provided to the employee, the employee's spouse, dependent child, or other person treated as an employee under Code Sec. 132(h). However, it can only be used for education below the graduate level unless it is for the education of an employee who is a graduate student and who is engaged in teaching or research activities for the employer (Code Sec. 117(d)(5)[4]).[97] Any qualified tuition reduction may be excluded only if it does not discriminate in favor of highly compensated employees (Code Sec. 117(d)(3)).[98]

The exclusions for qualified scholarships and qualified tuition reductions will not apply to amounts representing payments for teaching, research, or other services performed by the student that are required as a condition for receiving the qualified scholarship or qualified tuition reduction (Code Sec. 117(c)).[99] Presumably, athletic scholarships awarded to students who are expected, but not required, to participate in sports would, as they have in the past, qualify for exclusion.[100] Beginning after December 31, 2001, amounts received by degree candidates from the National Health Service Corps (NHSC) Scholarship Program or the Armed Forces Scholarship Program for tuition, fees, books, supplies and required equipment are excluded from the recipient's gross income, even though there is a future service obligation connected to these qualified scholarships (Code Sec. 117(c)(2)). Beginning after December 31, 2003,

---

Footnote references are to paragraphs of the 2008 Standard Federal Tax Reports.

[91] ¶ 6852.12
[92] ¶ 6852.31
[93] ¶ 14,050
[94] ¶ 7300, ¶ 7301
[95] ¶ 7170, ¶ 7172
[96] ¶ 7170
[97] ¶ 7170
[98] ¶ 7170
[99] ¶ 7170
[100] ¶ 7183.22

amounts received as repayments for NHSC Loan Program by health care professionals are excluded from gross income and employment taxes (Code Sec. 108(f)(4)). This provision extends to loan repayments received under similar state programs qualified for funds under the Public Health Service Act.

Government Cost-Sharing Payments

881. Certain Agricultural Cost-Sharing Payments Are Excludable. Agricultural and forestry cost-sharing payments made by state or federal governments may be excluded from gross income if (1) the Secretary of Agriculture determines that the payments were made primarily for soil and water conservation, environmental protection or restoration, wildlife habitat development, or forest improvement and (2) the Treasury Department determines that the payments do not result in a substantial increase in the annual income derived from the property with respect to which the payments were made. No adjustment to the basis of the property involved is made for the payments and, therefore, no income tax deduction or credit may be taken with respect to them (Code Sec. 126).[101] Further, if the property (or improvement) purchased with the payments is disposed of within 20 years, the payment amounts are recaptured as ordinary income. A 100% recapture rate applies if disposition occurs within the first 10 years, with an annual decrease of 10% thereafter (Code Sec. 1255).[102]

Small Business Stock

882. Exclusion for Gain from Small Business Stock. Noncorporate taxpayers may exclude 50% of any gain from the sale or exchange of qualified small business stock issued after August 10, 1993, and held for more than five years (see ¶ 2396).

Foster Care Payments

883. Income Received for Foster Care. Payments made by a state or qualified foster care placement agency as "difficulty of care payments" or to reimburse a foster home provider for the expenses of caring for individuals placed in the home by a state agency or a qualified foster care placement agency are excludable from gross income (Code Sec. 131).[103] A qualified foster care placement agency is a placement agency that is licensed or certified by a state or local government or an entity designated by such a government to make foster care payments. Foster care payments are excludable only for foster care individuals who live in the foster care provider's home. Regular foster care payments are not excludable to the extent made for more than five individuals over age 18. In the case of "difficulty of care payments" (i.e., payments for additional care required by a physically, mentally, or emotionally handicapped person), payments are not excludable to the extent made for more than 10 individuals under age 19 and more than five individuals over 18 years of age.

Energy Conservation Subsidies

884. Subsidies for Energy Conservation Measures. The value of any subsidy provided (directly or indirectly) by a public utility to a customer for the purchase or installation of energy conservation measures for a dwelling unit is excluded from the customer's gross income (Code Sec. 136).[104] Energy conservation measures are any installations or modifications designed to reduce the consumption of electricity or natural gas or to improve management of energy demand.

Cancellation of Debt

885. Income from Discharge of Debt. Generally, a taxpayer realizes income to the extent his debts are forgiven (Code Sec. 61(a)(12)). However, a taxpayer need not recognize income from the discharge of debts in bankruptcy proceedings under title 11 of the U.S. Code or when the taxpayer is insolvent outside bankruptcy (Code Sec. 108(a)(1)(A) and (B)). Certain taxpayers may also exclude from gross income amounts realized from the discharge of qualified real property business indebtedness, qualified farm indebtedness, and certain student loans (Code Sec. 108(c), (f) and (g)). For a more detailed discussion see ¶ 791.

Footnote references are to paragraphs of the 2008 Standard Federal Tax Reports.

[101] ¶ 7330

[102] ¶ 31,080, ¶ 31,081, ¶ 31,082

[103] ¶ 7400

[104] ¶ 7560

886. Debt Discharge for Victims of Terrorist Attacks. The Victims of Terrorism Tax Relief Act of 2001 (P.L. 107-134) provided an exclusion from gross income for certain cancellations of indebtedness (Code Sec. 101(i)).[105] Specifically, a discharge of debt is excluded from gross income if the indebtedness is discharged by reason of the death of an individual which was caused by the April 19, 1995 bombing of the federal building in Oklahoma City, the September 11, 2001 terrorist attacks or as a result of the terrorist attack involving anthrax occurring on or after September 11, 2001 and before January 1, 2002. The exclusion applies to discharges of debt made on or after September 11, 2001 and before January 1, 2002. The exclusion also applies to certain payments received by the survivors of those killed and disability payments received by those injured in the attacks.

Military Exemptions

889. Income Generally. Except as noted in the following paragraphs, members of the U.S. Armed Forces include the same items in income as civilians.

891. Armed Forces Benefits. A pension, annuity, or similar payment for *personal injuries* or *sickness* that resulted from combat-related service in the armed forces of *any* country or in the Coast and Geodetic Survey or the Public Health Service of the U.S., or a disability annuity under the provisions of section 808 of the Foreign Service Act of 1980, is exempt (see ¶ 851) (Code Sec. 104(a)(4); Reg. § 1.104-1(e)).[106]

Retirement pay received from the government by Armed Service members is not exempt (Code Sec. 61(a)(11)).[107] Disability retirement pay that is computed on the basis of the percentage of disability is fully excludable from gross income, but disability retirement pay that is computed by reference to years of service is excludable only to the extent allowed under the percentage-of-disability method (Code Sec. 104).[108]

Dividends and proceeds from maturing government endowment insurance contracts under the National Service Life Insurance Act of 1940 and all other acts relating to veterans are exempt.[109] Interest on dividends left on deposit with the Veterans Administration is exempt. If an individual uses accumulated dividends to buy additional paid-up National Service Life Insurance, neither the dividends nor the paid-up insurance is taxable (Rev. Rul. 91-14).

Veterans' benefits under any law administered by the U.S. Department of Veterans Affairs (VA) are not includible in income.[110] This includes amounts paid to veterans or their families in the form of educational, training, or subsistence allowances, disability compensation and pension payments for disabilities, compensation for participation in a work therapy program, grants for homes designed for wheelchair living, grants for motor vehicles for veterans who lost their sight or the use of their limbs, and veterans' pensions (38 USC § 5301 and following).

893. Armed Forces Allowances. Allowances for subsistence, quarters, travel, and moving furnished to a commissioned officer, chief warrant officer, warrant officer, or enlisted personnel of the Armed Forces, Coast and Geodetic Survey, or Public Health Service are not taxable income.[111]

Housing and cost-of-living allowances received by Armed Forces members to cover the excess cost of quarters and subsistence while on permanent duty at a post outside the U.S. are excludable from gross income (Rev. Rul. 61-5).[112] The same rule applies to family separation allowances received on account of overseas assignment.[113] The fact that a member of the military service, Coast and Geodetic Survey, or Public Health Service receives a tax-free housing allowance will not bar a deduction for mortgage interest or real property taxes on the member's home (Code Sec. 265(a)(6)).[114]

895. Combat Zone Compensation. Enlisted members of the Armed Forces and warrant officers (both commissioned and noncommissioned) may exclude from gross income all pay received for any month during any part of which they served in a combat

---

Footnote references are to paragraphs of the 2008 Standard Federal Tax Reports.

[105] ¶ 6502
[106] ¶ 6660, ¶ 6661
[107] ¶ 5502, ¶ 5507.121
[108] ¶ 6660, ¶ 6662.79

[109] ¶ 5504.74
[110] ¶ 5504.785
[111] ¶ 5506, ¶ 7222.79
[112] ¶ 5507.111

[113] ¶ 5507.110
[114] ¶ 14,050, ¶ 14,054.0662

zone or were hospitalized as a result of wounds, disease, or injury incurred while serving in a combat zone. The exclusion for months of hospitalization does not apply for any month beginning more than two years after the termination of combatant activities in the zone. The same exclusion applies to commissioned officers, but it is limited to "the maximum enlisted amount." This amount is the highest rate of basic pay at the highest pay grade that enlisted personnel may receive plus the amount of hostile fire/imminent danger pay that the officer receives (Code Sec. 112; Reg. § 1.112-1).[115]

The following areas, among others, have been designated combat zones qualifying American military personal serving in these areas for special tax benefits;

> (1) Bosnia, Herzegovina, Croatia and Macedonia, effective on November 21, 1995 (Notice 96-34),

> (2) the Kosovo region, effective on March 12, 1999 (Notice 99-30, supplementing Notice 96-34),

> (3) the Persian Gulf, the Red Sea, the Gulf of Oman, part of the Arabian Sea, the Gulf of Aden and the geographic areas of Iraq, Kuwait, Saudi Arabia, Oman, Bahrain, Qatar and the United Arab Emirates, effective on January 17, 1991 (Notice 2003-21),

> (4) Afghanistan (including Jordan, Pakistan and Tajikistan), effective on September 19, 2001,

> (5) Kyrgyzstan and Uzbekistan, effective on October 1, 2001 (Notice 2002-17), and

> (6) areas supporting Operation Iraqi Freedom, effective on April 10, 2003.

Exception to the exclusion. Combat pay excludible under Code Sec. 112 may nevertheless be included in earned income for purposes of the earned income tax credit and calculating the refundable portion of the child tax credit (Code Secs. 24(d)(1) and 32(c)(2)(B)).

Similarly, excludible combat pay is included in determining the amount military personnel can contribute to their individual retirement accounts (IRAs) (Code Sec. 219(f), as amended by the Heroes Earned Retirement Opportunities Act (P.L. 109-277)). This provision is retroactively effective for tax years beginning after December 31, 2003. Contributions for 2004 and 2005 may be made as late as May 28, 2009. Affected taxpayers will also have an additional year after making an IRA contribution to file a claim for refund of tax for those years in which the making of a deductible IRA contribution lower their tax liability.

896. Qualified Military Benefits. Before enactment of the Tax Reform Act of 1986, a variety of benefits for military personnel were excludable from gross income under a variety of statutes, regulations, and long-standing administrative practices. In the 1986 Act it was determined that, in the future, no such exclusions would be permitted except under some provision of the Internal Revenue Code. However, the Act added to the Code a provision that, in effect, "grandfathered" all of the previous non-Code exclusions (Code Sec. 134).[116] Under this provision, all such exclusions that were in effect on September 9, 1986, continue to be in effect. If a benefit in effect on September 9, 1986, is thereafter modified or adjusted for increases in the cost of living or the like under authority existing on that date, the adjustments are also excludable.

Benefits not otherwise categorized as qualified military benefits but provided in connection with an individual's status or service as a member of the uniformed services may be excluded from income under other Code sections if their requirements for exclusion are met.

Death Gratuity Payments. Section 1478, Title 10, of the U.S. Code provides that upon notification of the death of military personnel on active duty or on inactive duty training, a death gratuity will be paid to or for the survivor of the service member.

The Military Family Tax Relief Act of 2003 (MFTRA) (P.L. 108-121) increases the death gratuity payment from $6,000 to $12,000, effective for deaths occurring after September 10, 2001. An exemption from gross income is also allowed for any adjustment

---

Footnote references are to paragraphs of the 2008 Standard Federal Tax Reports.

[115] ¶ 7080, ¶ 7081   [116] ¶ 7500

¶896

in the amount of the death gratuity payments. The limitation on post-September 9, 1986 modifications does not apply to this benefit. Thus, cost-of-living adjustments or other increases in the gratuity amount will not be subject to tax.

Dependent Care Assistance Program. Qualified military benefits have been expanded under MFTRA to include dependent care assistance provided under a Code Sec. 129 dependent care assistance program for a current or former uniformed forces service member or for a dependent (Code Sec. 134(b)(4)). The exclusion is effective for tax years beginning after December 31, 2002.

Disaster Relief Payments

897. Disaster Relief Payments. The Victims of Terrorism Tax Relief Act of 2001 (P.L. 107-134) has provided an exclusion from gross income for qualified disaster relief payments, as well as payments received under Section 406 of the Air Transportation Safety and System Stabilization Act (Code Sec. 139). This exclusion also applies to self-employment and employment taxes, and as such no withholding is required for qualified disaster relief payments. However, the exclusion does not apply to any individual (or a representative) identified by the Attorney General to have been a participant or conspirator in a terrorist action.

Disaster Relief Payments Defined. Qualified disaster relief payments include payments, from any source, to or for the benefit of, an individual to reimburse or pay reasonable and necessary:

(1) personal, family, living or funeral expenses incurred as a result of a qualified disaster;

(2) expenses incurred for the repair or rehabilitation of a personal residence or for the repair or replacement of its contents to the extent attributable to a qualified disaster;

(3) payments made by a commercial airlines to families of passengers killed as a result of a qualified disaster; and

(4) payments made by a federal, state or local government in connection with a qualified disaster.

Taxpayers in a presidentially declared disaster area who receive grants from state programs, charitable organizations or employers to cover medical, transportation, or temporary housing expenses do not include these grants in gross income (Rev. Rul. 2003-12). However, qualified disaster relief payments do not include payments for any expense compensated for by insurance or otherwise, or payments in the nature of income replacement, such as payments to individuals of lost wages, unemployment compensation, or payments in the nature of business income replacement.

Code Sec. 139(c) defines a qualified disaster as:

(1) a disaster that results from a terroristic or military action (as defined under Code Sec. 692(c)(2));

(2) a presidentially declared disaster (as defined under Code Sec. 1033(h)(3));

(3) a disaster that results from an accident involving a common carrier, or from any other event, which is determined by the IRS to be of a catastrophic nature; or

(4) a disaster determined by an applicable federal, state or local authority (as determined by the IRS) to warrant assistance.

Air Transportation Safety Act. Taxpayers who are eligible to receive payments under Section 406 of the Air Transportation Safety and System Stabilization Act as a result of physical harm or death incurred from the terrorist-related aircraft crashes of September 11, 2001, can exclude these amounts (Code Sec. 139(f)).

Coverdell Education Savings Accounts

898. Coverdell Education Savings Accounts. Individuals may open a Coverdell Education Savings Account (ESA, formerly called an "education IRA") to help pay for the qualified education expenses of a designated beneficiary (Code Sec. 530(b)). A Coverdell ESA is a tax-exempt trust or custodial account organized exclusively in the United States. At the time it is organized the trust must be designated as an ESA and the

designated beneficiary must be under age 18 or a special needs beneficiary. Contributions to a Coverdell ESA must be made in cash and are not deductible. In addition, the maximum annual contribution that can be made is limited $2,000 a year (excluding rollovers). The annual contribution is phased out for joint filers with modified adjusted gross income at or above $190,000 and less than $220,000 (at or above $95,000 and less than $110,000 for single filers). The reduction in permitted contributions based on modified AGI applies only to individual contributors. Thus, contributions made by entities, such as a corporation or tax-exempt organization are not subject to the phase-out rules. Amounts remaining in the account must be distributed within: (1) 30 days after the beneficiary reaches age 30 or (2) 30 days after the death of the beneficiary (see "*Rollovers*," following) (Code Sec. 530(b)(1)(E)).

Coordination With Other Educational Benefits. Qualified expenses will first be reduced for tax-exempt scholarships or fellowship grants (see ¶ 879) and any other tax-free educational benefits, as required by Code Sec. 25A(g). Expenses will then be reduced for amounts taken into account in determining the Hope and Lifetime Learning credits (¶ 1303). Where a student receives distributions from both a Coverdell ESA and a qualified tuition program that together exceed these remaining expenses, the expenses must be allocated between the distributions (Code Sec. 530(d)(2)(C)).

Distributions. Generally, contributions to Coverdell ESAs are treated as gifts to the beneficiaries. Distributions from Coverdell ESAs are excludable from gross income to the extent that the distribution does not exceed the qualified higher education expenses incurred by the designated beneficiary during the year in which the distribution is made (Code Sec. 530(d)(2)(A)).[117] Qualified distributions, with the exception of room and board, are tax exempt regardless of whether the designated beneficiary attends an eligible educational institution on a full-time, half-time, or less than half-time basis. Room and board expenses constitute qualified higher education expenses only if the student is enrolled at an eligible institution on at least a half-time basis (see below).

Distributions are deemed paid from both contributions (which are always tax free) and earnings (which may be excludable). The amount of contributions distributed is determined by multiplying the distribution by the ratio that the aggregate amount of contributions bears to the total balance of the account at the time the distribution is made (Code Sec. 530(d)(1)).[118]

If aggregate distributions exceed expenses during the tax year, qualified education expenses are deemed to be paid from a pro rata share of both principal and interest. Thus, the portion of earnings excludable from income is based on the ratio that the qualified higher education expenses bear to the total amount of the distribution. The remaining portion of earnings are included in the income of the distributee.

Distributions Not Used for Education. The tax imposed on any taxpayer who receives a payment or distribution from a Coverdell ESA that is includible in gross income will be increased by an additional 10% (Code Sec. 530(d)(4)(A)).[119] The additional 10% penalty does not apply to distributions: (1) made to a designated beneficiary or the estate of a designated beneficiary after the designated beneficiary's death; (2) attributable to the designated beneficiary being disabled (as defined under Code Sec. 72(m)(7)); (3) made on account of a scholarship or allowance (as defined under Code Sec. 25A(g)(2))[120] received by the account holder to the extent the amount of the distribution does not exceed the amount of the scholarship or allowance; or (4) that constitute the return of excess contributions and earnings thereon (although earnings are includible in income) (Code Sec. 530(d)(2)(A)).[121]

Military Academy Attendance. Generally, since recipients of appointments to military academies are required to fulfill service obligations, the appointments are not considered scholarships and the 10% penalty applies. The Military Family Tax Relief Act of 2003 allows penalty-free withdrawals from Coverdell ESAs made on account of the beneficiary's attendance at a service academy to the extent the distribution is used for the costs of advanced education (Code Sec. 530(d)(4)). The penalty-waiver applies to tax

---

Footnote references are to paragraphs of the 2008 Standard Federal Tax Reports.

[117] ¶ 22,950   [119] ¶ 22,950   [121] ¶ 22,950
[118] ¶ 22,950   [120] ¶ 3820

years beginning after 2002 and covers appointments to the United States Military, Navy, Air Force, Coast Guard and Merchant Marine Academies.

Rollovers. Amounts held in a Coverdell ESA may be distributed and put into a Coverdell ESA for a member of the designated beneficiary's family. These distributions will not be included in the distributee's gross income provided the rollover occurs within 60 days of the distribution. Similarly, any change in the beneficiary of a Coverdell ESA does not constitute a distribution for gross income purposes if the new beneficiary is a member of the family of the original beneficiary and of the same or higher generation (Code Sec. 529(c)(5)(B)). A person's family members are determined under Code Sec. 529(e)(2) (Code Sec. 530(d)(2)(A)).[122] Amounts held in a Coverdell ESA may also be rolled over into another Coverdell ESA for the benefit of the same beneficiary.

Qualified Education Expenses. Tuition, fees, books, supplies and equipment fall under the definition of "education expenses" for the designated beneficiary to attend undergraduate or graduate level courses at an eligible education institution. The term also includes room and board provided that the student incurring the expense is enrolled at an eligible on at least a half-time basis (Code Sec. 530(b)(3)).[123]

Elementary and secondary education expenses are defined by reference to Code Sec. 529(e)(3) and include expenses for tuition, books, supplies, and equipment. Expenses for special needs services of a special needs beneficiary are also qualified expenses for both purposes (Code Sec. 529(e)(3)(A)). Qualified elementary and secondary expenses differ, however, in that they include expenses for academic tutoring, the purchase of computer technology or equipment or internet access or related services, room and board, uniforms, transportation and supplementary items and services such as extended day programs as required or provided by the school.

Eligible Educational Institution. An eligible educational institution is generally an accredited postsecondary educational institution offering credit toward a bachelor's degree, an associate's degree, a graduate-level or professional degree, or other recognized postsecondary credential. Generally, proprietary and postsecondary vocational institutions are eligible educational institutions (Code Sec. 530(b)(3)).[124] Elementary and secondary schools (i.e., kindergarten through grade 12) are also eligible institutions. Schools may be public, private or religious.

Account Requirements. A Coverdell ESA is a tax-exempt trust created in the United States exclusively for purposes of paying the qualified higher education expenses of the trust's designated beneficiary. The trust must be designated as a Coverdell ESA at the time it is created or organized (Code Sec. 530(b)(1)).[125]

Prohibited Uses of Accounts. A Coverdell ESA will lose its tax-exempt status if it engages in a prohibited transaction or is pledged as security for a loan. Prohibited transactions include loans and use of account assets by the beneficiary or a fiduciary (see Code Sec. 4975(c)).[126]

Transfers Upon Death or Divorce. Death or divorce of the designated beneficiary need not cause a taxable distribution to the spouse or ex-spouse. The transfer of a beneficiary's interest in a Coverdell ESA to a spouse or ex-spouse under a divorce or separation agreement is not a taxable transfer, and after the transfer the interest in the account is treated as belonging to the spouse/ex-spouse (Code Sec. 530(d)(7)).[127]

Estate and Gift Tax Treatment. Any contribution to a Coverdell ESA is treated as a completed gift of a present interest from the contributor to the beneficiary at the time of the contribution. Annual contributions are eligible for the gift tax exclusion under Code Sec. 2503(b) and are excludable for purposes of the generation-skipping transfer tax (Code Sec. 530(d)(3)).[128]

Footnote references are to paragraphs of the 2008 Standard Federal Tax Reports.

[122] ¶ 22,940	[125] ¶ 22,950	[128] ¶ 22,950
[123] ¶ 22,950	[126] ¶ 34,400	
[124] ¶ 22,950	[127] ¶ 22,950	

Qualified Tuition Programs

899. Qualified Tuition Programs. A qualified tuition program (QTP or Code Sec. 529 plan) is a program under which a person may prepay tuition credits or make cash contributions to an account on behalf of a beneficiary for payment of qualified higher education expenses. The program must be established and maintained by a state, state agency, or by an eligible educational institution (i.e., private college or university). Eligible schools generally include any accredited post-secondary educational institution, so long as contributions made to the program are held in a "qualified trust" (i.e., one which meets the requirements under Code Sec. 408(a)(2) and (5)).[129] A QTP is exempt from all federal income taxation, except for the tax imposed on unrelated business income (see ¶ 655 and following) (Code Sec. 529).[130]

Distributions. Distributions from a QTP, including cash, earnings, and in-kind distributions, may be excluded from a designated beneficiary's gross income to the extent that the distribution is used to pay for qualified higher education expenses (QHEEs). A 10-percent penalty will apply to any distribution which is not used to pay QHEEs for a reason other than the death or disability of the beneficiary, or to the extent that the distribution exceeds amounts not covered by scholarships (Code Sec. 529(c)(6)).[131] A distribution will not be considered to have occurred if:

- any amount received from a QTP is rolled-over (within 60 days) to the QTP of another beneficiary who is a family member of the first beneficiary;

- the contributor changes the designated beneficiary to another person who is a member of the family of the first beneficiary; and

- any amount is transferred from the QTP to another QTP of the same beneficiary, but only so long as there is only one such transfer within a 12-month period (Code Sec. 529(c)(3)).[132]

For this purpose, QHEEs include tuition, fees, books, supplies and equipment required by an educational institution for enrollment or attendance. They also include the reasonable cost of room and board (as determined by the school) if the beneficiary is enrolled at least half-time (Code Sec. 529(e)(3)).[133] Certain expenses of special needs beneficiaries may also be considered QHEEs. On the other hand, the amount of QHEEs must be reduced by the amount of any other tax free benefits (i.e., scholarship or fellowship grants excluded from gross income (¶ 879), or the Hope and Lifetime Learning credits (¶ 1303)).

Contributions. Contributions to a QTP on behalf of any beneficiary cannot exceed the necessary amount of QHEEs for the beneficiary. There are, however, no adjusted gross income phaseout limits. In addition, a taxpayer can contribute to both a QTP and a Coverdell account (¶ 898) in the same year for the same beneficiary.

Estate and Gift Tax Treatment. A contribution to a QTP is treated as a completed gift of a present interest for gift tax purposes (Code Sec. 529(c)(2)). Thus, the contribution qualifies for annual gift-tax exclusion (¶ 2905). If a donor's contribution exceeds the annual exclusion amount, then he or she may elect to take the excess into account ratably over five years. A QTP contribution does not qualify for the unlimited gift tax exclusion for money used to pay educational expenses (¶ 2907). In addition, no portion of a contribution is generally includible in the estate of a donor who dies after June 8, 1997, unless the donor dies during the five-year period in which excess contributions to a QTP are being ratably taken into account.

Footnote references are to paragraphs of the 2008 Standard Federal Tax Reports.

[129] ¶ 18,902   [131] ¶ 22,940   [133] ¶ 22,940
[130] ¶ 22,940   [132] ¶ 22,940

¶899

Chapter 9
BUSINESS EXPENSES

Trade or Business Expenses

901. Deductibility, Generally. A taxpayer, whether a corporation, an individual, a partnership, a trust, or an estate, generally may deduct from gross income the ordinary and necessary expenses of carrying on a trade or business that are paid or incurred in the tax year (Reg. § 1.162-1).[1] Business expenses incurred by a cash basis taxpayer while conducting a business but paid in a year after terminating the business are deductible as business expenses in the year paid (Rev. Rul. 67-12).[2] However, a deduction is not permitted for any expenditure that is a capital expense (see ¶ 903).

Expenses for property used for both business and personal activities must be allocated between the different activities. The origin and character of a claim control whether an expense is a deductible business expense or a nondeductible personal expense (*D. Gilmore*, SCt, 63-1 USTC ¶ 9285).[3]

A number of tax incentives (e.g., tax credits and increased Section 179 deductions) may be available for taxpayers who operate qualified businesses in areas designated as empowerment zones (¶ 999B), renewal communities (¶ 999C), the District of Columbia (¶ 999D), or the New York Liberty Zone (¶ 999E) (Code Sec. 1400E).[4] Special tax incentives for specific industries are also available. One such incentive is available for "qualified" film and television production costs paid or incurred after October 22, 2004 (¶ 1229) (Code Sec. 181).

Trade or Business. A "trade or business," although not defined in the tax law, has been characterized as an activity carried on for a livelihood or for profit. A profit motive must be present and some type of economic activity must be conducted.

902. Ordinary and Necessary. Whether an expense is ordinary and necessary is based upon the facts surrounding the expense. An expense is necessary if it is appropriate and helpful to the taxpayer's business. An expense is ordinary if it is one that is common and accepted in the particular business activity.[5]

Footnote references are to paragraphs of the 2008 Standard Federal Tax Reports.

[1] ¶ 8501
[2] ¶ 8520.1546
[3] ¶ 8526.4460
[4] ¶ 32,389.01, ¶ 32,423.01, ¶ 32,430, ¶ 32,435.01, ¶ 32,477.01
[5] ¶ 8520.026

903. Capital Expenditures. An expense that adds to the value or useful life of property is considered a capital expense or adapts property to a new or different use (Reg. § 1.263(a)-1(b)).[6] Generally, capital expenses must be deducted by means of depreciation, amortization or depletion. If the expense is not subject to depreciation, amortization or depletion, it is added to the cost basis of the property. Capital expenses include the cost of buildings, improvements or betterments of a long-term nature, machinery, architect's fees, and costs of defending or perfecting title to property (Reg. § 1.263(a)-2).[7] See Checklist at ¶ 57.

Expenses that keep property in an ordinarily efficient operating condition and do not add to its value or appreciably prolong its useful life are generally deductible as repairs (Reg. § 1.162-4).[8] Repairs include repainting, tuck-pointing, mending leaks, plastering, and conditioning gutters on buildings. However, the costs of installing a new roof and bricking up windows to strengthen a wall are capital expenditures.[9]

Legal fees, investment banker fees, and other expenses incurred by the target and acquiring corporations in a *friendly* takeover are capital expenses if they result in a long-term benefit. Expenses incurred in resisting a *hostile* takeover have been held to be currently deductible if the merger never took place.[10] Although the realization of future benefits is important to consider in determining whether an expense must be capitalized, the mere presence of some future benefit does not necessarily warrant capitalization. *Severance payments* made to employees in connection with a business downsizing, or an acquisition principally relate to previously rendered service, are therefore currently deductible (Rev. Rul. 94-77).[11]

904. Amortization of Start-Up Costs. Taxpayers who pay or incur business start-up costs and who subsequently enter the trade or business can elect to expense up to $5,000. However, the $5,000 deduction amount is reduced dollar-for-dollar when the start-up expenses exceed $50,000. The balance of start-up expenses, if any, are to be amortized over a period of not less than 180 months, starting with the month in which the business begins (Code Secs. 195(b) and 248).[12] The election must be made no later than the date (including extensions) for filing the return for the tax year in which the business begins or is acquired (Code Secs. 195(c) and 195(d)). The election is made by completing Part VI of Form 4562, Depreciation and Amortization, and attaching a separate statement that provides such information as total start-up costs, date each cost was incurred, and a description of each cost.[13] A taxpayer who does not make the election must capitalize the expenses (Code Sec. 195(a)).[14]

To qualify for amortization, the expense must be paid or incurred in connection with (1) investigating the creation or acquisition of an active trade or business, (2) creating an active trade or business, or (3) any activity engaged in for profit and for the production of income before the day on which the active trade or business begins, in anticipation of such activity becoming an active trade or business. In addition, the start-up expense must be a cost that would be allowable as a deduction if it were paid or incurred in connection with an existing active business in the same field as that entered into by the taxpayer (Code Sec. 195(c)).[15]

The term "start-up costs" does not include any amount with respect to which a deduction is allowable under Code Sec. 163(a) (interest on indebtedness), Code Sec. 164 (taxes), or Code Sec. 174 (research and experimental expenditures) (Code Sec. 195(c)).[16]

If the trade or business is disposed of completely by the taxpayer before the end of the 180-month (or longer) period, any remaining deferred expenses may be deductible as a loss under Code Sec. 165 (Code Sec. 195(b)(2)).[17]

Corporate organization fees are discussed at ¶ 243. Costs of organizing a partnership are discussed at ¶ 477 and ¶ 481.

Footnote references are to paragraphs of the 2008 Standard Federal Tax Reports.

[6] ¶ 13,701	[10] ¶ 8526.4234	[14] ¶ 12,370
[7] ¶ 13,703	[11] ¶ 8752.676	[15] ¶ 12,370
[8] ¶ 8620	[12] ¶ 12,370	[16] ¶ 12,370
[9] ¶ 13,701	[13] ¶ 12,371.06	[17] ¶ 12,370

Prior Law. For start-up and organizational expenses incurred prior to October 22, 2004, an election could be made to amortize these costs over a period of not less than 60 months. All other definitions, requirements and election deadlines remain applicable.

905. Expenses, Interest Deductions and Losses—Related Taxpayers. When the payor and payee are related taxpayers (see ¶ 1717), and the payor is on the accrual method of accounting and the payee is on the cash method, no deduction will be allowed for any expense or interest payable to the payee until the payee includes the payment in income (Code Sec. 267(a)(2)).[18]

A similar rule denies a deduction for a loss (except for a loss from a distribution in corporate liquidation) for property sold or exchanged between related taxpayers. However, upon later sale or exchange of the property by the transferee at a gain, the gain is recognized only to the extent it exceeds the previously disallowed loss (Code Sec. 267(a) and (d)).[19]

Compensation Paid

906. Compensation for Personal Service. A taxpayer carrying on a trade or business is entitled to deduct a *reasonable* allowance for salaries or other compensation for personal services. The deduction is allowable for the year in which the salary is paid or incurred (Reg. § 1.162-7).[20] However, publicly held corporations are generally not able to deduct compensation paid to certain covered employees to the extent that the compensation exceeds $1 million per tax year (Code Sec. 162(m)(1); Reg. § 1.162-27).[21] The $1 million limit does not apply to certain "performance-based compensation" (Code Sec. 162(m)(4)(C)).[22] A "covered employee", for purposes of Code Sec. 162(m), means any employee of the taxpayer who, as of the close of the taxable year, is (Notice 2007-49):

(1) the principal executive officer of the taxpayer;

(2) an individual acting in a capacity as principal executive officer; or

(3) required to have his or her compensation reported to shareholders under SEC rules by reason of the individual's being among the three highest compensated officers for the tax year.

A bonus is deductible if paid for services performed and if, when added to other salaries, it does not exceed reasonable compensation (Reg. § 1.162-9).[23]

Compensation paid to a relative is deductible if the relative performs needed services that would otherwise be performed by an unrelated party. The deduction is limited to the amount that would have been paid to a third party.[24]

Court decisions dealing with the question of excessive salaries, arising almost exclusively with closely held companies, show that each case is decided upon its particular facts. The IRS test is that *reasonable* compensation is the amount that would ordinarily be paid for like services by like enterprises in like circumstances. Additional factors are personal ability, responsibility of the position, and economic conditions in the locality.[25] The U.S. Court of Appeals for the Seventh Circuit has used an "independent-investor" test. This test presumes that compensation is reasonable if the company's investors earn their expected rate of return (*Exacto Spring Corporation,* 99-2 USTC ¶ 50,964).[26]

Officer-stockholders of closely held corporations may deduct repayments of salary to their corporation that are made pursuant to an agreement requiring such repayments in the event that the IRS determines the salaries to be excessive. However, the officer-stockholders may claim the deduction only if the agreement is legally enforceable and was in existence *before* the payment of the amounts.[27]

Deferred Compensation Plans. For unfunded deferred compensation plans, the employer's deduction for compensation is claimed when the compensation (or amount attributable to it) is included in the gross income of the recipient (Code Sec. 404(a)(5)

Footnote references are to paragraphs of the 2008 Standard Federal Tax Reports.

[18] ¶ 14,150
[19] ¶ 14,150
[20] ¶ 8635
[21] ¶ 8500, ¶ 9051B

[22] ¶ 8500
[23] ¶ 8641
[24] ¶ 8637.752, ¶ 8638.01
[25] ¶ 8637.744, ¶ 8637.021

[26] ¶ 8637.227, ¶ 8637.57
[27] ¶ 8637.022, ¶ 8640.021

and (b)(1)).[28] For the time of inclusion, see ¶ 723. Other benefits that are excluded from the recipient's gross income are deductible when they otherwise would have been includible in the recipient's gross income but for the exclusion (Code Sec. 404(b)(2)).[29] This rule also applies to compensation paid to independent contractors (Code Sec. 404(d)).[30]

A plan is unfunded if it consists of an unsecured promise to pay compensation at some time in the future. If the employer sets aside a reserve for the future obligation, the plan is unfunded if the employee has no rights in the reserve or its earnings and if the reserve remains solely the property of the employer or other payor, subject to the claims of creditors.[31]

A plan is presumed to defer compensation if the compensation is received after the 15th day of the third calendar month after the end of the employer's tax year in which the related services are rendered. This presumption may be overcome if the employer establishes that it was administratively or economically impractical to avoid the deferral of compensation beyond the 2½-month period. Payments within the 2½-month period are not treated as deferred compensation and may be accrued by an accrual-method employer in the year earned by the employee (Temp. Reg. § 1.404(b)-1T, Q&A-2).[32]

For a discussion of rules governing the employer's deduction for compensation for deferred compensation plans, see ¶ 2147–¶ 2151, ¶ 2197 and ¶ 2197A.

907. Golden Parachutes. A corporation that enters into a contract agreeing to pay an employee additional compensation in the event that control or ownership of the corporation changes is barred from taking a deduction for an "excess parachute payment" made to a "disqualified individual" Code Sec. 280G. The disqualified individual is subject to an excise tax of 20 percent of the excess parachute payment in addition to the income tax due (Code Sec. 4999(a)).[33] A disqualified individual is an employee or independent contractor who performs personal services for any corporation and is an officer, shareholder, or highly compensated person. A personal service corporation is treated as an individual (Code Sec. 280G(c)).[34]

Parachute Payment Defined. A parachute payment is any payment in the nature of compensation to a disqualified individual if: (1) the payment is contingent on a change in the ownership or effective control of the corporation or a substantial portion of the corporation's assets and (2) the aggregate present value of such contingent payments equals or exceeds three times an individual's base amount. Any payment in the nature of compensation to a disqualified individual that violates any securities law or regulations is also considered a parachute payment. Reasonable compensation for personal services to be rendered on or after the date of change or for personal services actually rendered before the date of change are not treated as parachute payments. Additionally, parachute payments do not include payments to or from certain qualified plans (Code Sec. 280G(b)).[35]

Base Amount. The base amount is the individual's annualized includible compensation for the base period (the most recent five taxable years ending before the date on which the ownership of control changed, or that portion of the period during which the disqualified individual performed personal services for the corporation (Code Sec. 280G(b)(3)(A); Code Sec. 280G(d)(2)).[36]

Exceptions. Generally, a parachute payment does not include any payment made to a disqualified individual by (1) a small business corporation or (2) other corporations, if, immediately before the change, none of their stock was readily tradable on an established securities market and shareholder approval requirements are met (Code Sec. 280G(b)(5)).[37]

"Excess Parachute Payment." An "excess parachute payment" is an amount equal to the excess of any parachute payment over the portion of the base amount allocated to the payment. The allocable base amount is subtracted from the parachute payment, and the remainder is the excess parachute payment (Code Sec. 280G(b)).[38]

Footnote references are to paragraphs of the 2008 Standard Federal Tax Reports.

[28] ¶ 18,330
[29] ¶ 18,330
[30] ¶ 18,330
[31] ¶ 18,352.027

[32] ¶ 18,354
[33] ¶ 34,940
[34] ¶ 15,150
[35] ¶ 15,150

[36] ¶ 15,150
[37] ¶ 15,150
[38] ¶ 15,150

Reporting Requirement. The excise tax is reported on Line 63 of the 2007 Form 1040 by writing the amount of the tax and "EPP" (excess parachute payment) on the dotted line.

908. Disability Payments; Contributions for Employee Benefits. An employer's deduction for contributions to a funded welfare benefit plan for sickness, accident, hospitalization or medical benefits is governed by Code Sec. 419 (see ¶ 2198–¶ 2199) (Temp. Reg. § 1.162-10T).[39] Although amounts that are added to a self-insurance reserve account are not currently deductible, actual claims charged to the account are deductible.[40]

Group health plans that fail to provide continuing coverage to qualified beneficiaries may subject employers to an excise tax (Code Sec. 4980B).[41]

Self-Employed Persons. Self-employed persons may deduct from gross income 100 percent of amounts paid during the year for health insurance for themselves, spouses, and dependents (Code Sec. 162(l)(1)).[42] The deduction cannot exceed the taxpayer's net earned income derived from the trade or business for which the insurance plan was established, minus the deductions for 50 percent of the self-employment tax and/or the deduction for contributions to qualified retirement plans, self-employed SEP or SIMPLE plans. Amounts eligible for the deduction do not include amounts paid during any month, or part of a month, that the self-employed individuals were able to participate in a subsidized health plan maintained by their employers or their spouses' employers (Code Sec. 162(l)(2)(B)).

909. Life Insurance Premiums. Premiums paid by an employer for insurance on the life of an officer or employee are deductible only if it can be shown that: (1) premium payments are in the nature of additional compensation; (2) total compensation, including premiums, is not unreasonable; and (3) the employer is not directly or indirectly a beneficiary under the policy.[43] However, no deduction is allowed an employer for premiums paid under a split dollar arrangement (see ¶ 721).[44]

Premiums on group-term life insurance covering the lives of employees are deductible by the employer if the employer is not a direct or indirect beneficiary.[45] The payment of such premiums generally represents income to the employee to the extent that the coverage provided exceeds $50,000 (see ¶ 721).

Generally, no deduction is allowed for interest paid or accrued on a debt incurred or continued to purchase or carry any single premium life insurance, endowment or annuity contract. If substantially all the premiums on a life insurance or endowment contract are paid within four years from date of purchase, or if an amount is deposited with the insurer for payment of a substantial number of future premiums on the contract, it is regarded as a single premium contract (Code Sec. 264(a)(2) and (c)).[46]

Interest on a debt incurred to purchase or continue a life insurance, endowment, or annuity contract pursuant to a plan of purchase contemplating the systematic borrowing of part or all of the increases in cash value is not deductible (Code Sec. 264(a)(3)).[47] However, Code Sec. 264(d) allows an interest deduction in limited situations.[48] Special rules may permit the deduction of interest incurred for key person policies owned by corporations (Code Sec. 264(e)).[49]

Entertainment, Meal and Gift Expenses

910. Entertainment Expenses. Special limits are imposed by Code Sec. 274 on the deduction of business-related entertainment, meals and gift expenses. These limits are in addition to those imposed by other Code sections. For example, no deduction is allowed for the cost of entertainment, amusement, or recreation unless that cost is either (1) *directly related* to the active conduct of a trade or business or (2) for entertainment directly before or after a substantial and bona fide business discussion *associated with* the conduct of that trade or business. Specific exceptions to these general requirements are discussed at ¶ 915. Entertainment includes entertaining guests at nightclubs, sport-

---

Footnote references are to paragraphs of the 2008 Standard Federal Tax Reports.

[39] ¶ 8751	[43] ¶ 8522.386, ¶ 14,002,	[46] ¶ 14,002, ¶ 14,008.021
[40] ¶ 8522.3947	¶ 14,008.03, ¶ 14,008.12	[47] ¶ 14,002, ¶ 14,008.021
[41] ¶ 34,600	[44] ¶ 5907.052, ¶ 5508.24	[48] ¶ 14,002, ¶ 14,008.023
[42] ¶ 8500	[45] ¶ 6360, ¶ 14,003	[49] ¶ 14,002, ¶ 14,008.023

ing events, theaters, etc. A taxpayer's trade or business is considered in applying an objective test as to what constitutes entertainment. For example, if an appliance distributor conducts a fashion show for the spouses of retailers, the show would generally be considered entertainment (Code Sec. 274(a)(1)(A); Reg. § 1.274-2(b)(1)(ii)).[50]

The deduction for entertainment expenses may not exceed the portion that is related to the business. If there are business and nonbusiness expenses at the same event, an allocation must be made, and only the business portion is deducted.

Generally, only 50 percent of otherwise allowable meal and entertainment expenses are deductible (see ¶ 916) (Code Sec. 274(n)).[51] There are numerous exceptions to the 50-percent limitation rule which are discussed at ¶ 917.

Two-Percent of Adjusted Gross Income Floor. In most situations, an employee's unreimbursed business expenses must be claimed as a miscellaneous itemized deduction, subject to the 2-percent-of-adjusted-gross-income (AGI) floor, on Schedule A (Form 1040) (see ¶ 1011). The percentage limit (e.g., 50 percent) on meal and entertainment expenses must be taken into account prior to application of the two percent of AGI floor (see ¶ 916) (Code Sec. 67; Temp. Reg. § 1.67-1T(a)).[52] Certain employees defined by the Code may deduct their unreimbursed expenses directly from gross income (see ¶ 941).

911. Directly Related Test. For an entertainment expense to meet the directly related test, the taxpayer must have had more than a general expectation of deriving income, or some other specific business benefit, at some indefinite future time. The taxpayer must engage in the active conduct of business with the person being entertained. In addition, the active conduct of business must be the principal aspect of the combined business and entertainment (Reg. § 1.274-2(c)).[53]

912. Associated Entertainment. Entertainment expenses associated with the active conduct of the taxpayer's business are deductible if they directly precede or follow a bona fide and substantial business discussion. This includes goodwill expenditures to obtain new business or encourage continuation of existing business relationships. The business discussion must be the principal aspect of the combined entertainment and business and must represent an active effort by the taxpayer to obtain income or other specific business benefit (Reg. § 1.274-2(d)).[54]

913. Entertainment Facility. No deduction is generally allowed for any expense for entertainment facilities, such as yachts, hunting lodges, swimming pools, tennis courts, or bowling alleys (Code Sec. 274(a)(1)(B)).[55] However, expenses for recreational facilities primarily for the benefit of employees generally are deductible (Reg. § 1.274-2(f)(2)(v)).[56]

913A. Club Dues. As a general rule, no business deduction is permitted for club dues. This rule extends to business, social, athletic, luncheon, sporting, airline and hotel clubs (Code Sec. 274(a)(3)). However, dues paid to professional or public service organizations (e.g., accounting associations, or Kiwanis and Rotary clubs) are deductible if paid for business reasons and the organization's principal purpose is *not* to conduct entertainment activities for members or their guests or to provide those parties with access to entertainment facilities (Reg. § 1.274-2(a)(2)(iii) and Code Sec. 1.274-2(b)).[57]

914. Entertainment-Related Meals. Generally, an entertainment-related meal expense is *not* deductible unless the taxpayer establishes that the expense is directly related to the active conduct of a trade or business. However, if a meal expense directly precedes or follows a substantial and bona fide business discussion (including a business meeting at a convention), then it is deductible if it is established that the expense was associated with the active conduct of a trade or business. The taxpayer must be able to substantiate the expense (see ¶ 953) (Code Sec. 274(d); Temp. Reg. § 1.274-5T(c), (f)).[58]

There are two additional restrictions placed on the deduction of meal expenses: (1) meal expenses generally are not deductible if neither the taxpayer nor the taxpayer's

---

Footnote references are to paragraphs of the 2008 Standard Federal Tax Reports.

[50] ¶ 14,402, ¶ 14,405
[51] ¶ 14,402
[52] ¶ 6060, ¶ 6061
[53] ¶ 14,405
[54] ¶ 14,405
[55] ¶ 14,402
[56] ¶ 14,405
[57] ¶ 14,402, ¶ 14,405, ¶ 14,408A.035
[58] ¶ 14,402, ¶ 14,410

employee is present at the meal, and (2) a deduction will not be allowed for food and beverages to the extent that such expense is lavish or extravagant under the circumstances. These restrictions do not apply to the expenses described in exceptions (2), (3), (4), (7), (8), and (9) at ¶ 915 (Code Sec. 274(k)).[59]

915. Exceptions to Entertainment Rules. The following entertainment expenses are not subject to the special rules for entertainment expenses described in the preceding sections. They are deductible provided that they meet the ordinary and necessary requirements and are properly substantiated (Code Sec. 274(e); Reg. § 1.274-2(f)(2)).[60] However, they may be subject to the 50-percent limit rule (see ¶ 916 and ¶ 917).

(1) Food and beverages for employees furnished on the business premises.

(2) Expenses for services, goods, and facilities that are treated as compensation and as wages for withholding tax purposes. Note that if the recipient is a specified individual (generally, an officer, director, or 10-percent shareholder or a related person), the employer's deduction cannot exceed the amount of compensation reported.

(3) Reimbursed expenses, but only:

(a) if the services relating to the expenses for which reimbursement is made are performed for an employer and the employer has not treated the expenses as wages subject to withholding; or

(b) if the services are performed for a person other than an employer and the taxpayer incurring the reimbursed expenses accounts to that person.

(4) Recreational expenses primarily for employees who, for this purpose, are not highly compensated (within the meaning of Code Sec. 414(q)). An example of such an expense is a company picnic.

(5) Expenses of employees', stockholders', agents' or directors' *business* meetings.

(6) Expenses directly related and necessary to attendance at a *business* meeting of a tax-exempt business league, including a real estate board, chamber of commerce or board of trade.

(7) Expenses for goods, services and facilities made available to the public.

(8) Expenses for entertainment sold to customers in a bona fide transaction for adequate consideration.

(9) Goods, services, and facilities that are furnished to nonemployees as entertainment, amusement or recreation expenses and that are includible in the recipients' incomes and reported on a Form 1099-MISC by the taxpayer.

916. 50-Percent Limitation Rule. The amount allowable as a deduction for meal and entertainment expenses is generally limited to 50 percent of such expenses. Food and beverage costs incurred in the course of travel away from home fall within the scope of this rule. The 50-percent rule is applied only after determining the amount of the otherwise allowable deductions. For instance, the portion of a travel meal that is lavish and extravagant must first be subtracted from the meal cost before the 50-percent reduction is applied. Related expenses, such as taxes and tips in the case of meals and other charges, and room rental and parking fees in the case of entertainment expenses, must be included in the total expense before applying the 50-percent reduction. Allowable deductions for transportation costs to and from a business meal are not reduced (Code Sec. 274(n)).[61]

Transportation Workers. The deductible percentage of the cost of meals consumed while away from home by individuals subject to Department of Transportation hours of service rules (e.g., interstate truck and bus drivers and certain railroad, airline, and merchant marine employees) is 75 percent for tax year 2007 and 80 percent for tax years 2008 and thereafter (Code Sec. 274(n)(3)).

917. Exceptions to 50-Percent Limitation Rule. The following expenses are *not* subject to the 50-percent limit on meal and entertainment expense deductions:

Footnote references are to paragraphs of the 2008 Standard Federal Tax Reports.

[59] ¶ 14,402   [60] ¶ 14,402, ¶ 14,405   [61] ¶ 14,402

(1) Expenses described in categories (2), (3), (4), (7), (8), and (9) at ¶ 915.

(2) Food and beverage expenses associated with benefits that are excludable from the recipient's gross income as a *de minimis* fringe benefit (Code Sec. 274(n)(2)(B)).[62]

(3) The cost of a ticket package to a sporting event and related expenses if the event is organized to benefit a tax-exempt organization, all net proceeds of the event are contributed to such organization, and volunteers perform substantially all of the work in carrying out the event (Code Sec. 274(n)(2)(C)).[63] In other situations, a deduction for a ticket may not exceed the ticket's face value (Code Sec. 274(l)(1)).[64]

(4) An employee's meal expenses incurred while moving that are reimbursed by the employer and includible in the employee's gross income (see ¶ 1073).

(5) Expenses for food and beverages provided to employees on certain (a) vessels and (b) oil or gas platforms and drilling rigs and their support camps (Code Sec. 274(n)(2)(E)).[65]

See ¶ 916 for the special rules that apply to transportation workers subject to the Department of Transportation service limitation restrictions.

Skyboxes. When a skybox is rented for more than one event, the deduction may not exceed the price of non-luxury box seats (subject to the usual 50-percent limit) (Code Sec. 274(l)(2)).[66]

918. Business Gifts. Deductions for business gifts, whether made directly or indirectly, are limited to $25 per recipient per year. Items clearly of an advertising nature that cost $4 or less and signs, display racks, or other promotional materials given for use on business premises are not gifts (Code Sec. 274(b)(1) and Reg. § 1.274-3).[67]

919. Employee Achievement Awards. An employer may deduct the cost of an employee achievement award up to $400 for all *nonqualified plan awards* to each employee. The employer's deduction for the cost of *qualified plan awards* made to a particular employee is limited to $1,600 per year, taking into account all other qualified and nonqualified awards made to that employee during the tax year (Code Sec. 274(j)(2)).[68]

An employee achievement award is an item of tangible personal property awarded to an employee as part of a meaningful presentation for length of service or safety achievement and under circumstances that do not create a significant likelihood of disguised compensation (Code Sec. 274(j)(3)(A)).[69]

A qualified plan award is an employee achievement award provided under an established written plan or program that does not discriminate in favor of highly compensated employees (within the meaning of Code Sec. 414(q)) as to eligibility or benefits. An employee achievement award is not a qualified plan award if the average cost of all employee achievement awards under the plan exceeds $400. This average cost calculation includes the entire cost of all qualified plan awards, ignoring employee achievement awards of nominal value (Code Sec. 274(j)(3)(B)).[70]

A length of service award will not qualify if it is received during the employee's first five years of service or if the employee has received another length of service award (other than an award excludable under Code Sec. 132(e), relating to *de minimis* fringe benefits) during the year or within the last four years. An award will not be considered a safety achievement award if made to a manager, administrator, clerical employee, or other professional employee or if, during the tax year, awards for safety achievement previously have been made to more than 10 percent of the employees, excluding managers, administrators, clerical employees, or other professional employees (Code Sec. 274(j)(4)).[71]

Footnote references are to paragraphs of the 2008 Standard Federal Tax Reports.

[62] ¶ 14,402
[63] ¶ 14,402
[64] ¶ 14,402
[65] ¶ 14,402

[66] ¶ 14,402
[67] ¶ 14,402, ¶ 14,406
[68] ¶ 14,402
[69] ¶ 14,402

[70] ¶ 14,402
[71] ¶ 14,402

Taxes

920. Taxes Directly Attributable to Business. Business taxpayers can deduct the taxes listed at ¶ 1021 and any other state, local, and foreign taxes paid or accrued within the tax year to the extent that they are directly attributable to a trade or business or to property held for the production of rents or royalties. Any tax not listed at ¶ 1021 that is paid or accrued by the taxpayer in connection with the acquisition of property is treated as part of the cost of the acquired property or, if in connection with the disposition of property, as a reduction in the amount realized (Code Sec. 164(a)).[72]

The uniform capitalization rules require some taxpayers to capitalize certain taxes that would otherwise be deductible (see ¶ 990–¶ 999).

921. Unemployment Insurance Tax. The federal unemployment insurance tax is deductible as a business expense by the employer after application of state credits. On the accrual basis, the deduction may be accrued for the calendar year in which the wages were paid even though payment of the tax is not due until the following year. On the cash basis, the tax is deductible when paid.[73]

922. State Unemployment Insurance and Disability Fund Contributions. An employer covered by state unemployment insurance laws is entitled to deduct as taxes only those contributions that are classified as taxes under state law and are incurred in carrying on a trade or business or in the production of income.[74] In states that require employees to contribute to state unemployment compensation funds, such contributions may be claimed as *itemized* deductions (as state income taxes). Also, compulsory employee contributions to *state* disability funds (e.g., California, New Jersey, New York, Rhode Island, Washington and West Virginia) are deductible as itemized deductions (as state income taxes). However, employee contributions to *private* disability benefit plans (e.g., California, New Jersey and New York) are not deductible by employees.[75] See also the checklist at ¶ 57.

923. Social Security Tax. The federal social security tax on an employer is deductible by the employer as a business expense. The contribution of an employer on wages paid to a domestic worker is not deductible unless it is classified as a business expense.[76]

The tax imposed on employees by the Social Security Act is not deductible by the employee. If the employer pays the tax without deduction from the employee's wages under an agreement with the employee, the amount is deductible by the employer and is income to the employee (Rev. Rul. 86-14).[77]

A self-employed individual may deduct from gross income 50 percent of the self-employment tax imposed for the same tax year (see ¶ 2670) (Code Sec. 164(f)).[78]

924. Federal and State Income Tax. Federal income taxes are not deductible in determining taxable income (Code Sec. 275).[79] However, they are deductible in determining the amount of a corporation's income subject to the accumulated earnings tax (¶ 251) (Reg. § 1.535-2) and the personal holding company tax (¶ 275) (Reg. § 1.545-2).[80] Corporations and partnerships may deduct their state income taxes as business expenses. State income taxes that are based on net business income may only be deducted by self-employed individuals on Schedule A (Form 1040) as an itemized deduction. However, if the state income tax is based on gross business income, the tax may be deducted as a business expense (Temp. Reg. § 1.62-1T(d)).[81]

Charitable Contributions

927. Corporate Limits. The deduction of a corporation for charitable contributions is limited to 10 percent of its taxable income for the year, computed without regard to (1) the deduction for charitable contributions, (2) the deductions for dividends received and for dividends paid on certain preferred stock of public utilities, (3) any net operating

---

Footnote references are to paragraphs of the 2008 Standard Federal Tax Reports.

[72] ¶ 9500
[73] ¶ 9502.31
[74] ¶ 9502.0425
[75] ¶ 9502.0425, ¶ 9502.31

[76] ¶ 9502.30, ¶ 9502.032, ¶ 9502.042
[77] ¶ 5508.0146
[78] ¶ 9500

[79] ¶ 14,500
[80] ¶ 23,042, ¶ 23,252
[81] ¶ 6003

loss carryback to the tax year, (4) the manufacturer's deduction, and (5) any capital loss carryback to the tax year (Code Sec. 170(b)(2); Reg. § 1.170A-11(a)).[82]

Conservation contribution. Corporate donors that qualified as farmers or ranchers could deduct up to 100 percent of their contribution base (adjusted gross income computed without regard to any net operating loss carryback) for qualified conservation contributions of capital gain real estate made in 2006 or 2007 (Code Sec. 170(b)(2)(B)). The special deduction for conservation contributions is no longer available as of January 1, 2008.[83]

928. Five-Year Carryover for Corporations. A corporation is permitted to carry over to the five succeeding tax years contributions that exceed the 10-percent limitation, but deductions in those years are also subject to the maximum limitation (Code Sec. 170(d)(2); Reg. § 1.170A-11(c)).[84]

929. Accrual-Basis Corporations. Except for the carryover rule (¶ 928), a deduction is allowed only for a contribution paid during the tax year. An accrual-basis corporation may elect to treat as paid during the tax year all or a portion of a contribution that is actually paid within two and one-half months after the close of the tax year if it was authorized by the board of directors during the year (Code Sec. 170(a)(2); Reg. § 1.170A-11(b)).[85]

930. Contributions of Inventory or Scientific Property. Generally, the deduction for a charitable contribution of ordinary income property is the fair market value of that property less the amount that would have been ordinary income if the property had been sold at its fair market value on the date of the contribution (see ¶ 1062). There are, however, three exceptions to this rule in the case of contributions by corporations.

Inventory-Type Property. If a corporation (other than an S corporation) makes a gift of inventory, property held for sale to customers in the ordinary course of business, or depreciable or real property used in the trade or business, it may—if certain conditions are met—deduct its basis for the property plus one-half of the property's unrealized appreciation. However, the claimed deduction may not exceed twice the basis of the property (Code Sec. 170(e)(3)).[86] Moreover, no deduction is allowed for any part of the appreciation that would be ordinary income resulting from recapture. To qualify, the gift must be made to a qualified public charity or a private operating foundation and the donee's use of the property must be for the care of infants, the ill or needy. Noncorporate, as well as corporate, taxpayers can claim an enhanced deduction for donations of food inventory through the end of 2007 (Code Sec. 170(e)(3)(C)). The food inventory must consist of items fit for human consumption and must be contributed to a qualified charity or private operating foundation for use in the care of the ill, the needy or infants.

C corporations can claim an enhanced deduction for donations of book inventories to public schools through the end of 2007 (Code Sec. 170(e)(3)(D)). This provision essentially takes the present-law enhanced deduction for donations of inventory to a qualified charity or private operating foundation and extends it to qualified donations of book inventory to public schools. The enhanced deduction generally increases the deductible amount from the donated inventory item's basis to the lesser of (1) the donated inventory item's basis plus one-half of the item's appreciation or (2) two times the donated inventory item's basis.

Scientific Research Property. A corporation (other than an S corporation, a personal holding company, or a service organization) is entitled to the same deduction for a qualified research contribution of certain ordinary income property to an institution of higher education or to an exempt scientific research organization for research purposes as that described above for inventory-type property (Code Sec. 170(e)(4)).[87]

The three main requirements for a contribution to qualify as a research contribution are: (1) the contributed property must have been constructed or assembled by the donor, (2) the contribution must be made within two years of construction or assembly,

---

Footnote references are to paragraphs of the 2008 Standard Federal Tax Reports.

[82] ¶ 11,600, ¶ 11,672
[83] ¶ 11,680.033
[84] ¶ 11,600, ¶ 11,672
[85] ¶ 11,600, ¶ 11,672
[86] ¶ 11,600, ¶ 11,672
[87] ¶ 11,600

¶928

and (3) the original use of the property must be by the donee. There are several additional requirements that must also be satisfied (Code Sec. 170(e)(4)(B)).[88]

Computer Equipment. For tax years beginning before January 1, 2008, a corporation is entitled to an increased deduction for a charitable contribution of computer technology or equipment to an elementary or secondary school or public library. The amount of the deduction is equal to the taxpayer's basis in the donated property plus one-half of the amount of ordinary income that would have been realized if the property had been sold. The deduction may not exceed twice the taxpayer's basis in the donated property. The contribution must be made within three years of the property's acquisition or substantial completion of its construction or assembly, and the original use of the property must be by the donor or the donee (Code Sec. 170(e)(6)).

931. Contribution Rules. The rules concerning a deduction for the following charitable contributions are the same regardless of whether the contribution is made by a corporate or a noncorporate taxpayer: (1) gifts of appreciated property (¶ 1062), (2) use of property—partial interests (¶ 1063), (3) reduction for interest (¶ 1065), (4) gift of future interest in tangible personal property (¶ 1069), (5) transfers in trust (¶ 1070), (6) appraisals (¶ 1071), and (7) denial of deduction (¶ 1068).

Interest

937. Business Expense. Interest expense incurred in a trade or business or in the production of rental or royalty income is deductible from gross income (Code Sec. 163). See ¶ 1055 and ¶ 1056 for the rules on prepaid interest and ¶ 1094 for the rules on investment interest paid by noncorporate taxpayers.

937A. Interest on Income Tax Liability. Interest paid or accrued on income tax assessed on an individual's federal, state or local income tax liability is not a business deduction even though the tax due is related to income from a trade or business (Temp. Reg. § 1.163-9T(b)(2)(i)(A)).[89] This rule also applies to an individual's partnership and S corporation activities. See ¶ 2723 and ¶ 2724 for interest allocations pursuant to compromise and partial payments. Penalties on deficiencies and underestimated tax cannot be deducted.

938. Bank. A bank or trust company may deduct interest paid during the year on deposits and certificates of indebtedness (Reg. § 1.163-1(c)).[90]

939. Margin Account. Interest on a margin account is deductible by a cash basis investor when it is paid to the broker or when the interest becomes available to the broker through the investor's account.[91] See ¶ 1094 for investment interest.

940. Exceptions and Limitations. There are a number of Code sections which limit or preclude a taxpayer from claiming an interest deduction on certain types of indebtedness. See also ¶ 1045 for limits on personal interest.

Original Issue Discount Bonds. The interest deduction is generally limited (see ¶ 1952) (Code Sec. 163(e)).[92]

Bonds Not in Registered Form. Failure to meet the registration requirement generally results in a denial of an interest deduction (see ¶ 1963) (Code Sec. 163(f)).[93]

Commodity Straddles. Interest on debt incurred to purchase or carry commodity investments that are part of a straddle is not currently deductible. The interest must be added to the basis of the commodity. Hedging transactions, however, are exempted from this capitalization rule (see also ¶ 1948 and ¶ 1949) (Code Sec. 263(g)).[94]

Earnings Stripping. A corporation is not allowed a deduction for excessive interest paid if the interest will not be taxed as income to the recipient. A corporate partner's share of interest paid or accrued to or by the partnership is treated as paid or accrued by or to the corporation directly (Code Sec. 163(j)).[95]

Corporate Indebtedness Incurred to Acquire Another Corporation's Stock. Generally, there is a $5 million annual limit on the interest deductible by a corporation on a debt

---

Footnote references are to paragraphs of the 2008 Standard Federal Tax Reports.

[88] ¶ 11,600
[89] ¶ 9400, ¶ 9400A.04
[90] ¶ 9103
[91] ¶ 9104.048
[92] ¶ 9102
[93] ¶ 9102
[94] ¶ 13,700
[95] ¶ 9406N.01

incurred to acquire stock or two-thirds of the operating assets of another corporation (Code Sec. 279).[96]

Uniform Capitalization Rules. Interest paid or incurred during the production period and allocable to real property or tangible personal property may be required to be capitalized (see ¶ 993) (Code Sec. 263A(f)).[97]

Employee's Expenses

941. Gross Income Deductions. The performance of services as an employee is considered to be a trade or business. Thus, employee business expenses are generally deductible. *Reimbursed* employee business expenses are deductible from gross income (Code Sec. 62(a)(2)(A)).[98] However, in actual practice, employees do not claim the deductions on their returns because employers are instructed not to report the reimbursed amount in the employee's gross income (¶ 942). Generally, *unreimbursed* employee business expenses are deductible as miscellaneous itemized deductions, subject to the 2-percent-of-adjusted-gross-income (AGI) floor (¶ 1011) and the 50-percent limit for meal and entertainment expenses (75 percent, in 2007, for employees subject to the Department of Transportation's hours of service limitations) (¶ 916).[99] Schedule A (Form 1040) is used. Special rules apply to qualified performing artists (¶ 941A), statutory employees (¶ 941B), impairment-related work expenses (¶ 1013), fee-based government employees (¶ 941D), schoolteachers (¶ 941C), and members of the National Guard and Reserves (¶ 941E). An employee is also allowed a deduction from gross income for jury duty pay surrendered to an employer in exchange for regular salary (¶ 1010) (Code Sec. 62(a)(13)).[100]

941A. Performing Artist. A qualified performing artist may deduct business expenses in arriving at adjusted gross income on Form 2106 or Form 2106-EZ. Generally, to qualify for this deduction an individual must: (1) render services in the performing arts during the tax year for at least two employers, (2) have total business deductions attributable to the performance of such services that exceed 10 percent of the income received from such services, and (3) have adjusted gross income of $16,000 or less (determined prior to the application of this provision) (Code Sec. 62(b)(1) and (2)).[101]

941B. Statutory Employees. Individuals who are considered to be "statutory employees" may deduct their allowable business expenses from gross income.[102] The term "statutory employees" includes:

(1) A full-time traveling or city salesperson who solicits orders from wholesalers, restaurants, or similar establishments on behalf of a principal. The merchandise sold must be for resale (e.g., food sold to a restaurant) or for supplies used in the buyer's business.

(2) A full-time life insurance agent whose principal business activity is selling life insurance and/or annuity contracts for one life insurance company.

(3) An agent-driver or commission-driver engaged in distributing meat, vegetables, bakery goods, beverages (other than milk), or laundry or dry cleaning services.

(4) A home worker performing work on material or goods furnished by the employer.

An employer should indicate on the worker's Form W-2 whether the worker is classified as a statutory employee. Statutory employees report their wages, income and allowable expenses on Schedule C (Form 1040) (or Schedule C-EZ (Form 1040). Statutory employees are not liable for self-employment tax because their employers are obligated to treat such individuals as employees for social security tax purposes.

941C. School Teachers. For tax years beginning in 2002 through 2007, eligible educators can deduct expenses paid or incurred, up to $250, for the purchase of supplies (see ¶ 1084 for a detailed discussion) (Code Sec. 62(a)(2)(D)). The "teacher's expense

---

Footnote references are to paragraphs of the 2008 Standard Federal Tax Reports.

[96] ¶ 14,700, ¶ 14,708.30   [99] ¶ 6004,   [102] ¶ 8524.2547
[97] ¶ 13,800   [100] ¶ 6002
[98] ¶ 6002   [101] ¶ 6002

¶941

deduction" was scheduled to terminate on December 31, 2005, but was extended for two years by the Tax Relief and Health Care Act of 2006.

941D. Fee-Based Government Officials. Expenses paid or incurred with respect to services performed by an official as an employee of a state or local government are deductible in computing adjusted gross income (Code Sec. 62(a)(2)(C)). The employee must be compensated in whole or in part on a fee basis.

941E. National Guard and Reserve Members. Members of the National Guard and the Reserves are allowed to deduct travel expenses while away from home to attend meetings and training sessions as an above-the-line deduction (Code Secs. 62 and 162). This type of travel has been deemed to be travel away from home in the pursuit of a trade or business when an individual is away from home overnight in connection with their service as a member of the guard or reserves. Expenses incurred in connection with the performance of such service are deductible as an above-the-line deduction only when the taxpayer is more than 100 miles away from home. The amount of deductible expenses is limited to the federal per diem rate for the locality of the meeting or training session.[103]

941F. Daycare. Payments to a daycare center have been determined to be a deductible business expense where the purpose of providing the availability of the day care center was (Rev. Rul. 73-348):

(1) to provide an employee with a place to send his or her child while at work knowing that the child is receiving proper care;

(2) to reduce absenteeism, increase productivity, and reduce company training costs; and

(3) to reduce employee turnover.

However, an S corporation was not allowed to deduct amounts it paid for daycare for its sole shareholder's preschool children where there was no evidence that indicated that the daycare expenses were directly related to the taxpayer's business and, despite the S corporation employing over 20 individuals, the S corporation only paid daycare expenses for the taxpayer's children (*F.M. Settimo,* TC Memo. 2006-261, Dec. 56,694(M)).

942. Reimbursed and Unreimbursed Business Expenses of Employee. The tax treatment of an employee's reimbursed business expenses depends on whether the employer's reimbursement or expense allowance arrangement is an accountable or nonaccountable plan (¶ 952A).[104] If expenses are reimbursed under an *accountable* plan, neither the expense nor the reimbursement is claimed on the employee's tax return. The reimbursement is not reported as income on the employee's Form W-2 (Reg. § 1.62-2(c)(4)).[105] In this situation, the percentage limit on deductions for meals and entertainment applies to the employer (¶ 916). If the employee's deductible business expenses exceed the amounts paid by the accountable plan, and these expenses are adequately substantiated (¶ 943), then the excess expenses are deductible as miscellaneous itemized deductions, subject to the 2-percent-of-adjusted-gross-income (AGI) floor (¶ 1011) and the 50-percent limit for meals and entertainment (¶ 916) (Code Sec. 62; Reg. § 1.62-1(e)).[106] If expenses are reimbursed under a *nonaccountable* plan, the reimbursements are included in the employee's income (Reg. § 1.62-2(c)(5)). Business expenses that are reimbursed under a nonaccountable plan or not reimbursed at all can be deducted, to the extent they can be adequately substantiated, as miscellaneous itemized deductions, subject to the 2-percent-of-adjusted-gross-income (AGI) floor (¶ 1011) and the 50-percent limit for meals and entertainment (¶ 916). The employee reports the expenses on Form 2106 or Form 2106-EZ.

943. Substantiation for Employees' Returns. Business expenses which exceed the reimbursements received under an accountable plan, which are reimbursed under a nonaccountable plan, or which are not reimbursed at all may be deducted by the employee (¶ 942). As with any other deductible expense, an employee must adequately substantiate business expenses in order to deduct them.

Footnote references are to paragraphs of the 2008 Standard Federal Tax Reports.

[103] ¶ 6005.0295
[104] ¶ 6004
[105] ¶ 6004
[106] ¶ 6004

More specific substantiation requirements apply with respect to the following expenses, which are deemed particularly susceptible to abuse: expenses with respect to travel away from home (including meals and lodging), entertainment expenses, business gifts, and expenses in connection with the use of "listed property" (such as cars, computers and cellphones—see ¶ 1211). These expenses must generally be substantiated by adequate records or other sufficient evidence corroborating the taxpayer's own statement (Code Sec. 274(d); Temp. Reg. § 1.274-5T(c)). The expenses must be substantiated as to: (1) amount, (2) time and place, and (3) business purpose. For entertainment and gift expenses, the business relationship of the person being entertained or receiving the gift must also be substantiated (Temp. Reg. § 1.274-5T(b)).[107]

Substantiation by Adequate Records. A contemporaneous log is not required, but a record of the elements of the expense or use of the listed property made at or near the time of the expenditure or use, supported by sufficient documentary evidence, has a high degree of credibility. Adequate accounting generally requires the submission of an account book, expense diary or log, or similar record maintained by the employee and recorded at or near the time of incurrence of the expense. Documentary evidence, such as receipts or paid bills, is not generally required for expenses that are less than $75. Documentary evidence for lodging expenses is required (Reg. § 1.274-5(c)(2)(iii)).[108] The employee should also maintain a record of any amounts charged to the employer.

Substantiation of Amount of Meal and Incidental Expenses. The amount of meal and/ or incidental expenses deducted by an employee can be substantiated either by retaining evidence of the actual expenses or by use of the standard meal allowance (¶ 954B). The amount of the standard meal allowance varies by location, and for some locations, by the time of year. An individual using the standard meal allowance must still keep records, such as a daily planner or log, to prove the time, place and business purpose of the expenses. There is no standard lodging amount similar to the standard meal allowance. Employees must be able to substantiate the actual cost of their lodging in order to deduct it.

Transportation and Car Expenses

945. Local Transportation Expenses. Local transportation expenses are generally those incurred for the business use of a car. However, they also include the cost of travel by rail, bus, or taxi. Businesses (including self-employed persons and statutory employees) may deduct ordinary and necessary local transportation expenses from gross income (Reg. § 1.162-1(a)).[109] The manner of an employee's deduction for transportation expenses generally depends on whether the employee is reimbursed under an accountable plan (see ¶ 943).

Commuting Expenses. Commuting expenses between a taxpayer's residence and a business location within the area of the taxpayer's tax home generally are not deductible.[110] However, a deduction is allowed for expenses incurred in excess of ordinary commuting expenses for transporting job-related tools and materials.[111] An individual who works at two or more different places in a day may deduct the costs of getting from one place to the other.[112]

There is an exception to the general rule that commuting expenses are not deductible. If a taxpayer has at least one regular place of business away from home, then daily transportation expenses for commuting between the taxpayer's residence and a *temporary* work location in the same trade or business can be deducted (see ¶ 951) (Rev. Rul. 99-7).[113] For this purpose, a temporary work location is defined using a one-year standard. If employment at a work location is realistically expected to last (and does in fact last) for one year or less, the employment is temporary, absent facts and circumstances to the contrary. Employment at a work location is not temporary, regardless of whether or not it lasts for more than one year, if it is realistically expected to last more than one year or there is no realistic expectation that employment will last for one year or less. A taxpayer may at first realistically expect that employment at a work location will last one year or less, but, at a later date, realistically expect that the work

---

Footnote references are to paragraphs of the 2008 Standard Federal Tax Reports.

[107] ¶ 14,410
[108] ¶ 14,410
[109] ¶ 8501

[110] ¶ 8550.269
[111] ¶ 8590.25
[112] ¶ 8570.175

[113] ¶ 8570.146

will last for more than one year. In this situation, the employment will be treated as temporary until the date that the taxpayer's realistic expectation changes and will be treated as not temporary after that date (unless facts and circumstances indicate otherwise).

For the rules concerning deductions while on a temporary assignment "away from home," see ¶ 951.

Travel from a Home Office. Individuals who use their homes as their principal place of business (¶ 961) are permitted to deduct transportation expenses between their homes and another work location in the same trade or business (Rev. Rul. 99-7).[114] This rule applies regardless of whether the work location is temporary or regular and regardless of the distance. See ¶ 961 for a discussion of home office expenses.

946. Car Expense. Expenses for gasoline, oil, tires, repairs, insurance, depreciation, parking fees and tolls, licenses, and garage rent incurred for cars used in a trade or business are deductible. The deduction is allowed only for that part of the expenses that is attributable to business.[115] Generally, an employee's unreimbursed expenses can be deducted only as a miscellaneous itemized deduction subject to the 2-percent-of-adjusted-gross-income (AGI) floor (see ¶ 941) (Code Sec. 67).[116] See ¶ 1208–¶ 1215 concerning the expensing election and depreciation of a car.

947. Substantiation of Car Expenses. A taxpayer can substantiate car expenses by keeping an exact record of the amount paid for gasoline, insurance, and other costs. However, the standard mileage rate method is a simplified method available to both employees and self-employed persons in computing deductions for car expenses in lieu of calculating the operating and fixed costs allocable to business purposes.[117]

Standard Mileage Rate. Under the standard mileage method, the taxpayer determines the amount of the allowable deduction by multiplying all the business miles driven during the year by the standard mileage rate. For 2007 the standard mileage rate for business miles is 48.5 cents a mile (Rev. Proc. 2006-49). The business portion of parking fees and tolls may be deducted in addition to the standard mileage rate.

Rural mail carriers receive a qualified reimbursement for expenses incurred for the use of their vehicles for performing the collection and delivery of mail in a rural route. They are allowed an itemized deduction, subject to the 2-percent-of-adjusted-gross-income limitation, for their automobile expenses that exceed their qualified reimbursement (Code Sec. 162(o)).[118] Qualified reimbursements in excess of actual automobile expenses continue to be excluded from gross income (H.R. Conf. Rep. No. 108-755).

The standard mileage rate method may be used in 2007 by businesses, self-employed individuals or employees in computing the deductible costs of operating automobiles they own or lease for business purposes (Rev. Proc. 2006-49). The business standard mileage rate may not be used to compute the deductible expenses of automobiles used for hire, such as taxicabs, or five or more automobiles owned or leased by a taxpayer and used simultaneously (such as in fleet operations). Use of the standard mileage rate in the first year of business use is considered an election to exclude the car from MACRS depreciation (¶ 1236).

For owned automobiles placed in service for business purposes, and for which the business standard mileage rate has been used for any year, depreciation is considered to have been allowed at the rate of 19 cents per mile for 2007 for those years in which the business standard mileage rate was used (Rev. Proc. 2006-49). If actual costs were used for one or more of those years, these rates do not apply to any year in which actual costs were used. The depreciation described above reduces the basis of the automobile (but not below zero) in determining adjusted basis as required by Code Sec. 1016.

Fixed and Variable Rate (FAVR) Method. The maximum standard automobile cost for purposes of the alternative fixed and variable rate (FAVR) allowance is $27,600 for 2007 (Rev. Proc. 2006-49). Under the FAVR method, an employer reimburses its employee's expenses with a mileage allowance using a flat rate or a stated schedule that combines periodic fixed and variable payments. An employee's car expenses will be

---

Footnote references are to paragraphs of the 2008 Standard Federal Tax Reports.

[114] ¶ 8570.012   [116] ¶ 6060   [118] ¶ 8500
[115] ¶ 8501   [117] ¶ 8590.55

deemed substantiated if the payor (usually the employer) reimburses the employee's expenses with the FAVR mileage allowance using a flat rate or a stated schedule that combines periodic fixed and variable payments. At least five employees must be covered by such an arrangement at all times during the calendar year, but at no time can the majority of covered employees be management employees. There are additional requirements that must be met (Rev. Proc. 2006-49).

948. Interest on Car Loans. Interest paid by an employee on a car loan is nondeductible personal interest (see ¶ 1045). A self-employed taxpayer may claim the interest paid on the business portion of a car as a business expense. The nonbusiness portion is nondeductible personal interest (Code Sec. 163(a)).[119]

Traveling Expenses Away from Home

949. Traveling Expenses Generally. A deduction is allowed for ordinary and necessary traveling expenses incurred by a taxpayer while *away from home* in the conduct of a trade or business (Code Sec. 162(a)(2); Reg. § 1.162-2).[120] Individuals are not "away from home" unless their duties require them to be away from the general area of their tax homes for a period substantially longer than an ordinary workday and it is reasonable for them to need to sleep or rest. In some cases, then, travel expenses may be deductible even though the taxpayer is away from home for a period of less than 24 hours.[121]

Local lodging. The IRS will no longer contest an employer's deduction of the cost of employee lodging that is located in the same town as the employer, provided that the lodging is necessary for the employee to take part in a meeting or function of the employer (Notice 2007-47). The rule will apply to lodging provided by the employer or lodging that the employer requires the employee to obtain and must meet the following conditions:

(1) the lodging must be on a temporary basis;

(2) the lodging must be necessary for the employee to participate in or be available for a business meeting or function of the employer; and

(3) the expenses must be otherwise deductible by the employee, or would be deductible if paid by the employee under Code Sec. 162.

950. "Home" Defined. A taxpayer's "home" is considered to be: (1) the taxpayer's regular or principal (if there is more than one regular) place of business or (2) if the taxpayer has no regular or principal place of business because of the nature of the work, the taxpayer's regular place of abode in a real and substantial sense.[122]

If a taxpayer fails to fall within either category, the taxpayer is an itinerant (i.e., one who has a home wherever one happens to be working) and, thus, is never "away from home" for purposes of deducting traveling expenses.[123]

When there are multiple areas of business activity or places of regular employment, the principal place of business is treated as the tax home. In determining the principal place of business, the following factors are considered: (1) the time spent on business activity in each area, (2) the amount of business activity in each area, and (3) the amount of the resulting financial return in each area. Business travel expenses incurred while away from the principal place of business are deductible.[124]

The tax home of a member of the U.S. Congress is the member's residence in the state or district that the member represents. However, deductions for meals and lodging while in Washington, DC, are limited to $3,000 per year, after applying the 2-percent-of-adjusted-gross-income (AGI) floor (Code Sec. 162(a)).[125]

The Supreme Court has held that a member of the Armed Forces is not "away from home" while at the individual's permanent duty station.[126] However, members of the National Guard and Reserves can deduct qualifying expenses as an above-the-line deduction when attending meetings or training sessions (see ¶ 941E).

Footnote references are to paragraphs of the 2008 Standard Federal Tax Reports.

[119] ¶ 9102
[120] ¶ 8500, ¶ 8527
[121] ¶ 8550.269, ¶ 8550.4661, ¶ 8570.154

[122] ¶ 8570.1327
[123] ¶ 8570.1327
[124] ¶ 8570.1327

[125] ¶ 8500
[126] ¶ 8570.0652

951. Temporary v. Indefinite Test. In determining when an individual is "away from home," the nature of the stay and the length of time away from the individual's principal place of business are of prime importance. If the assignment is *temporary* in nature, the taxpayer is considered "away from home" and a traveling expense deduction is allowed. If the assignment is for an *indefinite* period of time, the location of the assignment becomes the individual's new "tax home," and the individual may not deduct traveling expenses while there. When an individual works away from home, at a single location, for more than one year, the employment will be treated as indefinite and related travel expenses will not be deductible (Code Sec. 162(a)).[127] Employment expected to last more than one year is classified as indefinite, regardless of whether the work actually exceeds a year (Rev. Rul. 93-86). Employment that is expected to and does last for one year or less is temporary (Rev. Rul. 99-7).

The one-year rule does not apply to federal employees certified by the Attorney General as traveling on behalf of the United States in temporary duty status to investigate or prosecute, or to provide support services for the investigation or prosecution of, a federal crime. Such employees may deduct their travel expenses even if their assignment is expected to last for more than one year (Code Sec. 162(a)).

952. Deductible Travel Expenses. The costs of the following items are ordinarily deductible, if paid or incurred while a business owner or employee is traveling away from home on business: meals and lodging; transportation, including a reasonable amount for baggage, necessary samples and display materials; hotel rooms, sample rooms, telephone and fax services, and public stenographers; and the costs (including depreciation—see ¶ 1211) of maintaining and operating a car for business purposes.[128]

No deduction is allowed for the travel expenses of a spouse, dependent, or other individual who accompanies the taxpayer or employee on a business trip unless such person is an employee of the person who is paying or reimbursing the expenses, the travel of such person serves a bona fide business purpose, and the expenses of such person are otherwise deductible (Code Sec. 274(m)(3)).[129]

A taxpayer may deduct traveling expenses between the principal place of business and place of business at a temporary or minor post of duty. When the taxpayer's family lives at the temporary or minor post of duty, the taxpayer may still claim travel expenses. However, the deduction for meal and lodging is limited to the portion of the taxpayer's expenses that are allocable to the taxpayer's presence there in the actual performance of the taxpayer's duties (Rev. Rul. 55-604).[130]

The deduction for the cost of meals and lodging while away from home on business is limited to amounts that are not lavish or extravagant under the circumstances (Code Sec. 162(a)(2)).[131] The deduction for meals is limited to 50 percent of the total expenses (see ¶ 916).

952A. Accountable v. Nonaccountable Plans. The arrangement under which an employer reimburses business expenses incurred by employees (or provides advances to cover such expenses) is either an accountable plan or a nonaccountable plan. Amounts paid under an accountable plan are deductible by the employer and not reported as income to the employee. Amounts paid under a nonaccountable plan are deductible by the employer as compensation reportable on the employee's Form W-2 and subject to withholding requirements. Withholding rules relating to employee expense reimbursements are explained at ¶ 2662 and ¶ 2663. The tax treatment of an employee's business expenses and reimbursements under each type of plan is explained at ¶ 942.

A plan is an *accountable* plan only if it satisfies the following three conditions:

    (1) the expenses covered under the plan must have a business connection;

    (2) the plan must require employees to substantiate the covered expenses; and

    (3) the plan must require employees who receive advances to return any amounts in excess of their substantiated expenses (Reg. § 1.62-2(c)).[132]

Footnote references are to paragraphs of the 2008 Standard Federal Tax Reports.

[127] ¶ 8500
[128] ¶ 8527

[129] ¶ 14,402
[130] ¶ 8570.175

[131] ¶ 8500
[132] ¶ 6004

If a plan satisfies these requirements, but an employee fails to return an excess advance to the employer within a reasonable period, only the amount of the substantiated expenses is treated as paid under an accountable plan. The retained excess is treated as paid under a nonaccountable plan. If a plan does not satisfy these requirements, an employee cannot force the employer to treat it as an accountable plan by substantiating the expenses and returning the excess (Reg. § 1.62-2(c)).

Business Connection. The business connection requirement is satisfied if the expenses are deductible business expenses of the employer, paid or incurred in connection with the performance of services as an employee. If a plan also covers bona fide expenses that are related to the employer's business but not deductible, such as travel that is not away from home, the plan is treated as two separate arrangements, one accountable, the other nonaccountable (Reg. § 1.62-2(d)).[133]

Substantiation. The substantiation an accountable plan must require for the expenses it covers must be sufficient to substantiate the expense under the general substantiation rules (Reg. § 1.62-2(e)), which vary depending on the type of expense. If the expense is for travel, meals, lodging, entertainment, gifts, or attributable to the use of "listed property" (which includes cars, computers and cellphones) (¶ 1211), the substantiation requirement is satisfied if enough information is submitted to the employer to satisfy the substantiation requirements of Code Sec. 274(d) (¶ 953), including travel and car expenses deemed substantiated.

If the expense is not in one of the categories stated above, such as expenses for printing a report, then the expense is considered substantiated if enough information is submitted to the employer to enable the employer to identify the specific nature of each expense and to conclude that the expense was attributable to the employer's business activities. The elements of each expense should be substantiated, including the amount, place, time or date, and business purpose (Reg. § 1.62-2(e)(3)).[134]

Deemed Substantiation of Employee's Reimbursed Expenses. An employee's expenses are deemed to be substantiated, for purposes of the accountable plan requirements, if the employee provides an adequate accounting of the expenses to the employer in the form of adequate records (Reg. § 1.274-5(f)(4)).[135] The adequate accounting requirement can be satisfied as to the amount of car expenses and lodging and/or meals and incidental expenses by using the per diem allowances discussed at ¶ 947 (car expenses) and ¶ 954-¶ 954B (meals and incidental expense only). Note that in order to deduct unreimbursed expenses for lodging on their own return, an employee or self-employed individual must have evidence of the actual costs.

Return of Excess Advances. The return of excess advances requirement is satisfied if employees are required to return amounts received in excess of the expenses that are substantiated or deemed substantiated within a reasonable period of time.[136] Advances must be provided within a reasonable period before the covered expenses are anticipated to be paid or incurred and must be reasonably calculated not to exceed the anticipated expenses. If an employee fails to return the excess within a reasonable period of time, only amounts paid that are not in excess of the amounts substantiated will be treated as paid under an accountable plan. Excess amounts retained will be treated as paid under a nonaccountable plan and must be included in income by the employee. An accountable plan that reimburses expenses pursuant to an IRS-approved mileage (see ¶ 947) or per diem allowance (see ¶ 954-¶ 954B) must require the return of the portion that relates to days or miles of travel not substantiated.

Reasonable Period of Time. The provision of advances, the substantiation of expenses and the return of excess advances must each take place within a reasonable period of time. A reasonable period depends on facts and circumstances, but the IRS has provided two safe harbor methods: the fixed date method and the periodic statement method (Reg. § 1.62-2(g)).[137] Under the fixed date method, the following are treated as occurring within a reasonable period of time:

(1) advance payments made no more than 30 days before expenses are reasonably anticipated to be paid or incurred;

Footnote references are to paragraphs of the 2008 Standard Federal Tax Reports.

[133] ¶ 6004   [135] ¶ 14,410   [137] ¶ 6004
[134] ¶ 6004   [136] ¶ 6004

¶952A

(2) substantiation provided no more than 60 days after expenses are paid or incurred; and

(3) return of excess amounts made no more than 120 days after expenses are paid or incurred.

The periodic statement method is a safe harbor for determining reasonable time for the provision of substantiation and the return of excess advances. Under this method, the employer must:

(1) give each employee periodic statements (no less than quarterly) that set forth the amounts paid under the reimbursement arrangement in excess of the substantiated amount; and

(2) request that the employee either substantiate or return the excess amounts within 120 days of the statement date. An expense substantiated or amount returned within that period will satisfy the reasonable period requirement.

953. Substantiation Requirements. In order to claim any deduction, a taxpayer must be able to prove, if the return is audited, that the expenses were in fact paid or incurred. Small expenses and those which are clearly related to the business may be substantiated by the taxpayer's statement or by keeping receipts, sales slips, invoices, or cancelled checks or other evidence of payments. The following expenses, which are deemed particularly susceptible to abuse, must generally be substantiated by adequate records or sufficient evidence corroborating the taxpayer's own statement: expenses with respect to travel away from home (including meals and lodging), entertainment expenses, business gifts, and expenses in connection with the use of "listed property" (such as cars, computers and cellphones–see ¶ 1211) (Code Sec. 274(d)). The expenses must be substantiated as to (1) amount, (2) time and place, and (3) business purpose. For entertainment and gift expenses, the business relationship of the person being entertained or receiving the gift must also be substantiated (Temp. Reg. § 1.274-5T(a)–(c)).[138] An employer's reimbursement arrangement must require employees to satisfy these substantiation requirements in order to be treated as an accountable plan (¶ 952A).

Substantiation by Adequate Records. A contemporaneous log is not required, but a record of the elements of the expense or use of the listed property made at or near the time of the expenditure or use, supported by sufficient documentary evidence, has a high degree of credibility. Adequate accounting generally requires the submission of an account book, expense diary or log, or similar record maintained by the employee and recorded at or near the time of incurrence of the expense. Documentary evidence, such as receipts or paid bills, is not generally required for expenses that are less than $75. However, documentary evidence is required for all lodging expenses (Reg. § 1.274-5(c)(2)(iii)).[139] The employee should also maintain a record of any amounts charged to the employer.

The *Cohan* rule, which allows the courts to estimate the amount of a taxpayer's expenses when adequate records do not exist, does not apply for the expenses covered by the substantiation rules of Code Sec. 274(d) (Temp. Reg. § 1.274-5T(a)(1)).[140] However, if a taxpayer has established that the records have been lost due to circumstances beyond the taxpayer's control, such as destruction by fire or flood, then the taxpayer has a right to substantiate claimed deductions by a reasonable construction of the expenditures or use (Temp. Reg. § 1.274-5T(c)(5)).[141]

Employees of the executive and judicial branches and certain employees of the legislative branch of the federal government may substantiate their requests for reimbursement of ordinary and necessary business expenses with an account book or expense log instead of submitting documentary evidence (e.g., receipts or bills) (Rev. Proc. 97-45).

954. Per Diem Methods for Substantiating Employers' Meals and Lodging Expenses. A taxpayer must substantiate the amount, time, place, and business purpose of expenses paid or incurred in traveling away from home. Although the taxpayer has the

---

Footnote references are to paragraphs of the 2008 Standard Federal Tax Reports.

[138] ¶ 14,410
[139] ¶ 14,410
[140] ¶ 14,410
[141] ¶ 14,410

option of keeping the actual records of travel expenses, the IRS has provided per diem allowances under which the *amount* of away-from-home meals and incidental expenses may be deemed to be substantiated. These per diem allowances eliminate the need for substantiating actual costs (Rev. Proc. 2007-63).[142] If per diem allowances are used to calculate the deductible amount, the time, place and business purpose of the travel must still be substantiated by adequate records or other evidence.

Although most frequently used in the employer-employee relationship, per diem allowances may be used in connection with arrangements between any payor and payee, such as between independent contractors and those contracting with them. However, employees related to the payor within the related party rules of Code Sec. 267(b) (using a 10-percent common ownership standard) cannot use per diem substantiation methods.

Employees. The per diem method can be used to substantiate an employee's *reimbursed* expenses (for purposes of the employer's return) only if the arrangement is considered an accountable plan and the allowance: (1) is paid with respect to ordinary and necessary expenses incurred or which the employer reasonably expects to be incurred by an employee for lodging, meal and/or incidental expenses while traveling away from home in connection with the performance of services as an employee, (2) is reasonably calculated not to exceed the amount of the expense or the anticipated expenses, and (3) is paid at the applicable federal per diem rate, a flat rate or stated schedule.

Types of Per Diem Allowances. There are three types of per diem allowances: (1) M&IE only, which provides a per diem allowance for meals and incidental expenses only, (2) lodging plus M&IE, which provides a per diem allowance to cover lodging as well as meals and incidental expenses, and (3) incidental expenses only, to be used when no meal or lodging expenses are incurred.

Incidental expenses include tips given to bellhops, hotel maids, and other service providers; taxis or other transportation; and the mailing costs associated with filing travel vouchers and payment of employer-sponsored charge card billings (Rev. Proc. 2007-63).

Expenses of laundry, lodging taxes, and telephone calls are not incidental expenses (IRS Pub. 463). Lodging taxes for travel within the continental United States and for nonforeign travel outside the continental United States are not considered incidental expenses but rather reimbursable miscellaneous expenses. However, lodging taxes are considered incidental expenses for foreign travel (41 C.F.R. 301-11.27 (2004)). Finally, under 41 C.F.R. 301-12.1, energy surcharges are to be considered reimbursable miscellaneous expenses.

Allowances Exceeding Federal Rates. If expenses are substantiated using a per diem amount, regardless of whether it covers lodging plus M&IE or only M&IE, and the reimbursement exceeds the relevant federal per diem rates for that type of allowance, then the employee (or independent contractor) is required to include the excess in gross income. The excess portion is treated as paid under a nonaccountable plan; thus, it must be reported on the employee's W-2 and is subject to withholding.

954A. Lodging Plus Meals and Incidental Expenses Per Diem. Under the lodging plus M&IE per diem method, the amount of an employee's (or other payee's) *reimbursed* expenses that is deemed substantiated (for purposes of the employer's return) is equal to the lesser of the employer's per diem allowance or the federal per diem amount for the locality of travel for the period in which the employee is away from home (Rev. Proc. 2007-63). The employer is not required to produce lodging receipts if per diem allowances are used to substantiate such expenses. The locality of travel is the place where the employee stops for sleep or rest. Employees and self-employed individuals may determine their allowable deductions for *unreimbursed* meals and incidental expenses while away from home by using the applicable federal M&IE rate (¶ 954B). However, unreimbursed *lodging* costs must be substantiated by required records (e.g., hotel receipts).

Per Diem Rates. The federal per diem rate for lodging plus M&IE depends upon the locality of travel. For various geographic areas within the continental United States (the

---

Footnote references are to paragraphs of the 2008 Standard Federal Tax Reports.

[142] ¶ 14,417.421

¶954A

48 contiguous states plus the District of Columbia) (CONUS), the federal per diem rate for a given locality is equal to the sum of a maximum lodging amount and the M&IE rate for that locality.

Federal per diem rates have also been established for nonforeign localities outside of the continental United States (OCONUS). These areas include Alaska, Hawaii, Puerto Rico, and possessions of the United States. Rates are also established for foreign travel (foreign OCONUS).

Rates for CONUS, OCONUS and foreign travel are published under the Federal Travel Regulations for government travel and are updated periodically. Per diem tables appear at ¶ 180.01 and following of the 2008 STANDARD FEDERAL TAX REPORTER. The travel rates are issued to coincide with the government's fiscal year of October to September. For a discussion of the transitional rules for using the per diem rates, see *Transition Rules*, below.

High-Low Method. In lieu of using the maximum per diem rates from the CONUS table, the high-low method, which is a simplified method for determining a lodging plus M&IE per diem, can be used to compute per diem allowances for travel within the continental United States. This method divides all CONUS localities into two categories: low-cost or high-cost localities.

For travel on or after October 1, 2007, the following per diem rates for lodging expenses and M&IE were set by the IRS for high-cost and low-cost localities (Rev. Proc. 2007-63):[143]

	Lodging expense rate	M&IE rate	Maximum per diem rate
High-cost locality	$179	$58	$237
Low-cost locality	107	45	152

For travel on or after October 1, 2006 and through September 30, 2007, the following per diem rates for lodging expenses and M&IE were set by the IRS for high-cost and low-cost localities (Rev. Proc. 2006-41):

	Lodging expense rate	M&IE rate	Maximum per diem rate
High-cost locality	$188	$58	$246
Low-cost locality	103	45	148

For travel on or after January 1, 2006, the following per diem rates for lodging expenses and M&IE were set by the IRS for high-cost and low-cost localities (Rev. Proc. 2005-67):

	Lodging expense rate	M&IE rate	Maximum per diem rate
High-cost locality	$168	$58	$226
Low-cost locality	96	45	141

Certain areas are treated as high-cost only during designated periods of the year (e.g., a peak tourist season) and as low-cost during other periods of time. Thus, employers who use the high-low method must determine whether the employee traveled in a high-cost area and if the area was classified as high-cost during the actual period of travel.

If the high-low method is used for an employee, then the payor may not use the actual federal maximum per diem rates for that employee during the calendar year for travel within the continental United States. However, the applicable federal rates for travel outside the continental United States (OCONUS rates) may be used, and the M&IE-only rate may be used or the reimbursement of actual expenses may be made.

Proration of M&IE Allowance. If an individual is traveling away from home for only a portion of the day, there are two alternative methods that may be used to prorate the per diem rate or the M&IE rate. Under the first method, 75 percent of the M&IE rate (or the M&IE portion of the per diem rate) is allowed for each partial day during which an

---

Footnote references are to paragraphs of the 2008 Standard Federal Tax Reports.

[143] ¶ 14,417.421

employee or self-employed individual is traveling on business. Under the second method ("the reasonable business practice method"), the M&IE rate may be prorated using any method that is consistently applied and in accordance with reasonable business practice. For example, if an employee travels from 9 a.m. one day until 5 p.m. the next day, a proration method that gives an amount equal to 2 times the M&IE rate will be treated as in accordance with reasonable business practice (Rev. Proc. 2007-63).

Transition Rules. Taxpayers are allowed to continue to use the per diem rates effective prior to October 1, 2007, for the remainder of 2007 or they may begin to use the new per diem rates for reimbursement for travel as long as the rates and method used are consistent for all employees and from year to year.

Taxpayers who used the standard federal per diem substantiation method for reimbursement of an individual's travel expenses during the first nine months of calendar-year 2007 may not use the high-low substantiation method for reimbursement until January 1, 2008. Likewise, taxpayers who used the high-low substantiation method for reimbursement of an individual's travel expenses during the first nine months of calendar-year 2007 must continue to use that method for the remainder of calendar-year 2007. However, taxpayers who use the high-low method of substantiation during the first nine months of calendar-year 2007 to reimburse an individual's travel expenses have the option of either continuing to use the rates and localities in effect for travel on or after January 1, 2007, or to use the rates and localities in effect for travel on or after October 1, 2007. The rates and localities that the taxpayer elects to use for reimbursement of an individual's travel expense must be used consistently during this October-December period (Rev. Proc. 2007-63).

954B. Meals-and-Incidental-Expense-Only Per Diem Allowances. An M&IE-only per diem allowance may be used to substantiate an employee's (or other payee's) meal and incidental expenses (for purposes of the employer's return). The amount that is deemed substantiated is equal to the lesser of the per diem allowance or the amount computed at the federal M&IE rate for the locality of travel for the period that the employee is away from home.

Detailed per diem tables appear at ¶ 180.25 and following of the 2008 STANDARD FEDERAL TAX REPORTER.

If meal and incidental expenses are substantiated using a per diem allowance, the entire amount is treated as a food and beverage expense subject to the 50-percent limitation on meal and entertainment expenses.

The M&IE rate must be prorated for partial days of travel away from home. See the discussion of proration at ¶ 954A.

Self-Employed Persons and Employees. Self-employed individuals and employees whose expenses are not reimbursed may also use the M&IE-only rate to substantiate meal and incidental expenses while traveling away from home. The taxpayer must actually prove (through adequate records or sufficient corroborative evidence (¶ 953)) the time, place and business purpose of the travel (Rev. Proc. 2007-63). While the M&IE rate may be used by an employee or self-employed person to substantiate meal and incidental expenses, the amount of lodging costs must be proven by documentary evidence (e.g., a receipt).

Optional Method for Incidental Expenses Only Deduction. Effective for travel on or after October 1, 2007, taxpayers have available an optional method for claiming the deduction for only incidental expenses in lieu of using actual expenses. Taxpayers who do not incur any meal expenses may deduct $3 per calendar day (or partial day) as ordinary and necessary incidental expenses, paid or incurred, while traveling to any CONUS or OCONUS localities. The optional method is subject to the proration rules for partial days and substantiation requirements for taxpayers who use the per diem method for substantiation. The optional method for incidental expenses only cannot also be used by taxpayers already using the following per diem methods: (1) the lodging plus meal and incidental expenses per diem method; (2) the meal and incidental expenses only method; or (3) the high-low method and the optional meal and incidental expenses only method (¶ 954) (Rev. Proc. 2007-63).

Transportation Workers. The M&IE rates for travel away from home on or after October 1, 2007, for both self-employed persons and employees in the transportation industry are $52 for CONUS localities and $58 for OCONUS localities (Rev. Proc.

¶954B

2007-63). An individual is in the transportation industry only if the individual's work: (1) directly involves moving people or goods by airplane, barge, bus, ship, train, or truck and (2) regularly requires travel away from home that involves travel to localities with differing federal M&IE rates during a single trip.

Transition Rules. Taxpayers under the calendar-year convention for the transportation industry, who used the federal M&IE rates during the first nine months of calendar year 2007 to substantiate the amount of an individual's travel expense, may not use the special transportation industry rates until January 1, 2008. Likewise, taxpayers who used the special transportation industry rates for the first nine months of calendar year 2007 to substantiate the amount of an individual's travel expenses may not use the federal M&IE rates until January 1, 2008 (Rev. Proc. 2007-63).

955. Foreign Travel. Generally, traveling expenses (including meals and lodging) of a taxpayer who travels outside of the United States away from home must be allocated between time spent on the trip for business and time spent for pleasure. However, when the trip is for not more than one week or when the time spent on personal activities on the trip is less than 25 percent of the total time away from home, no allocation is required and all expenses are deductible (Code Sec. 274(c)(2)).[144] Also, no allocation is required when the traveling expenses are incurred for a trip within the United States and the trip is entirely for business reasons (Reg. § 1.162-2(b)).[145] If, however, expenses were incurred on a purely personal side trip, they would be nondeductible even though all the travel was within the U.S.

When the foreign trip is longer than a week (seven consecutive days counting the day of return but not the day of departure) or 25 percent or more of the time away from home is spent for personal reasons, a deduction for travel expenses will be denied to the extent that they are not allocable to the taxpayer's business (or the taxpayer's management of income-producing property) (Code Sec. 274(c)(2)).[146]

No allocation is required on a foreign trip when (1) the individual traveling had no substantial control over the arranging of the business trip or (2) a personal vacation was not a major consideration in making the trip. An employee traveling under a reimbursement or expense account allowance arrangement is not considered as having substantial control over the arranging of a business trip unless the employee is a managing executive (an employee who can, without being vetoed, decide on whether and when to make the trip) or is a 10 percent-or-more owner of the employer (Reg. § 1.274-4(f)(5)).[147]

If the trip is primarily personal in nature, travel expenses are not deductible even though the taxpayer engages in some business activities while at the destination. However, business expenses incurred while at the destination are deductible even though the travel expenses are not (Reg. § 1.162-2(b)).[148]

For special rules governing expenses of attending foreign conventions, seminars, and other similar meetings, see ¶ 959 and ¶ 960.

956. State Legislators. A state legislator whose residence is further than 50 miles from the state capitol building may elect to be deemed to be away from home in the pursuit of a trade or business on any day that the legislature is in session (including periods of up to four consecutive days when the legislature is not in session) or on any day when the legislature is not in session but the legislator's presence is formally recorded at a committee meeting (Code Sec. 162(h)).[149]

957. Luxury Water Travel. A deduction for transportation by ocean liner, cruise ship, or other form of water transportation is limited to a daily amount equal to twice the highest per diem travel amount allowable to employees of the federal government while on official business away from home, but within the U.S. However, the limitation does not apply to any expense allocable to a convention, seminar, or other meeting that is held on a cruise ship (¶ 959). Separately stated meal and entertainment expenses are subject to the 50-percent limitation rule (¶ 916), prior to the application of the per diem

---

Footnote references are to paragraphs of the 2008 Standard Federal Tax Reports.

[144] ¶ 14,402	[146] ¶ 14,402	[148] ¶ 8527
[145] ¶ 8527	[147] ¶ 14,408	[149] ¶ 8500

limitation. Statutory exceptions to the percentage limitation rule (¶ 917) are applicable (Code Sec. 274(m)).[150]

958. Travel as a Form of Education. A deduction for travel expenses is not allowed if the expense would be deductible only on the basis that the travel itself constitutes a form of education (Code Sec. 274(m)).[151] See also ¶ 1082.

959. Convention Expenses. Deductible travel expenses include those incurred in attending a convention related to the taxpayer's business, even though the taxpayer is an employee (Code Sec. 274(h)).[152] The fact that an employee uses vacation or leave time or that attendance at the convention is voluntary will not necessarily negate the deduction (Reg. § 1.162-2(d)).[153] See also ¶ 960.

Production-of-Income Expenses. Expenses for a convention or meeting in connection with investments, financial planning, or other income-producing property are not deductible (Code Sec. 274(h)(7)).[154]

Cruise Ships. A limited deduction is available for expenses incurred for conventions on U.S. cruise ships. This deduction (limited to $2,000 with respect to all cruises beginning in any calendar year) applies only if: (1) all ports of such cruise ship are located in the U.S. or in U.S. possessions, (2) the taxpayer establishes that the convention is directly related to the active conduct of his trade or business, and (3) the taxpayer includes certain specified information in the return on which the deduction is claimed (Code Sec. 274(h)(2)).[155]

960. Foreign Conventions. No deduction is allowed for expenses allocable to a convention, seminar or meeting held outside the "North American area" unless the taxpayer establishes that the meeting is directly related to the active conduct of his trade or business and that it is as reasonable for the meeting to be held outside the North American area as within it. The factors to be taken into account are: (1) the purpose of the meeting and the activities taking place at such meeting, (2) the purposes and activities of the sponsoring organization or group, (3) the places of residence of the active members of the sponsoring organization or group and the places at which other meetings of the organization or group have been held or will be held, and (4) such other relevant factors as the taxpayer may present.

The term "North American area" means the fifty states of the United States and the District of Columbia, the possessions of the United States, Canada, Mexico, the Republic of the Marshall Islands, the Federated States of Micronesia, and the Republic of Palau. Costs incurred in attending conventions held in the Caribbean or on certain Pacific Islands may also be deductible if the host country is a designated beneficiary country, there is a bilateral or multilateral agreement in effect providing for the exchange of tax information with the United States, and the country has not been found to discriminate in its tax laws against conventions held in the U.S. (Code Sec. 274(h)). A list of qualifying countries is provided in Rev. Rul. 2007-28.[156] Expenses for foreign conventions on cruise ships are not deductible.

Home Office and Vacation Home Expenses

961. Business Use of Home. Taxpayers are not entitled to deduct any expenses for using their homes for business purposes unless the expenses are attributable to a portion of the home (or separate structure) *used exclusively on a regular basis:*

    (1) as the *principal place* of any business carried on by the taxpayer;

    (2) as a place of business that is used by patients, clients, or customers in meeting or dealing with the taxpayer in the normal course of business; or

    (3) in connection with the taxpayer's business if the taxpayer is using a separate structure that is appurtenant to, but not attached to, the home (Code Sec. 280A(c)).[157]

Footnote references are to paragraphs of the 2008 Standard Federal Tax Reports.

[150] ¶ 14,402	[153] ¶ 8527	[156] ¶ 14,402
[151] ¶ 14,402	[154] ¶ 14,402	[157] ¶ 14,850
[152] ¶ 14,402	[155] ¶ 14,402	

If the taxpayer is an employee, the business use of the home must also be for the convenience of the employer. The allowable deduction is computed on Form 8829, Expenses for Business Use of Your Home.

Generally, a specific portion of the taxpayer's home must be used solely for the purpose of carrying on a trade or business in order to satisfy the exclusive use test. This requirement is not met if the portion is used for both business and personal purposes. However, an exception is provided for a wholesale or retail seller whose dwelling unit is the sole fixed location of the trade or business. In this situation, the ordinary and necessary expenses allocable to space within the dwelling unit that is used as a storage unit for inventory or product samples are deductible provided that the space is used on a regular basis and is a separately identifiable space suitable for storage (Code Sec. 280A(c)(2)).[158] Another special exception applies to licensed day care operators (see ¶ 964) (Code Sec. 280A(c)(4)).[159] See ¶ 964.

The phrase "principal place of business" includes a place of business that is used by the taxpayer for the administrative or management activities of any trade or business of the taxpayer if there is no other fixed location where the taxpayer conducts substantial administrative or management activities (Code Sec. 280A(c)(1)).

Taxpayers who perform administrative or management activities for their trade or business at places other than the home office are not automatically prohibited from taking the deduction based on failure to meet the principal place of business require-ment. According to the House Committee Report to P.L. 105-34, the following taxpayers are *not* prevented from taking a home office deduction under the new definition:[160]

(1) taxpayers who do not conduct substantial administrative or management activities at a fixed location other than the home office, even if administrative or management activities (e.g., billing activities) are performed by other people at other locations;

(2) taxpayers who carry out administrative and management activities at sites that are not fixed locations of the business (e.g., cars or hotel rooms) in addition to performing the activities at the home office;

(3) taxpayers who conduct an insubstantial amount of administrative and management activities at a fixed location other than the home office (e.g., occasion-ally doing minimal paperwork at another fixed location); and

(4) taxpayers who conduct substantial nonadministrative and nonmanage-ment business activities at a fixed location other than the home office (e.g., meeting with, or providing services to customers, clients or patients at a fixed location other than the home office).

Residential Telephone. Basic local telephone service charges on the first line in a residence are not deductible as business expenses. Additional charges for long-distance calls, equipment, optional services (e.g., call waiting), or additional telephone lines may be deductible (Code Sec. 262(b)).[161]

963. Limitation on Deduction. The home office deduction cannot exceed the gross income from the activity, reduced by the home expenses that would be deductible in the absence of any business use (mortgage interest, property taxes, etc.) and the business expenses not related to the use of the home. The business related expenses are deducted in a specific order, as follows:

(1) expenses that are required by the business but not allocable to the use of the home (such as office supplies);

(2) expense that would be deductible even if the home was not used as a place of business (such as mortgage interest and real estate taxes);

(3) expenses related to the household that are allocable to the business use (such as utilities and insurance); and

(4) the allocable depreciation expenses.

Footnote references are to paragraphs of the 2008 Standard Federal Tax Reports.

[158] ¶ 14,850
[159] ¶ 14,850
[160] ¶ 14,850.017
[161] ¶ 13,600

¶963

However, the deduction of the expenses under items (3) and (4) above cannot create a loss. Unused expenses under items (3) and (4) are carried over to the next year but are still subject to the same limitation rules (Code Sec. 280A(c)(5)).[162]

Example: A teacher operates a retail sales business, in which she makes a qualified business use of a home office. Assume that 25 percent of the general expenses for the dwelling unit are allocable to the home office. The taxpayer's gross income and expenses from the retail sales business are:

		Gross income		$25,000

Home Office Expenses	Total	Allocable to Office	
Interest and property taxes	$8,000	$2,000	
Insurance, maintenance, utilities	2,000	500	
Depreciation	6,000	1,500	
Total home office expenses			$4,000
Expenses allocable to retail sales business, but not allocable to home office use (e.g., supplies, wages paid)			$24,000
Total expenses			$28,000

For the teacher to determine the amount of the home office deduction, the business related expenses must be applied against the gross income in the prescribed order. The teacher must first reduce her gross income by the expenses directly related to the retail sales business but not allocable to the business use of the home ($24,000). Next, the teacher applies those expenses allocable to the business use of the home but which are deductible even if there was no retail sales business ($2,000). Since the gross income from the activity is reduced less than zero (–$1,000), the allocable expenses of insurance, maintenance and utilities and depreciation are carried over to the next tax year. The carryover amounts ($500 and $1,500) will be subject to the same limitation rules for the determining the amount of the home office deduction. Thus, the school teacher has a business loss of $1,000 from the retail sales business for the current tax year and a carryforward amount of $2,000 of unused home office expenses to the next tax year.

964. Day Care Services. Taxpayers who use their personal residences on a regular basis in the trade or business of providing qualifying day care services (for the care of children, handicapped persons, or the elderly) do not have to meet the "exclusive use" test (¶ 961) in order to deduct business-related expenses. However, the deduction is available only if the taxpayer has applied for, has been granted, or is exempt from having a license, certification, or approval as a day care center or as a family or group day care home under the provisions of applicable state law (Code Sec. 280A(c)(4)).[163]

The deduction of expenses allocable to day care use is limited as described at ¶ 963. Form 8829, Expenses for Business Use of Your Home, must be filed.

965. Home Office Deduction by Employees. In order for employees to qualify for the home office deduction, they must meet the "exclusive use" requirements cited at ¶ 961. In addition, the exclusive use of the home office must be for the convenience of their employers (Code Sec. 280A(c)(1)).[164] However, regardless of whether or not an employee meets the "exclusive use" requirements, an employee is denied a home office deduction for any portion of the home rented to the employer (except for expenses such as home mortgage interest and real property taxes that are deductible absent business use) (Code Sec. 280A(c)(6)).[165] Generally, an employee's home office expenses must be taken as a miscellaneous itemized deduction subject to the two percent of adjusted gross income floor on Schedule A (Form 1040) (¶ 941). However, statutory employees claim their allowable home office deductions on Schedule C (Form 1040) (Schedule C-EZ (Form 1040) may not be used) (¶ 941B).

966. Deductions on Rental Residence or Vacation Home. Special rules limit the amount of deductions that may be taken by an individual or an S corporation in connection with the rental of a residence or vacation home, or a portion thereof, that is also used as the taxpayer's residence (Code Sec. 280A).[166] Deductions that may be

---

Footnote references are to paragraphs of the 2008 Standard Federal Tax Reports.

[162] ¶ 14,850
[163] ¶ 14,850
[164] ¶ 14,850
[165] ¶ 14,850
[166] ¶ 14,850

claimed without regard to whether or not the home is used for trade or business, or the production of income (e.g., mortgage interest, property taxes, or a casualty loss) are not limited.

Personal Usage Defined. A vacation home is deemed to have been used by the taxpayer for personal purposes on a particular day if, for any part of the day, the home is used (Code Sec. 280A(d)(2)):

(1) for personal purposes by the taxpayer, any other person who owns an interest in the home, or the relatives (spouses, brothers, sisters, ancestors, lineal descendants, and spouses of lineal descendants) of either;

(2) by any individual who uses the home under a reciprocal arrangement, whether or not a rental is charged; and

(3) by any other individual who uses the home unless a fair rental is charged.

If the taxpayer rents the home at a fair rental value to any person (including a relative listed above), for use as that person's principal residence, the use by that person is not considered personal use by the taxpayer. This exception applies to a person who owns an interest in the home only if the rental is under a shared equity financing agreement.

The term "vacation home" means a dwelling unit, including a house, apartment, condominium, house trailer, boat, or similar property (Code Sec. 280A(f)(1)).

Rental Use of Fewer Than 15 Days. If the property is rented for fewer than 15 days during the year, no deductions attributable to such rental are allowable and no rental income is includible in gross income (Code Sec. 280A(g)).

Rental Use Exceeding 14 Days. If the property is rented for more than 14 days during the year, deductions are available. If the home is used as a personal residence, that is, used by the taxpayer for personal purposes for more than the greater of (a) 14 days or (b) 10 percent of the number of days during the year for which the home is rented at a fair market rental, the amount of rental deductions is limited to the gross rental income. If the home is not used as a personal residence by the taxpayer, the deduction is not limited to the rental income. The deduction may also be reduced or eliminated under the passive activity loss rules (see ¶ 2053) or the hobby loss rules if the rental of the residence is not engaged in for profit (see ¶ 1195).

Ordering of Deduction. Rental expenses are deducted in a specific order from gross rental income. Mortgage interest, real property taxes, and casualty losses attributable to the rental use are deducted first. Next, operating expenses other than depreciation attributable to the rental use are deducted. Last, depreciation and other basis adjustments attributable to rental income are deducted. To determine the amount of these expenses attributable to rental use, the expenses are allocated based on a ratio that the total number of rental days bears to the total days used for all purposes during the year (Code Sec. 280A(e)).[167] When the personal usage exceeds the greater of either 14 days or 10 percent of the rental days, according to the IRS, expenses attributable to the use of the rental unit are limited in the same manner as that prescribed under the hobby loss rules at ¶ 1195 (i.e., the total deductions may not exceed the gross rental income, as well as the expenses being limited to a percentage that represents the total days rented divided by the total days used).

However, the Tax Court has rejected this formula (in decisions that have been affirmed on appeal by both the Ninth and Tenth Circuit Courts of Appeals).[168] It is the Tax Court's position that mortgage interest and real estate taxes are not subject to the same percentage limitations as are other expenses because they are assessed on an annual basis without regard to the number of days that the property is used. As a result, the formula employed by the Tax Court computes the percentage limitation for interest and taxes by dividing the total days rented by the total days in the year. This creates the potential of leaving more gross rental income to offset allocated rental expenses. The following example illustrates the operation of the two methods for allocating rental unit expenses.

Footnote references are to paragraphs of the 2008 Standard Federal Tax Reports.

[167] ¶ 14,850   [168] ¶ 14,854.15

Example: During the year an individual rents out his vacation home for 91 days and uses the home for personal purposes for 30 days. The gross rental income from the unit is $2,700 for the year. He pays $621 of real property taxes and $2,854 of mortgage interest on the property for the year. The additional expenses for maintenance, repair and utilities total $2,693.

The IRS allocation of all expenses would be based on 75 percent (91 days rented ÷ 121 days used). In contrast, the Tax Court would allocate taxes and interest based on 25 percent (91 days rented ÷ 365 days) and use the 75-percent limitation for the additional expenses for maintenance, repair, etc.

	IRS	Tax Court
1. Gross rental income	$2,700	$2,700
2. Less: Interest ($2,854)	− 2,141	− 714
Property tax ($621)	− 466	− 155
3. Remaining available income	$93	$1,831
4. Utilities, maintenance, etc.	− 93	− 1,831
5. Net income	$0	$0
6. Unused expense allowable as itemized deductions:		
Interest	$713	$2,140
Property tax	155	466
7. Total allowable deductions	$3,568	$5,306

Bed and Breakfast Inns. The special restrictions on deductions related to a residence used for business and personal purposes do not apply to the portion of the residence used exclusively as a bed and breakfast inn. Expenses related to that portion of a residence may be limited under the hobby loss rules (see ¶ 1195) (Code Sec. 280A(f); IRS Letter Ruling 8732002).[169]

967. Conversion of Property. Individuals who convert their principal residences into rental units (or vice versa) will not be considered to have used the unit for personal purposes for any day during the tax year which occurs before (or after) a qualified rental period for purposes of applying the deduction limitation (¶ 966) allocable to the qualified rental period. However, the expenses must be allocated between the periods of rental and personal use. A qualified rental period is a consecutive period of 12 or more months, beginning (or ending) during the tax year, during which the unit is rented or held for rental at its fair market value. The 12-month rental requirement does not apply if the residence is sold or exchanged before it has been rented or held for rental for the full 12 months (Code Sec. 280A(d)(4)).[170]

Example: A taxpayer moved out of his principal residence on February 28, 2006, to accept employment in another town. The house was rented at its fair market value from March 15, 2006, through May 14, 2007. The use of the house as a principal residence from January 1 through February 28, 2006 is not counted as personal use. If, on June 1, 2007, the taxpayer moved back and reoccupied the home, the use of the house as a principal residence from June 1 through December 31, 2007, is not counted as personal use.

Other Business Expenses

968. Fire and Casualty Insurance Premiums. A premium paid for insurance against losses from fire, accident, storm, theft, or other casualty is deductible if it is an ordinary and necessary expense of a business (Reg. § 1.162-1).[171] However, the uniform capitalization rules may require that insurance costs on real or tangible personal property produced or acquired for resale be included in inventory or capitalized, rather than being deducted (see ¶ 990–¶ 999).

A premium on a personal disability insurance policy is not deductible. A business or professional person may deduct premiums on a policy that pays overhead expenses during a period of disability, but the proceeds under such a policy are includible in gross income.[172] When an insurance premium is paid in advance for more than one year, only

---

Footnote references are to paragraphs of the 2008 Standard Federal Tax Reports.

[169] ¶ 14,854.585
[170] ¶ 14,850
[171] ¶ 8501
[172] ¶ 8522.385

a pro rata portion of the premium is deductible for each year, regardless of the taxpayer's method of accounting (Reg. § 1.461-1; Rev. Rul. 70-413).[173]

An arrangement between a business and an insurance company that provides for the reimbursement of future remediation costs the business is certain to incur does not constitute an insurance contract for federal income tax purposes, the IRS has determined. The arrangement does not involve the requisite risk shifting to constitute "insurance" and, therefore, payments made by the business are not deductible as insurance premiums under Code Sec. 162 (Rev. Rul. 2007-47, amplifying Rev. Rul. 89-96),

969. Advertising Expenses. Advertising expenses are deductible if they are reasonable in amount and bear a reasonable relation to the business. Deductible expenses may be for the purpose of developing goodwill as well as gaining immediate sales. The cost of advertising is deductible when paid or incurred, even though the advertising program extends over several years or is expected to result in benefits extending over a period of years (Rev. Rul. 92-80).[174] The Tax Court and the IRS require that the cost of printing a catalog that is not replaced annually be amortized over the expected life of the catalog. However, some courts have held to the contrary, taking the view that catalog costs are in the nature of an advertising expense.[175] The cost of public service or other impartial advertising, such as advertising designed to encourage the public to register and to vote, are deductible.[176]

Design Costs. The Tax Court has held that packaging design costs were a deductible advertising expense even though the design provided the company with significant future benefits (*RJR Nabisco*, 76 TCM 71, CCH Dec. 52,786(M) (Nonacq.)).[177]

No deduction may be claimed for expenses of advertising in political programs or for admission to political fund-raising or inaugural functions and similar events (Code Sec. 276).[178] This includes admission to any dinner or program if any part of the proceeds of the event directly or indirectly inures to or for the use of a political party or a political candidate.

970. Expenses of Earning Tax-Exempt Income. No deduction is allowed for any expense allocable to the earning of tax-exempt income.[179] No deduction is allowed for interest paid on a debt incurred or continued in order to purchase or carry tax-exempt bonds or other obligations, regardless of whether the interest expense was incurred in business, in a profit-inspired transaction, or in any other connection (Code Sec. 265(a)(2)).[180]

Generally, banks, thrift institutions, and all other financial institutions may not deduct any portion of their interest expenses allocable to tax-exempt interest on obligations acquired after August 7, 1986.[181] This includes amounts paid in respect of deposits, investment certificates, or withdrawable or repurchasable shares.

971. Circulation Expenses. Any expenditure to establish, maintain, or increase the circulation of a newspaper, magazine, or other periodical may be deducted in the year paid or incurred (Code Sec. 173; Reg. § 1.173-1),[182] even though the taxpayer reports only an allocable portion of the subscription income for each year of the subscription period (see ¶ 1537).[183] See ¶ 1435 for adjustments that may be required in computing alternative minimum taxable income.

972. Fines, Penalties, Kickbacks, Drug Trafficking. A fine or a penalty paid to a government for the violation of any law is not a deductible business expense (Code Sec. 162(f)).[184] Also, any illegal bribe or kickback paid directly or indirectly to a domestic government official or employee is nondeductible.[185] Bribes and kickbacks paid directly or indirectly to an employee or official of a foreign government are nondeductible if they are unlawful under the federal Foreign Corrupt Practices Act of 1977. No deduction is allowed for any payment made directly or indirectly to any person if the payment is a bribe, kickback, or other illegal payment under any U.S. law or under any generally

---

Footnote references are to paragraphs of the 2008 Standard Federal Tax Reports.

[173] ¶ 21,805, ¶ 21,817.21
[174] ¶ 8851.152
[175] ¶ 21,817.206
[176] ¶ 8952.40
[177] ¶ 8851.028
[178] ¶ 14,550
[179] ¶ 14,050, ¶ 14,051
[180] ¶ 14,050
[181] ¶ 14,050
[182] ¶ 12,030, ¶ 12,031
[183] ¶ 12,032.01
[184] ¶ 8500
[185] ¶ 8500

enforced state law that subjects the payor to a criminal penalty or to the loss of license or privilege to engage in a trade or business (Code Sec. 162(c)(2); Reg. § 1.162-18).[186] A deduction is also denied for any kickback, rebate or bribe made by any provider of services, supplier, physician, or other person who furnished items or services for which payment is or may be made under the Social Security Act, or in whole or in part out of federal funds under a state plan approved under the Act, if the kickback, rebate or bribe is made in connection with the furnishing of such items or services or the making or receiving of such payments. For all the above purposes, a kickback includes a payment in consideration of the referral of a client, patient or customer (Code Sec. 162(c)(3); Reg. § 1.162-18).[187]

If a taxpayer is convicted of a criminal violation of the antitrust laws, which contain a treble damage provision, or enters a plea of guilty or "no contest" to a charged violation, no deduction is allowed for two-thirds of the amount paid to satisfy the judgment or in settlement of a suit brought under section 4 of the Clayton Act (Code Sec. 162(g); Reg. § 1.162-22).[188]

No deduction is allowed for a federal tax penalty.[189] No deduction or credit is allowed for amounts paid or incurred in the illegal trafficking in drugs listed in the federal Controlled Substances Act. However, a deduction for the cost of goods sold is permitted (Code Sec. 280E).[190] Damage awards paid in connection with the violation of a federal civil statute and similar penalties may be deductible if they are compensatory, rather than punitive, in nature.[191]

973. Legal Expenses. Legal expenses paid or incurred in connection with a business transaction or primarily for the purpose of preserving existing business reputation and goodwill are ordinarily deductible. The deductibility tests are substantially the same as those for other business expenses and preclude a current deduction for a legal expense incurred in the acquisition of capital assets.[192] It is not necessary that litigation be involved for legal fees to be deductible. In addition to attorney fees, legal expenses include fees or expenses of accountants and expert witnesses, as well as court stenographic and printing charges.[193]

A taxpayer may deduct, as a business expense, that part of the cost of tax return preparation that is properly allocable to the business, as well as expenses incurred in resolving asserted tax deficiencies relating to the business.[194]

For the deductibility of legal expenses arising from the determination of nonbusiness taxes or income-producing property, see ¶ 1092 and ¶ 1093.

974. Lobbying Expenses. Lobbying expenses directed towards influencing federal or state legislation are generally not deductible (Code Sec. 162(e)(1) and (2); Reg. § 1.162-20(c)).[195] However, the prohibition does not generally apply to in-house expenses that do not exceed $2,000 for a tax year (Code Sec. 162(e)(5)(B)).[196] Lobbying expenses pertaining to local legislation are deductible.[197]

975. Federal National Mortgage Association Stock. Initial holders of stock issued by the Federal National Mortgage Association may deduct, as a business expense, the excess of the price paid over the market price of the stock on the date of issuance (Code Sec. 162(d)).[198] The basis in the stock is reduced to reflect the deduction.

976. Political Contributions. Contributions made to a political candidate or party are not deductible as a business expense (Code Sec. 162(e)(2)(A)).[199]

977. Environmental Clean-Up Costs. Taxpayers may elect to currently deduct certain environmental cleanup costs (Code Sec. 198).[200] This deduction only pertains to the cleanup of hazardous substances located on sites within areas that meet specific requirements (Code Sec. 198(c)(2)(A)).[201] The expenses must have been paid or incurred before January 1, 2008 (Code Sec. 198(h)). The IRS has provided guidance for

---

Footnote references are to paragraphs of the 2008 Standard Federal Tax Reports.

[186] ¶ 8500, ¶ 8857
[187] ¶ 8500, ¶ 8857
[188] ¶ 8500, ¶ 8955
[189] ¶ 8500 and following
[190] ¶ 15,050
[191] ¶ 8953

[192] ¶ 12,521
[193] ¶ 8526.4035
[194] ¶ 8520.73
[195] ¶ 8500, ¶ 8951, ¶ 8952
[196] ¶ 8500
[197] ¶ 8500

[198] ¶ 8500, ¶ 8859
[199] ¶ 8500
[200] ¶ 12,460
[201] ¶ 12,460

taxpayers who want to make this election (Rev. Proc. 98-47).[202] Individuals must include the total amount of the expenses on the line for "other expenses" on Schedule C, E, or F (as appropriate) for Form 1040.

Before the enactment of Code Sec. 198, the IRS ruled that a corporation that discharged hazardous waste as part of its manufacturing process could deduct for ongoing soil remediation and groundwater treatment costs because the costs did not produce permanent improvements or otherwise provide significant future benefits. However, the costs of constructing groundwater treatment facilities, having a useful life substantially beyond the tax year, are required to be capitalized (Rev. Rul. 94-38).[203]

977A. Small Refiners' Deduction for Upgrades to Produce Low Sulfur Fuels. Small refiners that invest in upgrading their facilities to produce low-sulfur fuels are allowed to elect to deduct a portion of the costs (Code Sec. 179B). Qualified small refiners may deduct up to 75 percent of the capital costs paid or incurred for the purposes of complying with the Highway Diesel Fuel Sulfur Control Requirements of the Environmental Protection Agency (¶ 1285).[204]

977B. Domestic Film and Television Productions Deduction. Film and television producers are allowed to elect to immediately deduct the cost of a production if the cost does not exceed $15 million ($20 million if the costs are significantly incurred in a low-income community or distressed area). At least 75 percent of the compensation paid in the production must be for services performed in the United States (Code Sec. 181). See ¶ 1229 for general discussion of the amortization of film and television production costs.[205]

977C. New Refinery Property Deduction. The builders of new liquid fuel refineries may elect to deduct up to 50 percent of the cost of building a qualified refinery property in the year it is placed in service (Code Sec. 179C). This deduction is available to taxpayers who place a qualified refinery property in service after August 8, 2005 and before January 1, 2012 (¶ 1285A).[206]

977D. Energy-Efficient Commercial Buildings Deduction. Taxpayers may deduct a portion of the costs of installation of energy-efficient systems into commercial buildings (Code Sec. 179D). The maximum deduction is generally $1.80 per square foot of a qualified commercial property, less the total amount of deductions under this provision taken in prior tax years. Qualified systems include interior lighting, heating, cooling, ventilation and hot water systems, and the building envelope. The deduction is available for qualified commercial property placed in service after December 31, 2005 but before January 1, 2009 (see ¶ 1286A).[207]

978. Expenses of Mercantile and Manufacturing Businesses. Merchants and manufacturers generally are subject to the uniform capitalization rules. See the discussion at ¶ 990—¶ 999. However, ordinary and necessary business expenses not covered by such rules may be currently deducted (Reg. § 1.162-1).[208]

979. Research Expenditures. A taxpayer may elect to currently deduct certain research and experimental costs by claiming the deduction on the income tax return for the first tax year in which the costs are paid or incurred in connection with its business (Code Sec. 174). Only costs of research in the laboratory or for experimental purposes, whether carried on by the taxpayer or on behalf of the taxpayer by a third party, are deductible. Market research and normal product testing costs are not considered research expenditures. Once made, the election is applicable to all research costs incurred in the project for the current and all subsequent years.

As an alternative, a taxpayer can elect to capitalize the costs and amortize them ratably over a period of at least 60 months beginning with the month when benefits are first realized from them, assuming that the property created does not have a determinable useful life at that time. Costs associated with property that has a determinable useful life must be amortized or depreciated over its useful life.

Footnote references are to paragraphs of the 2008 Standard Federal Tax Reports.

[202] ¶ 12,465.30
[203] ¶ 8630.1242
[204] ¶ 12,136.01
[205] ¶ 12,146.01
[206] ¶ 12,137E.01
[207] ¶ 12,138D.01
[208] ¶ 8501

The election to amortize must be made no later than the due date of the return for the tax year for which the election is made by attaching a statement to the return. The elections are not available for expenditures for land, oil or gas exploration, or for depreciable and depletable property used in experimental work (Code Sec. 174).[209] Amortization is claimed on Form 4562, Depreciation and Amortization. Both elections are available for research costs incurred before a trade or business begins.[210]

The costs of obtaining a patent, including attorneys' fees paid or incurred in making and perfecting a patent application, qualify as research or experimental expenditures, but the costs of acquiring another's patent, model, production or process do not qualify (Reg. § 1.174-2(a)(1)).[211] When the election to defer expenses has been made, the right to amortize ceases when the patent issues. Unrecovered expenditures are recovered through depreciation over the life of the patent (Reg. § 1.174-4(a)(4)).[212] There is a credit for increased research and experimental expenses (see ¶ 1330). A purchased patent may qualify as a Section 197 intangible to be amortized over 15 years (see ¶ 1288).

980. Computer Software Costs. The costs of developing software (for taxpayer's own use or for sale or lease to others) may be deducted currently or amortized over a five-year period (or shorter if established as appropriate), so long as such costs are treated consistently (Rev. Proc. 2000-50).[213]

Computer software which is not amortizable over 15 years as a Section 197 intangible (as defined at ¶ 1288) is depreciated using the straight-line method over three years beginning in the month it is placed in service (Code Sec. 167(f)). The cost of computer software that is included as part of the cost of computer hardware, and is not separately stated, is treated as part of the cost of the hardware (Reg. § 1.167(a)-14(b)).[214]

Computer software with a useful life of less than one year is currently deductible. A deduction is allowed for rental payments made for software leased for use in a trade or business.[215]

Web Site Development Costs. The IRS has yet to issue formal guidance on the treatment of web site development costs.

Domestic Production Activities

980A. Deduction for Domestic Production Activities. For tax years beginning after December 31, 2004, a taxpayer may claim a deduction against gross income equal to the applicable percentage of its qualified production activities income (QPAI) or its taxable income without regard to the deduction (whichever is less) (Code Sec. 199).[216] The amount of this "manufacturer's deduction" for any tax year, however, may not exceed 50 percent of the W-2 wages paid by the taxpayer. For tax years beginning after May 17, 2006, the deduction may not exceed 50 percent of the W-2 wages allocable to the taxpayer's domestic production gross receipts (see ¶ 980C).

For tax years beginning in 2005 and 2006 the applicable percentage was three percent. The percentage increases to six percent in 2007, 2008, and 2009 and to nine percent thereafter. In the case of an individual, adjusted gross income is used to calculate the deduction rather than taxable income. Form 8903, Domestic Production Activities Deduction, is used to calculate the deduction.

The IRS has issued guidance regarding the manufacturer's deduction. Final regulations apply generally to tax years beginning on or after June 1, 2006. For tax years beginning before June 1, 2006, generally a taxpayer could either apply the final regulations in full or apply Notice 2005-14 and the proposed regulations (Reg. § 1.199-8(i)).

980B. Qualified Production Activities Income. A taxpayer's qualified production activities income (QPAI) is its "domestic production gross receipts" (DPGR) attributable to the actual conduct of a trade or business during the tax year, reduced by: (1) the cost of goods sold allocable to DPGR; (2) other deductions, expenses and losses that are directly allocable to DPGR; and (3) a ratable share of other deductions, expenses and losses that are not directly allocable to DPGR or another class of income (Code Sec. 199(c)(1)).[217]

Footnote references are to paragraphs of the 2008 Standard Federal Tax Reports.

[209] ¶ 12,040, ¶ 12,047	[212] ¶ 12,046	[215] ¶ 8754.1695
[210] ¶ 12,047.1805	[213] ¶ 8754.1695	[216] ¶ 12,468
[211] ¶ 12,043	[214] ¶ 11,030D	[217] ¶ 12,468

QPAI must be determined on an item-by-item basis and is the sum of QPAI from each item (whether positive or negative) (Proposed Reg. § 1.199-1(c); Reg. § 1.199-3(d); Notice 2005-14, Section 4.03(1)).[218] Thus, a taxpayer cannot determine QPAI on a division-by-division, product-line-by-product-line, or transaction-by-transaction basis. This prevents a taxpayer from isolating loss activities from other activities in order to maximize their deduction. An "item" is defined as property, or any portion of property, that is offered to sale to customers that meets all of the requirements of the manufacturer's deduction.

980C. W-2 Wage Limitation. The deduction for domestic production activities may not exceed 50 percent of the W-2 wages paid by the taxpayer to its employees for the calendar year ending during the tax year (Code Sec. 199(b)(2); Proposed Reg. § 1.199-2; Reg. § 1.199-2; Notice 2005-14, Section 4.02).[219] For tax years beginning after May 17, 2006, the wage limitation includes only the W-2 wages properly allocable to the taxpayer's domestic gross production receipts, which are the wages the taxpayer deducts in calculating its qualified production activities income.

W-2 wages are defined as amounts required to be reported for wages and compensation on Form W-2, plus compensation deferred under Code Sec. 457 plans and elective deferrals under other employer plans (i.e., 401(k), 403(b), SIMPLEs and SEPs, as well as designated Roth contributions) (Proposed Reg. § 1.199-2(f); Reg. § 1.199-2(e); Notice 2005-14, Section 4.02(2)).[220] While all of these payments are reported on Form W-2, no single box includes all types of payments. Thus, taxpayers may use one of three safe harbors for computing W-2 wages (Rev. Proc. 2006-47):

(1) **Unmodified box method:** Under the unmodified box method, W-2 wages are the *lesser of:* (a) the total amount entered for all employees in Box 1 (wages, tips, other compensation) or (b) the total amount entered for all employees in Box 5 (Medicare wages and tips).

(2) **Modified box 1 method:** Under the modified Box 1 method, the total amount reported in Box 1 for all employees is reduced by the total amount included in Box 1 for all employees that are: (a) not wages subject to federal income tax withholding and (b) amounts that are not wages but the taxpayer has elected to withhold income on (e.g., supplemental unemployment compensation benefits and certain sick pay). The result is then increased by the total amount reported in Box 12 for all employees which are coded D, E, F, G, or S to arrive at the taxpayer's W-2 wages.

(3) **Tracking wages method:** Under the tracking wages method, the taxpayer actually tracks total wages paid to its employees that are subject to federal income tax withholding and that are reported on Form W-2 (not including supplemental unemployment benefits). The result is then increased by the amount reported in Box 12 and coded D, E, F, G, or S to arrive at the taxpayer's W-2 wages.

Amounts that are treated by a taxpayer as W-2 wages in one tax year (e.g., nonqualified deferred compensation) may not be treated as W-2 wages in another tax year or as W-2 wages of another taxpayer. In addition, an employer with a short-tax year must use a modified version of the tracking wages method. A taxpayer that acquires a major portion of a trade or business may not take into account wages paid to common law employees of the predecessor employer for services rendered to the predecessor employer, even if those wages are reported on Forms W-2 furnished by the taxpayer.

980D. Domestic Production Gross Receipts. Domestic production gross receipts (DPGR) are the gross receipts of the taxpayer that are derived from:

(1) the lease, rental, license, sale, exchange or other disposition of:

• qualifying production property (generally, tangible personal property, computer software, and sound recordings) manufactured, produced, grown, or extracted by the taxpayer in whole or in significant part within the United States,

---

Footnote references are to paragraphs of the 2008 Standard Federal Tax Reports.

[218] ¶ 12,472, ¶ 12,476.15   [219] ¶ 12,468, ¶ 12,472A, ¶ 12,476.15   [220] ¶ 12,472A, ¶ 12,476.15

¶980D

- any qualified film produced by the taxpayer in the United States, or
- electricity, natural gas, or potable water produced by the taxpayer in the United States;

(2) construction performed within the United States; and

(3) engineering or architectural services performed in the United States for construction projects located in the United States (Code Sec. 199(c)(4)).[221]

DPGR does not include gross receipts from (Code Sec. 199(c)(4)(B)):

(1) the sale of food and beverages prepared by the taxpayer at a retail establishment;

(2) transmission or distribution of electricity; or

(3) distribution of electricity, natural gas or potable water.

For this purpose, the "United States" is defined as including all 50 states and the District of Columbia, as well as the territorial waters of the United States, and the seabed and subsoil of those submarine areas that are adjacent to the territorial waters of the United States and over which the U.S. has exclusive rights, in accordance with international law, with respect to the exploration and exploitation of natural resources (Reg. § 1.199-3(h), effective for tax years beginning after May 31, 2006; Notice 2005-14, and Proposed Reg. § 1.199-3(g), effective for tax years beginning before June 1, 2006). The "United States" generally does not include possessions and territories of the United States or the airspace or space over the United States and these areas. However, a taxpayer may take into account its Puerto Rico business activity in calculating its DPGR and qualified production activities income (QPAI), if all of the taxpayer's gross receipts from Puerto Rican sources are subject to U.S. income taxation. For purposes of the 50-percent W-2 wage limitation, those taxpayers can take into account wages paid to U.S. citizens who are bona fide residents of Puerto Rico. This expansion of the definition of the United States is only effective for the first two tax years beginning after 2005 and before 2008 (Code Sec. 199(d)(8)).

Generally, a taxpayer may allocate which of its gross receipts are DPGR and non-DPGR using any reasonable method. A specific identification method must be used only if that method is used for other purposes and it can be used without undue burden or expense (Proposed Reg. § 1.199-1(d); Reg. § 1.199-1(d)).[222] A similar rule applies in determining when a taxpayer takes gross receipts into account. For example, in circumstances where gross receipts and expenses may be recognized in different tax years (e.g., advanced payments, long-term contracts), the taxpayer may recognize DPGR and related expenses in the tax year such items are recognized under the taxpayer's method of accounting (Proposed Reg. § 1.199-1(e); Reg. § 1.199-1(e)). If a taxpayer has a de minimis amount of non-DPGR (less than five percent of total gross receipts), then all of the taxpayer's gross receipts may be treated as DPGR.

Generally, gross receipts derived from the performance of a service other than construction, engineering and architectural activities do not qualify as DPGR (Proposed Reg. § 1.199-3(h)(4); Reg. § 1.199-3(i)(4); Notice 2005-14, Section 4.04(7)(b)).[223] There are five exceptions to this rule. A taxpayer may include in DPGR the gross receipts derived from a qualified warranty, delivery or distribution, installation, the provision of operating manuals and a de minimis amount of embedded services (less than five percent of the gross receipts) with respect to an underlying item of qualifying property. A service is considered embedded if its price is not separately stated from the amount charged for the qualified property.

If a taxpayer exchanges qualified production property it manufactured, produced, etc., for other property in a taxable or nontaxable exchange, the value of the property received may be treated as DPGR (Proposed Reg. § 1.199-3(h)(2); Reg. § 1.199-3(i)(1)). However, unless the taxpayer further manufactures, produces, etc., the property received, any gross receipts from the subsequent sale will not be DPGR even if the property was qualified property in the hands of the other person. Generally, DPGR will also not include any gross receipts derived by the taxpayer from the lease, rental, or

---

Footnote references are to paragraphs of the 2008 Standard Federal Tax Reports.

[221] ¶ 12,468   [222] ¶ 12,472   [223] ¶ 12,472B, ¶ 12,476.15

license of qualified production property for use by any related person (Code Sec. 199(c)(7)).[224]

980E. Qualified Production Property. Generally, only one taxpayer may claim the domestic production activities deduction with respect to the manufacture, production, growth, or extraction (MPGE) of qualifying production property (QPP) (i.e., tangible personal property, computer software, and sound recordings) (Proposed Reg. § 1.199-3(e); Reg. § 1.199-3(f)(1); Notice 2005-14, Section 4.04(4)).[225] The deduction is claimed by the taxpayer who has the benefits and burdens of ownership of the property (i.e., bears the risk of loss) under federal income tax principles during the period that the qualifying MPGE activity occurs.

The QPP must be MPGE by the taxpayer in whole or in significant part within the United States. QPP will be treated as having been MPGE in significant part in the United States if the MPGE activity performed within the United States is substantial in nature. This is determined on a facts and circumstances basis taking into account the nature and relative value added by the taxpayer's U.S. activity (Proposed Reg. § § 1.199-3(d) and (f); Reg. § § 1.199-3(e) and (g); Notice 2005-14, Section 4.04(5)).[226] A safe harbor provides that the significant part requirement will be satisfied if conversion costs (i.e., direct labor and related factory expenses) to MPGE the property are incurred by the taxpayer within the United States and such costs account for 20 percent or more of the total cost of goods sold of the property. For this purpose, packaging, repackaging, labeling, and minor assembly operations are not considered so substantial in nature as to qualify as the MPGE of QPP. In addition, research and experimental activities and the creation of intangibles (other than computer software and sound recordings) do not qualify as substantial activities and may be excluded in calculating the safe harbor.

980F. Construction, Engineering, or Architectural Activities. The domestic production gross receipts (DPGR) of a taxpayer includes the proceeds from the sale, exchange or other disposition of real property constructed by the taxpayer in the United States (whether or not sold or completed), including compensation for the performance of construction services by the taxpayer and any qualified construction warranty (Proposed Reg. § 1.199-3(l); Reg. § 1.199-3(m); Notice 2005-14, Section 4.04(11)).[227] It also includes proceeds derived from engineering or architectural services performed in the United States for real property construction projects. DPGR does not include proceeds from the lease or rental of real property constructed by the taxpayer. Nor does it include gross receipts attributable to the sale or other disposition of land (though the taxpayer may reduce its cost related to DPGR by the cost of the land).

980G. Allocation of Costs and Deductions. If a taxpayer can specifically identify from its books and records the cost of goods sold (CGS) allocable to its domestic production gross receipts (DPGR) (without undue burden or expense), then CGS allocable to DPGR is that amount regardless of whether the taxpayer uses another allocation method to allocate gross receipts (Proposed Reg. § 1.199-4(b); Reg. § 1.199-4(b); Notice 2005-14, Section 4.05(2)).[228] If a taxpayer cannot specifically identify CGS allocable to DPGR (e.g., inventory accounted for under the LIFO method), the taxpayer may use any reasonable method. This includes allocation based on gross receipts, number of units produced, or total production costs. An allocation of CGS between DPGR and non-DPGR that is different from the taxpayer's method for allocating gross receipts will ordinarily *not* be considered reasonable unless the method used for allocating CGS is demonstrably more accurate. However, a qualifying small taxpayer may use the small business simplified overall method to allocate CGS and other deductions (see below).

Three methods are provided for apportioning deductions directly allocable to DPGR and a ratable portions of deductions not directly allocable to DPGR or another class of income. For purposes of all three methods, net operating losses (NOLs) and deductions not attributable to the actual conduct of a trade or business (i.e., standard deduction, exemptions) may not be allocated or apportioned to DPGR.

Footnote references are to paragraphs of the 2008 Standard Federal Tax Reports.

[224] ¶ 12,468
[225] ¶ 12,472B, ¶ 12,476.15
[226] ¶ 12,472B, ¶ 12,476.15
[227] ¶ 12,472B, ¶ 12,476.15
[228] ¶ 12,472C, ¶ 12,476.15

¶980G

(1) The *Section 861* method is required to be used by a taxpayer unless it is eligible and chooses to use one of the other methods. Under the Section 861 method, a taxpayer must allocate a deduction to the relevant class of gross income to which the deduction relates, and then apportion the deduction within each class between DPGR and non-DPGR (Proposed Reg. §1.199-4(d); Reg. §1.199-4(d); Notice 2005-14, Section 4.05(3)(c)).[229] If non-DPGR is treated as DPGR by reason of a safe harbor or de minimis rule, then deductions related to such non-DPGR may be apportioned to DPGR.

(2) Under the *simplified deduction method*, deductions other than CGS may be ratably apportioned between DPGR and non-DPGR based on relative gross receipts. A taxpayer is eligible to use this method at any time if: (a) its average annual gross receipts during the three year period prior to the tax year is $25 million or less or (b) its total assets at the end of the tax year attributable to its trade or business is $10 million or less (Proposed Reg. §1.199-4(e); Reg. §1.199-4(e)). In the case of a pass-through entity, eligibility to use this method is determined at the owner level. The method is also applied at the owner level, except for trusts and estates.

(3) Under the *small business simplified overall method*, a qualifying small taxpayer may ratably apportion its total costs for the tax year (including CGS and other deductions) between DPGR and non-DPGR based on relative gross receipts (Proposed Reg. §1.199-4(f); Reg. §1.199-4(f)). A taxpayer is eligible to use this method if: (a) its average annual gross receipts during the three year period prior to the tax year is $5 million or less, and its total costs for the tax year are less than $5 million; (b) it is engaged in the business of farming and is not required to use the accrual method of accounting; or (c) is eligible to use the cash method of accounting under Rev. Proc. 2002-28 (see ¶ 1515). In the case of a pass-through entity, eligibility to use the method is determined (and application is made) at the entity level.

980H. Application to Pass-Through Entities. The deduction for domestic production activities is generally applied at the shareholder, partner or similar level of a pass-through entity (Code Sec. 199(d)(1)).[230] The IRS has issued guidance permitting a partnership or S corporation to calculate a partner's or shareholder's share of QPAI and W-2 wages at the entity level (Rev. Proc. 2007-35). The entity would then allocate to each partner or shareholder its share of QPAI and W-2 wages from the entity. Only an "eligible entity" may calculate QPAI and W-2 wages at the entity level. An "eligible entity" is:

(1) an eligible Code Sec. 861partnership;

(2) an eligible widely-held pass-thru entity; or

(3) an eligible small pass-thru entity.

Entities that are ineligible to calculate QPAI and W-2 wages at the entity level include qualifying in-kind partnerships (under Temporary Reg. §1.199-3T(i)(7)) and EAG partnerships (as described in Temporary Reg. §1.199-3T(i)(8)).

In addition, special rules permit patrons of agricultural or horticultural cooperatives to claim the deduction for their portion of any patronage dividend or per-unit allocation received which is allocable to the QPAI of the cooperative (Code Sec. 199(d)(3); Proposed Reg. §1.199-6; Reg. §1.199-6).[231] For a discussion of the application of the deduction to S corporations, see ¶ 312; for partnerships, see ¶ 431A; and for nongrantor trusts and estates, see ¶ 536.

Expenses of Professional Persons

981. Professional Persons. Expenses incurred for operating a car used in making professional calls, dues to professional organizations, rent paid for office space, and other ordinary and necessary business expenses are deductible by a professional person. Amounts for books and equipment may be deducted if the useful life of the item is not more than one year (Reg. §1.162-6).[232]

Footnote references are to paragraphs of the 2008 Standard Federal Tax Reports.

[229] ¶ 12,472C, ¶ 12,476.15   [231] ¶ 12,468, ¶ 12,472E,   [232] ¶ 8633
[230] ¶ 12,468   ¶ 12,476.15

No deduction is allowed for dues paid to any club organized for business, pleasure, recreation, or other social purposes (Code Sec. 274(a)(3)).[233] However, this disallowance does not extend to professional organizations (e.g., bar and accounting associations) or public service organizations (e.g., Kiwanis and Rotary clubs) (see ¶ 913A) (Reg. § 1.274-2(a)(2)(iii)(b)).[234]

A professional who performs services as an employee and who incurs unreimbursed related expenses may deduct such expenses only as itemized deductions subject to the 2-percent-of-adjusted-gross-income floor (see ¶ 941 and ¶ 1011).

Information Services. Amounts paid for subscriptions to professional journals, and the cost of information services such as Federal or State Tax Reporters, Unemployment Reporters, Labor or Trade Regulation Reporters, Estate Tax Reporters, and other law reporters that have a useful life of one year or less, are deductible by a lawyer, accountant or an employee who buys a service in connection with the performance of his duties.[235] The cost of a professional library having a more permanent value should be capitalized.

Other Expenses. A deduction is allowed to members of the clergy, lawyers, merchants, professors, and physicians for expenses incurred in attending business conventions (¶ 959).[236] (For foreign conventions, see ¶ 960.) A member of the medical profession is allowed a deduction for business entertainment, subject to the rules discussed at ¶ 910, so long as there is a direct relationship between the expense and the development or expansion of a medical practice.[237] A doctor's staff privilege fee paid to a hospital is a capital expenditure.[238] For other deductions, see the Checklist at ¶ 57.

Farmer's Expenses

982. Expenses. Deductions are permitted for expenses incurred in carrying on the business of farming, including a horticultural nursery business (Reg. § 1.162-12).[239] Special rules, however, apply to certain property produced in a farming business (see ¶ 999) and to farm tax shelters (see ¶ 2028). See ¶ 767 for income averaging rules.

Among allowable deductions are the following: cost of tools, cost of feeding and raising livestock (excluding produce grown on the farm and labor of the taxpayer), and cost of gasoline, repairs, and upkeep of a car or truck used wholly in the business of farming, or a portion of the cost if used for both farming and personal use.

For the accounting methods available to farmers, see ¶ 767. Special rules apply to deductions for prepaid feed and other supply costs of cash-basis farmers (see ¶ 1539). Farming syndicates are discussed at ¶ 2032.

Expenses for the purchase of farm machinery or equipment, breeding, dairy or work animals, a car, and drilling water wells for irrigation purposes are capital items usually subject to depreciation (Reg. § 1.162-12).[240]

Conservation Expenses. A farmer may generally deduct soil and water conservation expenditures that do not give rise to a deduction for depreciation, that are not otherwise deductible and that would increase the basis of the property absent the election to deduct them. However, current deductions for soil and water conservation expenses are limited to those that are consistent with a conservation plan approved by the Soil Conservation Service of the U.S.D.A. or, in the absence of a federally approved plan, a soil conservation plan of a comparable state agency. Expenses related to the draining or filling of wetlands or to land preparation for the installation or operation of center pivot irrigation systems may not be deducted under this provision (Code Sec. 175(c)(3)).[241] The deduction is limited annually to 25 percent of the taxpayer's *gross* income from farming. Excess expenses can be carried over to succeeding tax years, without time limitation, but in each year the total deduction is limited to 25 percent of that year's gross income from farming (Code Sec. 175; Reg. §§ 1.175-1-1.175-6).[242]

Deductible soil and water conservation expenses include such costs as leveling, grading, construction, control and protection of diversion channels, drainage ditches,

---

Footnote references are to paragraphs of the 2008 Standard Federal Tax Reports.

[233] ¶ 14,402	[237] ¶ 8523.2717	[241] ¶ 12,060
[234] ¶ 14,405	[238] ¶ 8634.043	[242] ¶ 12,060—¶ 12,066
[235] ¶ 8634.02	[239] ¶ 8755	
[236] ¶ 8527	[240] ¶ 8755	

outlets and ponds, planting of windbreaks, and other treatment or moving of earth. No current deduction is allowed for the purchase, construction, installation or improvement of depreciable masonry, tile, metal or wood structures, appliances and facilities such as tanks, reservoirs, pipes, canals and pumps (Reg. § 1.175-2).[243] Assessments levied by a soil or water conservation or drainage district in order to defray expenses made by the district may also be deductible.

983. Land Clearing Expenses. Land clearing expenditures must be capitalized and added to the farmer's basis in the land. However, business expenses for ordinary maintenance activities related to property already used in farming (e.g., brush clearing) are currently deductible.[244]

984. Development Costs. Generally, farmers have the option of deducting or capitalizing developmental expenses that are ordinary and necessary business expenses (Reg. § 1.162-12).[245] However, plants produced by farms that have a preproductive period of more than two years must be capitalized. For certain farms (corporations, partnerships, and tax shelters) that are required to use the accrual method, the expenses must be capitalized regardless of the length of the preproductive period (¶ 999). Special rules apply to farming syndicates (¶ 2032).

985. Expensing Fertilizer Costs. A farmer, other than a farm syndicate, may elect to deduct current expenses otherwise chargeable to capital account made for fertilizer, lime, ground limestone, marl, or other materials for enriching, neutralizing, or conditioning land used in farming. If no election is made, expenditures producing benefits extending over more than one year are capitalized and recovered by amortization (Reg. § 1.180-1).[246] The election, which is effective only for the tax year claimed, is made by claiming the deduction on the return (Reg. § 1.180-2).[247] For farm syndicates and prepayments by cash-basis farmers, see ¶ 1539, ¶ 2028 and ¶ 2032.

Landlord or Tenant Expenses

986. Landlord or Tenant. A tenant may deduct rent paid for business property as well as any amounts, such as property taxes and interest, that the lease requires the tenant to pay on behalf of the landlord (Reg. § 1.162-11).[248]

An amount paid by a *lessee* for cancellation of a lease on business property is generally deductible.[249] However, payments by the *lessor* for the cancellation of a lease have generally been regarded as capital expenditures.[250] If rent is prepaid, the lessee may only deduct that portion of the rent that pertains to the current tax year.[251] Some rental payments are subject to the uniform capitalization rules (see ¶ 990). For an improvement made by the lessee on leased premises, see ¶ 1234.

If an owner of property occupies part of the property as a personal residence and rents part of it, expenses and depreciation allocable to the rented space may be deductible (see ¶ 966).

Payments made under a conditional sales contract are not deductible as rent. A conditional sales contract generally exists when at least a portion of the rental payments is applied to the purchase of the property under advantageous terms (IRS Fact Sheet FS-2007-14, 2-23-07).

Under certain conditions, taxpayers who are in the business of producing real property or tangible personal property for resale, or who purchase property for resale, may not claim rental or lease expenses as a current deduction. Instead, they must include some or all of these costs in the basis of the property they produce or acquire for resale under the uniform capitalization rules. These costs are recovered when the property is sold (IRS Fact Sheet FS-2007-14, 2-23-07).

Mining Company's Expenses

987. Mine Exploration. Mining companies may elect to deduct domestic exploration expenses (except for oil or gas), provided that the amount deducted is recaptured

---

Footnote references are to paragraphs of the 2008 Standard Federal Tax Reports.

[243] ¶ 12,062	[246] ¶ 12,141	[249] ¶ 8754.06
[244] ¶ 12,160.01	[247] ¶ 12,142	[250] ¶ 13,709.307
[245] ¶ 8755	[248] ¶ 8753	[251] ¶ 8754.01, ¶ 21,817.635

once the mine reaches production stage or is sold (Code Sec. 617).[252] Recapture is accomplished by a company's electing either to (1) include in income for that year the previously deducted exploration expenditures chargeable to the mine, increase the basis of the property by the amount included in income, and subsequently recover this amount through depletion or (2) forgo depletion from the property which includes or comprises the mine until deductions forgone equal exploration expenditures previously deducted. Expenses not recaptured by one of these methods are recaptured on the sale or other disposition of the mining property with the amount recaptured treated as ordinary income. Certain transfers are not subject to these recapture rules (Code Sec. 617(b) and (d)(3)).[253]

Deductions allowed a corporation (other than an S corporation) for mineral exploration and development costs under Code Sec. 616(a) and 617(a) must be reduced by 30 percent (Code Sec. 291(b)).[254] The 30 percent of expenses that cannot be deducted must be capitalized and amortized over a 60-month period on Form 4562, Depreciation and Amortization. Taxpayers may also elect to capitalize mine exploration expenses and amortize them over a 10-year period (Code Sec. 59(e)).[255] If the election is made, the expenses will not be tax preference items under the alternative minimum tax (see ¶ 1430).

For amounts paid or incurred in tax years beginning after August 8, 2005, geological and geophysical (G&G) expenditures paid or incurred in connection with oil and gas exploration or development in the United States must be amortized ratably over a 24-month period beginning on the mid-point of the tax year that the expenses were paid or incurred. If a property or project is abandoned or retired during the 24-month amortization period, any remaining basis must continue to be amortized (Code Sec. 167(h)). "Major integrated oil companies" must ratably amortize any G&G costs incurred after May 17, 2006 over five years (Code Sec. 167(h)(5)).[256]

988. Mine Development. Expenses paid or incurred with respect to a domestic mine or other natural deposit (other than oil or gas) after the existence of ores or minerals in commercially marketable quantities has been discovered can be deducted currently unless the taxpayer elects to treat them as deferred expenses and deduct them ratably as the ore or mineral is sold. Such expenses do not include those made for the acquisition or improvement of depreciable property. However, depreciation allowances are considered as development costs (Code Sec. 616; Reg. § 1.616-1).[257]

The 30 percent reduction in the allowable deduction and the election to amortize over a 10-year period (discussed at ¶ 987 in the case of exploration expenses) applies also to mine development expenses (Code Sec. 291(b)).[258]

988A. Foreign Mine Exploration and Development. Foreign mining exploration and development expenses (other than oil, gas, or geothermal wells) are to be recovered over a 10-year, straight-line amortization schedule beginning with the tax year in which the costs were paid or incurred. However, the taxpayer may elect to add such expenses to the adjusted basis of the property for purposes of computing cost depletion (Code Secs. 616(d) and 617(h)).[259]

989. Oil, Gas, or Geothermal Well Drilling Expense. Operators of a domestic oil, gas, or geothermal well may elect to currently deduct intangible drilling and development costs (IDCs) rather than charge such costs to capital, recoverable through depletion or depreciation. The election is binding upon future years. IDCs generally include all expenses made by the operator incident to and necessary for the drilling of wells and the preparation of wells for the production of oil, gas, or geothermal energy that are neither for the purchase of tangible property nor part of the acquisition price of an interest in the property. IDCs include labor, fuel, materials and supplies, truck rent, repairs to drilling equipment, and depreciation for drilling equipment (Code Sec. 263(c); Reg. § 1.612-4).[260]

Footnote references are to paragraphs of the 2008 Standard Federal Tax Reports.

[252] ¶ 24,110
[253] ¶ 24,110
[254] ¶ 15,190
[255] ¶ 5400
[256] ¶ 11,009.047
[257] ¶ 24,090, ¶ 24,091
[258] ¶ 15,190
[259] ¶ 24,090, ¶ 24,110
[260] ¶ 13,700, ¶ 23,949

An integrated oil company (generally, a producer that is not an independent producer) must reduce the deduction for IDCs otherwise allowable by 30 percent. The amount disallowed as a current expense deduction must be amortized over a 60-month period (Code Sec. 291(b)).[261] Taxpayers may elect to capitalize, rather than currently deduct, IDCs and amortize these expenditures over a 60-month period. If amortization is elected, the expenses will not constitute tax preference items (see ¶ 1430) (Code Sec. 59(e)(1), (6)).[262]

If the operator has elected to capitalize intangible drilling and development costs, and the well later proves to be nonproductive (a dry hole), the operator may elect to deduct those costs as an ordinary loss. The election, once made, is binding for all years (Reg. § 1.612-4(b)(4)).[263] As to the recapture of intangible drilling expenses upon sale of oil, gas, or geothermal property, see ¶ 2025.

Foreign Wells. Operators may not opt to currently deduct IDCs for wells located outside the U.S. Such costs must be recovered over a 10-year straight-line amortization schedule or, at the operator's election, added to the adjusted basis of the property for cost depletion. Dry hole expenses incurred outside the U.S. are currently deductible (Code Sec. 263(i)).[264]

989A. Advanced Mine Safety Equipment Expensing. A taxpayer may make an election to expense 50 percent of the cost of advanced mine safety equipment paid or incurred after December 20, 2006 (Code Sec. 179E). The cost of any eligible equipment that is expensed under Code Sec. 179 cannot be taken into account in calculating this special deduction for mine safety equipment. The election is available only with respect to the cost of new advanced mine safety equipment placed in service after December 20, 2006, and before January 1, 2009. The deduction is subject to recapture as ordinary income under the Code Sec. 1245 depreciation recapture rules.[265]

Advanced mine safety equipment includes:

(1) emergency communication technology or devices which allow a miner to maintain constant communication with an individual who is not in the mine;

(2) electronic identification and location devices which allow an individual who is not in the mine to track at all times the movements and location of miners working in or at the mine;

(3) emergency oxygen-generating, self-rescue devices which provide oxygen for at least 90 minutes;

(4) pre-positioned supplies of oxygen which in combination with self-rescue devices can be used to provide each miner on a shift the ability to survive for at least 48 hours if trapped in the mine; and

(5) comprehensive atmospheric monitoring systems which monitor the levels of carbon monoxide, methane, and oxygen that are present in all areas of the mine and which can detect smoke in the case of a fire in a mine.

Uniform Capitalization Rules

990. Uniform Capitalization Rules. Taxpayers subject to the uniform capitalization rules are required to capitalize all direct costs and an allocable portion of most indirect costs that are associated with production or resale activities. The uniform capitalization rules apply to the following (Code Sec. 263A(a), (b), (c), and (g)):[266]

(1) real or tangible personal property *produced* by the taxpayer for *use* in a trade or business or in an activity engaged in for profit;

(2) real or tangible personal property *produced* by the taxpayer for *sale* to customers; or

(3) real or personal property (both tangible and intangible) *acquired* by the taxpayer for *resale*. However, the uniform capitalization rules do not apply to *tangible* or *intangible* personal property acquired for resale if the taxpayer's annual gross receipts for the preceding three tax years do not exceed $10 million.

Footnote references are to paragraphs of the 2008 Standard Federal Tax Reports.

[261] ¶ 15,190   [263] ¶ 23,949   [265] ¶ 12,139
[262] ¶ 5400   [264] ¶ 13,700   [266] ¶ 13,800

¶989A

Costs attributable to producing or acquiring property generally are capitalized by charging them to capital accounts or basis, and costs attributable to property that is inventory in the hands of the taxpayer generally are capitalized by including them in inventory.

Property Excepted from Rules. Among the classes of property excepted from the rules are: (1) property produced by the taxpayer for its own use other than in a trade or business or in an activity conducted for profit; (2) research and experimental expenditures (see ¶ 979); (3) capital costs incurred in complying with EPA sulfur regulations under Code Sec. 179B, intangible drilling and development costs under Code Secs. 263(c), (i), and 291(b)(2), and mine development and exploration costs pursuant to Code Secs. 616 and 617; (4) any property produced by the taxpayer pursuant to a long-term contract; (5) any costs incurred in raising, growing or harvesting trees (including the costs associated with the real property underlying such trees) other than trees bearing fruit, nuts or other crops and ornamental trees (those which are six years old or less when severed from the roots); and (6) costs (other than circulation expenditures) subject to amortization pursuant to Code Sec. 59(e) (Code Sec. 263A(c)).[267]

990A. Writers, Photographers, and Artists. Expenses paid or incurred by a self-employed individual (including expenses of a corporation owned by a free-lancer and directly related to the activities of a qualified employee-owner) in the business of being a writer, photographer, or artist whose personal efforts create or may reasonably be expected to create the product are exempt from uniform capitalization (Code Sec. 263A(h)).[268] Generally, expenses for producing jewelry, silverware, pottery, furniture and similar household items are not exempt.[269]

991. Costs Required To Be Capitalized. Generally, direct material and labor costs and indirect costs must be capitalized with respect to property that is produced or acquired for resale. Direct material costs include the costs of those materials that become an integral part of the subject matter and of those materials that are consumed in the ordinary course of the activity. Direct labor costs include the cost of labor that can be identified or associated with a particular activity such as basic compensation, over-time pay, vacation pay, and payroll taxes.

Indirect costs include all costs other than direct material and labor costs. Indirect costs require a reasonable allocation to determine the portion of such costs that are attributable to each activity of the taxpayer. Indirect costs include: repair and maintenance of equipment or facilities; utilities; rental of equipment, facilities, or land; indirect labor and contract supervisory wages; indirect materials and supplies; depreciation, amortization and cost recovery allowance on equipment and facilities (to the extent allowable as deductions under Chapter 1 of the Code); certain administrative costs; insurance; contributions paid to or under a stock bonus, pension, profit-sharing, annuity, or other deferred compensation plan; rework labor, scrap and spoilage; and certain engineering and design expenses (Code Sec. 263A(a)(2); Reg. § 1.263A-1(e)).[270]

992. Costs Not Required To Be Capitalized. Costs that are not required to be capitalized with respect to property produced or acquired for resale include marketing, selling, advertising and distribution expenses. The IRS has established procedures that allow for the capitalization or amortization of package design costs (Rev. Proc. 98-39).[271] Other costs that need not be capitalized include bidding expenses incurred in the solicitation of contracts not awarded the taxpayer; certain general and administrative expenses; and compensation paid to officers attributable to the performance of services that do not directly benefit or are not incurred by reason of a particular production activity (Reg. § 1.263A-1(e)(4)(iv)).[272]

993. Interest Capitalization Rules. Interest costs paid or incurred during the production period and allocable to real property or tangible personal property produced by the taxpayer which has a class life of at least 20 years, an estimated production period exceeding two years, or an estimated production period exceeding one year and a cost exceeding $1 million must be capitalized (Code Sec. 263A(f)).[273]

Footnote references are to paragraphs of the 2008 Standard Federal Tax Reports.

[267] ¶ 13,800
[268] ¶ 13,800
[269] ¶ 13,800.072

[270] ¶ 13,800, ¶ 13,811
[271] ¶ 13,709.469
[272] ¶ 13,811

[273] ¶ 13,800, ¶ 13,856

994. Property Acquired for Resale. Unless an election is made to use the simplified resale method at ¶ 995, the rules applicable to the production of property apply to costs incurred with respect to property acquired for resale in a trade or business or in an activity conducted for profit. Property held for resale may include literary, musical or artistic compositions, stocks, certificates, notes, bonds, debentures or other evidence of indebtedness or an interest in, right to subscribe to or purchase of any of the foregoing, and other intangible properties. However, in the case of personal property acquired for resale, a taxpayer is not subject to the uniform capitalization rules if its average annual gross receipts for the three preceding tax years (or, if less, the number of preceding tax years the taxpayer (and any predecessor) has been in existence) do not exceed $10 million. The uniform capitalization rules apply in the case of real property acquired for resale, regardless of the taxpayer's gross receipts (Code Sec. 263A(b)).[274]

995. Simplified Methods of Accounting for Resale Costs. Generally, taxpayers may elect to use one of the simplified resale methods for allocating costs to property acquired for resale. However, in the case of a single trade or business that consists of both production and resale activities, only the simplified production method (¶ 996) is available. Under the simplified resale methods, preliminary inventory balances are calculated without the inclusion of the additional costs (listed below) required to be capitalized. The amount of additional costs attributable to prior periods and the amount of additional costs determined to be capitalized for the current period are then taken into account with the inventory balances as initially calculated in order to arrive at an ending inventory balance.

The following categories of costs are required to be capitalized with respect to property acquired for resale, regardless of whether a taxpayer elects one of the simplified resale methods: (1) off-site storage or warehousing, (2) purchasing, (3) handling, processing, assembly, and repackaging, and (4) certain general and administrative expenses (Reg. § 1.263A-3(c)).[275]

996. Simplified Method of Accounting for Production Costs. An election to use the simplified production method may be made to account for the additional costs required to be capitalized with respect to property produced by the taxpayer that is: (1) stock in trade or other property properly includible in inventory; or (2) property held primarily for sale to customers in the ordinary course of business.

Categories of property eligible for the simplified production method also include properties constructed by a taxpayer for use in its trade or business if the taxpayer: (1) is also producing inventory property and the constructed property is substantially identical in nature and is produced in the same manner as the inventory property; or (2) produces such property on a routine and repetitive basis (Reg. § 1.263A-2(b)(2)(i)).[276]

997. Simplified Service Cost Method. A simplified method is available for determining capitalizable mixed service costs for eligible property (Reg. § 1.263A-1).[277]

The election to use the simplified method must be made independently from other allowable simplified methods (Reg. § 1.263A-1(h)).[278]

999. Farming Business. The uniform capitalization rules apply to plants and animals produced by certain farming businesses (corporations, partnerships, and tax shelters) that are required to use the accrual method. For other farming businesses, the uniform capitalization rules apply only to plants produced in the farming business that have a preproductive period of more than two years (Code Sec. 263A(d)(1)).[279]

Generally, the rules do not apply to costs that are attributable to the replanting, cultivation, maintenance, and development of any plants (of the same type of crop) bearing an edible crop for human consumption (normally eaten or drunk by humans) that were lost or damaged as the result of freezing temperatures, disease, drought, pests, or casualty. Replanting or maintenance costs may be incurred on property other than the damaged property if the acreage is not in excess of the acreage of the damaged property (Code Sec. 263A(d)(2)).[280]

Footnote references are to paragraphs of the 2008 Standard Federal Tax Reports.

[274] ¶ 13,800
[275] ¶ 13,824
[276] ¶ 13,817
[277] ¶ 13,811, ¶ 13,815.09
[278] ¶ 13,811, ¶ 13,815.09
[279] ¶ 13,800
[280] ¶ 13,800

A farming business is a trade or business involving the cultivation of land or the raising or harvesting of any agricultural or horticultural commodity. Examples include a nursery or sod farm, the raising of ornamental trees (including evergreen trees six years old or less when severed from their roots), the raising or harvesting of trees bearing fruit, nuts, or other crops, and the raising, shearing, feeding, caring for, training, and managing of animals (Code Sec. 263A(e)(4)).[281]

Any farmer (other than a corporation, partnership, or tax shelter required to use the accrual method) may elect *not* to have the uniform capitalization rules made applicable to any plant produced in his business. However, such election may *not* be made for any costs incurred within the first four years in which any almond or citrus trees were planted (Code Sec. 263A(d)(3) and (e); Reg. § 1.263A-1(b)(3)).[282]

Unless IRS consent is obtained, farmers may only make the election not to have the uniform capitalization rules apply for the first tax year during which the farmer produces property to which the uniform capitalization rules apply. Once the election is made, it is revocable only with the consent of the IRS (Code Sec. 263A(d)(3)).[283]

Incentives for Economically Distressed Communities

999A. Empowerment Zones, Renewal Communities, and District of Columbia Tax Incentives, Generally. Special tax incentives encourage the development of economically distressed areas by businesses located in empowerment zones (¶ 999B), renewal communities (¶ 999C), and the District of Columbia Enterprise Community Zone (¶ 999D). The locations of qualifying empowerment zones and renewal communities are listed in the instructions to Form 8844, Empowerment Zone and Renewal Community Employment Credit. Also, they can be found in IRS Pub. 954 (Tax Incentives for Empowerment Zones and Other Distressed Communities).

999B. Empowerment Zones. Status as an empowerment zone generally terminates after December 31, 2009 (Code Sec. 1391(d)).

Employment Credit. For qualified zone wages paid or incurred during the tax year, employers are entitled to a credit equal to 20 percent of the first $15,000 of wages paid per calendar year to each full- or part-time qualified zone employee who is a resident of an empowerment zone and performs substantially all of his work in the zone in the employer's trade or business (Code Sec. 1396).[284]. The $15,000 figure is reduced by wages taken into account in computing the work opportunity credit (¶ 1342).

The credit is claimed on Form 8844, Empowerment Zone and Renewal Community Employment Credit, and is a component of the general business credit but not subject to the general business credit limitation rules (see ¶ 1323 for limits). The amount of the credit claimed may not be deducted as wages.

Work Opportunity Credit. The work opportunity credit may be claimed for "high-risk youth" and "qualified summer youth employees" living within an empowerment zone or enterprise community (see ¶ 1342) (Code Sec. 51(d)). Claiming the credit may reduce or eliminate the employment credit, as discussed above. This credit is available for employees hired through August 31, 2011 (Code Sec. 51(c)(4)(B)).

Increased Section 179 Expense Allowance. In the case of a qualifying business (Code Sec. 1397C), the basic Code Sec. 179 expense allowance ($125,000 for 2007) (¶ 1208) for qualified zone property (Code Sec. 1397D) used in an empowerment zone is increased by the lesser of (1) $35,000 or (2) the cost of section 179 property which is qualified zone property placed in service during the tax year. A number of special rules apply (Code Sec. 1397A)[285] and the increased deduction is claimed on Form 4562, Depreciation and Amortization.

Nonrecognition of Capital Gain on Rollover of Empowerment Zone Investments. An election allows the rollover of capital gain from the sale of a qualified empowerment zone asset (Code Sec. 1397B(b)(1)(A)) acquired after December 21, 2000 and before January 1, 2010 and held for more than one year if another qualified empowerment zone asset is purchased in the same zone within 60 days (Code Sec. 1397B(a)). Gain is recognized to the extent that the amount realized on the sale exceeds the cost of the replacement

---

Footnote references are to paragraphs of the 2008 Standard Federal Tax Reports.

[281] ¶ 13,800
[282] ¶ 13,800, ¶ 13,811

[283] ¶ 13,800
[284] ¶ 32,394.01

[285] ¶ 32,398.01

property. The gain is deferred until the sale of the replacement property by reducing its basis by the unrecognized gain.[286]

Ordinary income is not eligible for rollover. Thus, gain recaptured as ordinary income under the depreciation recapture rules may not be rolled over. Gain attributable to real property, or an intangible asset, that is not an integral part of an enterprise zone business does not qualify for the rollover election (Code Sec. 1397B(b)(2)). This rollover provision does not apply to the District of Columbia empowerment zone (Code Sec. 1397B(b)(1)(B)).

60-Percent Gain Exclusion for Small Business Stock. Taxpayers other than corporations may exclude 50 percent of the gain on the sale or exchange of qualified small business stock (see ¶ 2396) (Code Sec. 1202(a)(1)). In the case of a qualified business entity (Code Sec. 1397C(b)) that acquired small business stock after December 21, 2000 and holds it for more than 5 years, the exclusion percentage is increased to 60 percent (Code Sec. 1202(a)(2)).[287] Gain attributable to periods after December 31, 2014 does not qualify (Code Sec. 1202(a)(2)(C)). Gain from the sale of small business stock of a qualified business entity in the District of Columbia enterprise zone is not eligible for the increased exclusion (Code Sec. 1202(a)(2)(D)).

If a corporation ceases to be a qualifying business after the five-year holding period, the exclusion applies to the gain that would have been recognized if the stock had been sold on the date the corporation ceased to qualify.

999C. Renewal Communities. The tax benefits for renewal communities are available January 1, 2002, through December 31, 2009.

Employment Credit. The employment credit for empowerment zones (¶ 999B) is also available in renewal communities, effective for qualified wages paid or incurred after December 31, 2001. The credit, however, is 15 percent of the first $10,000 of wages paid to each qualifying full- or part-time employee who is a resident of the renewal community (Code Sec. 1400H(b)).[288] The credit is claimed on Form 8844, Empowerment Zone and Renewal Community Employment Credit.

Work Opportunity Credit. The work opportunity credit may be claimed for "high-risk youth" and "qualified summer youth employees" living within a renewal community (see also ¶ 1342) (Code Sec. 51(d)). Claiming either the work opportunity credit or the welfare-to-work credit may reduce or eliminate the employment credit, as discussed at ¶ 999B.

Increased Code Sec. 179 Expense Allowance. The $35,000 increase in the standard Code Sec. 179 deduction amount for empowerment zones (¶ 999B) also applies for investments in renewal communities (Code Sec. 1400J). Similar limitations apply (Code Sec. 1400J).

The rules that apply to empowerment zones are applied by treating a renewal community as an empowerment zone, a renewal community business as an enterprise zone business, and qualified renewal property as qualified zone property (Code Sec. 1400J(a)).[289]

Revitalization Deduction for Commercial Buildings. A taxpayer who receives a revitalization allocation from a state agency may elect to either: (1) deduct one-half of any qualified revitalization expenditures (Code Sec. 1400I(b)(2)) otherwise chargeable to the capital account with respect to any qualified revitalization building (Code Sec. 1400I(b)(1)) in the tax year that the building is placed in service or (2) amortize all such expenditures ratably over 120 months beginning in the month that the building is placed in service (Code Sec. 1400I(a)).[290] The deduction does *not* apply to buildings placed in service after December 31, 2009 (Code Sec. 1400I(g)).

A taxpayer who claims a deduction for one-half of its expenditures may only claim depreciation deductions on the remaining half. No depreciation deductions are allowed for expenditures amortized over five years. The deduction is treated as depreciation for purposes of the Code Sec. 1250 depreciation recapture rules and is allowed in full for alternative minimum tax purposes (Code Sec. 1400I(f)).

Footnote references are to paragraphs of the 2008 Standard Federal Tax Reports.

[286] ¶ 32,398B.01   [288] ¶ 32,458.01   [290] ¶ 32,465.01
[287] ¶ 30,375.01   [289] ¶ 32,472.01

Expenditures taken into account in computing any tax credit (for example, the rehabilitation credit) cannot be taken into account in computing the deduction (Code Sec. 1400I(b)(2)(B)(ii)) and special passive activity loss rules apply (Code Sec. 469(i)(3)(C) and (i)(6)(B)(iii)).[291]

Renewal Community Capital Gain Exclusion. Gross income does not include capital gain (or section 1231 gain) from the sale or exchange of a "qualified community asset" (Code Sec. 1400F(b)) held for more than five years and acquired after December 31, 2001 and before January 1, 2010 (Code Sec. 1400F(a)). Gain attributable to periods before 2002 and after 2014 does not qualify for the exclusion (Code Sec. 1400F(c)(2)).[292]

If a qualified community asset is sold (or otherwise transferred) to a subsequent purchaser, it will qualify for the capital gain exclusion for the purchaser provided that the stock or partnership interest continues to represent an interest in a renewal community business or the tangible property continues to be used in a renewal community business (Code Sec. 1400F(d); Code Sec. 1400B(b)(6)).

Gain on tangible property which is substantially improved by a taxpayer before January 1, 2010 and any land on which such property is located qualifies for the exclusion if during any 24-month period beginning after December 31, 2001, additions to the basis of the property exceed the greater of the adjusted basis of the property at the start of the 24-month period or $5,000 (Code Sec. 1400F(b)(4)(B); Code Sec. 1400B(b)(4)(B)(ii)).

Special rules apply that limit the exclusion in the same way as with DC Zone assets (¶ 999D) (Code Sec. 1400F(c)(3), Code Sec. 1400B(e)).

999D. District of Columbia. The District of Columbia Enterprise Zone (DC Zone) is treated as an empowerment zone and qualifying taxpayers are entitled to the same wage credit, work opportunity credit, and increased expense allowance (¶ 999B) applicable to other empowerment zones (Code Sec. 1400). In addition, the capital gain exclusion described below is available. A $5,000 credit is available to certain first-time homebuyers within the District of Columbia (see ¶ 1310).

Capital Gain Exclusion for DC Zone Assets. Gross income does not include qualified capital gain from the sale or exchange of any DC Zone asset held for more than five years (Code Sec. 1400B(a)). In general, a DC Zone asset includes only (Code Sec. 1400B(b)):

(1) DC Zone business stock—stock acquired for cash at original issue after 1997 and before 2008 from a domestic corporation that is a DC Zone business;

(2) a DC Zone partnership interest—a capital or profits interest in a domestic partnership interest originally issued after 1997 and acquired before 2008 for cash from a partnership that is a DC Zone business; and

(3) DC Zone business property—tangible property acquired by purchase (as defined in Code Sec. 179(d)(2)) after December 31, 1997 and before January 1, 2008, the original use of which commences with the taxpayer in the taxpayer's DC Zone business. The property may not be acquired from a related person or another member of a controlled group.[293]

A taxpayer who acquires stock, a partnership interest, or tangible property from another person in whose hands the asset was a DC Zone asset may also qualify for the exclusion (Code Sec. 1400B(b)(6)).

Qualified capital gain is gain recognized on the sale or exchange of a DC Zone asset that is a capital asset or that is a Section 1231 asset (i.e., depreciable personal property and real property). It does not include gain attributable to periods before January 1, 1998 or after December 31, 2012, gain which would be recaptured as ordinary income under the Code Sec. 1245 depreciation recapture rules, gain which would be recaptured as ordinary income under the Code Sec. 1250 recapture rules if all depreciation on real property (rather than depreciation in excess of straight-line) was subject to recapture, and gain attributable to a transaction with a related person within the meaning of Code Sec. 267(b) or Code Sec. 707(b)(1) (Code Sec. 1400B(e)).

Footnote references are to paragraphs of the 2008 Standard Federal Tax Reports.

[291] ¶ 21,966.0355   [292] ¶ 32,442.01   [293] ¶ 32,427.01

999E. New York Liberty Zone. Several tax incentives are available in the New York Liberty Zone (NYLZ/Liberty Zone)—the portion of Manhattan directly affected by the September 11, 2001 terrorist attack. The NYLZ is the area on or south of Canal Street, East Broadway (east of its intersection with Canal Street), or Grand Street (east of its intersection with East Broadway) (Code Sec. 1400L(h)).

Work Opportunity Credit. An employee of a NYLZ business is treated as a targeted group member for purposes of the work opportunity credit (¶ 1342). The credit was available for the first $6,000 of wages paid or incurred for work performed during calendar year 2002 or 2003 (Code Sec. 1400L(a)).[294]

30-Percent First-Year Bonus Depreciation Allowance. The NYLZ has a separate 30-percent bonus depreciation provision for property acquired after September 10, 2001. This allowance can only be claimed on property which did not qualify for the special bonus depreciation allowance that was available before 2005 (Code Sec. 168(k)) described at ¶ 1237. The main differences between the NYLZ allowance and the former general rule is that the NYLZ allowance can also apply to used property (provided its first use is in the NYLZ) and real property that rehabilitates damaged property or replaces destroyed or condemned property. A taxpayer generally has until December 31, 2006 to place qualifying NYLZ personal property in service. The deadline to place nonresidential real property and residential rental property into service is December 31, 2009 (Code Sec. 1400L(b)(2)).[295]

Increased Code Sec. 179 Expense Allowance. The Code Sec. 179 expense allowance (¶ 1208) ($125,000 for 2007) is increased by the lesser of (1) $35,000 or (2) the cost of section 179 property that is qualified NYLZ property placed in service during the tax year. Only 50 percent of the cost of NYLZ property is taken into account in applying the Code Sec. 179(b)(2) investment limitation ($450,000 for 2007) (Code Sec. 1400L(f)).[296]

Depreciation of Leasehold Improvements. Qualified NYLZ leasehold improvements placed in service after September 10, 2001 and before January 1, 2007 are depreciated as five-year MACRS property using the straight-line method (Code Sec. 1400L(c)).[297]

Rollover Period for Involuntary Conversions Extended to Five Years. The Code Sec. 1033 replacement period (¶ 1713 and following) for property that was compulsorily or involuntarily converted in the NYLZ as a result of the September 11, 2001 attack is five years, provided that substantially all of the use of the replacement property is in New York City (Code Sec. 1400L(g)).[298]

Tax-Exempt Bonds. An aggregate of $8 billion in additional tax-exempt private activity bonds, called New York Liberty bonds, are authorized during calendar years 2002 through 2009 to finance the construction and repair of real estate and infrastructure in the NYLZ (Code Sec. 1400L(d)).[299] In addition, advance refunding may be available with respect to certain tax-exempt bonds issued for facilities located in New York City (Code Sec. 1400L(e)(1)).[300]

Footnote references are to paragraphs of the 2008 Standard Federal Tax Reports.

[294] ¶ 32,477.021
[295] ¶ 32,477.026
[296] ¶ 32,477.028
[297] ¶ 32,477.032
[298] ¶ 32,477.034
[299] ¶ 32,477.037
[300] ¶ 32,477.039

Chapter 10

NONBUSINESS EXPENSES

Deductions, Generally

1001. Major Classifications. Deductions for individuals fall into two basic categories: (1) those taken from adjusted gross income if an eligible taxpayer elects to itemize deductions, and (2) those taken from gross income regardless of whether the taxpayer itemizes. Itemized deductions should be claimed only if they exceed the taxpayer's standard deduction.[1]

1002. Standard Deduction. Individuals who do not itemize their deductions are entitled to a standard deduction amount which varies according to filing status. This amount, along with the taxpayer's personal and dependency exemptions, reduces adjusted gross income to arrive at taxable income.[2] See ¶ 126.

1003. Personal Expense. A personal, living or family expense is not deductible unless the Code specifically provides otherwise (Reg. § 1.262-1).[3] Nondeductible expenses include rent and insurance premiums paid for the taxpayer's own dwelling, life insurance premiums paid by the insured, and payments for food, clothing, domestic help, and upkeep of an automobile.

Adjusted Gross Income

1005. Deductions Allowed. Adjusted gross income (AGI),[4] an intermediate figure between gross income and taxable income, is the starting point for computing deductions, credits and other tax benefits that are based on or limited by income (Reg. § 1.62-1T).[5] See the chart at ¶ 88A for a listing of the 2007 AGI phaseout thresholds.

"Adjusted gross income" means gross income minus deductions (Code Sec. 62):[6]

(1) on account of a trade or business carried on by the taxpayer (except for services as an employee) (¶ 1006);

(2) for trade or business expenses paid or incurred by a qualified performing artist for services in the performing arts as an employee (¶ 941A);

(3) allowed as losses from the sale or exchange of property (see ¶ 1007, ¶ 1701 and following);

(4) for expenses paid or incurred in connection with the performance of services as an employee that are not reimbursed under a reimbursement or other expense allowance arrangement with the employer or third party (¶ 942);

Footnote references are to paragraphs of the 2008 Standard Federal Tax Reports.

| [1] ¶ 6020 | [3] ¶ 13,601 | [5] ¶ 6003 |
| [2] ¶ 6020 | [4] ¶ 6002 | [6] ¶ 6002 |

(5) attributable to rental or royalty property (¶ 1089);

(6) for depreciation or depletion allowed to a life tenant of property or to an income beneficiary of property held in trust, or to an heir, legatee, or devisee of an estate (¶ 1090);

(7) for contributions by self-employed persons to pension, profit-sharing, and annuity plans (¶ 2113, ¶ 2152);

(8) for cash payments to individual retirement accounts (IRAs), and to retirement savings plans of certain married individuals to cover a nonworking spouse (¶ 2170, ¶ 2172);

(9) for interest forfeited to a bank, savings association, etc., on premature withdrawals from time savings accounts or deposits (¶ 1120);

(10) for alimony payments (¶ 1008);

(11) for the amortization of reforestation expenses (¶ 1287);

(12) for certain repayments of supplemental unemployment compensation benefits to a trust described in Code Sec. 501(c)(9) or (17), required because of receipt of trade readjustment allowances (¶ 1009);

(13) for jury duty pay remitted to employer (¶ 1010);

(14) for moving expenses (¶ 1073);

(15) for interest on education loans (¶ 1082);

(16) for contributions to an Archer medical savings account (¶ 1020);

(17) for expenses paid or incurred by a fee-basis state or local government official for services performed (¶ 941D);

(18) for unreimbursed classroom expenses incurred by eligible educators (¶ 1084);

(19) for post-secondary tuition and related expenses (¶ 1082);

(20) for contributions to a health savings account (HSA) (¶ 1020A);

(21) for attorney fees and court costs arising from unlawful federal discrimination claims (¶ 1010A);

(22) for travel expenses of National Guard and Reserve members while away from home to attend meetings and training sessions (¶ 941E);

(23) for costs and attorney's fees paid in connection with any whistleblower award for providing information regarding tax law violations (¶ 1010A); and

(24) for domestic production activities ("manufacturer's deduction") (¶ 980A).

Employee expenses at (4), above, that are reimbursed under an accountable plan are not deductible from gross income (see ¶ 942 and ¶ 943).

1006. Trade or Business Deductions. Expenses directly attributable to a trade or business carried on by a taxpayer are deducted from gross income. For this purpose, the performance of services as an employee is not considered to be a trade or business. However, the practice of a profession, not as an employee, is considered the conduct of a trade or business (Reg. § 1.62-1T(d)).[7] See ¶ 941 and following for business deductions that are available to employees.

1007. Losses from Sales or Exchanges. Any allowable loss from the sale or exchange of property may be claimed as a deduction in arriving at adjusted gross income (Reg. § 1.62-1T(c)(4)).[8] This includes allowable losses from sales or exchanges of capital assets; losses that are *treated* as losses from sales or exchanges of capital assets, such as losses on worthless stocks and bonds and on nonbusiness bad debts; and any allowable losses from sales or exchanges of noncapital assets (see ¶ 1701, and ¶ 1735 and following). These deductions are allowed in addition to any losses attributable to a trade or business, or to losses incurred in connection with property held for the production of rents or royalties. An individual's capital loss deduction is generally limited to the individual's capital gains plus $3,000 (see ¶ 1752).

Footnote references are to paragraphs of the 2008 Standard Federal Tax Reports.

[7] ¶ 6003   [8] ¶ 6003

A loss on an involuntary conversion *as such* is deductible in computing adjusted gross income only if it is attributable to property used in a trade or business or to property held for the production of rents or royalties. However, a taxpayer may be entitled to an itemized deduction for the involuntary conversion of property used for personal purposes if such loss arises from a casualty (see ¶ 1713).[9]

1008. Deduction for Alimony Paid. Alimony payments[10] are deductible from gross income in the year paid whether the taxpayer uses the cash or accrual method of accounting. Back alimony is deductible in the year paid if it would have been deductible if paid on schedule (see ¶ 771 and following for details).[11]

1009. Repayment of Supplemental Unemployment Compensation Benefits. Repayments of supplemental unemployment compensation benefits to trusts or voluntary employees' beneficiary associations required because of subsequent receipt of trade readjustment allowances under the Trade Act of 1974 are deductible from gross income.[12] Repayment of most other unemployment compensation benefits in a year after the year of receipt are deductible as an itemized deduction on Schedule A of Form 1040 (IRS Pub. 525). If the repayment of either type of unemployment compensation exceeds $3,000, the taxpayer may compute tax for the tax year of the repayment by using the claim-of-right method provided by Code Sec. 1341 (¶ 1543; IRS Pub. 525).[13]

1010. Jury Pay. An employee can deduct jury pay surrendered to an employer who continued to pay the employee's normal salary while the employee was on jury duty.[14]

1010A. Legal Fees and Costs. An individual can deduct from gross income attorney fees and court costs incurred in connection with an action involving: (1) a claim of unlawful discrimination; (2) certain claims against the federal government; or (3) a private cause of action under the Medicare Secondary Payer statute. The deduction is limited to the amount includible in gross income on account of a judgment or settlement, whether as a lump sum or in periodic payments (Code Sec. 62(a)(20)).[15] This deduction is claimed by entering the amount and "UDC" on the dotted line next to line 36 of Form 1040 and by including the amount in the line 36 total.

An "above-the-line" deduction is also allowed for court costs and attorney's fees paid by or on behalf of the taxpayer in connection with any whistleblower award under Code Sec. 7623(b) for providing information regarding tax law violations. The deduction cannot exceed the amount includible in gross income as a result of the award (Code Sec. 62(a)(21)).[16] The taxpayer claims this deduction by entering the amount and "WBF" on the dotted line next to line 36 of Form 1040 and by including the amount in the line 36 total.

For deductibility of legal fees associated with the production of income, see ¶ 1093.

Floor on Miscellaneous Itemized Deductions

1011. Two-Percent Floor on Itemized Deductions. Many expenses that are not deductible from gross income (¶ 1005) may be deductible from adjusted gross income (AGI) as itemized deductions, which are reported on Schedule A of Form 1040. A taxpayer should elect to itemize deductions if they exceed the applicable standard deduction (¶ 126) (Code Sec. 63(d)).[17] However, most itemized deductions are treated as miscellaneous itemized deductions, which are allowed only to the extent that their total exceeds two percent of the individual's AGI (Code Sec. 67(a)).[18] Any limitation or restriction placed upon an itemized deduction, such as the 50-percent reduction for meals, generally applies prior to the two-percent floor (Reg. § 1.67-1T(a)(2)).[19]

Indirect deductions from pass-through entities are subject to the floor because they are treated as if they were incurred by the individual taxpayer. This rule applies to nonpublicly offered mutual funds, but does not apply to estates, certain trusts, cooperatives, certain publicly offered mutual funds (RICs), and real estate investment trusts (REITs) (Code Sec. 67(c)).[20] Estates and trusts are generally treated as individuals (see ¶ 528).

Footnote references are to paragraphs of the 2008 Standard Federal Tax Reports.

[9] ¶ 9802
[10] ¶ 6090, ¶ 12,570
[11] ¶ 6094.80
[12] ¶ 6002

[13] ¶ 31,880
[14] ¶ 6002
[15] ¶ 6002
[16] ¶ 6002

[17] ¶ 6020
[18] ¶ 6060
[19] ¶ 6061
[20] ¶ 6060

Statutory employees, such as full-time life insurance salespersons, are not treated as employees for purposes of deducting expenses incurred in their business. Thus, such expenses may be claimed as trade or business expenses on Form 1040, Schedule C, and are not treated as miscellaneous itemized deductions (see ¶ 941B).[21]

1012. Itemized Deductions Not Subject to the Two-Percent Floor. The following itemized deductions (reported on Schedule A of Form 1040) are not subject to the two-percent floor discussed at ¶ 1011 (Code Sec. 67(b)):[22]

(1) interest (¶ 1043 and following);

(2) taxes (¶ 1021 and following, and ¶ 1028 and following);

(3) personal casualty losses, such as theft (¶ 1101 and following);

(4) charitable contributions (¶ 1058 and following);

(5) medical and dental expenses (¶ 1015 and following);

(6) impairment-related work expenses (¶ 1013);

(7) estate tax in the case of income in respect of a decedent (¶ 191);

(8) deductions allowable in connection with personal property used in a short sale (¶ 1944);

(9) deductions relating to computation of tax when the taxpayer restores an amount in excess of $3,000 held under claim of right (¶ 1543);

(10) deductions where annuity payments cease before an investment is recovered pursuant to Code Sec. 72(b)(3) (¶ 817);

(11) amortizable bond premiums (¶ 1967);

(12) deductions of taxes, interest, and business depreciation by a cooperative housing corporation tenant-stockholder (¶ 1040); and

(13) gambling losses (¶ 788).

For a chart listing the average itemized deductions by AGI ranges, see ¶ 88.

1013. Impairment-Related Work Expenses. Ordinary and necessary business expenses incurred by a handicapped worker for attendant care services at the place of employment, or for other expenses in connection with the place of employment that are necessary for the individual to be able to work, are not subject to the two-percent floor. Handicapped persons include individuals who have a physical or mental disability (including blindness or deafness) that limits employment, or a physical or mental impairment (including sight or hearing impairment) that substantially limits one or more major life activities (Code Sec. 67(d)).[23]

Phaseout of Itemized Deductions

1014. When AGI Exceeds Inflation-Adjusted Dollar Amount. An individual whose adjusted gross income exceeds a threshold amount must reduce the amount of allowable itemized deductions by a reduction equal to the *lesser* of: (1) three percent of the excess over the threshold amount; or (2) 80 percent of allowable deductions (Code Sec. 68).[24] (This reduction is being phased out; see *"Phaseout of Deduction Limit,"* following.) The 2007 threshold amount is $156,400 ($78,200 for married filing separately) (Rev. Proc. 2006-53). The phaseout threshold amount for 2008 will be $159,950 ($79,975 for married filing separately) (Rev. Proc. 2007-66). No reduction is required, however, in the case of deductions for medical expenses, investment interest, and casualty, theft or wagering losses.

This limitation is applied after any disallowance of miscellaneous itemized deductions subject to the two-percent floor (¶ 1011) has been taken into account (Code Sec. 68(d)). The reduced amount is reported on Schedule A of Form 1040.[25]

Phaseout of Deduction Limit. Starting in 2006, the reduction in the amount of itemized deductions that high-income taxpayers may claim is being phased out. For 2006 and 2007, only two-thirds of the reduction applies. In 2008 and 2009, only one-third of the reduction will apply (Code Sec. 68(f) and (g)). In 2010, high-income taxpayers will

---

Footnote references are to paragraphs of the 2008 Standard Federal Tax Reports.

21 ¶ 6006.107   23 ¶ 6060   25 ¶ 6080
22 ¶ 6060   24 ¶ 6080

not be required to reduce the amount of itemized deductions they can claim. However, barring further Congressional action, the full limit on itemized deductions will apply for tax years after 2010.

Medical Expenses

1015. Medical and Dental Expenses. An itemized deduction is allowed for expenses paid during the tax year for the medical care of the taxpayer, the taxpayer's spouse, or a dependent to the extent that such expenses exceed 7.5 percent of adjusted gross income (AGI) (Code Sec. 213(a)).[26] These expenses are reported on Schedule A of Form 1040. On a joint return, the percentage limitation is based on the total AGI of both spouses. The deduction may be taken for any person who was the taxpayer's dependent or spouse when the services were rendered or the expenses were paid (Reg. § 1.213-1(e)(3)).[27] For purposes of this deduction, "dependent" is defined at Code Sec. 152 (see ¶ 137), except that (1) dependent status is determined without regard to whether the dependent claims dependency exemptions, files a joint return or has gross income in excess of the exemption amount (Code Sec. 213(a); Reg. § 1.213-1(a)(3))[28] and (2) a child of divorced parents is treated as the dependent of both parents (Code Sec. 213(d)(5)).[29] The deduction is limited to unreimbursed medical expenses (Code Sec. 213(a)).[30] Reimbursement received for expenses deducted in a previous tax year is includible in gross income in the year received to the extent the expenses were previously deducted. Reimbursement for an earlier tax year in which no deduction was claimed is excludable (Reg. § 1.213-1(g)).[31]

See ¶ 1016 for the definition of medical expenses, ¶ 1017 for the treatment of drugs and supplies, ¶ 1018 for the treatment of medical expenses paid after death, ¶ 1019 for health insurance premiums, ¶ 1020 for medical savings accounts, and ¶ 1020A for health savings accounts.

Although medical expenses are generally deductible in the year paid (Reg. § 1.213-1(a)),[32] advance payments generally are not deductible until services are rendered. However, prepayments for lifetime care in a retirement home, nursing center or similar institution are deductible in the year paid if the obligation to pay was incurred at the time the payment was made, and the promise to provide lifetime care was conditioned on the payment.[33] Charges to credit cards qualify as payment of medical expenses in the year the expenses are charged, regardless of when the credit card company is paid (Rev. Rul. 78-39).[34]

1016. Medical Expenses Defined. Medical expenses include amounts paid for the diagnosis, cure, mitigation, treatment, or prevention of disease or for the purpose of affecting any structure or function of the body; transportation and lodging costs incurred on trips primarily for and essential to medical care; qualified long-term care services; and medical insurance (including premiums paid under the Social Security Act, relating to supplementary medical insurance for the aged or for any qualified long-term care insurance contracts that do not exceed certain limits) (Code Sec. 213(d)).[35] The lodging deduction is limited to amounts that are not lavish or extravagant and cannot exceed $50 per night for each individual (Code Sec. 213(d)(2)).[36] The lodging deduction may also be claimed for a person who must accompany the individual seeking medical care, but meals are not deductible.[37]

The costs of birth control pills prescribed by a physician, a legal abortion or a vasectomy are deductible.[38] Payments for psychiatric treatment of sexual inadequacy are medical expenditures, but marriage counseling fees are not.[39] The cost of fertility enhancement procedures are deductible if incurred in connection with *in vitro* fertilization or surgery (IRS Pub. 502). Costs incurred to obtain donated eggs, including donor, agency, testing and legal expenses, are also deductible (IRS Letter Ruling 200318017).

Footnote references are to paragraphs of the 2008 Standard Federal Tax Reports.

[26] ¶ 12,540	[31] ¶ 12,541	[36] ¶ 12,540
[27] ¶ 12,541	[32] ¶ 12,541	[37] ¶ 12,543.82
[28] ¶ 12,540, ¶ 12,541	[33] ¶ 12,543.794	[38] ¶ 12,543.115
[29] ¶ 12,540	[34] ¶ 12,543.175	[39] ¶ 12,543.7055,
[30] ¶ 12,540	[35] ¶ 12,540	¶ 12,543.7869

Expenses for elective cosmetic surgery are not deductible. Cosmetic surgery includes any procedure directed at improving the patient's appearance that does not meaningfully promote the proper function of the body or prevent or treat illness or disease (Code Sec. 213(d)(9)). Thus, costs to whiten teeth discolored by age are not deductible medical expenses, but costs for breast reconstruction after a mastectomy and vision correction by laser surgery are deductible expenses (Rev. Rul. 2003-57).[40] A weight-loss program is a medical expense if undertaken to relieve a disease or defect, such as obesity or hypertension (Rev. Rul. 2002-19).[41] Smoking-cessation programs (whether or not prescribed) and prescription drugs to alleviate symptoms of nicotine withdrawal are also medical expenses, but over-the-counter gums or patches are not (Rev. Rul. 99-28).[42]

The Supreme Court denied a medical expense deduction for rent paid on an apartment for a patient who spent the winter months in Florida on the advice of his doctor. But the Court of Appeals for the Seventh Circuit allowed a medical expense deduction for a hotel bill incurred by a patient who was too weak to travel to his home town after being discharged from a hospital due to overcrowding.[43] Medical expenses do not include amounts allowable as a child care credit (¶ 1301) (Code Sec. 213(e))[44] or funeral expenses.[45]

When transportation expenses are deductible as a medical expense, the cost of operating a car in 2007 may be calculated at a standard rate of 20 cents per mile (plus parking fees and tolls) (Rev. Proc. 2006-49).[46]

Special schooling for a physically or mentally handicapped child or one needing psychiatric treatment is deductible.[47] Amounts paid for inpatient treatment of alcoholism or drug addiction at a therapeutic center and for meals and lodging furnished as a necessary incident to the treatment are deductible.[48] Amounts paid to acquire, train, and maintain a dog or other service animal for assisting a blind, deaf or physically disabled individual are deductible.[49]

The entire cost of maintenance in a nursing home or home for the aged, including meals and lodging, is a medical expense if an individual is there because of a physical condition and the availability of medical care is a principal reason for the individual's residence. If an individual is in such an institution primarily for personal or family reasons, then only that portion of the cost attributable to medical or nursing care (excluding meals and lodging) is deductible. Payments to perform both nursing care and housework may be deducted only to the extent of the nursing cost.[50]

Capital expenditures for home improvements and additions that are primarily for medical care qualify as a medical expense only to the extent that the cost of the improvement exceeds any increase in the value of the affected property (Reg. § 1.213-1(e)(1)).[51] The entire cost of any improvement that does not increase the value of the property is deductible. Deductions have been allowed for the installation of an elevator, a swimming pool, and a central air-conditioning system. Capital expenditures incurred to remove structural barriers to accommodate the condition of a physically handicapped person generally do not improve the value of the residence and, therefore, are fully deductible (Rev. Rul. 87-106).[52] The entire cost of special equipment used to mitigate the effects of a physical impairment is also deductible.

See ¶ 59 for a checklist of medical expenses.

1017. Medicines and Drugs. In computing the deduction for medicine and drugs, only amounts paid for insulin and prescription medications may be taken into account (Code Sec. 213(b)). Although amounts paid for over-the-counter (OTC) medicines or drugs are not taken into account in calculating the deduction, amounts paid for OTC equipment, supplies, or diagnostic devices may be deductible medical expenses (Rev. Rul. 2003-58).[53]

Footnote references are to paragraphs of the 2008 Standard Federal Tax Reports.

[40] ¶ 12,543.189, ¶ 12,543.404
[41] ¶ 12,543.865
[42] ¶ 12,543.7877
[43] ¶ 12,543.67
[44] ¶ 12,540

[45] ¶ 12,543.452
[46] ¶ 12,543.82
[47] ¶ 12,543.786
[48] ¶ 12,543.355
[49] ¶ 12,543.138

[50] ¶ 12,543.726, ¶ 12,543.727
[51] ¶ 12,541
[52] ¶ 12,543.48
[53] ¶ 12,540, ¶ 12,543.023

Example: In 2007, a taxpayer with an adjusted gross income of $38,000 paid $1,750 to a doctor for medical services, $1,325 to a hospital, $340 for prescription drugs, and $250 for OTC cold remedies and vitamins. His medical expense deduction is computed as follows:

Doctor	$1,750
Hospital	1,325
Medicine and drugs	340
OTC remedies and vitamins	0
2007 medical expenses	$3,415
Less: 7.5% of $38,000 (adjusted gross income)	2,850
Allowable deduction for 2007	$565

1018. Medical Expenses Paid After Death. A decedent's own medical expenses that are paid by the decedent's estate within one year (beginning on the day after the decedent's death) are treated as paid when incurred and may be deducted on the decedent's income tax return for the year incurred if the estate waives an estate tax deduction for these expenses (Reg. § 1.213-1(d)).[54] Alternatively, the estate may deduct the medical expenses as a claim against the estate for federal estate tax purposes (Code Sec. 2053; Reg. § 20.2053-4). Medical expenses disallowed for income tax purposes because of the 7.5-percent limitation (¶ 1015) may not be claimed on the estate tax return when the estate allocates medical expenses between a decedent's final income tax and estate tax returns.[55]

1019. Health and Accident Insurance Premiums. A medical expense deduction is allowed for premiums paid for medical care insurance (including contact lens insurance),[56] subject to the 7.5-percent limitation (¶ 1015).[57] If the insurance contract provides payments for more than medical care (such as indemnity for loss of income or life, limb, or sight), premiums are deductible only to the extent a reasonable charge for the medical care is stated separately in the contract or in a separate statement from the insurer. Premiums paid by a taxpayer under age 65 for insurance covering medical care expenses of the taxpayer, the taxpayer's spouse, or a dependent after the taxpayer turns 65 are considered to be medical expenses in the year paid if the premiums are payable (on a level payment basis) under the contract: (1) for a period of 10 years or more or (2) until the year the taxpayer reaches age 65 (but in no case for a period of less than five years) (Reg. § 1.213-1(e)(4)).[58]

Premiums paid for a qualified long-term care insurance contract are a medical expense, but the deductible amount of the premium is limited by the age of the individual at the close of the tax year. The inflation-adjusted maximum deductible amount for 2007 is:

- age 40 or less, $290;
- age 41 through 50, $550
- age 51 through 60, $1,110;
- age 61 through 70, $2,950; and
- age 71 or older, $3,680 (Code Sec. 213(d)(10); Rev. Proc. 2006-53).

The inflation-adjusted maximum deductible amount for 2008 will be:

- age 40 or less, $310;
- age 41 through 50, $580
- age 51 through 60, $1,150;
- age 61 through 70, $3,080; and
- age 71 or older, $3,850 (Rev. Proc. 2007-66).

Amounts paid as self-employment tax (¶ 2664) or as employee tax (¶ 2648) for hospital insurance under the Medicare program are not medical expenses. Similarly, the basic cost of Medicare insurance (Medicare A) is not deductible unless voluntarily paid

---

Footnote references are to paragraphs of the 2008 Standard Federal Tax Reports.

[54] ¶ 12,541
[55] ¶ 12,543.185
[56] ¶ 12,543.165
[57] ¶ 12,543.77
[58] ¶ 12,541

by the taxpayer for coverage. However, the cost of extra Medicare (Medicare B) is deductible.[59]

Self-employed persons can deduct from gross income 100 percent of amounts paid for health insurance coverage. For details, see ¶ 908.

1020. Archer Medical Savings Accounts. Eligible individuals may claim an "above the line" deduction for contributions they make during the tax year to their Archer medical savings account (Archer MSA). Individuals who are self-employed or who work for small employers may be able to maintain Archer MSAs to pay medical expenses, provided that the accounts are used in conjunction with high deductible health insurance (Code Sec. 220; Notice 96-53).[60] For 2007, a high deductible health insurance plan has the following deductibles and limitations: (1) for individual coverage, the minimum deductible is $1,900, maximum deductible is $2,850 and maximum out-of-pocket limitation is $3,750 and (2) for family coverage, the minimum deductible is $3,750, maximum deductible is $5,650 and maximum out-of-pocket limitation is $6,900 (Code Sec. 220(c)(2); Rev. Proc. 2006-53). In 2008, the deductibles and limitations are as follows: (1) for individual coverage: minimum deductible is $1,950, maximum deductible is $2,900 and maximum out-of-pocket limitation is $3,850, and (2) for family coverage: minimum deductible is $3,850, maximum deductible is $5,800 and maximum out-of-pocket limitation is $7,050 (Rev. Proc. 2007-66).

An Archer MSA is a tax-exempt trust or custodial account with a financial institution that is used solely to pay the unreimbursed health care expenses of the account holder or the account holder's spouse or dependents (IRS Pub. 969). Within the limits, contributions to an Archer MSA are deductible if made by an eligible individual, and excludable from income if made by an employer on behalf of an eligible individual (employer contributions must be reported on the employee's W-2). Annual contributions to an Archer MSA are limited to 75 percent of the deductible of the required health insurance plan (65 percent if a self-only plan). Contributions are also limited by an employee's compensation or the income earned from a self-employed individual's business (Code Sec. 220(b)). New Archer MSAs may not be established after 2007 (Code Sec. 220(i)(2)). However, all eligible individuals who previously made or received Archer MSA contributions, or who work for employers whose employees previously used Archer MSAs, can make or receive such contributions if they remain eligible individuals. Individuals can also continue to receive distributions from Archer MSAs (Notice 96-53).

Distributions from an Archer MSA are tax free when used to pay qualified medical expenses. Other distributions are included in income and subject to an additional 15-percent tax unless made after the participant reaches age 65, dies or becomes disabled (Code Sec. 220(f)(4)). The 15-percent additional tax is not treated as a tax liability for purposes of the alternative minimum tax (Code Secs. 26(b)(2)(Q) and 55(c)(1)). Individuals use Form 8853, Archer MSAs and Long-Term Care Insurance Contracts, to calculate their Archer MSA deductions and any taxable distributions.

Eligible seniors may establish medical savings accounts called Medicare Advantage MSAs. The government makes contributions directly to the individual's MSA, and income earned on the account and withdrawals used to pay health care expenses are not included in the individual's income. Medicare Advantage MSAs must be used in conjunction with a high deductible Medicare Advantage MSA health plan (Code Sec. 138).[61] It should be noted that, since no health insurance plans have been designated as a high deductible Medicare insurance policy, no Medicare Advantage MSAs have been established as of January, 2007 (IRS Pub. 969).

1020A. Health Savings Accounts. Eligible individuals may claim an "above the line" deduction for contributions they make during the tax year to their health savings account (HSA). Individuals and employees, through an employer's cafeteria plan, can establish HSAs to reimburse them for qualified medical expenses paid during the year (Code Sec. 223).[62] These accounts allow taxpayers with high deductible health insur-

---

Footnote references are to paragraphs of the 2008 Standard Federal Tax Reports.

[59] ¶ 12,543.49
[60] ¶ 12,670, ¶ 12,675.25

[61] ¶ 7630
[62] ¶ 12,776

¶1020

ance to make contributions in 2007 of up to $2,850 for self-coverage, $5,650 for family coverage, to cover health care costs. In 2008, the contribution limits will be $2,900 for self-coverage, $5,800 for family coverage (Rev. Proc. 2007-36). Amounts are excluded from gross income if paid or distributed from an HSA that is used exclusively to pay the qualified medical expenses of the account beneficiary, his or her spouse or dependents (Notice 2004-2).[63] For purposes of an HSA, a "dependent" is as defined in Code Sec. 152 (see ¶ 137), but without regard to whether the dependent claims dependency exemptions, files a joint return or has gross income in excess of the exemption amount (Code Sec. 223(d)(2)(A)).[64] Excess distributions are subject to income tax and a 10-percent penalty, unless made after the beneficiary reaches age 65, dies or becomes disabled (Code Sec. 223(f)(4)). The 10-percent additional tax is not treated as a tax liability for purposes of the alternative minimum tax (Code Secs. 26(b)(2)(S) and 55(c)(1)). Qualified medical expenses are generally the same expenses that qualify for the medical expenses deduction. Premiums for long-term care and coverage during periods of unemployment, whether through COBRA or not, also qualify.

In order for an individual to be eligible for an HSA, on the first day of each month the individual must be covered by a high deductible health plan and not covered by any other health plan that is not a high deductible health plan. However, the individual is still eligible if he or she is covered for any benefit provided by permitted insurance, or has permitted coverage by insurance or otherwise. "Permitted insurance" is generally limited to insurance related to workers' compensation liabilities, tort liabilities and liabilities arising from property ownership (such as automobile insurance); insurance for a specified disease or illness; or insurance that provides a fixed payment for each period of hospitalization. "Permitted coverage" is coverage for accidents, disability, dental care, vision care or long-term care. Individual eligibility for an HSA is determined on a monthly basis (Code Sec. 223(c)(1)).[65] Starting in 2007, coverage under a health flexible spending arrangement (FSA) (¶ 861) is disregarded for purposes of determining an individual's HSA eligibility after the end of the FSA plan year, if (1) the balance in the individual's FSA at the end of the plan year is zero; or (2) the individual is making a qualified HSA distribution equal to the remaining balance (Code Sec. 223(c)(1)(B)(iii)).[66]

A high deductible health plan (HDHP) is a plan that has at least a $1,000 annual deductible for self-only coverage and a $2,000 deductible for family coverage. In addition, annual out-of-pocket expenses paid under the plan must be limited to $5,000 for individuals and $10,000 for families. These amounts are indexed annually for inflation. For 2007, the minimum deductible is $1,100 for individual coverage and $2,200 for family coverage, and the out-of-pocket expense maximum is $5,500 for individuals and $11,000 for families (Rev. Proc. 2006-53). For 2008, the minimum deductible again is $1,100 for individual coverage and $2,200 for family coverage, but the out-of-pocket expense maximum is $5,600 for individuals and $11,200 for families (Rev. Proc. 2007-36). Out-of-pocket expenses include deductibles, co-payments and other amounts (other than premiums) that must be paid for plan benefits (Code Sec. 223(c)(2)(A); Notice 2004-2).[67]

Generally, for married taxpayers, if either spouse has family coverage under any health plan, then both will be treated as having family coverage under the plan. If each spouse has family coverage under different plans, then both spouses are treated as having coverage under the plan with the lowest deductible (Code Sec. 223(b)(5)). However, a married taxpayer covered under an HDHP can contribute to an HSA for use with qualifying out-of-pocket medical expenses even if his or her spouse's coverage is nonqualifying family coverage, as long as the taxpayer is not covered by the spouse's policy (Rev. Rul. 2005-25).[68]

Contributions to HSAs are deductible in determining adjusted gross income. Starting in 2007, HSA contributions are no longer limited to the annual deductible under the HDHP; instead, the maximum aggregate annual contribution is $2,250 for an individual with self-only coverage, and $4,500 for an individual with family coverage (Code Sec.

Footnote references are to paragraphs of the 2008 Standard Federal Tax Reports.

[63] ¶ 12,785.25
[64] ¶ 12,776

[65] ¶ 12,776
[66] ¶ 12,776

[67] ¶ 12,776, ¶ 12,785.25
[68] ¶ 12,785.25

223(b)).[69] These amounts are adjusted annually for inflation: for 2007, the limit is $2,850 for individuals and $5,650 for families; in 2008, the limit will be $2,900 for individuals and $5,800 for families (Rev. Proc. 2007-36). Excess contributions are subject to a six-percent excise tax and includible in gross income. Individuals who reach age 55 by the end of the tax year can increase their annual contributions by $800 for 2007, $900 for 2008 and $1,000 for 2009 and later years. Contributions, including catch-up contributions, cannot be made to a HSA after the participant attains age 65 and is eligible for Medicare (Notice 2004-2).[70] However, distributions for qualified medical expenses continue to be excludable from gross income and premiums for health insurance other than for a Medicare supplemental policy are considered qualified medical expenses. Individuals use Form 8889, Health Savings Accounts (HSAs), to report contributions to or distributions from their HSA and to calculate their HSA deduction.

Starting in 2007, a taxpayer who is an eligible individual for an HSA during the last month of a tax year is treated as eligible during every month of that tax year, so the annual limit on deductible contributions for that taxpayer is not reduced. A recapture provision applies if the taxpayer ceases to be eligible during the period beginning with the last month of the tax year and ending on the last day of the 12th month following that month. If recapture applies, the taxpayer must include in gross income the amount of otherwise deductible contributions attributable to the months preceding the month in which the taxpayer was an eligible individual, and an additional 10-percent tax is imposed. Recapture does not apply if the taxpayer is ineligible due to death or disability (Code Sec. 223(b)(8)).[71]

Contributions made by a partnership or S corporation to a partner's or shareholder's HSA are generally treated as payments to the partner or shareholder and are includible in gross income. The individual partner or shareholder may treat the contribution as an above-the-line deduction. However, a contribution to the partner's HSA by the partnership for services rendered is treated as a guaranteed payment, and the partnership may deduct the contribution as a business expense. Similarly, a contribution by the S corporation to a two-percent shareholder's HSA for services rendered is deductible by the S corporation and included in the shareholder's income (Notice 2005-8).[72]

Distributions to HSAs. On or after December 20, 2006, an employer can make a one-time "qualified HSA distribution" from an employee's health flexible spending arrangement (FSA) or health reimbursement account (HRA) to the employee's HSA (see ¶ 859A and ¶ 861). Also, starting in 2007, an eligible individual can elect a one-time rollover distribution from his or her individual retirement arrangement (IRA) to his or her HSA (see ¶ 2178). The amount that can otherwise be contributed to the HSA for the tax year of the distribution is reduced by the amount contributed from the IRA, and the individual cannot deduct the distribution amount as an HSA contribution (Code Sec. 223(b)(4)(C)).[73]

HSAs v. MSAs. HSAs differ from Archer medical savings account (MSAs) in several ways. MSAs are limited to individuals who work for small employers or are self-employed, while there is no such limitation for HSAs. HSAs are available for a wider range of high deductible plans than are MSAs. In addition, contributions for MSAs must be made by the self-employed individual or the taxpayer's employer, while contributions to HSAs may be made by the taxpayer, his or her family or employer. Contributions to HSAs may be made even if the individual on whose behalf they are made has no compensation, or the contribution exceeds that individual's compensation. Finally, Archer MSAs generally cannot be established after 2007, although eligible individuals can still make and receive Archer MSA contributions, and individuals can still receive Archer MSA distributions (see ¶ 1020).[74]

Taxes, Generally

1021. Deductible Taxes. Taxes not directly connected with a trade or business or with property held for production of rents or royalties may be deducted only as an

---

Footnote references are to paragraphs of the 2008 Standard Federal Tax Reports.

[69] ¶ 12,776	[71] ¶ 12,776	[73] ¶ 12,776
[70] ¶ 12,785.25	[72] ¶ 12,785.25	[74] ¶ 12,785.25

itemized deduction on Schedule A of Form 1040. These include the following (Code Sec. 164(a)):[75]

    (1) State, local or foreign real property tax. (However, see ¶ 1026.)

    (2) State or local personal property tax (Reg. § 1.164-3(c)).[76]

    (3) State, local or foreign income, war profits, or excess profits tax (¶ 1023 and ¶ 2475).

    (4) Generation-skipping transfer tax imposed on income distributions (¶ 2942).

    (5) State and local general sales tax (at the taxpayer's election, and in lieu of state and local income taxes) (Code Sec. 164(b)(5)).

State and local taxes imposed on personal property are deductible if three conditions are met: the tax must be (1) *ad valorem* (substantially in proportion to the value of the property), (2) imposed on an annual basis, and (3) imposed with respect to personal property (Reg. § 1.164-3(c)).[77] Payment for car registration and licensing or a motor vehicle tax may be deductible as a personal property tax if it is imposed annually and assessed in proportion to the value of the car.

For 2007, taxpayers may elect to *either* deduct state and local income tax paid or general state and local sales taxes paid. If they elect to deduct the general state and local sales taxes paid, they may claim either the total amount paid by substantiation with receipts, or the amount from IRS tables plus the amounts of general state and local sales taxes paid on the purchase a motor vehicle, boat or other items to be determined by the IRS. The sales tax deduction is subject to the phase-out limitations (see ¶ 1014). The election does not apply to tax years after 2007 (Code Sec. 164(b)(5)).[78]

See ¶ 1022 for when a tax is deductible, ¶ 1023 for the deductibility of foreign income and profits taxes, ¶ 1024 for the deductibility of advance payments of state income taxes, ¶ 1025 for nondeductible taxes, ¶ 1026 for the deductibility of taxes used to pay for local improvements, and ¶ 1027 for the deductibility of self-employment taxes. For discussion of real property taxes, see ¶ 1028 and following.

1022. Taxes Deductible When Paid or Accrued. The deduction for taxes is allowed only for the year in which the taxes are paid or accrued (Code Sec. 164(a)).[79] Cash-basis taxpayers deduct taxes in the year paid, including amounts withheld from wages, payments of estimated tax, and payments applicable to other tax years. Accrual-basis taxpayers may generally deduct taxes in the year they accrue.[80] See ¶ 1515. A failure to deduct taxes in the proper year does not allow the taxpayer to deduct the taxes in a subsequent year; instead, the taxpayer must file an amended return for the year the taxes were paid or accrued.

The date when a tax becomes due and payable is not necessarily its accrual date.[81] State income taxes accrue during the year in which the income is earned.[82] Uncontested additional assessments accrue at the same time they would have accrued upon a correct original assessment.[83] For accrual of real estate taxes, see ¶ 1031 and ¶ 1036.

A contested tax accrues when the taxpayer transfers cash or property to satisfy the tax, if the contest exists after the transfer and a deduction would have otherwise been allowed for the year of transfer. This rule does not apply to taxes imposed by a foreign country or U.S. possession (Code Sec. 461(f)).[84]

1023. Deduction of Foreign Income and Profits Taxes. Foreign income and profits taxes are deductible only if no credit is claimed for them on the taxpayer's U.S. income tax return. The taxpayer must choose either the credit or the deduction; the taxes cannot be divided to support both a credit and a deduction. Foreign taxes accrue in the period for which they are imposed (see ¶ 2475–¶ 2485).[85]

Footnote references are to paragraphs of the 2008 Standard Federal Tax Reports.

[75] ¶ 9500
[76] ¶ 9506
[77] ¶ 9506
[78] ¶ 9500

[79] ¶ 9500
[80] ¶ 9502.195, ¶ 9502.23
[81] ¶ 9502.04
[82] ¶ 9502.445

[83] ¶ 9502.10
[84] ¶ 21,802
[85] ¶ 9500, ¶ 9503

1024. Deduction of Advance Payments of State Income Taxes. Advance payments of estimated state income taxes made by a cash-basis taxpayer pursuant to state law are deductible in the year paid unless, on the date of payment, the taxpayer cannot reasonably determine that there was an additional amount owing.[86]

1025. Nondeductible Taxes. The taxes that cannot be deducted either as taxes or as business expenses are (Code Sec. 275):[87]

(1) federal income taxes, including social security and railroad retirement taxes paid by employees and one-half of the self-employment tax imposed by Code Sec. 1401[88] (¶ 2664);

(2) federal war profits and excess profits taxes;[89]

(3) estate, inheritance, legacy, succession, and gift taxes (¶ 2901);

(4) income, war profits, and excess profits taxes imposed by a foreign country or a U.S. possession, if the taxpayer chooses to take a foreign tax credit for these taxes or they are paid or accrued with respect to foreign trade income of a foreign sales corporation (¶ 2470);[90]

(5) taxes on real property that must be treated as imposed on another taxpayer because of apportionment between buyer and seller (see ¶ 1032); and

(6) certain additions to taxes imposed under Chapters 41, 42, 43, 44, 45, 46 and 54 of the Internal Revenue Code on public charities, private foundations, qualified pension plans, real estate investment trusts, stock compensation of insiders in expatriated corporations, golden parachute payments and greenmail.

1026. Improvement Tax. Any tax that is in reality an assessment for local benefits such as streets, sidewalks, and similar improvements is not deductible by a property owner, except where it is levied for the purpose of maintenance and repair or of meeting interest charges on local benefits. It is the taxpayer's burden to show the allocation of amounts assessed to the different purposes (Code Sec. 164(c)(1); Reg. § 1.164-4).[91]

1027. Self-Employment Tax. A taxpayer can deduct one-half of the self-employment taxes paid in the computation of the taxpayer's adjusted gross income for income tax purposes (Code Sec. 164(f)) (see ¶ 2664).

Real Property Taxes

1028. Deductibility. Local, state, and foreign real property taxes are generally deductible only by the person upon whom they are imposed in the year in which they were paid or accrued (Code Sec. 164(a)(1); Reg. § 1.164-1(a)).[92] Real property taxes are taxes imposed on interests in real property and levied for the general public welfare. Such taxes do not include taxes assessed for local benefits (Reg. § 1.164-3(b)).[93] See ¶ 1026. State or local tax includes only taxes imposed by a state, the District of Columbia, possessions of the U.S., or a political subdivision thereof. Foreign tax includes taxes imposed by the authority of a foreign country or its political subdivisions (Reg. § 1.164-3(a) and (d)).[94]

Stockholder-owners in a cooperative housing corporation may deduct their proportionate shares of the taxes paid by the corporation (Code Sec. 216). See ¶ 1040. Condominium unit owners may also deduct real property taxes paid on their personal interests in the property (Rev. Rul. 64-31). However, their homeowner association assessments are not deductible as real property taxes because the assessments are not paid to the state or a political subdivision (Rev. Rul. 76-495).[95]

Ministers and military personnel (see ¶ 1050) are allowed to deduct taxes paid on their homes even if they receive a parsonage or military allowance excludable from gross income (Code Sec. 265(a)(6)).[96] Cash-basis mortgagors that pay taxes directly to the mortgagee are entitled to deduct the taxes when the mortgagee pays the taxing authority.[97]

Footnote references are to paragraphs of the 2008 Standard Federal Tax Reports.

[86] ¶ 9502.22
[87] ¶ 14,500
[88] ¶ 32,541
[89] ¶ 14,500

[90] ¶ 27,820, ¶ 28,080
[91] ¶ 9500, ¶ 9508
[92] ¶ 9500, ¶ 9501
[93] ¶ 9506

[94] ¶ 9506
[95] ¶ 9502.422, ¶ 9502.515
[96] ¶ 14,050
[97] ¶ 9502.225

1029. Real Property Construction Period Interest and Taxes. Interest and taxes on real property paid or incurred during the construction period generally must be capitalized (see ¶ 991 and ¶ 993) (Code Sec. 263A).[98]

1030. Carrying Charges on Real Property. If a taxpayer elects to capitalize taxes on unimproved and unproductive real property, no deduction is allowed for such taxes (Code Sec. 266).[99] See ¶ 1614.

1031. Alternative Elections to Accrue Real Property Taxes for Accrual-Method Taxpayers. Generally, the economic performance rule delays an accrual-method taxpayer's deduction for real property taxes until they are paid. However, if such taxes are a "recurring item" (see ¶ 1539) and certain requirements are met, a taxpayer may elect to accrue real property taxes which allows the taxpayer to claim the deduction on the date the tax is assessed or becomes a lien against the property (Reg. § § 1.461-4(g)(6) and 1.461-5).[100] Alternately, an accrual-basis taxpayer may elect to accrue real property taxes that are related to a definite period of time ratably over that period. Either election may be made without IRS consent for the first tax year in which a taxpayer incurs real property taxes, or at any other time with IRS consent (Code Sec. 461(c); Reg. § 1.461-1(c); Code Sec. 461(h)(3); Reg. § 1.461-5(d)).[101]

Should Election Be Made? Whether a taxpayer should make a Code Sec. 461(c) election or adopt the recurring item exception for real property taxes depends on the taxpayer's tax year and the tax year and lien date of the jurisdiction in which the real property is located. Except where taxes are prepaid, either option is more favorable than the payment rule.

> **Example 1:** X is a calendar-year, accrual-method taxpayer who owns Blackacre in Cook County, Illinois, where the real property tax year is the calendar year and 2007 real property taxes were assessed and became a lien on the property on January 1, 2007. Taxes are due as follows: ½ on March 1, 2008, and ½ on August 1, 2008.

Under its three options for accruing real property taxes, X would allocate its deduction between 2006 and 2007 as follows:

> (1) *Payment rule.* 2007: none. 2008: $^{12}/_{12}$.

> (2) *Ratable accrual.* 2007: $^{12}/_{12}$. 2008: none.

> (3) *Recurring item exception.* 2007: $^{12}/_{12}$ (provided that X adopted the recurring item exception on either a timely filed original return or on an amended return filed after paying the second installment but before September 15, 2008). 2008: none.

> **Example 2:** Assume X owns Greenacre in Alabama, where taxes for the fiscal year from October 1, 2007, to September 30, 2008, were assessed and became a lien on the property on October 1, 2007. Taxes are due on October 1, 2008.

Under its three options for accruing real property taxes, X would allocate its deduction between 2007 and 2008 as follows:

> (1) *Payment rule.* 2007: none. 2008: $^{12}/_{12}$.

> (2) *Ratable accrual.* 2007: $^{3}/_{12}$. 2008: $^{9}/_{12}$.

> (3) *Recurring item exception.* 2007: none (because taxes are not due until more than 8½ months after end of 2007). 2008: $^{12}/_{12}$. However, X could advance its entire deduction into 2007 by prepaying its real property taxes on or before September 15, 2008.

1032. Apportionment of Real Property Tax Upon Sale. The real property tax deduction must be apportioned between the seller and the buyer according to the number of days in the real property tax year (¶ 1033) that each holds the property. When property is sold during any real property tax year, the taxes are imposed upon the seller up to, but not including, the date of sale. The taxes are imposed on the buyer beginning with the date of sale. Proration is required whether or not the seller and

Footnote references are to paragraphs of the 2008 Standard Federal Tax Reports.

[98] ¶ 13,800	[100] ¶ 21,810, ¶ 21,811	[101] ¶ 21,802, ¶ 21,805,
[99] ¶ 14,100		¶ 21,811

purchaser actually apportion the tax (Reg. §1.164-6(a) and (b)(1)).[102] However, when property is sold subsequent or prior to the real property tax year, see ¶ 1038.

> **Example 1:** A sells his farm to B on August 1, 2006. Both use the cash- and calendar-year basis of accounting. Taxes for the real property tax year, April 1, 2007, to March 31, 2008, become due and payable on May 15, 2008. B pays the real estate taxes when they fall due. Regardless of any agreement between the parties, for federal income tax purposes $^{122}/_{366}$ of the real estate taxes are treated as imposed upon A and are deductible by him.

> **Example 2:** Assume the same facts as in Example 1, except that A uses the accrual basis of accounting. If A has not elected to accrue the real property taxes ratably, he will be treated as having accrued $^{122}/_{366}$ of the taxes on the date of sale. The balance is deductible by B when she pays the taxes, if she is on the cash basis, unless the rule at ¶ 1035 applies because the seller (A) is personally liable for the taxes. If B is on the accrual basis, she follows the rules explained at ¶ 1031.

1033. Real Property Tax Year Defined. The real property tax year is the period to which the tax relates under state law, local law or the law imposing the tax. If a state and one or more local governmental units each imposes a tax, the real property tax year for each tax must be determined (Reg. §1.164-6(c)).[103]

1034. Cash-Basis Sellers. The real estate tax apportioned to a cash-basis seller under the rules described at ¶ 1032 may be deducted by the seller in the tax year of the sale (whether or not actually paid in that tax year) if: (1) the buyer is liable for the real estate tax for the real property tax year or (2) the seller is liable for the real estate tax for the real property tax year and the tax is not payable until after the date of sale. When the tax is not a liability of any person, the person who holds the property at the time the tax becomes a lien on the property is considered liable for the tax (Reg. §1.164-6(d)(1) and (3)).[104]

1035. Cash-Basis Buyers. The real estate tax apportioned to a cash-basis buyer under the rules described at ¶ 1032 may be deducted by the buyer in the tax year of the sale, whether or not the tax is actually paid by the buyer in the tax year of the sale, if the seller is liable for the real estate tax. When the tax is not a liability of any person, the person who holds the property at the time the tax becomes a lien on the property is considered liable for the tax (Reg. §1.164-6(d)(2) and (3)).[105]

1036. Accrual-Basis Buyers and Sellers. For accrual-basis buyers or sellers who do not elect ratable accrual for property taxes (see ¶ 1031), the portion of their tax liability (see ¶ 1032) that may not be deducted for any tax year by reason of their accounting method is treated as if accrued on the date of sale (Reg. §1.164-6(d)(6)).[106]

1037. Excess Deduction. If a taxpayer deducted taxes in excess of the portion of such tax treated as imposed upon the taxpayer under the rules discussed at ¶ 1032 in a tax year prior to the year of sale, the excess amount is included in the taxpayer's gross income in the year of sale, subject to the tax benefit rule (¶ 799) (Reg. §1.164-6(d)(5)).[107]

> **Example:** A is a cash-basis taxpayer whose real property tax is due and payable on November 30 for the succeeding calendar year, which is also the real property tax year. A paid the 2007 real property taxes on November 30, 2006, and deducted them on his 2006 income tax return. On June 30, 2007, A sold the real property. The taxes from January 1 through June 29, 2007, i.e., the $^{180}/_{365}$ portion, are treated as imposed on A. The excess amount deducted by A on his 2006 income tax return is includible in his gross income in 2007.

1038. Property Sold Prior or Subsequent to Real Property Tax Year. If property is sold subsequent to the time the real property tax becomes a personal liability or a lien but prior to the beginning of the related real property tax year, the seller may not deduct any amount for real property taxes for the related real property tax year. To the extent that the buyer holds the property for that real property tax year, the buyer may deduct the amount of the taxes for the tax year in which they are paid or accrued. Conversely,

---

Footnote references are to paragraphs of the 2008 Standard Federal Tax Reports.

[102] ¶ 9603
[103] ¶ 9603
[104] ¶ 9603
[105] ¶ 9603
[106] ¶ 9603
[107] ¶ 9603

where the property is sold prior to the time the tax becomes a personal liability or a lien but after the end of the related real property tax year, the buyer cannot deduct any amount for taxes for the related real property tax year. To the extent that the seller holds the property for that real property tax year, the seller may deduct the amount of the taxes for the tax year they are paid or accrued (Reg. § 1.164-6(b)(1)(ii) and (iii)).[108]

1040. Cooperative Housing Corporation. A tenant-stockholder may deduct amounts paid or accrued to the cooperative housing corporation (CHC) to the extent that they represent the tenant's proportionate share of: (1) real estate taxes on the apartment building or houses and the land on which they are situated or (2) interest on debt contracted in the acquisition, construction, alteration, rehabilitation, or maintenance of such building, houses or land (Code Sec. 216; Reg. § 1.216-1).[109] The limitations on deductible residential interest apply. See ¶ 1048A.

Eighty percent or more of CHC gross income must come from its tenants before a tenant may deduct a share of the taxes and interest. For purposes of this 80-percent test, amounts received from tenant-stockholders to defray expenses for items like secretarial services, parking, utilities, recreation facilities, cleaning and related services are included in gross income derived from tenants, while amounts received from commercial leases and the operation of a business other than housing are excluded.[110] Income attributable to a unit that a governmental entity is entitled to occupy pursuant to a lease or stock ownership is also excluded (Code Sec. 216(b)(4); Reg. § 1.216-1(e)(4)).[111]

Interest

1043. Interest Paid or Accrued. A taxpayer may generally deduct interest paid or accrued during the tax year (Code Sec. 163(a)).[112] The interest is reported on Schedule A of Form 1040. Deductible interest must pertain to a debt of the taxpayer and result from a debtor-creditor relationship based upon a valid and enforceable obligation to pay a fixed or determinable sum of money.[113] For example, interest paid by children on their parent's mortgage was not deductible.[114] There are numerous exceptions to and limitations on the deductibility of interest. See ¶ 940 and ¶ 1044–¶ 1056.

1044. Exceptions and Limitations. Interest deductions are limited or precluded for certain types of indebtedness. See ¶ 940.

Investment Indebtedness Interest. The deduction by noncorporate taxpayers is limited to net investment income (Code Sec. 163(d)).[115] See ¶ 1094.

Life Insurance. Interest on loans incurred or continued to pay premiums on certain insurance contracts is nondeductible (Code Sec. 264(a)).[116] See ¶ 909.

Mortgage Credit Certificates. The deduction for interest paid or accrued on indebtedness with respect to which a mortgage credit certificate has been issued is reduced by the amount of credit allowable (Code Sec. 163(g)).[117] See ¶ 1308.

Personal Interest. Personal interest is not deductible (Code Sec. 163(h)).[118] See ¶ 1045.

Prepaid Interest. Cash-basis taxpayers generally must capitalize prepaid interest and deduct it as if on the accrual basis (Code Sec. 461(g)).[119] See ¶ 1055.

Loan to Purchase and Carry Tax-Exempt Securities. A deduction for interest paid on a debt incurred or continued to purchase or carry tax-exempt bonds or other tax-exempt obligations is generally denied (Code Sec. 265(a)).[120] See ¶ 970.

Related Taxpayers. Accrual-basis taxpayers are placed on the cash basis for interest owed to related cash-basis taxpayers (Code Sec. 267(a)).[121] A corporation is not allowed a deduction for excessive interest paid to a tax-exempt related person or on a loan guaranteed by certain tax-exempt or foreign related persons. For purposes of the disallowance, for tax years beginning on or after May 17, 2006, a corporate partner's

---

Footnote references are to paragraphs of the 2008 Standard Federal Tax Reports.

[108] ¶ 9603
[109] ¶ 12,600, ¶ 12,601
[110] ¶ 12,603.13
[111] ¶ 12,600, ¶ 12,601
[112] ¶ 9102

[113] ¶ 9104.264, ¶ 9104.344
[114] ¶ 9104.728
[115] ¶ 9102
[116] ¶ 14,002
[117] ¶ 9102

[118] ¶ 9102
[119] ¶ 21,802
[120] ¶ 14,050
[121] ¶ 14,150

distributive share of a partnership's interest income or expense is treated as the partner's interest income or expense, and its share of the partnership's liabilities is treated as the partner's liabilities (Code Sec. 163(j)).[122]

Judicial Exceptions. The courts have denied a deduction for the interest charged upon conversion of a life insurance policy to a higher-premium policy,[123] and for interest paid on loans to buy U.S. Treasury notes where there was nothing to be realized from the transaction beyond a tax deduction.[124]

1045. Personal Interest. Personal interest is not deductible (Code Sec. 163(h)).[125] Personal interest is any interest incurred by an individual other than:

(1) interest paid or accrued on indebtedness properly allocable to a trade or business (other than services as an employee) (¶ 937);

(2) investment interest (¶ 1094);

(3) interest taken into account in computing income or loss from a passive activity of the taxpayer (¶ 2053);

(4) qualified residence interest (¶ 1047);

(5) interest on the unpaid portion of the estate tax for the period during which there is an extension of time for payment of the tax either: (i) on the value of a reversionary or remainder interest in property or (ii) when an estate of a decedent who died before 1998 consists largely of an interest in a closely-held business (¶ 1051); and

(6) interest on qualified education loans (¶ 1082).

1047. Qualified Residence Interest Defined. Qualified residence interest is interest that is paid or accrued during the tax year on acquisition or home equity indebtedness with respect to any qualified residence (Code Sec. 163(h)(3)). Qualified residence interest also can include interest on a loan secured by a qualified residence in a state where the security instrument is otherwise restricted by a debtor protection law. Interest paid or accrued by a trust or estate is deductible if the debt is secured by a beneficiary's qualified residence (Code Sec. 163(h)(4)(C) and (D)). A qualified residence includes the principal residence of the taxpayer, and one other residence (i.e., vacation home) that is not rented out at any time during the tax year, or that is used by the taxpayer for a number of days exceeding the greater of 14 days or 10 percent of the number of days that it is rented out at a fair rental value. Married taxpayers who file separate returns are treated as one taxpayer, with each entitled to take into account one residence unless both consent in writing to having only one taxpayer take into account both residences (Code Sec. 163(h)(4)(A)).[126] For seller-provided financing, taxpayers deducting qualified residence interest must include on their Form 1040, Schedule A, the name, address and TIN of the person to whom interest is paid or accrued (Code Sec. 6109(h)).[127]

Mortgage Insurance Premiums. Certain premiums paid during 2007 for qualified mortgage insurance in connection with acquisition indebtedness are deductible as qualified residence interest. However, for every $1,000 by which the taxpayer's adjusted gross income (AGI) exceeds $100,000, the amount of premiums treated as interest is reduced by 10 percent; for married taxpayers filing separately, the 10-percent phase-out applies to every $500 that AGI exceeds $50,000. The deduction does not apply to mortgage insurance contracts issued prior to January 1, 2007, or to premiums paid or accrued after December 31, 2007, or allocable to any period after December 31, 2007 (Code Sec. 163(h)(3)(E)). Qualified mortgage insurance is that provided by the Veterans Administration (VA), the Federal Housing Administration (FHA), the Rural Housing Administration (RHA) and private mortgage insurance. For prepaid mortgage insurance (except VA or RHA contracts), amounts paid that are allocable to periods after the payment year are capitalized and treated as paid in the allocable year. If the mortgage is satisfied before the end of its term, no deduction is allowed for the unamortized capital account balance (Code Sec. 163(h)(4)(E) and (F)).

Footnote references are to paragraphs of the 2008 Standard Federal Tax Reports.

[122] ¶ 9102
[123] ¶ 9104.45
[124] ¶ 9104.364
[125] ¶ 9102
[126] ¶ 9102
[127] ¶ 9102, ¶ 36,960

1048. Acquisition and Home Equity Indebtedness. Acquisition indebtedness is debt incurred in acquiring, constructing, or substantially improving a qualified residence and secured by such residence. Refinanced debt remains acquisition debt to the extent that it does not exceed the principal amount of acquisition debt immediately before refinancing (Code Sec. 163(h)(3)(B)).

Home equity indebtedness is all nonacquisition debt that is secured by a qualified residence to the extent it does not exceed the fair market value of the residence reduced by any acquisition indebtedness (Code Sec. 163(h)(3)(C)). Interest on such debt is deductible even if the proceeds are used for personal expenditures (IRS Pub. 936).[128]

1048A. Limits on Acquisition and Home Equity Indebtedness. There is a limit to the amount of qualified residence interest that is deductible. The aggregate amount of acquisition indebtedness may not exceed $1 million and the aggregate amount of home equity indebtedness may not exceed $100,000; interest attributable to debt over these limits is nondeductible personal interest (¶ 1045). These amounts are halved for a married individual filing a separate return (Code Sec. 163(h)(3)).[129] See ¶ 1048B for rules applicable to debt incurred on or before October 13, 1987.

> **Example 1:** In 2007, A buys a home to be used as her principal residence for $175,000 that is secured by a mortgage in the amount of $150,000. The mortgage qualifies as home acquisition debt because the loan amount does not exceed the home's cost. Thus, because the acquisition indebtedness is less than $1 million, the entire amount of the interest payments is deductible.

> **Example 2:** In 2007, the fair market value of B's home is $110,000, and the balance of the mortgage (home acquisition debt) is $95,000. B takes out a home equity loan in the amount of $42,500. B's home equity debt, on which interest payments will be deductible as qualified home equity indebtedness, is limited to $15,000—the smaller of (1) the $100,000 maximum limit or (2) the excess of the home's fair market value ($110,000) over the home acquisition debt ($95,000).

1048B. Special Rules for Pre-October 13, 1987, Indebtedness. Interest on acquisition indebtedness incurred on or before October 13, 1987, is fully deductible, and is not subject to the $1 million limitation at ¶ 1048A. The amount of this grandfathered debt reduces the amount of the $1 million limitation available for new acquisition debt (e.g., for improvements).

Grandfathered debt is any debt incurred on or before October 13, 1987, that is secured by a qualified residence on that date and at all times thereafter before the interest is paid or accrued. It also includes debt secured by a qualified residence to refinance existing pre-October 13 debt, to the extent that the refinancing does not increase the principal amount or extend the term of the debt beyond the existing term of the acquisition debt immediately before the refinancing. If acquisition debt is not amortized over its term, as in the case of a balloon note, interest on any otherwise qualified refinancing is deductible for the term of the first refinancing for up to 30 years (Code Sec. 163(h)(3)(D)).[130]

1049. Redeemable Ground Rents. Annual or periodic payments of redeemable ground rent (except amounts paid in redemption of this rent) are treated as interest paid on mortgage indebtedness (Code Sec. 163(c)).[131] Therefore, it seems that such ground rents are subject to the rules pertaining to qualified residences. See ¶ 1047. A redeemable ground rent is a ground rent payable under a freely assignable lease that (including possible renewal periods) is for a term in excess of 15 years (Code Sec. 1055(c)(1); Reg. § 1.1055-1).[132]

1050. Ministers and Military Personnel. Ministers and military personnel are allowed to deduct mortgage interest on their qualified residences (see ¶ 1047) even though they receive a parsonage or military allowance that is excludable from gross income (Code Sec. 265(a)(6)).[133] Military personnel includes members of the Army,

---

Footnote references are to paragraphs of the 2008 Standard Federal Tax Reports.

[128] ¶ 9102
[129] ¶ 9102, ¶ 9402.15
[130] ¶ 9102
[131] ¶ 9102
[132] ¶ 29,940, ¶ 29,941
[133] ¶ 14,050

Navy, Air Force, Marine Corps, Coast Guard, National Oceanic and Atmospheric Administration, and Public Health Service (Rev. Rul. 87-32).[134]

1051. Interest Paid on Delinquent Taxes. Interest imposed on delinquent taxes is generally nondeductible personal interest (Temp. Reg. §1.163-9T(b)(2)(i)(A)). See ¶1045. However, any interest expense accrued for federal estate taxes during an extension for payment of tax under Code Sec. 6163 (or under Code Sec. 6166 for estates of decedents who died before 1998) may be claimed as either a deduction from federal estate tax as an administrative expense, or an income tax deduction under Code Sec. 163(h)(2)(E)[135] provided that the right to an estate tax deduction for the interest expense has been waived (Code Sec. 642(g)).[136] Further, interest on federal and state income tax deficiencies accruing after death is generally deductible by the estate as an administration expense.[137] Interest paid on an individual's federal, state, or local income tax deficiencies is nondeductible interest regardless of the source of the income generating the tax liability (Temp. Reg. §1.163-9T(b)(2)(i)(A)).[138]

Interest paid on sales and excise taxes incurred in connection with a trade or business or investment activity, and interest paid by a transferee for a C corporation's delinquent taxes, is not personal interest (Temp. Reg. §1.163-9T(b)(2)(iii)).[139]

1052. Consumer Debt. Interest on consumer debt is nondeductible personal interest. See ¶1045.

Prepaid Interest

1055. Deductibility of Prepaid Interest by Cash-Basis Taxpayers. All cash-basis taxpayers must deduct prepaid interest over the period of the loan to the extent that the interest represents the cost of using the borrowed funds during each tax year in the period. Points paid on loans (other than certain home mortgage loans) are deducted ratably over the term of the loan (Code Sec. 461(g)).[140] Penalty payments made for the privilege of prepaying mortgage indebtedness are currently deductible as interest.[141]

The prepaid interest rule does not contemplate that interest will be treated as paid in equal payments over the term of the loan. Thus, interest paid on an amortizing loan as part of an equal constant payment (including principal and interest) is not subject to the prepaid interest rule merely because the payments consist of a larger interest portion in the earlier years of the loan than in later years.[142]

Points on a home mortgage loan for the purchase or improvement of, and secured by, a principal residence are deductible in the year paid to the extent that the payment of points is an established practice in the area, and the amount paid does not exceed the points generally charged in the area for a home loan (Code Sec. 461(g)(2)).[143] Taxpayers may also choose to amortize points over the life of their loan if, for instance, the standard deduction in the year the points were paid exceeds the taxpayer's itemized deductions, including the points (IRS Letter Ruling 199905033).[144]

As a matter of administrative practice, the IRS treats as deductible in the year paid any points paid by a cash-basis taxpayer that (Rev. Proc. 94-27):[145]

(1) are designated as points on the RESPA settlement statement (Form HUD-1), for example, as "loan origination fees" (including amounts so designated on VA and FHA loans), "loan discount," "discount points," or "points";

(2) are calculated as a percentage of the principal loan amount;

(3) are paid to acquire the taxpayer's principal residence in connection with a loan secured by that residence;

(4) are paid directly by the taxpayer (which may include earnest money, an escrow deposit, or down payment applied at closing) and not derived from loan proceeds; points paid by a seller (including points charged to the seller) are considered directly paid by the taxpayer from funds not derived from loan pro-

---

Footnote references are to paragraphs of the 2008 Standard Federal Tax Reports.

134 ¶14,054.54
135 ¶9102
136 ¶24,280
137 ¶24,308.1488
138 ¶9400
139 ¶9400
140 ¶21,802
141 ¶9402.68
142 ¶21,802.05
143 ¶21,802
144 ¶9402.55
145 ¶9402.65

ceeds if they are subtracted by the taxpayer from the purchase price of the residence in computing its basis; and

(5) conform to an established business practice of charging points for loans for the acquisition of personal residences in the area. No part of the points may be in lieu of appraisal, inspection, title, and attorney fees, property taxes, or other amounts that are ordinarily stated separately on the settlement statement.

The above safe harbor does not apply to points paid for a loan to acquire a principal residence to the extent the principal amount exceeds the limit on acquisition indebtedness discussed at ¶ 1048A. Nor does it apply to points paid on home improvement loans, second or vacation home loans, refinancing or home equity loans, or lines of credit. The fact that a taxpayer cannot satisfy the requirements of the safe harbor does not necessarily mean that points are not currently deductible; it does mean that the IRS will not automatically consider them to be currently deductible.

Points paid to refinance a home mortgage are not deductible in full in the year paid but must be deducted ratably over the period of the loan because they are incurred for the repayment of the taxpayer's existing indebtedness and are not paid in connection with the purchase or improvement of the home. However, the U.S. Court of Appeals for the Eighth Circuit allowed full deduction in the year paid for points on a long-term home mortgage loan refinancing a short-term balloon loan used to acquire the home (*J.R. Huntsman*, 90-2 USTC ¶ 50,340).[146] Also, the portion of the points allocable to the proceeds of a refinancing that are used for improvements may be deducted in the year paid. However, the portion allocable to the repayment of existing indebtedness or other purposes is deducted ratably over the period of the loan (Rev. Rul. 87-22).[147]

A loan discount (where a lender delivers to an individual borrower an amount smaller than the face amount of the loan and the difference is the agreed charge for the use of borrowed money) is interest.[148]

1056. Deductibility of Prepaid Interest by Accrual-Basis Taxpayers. Taxpayers who use the accrual method accrue and deduct interest ratably over the loan period, regardless of whether the interest is prepaid (Rev. Rul. 68-643).[149]

Charitable Contributions

1058. Contributions by Individuals, Generally. Contributions to charitable organizations are deductible, subject to certain limits. The charitable deduction for any one tax year is limited to a percentage of the individual taxpayer's contribution base, which is the taxpayer's adjusted gross income (AGI), computed without regard to any net operating loss carryback (Code Sec. 170(b)(1)(G)).[150] The percentage limitation is determined by two factors: the type of organization receiving the donation and the type of property donated (Code Sec. 170(b)(1)).[151] Any amount in excess of the percentage limitation for the tax year may be carried forward for a period of five years (Code Sec. 170(d)).[152] See ¶ 1060. When spouses file a joint return, the percentage limitation depends on their aggregate contribution base (Reg. § 1.170A-8(a)).[153] A limit also applies to the amount of a charitable deduction allowed for gifts of appreciated property (see ¶ 1062), and is imposed before applying the percentage limitation (Code Sec. 170(e); Reg. § 1.170A-4).[154] Contributions are reported on Schedule A of Form 1040. See ¶ 1061 for discussion of what contributions are deductible.

Except for the carryover rule at ¶ 1060, a contribution is generally deductible only in the year of payment (Reg. § 1.170A-1(a)).[155] However, contributions charged to a bank credit card are deductible in the year charged even though paid in a later year (Rev. Rul. 78-38).[156]

Taxpayers who are recognized by the Alaska Eskimo Whaling Commission as whaling captains can claim a charitable contribution deduction of up to $10,000 per tax

---

Footnote references are to paragraphs of the 2008 Standard Federal Tax Reports.

[146] ¶ 9402.62	[150] ¶ 11,600	[154] ¶ 11,600, ¶ 11,632
[147] ¶ 9402.60	[151] ¶ 11,600	[155] ¶ 11,615
[148] ¶ 9104.586	[152] ¶ 11,600	[156] ¶ 11,620.691
[149] ¶ 21,817.3253	[153] ¶ 11,661	

year for reasonable and necessary expenses paid in carrying out sanctioned Alaskan subsistence whale hunting activities (Code Sec. 170(n)).[157]

In 2006 and 2007, individuals age 70½ or older can distribute up to $100,000 tax-free annually from their individual retirement account (IRA) to certain charitable organizations without taking a charitable deduction or including the distribution in gross income. To qualify, the distribution must be made directly by the trustee to a 50-percent organization (see ¶ 1059), but not to a supporting organization or a donor advised fund (see ¶ 1061), and the entire distribution must otherwise be deductible under Code Sec. 170 (disregarding the percentage limitations). The distribution may be delivered to the charity by the IRA owner provided that the check from the IRA is payable to the charity (Code Sec. 408(d)(8); Notice 2007-7).[158] See ¶ 2178.

1059. Limits on Individuals' Contributions. Charitable contribution deduction limits depend, in part, on whether the donation is made to the charitable organization or for its use. A donation is made for the use of the organization if it is transferred in trust to be held and administered for the organization (Reg. § 1.170A-8(a)(2)).[159]

Contributions *to* the following types of tax-exempt organizations qualify for the maximum deduction of 50 percent of a taxpayer's contribution base (see ¶ 1058) for the tax year: (1) churches or conventions or associations of churches (see ¶ 604); (2) educational institutions; (3) hospital or medical research organizations (not including home health care organizations,[160] convalescent homes, homes for children or the aged, or vocational institutions that train handicapped individuals); (4) endowment foundations in connection with a state college or university; (5) state, federal or local government units, if the contribution is made for exclusively public purposes; (6) organizations normally receiving a substantial part of their support from the public or a governmental unit; (7) private operating foundations; (8) a private nonoperating foundation that distributes all contributions received to public charities and private operating foundations (or makes certain other qualifying distributions) within 2½ months after the end of its tax year; (9) organizations normally receiving (a) more than ⅓ of their support in each tax year from the public and organizations listed at (1)-(6), above, in the form of grants, gifts, contributions, or membership fees, and gross receipts from an activity that is not an unrelated trade or business (less certain receipts), and (b) not more than ⅓ of their support from gross investment income and unrelated business taxable income (less taxes); and (10) private foundations that pool all contributions into a common fund and allow a substantial contributor to designate a recipient charity, where income from the pool is distributed within 2½ months after the tax year in which it was realized and corpus attributable to any donor's contribution is distributed to a charity not later than one year after the death of the donor (or surviving spouse with the right to designate the recipients of the corpus) (Code Sec. 170(b)(1)(A) and (F); Reg. § 1.170A-9).[161]

There is a special 30-percent limitation on certain capital gain property contributed by an individual to the 10 types of organizations listed above (Code Sec. 170(b)(1)(C)).[162] See ¶ 1062.

The deduction limitation on contributions of ordinary income property to nonoperating foundations and organizations, such as war veterans' and fraternal organizations, public cemeteries, and gifts *for the use of* 50-percent organization donees, is the lesser of: (1) 30 percent of the taxpayer's contribution base or (2) the excess of 50 percent of the taxpayer's contribution base for the tax year over the amount of charitable contributions qualifying for the 50-percent deduction ceiling, including carryovers (Code Sec. 170(b)(1)(B)).[163] Gifts of capital gain property to these organizations are subject to a 20-percent contribution base limitation (Code Sec. 170(b)(1)(D)).[164] See ¶ 1062.

For deduction limitations on charitable contributions by corporations, see ¶ 927.

In 2006 and 2007, individual donors are allowed to take charitable deductions of up to 50 percent of their contribution base for a qualified conservation contribution (QCC) of real property (see ¶ 1063). Thus, the individual donor making a QCC will have a

---

Footnote references are to paragraphs of the 2008 Standard Federal Tax Reports.

[157] ¶ 11,600
[158] ¶ 18,902, ¶ 18,922.745
[159] ¶ 11,661

[160] ¶ 11,670.562
[161] ¶ 11,600, ¶ 11,662
[162] ¶ 11,600

[163] ¶ 11,600
[164] ¶ 11,600

50-percent contribution base, rather than the 20- or 30-percent base generally applicable to donations of capital gain appreciated property. Any excess over the 50-percent contribution base may be carried forward for 15 years (see ¶ 1060). For qualified farmers and ranchers (i.e., individual taxpayers with more than 50 percent of gross income from farming), the QCC deduction limit is 100 percent of the contribution base; for contributions made after August 17, 2006, the 100-percent limit applies only if the contribution includes a restriction that the property must remain generally available for agriculture or livestock production. These rules are applied separately from the rules that apply to other donations (Code Sec. 170(b)(1)(E)).[165]

Temporary Suspension of Contribution Limits. In response to the Hurricane Katrina, Rita and Wilma disasters, the income limits were temporarily waived for certain cash contributions made for any purpose by individuals to "50-percent" charities (but not Code Sec. 509(a)(3) supporting organizations). These qualified contributions were not subject to the phaseout for high-income taxpayers (see ¶ 1014). Donors who made these donations from August 28, 2005, through December 31, 2005, and elected qualified contribution treatment were allowed a charitable deduction up to the amount by which the taxpayer's contribution base (see ¶ 1058) exceeded the amount of all other allowable contributions during the rest of the tax year. Excess qualified contributions may be carried over to the succeeding five tax years (see ¶ 1060). Qualified contributions were not included in determining the 50-percent limit or the carryover limit for other contributions (Code Sec. 1400S(a)).[166]

1060. Individuals' Five-Year Carryover. Individuals may carry forward for five years their charitable contributions that exceed the deductible ceiling for the year of the contribution (Code Sec. 170(b)(1)(D)(ii) and (d); Reg. § 1.170A-10).[167] The amount of the excess that may be deducted in any carryover year is limited to the lesser of: (1) the remaining portion of any excess contribution not already deducted or (2) an amount equal to 50 percent (or 30 percent for capital gain carryover) of the taxpayer's contribution base (see ¶ 1058) after first deducting the sum of the charitable contributions (to which the 50- or 30-percent limitation applies) paid in the carryover year and any excess contributions that have precedence in order of time over the present carryover. "Qualified contributions" are not taken into account when calculating the carryover limits (see ¶ 1059, *"Temporary Suspension of Contribution Limits"*).

If the value of an taxpayer's qualified conservation contribution of real property (see ¶ 1059) exceeds the special 50-percent contribution base for such a donation, the excess may be carried forward for 15 years (Code Sec. 170(b)(1)(E)(ii)).

1061. Contributions That Are Deductible. A contribution is deductible only if made to, or for the use of, the following qualified organizations:

(1) The United States, a state, a local government, the District of Columbia, or a U.S. possession, for exclusively public purposes.

(2) A corporation, trust, or community chest, fund, or foundation, created or organized in the United States or a possession or under the law of the United States, a possession, a state, or the District of Columbia, organized and operated exclusively for religious, charitable, scientific, literary or educational purposes, or to foster national or international amateur sports competition, or for the prevention of cruelty to children or animals. No part of the charity's net earnings may inure to the benefit of any private shareholder or individual. Also, the organization must not be disqualified for tax exemption under Code Sec. 501(c)(3) by attempting to influence legislation.

(3) A cemetery company owned and operated exclusively for the benefit of its members or any corporation chartered solely for burial purposes as a cemetery corporation and not operated for profit or for the benefit of any private shareholder or individual.

(4) A post or organization of war veterans, or its auxiliary society or unit, organized in the United States or its possessions, if no part of the net earnings inures to the benefit of any private shareholder or individual.

Footnote references are to paragraphs of the 2008 Standard Federal Tax Reports.

[165] ¶ 11,600   [166] ¶ 32,508   [167] ¶ 11,600, ¶ 11,663

(5) For individual donors only, a domestic fraternal society, order, or association, operating under the lodge system, if the contributions are used exclusively for religious, charitable, scientific, literary, or educational purposes, or for the prevention of cruelty to children or animals (Code Sec. 170(c)).[168]

Clothing and Household Items. For contributions made after August 17, 2006, the deduction for a donation of clothing and household items will be allowed only if the donated property is in good used condition or better. "Household items" do not include food, paintings, antiques, other objects of art, jewelry, gems or collections. The IRS can deny a deduction for such donated property that is of minimal value. These restrictions do not apply if: (1) a deduction of more than $500 is claimed for the single clothing or household item and (2) a qualified appraisal for that item is attached to the return (see ¶ 1071). For partnerships and S corporations, the restrictions are applied at the entity level, and denial of the deduction is at the partner or shareholder level (Code Sec. 170(f)(16)).[169]

Services. The value of service rendered to a charitable organization is not deductible as a contribution,[170] nor is the value of a blood donation, which is in the nature of service rendered.[171] But an out-of-pocket, unreimbursed expense (such as for uniforms, telephone or equipment) incurred in rendering such service is a deductible contribution.[172] No deduction is allowed for an out-of-pocket expenditure made by any person on behalf of a charitable organization other than an organization described in Code Sec. 501(h)(5) (churches, etc.) if the expenditure is made for the purpose of influencing legislation (Code Sec. 170(f)(6)). No charitable or business deduction is allowed for contributions made to organizations that conduct lobbying activities relating to matters of direct financial interest to the donor, unless the donor's direct conduct of the activities would have given rise to a business expense deduction (see ¶ 974) (Code Sec. 170(f)(9)).[173] Payments made before 2003 under leave-based donation programs, in which an employer makes charitable donations in exchange for an employee's election to forego paid leave, are deductible by the employer as compensation (¶ 906) but are not includible in the employee's income or deductible by the employee as a charitable contribution (Notice 2001-69). Similar treatment applies to payments made before 2007 under leave-donation programs to charities providing relief for Hurricane Katrina victims (Notice 2005-68).

Travel Expenses. Deductions are allowed for transportation or other travel expenses (including meals and lodging) incurred in the performance of services away from home on behalf of a charitable organization if there is no significant element of personal pleasure, recreation, or vacation. If there is such an element, deductions are denied even though the expenses are paid directly by the individual, indirectly through a contribution to the organization, or by reimbursement by the organization. This rule does not apply to the extent that an individual pays for travel for third parties who are participants in the charitable activity. However, deductions are disallowed where two unrelated taxpayers pay each other's travel expenses or members of a group contribute to a fund that pays for all travel expenses (Code Sec. 170(j)).[174] Individuals who qualify for a deduction for the use of an automobile in 2007 may use the statutory standard mileage rate of 14 cents per mile, plus parking fees and tolls, in lieu of a deduction based on the actual expenses incurred (Rev. Proc. 2006-49). Depreciation and insurance are not includible in the deductible contribution (Code Sec. 170(i)).[175]

Hurricane Katrina Relief. In response to the Hurricane Katrina disaster, the statutory standard mileage rate for charity work related to Hurricane Katrina was raised to 70 percent of the standard business mileage rate for the period beginning on August 25, 2005, and ending on December 31, 2006, rounded up to the next highest cent (Sec. 303 of the Katrina Emergency Tax Relief Act of 2005 (P.L. 109-73)). Therefore, the increased mileage rate for Katrina-related charity work was 29 cents-per-mile during the period of August 25, 2005 through August 31, 2005, and 34 cents-per-mile from September 1, 2005

Footnote references are to paragraphs of the 2008 Standard Federal Tax Reports.

[168] ¶ 11,600
[169] ¶ 11,600
[170] ¶ 11,620.655

[171] ¶ 11,620.65
[172] ¶ 11,620.67
[173] ¶ 11,600

[174] ¶ 11,600
[175] ¶ 11,600

through December 31, 2005. For 2006, the increased Hurricane Katrina charity rate was 32 cents-per-mile.

Fund-Raising Activities. An amount paid for a ticket to a charity event—e.g., a ball, bazaar, show, or athletic event—is presumed to represent the purchase price for an item of value. The burden is on the taxpayer to show either that the payment is not a purchase or that the payment exceeds the fair market value of the admission or other privileges associated with the event. The purchase price of a raffle ticket is not deductible.[176]

> **Example:** A pays $20 to see a special showing of a motion picture, the net proceeds of which go to a qualified charitable organization. Printed on the ticket is "Contribution—$20." If the regular price for the movie is $9, A made a contribution of $11 to a qualified charitable organization.

A fund-raising organization that provides token benefits to contributors can advise them that their donations are fully deductible only if the token benefits have an insubstantial value. If items are mailed to potential donors, the organization can advise that a contribution is fully deductible only if the items are low cost, provided for free, and not distributed at the donor's request or consent (Rev. Proc. 92-49).[177] A charity that receives a *quid pro quo contribution* in excess of $75 must provide a statement to the donor describing what portion of the donation represents consideration for goods or services (Code Sec. 6115).[178] See ¶ 620.

Eighty percent of an otherwise deductible payment made to a college or university for the right to purchase tickets to an athletic event, including tickets to skyboxes, is treated as a charitable contribution regardless of whether the tickets would have been available if the payment had not been made (Code Sec. 170(l); IRS Letter Ruling 200004001).[179]

Transfers of property to a charitable organization that are directly related to the donor's business and made with a reasonable expectation of financial return equivalent to value of the transfers do not qualify for a charitable deduction but may qualify as a trade or business expense (Reg. § 1.170A-1(c)(5)).[180]

Donor Advised Funds. The deduction for a contribution made to a donor advised fund after February 13, 2007 is allowed only if: (1) the fund's sponsoring organization is not described in Code Sec. 170(c)(3), (4) or (5) (i.e., a cemetery, war veterans' organization, or lodge) or a "Type III supporting organization" that is not a "functionally integrated Type III supporting organization" (both as described in Code Sec. 4943(f)(5)), and (2) the donor obtains a contemporaneous written acknowledgement from the sponsoring organization that the organization has exclusive legal control over the assets contributed (Code Sec. 170(f)(18)).[181] After August 17, 2006, distributions from donor advised funds that are for noncharitable purposes are taxable, as are certain transactions between a donor advised fund and its donors, donor advisors, or related persons (Code Secs. 4966 and 4967).[182]

A donor advised fund is a fund: (1) separately identified by reference to contributions of a donor or donors, (2) owned and controlled by a sponsoring organization, and (3) with respect to which a donor (or person appointed by the donor) reasonably expects to have advisory privileges regarding the distribution or investment of amounts in the fund. It does not include a fund (1) that makes distributions only to a single identified organization or governmental entity, or (2) with respect to which a donor or donor advisor provides advice as to which individuals receive grants for travel, study, or other similar purposes (provided certain conditions are met). The IRS may exempt a fund from donor advised fund treatment (Code Sec. 4966(d)(2)). A sponsoring organization is an organization that: (1) is a Code Sec. 170(c) organization (see above), other than the United States, a U.S. possession, the District of Columbia, or a state or local government, and without regard to whether it was created or organized in any of those

---

Footnote references are to paragraphs of the 2008 Standard Federal Tax Reports.

[176] ¶ 11,620.511
[177] ¶ 11,620.512
[178] ¶ 37,065

[179] ¶ 11,600, ¶ 11,680.10
[180] ¶ 11,615
[181] ¶ 11,600

[182] ¶ 34,317, ¶ 34,319

governmental entities, (2) is not a private foundation (see ¶ 631), and (3) maintains one or more donor advised funds (Code Sec. 4966(d)(1)).

1062. Gifts of Appreciated Property. The amount of a noncash charitable contribution is generally the property's fair market value at the time of the contribution, reduced by limitations that apply to certain appreciated property (Reg. § 1.170A-1(c)). The deductible amount for appreciated property depends on whether it is ordinary income property, capital gain property, or a combination of both. The reduction rules described below do not apply if, due to the transfer of the contributed property , the donor recognizes income or gain in the same tax year in which the contribution is made (Code Sec. 170(b) and (e); Reg. § 1.170A-4).[183]

Ordinary Income Property. Ordinary income property is property that, if sold at its fair market value on the date of contribution, would give rise to ordinary income or short-term capital gain. The deduction for such property is limited to the fair market value of the property less the amount that would be ordinary income. Such property includes inventory and stock in trade, artworks and manuscripts created by the donor, letters and memoranda, capital assets held for less than the required holding period for long-term capital gain treatment, and Code Sec. 306 stock (see ¶ 739 and ¶ 740) (Code Sec. 170(e)(1)(A); Reg. § 1.170A-4).[184]

Capital Gain Property. Capital gain property includes any asset on which a long-term capital gain would be realized if the taxpayer sold the asset for its fair market value on the date of contribution. As a general rule, gifts of capital gain property are deductible at their fair market value on the date of contribution. However, the individual's contribution must be reduced by the potential long-term gain (appreciation) if:

(1) the property is contributed to certain private nonoperating (grant-making) foundations (Code Sec. 170(e)(1)(B)(ii)) (however, a deduction is allowed for the fair market value of qualified appreciated stock, which is publicly traded stock that would produce long-term capital gain if sold (Code Sec. 170(e)(5)));

(2) the gift is tangible personal property put to a use that is unrelated to the purpose or function upon which the organization's exemption is based (Code Sec. 170(e)(1)(B)(i)(I));

(3) the gift is tangible personal property which is "applicable property" that the organization sells, exchanges, or disposes of in the tax year when the contribution was made, and the organization has not made a certification regarding the property (see *"Recapture of Charitable Tax Benefits,"* following); this treatment applies to contributions made after September 1, 2006 (Code Sec. 170(e)(1)(B)(i)(II));

(4) the donation consists of patents, certain copyrights, trademarks, trade names, trade secrets, know-how, certain software, or similar intellectual property or applications or registrations of such property (Code Sec. 170(e)(1)(B)(iii));

(5) the donation consists of taxidermy property contributed after July 25, 2006, by the person who prepared, stuffed or mounted the property, or who paid or incurred the cost of preparation, stuffing or mounting (Code Sec. 170(e)(1)(B)(iv)); or

(6) the taxpayer elects to disregard the special 30% capital gains limitation in favor of the 50% limitation (Reg. § 1.170A-4(b)(2)).[185]

Combination Property. The charitable contribution deduction is specially computed if the donor's sale of the property at fair market value would have produced both ordinary income and capital gain (Code Sec. 170(e)). The fair market value is reduced by the ordinary income that would have resulted from the sale, and the remainder of the fair market value is treated as capital gain property, subject to the above rules. The types of property to which this special computation applies include property subject to depreciation recapture (¶ 1779–¶ 1788) and to recapture of farmland expenditures (¶ 1797), as well as interests in oil, gas, or geothermal property (¶ 2025).

Footnote references are to paragraphs of the 2008 Standard Federal Tax Reports.

[183] ¶ 11,600, ¶ 11,615, ¶ 11,632

[184] ¶ 11,600, ¶ 11,632

[185] ¶ 11,600, ¶ 11,632

Recapture of Charitable Tax Benefits. If a donee organization disposes of applicable property within three years of the contribution and does not provide certification regarding the property, the donor taxpayer will be required to include as ordinary income for the year of the disposition the difference between the fair market value of the donated capital gains property and the donor's basis. "Applicable property" is appreciated tangible personal property with a claimed value over $5,000, the use of which the donee certifies as related to its exempt function or purpose, and for which a deduction greater than the donor's basis is allowed. The certification is a written statement, signed under penalty of perjury by an officer of the donee, which either: (1) certifies that the property's use was related to the donee's exempt purpose and describes how the property was used and how such use furthered the exempt purpose or (2) states the donee's intended use of the property at the time of the contribution and certifies that such use became impossible or infeasible to implement. This treatment applies to contributions made after September 1, 2006 (Code Sec. 170(e)(7)).[186]

Food Inventories. In 2006 and 2007, noncorporate and corporate taxpayers can claim an enhanced deduction for certain donations of food inventories (see ¶ 930). For a taxpayer other than a C corporation, the total deduction for food inventory donations during the tax year is limited to a maximum of 10 percent of the taxpayer's net income from those trades or businesses making such donations (Code Sec. 170(e)(3)(C)).[187]

1062A. Donee Income from Intellectual Property. A donor is allowed an additional charitable deduction based on a sliding-scale percentage of qualified donee income from donated qualified intellectual property over a 10-year period. "Qualified donee income" is any net income received by or accrued to the donee that is allocable to qualified intellectual property. "Qualified intellectual property" includes patents and other intellectual property (see ¶ 1062) but does not include property donated to certain private nonoperating (grant-making) foundations. This additional deduction is allowed only to the extent that the total of the amounts calculated using the sliding scale exceeds the deduction amount claimed on the property contribution without regard to the additional amount. The donor must inform the donee at the time of the contribution of its intent to treat the donation as a qualified intellectual property contribution (Code Secs. 170(m) and 6050L(b); Notice 2005-41).[188]

1063. Use of Property—Partial Interests. Generally, no charitable deduction is allowed for gifts to charity of the rent-free use of property and other nontrust gifts where less than the taxpayer's entire interest in the property is contributed, except in the following cases: (1) a contribution of an undivided portion of a taxpayer's entire interest in property—for example, a one-fourth interest in property; (2) a contribution of a remainder interest in a personal residence or farm; (3) a qualified conservation contribution; and (4) where a charitable deduction would have been allowed had the interest been transferred in trust (Code Sec. 170(f)(3); Reg. § 1.170A-7).[189] See ¶ 538 and ¶ 1070.

Additional Fractional Interest Charitable Contributions. The charitable deduction for additional contributions of tangible personal property in which the donor has previously contributed an undivided fractional interest is equal to the lesser of the fair market value of: (1) the property used to determine the deduction for the initial fractional contribution or (2) the property at the time of the additional contribution. The deduction will be recaptured if, before the earlier of the 10th anniversary of the initial fractional contribution or the donor's date of death, either: (1) the donor fails to contribute the remaining interests to the donee or (2) the donee fails to take substantial physical possession of the property and use it in a manner related to its exempt purpose. The recaptured amount will be subject to interest and an additional 10 percent tax. These rules apply to contributions made after August 17, 2006 (Code Sec. 170(o)).[190]

Qualified Conservation Contributions. A qualified conservation contribution (QCC) is a contribution of a qualified real property interest to a qualified organization exclusively for conservation purposes that are protected in perpetuity. Qualified real property includes a donor's entire interest in real property (other than an interest in subsurface

---

Footnote references are to paragraphs of the 2008 Standard Federal Tax Reports.

[186] ¶ 11,600
[187] ¶ 11,600

[188] ¶ 11,600, ¶ 36,260, ¶ 11,660.32

[189] ¶ 11,600, ¶ 11,651
[190] ¶ 11,600

oil, gas or other minerals, and the right to access to such minerals), a remainder interest, and a restriction granted in perpetuity on the property's use (i.e., an easement). A qualified organization includes certain governmental units, public charities that meet certain public support tests, and certain supporting organizations. A qualified conservation purpose includes: (1) preserving land, for outdoor recreation by or the education of the general public; (2) protecting a relatively natural habitat of fish, wildlife, or plants; (3) preserving open space for the public's scenic enjoyment or under a governmental conservation policy that will yield significant public benefit; and (4) preserving an historically important land area or a certified historic structure (Code Sec. 170(h)).[191] A facade easement may qualify as a QCC (IRS Letter Ruling 199933029).

For any QCC made after August 17, 2006, the deduction is reduced by an amount equal to the contribution's fair market value multiplied by a fraction: the sum of the rehabilitation credits (see ¶ 1347) allowed to the taxpayer for the five preceding tax years on any building that is part of the donation, over the building's fair market value on the contribution date (Code Sec. 170(f)(14)). Additionally, the QCC amount that may be deducted in 2006 and 2007 has been increased (see ¶ 1059).

Facade Easement Restrictions. There are several requirements for contributions of facade easements, made after July 26, 2006, regarding buildings located in registered historic districts and certified as being of historic significance. The easement must preserve the building's entire exterior and prohibit any change that is inconsistent with the exterior's historical character. Both the donor and donee must certify in writing that the donee: (1) is a qualified organization whose purpose is environmental protection, land conservation, or open space or historic preservation and (2) has the resources and a commitment to manage and enforce the restriction. If the donation is made in a *tax year* beginning after July 26, 2006, the donor's return must include: (1) a qualified appraisal of the qualified property interest (see ¶ 1071); (2) photographs of the building's entire exterior; and (3) a description of all restrictions on the building's development (Code Sec. 170(h)(4)(B)). For contributions made after February 12, 2007, taxpayers who seek deductions over $10,000 for such contributions must submit a $500 filing fee with their return (Code Sec. 170(f)(13)).

1064. Care of Unrelated Student in the Home. Charitable contributions include unreimbursed amounts spent to maintain an elementary or high school student (who is *not* a dependent or relative) in the taxpayer's home under a written agreement with a program sponsored by a charitable organization providing educational opportunities for students. The deduction is limited to actual expenditures, up to $50 per month while the student is a member of the taxpayer's household. "Dependent" is defined at Code Sec. 152 (see ¶ 137 and following), but without regard to whether the dependent claims dependency exemptions, files a joint return or has gross income in excess of the exemption amount (Code Sec. 170(g); Reg. § 1.170A-2).[192]

1065. Reduction for Interest. If a liability is assumed by the recipient or by any other person, or if the contributed property is subject to a liability, the contribution must be reduced by the interest paid by the taxpayer-donor (whether prepaid or to be paid in the future) attributable to any period after the contribution. If the gift is a bond, note or other evidence of indebtedness, the amount of the contribution is further reduced by the interest that is paid (or to be paid) by the taxpayer-donor on indebtedness incurred or continued to purchase or carry such bond that is attributable to any period prior to the contribution (Code Sec. 170(f)(5); Reg. § 1.170A-3).[193]

1066. Contribution by Partnership. Although a partnership cannot claim a charitable deduction in figuring its taxable income, each partner is allowed a deduction for the partner's distributive share of the partnership's charitable contribution (see ¶ 417) (Code Secs. 702(a) and 703(a); Reg. § 1.702-1(a)).[194] See ¶ 1061 for special rules regarding partnership donations of clothing and household items.

1068. Denial of Deduction. A contribution is not deductible unless it is made to, or for the use of, an organization that qualifies as one of the types described at ¶ 1061.

Footnote references are to paragraphs of the 2008 Standard Federal Tax Reports.

[191] ¶ 11,600

[192] ¶ 11,600, ¶ 11,621

[193] ¶ 11,600, ¶ 11,631

[194] ¶ 25,080, ¶ 25,081, ¶ 25,100

Contributions made directly to an individual or to groups of individuals are not deductible, including those made directly to individuals in the military.[195] Gifts to private schools and organizations, including churches, that practice racial discrimination in their admissions policies are not deductible.[196]

If a taxpayer makes a gift to a private foundation or a nonexempt trust (an annuity trust or unitrust), a deduction will be allowed only if the governing instrument specifically prohibits income accumulations and certain conflict-of-interest activities (¶ 635–¶ 644) (Code Sec. 508(d)).[197] The IRS has issued sample acceptable governing instrument clauses.[198] Many states have enacted statutes that accomplish the required governing instrument adjustments, and the IRS has published a list of those that satisfy the Code requirements.[199] See also ¶ 538 and ¶ 631.

An organization formed after October 9, 1969, and claiming exemption under Code Sec. 501(c)(3) (see ¶ 1061, item (2)) must file notice of intent to be exempt (¶ 616), the exemption being retroactive to the date of organization only if the notice was timely. Contributions to such an organization are deductible only if the notice is filed. Contributions made to a late-filing organization are not deductible if made before the date of filing (Code Secs. 170(f)(1) and 508(d); Reg. § 1.508-1).[200] The IRS periodically updates and publishes a cumulative list of eligible organizations which may be searched on the IRS website, at http://apps.irs.gov/app/pub78. IRS Publication 78, Cumulative List of Organizations, is available only online, and may be downloaded from the IRS website, at http://www.irs.gov.[201]

Deductions are disallowed for contributions by a "substantial contributor" (¶ 635) to a foundation in a tax year in which there is an action resulting in a Code Sec. 507(c) termination tax (¶ 649) (Code Secs. 170(f)(1) and 508(d); Reg. § 1.508-1).[202] Deductions are also denied for contributions made in connection with church-related tax avoidance schemes, such as the "donation" of assets to a personal "church" that effectively redistributes them to the donor. Deficiencies arising from the denial of deduction based on these schemes usually result in assessment of interest and penalties.[203]

1069. Gift of Future Interest in Tangible Personal Property. When a taxpayer transfers to a charitable organization a future interest in tangible personal property, such as a painting, manuscript, sculpture, or other art object, a charitable contribution deduction is not allowed until all intervening interests in, and rights to, the actual possession or enjoyment of the property have expired or are held by persons other than the taxpayer, related taxpayers and controlled partnerships (Code Sec. 170(a)(3); Reg. § 1.170A-5).[204]

1070. Transfer in Trust. No deduction is allowed for the value of a contribution of a remainder interest that the donor transfers in trust unless the trust is a pooled income fund (¶ 593), a charitable remainder annuity trust, or a charitable remainder unitrust (¶ 590) (Code Sec. 170(f)(2); Reg. § 1.170A-6).[205]

1070A. Reporting, Recordkeeping and Substantiation. Taxpayers report their charitable contributions by entering the total amount contributed on Form 1040, Schedule A, but written records are required to substantiate the deductions. In general, a taxpayer making a contribution of money of less than $250 must keep a cancelled check, a receipt from the donee or, in the absence of these, other reliable written records showing the name of the donee and the amount and date of the contribution (Reg. § 1.170A-13(a)). (But see *"Cash Donations,"* below.) For a noncash donation for which a deduction of less than $250 is claimed, the taxpayer generally must maintain a receipt from the donee indicating the donee's name, the date and location of the donation, and a detailed description (but not the value) of the donated property. If it would be impracticable to obtain a receipt, the donor must maintain reliable written records regarding the noncash contribution (Reg. § 1.170A-13(b)).[206]

Footnote references are to paragraphs of the 2008 Standard Federal Tax Reports.

[195] ¶ 11,620.111
[196] ¶ 11,620.32
[197] ¶ 22,790
[198] ¶ 22,795.75
[199] ¶ 22,795.79

[200] ¶ 11,600, ¶ 22,790, ¶ 22,791
[201] ¶ 11,620.103
[202] ¶ 11,600, ¶ 22,790, ¶ 22,791

[203] ¶ 39,651G.225
[204] ¶ 11,600, ¶ 11,634
[205] ¶ 11,600, ¶ 11,635
[206] ¶ 11,685

Cash Donations. In tax years beginning after August 17, 2006, no deduction will be allowed for contributions of cash, checks or other monetary gifts, *regardless of the amount*, unless the donor maintains either: (1) a bank record or (2) a receipt, letter, or other written communication from the donee, indicating the donee's name and the contribution date and amount (Code Sec. 170(f)(17)).[207]

Contributions of $250 or More. Charitable contributions of $250 or more must be substantiated by a contemporaneous written acknowledgment from the donee organization unless the donee files a return with the IRS reporting the information that would be included in the written acknowledgment. Generally, the acknowledgment must include the amount of cash and a description of noncash contributions, together with a description and good-faith estimate of the value of any goods or services with more than insubstantial value received in exchange for the contributions (Code Sec. 170(f)(8); Reg. § 1.170A-13(f)).[208] Contributions made by payroll deduction may be substantiated with an employer-provided document, such as a pay stub or Form W-2, showing the amount deducted, or with a donee-prepared pledge card or other document stating that the donee does not provide goods or services as whole or partial consideration for contributions made by payroll deduction. Substantiation is required only if $250 or more is deducted from a single paycheck (Reg. § 1.170A-13(f)(11)).[209]

Noncash Donations of More Than $500. For contributions of property made after June 3, 2004 and for which a deduction of more than $500 is claimed, the taxpayer (other than a C corporation that is not a personal service corporation or closely-held C corporation) must include with its return for the tax year in which the contribution is made a written description of the donated property and any other required information as the IRS may prescribe by regulation. If the documentation requirement is not met, the deduction will be denied unless the failure is due to reasonable cause and not to willful neglect. To determine the $500 threshold, all similar items of property donated to one or more donees are treated as a single item of property (Code Sec. 170(f)(11)).[210] Noncash contributions over $500 (over $5,000 for C corporations other than closely-held or personal service corporations) must be described in Section A of Form 8283, Noncash Charitable Contributions, which is attached to the taxpayer's return. A noncash contribution that exceeds $5,000 must also be appraised and must be described in Section B of Form 8283 (see ¶ 1071) (Reg. § 1.170A-13(c)).[211]

Donations of Clothing or Household Items. Donations of clothing or household items made after August 17, 2006, that are not "in good used condition or better" will be allowed only if a deduction of more than $500 is claimed for the single item and a qualified appraisal for that item is attached to the return (see ¶ 1061).

Vehicle Donations. Taxpayers donating to a charity a qualified vehicle (e.g., car, truck, boat, aircraft) valued at over $500 must obtain from the charity and attach to his or her return either a Form 1098-C or a similar contemporaneous written acknowledgement of the contribution. The acknowledgment must identify the donor taxpayer, list the taxpayer's and the vehicle's identification numbers, and include a description and good faith estimate of the value of any goods or services provided by the charity in exchange for the vehicle. If the goods or services consist solely of intangible religious benefits, the acknowledgment must say so. If the charity sells the vehicle without significant intervening use or material improvement, the acknowledgment must also certify that the vehicle was sold in an arm's length transaction between unrelated parties, list the gross proceeds, and state that the deduction may not exceed the gross proceeds. If the charity retains the vehicle for its significant use or makes a material improvement, the acknowledgment must certify the use or improvement, the time frame the charity will use the vehicle, and that the vehicle will not be transferred before the use or improvement is completed. The taxpayer will then be allowed to claim the fair market value of the vehicle as a charitable donation (Code Sec. 170(f)(12)).[212]

If the charity sells the vehicle for a significantly low fair market value (or gratuitously transfers the vehicle) to a needy individual, the taxpayer can claim the donated vehicle's fair market value only if the sale or transfer directly furthers the charity's

---

Footnote references are to paragraphs of the 2008 Standard Federal Tax Reports.

[207] ¶ 11,600
[208] ¶ 11,600, ¶ 11,685
[209] ¶ 11,685
[210] ¶ 11,600
[211] ¶ 11,685
[212] ¶ 11,600

purpose (Notice 2005-44). However, if a charity sells the vehicle at auction, the IRS will not accept as substantiation an acknowledgment stating that the vehicle is to be transferred to a needy individual for significantly below fair market value. In that case, the donor taxpayer may claim a deduction greater than $500, but only to the extent that the gross sale proceeds exceed that amount and the donor substantiates the contribution with an acknowledgment listing the gross proceeds (IRS News Release IR-2005-145).[213]

Qualified Conservation Contributions. Documentation and certification requirements must be met for certain qualified conservation contributions of facade easements (see ¶ 1063).

1071. Appraisals for Noncash Contributions. For certain noncash contributions made after June 3, 2004, a charitable deduction will be denied to any taxpayer that fails to meet specific appraisal requirements. (See ¶ 1070A for documentation requirements.) An exception exists if the failure is due to reasonable cause and not to willful neglect. For purposes of determining the threshold dollar amounts for the reporting requirements (described below), all similar items of noncash property, whether donated to a single donee or multiple donees, are aggregated and treated as a single property donation. For partnerships and S corporations, the requirements are applied at the entity level, but if the entities fail to meet the requirements, denial of the deduction will be made at the partner or shareholder level (Code Sec. 170(f)(11)).[214]

If a deduction of more than $5,000 is being claimed for a noncash donation, the taxpayer (including a C corporation) must obtain a qualified appraisal of the property and attach to its return for the tax year in which the donation is made whatever information about the property and the appraisal that the IRS prescribes by regulations. If a deduction of $500,000 or more is being claimed, the qualified appraisal itself must be attached to the return when filed (Code Sec. 170(f)(11)(C) and (D)). These substantiation requirements do not apply to donations of: (1) cash; (2) patents and other intellectual property (see ¶ 1062); (3) publicly-traded securities for which market quotations are readily available on an established securities market; (4) inventory or property held by the taxpayer primarily for sale to customers in the ordinary course of his trade or business (see ¶ 1741); and (5) a qualified vehicle sold by the donee organization without any significant intervening use or material improvement and for which an acknowledgment is provided (see ¶ 1070A) (Code Sec. 170(f)(11)(A)(ii)).[215]

A "qualified appraisal" is one which: (1) is treated as a qualified appraisal under regulations or other guidance prescribed by the IRS, and (2) for returns or submissions filed after August 17, 2006, is conducted by a qualified appraiser under generally-accepted appraisal standards and any regulations or other IRS guidance. A "qualified appraiser" is an individual who: (1) has earned an appraisal designation from a recognized professional appraiser organization, or has otherwise met minimum education and experience requirements set forth in the regulations, (2) regularly performs appraisals for pay, and (3) meets other requirements prescribed in the regulations or other guidance. An individual cannot be a qualified appraiser regarding any specific appraisal unless he or she demonstrates verifiable education and experience in valuing the property type being appraised, and has not been prohibited from practicing before the IRS under 31 U.S.C. Sec. 330(c) at any time during the three-year period ending on the appraisal date (Code Sec. 170(f)(11)(E); Notice 2006-96).

An appraisal summary, made on Section B, Form 8283, must be attached to the tax return on which the deduction of more than $5,000 is first claimed. Appraisals are also required if a taxpayer donates a number of similar items (whether or not to the same donee), such as stamps or coins, with a total value in excess of $5,000. For publicly traded securities for which market quotations are *not* readily available on an established securities market, a partially completed appraisal summary is required if the claimed value exceeds $5,000. The appraisal summary also need be only partially completed for nonpublicly traded stock with a claimed value between $5,000 and $10,000 (Reg. § 1.170A-13(c)).[216] The qualified appraisal requirement is waived for closely held and

---

Footnote references are to paragraphs of the 2008 Standard Federal Tax Reports.

[213] ¶ 11,660.515 [215] ¶ 11,600
[214] ¶ 11,600 [216] ¶ 11,685

personal service corporations that contribute inventory, stock in trade, or other property normally held for sale in its business for the ill, needy, or infants.[217]

Appraisal fees incurred by an individual in determining the fair market value of donated property are not treated as part of the charitable contribution, but they may be claimed as a miscellaneous deduction on Schedule A of Form 1040 (Rev. Rul. 67-461).[218]

Accuracy-Related Penalties. Appraisers are subject to a civil penalties for certain appraisals that result in substantial or gross valuation misstatements (Code Sec. 6695A).

Moving Expense

1073. Moving Expense Deduction. Employees and self-employed individuals may deduct as an adjustment to gross income the reasonable expenses of moving themselves and their families if the move is related to starting work in a new location (Code Sec. 217).[219] The deduction is computed on Form 3903, Moving Expenses, and reported on Form 1040.

Deductible moving expenses are limited to the cost of: (1) transportation of household goods and personal effects and (2) travel (including lodging but not meals) to the new residence (Code Sec. 217(b)).[220]

Where an automobile is used in making the move, a taxpayer may deduct either: (1) the actual out-of-pocket expenses incurred (gasoline and oil, but not repairs, depreciation, etc.) or (2) a standard mileage allowance of 20 cents per mile in 2007 (plus parking fees and tolls) (Rev. Proc. 2006-49).[221]

1075. Eligibility for Deduction. To deduct moving expenses, a taxpayer must meet a distance test, a length-of-employment test and a commencement-of-work test.

The new principal place of work must be at least 50 miles farther from the taxpayer's old residence than the old residence was from the taxpayer's old place of work. If there was no old place of work, the new place of work must be at least 50 miles from the old residence (Code Sec. 217(c)).[222]

During the 12-month period immediately following the move, the taxpayer must be employed full time for at least 39 weeks. A self-employed taxpayer must be employed or performing services full time for at least 78 weeks of the 24-month period immediately following the move and at least 39 weeks during the first 12 months. The full-time work requirement is waived, however, due to death, disability, involuntary separation from work (other than for willful misconduct), or transfer to another location for the benefit of the employer (Code Secs. 217(c) and (d)).[223]

In general, the move must be in connection with the commencement of work at the new location and the moving expenses must be incurred within one year from the time the taxpayer first reports to the new job or business. If the move is not made within one year, the expenses ordinarily will not be deductible unless it can be shown that circumstances prevented the taxpayer from incurring the expenses within that period (Reg. § 1.217-2(a)(3)).[224]

An eligible taxpayer is permitted to deduct moving expenses even though the 39- or 78-week residence requirement has not been satisfied by the due date for the return (including extensions) for the tax year in which the moving expenses were incurred and paid. However, a taxpayer who fails to meet the requirements must either file an amended return or include as gross income on the next year's return the amount previously claimed as expenses (Code Sec. 217(d); Reg. § 1.217-2(d)(3)).[225]

An individual who retires from an overseas job may deduct moving expenses incurred in returning to the United States. A surviving spouse or dependent who shared the residence of a decedent who worked outside the U.S. at the time of death may also deduct moving expenses incurred in returning to the U.S. within six months after the death (Code Sec. 217(i)).[226]

Footnote references are to paragraphs of the 2008 Standard Federal Tax Reports.

[217] ¶ 11,700.45   [221] ¶ 12,623.11   [225] ¶ 12,620, ¶ 12,622
[218] ¶ 11,700.10   [222] ¶ 12,620   [226] ¶ 12,620
[219] ¶ 12,620   [223] ¶ 12,620
[220] ¶ 12,620   [224] ¶ 12,622

1076. Reimbursement by Employer. Gross income does not include qualified moving expense reimbursements, which are amounts received directly or indirectly by an individual employee from an employer as a payment for or reimbursement of expenses that would be deductible as a moving expense if directly paid or incurred by the employee (Code Sec. 132(a)(6) and (g)).[227] See ¶ 863.

Any amount (other than a qualified reimbursement) received or accrued, directly or indirectly, from the employer as a payment for or reimbursement of moving expenses must be included in the employee's gross income as compensation for services (Code Sec. 82)[228] and is considered wages subject to withholding (Code Sec. 3401(a)(15); Reg. § 31.3401(a)(15)-1).[229]

1077. Foreign Moves. The rules governing moving expenses incurred in connection with the commencement of work outside the U.S. and its possessions are similar to those discussed in ¶ 1073 and ¶ 1075. However, a deduction is also allowed for reasonable expenses of moving household goods and personal effects to and from storage, and of storing them while the new place of work abroad is the taxpayer's principal place of work (Code Sec. 217(h)).[230]

1078. Moves of Armed Forces Members. Gross income does not include moving and storage expenses that are furnished in kind by the military or cash reimbursements or allowances to the extent of expenses actually paid or incurred incident to a permanent change of station for a member of the U.S. Armed Forces on active duty. Such expenses need not be reported and such moves are exempt from the time and mileage requirements (see ¶ 1075). An income exclusion is also provided for moving and storage expenses incurred by the spouse or dependents of a member of the Armed Forces even if they do not reside with the member either before or after the move (Code Sec. 217(g)). Reimbursements in excess of actual expenses are included in the member's income as wages, while expenses in excess of reimbursements are deductible (Reg. § 1.217-2(g)(2)(ii)).[231]

Dues, Education, and Other Expenses

1080. Union Dues. Union dues, initiation fees and out-of-work-benefit assessments are deductible as an itemized deduction on Schedule A of Form 1040, subject to the two-percent floor (¶ 1011).[232] The self-employed may deduct union dues as a business expense (see ¶ 1005).

1081. Job-Hunting Expenses. Individuals may deduct all expenses incurred in seeking employment in the *same* trade or business regardless of whether or not the search is successful. Such expenses include the typing, printing, and mailing of resumes, and travel and transportation expenses. Travel and transportation expenses to and from an area are deductible only if the trip relates primarily to seeking new employment. If the travel is primarily personal in nature, only the actual expenses of the search at the destination are deductible.[233]

Expenses are not deductible if an individual is seeking employment in a *new* trade or business even where employment is secured. Individuals seeking their first job, entering a new trade or business, or working after a long period of unemployment cannot deduct job-hunting expenses.[234]

Job-hunting expenses are deductible only as an itemized deduction on Schedule A of Form 1040, subject to the two-percent floor (see ¶ 1011). Individuals generally must complete Form 2106, Employee Business Expenses, if they were reimbursed by an employer or a third party or if they claim any meal, entertainment, travel or transportation expenses.

1082. Education and Related Expenses. There are several types of deductions for education expenses. First, interest paid during the tax year on any qualified education loan is deductible as an adjustment to gross income on Form 1040 or 1040A. The debt must be incurred by the taxpayer solely to pay qualified higher education expenses

---

Footnote references are to paragraphs of the 2008 Standard Federal Tax Reports.

[227] ¶ 7420
[228] ¶ 6374
[229] ¶ 33,502, ¶ 33,528
[230] ¶ 12,620
[231] ¶ 12,620, ¶ 12,622
[232] ¶ 6006.16
[233] ¶ 8524.25
[234] ¶ 8524.25

(Code Sec. 221(d)(1)). The maximum deductible amount of interest is $2,500, but the amount of any deduction is reduced by an amount that equals the otherwise allowable deduction times a fraction, the numerator being the excess of modified adjusted gross income (AGI) over $50,000 ($100,000 if married filing jointly) and the denominator being $15,000 ($30,000 if married filing jointly). The deductible amount cannot be reduced below zero (Code Sec. 221(b)(1)).[235] The phaseout amounts are indexed annually for inflation. For 2007, the maximum deduction is reduced when modified AGI exceeds $55,000 ($110,000 for joint returns) and is completely eliminated when modified AGI is $70,000 ($140,000 for joint returns) (Rev. Proc. 2006-53). For 2008, the maximum deduction is reduced when modified AGI exceeds $55,000 ($115,000 for joint returns) and is completely eliminated when modified AGI is $70,000 ($145,000 for joint returns) (Rev. Proc. 2007-66).

Second, there is an "above-the-line" deduction for qualifying tuition and related expenses paid for enrollment or attendance by the taxpayer or the taxpayer's spouse or dependent at any accredited post-secondary institution. For 2007, the maximum deductible amount is $4,000 for taxpayers with AGI at or below $65,000 ($130,000 for joint filers). For taxpayers with AGI above $65,000 but less than or equal to $80,000 ($130,000 and $160,000, respectively, for joint filers), the maximum deductible amount is $2,000. No deduction is available to taxpayers with AGI above $80,000 ($160,000 for joint filers). The taking of the tuition and fees deduction must be coordinated with other educational exclusions and cannot be taken if the taxpayer claims either of the educational credits (see ¶ 1303). This deduction does not apply to tax years beginning after 2007 (Code Sec. 222).[236]

Finally, the taxpayer's own education expenses may also be deducted as a business expense (even if they lead to a degree) if the education: (1) maintains or improves a skill *required* in the taxpayer's employment or other trade or business or (2) meets the express *requirements* of the taxpayer's employer, laws or regulations, *imposed* as a condition to the taxpayer's retention of an established employment relationship, status, or rate of compensation (Reg. § 1.162-5).[237]

The business expense deduction does not apply to educational expenses that are personal or constitute an inseparable aggregate of personal and capital expenditures, even though they may maintain or improve a skill or may meet the express requirements of the taxpayer's employer. Nondeductible capital or personal education expenses are those that: (1) are required of the taxpayer in order to meet the minimum educational requirements for qualification in the taxpayer's present employment, trade, or business or (2) qualify the taxpayer for a new trade or business.

The minimum education necessary to qualify for a position or other trade or business is determined from a consideration of such factors as requirements of the employer, laws or regulations, and the standards of the profession, trade, or business involved. A currently employed taxpayer does not necessarily meet the minimum requirements for qualification in that employment so as to be entitled to a educational deduction under the improving-of-skills test. However, educational expenses are deductible if they are incurred in meeting new education requirements that are established after a taxpayer has met the minimum requirements for qualification in a current position.

A change of duties is not a new trade or business if the new duties and the taxpayer's present employment involve the same general work. Thus, there is no new trade or business when a teacher moves from an elementary to a secondary school, from one subject to another, or from a teaching position to a principal's position (Reg. § 1.162-5(b)(3)).[238]

Unreimbursed expenditures for such items as tuition, books, laboratory fees, dues paid to professional societies, fees paid for professional journals, etc., are deducted by an employee as an itemized deduction, subject to the two-percent floor (¶ 1011) (Reg. § 1.162-6; IRS Pub. 970).[239] The cost of technical books of relatively permanent value

---

Footnote references are to paragraphs of the 2008 Standard Federal Tax Reports.

[235] ¶ 12,692   [237] ¶ 8631   [239] ¶ 8633
[236] ¶ 12,770   [238] ¶ 8631

used in connection with professional work is a capital expenditure and must be depreciated (IRS Pub. 946) (¶ 1240).[240]

Travel as a Form of Education. Generally, no deduction is allowed for travel as a form of education, such as when a French teacher spends summers in Paris to maintain familiarity with the language (Code Sec. 274(m)(2)).[241] However, travel in pursuit of an education may be deductible if the education expense itself is deductible as a business expense or as a higher education expense; if, for example, a French teacher travels to Paris to take otherwise deductible classes that are offered only at the Sorbonne.[242]

1083. Uniforms and Special Clothing. The cost and upkeep of a uniform, including laundering and cleaning, are deductible only if the uniform is required as a condition of employment and is not adaptable to general wear. Uniform expense reimbursements paid under an accountable plan (¶ 943) are not reported on the employee's Form W-2 or included in the employee's income (Reg. § 1.62-2(c)(4)).[243] Costs that exceed the reimbursement are deductible as an itemized deduction, subject to the two-percent floor (¶ 1011). Reimbursement made under a nonaccountable plan (¶ 943) must be included in income but may be deducted as an itemized deduction on Schedule A of Form 1040, subject to the two-percent floor and limitations (Reg. § 1.62-2(c)(5)).[244] Armed Forces reservists may deduct the unreimbursed cost (less nontaxable uniform allowance) of a uniform required at drills or other functions if they are prohibited from wearing it for regular use.[245]

A deduction is allowed for special items required in the employee's work that do not replace items of ordinary clothing, such as special work shoes and gloves, shop caps, and protective clothing.[246]

1084. Teachers' Classroom Expenses. Eligible educators are permitted an "above-the-line" deduction in 2007 of up to $250 for unreimbursed expenses incurred in connection with books, supplies (other than nonathletic supplies for courses in health or physical education), computer equipment and supplementary materials used in the classroom (Code Sec. 62(a)(2)(D)).[247] An eligible educator is an individual who, for at least 900 hours during a school year, is a kindergarten through grade 12 teacher, instructor, counselor, principal or aide in a school that provides elementary or secondary education as determined under state law (Code Sec. 62(d)(1)). After 2007, barring further Congressional action, these expenses will be deductible only as miscellaneous itemized deductions subject to the two-percent of adjusted gross income floor.

Production of Income

1085. Nontrade or Nonbusiness Expenses. An individual may deduct ordinary and necessary expenses paid or incurred for the production or collection of income or for the management, conservation, or maintenance of property held for the production of income, as long as they are proximately related to these purposes and reasonable in amount (Code Sec. 212; Reg. § 1.212-1(d)).[248] The expenses are an itemized deduction on Schedule A of Form 1040, subject to the two-percent floor (¶ 1011). Expenses attributable to property held for rents or royalties are deductible from gross income and are not subject to the two-percent floor (¶ 1089). No deduction is allowed for interest on indebtedness incurred or continued to purchase or carry obligations earning fully tax-exempt interest or other exempt income (Code Sec. 265(a)).[249] See also ¶ 1970.

1086. Investor's Expenses. Investment counsel fees, custodian fees, fees for clerical help, office rent, state and local transfer taxes, and similar expenses paid or incurred by individuals in connection with their investments are deductible as itemized deductions on Schedule A of Form 1040, subject to the two-percent floor (¶ 1011) (Reg. § 1.212-1(g)),[250] except where they relate to rents and royalties (¶ 1089). A dealer or trader in securities is not an investor and may deduct these items as business expenses (subject to the uniform capitalization rules; see ¶ 990 and following).[251]

Footnote references are to paragraphs of the 2008 Standard Federal Tax Reports.

[240] ¶ 8634.01	[244] ¶ 6004	[248] ¶ 12,520, ¶ 12,521
[241] ¶ 14,402	[245] ¶ 8524.2652	[249] ¶ 14,050
[242] ¶ 14,402.018	[246] ¶ 8524.2658	[250] ¶ 12,521
[243] ¶ 6004, ¶ 6006.15	[247] ¶ 6002	[251] ¶ 8521.1475, ¶ 8521.148

¶1086

1089. Deductions Attributable to Rental or Royalty Property. Ordinary and necessary expenses attributable to property held for the production of rents or royalties may be deducted in determining adjusted gross income (Reg. § 1.62-1T(c))[252] even if the property is not actually producing income.[253] These deductions include interest, taxes, depreciation, depletion, losses, etc. (Reg. § 1.212-1).[254]

Property held for the production of royalties includes intangible as well as tangible property. Therefore, depreciation on a patent or copyright may be deducted. Similarly, operating owners, lessees, sublessors or sublessees, or purchasers of royalty interests can deduct their shares of a depletion allowance on natural resources. See ¶ 1201 and ¶ 1289, respectively.

Expenses must be prorated if a property is devoted to rental purposes for part of a year and to personal use for the other part. See the example on proration at ¶ 963. See also ¶ 966 for special rules governing the deduction of expenses of rental vacation homes. For the applicability of the at-risk and passive activity rules, see ¶ 2045 and ¶ 2053.

1090. Deductions of Life Tenant or Income Beneficiary. When property is held by one person for life, with the remainder to another person, the deduction for depreciation or depletion is allowed to the life tenant and is computed as if the life tenant were the absolute owner of the property (Reg. §§ 1.167(h)-1 and 1.611-1(c)).[255] After the life tenant's death, the deduction, if any, is allowed to the remainderman. For property held in trust or by an estate, the deduction is apportioned as explained at ¶ 530.

1091. Guardianship Expenses. A deduction is permitted for a reasonable amount paid or incurred for the services of a guardian or committee for a ward or minor and for other ordinary and necessary expenses incurred in connection with the production or collection of income inuring to the ward or minor, or in connection with the management, conservation, or maintenance of income-producing property belonging to the ward or minor (Reg. § 1.212-1(j)).[256] Expenses of a competency proceeding are deductible if the purpose of the proceeding is the management and conservation of income-producing property owned by the taxpayer.[257]

1092. Expenses Connected with the Determination of Tax. Any ordinary and necessary expense incurred in connection with the determination, collection, or refund of any tax is deductible as an itemized deduction on Schedule A of Form 1040, subject to the two-percent floor (¶ 1011) (Code Sec. 212(3)).[258] This includes tax return preparation fees allocable to an individual's Form 1040 and Schedules A and B. However, Form 1040 expenses attributable to a trade or business, including Schedules C, C-EZ, E and F, are deductible from gross income and are not itemized deductions.[259] See ¶ 973.

This provision applies to income, estate, gift, property and other taxes imposed at the federal, state or local level (Reg. § 1.212-1(l)).[260] Legal expenses incurred in determining tax liability include legal fees paid for obtaining a ruling on a tax question[261] and defending against a criminal indictment for tax evasion.[262] Expenses that pertain to both tax and nontax matters must be allocated and substantiated because only the tax element of the expense is deductible (Rev. Rul. 72-545).[263]

Appraisal fees may be deductible as an expense paid in connection with the determination of income tax liability. For example, appraisal fees incurred in determining the fair market value of property donated to a charity or to establish the amount of loss are deductible expenses.[264]

1093. Legal Expenses. Legal expenses are deductible as miscellaneous itemized deductions on Schedule A of Form 1040, subject to the two-percent floor (¶ 1011), if they are paid or incurred for the production of income or for the management, conservation, or maintenance of income-producing property.[265] Generally, legal expenses paid or

---

Footnote references are to paragraphs of the 2008 Standard Federal Tax Reports.

[252] ¶ 6003
[253] ¶ 6005.03, ¶ 12,523.035
[254] ¶ 12,521
[255] ¶ 11,048, ¶ 23,922
[256] ¶ 12,521

[257] ¶ 12,523.13, ¶ 12,523.33
[258] ¶ 12,520
[259] ¶ 6005.109
[260] ¶ 12,521
[261] ¶ 12,523.421

[262] ¶ 12,523.3264
[263] ¶ 12,523.3273
[264] ¶ 12,523.3848
[265] ¶ 12,521

incurred in recovering investment property and amounts of income includible in gross income are deductible (Reg. § 1.212-1(k)).[266] However, the U.S. Court of Appeals for the Sixth Circuit has ruled that legal expenses incurred in recovering stock were deductible only to the extent that they were allocable to the recovery of interest and dividends (*J.K. Nickell*, 87-2 USTC ¶ 9585).[267] Legal expenses incurred in defending or perfecting title to property, in the acquisition or disposition of property, or in developing or improving property are not deductible and must be capitalized.

Divorce and Separation. Generally, legal expenses paid by one spouse in resisting the other's monetary demands in divorce, separation or support decree are nondeductible personal expenses (¶ 1003). However, legal expenses for producing or collecting alimony under a divorce decree, separation agreement or support decree are deductible as a miscellaneous itemized deduction, subject to the two-percent floor (¶ 1011).[268]

1094. Limitation on Deduction of Investment Interest. The deduction by a noncorporate taxpayer for interest on investment indebtedness that is reported on Form 4952 is limited to the taxpayer's net investment income (Code Sec. 163(d)).[269] Net investment income is the excess of investment income over investment expenses. The disallowed investment interest can be carried over to a succeeding tax year (Rev. Rul. 95-16).[270]

Interest subject to the investment interest limitation is interest on debt properly allocable to property held for investment, which is generally defined as:

    (1) property that produces interest, dividends, annuities, or royalties that are not derived in the ordinary course of a trade or business;

    (2) property that produces gain or loss not derived in the ordinary course of a trade or business from the sale or exchange of property that either produces item (1) types of income or that is held for investment (but which is not an interest in a passive activity); and

    (3) an interest in a trade or business activity that is not a passive activity and in which the taxpayer did not materially participate (Code Sec. 163(d)(5)(A); IRS Pub. 550).

It does not include qualified residence interest (¶ 1047), interest properly allocable to a rental real estate activity in which the taxpayer actively participates (within the meaning of the passive loss rule) (¶ 2062), or interest that is taken into account in computing income or loss from a passive activity (¶ 2053).

Net capital gain from the disposition of investment property is not considered investment income. However, individuals may elect to treat all or any portion of such net capital gain as investment income by paying tax on the elected amounts at their ordinary income rates. The taxpayer may elect similar treatment for qualified dividend income (Code Sec. 163(d)(4)(B)).[271] Thus, the taxpayer loses the benefit of the otherwise applicable maximum capital gains tax rate with respect to the elected amount (Code Sec. 1(h)).[272] The election must be made on Form 4952, Investment Interest Expense Deduction, on or before the due date of the return for the tax year in which the net capital gain or the qualified dividend income is recognized. Once made, the election is revocable with the consent of the IRS (Reg. § 1.163(d)-1).[273]

Footnote references are to paragraphs of the 2008 Standard Federal Tax Reports.

[266] ¶ 12,521
[267] ¶ 12,523.35
[268] ¶ 12,523.3273

[269] ¶ 9102
[270] ¶ 9403.10
[271] ¶ 9102

[272] ¶ 3260
[273] ¶ 9402B

Chapter 11

LOSSES

Overview of Losses

1101. Losses, Generally. In general, a taxpayer may deduct losses that occur during the tax year and have not been compensated for by insurance or otherwise (Code Sec. 165(a)).[1] Tax treatment of a loss depends upon the nature of the activity in which the loss was incurred. To be deductible, a loss must be evidenced by closed and completed transactions, fixed by identifiable events. Only a bona fide loss is allowable, and substance governs over mere form in the determination (Reg. § 1.165-1(b)).[2]

In computing adjusted gross income (¶ 1005), individual taxpayers can deduct *allowable* losses that: (1) are incurred in a trade or business; (2) result from a sale or exchange of property; (3) are attributable to property held for the production of rents or royalties; or (4) are penalties for premature withdrawals of funds. However, an individual's allowable losses are specifically limited to:

(1) loss incurred in a trade or business;

(2) loss incurred in a transaction entered into for profit; or

(3) loss of property that arises from fire, storm, shipwreck or other casualty, or from theft (Code Sec. 165(c)).[3]

The basis for determining the amount of the loss deduction is the taxpayer's adjusted basis as calculated under Code Sec. 1011 (Code Sec. 165(b)).[4] The deduction for a loss cannot exceed the taxpayer's adjusted basis in the property (Reg. § 1.165-1(c)(1)).[5] In addition, the deduction must be reduced by any salvage value and any amount recovered from insurance or another source (Reg. § 1.165-1(c)(4)).[6]

For the treatment of a loss on stock in a small business company, see ¶ 2395. For losses on worthless securities, see ¶ 1764 and ¶ 1915. For losses on wash sales of securities, see ¶ 1935. For the disallowance of losses on the sale, exchange, or worthlessness of bonds not issued in registered form, see ¶ 1963. For losses limited by the "at-risk" rules, see ¶ 2045. For losses from passive activities, see ¶ 2053.

1104. When Is a Loss Sustained. Generally, a loss is deductible only for the tax year in which it is sustained, i.e., the tax year in which its occurrence is evidenced by closed and completed transactions and is fixed by identifiable events occurring in such tax year (Reg. § 1.165-1(b), (d)(1)).[7] No deduction may be claimed in the year of loss for any portion of the loss for which there remains a reasonable prospect of recovery. A deduction may be taken in the year in which it becomes reasonably certain that there will be no recovery (Reg. § 1.165-1(d)(2)).[8] A special election exists for determining when to deduct disaster losses (see ¶ 1141).

No deduction is available for a *partial* loss resulting from the shrinkage in value of property, except as reflected in an inventory.[9] An exception to this rule is the charge-off

---

Footnote references are to paragraphs of the 2008 Standard Federal Tax Reports.

[1] ¶ 9802	[4] ¶ 9802, ¶ 29,310	[7] ¶ 9803, ¶ 9805.996
[2] ¶ 9803	[5] ¶ 9803	[8] ¶ 9803, ¶ 9805.575
[3] ¶ 9802	[6] ¶ 9803	[9] ¶ 9805.01

of the worthless part of a business debt (see ¶ 1145). See ¶ 1157 regarding bad debt reserves.

1107. Loss on Sale of Residence. A loss from a sale of residential property acquired and held as a personal residence is not deductible by an individual. But loss on the sale of such property at the time it is being rented or otherwise used for income-producing purposes is deductible (Reg. § 1.165-9(a) and (b)).[10] As to the basis for such a loss, see ¶ 1626. If the property is used as the taxpayer's personal residence after having been acquired as income-producing property, loss on its sale at the time it is being used as a residence is not deductible.[11]

1112. Capitalization of Demolition Costs and Losses. Any amount expended or loss sustained by an owner or lessee on account of the demolition of any structure (including a certified historic structure) must be capitalized as part of the basis of the land on which the structure was located (Code Sec. 280B).[12]

A taxpayer can claim a 50-percent deduction for qualified Gulf Opportunity Zone clean-up costs paid or incurred after August 27, 2005 and before January 1, 2008 (Code Secs. 1400M and 1400N(f)). A qualified cost is an amount paid or incurred for the removal of debris from, or the demolition of structures on, real property which is located in the Gulf Opportunity Zone if the real property is either: (1) held by the taxpayer for use in a trade or business or for the production of income; or (2) inventory in the hands of the taxpayer.[13]

1115. Foreclosure Loss or Tax Sale. Where the owner of an equity interest receives less than his or her basis in real estate when it is sold upon foreclosure of the mortgage, his or her investment may represent a deductible loss only if the property foreclosed upon is business or investment property.[14] The nature of the loss—capital loss or ordinary loss—depends in each case upon the nature of the property foreclosed upon, i.e., whether it is a capital asset or required to be treated as a capital asset under Code Sec. 1231 (¶ 1747). The loss occurs when the redemption period expires or in the year the property became worthless where such property became worthless in an earlier year.[15] However, if there is no equity of redemption, the loss is fixed by the foreclosure sale and not by the decree of foreclosure that ordered the sale.[16] These principles also apply to a sale for delinquent taxes.[17]

If real property is disposed of by reason of foreclosure or similar proceedings, the monthly percentage reduction of the amount of accelerated depreciation subject to recapture (see ¶ 1779) is determined as if the taxpayer ceased to hold the property on the date on which such proceedings were begun.[18]

1118. Abandonment and Obsolescence Losses. A loss may be allowed for the abandonment of a depreciable asset in the amount of its adjusted basis if the owner manifests an irrevocable intent to abandon (discard) the asset so that it will neither be used again by the taxpayer nor retrieved for sale, exchange, or other disposition (Reg. § 1.167(a)-8(a)).[19] An abandonment loss is an ordinary loss (whether or not the aban-doned asset is a capital asset) and is reported on Form 4797, Sales of Business Property (IRS Pub. 544).

A taxpayer cannot deduct the costs of acquiring and developing creative property (screenplays, scripts, story outlines, and similar property for film development or production) as an abandonment loss unless the taxpayer establishes either: (1) an intent to abandon the property and an affirmative act of abandonment or (2) identifiable events which show a closed and completed transaction establishing the property's worthless-ness (Rev. Rul. 2004-58). This is so even though, for financial accounting purposes, a taxpayer should change its income statement to recognize loss if the creative property will not be used, and it is presumed that property not set for film production after three years will be disposed. To minimize accounting disputes, the IRS has provided a safe

---

Footnote references are to paragraphs of the 2008 Standard Federal Tax Reports.

[10] ¶ 10,102, ¶ 10,103.383
[11] ¶ 10,102
[12] ¶ 14,900
[13] ¶ 32,478, ¶ 32,483

[14] ¶ 9805.155, ¶ 10,103.54
[15] ¶ 21,817.45
[16] ¶ 21,817.451
[17] ¶ 9808.453

[18] ¶ 31,000, ¶ 31,006.032
[19] ¶ 11,020, ¶ 11,021.021

harbor allowing taxpayers to amortize ratably over a 15-year period any creative property costs that have been properly written off by the taxpayer under generally accepted accounting principles for financial reporting purposes (Rev. Proc. 2004-36).[20]

If a nondepreciable asset is abandoned following a sudden termination of its usefulness, an obsolescence loss is allowed in an amount equal to its adjusted basis. An obsolescence loss, in the case of nondepreciable property, is deductible in the tax year in which it is sustained, even though the overt act of abandonment or the loss of title to the property may not occur in that year (Reg. § 1.165-2).[21]

1120. Interest Forfeited on Premature Withdrawals. Interest that was previously earned on a time savings account or deposit with a savings institution and that is later forfeited because of premature withdrawals is deductible from gross income in the year when the interest is forfeited (Code Sec. 62(a)(9)).[22]

> **Example:** Tom Smith opened a four-year time savings account in January 2006. He was credited with $400 in interest earned for 2006 and reported this income on his 2006 return. He withdrew the funds in October 2007. This premature withdrawal triggered a penalty provision so that he received only $230 of interest for 2006, plus $195 in interest earned on the account for 2007. Thus, he has incurred a loss of $170 ($400 of interest reported for 2006 less $230 actually received with respect to that year). This $170 loss should be claimed on his 2007 return. He should also report the $195 in interest earned for 2007 on his 2007 return.

The necessary information is provided on Form 1099-INT. In addition, the deduction must be claimed on Form 1040 or 1040A; no deduction is available on Form 1040EZ.

1121. Wagering Loss. Losses from wagering are deductible to the extent of the gains from wagering, regardless of the legality of the activity under local law (Code Sec. 165(d)).[23] A professional gambler may deduct losses directly from gambling income. A nonprofessional gambler must include all gambling income in gross income but can claim the losses only as an itemized deduction on Schedule A (Form 1040).[24]

Casualty Losses

1124. Casualty Loss. Code Sec. 165(c)(3) limits any loss, in the case of nonbusiness property of individuals, to that arising from fire, storm, shipwreck or other casualty, or from theft.[25] Each loss is subject to a $100 floor (see ¶ 1134), and total losses are deductible only to the extent that the total loss amount for the year exceeds 10 percent of adjusted gross income (AGI) (see ¶ 1137). Additionally, an individual cannot claim a casualty loss deduction for damage to insured property unless a timely insurance claim is filed (Code Sec. 165(h)(4)(E)).[26] Casualty and theft losses are reported on Form 4684, Casualties and Thefts.

A loss from a casualty arises from an event due to some sudden, unexpected, or unusual cause.[27] Damage to nonbusiness property caused by hurricane,[28] flood,[29] quarry blast,[30] vandalism,[31] sonic boom,[32] earthquake,[33] or earthslide[34] is deductible. Loss to shoreline buildings and structures from battering by waves and winds or flooding of buildings, but not damage from gradual erosion or inundation, is a casualty loss.[35] Damage or loss to property caused by an unusual and unprecedented drought can be treated as a casualty loss.[36] Although cash or property received as compensation for, or to repair or replace, damaged property reduces the amount of the loss,[37] the deduction will not be reduced by excludable gifts received by a disaster victim, even if such gifts are used to rehabilitate the property.[38]

Footnote references are to paragraphs of the 2008 Standard Federal Tax Reports.

[20] ¶ 9902.27, ¶ 20,620.627
[21] ¶ 9901
[22] ¶ 6002
[23] ¶ 9802, ¶ 10,105.30
[24] ¶ 10,105.01
[25] ¶ 9802
[26] ¶ 9802, ¶ 10,005.051

[27] ¶ 10,005.023
[28] ¶ 10,005.42
[29] ¶ 10,005.33
[30] ¶ 10,005.56
[31] ¶ 10,005.85
[32] ¶ 10,005.4645
[33] ¶ 10,005.18

[34] ¶ 10,005.63
[35] ¶ 10,005.466
[36] ¶ 10,005.17
[37] ¶ 10,005.039
[38] ¶ 10,005.117

A casualty includes damage to an automobile resulting from a collision, whether due to the faulty driving of another or the taxpayer, unless caused by the taxpayer's willful act (Reg. § 1.165-7(a)(3)).[39] The IRS takes the position that a casualty loss deduction for termite damage is not permitted because the "suddenness" test is not met, but some courts have allowed the deduction.[40] Storm damage to ornamental trees, as well as to orchards, is deductible as a casualty loss; however, loss of ornamental trees from Dutch elm or other diseases or insects lacks the "sudden force" requirement for classification as a casualty.[41] A loss sustained as a result of negligent workmanship in repairing a leaky roof is a casualty loss.[42]

A casualty loss of nonbusiness property, as well as of business property, can result in a net operating loss (NOL) (see ¶ 1176). The $100 floor and the 10-percent-of-AGI limitation are applied in the nonbusiness situation in determining an NOL.

If, as the result of insurance or other reimbursement, a taxpayer realizes a gain from a casualty or theft loss, recognition of the gain can be deferred under the involuntary conversion rules by making an election and purchasing qualifying replacement property within the applicable replacement period (see ¶ 1713).

1125. Embezzlement or Theft Loss. A loss from theft or embezzlement is generally deductible for the tax year in which the taxpayer discovers the loss (Code Sec. 165(e); Reg. § 1.165-8(a)(2)).[43] However, no deduction may be claimed in the year of discovery if a reimbursement claim exists with respect to which there is a reasonable prospect of recovery (Reg. § 1.165-1(d)(3)).[44] As with casualty losses, an individual cannot claim a deduction for theft of insured property unless a timely insurance claim is filed (Code Sec. 165(h)(4)(E)).[45] No deduction is available for lost or mislaid articles.[46] The deduction of theft losses is determined in the same way as other casualty losses (see ¶ 1131).

1128. Loss on Bank Deposits. Individuals may elect to treat the loss on a nonbusiness account in an insolvent or bankrupt financial institution as a personal casualty loss in the year in which the loss can reasonably be estimated (Code Sec. 165(l)).[47] If elected, the casualty loss is subject to the deduction limitations at ¶ 1134 and ¶ 1137. The election is made on Form 4684, Casualties and Thefts.

In lieu of the above election, an individual can elect to treat the loss as an ordinary loss arising from a transaction entered into for profit in the year the loss can be reasonably estimated, provided that no portion of the deposit is federally insured. The aggregate amount of such losses for any tax year with respect to which the ordinary loss election may be made is limited to $20,000 ($10,000 in the case of a married individual filing separately) for each financial institution and must be reduced by the amount of insurance proceeds that the taxpayer can reasonably expect to receive under state law (Code Sec. 165(l)(5)). The loss is deducted on Schedule A (Form 1040) as a miscellaneous itemized deduction subject to the two-percent-of-adjusted-gross-income floor (see ¶ 1011). The name of the financial institution and "Insolvent Financial Institution" should be written on the appropriate line of Schedule A. The calculation of the deducted loss should be included with the return (IRS Pub. 529).

Once made, these elections apply to all losses on deposits in the financial institution during the tax year and are revocable only with IRS consent. Taxpayers making the elections are prohibited from deducting such losses as bad debts (Code Sec. 165(l)(6) and (7)).[48] The elections cannot be made by an individual who is an owner of one percent or more of the value of the institution's stock, an officer of the institution, or a relative of an owner or officer (Code Sec. 165(l)(2)).

If these elections are not made, the loss is treated as a nonbusiness bad debt in the year of final determination of the actual loss and is deducted on Schedule D (Form 1040) as a short-term capital loss subject to the $3,000 ($1,500 for married individuals filing

---

Footnote references are to paragraphs of the 2008 Standard Federal Tax Reports.

[39] ¶ 10,004

[40] ¶ 10,005.671

[41] ¶ 10,005.68, ¶ 10,005.80— ¶ 10,005.817

[42] ¶ 10,005.904

[43] ¶ 9802, ¶ 10,100

[44] ¶ 9803

[45] ¶ 9802, ¶ 10,005.051

[46] ¶ 10,101.021

[47] ¶ 9802

[48] ¶ 9802

separate returns) annual limit (¶ 1145). See ¶ 1752 for the discussion of the limitation of capital losses.

1131. Amount of Casualty or Theft Loss. The amount of a casualty loss (business/income-producing property or nonbusiness) is the *lesser* of:

(1) the difference between the fair market value (FMV) of the property immediately before the casualty and its FMV immediately after; or

(2) the adjusted basis of the property immediately before the casualty (Reg. § 1.165-7(b)).[49]

However, if business or income-producing property is totally destroyed, and if the property's FMV immediately before the casualty is less than its adjusted basis, then the casualty loss is the adjusted basis of the property (Reg. § 1.165-7(b)).

When money is stolen, the theft loss is the amount stolen. The amount of a theft loss in the case of nonbusiness property other than money is the lesser of the value of the property or its adjusted basis. In the case of stolen business or income-producing property, the theft loss is the adjusted basis of the property stolen (Reg. § § 1.165-7(b) and 1.165-8(c)).[50]

A casualty loss is reduced by any salvage received. A casualty or theft loss is also reduced by any insurance or other compensation received (Code Sec. 165(a)). An individual cannot claim a personal casualty or theft loss to the extent the loss is covered by insurance unless a timely insurance claim is filed with respect to the loss (Code Sec. 165(h)(4)(E)).[51]

A personal casualty loss is subject to a $100 floor and to a 10-percent-of-adjusted-gross-income limitation in determining the allowable deduction (see ¶ 1134 and ¶ 1137). The $100 floor and AGI limitations do not apply to a business or income-producing property casualty or theft loss.

When there is damage to different kinds of *business* property, losses must be computed separately for each single, identifiable property damaged or destroyed. This rule does not apply to *nonbusiness* property. Thus, if a tree is blown down in the front yard of a taxpayer's residence, the loss is the difference in the FMV of the taxpayer's whole property before and after damage to the tree (Reg. § 1.165-7(b)).[52]

Hurricane Relief. Individuals who realized losses to their residences and personal belongings due to Hurricanes Katrina, Rita and Wilma can use a safe harbor method to determine their casualty or theft loss deduction (Rev. Proc. 2006-32).[53] There are three safe harbors available for personal-use residential real property: (1) the *insurance safe harbor method*, which uses the estimated loss determined in reports prepared by the taxpayer's insurance company; (2) the *contractor safe harbor method*, which uses the repair price specified in an itemized contract prepared by a licensed or registered contractor, but excluding the cost of improvements that increase the residence's value over its pre-hurricane value; and (3) the *cost indexes safe harbor method*, which uses one or more indexes provided by the IRS to determine the loss amount, reduced by the value of any no-cost repairs provided. For losses to personal belongings, the taxpayer may use the *personal belongings safe harbor method*, under which an item's replacement cost is determined and then reduced by 10 percent for every year the taxpayer owned the item; if an item is owned nine years or longer, its pre-hurricane FMV is 10 percent of the replacement cost. The personal belongings safe harbor is not allowed for certain vehicles or for antiques or other assets that maintain or increase their value over time.

The safe harbors are not mandatory, and a taxpayer can use the actual reduction in value if he or she has adequate substantiation. Taxpayers who use a residential safe harbor method should attach a statement to Form 4684, Casualties and Thefts. The safe harbors are effective for losses that arose in: (1) the Hurricane Katrina disaster area on or after August 25, 2005, and are due to Hurricane Katrina; (2) the Hurricane Rita disaster area on or after September 23, 2005, and are due to Hurricane Rita; or (3) the

---

Footnote references are to paragraphs of the 2008 Standard Federal Tax Reports.

[49] ¶ 10,004
[50] ¶ 10,004, ¶ 10,100, ¶ 10,101.113
[51] ¶ 9802
[52] ¶ 10,004
[53] ¶ 10,005.10

Hurricane Wilma disaster area on or after October 23, 2005, and are due to Hurricane Wilma.

1134. $100 Floor for Personal Casualty or Theft Loss. The deduction for a personal casualty or theft loss is limited to the amount that the loss from each casualty or theft exceeds $100 (Code Sec. 165(h)(1); Reg. § 1.165-7).[54] The $100 floor applies separately to the loss from each single casualty or theft. If several items of nonbusiness property are damaged or stolen in the course of a single casualty or theft, the $100 floor is applied only once against the sum of the allowable losses established for each item (Reg. § 1.165-7(b)(4)(ii)).[55] In the case of married taxpayers filing a joint return, *only one* $100 floor applies to each casualty or theft loss; if married taxpayers file separate returns, each spouse is subject to the $100 limitation for each casualty or theft loss (Reg. § 1.165-7(b)(4)(iii)).[56] When property is used for both business and personal purposes, the $100 floor applies only to the net loss attributable to that portion of the property used for personal purposes (Reg. § 1.165-7(b)(4)(iv)).[57]

Hurricane Relief. The $100 floor does not apply to personal casualty and theft losses which arose in: (1) the Hurricane Katrina disaster area on or after August 25, 2005, and are due to Hurricane Katrina; (2) the Hurricane Rita disaster area on or after September 23, 2005, and are due to Hurricane Rita; or (3) the Hurricane Wilma disaster area on or after October 23, 2005, and are due to Hurricane Wilma (Code Secs. 1400M and 1400S(b)).[58]

1137. Ten-Percent-of-Adjusted-Gross-Income Limitation. Gains and losses from personal casualties and thefts are separately netted without regard to holding periods for the initial determination of whether there was a gain or loss (Code Sec. 165(h)).[59] The $100 floor is applied before the above netting occurs. If the recognized gains exceed the recognized losses, all such gains and losses are treated as capital gains and losses; the gains must be recalculated by combining short-term gains with short-term losses and long-term gains with long-term losses. If the recognized losses exceed the recognized gains after netting, all gains and losses will be treated as ordinary gains and losses. Net personal casualty and theft losses are deductible for the tax year to the extent that they exceed the sum of personal casualty or theft gains plus 10 percent of adjusted gross income (AGI).

Form 4684, Casualties and Thefts, must be used to calculate and report gain or loss from a casualty or theft of nonbusiness property, and the calculated amounts must be entered on the appropriate Form 1040 schedule. Allowable personal casualty or theft gains are entered on Schedule D, while allowable losses are entered as an itemized deduction on Schedule A.

> **Example 1:** A taxpayer who has AGI of $50,000 (without regard to casualty gains or losses), a $25,000 casualty gain, and a $15,000 casualty loss (after the $100 floor) will report a $10,000 capital gain on Schedule D. The 10-percent floor does not apply in this computation.

> **Example 2:** A taxpayer who has AGI of $40,000, a $25,000 casualty loss (after the $100 floor), and a $15,000 casualty gain is allowed a $6,000 itemized deduction. The $10,000 loss resulting from netting the casualty gains against the casualty losses is deductible only to the extent that it exceeds 10 percent of AGI ($10,000 – $4,000 = $6,000).

Limitation for Estates and Trusts. The 10-percent-of-AGI limitation on personal casualty and theft losses applies to estates and trusts. AGI is computed in the same manner as it is for individuals, except that estates and trusts are allowed to deduct their administration expenses in arriving at AGI (Code Sec. 165(h)(4)(C)).[60] No deduction for a personal casualty or theft loss may be taken if, at the time of filing a decedent's return, the loss has been claimed for estate tax purposes (Code Sec. 165(h)(4)(D)).[61] See ¶ 531.

Footnote references are to paragraphs of the 2008 Standard Federal Tax Reports.

[54] ¶ 9802, ¶ 10,004   [57] ¶ 10,004   [60] ¶ 9802
[55] ¶ 10,004   [58] ¶ 32,478, ¶ 32,508   [61] ¶ 9802
[56] ¶ 10,004   [59] ¶ 9802

Hurricane Relief. The 10-percent-of-AGI floor does not apply to personal casualty and theft losses which arose in: (1) the Hurricane Katrina disaster area on or after August 25, 2005, and are due to Hurricane Katrina; (2) the Hurricane Rita disaster area on or after September 23, 2005, and are due to Hurricane Rita; or (3) the Hurricane Wilma disaster area on or after October 23, 2005, and are due to Hurricane Wilma. The 10-percent floor must still be determined for other losses, but without regard to Hurricane Katrina, Rita or Wilma disaster area losses (Code Secs. 1400M and 1400S(b)).[62]

1139. Basis of Damaged Property. The basis of damaged property is decreased by: (1) the amount of any insurance or other reimbursement and (2) the amount of the *deductible* loss (Rev. Rul. 71-161).[63] Any amount spent to restore the property is added back to basis (Reg. § 1.165-1(c); IRS Pub. 547).[64]

1141. Disaster Loss. If a taxpayer sustains a loss from a disaster in an area subsequently determined by the President of the United States to warrant federal assistance, a special rule may help the taxpayer to cushion his or her loss (Code Sec. 165(i)).[65] This special disaster loss treatment is also available with respect to a personal residence rendered unsafe by a disaster in a presidentially-designated area and ordered to be demolished or relocated by the state or local government (Code Sec. 165(k)).[66]

The taxpayer has the option of:

(1) deducting the loss on the tax return for the year in which the loss occurred or

(2) electing to deduct the loss on the return for the preceding tax year.

The election to deduct a 2007 disaster loss in 2006 must be made on or before the due date (without extensions) of the taxpayer's 2007 return (April 15, 2008, for calendar-year individuals; March 17, 2008, for calendar-year corporations). The loss may be claimed by filing an amended 2006 return (see ¶ 2759). Although Reg. § 1.165-11(e) states that revocation must be made within 90 days after election, the Tax Court has held that revocation of such an election may be made any time before expiration of the time for filing the return for the year of the loss.[67]

The calculation of the deduction for a disaster loss follows the same rules as those for any other personal casualty loss. (See ¶ 1134 and ¶ 1137 for special calculation rules regarding the Hurricane Katrina, Rita and Wilma disaster areas.) However, if the taxpayer elects to claim a disaster loss on the return for the year immediately preceding the loss year, the 10-percent-of-adjusted-gross-income (AGI) limitation is determined with respect to the preceding year's AGI.

The IRS is not prohibited from issuing guidance or other rules allowing an appraisal used to secure a loan or loan guarantee from the federal government to be used to establish the amount of a disaster loss for tax purposes. Should the IRS authorize a new valuation method, it would apply in a presidentially-declared disaster area (Code Sec. 165(i)(4)).

Gulf Opportunity (GO) Zone Public Utility Disaster Losses. A taxpayer can elect to deduct a disaster loss for public utility property located in the GO Zone that was damaged by Hurricane Katrina in the fifth tax year before the tax year in which the disaster occurred (Code Secs. 1400M and 1400N(o)).[68] An application for a tentative carryback adjustment for any prior tax year affected by the carryback may be made (see ¶ 1173). The statute of limitations on any resulting refund or credit claim will not expire earlier than one year after December 21, 2005. The taxpayer is not entitled to interest on any resulting overpayment. If eligible, the taxpayer can elect either the five-year carryback or specified loss treatment for NOL purposes (see ¶ 1179), but not both. The treatment applies to tax years ending on or after August 28, 2005.

Footnote references are to paragraphs of the 2008 Standard Federal Tax Reports.

[62] ¶ 32,478, ¶ 32,508
[63] ¶ 10,005.16
[64] ¶ 9803
[65] ¶ 9802, ¶ 10,201.25
[66] ¶ 9802
[67] ¶ 10,200, ¶ 10,201.13
[68] ¶ 32,478, ¶ 32,483

Bad Debts

1145. Business Bad Debts. Business bad debts, which arise from the taxpayer's trade or business, differ from nonbusiness bad debts (see ¶ 1169). Debts from a trade or business can be deducted when and to the extent that they become partly or totally worthless and are generally deductible from gross income (Code Sec. 166).[69] A "business debt" is a debt: (1) created or acquired in connection with the trade or business of the taxpayer who is claiming the deduction or (2) the worthlessness of which has been incurred in the taxpayer's trade or business (Reg. § 1.166-5(b)).[70] A business bad debt deduction, however, is not available to shareholders who have advanced money to a corporation as a contribution to capital,[71] or to creditors who hold a debt that is evidenced by a bond, debenture, note, or other evidence of indebtedness that is issued by a corporation or by a governmental unit, with interest coupons or in registered form (Code Secs. 165(g)(2)(C) and 166(e)).[72] (See ¶ 1764 for discussion of loss from worthless securities.) Nonbusiness bad debts are treated as short-term capital losses, subject to a $3,000 per year deduction limitation ($1,500 per year for married individuals filing separate returns) (see ¶ 1752 and ¶ 1757), and are deductible only when totally worthless.

Guarantors. A noncorporate taxpayer who incurs a loss arising from his or her guaranty of a loan is entitled to deduct the loss only if the guaranty arose out of his or her trade or business or in a transaction entered into for profit. If the guaranty was connected with a trade or business, the resulting loss is an ordinary loss (business bad debt). If the guaranty was not connected with a true trade or business but was profit inspired, the resulting loss is a short-term capital loss (nonbusiness bad debt). No deduction is available if the guaranty payment does not fall within the above categories, if there is no legal obligation on the taxpayer to make the guaranty payment, or if the guaranty was entered into after the debt became worthless (Reg. § 1.166-9).[73]

Employee Loans. An employee's rendering of services for pay is a trade or business for purposes of the bad debt provisions. Therefore, a loan to an employer to protect a job can give rise to a business bad debt deduction if the employer defaults. If a loan by a shareholder-employee is intended to protect the shareholder's job rather than to protect the shareholder's investment in the company, the failure to repay the loan results in a business bad debt deduction. The larger the shareholder's investment, the smaller his or her salary, and the larger his or her other sources of income, the more likely that a dominant nonbusiness motive existed for making the loan.[74]

Dominant Motivation Test. Since the tax treatment accorded business bad debts and nonbusiness bad debts differs, the taxpayer must show that his or her dominant motivation in making the payment was business related in order to obtain the more favorable tax treatment.[75]

1148. Time and Method of Deduction. Generally, bad debts are deductible in the tax year in which they become worthless (Code Sec. 166(a)).[76] A cash-basis taxpayer can deduct a bad debt only if an actual cash loss has been sustained or if the amount deducted was included in income. Nearly all accrual-basis taxpayers must use the specific chargeoff method to deduct business bad debts, which is based on actual worthlessness and is not applicable merely because the taxpayer gives up attempts to collect (see ¶ 1157). A worthless debt arising from unpaid wages, rent, interest, or a similar item is not deductible unless the income that such item represents has been reported for income tax purposes by a taxpayer (Reg. §§ 1.166-1(e), 1.166-3 and 1.166-6(a)(2); *Federal Home Loan Mortgage Corporation*, 121 TC 279, CCH Dec. 55,333).[77]

1151. Secured Bad Debt. When secured or mortgaged property is sold either to the secured party or to a third party for less than the amount of the debt, the creditor is

---

Footnote references are to paragraphs of the 2008 Standard Federal Tax Reports.

[69] ¶ 10,602
[70] ¶ 10,691
[71] ¶ 10,650.7301
[72] ¶ 9802, ¶ 10,602

[73] ¶ 10,753
[74] ¶ 10,700.241
[75] ¶ 10,700.241, ¶ 10,700.62
[76] ¶ 10,602

[77] ¶ 10,603, ¶ 10,605, ¶ 10,650.023, ¶ 10,701, ¶ 10,750.16

entitled to a bad debt deduction in an amount equal to the difference between the sale price and the amount of the debt, to the extent that the creditor can show that such difference is wholly or partially uncollectible. No bad debt deduction is allowed if a mortgage is foreclosed and the creditor buys the mortgaged property at a price equal to the unpaid indebtedness. However, loss or gain is realized on the transaction and is measured by the difference between the amount of the obligations of the debtor that are applied to the purchase or bid price of the property and the fair market value of the property, to the extent that the obligations are capital or represent items the income from which has been returned by the creditor (Reg. § 1.166-6).[78] As to repossession of property sold on the installment plan, see ¶ 1838 and ¶ 1841.

1157. Reserve for Bad Debts. Nearly all accrual-basis taxpayers must use the specific chargeoff method for receivables that become uncollectible in whole or in part. Small banks can deduct a reasonable addition to a reserve for bad debts, in lieu of any bad debt deduction under Code Sec. 166(a). Small banks and thrift institutions that qualify as small banks can use the experience method of accounting. Large banks and thrift institutions that are treated as large banks must use the specific chargeoff method (Code Secs. 585 and 593(f), (g)).[79]

1160. Guarantor's Reserve for Bad Debts. The reserve method is not available to dealers who guarantee, endorse, or provide indemnity agreements with respect to debts owed to others. Their losses are not deductible until sustained. If the dealer is subrogated to the rights of the original creditor, the loss will be deductible at the time the subrogation rights become wholly or partially worthless.[80]

1166. Debts Owed by Political Parties. Generally, no deduction is allowable for a worthless debt owed by a political party. However, banks and accrual-basis taxpayers who are in the business of providing goods and services (such as polling, media, or organizational services) to political campaigns and candidates may be allowed to deduct such bad debts (Code Sec. 271).[81]

1169. Nonbusiness Bad Debts. Nonbusiness bad debts do not include debts created or acquired in connection with a trade or business of the taxpayer, or losses from worthless debts incurred in the taxpayer's trade or business (Code Sec. 166(d); Reg. § 1.166-5).[82] (See ¶ 1145 for a discussion of business bad debts.) If a nonbusiness bad debt becomes *entirely* worthless within the tax year, the loss is treated as a short-term capital loss, regardless of how old the debt is. No deduction is permitted unless and until the debt becomes totally worthless.[83] For limitations on deduction of a capital loss, see ¶ 1752. For worthlessness of a debt evidenced by a bond or other security of a corporation or a government, see ¶ 1917.

Net Operating Losses

1173. Application of Net Business Loss. Nearly every taxpayer is allowed to carry back a net operating loss (NOL) from a trade or business to apply as a deduction against prior income and to deduct from succeeding years' income any unabsorbed loss (Code Sec. 172(b)).[84] Taxpayers entitled to the carryback and carryover privilege include:

    (1) corporations, other than the exceptions noted below;

    (2) individuals;

    (3) estates and trusts;

    (4) common trust fund participants; and

    (5) partners who may deduct allocable partnership loss.

Among those entities excepted from this privilege are regulated investment companies (Code Sec. 852(b)(2)(B)) and life insurance companies (Code Sec. 805(b)(4)).[85] Generally, no NOL deductions are available to partnerships and S corporations, but their

---

Footnote references are to paragraphs of the 2008 Standard Federal Tax Reports.

[78] ¶ 10,701, ¶ 10,670.01, ¶ 10,750.01

[79] ¶ 10,690.01, ¶ 23,650, ¶ 23,710

[80] ¶ 10,690.01, ¶ 10,800.01

[81] ¶ 14,306, ¶ 14,308.01

[82] ¶ 10,602, ¶ 10,691

[83] ¶ 10,602, ¶ 10,691

[84] ¶ 12,002

[85] ¶ 25,770, ¶ 26,420

investors may use their distributive shares to calculate individual NOLs (see ¶ 321 and ¶ 417).

Forms. Individuals, estates, and trusts compute the NOL for the loss year and the carrybacks and any carryforward on Form 1045, Application for Tentative Refund (Code Sec. 6411; Reg. § 1.6411-1). Form 1045 is filed to claim a quick refund for the excess taxes paid in the carryback years that are attributable to the NOL. Form 1045, however, may be used only if filed within one year after the close of the NOL year (but not before Form 1040 or Form 1041 for the NOL year is filed). Form 1045 is processed within the later of 90 days after being filed or 90 days after the last day of the month that includes the due date (including extensions) for filing Form 1040 or Form 1041 for the loss year (Code Sec. 6411(b)).[86]

As an alternative to Form 1045, an individual may file Form 1040X for each carryback year to claim a refund. Form 1040X must generally be filed within three years after the due date of the return for the NOL year. Estates and trusts file an amended Form 1041, U.S. Income Tax Return for Estates and Trusts. (There is no Form "1041X"; use Form 1041 as issued for the carryback year and check the "amended return" box.) If an amended return is filed the taxpayer must still attach the NOL computations using the Form 1045 computation schedules. The IRS generally processes an amended return within six months after filing.

Corporations may file for a quick refund using Form 1139, Corporation Application for Tentative Refund.[87] Form 1139 also needs to be filed within one year after the close of the NOL year (but not before the return for the NOL year is filed). A separate Form 1120X may be filed in place of Form 1139 for each carryback year, generally within three years after the due date of the return for the NOL year.

A corporation that expects an NOL in the current tax year may file Form 1138, Extension of Time for Payment of Taxes by a Corporation Expecting a Net Operating Loss Carryback, to extend the time for payment of the tax for the immediately preceding tax year (Code Sec. 6164; Reg. § 1.6164-1).[88] The extension applies only to payments of tax that are required to be paid after Form 1138 is filed. The extension expires at the end of the month in which the return for the tax year of the expected NOL is required to be filed (including extensions). However, if the corporation files Form 1139 before the extension period ends, the time for payments is further extended until the date that the IRS mails notice that it has allowed or disallowed the application (Reg. § 1.6164-5).[89]

Forms 1045 and 1139 may also be used to claim a quick refund of taxes from the carryback of a net *capital* loss (corporations only), unused general business credit, or claim of right adjustment under Code Sec. 1341(b)(1).

For additional information on Forms 1045 and 1139, see ¶ 2773.

1176. Net Operating Loss Defined. Simply stated, an NOL is the excess of allowable deductions over gross income, computed under the law in effect for the loss year, with the required adjustments (Code Sec. 172(c) and (d); Reg. §§ 1.172-2 and 1.172-3).[90]

Noncorporate Taxpayers. The following adjustments are made with respect to noncorporate taxpayers:

(1) No deduction for NOL carryovers or carrybacks from other years is allowed.

(2) An individual may not take any personal or dependency exemptions into account, and an estate or a trust cannot take the deduction available to it in lieu of the deduction for personal exemptions.

(3) Nonbusiness capital losses are deductible only to the extent of nonbusiness capital gains. Business capital losses are deductible only to the extent of the sum of (a) business capital gains and (b) any nonbusiness capital gains that remain

---

Footnote references are to paragraphs of the 2008 Standard Federal Tax Reports.

[86] ¶ 12,014.075, ¶ 38,720, ¶ 38,722
[87] ¶ 12,014.075

[88] ¶ 12,014.0751, ¶ 37,240, ¶ 37,241
[89] ¶ 37,247

[90] ¶ 12,002, ¶ 12,004, ¶ 12,005

after deducting nonbusiness capital losses and other nonbusiness deductions (item (4), below) (Reg. § 1.172-3(a)(2)).[91] The 50-percent exclusion for gain from qualified small business stock under Code Sec. 1202 is not allowed (Code Sec. 172(d)(2)(B)).

(4) Nonbusiness deductions are allowed only to the extent of nonbusiness income (including net nonbusiness capital gains). Further, any excess may not be allowed against business capital gains (and thereby increase the NOL). Generally, nonbusiness income includes income from passive investments, such as interest, dividends, annuities, endowment income, etc. Salary is considered business income. A loss on a rental property is considered a business loss.[92] The nonbusiness deduction for a taxpayer who itemizes is the total of his or her itemized deductions other than the personal or business-related casualty loss deduction. For one who does not itemize, the standard deduction is a nonbusiness deduction. Deductible contributions to a retirement plan by a self-employed individual on his or her own behalf are considered nonbusiness deductions (Code Sec. 172(d)(4); Reg. § 1.172-3(a)(3)(iv)).[93]

(5) The domestic production activities deduction (i.e., the manufacturer's deduction) (see ¶ 980A and following) is not allowed (Code Sec. 172(d)(7)).[94]

Corporations. The following adjustments are made with respect to corporations:

(1) No deduction for NOL carryovers or carrybacks from other years is allowed.

(2) A corporation is entitled to deductions for dividends received from a domestic corporation, those received on certain preferred stock of public utilities, those received from certain foreign corporations, and those paid on certain preferred stock of public utilities, without regard to the limitations (based on taxable income) imposed on such deductions in computing taxable income (see ¶ 237 and ¶ 241) (Code Sec. 172(d)(5); Reg. § 1.172-2).[95]

(3) The domestic production activities deduction (i.e., the manufacturer's deduction) (see ¶ 980A and following) is not allowed (Code Sec. 172(d)(7)).[96]

1179. Carryover and Carryback. The NOL carryback or carryover is generally that part of the NOL that has not previously been applied against income for other carryback or carryover years (Code Sec. 172(b)(2); Reg. § 1.172-4).[97] In computing the taxable income of an intervening year that must be subtracted from an NOL to determine the portion still available to carry to a subsequent year, the following adjustments must be made (Reg. § 1.172-5):[98]

(1) The NOL deduction for the intervening year is computed by taking into account only carrybacks and carryovers from tax years *preceding* the loss year.

(2) For taxpayers other than corporations, capital losses are deductible only to the extent of capital gains.

(3) Personal and dependency exemptions are not allowed.

(4) The domestic production activities deduction (i.e., the manufacturer's deduction) (see ¶ 980A and following) is not allowed (Code Sec. 172(d)(7)).

Generally, net operating losses can be carried back to the two years preceding the loss year and then forward to the 20 years following the loss year. Further, for net operating losses that arose in tax years beginning before August 6, 1997, taxpayers could have carried back an NOL to the three years preceding the loss year and then forward to 15 years following the loss year. No deduction is allowed in the year the loss is incurred (Code Sec. 172(b); Reg. § 1.172-4).[99] A three-year carryback period is retained for: (1) the portion of an NOL that relates to casualty and theft losses of individual taxpayers and (2) NOLs that are attributable to presentially-declared disas-

---

Footnote references are to paragraphs of the 2008 Standard Federal Tax Reports.

[91] ¶ 12,005, ¶ 12,014.031
[92] ¶ 12,014.5085
[93] ¶ 12,002, ¶ 12,005, ¶ 12,014.033
[94] ¶ 12,002
[95] ¶ 12,002, ¶ 12,004
[96] ¶ 12,002
[97] ¶ 12,002, ¶ 12,006, ¶ 12,014.037
[98] ¶ 12,007, ¶ 12,014.041
[99] ¶ 12,002, ¶ 12,006

ters in the case of a small business or of a farming business that elects to forgo the five-year carryback period for a farming loss (Code Sec. 172(b)(1)(F)). See *"Farming Loss,"* below.

Election to Forgo Carryback. A taxpayer may elect to waive the entire carryback period (Code Sec. 172(b)(3)).[100] If the election is made, the loss may be carried forward only. The election must be made by the return due date (including extensions) for the tax year of the NOL. The election is irrevocable. The election may also be made on an amended return filed within six months of the due date of an original timely return (excluding extensions). Refer to the instructions for Form 1139, Corporation Application for Tentative Refund, or Form 1045, Application for Tentative Refund, for specific statement requirements.

Special Rules for Gulf Opportunity (GO) Zone Losses. A five-year NOL carryback period is available for qualified Gulf Opportunity Zone ("GO Zone") losses in any tax year ending on or after August 28, 2005 (Code Secs. 1400M and 1400N(k)).[101] A "qualified GO Zone loss" is the *lesser* of:

(1) the excess of the NOLs for the tax year, over the specified liability loss for the tax year to which a 10-year carryback applies or

(2) the total amount of deductions in the tax year for:

(a) a qualified GO Zone casualty loss, which is any uncompensated Section 1231 loss (see ¶ 1747) of property in the GO Zone, which is due to Hurricane Katrina and for which a deduction is allowed for the tax year;

(b) moving expenses paid or incurred after August 27, 2005, and before January 1, 2008, of the taxpayer's employee or prospective employee who (i) lived in the GO Zone before August 28, 2005; (ii) could not stay in his or her abode due to Hurricane Katrina; and (iii) after the moving expense, has his or her principal workplace in the GO Zone;

(c) temporary housing expenses paid or incurred after August 27, 2005, and before January 1, 2008, to house any employee of the taxpayer whose principal workplace is in the GO Zone;

(d) depreciation or amortization of certain qualified GO Zone property (see ¶ 1237) for the tax year placed in service; and

(e) repair expenses (including debris removal expenses) paid or incurred after August 27, 2005, and before January 1, 2008, due to Hurricane Katrina damage and in connection with property in the GO Zone (Code Sec. 1400N(k)(2)).

Qualified GO Zone losses are not included in determining any three-year carryback (discussed above) for the tax year and are not subject to the 90-percent alternative tax net operating loss limitation (see ¶ 1430). Qualified GO Zone losses are treated as separate NOLs for ordering purposes, and the taxpayer can elect out of five-year carryback treatment.

For purposes of the qualified GO Zone casualty loss, and the depreciation or amortization of qualified GO Zone property, the affected property does not include property used in connection with golf courses, country clubs, massage parlors, hot tub or suntan facilities, liquor stores, or gambling or animal racing property (Code Sec. 1400N(p)).

Short Tax Years. If a NOL arising in a short tax year that results from a change in accounting period is greater than either $50,000 or the NOL for a full 12-month period beginning with the first day of the short period, a taxpayer may be prevented from carrying the NOL back to earlier years (Rev. Proc. 2003-34, Sec. 4.01, modifying Rev. Proc. 2002-37, Sec. 6.08 and Rev. Proc. 2002-39, Sec. 5.04).[102]

Specified Liability Losses. Special carryback periods apply in the case of specified liability losses. A specified liability loss (product liability loss) is a separate NOL that can be carried back 10 years from the tax year of the loss (Code Sec. 172(b)(1)(C); Notice

---

Footnote references are to paragraphs of the 2008 Standard Federal Tax Reports.

[100] ¶ 12,002   [101] ¶ 32,478, ¶ 32,483   [102] ¶ 12,014.30

2005-20).[103] For ordering purposes, the specified liability loss is treated as a separate NOL to be taken into account *after* the remaining portion of the NOL for the tax year (Code Sec. 172(f)(5)). A casualty loss of certain public utility property located in the GO Zone, and arising in tax years ending on or after August 28, 2005, can be treated as a specified liability loss if: (1) a deduction for the loss is allowed for the tax year; (2) the loss is due to Hurricane Katrina; and (3) the taxpayer elects this treatment (Code Secs. 1400M and 1400N(j)).[104] A taxpayer that elects this treatment is not eligible for the five-year NOL carryback for qualified GO Zone losses (see *"Special Rules for Gulf Opportunity (GO) Zone Losses,"* above), and cannot elect the five-year carryback for GO Zone public utility disaster losses (see ¶ 1141).

Real Estate Investment Trusts. A real estate investment trust (REIT) generally cannot carry back an NOL to a tax year in which the entity operated as a REIT (Code Sec. 172(b)(1)(B); Reg. § 1.172-10).[105]

Corporate Equity Reduction Transactions (CERTs). A C corporation may not carry back a portion of its NOL if $1 million or more of interest expense is incurred in a "major stock acquisition" of another corporation or in an "excess distribution" by the corporation (Code Sec. 172(b)(1)(E) and (h)).[106] The amount subject to the limitation is the lesser of: (1) the corporation's deductible interest expense allocable to the CERT or (2) the amount by which the corporation's interest expense for the current tax year exceeds the average interest expense for the three tax years preceding the tax year in which the CERT occurs. The portion of the NOL that cannot be carried back may be carried forward.

Farming Loss. Effective for NOLs for tax years beginning after 1997, a farming loss may be carried back for five years (Code Sec. 172(b)(1)(G) and (i)). This loss is the amount of *any* NOL attributable to the income and deductions of a farming business. A taxpayer may elect to treat a farming loss as if it were not a farming loss. In this case, the two-year carryback period generally applies (Code Sec. 172(i)(3)).[107] For ordering purposes, the farming loss is treated as a separate NOL to be taken into account *after* the remaining portion of the NOL for the tax year (Code Sec. 172(i)(2)).

Timber Property in Gulf Hurricane Zones. Certain taxpayers may treat a loss attributable to a qualified timber property as a farming loss eligible for the five-year NOL carryback for property located in the GO Zone, the portion of the Rita GO Zone that is not part of the main GO Zone, or the Wilma GO Zone (Code Secs. 1400M and 1400N(i)).[108] The taxpayer must have held the property on: (1) August 28, 2005, for property in the GO Zone; (2) September 23, 2005, for property (other than property in the GO Zone) in the portion of the Rita GO Zone that is not part of the GO Zone; or (3) October 23, 2005, for property (other than property in the GO Zone or Rita GO Zone) in the Wilma GO Zone. Attributable income and deductions are accounted for to the extent they are allocable to the portion of the tax year that begins on or after the zone's applicable date and before January 1, 2007. This treatment does not apply publicly-traded corporations, real estate investment trusts, or taxpayers that held more than 500 acres of qualified property on the applicable date.

Electric Utilities. Electric utilities can elect a five-year carryback period for NOLs generated for tax years ending in 2003, 2004, and 2005, in an amount based on the taxpayer's pre-election investment in certain electric transmission or pollution control equipment. A taxpayer can make the election for any tax year ending after 2005 and before 2009. If the five-year period is elected, the carried-back NOL amount is limited to 20 percent of the sum of electric transmission property capital expenditures and pollution control facility capital expenditures for the tax year preceding the tax year for which the election is made. Only one election can be made with respect to any NOL for a tax year, and an election cannot be made for more than one tax year beginning in any calendar year (Code Sec. 172(b)(1)(I)).[109]

Footnote references are to paragraphs of the 2008 Standard Federal Tax Reports.

[103] ¶ 12,002, ¶ 12,014.3103   [106] ¶ 12,002   [109] ¶ 12,002
[104] ¶ 32,478, ¶ 32,483   [107] ¶ 12,002
[105] ¶ 12,002, ¶ 12,012   [108] ¶ 32,478, ¶ 32,483

1182. Net Operating Loss Deduction. The NOL deduction that is subtracted from gross income is simply the sum of the carrybacks and carryovers to the tax year (Reg. § 1.172-1).[110] No adjustments need be made. However, certain adjustments must be made in determining the income for any year that must be offset against carryovers or carrybacks to find the portion of the loss that will still be available to carry to a later year (see ¶ 1179).

1185. Carryovers and Carrybacks Between Predecessors and Successors. As a general rule, an NOL may be carried back or carried over only by the taxpayer who sustained the loss. A beneficiary of an estate or trust, however, is entitled to any carryover amount remaining unused after the last tax year of the estate or trust (Code Sec. 642(h); Reg. § 1.642(h)-1; Code Sec. 1398(g) and (j)).[111] A successor corporation is allowed to carry over the NOL and certain other items of its predecessor under specified conditions (see ¶ 2277).

A divorced taxpayer who suffered an NOL in a year when he or she was single can carry it back to his or her portion of income in previous years when a joint return was filed. Only the taxpayer's signature is necessary for a valid refund claim.[112]

1188. Recomputation After Carryback. In a year in which an NOL is carried back, any income, deductions, or credits that are based on or limited to a percentage of adjusted gross income (AGI) must be recomputed based on AGI after applying the NOL deduction for the carryback year. The charitable contribution deduction, however, is not recomputed. Taxable income is recomputed taking into account the NOL and the preceding adjustments. Income tax, alternative minimum tax, and any credits that are based on or limited to the amount of tax are then recomputed (Reg. § 1.172-5).[113]

Hobby Losses

1195. Hobby Expenses and Losses. Losses incurred by individuals, S corporations, partnerships, and estates and trusts that are attributable to an activity not engaged in for profit—so-called "hobby losses"—are generally deductible only to the extent of income produced by the activity (Code Sec. 183; Reg. § 1.183-1—Reg. § 1.183-4).[114] Some expenses that are deductible whether or not they are incurred in connection with a hobby, such as taxes, interest, and casualty losses, are deductible even if they exceed hobby income. These expenses, however, reduce the amount of hobby income against which hobby expenses can be offset (Code Sec. 183(b)(1)).[115] The hobby expenses then offset the reduced income, in the following order: (1) operating expenses other than amounts resulting in a basis adjustment and (2) depreciation and other basis adjustment items (Reg. § 1.183-1).[116] The itemized deduction for hobby expenses to the extent of income derived from the activity is subject to the two-percent floor on miscellaneous itemized deductions (see ¶ 1011).

An activity is presumed not to be a hobby if profits result in any three of five consecutive tax years ending with the tax year in question, unless the IRS proves otherwise (Code Sec. 183(d)).[117] An activity involving the breeding, training, showing, or racing of horses is presumed not to be a hobby if profits result in two out of seven consecutive years. A special election on Form 5213, Election to Postpone Determination as To Whether the Presumption Applies That an Activity Is Engaged in for Profit, permits suspension of the presumption until after the fourth (or sixth, for horse breeding, training, showing or racing) tax year after the tax year in which the taxpayer first engages in the activity. A taxpayer need not waive the statute of limitations for unrelated items on the return in order to take advantage of the presumption (Code Sec. 183(e)).[118]

Footnote references are to paragraphs of the 2008 Standard Federal Tax Reports.

[110] ¶ 12,003
[111] ¶ 24,280, ¶ 24,301, ¶ 32,410
[112] ¶ 12,014.443

[113] ¶ 12,007, ¶ 12,014.041
[114] ¶ 12,170, ¶ 12,171— ¶ 12,176
[115] ¶ 12,170, ¶ 12,177.01

[116] ¶ 12,171, ¶ 12,177.035
[117] ¶ 12,170
[118] ¶ 12,170, ¶ 12,177.045

Chapter 12

DEPRECIATION, AMORTIZATION AND DEPLETION

Allowance for Depreciation

1201. Property Subject to Depreciation. Taxpayers may deduct a reasonable allowance for the exhaustion, wear and tear of property used in a trade or business, or of property held for the production of income (Reg. § 1.167(a)-1).[1] Depreciation is not allowable for property used solely for personal purposes, such as a residence.

Converted Residence. When an individual vacates a principal residence and offers it for sale, it may be depreciable for the period before the sale if the individual is seeking a profit based on the post-conversion appreciation in value.[2] MACRS must be used to depreciate a residence converted to business use after 1986. For computation of depreciation when a home is used partly for business or rental purposes, see ¶ 961 and following. For depreciable basis, see ¶ 1203.

Estates and Trusts. For depreciation by an estate or trust, see ¶ 530.

Inventory. Depreciation is allowed for tangible property, but not for inventories, stock in trade, land apart from its improvements, or a depletable natural resource (Reg. § 1.167(a)-2).[3]

Farmers. Farm buildings and other physical farm property (except land) are depreciable. Livestock acquired for work, breeding, or dairy purposes may be depreciated unless included in inventory (Reg. § 1.167(a)-6(b)).[4]

Footnote references are to paragraphs of the 2008 Standard Federal Tax Reports.

[1] ¶ 11,003
[2] ¶ 11,007.512
[3] ¶ 11,006
[4] ¶ 11,015

Intangibles. An intangible business asset that is not amortizable over 15 years under Code Sec. 197 (see ¶ 1288) may be amortized under Code Sec. 167, generally using the straight-line method, provided that it has an ascertainable value and useful life that can be measured with reasonable accuracy.[5] Certain intangibles with no ascertainable useful life that are created by a taxpayer on or after December 31, 2003 may be amortized over 15 years (Reg. § 1.167(a)-3(b)). See ¶ 1288A.

Software. Certain depreciable computer software generally acquired after August 10, 1993, that is not an amortizable Code Sec. 197 intangible may be depreciated using the straight-line method over 36 months (Code Sec. 167(f)(1)).[6] See ¶ 980. Off-the-shelf computer software may be expensed under Code Sec. 179. See ¶ 1208.

Web Site Development Costs. The IRS has not issued formal guidance on the treatment of web site development costs. However, informal internal IRS guidance suggests that one appropriate approach is to treat these costs like an item of software and depreciate them over three years. It is clear, however, that taxpayers who pay large amounts to develop sophisticated sites have been allocating their costs to items such as software development (currently deductible like research and development costs under Code Sec. 174) and currently deductible advertising expense.[7]

Residential Mortgage Servicing Rights. Depreciable residential mortgage servicing rights that are not Code Sec. 197 intangibles may be depreciated under the straight-line method over 108 months (Code Sec. 167(f)(3)).[8]

Term Interests. No depreciation or amortization deduction is allowed for certain term interests in property for any period during which the remainder interest is held directly (or indirectly) by a related person (Code Sec. 167(e)).[9]

Methods. The Modified Accelerated Cost Recovery System (MACRS) (¶ 1236) applies to tangible property generally placed in service after 1986 and the Accelerated Cost Recovery System (ACRS) applies to property placed in service after 1980 and before 1987 (¶ 1252). Under MACRS and ACRS, the cost or other basis of an asset is generally recovered over a specific recovery period. Post-1980 depreciation on tangible assets first placed in service before 1981 is computed under the method elected for the years they were placed in service. For assets placed in service after 1970 and before 1981, the taxpayer had a choice of the Asset Depreciation Range (ADR) System[10] (¶ 1282) or the general depreciation rules (¶ 1216). For tangible assets first placed in service before 1971, the taxpayer could have elected the Class Life System (CLS)[11] for pre-1971 assets or the general depreciation rules. In no event may an asset that is not subject to MACRS or ACRS be depreciated below a reasonable salvage value (Reg. § 1.167(a)-1(a)).[12]

Depreciation based on a useful life is calculated over the estimated useful life of the asset while actually used by the taxpayer and not over the longer period of the asset's physical life (Reg. § 1.167(a)-1(b)).[13] For rules governing the depreciation of self-constructed assets, see the uniform capitalization rules at ¶ 990–¶ 999.

Form. Form 4562 is generally used to claim the depreciation or amortization deduction and is attached to the taxpayer's tax return. However, individuals and other noncorporate taxpayers (including S corporations) need not complete Form 4562 if their only depreciation (or amortization) deduction is for property (other than listed property (¶ 1211)) placed in service before the current tax year.

Basis for Depreciation

1203. Cost or Other Basis Recoverable Through Depreciation Allowance. Generally, the cost of a depreciable asset reduced by any amount claimed as an expense deduction under Code Sec. 179 or as first-year bonus depreciation may be recovered through depreciation. Other downward adjustments to cost to prevent a duplication of

---

Footnote references are to paragraphs of the 2008 Standard Federal Tax Reports.

[5] ¶ 11,009.015
[6] ¶ 11,002, ¶ 11,009.027
[7] ¶ 11,009.027, ¶ 13,709

[8] ¶ 11,002, ¶ 11,009.03
[9] ¶ 11,002, ¶ 11,049.035
[10] ¶ 11,029.021

[11] ¶ 11,031.021
[12] ¶ 11,003, ¶ 11,009.04
[13] ¶ 11,003, ¶ 11,005.021

benefits received from credits and deductions claimed with respect to the property in the tax year of purchase may also be necessary. For example, for the effect of the investment credit on depreciable basis, see ¶ 1360. When property held for personal use, such as a residence, is converted to business or income-producing use, the basis for depreciation is the lesser of the property's fair market value or adjusted basis on the date of conversion (Reg. § 1.167(g)-1; Reg. § 1.168(i)-4(b)).[14] In the case of a residence converted to business use after 1986, MACRS must be used.

When a building and land have been acquired for a lump sum, only the building is depreciated. The basis for depreciation cannot exceed the same proportion of the lump sum as the value of the building bore to the value of the entire property at the time of acquisition.

If property is subject to both depreciation and amortization, depreciation is allowable only for the portion that is not subject to the allowance for amortization and may be taken concurrently with amortization (Reg. § 1.167(a)-5).[15]

Proration of Depreciation Allowance

1206. Sale or Purchase During Tax Year. Depreciation begins in the tax year that an asset is placed in service and ends in the tax year that it is retired from service or is fully depreciated (Reg. § 1.167(a)-10).[16] Generally, an asset is considered placed in service when it is in a condition or state of readiness and availability for a specifically assigned function.

MACRS Depreciable Property. For tangible depreciable personal property placed in service after 1986, one-half year's depreciation is generally allowed, regardless of how long the property is held in the year it is placed in service or disposed of, unless the mid-quarter convention applies (¶ 1245). Special prorations by month (using a mid-month convention) are provided for depreciable real property (¶ 1243).

ACRS Recovery Property. For personal recovery property placed in service after 1980 and before 1987, one-half year's depreciation is allowed, regardless of how long it is held in the year that it is placed in service (see ¶ 1252). No deduction is allowed in the year of disposition of personal recovery property. Special prorations by month (using a mid-month convention) are provided for real recovery property (¶ 1261).

Pre-1981 Assets. For an asset purchased before 1981, only a part of a full year's depreciation was allowed in the year it was placed in service. The allowable deduction was computed by multiplying the first full year's depreciation allowance by the months the property was owned and dividing by 12. The same rule applies in the year of sale.[17]

Section 179 Expense Election

1208. Election to Expense Certain Depreciable Business Assets. An expense deduction is provided for taxpayers (other than estates, trusts or certain noncorporate lessors) who elect to treat the cost of qualifying property, called section 179 property, as an expense rather than a capital expenditure (Code Sec. 179).[18] The election, which is made on Form 4562, is generally attached to the taxpayer's original return (including a late-filed original return). However, for tax years beginning in 2003 through 2010, a taxpayer may make, revoke, or change an election without IRS consent on an amended return filed during the period prescribed for filing an amended return (i.e., generally, three years from the filing of the original return) (Code Sec. 179(c)(2), as amended by the Small Business and Work Opportunity Tax Act of 2007 (P.L. 110-28); Reg. § 1.179-5).[19]

For tax years beginning after 2010, an election not made on an original return must be made on an amended return filed by the due date of the original return (including extensions) unless permission is obtained. Permission to revoke or change an election is also required.

Footnote references are to paragraphs of the 2008 Standard Federal Tax Reports.

[14] ¶ 11,046, ¶ 11,007.045   [16] ¶ 11,024   [18] ¶ 12,120, ¶ 12,126
[15] ¶ 11,012, ¶ 11,014.021 [17] ¶ 11,025.03   [19] ¶ 12,120, ¶ 12,126.073

Dollar Limitation. The maximum Code Sec. 179 deduction is $125,000 for tax years beginning in 2007 and $128,000 for tax years beginning in 2008 (Code Sec. 179(b)(1), as amended by the Small Business and Work Opportunity Tax Act of 2007 (P.L. 110-28); Rev. Proc. 2007-66). The dollar limitation is adjusted for inflation for tax years beginning in 2008, 2009, and 2010. However for tax years beginning in 2011 and thereafter, the maximum deduction is reduced to $25,000 per year and not adjusted for inflation.

See ¶ 1214 below for a $25,000 Code Sec. 179 expensing limitation on certain sport utility vehicles, trucks, and vans.

Investment Limitation. The maximum Code Sec. 179 limitation is reduced dollar for dollar by the cost of qualified property placed in service during the tax over an investment limitation. For tax years beginning in 2007, the investment limitation is $500,000 (Code Sec. 179(b)(2), as amended by the Small Business and Work Opportunity Tax Act of 2007 (P.L. 110-28)). The investment limitation is $510,000 for tax years beginning in 2008 (Rev. Proc. 2007-66). The investment limit is adjusted for inflation in 2008, 2009, and 2010. However, for tax years beginning in 2011 and thereafter, the investment limitation is reduced to $200,000 per year and is not adjusted for inflation.

Taxable Income Limitation. The total cost of property that may be expensed for any tax year cannot exceed the total amount of taxable income derived from the active conduct of any trade or business during the tax year, including salaries and wages. An amount disallowed as the result of the taxable income limitation is carried forward. The deduction for carryforwards and the amounts expensed for qualifying property placed in service in a carryforward year, however, may not exceed the maximum annual dollar cost ceiling, investment limitation, or, if lesser, the taxable income limitation.

Qualifying Property. To qualify as section 179 property, the property must be tangible section 1245 property (new or used), depreciable under MACRS, and acquired by purchase for use in the active conduct of a trade or business (Code Sec. 179(d)).[20] Code Sec. 50(b) property and air conditioning or heating units do not qualify as section 179 property. Code Sec. 50(b) property includes property used predominantly outside of the U.S., property used with respect to lodging such as apartment buildings but not hotels and motels, and property used by tax-exempt organizations (unless the property is used predominantly in connection with an unrelated business income activity).

Depreciable off-the-shelf computer software placed in service in tax years beginning in 2003 through 2010 may be expensed under Code Sec. 179 (Code Sec. 179(d)(1)(A), as amended by the Small Business and Work Opportunity Tax Act of 2007 (P.L. 110-28)). This is software described in Code Sec. 197(e)(3)(A)(i) (i.e., software that is readily available for purchase by the general public, is subject to a nonexclusive license, and has not been substantially modified) which is depreciable over three years under Code Sec. 167(f)(1)(A).[21]

Purchase Defined. Property is acquired by purchase unless it (1) is acquired from certain related persons, (2) is transferred between members of a controlled group, (3) has a substituted basis in whole or in part, or (4) is acquired from a decedent and has a basis determined under Code Sec. 1014(a) (i.e., a fair-market value basis) (Code Sec. 179(d)(2)).

Recapture. The Code Sec. 179 expense deduction is treated as depreciation for recapture purposes. Thus, gain on a disposition of section 179 property is generally treated as ordinary income to the extent of the Code Sec. 179 expense allowance claimed plus any depreciation claimed.

If business use of section 179 property fails to exceed 50 percent during any year of the property's depreciation period, a portion of the amount expensed is recaptured as ordinary income (Code Sec. 179(d)(10); Reg. §1.179-1(e)). The recapture amount is the difference between the expense claimed and the depreciation that would have been allowed on the expensed amount for prior tax years and the tax year of recapture. Recapture is computed on Form 4797.

Footnote references are to paragraphs of the 2008 Standard Federal Tax Reports.

[20] ¶ 12,120, ¶ 12,126.021   [21] ¶ 12,126.021

In the case of a listed property, such as a passenger automobile, the recapture rules described at ¶ 1211 for property used 50 percent or less for business apply in place of the above Code Sec. 179 recapture rule.

Gulf Opportunity Zone Property—Hurricane Relief. The otherwise applicable dollar limitation for section 179 property (i.e., $125,000 in 2007 and $128,000 in 2008) that is also qualified Gulf Opportunity Zone property (as defined at ¶ 1237) is increased by $100,000 (or, if less, the cost of qualified zone property placed in service in the tax year). The otherwise applicable investment limitation ($500,000 in 2007 and $510,000 in 2008) is increased by an additional $600,000 (or, if less, the cost of qualified zone property placed in service during the tax year). The original use of the property must commence with the taxpayer in the Gulf Opportunity Zone after August 27, 2005 and the property must be placed in service before January 1, 2009 (Code Sec. 1400N(e)).[22]

Empowerment Zones, Renewal Communities, District of Columbia, and New York City Liberty Zone. The expense allowance is increased an additional $35,000 for qualifying assets placed in service in certain distressed communities.[23] See ¶ 999A and following.

Capitalization v. Expensing Policy—Low-Cost Items. The IRS approves an expensing policy followed by its auditors that allows taxpayers to expense, apart from Code Sec. 179, low-cost items on the basis of risk analysis and/or materiality. Although not included in proposed regulations, final regulations under Code Sec. 263 may include such a de minimis rule (NPRM REG-168745-03, published in the Federal Register on August 21, 2006).[24]

Limitations on Automobiles and Other Listed Property

1211. Business Usage Requirement for Listed Property. Depreciation deductions for "listed property" are subject to special rules (Code Sec. 280F).[25] Listed property includes "passenger automobiles" (as defined at ¶ 1214), other forms of transportation if the property's nature lends itself to personal use (e.g., airplanes, boats, vehicles excluded from the definition of a passenger automobile, etc.), entertainment, recreational and amusement property, computers and peripheral equipment, cellular telephones and similar telecommunications equipment, and any other property specified by regulation. Unless used more than 50% for business, MACRS deductions on listed property must be determined under the MACRS alternative depreciation system (ADS) (see ¶ 1247).

If the listed property satisfies the more-than-50% business use requirement in the year it is placed in service but fails to meet that test in a later tax year, depreciation deductions previously taken are subject to recapture in such later year. MACRS depreciation for years preceding the year in which the business use fell to 50% or less is recaptured to the extent that the MACRS depreciation for such years exceeds the depreciation that would have been allowed under ADS. Depreciation thereafter must be computed using ADS.

If the more-than-50% business use test is not satisfied in the year the property is placed in service, the property does not qualify for the Code Sec. 179 expensing election (¶ 1208). If the more-than-50% business use test is initially satisfied but is not met in a later tax year, the deduction taken under the Code Sec. 179 election is treated as a depreciation deduction for purposes of the listed property depreciation recapture rule. For example, if a taxpayer expenses the entire cost of a listed property, the difference between the amount expensed and the ADS deductions that would have been allowed on that amount prior to the recapture year are recaptured as ordinary income.

See ¶ 1214 for additional limits on passenger automobiles.

Reporting. Form 4797 is used to calculate any recapture amount.

Footnote references are to paragraphs of the 2008 Standard Federal Tax Reports.

[22] ¶ 32,487.032

[23] ¶ 32,398.01, ¶ 32,423.02, ¶ 32,472.01, ¶ 32,477.028

[24] ¶ 12,126.01

[25] ¶ 15,100, ¶ 15,108

1214. Limitations on Passenger Automobiles, Including Trucks, SUVs, and Vans. Even though a "passenger automobile" (as defined below) is used more than 50% for business purposes, there is an additional limit on the annual depreciation that may be claimed (Code Sec. 280F(a)).[26] The maximum MACRS deductions (including the Code Sec. 179 expensing deduction (¶ 1208) and first-year bonus depreciation allowance (¶ 1237)) that may be claimed for a passenger automobile (other than a truck or van placed in service in calendar year 2003 or later) are shown in the following chart:

For Cars Placed in Service After	Before	Year 1	Year 2	Year 3	Year 4, etc.	Authority
			Depreciation Allowable in—			
12/31/94	1/01/97	3,060	4,900	2,950	1,775	Rev. Proc. 95-9
						Rev. Proc. 96-25
12/31/96	1/01/98	3,160	5,000	3,050	1,775	Rev. Proc. 97-20
12/31/97	1/01/99	3,160	5,000	2,950	1,775	Rev. Proc. 98-30
12/31/98	1/01/00	3,060	5,000	2,950	1,775	Rev. Proc. 99-14
12/31/99	9/11/01	3,060	4,900	2,950	1,775	Rev. Proc. 2000-18
9/10/01	5/06/03	7,660 * 3,060 *	4,900	2,950	1,775	Rev. Proc. 2003-75
5/05/03	1/01/04	10,710 ** 3,060 **	4,900	2,950	1,775	Rev. Proc. 2003-75
12/31/03	1/01/05	10,610 *** 2,960 ***	4,800	2,850	1,675	Rev. Proc. 2004-20
12/31/04	1/01/06	$2,960	$4,700	$2,850	$1,675	Rev. Proc. 2005-13
12/31/05	1/01/07	$2,960	$4,800	$2,850	$1,775	Rev. Proc. 2006-18
12/31/06	1/01/08	$3,060	$4,900	$2,850	$1,775	Rev. Proc. 2007-30

* The $7,660 limit applies if the vehicle qualifies for the 30-percent bonus depreciation under Code Sec. 168(k) and no election out is made (¶ 1237). The $3,060 limit applies if the vehicle does not qualify for bonus depreciation or the election out is made.
** The $10,710 limit applied if the vehicle qualified for the 50-percent bonus depreciation under Code Sec. 168(k) and no election out was made, or the 30-percent bonus depreciation was elected in lieu of the 50-percent rate. The $3,060 limit applied if the vehicle did not qualify for bonus depreciation or the election out was made.
*** The $10,610 limit applied if the vehicle qualified for the 50-percent bonus depreciation under Code Sec. 168(k) and no election out was made, or the 30-percent bonus depreciation was elected in lieu of the 50-percent rate. The $2,960 limit applied if the vehicle did not qualify for bonus depreciation or the election out was made.
The increased limits did not apply if 30 percent bonus depreciation was claimed on a vehicle that was qualified New York Liberty Zone property. Increased limits are not provided for vehicles that are qualified Gulf Opportunity Zone property. See ¶ 1237.

Trucks and vans (including SUVs and minivans built on a truck chassis) are subject to their own set of depreciation caps if placed in service after 2002. These caps (reproduced in the table below) reflect the higher costs associated with such vehicles. Keep in mind, however, that trucks and vans (including SUVs and minivans built on a truck chassis) that have a loaded gross vehicle weight rating greater than 6,000 pounds are not subject to any caps (see below). *Also, certain trucks and vans placed in service after July 6, 2003 are not subject to the caps if, because of their design, they are not likely to be used for personal purposes (see below).*

Footnote references are to paragraphs of the 2008 Standard Federal Tax Reports.

[26] ¶ 15,100, ¶ 15,108

For Trucks and Vans Placed in Service After	Before	Depreciation Allowable in—				
		Year 1	Year 2	Year 3	Year 4, etc.	Authority
12/31/02	1/01/04	11,010 * 7,960 * 3,360 *	5,400	3,250	1,975	Rev. Proc. 2003-75
12/31/03	1/01/05	10,910 ** 3,260 **	5,300	3,150	1,875	Rev. Proc. 2004-20
12/31/04	1/01/06	$3,260	$5,200	$3,150	$1,875	Rev. Proc. 2005-13
12/31/05	1/01/07	$3,260	$5,200	$3,150	$1,875	Rev. Proc. 2006-18
12/31/06	1/01/08	$3,260	$5,200	$3,050	$1,875	Rev. Proc. 2007-30

* The $11,010 limit applied if the vehicle qualified for the 50-percent bonus depreciation rate and no election out was made, or the 30-percent bonus depreciation was elected in lieu of the 50-percent rate (¶ 1237). The $7,960 limit applied for vehicles acquired prior to May 6, 2003, if the vehicle qualified for 30-percent bonus depreciation rate and no election out was made. The $3,360 limit applied if the vehicle did not qualify for bonus depreciation or the election out was made.

** The $10,910 limit applied if the vehicle qualified for the 50-percent bonus depreciation and no election out was made, or the 30-percent bonus depreciation was elected in lieu of the 50-percent rate. The $3,260 limit applied if the vehicle did not qualify for bonus depreciation or the election out was made.

The increased limits did not apply if 30 percent bonus depreciation was claimed on a vehicle that was qualified New York Liberty Zone property. Increased limits are not provided for vehicles that are qualified Gulf Opportunity Zone property. See ¶ 1237.

The above maximum annual limits (often referred to as the luxury car limits) are based on 100% business use. If business use is less than 100%, the limits must be reduced to reflect the actual business use percentage.

For electric passenger automobiles built by an original equipment manufacturer and placed in service after August 5, 1997 and before 2007, the yearly statutory limits that apply to depreciation for luxury cars (¶ 1214) are tripled and then adjusted for inflation (Code Sec. 280F(a)(1)(C)(ii)). The annual limits above apply to electric vehicles placed in service after 2006.[27]

Footnote references are to paragraphs of the 2008 Standard Federal Tax Reports.

[27] ¶ 15,100, ¶ 15,108.025

¶1214

The following chart provides the applicable depreciation caps for electric passenger automobiles placed in service before 2007:

Depreciation Caps for Electric Vehicles
Placed in Service before 2007

| For Electric Vehicles Placed in Service | | | Depreciation Allowable in— | | | |
After	Before	Year 1	Year 2	Year 3	Year 4, etc.	Authority
8/05/97	1/01/98	$9,480	$15,100	$9,050	$5,425	Rev. Proc. 98-24
12/31/97	1/01/99	$9,380	$15,000	$8,950	$5,425	Rev. Proc. 98-30
12/31/98	1/01/00	$9,280	$14,900	$8,950	$5,325	Rev. Proc. 99-14
12/31/99	1/01/01	$9,280	$14,800	$8,850	$5,325	Rev. Proc. 2000-18
12/31/00	9/11/01	$9,280	$14,800	$8,850	$5,325	Rev. Proc. 2001-19
9/10/01	1/01/02	$23,080*	$14,800	$8,850	$5,325	Rev. Proc. 2003-75
12/31/01	1/01/03	$22,980*	$14,700	$8,750	$5,325	Rev. Proc. 2003-75
12/31/02	5/06/03	$22,880*	$14,600	$8,750	$5,225	Rev. Proc. 2003-75
5/05/03	1/01/04	$32,030*	$14,600	$8,750	$5,225	Rev. Proc. 2003-75
12/31/03	1/01/05	$31,830*	$14,300	$8,550	$5,125	Rev. Proc. 2004-20
12/31/04	1/01/06	$8,880	$14,200	$8,450	$5,125	Rev. Proc. 2005-13
12/31/05	1/01/07	$8,980	$14,400	$8,650	$5,225	Rev. Proc. 2006-18

* These figures applied if the car qualified for the additional bonus depreciation allowance under Code Sec. 168(k) and no election out was made (¶ 1237). If the vehicle did not qualify for bonus depreciation under Code Sec. 168(k) or the election out was made, then the limit was $9,280 if the vehicle was placed in service after September 10, 2001 and before January 1, 2002; $9,180 if the vehicle was placed in service in 2002; $9,080 if the vehicle was placed in service in 2003; and $8,880 if the vehicle was placed in service in 2004. If an election was made to claim 30 percent bonus depreciation in lieu of 50 percent bonus depreciation, the 50 percent bonus depreciation cap still applied (viz., $32,030 if the vehicle was placed in service after May 5, 2003 and before January 1, 2004 and $31,830 if placed in service in 2004).

For passenger vehicles that initially used nonclean-burning fuel, but were modified to allow them to be propelled by clean-burning fuel, the Code Sec. 280F limits do not apply to the cost of the installed device that equips the car to use clean-burning fuel. The balance of the car's cost remains subject to the Code Sec. 280F limits (Code Sec. 280F(a)(1)(C)).[28]

If, after the normal recovery period for automobiles, the taxpayer continues to use the car in its trade or business, the unrecovered basis (referred to as "Sec. 280F unrecovered basis") may be deducted at the maximum annual rate provided in the chart for the fourth and succeeding years. This rule permits depreciation deductions beyond the normal recovery period. Unrecovered basis is determined as if business use had been 100 percent during each year of the recovery period.

Example: On April 5, 2007, a calendar-year taxpayer purchased a car for $30,000. Business use of the car each year is 80%. Depreciation is computed under the general MACRS 200% declining-balance method over a five-year recovery period using a half-year convention subject to the luxury car limitations. Allowable depreciation during the regular recovery period (2007 through 2012) is computed as follows:

Year	100% Business-Use MACRS Depreciation	Luxury Car Limit	Deduction: 80% of Lesser	Sec. 280F Unrecovered Basis
2007	$6,000	$3,060	$2,448	$26,940
2008	9,600	4,900	3,920	22,040
2009	5,760	2,850	2,280	19,190
2010	3,456	1,775	1,420	17,415
2011	3,456	1,775	1,420	15,640
2012	1,728	1,775	1,382	13,912

Note that the unrecovered basis is computed by subtracting the depreciation that would have been allowed (taking the applicable cap into consideration) if

Footnote references are to paragraphs of the 2008 Standard Federal Tax Reports.

[28] ¶ 15,100, ¶ 12,133.029

business use was 100%. Thus, for example, the unrecovered basis at the close of 2007 is $26,940 ($30,000 − $3,060). The $13,912 unrecovered basis at the close of the regular recovery period is deducted in the post recovery period years as follows:

Year	Unrecovered basis at beginning of year	Luxury Car Limit	Deduction: 80% of Lesser	Unrecovered basis at end of year
2013	$13,912	$1,775	$1,420	$12,137
2014	12,137	1,775	1,420	10,362
2015	10,362	1,775	1,420	8,587
2016	8,587	1,775	1,420	6,812
2017	6,812	1,775	1,420	5,037
2018	5,037	1,775	1,420	3,262
2019	3,262	1,775	1,420	1,487
2020	1,487	1,775	1,190	0

Passenger Automobile Defined. For purposes of the depreciation caps, a passenger automobile includes any four-wheeled vehicle manufactured primarily for use on public streets, roads, and highways that has an *unloaded* gross vehicle weight rating (i.e., curb weight fully equipped for service but without passengers or cargo) of 6,000 pounds or less (Code Sec. 280F(d)(5)(A)). However, a truck (including a sport utility vehicle built on a truck chassis or a van or minivan built on a truck chassis) is treated as a passenger automobile subject to the caps if it has a *gross* vehicle weight rating (i.e., maximum total weight of a loaded vehicle as specified by the manufacturer) of 6,000 pounds or less. Such a vehicle is not subject to the depreciation caps if its GVWR exceeds 6,000 pounds. Ambulances or hearses and vehicles used directly in the trade or business of transporting persons or property for hire (e.g., taxis and limousines) are not considered passenger automobiles subject to the caps regardless of their weight.

$25,000 Section 179 Expensing Cap on Sport Utility Vehicles, Certain Trucks, and Certain Vans That Are Exempt from Luxury Car Depreciation Caps. The maximum amount of the cost of an SUV that may be expensed under Code Sec. 179 if the SUV is exempt from the luxury car caps (e.g., is built on a truck chassis and has a GVWR in excess of 6,000 pounds) is limited to $25,000, effective for SUVs placed in service after October 22, 2004. The $25,000 limitation also applies to exempt trucks with an interior cargo bed length of less than six feet and exempt passenger vans that seat fewer than ten persons behind the driver's seat. Exempt cargo vans are generally not subject to the $25,000 limitation (Code Sec. 179(b)(6)).

Exclusion from Depreciation Caps for Certain Trucks and Vans Not Likely To Be Used for Personal Purposes. Effective for trucks and vans placed in service after July 6, 2003, a truck or van that is a qualified nonpersonal use vehicle as defined in Temporary Reg. §1.274-5T(k) is excluded from the definition of a passenger automobile and is not subject to the annual depreciation limits (Reg. §1.280F-6(c)(3)(iii)). In general, a qualified nonpersonal use vehicle is one that has been specially modified in such a way that it is not likely to be used more than a *de minimis* amount for personal purposes.[29]

Reporting. The allowable depreciation deduction for any listed property, including automobiles, is reported on Form 4562 (Part V).

1215. Leased Listed Property Inclusion Amounts. The lessee of a passenger automobile (as defined for depreciation cap purposes at ¶ 1214) used for business is required to include an additional amount in income to offset rental deductions for each tax year during which the vehicle is leased (Code Sec. 280F(c)(2); Reg. §1.280F-7).[30] The inclusion amount is based on the cost of the vehicle and generally applies to a vehicle with a fair market value exceeding an inflation-adjusted dollar amount. The inclusion amount is not required on trucks, vans, and SUVs that would be exempt from the depreciation caps if owned by the lessee (e.g., an SUV built on a truck chassis with a GVWR in excess of 6,000 pounds).

Footnote references are to paragraphs of the 2008 Standard Federal Tax Reports.

[29] ¶ 15,108.042   [30] ¶ 15,100, ¶ 15,107

Lease inclusion tables are issued annually by the IRS in the same revenue procedure in which the annual depreciation caps are issued (see list of these revenue procedures at ¶ 1214). The appropriate table is based on the calendar year that the vehicle was first leased. The same table is used for each year of the lease term.

Each revenue procedure includes a lease inclusion table for passenger automobiles and a lease inclusion table for trucks and vans (including SUVs and minivans that are built on a truck chassis). Prior to 2003 trucks and vans used the same table that applied to other passenger automobiles. Prior to 2007 electric vehicles had a separate lease inclusion table. Electric vehicles first leased in 2007 are now subject to the table that applies to passenger automobiles or trucks and vans, as appropriate. The inclusion tables for vehicles first leased in 2007 are reproduced below (Rev. Proc. 2007-30). For tables for vehicles first leased in earlier calendar years, see the STANDARD FEDERAL TAX REPORTER ¶ 15,108.048 or IRS Publication 463.

A lessee's inclusion amount for each tax year that the vehicle is leased is computed as follows: (1) use the fair market value of the vehicle on the first day of the lease term to find the appropriate dollar (inclusion) amounts on the IRS table (see below); (2) prorate the dollar amount from the table for the number of days of the lease term included in the tax year; and (3) multiply the prorated amount by the percentage of business and investment use for the tax year. For the last tax year during any lease that does not begin and end in the same tax year, the dollar amount for the preceding tax year should be used.

> **Example:** A car costing $25,500 is leased for four years by a calendar-year taxpayer beginning on April 1, 2007 and is used 100% for business. The annual dollar amounts from the table (Rev. Proc. 2007-30) for leases beginning in 2007 are: $70 for the first tax year during the lease, $153 for the second tax year, $229 for the third tax year, $275 for the fourth tax year, and $316 for the fifth and following tax years. In 2007, the inclusion amount is $53 ($275/365 \times 70). The inclusion amounts for 2008, 2009, and 2010 are $153, $229, and $275 respectively since the vehicle is leased for the entire year during these tax years. In 2011, the inclusion amount is $68 ($90/365 \times 275 (the dollar amount for 2010, the preceding tax year, is used in the last year of the lease)).

Listed Property Other Than Passenger Automobiles. Lessees of listed property (other than passenger automobiles) are required to include in income a usage-based inclusion amount in the first tax year that the business use percentage of such property is 50% or less (Code Sec. 280F(c); Reg. § 1.280F-7(b)).[31]

Reporting. The inclusion amount is reported on Form 2106 by employees, Schedule C (Form 1040) by the self-employed, and Schedule F by farmers.

Footnote references are to paragraphs of the 2008 Standard Federal Tax Reports.

[31] ¶ 15,108.054

Dollar Amounts for Passenger Automobiles
(That are not Trucks or Vans, including SUVs and minivans built on a truck chassis)
With a Lease Term Beginning in Calendar Year 2007
[Rev. Proc. 2007-30, I.R.B. 2007-18]

Fair Market Value of Passenger Automobile		Tax Year During Lease				
Over	Not Over	1st	2nd	3rd	4th	5th and Later
$15,500	$15,800	2	5	11	11	13
15,800	16,100	4	10	17	19	22
16,100	16,400	6	14	24	28	31
16,400	16,700	9	18	31	35	41
16,700	17,000	11	23	37	43	50
17,000	17,500	13	29	46	54	62
17,500	18,000	17	37	56	68	77
18,000	18,500	20	44	68	81	93
18,500	19,000	24	51	80	94	108
19,000	19,500	27	59	90	108	124
19,500	20,000	30	67	101	121	139
20,000	20,500	34	74	113	134	154
20,500	21,000	37	82	123	148	170
21,000	21,500	41	89	135	161	185
21,500	22,000	44	97	146	174	201
22,000	23,000	49	108	163	194	224
23,000	24,000	56	123	185	221	255
24,000	25,000	63	138	207	248	285
25,000	26,000	70	153	229	275	316
26,000	27,000	77	168	251	302	347
27,000	28,000	83	183	274	328	378
28,000	29,000	90	198	296	355	409
29,000	30,000	97	213	318	382	439
30,000	31,000	104	228	341	408	470
31,000	32,000	111	243	363	435	501
32,000	33,000	118	258	385	461	532
33,000	34,000	125	273	407	488	563
34,000	35,000	131	288	430	515	593
35,000	36,000	138	303	452	542	624
36,000	37,000	145	318	474	568	656
37,000	38,000	152	333	496	595	686
38,000	39,000	159	348	519	621	717
39,000	40,000	166	363	541	648	748
40,000	41,000	172	378	564	674	779
41,000	42,000	179	393	586	701	810
42,000	43,000	186	408	608	728	840
43,000	44,000	193	423	630	755	871
44,000	45,000	200	438	652	782	902
45,000	46,000	207	453	674	809	933
46,000	47,000	213	468	697	835	964
47,000	48,000	220	483	719	862	995
48,000	49,000	227	498	742	888	1,025
49,000	50,000	234	513	764	915	1,056
50,000	51,000	241	528	786	942	1,087
51,000	52,000	248	543	808	969	1,117
52,000	53,000	254	558	831	995	1,148
53,000	54,000	261	573	853	1,022	1,179
54,000	55,000	268	588	875	1,049	1,210
55,000	56,000	275	603	897	1,076	1,241
56,000	57,000	282	618	920	1,102	1,271
57,000	58,000	289	633	942	1,128	1,303
58,000	59,000	296	648	964	1,155	1,334
59,000	60,000	302	663	987	1,182	1,364
60,000	62,000	313	685	1,020	1,222	1,411
62,000	64,000	326	716	1,064	1,276	1,472
64,000	66,000	340	746	1,108	1,329	1,534
66,000	68,000	354	775	1,154	1,382	1,595
68,000	70,000	367	806	1,198	1,435	1,657
70,000	72,000	381	836	1,242	1,489	1,719
72,000	74,000	395	865	1,287	1,543	1,780
74,000	76,000	408	896	1,331	1,596	1,842

Dollar Amounts for Passenger Automobiles
(That are not Trucks or Vans, including SUVs and minivans built on a truck chassis)
With a Lease Term Beginning in Calendar Year 2007
[Rev. Proc. 2007-30, I.R.B. 2007-18]

Fair Market Value of Passenger Automobile		*Tax Year During Lease*				
Over	Not Over	1st	2nd	3rd	4th	5th and Later
76,000	78,000	422	926	1,376	1,649	1,903
78,000	80,000	436	955	1,421	1,703	1,965
80,000	85,000	460	1,008	1,498	1,796	2,074
85,000	90,000	494	1,083	1,610	1,929	2,228
90,000	95,000	528	1,158	1,721	2,063	2,382
95,000	100,000	562	1,233	1,833	2,196	2,536
100,000	110,000	614	1,346	1,999	2,396	2,767
110,000	120,000	682	1,496	2,222	2,663	3,075
120,000	130,000	750	1,646	2,444	2,931	3,383
130,000	140,000	819	1,796	2,667	3,197	3,692
140,000	150,000	887	1,946	2,890	3,464	4,000
150,000	160,000	956	2,096	3,112	3,731	4,308
160,000	170,000	1,024	2,246	3,335	3,998	4,616
170,000	180,000	1,093	2,396	3,557	4,266	4,924
180,000	190,000	1,161	2,546	3,780	4,532	5,233
190,000	200,000	1,229	2,696	4,003	4,799	5,541
200,000	210,000	1,298	2,846	4,225	5,067	5,848
210,000	220,000	1,366	2,996	4,448	5,333	6,157
220,000	230,000	1,435	3,146	4,671	5,600	6,465
230,000	240,000	1,503	3,296	4,893	5,867	6,774
240,000	and up	1,571	3,446	5,116	6,134	7,082

Dollar Amounts for Trucks and Vans (including SUVs and minivans built on a truck chassis)
With a Lease Term Beginning in Calendar Year 2007
[Rev. Proc. 2007-30, I.R.B. 2007-18]

Fair Market Value of Truck or Van		*Tax Year During Lease*				
Over	Not Over	1st	2nd	3rd	4th	5th and later
$16,400	$16,700	2	4	8	10	11
16,700	17,000	4	9	15	17	21
17,000	17,500	6	15	24	28	33
17,500	18,000	10	22	35	42	48
18,000	18,500	13	30	46	55	64
18,500	19,000	17	37	57	69	79
19,000	19,500	20	45	68	82	94
19,500	20,000	24	52	80	95	109
20,000	20,500	27	60	90	109	125
20,500	21,000	30	67	102	122	141
21,000	21,500	34	75	113	135	156
21,500	22,000	37	82	124	149	171
22,000	23,000	42	94	140	169	194
23,000	24,000	49	109	163	195	225
24,000	25,000	56	123	186	222	256
25,000	26,000	63	138	208	249	286
26,000	27,000	70	153	230	276	317
27,000	28,000	77	168	252	302	349
28,000	29,000	83	184	274	329	379
29,000	30,000	90	199	296	356	410
30,000	31,000	97	214	318	383	440
31,000	32,000	104	228	342	408	472
32,000	33,000	111	243	364	435	503
33,000	34,000	118	258	386	462	534
34,000	35,000	125	273	408	489	564
35,000	36,000	131	289	430	515	595
36,000	37,000	138	304	452	542	626
37,000	38,000	145	318	475	569	657
38,000	39,000	152	333	497	596	688
39,000	40,000	159	348	520	622	718
40,000	41,000	166	363	542	649	749
41,000	42,000	172	379	563	676	780
42,000	43,000	179	394	586	702	811

Dollar Amounts for Trucks and Vans (including SUVs and minivans built on a truck chassis)
With a Lease Term Beginning in Calendar Year 2007
[Rev. Proc. 2007-30, I.R.B. 2007-18]

Fair Market Value of Truck or Van		Tax Year During Lease				
Over	Not Over	1st	2nd	3rd	4th	5th and later
43,000	44,000	186	409	608	729	842
44,000	45,000	193	423	631	756	872
45,000	46,000	200	438	653	783	903
46,000	47,000	207	453	675	810	934
47,000	48,000	213	469	697	836	965
48,000	49,000	220	484	719	863	996
49,000	50,000	227	499	741	890	1,026
50,000	51,000	234	514	764	916	1,057
51,000	52,000	241	528	787	943	1,088
52,000	53,000	248	543	809	969	1,119
53,000	54,000	254	559	831	996	1,150
54,000	55,000	261	574	853	1,023	1,180
55,000	56,000	268	589	875	1,050	1,211
56,000	57,000	275	604	897	1,076	1,243
57,000	58,000	282	618	920	1,103	1,273
58,000	59,000	289	633	943	1,129	1,304
59,000	60,000	296	648	965	1,156	1,335
60,000	62,000	306	671	998	1,196	1,381
62,000	64,000	319	701	1,043	1,249	1,443
64,000	66,000	333	731	1,087	1,303	1,504
66,000	68,000	347	761	1,131	1,357	1,566
68,000	70,000	361	791	1,176	1,410	1,627
70,000	72,000	374	821	1,221	1,463	1,689
72,000	74,000	388	851	1,265	1,517	1,751
74,000	76,000	402	881	1,309	1,570	1,813
76,000	78,000	415	911	1,354	1,624	1,874
78,000	80,000	429	941	1,399	1,676	1,936
80,000	85,000	453	994	1,476	1,770	2,044
85,000	90,000	487	1,069	1,587	1,904	2,198
90,000	95,000	521	1,144	1,699	2,037	2,352
95,000	100,000	555	1,219	1,810	2,171	2,506
100,000	110,000	607	1,331	1,977	2,371	2,737
110,000	120,000	675	1,481	2,200	2,638	3,045
120,000	130,000	744	1,631	2,423	2,904	3,354
130,000	140,000	812	1,781	2,646	3,171	3,662
140,000	150,000	880	1,932	2,867	3,439	3,970
150,000	160,000	949	2,081	3,091	3,705	4,279
160,000	170,000	1,017	2,232	3,313	3,972	4,586
170,000	180,000	1,086	2,381	3,536	4,239	4,895
180,000	190,000	1,154	2,532	3,758	4,506	5,203
190,000	200,000	1,222	2,682	3,981	4,773	5,511
200,000	210,000	1,291	2,831	4,204	5,040	5,820
210,000	220,000	1,359	2,982	4,426	5,307	6,128
220,000	230,000	1,428	3,131	4,649	5,575	6,435
230,000	240,000	1,496	3,282	4,871	5,841	6,744
240,000	and up	1,565	3,431	5,095	6,108	7,052

Depreciation Methods

1216. Methods of Computing Depreciation. Most tangible property placed in service after 1986 must be depreciated using MACRS (¶ 1243). Depreciation for tangible property placed in service after 1980 and before 1987 is computed under ACRS (¶ 1252).

For tangible property placed in service before 1981, post-1980 depreciation may be computed under the straight-line method (¶ 1224), the double declining-balance method (¶ 1226), the sum-of-the-years-digits method (¶ 1228), and other "consistent methods" (¶ 1231) (former Code Sec. 167(b)), depending on the taxpayer's election in the year the

property was placed in service.[32] However, accelerated depreciation for pre-1981 realty is limited (former Code Sec. 167(j)).[33]

1218. Methods for Depreciating Real Estate. Real property placed in service after 1986 is depreciated under MACRS (¶ 1236). Real property placed in service after 1980 and before 1987 is depreciated under ACRS (¶ 1252). Additions and improvements to a building, including structural components of a building, placed in service after 1986 are depreciated under MACRS (see ¶ 1240). Post-1986 rehabilitation expenditures are also depreciated using MACRS (¶ 1236). Elements of a building which qualify as personal property may be separately depreciated under the cost segregation rules using shortened MACRS recovery periods (¶ 1240). Real property which is converted from personal use to residential rental property or nonresidential real property is depreciated as MACRS 27.5-year residential rental property or MACRS 39-year nonresidential real property even if the property was acquired for personal use prior to 1987.

1221. Change in Depreciation Method. A change in the method of computing depreciation is generally a change in accounting method that requires the consent of the IRS and the filing of Form 3115 (Reg. § 1.167(e)-1).[34] If the change from an impermissible accounting method to a permissible accounting method results in a negative (taxpayer favorable) Code Sec. 481(a) adjustment, the adjustment is taken into account in a single tax year. A positive adjustment is taken into account over four tax years (one-year if the positive adjustment is less than $25,000 and the taxpayer makes an election to include it in income in one year). No Code Sec. 481(a) adjustment is allowed when a taxpayer changes from one permissible method to another permissible method. These changes are applied on a "cut-off" basis.[35] Reg. § 1.446-1(e)(2)(ii)(d)(2) and (3) list changes in depreciation or amortization that are or are not considered a change in accounting method.[36]

Although a taxpayer has not adopted an accounting method unless two or more returns have been filed, the IRS will allow a taxpayer who has only filed one return on which incorrect depreciation has been claimed to either file Form 3115 and claim a Code Sec. 481(a) adjustment on the current-year return or file an amended return. The asset must have been placed in service in the tax year immediately preceding the tax year of the change. This rule is effective for a Form 3115 filed for a tax year ending on or after December 30, 2003 (Rev. Proc. 2002-9, as modified and amplified by Rev. Proc. 2007-16, I.R.B. 2007-4).

For changes that are not a change in accounting method, such as mathematical or posting errors, a taxpayer may only file amended returns for open years. Changes in accounting method are generally made by filing Form 3115. Procedures for changing from an impermissible method (e.g., where incorrect or no depreciation has been claimed) to a permissible method and from permissible to permissible methods with respect to pre-1986 (i.e., pre-ACRS) property are generally governed by the automatic consent procedures of Rev. Proc. 2002-9 (Appendix 2.01). Otherwise, the advance consent procedures of Rev. Proc. 97-27 are followed.[37]

A taxpayer who has sold depreciable property without claiming any depreciation or all of the depreciation allowable may claim the depreciation by filing Form 3115 by the expiration of the period of limitations for filing an amended return for the year of the sale. The Form 3115 may be filed with the original federal tax return for the tax year in which the depreciable property is disposed of (Rev. Proc. 2007-16).[38]

1224. "Straight-Line" or "Fixed-Percentage" Method of Depreciation. The "straight-line" method of computing the depreciation deduction assumes that the depreciation sustained is uniform during the useful life of the property. The cost or other basis, less estimated salvage value, is deductible in equal annual amounts over the estimated useful life (Reg. § 1.167(b)-1).[39] An asset may not be depreciated below its

---

Footnote references are to paragraphs of the 2008 Standard Federal Tax Reports.

[32] ¶ 11,037.021
[33] ¶ 11,059.01
[34] ¶ 11,043.01

[35] ¶ 11,043.021
[36] ¶ 11,043.015
[37] ¶ 11,043.021

[38] ¶ 11,043.021
[39] ¶ 11,033, ¶ 11,037.022

salvage value. Straight-line depreciation under MACRS and ACRS is generally computed in this manner, except that a recovery period is used instead of the useful life and salvage value is not considered (Code Sec. 168(b)(4))[40] (¶ 1243 and ¶ 1252).

1226. Declining-Balance Method of Depreciation. Under this method, depreciation is greatest in the first year and smaller in each succeeding year (Reg. § 1.167(b)-2).[41] The depreciable basis (e.g., cost) is reduced each year by the amount of the depreciation deduction, and a uniform rate of 200% of the straight-line rate ("double-declining balance" or "200% declining balance" method) or 150% of the straight-line rate ("150% declining balance" method) is applied to the resulting balances (Reg. § 1.167(b)-2).[42] Under the MACRS rules, the double declining-balance method is used to depreciate 3-, 5-, 7-, and 10-year property and the 150% declining balance method is used to depreciate 15- and 20-year property (¶ 1243).

1228. Sum-of-the-Years-Digits Method. Under the sum-of-the-years-digits method, changing fractions are applied each year to the original cost or other basis, less salvage. The numerator of the fraction each year represents the remaining useful life of the asset and the denominator, which remains constant, is the sum of the numerals representing each of the years of the estimated useful life (the sum-of-the-years digits). This method, if elected, may be used for group, classified or composite accounts (Reg. § 1.167(b)-3).[43]

1229. Income Forecast Method. For property placed in service after August 5, 1997, the use of the income forecast method only applies to film, videotape, sound recordings, copyrights, books, patents, and other property that may be specified by IRS regulations. (The IRS has issued proposed regulations that would apply to property placed in service on or after the date final regulations are published (Prop. Reg. § 1.167(n)-1)). The income forecast method may not be used to depreciate intangible property that is amortizable under Code Sec. 197 (¶ 1288) or consumer durables subject to rent-to-own contracts (¶ 1240) (Code Sec. 167(g)(6); Rev. Rul. 60-358).[44]

Under the income forecast method, the cost of an asset (less any salvage value) placed in service after September 13, 1995, is multiplied by a fraction, the numerator of which is the net income from the asset for the tax year and the denominator of which is the total net income forecast to be derived from the asset before the close of the 10th tax year following the tax year in which the asset is placed in service. The unrecovered adjusted basis of the property as of the beginning of the 10th tax year is claimed as a depreciation deduction in the 10th tax year following the tax year in which the asset was placed in service.

If the income forecast changes during the 10-year period, the formula is as follows: the unrecovered depreciable cost of the asset at the beginning of the tax year of revision multiplied by a fraction, the numerator of which is the net income from the asset for the tax year of revision and the denominator of which is the revised forecasted total net income from the asset for the year of revision and the remaining years before the close of the 10th tax year following the tax year in which the asset was placed in service.

Generally, during the 3rd and 10th tax years after the asset is placed in service, a taxpayer is required to pay or may receive interest based on the recalculation of depreciation using actual income figures. This look-back rule does not apply to property that has a cost basis of $100,000 or less or if the taxpayer's income projections were within 10 percent of the income actually earned.

Effective for property placed in service after October 22, 2004, residuals and participations may be included in the adjusted basis of a property in the tax year that it is placed in service or excluded from adjusted basis and deducted in the year of payment (Code Sec. 167(g)(7)). Election guidance is provided in Notice 2006-47.

Reporting. Form 8866 is used to compute the look-back interest due or owed.

Footnote references are to paragraphs of the 2008 Standard Federal Tax Reports.

[40] ¶ 11,250
[41] ¶ 11,034, ¶ 11,037.023
[42] ¶ 11,034
[43] ¶ 11,035, ¶ 11,037.025
[44] ¶ 11,002, ¶ 11,037.036

¶1226

Creative Property Costs of Film Makers. A taxpayer may choose to amortize creative property costs ratably over 15 years beginning on the first day of the second half of the tax year in which the cost is written off for financial accounting purposes in accordance with Statement of Position 00-2 (SOP 00-2), as issued by the American Institute of Certified Public Accountants (AICPA) on June 12, 2000 (Rev. Proc. 2004-36).[45] Creative property costs are costs to acquire and develop for purposes of potential future film development, production, and exploitation; (1) screenplays; (2) scripts; (3) story outlines: (4) motion picture production rights to books and plays; and (4) similar properties. If the election is not made, these costs are generally recovered under the income forecast method only if a film is actually produced. If a film is not made, deduction of the costs as a loss is usually denied (Rev. Rul. 2004-58).

Election to Expense Films Costing $15 Million or Less. In the case of qualified film and television productions that commence after October 22, 2004 and before January 1, 2009, a taxpayer may elect to expense productions with an aggregate cost that does not exceed $15,000,000 (Code Sec. 181). Election guidance is provided in Temporary Reg. § 1.181-2T.

1231. Other Consistent Methods. In addition to the depreciation methods explained at ¶ 1224–¶ 1228, a taxpayer may use any other consistent method, such as the sinking fund method, if the total deductions during the first two-thirds of the useful life are not more than the total allowable under the declining-balance method (Reg. § 1.167(b)-4).[46]

Leased Property

1234. Lessee/Lessor Improvements, Lease Acquisition Costs. Unless a leasehold improvement qualifies as "15-year leasehold improvement property" under the rule described below, the cost of an addition or improvement made by the lessee or lessor to real property that is a structural component of the building is depreciated under MACRS in the same manner as the MACRS deduction for the real property would be calculated if the real property had been placed in service at the same time as the addition or improvement (Code Sec. 168(i)(6) and (8)(A)).[47] For example, permanent walls installed in a commercial building (structural components) are separately depreciated as 39-year real property beginning in the month that the walls are placed in service using the mid-month convention. If, upon termination of the lease, a lessee does not retain an improvement (made by the lessee), loss is computed by reference to the improvement's adjusted basis at the time of the lease termination. A lessor that disposes of or abandons a leasehold improvement (made by the lessor) upon termination of the lease may use the adjusted basis of the improvement at such time to determine gain or loss (Code Sec. 168(i)(8)(B)).

"Qualified leasehold improvement property" placed in service after October 22, 2004, and before January 1, 2008, is 15-year MACRS property with a 15-year recovery period (39-years if ADS is elected), depreciable using the straight-line method, and the half-year or mid-quarter convention, as applicable (Code Sec. 168(e)(3)(E)(iv) as amended by P.L. 109-432, (b)(3)(G), and (g)(3)(B)). Qualified leasehold improvement property is defined the same way as the term is defined in Code Sec. 168(k)(3) for purposes of the bonus depreciation deduction (Code Sec. 168(e)(6)). Thus, the improvements must be made to the interior portion of nonresidential real property that is at least three years old by the lessor or lessee under or pursuant to the terms of a lease.

Leasehold additions and improvements that are not structural components are generally depreciated as MACRS personal property. See, *Cost segregation*, at ¶ 1240.

Lease Acquisition Costs. In amortizing the cost of acquiring a lease over the lease term, a renewal period is counted as part of the lease term if less than 75% of the acquisition cost is attributable to the unexpired lease period (not counting the renewal period) (Code Sec. 178).[48]

Footnote references are to paragraphs of the 2008 Standard Federal Tax Reports.

[45] ¶ 11,009.046
[46] ¶ 11,036, ¶ 11,037.031

[47] ¶ 11,250, ¶ 11,011.021
[48] ¶ 12,100, ¶ 12,105.021

Construction Allowances. A lessor must depreciate improvements made by the lessee with a qualified construction allowance (Code Sec. 110) as nonresidential real property. See ¶ 764.

1235. Sale v. Lease of Property. Whether a transaction is treated as a lease or as a purchase for tax purposes is important in determining who is entitled to claim depreciation and other deductions for related business expenses.[49] In most situations, the rules for determining whether a transaction is a lease or a purchase evolved from a series of court decisions and IRS rulings. Basically, the rules look to the economic substance of a transaction, not its form, to determine who is the owner of the property for tax purposes when the parties characterize it as a lease (Rev. Proc. 2001-28, Rev. Proc. 2001-29).

Motor Vehicle Leases. A qualified motor vehicle lease agreement that contains a terminal rental adjustment clause (a provision permitting or requiring the rental price to be adjusted upward or downward by reference to the amount realized by the lessor upon the sale of the vehicle) is treated as a lease if, but for the clause, it would have been treated as a lease for tax purposes (Code Sec. 7701(h)). This provision applies only to qualified agreements with respect to a motor vehicle (including a trailer).[50]

Modified Accelerated Cost Recovery System (MACRS)

1236. MACRS in General. MACRS is mandatory for most tangible depreciable property placed in service after December 31, 1986, unless transitional rules apply (Code Sec. 168).[51] Under MACRS, the cost of eligible property is recovered over a 3-, 5-, 7-, 10-, 15-, 20-, 27.5-, 31.5- or 39-year period, depending upon the type of property (see ¶ 1240) by using statutory recovery methods (see ¶ 1243) and conventions (see ¶ 1245). Special transferee rules apply to property received in specified nonrecognition transactions (see Code Sec. 168(i)(7)) (see ¶ 1248).[52]

1237. MACRS Bonus Depreciation. A bonus depreciation deduction was allowed for qualifying MACRS property placed in service after September 10, 2001 and before January 1, 2005 (Code Sec. 168(k); Reg. § 1.168(k)-1).[53] A 30 percent rate applied to property acquired after September 10, 2001 and before May 6, 2003, and placed in service before January 1, 2005. A 50 percent rate applied to property acquired after May 5, 2003 and placed in service before January 1, 2005. The placed in service deadline for the 30 and 50 percent rates was extended one year to January 1, 2006 for property which (a) was produced by a taxpayer and was subject to the Code Sec. 263A uniform capitalization rules, (b) had a production period greater than two years, or greater than one year and a cost exceeding $1 million, and (c) had an MACRS recovery period of at least 10 years or was used in the trade or business of transporting persons for hire, such as commercial aircraft (Code Sec. 168(k)(2)(B)). However, only pre-2005 expenditures were taken into account if the extended placed in service deadline applied. The extended January 1, 2006 placed-in-service deadline also applied to certain noncommercial aircraft acquired by purchase. In contrast, pre-January 1, 2006 expenditures on noncommercial aircraft were eligible for bonus depreciation (Code Sec. 168(k)(2)(C)). The January 1, 2006 placed-in-service deadline was extended an additional year if the inability to place the property in service before January 1, 2006 was caused by Hurricane Katrina, Rita, or Wilma. (Act Sec. 105 of the Gulf Opportunity Zone Act of 2005 (P.L. 109-135); Announcement 2006-29, I.R.B. 2006-19).[54]

Bonus depreciation was treated as depreciation for recapture purposes upon the sale of the property. Unlike the Code Sec. 179 allowance, there is no taxable income limitation or investment limitation on the bonus allowance.

AMT. Bonus depreciation was allowed in full for alternative minimum tax purposes. If bonus depreciation was claimed, no AMT adjustment is required on the regular MACRS deductions claimed during an asset's recovery period (i.e., the deductions are allowed in full for AMT purposes) (Code Sec. 168(k)(2)(F); Reg. § 1.168(k)-1(d)(1)(iii)).

Footnote references are to paragraphs of the 2008 Standard Federal Tax Reports.

[49] ¶ 8754.022
[50] ¶ 11,274.023
[51] ¶ 11,250, ¶ 11,279
[52] ¶ 11,250, ¶ 11,279.054
[53] ¶ 11,250, ¶ 11,277E, ¶ 11,279.058
[54] ¶ 11,279.058

Computation. The deduction was claimed on the cost of the property after reduction by any Code Sec. 179 allowance (¶ 1208) claimed. Regular MACRS deductions are claimed on the cost as reduced by any Code Sec. 179 allowance and bonus depreciation.

Example: Taxpayer purchases qualifying 5-year MACRS property subject to the half-year convention for $1,500 and claims a $600 Code Sec. 179 allowance. Using the 50-percent rate, bonus depreciation is $450 (($1,500 – $600) × 50%). Regular MACRS depreciation deductions are computed on a depreciable basis of $450 ($1,500 – $600 – $450). The regular first-year MACRS allowance is $90 ($450 ×20% (first-year table percentage)).

50 percent bonus allowance for Gulf Opportunity Zone property. Taxpayers may claim a bonus depreciation allowance equal to 50 percent of the adjusted basis of qualified Gulf Opportunity Zone property acquired after August 27, 2005 and placed in service before January 1, 2008 (Code Sec. 1400N(d); Notice 2006-67, providing extensive regulatory type guidance).[55] No binding acquisition contract may be in effect before August 28, 2005. The original use of the property in the Gulf Opportunity Zone (as defined in Code Sec. 1400M(1)) must commence with the taxpayer after August 27, 2005. The property must be acquired by purchase (as defined in Code Sec. 179(d) (see ¶ 1208)) and substantially all use of the property (80 percent or more) must be in an active trade or business within the Zone.

The additional depreciation allowance applies to MACRS property with a recovery period of 20 years or less, off-the-shelf computer software that is amortizable over three years, MACRS 25-year water utility property, qualified leasehold improvement property, new nonresidential real property, and new residential rental property.

The cost of rehabilitating or improving an existing building located in the GO Zone is generally eligible for bonus depreciation. A taxpayer who acquires a damaged building for rehabilitation may also claim bonus depreciation on the cost of the building if the cost of building is not more than 20 percent of the sum of the cost of the building and the rehabilitation expenditures. If the owner of a damaged building that was taken out of service rehabilitates the building and before placing it back into service sells the property, the purchaser may claim bonus depreciation on the cost attributable to the rehabilitation expenditures and, also, the cost attributable to the damaged building if the 20 percent test is satisfied. Similar rules apply to damaged personal property (Notice 2007-36).

The placed-in-service deadline for nonresidential and residential property is December 31, 2008. The deadline is extended to December 31, 2010 if the building is located in the Louisiana parishes of Calcasieu, Cameron, Orleans, Plaquemines, St. Bernard, St. Tammany, or Washington or the Mississippi counties of Hancock, Harrison, Jackson, Pearl River, or Stone. However, bonus depreciation may only be claimed on pre-January 1, 2010 progress expenditures. Personal property used in a building that meets the December 31, 2010 placed-in-service deadline, such as furniture or personal property identified in a cost segregation study, will qualify for the 50 percent allowance if placed in service not later than 90 days after the building is placed in service. Bonus depreciation may be claimed on portions of buildings (e.g., floors of multi-story buildings) that are placed in service by the December 31, 2010 deadline (Code Sec. 1400N(d)(6), as added by the Tax Relief and Health Care Act of 2006 (P.L. 109-432); Notice 2007-36).

The allowance may not be claimed on property required to be depreciated using the MACRS alternative depreciation system (ADS) (i.e., mandatory ADS property). An election to use ADS does not disqualify property. See ¶ 1247. Exclusions also apply to tax-exempt bond financed property, qualified revitalization buildings and rehabilitation expenditures for which a deduction under Code Sec. 1400I(a) is claimed (¶ 999C), and property used in connection with a golf course, country club, massage parlor, hot tub or suntan facility, liquor store, gambling or animal racing establishment (Code Sec. 1400N(p)).

Footnote references are to paragraphs of the 2008 Standard Federal Tax Reports.

[55] ¶ 32,487.031

A taxpayer may elect out of the provision on a property class basis. A deemed election out may apply to a taxpayer that filed its 2004 or 2005 federal income tax return before September 13, 2006 and did not claim the deduction (Notice 2006-67). If the Gulf Zone bonus allowance is claimed, the bonus allowance and regular depreciation deductions on the property are allowed in full for AMT purposes. If business use drops to less than 80 percent, the deduction is subject to recapture under rules similar to those that apply to the Code Sec. 179 allowance (¶ 1208). If the property is disposed of, the bonus allowance is treated as a depreciation allowance for purposes of the recapture rules. See ¶ 1779. Qualified Gulf Opportunity Zone property is also eligible for an increased section 179 expense allowance. See ¶ 1208.

New York Liberty Zone Incentives. See ¶ 999E for special incentives, including a 30 percent bonus depreciation allowance, that apply to property placed in service in the New York Liberty Zone (Code Sec. 1400L).

50 percent bonus allowance for mine safety equipment. A taxpayer may elect to deduct 50 percent of the cost of qualified advanced mine safety equipment paid or incurred after December 20, 2006 if the equipment is placed in service before January 1, 2009 (Code Sec. 179E, as added by the Tax Relief and Health Care Act of 2006 (P.L. 109-432)).

50 percent bonus allowance for cellulosic biomass ethanol plant property. A 50-percent additional depreciation allowance may be claimed on the adjusted basis of qualified cellulosic biomass ethanol plant property (QCBEPP) acquired and placed in service after December 20, 2006 and before January 1, 2013 (Code Sec. 168(l), as added by the Tax Relief and Health Care Act of 2006 (P.L. 109-432)).

1238. Property Subject to MACRS. Generally, most tangible depreciable property placed in service after 1986 is depreciated under MACRS. MACRS property is depreciable if it wears out, has a useful life that exceeds one year, and is used in a trade or business or for the production of income. Such property does not include property for which an election was made to use a depreciation method not expressed in terms of years, such as the unit of production or income forecast method; public utility property (unless a normalization method of accounting is used); motion picture films and videotapes; sound recordings; intangible property; and property placed in service before 1987 that is excluded from MACRS under the anti-churning rules (Code Sec. 168(f)).[56] Public utility property that does not qualify under MACRS (Code Sec. 168(f)(2))[57] is depreciated under Code Sec. 167(a)[58] using the same depreciation method and useful life as is used to compute the ratemaking depreciation allowance for the property.[59]

1240. MACRS Depreciation Periods. The MACRS depreciation (recovery) period for an asset is based on its class life as of January 1, 1986 or is specifically prescribed by Code Sec. 168.[60] The recovery periods for MACRS assets can be found in a table that appears in IRS Publication 946. This table is an updated version of the table that appears in Rev. Proc. 87-56. Under MACRS, assets are classified according to their class life as follows:

Three-Year Property. Three-year property includes property with a class life of four years or less. Any race horse over two years old or any other horse over 12 years old at the time it is placed in service is also classified as three-year property (Code Sec. 168(e)(1) and (3)).[61] For property placed in service after August 5, 1997, certain "rent-to-own" consumer durable property (e.g., televisions and furniture) is three-year property (Code Sec. 168(e)(3)(iii)).[62] Breeding hogs (Rev. Proc. 87-56 Asset Class 01.236) and tractor units for use over the road (Rev. Proc. 87-56 Asset Class 00.26) are three-year property. A tractor unit is a highway truck designed to tow a trailer or semitrailer and which does not carry cargo on the same chassis as the engine (Reg. § 145.4051-1(e)(1)).

Five-Year Property. Five-year property generally includes property with a class life of more than four years and less than 10 years. This property includes: (1) cars, (2) light

Footnote references are to paragraphs of the 2008 Standard Federal Tax Reports.

[56] ¶ 11,250, ¶ 11,279.021   [59] ¶ 11,070.01   [62] ¶ 11,250, ¶ 11,279.023
[57] ¶ 11,250   [60] ¶ 163.01, ¶ 11,279.021
[58] ¶ 11,002   [61] ¶ 11,250, ¶ 11,279.023

and heavy general-purpose trucks, (3) qualified technological equipment, (4) computer-based telephone central office switching equipment, (5) research and experimentation property that is Sec. 1245 property, (6) semi-conductor manufacturing equipment, (7) geothermal, solar and wind energy properties, (8) certain biomass properties that are small power production facilities, (9) computers and peripheral equipment, and (10) office machinery (typewriters, calculators, etc.) (Code Sec. 168(e)(1) and (3)).[63]

Furniture, appliances, window treatments, and carpeting used in residential rental property are five-year property (Announcement 99-82). Personal property used in wholesale or retail trade or in the provision of personal and professional services for which a specific recovery period is not otherwise provided is five-year property (Asset Class 57.0 of Rev. Proc. 87-56). For example, a professional library used by an accountant or attorney is five-year property. Examples of *personal* service businesses include hotels and motels, laundry and dry cleaning establishments, beauty and barber shops, photographic studios and mortuaries (Rev. Proc. 77-10). Examples of *professional* service businesses include services offered by doctors, dentists, lawyers, accountants, architects, engineers, and veterinarians (Rev. Proc. 77-10).

Five-year property also includes taxis (Rev. Proc. 87-56 Asset Class 00.22), buses (Rev. Proc. 87-56 Asset Class 00.23), airplanes not used in commercial or contract carrying of passengers or freight and all helicopters (Rev. Proc. 87-56 Asset Class 00.21), trailers and trailer-mounted containers (Rev. Proc. 87-56 Asset Class 00.27), breeding cattle and dairy cattle (Rev. Proc. 87-56 Asset Class 01.21), breeding sheep and breeding goats (Rev. Proc. 87-56 Asset Class 01.21), and assets used in construction by certain contractors, builders, and real estate subdividers and developers (Rev. Proc. 87-56 Asset Class 15.0).

Seven-Year Property. Seven-year property includes property with a class life of 10 years or more but less than 16 years (Code Sec. 168(e)(1)). This property includes office furniture, equipment and fixtures that are not structural components (Rev. Proc. 87-56 Asset Class 00.11). Desks, files, safes, overhead projectors, cell phones, fax machines and other communication equipment not included in any other class fall within this category. Seven-year property also includes: assets (except helicopters) used in commercial and contract carrying of passengers and freight by air (Rev. Proc. 87-56 Asset Class 45.0); certain livestock (Rev. Proc. 87-56 Asset Class 01.1); breeding or work horses 12 years old or less when placed in service (Rev. Proc. 87-56 Asset Class 01.221); other horses that are not three-year property (Rev. Proc. 87-56 Asset Class 01.225); machinery and equipment, grain bins, and fences used in agricultural activities (Rev. Proc. 87-56 Asset Class 01.1); assets used in recreation businesses (Rev. Proc. 87-56 Asset Class 80.0); and assets used in theme and amusement parks (Rev. Proc. 87-56 Asset Class 80.0). Railroad track and property (such as a fishing vessel) that does not have a class life and is not otherwise classified is seven-year property (Code Sec. 168(e)(3)(C)).[64]

10-Year Property. Ten-year property is property with a class life of 16 years or more and less than 20 years (Code Sec. 168(e)(1)).[65] Ten-year property includes vessels, barges, tugs, and similar means of water transportation not used in marine construction or as a fishing vessel (Rev. Proc. 87-56 Asset Class 00.28). MACRS deductions for trees or vines bearing fruit or nuts that are placed in service after 1988 are determined under the straight-line method over a 10-year recovery period (Code Sec. 168(b)(1)).[66] Single purpose agricultural or horticultural structures placed in service after 1988 are ten-year property (Code Sec. 168(e)(3)(D)(i)).

15-Year Property. Property with a class life of 20 years or more but less than 25 years is generally considered 15-year property (Code Sec. 168(e)(1)). It includes municipal wastewater treatment plants and telephone distribution plants and other comparable equipment used for the two-way exchange of voice, data communications, and retail motor fuels outlets (Code Sec. 168(e)(3)(E)).[67] A property qualifies as a retail motor

---

Footnote references are to paragraphs of the 2008 Standard Federal Tax Reports.

[63] ¶ 11,250, ¶ 11,279.023   [65] ¶ 11,250, ¶ 11,279.023   [67] ¶ 11,250, ¶ 11,279.023
[64] ¶ 11,250, ¶ 11,279.023   [66] ¶ 11,250, ¶ 11,279.023

fuels outlet (as opposed, for example, to a convenience store which is 39-year real property) if (1) 50 percent or more of gross revenues are derived from petroleum sales, or (2) 50 percent or more of the floor space is devoted to petroleum marketing sales, or (3) the property is 1,400 square feet or less (Rev. Proc. 97-10).[68]

15-year property includes car wash buildings (and related land improvements), billboards, and section 1250 real property (including service station buildings) and depreciable land improvements used in marketing petroleum and petroleum products (Rev. Proc. 87-56 Asset Class 57.1). Water transportation assets (other than vessels) used in the commercial and contract carrying of freight and passengers by water are 15-year property (Rev. Proc. 87-56 Asset Class 44.0).

Land improvements not specifically included in any other asset class and otherwise depreciable are 15-year property (Rev. Proc. 87-56 Asset Class 00.3). Examples of land improvements include sidewalks, driveways, curbs, roads, parking lots, canals, waterways, drainage facilities, sewers (but not municipal sewers), wharves and docks, bridges, and nonagricultural fences. Landscaping and shrubbery is a depreciable land improvement if it is located near a building and would be destroyed if the building were replaced (Rev. Rul. 74-265; IRS Publication 946). Playground equipment is a land improvement (IRS Letter Ruling 8848039).[69]

Depreciable gas utility clearing and grading costs incurred after October 22, 2004 to place pipelines into service are 15-year property (Code Sec. 168(e)(3)(E)(vi)).

Restaurant Improvements. Qualified restaurant property placed in service after October 22, 2004 and before January 1, 2008 is 15-year MACRS property, depreciable using the straight-line method using the half-year or mid-quarter convention, as applicable. If ADS is elected a 39-year recovery period applies. Qualified restaurant property is section 1250 property which is an improvement to a building if the improvement is placed in service more than three years after the date the building was first placed in service. More than 50 percent of the building's square footage must be devoted to preparation of and seating for on-premises consumption of prepared meals (Code Sec. 168(e)(7)).

20-Year Property. Twenty-year property includes property with a class life of 25 years and more, other than Code Sec. 1250 real property with a class life of 27.5 years or more. Water utility property and municipal sewers placed in service before June 13, 1996, and farm buildings (e.g., barns and machine sheds) are included within this class (Code Sec. 168(e)(1) and (3)).[70]

Depreciable electric utility clearing and grading costs incurred after October 22, 2004 to place transmission and distribution line into service are 20-year property (Code Sec. 168(e)(3)(F)).

25-Year Property. Water utility property and municipal sewers placed in service after June 12, 1996 are included in this class (Code Sec. 168(c) and (e)(5)). The straight-line depreciation method is mandatory for 25-year property (Code Sec. 168(b)(3)(F)).

27.5-Year Residential Rental Property. Residential rental property (Code Sec. 168(e)(2)(A))[71] includes buildings or structures with respect to which 80% or more of the gross rental income is from dwelling units. It also includes manufactured homes that are residential rental property and elevators and escalators.

Nonresidential Real Property. Nonresidential real property is Code Sec. 1250 real property (see ¶ 1786) that is not (1) residential rental property or (2) property with a class life of less than 27.5 years. It includes property that either has no class life or whose class life is 27.5 years or more, including elevators and escalators (Code Sec. 168(e)(2)(B)).[72] The cost of nonresidential real property generally placed in service after May 12, 1993, is recovered over 39 years. For property placed in service after 1986 and before May 13, 1993, cost is recovered over 31.5 years.

Footnote references are to paragraphs of the 2008 Standard Federal Tax Reports.

[68] ¶ 11,279.023
[69] ¶ 11,279.0518

[70] ¶ 11,250, ¶ 11,279.023
[71] ¶ 11,250, ¶ 11,279.023

[72] ¶ 11,250, ¶ 11,279.023

Indian Reservation Property. For qualified Indian reservation property that is placed in service after 1993 and before 2008, special MACRS recovery periods are provided for both regular tax and alternative minimum tax purposes that permit faster write-offs (Code Sec. 168(j), as amended by P.L. 109-432).[73]

Additions and Improvements. Additions and improvements made to an existing property are depreciated under MACRS in the same way that the existing property would be depreciated if it were placed in service at the same time as the addition or improvement (Code Sec. 168(i)(6)). For example, a window added to a commercial building in 2007 is treated as 39-year MACRS nonresidential real property even if the building is depreciated under a pre-MACRS method.[74] However, any elements of an addition or improvement to a building that qualify as personal property may be depreciated as personal rather than real property by reason of the cost segregation rule described below. Special rules apply to leasehold improvement property (see ¶ 1234) and restaurant improvements, as explained above.

Roofs. The IRS maintains that the replacement of all of the shingles on a roof or the asphalt and gravel on a flat roof is a capital expenditure. Although the IRS position is supported by many court decisions, the Tax Court has held that the cost of removing and replacing the entire perlite and asphalt and gravel covering on a leaky roof (as well as replacing an expansion joint to prevent further leaking) was a deductible repair (*Oberman Manufacturing Co.*, 47 TC 471, CCH 28,334 (1967)). Two Tax Court summary opinions, citing *Oberman*, have also allowed a current repair deduction for the cost of replacing the roofing shingles on an apartment house (*N. Campbell*, T.C. Summary Opinion 2002-117) and a tar and gravel roof on a commercial building (*T.J. Northen Jr. and S. Cox* T.C. Summary Opinion 2003-113).[75]

Cost Segregation. The Tax Court has ruled that elements of a building that are treated as personal property under the former investment tax credit rules (Reg. § 1.48-1(c)) may be separately depreciated under MACRS and ACRS as personal property (*Hospital Corp. of America*, 109 TC 21, Dec. 52,163). The IRS has acquiesced to the court's holding that the former investment tax credit rules apply in determining whether an item is a structural component (i.e., real property) or personal property but nonacquiesced to its finding that various disputed items were in fact personal property under these rules (Notice of Acquiescence, 1999-35 I.R.B. 314). The separate depreciation of personal property elements of a building is referred to as cost segregation.[76]

The determination of whether an item is personal property or a structural component will often depend upon the specific facts. However, the following items, if related to the operation and maintenance of a building, are examples of structural components: bathtubs, boilers, ceilings (including acoustical ceilings), central air conditioning and heating systems, chimneys, doors, electrical and wiring, fire escapes, floors, hot water heaters, HVAC units, lighting fixtures, paneling, partitions (if not readily removable), plumbing, roofs, sinks, sprinkler systems, stairs, tiling, walls, and windows (Reg. § 1.48-1(e)(2)).

1243. MACRS Recovery Methods. Under MACRS, the cost of depreciable property is recovered using (1) the applicable depreciation method, (2) the applicable recovery period, and (3) the applicable convention (Code Sec. 168(a)). Instead of the applicable depreciation method, taxpayers may irrevocably elect to claim straight-line MACRS deductions over the regular recovery period. The election applies to all property in the MACRS class for which the election is made that is placed in service during the tax year and is made on the return for the year the property is first placed in service (Code Sec. 168(b)(5)). For example, if the election is made for 3-year property, it applies to all 3-year property placed in service in the tax year of the election.[77] A taxpayer may also elect the MACRS alternative depreciation system (ADS) with respect to any class of property. ADS uses the straight-line method over recovery periods that are usually longer than those that normally apply under MACRS. See ¶ 1247.

Footnote references are to paragraphs of the 2008 Standard Federal Tax Reports.

[73] ¶ 11,250, ¶ 11,279.031   [75] ¶ 13,709.0575   [77] ¶ 11,279.033
[74] ¶ 11,279.05   [76] ¶ 11,279.051

The cost of property in the 3-, 5-, 7-, and 10-year classes is recovered using the 200% declining-balance method over three, five, seven, and ten years, respectively, and the half-year convention (unless the mid-quarter convention applies), with a switch to the straight-line method in the year that maximizes the deduction (Code Sec. 168(b)(1)).[78] The cost of 15- and 20-year property is recovered using the 150% declining-balance method over 15 and 20 years, respectively, and the half-year convention (unless the mid-quarter convention applies), with a switch to the straight-line method to maximize the deduction (Code Sec. 168(b)(2)).[79] The cost of residential rental and nonresidential real property is recovered using the straight-line method and the mid-month convention over 27.5- and 39-year recovery periods, respectively (Code Sec. 168(b)(3)).[80]

An election may be made to recover the cost of 3-, 5-, 7-, and 10-year property using the 150% declining-balance method over the regular recovery periods (the ADS recovery period for property placed in service before 1999) (see ¶1247) (Code Sec. 168(b)(2)(C)). This election, like the straight-line election described above, is made separately for each property class placed in service during the tax year of the election.[81] Generally, 3-, 5-, 7-, and 10-year property used in the trade or business of farming must be depreciated under the 150% declining balance method unless an election was made to deduct preproductive period expenditures, in which case the ADS must be used (Code Sec. 168(b)(2)(B)). Consequently, Tables 1-8, below, may not be used for such property.

Computation of Deduction Without Tables. The MACRS deduction on personal property is computed by first determining the rate of depreciation (dividing the number one by the recovery period).[82] This basic rate is multiplied by 1.5 or 2 for the 150% or 200% declining-balance method, as applicable, to determine the declining balance rate. The adjusted basis of the property is multiplied by the declining-balance rate and the half-year or mid-quarter convention (whichever is applicable) is applied in computing depreciation for the first year. The depreciation claimed in the first year is subtracted from the adjusted basis before applying the declining-balance rate in determining the depreciation deduction for the second year.

Under the MACRS straight-line method (used, for example, on real property or if ADS applies), a new applicable depreciation rate is determined for each tax year in the applicable recovery period. For any tax year, the applicable depreciation rate (in percentage terms) is determined by dividing one by the length of the applicable recovery period remaining as of the beginning of such tax year. The rate is applied to the unrecovered basis of such property in conjunction with the appropriate convention. If as of the beginning of any tax year the remaining recovery period is less than one year, the applicable depreciation rate under the straight-line method for that year is 100%.

Example 1: An item of 5-year property is purchased by a calendar-year taxpayer in January ("Year 1") at a cost of $10,000. No Code Sec. 179 expense allowance is claimed. The 200% declining-balance method and half-year convention apply. Depreciation computed without the use of the IRS tables is determined as follows: the declining-balance depreciation rate is determined and compared with the straight-line rate. A switch is made to the straight-line rate in the year depreciation equals or exceeds that determined under the declining-balance method. The applicable rate is applied to the unrecovered basis. The 200% declining-balance depreciation rate is 40% (1 divided by 5 (recovery period) times 2). The straight-line rate (which changes each year) is 1 divided by the length of the applicable recovery period remaining as of the beginning of each tax year (after considering the applicable convention for purposes of determining how much of the applicable recovery period remains as of the beginning of the year). For year four, the straight-line rate is .40 (1 divided by 2.5). For year five, the straight-line rate is .6667 (1 divided by 1.5). For year six, the straight-line rate is 100% because the remaining recovery period is less than one year.

Footnote references are to paragraphs of the 2008 Standard Federal Tax Reports.

[78] ¶11,250, ¶11,279.03   [80] ¶11,250, ¶11,279.03   [82] ¶11,279.027
[79] ¶11,250, ¶11,279.03   [81] ¶11,279.035

Year	Method	Rate	Unrecovered Basis			Depreciation
1	DB	.40	× $ 10,000 × .5 (half-yr. conv.)		....	= $ 2,000
2	DB	.40	× (10,000 – 2,000)	= $8,000	..	= 3,200
3	DB	.40	× (8,000 – 3,200)	= 4,800	..	= 1,920
4	SL	.40	× (4,800 – 1,920)	= 2,880	..	= 1,152
5	SL	.6667	× (2,880 – 1,152)	= 1,728	..	= 1,152
6	SL	1.000	× (1,728 – 1,152)	= 576	..	= 576
					0	
				Total	..	$10,000

The computation of MACRS without tables is discussed in detail by the IRS in Rev. Proc. 87-57.

Computation of Deduction Using Tables. MACRS depreciation tables, which contain the annual percentage depreciation rates to be applied to the unadjusted basis of property in each tax year, may be used to compute depreciation instead of the above rules.[83] The tables incorporate the appropriate convention and a switch from the declining-balance method to the straight-line method in the year that the latter provides a depreciation allowance equal to, or larger than, the former. The tables may be used for any item of property (that otherwise qualifies for MACRS) placed in service in a tax year.

Selected MACRS depreciation tables are reproduced below. A complete set of tables is at ¶ 164.01 of the STANDARD FEDERAL TAX REPORTER. Tables for the TAX RESEARCH CONSULTANT are located in the "Practice Aids" tab of the Tax Research Network at ¶ 470 of the "Tax Rates and Tables" publication.

If a table is used to compute the annual depreciation allowance for any item of property, it must be used throughout the entire recovery period of such property. However, a taxpayer may not continue to use a table if there are any adjustments to the basis of the property for reasons other than (1) depreciation allowances or (2) an addition or improvement to such property that is subject to depreciation as a separate item of property.

The IRS MACRS depreciation tables may not be used in situations involving short tax years (see ¶ 1244).

Example 2: Depreciation on 5-year property purchased by a calendar-year taxpayer in January of the current tax year at a cost of $10,000 is computed under the general MACRS 200% declining-balance method over a five-year recovery period using the half-year convention. No amount is expensed under Code Sec. 179 or claimed as a bonus deduction.

If the depreciation tables provided by the IRS are used, depreciation is computed as follows: the applicable depreciation rate in Table 1 under the column for a 5-year recovery period for the applicable recovery year is applied to the cost of the property.

Year	Rate	Unadj. Basis	Depreciation	Basis			
1	.20 ×	$ 10,000 =	$ 2,000	($10,000 –	$2,000)	=	$8,000
2	.32 ×	10,000 =	3,200	(8,000 –	3,200)	=	4,800
3	.192 ×	10,000 =	1,920	(4,800 –	1,920)	=	2,880
4	.1152 ×	10,000 =	1,152	(2,880 –	1,152)	=	1,728
5	.1152 ×	10,000 =	1,152	(1,728 –	1,152)	=	576
6	.0576 ×	10,000 =	576	(576 –	576)	=	0
		Total	$10,000				

Footnote references are to paragraphs of the 2008 Standard Federal Tax Reports.

[83] ¶ 164.01

Table 1. General Depreciation System
Applicable Depreciation Method: 200 or 150 Percent
Declining Balance Switching to Straight Line
Applicable Recovery Periods: 3, 5, 7, 10, 15, 20 years
Applicable Convention: Half-year

If the Recovery Year is:	\ 3-year	\ 5-year	and the Recovery Period is: \ 7-year	\ 10-year	\ 15-year	\ 20-year
			the Depreciation Rate is:			
1	33.33	20.00	14.29	10.00	5.00	3.750
2	44.45	32.00	24.49	18.00	9.50	7.219
3	14.81	19.20	17.49	14.40	8.55	6.677
4	7.41	11.52	12.49	11.52	7.70	6.177
5		11.52	8.93	9.22	6.93	5.713
6		5.76	8.92	7.37	6.23	5.285
7			8.93	6.55	5.90	4.888
8			4.46	6.55	5.90	4.522
9				6.56	5.91	4.462
10				6.55	5.90	4.461
11				3.28	5.91	4.462
12					5.90	4.461
13					5.91	4.462
14					5.90	4.461
15					5.91	4.462
16					2.95	4.461
17						4.462
18						4.461
19						4.462
20						4.461
21						2.231

Table 2. General Depreciation System
Applicable Depreciation Method: 200 or 150 Percent
Declining Balance Switching to Straight Line
Applicable Recovery Periods: 3, 5, 7, 10, 15, 20 years
Applicable Convention: Mid-quarter (property placed in service in first quarter)

If the Recovery Year is:	\ 3-year	\ 5-year	and the Recovery Period is: \ 7-year	\ 10-year	\ 15-year	\ 20-year
			the Depreciation Rate is:			
1	58.33	35.00	25.00	17.50	8.75	6.563
2	27.78	26.00	21.43	16.50	9.13	7.000
3	12.35	15.60	15.31	13.20	8.21	6.482
4	1.54	11.01	10.93	10.56	7.39	5.996
5		11.01	8.75	8.45	6.65	5.546
6		1.38	8.74	6.76	5.99	5.130
7			8.75	6.55	5.90	4.746
8			1.09	6.55	5.91	4.459
9				6.56	5.90	4.459
10				6.55	5.91	4.459
11				0.82	5.90	4.459
12					5.91	4.460
13					5.90	4.459
14					5.91	4.460
15					5.90	4.459
16					0.74	4.460
17						4.459
18						4.460
19						4.459
20						4.460
21						0.557

Table 3. General Depreciation System
Applicable Depreciation Method: 200 or 150 Percent
Declining Balance Switching to Straight Line
Applicable Recovery Periods: 3, 5, 7, 10, 15, 20 years
Applicable Convention: Mid-quarter (property placed in
service in second quarter)

If the Recovery Year is:	and the Recovery Period is:					
	3-year	5-year	7-year	10-year	15-year	20-year
	the Depreciation Rate is:					
1 ..	41.67	25.00	17.85	12.50	6.25	4.688
2 ..	38.89	30.00	23.47	17.50	9.38	7.148
3 ..	14.14	18.00	16.76	14.00	8.44	6.612
4 ..	5.30	11.37	11.97	11.20	7.59	6.116
5		11.37	8.87	8.96	6.83	5.658
6		4.26	8.87	7.17	6.15	5.233
7			8.87	6.55	5.91	4.841
8			3.33	6.55	5.90	4.478
9				6.56	5.91	4.463
10				6.55	5.90	4.463
11				2.46	5.91	4.463
12					5.90	4.463
13					5.91	4.463
14					5.90	4.463
15					5.91	4.462
16					2.21	4.463
17						4.462
18						4.463
19						4.462
20						4.463
21						1.673

Table 4. General Depreciation System
Applicable Depreciation Method: 200 or 150 Percent
Declining Balance Switching to Straight Line
Applicable Recovery Periods: 3, 5, 7, 10, 15, 20 years
Applicable Convention: Mid-quarter (property placed in
service in third quarter)

If the Recovery Year is:	and the Recovery Period is:					
	3-year	5-year	7-year	10-year	15-year	20-year
	the Depreciation Rate is:					
1 ..	25.00	15.00	10.71	7.50	3.75	2.813
2 ..	50.00	34.00	25.51	18.50	9.63	7.289
3 ..	16.67	20.40	18.22	14.80	8.66	6.742
4 ..	8.33	12.24	13.02	11.84	7.80	6.237
5		11.30	9.30	9.47	7.02	5.769
6		7.06	8.85	7.58	6.31	5.336
7			8.86	6.55	5.90	4.936
8			5.53	6.55	5.90	4.566
9				6.56	5.91	4.460
10				6.55	5.90	4.460
11				4.10	5.91	4.460
12					5.90	4.460
13					5.91	4.461
14					5.90	4.460
15					5.91	4.461
16					3.69	4.460
17						4.461
18						4.460
19						4.461
20						4.460
21						2.788

Table 5. General Depreciation System
Applicable Depreciation Method: 200 or 150 Percent
Declining Balance Switching to Straight Line
Applicable Recovery Periods: 3, 5, 7, 10, 15, 20 years
Applicable Convention: Mid-quarter (property placed in
service in fourth quarter)

If the Recovery Year is:	and the Recovery Period is:					
	3-year	5-year	7-year	10-year	15-year	20-year
	the Depreciation Rate is:					
1 ..	8.33	5.00	3.57	2.50	1.25	0.938
2 ..	61.11	38.00	27.55	19.50	9.88	7.430
3 ..	20.37	22.80	19.68	15.60	8.89	6.872
4 ..	10.19	13.68	14.06	12.48	8.00	6.357
5		10.94	10.04	9.98	7.20	5.880
6		9.58	8.73	7.99	6.48	5.439
7			8.73	6.55	5.90	5.031
8			7.64	6.55	5.90	4.654
9				6.56	5.90	4.458
10				6.55	5.91	4.458
11				5.74	5.90	4.458
12					5.91	4.458
13					5.90	4.458
14					5.91	4.458
15					5.90	4.458
16					5.17	4.458
17						4.458
18						4.459
19						4.458
20						4.459
21						3.901

Table 6. General Depreciation System
Applicable Depreciation Method: Straight Line
Applicable Recovery Period: 27.5 years
Applicable Convention: Mid-month

If the Recovery Year is:	And the Month in the First Recovery Year the Property is Placed in Service is:											
	1	2	3	4	5	6	7	8	9	10	11	12
	the Depreciation Rate is:											
1 ..	3.485	3.182	2.879	2.576	2.273	1.970	1.667	1.364	1.061	0.758	0.455	0.152
2 ..	3.636	3.636	3.636	3.636	3.636	3.636	3.636	3.636	3.636	3.636	3.636	3.636
3 ..	3.636	3.636	3.636	3.636	3.636	3.636	3.636	3.636	3.636	3.636	3.636	3.636
4 ..	3.636	3.636	3.636	3.636	3.636	3.636	3.636	3.636	3.636	3.636	3.636	3.636
5 ..	3.636	3.636	3.636	3.636	3.636	3.636	3.636	3.636	3.636	3.636	3.636	3.636
6 ..	3.636	3.636	3.636	3.636	3.636	3.636	3.636	3.636	3.636	3.636	3.636	3.636
7 ..	3.636	3.636	3.636	3.636	3.636	3.636	3.636	3.636	3.636	3.636	3.636	3.636
8 ..	3.636	3.636	3.636	3.636	3.636	3.636	3.636	3.636	3.636	3.636	3.636	3.636
9 ..	3.636	3.636	3.636	3.636	3.636	3.636	3.636	3.636	3.636	3.636	3.636	3.636
10 ..	3.637	3.637	3.637	3.637	3.637	3.637	3.636	3.636	3.636	3.636	3.636	3.636
11 ..	3.636	3.636	3.636	3.636	3.636	3.636	3.637	3.637	3.637	3.637	3.637	3.637
12 ..	3.637	3.637	3.637	3.637	3.637	3.637	3.636	3.636	3.636	3.636	3.636	3.636
13 ..	3.636	3.636	3.636	3.636	3.636	3.636	3.637	3.637	3.637	3.637	3.637	3.637
14 ..	3.637	3.637	3.637	3.637	3.637	3.637	3.636	3.636	3.636	3.636	3.636	3.636
15 ..	3.636	3.636	3.636	3.636	3.636	3.636	3.637	3.637	3.637	3.637	3.637	3.637
16 ..	3.637	3.637	3.637	3.637	3.637	3.637	3.636	3.636	3.636	3.636	3.636	3.636
17 ..	3.636	3.636	3.636	3.636	3.636	3.636	3.637	3.637	3.637	3.637	3.637	3.637
18 ..	3.637	3.637	3.637	3.637	3.637	3.637	3.636	3.636	3.636	3.636	3.636	3.636
19 ..	3.636	3.636	3.636	3.636	3.636	3.636	3.637	3.637	3.637	3.637	3.637	3.637
20 ..	3.637	3.637	3.637	3.637	3.637	3.637	3.636	3.636	3.636	3.636	3.636	3.636
21 ..	3.636	3.636	3.636	3.636	3.636	3.636	3.637	3.637	3.637	3.637	3.637	3.637
22 ..	3.637	3.637	3.637	3.637	3.637	3.637	3.636	3.636	3.636	3.636	3.636	3.636
23 ..	3.636	3.636	3.636	3.636	3.636	3.636	3.637	3.637	3.637	3.637	3.637	3.637
24 ..	3.637	3.637	3.637	3.637	3.637	3.637	3.636	3.636	3.636	3.636	3.636	3.636
25 ..	3.636	3.636	3.636	3.636	3.636	3.636	3.637	3.637	3.637	3.637	3.637	3.637
26 ..	3.637	3.637	3.637	3.637	3.637	3.637	3.636	3.636	3.636	3.636	3.636	3.636
27 ..	3.636	3.636	3.636	3.636	3.636	3.636	3.637	3.637	3.637	3.637	3.637	3.637
28 ..	1.970	2.273	2.576	2.879	3.182	3.485	3.636	3.636	3.636	3.636	3.636	3.636
29 ..	0.000	0.000	0.000	0.000	0.000	0.000	0.152	0.455	0.758	1.061	1.364	1.667

Table 7. General Depreciation System
Applicable Depreciation Method: Straight Line
Applicable Recovery Period: 31.5 years
Applicable Convention: Mid-month

If the Recovery Year is:	And the Month in the First Recovery Year the Property is Placed in Service is:											
	1	2	3	4	5	6	7	8	9	10	11	12
	the Depreciation Rate is:											
1	3.042	2.778	2.513	2.249	1.984	1.720	1.455	1.190	0.926	0.661	0.397	0.132
2	3.175	3.175	3.175	3.175	3.175	3.175	3.175	3.175	3.175	3.175	3.175	3.175
3	3.175	3.175	3.175	3.175	3.175	3.175	3.175	3.175	3.175	3.175	3.175	3.175
4	3.175	3.175	3.175	3.175	3.175	3.175	3.175	3.175	3.175	3.175	3.175	3.175
5	3.175	3.175	3.175	3.175	3.175	3.175	3.175	3.175	3.175	3.175	3.175	3.175
6	3.175	3.175	3.175	3.175	3.175	3.175	3.175	3.175	3.175	3.175	3.175	3.175
7	3.175	3.175	3.175	3.175	3.175	3.175	3.175	3.175	3.175	3.175	3.175	3.175
8	3.175	3.174	3.175	3.174	3.175	3.174	3.175	3.175	3.175	3.175	3.175	3.175
9	3.174	3.175	3.174	3.175	3.174	3.175	3.174	3.175	3.174	3.175	3.174	3.175
10	3.175	3.174	3.175	3.174	3.175	3.174	3.175	3.174	3.175	3.174	3.175	3.174
11	3.174	3.175	3.174	3.175	3.174	3.175	3.174	3.175	3.174	3.175	3.174	3.175
12	3.175	3.174	3.175	3.174	3.175	3.174	3.175	3.174	3.175	3.174	3.175	3.174
13	3.174	3.175	3.174	3.175	3.174	3.175	3.174	3.175	3.174	3.175	3.174	3.175
14	3.175	3.174	3.175	3.174	3.175	3.174	3.175	3.174	3.175	3.174	3.175	3.174
15	3.174	3.175	3.174	3.175	3.174	3.175	3.174	3.175	3.174	3.175	3.174	3.175
16	3.175	3.174	3.175	3.174	3.175	3.174	3.175	3.174	3.175	3.174	3.175	3.174
17	3.174	3.175	3.174	3.175	3.174	3.175	3.174	3.175	3.174	3.175	3.174	3.175
18	3.175	3.174	3.175	3.174	3.175	3.174	3.175	3.174	3.175	3.174	3.175	3.174
19	3.174	3.175	3.174	3.175	3.174	3.175	3.174	3.175	3.174	3.175	3.174	3.175
20	3.175	3.174	3.175	3.174	3.175	3.174	3.175	3.174	3.175	3.174	3.175	3.174
21	3.174	3.175	3.174	3.175	3.174	3.175	3.174	3.175	3.174	3.175	3.174	3.175
22	3.175	3.174	3.175	3.174	3.175	3.174	3.175	3.174	3.175	3.174	3.175	3.174
23	3.174	3.175	3.174	3.175	3.174	3.175	3.174	3.175	3.174	3.175	3.174	3.175
24	3.175	3.174	3.175	3.174	3.175	3.174	3.175	3.174	3.175	3.174	3.175	3.174
25	3.174	3.175	3.174	3.175	3.174	3.175	3.174	3.175	3.174	3.175	3.174	3.175
26	3.175	3.174	3.175	3.174	3.175	3.174	3.175	3.174	3.175	3.174	3.175	3.174
27	3.174	3.175	3.174	3.175	3.174	3.175	3.174	3.175	3.174	3.175	3.174	3.175
28	3.175	3.174	3.175	3.174	3.175	3.174	3.175	3.174	3.175	3.174	3.175	3.174
29	3.174	3.175	3.174	3.175	3.174	3.175	3.174	3.175	3.174	3.175	3.174	3.175
30	3.175	3.174	3.175	3.174	3.175	3.174	3.175	3.174	3.175	3.174	3.175	3.174
31	3.174	3.175	3.174	3.175	3.174	3.175	3.174	3.175	3.174	3.175	3.174	3.175
32	1.720	1.984	2.249	2.513	2.778	3.042	3.175	3.174	3.175	3.174	3.175	3.174
33	0.000	0.000	0.000	0.000	0.000	0.000	0.132	0.397	0.661	0.926	1.190	1.455

Table 7A. General Depreciation System
Applicable Depreciation Method: Straight-Line
Applicable Recovery Period: 39 years
Applicable Convention: Mid-month—taken from the IRS Pub. 946—CCH.

If the Recovery Year is:	And the Month in the First Recovery Year the Property is Placed in Service is:											
	1	2	3	4	5	6	7	8	9	10	11	12
	the Depreciation Rate is:											
1	2.461	2.247	2.033	1.819	1.605	1.391	1.177	0.963	0.749	0.535	0.321	0.107
2—39	2.564	2.564	2.564	2.564	2.564	2.564	2.564	2.564	2.564	2.564	2.564	2.564
40	0.107	0.321	0.535	0.749	0.963	1.177	1.391	1.605	1.819	2.033	2.247	2.461

Table 7B. Alternative Depreciation System
Applicable Depreciation Method: Straight-Line
Applicable Recovery Period: 40 years
Applicable Convention: Mid-month

If the Recovery Year is:	and the Month in the First Recovery Year the Property is Placed in Service is:											
	1	2	3	4	5	6	7	8	9	10	11	12
	the Depreciation Rate is:											
1	2.396	2.188	1.979	1.771	1.563	1.354	1.146	0.938	0.729	0.521	0.313	0.104
2—40	2.500	2.500	2.500	2.500	2.500	2.500	2.500	2.500	2.500	2.500	2.500	2.500
41	0.104	0.312	0.521	0.729	0.937	1.146	1.354	1.562	1.771	1.979	2.187	2.396

¶1243

Table 8. General and Alternative Depreciation Systems
Applicable Depreciation Method: Straight Line
Applicable Recovery Periods: 2.5 — 50 years
Applicable Convention: Half-year

If the Recovery Year is:	2.5	3.0	3.5	4.0	4.5	5.0	5.5	6.0	6.5	7.0	7.5	8.0	8.5	9.0	9.5
1	20.00	16.67	14.29	12.50	11.11	10.00	9.09	8.33	7.69	7.14	6.67	6.25	5.88	5.56	5.26
2	40.00	33.33	28.57	25.00	22.22	20.00	18.18	16.67	15.39	14.29	13.33	12.50	11.77	11.11	10.53
3	40.00	33.33	28.57	25.00	22.22	20.00	18.18	16.67	15.38	14.29	13.33	12.50	11.76	11.11	10.53
4		16.67	28.57	25.00	22.23	20.00	18.18	16.67	15.39	14.28	13.33	12.50	11.77	11.11	10.53
5				12.50	22.22	20.00	18.19	16.66	15.38	14.29	13.34	12.50	11.76	11.11	10.52
6						10.00	18.18	16.67	15.39	14.28	13.33	12.50	11.77	11.11	10.53
7								8.33	15.38	14.29	13.34	12.50	11.76	11.11	10.52
8										7.14	13.33	12.50	11.77	11.11	10.53
9												6.25	11.76	11.11	10.52
10														5.56	10.53

If the Recovery Year is:	10.0	10.5	11.0	11.5	12.0	12.5	13.0	13.5	14.0	14.5	15.0	15.5	16.0	16.5	17.0
1	5.00	4.76	4.55	4.35	4.17	4.00	3.85	3.70	3.57	3.45	3.33	3.23	3.13	3.03	2.94
2	10.00	9.52	9.09	8.70	8.33	8.00	7.69	7.41	7.14	6.90	6.67	6.45	6.25	6.06	5.88
3	10.00	9.52	9.09	8.70	8.33	8.00	7.69	7.41	7.14	6.90	6.67	6.45	6.25	6.06	5.88
4	10.00	9.53	9.09	8.69	8.33	8.00	7.69	7.41	7.14	6.90	6.67	6.45	6.25	6.06	5.88
5	10.00	9.52	9.09	8.70	8.33	8.00	7.69	7.41	7.14	6.90	6.67	6.45	6.25	6.06	5.88
6	10.00	9.53	9.09	8.69	8.33	8.00	7.69	7.41	7.14	6.89	6.67	6.45	6.25	6.06	5.88
7	10.00	9.52	9.09	8.70	8.34	8.00	7.69	7.41	7.14	6.90	6.67	6.45	6.25	6.06	5.88
8	10.00	9.53	9.09	8.69	8.33	8.00	7.69	7.41	7.15	6.89	6.66	6.45	6.25	6.06	5.88
9	10.00	9.52	9.09	8.70	8.34	8.00	7.69	7.41	7.14	6.90	6.67	6.45	6.25	6.06	5.88
10	10.00	9.53	9.09	8.69	8.33	8.00	7.70	7.40	7.15	6.89	6.66	6.45	6.25	6.06	5.88
11	5.00	9.52	9.09	8.70	8.34	8.00	7.69	7.41	7.14	6.90	6.67	6.45	6.25	6.06	5.89
12			4.55	8.69	8.33	8.00	7.70	7.40	7.15	6.89	6.66	6.45	6.25	6.06	5.88
13					4.17	8.00	7.69	7.41	7.14	6.90	6.67	6.45	6.25	6.06	5.89
14							3.85	7.40	7.15	6.89	6.66	6.46	6.25	6.06	5.88
15									3.57	6.90	6.67	6.45	6.25	6.06	5.89
16											3.33	6.46	6.25	6.06	5.88
17													3.12	6.07	5.89
18															2.94

If the Recovery Year is:	17.5	18.0	18.5	19.0	19.5	20.0	20.5	21.0	21.5	22.0	22.5	23.0	23.5	24.0	24.5
1	2.86	2.78	2.70	2.63	2.56	2.500	2.439	2.381	2.326	2.273	2.222	2.174	2.128	2.083	2.041
2	5.71	5.56	5.41	5.26	5.13	5.000	4.878	4.762	4.651	4.545	4.444	4.348	4.255	4.167	4.082
3	5.71	5.56	5.41	5.26	5.13	5.000	4.878	4.762	4.651	4.545	4.444	4.348	4.255	4.167	4.082
4	5.71	5.55	5.41	5.26	5.13	5.000	4.878	4.762	4.651	4.545	4.445	4.348	4.255	4.167	4.082
5	5.72	5.56	5.40	5.26	5.13	5.000	4.878	4.762	4.651	4.546	4.444	4.348	4.255	4.167	4.082
6	5.71	5.55	5.41	5.26	5.13	5.000	4.878	4.762	4.651	4.545	4.445	4.348	4.255	4.167	4.082
7	5.72	5.56	5.40	5.26	5.13	5.000	4.878	4.762	4.651	4.545	4.444	4.348	4.255	4.167	4.082
8	5.71	5.55	5.41	5.26	5.13	5.000	4.878	4.762	4.651	4.545	4.445	4.318	4.255	4.167	4.082
9	5.72	5.56	5.40	5.27	5.13	5.000	4.878	4.762	4.651	4.546	4.444	4.348	4.255	4.167	4.081
10	5.71	5.55	5.41	5.26	5.13	5.000	4.878	4.762	4.651	4.545	4.445	4.348	4.255	4.167	4.082
11	5.72	5.56	5.40	5.27	5.13	5.000	4.878	4.762	4.651	4.546	4.444	4.348	4.256	4.166	4.081
12	5.71	5.55	5.41	5.26	5.13	5.000	4.878	4.762	4.651	4.545	4.445	4.348	4.255	4.167	4.082
13	5.72	5.56	5.40	5.27	5.13	5.000	4.878	4.762	4.651	4.546	4.444	4.348	4.256	4.166	4.081
14	5.71	5.55	5.41	5.26	5.13	5.000	4.878	4.762	4.651	4.545	4.445	4.348	4.255	4.167	4.082
15	5.72	5.56	5.40	5.27	5.13	5.000	4.878	4.762	4.651	4.546	4.444	4.348	4.256	4.166	4.081
16	5.71	5.55	5.41	5.26	5.12	5.000	4.878	4.762	4.651	4.545	4.445	4.348	4.255	4.167	4.082
17	5.72	5.56	5.40	5.27	5.13	5.000	4.878	4.762	4.652	4.546	4.444	4.347	4.256	4.166	4.081
18	5.71	5.55	5.41	5.26	5.12	5.000	4.878	4.762	4.651	4.545	4.445	4.348	4.255	4.167	4.082
19		2.78	5.40	5.27	5.13	5.000	4.878	4.761	4.652	4.546	4.444	4.347	4.256	4.166	4.081
20				2.63	5.12	5.000	4.879	4.762	4.651	4.545	4.445	4.348	4.255	4.167	4.082
21						2.500	4.878	4.761	4.652	4.546	4.444	4.347	4.256	4.166	4.081
22								2.381	4.651	4.545	4.445	4.348	4.255	4.167	4.082
23										2.273	4.444	4.347	4.256	4.166	4.081
24												2.174	4.255	4.167	4.082
25														2.083	4.081

If the Recovery Year is:	and the Recovery Period is:														
	25.0	25.5	26.0	26.5	27.0	27.5	28.0	28.5	29.0	29.5	30.0	30.5	31.0	31.5	32.0
	the Depreciation Rate is:														
1	2.000	1.961	1.923	1.887	1.852	1.818	1.786	1.754	1.724	1.695	1.667	1.639	1.613	1.587	1.563
2	4.000	3.922	3.846	3.774	3.704	3.636	3.571	3.509	3.448	3.390	3.333	3.279	3.226	3.175	3.125
3	4.000	3.922	3.846	3.774	3.704	3.636	3.571	3.509	3.448	3.390	3.333	3.279	3.226	3.175	3.125
4	4.000	3.922	3.846	3.774	3.704	3.636	3.571	3.509	3.448	3.390	3.333	3.279	3.226	3.175	3.125
5	4.000	3.922	3.846	3.774	3.704	3.636	3.571	3.509	3.448	3.390	3.333	3.279	3.226	3.175	3.125
6	4.000	3.921	3.846	3.774	3.704	3.636	3.571	3.509	3.448	3.390	3.333	3.279	3.226	3.175	3.125
7	4.000	3.922	3.846	3.773	3.704	3.636	3.572	3.509	3.448	3.390	3.333	3.279	3.226	3.175	3.125
8	4.000	3.921	3.846	3.774	3.704	3.636	3.571	3.509	3.448	3.390	3.333	3.279	3.226	3.175	3.125
9	4.000	3.922	3.846	3.773	3.704	3.637	3.572	3.509	3.448	3.390	3.333	3.279	3.226	3.175	3.125
10	4.000	3.921	3.846	3.774	3.704	3.636	3.571	3.509	3.448	3.390	3.333	3.279	3.226	3.174	3.125
11	4.000	3.922	3.846	3.773	3.704	3.636	3.572	3.509	3.448	3.390	3.333	3.279	3.226	3.174	3.125
12	4.000	3.921	3.846	3.774	3.704	3.636	3.571	3.509	3.448	3.390	3.333	3.279	3.226	3.174	3.125
13	4.000	3.922	3.846	3.773	3.703	3.637	3.572	3.509	3.448	3.390	3.334	3.279	3.226	3.175	3.125
14	4.000	3.921	3.846	3.774	3.704	3.636	3.571	3.509	3.448	3.390	3.333	3.279	3.226	3.174	3.125
15	4.000	3.922	3.846	3.774	3.703	3.637	3.572	3.509	3.449	3.390	3.334	3.278	3.226	3.175	3.125
16	4.000	3.921	3.846	3.773	3.704	3.636	3.571	3.509	3.448	3.390	3.333	3.279	3.226	3.174	3.125
17	4.000	3.922	3.846	3.774	3.703	3.637	3.572	3.509	3.449	3.390	3.334	3.278	3.226	3.175	3.125
18	4.000	3.921	3.846	3.773	3.704	3.636	3.571	3.508	3.448	3.390	3.333	3.279	3.226	3.174	3.125
19	4.000	3.922	3.846	3.774	3.703	3.637	3.572	3.509	3.449	3.390	3.334	3.278	3.226	3.175	3.125
20	4.000	3.921	3.847	3.773	3.704	3.636	3.571	3.508	3.448	3.390	3.333	3.279	3.226	3.174	3.125
21	4.000	3.922	3.846	3.774	3.703	3.637	3.572	3.509	3.449	3.389	3.334	3.278	3.225	3.175	3.125
22	4.000	3.921	3.847	3.773	3.704	3.636	3.571	3.508	3.448	3.390	3.333	3.279	3.226	3.174	3.125
23	4.000	3.922	3.846	3.774	3.703	3.637	3.572	3.509	3.449	3.334	3.334	3.278	3.225	3.175	3.125
24	4.000	3.921	3.847	3.773	3.704	3.636	3.571	3.508	3.448	3.390	3.333	3.279	3.226	3.174	3.125
25	4.000	3.922	3.846	3.774	3.703	3.637	3.572	3.509	3.449	3.389	3.334	3.278	3.225	3.175	3.125
26	2.000	3.921	3.847	3.773	3.704	3.636	3.571	3.508	3.448	3.390	3.333	3.279	3.226	3.174	3.125
27			1.923	3.774	3.703	3.637	3.572	3.509	3.449	3.389	3.334	3.278	3.225	3.175	3.125
28					1.852	3.636	3.571	3.508	3.448	3.390	3.333	3.279	3.226	3.174	3.125
29							1.786	3.509	3.449	3.389	3.334	3.278	3.225	3.175	3.125
30									1.724	3.390	3.333	3.279	3.226	3.174	3.125
31											1.667	3.278	3.225	3.175	3.125
32													1.613	3.174	3.125
33															1.562

If the Recovery Year is:		32.5	33.0	33.5	34.0	34.5	35.0	35.5	36.0	36.5	37.0	37.5	38.0	38.5	39.0	39.5
and the Recovery Period is:																
the Depreciation Rate is:																
1	. .	1.538	1.515	1.493	1.471	1.449	1.429	1.408	1.389	1.370	1.351	1.333	1.316	1.299	1.282	1.266
2	. .	3.077	3.030	2.985	2.941	2.899	2.857	2.817	2.778	2.740	2.703	2.667	2.632	2.597	2.564	2.532
3	. .	3.077	3.030	2.985	2.941	2.899	2.857	2.817	2.778	2.740	2.703	2.667	2.632	2.597	2.564	2.532
4	. .	3.077	3.030	2.985	2.941	2.899	2.857	2.817	2.778	2.740	2.703	2.667	2.632	2.597	2.564	2.532
5	. .	3.077	3.030	2.985	2.941	2.899	2.857	2.817	2.778	2.740	2.703	2.667	2.632	2.597	2.564	2.532
6	. .	3.077	3.030	2.985	2.941	2.899	2.857	2.817	2.778	2.740	2.703	2.667	2.632	2.597	2.564	2.532
7	. .	3.077	3.030	2.985	2.941	2.898	2.857	2.817	2.778	2.740	2.703	2.667	2.632	2.597	2.564	2.532
8	. .	3.077	3.030	2.985	2.941	2.899	2.857	2.817	2.778	2.740	2.703	2.667	2.631	2.597	2.564	2.532
9	. .	3.077	3.030	2.985	2.941	2.898	2.857	2.817	2.778	2.740	2.703	2.667	2.632	2.597	2.564	2.532
10	. .	3.077	3.030	2.985	2.941	2.899	2.857	2.817	2.778	2.740	2.703	2.667	2.631	2.598	2.564	2.532
11	. .	3.077	3.030	2.985	2.941	2.898	2.857	2.817	2.778	2.740	2.703	2.667	2.632	2.597	2.564	2.532
12	. .	3.077	3.030	2.985	2.941	2.899	2.857	2.817	2.778	2.740	2.703	2.667	2.631	2.598	2.564	2.532
13	. .	3.077	3.030	2.985	2.941	2.898	2.857	2.817	2.778	2.740	2.703	2.667	2.632	2.597	2.564	2.532
14	. .	3.077	3.030	2.985	2.941	2.899	2.857	2.817	2.778	2.740	2.703	2.667	2.631	2.598	2.564	2.531
15	. .	3.077	3.031	2.985	2.941	2.898	2.857	2.817	2.778	2.740	2.703	2.666	2.632	2.597	2.564	2.532
16	. .	3.077	3.030	2.985	2.941	2.899	2.857	2.817	2.778	2.740	2.703	2.667	2.631	2.598	2.564	2.531
17	. .	3.077	3.031	2.985	2.941	2.898	2.857	2.817	2.778	2.740	2.703	2.666	2.632	2.597	2.564	2.532
18	. .	3.077	3.030	2.985	2.841	2.899	2.857	2.817	2.778	2.740	2.702	2.667	2.631	2.598	2.564	2.531
19	. .	3.077	3.031	2.985	2.941	2.898	2.857	2.817	2.778	2.739	2.703	2.666	2.632	2.597	2.564	2.532
20	. .	3.077	3.030	2.985	2.941	2.898	2.857	2.817	2.778	2.740	2.702	2.667	2.631	2.598	2.564	2.531
21	. .	3.077	3.031	2.985	2.941	2.899	2.857	2.817	2.778	2.739	2.703	2.666	2.632	2.597	2.564	2.532
22	. .	3.077	3.030	2.985	2.941	2.898	2.857	2.817	2.777	2.740	2.702	2.667	2.631	2.598	2.564	2.531
23	. .	3.077	3.031	2.985	2.941	2.899	2.857	2.817	2.778	2.739	2.703	2.666	2.632	2.597	2.564	2.532
24	. .	3.077	3.030	2.985	2.941	2.898	2.857	2.817	2.777	2.740	2.702	2.667	2.631	2.598	2.564	2.531
25	. .	3.077	3.031	2.985	2.942	2.899	2.857	2.817	2.778	2.739	2.703	2.666	2.632	2.597	2.564	2.532
26	. .	3.077	3.030	2.985	2.941	2.898	2.857	2.817	2.777	2.740	2.702	2.667	2.631	2.598	2.564	2.531
27	. .	3.077	3.031	2.985	2.942	2.899	2.857	2.817	2.778	2.739	2.703	2.666	2.632	2.597	2.564	2.532
28	. .	3.077	3.030	2.985	2.941	2.898	2.858	2.817	2.777	2.740	2.702	2.667	2.631	2.598	2.564	2.531
29	. .	3.077	3.031	2.985	2.942	2.899	2.857	2.817	2.778	2.739	2.703	2.666	2.632	2.597	2.564	2.532
30	. .	3.077	3.030	2.985	2.941	2.898	2.858	2.817	2.777	2.740	2.702	2.667	2.631	2.598	2.564	2.531
31	. .	3.076	3.031	2.986	2.942	2.899	2.857	2.817	2.778	2.739	2.703	2.666	2.632	2.597	2.564	2.532
32	. .	3.077	3.030	2.985	2.941	2.898	2.858	2.816	2.777	2.740	2.702	2.667	2.631	2.598	2.564	2.531
33	. .	3.076	3.031	2.986	2.942	2.899	2.857	2.817	2.778	2.739	2.703	2.666	2.632	2.597	2.565	2.532
34	. . . .		1.515	2.985	2.941	2.898	2.858	2.816	2.777	2.740	2.702	2.667	2.631	2.598	2.564	2.531
35	. . . .				1.471	2.899	2.857	2.817	2.778	2.739	2.703	2.666	2.632	2.597	2.565	2.532
36	. . . .						1.429	2.816	2.777	2.740	2.702	2.667	2.631	2.598	2.564	2.531
37	. . . .								1.389	2.739	2.703	2.666	2.632	2.597	2.565	2.532
38	. . . .										1.351	2.667	2.631	2.598	2.564	2.531
39	. . . .												1.316	2.597	2.565	2.532
40	. . . .														1.282	2.531

If the Recovery Year is:	and the Recovery Period is:														
	40.0	40.5	41.0	41.5	42.0	42.5	43.0	43.5	44.0	44.5	45.0	45.5	46.0	46.5	47.0
	the Depreciation Rate is:														
1	1.250	1.235	1.220	1.205	1.190	1.176	1.163	1.149	1.136	1.124	1.111	1.099	1.087	1.075	1.064
2	2.500	2.469	2.439	2.410	2.381	2.353	2.326	2.299	2.273	2.247	2.222	2.198	2.174	2.151	2.128
3	2.500	2.469	2.439	2.410	2.381	2.353	2.326	2.299	2.273	2.247	2.222	2.198	2.174	2.151	2.128
4	2.500	2.469	2.439	2.410	2.381	2.353	2.326	2.299	2.273	2.247	2.222	2.198	2.174	2.151	2.128
5	2.500	2.469	2.439	2.410	2.381	2.353	2.326	2.299	2.273	2.247	2.222	2.198	2.174	2.151	2.128
6	2.500	2.469	2.439	2.410	2.381	2.353	2.326	2.299	2.273	2.247	2.222	2.198	2.174	2.151	2.128
7	2.500	2.469	2.439	2.410	2.381	2.353	2.326	2.299	2.273	2.247	2.222	2.198	2.174	2.150	2.128
8	2.500	2.469	2.439	2.410	2.381	2.353	2.326	2.299	2.273	2.247	2.222	2.198	2.174	2.151	2.128
9	2.500	2.469	2.439	2.410	2.381	2.353	2.325	2.299	2.273	2.247	2.222	2.198	2.174	2.150	2.128
10	2.500	2.469	2.439	2.410	2.381	2.353	2.326	2.299	2.273	2.247	2.222	2.198	2.174	2.151	2.128
11	2.500	2.469	2.439	2.410	2.381	2.353	2.325	2.299	2.273	2.247	2.222	2.198	2.174	2.150	2.128
12	2.500	2.469	2.439	2.410	2.381	2.353	2.326	2.299	2.273	2.247	2.222	2.198	2.174	2.151	2.128
13	2.500	2.469	2.439	2.410	2.381	2.353	2.325	2.299	2.273	2.247	2.222	2.198	2.174	2.150	2.128
14	2.500	2.469	2.439	2.409	2.381	2.353	2.326	2.299	2.273	2.247	2.222	2.198	2.174	2.151	2.128
15	2.500	2.469	2.439	2.410	2.381	2.353	2.325	2.299	2.273	2.247	2.222	2.198	2.174	2.150	2.128
16	2.500	2.469	2.439	2.409	2.381	2.353	2.326	2.299	2.273	2.247	2.222	2.198	2.174	2.151	2.128
17	2.500	2.469	2.439	2.410	2.381	2.353	2.325	2.299	2.273	2.247	2.222	2.198	2.174	2.150	2.127
18	2.500	2.469	2.439	2.409	2.381	2.353	2.326	2.299	2.273	2.247	2.222	2.198	2.174	2.151	2.128
19	2.500	2.469	2.439	2.410	2.381	2.353	2.325	2.299	2.273	2.247	2.222	2.198	2.174	2.150	2.127
20	2.500	2.469	2.439	2.409	2.381	2.353	2.326	2.299	2.273	2.247	2.222	2.198	2.174	2.151	2.128
21	2.500	2.469	2.439	2.410	2.381	2.353	2.325	2.299	2.273	2.247	2.222	2.198	2.174	2.150	2.127
22	2.500	2.469	2.439	2.409	2.381	2.353	2.326	2.299	2.273	2.247	2.222	2.198	2.174	2.151	2.128
23	2.500	2.469	2.439	2.410	2.381	2.353	2.325	2.299	2.272	2.247	2.222	2.198	2.174	2.150	2.127
24	2.500	2.469	2.439	2.409	2.381	2.353	2.326	2.299	2.273	2.247	2.222	2.198	2.174	2.151	2.128
25	2.500	2.469	2.439	2.410	2.381	2.353	2.325	2.299	2.272	2.247	2.222	2.198	2.174	2.150	2.127
26	2.500	2.469	2.439	2.409	2.381	2.353	2.326	2.299	2.273	2.247	2.222	2.198	2.174	2.151	2.128
27	2.500	2.469	2.439	2.410	2.381	2.353	2.325	2.299	2.272	2.247	2.223	2.198	2.174	2.150	2.127
28	2.500	2.469	2.439	2.409	2.381	2.353	2.326	2.299	2.273	2.247	2.222	2.198	2.174	2.151	2.128
29	2.500	2.469	2.439	2.410	2.381	2.353	2.325	2.299	2.272	2.247	2.223	2.198	2.174	2.150	2.127
30	2.500	2.469	2.439	2.409	2.381	2.353	2.326	2.299	2.273	2.248	2.222	2.197	2.174	2.151	2.128
31	2.500	2.469	2.439	2.410	2.381	2.353	2.325	2.299	2.272	2.247	2.223	2.198	2.174	2.150	2.127
32	2.500	2.470	2.439	2.409	2.381	2.353	2.326	2.299	2.273	2.248	2.222	2.197	2.174	2.151	2.128
33	2.500	2.469	2.439	2.410	2.381	2.353	2.325	2.298	2.272	2.247	2.223	2.198	2.174	2.150	2.127
34	2.500	2.470	2.439	2.409	2.381	2.353	2.326	2.299	2.273	2.248	2.222	2.197	2.174	2.151	2.128
35	2.500	2.469	2.439	2.410	2.381	2.353	2.325	2.298	2.272	2.247	2.223	2.198	2.174	2.150	2.127
36	2.500	2.470	2.139	2.409	2.381	2.353	2.326	2.299	2.273	2.248	2.222	2.197	2.174	2.151	2.128
37	2.500	2.469	2.439	2.410	2.381	2.353	2.325	2.298	2.272	2.247	2.223	2.198	2.174	2.150	2.127
38	2.500	2.470	2.439	2.409	2.381	2.353	2.326	2.299	2.273	2.248	2.222	2.197	2.174	2.151	2.128
39	2.500	2.469	2.439	2.410	2.381	2.353	2.325	2.298	2.272	2.247	2.223	2.198	2.174	2.150	2.127
40	2.500	2.470	2.439	2.409	2.381	2.353	2.326	2.299	2.273	2.248	2.222	2.197	2.173	2.151	2.128
41	1.250	2.469	2.439	2.410	2.380	2.352	2.325	2.298	2.272	2.247	2.223	2.198	2.174	2.150	2.127
42			1.220	2.409	2.381	2.353	2.326	2.299	2.273	2.248	2.222	2.197	2.173	2.151	2.128
43					1.190	2.352	2.325	2.298	2.272	2.247	2.223	2.198	2.174	2.150	2.127
44							1.163	2.299	2.273	2.248	2.222	2.197	2.174	2.151	2.128
45									1.136	2.247	2.223	2.198	2.174	2.150	2.127
46											1.111	2.197	2.173	2.151	2.128
47													1.087	2.150	2.127
48															1.064

¶1243

If the Recovery Year is:		and the Recovery Period is:					
		47.5	48.0	48.5	49.0	49.5	50.0
				the Depreciation Rate is:			
1	. . . . . .	1.053	1.042	1.031	1.020	1.010	1.000
2	. . . . . .	2.105	2.083	2.062	2.041	2.020	2.000
3	. . . . . .	2.105	2.083	2.062	2.041	2.020	2.000
4	. . . . . .	2.105	2.083	2.062	2.041	2.020	2.000
5	. . . . . .	2.105	2.083	2.062	2.041	2.020	2.000
6	. . . . . .	2.105	2.083	2.062	2.041	2.020	2.000
7	. . . . . .	2.105	2.083	2.062	2.041	2.020	2.000
8	. . . . . .	2.105	2.083	2.062	2.041	2.020	2.000
9	. . . . . .	2.105	2.083	2.062	2.041	2.020	2.000
10	. . . . . .	2.105	2.083	2.062	2.041	2.020	2.000
11	. . . . . .	2.105	2.083	2.062	2.041	2.020	2.000
12	. . . . . .	2.105	2.083	2.062	2.041	2.020	2.000
13	. . . . . .	2.105	2.083	2.062	2.041	2.020	2.000
14	. . . . . .	2.105	2.083	2.062	2.041	2.020	2.000
15	. . . . . .	2.105	2.083	2.062	2.041	2.020	2.000
16	. . . . . .	2.105	2.083	2.062	2.041	2.020	2.000
17	. . . . . .	2.105	2.083	2.062	2.041	2.020	2.000
18	. . . . . .	2.105	2.083	2.062	2.041	2.020	2.000
19	. . . . . .	2.105	2.084	2.062	2.041	2.020	2.000
20	. . . . . .	2.105	2.083	2.062	2.041	2.020	2.000
21	. . . . . .	2.105	2.084	2.062	2.041	2.020	2.000
22	. . . . . .	2.105	2.083	2.062	2.041	2.020	2.000
23	. . . . . .	2.105	2.084	2.062	2.041	2.020	2.000
24	. . . . . .	2.105	2.083	2.062	2.041	2.020	2.000
25	. . . . . .	2.105	2.084	2.062	2.041	2.020	2.000
26	. . . . . .	2.106	2.083	2.062	2.041	2.020	2.000
27	. . . . . .	2.105	2.084	2.062	2.041	2.020	2.000
28	. . . . . .	2.106	2.083	2.062	2.041	2.020	2.000
29	. . . . . .	2.105	2.084	2.062	2.041	2.020	2.000
30	. . . . . .	2.106	2.083	2.062	2.041	2.020	2.000
31	. . . . . .	2.105	2.084	2.062	2.041	2.021	2.000
32	. . . . . .	2.106	2.083	2.062	2.041	2.020	2.000
33	. . . . . .	2.105	2.084	2.062	2.041	2.021	2.000
34	. . . . . .	2.106	2.083	2.062	2.040	2.020	2.000
35	. . . . . .	2.105	2.084	2.062	2.041	2.021	2.000
36	. . . . . .	2.106	2.083	2.062	2.040	2.020	2.000
37	. . . . . .	2.105	2.084	2.061	2.041	2.021	2.000
38	. . . . . .	2.106	2.083	2.062	2.040	2.020	2.000
39	. . . . . .	2.105	2.084	2.061	2.041	2.021	2.000
40	. . . . . .	2.106	2.083	2.062	2.040	2.020	2.000
41	. . . . . .	2.105	2.084	2.061	2.041	2.021	2.000
42	. . . . . .	2.106	2.083	2.062	2.040	2.020	2.000
43	. . . . . .	2.105	2.084	2.061	2.041	2.021	2.000
44	. . . . . .	2.106	2.083	2.062	2.040	2.020	2.000
45	. . . . . .	2.105	2.084	2.061	2.041	2.021	2.000
46	. . . . . .	2.106	2.083	2.062	2.040	2.020	2.000
47	. . . . . .	2.105	2.084	2.061	2.041	2.021	2.000
48	. . . . . .	2.106	2.083	2.062	2.040	2.020	2.000
49			1.042	2.061	2.041	2.021	2.000
50				1.020	2.020	2.000
51						1.000

1244. MACRS Short Tax Years. A short tax year is any tax year with less than 12 months. Special rules are provided for determining MACRS deductions when: (1) property is placed in service in a short tax year, (2) a short tax year occurs during the recovery period of property, or (3) a disposition of property occurs before the end of the recovery period (Rev. Proc. 89-15). If any of the above situations exist, refinements are made to the use of the applicable conventions and the IRS MACRS depreciation tables at ¶ 1243 may *not* be used.[84]

The mid-month convention is applied without regard to the length of the tax year. For example if residential rental property is placed in service in the first month of a six-month tax year, 5 ½ months depreciation is claimed.

Under the half-year convention, property placed in service or disposed of in a short tax year is deemed placed in service or disposed of on the midpoint of the short tax year, which always falls on either the first day or the midpoint of the month.

Under the mid-quarter convention, property is deemed placed in service or disposed of on the midpoint of the quarter, which always falls on either the first day or the midpoint of a month, in the short tax year that it is placed in service or disposed of.

Depreciation for the first recovery year in the recovery period is computed by multiplying the basis in the property by the applicable depreciation rate. The depreciation allowance allocable to the first tax year that includes a portion of the first recovery year is derived by multiplying the depreciation for the first recovery year by a fraction, the numerator of which is the number of months (including fractions of months) the property is deemed to be in service during the tax year under the applicable convention and the denominator of which is 12.

The correlation of a depreciation allowance between recovery years and tax years after the first tax year in the recovery period may be made under either an allocation or a simplified method.

1245. Applicable MACRS Conventions. Specified averaging conventions apply to depreciation computations made under MACRS (Code Sec. 168(d)).[85] The recovery period begins on the date on which the property is placed in service under the applicable convention. The depreciation table percentages take into account the applicable convention in the first and last year of the regular recovery period. However, if property is disposed of prior to the end of the regular recovery period, the result obtained by using the table percentage for the year of disposition must be adjusted to take into account the applicable convention.

Half-Year Convention. Under the half-year convention, which can apply to property other than residential rental property and nonresidential real property, property is treated as placed in service or disposed of in the middle of the tax year. Thus, one-half of the depreciation for the first year of the recovery period is allowed in the tax year in which the property is placed in service, regardless of when the property is placed in service during the year.

A half-year of depreciation is allowed in the tax year of disposition if there is a disposition of property before the end of the recovery period.[86] The table percentage for the year of disposition does not take this into account; therefore, only one-half of the depreciation as computed using the applicable table percentage is allowed.

> **Example 1:** Five-year property with a depreciable basis of $1,000 (after reduction by any amount expensed under Code Sec. 179 and claimed as bonus depreciation) and subject to the half-year convention is placed in service in 2005 and sold in 2007. Using Table 1 at ¶ 1243, 2005 depreciation is $200 ($1,000 × 20%); 2006 depreciation is $320 ($1,000 × 32%); and 2007 depreciation is $96 ($1,000 × 19.20% × 50% to reflect half-year convention in year of disposition).

Mid-Month Convention. A mid-month convention applies to residential rental property, including low-income housing, and nonresidential real property. Property is deemed placed in service or disposed of during the middle of the month. The deduction

---

Footnote references are to paragraphs of the 2008 Standard Federal Tax Reports.

[84] ¶ 11,279.053   [85] ¶ 11,250, ¶ 11,279.037   [86] ¶ 11,279.037

is based on the number of months the property was in service. Thus, one-half month's depreciation is allowed for the month the property is placed in service and for the month of disposition if there is a disposition of property before the end of the recovery period.

> **Example 2:** A commercial building costing $100,000 is purchased by a calendar-year taxpayer in February 2006 and sold in August 2007. Using Table 7A at ¶ 1243, 2006 depreciation is $2,247 ($100,000 × 2.247% (first-year percentage for property placed in service in second month of tax year)) and 2007 depreciation is $1,603 ($100,000 × 2.564% (second-year percentage for property placed in service in second month) × 7.5/12 to reflect 7.5 months in service in 2007 (January through mid-August) under the mid-month convention).

Mid-Quarter Convention. Under the mid-quarter convention, all property placed in service, or disposed of, during any quarter of a tax year is treated as placed in service at the midpoint of the quarter (Code Sec. 168(d)(3); Reg. § 1.168(d)-1).[87] Depreciation under the mid-quarter convention may be determined using Tables 2-5, above.

The mid-quarter convention applies to all property, other than nonresidential real property and residential rental property, if more than 40% of the aggregate bases of such property is placed in service during the last three months of the tax year. Property placed in service and disposed of within the same tax year is disregarded for purposes of the 40% test.

In determining whether the mid-quarter convention is applicable, the aggregate basis of property placed in service in the last three months of the tax year must be computed regardless of the length of the tax year. Thus, if a short tax year consists of three months or less, the mid-quarter convention applies regardless of when the depreciable property is placed in service during the tax year.

Any amount properly expensed under Sec. 179 reduces the basis of the property for purposes of determining whether the mid-quarter convention applies. Thus, a taxpayer may be able to avoid the mid-quarter convention (if this is desirable) by allocating the Code Sec. 179 deduction to property placed in service in the last quarter. No similar reduction is made for the amount of bonus depreciation. Also, the mid-quarter convention does not operate to reduce the deduction otherwise allowable under Code Sec. 179 or for bonus depreciation (¶ 1237).

For purposes of the 40% test, depreciable basis does not include adjustments resulting from transfers of property between members of the same affiliated group filing a consolidated return.

If the MACRS deduction for property subject to the mid-quarter convention is computed without tables, depreciation for the first year is determined by computing the depreciation for the full tax year and then multiplying it by the following percentages for the quarter of the tax year the property is placed in service: first quarter, 87.5%; second quarter, 62.5%; third quarter, 37.5%; and fourth quarter, 12.5%.

1247. MACRS Alternative Depreciation System (ADS). ADS must be used for (1) tangible property used outside the U.S., (2) tax-exempt use property, (3) tax-exempt bond-financed property, (4) property imported from a foreign country for which an Executive Order is in effect because the country maintains trade restrictions or engages in other discriminatory acts, and (5) property for which an ADS election has been made (Code Sec. 168(g)).[88] Mandatory ADS property did not qualify for bonus depreciation (¶ 1237).

Under ADS, the deduction is computed by applying the straight-line method, the applicable convention and the applicable longer recovery period (12 years for personal property with no class life, 40 years for real property, 50 years for railroad grading and tunnel bores, and the class life for all other property) for the respective class of property (Code Sec. 168(g)(2)(C)).[89] ADS is also used to compute the earnings and profits of a foreign or domestic corporation. The allowable depreciation deductions for luxury cars

---

Footnote references are to paragraphs of the 2008 Standard Federal Tax Reports.

[87] ¶ 11,250, ¶ 11,279.037   [88] ¶ 11,250, ¶ 11,279.04   [89] ¶ 11,250, ¶ 11,279.04

and listed property used 50% or less in business are also determined under this method (see ¶ 1211 and ¶ 1214).

Electing ADS. In lieu of the regular MACRS deduction, taxpayers may irrevocably elect to apply the MACRS alternative depreciation system to any class of property for any tax year (Code Sec. 168(g)(7)).[90] If elected, ADS applies to all property in the MACRS class placed in service during the tax year. For example, if the election is made for five-year property, it applies to all five-year property placed in service in the tax year of the election. For residential rental property and nonresidential real property, the election is made on a property-by-property basis. Property for which ADS is elected may qualify for bonus depreciation (¶ 1237).

1248. Special Transferee Rules. A transferee in certain corporate and partnership transactions is treated as the transferor and must use the latter's recovery period and method in computing the MACRS deduction for the portion of the transferee's basis that does not exceed the transferor's adjusted basis in the property (Code Sec. 168(i)(7)).[91] This rule applies to nonrecognition transfers under Code Sec. 332 (subsidiary liquidations) (¶ 2261); transfers to a controlled corporation (¶ 1731); transfers related to certain reorganizations (¶ 2209); contributions to a partnership (¶ 443); certain partnership distributions (¶ 453); and transactions between members of the same affiliated group during any tax year for which a consolidated return is made by such group. It does not apply to transactions relating to the sale or exchange of 50% or more of the total interest in a partnership's capital and profits within a 12-month period (Code Sec. 708(b)(1)(B)).

1249. Disposition of Depreciable Property. See ¶ 1779.

1250. Like-Kind Exchanges and Involuntary Conversions. The exchanged basis (i.e., carryover basis) of MACRS property acquired in a like-kind exchange or involuntary conversion for other MACRS property is depreciated by applying the following rules (Reg. § 1.168(i)-6):[92]

(1) If the replacement MACRS property has the same or a shorter recovery period and the same or a more accelerated depreciation method than the relinquished MACRS property, the exchanged (carryover) basis is depreciated over the remaining recovery period of, and using the depreciation method and convention of, the relinquished MACRS property.

(2) If the recovery period of the replacement MACRS property is longer than that of the relinquished MACRS property, the exchanged basis is depreciated over the remainder of the recovery period that would have applied to the replacement MACRS property if the replacement MACRS property had originally been placed in service when the relinquished MACRS property was placed in service by the acquiring taxpayer.

(3) If the depreciation method of the replacement MACRS property is less accelerated than that of the relinquished MACRS property, the exchanged basis is depreciated beginning in the year of replacement using the less accelerated depreciation method of the replacement MACRS property that would have applied to the replacement MACRS property if the replacement MACRS property had originally been placed in service when the relinquished MACRS property was placed in service by the acquiring taxpayer.

The excess basis of the replacement property (i.e., the noncarryover basis usually attributable to additional cash paid for the replacement property) is separately depreciated as if originally acquired in the year of replacement.

These rules are effective for like-kind exchanges and involuntary conversions in which the time of disposition and replacement both occur after February 27, 2004. A taxpayer, however, may apply the regulations retroactively (Reg. § 1.168(i)-6(k)). A taxpayer may also elect not to apply the regulations to a post-effective date exchange or conversion and depreciate the entire basis of the acquired property as a single deprecia-

---

Footnote references are to paragraphs of the 2008 Standard Federal Tax Reports.

[90] ¶ 11,250, ¶ 11,279.04   [91] ¶ 11,279.054   [92] ¶ 11,279.0545

ble asset beginning in the tax year of replacement (Reg. § 1.168(i)-6(i); Reg. § 1.168(i)-6(j)).

Bonus depreciation may be claimed on the entire basis of qualifying acquired property (¶ 1237) (Reg. § 1.168(k)-1(f)(5)). However, only the excess basis (noncarryover basis) may qualify for expensing under Code Sec. 179 even if an election not to apply the temporary regulations is made (Reg. § 1.168(i)-6(g) and (i)).

Accelerated Cost Recovery System (ACRS)

1252. Pre-1987 ACRS in General. The Accelerated Cost Recovery System (ACRS) must be used to compute the depreciation deduction for most tangible depreciable property placed in service after 1980 and before 1987 (pre-1987 Code Sec. 168).[93] Cost recovery methods and periods are the same for both new and used property, and salvage value is disregarded in computing ACRS allowances. Post-1980 depreciation on tangible assets first placed in service before 1981 is computed using the method elected by the taxpayer when the property was placed in service (including the Class Life ADR depreciation system (¶ 1284) and other methods of depreciation discussed at ¶ 1216 and following).

Under ACRS, the cost of eligible property is recovered over a 3-year, 5-year, 10-year, 15-year, 18-year, or 19-year period, depending on the type of property. ACRS applies to recovery property, as defined at ¶ 1255. The deduction is determined by applying the statutory table percentage for the appropriate class of property to its unadjusted basis. The unadjusted basis of property under ACRS is the basis of the property (as determined for purposes of computing gain or loss), unadjusted for depreciation, amortization or depletion. It does not include that portion of the basis for which there is an election to amortize (¶ 1287) or to expense the cost of Code Sec. 179 property (¶ 1208) (pre-1987 Code Sec. 168(d)(1)).[94]

Straight-Line Election. An election to recover costs by using a straight-line method over the regular recovery period or a longer recovery period was also available under ACRS and was made on the taxpayer's return for the year in which the property was placed in service (pre-1987 Code Sec. 168(f)(4)).[95]

1255. ACRS Recovery Property. For ACRS purposes, recovery property is tangible depreciable property that is placed in service after 1980 and before 1987. It does not include property for which an election is made to compute depreciation on a method not based on a depreciation period (unit-of-production method, income forecast method, etc.), public utility property for which the normalization method of accounting is not used, intangible assets such as patents and copyrights (¶ 1201), property for which an election to amortize was made, or motion picture films and videotapes (pre-1987 Code Sec. 168(c), (e)).[96] For purposes of determining the class of recovery property into which an asset falls, recovery property is defined as either Code Sec. 1245 class property or Code Sec. 1250 class property.

Code Sec. 1245 class property includes tangible Code Sec. 1245 property, as defined at ¶ 1785, other than (1) elevators and escalators and (2) certain rapidly amortized realty. *Code Sec. 1250 class property* includes tangible Code Sec. 1250 property, as defined at ¶ 1786, and elevators and escalators.

1258. ACRS Personal Property. The ACRS statutory percentage for personal property placed in service after 1980 and before 1987 is determined using prescribed percentage tables based on the type of property (3-year, 5-year, 10-year or 15-year). These table percentages are not reproduced because such property should generally be fully depreciated at this time. The tables, however, are contained in ACRS Prop. Reg. § 1.168-2.

Generally, no recovery deduction is allowed in the year of disposition of personal property.

Footnote references are to paragraphs of the 2008 Standard Federal Tax Reports.

[93] ¶ 11,258.01
[94] ¶ 11,258.041
[95] ¶ 11,258.031
[96] ¶ 11,258.01, ¶ 11,258.045

1261. ACRS Real Property. Under ACRS, the unadjusted basis of real property is recovered over a period of 19 years for real property placed in service after May 8, 1985, and before 1987. For real property placed in service after March 15, 1984, and before May 9, 1985, unadjusted basis is recovered over a period of 18 years. A 15-year recovery period applies to real property placed in service after 1980 and before March 16, 1984, and to low-income housing.[97]

In computing the ACRS deduction, a full-month convention is used for real recovery property placed in service before March 16, 1984, and for low-income housing, and a mid-month convention is used for real recovery property (other than low-income housing) placed in service after March 15, 1984. Under the full-month convention, real property placed in service at any time during a particular month is treated as placed in service on the first day of such month, thereby permitting a full month's cost recovery for the month the property is placed in service. For a disposition at any time during a particular month before the end of a recovery period, no cost recovery is permitted for such month of disposition. Under the mid-month convention, real property placed in service at any time during a particular month is treated as placed in service in the middle of such month, thereby permitting one-half month's cost recovery for the month the property is placed in service. For a disposition of real property during a month before the end of a recovery period, one-half month's cost recovery is allowed for the month of disposition.

In using the following tables, there are separate rate schedules depending upon the month in the first tax year that the property is placed in service. Further, where real property is sold before the end of the recovery period, the ACRS deduction for the year of disposition is to reflect only the months of the year during which the property was in service. For a short tax year, appropriate adjustments must also be made to the table amounts (¶ 1270).

Footnote references are to paragraphs of the 2008 Standard Federal Tax Reports.

[97] ¶ 11,258.025

Table I *15-Year Real Property (other than low-income housing)*

Year	Month Placed in Service

Year	1	2	3	4	5	6	7	8	9	10	11	12
1st	12%	11%	10%	9%	8%	7%	6%	5%	4%	3%	2%	1%
2nd	10%	10%	11%	11%	11%	11%	11%	11%	11%	11%	11%	12%
3rd	9%	9%	9%	9%	10%	10%	10%	10%	10%	10%	10%	10%
4th	8%	8%	8%	8%	8%	8%	9%	9%	9%	9%	9%	9%
5th	7%	7%	7%	7%	7%	7%	8%	8%	8%	8%	8%	8%
6th	6%	6%	6%	6%	7%	7%	7%	7%	7%	7%	7%	7%
7th	6%	6%	6%	6%	6%	6%	6%	6%	6%	6%	6%	6%
8th	6%	6%	6%	6%	6%	6%	5%	6%	6%	6%	6%	6%
9th	6%	6%	6%	6%	5%	6%	5%	5%	5%	6%	6%	6%
10th	5%	6%	5%	6%	5%	5%	5%	5%	5%	5%	6%	5%
11th	5%	5%	5%	5%	5%	5%	5%	5%	5%	5%	5%	5%
12th	5%	5%	5%	5%	5%	5%	5%	5%	5%	5%	5%	5%
13th	5%	5%	5%	5%	5%	5%	5%	5%	5%	5%	5%	5%
14th	5%	5%	5%	5%	5%	5%	5%	5%	5%	5%	5%	5%
15th	5%	5%	5%	5%	5%	5%	5%	5%	5%	5%	5%	5%
16th	—	—	1%	1%	2%	2%	3%	3%	4%	4%	4%	5%

Table II *Low-Income Housing*
(placed in service before May 9, 1985)

Year	1	2	3	4	5	6	7	8	9	10	11	12
1st	13%	12%	11%	10%	9%	8%	7%	6%	4%	3%	2%	1%
2nd	12%	12%	12%	12%	12%	12%	12%	13%	13%	13%	13%	13%
3rd	10%	10%	10%	10%	11%	11%	11%	11%	11%	11%	11%	11%
4th	9%	9%	9%	9%	9%	9%	9%	9%	10%	10%	10%	10%
5th	8%	8%	8%	8%	8%	8%	8%	8%	8%	8%	8%	9%
6th	7%	7%	7%	7%	7%	7%	7%	7%	7%	7%	7%	7%
7th	6%	6%	6%	6%	6%	6%	6%	6%	6%	6%	6%	6%
8th	5%	5%	5%	5%	5%	5%	5%	5%	5%	5%	6%	6%
9th	5%	5%	5%	5%	5%	5%	5%	5%	5%	5%	5%	5%
10th	5%	5%	5%	5%	5%	5%	5%	5%	5%	5%	5%	5%
11th	4%	5%	5%	5%	5%	5%	5%	5%	5%	5%	5%	5%
12th	4%	4%	4%	5%	4%	5%	5%	5%	5%	5%	5%	5%
13th	4%	4%	4%	4%	4%	4%	5%	4%	5%	5%	5%	5%
14th	4%	4%	4%	4%	4%	4%	4%	4%	4%	5%	4%	4%
15th	4%	4%	4%	4%	4%	4%	4%	4%	4%	4%	4%	4%
16th	—	—	1%	1%	2%	2%	2%	3%	3%	3%	4%	4%

Table III *Low-Income Housing*
(placed in service after May 8, 1985)

Year	1	2	3	4	5	6	7	8	9	10	11	12
1st	13.3%	12.2%	11.1%	10%	8.9%	7.8%	6.6%	5.6%	4.4%	3.3%	2.2%	1.1%
2nd	11.6%	11.7%	11.9%	12%	12.1%	12.3%	12.5%	12.6%	12.7%	12.9%	13%	13.2%
3rd	10%	10.1%	10.2%	10.4%	10.5%	10.7%	10.8%	10.9%	11.1%	11.2%	11.3%	11.4%
4th	8.7%	8.8%	8.9%	9%	9.1%	9.2%	9.3%	9.5%	9.6%	9.7%	9.8%	9.9%
5th	7.5%	7.6%	7.7%	7.8%	7.9%	8%	8.1%	8.2%	8.3%	8.4%	8.5%	8.6%
6th	6.5%	6.6%	6.7%	6.8%	6.9%	6.9%	7%	7.1%	7.2%	7.3%	7.4%	7.4%
7th	5.7%	5.7%	5.8%	5.9%	5.9%	6%	6.1%	6.1%	6.2%	6.3%	6.4%	6.5%
8th	4.9%	5%	5%	5.1%	5.2%	5.2%	5.3%	5.3%	5.4%	5.5%	5.5%	5.6%
9th	4.6%	4.6%	4.6%	4.6%	4.6%	4.6%	4.6%	4.6%	4.6%	4.7%	4.8%	4.8%
10th	4.6%	4.6%	4.6%	4.6%	4.6%	4.6%	4.6%	4.6%	4.6%	4.6%	4.6%	4.6%
11th	4.6%	4.6%	4.6%	4.6%	4.6%	4.6%	4.6%	4.6%	4.6%	4.6%	4.6%	4.6%
12th	4.5%	4.6%	4.6%	4.6%	4.6%	4.6%	4.6%	4.6%	4.6%	4.6%	4.6%	4.6%
13th	4.5%	4.5%	4.6%	4.5%	4.6%	4.6%	4.6%	4.6%	4.6%	4.5%	4.6%	4.6%
14th	4.5%	4.5%	4.5%	4.5%	4.5%	4.5%	4.5%	4.6%	4.6%	4.5%	4.5%	4.5%
15th	4.5%	4.5%	4.5%	4.5%	4.5%	4.5%	4.5%	4.5%	4.5%	4.5%	4.5%	4.5%
16th	—	0.4%	0.7%	1.1%	1.5%	1.9%	2.3%	2.6%	3%	3.4%	3.7%	4.1%

¶1261

Table IV *18-Year Real Property*
(placed in service after June 22, 1984)

Year	Month Placed in Service											
	1	2	3	4	5	6	7	8	9	10	11	12
1st	9%	9%	8%	7%	6%	5%	4%	4%	3%	2%	1%	0.4%
2nd	9%	9%	9%	9%	9%	9%	9%	9%	9%	10%	10%	10%
3rd	8%	8%	8%	8%	8%	8%	8%	8%	9%	9%	9%	9%
4th	7%	7%	7%	7%	7%	8%	8%	8%	8%	8%	8%	8%
5th	7%	7%	7%	7%	7%	7%	7%	7%	7%	7%	7%	7%
6th	6%	6%	6%	6%	6%	6%	6%	6%	6%	6%	6%	6%
7th	5%	5%	5%	5%	6%	6%	6%	6%	6%	6%	6%	6%
8-12th	5%	5%	5%	5%	5%	5%	5%	5%	5%	5%	5%	5%
13th	4%	4%	4%	5%	4%	4%	5%	4%	4%	4%	5%	5%
14-17th	4%	4%	4%	4%	4%	4%	4%	4%	4%	4%	4%	4%
18th	4%	3%	4%	4%	4%	4%	4%	4%	4%	4%	4%	4%
19th		1%	1%	1%	2%	2%	2%	3%	3%	3%	3%	3.6%

Table V *18-Year Real Property*
(placed in service after March 15 and before June 23, 1984)

Year	Month Placed in Service										
	1	2	3	4	5	6	7	8	9	10-11	12
1st	10%	9%	8%	7%	6%	6%	5%	4%	3%	2%	1%
2nd	9%	9%	9%	9%	9%	9%	9%	9%	9%	10%	10%
3rd	8%	8%	8%	8%	8%	8%	8%	8%	9%	9%	9%
4th	7%	7%	7%	7%	7%	7%	8%	8%	8%	8%	8%
5th	6%	7%	7%	7%	7%	7%	7%	7%	7%	7%	7%
6th	6%	6%	6%	6%	6%	6%	6%	6%	6%	6%	6%
7th	5%	5%	5%	5%	6%	6%	6%	6%	6%	6%	6%
8-12th	5%	5%	5%	5%	5%	5%	5%	5%	5%	5%	5%
13th	4%	4%	4%	5%	5%	4%	4%	5%	4%	4%	4%
14-18th	4%	4%	4%	4%	4%	4%	4%	4%	4%	4%	4%
19th		1%	1%	1%	2%	2%	2%	3%	3%	4%

Table VI *19-Year Real Property*

Year	Month Placed in Service											
	1	2	3	4	5	6	7	8	9	10	11	12
1st	8.8%	8.1%	7.3%	6.5%	5.8%	5.0%	4.2%	3.5%	2.7%	1.9%	1.1%	0.4%
2nd	8.4%	8.5%	8.5%	8.6%	8.7%	8.8%	8.8%	8.9%	9.0%	9.0%	9.1%	9.2%
3rd	7.6%	7.7%	7.7%	7.8%	7.9%	7.9%	8.0%	8.1%	8.1%	8.2%	8.3%	8.3%
4th	6.9%	7.0%	7.0%	7.1%	7.1%	7.2%	7.3%	7.3%	7.4%	7.4%	7.5%	7.6%
5th	6.3%	6.3%	6.4%	6.4%	6.5%	6.5%	6.6%	6.6%	6.7%	6.8%	6.8%	6.9%
6th	5.7%	5.7%	5.8%	5.9%	5.9%	5.9%	6.0%	6.0%	6.1%	6.1%	6.2%	6.2%
7th	5.2%	5.2%	5.3%	5.3%	5.3%	5.4%	5.4%	5.5%	5.5%	5.6%	5.6%	5.6%
8th	4.7%	4.7%	4.8%	4.8%	4.8%	4.9%	4.9%	5.0%	5.0%	5.1%	5.1%	5.1%
9th	4.2%	4.3%	4.3%	4.4%	4.4%	4.5%	4.5%	4.5%	4.5%	4.6%	4.6%	4.7%
10-19th	4.2%	4.2%	4.2%	4.2%	4.2%	4.2%	4.2%	4.2%	4.2%	4.2%	4.2%	4.2%
20th	0.2%	0.5%	0.9%	1.2%	1.6%	1.9%	2.3%	2.6%	3.0%	3.3%	3.7%	4.0%

Table VII *18-Year Real Property*
(placed in service after June 22, 1984)
for Which Alternate ACRS Method Over an
18-Year Period Is Elected

Year	Month Placed in Service					
	1-2	3-4	5-7	8-9	10-11	12
1st	5%	4%	3%	2%	1%	0.2%
2-10th	6%	6%	6%	6%	6%	6%
11th	5%	5%	5%	5%	5%	5.8%
12-18th	5%	5%	5%	5%	5%	5%
19th	1%	2%	3%	4%	5%	5%

Table VIII *18-Year Real Property*
(placed in service after March 15 and before June 23, 1984)
for Which Alternate ACRS Method Over an
18-Year Period Is Elected

Year	Month Placed in Service						
	1	2-3	4-5	6-7	8-9	10-11	12
1st	6%	5%	4%	3%	2%	1%	0.5%
2-10th	6%	6%	6%	6%	6%	6%	6%
11th	5%	5%	5%	5%	5%	5%	5.5%
12-18th	5%	5%	5%	5%	5%	5%	5%
19th		1%	2%	3%	4%	5%	5%

Table IX *19-Year Real Property*
for Which Alternate ACRS Method Over a
19-Year Period Is Elected

Year	Month Placed in Service											
	1	2	3	4	5	6	7	8	9	10	11	12
1st	5.0%	4.6%	4.2%	3.7%	3.3%	2.9%	2.4%	2.0%	1.5%	1.1%	0.7%	0.2%
2-13th	5.3%	5.3%	5.3%	5.3%	5.3%	5.3%	5.3%	5.3%	5.3%	5.3%	5.3%	5.3%
14-19th	5.2%	5.2%	5.2%	5.2%	5.2%	5.2%	5.2%	5.2%	5.2%	5.2%	5.2%	5.2%
20th	0.2%	0.6%	1.0%	1.5%	1.9%	2.3%	2.8%	3.2%	3.7%	4.1%	4.5%	5.0%

Table X *18-Year Real Property*
(placed in service after June 22, 1984) for Which Alternate ACRS Method
Over a 35-Year Period Is Elected

Year	Month Placed in Service				
	1-2	3-6	7-10	11	12
1st	3%	2%	1%	0.4%	0.1%
2-30th	3%	3%	3%	3%	3%
31st	2%	2%	2%	2.6%	2.9%
32-35th	2%	2%	2%	2%	2%
36th		1%	2%	2%	2%

Table XI *18-Year Real Property*
(placed in service after March 15 and before June 23, 1984)
15-Year Real Property and Low-Income housing
(placed in service before May 9, 1985) for Which Alternate
ACRS Method Over a 35-Year Period Is Elected

Year	Month Placed in Service		
	1-2	3-6	7-12
1st	3%	2%	1%
2-30th	3%	3%	3%
31-35th	2%	2%	2%
36th		1%	2%

Table XII *Low-Income Housing (placed in service after May 8, 1985)*
for Which Alternate ACRS Method Over a 35-Year Period Is Elected

Year	Month Placed in Service											
	1	2	3	4	5	6	7	8	9	10	11	12
1st	2.9%	2.6%	2.4%	2.1%	1.9%	1.7%	1.4%	1.2%	1.0%	0.7%	0.5%	0.2%
2-20th	2.9%	2.9%	2.9%	2.9%	2.9%	2.9%	2.9%	2.9%	2.9%	2.9%	2.9%	2.9%
21-35th	2.8%	2.8%	2.8%	2.8%	2.8%	2.8%	2.8%	2.8%	2.8%	2.8%	2.8%	2.8%
36th		0.3%	0.5%	0.8%	1.0%	1.2%	1.5%	1.7%	1.9%	2.2%	2.4%	2.7%

Table XIII *19-Year Real Property*
for Which Alternate ACRS Method Over a 35-Year Period Is Elected

Year	Month Placed in Service											
	1	2	3	4	5	6	7	8	9	10	11	12
1st	2.7%	2.5%	2.3%	2.0%	1.8%	1.5%	1.3%	1.1%	0.8%	0.6%	0.4%	0.1%
2-20th	2.9%	2.9%	2.9%	2.9%	2.9%	2.9%	2.9%	2.9%	2.9%	2.9%	2.9%	2.9%
21-35th	2.8%	2.8%	2.8%	2.8%	2.8%	2.8%	2.8%	2.8%	2.8%	2.8%	2.8%	2.8%
36th	0.2%	0.4%	0.6%	0.9%	1.1%	1.4%	1.6%	1.8%	2.1%	2.3%	2.5%	2.8%

Table XIV *18-Year Real Property*
(placed in service after June 22, 1984) 19-Year Real Property for Which
Alternate ACRS Method Over a 45-Year Period Is Elected

Year	Month Placed in Service											
	1	2	3	4	5	6	7	8	9	10	11	12
1st	2.1%	1.9%	1.8%	1.6%	1.4%	1.2%	1%	0.8%	0.6%	0.5%	0.3%	0.1%
2-11th	2.3%	2.3%	2.3%	2.3%	2.3%	2.3%	2.3%	2.3%	2.3%	2.3%	2.3%	2.3%
12-45th	2.2%	2.2%	2.2%	2.2%	2.2%	2.2%	2.2%	2.2%	2.2%	2.2%	2.2%	2.2%
46th	0.1%	0.3%	0.4%	0.6%	0.8%	1%	1.2%	1.4%	1.6%	1.7%	1.9%	2.1%

Table XV *18-Year Real Property*
(placed in service after March 15 and before June 23, 1984) 15-Year Real Property
and Low-Income housing (placed in service after December 31, 1980) for Which
Alternate ACRS Method Over a 45-Year Period Is Elected

Year	Month Placed in Service											
	1	2	3	4	5	6	7	8	9	10	11	12
1st	2.3%	2%	1.9%	1.7%	1.5%	1.3%	1.2%	0.9%	0.7%	0.6%	0.4%	0.2%
2-10th	2.3%	2.3%	2.3%	2.3%	2.3%	2.3%	2.3%	2.3%	2.3%	2.3%	2.3%	2.3%
11-45th	2.2%	2.2%	2.2%	2.2%	2.2%	2.2%	2.2%	2.2%	2.2%	2.2%	2.2%	2.2%
46th		0.3%	0.4%	0.6%	0.8%	1%	1.1%	1.4%	1.6%	1.7%	1.9%	2.1%

1264. ACRS: Predominant Use Outside the U.S. Under ACRS, the unadjusted basis of personal property used outside the U.S. is recovered over a period equal to the ADR class life for that property as of January 1, 1981.[98] Generally, no recovery deduction is allowed in the year of disposition of personal recovery property used predominantly outside the U.S. The unadjusted basis of real property and low income housing used predominantly outside the U.S. is to be recovered over a period of 35 years. For real recovery property (other than low-income housing) placed in service after March 15, 1984, a mid-month convention is used. There are separate rate schedules depending on the month in the first tax year that the property is placed in service.

1267. ACRS: Components of Sec. 1250 Class Property. Under ACRS, structural components of Sec. 1250 class property may not be depreciated separately. Composite depreciation is required on the entire building, unless the components qualify for amortization elections (pre-1987 Code Sec. 168(f)(1)).[99] Components which are considered personal property can be separately depreciated under the cost segregation rules. See ¶ 1240.

Substantial Improvements. If a taxpayer made a substantial improvement to a building, it was treated as a separate building rather than as one or more components. The taxpayer could use the regular ACRS deduction or may elect the straight-line ACRS deduction for the improvement over the regular or a longer recovery period regardless of the ACRS method that is used for the rest of the building.

Components and improvements placed in service after 1986 are depreciated using MACRS even if the building is not MACRS property. See *"Additions and improvements"* at ¶ 1240.

1270. ACRS: Short Tax Years. For a tax year of less than 12 months, the amount of the ACRS deduction is the amount that bears the same relationship to the amount of the deduction as the number of months and partial months in the short year bears to 12 (pre-1987 Code Sec. 168(f)(5)).[100] Generally, for real property and low-income housing placed in service or disposed of in a short tax year, the above rule does not apply and the deduction is based on the number of months the property is in service during the year, regardless of the length of the tax year and regardless of the recovery period and method used.

Any unrecovered allowance (the difference between the recovery allowance properly allowable for the short tax year and the recovery allowance that would have been allowable if such year were not a short tax year) is claimed in the tax year following the last year in the recovery period (Prop. Reg. § 1.168-2(f)(3)).[101] However, there is a maximum limitation on the amount of an unrecovered allowance that may be claimed as a recovery allowance in a tax year. The unrecovered allowance claimed as a recovery allowance in the tax year following the last year of the recovery period may not exceed the amount of the recovery allowance permitted for the last year of the recovery period, assuming that such year consists of 12 months. Any remainder is carried forward until exhausted.

Class Life ADR System

1282. Post-1980 Depreciation Under ADR. If the Asset Depreciation Range (ADR) System was elected for tangible assets first placed in service after 1970 and before 1981, post-1980 depreciation on such assets must be computed under the ADR System.[102]

1284. ADR in General. Under ADR, all tangible assets were placed in specific classes. A class life (called "asset guideline period" in the regulations[103]) was given for each class of assets. In addition, each class of assets other than land improvements and buildings was given a range of years (called "asset depreciation range") that was about

---

Footnote references are to paragraphs of the 2008 Standard Federal Tax Reports.

[98] ¶ 162.01
[99] ¶ 11,258.05

[100] ¶ 11,258.055
[101] ¶ 11,252, ¶ 11,258.055

[102] ¶ 11,029.01
[103] ¶ 11,026, ¶ 11,029.01

20 percent above and below the class life. For details on the ADR system, see ¶ 11,029.01 and following of the STANDARD FEDERAL TAX REPORTER.

Deductions for Refiners

1285. Deduction for EPA Sulfur Regulation Compliance Costs of Small Refiners. Small business refiners may elect to immediately deduct as an expense up to 75 percent of the qualified capital costs paid or incurred during the tax year for the purpose of complying with the Highway Diesel Fuel Sulfur Control Requirements of the Environmental Protection Agency (EPA) (Code Sec. 179B). Costs paid or incurred with respect to any facility of a small business refiner during the period beginning on January 1, 2003 and ending on the earlier of the date that is one year after the date on which the taxpayer must comply with the applicable EPA regulations or December 31, 2009 qualify for the deduction. Election guidance is provided in Notice 2006-47.

1285A. Expensing election for new or expanded refineries. A taxpayer may elect to expense 50 percent of the cost of qualified refinery property placed in service after August 8, 2005 and before January 1, 2012. The original use of the refinery property must commence with the taxpayer. An improvement to an existing refinery can qualify if the improvement increases production capacity by specified levels (Code Sec. 179C).

Deduction for Clean Fuel Vehicles and Refueling Property

1286. Clean Fuel Vehicle Property Deduction. A deduction from gross income was allowed for up to $2,000 of the cost of a new clean fuel motor vehicle. The deduction applied to vehicles placed in service after June 30, 1993, and before January 1, 2006 (Code Sec. 62(a)(14) and Code Sec. 179A).[104]

Cars certified as qualifying for a $2,000 deduction are the 2006 Toyota Highlander Hybrid, Lexus RX 400h, Ford Escape Hybrid, Mercury Mariner Hybrid, and Toyota Prius and the 2005 Toyota Prius, Ford Escape Hybrid, Honda Insight, Honda Civic Hybrid, and Honda Accord Hybrid (IRS News Releases IR-2006-26, IR-2005-132, IR-2005-69, IR-2005-57, IR-2005-14, IR-2004-147, and IR-2004-125), as well as the Toyota Prius, Honda Insight, and Honda Civic Hybrid for model years 2004, 2003 and earlier (IRS News Releases IR-2004-16, IR-2003-114, IR-2002-97, and IR-2002-93). Hybrid vehicles placed in service after December 31, 2005 will generally qualify for a tax credit. See ¶ 1315D

The deduction was increased for certain clean-fuel trucks, vans, and buses (Code Sec. 179A(b)(1)(A)).

A deduction from gross income was also allowed for the aggregate cost of qualified clean fuel vehicle refueling property up to $100,000 per location minus the aggregate amount of such property at such location previously deducted by the taxpayer or a related person (Code Sec. 179A(b)(2)).[105] This property must also be placed in service before January 1, 2006.

Qualified clean fuel vehicle refueling property is depreciable property (other than a building and its structural components) the original use of which begins with the taxpayer that either (a) stores or dispenses clean-burning fuel into the fuel tank of a clean fuel vehicle at a refueling location or (b) recharges electric vehicles at a recharging location (Code Sec. 179A(d)).[106]

These deductions are recaptured when property ceases to be eligible for them (Code Sec. 179A(e)(4); Reg. § 1.179A-1).[107] If the recapture event occurs within one, two, or three years after the property is placed in service, the portion of the deduction for clean-fuel vehicles recaptured is 100, 67, and 33 percent, respectively. The deduction for refueling property is recaptured ratably if such property ceases to be eligible during the recovery period for such property. For depreciable property, these deductions are treated as depreciation deductions and may be recaptured as ordinary income upon the sale or disposition of the property at a gain.

Footnote references are to paragraphs of the 2008 Standard Federal Tax Reports.

[104] ¶ 6002, ¶ 12,130, ¶ 12,133 [106] ¶ 12,130, ¶ 12,133.022
[105] ¶ 12,130, ¶ 12,133 [107] ¶ 12,133.03

Deduction for Energy Efficiency Improvements

1286A. Deduction for Energy Efficiency Improvements to Depreciable Buildings. A taxpayer may deduct the cost of certain energy efficiency improvements installed on or in a depreciable building located in the U.S., effective for improvements placed in service after December 31, 2005 and before January 1, 2009 (Code Sec. 179D, as amended by P.L. 109-432). The deduction applies to "energy efficient commercial building property," which is defined as depreciable property installed as part of a building's (1) interior lighting systems, (2) heating, cooling, ventilation, and hot water systems, or (3) envelope as part of a certified plan to reduce the total annual energy and power costs of these systems by at least 50 percent in comparison to a reference building that meets specified minimum standards. The deduction is limited to the product of $1.80 and the total square footage of the building, reduced by the aggregate amount deducted in any prior tax year.

A taxpayer may also claim a partial deduction for the costs of property that meet energy savings targets set by the IRS in Notice 2006-52. The deduction is determined by substituting $.60 for $1.80.

Generally, the deduction is claimed by the building's owner. However, in the case of a public building, the person primarily responsible for designing the property may claim the deduction. The deduction reduces the depreciable basis of the building and is treated as a depreciation deduction for section 1245 recapture purposes (Code Sec. 1245(a)(3)(C).

The Department of Energy maintains a list of the software that must be used to calculate power consumption and energy costs for purposes of certifying the required energy savings necessary to claim the deduction (Notice 2006-52). The certification is not attached to the taxpayer's return but must be retained as part of the taxpayer's books and records.

Allowance for Amortization

1287. Property Subject to Amortization. Amortization is the recovery of certain capital expenditures, that are not ordinarily deductible, in a manner that is similar to straight-line depreciation. That portion of the basis of property that is recovered through amortization deductions may not also be depreciated.

Pollution Control Facilities. Taxpayers may elect to amortize over a 60-month period the cost of certified pollution control facilities added to or used in connection with a plant in operation before 1976. The amortization deduction is available only for the portion of the facility's basis attributable to the first 15 years of its recovery period if it has an MACRS recovery period in excess of 15 years. The remaining basis is depreciable. An air pollution control facility placed in service after April 11, 2005 in connection with a coal-fired plant placed in operation after 1975 qualifies for an 84-month amortization period (Code Sec. 169). The 60-month amortization period continues to apply to an air pollution facility placed in service after April 11, 2005 in connection with a coal-fired plant placed in operation before 1976 (Code Sec. 169).[108]

Architectural and Transportation Barriers. Business taxpayers can elect to deduct up to $15,000 of the costs of removing certain architectural and transportation barriers for handicapped or elderly persons in the year paid or incurred instead of capitalizing and depreciating such costs (Code Sec. 190).[109]

Reforestation Expenditures. In the case of expenditures paid or incurred after October 22, 2004, a taxpayer (other than a trust) may elect to expense up to $10,000 of qualified reforestation expenditures each tax year for each qualified timber property. A taxpayer may elect to amortize over 84 months amounts for which a current deduction is not elected (Code Sec. 194).[110] The expense election may be made by estates. Trusts and estates may make the amortization election. Election guidance is provided in Notice 2006-47.

Footnote references are to paragraphs of the 2008 Standard Federal Tax Reports.

[108] ¶ 11,502, ¶ 11,517   [109] ¶ 12,260, ¶ 12,264   [110] ¶ 12,330, ¶ 12,335

The $10,000 maximum annual per-property expensing limitation for reforestation expenditures paid or incurred after August 27, 2005 in the Gulf Opportunity Zone, after September 22, 2005 in the Rita GO Zone, and after October 22, 2005 in the Wilma GO Zone is temporarily increased by the lesser of (1) $10,000 ($5,000 if married filing separately) or (2) the amount of reforestation expenditures paid or incurred during the tax year with respect to qualified timber property located in these zones (Code Sec. 1400N(i)). The provision does not apply to taxpayers that hold more than 500 acres of qualified timber property or to corporations with stock traded on an established securities market. To qualify, the expenditures must be paid or incurred before January 1, 2008.[111]

Start-Up and Organizational Costs. See ¶ 904.

Oil and Gas Geological and Geophysical Expenditures. Effective for amounts paid or incurred in tax years beginning after August 8, 2005, geological and geophysical ("G&G") expenditures paid or incurred in connection with oil and gas exploration or development in the United States must be amortized ratably over a 24-month period beginning on the mid-point of the tax-year that the expenses were paid or incurred. If a property or project is abandoned or retired during the 24-month amortization period, any remaining basis must continue to be amortized (Code Sec. 167(h)). Major integrated oil companies, however, must ratably amortize any G&G costs incurred after May 17, 2006 over five years (Code Sec. 167(h)(5), as added by the Tax Increase Prevention and Reconciliation Act of 2005 (P.L. 109-222)).[112]

Musical compositions and copyrights. A taxpayer may elect five-year ratable amortization of capitalized expenses paid or incurred in creating or acquiring a musical composition (including the accompanying words) or a copyright to a musical composition if the expenses are not exempt from capitalization as the qualified creative expenses of an individual (¶ 990A), the expenses are not amortizable under Code Sec. 197 because acquired as part of the acquisition of a trade or business, or the taxpayer uses a simplified UNICAP method for property acquired for resale (¶ 995) (Code Sec. 167(g)(8), as added by the Tax Increase Prevention and Reconciliation Act of 2005 (P.L. 109-222)). The provision is effective for expenses paid or incurred with respect to property placed in service in tax years beginning after December 31, 2005. It terminates in tax years beginning after 2010.

1288. Amortization of Section 197 Intangibles. The capitalized cost of goodwill and most other intangibles acquired after August 10, 1993, and used in a trade or business or for the production of income are ratably amortized over a 15-year period generally beginning in the month of acquisition (Code Sec. 197).[113] Intangibles amortizable under this provision are referred to as "section 197 intangibles."

The following intangibles are section 197 intangibles: (1) goodwill, going concern value, and covenants not to compete entered into in connection with the acquisition of a trade or business (¶ 1743); (2) workforce in place; (3) information base; (4) a patent, copyright, formula, design, or similar item; (5) any customer-based intangible; (6) any supplier-based intangible; (7) any license, permit, or other right granted by a governmental unit or agency; and (8) any franchise, trademark, or trade name (Code Sec. 197(d)).[114]

Generally, self-created intangibles are not amortized under Code Sec. 197 unless created in connection with the acquisition of a trade or business. Exceptions are provided for government-granted licenses, permits, and rights, covenants not to compete entered into in connection with the purchase of a business, and franchises, trademarks, and trade names (Code Sec. 197(c)(2)).[115] However, certain self-created intangibles without an ascertainable useful life may be amortized over 15-years under Reg. § 1.167(a)-3(b). See ¶ 1288A.

Footnote references are to paragraphs of the 2008 Standard Federal Tax Reports.

[111] ¶ 12,330, ¶ 12,335   [113] ¶ 12,450, ¶ 12,455   [115] ¶ 12,450, ¶ 12,455.033
[112] ¶ 11,009.047   [114] ¶ 12,450, ¶ 12,455.023

The following intangibles are specifically excluded from the definition of a section 197 intangible: (1) interests in a corporation, partnership, trust, or estate; (2) interests under certain financial contracts; (3) interests in land; (4) computer software not acquired in connection with the purchase of a business or which is readily available for purchase by the general public, is subject to a nonexclusive license, and has not been substantially modified (¶ 980); (5) certain separately acquired rights and interests, including an interest in a patent or copyright or an interest in a film, sound recording, videotape, book, or similar property; (6) interests under existing leases of tangible property; (7) interests under existing indebtedness; (8) sports franchises acquired on or before October 22, 2004; (9) residential mortgage servicing rights not acquired in connection with the acquisition of a business; and (10) professional fees and transaction costs incurred in a corporate organization or reorganization (Code Sec. 197(e)).[116]

No loss may be claimed when an amortizable section 197 intangible is disposed of if any other section 197 intangibles acquired in the same transaction are retained. The bases of the retained section 197 intangibles are increased by the amount of the unrecognized loss (Code Sec. 197(f)).[117]

Generally, Code Sec. 197 applies to acquisitions made after August 10, 1993, or, on an elective basis, to all property acquired after July 25, 1991.[118] However, antichurning rules prevent the provision from applying to section 197 intangibles that were not amortizable under prior law, if held or used by a taxpayer or a related person before the effective date and in certain other circumstances.[119]

1288A 15-Year Safe-Harbor Amortization for Certain Self-Created Intangibles. Effective for intangible assets created on or after December 31, 2003, a taxpayer is permitted to amortize certain created intangibles that do not have readily ascertainable useful lives over a 15-year period using the straight-line method and no salvage value (Reg. § 1.167(a)-3(b); Rev. Proc. 2006-12, providing change of accounting method procedures).[120] For example, amounts paid to acquire memberships or privileges of indefinite duration, such as a trade association membership, are covered by this safe harbor.

A taxpayer may use the 15-year amortization period on any intangible other than (1) any intangible acquired from another person; (2) created financial interests; (3) any intangible that has a useful life that can be estimated with reasonable accuracy; or (4) an intangible asset for which an amortization period or useful life is specifically prescribed or proscribed by the Code, regulations, or other published IRS guidance. In addition, amounts paid to facilitate an acquisition of a trade or business, a change in the capital structure of a business entity, and certain other similar transactions described in Reg. § 1.263(a)-5 do not qualify. The 15-year amortization period is extended to 25 years for an intangible benefit described in Reg. § 1.263(a)-4(d)(8). These are intangibles created by transferring ownership of real property to another person or by making a monetary contribution for the acquisition or improvement of real property owned by another person. However, for the treatment of impact fees, see Rev. Rul. 2002-9, which requires developers to allocate the cost of impact fees to the basis of the buildings constructed.

What Is Depletion?

1289. Deduction for Depletion. A deduction for depletion is allowed in determining the taxable income from natural resources. The deduction is similar to depreciation in that it allows the taxpayer to recover the cost of an asset over the resources' productive life. "Depletion" is the exhaustion of natural resources, such as mines, wells, and timberlands, as a result of production. The right to a depletion allowance is based upon the taxpayer's economic interest in the property (Reg. § 1.611-1(b)(i)).[121] An economic interest exists if the taxpayer (1) has acquired by investment any interest in minerals in place or in standing timber and (2) looks to the income from the extraction of the minerals or severance of the timber for a return on investment.[122]

Footnote references are to paragraphs of the 2008 Standard Federal Tax Reports.

[116] ¶ 12,450, ¶ 12,455.034   [119] ¶ 12,455.044   [122] ¶ 23,924.027
[117] ¶ 12,450, ¶ 12,455.035   [120] ¶ 11,009.045
[118] ¶ 12,455.06   [121] ¶ 23,922

The basic method of computing depletion is "cost depletion". (Code Sec. 612).[123] The basis upon which the deduction is allowed is the adjusted basis of the property (Reg. § 1.612-1).[124] Determination of cost depletion first requires an estimate of the number of units (tons, barrels, etc.) that make up the deposit. Then that part of the cost or other adjusted basis of the property that is allocable to the depletable reserves is divided by the number of units. The quotient is the cost depletion per unit. This amount, multiplied by the number of units extracted and sold during the year, determines the cost depletion deductible for the year. Each year the "cost basis" of the property is reduced, but not below zero, by the amount of depletion deducted for that year, whether cost or percentage depletion was used. The remaining basis is used in computing cost depletion for the next year.

An alternative method of computing depletion, known as percentage depletion, may be used for almost all depletable property. However, timber is excluded from this method (Reg. § 1.611-1(a)(1)).[125] Under this method, a flat percentage of *gross income* from the property is taken as the depletion deduction. The percentage depletion deduction may not exceed 50% (100% in the case of oil or gas properties) of the *taxable income* from the property (see ¶ 1294 for special rules concerning independent producers and royalty owners) computed without regard to the depletion allowance. In computing taxable income, the deductible mining expenses must be decreased by the amount of Sec. 1245 gains allocable to the property (Code Sec. 613(a)).[126] If cost depletion results in a greater deduction, cost depletion must be used (Reg. § 1.613-1).[127]

Ordinarily, the lease of a mineral property requires the lessee to make an advance payment, known as a bonus or advance royalty. In such a case, the lessor's cost depletion allowance must be allocated between the advance lump-sum payment and the royalties received during the period of extraction (Reg. § 1.612-3).[128] Unlike bonuses or advance royalties, "shut-in" oil payments and delay rentals are not depletable.[129]

Coal and iron ore royalties retained upon the disposition of coal and iron ore generally held for more than one year before mining are eligible for percentage depletion for any tax year in which the maximum rate of tax imposed on net capital gain equals or exceeds the maximum rate for ordinary income (Code Sec. 631(c)).[130]

Depletion is subject to recapture as ordinary income upon the sale or other disposition of an oil, gas, geothermal, or other mineral property at a gain (Code Sec. 1254).[131] Recapture is limited to the amount by which the depletion deduction reduced the adjusted basis of the disposed property.

Mineral Production Payments

1291. Mineral Production Payments. A mineral production payment is treated as a loan by the owner of the production payment to the owner of the mineral property (Code Sec. 636).[132] Thus, a carved-out mineral production payment—created when the owner of a mineral property sells or carves out a portion of the future production with payment secured by an interest in the minerals—is treated as a mortgage loan on the mineral property rather than as an economic interest in the property. All the income from the property is taxed to the seller (owner of the working interest) and is subject to depletion by him. The owner of the production payment does not get depletion.

When the owner of a mineral interest sells the working interest, a retained production payment is treated as a purchase money mortgage loan and not as an economic interest in the mineral property. Accordingly, all the income from the property is taxed to the purchaser and is subject to depletion by him. The seller who retains the production payment is not entitled to depletion.

Footnote references are to paragraphs of the 2008 Standard Federal Tax Reports.

[123] ¶ 23,940, ¶ 23,942	[126] ¶ 23,960, ¶ 23,963	[130] ¶ 24,150, ¶ 24,156.021
[124] ¶ 23,941, ¶ 23,942.021	[127] ¶ 23,961, ¶ 23,963.01	[131] ¶ 31,060, ¶ 31,066
[125] ¶ 23,922, ¶ 29,960, ¶ 23,963	[128] ¶ 23,946, ¶ 23,948.01	[132] ¶ 24,170, ¶ 24,176
	[129] ¶ 23,963.60	

Percentage Depletion

1294. Oil and Gas Production. A 22% depletion rate is allowed for oil and gas production in the case of regulated natural gas and natural gas sold under a fixed contract (but not certain casinghead gas contracts[133]); a 10% rate applies to geopressurized methane gas wells (Code Sec. 613A(b)).[134]

A 15% depletion rate applies to independent producers and royalty owners with limitations based on average daily production (Code Sec. 613A(c)).[135] The rate applies to an average daily production of 1,000 barrels of oil and six million cubic feet of gas. The percentage depletion deduction is generally limited to the lesser of 65% of the *taxable income* before the depletion allowance (Code Sec. 613A(d)(1))[136] or 100% of the *taxable income from the property* before the depletion allowance (see ¶ 1289). For purposes of the 65% limit, taxable income is computed without regard to any net operating loss carryback or capital loss carryback. Any portion of a depletion allowance disallowed under the 65% limit may be carried over. Percentage depletion is also denied for lease bonuses, advance royalty payments, or other amounts payable without regard to actual production from an oil, gas or geothermal property (see ¶ 1296) (Code Sec. 613(e)(3) and Code Sec. 613A(d)(5)).[137]

For tax years beginning after December 31, 1997, and before January 1, 2008, the 100% taxable income limit on percentage depletion deductions for oil and gas properties is suspended for marginal properties (Code Sec. 613A(c)(6)(H)).[138]

The 15% depletion rate for marginal oil or gas production properties held by independent producers or royalty owners increases by one percent (up to a maximum 25% rate) for each whole dollar that the reference price for crude oil for the preceding calendar year is less than $20 per barrel (Code Sec. 613A(c)(6)).[139] The allowance for depletion is computed using the increased rate with respect to the portion of the taxpayer's average daily marginal production of domestic crude oil and natural gas that does not exceed the taxpayer's depletable quantities of those products. An election may be made to have this rule apply to the pro rata portion of marginal production. The applicable percentage for marginal production for tax years beginning in 2003 through 2007 is 15% (Notice 2007-65).

1296. Geothermal Deposits. Geothermal deposits (geothermal reservoirs consisting of natural heat that is stored in rocks or in an aqueous liquid or vapor (whether or not under pressure)) are eligible for a 15% depletion allowance (Code Sec. 613(e)).[140]

1298. Coal or Other Minerals. Percentage depletion is allowed, under Code Sec. 613(b),[141] at the following percentages of "gross income from the property":

(a) 22%—sulphur and uranium; and, if from deposits in the United States, anorthosite, clay, laterite, and nephelite syenite (to the extent that alumina and aluminum compounds are extracted therefrom), asbestos, bauxite, celestite, chromite, corundum, fluorspar, graphite, ilmenite, kyanite, mica, olivine, quartz crystals (radio grade), rutile, block steatite talc, and zircon, and ores of the following metals: antimony, beryllium, bismuth, cadmium, cobalt, columbium, lead lithium, manganese, mercury, molybdenum, nickel, platinum and platinum group metals, tantalum, thorium, tin, titanium, tungsten, vanadium and zinc.

(b) 15%—if from deposits in the United States, gold, silver, copper, iron ore, and oil shale (except shale described in (e) below).

(c) 14%—metal mines (other than metals from deposits in the United States to which the 22% rate in (a) applies), rock asphalt, and vermiculite; if (a) above and (e) and (f) below do not apply, ball clay, bentonite, china clay, sagger clay, and clay used or sold for use for purposes dependent on its refractory properties.

Footnote references are to paragraphs of the 2008 Standard Federal Tax Reports.

[133] ¶ 23,924.039, ¶ 23,988.01
[134] ¶ 23,980, ¶ 23,988.021
[135] ¶ 23,980, ¶ 23,988.024
[136] ¶ 23,980, ¶ 23,988.024
[137] ¶ 23,960, ¶ 23,980, ¶ 23,988.036
[138] ¶ 23,980, ¶ 23,988.044
[139] ¶ 23,980, ¶ 23,988.044
[140] ¶ 23,960, ¶ 23,965.03
[141] ¶ 23,960, ¶ 23,965.01

(d) 10%—asbestos from deposits outside the United States, brucite, coal, lignite, perlite, sodium chloride, and wollastonite.

(e) 7½%—clay and shale used or sold for use in the manufacture of sewer pipe or brick, and clay, shale, and slate used or sold for use as sintered or burned lightweight aggregates.

(f) 5%—gravel, peat, pumice, sand, scoria, shale (except shale described in (b) and (e) above) and stone (except stone falling within the general 14% group described in (g)); clay used, or sold for use, in the manufacture of drainage and roofing tile, flower pots, and kindred products; also, if from brine wells, bromite, calcium chloride, and magnesium chloride.

(g) 14%—all other minerals not included in any of the categories listed above. For purposes of this paragraph, the term "all other minerals" does not include (A) soil, sod, dirt, turf, water, or mosses; (B) minerals from sea water, the air, or similar inexhaustible sources; or (C) oil and gas wells.

"Gross income from the property," on which percentage depletion is based, is that amount of income which comes from the extraction of the ores or minerals from the ground and the application of mining processes, including mining transportation (Code Sec. 613(c)).[142] Mining processes include certain specified treatment processes. In general, it can be said that the percentage depletion allowance is based on the mined product after application of those treatment processes applied by "ordinary" miners. Hence, an integrated miner-manufacturer computes gross income from mining at the point when the non-integrated miner disposes of the product. Gross income is computed by use of the representative market or field price. However, when it is impossible to determine such a field price, and where the IRS does not determine that a more appropriate method should be used, the proportionate profits method must be used (Reg. § 1.613-4(d)).[143]

Footnote references are to paragraphs of the 2008 Standard Federal Tax Reports.

[142] ¶ 23,960, ¶ 23,968.04   [143] ¶ 23,967, ¶ 23,968.04

Chapter 13
TAX CREDITS

Personal Credits

1301. Child and Dependent Care Credit. A nonrefundable credit is allowed for a portion of qualifying child or dependent care expenses paid for the purpose of allowing the taxpayer to be gainfully employed (Code Sec. 21).[1] The credit is computed on Form 2441, Child and Dependent Care Expenses, or Schedule 2, Child and Dependent Care Expenses for Form 1040A Filers, whichever is applicable. To be eligible for the credit, the taxpayer must incur employment-related expenses in providing care for one of the following qualified individuals:

(1) a dependent of the taxpayer as defined in Code Sec. 152(a)(1) who has not attained the age of 13 (see ¶ 137—¶ 137B);

(2) a dependent of the taxpayer (other than a married person filing a joint return, a person having at least $3,400 of gross income in 2007, and a person (or spouse if filing a joint return) who may be claimed as dependent on another taxpayer's return) who is physically or mentally incapable of caring for himself or herself and who has the same principal place of abode as the taxpayer for more than one-half of the year; or

(3) the taxpayer's spouse, if the spouse is physically or mentally incapable of caring for himself or herself and who has the same principal place of abode as the taxpayer for more than one-half of the year.

Qualifying expenses include expenses paid for household services and for the care of a qualifying individual. Services outside the home qualify if they involve the care of a qualified child or a disabled spouse or dependent who regularly spends at least eight hours a day in the taxpayer's home. Payments to a relative also qualify for the credit unless the taxpayer claims a dependency exemption for the relative or if the relative is the taxpayer's child and is under age 19. However, no credit is allowed for expenses incurred to send a child or other dependent to an overnight camp.

Amount of Credit. The maximum amount of employment-related expenses to which the credit may be applied is $3,000 if one qualifying individual is involved or $6,000 if two or more are involved less excludable employer dependent care assistance program payments (Code Sec. 21(c)). The credit amount is equal to the applicable percentage, as determined by the taxpayer's adjusted gross income (AGI), times the qualified employment expenses paid. Taxpayers with an AGI of $15,000 or less use the highest applicable

---

Footnote references are to paragraphs of the 2008 Standard Federal Tax Reports.

[1] ¶ 3502

¶1301

percentage of 35 percent. For taxpayers with adjusted gross income over $15,000, the credit is reduced by one percentage point for each $2,000 of adjusted gross income (or fraction thereof) over $15,000 (Code Sec. 21(a)(2)). The minimum applicable percentage of 20 percent is used by taxpayers with AGIs greater than $43,000. Thus, the maximum dependent care credit amount for one qualifying dependent is $1,050 and $2,100 for two or more qualifying dependents.

> **Example:** A widower pays a housekeeper $5,000 to take care of his home and 10-year-old daughter while he is working. For 2007, his adjusted gross income was $25,000. Since there is only one qualifying child, the maximum credit he can claim is $900 (30 percent of $3,000).

Qualifying employment-related expenses are considered in determining the credit only to the extent of earned income—wages, salary, remuneration for personal services, net self-employment income, etc. For married taxpayers, expenses are limited to the earned income of the lower-earning spouse. Generally, if one spouse is not working, no credit is allowed. However, if the nonworking spouse is physically or mentally incapable of caring for himself/herself or is a full-time student at an educational institution for at least five calendar months during the year, the law assumes an earned income amount— for each month of disability or school attendance—of $250 if there is one qualifying individual or of $500 if there are two or more (Code Sec. 21(d)(2)).

Generally, a married taxpayer *must* file a joint return to claim the credit. For this purpose, a married person living apart from his or her spouse under the circumstances described at ¶ 173 is considered unmarried. Also, a divorced or legally separated taxpayer having custody of child who is disabled or under the age 13 is entitled to the credit even though he or she has released the right to a dependency exemption for the child (Code Sec. 21(e)(5)). Taxpayers must provide each qualifying individual's taxpayer identification number in order to claim the credit as well as the identifying number of the dependent care service provider (Code Sec. 21(e)(9) and (e)(10)).

1302. Child Tax Credit. Taxpayers who have one or more qualifying children may be entitled to a child tax credit of $1,000 per child through 2010 (Code Sec. 24(a)).[2] However, the credit amount decreases to $500 per qualifying child beginning in 2011. The credit is allowed only for tax years consisting of 12 months (Code Sec. 24(f)).

Qualifying Child(ren). A qualifying child is defined under the uniform qualifying child definition (¶ 137A) except that the child must not have attained the age of 17 by the end of the year. In addition, the qualifying child must be either a U.S. citizen or national, or resident of the United States (Code Sec. 24(c)).

Limitation of Child Tax Credit Based on AGI. The child tax credit begins to phase out when modified adjusted gross income (AGI) reaches $110,000 for joint filers, $55,000 for married taxpayers filing separately, and $75,000 for single taxpayers. The credit is reduced by $50 for each $1,000, or fraction thereof, of modified AGI above the threshold amount (Code Sec. 24(b)). Modified AGI is defined as AGI determined without regard to the exclusions from gross income for foreign earned income, foreign housing expenses, and income of residents of U.S. possessions (Code Sec. 24(b)(1)).

Tax Liability Limitation. Beginning in 2007, barring Congressional action, the total amount of child tax credit claimed by the taxpayer cannot exceed the sum of their regular income tax liability (see ¶ 1420) and their alternative minimum tax liability, over the sum of the nonrefundable personal credits allowed to the taxpayer (other then the adoption credit, the retirement savings contribution credit and the child tax credit (Code Sec. 24(b)(3)).

Refundable Amount of Child Tax Credit. A portion of the child tax credit is refundable for all taxpayers, regardless of the amount of the taxpayer's regular tax or alternative minimum tax liability. The credit is refundable to the lesser of either the unclaimed portion of the nonrefundable credit amount or to the extent the taxpayer's earned income exceeds a specific earned income threshold amount times 15 percent. The threshold earned income amount is adjusted for inflation and will be $11,750 for 2007 (to increase to $12,050 in 2008). Military families may elect to include otherwise excludable combat zone pay in their earned income when calculating the refundable

---

Footnote references are to paragraphs of the 2008 Standard Federal Tax Reports.

[2] ¶ 3760

portion of the credit (Code Sec. 24(d)). Taxpayers with three or more children may use an alternative method to calculate their refundable child tax credit. Under this method, the refundable credit is the excess of the taxpayer's share of Social Security taxes (including one-half of any self-employment taxes) over his or her earned income credit for the tax year.

1303. Credits for Higher Education Tuition. There are two education-related credits: the Hope scholarship credit and the Lifetime Learning credit. These credits may be claimed by individuals for tuition expenses incurred by students pursuing college or graduate degrees or vocational training (Code Sec. 25A).[3] For 2007, the Hope scholarship credit provides a maximum allowable credit of $1,650 per student for each of the first two years of post-secondary education. The Lifetime Learning credit allows a credit of 20 percent of qualified tuition expenses paid by the taxpayer for any year the Hope credit is not claimed up to a maximum allowable credit of $2,000. Both of these credits are claimed on Form 8863, Educational Credits (Hope and Lifetime Learning Credits).

Specifically, the Hope scholarship credit allows taxpayers a credit per eligible student for 100 percent of the first $1,100 of qualified tuition expenses and a 50 percent for the second $1,100 of qualified tuition paid in 2007 (Rev. Proc. 2006-53). The amount of tuition expenses eligible for the Hope scholarship credit is to increase to $1,200 in 2008. The Lifetime Learning credit is equal to 20 percent of the amount of tuition paid by the taxpayer and is available for the first $10,000 of tuition (not adjusted for inflation).

Eligibility. Both credits are available for qualified tuition and related expenses incurred for the taxpayer, the taxpayer's spouse, or the taxpayer's dependent who is an eligible student at a qualified educational institution (Code Sec. 25A(b)(3) and (f)). Qualified tuition and related expenses does not include room and board, books (unless required for enrollment), student health fees, or transportation. The amount of qualified tuition and related expenses paid with any tax-free funds (i.e., scholarships or Pell grants) reduces the amount available for claiming the credits. A qualified educational institution is defined as any postsecondary educational institution eligible to participate in a student aid program administered by the Department of Education.

An eligible student for the Hope credit is any individual who: (1) has not elected to claim the Hope credit in any two earlier years, (2) has not completed the first two years of postsecondary education before the beginning of the current tax year, (3) is enrolled at least half-time in a program that leads to a degree, certificate, or other recognized educational credentials, and (4) has *not* been convicted of any Federal or State felony class drug offense for possession or distribution. An eligible student for the Lifetime Learning credit is a student who is enrolled in one or more courses at a qualified educational institution.

The maximum allowable Hope credit is allowed per student. In contrast, the $2,000 Lifetime Learning credit maximum is calculated per taxpayer and does not vary based on the number of students in the taxpayer's family. The credits are elective and nonrefundable (Code Sec. 25A(e)). The credits cannot be claimed using the same expenses for which another tax benefit is also received. The credits are also *not* permitted to be claimed by more than one taxpayer in the same year (i.e., either the parents or the dependent child (as defined under Code Sec. 152(a)(1)) can claim the credit). Higher income parents whose AGI would result in the phase out of the dependency exemption may waive claiming the dependency exemption to allow their student dependent to claim an educational credit assuming the student child has a sufficient tax liability to be offset by the educational credit (Reg. § 1.25A-1(f)(1)). However, this does not entitle the student dependent to claim a personal exemption on his or her tax return. Taxpayers need to be aware of the distinction between being entitled to claim your own personal exemption and the requirements for being claimed as a dependency exemption (see ¶ 135).

Income Limitations. The allowable amount of the credits is reduced for taxpayers who have modified adjusted gross income (AGI) above certain amounts. Modified AGI is defined as AGI determined without regard to the exclusions from gross income for foreign earned income, foreign housing expenses, and income of residents of U.S.

Footnote references are to paragraphs of the 2008 Standard Federal Tax Reports.

[3] ¶ 3820

possessions. The phaseout of the credits begins for single taxpayers in 2007 when modified AGI reaches $47,000 (to increase to $48,000 in 2008) and completely phases out when modified AGI reaches $57,000 (to increase to $58,000 in 2008). For joint filers, the phaseout range is $94,000 to $114,000 in 2007 (to increase to $96,000 to $116,000 in 2008) (Code Sec. 25A(d); Rev. Proc. 2006-53). The Hope credit and the Lifetime Learning credit are *not* available to married taxpayers who file separate returns (Code Sec. 25A(g)).

Schools Located in the GO Zone (Expired). The Hope and the Lifetime Learning credits were temporarily expanded for students attending (enrolled and paying tuition at) an eligible education institution located in the Gulf Opportunity Zone during 2005 or 2006 (Code Sec. 1400O).[4] Specifically, the amount of qualified tuition expenses eligible for the Hope scholarship credit was doubled. The Lifetime Learning credit rate was also doubled from 20 percent to 40 percent of eligible expenses for eligible students. Finally, the definition of qualified tuition and expenses was expanded to follow the definition of qualified higher education expenses used for qualified tuition programs (¶ 697), which includes room and board.

Coordination with Other Provisions. To coordinate the education credits with other provisions of the Code, educational expenses eligible for the credits must first be reduced by tax-free educational assistance such as scholarships or fellowships, veterans' educational assistance allowance, employer-provided educational assistance, or any other educational assistance excluded from gross income other than as gifts, bequests, devises, or inheritances (Reg. § 1.25A-5(c)). Taxpayers are then permitted to elect to claim either the Hope credit or the Lifetime Learning credit for a student in any tax year. The expenses used to claim an educational credit also reduce the amount of eligible expenses available for purposes of determining the exclusion of distributions from Coverdell educational savings accounts (ESAs) (¶ 898) or qualified tuition programs (QTPs) (¶ 899). Since any excess distributions from an ESA or a QTP over the eligible educational expenses are includible in gross income and subject to a 10 percent additional tax, not claiming an educational credit may result in a lower tax liability. However, taxpayers should be aware that the 10 percent additional tax for excess distributions from ESAs or QTPs is waived if the excess is caused by claiming an educational credit. Taxpayers who receive distributions in excess of eligible expense from both an ESA and a QTP in the same year must allocate the expenses between the two distributions. Finally, only after eligible expenses are reduced by an educational credit and distributions from ESAs or QTPs, the remaining expenses may be used to determine the exclusion amount for Series EE United States Savings Bonds (Code Secs. 25A(g)(2), 135(d)(2), 529(c)(3)(B), and 530(d)(2)(C)).[5]

1304. Credit for the Elderly or the Permanently and Totally Disabled. A tax credit is available to individuals who are: (1) 65 years of age before the close of the tax year or (2) under age 65 but are retired on disability, and were permanently and totally disabled when they retired (Code Sec. 22).[6] Married taxpayers must file a joint return to claim the credit, unless the spouses live apart throughout the tax year. The credit is computed on Schedule R of Form 1040.

The credit is 15 percent of an applicable initial amount based on an individual's filing status and reduced by certain income. For individuals age 65 or older, the applicable initial amount is as follows:

Single individual	$5,000
Married individuals, joint return, one spouse is a qualified individual	5,000
Married individuals, joint return, both spouses are qualified individuals	7,500
Married individual, separate return	3,750

This initial amount is then reduced by amounts received as pension, annuity or disability benefits that are excludable from gross income and are payable under the Social Security Act (Title II), the Railroad Retirement Act of 1974, or a Veterans Administration program or that are excludable under a non-Code provision. However, no

---

Footnote references are to paragraphs of the 2008 Standard Federal Tax Reports.

[4] ¶ 32,488   [5] ¶ 3820, ¶ 7550, ¶ 22,940, ¶ 22,950   [6] ¶ 3550

reduction is made for pension, annuity or disability benefits for personal injuries or sickness payable from a Veterans Administration program.

The maximum amount determined above is further reduced by one-half of the excess of the taxpayer's adjusted gross income (AGI) over the following levels, based on filing status (Code Sec. 22(d)):

Single taxpayer	$ 7,500
Married taxpayers, combined AGI on joint return	10,000
Married individual filing separately	5,000

For permanently and totally disabled individuals under age 65, the applicable initial amount noted above may not exceed the amount of disability income for the tax year. In determining their initial amounts, special rules apply to a married couple filing a joint return where both spouses qualify for the credit and at least one of them is under age 65. Disability income means the total amount that is includible in an individual's gross income for the tax year under Code Secs. 72 or 105(a) to the extent the amount constitutes wages (or payments in lieu of wages) for periods during which the individual is absent from work due to permanent and total disability (Code Sec. 22(c)(2)(B)).

An individual is considered permanently and totally disabled for this purpose if they are unable to engage in any substantial gainful activity by reason of any medically determinable physical or mental impairment that can be expected to result in death or to last for a continuous period of not less than 12 months. This impairment should be substantiated by a letter from a certified physician kept in the taxpayer's records (Code Sec. 22(a)(3)).

Example: Alex, age 66 and single, has AGI of $9,000 for 2007 and receives $4,000 of nontaxable Social Security benefits for the year. To determine his credit, he would make the following computation:

Initial amount	$5,000
Less: Social security benefits	4,000
Reduced initial amount	$1,000
Less: One-half of AGI above $7,500	750
Amount eligible for credit	$250
Credit: $250 × 15%	$ 38

1306. Adoption Credit. Taxpayers may claim a nonrefundable credit on Form 8839, Qualified Adoption Expenses, of up to $11,390 for qualified adoption expenses for each eligible child in 2007 (Code Sec. 23; Rev. Proc. 2006-53).[7] The credit is phased out ratably for taxpayers with a modified adjusted gross income (AGI) over $170,820 and no credit is allowed to taxpayers with a modified AGI of $210,820 or more. The credit amount and the phase out range are adjusted annually for inflation. In 2008, the credit amount will be $11,650 and the phase out range will be $174,730 to $214,730. For 2007, barring Congressional action, the total amount of adoption credit claimed by the taxpayer cannot exceed the sum of their regular income tax liability (see ¶ 1420) and alternative minimum tax liability, over the sum of the nonrefundable personal credits allowed to the taxpayer (other than the foreign tax credit and this credit) (Code Sec. 23(b)(4)). A five-year carryforward is provided for the unused portion of the credit that exceeds this limit. Taxpayers who adopt a child with special needs are allowed to claim the full amount of the credit regardless of actual expenses paid or incurred in the year the adoption becomes final. Married couples must file a joint return in order to claim the credit unless the special rules for married individuals who are separated or living apart apply (see ¶ 173).

Qualified Adoption Expenses. Qualified adoption expenses include reasonable and necessary adoption fees, court costs, attorney fees and other expenses which are directly related to the legal adoption of an eligible child. Expenses incurred in violation of state or federal law or in connection with the adoption of a child of the taxpayer's spouse are not eligible for the credit. Costs associated with a surrogate parenting arrangement are also ineligible for the credit (Code Sec. 23(d)(1)).

Footnote references are to paragraphs of the 2008 Standard Federal Tax Reports.

[7] ¶ 3700

Eligible Child and Special Needs Child. An eligible child is an individual who has not attained the age of 18 as of the time of the adoption or who is physically or mentally incapable of caring for himself or herself. A child with special needs is any child who cannot or should not be returned to the home of his or her parents and a specific factor or condition makes it reasonable to conclude that the child cannot be placed with adoptive parents unless assistance is provided as determined by a state. Also, to qualify as a child with special needs, the child must be a citizen or resident of the United States (Code Sec. 23(d)(2) and (d)(3)). The qualified adoption expenses of a child, regardless of need, who is not a citizen or resident of the United States will not qualify for the adoption credit until the adoption is final (Code Sec. 23(e)).

Adoption expenses that are incurred for a child who is either a U.S. citizen or resident incurred or paid during a tax year prior to the year in which the adoption is finalized may be claimed as a credit in the tax year following the year the expense were incurred. Adoption expenses incurred during the year the adoption becomes final or in the year following the finalization of the adoption will be claimed in the year they were incurred. However, adoption expenses for any foreign child that are incurred or paid cannot be claimed as a credit until the adoption is finalized (Code Sec. 23(e)).

Coordination with Employer Adoption Assistance Programs. Taxpayers may not claim the adoption credit for any expense for which another deduction or credit is allowed. This includes amounts excluded from gross income that are paid or incurred by an employer for the employee's qualified adoption expenses pursuant to an adoption assistance program (see ¶ 863). The dollar limitation for the exclusion is identical to the dollar limitation for the credit ($11,390 for 2007; to increase to $11,650 in 2008). However, any adoption expenses incurred in excess of the amount provided under an employer's adoption assistance program may be used to claim the adoption credit.

1307. Credit for Elective Deferrals and IRA Contributions (Retirement Savings Contributions Credit). Eligible taxpayers may claim a nonrefundable credit for their contributions to elective deferral plans or individual retirement accounts (IRAs) (Code Sec. 25B).[8] The credit amount equals the eligible taxpayer's applicable percentage, determined by filing status and adjusted gross income (AGI), multiplied by the total qualified retirement savings contributions (not to exceed $2,000) for the tax year. The maximum credit amount is $1,000. The credit is in addition to the exclusion or deduction from gross income for making elective deferrals and IRA contributions that are otherwise allowed.

To be eligible for the credit, an individual making a contribution to a qualified retirement savings plan, must be at least 18 years of age at the close of the tax year, must *not* be claimed as a dependent by someone else, and must *not* be a student as defined at Code Sec. 152(f)(2). A qualified retirement savings plan contribution is the sum of:

(1) contributions to a tradition or Roth IRA (other than rollover contributions) (Code Sec. 219(e)),

(2) any elective deferrals of compensation to a 401(k), 403(b) tax-sheltered annuity, SIMPLE or SEP plan (Code Sec. 402(g)(3)),

(3) any elective deferrals of compensation to a Code Sec. 457(b) plan of a state or local government or tax-exempt organization, and

(4) any voluntary employee contributions to any qualified retirement plan (Code Sec. 4974(c)).

The amount of contributions to be taken into account in determining the credit, however, must be reduced by any distributions from such qualified retirement plans over a test period (Code Sec. 25B(d)(2)). The test period is defined as the current tax year, the two preceding tax years, and the following tax year up to the due date of the return including extensions. However, distribution amounts that qualify as a trustee-to-trustee transfer or as a rollover distribution to another qualified retirement account are not included in the reduction calculation.

Footnote references are to paragraphs of the 2008 Standard Federal Tax Reports.

[8] ¶ 3838

Claiming the Credit. Form 8880, Credit for Qualified Retirement Savings Contributions, is used to calculate the amount of the credit, which is then reported on Line 53 of Form 1040. For 2007, the maximum applicable percentage is 50 percent which is completely phased out when AGI exceeds $52,000 for joint return filers, $39,000 for head of household filers, and $26,000 for single and married filing separately filers (Rev. Proc. 2006-53). The income limitations are adjusted for inflation for tax years after 2006 (Code Sec. 25B(b)(3)). The applicable percentage is the percentage as determined in accordance with the following table:

Adjusted Gross Income						Applicable percentage
Joint return		Head of a household		All other cases		
Over	Not over	Over	Not over	Over	Not over	
$0	$31,000	$0	$23,250	$0	$15,500	50
31,000	34,000	23,250	25,500	15,500	17,000	20
34,000	52,000	25,500	39,000	17,000	26,000	10
52,000	—	39,000	—	26,000	—	0

1308. Credit for Interest on Certain Home Mortgages. Low-income homeowners who obtain qualified mortgage credit certificates (MCCs) from state or local governments may claim a tax credit on Form 8396, Mortgage Interest Credit (For Holders of Qualified Credit Certificates Issued by State or Local Governmental Units or Agencies), during any tax year for which the certificate is in effect for a portion of the interest paid or incurred. An MCC is in effect for interest attributable to the period beginning on the date the certificate is issued and ending when either: (1) it is revoked by the issuing authority, or (2) the taxpayer sells the residence or ceases to use it as a personal residence (Code Sec. 25).[9] Any mortgage interest claimed as an itemized deduction must be reduced by any credit allowed under this provision (Code Sec. 163(g)).

The credit is an amount equal to the product of: (1) the certificate credit rate (which may not be less than 10 percent or more than 50 percent) and (2) the interest paid or accrued by the taxpayer for the year on the remaining principal of the certified indebtedness (plus, a limited carryforward, if any). If the credit rate exceeds 20 percent, the tax credit for any year may not exceed $2,000 (Code Sec. 25(a)(2)(A)). A three-year carryforward is provided for the unused portion of such credit caused by the limitation. The amount of any unused credit which may be applied in any tax year is also limited by Code Sec. 25(e)(1)(B) and (C).

1310. Credit for First-Time Homebuyers for District of Columbia. First-time homebuyers, who purchase a principal residence in the District of Columbia from an unrelated person, may claim a nonrefundable personal credit of up to $5,000 of the purchase price ($2,500 in the case of a married person filing separately) on Form 8859, District of Columbia First-Time Homebuyer Credit. To qualify, the taxpayer (and, if married, his or her spouse) cannot have had a present ownership interest in a principal residence in the District of Columbia during the one-year period ending on the date of purchase. The credit may only be claimed once. The credit is phased out ratably between adjusted gross income of $70,000 to $90,000 ($110,000 to $130,000 for married individuals filing jointly). The purchase must be before January 1, 2008 (Code Sec. 1400C(i)). Any unused credit amount may be carried forward indefinitely. The basis of the residence is reduced by the amount of the credit (including any carryforward portion) (Code Sec. 1400C(h)).[10]

Foreign Tax Credit

1311. Foreign Tax Credit. An individual taxpayer may either deduct foreign income taxes paid or accrued as an itemized deduction on Schedule A of Form 1040 or may apply them as a credit against his or her U.S. income tax liability (see ¶ 2475) (Code Sec. 27).[11] The credit is claimed by individuals on Form 1116, Foreign Tax Credit, unless the total foreign taxes paid are less than $300 for single filers ($600 for married filing jointly). For these taxpayers, the credit may be claimed directly on Form 1040 if all filing requirements are satisfied (see ¶ 2475). A corporate taxpayer also may either

---

Footnote references are to paragraphs of the 2008 Standard Federal Tax Reports.

[9] ¶ 3800   [10] ¶ 32,428   [11] ¶ 4002

deduct foreign income taxes paid or accrued or elect to claim such payments as a credit against its U.S. income tax liability. Form 1118, Foreign Tax Credit—Corporations, is used to calculate the amount of credit in a single tax year (see ¶ 2475).

Personal Energy Credits

1313. Nonbusiness Energy Property Credit. A tax credit is available to individuals for the installation of nonbusiness energy property, such as residential exterior doors and windows, insulation, heat pumps, furnaces, central air conditioners and water heaters (Code Sec. 25C). The credit is equal to the taxpayer's residential energy property expenditures, plus 10 percent of the cost of qualified energy efficiency improvements. The credit is limited to a lifetime maximum of $500 and no more than: $200 of the credit can be based on expenditures for windows; $50 of the credit on any advanced main air circulating fans; $150 of the credit on any qualified natural gas, propane, or oil furnace or hot water boiler; and $300 of the credit on any item of energy-efficient building property. The credit applies to qualified energy efficiency improvements and qualified energy property placed in service before January 1, 2008. The property must be installed in, or on, a dwelling unit in the United States that is owned and used by the taxpayer as the taxpayer's principal residence and originally placed in service by the taxpayer. Residential energy property expenditures (heat pumps, furnaces, central air conditioners and water heaters) may include labor costs. The credit is claimed on Form 5695, Residential Energy Credits.

1314. Residential Energy Efficient Property Credit. A tax credit is available to help individual taxpayers pay for residential alternative energy equipment (Code Sec. 25D). The credit is 30 percent of the cost of eligible solar water heaters, solar electricity equipment and fuel cell plants placed in service before January 1, 2009 (Code Sec. 25D). The maximum credit is $2,000 per tax year for each category of solar equipment and $500 for each half kilowatt of capacity of fuel cell plants installed per tax year. None of the systems may be used to heat a swimming pool or hot tub. Cooperative and condominium dwellers can claim the credit by splitting the cost of installing equipment with other unit owners. The credit is claimed on Form 5695, Residential Energy Credits.

Alternative Motor Vehicle Credit

1315. Alternative Motor Vehicle Credit. Effective for qualifying vehicles placed in service after 2005, a taxpayer may claim an alternative motor vehicle credit. The credit is the sum of the following component credits: (1) a qualified fuel cell motor vehicle credit (¶ 1315A); (2) an advanced lean burn technology motor vehicle credit (¶ 1315B); (3) a qualified hybrid motor vehicle credit (¶ 1315C); and (4) a qualified alternative motor vehicle credit (¶ 1315D) (Code Sec. 30B). The individual components comprising the alternative motor vehicle credit are calculated based on various factors such as vehicle weight, vehicle fuel efficiency, lifetime fuel savings, etc. The credit claimed is the sum of the components applicable to a particular vehicle, whether used for personal or business purposes. The credit is claimed on Form 8910, Alternative Motor Vehicle Credit.

There are distinct requirements for each of the four components of the credit, however, three requirements are common to each of the components: (1) the original use of the vehicle must commence with the taxpayer; (2) the vehicle must be acquired for use or lease by the taxpayer and not for resale; and (3) the vehicle must be made by a manufacturer.

Taxpayers with qualified motor vehicles that are used in a trade or business and subject to depreciation will claim the alternative motor vehicle credit as a part of, and subject to the rules of, the general business credit. Thus, any unused credit in a tax year will be eligible to be carried back three years (but not before 2006) and forward 20 years. If the alternative motor vehicle credit is claimed by an individual as a personal credit, the credit cannot exceed the excess of their regular income tax liability reduced by the sum of the nonrefundable personal credits, the foreign tax credit, and the credit for electric automobiles, over the individual's tentative minimum tax. A seller claiming the alternative motor vehicle credit for a vehicle sold to a tax-exempt entity can only claim the credit as a part of the general business credit (Code Sec. 30B(h)(6)).

Phaseout of credits. The advanced lean burn technology motor vehicle credit (see ¶ 1315B) and the qualified hybrid motor vehicle credit (see ¶ 1315C) begin to phase out after a manufacturer sells a specific quantity of qualified vehicles. When a particular

manufacturer has sold 60,000 combined units after December 31, 2005, the phaseout will be triggered for vehicles produced by that specific manufacturer. For purposes of this phaseout, consolidated groups of corporations and foreign controlled corporations will be considered one manufacturer. In addition, the 60,000 limit applies to all qualified vehicles sold by the manufacturer, not just a particular model. The phaseout period begins with the second calendar quarter following the calendar quarter which contains the date on which the 60,000th unit is sold. For the first two quarters of the phaseout period, the credit is reduced to 50 percent of the full credit amount. The credit is cut to 25 percent for the third and fourth quarters of the phaseout period. Thereafter, there is no credit allowed for the purchase of hybrid and advanced lean burn technology motor vehicles (Code Sec. 30B(f)).

1315A. Fuel Cell Motor Vehicle Credit. The first component of the alternative motor vehicle credit is a qualified fuel cell motor vehicle credit for qualifying vehicles placed in service during 2006 through 2014 (Code Sec. 30B(b)). In addition to the common requirements for qualifying vehicles (¶ 1315), there are specific requirements for a vehicle to be classified as a qualified fuel cell motor vehicle. The vehicle must be propelled by power derived from one or more cells which convert chemical energy directly into electricity by combining oxygen with hydrogen fuel. In addition, if the vehicle is a passenger vehicle or light truck it must be certified to meet specific environmental emission standards.

The amount of the credit is calculated based on the gross vehicle weight rating (GVWR) of the vehicle, supplemented by the fuel efficiency of the vehicle relative to the 2002 model year city fuel economy. The credit can range from $8,000 for vehicles under 8,500 pounds GVWR and up to $40,000 for vehicles over 26,000 pounds GVWR. Qualified fuel cell vehicles that meet the definition of either a "passenger automobile" or "light truck" and meet certain standards for increased fuel efficiency will be able to increase their credit amount based on the increase in fuel efficiency over the 2002 city fuel economy standards. The increase ranges from $1,000 up to $4,000.

1315B. Advanced Lean Burn Technology Vehicle Credit. The second component of the alternative motor vehicle credit is the advanced lean burn technology motor vehicle credit for qualifying vehicles placed in service during 2006 through 2010 (Code Sec. 30B(c)). In addition to the common requirements for qualifying vehicles (¶ 1315), there are specific requirements for classification as an advanced lean burn technology motor vehicle. An advanced lean burn technology motor vehicle is a passenger vehicle or light truck with an internal combustion engine that: (1) is designed to operate primarily using more air than is necessary for complete combustion of the fuel, (2) incorporates direct injection, and (3) achieves at least 125 percent of the 2002 model year city fuel economy. Additionally, year 2004 and later model vehicles must meet specified environmental emission standards based on gross vehicle weight rating (GVWR).

The credit amount is calculated based on the fuel efficiency of the vehicle relative to the 2002 model year city fuel economy supplemented by a conservation credit based on the vehicle's lifetime fuel savings. The range of the credit amount is from $400 to $2,400. The credit amount for new advanced lean burn technology motor vehicles may be increased by a conservation credit, which ranges from $250 to $1,000. The advance lean burn technology motor vehicle credit begins to phase out after a manufacturer sells a specific quantity of qualifying vehicles (see ¶ 1315).

1315C. Hybrid Motor Vehicle Credit. The third component of the alternative motor vehicle credit is the qualified hybrid motor vehicle credit for qualifying vehicles placed in service after December 31, 2005 (Code Sec. 30B(d)). The qualified hybrid motor vehicle credit for passenger automobiles or light trucks with a gross vehicle weight rating (GVWR) of no more than 8,500 pounds terminates for vehicles purchased after December 31, 2010. The credit for all other vehicles terminates after December 31, 2009. In addition to the common requirements for qualifying vehicles (¶ 1315), there are requirements specific to the qualified hybrid motor vehicle credit.

The vehicle must draw propulsion energy from both an internal combustion or heat engine and a rechargeable energy storage system. In addition, the vehicle must receive a certificate of conformity that it meets or exceeds specific environmental emission standards. The vehicle must also meet the maximum available power standards required

for the vehicle's GVWR. Passenger automobiles and light trucks with a GVWR of less than 8,500 pounds must have maximum available power of at least four percent. Vehicles with a GVWR of more than 8,500 and less than 14,000 pounds must have maximum available power of at least 10 percent. Vehicles with a GVWR of more than 14,000 pounds must have maximum available power of at least 15 percent.

The amount of the credit allowed for a qualified vehicle with a GVWR of 8,500 pounds or less is the sum of the amounts determined for fuel economy and the conservation credit. The credit amount ranges from $400 up to $2,400. The credit amount for qualified hybrid motor vehicles that are passenger automobiles or light trucks with a GVWR of no more than 8,500 pounds may be increased by a conservation credit, which ranges from $250 up to $1,000. Thus, the credit ranges from $250 to $3,500. The IRS has certified almost 50 hybrid vehicles to qualify for the alternative motor vehicle credit. A complete list may be found on the IRS website at www.irs.gov/newsroom/article/0,,id=157632,00.html.

The qualified hybrid motor vehicle credit begins to phase out after a manufacturer sells a specific quantity of qualifying vehicles (see ¶ 1315). Toyota Motor Sales, U.S.A., Inc., manufacturer of Toyota and Lexus automobiles reached the 60,000 unit mark to initiate the phase out of the credit for their hybrid vehicles in the second quarter of 2006. Thus, Toyota and Lexus hybrids placed into service on or after October 1, 2006, will only qualify for 50 percent of the certified credit amount; hybrids placed in service on or after April 1, 2007, will only qualify for 25 percent of the certified credit amount; and hybrids placed in service on or after October 1, 2007 will be ineligible to claim any credit amount (Notice 2006-78).

1315D. Alternative Fuel Motor Vehicle Credit. The fourth component of the alternative motor vehicle credit is the qualified alternative fuel motor vehicle credit for qualifying vehicles placed in service during 2006 through 2010 (Code Sec. 30B(e)). In addition to the common requirements of qualifying vehicles (¶ 1315), the vehicle must be capable of operating on an alternative fuel (e.g., compressed natural gas, liquefied natural gas, liquefied petroleum gas, hydrogen or any liquid consisting of at least 85 percent methanol). The amount of the credit allowed for a qualifying vehicle is calculated as the applicable percentage of the incremental cost of any new vehicle placed into service during the tax year. The applicable percentage is 50 percent, plus 30 percent if the vehicle has received a certificate of conformity that it meets or exceeds specific environmental emission standards.

The incremental cost of a new qualified alternative motor vehicle is the amount by which the manufacturer's suggested retail price (MSRP) of the vehicle exceeds the MSRP of a gasoline-or diesel-powered version of the same model. However, the incremental cost is limited with respect to the vehicle's gross vehicle weight rating (GVWR). The incremental cost may not exceed $5,000 for vehicles with a GVWR of 8,500 pounds; $10,000 for vehicles with a GVWR of more than 8,500 pounds and less than 14,001 pounds; $25,000 for vehicles with a GVWR of more than 14,000 pounds and less than 26,001 pounds; and $40,000 for vehicles with a GVWR of more than 26,000 pounds.

The IRS has certified three models of Honda that use compressed natural gas for propulsion for the alternative fuel motor vehicle credit. These models are the 2005 through 2007 Civic GS and they are assigned a credit amount of $4,000.

Credit for Mixed-Fuel Vehicles. The credit for qualified alternative fuel motor vehicles also applies to vehicles that qualify as mixed-fuel vehicles, but at a fraction of the credit amount. In addition to the common requirements of qualifying vehicles (see ¶ 1315), there are two additional requirements for qualification as a mixed-fuel vehicle. The vehicle must be certified by the manufacturer as being able to efficiently operate on a mixture of an alternative fuel (e.g., compressed natural gas, liquefied natural gas, liquefied petroleum gas, hydrogen or any liquid consisting of at least 85 percent methanol) and a petroleum-based fuel. The vehicle must also have received either a certificate of conformity that it meets or exceeds specific environmental emission standards.

The credit amount allowed for a mixed fuel vehicle is 70 percent of the credit allowed as if the vehicle qualified for the alternative fuel motor vehicle credit and is a 75/25 mixed-fuel vehicle or 90 percent of the credit allowed as if the vehicle qualified for the alternative fuel motor vehicle credit and is a 90/10 mixed-fuel vehicle. A 75/25

mixed-fuel vehicle operates using at least 75 percent alternative fuel and no more than 25 percent petroleum based fuel while a 90/10 mixed-fuel vehicle operates using at least 90 percent alternative fuel and no more than 10 percent petroleum based fuel.

1316. Alternative Fuel Vehicle Refueling Property Credit. Effective for qualified property placed in service after 2005, taxpayers are permitted a credit for the installation of alternative fueling stations (Code Sec. 30C). The credit replaces the deduction for the installation of clean-fuel refueling property under Code Sec. 179A. The credit requirements are largely the same as the deduction requirements. The credit is claimed on Form 8911, Alternative Fuel Vehicle Refueling Property Credit, regardless of whether the property is personal or used in a trade or business.

The credit is equal to 30 percent of the cost of the property placed into service. However, for property of a character that is subject to depreciation (such as a commercial or retail refueling station), the credit cannot exceed $30,000. For all other instances (such as residential), the credit cannot exceed $1,000. If the credit is attributable to property that is subject to the rules of depreciation, then it will be considered to be part of the general business credit (see ¶ 1323). However, the amount of the credit that is *not* attributable to depreciable property (such as in the case of a residence) cannot exceed the excess of the taxpayer's regular income tax liability reduced by the foreign tax credit, the credit for electric automobiles, and the alternative motor vehicle credit, over the taxpayer's tentative minimum tax. Credits for property sold to a tax-exempt entity are subject to the business tax credit limitation of up to $30,000, not the $1,000 limit that applies to noncommercial taxpayers (Code Sec. 30C(e)(2)).

Alternative Fuels Credit

1319. Fuel Production from Nonconventional Source. A tax credit is allowed for the domestic production of oil, gas, and synthetic fuels, or coke or coke gas derived from nonconventional sources (such as shale, tar sands, coal seams, and geopressured brine) or a qualified facility that are sold to unrelated persons (Code Sec. 45K).[12] The credit is part of the general business credit under Code Sec. 38 and is subject to the ordering, tax liability limitation, and carryover rules of the general business credit (see ¶ 1323). For calendar year 2006, the credit is $4.72 ($3.00 in case of a credit derived from gas from a tight formation) per 5.8 million BTUs (energy equivalent of one barrel of oil) produced and sold from facilities placed in service after 1979 and before 1993 or from wells drilled after 1979 and before 1993. Such fuels must be sold before 2008 (Code Sec. 45K(e) and (f)). The credit is reduced by an amount which bears the same ratio to the amount of the credit as the amount by which the reference price for the calendar year in which the sale occurs ($59.68 for calendar year 2006) exceeds $23.50 bears to $6. Since the reference price for 2006 does exceed $23.50 times the inflation factor, the credit amount has been reduced by $2.31 for 2006. The inflation adjustment factor for 2006 is 2.3429 (Notice 2007-38).

Credit for Qualified Electric Vehicles

1321. Credit for Qualified Electric Vehicles (Expired). A nonrefundable credit calculated on Form 8834, Qualified Electric Vehicle Credit, was allowed for 10 percent of the cost of a qualified electric vehicle that is placed in service after June 30, 1993, and before 2007 (Code Sec. 30; Reg. § 1.30-1).[13] The maximum credit was $4,000 per qualified electric vehicle. However, the portion of the cost of a qualified electric vehicle that was expensed under Code Sec. 179 was ineligible for the credit. In addition, for vehicles placed in service in 2006, the credit was reduced by 75 percent for a maximum credit amount of $1,000.

The credit applied to a motor vehicle powered primarily by an electric motor drawing current from rechargeable batteries, fuel cells, or other portable sources of electric current. The original use of the vehicle must have commenced with the taxpayer. The basis of a qualified electric vehicle was reduced by the amount of the credit allowed. The credit was recaptured as an increase in tax in the year in which the vehicle ceased to be a qualified electric vehicle.

Footnote references are to paragraphs of the 2008 Standard Federal Tax Reports.

[12] ¶ 4050   [13] ¶ 4053, ¶ 4054

Hurricane Relief

1322. Employee Retention Credit (Expired). A temporary tax credit was available to encourage small employers to keep employees on their payrolls following the destruction and evacuation caused by Hurricanes Katrina, Rita and Wilma. There were three separate retention credits depending on which hurricane caused the damage that forced the business to cease operations (Code Sec. 1400R(a) for Hurricane Katrina; Code Sec. 1400R(b) for Hurricane Rita; and Code Sec. 1400R(c) for Hurricane Wilma).[14] An eligible employer could claim a credit equal to 40 percent of qualified wages paid to each eligible employee during a specified time period ending on January 1, 2006. The amount of qualified wages taken into account for any employee could not exceed $6,000. The credit was claimed on Form 5884-A, Credits for Employers Affected by Hurricane Katrina, Rita, or Wilma, and was added to the current year general business credit subject to the tax liability limitation and carry over rules.

1322A. Hurricane Katrina Housing Credit (Expired). A temporary credit was available for employers providing housing to their employees affected by Hurricane Katrina. Qualified employers of the Gulf Opportunity Zone were entitled to a temporary credit of 30 percent of the value of lodging furnished in-kind to a qualified employee. The value of the furnished lodging was excludable from the income of that qualified employee (Code Sec. 1400P(b)).[15] The credit period began on January 1, 2006 and ended on July 1, 2006. An employer taking the Hurricane Katrina housing credit could not also take a deduction for wages equal to the credit amount claimed (Code Sec. 280C(a)). The Hurricane Katrina housing credit was included as part of the general business credit and subject to the tax limitation and carryover rules (Code Sec. 38). Unused business credits may be carried back one year and carried forward 20 years (Code Sec. 39). For purposes of this provision, a qualified employer was any employer with a trade or business located in the Gulf Opportunity Zone (Code Sec. 1400P(d)). A qualified employee, was an individual who, on August 28, 2005, had a principal residence in the Gulf Opportunity Zone and who performs substantially all of his or her employment services in the Gulf Opportunity Zone for the qualified employer furnishing the lodging (Code Sec. 1400P(d)). The credit was claimed using Form 5884-A, Credits for Employers Affected by Hurricane Katrina, Rita, or Wilma.

Business-Related Credits

1323. General Business Credit. The general business credit (Code Sec. 38)[16] is a limited nonrefundable credit against income tax that is claimed after all other nonrefundable credits (Code Secs. 21, 22, 23, 24, 25, 25A, 25B, 27, 30, the personal portion of 30B and 30C, and 1400C except the credit for prior year minimum tax (Code Sec. 53)). The general business credit for a tax year is the sum of: (1) the business credit carryforwards to the year; (2) the amount of the current year business credit; and (3) the business credit carrybacks to the year.

Generally, the current year general business credit is the sum of:

    (1) the investment credit (¶ 1345 and following);

    (2) the work opporunity credit (¶ 1342);

    (3) the alcohol fuels credit (¶ 1326);

    (4) the research activities credit (¶ 1330);

    (5) the low-income housing credit (¶ 1334);

    (6) the enhanced oil recovery credit (phased out for 2007) (¶ 1336);

    (7) the disabled access credit (¶ 1338);

    (8) the renewable electricity production credit (¶ 1339);

    (9) the empowerment zone employment credit (¶ 1339A);

    (10) the Indian employment credit (¶ 1340);

    (11) the employer social security credit (FICA tip credit) (¶ 1341);

    (12) the orphan drug credit (¶ 1344);

    (13) the new markets credit (¶ 1335);

Footnote references are to paragraphs of the 2008 Standard Federal Tax Reports.

[14] ¶ 32,503   [15] ¶ 32,493   [16] ¶ 4250

(14) the small employer pension plan startup costs credit (¶ 1344B);

(15) the employer-provided child care facilities and services credit (¶ 1344C);

(16) the qualified railroad track maintenance credit (¶ 1344D);

(17) the biodiesel and renewable diesel fuels credit (¶ 1329A);

(18) the low sulfur diesel fuel production credit (¶ 1344E);

(19) marginal oil and gas well production credit (phased out for 2007) (¶ 1344F);

(20) the distilled spirits credit (¶ 1344K);

(21) advanced nuclear power facility production credit (¶ 1344G);

(22) the nonconventional source fuels credit (¶ 1319);

(23) the energy efficient home credit (¶ 1344H);

(24) the energy efficient appliance credit (¶ 1344I);

(25) the alternative motor vehicle credit (portion allocable to a trade or business) (¶ 1315–¶ 1315D);

(26) the alternative fuel vehicle refueling property credit (portion allocable to a trade or business) (¶ 1316);

(27) the Hurricane Katrina housing credit (only for S corporations, partnerships, estates and cooperatives) (¶ 1322A);

(28) the Hurricane Katrina, Rita, and Wilma employee retention credit (¶ 1322);

(29) the mine rescue team training credit (¶ 1344L);

(30) the credit for contributions to selected community development corporations (CDC) (¶ 1325);

(31) general credits from an electing large partnership (see ¶ 482–¶ 488);

Each of these credits is computed separately. If more than one of these components is claimed, or if there is a general business credit carryback or carryforward, Form 3800, General Business Credit, along with the appropriate form must be filed with the return. For this purpose, components of the general business credit arising in a single year are deemed used in the same order in which they are listed above, with the following exceptions. The work opportunity credit, alcohol fuels credit, empowerment zone employment credit, renewable electricity credit, and FICA tip credit have special tax liability limitations and, while a part of the general business credit, are not reported on Form 3800.

Limitations. The general business credit may not exceed a limitation based on the amount of tax liability (Code Sec. 38(c)). Generally, the general business credit may not exceed net income tax less the greater of the taxpayer's tentative minimum tax liability or 25 percent of net regular tax liability above $25,000 (Code Sec. 38(c)(1)). However, the limitation is determined separately for the portion of the credit attributable to the work opportunity credit, alcohol fuels credit, empowerment zone employment credit, renewable electricity credit and FICA tip credit. When calculating the limitation as it applies to the work opportunity credit, alcohol fuels credit, renewable electricity credit and FICA tip credit, the tentative minimum tax is to be treated as zero, which results in these credits being fully allowable against both the regular and alternative minimum tax liabilities of the taxpayer (Code Sec. 38(c)(4), as amended by the Small Business and Work Opportunity Tax Act of 2007 (P.L. 110-28)). For the empowerment zone employment credit, the credit amount may not exceed the excess of the net income tax over the greater of 75 percent of the taxpayer's tentative minimum tax liability or 25 percent of net regular tax liability above $25,000. This result is then reduced by the general business credit allowed for the tax year other than the work opportunity credit, alcohol fuels credit, renewable electricity credit and FICA tip credit (Code Sec. 38(c)(2)).

For purposes of calculating these limitations, net regular income tax liability is the sum of the taxpayer's regular tax liability (see ¶ 1402) and alternative minimum tax liability, less all other nonrefundable credits (Code Secs. 21— 30, and 1400C except the credit for prior year minimum tax (Code Sec. 53)). Net regular tax liability is the regular tax liability reduced by these credits.

¶1323

For a married couple filing separate returns, the $25,000 figure above is limited to $12,500 for each spouse. If, however, one spouse has no current credit or unused credit, the spouse having current credit or unused credit may use the full $25,000 figure in determining his or her credit for the year. For a controlled group of corporations, the group may divide the $25,000 figure among its members in any way the members choose. For an estate or trust, the $25,000 figure is reduced to an amount that bears the same ratio to $25,000 as the portion of the estate's or trust's income that is not allocated to the beneficiaries bears to the total income of the estate or trust (Code Sec. 38(c)(4)(D)).

Carrybacks and Carryforwards of Unused Credits. When the credit exceeds the tax liability limitation in any year, the excess or unused amount may be carried back one year and forward 20 years (3-year carryback and 15-year carryforward for credits that arise in tax years beginning before 1998) (Code Sec. 39)).[17] The order in which these credits are claimed in any carryback or carryforward year is as follows: (1) carryforwards to that year on a first-in, first-out (FIFO) basis; (2) the business credit earned in that year; and (3) the carrybacks to that year on a FIFO basis.

Separate carryback and carryforward records must be maintained for the amount of the general business credit attributable to the empowerment zone employment credit, and each of the other components of the general business credit. Separate recordkeeping is necessary because the empowerment zone employment credit may offset up to 25 percent of the taxpayer's alternative minimum tax (Code Sec. 38(c)(2)(A)). Several of the credits that remain unused at the end of the carryforward period may be claimed as a deduction in the following year (Code Sec. 196).[18]

1325. Credit for Contributions to CDCs. A nonrefundable credit may be claimed on Form 8847, Credit for Contributions to Selected Community Development Corporations, for qualified cash contributions (including loans or investments) made to qualified community development corporations (CDCs) (Act Sec. 13311 of the Omnibus Budget Reconciliation Act of 1993 (P.L. 103-66)).[19] Five percent of the amount contributed may be claimed as a credit for each tax year during a 10-year credit period beginning with the tax year in which the contribution is made. This credit is claimed as one of the components of the general business credit.

1326. Alcohol Fuels Credit. The alcohol fuels credit is the sum of the alcohol mixture credit, the alcohol credit, and the small ethanol producer credit (Code Sec. 40).[20]

The alcohol mixture credit is 60 cents per gallon of nonethanol alcohol of at least 190 proof (45 cents per gallon of nonethanol alcohol of at least 150 proof but less than 190 proof) utilized in the production of a qualified mixture fuel that is used by the producer or that is sold in the producer's trade or business. For any sale or use after 2004, the alcohol mixture credit is 51 cents per gallon of ethanol alcohol of at least 190 proof (37.78 cents per gallon of ethanol alcohol of at least 150 proof but less than 190 proof) utilized in the production of a qualified mixture fuel that is used by the producer or that is sold in the producer's trade or business (Code Sec. 40(h)).

The alcohol credit is 60 cents per gallon of nonethanol alcohol of at least 190 proof (45 cents per gallon of nonethanol alcohol of at least 150 proof but less than 190 proof) that is *not* a mixture with gas or a special fuel (other than any denaturant) and that is used by a person as a fuel in a trade or business or that is sold at retail and placed in the fuel tank of the purchaser's vehicle. For any sale or use after 2004, the alcohol credit is 51 cents per gallon of ethanol alcohol of at least 190 proof (37.78 cents per gallon of nonethanol alcohol of at least 150 proof but less than 190 proof) that is *not* a mixture with gas or a special fuel (other than any denaturant) and that is used by a person as a fuel in a trade or business or that is sold at retail and placed in the fuel tank of the purchaser's vehicle.

An eligible small ethanol producer (a producer with a production capacity of up to 60 million gallons of alcohol per year) may claim the small ethanol producer credit of 10 cents per gallon on production of up to 15 million gallons per year of ethanol. The small

---

Footnote references are to paragraphs of the 2008 Standard Federal Tax Reports.

[17] ¶ 4300
[18] ¶ 12,400
[19] ¶ 4251.055
[20] ¶ 4302

ethanol producer credit is recaptured through a tax of 10 cents per gallon that is imposed if a producer fails to use the ethanol or ethanol mixture as fuel.

The alcohol fuels credit is computed on Form 6478, Credit for Alcohol Used as Fuel, and, although a part of the general business credit, is not reported on Form 3800 because the credit limitation is calculated separately from the general business credit limitation (¶ 1323). For tax years beginning after December 31, 2004, for purposes of calculating the limitation on the amount of alcohol fuels credit, the tentative minimum tax will be considered zero (Code Sec. 38(c)(4)). The result of designating the tentative minimum tax as zero will be to allow taxpayers to claim the credit fully against both the regular and the alternative minimum tax liabilities. For tax years beginning prior to January 1, 2005, the alcohol fuels credit is a component of the general business credit and subject to the overall limitation and the carryback and carryforward rules under Code Sec. 38(c)(1) prior to amendment by the American Jobs Creation Act of 2004 (P.L. 108-357). Taxpayers also have the option of electing to not claim the alcohol fuels credit. Any excise tax exemption for alcohol fuels reduces the amount of the income tax credit.

The carryforward period for the alcohol fuels credit is limited. Generally, the credit may not be carried forward to tax years beginning after 2013. An alcohol fuels credit carryforward that is unused at the end of the carryforward period would be deductible in the following tax year under Code Sec. 196. An earlier termination of the carryforward period may occur if the tax rates on fuels under Code Sec. 4081(a)(2)(A) are 4.3 cents per gallon (Code Sec. 40(e)(1)(B)). The tax rates for gasoline (other than aviation gasoline) and diesel fuel or kerosene will be reduced to 4.3 cents per gallon effective after September 30, 2011. The tax rate for aviation gasoline will be reduced to 4.3 cents per gallon effective November 16, 2007. This date will trigger the earlier termination of the alcohol credit under Code Sec. 40(e) and limit the carryforward period of any unused credits.

1329A. Biodiesel Fuels Credit. The biodiesel fuels credit was created to encourage the production and use of biodiesel fuels (Code Sec. 40A).[21] The credit is the sum of the biodiesel mixture credit, the biodiesel credit, and the small agri-biodiesel producers credit. The biodiesel mixture credit is 50 cents for each gallon of biodiesel used in the production of a qualified biodiesel fuel that is sold or used in the course of a trade or business. The biodiesel credit amount is 50 cents for each gallon of biodiesel not used in a mixture with diesel fuel either used in the taxpayer's trade or business or sold at retail. The credit amount increases to $1.00 per gallon if either the biodiesel or the biodiesel mixture fuel meets the definition as a agri-biodiesel fuel.

Biodiesel fuels are defined as monoalkyl esters of long chain fatty acids derived from plant or animal matter that meets the requirements for fuels or fuel additives imposed by the Environmental Protection Agency under section 211 of the Clean Air Act and the American Society of Testing and Materials S6751. Biodiesel fuel mixture is defined as biodiesel mixed with diesel fuel without regard to any use of kerosene. Agri-biodiesel is biodiesel derived solely from virgin oils, including esters derived from virgin vegetable oils from corn, soybeans, sunflower seeds, cottonseeds, canola, crambe, rapeseeds, safflowers, flaxseeds, rice bran, and mustard seeds, and animal fats. Tax penalties are imposed if the credit for biodiesel mixture is claimed and the fuels are later separated. The credit as part of the general business credit is claimed after the railroad track maintenance credit and subject to the tax limitation and carryover rules (¶ 1323). Any unused credit at the end of the carryforward period, or if the taxpayer ceases to exist, may be claimed as deduction under Code Sec. 196. The credit may be claimed on Form 8864, Biodiesel and Renewable Diesel Fuels Credit, for the fuels produced and sold or used after December 31, 2004, and before January 1, 2009 (Code Sec. 40A(g)).

Small Agri-biodiesel Producers. Effective for tax years ending after August 8, 2005, a third component to the biodiesel fuels credit is added for a credit amount for qualified small agri-biodiesel producers (Code Sec. 40A(b)(5)). The credit amount is 10 cents per gallon of qualified agri-biodiesel fuel produced by a qualified agri-biodiesel fuel producer. A qualified agri-biodiesel fuels producer's production of qualified agri-biodiesel

---

Footnote references are to paragraphs of the 2008 Standard Federal Tax Reports.

[21] ¶ 4310

¶1329A

cannot exceed 15 million gallon per year. This credit parallels the credit requirements for small alcohol fuel producers under Code Sec. 40.

1330. Credit for Increased Research Expenditures. A credit for incremental research expenses (computed on Form 6765, Credit for Increasing Research Activities) is claimed as one of the components of the general business credit (Code Sec. 41).[22] The credit is available for amounts paid or incurred through December 31, 2007 (Code Sec. 41(h)(1)(B), as amended by the Tax Relief and Health Care Act of 2006 (P.L. 109-432)).

The credit is subject to the limitation and the carryback and carryforward rules discussed at ¶ 1323. The research credit that remains unused at the end of the carryforward period is allowed as a deduction in the year following the expiration of such period (Code Sec. 196). The deduction does not apply to unused amounts claimed under the reduced research credit election.

Amount of Credit. Unless an election is made to use either the alternative incremental method or the alternative simplified credit computation, the research credit is the sum of: (1) 20 percent of the excess of qualified research expenses for the current tax year over a base period amount, (2) 20 percent of the basic research payments made to a qualified organization, and (3) 20 percent of the amounts paid or incurred by a taxpayer to an energy research consortium (Code Sec. 41(a)). Special base period adjustments are required where there is an acquisition or disposition of the major portion of a business that paid or incurred research expenses.

Base Amount. For purposes of calculating the credit, the base period amount is the product of the taxpayer's fixed-base percentage and average annual gross receipts for the four tax years preceding the credit period (Code Sec. 41(c)). The base amount may not be less than 50 percent of the qualified research expenses for the credit year. The fixed-base percentage (aggregate qualified research expenses compared to aggregate gross receipts for 1984 through 1988 tax years) may not exceed 16 percent.

Start-Up Company. A start-up company's fixed-base percentage is three percent for each of the first five tax years for which it has qualified research expenses. However, the fixed-base percentage for the sixth through tenth tax years in which qualified research expenses were incurred is a portion of the percentage which qualified research expenses bear to gross receipts for specified preceding years. For subsequent tax years, the fixed-base percentage is the whole percentage that qualified research expenses bear to gross receipts for any five years selected by the taxpayer from the fifth through tenth tax years. The definition of a start-up company includes a taxpayer who has both gross receipts and qualified research expenses for the first time in a tax year that begins after 1983 (Code Sec. 41(c)(3)(B)).

Alternative Incremental Computation. A taxpayer may elect to compute the research credit using the alternative incremental credit (Code Sec. 41(c)(4)). The election must be made in the first tax year and applies to all future tax years unless the election is revoked with the consent of the IRS. The alternative credit is equal to the sum of an increasing percentage of the amount of qualified research expenses in excess of a percentage of the base amount, divided into three tiers. For purposes of the alternative incremental computation, the base amount is the average gross receipts for the last four tax years. The tier one amount for tax years ending after December 31, 2006 is equal to three percent of qualified research expenditures in excess of one percent of the base amount but not more than 1.5 percent of the base amount. The tier two amount is equal to four percent of qualified research expenditures in excess of 1.5 percent of the base amount but not in excess of two percent of the base amount. The amount of tier three is equal to five percent of qualified research expenditures in excess of two percent of the base amount (Code Sec. 41(c)(4)(A)). For tax years ending before December 31, 2006, these percentages were as follows: for tier 1 – 2.65 percent; for tier 2 – 3.2 percent; and for tier 3 – 3.75 percent.

A transitional rule applies for fiscal year taxpayers in computing the amount of credit for 2006-2007 by adding (1) the credit calculated as if it were extended but the rates not increased, and multiplied by a fraction that is the number of days in the tax year before January 1, 2007, over the total number of days in the tax year, and (2) the

---

Footnote references are to paragraphs of the 2008 Standard Federal Tax Reports.

[22] ¶ 4350

credit calculated using the increased rated and multiplied by a fraction that is the number of days in the tax year after December 31, 2006, over the total number of days in the tax year (Act Sec. 104(b)(3) of the Tax Relief and Health Care Act of 2006 (P.L. 109-432)).

Alternative Simplified Credit. Effective for tax years ending after December 31, 2006, taxpayers may elect a third method to calculate the increased research activities credit amount using an alternative simplified credit (Code Sec. 41(c)(5), as added by the Tax Relief and Health Care Act of 2006 (P.L. 109-432)). Under the alternative simplified credit, a taxpayer can claim an amount equal to 12 percent of the amount by which the qualified research expenses exceeds 50 percent of the average qualified research expenses for the three preceding tax years. If the taxpayer has no qualified research expenses for any of the preceding three years, then the credit is equal to six percent of the qualified research expenses for the current tax year. If the taxpayer makes the election to use the alternative simplified credit method, the election will be effective for succeeding tax years unless revoked with the consent of the IRS.

Transitional rules are provided for fiscal year taxpayers wishing to make the election to use the alternative simplified credit method for 2006-2007 by adding (1) the credit calculated under the general rule or the alternative incremental credit method, if elected, as if it were extended but the rates not increased, and multiplied by a fraction that is the number of days in the tax year before January 1, 2007, over the total number of days in the tax year, and (2) the credit calculated using the increased rates and multiplied by a fraction that is the number of days in the tax year after December 31, 2006, over the total number of days in the tax year (Act Sec. 104(c)(4) of the Tax Relief and Health Care Act of 2006 (P.L. 109-432)).

Deduction for Research and Experimental Expenditures. A taxpayer claiming the credit must reduce the business deduction for research and experimental expenditures (see ¶ 979) by the amount of the research credit (Code Sec. 280C(c)). Capitalized expenses must also be reduced by the amount of the research credit that exceeds the amount otherwise allowable as a deduction for such expenses. An annual irrevocable election is available to claim a reduced research credit and thereby avoid reducing the research expense deduction (or capital expenditures). Under the election, the research credit must be reduced by the product of the research credit computed in the regular manner and the maximum corporate tax rate.

Qualified Research Expenses. Qualified research expenses for purposes of calculating the credit are the same as those for the business deduction (see ¶ 979) other than: expenses for foreign research; research in the social sciences, arts or humanities; or subsidized research. However, research eligible for the credit is limited to research undertaken to discover information that is technological in nature and intended to be useful in the development of a new or improved business component. Further, the research must relate to elements of a process of experimentation for a functional purpose (i.e., it must relate to a new or improved function, performance, reliability, or quality). Qualified research expenses cover in-house expenses for the taxpayer's own research (i.e., wages, including income from employees' exercise of stock options, for substantially engaging in or directly supervising or supporting research activities, supplies, and computer use charges) and 65 percent of amounts paid or incurred for qualified research done by a person other than an employee of the taxpayer. The percentage is increased to 75 percent of amounts paid or incurred for qualified research performed by a qualified research consortium. A qualified research consortium is a tax-exempt organization under either Code Sec. 501(c)(3) or 501(c)(6). The consortium must be operating primarily to conduct energy research and it must have at least five unrelated customers, with no single person accounting for more than 50 percent of the revenues of the organization.

Qualified Energy Research Expenditures. The 20 percent credit amount for qualified energy research applies to all expenditures to a energy research consortium. The percent limitation placed on outside research has been repealed for purposes of energy research. Amounts paid or incurred for any energy research conducted outside of the United States, Puerto Rico or any possession of the United States cannot be taken into account in determining the 20 percent of amounts paid or incurred by a taxpayer in carrying on any trade or business during the tax year to an energy research consortium under Code Sec. 41(a)(3) (Code Sec. 41(f)(6)(C)).

¶1330

Special Rule for Pass-Thru Entities. For individuals with interests in unincorporated businesses, partners, trust or estate beneficiaries, or S corporation shareholders, any allowable pass-through of the credit cannot exceed the amount of tax attributable to the individual's taxable income allocable to that individual's interest in the entity (Code Sec. 41(g)).

1334. Low-Income Housing Credit. A nonrefundable income tax credit is available on a per unit basis for low-income units in qualified low-income buildings in qualified low-income housing projects (Code Sec. 42).[23] The owner of a qualified low-income housing project that is constructed, rehabilitated, or acquired may claim the credit in each of 10 tax years in an amount equal to the applicable credit percentage appropriate to the type of project, multiplied by the qualified basis allocable to the low-income units in each qualified low-income building.

The credit is claimed over a 10-year period that begins with the tax year in which the project is placed in service or, at the taxpayer's election, the next tax year (but only if the building is a qualified low-income building as of the close of the first year of such period). The first-year credit is reduced to reflect the time during the year that any low-income units are unoccupied. If the reduction is made, a credit is allowed in the eleventh year in an amount equal to the reduction. The credit is calculated on Form 8586, Low-Income Housing Credit, and is claimed as a component of the general business credit.[24] As such, it is subject to the limitation and the carryback and carryforward rules discussed at ¶ 1323. The credit is denied to otherwise qualified buildings unless the owner of the building is subject to an enforceable 30-year low-income use agreement with the housing agency (Code Sec. 42(h)(6)). However, the credit is not limited or disallowed by the rules applicable to activities not entered into for profit (see ¶ 1195) (Reg. § 1.42-4).[25]

Usually, the applicable credit rates are the appropriate percentages issued by the IRS for the month in which the building is placed in service. Different percentages are provided for new construction or rehabilitation, subsidized construction or rehabilitation, and the acquisition of existing housing (see ¶ 86). An irrevocable election is available to determine the credit percentage applicable to a building in advance of the date that it is placed in service.

Generally, rehabilitation expenditures are treated as expenditures for a separate new building provided that the expenditures are allocable to, or substantially benefit, low-income units and that they are incurred during any 24-month period and the greater of $3,000 per low-income unit or 10 percent of the adjusted basis of the building.

A qualified low-income housing project is any project for residential rental property that meets requirements for low-income tenant occupancy, gross rent restrictions, state credit authority, and IRS certification. The project must continue to meet these requirements for 15 years or recapture of a portion of the credit may occur. A qualified low-income building must be subject to MACRS depreciation.

Credit Expanded for Gulf Opportunity (GO) Zone. Rules relating to the state housing credit ceiling, difficult development areas, and median gross income have been modified in order to facilitate use of the low-income housing credit for property in the Gulf Opportunity (GO) Zone (Code Sec. 1400N(c)). GO Zone property consists of that portion of the Hurricane Katrina disaster area which the President determines warrants individual or individual and public assistance from the federal government because of Hurricane Katrina damage. For calendar years 2006, through 2008, the population component of the state housing credit ceiling is modified to allow for increased ceilings for the GO Zone. The increase is the lesser of: (1) the aggregate housing credit dollar amount allocated by the state housing credit agency to buildings located in the GO Zone for such calendar year or (2) an amount equal to $18 multiplied by the portion of the state population located in the GO Zone according to the most recent census estimate released before August 28, 2005 (Code Sec. 1400N(c)(1)(A) and (B)). The time for making and claiming low-income housing credit allocations from calendar years 2006 through 2008 for housing placed in service within the GO Zone is extended until January

---

Footnote references are to paragraphs of the 2008 Standard Federal Tax Reports.

[23] ¶ 4380   [24] ¶ 4380   [25] ¶ 4384A

1, 2011 (Code Sec. 1400N(c), as amended by the Small Business and Work Opportunity Tax Act of 2007 (P.L. 110-28)).

1335. New Markets Tax Credit. The new markets tax credit was created to increase investments in low-income communities. The credit is equal to five percent of the investment in a qualified community development entity (CDE) for the first three allowance dates and six percent of the investment for the next four allowance dates (Code Sec. 45D(a)).[26] The total credit available is equal to 39 percent of the investment over seven years. Active involvement of the low-income communities is required with strict penalties if the investment is terminated before seven years. There are national limitations on the amount of investments which can be used to claim the new market tax credit for investments made after December 31, 2000, as well as allocation and carryover rules (Code Sec. 45D(f)). The new markets credit availability has been extended through 2008 and the national limitations is $3.5 billion for calendar years 2006 through 2008 (Code Sec. 45D(f)).

The new markets tax credit is a part of and subject to the limitations and carryover rules of the general business credit (¶ 1323). The credit is calculated on Form 8874, New Markets Credit. The credit may not be carried back to tax years ending before January 1, 2001. Any unused credit at the end of the carryforward period will be allowed as a deduction in the following tax year (Code Sec. 196). Any termination event will require recapture of the credit amount claimed that will be treated as an increase to tax in the termination year. Any amounts of credit carried forward or carried back will need to be adjusted accordingly. Finally, the claiming of the new markets tax credit will necessitate an adjustment in the basis of the investment in the CDE.

Hurricane Katrina Relief. An additional allocation of the new markets tax credit (NMTC) is provided in an amount equal to $300 million for 2005 and 2006, and $400 million for 2007, to be allocated among qualified community development entities (CDEs) to make qualified low-income community investments within the Gulf Opportunity (GO) Zone. To qualify for this allocation, a qualified CDE must have as a significant mission the recovery and redevelopment within the GO Zone. The carryover of any unused additional allocation is applied separately from the carryover with respect to allocations made under the carryover rules of Code Sec. 45D(f)(3) (Code Sec. 1400N(m)).

1336. Enhanced Oil Recovery Credit. An enhanced oil recovery (EOR) credit may be claimed for up to 15 percent of the eligible costs attributable to a qualified domestic EOR project for increasing the production of crude oil or to production of Alaskan natural gas for tax years beginning after 2004, unless an election is made not to claim the credit (Code Sec. 43(a) and (e)).[27] Any increase in basis of this property caused by the expenditures for an EOR project shall be reduced by the amount of EOR credit claimed (Code Sec. 43(d)(2)).

The amount of the credit allowable is phased out as the average wellhead price of uncontrolled domestic oil rises from $28 to $34 per barrel. The amount allowable as a credit is reduced by an amount that bears the same ratio to the amount of the credit as the amount by which the reference price for the calendar year before the calendar year in which the tax year begins exceeds $28 bears to $6. Since the reference price for the 2006 calendar year ($59.68) exceeds $28 multiplied by the inflation adjustment factor for the 2007 calendar year of 1.4222, the EOR credit for qualified costs paid or incurred in 2007 is phased out completely (Notice 2007-64). This credit was computed on Form 8830, Enhanced Oil Recovery Credit, and was claimed as one of the components of the general business credit. Accordingly, it was subject to the limitation and the carryback and carryforward rules discussed at ¶ 1323. Any unused credit remaining after the expiration of the carryforward period is deductible (Code Sec. 196).

1338. Disabled Access Credit. An eligible small business is entitled to a nonrefundable income tax credit for expenditures incurred to make a business accessible to disabled individuals (Code Sec. 44).[28] The amount of the credit is 50 percent of the amount of eligible access expenditures for a year that exceed $250 but that do not exceed $10,250. The credit is computed on Form 8826, Disabled Access Credit, and is

---

Footnote references are to paragraphs of the 2008 Standard Federal Tax Reports.

[26] ¶ 4480   [27] ¶ 4386   [28] ¶ 4400

claimed as one of the components of the general business credit. Thus, the credit is subject to the limitation and the carryback and carryforward rules discussed at ¶ 1323. Any unused credit remaining at the end of the carryforward period is lost (Code Sec. 196(c)). No other deduction or credit is permitted for any amount for which a disabled access credit is allowed.

An eligible small business is any person that elects to claim the disabled access credit that had gross receipts (less returns and allowances) for the preceding tax year that did not exceed $1 million, or no more than 30 full-time employees during the preceding tax year. Eligible access expenditures include reasonable and necessary amounts paid or incurred by an eligible small business for the purpose of enabling the business to comply with the requirements of the Americans with Disabilities Act of 1990.

Eligible expenditures also include expenditures: (1) for the purpose of removing architectural, communication, physical, or transportation barriers that prevent a business from being accessible to, or usable by, disabled individuals (other than amounts for new construction); (2) to provide qualified interpreters or other effective methods of making aurally delivered materials available to hearing-impaired individuals; (3) to provide qualified readers, taped texts, and other effective methods of making visually delivered materials available to visually impaired individuals; (4) to acquire or modify equipment or devices for disabled individuals; or (5) to provide other similar services, modifications, materials, or equipment.

1339. Credit for Electricity Produced from Renewable Sources. A nonrefundable credit is available for the domestic production of electricity from qualified energy resources at a qualified facility which is sold to an unrelated third party (Code Sec. 45).[29] The credit amount for electricity produced in a qualified wind, closed-loop biomass, geothermal energy, or solar facility is 2.0 cents per kilowatt hour in 2007. Electricity produced in qualified open-loop biomass, small irrigation power, landfill gas, trash combustion, or qualified hydroelectric facilities generate a credit amount of 1.0 cents per kilowatt hour in 2007. The credit amount for production of refined coal in 2007 is $5.877 per ton and for Indian coal $1.544 per ton (Notice 2007-40).

The credit will be reduced by an amount that bears the same ratio to the amount of the credit as the excess of the reference price for the calendar year in which the sale occurs as eight cents bears to three cents. The reference price and the eight-cent threshold amount are each adjusted annually by multiplying them by an inflation adjustment factor for the calendar year in which the sale occurs. For 2007, the inflation adjustment factor for qualified energy resources and refined coal is 1.3433 and for Indian coal is 1.0293. The reference price for electricity produced from wind is 3.29 cents per kilowatt-hour; for refined coal production the reference price for 2002 is 31.90 and for 2007 is $48.35 per ton; the reference prices for electricity produced from closed-loop biomass, open-looped biomass, geothermal energy, solar energy, small irrigation power, municipal solid waste, and qualified hydropower production facilities have not been determined for calendar year 2007. The IRS continues to explore methods to determine these reference prices for calendar year 2008. Since none of the reference price exceeds the base threshold amount per kilowatt-hour multiplied by the inflation adjustment factor, there is no reduction in the credit amounts for electricity sold in 2007 (Notice 2007-40).

The credit is claimed on Form 8835, Renewable Electricity, Refined Coal, and Indian Coal Production Credit, and is one of the components of the general business credit. For tax years ending after October 24, 2004, the credit limitation for the renewable energy source credit is determined separately from the other general business credits and, in the calculation of the credit limitation, the tentative minimum tax is to be treated as zero. The result of this treatment is that the renewable energy source credit amounts are available to be used against both the regular and the alternative minimum tax liabilities for the current year (Code Sec. 38(c)(4)). For tax years ending before October 23, 2004, it is subject to the overall limitation and the carryback and carryforward rules discussed at ¶ 1323.

Footnote references are to paragraphs of the 2008 Standard Federal Tax Reports.

[29] ¶ 4410

Qualified Energy Facilities. The credit for electricity from renewable energy sources can be claimed over a five- or ten-year period depending on the facility. The following facilities qualify for the five-year period: (1) open-loop biomass facilities that use agricultural livestock waste nutrients originally placed in service after October 22, 2004, and on or before August 8, 2005; (2) open-loop biomass facilities that do not use agricultural livestock waste nutrients originally placed in service before January 1, 2005; (3) geothermal facilities originally placed in service after October 22, 2004, and on or before August 8, 2005; (4) solar facilities originally placed in service after October 22, 2004, and on or before August 8, 2005; (5) small irrigation power facilities originally placed in service after October 22, 2004, and on or before August 8, 2005; (6) landfill gas facilities originally placed in service after October 22, 2004, and on or before August 8, 2005; and (7) trash combustion facilities (or certain new units placed in service in connection with an existing trash combustion facility) originally placed in service after October 22, 2004, and on or before August 8, 2005.

The following facilities qualify to claim the credit for the ten-year period for electricity from a renewable energy source: (1) wind facilities originally placed in service after December 31, 1993, and before January 1, 2008; (2) open-loop biomass facilities that use agricultural livestock waste nutrients originally placed in service after August 8, 2005, and before January 1, 2008; (3) open-loop biomass facilities that do not use agricultural livestock waste nutrients if placed in service on or after January 1, 2005, and before January 1, 2008; (4) closed-loop biomass facilities modified to use closed-loop biomass to co-fire with coal, other biomass, or both originally placed in service before January 1, 2008; (5) any other closed-loop biomass facilities originally placed in service after December 31, 1992, and before January 1, 2008; (6) geothermal facilities originally placed in service after August 8, 2005, and before January 1, 2008; (7) solar facilities originally placed in service after August 8, 2005, and before January 1, 2006; (8) small irrigation power facilities originally placed in service after August 8, 2005, and before January 1, 2008; (9) landfill gas facilities originally placed in service after August 8, 2005, and before January 1, 2008; (10) trash combustion facilities (or new units placed in service in connection with an existing trash combustion facility) originally placed in service after August 8, 2005, and before January 1, 2008; (11) refined coal production facilities placed in service after October 22, 2004, and before January 1, 2009; (12) hydroelectric dams placed in service on or before August 8, 2005 (credit is determined by reference to electricity attributable to improvements placed in service after August 8, 2005, and before January 1, 2008, and the 10-year period begins on the date such improvements are placed in service); and (13) nonhydroelectric dams placed in service before August 8, 2005 (credit is determined by reference to electricity attributable to turbines added after August 8, 2005, and, apparently, before January 1, 2008; no special date for start of 10-year period is provided; however, it seems that the 10-year period should begin on the date the generators were placed in service, rather than on the date the dam was placed in service).

Refined Coal. A producer of refined coal who sells the coal with the reasonable expectation that it will be used to produce steam may claim a credit under Code Sec. 45. This credit is available with respect to refined coal produced from a refined coal production facility placed in service after October 22, 2004, and before January 1, 2009, and sold after October 22, 2004. The credit only applies to United States production. The refined coal must be produced and sold during the 10-year period that begins on the date that the facility was originally placed in service. The credit amount will begin to phase out when the current reference price of fuel used as feedstock for refined coal exceeds the 2002 reference price times the inflation factor for the year time 1.7. The credit for refined coal production may not be claimed if production from the facility was eligible for the nonconventional fuel source credit for any tax year (see ¶ 1319) (Code Sec. 45(e)(9)(A)).

Indian Coal Production. Effective August 8, 2005, a new component is added to the renewable resources credit for Indian coal production (Code Sec. 45(e)(10)). The coal does not need to be sold for the production of electricity or any other particular purpose. The taxpayer may claim a credit for sales of Indian coal produced at an Indian coal production facility during the seven-year period beginning on January 1, 2006, and ending after December 31, 2012. The sales must be to an unrelated party. An Indian coal production facility is simply defined as a facility which was placed in service before

¶1339

January 1, 2009. The credit is available for each ton of coal sold during the first four years of the seven-year period, which increases for each ton of coal sold during the last three years of the seven-year period. These credit rates are indexed for inflation in calendar years after 2006. Indian coal is defined as coal produced from reserves that on June 14, 2005, were owned by a federally recognized tribe of Indians or were held in trust by the United States for a tribe or its members.

Hydropower Production. Effective August 8, 2005, a new component is added to the renewable resources credit for qualified hydropower production (Code Sec. 45(c)(1)(H)). The credit rate is one-half of the standard 1.5 cent credit rate per kilowatt-hour of qualifying electricity production. In the case of a hyrdroelectric dam that was placed in service on or before August 8, 2005, the credit is available for electricity attributable to "incremental hydropower production" for the tax year. In general, incremental hydropower production for a particular tax year is equal to the percentage of average annual hydroelectric power produced at the dam that is attributable to efficiency improvements or additions to capacity that are made after August 8, 2005, and before January 1, 2008.

The 10-year credit period begins on the date that the efficiency improvements or additions to capacity are placed in service. The credit is also available for a dam that was placed in service before August 8, 2005, and which did not produce electricity on August 8, 2005 (a nonhydroelectric dam), if turbines or other generating equipment are added to the dam after August 8, 2005 (and, presumably, before January 1, 2008) to produce hydroelectric power. However, the credit can only be claimed if the diversion structure is not enlarged, a bypass channel is not enlarged (or constructed), and no additional water is impounded or withheld from the natural stream channel. The facility must be licensed by the Federal Energy Regulatory Commission and meet all other applicable environmental, licensing, and regulatory requirements.

1339A. Empowerment Zone and Renewal Community Employment Credit. Employers located in empowerment zones are entitled to a 20-percent wage credit on the first $15,000 of annual wages paid to residents of the empowerment zone (Code Sec. 1396).[30] Employers located in renewal community zones are entitled to a 15-percent wage credit on the first $10,000 of annual wages paid to residents of the renewal community zone (Code Sec. 1400H) (see also ¶ 999C).[31] These credits are claimed on Form 8844, Empowerment Zone and Renewal Community Employment Credit, and, although part of the general business credit, they are not a part of the general business credit limitation computation. The credit amounts are calculated separately, as are the yearly limitations on the amount of each credit that may be claimed against a taxpayer's tax liability (see ¶ 999A and following).

1340. Indian Employment Credit. A nonrefundable credit is available to employers for certain wages and health insurance costs paid or incurred in a tax year that begins before 2008 for qualified full- or part-time employees who are enrolled members of an Indian tribe or their spouses (Code Sec. 45A, as amended by the Tax Relief and Health Care Act of 2006 (P.L. 109-432)).[32] The credit is equal to 20 percent of the excess of eligible employee qualified wages and health insurance costs paid or incurred during a tax year over the amount of these costs paid or incurred during 1993. However, the credit is available only for the first $20,000 of qualified wages and health insurance costs paid for each qualified employee. Also, no wage deduction is allowed for the portion of wages equal to the amount of the credit. Qualified wages are wages paid or incurred by an employer for services performed by a qualified employee excluding wages for which a work opportunity credit (see ¶ 1342) is allowed. Qualified health insurance costs are costs paid or incurred by an employer for a qualified employee, except for costs paid under a salary reduction agreement.

An individual who received more than 50 percent of wages from services performed in the trade or business of the employer is a qualified employee for any period *only* if: (1) the individual was an enrolled member of an Indian tribe or the spouse thereof; (2) substantially all of the services performed during the period by the employee for the employer were performed within an Indian reservation; and (3) the principal place of

---

Footnote references are to paragraphs of the 2008 Standard Federal Tax Reports.

[30] ¶ 32,393   [31] ¶ 32,453   [32] ¶ 4430

474   **U.S. Master Tax Guide**

abode of the employee while performing the services was on or near the reservation on which the services are performed. Ineligible employees include employees who receive wages exceeding $40,000 as adjusted for inflation (Code Sec. 45A(c)(3); Instructions to Form 8845).

The credit was calculated on Form 8845, Indian Employment Credit, and is claimed as one of the components of the general business credit. Thus, it was subject to the limitation and carryback and carryforward rules discussed at ¶ 1323. Any unused credit at the end of the carryforward period is allowed as a deduction in the year following the expiration of the period (Code Sec. 196(c)).

1341. Credit for Employer-Paid Social Security Taxes on Employee Cash Tips (FICA Tip Credit). An employer in the food and beverage business may claim a nonrefundable income tax credit for its portion of employer social security and Medicare taxes (FICA taxes) paid or incurred on employee cash tips (Code Sec. 45B).[33] The credit is equal to the employer's FICA obligation attributable to tips received by the employee exceeding those tips treated as wages for purposes of satisfying the minimum wage provisions of the Fair Labor Standards Act. For purposes of calculating the credit, the minimum wage has been permanently established at the rate in effect on January 1, 2007, or $5.15 per hour (Code Sec. 45B(b)(1)(B), as amended by the Small Business and Work Opportunity Tax Act of 2007 (P.L. 110-28)).The credit is available whether or not the employee reported the tips and regardless of when the services were performed. The credit is allowed for tips received from customers in connection with the providing, delivering, or serving of food or beverages for consumption if the tipping of employees delivering or serving food or beverages by customers is customary. The employer may not deduct any amount considered in determining this credit. An election may be made to have this credit not apply.

The credit is claimed on Form 8846, Credit for Employer Social Security and Medicare Taxes Paid on Certain Employee Tips. Although it is one of the components of the general business credit, it is not subject to the general business credit limitation rule. For tax years beginning after December 31, 2004, for purposes of determining the amount of the FICA tip credit that may be claimed in the current year, the tentative minimum tax is considered zero (Code Sec. 38(c)). The result of setting the minimum tax at zero allows taxpayers claiming the FICA tip credit to use the complete amount of the credit against both the regular and the alternative minimum tax liabilities. The new credit limitation rule will apply to any such carrybacks of credits generated after December 31, 2004. For tax years beginning before January 1, 2005, the FICA tip credit was subject to the overall general business credit limitation rule and the rules for carryforwards and carrybacks as discussed at ¶ 1323. Any credit that remains unused at the end of the carryover period is lost.

1342. Work Opportunity Tax Credit. Unless an election is made to have it not apply, a credit is available for wages paid by employers who hire individuals from certain targeted groups of hard-to-employee individuals. The credit is 40 percent of the first $6,000 of wages ($3,000 for qualified summer youth employees) paid to each member of a target group during the first year of employment and 25 percent in the case of wages attributable to individuals meeting only minimum employment levels. The credit is taken for first-year wages paid to eligible individuals who begin work after September 30, 1996, and before September 1, 2011 (Code Sec. 51(c)(4), as amended by the Small Business and Work Opportunity Tax Act of 2007 (P.L. 110-28)).[34] Any business deduction for such wages must be reduced by the amount of the credit, as computed on Form 5884, Work Opportunity Credit. Although the work opportunity credit is a component of the general business credit (¶ 1323), credit amounts generated by individuals beginning work after May 25, 2007, are no longer subject to the general business credit limitation rule but are to be calculated separately. The credit limitation formula is changed to treat the tentative minimum tax as zero, resulting in the allowing taxpayers to fully utilize the credit against both the regular and the alternative minimum tax liabilities (Code Sec. 38(c)(4), as amended by the Small Business and Work Opportunity Work Tax Act (P.L. 110-28)). The new credit limitation calculation will apply to any carrybacks of such credit

---

Footnote references are to paragraphs of the 2008 Standard Federal Tax Reports.

[33] ¶ 4450   [34] ¶ 4800

¶1341

amounts. For credit amounts generated by individuals beginning work on or before May 25, 2007, the credit amount to claim is subject to the tax limitation and the carry over rules discussed at ¶ 1323. No credit is allowed for wages paid to an individual for services rendered at the employer's plant or facility that are substantially similar to services performed by employees who are participants in a strike or who are affected by a lockout.

Target Groups. Wages paid to individuals who are certified members of one of the following groups qualify for the work opportunity credit: (1) qualified IV-A (Aid to Families with Dependent Children (AFDC)) recipient; (2) qualified veteran; (3) qualified ex-felon; (4) designated community resident (formally the high-risk youth group); (5) vocational rehabilitation referral; (6) qualified summer youth employee; (7) qualified food stamps recipient; (8) a qualified SSI recipient; or (9) long-term family assistance recipients, the former welfare-to-work individuals. An employer of an individual who is a member of one of these groups must either have the individual certified by an authorized local agency prior to the individuals first day of work or file an application for certification of the individual within 28 days of the first day of work (Code Sec. 51(d)(12), as amended by the Small Business and Work Opportunity Tax Act of 2007 (P.L. 110-28)).

Qualified Veterans Group. Effective for employees hired after May 25, 2007, the qualified veterans group has been expanded to include veterans that have certified service-connected disabilities. In addition, the maximum amount of wages for veterans with service-connected disabilities has been increased to the first $12,000 instead of the first $6,000. The maximum amount of credit is effectively doubled to $4,800 (Code Sec. 51(b)(3) and (d)(3), as amended by the Small Business and Work Opportunity Tax Act of 2007 (P.L. 110-28)).

Qualified Ex-Felons. Effective for employees hired after December 31, 2006, an employer only needs to certify that the individual has been convicted of a felony and the hire date is within one year of conviction or release from prison (Code Sec. 51(c)(4), as amended by the Tax Relief and Health Care Act of 2006 (P.L. 109-432)). The requirement that the individual be a member of an economically disadvantage family and meet certain income levels during the six months prior to the hire date has been removed.

Newly Designated Community Residents. Effective for employees hired after May 25, 2007, the high-risk youth groups has been redesignated. This group was created to help youth that lived and worked in empowerment zones, enterprises zones and renewal communities. Instead of the individual being at least 18 years of age but less than 25 years of age, the age ranges have been broadened to include individuals less than 40 years of age on the hiring date. In addition, the individual can live in a newly designated distress area entitled rural renewal county. A rural renewal county is an area located outside of a metropolitan that has suffered the loss of population in both the period of 1990 though 1994 and 1995 though 1999 (Code Sec. 51(d)(5), as amended by the Small Business and Work Opportunity Tax Act of 2007 (P.L. 110-28)).

Vocational Rehabilitation Referral Group. Effective for employees hired after May 27, 2007, the definition of vocational rehabilitation referral has been expanded to include individuals referred to employers while receiving, or after completing, an individual work plan that was developed and implemented by an employment network under the Social Security Administration's Ticket to Work and Self Sufficiency program (Code Sec. 51(d)(6), as amended by the Small Business and Work Opportunity Tax Act of 2007 (P.L. 110-28)).

Food Stamp Recipients. Effective for employees hired after December 31, 2006, the age range for individuals that receive food stamps has been increased from having attained 18 year of age but not yet 25 years of age to having attained 18 years of age but not yet 40 years of age (Code Sec. 51(8), as amended by the Tax Relief and Health Care Act of 2007 (P.L. 109-432)).

New Long-term Family Assistance Recipients. Effective for employees hired after December 31, 2006, the welfare-to-work credit has been repealed (see ¶ 1343). However, the incentives for employing long-term family assistant recipients have been added as a new targeted group for the work opportunity credit with certain adjustments (Code Sec. 51(c)(10), as amended by the Tax Relief and Health Care Act of 2006 (P.L. 109-432)). For qualifying individuals of the long-term family assistance recipient group the first

$10,000 of qualifying wages are used to determine the credit amount in the first year instead of the first $6,000 of qualifying wages. Normally, the work opportunity is only available for the first year of the employment but for long-term family assistance recipients, the work opportunity credit will be available for the second year, to remain consistent with the former welfare-to-work credit. Employers will again use the first $10,000 of qualifying wages paid but instead of multiplying by 40 percent, the percentage rises to 50 percent or a maximum second year credit of $5,000 (Code Sec. 51(e), as added by the Tax Relief and Health Care Act of 2006 (P.L. 109-432)).

Hurricane Katrina Relief (Expired). To assist businesses located in the core disaster area of Hurricane Katrina, a targeted group was created (i.e., Hurricane Katrina employees) for purposes of claiming the work opportunity credit. Hurricane Katrina employees are: (1) any individual who on August 28, 2005, had a principal place of abode in the core disaster area and who is hired during the two-year period beginning on August 28, 2005, for a position in a trade or business which has its principal place of employment located within the core disaster area, and (2) any individual who on August 28, 2005, had a principal place of abode in the core disaster area, who is displaced from their principal place of abode by reasons of Hurricane Katrina, and who is hired during the period beginning on August 28, 2005, and ending on December 31, 2005. Certification requirements are waived and replaced with a requirement that individuals only need to provide employers with reasonable evidence that they qualify as a Hurricane Katrina employee.

Minimum Employment Period. An employee must have completed a minimum of 120 hours of service for the wages to be taken into account for calculation of the work opportunity credit. The hours of service test is the only way the minimum employment period is measured for purposes of the credit. If the 120-hour test is met but the employee fails to perform at least 400 hours of service, the employer is entitled to a credit of 25 percent. For 400 or more hours of service, the percentage is 40 percent of the employee's wages.

1343. Welfare-to-Work Credit (Repealed). The welfare-to-work credit was available to employers for wages paid to long-term family assistance recipients who begin work before January 1, 2007 (Code Sec. 51A, as repealed by the Tax Relief and Health Care Act of 2006 (P.L. 109-432)).[35] The amount of the credit was 35 percent of the qualified first-year wages for such year plus 50 percent of the qualified second-year wages for the tax year. The credit applies only to the first $10,000 of wages in each year with respect to any individual. Thus, the maximum total credit per qualified employee was $8,500 for the two years. The term "wages" was given a broad meaning for purposes of the welfare-to-work credit. The credit was a component and subject to the limitation rule and carryover rules of the general business credit. Effective for employees hired after December 31, 2006, the incentives for employing long-term family assistant recipients have been added as a new targeted group for the work opportunity credit with certain adjustments (see ¶ 1342).

1344. Credit for Clinical Testing Expenses for Certain Drugs for Rare Diseases and Conditions (Orphan Drug Credit). A credit, commonly known as the orphan drug credit, is allowed for an amount equal to 50 percent, subject to limitations, of the clinical testing expenses to develop drugs to treat rare diseases and conditions. The credit is claimed on Form 8820, Orphan Drug Credit, and is a component of the general business credit. Thus, it is subject to the limitation rules and the carryback and carryforward rules discussed at ¶ 1323 (Code Sec. 45C).[36]

1344A. Qualified Zone Academy Bond Credit. An eligible taxpayer (including banks, insurance companies or other corporations actively engaged in the business of lending money) who is holding a qualified zone academy bond on a credit allowance date is entitled to a nonrefundable tax credit for each year in which the bond is held (Code Sec. 1397E).[37] The shareholder of an S corporation may claim the credit from an S corporation that is otherwise an eligible taxpayer. The credit rate is the percentage that the Treasury estimates will permit qualified academy zone bonds to be issued without discount and without interest cost to the issuer of the bonds. The credit amount

Footnote references are to paragraphs of the 2008 Standard Federal Tax Reports.

[35] ¶ 4820   [36] ¶ 4470   [37] ¶ 32,405

¶1343

is included in the gross income of the taxpayer. The credit amount is calculated on Form 8860, Qualified Zone Academy Bond Credit. Allocation and carryover rules also apply.

1344B. Small Employer Pension Plan Startup Costs Credit. Eligible small businesses may claim a credit for qualified startup costs incurred in establishing and administering an eligible employer benefit plan for their employees (Code Sec. 45E).[38] The credit amount equals 50 percent of the qualified startup costs incurred to create or maintain a new employee retirement plan. The credit is limited to $500 in any tax year and it may be claimed for qualified costs incurred in each of the three years beginning with the tax year in which the plan becomes effective. The credit is part of and subject to the limitations and carryover rules of the general business credit (¶ 1323), except that no portion of the credit may be carried back to a tax year beginning before 2002. Form 8881, Credit for Small Employer Plan Startup Costs, is used to calculate and claim the credit.

An eligible small business is one that has not employed more than 100 employees who received at least $5,000 of compensation from that employer in the preceding year. However, a business is not eligible if during the preceding three tax years it established or maintained a qualified employer plan with respect to which contributions were made, or benefits were accrued, for substantially the same employees as are in the new qualified employer plan. An eligible plan includes a new qualified defined benefit plan, defined contribution plan (including a 401(k) plan), savings incentive match plan for employees (SIMPLE), or simplified employee pension (SEP) plan. Qualified startup costs are any ordinary and necessary expenses incurred to establish or administer an eligible plan or to educate employees about retirement planning. Qualified costs are not deductible to the extent that they are effectively offset by the tax credit. The credit is limited to the first $1,000 of qualified costs incurred in the first year the new plan is effective and in each of the following two years. The employer may elect to take the credit in the year immediately preceding the first year the new plan is effective or elect not to claim the credit for a tax year.

1344C. Employer-Provided Child Care Credit. Businesses may claim a tax credit for qualified expenses related to either an employer-provided child care center or service related to locating qualified child care (Code Sec. 45F).[39] The amount of the credit for a given tax year is the sum of 25 percent of the qualified child care expenditures and 10 percent of the qualified resource and referral expenditures. The maximum amount of credit allowed in any given year is $150,000. Form 8882, Credit for Employer-Provided Child Care Facilities and Services, is to be used to calculate and claim the credit. The credit is part of and subject to the limitations and carryover rules of the general business credit (¶ 1323). No double benefit is allowed for expenditures used to claim the employer-provided child care credit and the basis of the qualified child care facility must be reduced by the amount of the credit taken. In addition, there is no deduction allowed in the year following the final year of any carryforward of unused employer-provided child care credit. If a qualified childcare facility ceases to operate as a qualified childcare facility (or there is a change in ownership), it may have to recapture part or all of credit claimed. In the event of recapture, the tax liability of that tax year must be increased by an amount equal to the applicable percentage (see Code Sec. 45F(d)(2)(A)) times the aggregate decrease in the general business credit as if all previously allowed employer-provided child care credits with respect to the employer's child care facility had been zero. Any carryforward or carryback amounts of the employer-provided child care credit must also be adjusted.

A qualified child care facility is a facility whose "principal use" is to provide child care assistance and that meets the requirements of all applicable laws and regulations of the state and local government in which it is located, including the licensing requirements applicable to a child care facility. The principal use requirement is waived for facilities located in the principal residence of the operator of the facility. Additional requirements include that: (1) enrollment must be open to the employees of the taxpayer during the tax year; (2) at least 30 percent of the enrollees at the facility are the dependents of the taxpayer's employees, in the event the facility is the principal trade or

---

Footnote references are to paragraphs of the 2008 Standard Federal Tax Reports.

[38] ¶ 4492   [39] ¶ 4494

business of the taxpayer; and (3) the use of the child care facility cannot discriminate in favor of highly-compensated employees (see ¶ 2111).

Qualified child care expenditures are any amounts paid or incurred: (1) to acquire, construct, rehabilitate or expand property which is to used as a qualified child care facility of the taxpayer; (2) for the operating costs of a qualified child care facility, including the costs related to the training of employees, scholarship programs, and providing increased compensation for employees with high levels of child care training; or (3) under a contract with a qualified child care facility to provide child care services to the taxpayer's employees. Costs associated with item (1) must qualify for a depreciation or amortization deduction and must not be the principal residence of the taxpayer. Expenses for items (2) and (3) cannot exceed the fair market value of such care. Further, qualified child care resources and referral expenditures are expenses paid or incurred by the taxpayer under a contract to provide child care services to the taxpayer's employees. These expenditures cannot discriminate in favor of highly-compensated employees. Finally, special rules will be set forth by the IRS for allocation of the credits to pass-thru entities and estates and trusts.

1344D. Railroad Track Maintenance Credit. An income tax credit is available to small and mid-sized railroad companies for qualified railroad track maintenance expenses (Code Sec. 45G).[40] The credit is equal to 50 percent of the qualified expenses paid or incurred by an eligible taxpayer after December 31, 2004, and before January 1, 2008. The credit cannot exceed $3,500 multiplied by the number of miles of railroad track owned or leased by the eligible taxpayer as of the close of the tax year. Eligible taxpayers are Class II and Class III railroad companies and persons who operate over their rail lines or provide related rail services. The credit is a part of the general business credit and subject to the tax liability limitation and carryover rules (see ¶ 1323). The credit is claimed on Form 8900, Qualified Railroad Track Maintenance Credit. No provision is made for deduction of unused credits at the end of the carryforward period or if the taxpayer ceases to exist.

1344E. Low Sulfur Diesel Fuel Production Credit. Qualified small business refiners may claim a credit for qualified expenditures to produce low sulfur diesel fuel (Code Sec. 45H).[41] The credit is equal to five cents per gallon of qualified low sulfur diesel fuel produced during the tax year at a qualified facility. The fuel must contain no more sulfur than 15 parts per million and comply with the Environmental Protection Act (EPA) Highway Diesel Fuel Sulfur Control Requirements. To qualify as a small business refiner, the taxpayer cannot employ more than 1,500 individuals on any day during the tax year and its average daily refinery production of the one-year period ending on December 31, 2002, cannot exceed 205,000 barrels.

Qualifying capital costs eligible for the credit are: (1) expenditures for the construction of new process operation units, (2) expenditures for the dismantling and reconstruction of existing process units to be used in the production of low sulfur diesel fuel, (3) costs of associated adjacent or offsite equipment, and (4) engineering, construction period interest, and sitework expenses. Other qualifying costs are those that are paid or incurred on a qualified facility beginning January 1, 2003, and before the earlier of one year after the date the taxpayer must comply with EPA regulations or December 31, 2009.

The credit amount will begin phasing out for refiners whose production exceeds 155,000 barrels and the credit amount will be completely phased out when production equals 205,000 barrels. Any credit amount claimed reduces the basis to the taxpayer of the property. Expenditures used to claim the credit cannot be used to claim any other deduction or credit. Cooperatives that own a qualified small business refinery may elect to apportion the credit to its patrons but the election, if made, is irrevocable. Finally, as part of the general business credits, it is subject to the tax limitation and carryover rules (see ¶ 1323). The credit is claimed on Form 8896, Low Sulfur Diesel Fuel Production Credit. No provision under Code Sec. 196 is made for this credit if there remains any unused credit amounts at the end of the carryforward period or the taxpayer ceases to exist.

Footnote references are to paragraphs of the 2008 Standard Federal Tax Reports.

[40] ¶ 4151.01   [41] ¶ 4151.01

1344F. Credit for Producing Oil and Gas from Marginal Wells. Taxpayers owning interest in qualified marginal wells producing crude oil or natural gas may claim a credit for the amount of oil and gas produced (Code Sec. 45I).[42] The credit is equal to $3 per barrel of qualified crude oil or 50 cents per 1000 cubic feet of qualified natural gas production. The credit begins to phase out when the reference price of crude oil exceeds $15 per barrel and $1.67 per metric cubic foot (mcf). The credit is completely phased out if the reference price exceeds $18 per barrel or $2.00 per mcf, respectively (both adjusted for inflation after 2005). The credit for producing oil and gas from marginal wells is completely phased out and unavailable to taxpayers.

1344G. Advanced Nuclear Power Facilities Production Credit. A business tax credit is available to taxpayers that produce electricity from an advanced nuclear power facility (Code Sec. 45J). The credit is equal to 1.8 cents times the number of kilowatt hours of electricity produced at a qualifying advanced nuclear power facility and sold to an unrelated person during the tax year. It may only be claimed during the eight-year period beginning on the date the facility was originally placed in service. A qualifying advanced nuclear power facility is any advanced nuclear facility owned by the taxpayer, uses nuclear energy to produce electricity and was placed in service after August 8, 2005, and before January 1, 2021. Any nuclear facility with a reactor design (or a substantially similar design of comparable capacity) approved before 1994 by the Nuclear Regulatory Commission is not a qualifying advanced nuclear power facility. Certain limitations restrict the amount of credit that may be claimed in any tax year, including that the credit is part of the general business credit and as such is subject to the tax limitation and carryover rules (see ¶ 1323).

1344H. Energy Efficient Home Credit. Eligible contractors who build an energy-efficient home acquired by a person for use as a residence before 2009 may claim an income tax credit of up to $2,000 for tax years beginning after 2005 (Code Sec. 45L). Eligible contractors also include manufacturers of energy-efficient manufactured homes. A residence qualifies as an energy-efficient home if it is: (1) located in the United States, (2) substantially completed after August 8, 2005, and (3) certified to have an annual heating and/or cooling saving at least 50 percent less than a comparable house and that at least 10 percent of the 50 percent saving must come from the building envelope. This credit is a part of and subject to the limitation of the general business credit (¶ 1323). The credit is claimed on Form 8908, Energy Efficient Home Credit.

1344I. Energy Efficient Appliance Credit. An income tax credit is available to manufacturers of energy-efficient home appliances for tax years after 2005 (Code Sec. 45M). The total amount of credit available for a tax year is equal to the sum of the credit amount separately calculated for each type of qualified energy-efficient appliance (dishwashers, clothes washers and refrigerators) produced by the taxpayer during the calendar year ending with or within that tax year. The credit amount for each type of qualified appliance is determined by multiplying the eligible production for that type of appliance by the type's applicable amount. The total amount of the credit that may be claimed by a home appliance manufacturer is $75 million. In addition, there are sublimits within that $75 million for each type of home appliance. This credit is a part of and subject to the limitation under the general business credit (¶ 1323).

1344J. Clean Renewable Energy Bond Credit. Effective for tax years beginning after 2005 and before 2009, a taxpayer holding a clean renewable energy bond (CREB) on one or more credit allowance dates may claim an annual income tax credit in lieu of any periodic interest payments from the issuer (Code Sec. 54). The credit accrues quarterly (reported on Form 1099-INT) and is generally equal to 25 percent of the annual credit for the bond, though a pro rata reduction applies for the quarters in which the bond is issued, redeemed or matures. The annual credit is equal to the face amount of the bond multiplied by a credit rate determined by the IRS. The credit rate is the rate that the IRS estimates will allow the issuance of bonds with a specified maturity without discount and without interest cost to the issuer. The credit is calculated on Form 8912, Credit for Clean Renewable Energy and Gulf Tax Credit Bonds. However, the amount of the credit allowed to the taxpayer must be included in gross income and treated as

---

Footnote references are to paragraphs of the 2008 Standard Federal Tax Reports.

[42] ¶ 4151.01

interest income. For this purpose, CREBs are bonds that generally allow non-profit electricity providers, including cooperatives and government-owned utilities, to compete more evenly with for-profit companies. The issuer must designate the bond as a CREB but only if it applied for and received a CREB allocation from the IRS.

1344K. Distilled Spirits Excise Tax Carrying Credit. An income tax credit is available for wholesalers, qualified distillers and importers that carry distilled spirits subject to excise taxes in inventory for tax years beginning after September 30, 2005 (Code Sec. 5011). The credit amount is calculated to generally equal the approximate interest charges that the eligible taxpayer would incur while holding the distilled spirits in inventory. This credit is a part of and subject to the limitations of the general business credit (¶ 1323). The credit is claimed on Form 8906, Distilled Spirits Credit.

1344L. Mine Rescue Team Training Credit. Eligible employers are entitled to a credit for mine rescue team training expenses incurred in tax years beginning after December 21, 2005, but before January 1, 2009. The credit amount is equal to the lesser of (1) 20 percent of the training program costs paid or incurred during the tax year for each qualified mine rescue team employee, including wages paid while attending the training program, or (2) $10,000 (Code Sec. 45N). An eligible employer is any taxpayer that employs individuals as miners in underground mines located in the United States. A qualified mine rescue team employee is a full-time miner employee who is eligible for more than six months of the tax year to serve as a mine rescue team member because he or she has either: (1) completed at minimum an initial 20 hour instruction course as approved by the Mine Safety and Health Administration's Office of Education Policy and Development; or (2) received at least 40 hours of refresher training. Wages are defined as all compensation including noncash benefits under Code Sec. 3306(b) but without regard to any dollar limitation stated therein. To prevent any double benefits that may arise from the claiming of this credit, Code Sec. 280C is amended to disallow a wage deduction equal to the amount of credit claimed for the tax year. The mine rescue team training credit is claimed on Form 8923, Mine Rescue Team Training Credit, and is a component of and subject to the limitation and carryover rules of the general business credit (¶ 1323).

Investment Credit

1345. Investment Credit Components. Taxpayers may claim an investment credit which is the sum of the rehabilitation credit (¶ 1347), the energy credit (¶ 1351), the qualified advanced coal project credit (¶ 1354), and the qualified gasification project credit (¶ 1355) (Code Sec. 46).[43] The investment credit is claimed on Form 3468, Investment Credit, and is one of the components of the general business credit, subject to the limitation and the carryover rules discussed at ¶ 1323.

The amount of investment credit allowed on investment credit property of a partnership for a tax year is generally apportioned among partners according to the ratio in which the partners divide the general profits of the partnership. The investment credit amount on a S corporation's investment credit property for a tax year is apportioned among the shareholders on a daily basis according to each shareholder's proportion of ownership. The investment credit amount allowed on investment credit property of an estate or trust is apportioned between the estate or trust and the beneficiaries on the basis of the income allocable to each.

1347. Rehabilitation Credit. As part of the investment credit (see ¶ 1345), the rehabilitation investment credit is 20 percent of qualified rehabilitation expenses (QRE) for certified historic structures and 10 percent of QRE for qualified rehabilitated buildings (QRB) first placed in service before 1936 (other than certified historic structures) (Code Sec. 47).[44] An election may also be made to claim an advance rehabilitation investment credit (¶ 1349). No energy credit (¶ 1351) is allowed on that portion of the basis of property that is attributable to QRE (Code Sec. 48(a)(2)(B)). Certain restrictions apply to property which is used as lodging (Code Sec. 50(b)).

A building and its structural components constitute a QRB if they are substantially rehabilitated for the tax year and placed in service by any person before the beginning of

---

Footnote references are to paragraphs of the 2008 Standard Federal Tax Reports.

[43] ¶ 4502   [44] ¶ 4600

¶1344K

the rehabilitation. Property other than a certified historic structure must also satisfy: (1) the applicable wall retention test, (2) an age requirement, and (3) a location-of-rehabilitation requirement (Code Sec. 47(c)(1); Reg. § 1.48-12(b)).[45] Property is considered substantially rehabilitated only if the expenditures during an elected 24-month measurement period (60-month period for phased rehabilitations) ending with or within the tax year are greater then the adjusted basis of the property or $5,000.

QRE does not include: an enlargement or new construction; the cost of acquisition; noncertified rehabilitation of a certified historic structure; rehabilitation of tax-exempt use property; expenditures, generally, that are not depreciated under the MACRS straight-line method over specified recovery periods; and a lessee-incurred expenditure if, on the date the rehabilitation of the building is completed, the remaining term of the lease (determined without regard to renewal periods) is less than the applicable recovery period (Reg. § 1.48-12(c)).

Generally, the rehabilitation investment credit for QRE must be claimed in the tax year in which the property attributable to the expenditures is placed in service, provided that the building is a QRB for such tax year (Code Sec. 47(b)). However, the credit may be claimed before the date the property is placed in service under the rules for qualified progress expenditures (Code Sec. 47(d)).

Buildings in the Gulf Opportunity Zone. The rehabilitation tax credit percentage is increased for certified historic structures or qualified rehabilitated buildings in the Gulf Opportunity (GO) Zone. The tax credit percentage is increased from 20 to 26 percent for any certified historic structure and from 10 to 13 percent for qualified rehabilitated buildings provided the structure or building is located in the GO Zone. The increased credit is applicable to qualified rehabilitation expenditures that are paid or incurred on or after August 28, 2005, and before January 1, 2009 (Code Sec. 1400N(h)).

1349. Advance Credits for Progress Expenditures. An election may be made to claim an advance rehabilitation investment credit (¶ 1347) for progress expenditures on certain rehabilitated buildings before such property is placed in service (Code Sec. 47(d)).[46] Property qualifying for an advance rehabilitation investment credit on progress expenditures includes a building that is being rehabilitated by or for the taxpayer if the normal rehabilitation period for the building is two or more years and it is reasonable to expect that the building will be a qualified rehabilitated building when it is placed in service.

The amount of qualified rehabilitation expenses (QRE) that are considered progress expenditures for which an advance rehabilitation investment credit may be claimed is the amount of QRE properly chargeable to the capital account for self-rehabilitated buildings. For non-self-rehabilitated buildings, the amount is the lesser of: (a) the QRE paid to another person for the rehabilitation of the building during the tax year or (b) the portion of the overall cost of the rehabilitation completed during the tax year.

1351. Energy Credit. As part of the investment credit (see ¶ 1345) the business energy investment credit is generally equal to 10 percent of the taxpayer's basis in qualified energy property placed in service during the tax year. However, effective for property placed in service before 2009, the credit percentage is increased to 30 percent for (1) qualified fuel cell property, (2) equipment that uses solar energy to generate electricity to heat or cool a structure, or provide solar process heat (except used to heat a swimming pool), and (3) equipment that uses solar energy to illuminate the inside of a structure using fiber-optic distributed sunlight. To qualify for the credit, the energy property must be depreciable (or amortizable) and must meet performance and quality standards prescribed by IRS regulations. In addition, the taxpayer must complete the construction, reconstruction or erection of the property or, if the property is acquired, the taxpayer must be the first person to use it. The basis of all energy property prior to the credit determination is reduced by any tax-exempt or subsidized financing (Code Sec. 48).[47] No energy credit is allowed for that portion of the basis of property for which a rehabilitation investment credit (¶ 1347) is claimed. An advance energy investment credit may be claimed under special rules for progress expenditures.

Footnote references are to paragraphs of the 2008 Standard Federal Tax Reports.

[45] ¶ 4600, ¶ 4609   [46] ¶ 4600   [47] ¶ 4651

Energy property that qualifies for the ten percent energy percentage includes equipment that produces, distributes, or uses energy derived from geothermal deposits (but only, in the case of electricity generated by geothermal power, up to the electrical transmission stage). Effective for property placed in service before 2009, it also includes qualified microturbine property which is a stationary microturbine power plant with a nameplate capacity of less than 2,000 kilowatts and an electricity-only generation efficiency of not less than 26 percent at International Standard Organization conditions. Qualified microturbine property is subject to an additional limitation in that the credit amount cannot exceed $200 for each kilowatt of capacity in a tax year. Effective for property placed in service before 2009, qualified fuel cell property that qualifies for the 30 percent energy percentage is a fuel cell power plant with a nameplate capacity of at least 0.5 kilowatt of electricity using an electrochemical process and has an electricity-only generation efficiency greater than thirty percent. Such property is also subject to an additional limitation in that the credit amount cannot exceed $500 for each 0.5 kilowatt of capacity.

1354. Advanced Clean Coal Project Credit. Effective for periods after August 8, 2005, a qualifying advanced coal project credit has been added to the investment credit provisions (see ¶ 1345) (Code Sec. 46(3)). The credit is available only to taxpayers who have applied for and received certification that their project satisfies the relevant requirements outlined by the IRS, in consultation with the Secretary of Energy. Up to $1.3 billion in credits will be allocated among taxpayers whose applications for certification are approved. The IRS is authorized to allocate a maximum of $800 million in credits for integrated gasification combined cycle (IGCC) projects and a maximum of $500 million in credits for projects using other advanced coal-based generation technologies. The amount of the qualifying advanced coal project credit for a tax year is: (1) 20 percent of the qualified investment for the tax year for IGCC projects certified by the IRS and (2) 15 percent of the qualified investment for the tax year for projects using other technologies.

1355. Gasification Project Credit. Effective for periods after August 8, 2005, a qualifying gasification project credit has been added to the investment credit provisions (see ¶ 1345) (Code Sec. 48B). This credit is an extension of the clean coal project credit and was enacted to encourage investment in coal gasification facilities. A coal gasification facility is one that combines coal with steam under high pressure to create a synthetic gas or syngas. The credit amount per year is equal to 20 percent of the qualified investments for an eligible facility limited to a maximum credit amount of $130 million. To claim the credit, a certification must be obtained from the IRS (in consultation with the Department of Energy) during the next ten fiscal years beginning after October 1, 2005.

1356. Investment Credit At-Risk Limitation. No investment credit is allowed for investment credit property to the extent that the property is financed with nonqualified nonrecourse borrowing (Code Sec. 49).[48] Thus, the credit base of investment credit property is reduced by the amount of nonqualified nonrecourse financing regarding the property as determined at the close of the tax year in which the property is placed in service. Decreases in nonqualified recourse financing on the property in tax years following the year in which the property was placed in service increase the credit base of the property. This rule does not apply if the decrease occurs through the surrender or other use of property financed by nonqualified nonrecourse financing. Similarly, increases in nonqualified nonrecourse financing on the property in tax years following the year in which the property was placed in service decrease the credit base of the property and trigger recapture.

The limitation applies to investment credit property placed in service by individuals and by certain closely held corporations engaged in business activities that are subject to the loss limitation rules of the at-risk rules (see ¶ 2045). For a partnership or S corporation, the investment credit at-risk limitation applies at the partner or shareholder level.

Footnote references are to paragraphs of the 2008 Standard Federal Tax Reports.

[48] ¶ 4750

The investment credit at-risk limitation does not apply to certain energy property. To come within this exception, nonqualified nonrecourse financing may not exceed 75 percent of the basis of energy property at the close of the tax year in which the property is placed in service. In addition, any nonqualified nonrecourse financing for such property must be a level payment loan (a loan repaid in substantially equal installments, including both principal and interest).

An increase in the amount at risk is treated as if it occurred in the year that the property was first placed in service for purposes of computing the investment credit and for computing any recapture of such credit. However, the investment credit attributable to the increase in the amount at risk is claimed by the taxpayer during the tax year in which the decrease in the amount of nonqualified nonrecourse financing occurs.

If at the close of a tax year there is a net increase in the amount of nonqualified nonrecourse financing regarding such property, thereby causing a decrease in the taxpayer's amount at risk, the investment credit must be recomputed and the decrease in investment credits for previous tax years is recaptured as additional tax in the year that the net increase in nonqualified nonrecourse financing occurs.

1358. Ineligible Property. No investment credit is allowed for the following types of property (Code Sec. 50(b)):[49] (1) property used predominantly outside the United States is subject to limited exceptions; (2) property used predominantly to furnish lodging (or in connection with the furnishing of lodging) is ineligible except in the case of nonlodging commercial facilities, a hotel or motel furnishing accommodations predominantly to transients, certified historic structures to the extent of that portion of the basis attributable to qualified rehabilitation expenditures, and energy property; and (3) property used by a tax-exempt organization (other than a farmers' cooperative) is ineligible unless it is used predominantly in an unrelated trade or business. Generally, property used by, or leased to, a governmental unit, foreign person, or foreign entity is not eligible for the investment credit. However, the portion of the property attributable to qualified rehabilitation expenditures or held under a short-term lease (generally under six months) does qualify for the investment credit.

1360. Basis Reduction. The basis of property for which an investment credit is claimed is reduced by the full amount of the credit except for the energy credit property whose basis is reduced by 50 percent of the credit amount (¶ 1351) (Code Sec. 50(c)).[50] The reduced basis is used to compute depreciation and any gain or loss on the disposition of property.

If the investment credit is recaptured on property for which an investment credit downward basis adjustment was made, the basis of the property immediately before the event resulting in recapture must be increased by the recapture amount (see ¶ 1364) and by 50 percent of the recapture amount for an energy credit. In determining the amount of gain that is recaptured as ordinary income on a sale or disposition of depreciable personal property (Code Sec. 1245) or depreciable realty (Code Sec. 1250), the amount of the investment credit downward basis adjustment is treated as a deduction allowed for depreciation. Thus, the basis adjustment is treated as depreciation subject to ordinary income recapture. For Code Sec. 1250 property, the recapture applies only to the excess of depreciation claimed, over depreciation computed under the straight-line method, with the latter computed on the basis without reduction for the applicable investment credit downward basis adjustment.

If an investment credit for which a downward basis adjustment was made does not result in a tax benefit because it remains unused at the end of the 20-year credit carryover period for tax years after December 31, 1997 (15-year general business credit carryover period for tax years prior to January 1, 1998), a deduction is allowed under Code Sec. 196 to the taxpayer for 50 percent of the unused energy and 100 percent of any other unused investment credit attributable to the basis reduction.

1362. Special Investment Credit Rules. Special limitations apply to the amount of investment credit that may be claimed by mutual funds (regulated investment companies), real estate investment trusts, noncorporate lessors, and certain other regulated companies (Code Sec. 50).[51]

Footnote references are to paragraphs of the 2008 Standard Federal Tax Reports.

[49] ¶ 4752   [50] ¶ 4752   [51] ¶ 4752

¶1362

1364. Early Disposition. When investment credit property is disposed of (including dispositions due to casualties or thefts), or ceases to be investment credit property before the end of its recapture period, the tax for the year of disposal or cessation is increased by the amount of the credit that is recaptured (Code Sec. 50).[52]

The amount of the recapture is a percentage of the original credit claimed, depending on how long the property is held before recapture is required. The recapture percentages are 100 percent within the first full year after placement in service, 80 percent within the second full year, 60 percent within the third full year, 40 percent within the fourth full year, 20 percent within the fifth full year, and zero thereafter. Advance rehabilitation or energy credits on progress expenditures are also subject to recapture. For investment credit at-risk recapture, see ¶ 1356. Special recapture rules apply to certain energy property.

The recapture rules do not apply to the following transfers: (1) a transfer between spouses or incident to divorce (¶ 778) (but a later disposition by the transferee will result in recapture to the same extent as if the disposition had been made by the transferor at that later date), (2) a transfer because of death, and (3) a transfer to which Code Sec. 381(a) (relating carryovers in corporate acquisitions) applies. Similarly, the recapture rules do not apply where there is a mere change in the form of operating a business, provided that the property is retained in the business and the taxpayer retains a substantial interest in the business.

Credit for Prior Year Minimum Tax

1370. Credit Against Regular Tax for Prior Year Minimum Tax Liability. Taxpayers are permitted a tax credit against their regular income tax liability for some or all of alternative minimum tax (AMT) paid in previous years. The credit is allowed for the amount of "adjusted net minimum tax" for all tax years reduced by the minimum tax credit for all prior tax years (Code Sec. 53).[53] The credit may be carried forward indefinitely as a credit against regular tax liability. However, it is limited to the extent that the regular tax liability reduced by other nonrefundable credits exceeds the tentative minimum tax for the tax year. The credit may also not be used to offset any future AMT liability. The credit is claimed on Form 8801, Credit for Prior Year Minimum Tax—Individuals, Estates and Trusts.

The adjusted net minimum tax is the net minimum tax reduced by the amount that would have been the net minimum tax if only certain specified preferences and adjustments had been taken into account (Code Sec. 53(d)(1)). The adjustments are those described in Code Sec. 56(b)(1),[54] including the standard deduction, personal exemptions, medical and dental expenses, miscellaneous itemized deductions, taxes, and interest expenses. The exclusion-type preference items are certain depletion deductions exceeding adjusted basis, tax-exempt interest on specified private activity bonds, and one-half of the exclusion for gains on the sale of certain small business stock issued after August 10, 1993. Adjusted net minimum tax is increased by the amount of the credit for qualified electric vehicles (¶ 1321) that is not allowed for a tax year because of the limitation based on a taxpayer's tentative minimum tax (Code Sec. 53(d)).

In determining corporate credits for prior year minimum tax liability, adjusted net minimum tax is the sum of: (a) the corporate net minimum tax liability (including such tax attributable to corporate exclusion preferences) and (b) the credit for electric vehicles producing fuels from nonconventional sources that is not allowed because of the limitation based on a taxpayer's tentative minimum tax (Code Sec. 53(d)(1)(B)(iv)).

1370A. Refundable Long-Term Unused Minimum Tax Credit. Individuals with long-term unused minimum tax credit for any tax year after December 20, 2006, but before January 1, 2013, are allowed to claim an amount not less than the AMT refundable credit amount for that tax year regardless of the minimum tax credit otherwise allowed to the taxpayer (Code Sec. 53(e), as added by the Tax Relief and Health Care Act of 2006 (P.L. 109-432)). The AMT refundable credit amount is the greater of: (1) the lesser of $5,000 or the taxpayer's long-term unused minimum tax credit for the tax year; or (2) 20 percent of such credit. The long-term unused minimum

---

Footnote references are to paragraphs of the 2008 Standard Federal Tax Reports.

[52] ¶ 4752   [53] ¶ 5002   [54] ¶ 5200

¶1364

tax credit for a tax year is the portion of the minimum tax credit attributable to the adjusted net minimum tax for tax years before the third tax year immediately preceding such tax year. The credits are treated as allowed on a first-in, first-out basis. The AMT refundable credit amount is phased out at the income levels applicable to the phase out of the personal exemption deduction. The credit amount is reduced by two percent for every $2,500 or part thereof by which the modified adjust gross income of the individual exceeds the appropriate phase out threshold amount. Modified adjusted gross income (MAGI) is adjusted gross income (AGI) determined with taking into account the exclusions from gross income for foreign earned income, foreign housing expenses, and income of residents of U.S. possessions. The credit is also claimed on Form 8801, Credit for Prior Year Minimum Tax—Individuals, Estates and Trusts.

Limitations on Nonrefundable Credits

1371. Credit Limits. In addition to the limitations imposed on each credit, the aggregate amount of the nonrefundable personal credits, other than the adoption, child tax and retirement savings contributions credits, cannot exceed the excess, if any, of the regular tax liability over the tentative alternative minimum tax (AMT) liability determined without regard to the AMT foreign tax credit (Code Sec. 26).[55] Because of this limitation, it is important to note the order in which the nonrefundable personal credits are claimed since certain credits may be carried forward to future years while other credits are lost if not used in the current year. The nonrefundable credits are claimed in the following order: (1) child and dependent care credit (¶ 1301), (2) credit for the elderly or the permanently and totally disabled (¶ 1304), (3) educational credits (¶ 1303), (4) residential energy credits (¶ 1313 and ¶ 1314), and (5) foreign tax credit.

Credit for Taxes Withheld

1372. Credit for Taxes Withheld on Wages. A taxpayer is allowed a credit against income tax liability for income taxes withheld from his or her salary or wages (Code Sec. 31).[56] A taxpayer is also allowed a "special refund" of any Social Security taxes which were over withheld from his or her wages. Excess Social Security taxes may be withheld where an individual works for more than one employer during the year and, in total, earns more than the Social Security wage base of $97,500 in 2007. The maximum amount of Social Security taxes that may be withheld is 6.2 percent of the wage base. The same rule applies to excess withheld railroad retirement taxes. However, since there is no wage base for calculating Medicare taxes, there can be no over withholding of such taxes. The "special refund" for over withheld Social Security taxes may be claimed as a credit on Form 1040. However, if the individual is not required to file an income tax return, he or she may file a "special refund" claim (Reg. § 31.6413(c)-1).[57] A nonresident alien (or foreign corporation) is allowed a credit against income tax liability for taxes withheld on U.S. source income that is not effectively connected with a U.S. trade or business. For a discussion on the withholding of tax on payments other than wages to nonresident aliens, see ¶ 2447 (Code Sec. 33).[58]

Earned Income Credit

1375. Earned Income Credit. A refundable earned income credit is available to certain low-income individuals who have earned income, meet adjusted gross income (AGI) thresholds, do not have more than a certain amount of disqualified income, have no foreign income, have a valid Social Security number, use a filing status other than married filing separately, and are U.S. citizens or resident aliens (Code Sec. 32).[59] Taxpayers, to be eligible to claim the earned income tax credit, must have earned income with an adjusted gross income below a certain level, a valid Social Security number, use a filing status other than married filing separately, must be a U.S. citizen or resident alien, have no foreign income, and investment income less than a certain amount. The amount of credit varies depending on the number of the taxpayer's qualifying children.

Amount of Credit. The credit amount is determined by multiplying an individual's earned income that does not exceed a maximum amount (called the earned income

---

Footnote references are to paragraphs of the 2008 Standard Federal Tax Reports.

[55] ¶ 3850
[56] ¶ 4060
[57] ¶ 38,754
[58] ¶ 4100
[59] ¶ 4080

amount) by the applicable credit percentage. The maximum earned income amount for taxpayers with one qualifying child is $8,390 for 2007 (to increase to $8,580 in 2008), with two or more qualifying children is $11,790 for 2007 (to increase to $12,060 in 2008), and with no qualifying child is $5,590 for 2007 (to increase to $5,720 in 2008). The credit is reduced by a limitation amount determined by multiplying the applicable phaseout percentage by the excess of the amount of the individual's adjusted gross income (or earned income, if greater) over a phaseout amount. The earned income amount and the phaseout amount are adjusted yearly for inflation. The amount of allowable credit is determined through the use of the tables that appear at ¶ 87.

Credit percentages and phaseout percentages limit the maximum amount of credit that may be claimed. The maximum earned income credit for 2007 with one qualifying child is $2,853, with two or more qualifying children is $4,716, and with no qualifying children is $428 (Rev. Proc. 2006-53). The maximum earned income credit in 2008 with one qualifying child will increase to $2,917, with two or more qualifying children will increase to $4,824, and with no qualifying children will increase to $438.

For 2007, the earned income credit begins to phase out for taxpayers whose filing status is single, surviving spouse or head or household with one qualifying child at $15,390, with two or more qualifying children at $15,390, and with no qualifying child at $7,000. The credit for these taxpayers is completely phased out with one qualifying child at $33,241, with two or more qualifying children at $37,783, and with no qualifying children at $12,590. In 2008, the phaseout for these taxpayers will increase to $15,740 with one qualifying child, $15,740 with two or more qualifying children, and $7,160 with no qualifying children. The credit phases out completely in 2008 at $33,995, $38,646 and $12,880, respectively.

The threshold amount at which the phaseout of the earned income credit begins for taxpayers whose filing status is married, filing jointly increases by $2,000 for tax years 2005 through 2007 and by $3,000 for tax years 2008 and thereafter. Thus, the phaseout of the earned income credit for taxpayers whose filing status is married, filing jointly for 2007 with one qualifying child begins at $17,390, with two or more qualifying children at $17,390, and with no qualifying children at $9,000. The phaseout is complete at $35,241, $39,783 and $14,590, respectively (Code Sec. 32(b); Rev. Proc. 2006-53). In 2008, the phaseout will begin for married taxpayers filing jointly at $18,740 for one qualifying child, $18,740 for two or more qualifying children and $10,160 for no qualifying children and completely phased out at $36,995, $41,646 and $15,880, respectively.

Earned Income. The credit is based on earned income, which includes all wages, salaries, tips, and other employee compensation (including union strike benefits), plus the amount of the taxpayer's net earnings from self-employment (determined with regard to the deduction for one-half of self-employment taxes (see ¶ 923)). Earned income is determined without regard to community property laws (Code Sec. 32(c)(2)). Earned income does not include: (1) interest and dividends; (2) welfare benefits (including AFDC payments); (3) veterans' benefits; (4) pensions or annuities; (5) alimony; (6) Social Security benefits; (7) workers' compensation; (8) unemployment compensation; (9) taxable scholarships or fellowships that are not reported on Form W-2; (10) amounts that are subject to Code Sec. 871(a) (relating to income of nonresident alien individuals not connected with U.S. business); (11) amounts received for services performed by prison inmates while in prison; or (12) payments received from work activities (including work associated with the refurbishing of public housing) if sufficient private sector employment is not available and from community service programs (Sections 407(d)(4) and (7) of the Social Security Act). Effective for tax years 2004 through 2007, a taxpayer may also elect to treat combat pay that is otherwise excluded from gross income (see ¶ 895) as earned income for purposes of the earned income credit (Code Sec. 32(c)(2)(B)(vi)). The election applies to all excludable combat pay received by the taxpayer.

Modified Adjusted Gross Income. The calculation to determine the modified adjusted gross income for earned income tax purposes has been repealed. The earned income credit calculation is based on the taxpayer's adjusted gross income (Code Sec. 2(a)(2)(B) and (c)(2)).

Qualifying Child. The earned income credit has adopted the uniform definition of a qualifying child (see ¶ 137A). For the purposes of a claiming the earned income credit, a qualifying child is defined in Code Sec. 152(c) without regard to the support test (Code

¶1375

Sec. 32(c)(3)). A qualifying child must meet the relationship, residency, and age test with the following modifications. For the residency test, the child must have the same principal place of abode as the taxpayer for more than one-half of the tax year and the abode must be located within the United States. Also, a qualifying child for the earned income credit does not include a child who is married unless the taxpayer is entitled to claim an exemption for them. Additionally, the taxpayer claiming the qualifying child must include the name, age and taxpayer identification number of the qualifying on the return. Finally, the rules for determining among several taxpayers who may claim a child as a qualifying child for purposes of the earned income credit are the same as for who may claim a qualifying child for the dependency exemption (see ¶ 137).

No Qualifying Child. An individual who does not have a qualifying child may be eligible for the credit if: (1) the principal residence of such individual is in the United States for more than one-half of the tax year, (2) the individual (or the spouse of the individual) is at least age 25 and under age 65 before the close of the tax year, and (3) the individual is not claimed as a dependent by another (Code Sec. 32(c)(1)(A)(ii)).

Disqualifying Income. The earned income credit may not be claimed by taxpayers whose investment income is in excess of $2,900 in 2007 (to increase to $2,950 in 2008) (Code Sec. 32(i); Rev. Proc. 2006-53). Disqualified income includes an individual's capital gain net income and net passive income in addition to interest, dividends, tax-exempt interest, and non-business rents or royalties. The credit may also not be claimed by taxpayers who are not eligible to work in the United States. For example, a nonresident alien usually cannot claim an earned income credit (Code Sec. 32(c)(1)(E)). Also, a person who claims a foreign earned income exclusion cannot claim an earned income credit (Code Sec. 32(c)(1)(D)).

Advance Payments. The earned income credit is refundable to the extent that it reduces the tax below zero. An eligible taxpayer may elect to receive advance payment of the credit through his or her paychecks. Form W-5 is to be used by eligible employees in order to notify their employers that they choose to receive advance payments instead of waiting until they file their annual tax returns.

The amount of the earned income credit that may be received as an advance payment for individuals who have one or more qualifying children is limited to 60 percent of the maximum credit available to an individual with one qualifying child. The advance payment of the earned income credit is not available to an individual who does not have a qualifying child (Code Sec. 3507(b)).[60]

The advance payment is included on the taxpayer's Form W-2 and is shown on the return as part of the tax liability on Form 1040A and as an "other" tax due on Form 1040. The actual credit to which the taxpayer is entitled is treated as a payment. Any difference will be refunded to the taxpayer or has to be paid to the IRS by the taxpayer. Earned income credit payments due a taxpayer are subject to interception by the Treasury Department to reimburse a state for any unpaid child-support obligations that have been assigned to the state, the U.S. Supreme Court has ruled.[61]

Claiming the Credit. Taxpayers claiming the credit must provide their Social Security (or taxpayer identification) number and the Social Security (or taxpayer identification) numbers of their spouse and dependents, if any. Failure to provide all required Social Security numbers is treated as a mathematical error (Code Sec. 6213(g)(2)).[62] Married persons must file a joint return in order to claim the credit. However, a married person living apart from a spouse under circumstances described at ¶ 173 need not file a joint return to claim the credit. Taxpayers with one or more qualifying children should complete Schedule EIC for Forms 1040 or 1040A. Taxpayers with no qualifying children may use Form 1040EZ to determine whether they are eligible to claim the earned income credit. Credit amounts are determined by using the tables at ¶ 87. Finally, the credit may be claimed only for a full 12-month tax year, except in the case of death.

Footnote references are to paragraphs of the 2008 Standard Federal Tax Reports.

[60] ¶ 33,780   [61] ¶ 4082.38   [62] ¶ 37,545

Health Insurance Costs Credit

1377. Health Insurance Costs Credit. Individual taxpayers may claim a refundable tax credit tax years beginning after December 31, 2001, equal to 65 percent of the premiums paid for qualified health insurance costs for each eligible coverage month for themselves and qualified family members (Code Sec. 35).[63] Taxpayers will determine their eligibility and claim the credit by filing Form 8885, Health Insurance Credit for Eligible Recipients, along with Form 1040 and attaching copies of the required documentation.

Definitions. An eligible coverage month occurs when, on the first day of the month during the taxpayer's tax year, the taxpayer: (1) is an eligible individual; (2) is covered by a qualified health insurance plan on which the taxpayer paid the premiums; (3) has no other specified coverage; and (4) is not imprisoned by any federal, state or local authority (Code Sec. 35(b)).

Eligible individuals are: (1) eligible trade adjustment assistance (TAA) recipients; (2) eligible alternative TAA recipients as defined under Act Sec. 246 of the Trade Act of 1974 (P.L. 93-618), as amended by the Trade Act of 2002 (P.L. 107-210); and (3) eligible Pension Board Guaranty Corporation (PBGC) recipients (Code Sec. 35(c)). A qualifying family member of an eligible individual includes the taxpayer's spouse and any dependents to which the taxpayer is entitled to a dependency exemption (Code Sec. 35(d)). A spouse will not be considered a qualifying family member if the taxpayers are married at the end of the year, both are considered eligible individuals and each files a separate income tax return (Code Sec. 35(g)(5)). However, the rules for head of household will apply (Code Sec. 35(g)(6)). Dependents will be considered qualifying family members only for the custodial parent in the case of separated or divorced parents (Code Sec. 35(d)(2)). Both eligible TAA and alternative TAA recipients will be considered eligible individuals for the first month following the month the recipients cease to qualify for TAA or alternative TAA. Certification of groups of individuals for trade adjustment assistance benefit programs is set to terminate on September 30, 2007, and the benefits, including the health insurance costs credit, will be available only to individuals certified prior to the termination date.

Premiums paid by taxpayers for coverage under the following qualified health insurance plans are to be taken into account in determining the health insurance costs credit: (1) COBRA continuation; (2) state-based continuation coverage; (3) a qualified state high-risk pool; (4) health insurance programs offered to state employees; (5) health insurance programs equivalent to item (4); (6) an arrangement entered into by the state and a group health plan, an issuer of health insurance coverage, an administrator, or an employer; (7) a state arrangement with a private sector health care coverage purchasing pool; (8) a state-operated health plan that does not receive any federal funding; (9) a group health plan available through the employer of an eligible spouse; or (10) an individual health insurance policy not defined above, that was in effect for the entire 30 days prior to the taxpayer's separating from employment and that qualified the taxpayer as an eligible individual under the health insurance costs credit (Code Sec. 35(e)). Qualified health insurance does *not* include either a flexible spending or similar arrangement (see ¶ 861) or any insurance whose coverage is substantially for "excepted benefits" under Code Sec. 9832(c) (Code Sec. 35(e)(3)).

Insurance coverage that qualifies as "other specified coverage" includes: (1) any insurance which is considered to be for medical care under a health plan maintained by the employer of the taxpayer or the taxpayer's spouse and at least 50 percent of the cost is paid or incurred by the employer; (2) any insurance coverage under a cafeteria plan in which the premiums are paid or incurred by the employer in lieu of a right to receive cash benefits or other qualified benefits under a cafeteria plan; (3) participation in Medicare, Medicaid, or State Child Health Insurance Program (SCHIP), and (4) participation in a health benefits plan for federal employees and military personnel (Code Sec. 35(f)).

Footnote references are to paragraphs of the 2008 Standard Federal Tax Reports.

[63] ¶ 4170

Coordination with Other Provisions. Amounts taken into account for the determination of the health insurance costs credit may not be used in computing either the health insurance costs for the self-employed deduction (see ¶ 908) or the itemized deduction for medical/dental costs (¶ 1015–¶ 1019). Amounts received from Archer Medical Saving Accounts (¶ 1020) or Health Saving Accounts (¶ 1020A) may not be used to compute the health insurance costs credit. Payment made for the benefit of a third party who is not a qualifying family member cannot be included in the amount of premiums paid for qualified health insurance in determining the credit (Code Sec. 35(g)(1), (2), and (3)).

Advanced Payments. The Secretary of the Treasury is required to establish a program that allows for the making of payments on behalf of eligible individuals toward their qualified health insurance costs in eligible months. The advanced payments cannot equal more than 65 percent of the anticipated health insurance costs of the eligible taxpayer. The aggregate amount of all advanced payments during the tax year reduces the health insurance costs credit amount dollar for dollar but not below zero (Code Secs. 35(g)(8)(A) and 7527).

Additional State Requirements. State health plans, (2) through (8) above, must make an election to be considered a qualified health insurance plan for the health insurance costs credit. In addition to the election, several additional requirements must be satisfied (Code Sec. 35(e)(2)).

Gasoline Tax Credit

1379. Credit for Federal Tax on Gasoline, Special Fuels. A credit for federal excise taxes on gasoline and special fuels may be taken where the fuel item is used for: (1) farming purposes; (2) nonhighway purposes of a trade or business; (3) operation of intercity, local, or school buses; and (4) certain nontaxable purposes (Code Sec. 34).[64] The above credits are computed on Form 4136, Credit for Federal Tax Paid on Fuels, which is attached to Form 1040 or Form 843, Claim for Refund.

Regulated Investment Company Credit

1384. Credit for Capital Gain Tax. Undistributed capital gain of a mutual fund (regulated investment company) must be included proportionately in the gross income of its shareholders. The capital gain tax that the company pays on this gain is treated as having been paid by the shareholders and is allowed as a credit against the tax (Code Sec. 852(b)(3)(D)(ii)).[65] In order to claim the credit, Copy B of Form 2439, Notice to Shareholders of Undistributed Long-Term Capital Gains, must be attached to the taxpayer's return (see ¶ 2305).

Footnote references are to paragraphs of the 2008 Standard Federal Tax Reports.

[64] ¶ 4150   [65] ¶ 26,433.022

Chapter 14
MINIMUM TAX

Calculating Alternative Minimum Tax

1401. The Minimum Tax Equation. The alternative minimum tax (AMT) is a separate method of determining income tax devised to ensure that at least a minimum amount of tax is paid by high-income corporate and individual taxpayers (including estates and trusts) who reap large tax savings by making use of certain tax deductions, exemptions, losses and credits. Without the AMT, some of these taxpayers might be able to escape income taxation entirely. In essence, the AMT functions as a recapture mechanism, reclaiming some of the tax breaks primarily available to high-income taxpayers, and represents an attempt to maintain tax equity.

Generally, all taxpayers subject to regular income tax are subject to the AMT as well, although small corporations are exempt. A taxpayer's AMT for a tax year is the excess of the tentative minimum tax over the regular tax liability. AMT must be paid in addition to the regular tax liability (Code Sec. 55(a))[1] (regular tax is discussed at ¶ 1420). Thus, if a taxpayer's tentative minimum tax for a tax year is $75,000 while his regular tax is $50,000, he must pay an AMT of $25,000 in addition to the $50,000 regular tax for a total tax of $75,000. Form 6251, Alternative Minimum Tax—Individuals, must be used by individuals to compute the AMT, while corporations must use Form 4626, Alternative Minimum Tax—Corporations. Estates and trusts must use Schedule I of Form 1041, U.S. Income Tax Return for Estates and Trusts.

To calculate the tentative minimum tax, the taxpayer must first determine alternative minimum taxable income (AMTI) and then subtract the AMTI exemption amount. The difference is then multiplied by the appropriate AMT rate. The product of this computation is the tentative minimum tax. The AMTI, as discussed below, is taxable income recomputed taking into account adjustments and preferences.

AMT is computed at rates of 26 and 28 percent. The 26-percent rate applies to the first $175,000 ($87,500, in the case of married individuals filing separately) of AMTI in excess of the applicable exemption amount and the 28-percent rate applies to any additional AMTI (¶ 1405). However, special rates apply to net long-term capital gain and qualified dividends. Any AMT foreign tax credit (¶ 1410) is subtracted, as are two specified energy credits, the alcohol fuels credit (Code Sec. 40) and the credit for electricity or refined coal (Code Sec. 45), to arrive at the tentative minimum tax (see ¶ 1415).

Net Capital Gain and Qualified Dividends. The maximum rate of AMT on net capital gain is limited (Code Sec. 55(b)(3)), as it is limited for regular tax purposes (Code Sec. 1(h)). The maximum rate on the adjusted net capital gain of an individual is 15 percent, and any adjusted net capital gain which would otherwise be taxed at a rate below 25 percent (i.e., the 10-percent and 15-percent brackets) is taxed at 5 percent. (Higher rates of 25 and 28 percent apply in some instances, as discussed below.) A rate of zero percent replaces the 5-percent rate beginning in 2008 (¶ 1736).

Footnote references are to paragraphs of the 2008 Standard Federal Tax Reports.

[1] ¶ 5100

¶1401

Mutual funds and other types of pass-through entities must determine the date when capital gain or loss is to be properly taken into account. The entity would then notify its shareholders or other distributees whether the distributions were determined under the reduced rates that went into effect after May 5, 2003 or under the former rates.

The adjusted net capital gain of an individual is the net capital gain reduced (but not below zero) by the sum of the unrecaptured section 1250 gain (¶ 1736) (which is taxed at a maximum rate of 25 percent) and the 28-percent rate gain. The net capital gain is reduced by the amount of gain that the individual treats as investment income for purposes of determining the investment interest limitation. The term "28-percent rate gain" means the amount of net gain attributable to long-term capital gains and losses from the sale or exchange of collectibles, the amount of gain excluded from gross income relating to certain small business stock (¶ 1425), the net short-term capital loss for the tax year, and any long-term capital loss carryover to the tax year.

From 2003 through 2008, qualified dividends are taxed at the net capital gains rates (Code Sec. 55(b)(3)(C)) (¶ 733). Under current sunset provisions (as extended by the Tax Increase Prevention and Reconciliation Act of 2005 (P.L. 109-222)), the 15-percent and five-percent reduced net capital gains rates and the treatment of qualified dividend income introduced under the Jobs and Growth Tax Relief Reconciliation Act of 2003 (P.L. 108-27) will expire at the end of 2010 and the previous net capital gains rates will again apply for regular tax and AMT purposes. The five-percent rate will be reduced to zero percent for tax years beginning in 2008, 2009, or 2010. Similarly, the special qualified five-year gain rates will be reinstated.

Small Corporations. For tax years beginning in 1998 or later, a corporation that meets certain gross receipts tests is considered to be a small corporation and, as a result, will not be subject to the alternative minimum tax (its tentative minimum tax is treated as zero) as long as it remains a small corporation (Code Sec. 55(e)).[2] For a corporation to qualify as an exempt small corporation, its average gross receipts must not exceed $7,500,000 for all three-tax-year periods prior to the year for which qualification is sought. However, this amount is reduced to $5,000,000 for the first three-year-period following 1993 (or portion of that period, if the corporation has not been in existence for that long) that is taken into account for this purpose. Once a corporation qualifies as a small corporation, it will continue to be exempt from the AMT for so long as its average annual gross receipts for the prior three-year period does not exceed $7,500,000. If the corporation was in existence for less than three years at the time it seeks to qualify for the exemption, then the gross receipts test is applied based on the period during which it has existed.

A new corporation is treated as having a tentative minimum tax of zero and thus is not subject to the AMT for the first tax year that the corporation is in existence (regardless of its gross receipts for the year). The allowable credit against the regular tax for prior year minimum tax liability (¶ 1370) of a small corporation is limited to the amount by which the corporation's regular tax liability (reduced by other credits) exceeds 25 percent of the excess (if any) of the corporation's regular tax (reduced by other credits) over $25,000. If a corporation ceases to be a small corporation, it cannot qualify as such for any subsequent tax year and the AMT will apply only prospectively. In applying the small corporation exemption, any reference to the corporation includes its predecessors.

> **Example:** XYZ corporation came into existence in 2006 and is neither aggre-
> gated with a related, existing corporation nor treated as having a predecessor
> corporation. It will qualify as a small corporation for its first year of existence, 2006,
> regardless of its gross receipts for that year. In order to qualify as a small
> corporation for 2007, XYZ's gross receipts for 2006 must be $5 million or less. If
> XYZ qualifies for 2007, it will also qualify for 2008 if its average gross receipts for
> the two-taxable-year period including 2006 and 2007 is $7.5 million or less. If XYZ
> does not qualify for 2007, it cannot qualify for 2008 or any subsequent year. If XYZ
> qualifies for 2008, it will qualify for 2009 if its average gross receipts for the three-
> taxable-year period including 2006, 2007, and 2008 is $7.5 million or less.

Footnote references are to paragraphs of the 2008 Standard Federal Tax Reports.

[2] ¶ 5100

Other Corporations. In the case of other corporations, the tentative minimum tax for the tax year is 20 percent of the excess of the alternative minimum taxable income over the AMTI exemption amount, reduced by the alternative minimum tax foreign tax credit.

Alternative Minimum Taxable Income. AMTI is the heart of minimum taxation. It is through this figure that excessive tax savings are recaptured. The base for computing AMTI is regular taxable income (including unrelated business taxable income, real estate investment trust taxable income, life insurance company taxable income, or any other income base, other than income allocated to the alcohol and biodiesel fuels credits, used to calculate regular tax liability). This amount is then increased by a body of tax items, known as tax preference items (TPIs), which are the ultimate target of the minimum tax recapture apparatus. These items make up only a portion of the Code's available tax benefits but have been identified as a potential source of inordinate tax savings.

There are two ways in which TPIs are used to compute AMTI. In the first approach, all or a portion of the deductions or exclusions that have been claimed in computing regular taxation are directly added back to the regular taxable income base that makes up AMTI (Code Sec. 57).[3] For example, the excess of a depletion deduction for an interest in a mineral deposit over the adjusted basis of the interest must be added to the regular taxable income base (Code Sec. 57(a)(1)).[4] In the second form of recapture, the method used to compute a deduction for regular taxation is changed for minimum taxation (Code Secs. 56 and 58).[5] A change in methods will often, but not always, reduce the amount of a deduction originally claimed in regular taxation (or increase the amount of income originally subject to regular taxation) and thereby increase the taxable income base used in AMTI. For example, a corporation that uses the MACRS 200-percent declining balance method to compute a property's depreciation deduction for regular tax purposes may have to use the 150-percent declining balance method to compute AMTI (Code Sec. 56(a)(1)).[6] In the early years of that property's life, the regular tax MACRS deduction will exceed the deduction allowed for purposes of AMTI. For a given tax year, the excess of MACRS deductions over AMT deductions, if any, must be added back to the AMTI base. Tax preference items are discussed at ¶ 1425 and adjustments are covered at ¶ 1430–¶ 1440.

> **Example:** Jennifer, a single individual, has regular taxable income of $80,000 in 2007 and TPIs totaling $125,000. Her regular tax on the regular taxable income using tax rate schedules is $16,732. To compute her AMT, she must first establish her AMTI by adding the TPIs to regular taxable income ($205,000). Next, her tentative minimum tax must be computed by first subtracting her exemption amount of $19,375 (see ¶ 1405) from AMTI of $205,000 to arrive at the amount of $185,625. Since $185,625 exceeds $175,000, 28 percent of the $10,625 excess ($185,625 – $175,000), or $2,975, is added to 26 percent of $175,000, or $45,500, to arrive at a $48,475 tentative minimum tax from which any available alternative minimum tax foreign tax credit (AMT-FTC) is then subtracted. Assuming that there is no AMT-FTC, the $31,743 excess of the $48,475 tentative minimum tax over the $16,732 regular tax is the individual's AMT and must be paid in addition to her regular tax.

Minimum Tax on a Minor Child. A child under age 18 who is subject to the "kiddie tax" (¶ 114 and ¶ 706) will be subject to the alternative minimum tax. The child will compute a tentative minimum tax in the same manner as any individual taxpayer. However, the AMT exemption amount for the child will be the sum of the child's *earned income,* plus $6,300 for 2007 (Code Sec. 59(j); Rev. Proc. 2006-53) ($6,400 for 2008 (Rev. Proc. 2007-66)).[7] The child's exemption amount, and their ultimate AMT liability, is not dependent upon the computation of the parent's alternative minimum taxable income or AMT exemption amount.

Footnote references are to paragraphs of the 2008 Standard Federal Tax Reports.

[3] ¶ 5300	[5] ¶ 5200, ¶ 5350	[7] ¶ 5400
[4] ¶ 5300	[6] ¶ 5200	

Exemption Amount

1405. Amount Excluded from Minimum Taxation. A specified amount of AMTI is exempt from alternative minimum taxation (Code Sec. 55(d)).[8] The amount varies according to the taxpayer's filing status and the tax year at hand.

Absent Congressional action, for the 2007 tax year the AMT exemption amounts will revert to pre-2001 levels. These exemption amounts are $45,000 for married individuals filing a joint return and surviving spouses; $33,750 for a single individual who is not a surviving spouse; and $22,500 for a married individual filing a separate return. The AMT exemption amount of an estate or trust (other than electing small business trusts) is $22,500 (Code Sec. 55(d)(1)).

For the 2006 tax year, the AMT exemption amount was $62,550 for married individuals filing a joint return and surviving spouses; $42,500 for a single individual who is not a surviving spouse; and $31,275 for a married individual filing a separate return. The AMT exemption amount of an estate or trust (other than electing small business trusts) was $22,500 (Code Sec. 55(d)(1)).

The AMT exemption amount of a corporation is $40,000 (Code Sec. 55(d)(2)). In the case of a controlled group of corporations (see ¶ 34, ¶ 289 and ¶ 291), the single $40,000 exemption is shared by all members of the group (Code Sec. 1561(a)(3)).

The AMTI exemption amount is zero in the case of the portion of an electing small business trust that is treated as a separate trust (Code Sec. 641(c)(2)(B)). The portion of an electing small business trust that is used to hold the stock of an S corporation is taxed as a separate trust (Code Sec. 641(c)(1)(A)).

The exemption amounts are phased out for taxpayers with high AMTI. The threshold at which the AMT exemption begins to phase out is set by statute, and has remained unchanged after legislative increases in the exemption amount in 2001 through 2006. The exemption amounts are still reduced by 25 cents for each $1 of AMTI in excess of (1) $150,000 for married individuals filing a joint return, surviving spouses, and corporations; (2) $112,500 for single individuals other than surviving spouses; and (3) $75,000 for married individuals filing a separate return and estates and trusts (Code Sec. 55(d)(3).

> **Example 1:** For tax year 2007, a single individual with AMTI of $150,000 may claim an exemption amount of only $24,375, rather than the full $33,750 available to individuals with AMTI of $112,500 or less. The exemption amount is determined by finding the excess of the individual's AMTI ($150,000) over $112,500, which is $37,500, multiplying the difference by 25% ($37,500 × .25 = $9,375), and subtracting the product from $33,750 ($33,750 − $9,375 = $24,375).

> **Example 2:** For tax year 2007, married individuals have a regular taxable income of $100,000 and tax preferences and adjustments totaling $40,000. Assume that the regular tax on $100,000 is $17,848. Their AMTI (regular taxable income plus tax preferences and adjustments) is $140,000 ($100,000 + $40,000). The AMTI is reduced by the applicable exemption amount of $45,000 and their tentative minimum tax is $24,700 ($95,000 × 26%). Thus, their AMT liability is $6,852 ($24,700 − $17,848).

Since, in the absence of Congressional action, the AMT exemption amount for individuals has decreased in the 2007 tax year and the phaseout triggers have remained the same, the maximum amount of AMTI that an individual taxpayer may have before the exemption amount is fully phased out has also decreased. For married taxpayers filing joint returns and surviving spouses, the decreased AMT exemption amount of $45,000 is completely phased out when AMTI reaches $330,000, down from $400,200. For single taxpayers, the exemption amount of $33,750 is completely phased out when AMTI reaches $247,500, down from $282,500. Similarly, for married taxpayers filing a separate return, the exemption amount of $22,500 is completely phased out when AMTI reaches $165,000, down from $200,100. For married individuals filing a separate return, the maximum exemption phaseout amount is, in effect, the same as the $45,000 maximum exemption phaseout amount for married individuals filing jointly. This is accomplished by not only phasing out the otherwise applicable $22,500 exemption, but

---

Footnote references are to paragraphs of the 2008 Standard Federal Tax Reports.

[8] ¶ 5100

also by increasing the AMTI of the married individual filing a separate return by the lesser of (1) the $22,500 married filing separately AMT exemption or (2) 25 percent of the excess of AMTI (as determined before this adjustment) over the $165,000 phaseout ceiling. Thus, the ceiling on the amount of AMTI that would subject a married filing separate taxpayer to the full $22,500 add-back and $22,500 exemption phaseout is $255,000, down from $325,200.

The $40,000 exemption amount of a corporate taxpayer is not completely phased out until AMTI reaches $310,000.

None of the above exemption or phaseout amounts is adjusted for inflation in the annual IRS revenue procedure. However, the statutorily provided exemption amounts are modified periodically by Congress (see the history of Code Sec. 55(d)(1), as amended by various tax acts since 2001).

Special Exemption Amounts for Certain Minor Children. The AMTI exemption amount of a minor child under age 18 is equal to the sum of the child's earned income plus $6,300 in 2007 (Code Sec. 59(j); Rev. Proc. 2006-53).

Credits Against Minimum Tax

1410. Alternative Minimum Tax Foreign Tax Credit. One tax credit that may be applied fully against the AMT is the alternative minimum tax foreign tax credit (AMT-FTC) (¶ 1401 and Code Sec. 59(a)(2). (Prior to 2005, this credit was limited to 90 percent of the tentative minimum tax.) For purposes of this tentative minimum tax computation, AMTI is determined without including the alternative tax net operating loss deduction or intangible drilling cost preference exception for independent producers (see ¶ 1425 and ¶ 1430) and is determined after subtracting the AMTI exemption amount (Code Secs. 55(b)(1) and 59(a)).[9] An excess AMT-FTC for a tax year may be carried back or forward under the same ordering scheme allowed for carrybacks or carryforwards of regular tax FTCs, namely, to the second preceding tax year, the first preceding tax year, and then to the first through fifth succeeding tax years (Code Sec. 59(a)(2)(B)). The AMT-FTC for a tax year is determined by calculating the amount of foreign taxes on foreign source AMTI and then finding the limit on the size of an FTC that may be claimed during a tax year, which is accomplished by multiplying the tentative minimum tax by the ratio of a taxpayer's foreign source AMTI to worldwide AMTI. Alternatively, the taxpayer may elect to compute the AMT-FTC limit by multiplying the tentative minimum tax by the ratio of the taxpayer's foreign source regular taxable income to worldwide AMTI.

1415. Other Credits. In addition to the AMT foreign tax credit, four other specified credits, the alcohol fuels credit (Code Sec. 40) (see ¶ 1326), the credit for electricity or refined coal (Code Sec. 45) (see ¶ 1339), the FICA employer tip credit (Code Sec. 45B) (see ¶ 1341), and the work opportunity credit (Code Sec. 51) (see ¶ 1342) are fully taken into account in computing the AMT (Code Sec. 38(c)(4), as amended by the Small Business and Work Opportunity Tax Act of 2007 (P.L. 110-28)).

Tax Liability Limitations. For taxpayers subject to AMT, the full benefit of other tax credits may be denied. For tax years beginning in 2000 through 2006, the nonrefundable personal credits could offset both the regular tax liability and the alternative minimum tax. Nonrefundable credits that were allowed in those years in computing the AMT included the dependent care credit (¶ 1301), the credit for home mortgage interest (¶ 1308), the credit for residential energy efficient property (¶ 1314), the retirement savings contributions credit (formerly known as the "savers' credit") (¶ 1307), the credit for certain nonbusiness energy property (¶ 1313), the education credits (¶ 1303), and the District of Columbia first-time homebuyer credit (¶ 1310) (see ¶ 1371 regarding limitations on nonrefundable credits). However, absent Congressional action, a more restrictive general limitation rule applies to the 2007 tax year. In 2007, nonrefundable personal tax credits, other than the adoption credit, the child tax credit, and the credit for qualified retirement savings contributions, will reduce an individual's regular tax liability only to the extent that the regular tax exceeds the taxpayer's tentative minimum tax liability (determined without regard to the foreign tax credit) (Code Sec. 26(a)).

Footnote references are to paragraphs of the 2008 Standard Federal Tax Reports.

[9] ¶ 5100, ¶ 5400

Regular Tax

1420. Regular Tax Compared with Tentative Minimum Tax. The tentative minimum tax is compared to a taxpayer's regular tax liability reduced by any foreign tax credit, Puerto Rico and possessions tax credit and Puerto Rico economic activity credit (Code Sec. 55(c)).[10] Among other taxes, the following are not included in the regular tax (Code Sec. 26(b)):

(1) accumulated earnings taxes (Code Sec. 531);

(2) personal holding company taxes (Code Sec. 541);

(3) alternative minimum taxes (Code Sec. 55);

(4) 30-percent withholding taxes against the investment income of nonresident aliens and foreign corporations (Code Secs. 871(a) and 881);

(5) foreign corporations' branch profits taxes (Code Sec. 884);

(6) taxes on built-in gains of S corporations (Code Sec. 1374);

(7) taxes on an S corporation's passive investment income (Code Sec. 1375);

(8) taxes on early distributions from retirement plans (Code Sec. 72(m)(5)(B), (q), (t), and (v));

(9) excise taxes on the transfer of residual interests in REMICs to "disqualified organizations" (Code Sec. 860E(e));

(10) taxes on foreign expropriation loss recoveries (Code Sec. 1351(d));

(11) taxes on nonqualified withdrawals from certain Merchant Marine capital construction funds (Code Sec. 7518(g)(6));

(12) taxes that arise out of the recapture of investment tax credits (Code Sec. 49(b) or Code Sec. 50(a)) or low-income housing credits (Code Sec. 42(j) and (k));

(13) taxes that arise out of the recapture of mortgage bond federal subsidies (Code Sec. 143(m));

(14) interest on tax liabilities deferred under the installment method (Code Sec. 453(l)(3) and Code Sec. 453A(c));

(15) the additional tax on medical savings account distributions not used for qualified medical expenses (Code Sec. 220(f)(4));

(16) the additional tax on certain distributions from Coverdell education savings accounts (Code Sec. 530(d)(3));

(17) the "tax" on certain transfers of high-yield interests to disqualified holders (Code Sec. 860K);

(18) the penalty imposed for distributions from Medicare Advantage medical savings accounts that were not used for qualified medical expenses (Code Sec. 138(c)(2));

(19) the additional tax on health savings account distributions not used for qualified medical expenses; and

(20) the additional tax under Code Sec. 409(a)(1)(B) on income from nonqualified deferred compensation plans.

Tax Preference Items

1425. TPIs Added Back to AMTI. Among the tax items that have been singled out as potential sources of extraordinary tax savings are tax preference items (TPIs) (Code Sec. 57).[11] Because these items are instrumental in generating tax savings by reducing a taxpayer's taxable income, they must be added back to the taxable income of either corporate or noncorporate taxpayers in computing AMTI so that unreasonably high tax breaks may be recaptured. The following is a complete list of TPIs:

(1) The amount by which the depletion deduction claimed by a taxpayer (other than an independent oil and gas producer) for an interest in a property exceeds the adjusted basis of the interest at the end of a tax year;

Footnote references are to paragraphs of the 2008 Standard Federal Tax Reports.

[10] ¶ 5100   [11] ¶ 5300

(2) The amount by which an integrated oil company's excess intangible drilling costs (i.e., the excess of the IDC deduction over the deduction that would have been allowed if the costs had been capitalized and ratably amortized over a 120-month period) is greater than 65 percent of the taxpayer's net income from oil, gas, and geothermal properties. Independent producers are not subject to this preference. Their AMTI, however, may not be reduced by more than 40 percent of the AMTI that would otherwise be determined if the taxpayer were subject to this intangible drilling cost preference and did not compute an alternative tax net operating loss deduction;

(3) Tax-exempt interest (less any related expenses) on specified private activity bonds, which generally are issued after August 7, 1986;

(4) For most property placed in service prior to 1987, the excess of accelerated depreciation on nonrecovery real property over straight-line depreciation;

(5) For most property placed in service by noncorporate taxpayers and personal holding companies prior to 1987, the excess of accelerated depreciation on leased personal property over straight-line depreciation;

(6) For most property placed in service prior to 1987, the excess of rapid amortization of pollution control facilities under Code Sec. 169 over the depreciation that would be allowed under Code Sec. 167;

(7) For most property placed in service by noncorporate taxpayers and personal holding companies prior to 1987, the excess of the ACRS deduction for leased recovery property (other than 19-year real property and low-income housing) over the straight-line depreciation deduction that would have been allowed if a half-year convention had been used, salvage value had been disregarded, and the following recovery periods had been used:

In the case of:	The recovery period is:
3-year property	5 years
5-year property	8 years
10-year property	15 years
15-year public utility property	22 years

(8) For most property placed in service prior to 1987, the excess of the ACRS deduction for 19-year real property or low-income housing over the deduction that would have been allowed if straight-line depreciation, with a 19-year recovery period for real property and a 15-year recovery period for low-income housing, had been used and computed without considering salvage value; and

(9) An amount equal to 7 percent of the amount excluded from gross income under Code Sec. 1202. Since that section allows exclusion of 50 percent of gross income, only 3.5 percent of the gross income realized by the sale or exchange of small business stock will be treated as a tax preference item (¶ 2396).

Adjustments to Selected Tax Items

1430. Adjustments Affecting Corporate and Noncorporate Taxpayers. In addition to TPIs, the AMT is aimed at recovering some of the tax savings generated by other deductions and methods for computing tax liability. This is achieved by requiring taxpayers to recompute certain regular tax deductions in a less preferential manner. Adjustments are usually required in order to eliminate "time value" tax savings that result from tax laws allowing the acceleration of deductions (e.g., the MACRS depreciation) or the deferral of income (e.g., the completed-contract method of determining income from long-term contracts). Thus, the recomputation for AMT purposes usually results in an increase to AMTI.

Some adjustments have to be made solely by noncorporate taxpayers (see ¶ 1435), while others have to be made solely by corporate taxpayers (see ¶ 1440). All taxpayers, whether corporate or noncorporate, must make the following adjustments when determining AMTI:

Depreciation. For property placed in service after 1998, if the 200-percent declining balance method is used for regular tax purposes for 3-, 5-, 7-, or 10-year property, then the 150-percent declining balance method and regular tax depreciation period must be

used for AMT purposes (Code Sec. 56(a)(1)).[12] For all other property placed in service after 1998, no AMT adjustment is required, as AMT and regular tax depreciation are identical.

For property placed in service after 1986 and before 1999, if the 200-percent declining balance method is used for regular tax purposes for 3-, 5-, 7-, or 10-year property, then the 150-percent declining balance method and the ADS recovery period must be used for AMT purposes (Code Sec. 56(a)(1), prior to amendment by P.L. 105-34). If the 150-percent declining balance method is used for 15-or 20-year property, then the 150-percent declining balance method and the ADS recovery period is used for AMT purposes. If the 150-percent declining balance method election is in effect for regular tax purposes for 3-, 5-, 7-, 10-, 15-, or 20-year property, then no adjustment is required for AMT purposes, as the AMT and regular tax depreciation are computed the same way (i.e., using the 150-percent declining balance method over the ADS recovery period). In the case of 27.5-year residential real property, or in the case of 31.5- or 39-year real property, AMT depreciation is computed using the straight-line method and ADS recovery period (40 years). If the straight-line election is in effect for regular tax purposes for 3-, 5-, 7-, 10-, 15-, or 20-year property, then for AMT purposes the straight-line method and ADS recovery period must be used. If the MACRS ADS method (elective or nonelective) is used for regular tax purposes, then no adjustment is required for AMT purposes, as AMT and regular tax depreciation are computed the same way on real and personal property subject to such method.

Adjusting MACRS depreciation deductions, rather than treating them as TPIs, may provide taxpayers with some major benefits as they compute AMTI in the later years of a property's use. Although MACRS deductions will exceed AMT deductions in the early years of a property's use (assuming that AMT and MACRS deductions are not computed in the same manner), the reverse will be true in the later years. Thus, the higher deductions produced under the applicable AMT method in later years may be used to reduce AMTI and, therefore, reduce the potential for alternative minimum taxation. Another benefit from the adjustment approach to depreciation is that depreciation for all property is combined in calculating AMTI, allowing for the netting of excess MACRS deductions with excess alternative deductions. Consequently, a taxpayer who has excess MACRS deductions on a new piece of property may be able to avoid paying an AMT on the excess deductions by offsetting them with excess alternative deductions generated by an older piece of property.

No AMT adjustments have to be made to the amount expensed under Code Sec. 179; motion pictures, video tapes, and public utility property for which the normalization method of accounting is not used; property which is depreciated under the units of production method or under a depreciation method which is not based on a term of years (other than the retirement-replacement-betterment method or similar method); or natural gas gathering lines placed in service after April 11, 2005 (Code Sec. 56(a)(1)(B)).

When property that generated depreciation deductions is sold, its adjusted basis must be computed under the AMT rules in order to determine the gain or loss from the sale for AMT purposes (Code Sec. 56(a)(7)).[13] The difference between the regular tax gain or loss and the recomputed AMT gain or loss is a tax preference adjustment in the year of sale.

> **Example 1:** A taxpayer has purchased a piece of property for $100,000 and, over several tax years, has claimed a total of $25,000 of depreciation deductions in regular tax calculations. In AMTI calculations made during the same tax years, he has claimed adjusted depreciation deductions totaling $10,000. He sells the property in the current tax year for $150,000. The adjusted basis of the property in regular tax calculations is $75,000 ($100,000 – $25,000), leaving him with a regular tax gain of $75,000 ($150,000 – $75,000). The AMT adjusted basis is $90,000 ($100,000 – $10,000). The amount of gain that must be included in his AMTI calculations is only $60,000 ($150,000 – $90,000).

Mining Exploration and Development Costs. Taxpayers who have expensed mining exploration and development expenditures (or amortized these costs under Code Sec. 291) in computing their regular tax must, in calculating AMTI, capitalize and amortize

---

Footnote references are to paragraphs of the 2008 Standard Federal Tax Reports.

[12] ¶ 5200   [13] ¶ 5200

these costs over a 10-year period, beginning with the tax year in which the expenditures were made (Code Sec. 56(a)(2)).[14] If a tax loss is incurred from a mine, all expenditures which have been capitalized but not yet amortized may be deducted from AMTI.

When property that generated mining exploration and development deductions is sold, its adjusted basis must be computed under the AMT rules in order to determine the gain or loss from the sale for AMT purposes (Code Sec. 56(a)(7)).[15] The difference between the regular tax gain or loss and the recomputed AMT gain or loss is a tax preference adjustment in the year of sale.

Long-Term Contracts. The percentage-of-completion method of accounting for gain or loss from long-term contracts (other than home construction contracts) must be substituted for any other accounting method, such as the completed contract method or the cash basis method, to determine AMTI for long-term contracts (Code Sec. 56(a)(3)).[16] The percentage of completion is determined using simplified cost allocation procedures in the case of construction contracts of certain small contractors if the contract has an estimated duration of less than two years (Code Secs. 56(a)(3) and 460(e)(1)(B)).

Alternative Tax Net Operating Loss Deduction. Net operating loss (NOL) deductions must be recomputed so that tax preferences (including TPIs and items that are subject to adjustment for AMTI) that make up an NOL are not a factor in reducing AMTI (Code Sec. 56(a)(4) and (d)).[17] A recomputed NOL, termed an alternative tax NOL, may not offset more than 90 percent of AMTI (computed without the alternative tax NOL deduction). The 90-percent limitation is increased to 100 percent for NOLs generated or taken as carryovers in tax years ending in 2001 or 2002 (Code Sec. 56(d)(1)(A)). An alternative tax NOL is computed in the same manner as an ordinary NOL, except that it is reduced by TPIs (items listed in Code Sec. 57), and tax items that must be adjusted for AMTI calculations (items listed in Code Sec. 56 and Code Sec. 58) must also be adjusted for NOL calculations. It does not have to be reduced by the TPIs listed in Code Sec. 57 if those items did not increase the amount of a regular tax NOL deduction.

> **Example 2:** A taxpayer's income for a tax year is $75,000, while her losses total $100,000, of which $20,000 is from TPIs. Her NOL for regular taxation is $25,000. In computing AMTI, TPIs cannot be used. Consequently, only $80,000 of the losses may offset income, leaving the taxpayer with an alternative tax NOL of $5,000.

Pollution Control Facilities. For property placed in service after 1986 and before 1999, the five-year amortization method for depreciating pollution control facilities under Code Sec. 169 must be replaced by the alternative depreciation system in Code Sec. 168(g) (see Code Sec. 56(a)(5)).[18] The pollution control facility adjustment is computed under MACRS using the straight-line method for property placed in service after 1998.

When the pollution control facility is sold, its adjusted basis must be computed under the AMT rules in order to determine the gain or loss from the sale for AMT purposes (Code Sec. 56(a)(6)).[19] The difference between the regular tax gain or loss and the recomputed AMT gain or loss is a tax preference adjustment in the year of sale.

Domestic Production Activities Deduction. This deduction (see ¶ 245) is allowed for both individuals and corporations against the AMT. For individuals, the calculation of the deduction is the same for both regular income tax and AMT liability. For other taxpayers, however, the deduction for AMT purposes is calculated as a stated percentage (six percent for 2007) of the lesser of (1) the taxpayer's qualified production activities income (determined without regard to available AMT adjustments) or (2) the taxpayer's alternative minimum taxable income (determined without regard to this deduction) (Code Sec. 199(a) and (d)(6)).

1435. Adjustments Affecting Noncorporate Taxpayers. In addition to adjustments that affect all taxpayers, individuals and other noncorporate taxpayers must make a number of adjustments that only pertain to them.

Footnote references are to paragraphs of the 2008 Standard Federal Tax Reports.

[14] ¶ 5200	[16] ¶ 5200	[18] ¶ 5200
[15] ¶ 5200	[17] ¶ 5200	[19] ¶ 5200

Itemized Deductions. Individuals are entitled to claim itemized deductions in calculating AMTI with certain adjustments (Code Sec. 56(b)).[20] For example, an individual cannot claim any miscellaneous itemized deductions (subject to the two percent AGI floor). Similarly, state, local and foreign taxes on real property, personal property, as well as income and sales taxes may not be claimed (Code Sec. 56(b)(1)(A)(ii)). This means that any of these deductions claimed in computing regular tax liability must be added back to AMTI. Refunds of taxes that are deductible for regular tax purposes must also be excluded in determining AMTI.

Deductions may be claimed for medical expenses, but the expenses must exceed 10 percent of the taxpayer's AGI, rather than 7.5 percent. Investment interest expenses are limited to the size of a taxpayer's net investment income. Tax-exempt interest on private activity bonds is included in investment income for this purpose, and interest expended to carry the bonds is included in investment interest expenses. The limitation on itemized deductions of high-income taxpayers that applies for regular tax purposes (Code Sec. 68) does not apply for AMTI purposes (Code Sec. 56(b)(1)(F)).[21]

Among the itemized interest deductions that may be claimed against AMTI is qualified housing interest, which is similar to the qualified residence interest deduction that may be claimed against regular tax (Code Sec. 56(e)).[22] Qualified housing interest is interest paid on a loan used to purchase, build, or substantially improve:

    (1) a taxpayer's principal residence and

    (2) another dwelling (i.e., a house, apartment, condominium, or mobile home that is not used on a transient basis) personally used by the taxpayer during a tax year for the greater of:

        (a) 14 days or

        (b) 10 percent of the number of days during which the dwelling is leased (see Code Secs. 163(h)(4) and 280A(d)(1)).

It is not subject to the limitation on investment interest deductions. Interest on a refinanced loan is also deductible if the loan does not exceed the balance remaining on the original loan.

Personal Exemptions and the Standard Deduction. No deduction for or in lieu of personal exemptions may be claimed against AMTI, and the standard deduction may not be claimed for AMTI purposes (Code Sec. 56(b)(1)(E)).[23]

Circulation and Research and Experimental Expenditures. Circulation expenditures (i.e., the costs, deductible under Code Sec. 173, of establishing, maintaining, or increasing a newspaper's, magazine's, or other periodical's circulation), which are expensed for regular tax calculations, must be capitalized for AMTI calculations and ratably amortized over a three-year period, which starts with the tax year in which the expenditures are made (Code Sec. 56(b)(2));[24] research and experimental expenditures (Code Sec. 174) must be ratably amortized over a 10-year period. These adjustments, in effect, treat the excess of expense deductions over amortization deductions as a tax preference. Besides noncorporate taxpayers, personal holding companies must also recompute circulation expenditures for AMTI. No recomputation of research and experimental costs is required if a taxpayer has materially participated (i.e, regular, continuous, and substantial involvement) in the activity that generated the costs. If a loss is sustained on property that generated these research and experimental deductions or circulation expenditures, a deduction is allowed equal to the lesser of (1) the unamortized expenditures or (2) the amount that would be allowed as a loss had the expenditures remained capitalized. The adjusted basis of such property must be computed under the AMT rules in order to determine the gain or loss from the sale for AMT purposes (Code Sec. 56(a)(6)).[25] The difference between the regular tax gain or loss and the recomputed AMT gain or loss is a tax preference adjustment in the year of sale.

Incentive Stock Options. AMTI must be increased by the amount by which the price actually paid by an individual for an incentive stock option is exceeded by the option's

---

Footnote references are to paragraphs of the 2008 Standard Federal Tax Reports.

| [20] ¶ 5200 | [22] ¶ 5200 | [24] ¶ 5200 |
| [21] ¶ 5200 | [23] ¶ 5200 | [25] ¶ 5200 |

fair market value at the time his rights to the stock are freely transferable or are not subject to a substantial risk of forfeiture (Code Sec. 56(b)(3)).[26]

> **Comment:** In a case where an individual purchased an incentive stock option and exercised it when the fair market value had risen substantially, but where the stock's value had decreased substantially by the time the stock was sold, to a value below that existing at the time the stock was paid for, the individual, for AMT purposes, would be considered to have received ordinary income in the amount of the difference between the fair market value at the time the option was purchased and the time it became freely transferable. As a result, the taxpayer could have a large tax liability without ever having realized any actual income from the stock. If the stock was sold at a loss, the taxpayer would be subject to the $3,000 limit on the deductibility of net capital losses. Therefore, the excess of the regular tax over the tentative minimum tax might not reflect the full amount of the loss, and a portion of the minimum tax credit generated by the adjustment would remain unused. Congress has provided some relief to those in this situation by increasing the amount of minimum tax credit available to the taxpayer, and by providing that the additional amount of the credit allowed by the new law is refundable. See Code Sec. 53(e), as added by the Tax Relief and Health Care Act of 2006 (P.L. 109-432) and ¶ 1370A.

Passive Farm Tax Shelter Losses. Noncorporate taxpayers, including personal service corporations (see Code Sec. 469(j)(2)), who are not material participants in a farming business but use a farming tax shelter to avoid regular tax liability may not deduct passive farming losses in computing AMTI (Code Sec. 58(a)).[27] Farm tax shelters are farm syndicates (see Code Sec. 464(c)) or passive farm activities in which the taxpayer (or his spouse) is not a material participant (see Code Sec. 469(c)). The amount of denied losses must be reduced by the amount of a taxpayer's insolvency during a tax year. Insolvency is defined as the excess of a taxpayer's liabilities over the fair market value of his assets. Taxpayers may not net income and losses from various farming tax shelters to determine an overall loss or gain. Each tax shelter must be regarded separately. Thus, a taxpayer who suffers a $1,000 loss from one tax shelter, but has a $1,000 gain from another, must include a $1,000 gain in AMTI calculations. Also, tax preferences included in losses must be adjusted so that their preference is eliminated.

Farm losses that have been disallowed as deductions from AMTI in one tax year may be claimed as deductions from farm income from that activity in the succeeding tax year. Taxpayers who dispose of their interest in a farm tax shelter are allowed to claim their losses against AMTI.

Other Passive Business Activity Losses. With some modifications, the regular tax rules limiting the deductibility of losses from passive, nonfarm business activities must be followed in finding the AMT of individuals, trusts, estates, closely held C corporations, and personal service corporations. Thus, deductions for passive losses may be claimed only against passive income. One modification requires a taxpayer to reduce the amount of denied losses by the amount of his insolvency during a tax year. Furthermore, the passive activity loss is determined without regard to any qualified housing interest. Finally, passive losses must be adjusted, as they would be under other AMT rules, to eliminate tax preferences.

> **Example:** In calculating his regular tax, Doug Pratt has a passive loss deduction of $15,000 for net losses from real estate rentals. The losses are partially based on MACRS deductions, a tax preference (see ¶ 1430). His minimum tax liability must be determined by computing depreciation deductions under the alternative depreciation system. This leaves him with a passive loss deduction of only $5,000 against AMTI. Since he already has adjusted his depreciation deductions in determining whether there is a passive loss tax preference, he does not have to include them as part of any adjustment for depreciation tax preferences.

Unlawful Discrimination Damages. Gross income generally does not include the amount of any damages received by individuals (other than punitive damages) due to personal physical injuries, including death (Code Sec. 104(a)(2)). Other damages are usually included in gross income. Expenses, such as costs and fees, that are incurred in

---

Footnote references are to paragraphs of the 2008 Standard Federal Tax Reports.

[26] ¶ 5200   [27] ¶ 5350

¶1435

recovering damages are treated as miscellaneous itemized deductions, which are not taken into account in computing the AMT. However, an above-the-line deduction is allowed for fees and costs paid in connection with certain civil rights claims, most notably a claim of unlawful discrimination. The amount so excluded from gross income is limited to the amount of the judgment or settlement that was includible in the taxpayer's gross income (Code Sec. 62(a)(20)). Because this amount is allowed as an above-the-line deduction, it is not taken into account in computing the AMT.

Income Averaging for Farmers and Fishermen. Individuals engaged in the farming or fishing business may elect to average their income over three years in order to reduce their regular tax liability (see ¶ 767). This reduction in the regular tax could lead to a higher AMT, which is computed without income averaging. Thus, for tax years after 2003, solely for purposes of computing the AMT, the regular income tax liability of a farmer or fisherman is computed without income averaging. Consequently, the AMT will be reduced by nonapplication of the income averaging rules when computing AMT (Code Sec. 55(c)(2)).

State Taxes. In computing the AMT, no deduction is allowed for state or local property or income taxes (Code Sec. 56(b)(1)(A)(ii)). However, state and local property and income taxes are taken into account in computing adjusted gross income (AGI) if the taxes arose from the operation of a business (Code Sec. 56(b)(1)(A) (see ¶ 235)). This exception for use in computing the AGI does not apply to state or local sales taxes, which are deductible as an itemized deduction in the computation of the regular tax for tax years beginning after 2003 and before 2008 (see ¶ 1021) (Code Sec. 164(b)(5), as amended by the Tax Relief and Health Care Act of 2006 (P.L. 109-432)). Therefore, an individual who elected to deduct state sales taxes rather than state income taxes when computing AMT might not achieve the lowest total tax liability, if the income taxes paid were allowable in the computation of the taxpayer's adjusted gross income.

1440. Adjustments Affecting Corporate Taxpayers. Corporations must make the following adjustments to AMTI:

Adjusted Current Earnings. A portion of the difference between the AMTI and the adjusted current earnings (ACE) of corporations other than S corporations, regulated investment companies, real estate investment trusts, or real estate mortgage investment conduits is treated as a tax preference for tax years beginning after 1989. This preference does not attempt to recapture the tax benefit derived by a corporation from the use of a particular tax deduction or exclusion, such as the depletion deduction described at ¶ 1425. Instead, it is aimed at recapturing some of the overall tax savings enjoyed by corporations that report large earnings to their shareholders and creditors but, due to a variety of tax benefits, pay little or no tax. To achieve recapture, a corporation's AMTI must be increased by 75 percent of the amount by which its ACE exceeds its AMTI, computed without the adjustments for either the ACE preference or alternative tax NOLs (Code Secs. 56(c)(1) and (g)).[28]

> **Example 1:** A corporation has AMTI of $100,000 before it makes adjustments for alternative tax NOLs or ACE. The current tax year's ACE amounts to $200,000, leaving the corporation with an ACE preference of $75,000 (.75 ($200,000 − $100,000)), which increases AMTI to $175,000 ($100,000 + $75,000).

In some years, AMTI may be decreased, rather than increased, by the ACE preference. If a corporation's ACE is less than its AMTI, ACE may reduce AMTI by 75 percent of the amount by which AMTI exceeds ACE (.75 (AMTI − ACE)). The overall amount by which the ACE preference may decrease AMTI over a period of years may not be greater than the overall amount by which the ACE preference has increased AMTI over that period. In a given tax year, this ceiling is determined by limiting the amount of AMTI available for reduction to the excess of prior year increases in AMTI caused by the ACE preference over prior year reductions caused by an ACE shortfall.

> **Example 2:** In a corporation's current tax year, it calculates ACE of $50,000 and AMTI of $70,000. Multiplying the difference between AMTI and ACE by 0.75 leaves the corporation with $15,000, an amount that may possibly be used to reduce AMTI and thereby reduce the amount of minimum tax to which AMTI may

---

Footnote references are to paragraphs of the 2008 Standard Federal Tax Reports.

[28] ¶ 5200

be subjected for other tax preferences. In its prior tax years, the corporation calculated an overall positive ACE preference of $10,000. This amount serves as a limit on the amount by which ACE may reduce AMTI in the current year, leaving the corporation with only a $10,000 reduction of AMTI rather than a $15,000 reduction. The possible reduction of $5,000 that remains may not be carried over to later tax years.

A quick look at the rather simple ACE preference formula makes it clear that the most important factor in establishing the size of the preference is determining what makes up a corporation's adjusted current earnings. In a broad view, ACE is made up of a corporation's earnings and profits—with a twist. The earnings and profits figure must be adjusted so that it takes on some of the principles used to calculate income for tax returns, including some of the principles for calculating the earnings and profits figure used to determine the taxation of dividend distributions to shareholders. Thus, the computation of ACE starts with AMTI as a base, which carries with it the built-in income, deductions, and exclusions used to determine regular as well as alternative taxable income.

For depreciable property placed into service before 1994, AMTI must be adjusted using the applicable ACE depreciation method, a method that may differ from that used for regular tax reporting, for corporate books, or even for the portion of AMTI that does not include the ACE preference. No ACE depreciation adjustment is made for property placed in service after 1993. The alternative (straight-line) MACRS method is used to determine allowable ACE depreciation for property placed in service after 1989 and before 1994 (Code Sec. 56(g)(4)(A)).

Income, other than exempt discharge of indebtedness income, that is exempt from regular or minimum taxation but that is included in the computation of earnings and profits must be included in the computation of ACE. This includes items such as interest payments on state and local bonds that are excluded from regular taxation but typically are included in the earnings and profits corporations report in financial sheets disclosed to the public. Expenses incurred in earning this kind of income, while not deductible in determining regular or minimum taxation, are deductible in determining ACE.

Here is a sampling of other adjustments:

(1) if a corporation does not claim a deduction against earnings and profits, it may not claim the deduction in the computation of ACE (except for certain dividends);

(2) while they may be expensed or amortized in regular taxation, intangible drilling costs (other than the costs of a nonproductive well or costs incurred by independent producers related to oil or gas wells), the costs of organizing a corporation, and the costs of circulating periodicals must, in computing ACE, be capitalized;

(3) ACE must be increased or decreased by an increase or decrease in a corporation's LIFO recapture amount, which is the amount by which the value of the corporation's inventory under the FIFO method of inventory valuation exceeds the value under the LIFO method;

(4) the installment method of accounting, in most cases, may not be used in the computation of ACE to report income from installment sales;

(5) income that has built up on a life insurance contract must be included in a corporation's ACE;

(6) the cost depletion method must be used to determine depletion deductions of corporations other than independent oil and gas producers and royalty owners;

(7) a corporation that has undergone an ownership change in which new shareholders have acquired more than half of the value of the corporation's stock must undertake a wholesale recomputation of the bases of its assets so that the basis of each asset takes on the value of the asset at the time of the corporation's acquisition by the new shareholders;

(8) ACE may not include loss from the exchange of one pool of debt obligations for another pool that consists of obligations with the same effective interest rates and maturities as obligations in the first pool;

¶1440

(9) the adjusted basis of assets for purposes of making ACE preference adjustments is determined under these ACE preference rules; and

(10) no adjustment related to the earnings and profits effect of charitable contributions is made to ACE.

Merchant Marine Capital Construction Funds. Contributions made by shipping companies to capital construction funds (established under §607 of the Merchant Marine Act of 1936, 46 U.S.C. 1177) may not be deducted from AMTI, and a fund's earnings (including gains or losses) may not be excluded from AMTI (Code Sec. 56(c)(2)).[29] No reduction in the basis of a vessel, barge, or container need be made to reflect amounts withdrawn from a fund if the amounts have been included in AMTI.

Blue Cross and Blue Shield Organizations. The special deduction from regular tax allowed to Blue Cross and Blue Shield organizations, under Code Sec. 833, for one-fourth of their annual claims and administrative expenses (less the prior tax year's adjusted surplus) may not be claimed against AMTI (Code Sec. 56(c)(3)).[30]

Property and Casualty Insurance Companies. A property and casualty insurance company that elects to be taxed only on taxable investment income for regular tax purposes determines its ACE without regard to underwriting income or underwriting expense in tax years beginning after 1997 (Code Sec. 56(g)(4)(B)(i)).

Cutbacks of Certain Corporate Tax Benefits

1445. Reductions in Tax Benefits v. Minimum Taxation. Under Code Sec. 291, several tax benefits that may be claimed by corporations must be reduced, in most cases, by 20 percent.[31] Like tax preferences that are subject to minimum taxation, these tax items have been selected for reduction in order to prevent excessive tax benefits. However, the approach adopted under the preference cutback rules differs from the minimum tax principles. Rather than being subject to the minimum tax after they have been claimed against regular taxable income, these items are reduced in size before they may offset income. Some of these items are also tax preferences subject to minimum taxation, and, therefore, the AMT may be imposed if the tax benefit produced by these items after reduction remains too large (Code Sec. 59(f)).

The following reductions must first be made to these tax preferences:

(1) Corporations that have sold or otherwise disposed of Code Sec. 1250 property (depreciable real property) must provide ordinary income treatment to 20 percent of the portion of the gain on the disposition that has not been treated as ordinary income. The 20-percent treatment does not have to be applied if Code Sec. 1250 property was part of a certified pollution control facility (described in Code Sec. 169). Also, if a real estate investment trust (REIT) (Code Sec. 856) disposes of Code Sec. 1250 property, Code Sec. 1250 gain which is treated as not coming from ordinary income and is distributed to shareholders as a capital gain dividend is excluded from ordinary income treatment. Corporate shareholders of a REIT must treat capital gain dividends as subject to the 20-percent ordinary income treatment.

(2) The percentage depletion deduction (Code Sec. 613) for iron ore and coal (including lignite) must be reduced by 20 percent of the excess of (a) the percentage depletion deduction (determined before the 20-percent reduction is made) over (b) the adjusted basis (determined without including the depletion deduction claimed in a tax year) of the minerals at the close of the tax year.

(3) There must be a 20-percent reduction in the amount of deductions claimed by a financial institution (subject to Code Sec. 585 or Code Sec. 593) for certain interest expenses on debts incurred to purchase tax-exempt obligations acquired after December 31, 1982, and before August 8, 1986.

(4) The basis of certified pollution control facilities that is used under Code Sec. 169 for computing rapid amortization deductions must be reduced by 20 percent. ACRS depreciation must be used to depreciate the reduced basis.

(5) A corporation's (including an integrated oil company's) deductions for intangible drilling costs and mineral exploration and development costs (see Code

---

Footnote references are to paragraphs of the 2008 Standard Federal Tax Reports.

[29] ¶5200   [30] ¶5200   [31] ¶15,190

Sec. 263, Code Sec. 616, and Code Sec. 617) must be reduced by 30 percent. Reduced deductions may be deducted ratably over a 60-month period that starts with the month in which costs are paid or incurred. If the related property is disposed of, these deductions may be recaptured under Code Sec. 1254.

(6) Rapid amortization deductions by pollution control facilities, bad debt reserve deductions claimed by financial institutions, percentage depletion deductions, and deductions for intangible drilling costs and mineral explorations and development costs are also subject to the minimum tax. They must be reduced before, rather than after, the minimum tax is imposed so that a double cutback of these items does not occur (Code Sec. 59(f)).[32]

Miscellaneous Rules

1450. Election to Avoid Tax Preference Status. Deductions for certain expenditures that are treated as tax preferences will not be treated as tax preferences, and therefore will not be subject to minimum taxation, if a taxpayer elects to claim these deductions ratably over a 3-year, 60-month, or 10-year period, beginning with the tax year (or month) in which the expenditures were made, rather than entirely in one tax year (Code Sec. 59(e)).[33] Taxpayers may limit their elections to only a portion of their deductions, leaving the remaining deductions subject to minimum taxation. The 3-year period may be claimed for circulation expenditures, the 60-month period may be claimed for intangible drilling and development expenditures, and the 10-year period may be claimed for research and experimental, mine development, and mining exploration expenditures. Partners and S corporation shareholders must make elections separately.

1455. S Corporations and Partnerships. S corporations and partnerships are not subject to the minimum tax (Code Secs. 701 and 1363(a)).[34] Shareholders and partners must compute their minimum tax liability separately. In determining the AMTI of a partner in an electing large partnership, the partner must take into account his distributive share of the partnership's applicable net AMT adjustment, separately computed for passive loss limitation activities and other activities (Code Sec. 722), instead of making the separate adjustments provided in the AMT rules with respect to the items of the partnership. The net AMT adjustment is determined by using the adjustments applicable to individuals (in the case of noncorporate partners) and the adjustments applicable to corporations (in the case of corporate partners). Except as provided in regulations, the applicable net AMT adjustment is treated as a deferral tax preference for purposes of computing the minimum tax credit (¶ 1370).

1460. Possessions Tax Credit. Corporate income for which the Puerto Rican economic activity credit of Code Sec. 30A or the possessions tax credit of Code Sec. 936 may be claimed is not includible in AMTI and therefore is not subject to the minimum tax (Code Sec. 59(b)).[35]

1465. REITs, RICs, and Common Trust Funds. Tax items which are treated differently for minimum taxation and regular taxation must be apportioned between REITs or RICs and their shareholders and holders of beneficial interests. Participants in common trust funds must apportion these items among themselves on a pro rata basis (Code Sec. 59(d)).[36]

1470. Corporate Preference Cutbacks. Minimum tax calculations may be performed only after specified corporate tax preferences have been reduced in accordance with Code Sec. 291 (Code Sec. 59(f)). See ¶ 1445.[37]

1475. Credit for Minimum Tax Payments. For details on the tax credit carryforward allowed against regular tax liability for minimum tax payments, see Code Sec. 53 and ¶ 1370.[38]

1480. Limitations on Certain Losses Recomputed for Minimum Taxation. The loss limitations on at-risk amounts (Code Sec. 465), on a partner's distributive share of partnership losses (Code Sec. 704(d)), and on an S corporation shareholder's losses (Code Sec. 1366(d)) are applied for purposes of computing AMTI (see Code Sec. 59(h)).[39]

Footnote references are to paragraphs of the 2008 Standard Federal Tax Reports.

[32] ¶ 5400
[33] ¶ 5400
[34] ¶ 25,060, ¶ 32,060
[35] ¶ 5400
[36] ¶ 5400
[37] ¶ 5400
[38] ¶ 5002
[39] ¶ 5400

Chapter 15

TAX ACCOUNTING

Accounting Period

1501. Tax Year. Taxable income is computed on the basis of a period called a tax year. A tax year is the annual accounting period regularly used by a taxpayer in keeping its books and records to compute income. This period is usually a calendar year or a fiscal year (IRS Pub. 538). Special rules exist when:

(1) a taxpayer has no annual accounting period or keeps no books and records;

(2) a 52-53-week fiscal-year period is elected (¶ 1503);

(3) a foreign sales corporation (FSC) (¶ 2470) or domestic international sales corporation (DISC) (¶ 2468) files a return for a period of at least 12 months; or

(4) a taxpayer must file a return for a period that is less than 12 months (short-period return) (¶ 1505) (Code Sec. 441).[1]

Calendar v. Fiscal Year. A calendar year is a period of 12 months ending on December 31. A fiscal year is a period of 12 months ending on the last day of any month other than December or a 52-53-week tax year (see ¶ 1503). A *new* taxpayer may adopt either a calendar or a fiscal year on the first return (Reg. § 1.441-1).[2] A fiscal year will be recognized only if it is established as the taxpayer's annual accounting period and only if the taxpayer keeps his books accordingly. A taxpayer who has no annual accounting period, does not keep adequate records, or whose present tax year does not qualify as a fiscal year must compute taxable income on a calendar-year basis. Adoption of a tax year of exactly 12 months from the date business was begun is not permitted when the tax year does not begin on the first day of a calendar month (Rev. Rul. 85-22).[3] The IRS has issued procedures for changing from such an impermissible tax year to a calendar year (Rev. Proc. 85-15).[4]

Example 1: A corporation began doing business on August 15, 2007. The end of its first tax year cannot be later than July 31, 2008, since a tax year may not cover more than a 12-month period and it must end on the last day of a month, unless it is a 52-53-week tax year.

Example 2: Assume that the new corporation in Example 1 determines there is no advantage in keeping its books on the basis of any year other than the calendar year. Therefore, it adopts the calendar-year basis. It should close its

Footnote references are to paragraphs of the 2008 Standard Federal Tax Reports.

[1] ¶ 20,302
[2] ¶ 20,303
[3] ¶ 20,307.70
[4] ¶ 20,406.15

books as of December 31, 2007, and file its first return for the short period from August 15, 2007, through December 31, 2007. This is its first tax year. All its later tax years will be full calendar years until its dissolution or until it changes to a fiscal year.

A partnership generally must use the same tax year as that of its owners, unless the partnership can establish a business purpose for having a different tax year (Code Sec. 706(b)).[5] An S corporation or a personal service corporation (¶ 219) must generally use the calendar year, unless the entities can establish a business purpose for having a different tax year (Code Sec. 441(i) and Code Sec. 1378(b)).[6] For this purpose, a corporation is not considered a personal service corporation (PSC) unless more than 10 percent of its stock (by value) is held by employee-owners. An employee-owner for this purpose is any employee that owns any stock of the PSC. If a corporation is a member of an affiliated group filing a consolidated return, all members of such group must be considered in determining whether such corporation is a PSC (Code Sec. 441(i)).[7]

A partnership must use the same tax year as the partner(s) owning the majority interest in the partnership (i.e., that own in total more than a 50-percent interest in partnership profits and capital) (Code Sec. 706(b)). If there is no majority interest tax year, the partnership must adopt the same tax year as that of its principal partners each of whom has at least a 5-percent interest in partnership profits or capital. When neither condition is met, a partnership must use the calendar year.

Certain partnerships, S corporations, and personal service corporations may elect on Form 8716, Election to Have a Tax Year Other than a Required Tax Year, to use a tax year other than a required tax year (Code Sec. 444).[8] To neutralize tax benefits resulting from such a tax year, electing partnerships and S corporations must compute and make any required payments (i.e., the amount of tax that would otherwise be due from partners and stockholders had such entities used the required tax year) exceeding $500 (Code Sec. 7519).[9] The required payment is due on or before May 15 of the calendar year following the calendar year in which the election year begins (Temp. Reg. § 1.7519-2T(a)(4)).[10] Electing personal service corporations must make minimum distributions to their employee-owners by the end of a calendar year falling within a tax year to avoid certain deduction deferrals for amounts paid to employee-owners (Code Sec. 280H).

Generally, such an election must be made by the earlier of: (1) the 15th day of the fifth month following the month that includes the first day of the tax year for which the election is first effective or (2) the due date (without extensions) of the return that results from the election (Temp. Reg. § 1.444-3T(b)(1)).[11] The election remains in effect until an entity changes its tax year or otherwise terminates such an election (Code Sec. 444(d)(2)).[12]

Such an election may not be made by an entity that is a member of a tiered structure unless the tiered structure consists only of partnerships or S corporations (or both), all of which have the same tax year (Code Sec. 444(d)(3)).[13]

Common trust funds (certain investment funds maintained by a bank) are required to adopt the calendar year as their tax year (Code Sec. 584(h)).[14]

Qualifying Electric Transmission Transaction. Special rules are provided for determining the tax year of inclusion of certain income arising from a qualifying electric transmission transaction. A taxpayer may elect to defer the gain from such a transaction if the taxpayer purchases replacement utility property within four years of the date of the sale (Code Sec. 451(i)).[15] A "qualifying electric transmission transaction" is a sale or other disposition to an independent transmission company, before January 1, 2008, of property used in the trade or business of providing electric transmission services or any stock or partnership interest in an entity whose principal trade or business consists of providing such services (Code Sec. 451(i)(3)).

Footnote references are to paragraphs of the 2008 Standard Federal Tax Reports.

[5] ¶ 25,160
[6] ¶ 20,302, ¶ 32,260
[7] ¶ 20,302
[8] ¶ 20,600
[9] ¶ 42,770
[10] ¶ 42,774
[11] ¶ 20,604
[12] ¶ 20,600
[13] ¶ 20,600
[14] ¶ 23,630
[15] ¶ 21,030.001, ¶ 21,030.022

¶1501

Tax Year of FSC and DISC. The tax year of an FSC (¶ 2470) or a DISC (¶ 2468) must be the same as that of the shareholder or group of shareholders with the same tax year who have the highest percentage of voting power. Voting power is determined on the basis of total combined voting power of all classes of stock of the corporation entitled to vote. If two or more shareholders or groups are tied for the highest percentage, the tax year used shall be that of any such shareholder or group (Code Sec. 441(h)).[16]

1503. 52- or 53-Week Accounting Period. A taxpayer may elect to use a fiscal tax year that varies from 52 to 53 weeks if such period always ends on the same day of the week (Monday, Tuesday, etc.), either the last such day in a calendar month or the closest such day to the last day of a calendar month (Code Sec. 441(f); Reg. § 1.441-2).[17]

> **Example:** A new taxpayer wishes to have its accounting period end on the last Saturday in September. In 2007, its tax year ends on September 25, completing a 52-week year (September 27, 2006 through September 25, 2007). In 2008, its tax year ends on September 24, completing a 52-week year (September 25, 2007 through September 24, 2008). With this type of tax year, most of the taxpayer's tax years are 52 weeks long. As an alternative, the taxpayer could select a tax year that ends on the Saturday that is nearest to the end of September. In 2007, therefore, the tax year ends on September 29 (the Saturday nearest the end of September). In 2008, the tax year will end on September 27.

If a pass-through entity or an owner of a pass-through entity, or both, use a 52-53-week tax year and the tax year of the entity and owner end with reference to the same calendar month, then for purposes of determining the tax year in which items of income, gain, loss, deductions or credits from the entity are taken into account by the owner of the passthrough, the owner's tax year will be deemed to end on the last day of the entity's tax year. Under this rule, a passthrough entity is a partnership, S corporation, trust, estate, closely held real estate investment trust, common trust, controlled foreign corporation, foreign personal holding company or passive foreign investment company that is a qualified electing fund (Reg. § 1.441-2(e)(3)).[18]

Short-Period Return

1505. Tax for Portion of Year. Ordinarily no return may be made for a period of more than 12 months, except in the case of a 52-53-week tax year (Reg. § 1.441-1).[19] However, a return for a period of less than 12 months may need to be filed (Code Sec. 443; Reg. § 1.443-1)[20] by a taxpayer who:

> (1) changes its annual accounting period, e.g., from fiscal to calendar year (see ¶ 1513), or

> (2) is in existence during only part of what would otherwise be the tax year.

Taxpayers who are not in existence for a full 12-month period include:

> (a) a corporation that begins business or goes out of business at any time other than the beginning or end of its accounting period,

> (b) an individual taxpayer who dies prior to the end of the accounting period, and

> (c) a decedent's estate that comes into existence on the date of the decedent's death and adopts an accounting period ending less than 12 months from that date.

If the taxpayer is not in existence for a full tax year, the tax is computed as if the return had actually covered a full tax year. When a short period occurs as a result of a change in accounting period, the tax is computed on an annualized basis (see ¶ 1507). An alternative relief method is also available for taxpayers that change their accounting period (¶ 1509).

Special rules apply to taxpayers that change to or from a 52-53-week tax year (Code Sec. 441(f)(2)).[21] If such a change results in a short period of 359 days or more, the tax is computed as if the return had actually covered a full tax year. If the short period is less than seven days, the short period becomes a part of the following tax year. If the short

---

Footnote references are to paragraphs of the 2008 Standard Federal Tax Reports.

[16] ¶ 20,302
[17] ¶ 20,302, ¶ 20,304
[18] ¶ 20,304
[19] ¶ 20,303
[20] ¶ 20,500, ¶ 20,501
[21] ¶ 20,302

period is more than six days but less than 359 days, the tax is computed under the annualized method discussed at ¶ 1507.

1507. Tax Recomputed on Annual Basis. When there has been a change in an accounting period that necessitates the filing of a short-period return, income for the period must be converted to an annual basis. This conversion is accomplished by: (1) multiplying the modified taxable income for the short period by 12 and (2) dividing the result by the number of months in the short period. Then the tax is computed on the resulting taxable income by using the tax rate schedules and not the tax tables for individuals. The tax so computed is divided by 12 and multiplied by the number of months in the short period.

The modified taxable income for the short period is the gross income for the period less any allowable deductions (other than the standard deduction amount) and an adjusted personal exemption amount. Actual itemized deductions for the short period are allowed in lieu of the standard deduction amount. The adjusted personal exemption amount mentioned above is the total of an individual taxpayer's personal exemptions times the ratio of the number of months in the short period to 12 (Code Sec. 443).[22]

> **Example:** Tom has been making his returns on the basis of a fiscal year ending April 30. He changes to a year ending June 30 in 2007. He must file his return for the year ending April 30, 2007, on or before August 15, 2007. On or before October 16, 2007, he must file his return for the short period of two months beginning May 1, 2007, and ending June 30, 2007. His gross income for the short period is $9,600, and his itemized deductions total $600. He is married, age 60, and has no dependents. His wife has no income or deductions. The tax before credits on their joint return is computed as follows:

Gross income	$9,600
Itemized deductions*	600
Net income	$9,000
Less 2/12 of $6,800 (2 × $3,400) exemptions	1,133
Modified taxable income for short period	$7,867
Annualized taxable income—$7,867 × 12/2	$47,202
Tax on $47,202	$6,298
Tax for short period, 2/12 of $6,298	$1,050

> * Assume that the itemized deductions are not miscellaneous itemized deductions under Code Sec. 67 and that amounts are rounded up to the nearest dollar. An individual making a return under Code Sec. 443(a)(1) for a period of less than 12 months because of a change in annual accounting period is not eligible for the standard deduction (Code Sec. 63(c)(6)(C)).

When a short-period return is filed, the self-employment tax (¶ 2664) should be computed on the actual self-employment income for the short-period and not prorated for a portion of a 12-month period.[23] A net operating loss deduction should be applied against actual income for the short period before annualizing (Rev. Proc. 2002-39, modified by Rev. Proc. 2003-34 and Rev. Proc. 2003-79).[24]

A taxpayer that is changing to or from a 52-53-week fiscal tax year and that must annualize income will apply the same rules as other taxpayers in determining the income of the short period, but will calculate income on an annual basis by multiplying the income of the short period by 365 and dividing the result by the number of days in the short period (Code Sec. 441(f)(2)(B)(iii)). Tax is computed on such annualized income and, as computed, is multiplied by the ratio of the number of days in the short period to 365; the resulting figure is the tax for the short year.

Footnote references are to paragraphs of the 2008 Standard Federal Tax Reports.

[22] ¶ 20,500   [23] ¶ 35,203.30   [24] ¶ 20,406

1509. Relief from Annual Basis. Code Sec. 443(b)(2)[25] provides an alternative method for computing the short-period tax. Under this method, the tax for the short period is the greater of:

(1) a tax on the actual taxable income for the 12-month period beginning with the start of the short period (using the law in effect for that 12-month period) multiplied by the modified taxable income (¶ 1507) for the short period and divided by the modified taxable income for the 12-month period or

(2) a tax on the modified taxable income for the short period.

If a taxpayer does not exist at the end of the 12-month period described in (1), above, or if a corporate taxpayer has distributed substantially all its assets before the end of that period, the tax is computed by using a 12-month period ending with the last day of the short period (Code Sec. 443(b)(2)(B)(ii)).[26] In such cases, in order to claim the benefits of the alternative method, the taxpayer must attach a return covering the 12-month period ending on the last day of the short year to the return initially computed for the short period.

If there was a change in accounting period, with a resultant short period, the taxpayer must first compute the tax using the annualization method (¶ 1507) and file the return. If the alternate method would result in lower taxes, a claim for credit or refund must be filed no later than the due date by which a return would have been required to be filed if the 12-month period beginning with the short period were considered a tax year (Reg. § 1.443-1(b)(2)(v)(a)).[27] The application of the taxpayer for use of the alternate method is considered as a claim for credit or refund (Code Sec. 443(b)(2)(C)).[28]

1511. Returns of Decedents, New Corporations or Dissolving Corporations. Short-period returns of decedents and dissolving corporations and the first return of a new corporation are not required to be annualized (Reg. § 1.443-1).[29]

Change of Accounting Period

1513. IRS's Consent Generally Required. The change from one accounting period to another generally requires prior permission of the IRS and requires the filing of a return for the short period under the rules discussed at ¶ 1505–¶ 1509. To effect the change in cases where prior approval is required, Form 1128, Application to Adopt, Change, or Retain a Tax Year, generally must be filed by the 15th day of the second calendar month following the close of the short period for which a return is required. A change in the accounting period will be approved where it is established that a substantial business purpose exists for making the change (Reg. § 1.442-1(b)(2))[30] but generally will not be approved where the sole purpose of the change is to maintain or obtain a preferential tax status.[31] The IRS will consider all the facts and circumstances relating to the change, including the tax consequences. Among the nontax factors is the effect of the change on the taxpayer's annual cycle of business activity. The agreement between the taxpayer and the IRS under which the change is carried out will, in appropriate cases, provide terms, conditions, and adjustments necessary to prevent a substantial distortion of income that would otherwise result from the change. The following are examples of effects that would constitute substantial distortions of income:

(1) deferring a substantial portion of the taxpayer's income or shifting a substantial portion of deductions from one year to another so as to reduce substantially the taxpayer's tax liability;

(2) causing a similar deferral or shift in the case of any other person, such as a partner, a beneficiary, or an S corporation shareholder; or

(3) creating a short period in which there is either:

(a) a substantial net operating loss, capital loss or credit (including a general business credit) or

(b) a substantial amount of income to offset an expiring net operating loss, capital loss or credit (Reg. § 1.442-1(b)(3)).[32]

Footnote references are to paragraphs of the 2008 Standard Federal Tax Reports.

[25] ¶ 20,500
[26] ¶ 20,500
[27] ¶ 20,501
[28] ¶ 20,500
[29] ¶ 20,501
[30] ¶ 20,401
[31] ¶ 20,406.41
[32] ¶ 20,401

Corporations. Automatic approval procedures are provided for certain corporations that have not requested a tax year change within the most recent 48-month period ending with the last month of the requested tax year (Rev. Proc. 2006-45). Automatic approval procedures are also provided for certain partnerships, S corporations, electing S corporations and personal service corporations that have not requested a tax year change within the most recent 48-month period ending with the last month of the requested tax year and that meet other conditions (Rev. Proc. 2006-46). If a change in accounting period under the automatic approval procedures results in a short tax year, certain partners or S corporation shareholders may elect to take into account, ratably over four years, the partner's or shareholder's share of income from the entity that is attributable to a short tax year ending on or after May 10, 2002, but before June 1, 2004, that is a result of the change (Rev. Proc. 2003-79). If the automatic approval procedures do not apply, the IRS has provided other procedures for taxpayers to follow in order to obtain the IRS's prior approval of an adoption, change or retention in an annual accounting period through application to the IRS national office (Reg. § 1.442-1(b)(3); Rev. Proc. 2002-39, modified by Rev. Proc. 2003-34).[33]

Individuals. Certain individuals may also follow automatic approval procedures (Reg. § 1.442-1(b)(3); Rev. Proc. 2003-62). The only individual who may change his or her tax year without IRS consent is a newly married individual who is adopting the annual accounting period of his or her spouse to file a joint return (Reg. § 1.442-1(d)).[34]

Accounting Method

1515. Cash v. Accrual Basis. Taxable income must be computed not only on the basis of a fixed accounting *period* but also in accordance with a *method* of accounting regularly employed in keeping the taxpayer's books. A "method of accounting" includes the overall method of accounting for income and expenses and the method of accounting for special items such as depreciation (Reg. § 1.446-1(a)).[35] There are two common overall methods of accounting for income: (1) the cash basis and (2) the accrual basis.

The cash basis (cash receipts and disbursements) is the method of accounting used by most individuals. Income is generally reported in the year that it is actually or constructively received in the form of cash or its equivalent or other property. The constructive receipt of income is income not actually received but within the taxpayer's control. However, there is no constructive receipt if there are substantial limits or restrictions on the right to receive it. Deductions or credits are generally taken for the year in which the related expenditures were actually paid, unless they should be taken in a different period to more clearly reflect income (such as depreciation allowances and prepaid expenses).

Under the accrual method, income is accounted for when the taxpayer has the right to receive it—i.e., when all the events that determine that right have occurred. It is not the actual receipt but the *right to receive* that governs. Expenses are deductible on the accrual basis in the year incurred—i.e., when all the events have occurred that fix the amount of the item and determine the liability of the taxpayer to pay it. See ¶ 1539 for a discussion of this "all-events test" as it relates to economic performance.

When no books are kept, an individual not engaged in business must report income on the cash basis.[36] In other cases, the accounting method used must clearly reflect income. An approved standard method of accounting (such as the cash basis or the accrual basis) ordinarily is regarded as clearly reflecting income. A taxpayer may use one accounting method to keep his personal books and another for the books of his trade or business. A taxpayer may use different accounting methods if the taxpayer has two or more separate businesses as long as separate and distinct sets of records are maintained. However, the use of multiple accounting methods is not permitted if there is a creation or shifting of profits or losses between the taxpayer's various trades or businesses (Reg. § 1.446-1(d)(3)).

Footnote references are to paragraphs of the 2008 Standard Federal Tax Reports.

[33] ¶ 20,401
[34] ¶ 20,401
[35] ¶ 20,607
[36] ¶ 20,620.0254

Taxpayers that are required to use inventories must use the accrual method to account for purchases and sales (Reg. § 1.446-1(c)(2)).[37] Furthermore, the following taxpayers must generally use the accrual method of accounting as their overall method of accounting for tax purposes:

    (1) C corporations,

    (2) partnerships that have a C corporation as a partner,

    (3) trusts that are subject to the tax on unrelated trade or business income (charitable trusts), but only for such income, and

    (4) tax shelters (Code Sec. 448(a) and (d)(6)).[38]

Qualified personal service corporations (¶ 219) are treated as individuals rather than as corporations for purposes of category (2), above.

Notwithstanding the general requirement that these taxpayers use the accrual method, the cash method of accounting may be used instead if the entity is not a tax shelter and:

    (1) is engaged in a farming or tree-raising business,

    (2) is a qualified personal service corporation, or

    (3) is an entity that has met the $5 million or less gross receipts test for all prior tax years beginning after 1985.

An entity meets the $5 million gross receipts test if the average annual gross receipts for the three tax years ending with the prior tax year does not exceed $5 million. Furthermore, the cash method may also be used by most other taxpayers whose average annual gross receipts do not exceed $1,000,000 (Rev. Proc. 2001-10) and may be used by select taxpayers whose average annual gross receipts do not exceed $10,000,000 (Rev. Proc. 2002-28).

Certain farming corporations must use the accrual method (Code Sec. 447)[39] (see ¶ 2028).

An accrual-method publisher of magazines, paperbacks, or records may elect to exclude from gross income the income attributable to the qualified sale of magazines, paperbacks, or records that are returned before the close of the merchandise return period (Code Sec. 458).[40]

1517. Accruing Income Doubtful of Collection. On the accrual basis, income, such as interest, is taxable as it accrues even though it is received at a later date. However, if there is a real doubt that the interest is collectible when it becomes due, it need not be accrued.[41] But where the uncollectible item arises from a sale of property, the proper procedure is to report the sale and then take a bad debt deduction as appropriate.[42]

Generally, an accrual-basis taxpayer is not required to accrue as income any amount to be received for the performance of services that, based on experience, will not be collected (Code Sec. 448(d)(5); Reg. § 1.448-2(a)).[43] This treatment with respect to such amounts is a method of accounting that must be elected by the taxpayer. The nonaccrual experience method of accounting is limited to amounts to be received for the performance of qualified services (health, law, engineering, architecture, accounting, actuarial science, performing arts or consulting) and for services provided by certain small businesses (Code Sec. 448(d)(5)).

1519. Liability Uncertain or Unascertained. There can be no accrual of an expense until any contingency disappears and liability becomes fixed and certain (Reg. § 1.461-1(a)(2)(ii)).[44] See also ¶ 1539 on the economic performance rule. But when the taxpayer, while denying liability, has paid a claim, the entire amount may be deductible when paid. See ¶ 1521. For treatment of estimated expenses, see ¶ 1547.

Footnote references are to paragraphs of the 2008 Standard Federal Tax Reports.

[37] ¶ 20,607	[40] ¶ 21,540	[43] ¶ 20,800, ¶ 20,802
[38] ¶ 20,800	[41] ¶ 5704.32	[44] ¶ 21,805
[39] ¶ 20,700	[42] ¶ 21,005.20	

1521. Accruing Contested Liability. If money or property is transferred to provide for the satisfaction of certain contested liabilities, the taxpayer can take a deduction in the year of the transfer if:

>   (1) the taxpayer contests an asserted liability,

>   (2) the contest exists after the transfer, and

>   (3) the liability would otherwise be allowed as a deduction in the year of transfer (or an earlier tax year).

Thus, the taxpayer must meet the economic performance requirement of the all-events test, discussed at ¶ 1539 (Code Sec. 461(f)).[45]

1523. Hybrid Accounting Methods. Under Code Sec. 446(c),[46] one or more hybrid methods of accounting may be authorized by regulation. The regulations allow use of a combination of methods if the combination clearly reflects income and is consistently used (Reg. § 1.446-1(c)(1)(iv)).[47] A taxpayer engaged in more than one business is permitted to use a different method for each trade or business.

1525. Method Prescribed by IRS. The IRS can prescribe a method of accounting that will clearly reflect income if, in the IRS's opinion, the method used by the taxpayer fails to do so (Code Sec. 446(b)).[48] If the IRS requires a change in accounting methods, the taxpayer must compute an income adjustment due to the change (Code Sec. 481(a)).[49] See ¶ 1531.

1527. Interest and Expenses Owed to Related Taxpayers. When different methods of accounting are used by related taxpayers, accrued interest and expenses owed to a related taxpayer may not be deducted until the time that the interest or expense payment is includible in the gross income of the cash-basis payee (Code Sec. 267(a)(2)).[50] Thus, an accrual-basis payor is placed on the cash basis for the purpose of deducting business expenses and interest owed to a related cash-basis taxpayer. The deduction is deferred until the cash-basis payee takes the item into income.

The related taxpayers covered by this rule are described in Code Sec. 267(b) and Code Sec. 267(e). Related taxpayers include certain family members, members of a controlled group of corporations, controlling shareholders and controlled corporations, and owners of pass-through entities, such as a partnership and its partners and an S corporation and its shareholders.

A personal service corporation may not deduct payments made to owner-employees before the tax year in which such persons must include the payment in gross income. For this purpose, a personal service corporation and any employee-owner are considered related taxpayers (Code Sec. 267(a)(2)).[51]

Change of Accounting Method

1529. IRS Permission Needed. As a general rule, a taxpayer may not change his method of accounting without obtaining advance permission from the IRS (Code Sec. 446(e); Reg. § 1.446-1(e)).[52]

A change of accounting method includes a change in the overall plan of accounting as well as a change in the treatment of any material item. In most cases, a method of accounting is not established for an item unless there is a pattern of consistent treatment. A change in the treatment of a material item is one involving the timing of its inclusion in income or deduction (not the traditional accounting meaning dealing with the relationship of amounts). Consent is required whether the change is made from an acceptable or an unacceptable method, and, if the taxpayer fails to file a request to change his method of accounting, the absence of IRS consent to the change will not be taken into account in order to prevent the imposition of penalties (or additions to tax) or to diminish such penalties (or additions to tax) (Code Sec. 446(f)).[53] Changes in accounting method include, but are not limited to:

Footnote references are to paragraphs of the 2008 Standard Federal Tax Reports.

[45] ¶ 21,802   [48] ¶ 20,606   [51] ¶ 14,150
[46] ¶ 20,606   [49] ¶ 22,270   [52] ¶ 20,606, ¶ 20,607
[47] ¶ 20,607   [50] ¶ 14,150   [53] ¶ 20,606

(1) a change from the cash to the accrual basis (see Rev. Proc. 2002-9) or vice versa,

(2) any change in the method of valuing inventories (¶ 1571),

(3) a change from the cash or accrual basis to one of the long-term contract methods (percentage-of-completion capitalized-cost and percentage-of-completion), or vice versa, or from one long-term contract method to the other (¶ 1551),

(4) a change involving the adoption, use or discontinuance of any other specialized basis, such as the crop method (¶ 1569), and

(5) a change where the Code and regulations specifically require that IRS consent be obtained.

The IRS will automatically approve certain taxpayers' changes of accounting method. This approval is granted for the tax year for which the taxpayer requests the change if the taxpayer complies with the automatic change procedures (Rev. Proc. 2002-9, Rev. Proc. 2002-19, Rev. Proc. 2002-28, Rev. Proc. 2002-54, Announcement 2002-17).

Application for permission to change the method of accounting must generally be filed on Form 3115 during the tax year in which the taxpayer desires to make the proposed change (Reg. § 1.446-1(e)(3)(i)).[54] Requests for consent to a change in accounting method under a number of regulations were required to be made within a 90-day period after the beginning of the relevant tax year. However, that requirement has been eliminated (Rev. Proc. 2005-63).

1531. Adjustments Required by Changes in Method of Accounting. Taxpayers who voluntarily change their method of accounting with the IRS's permission, or who are compelled by the IRS to make a change because the method used does not clearly reflect income, must make certain adjustments to income in the year of the change (Code Sec. 481(a); Reg. § 1.481-1).[55] The adjustments are those determined to be necessary to prevent duplication or omission of items.

Since the adjustments for the year of change might result in the bunching of income, two statutory methods of limiting the tax in the changeover year may be applied if the adjustments for the changeover year increase taxable income by more than $3,000 (Reg. § 1.481-2).[56] If both limitations apply, the one resulting in the lower tax should be used. In order for the first of these methods to be used, the old method of accounting must have been used in the two preceding years; if so, the tax increase in the changeover year is limited to the tax increases that would result if the adjustments were spread ratably over that year and the two preceding years.

Under the second method, the taxpayer must be able to reconstruct his income under the new method of accounting for one or more consecutive years immediately preceding the changeover year. The increase in the changeover year's tax because of the adjustments may not be more than the net tax increases that would result if the adjustments were allocated back to those preceding years under the new method. Any amounts that cannot be allocated back must be included in the changeover year's income for purposes of computing the limitation.

In addition to the statutorily prescribed methods of allocation limiting the tax in the changeover year described above, the IRS has prescribed conditions under which accounting change adjustments must be made as well as favorable "spread of adjustment" provisions for taxpayers that agree to the IRS conditions (Rev. Proc. 2002-9 or Rev. Proc. 2002-19, modified by Rev. Proc. 2002-54; Reg. §§ 1.263A-7(b)(2) and 1.448-1(g)(2)).[57] Moreover, a taxpayer may request approval of an alternative method of allocating the amount of the adjustments (Reg. § 1.481-4).[58]

A change in accounting method resulting from limitations placed on the use of the cash method of accounting under Code Sec. 448 (¶ 1501) is treated as a change initiated by the taxpayer with the consent of the IRS. The related Code Sec. 481 adjustment is

---

Footnote references are to paragraphs of the 2008 Standard Federal Tax Reports.

[54] ¶ 20,607
[55] ¶ 22,270, ¶ 22,271

[56] ¶ 22,272
[57] ¶ 20,620

[58] ¶ 22,275

includible in income over a period not generally exceeding four years (Code Sec. 448(d)(7)).[59]

Constructive Receipt and Payment

1533. Cash Basis and Constructive Receipt. It is not always necessary that a taxpayer take possession of money or property representing income before it is considered received. Income that is constructively received is taxed to the cash-basis taxpayer as though it had been actually received.

There is constructive receipt when income is credited without restriction and made available to the taxpayer. There must be no substantial limitation or condition on the taxpayer's right to bring the funds within his control. An insubstantial forfeiture provision, a notice requirement, or the loss of bonus interest for deposits or accounts in certain financial institutions is not a substantial limitation (Reg. § 1.451-2(a)).[60]

Common examples of constructive receipt include matured and payable interest coupons, interest credited on savings bank deposits, and dividends unqualifiedly made subject to a stockholder's demand. However, if a dividend is declared payable on December 31 and the corporation follows a practice of paying the dividend by checks mailed so that the shareholders will not receive them until January of the following year, the dividend is not considered to be constructively received by the stockholders in December.[61] For the time of receipt by shareholders of certain mutual fund dividends, see ¶ 2309. Accrued interest on an unwithdrawn insurance policy dividend is gross income to the taxpayer for the first tax year during which the interest may be withdrawn.[62]

Salaries credited on corporate books are taxable to an officer in the year when the officer may withdraw the compensation at will if the corporation has funds available to pay the salaries without causing financial difficulties. Bonuses that are based on yearly sales and that are otherwise not available to an officer are taxable in the year of receipt.[63]

Accrued interest on a deposit that may not be withdrawn at the close of an individual's tax year because of an institution's actual or threatened bankruptcy or insolvency is not includible in the depositor's income until the year in which such interest is withdrawable (Code Sec. 451(g)).[64]

Any option to accelerate the receipt of any payment under a production flexibility contract (between certain eligible owners and producers and the Secretary of Agriculture) which is payable under the Federal Agriculture Improvement and Reform Act of 1996 (the FAIR Act) is to be disregarded in determining the tax year in which such payment is properly included in gross income (Act Sec. 525 of P.L. 106-170).

1535. Notes as Income and Payment. The fact that the negotiable note of a responsible and solvent maker, received in payment of salary, interest, rent, etc., must be reported by a recipient on the cash basis as income to the extent of its fair market value when received does not mean that the maker (on a cash basis) may also deduct the same amount at that time.

The Supreme Court has held that delivery of a note is not a payment on the cash basis, and the deduction may be taken only in the year when the note is paid. Giving collateral to secure the note does not change the promise to pay into an actual payment.[65]

Deferred and Accrued Income and Expense

1537. Deferred and Accrued Income. Payments received in advance are usually income to an accrual-basis taxpayer as well as to a cash-basis taxpayer in the year of receipt, provided that there is no restriction on the use of such payments. This is true even though the payments are returnable upon the happening of some specified event. A distinction must be made, however, between prepayments that may be refunded for services or goods and deposits over which the taxpayer does not have complete

---

Footnote references are to paragraphs of the 2008 Standard Federal Tax Reports.

[59] ¶ 20,800
[60] ¶ 21,007
[61] ¶ 21,007, ¶ 21,009.1235

[62] ¶ 21,007
[63] ¶ 21,007, ¶ 21,009.17
[64] ¶ 21,002

[65] ¶ 21,817.185

dominion and control upon receipt.[66] A utility company was not required to include deposits from uncreditworthy customers in income upon receipt since the utility was required to return the deposit upon request by a customer who established creditworthiness.

Prepaid merchandise. Inclusion in the year of receipt is also required for advance payments received on the sale of merchandise. However, under certain circumstances the IRS permits accrual-basis sellers to include certain advance payments in income in the tax year in which such payments are properly accruable under the method of accounting used for tax purposes if they are reported at that time or later for financial reporting purposes (Reg. § 1.451-5).[67] If the method used for financial reporting results in an earlier accrual, then the advance payments are taxed according to the financial reporting method. When a long-term contract method of accounting (¶ 1551) is used, advances are included in income under that method without regard to how the income from these payments is accounted for in the seller's financial reports.

An advance payment for the above purposes is any amount received by an accrual-basis taxpayer under an agreement (1) for the sale or other disposition in a future tax year of goods held by the taxpayer primarily for sale to customers in the ordinary course of his trade or business or (2) for the building, installation, construction or manufacture of items by the taxpayer where the agreement is not completed within such tax year. An exception exists where substantial advance payments for inventoriable goods have been received and goods are on hand or available to satisfy the agreement in the year of receipt. Payments for gift certificates are substantial when received, but in other cases, advance payments are not substantial until they exceed the cost of goods to be sold. In such cases, all advance payments received by the last day of the second tax year following the year in which the substantial advance payments are received and not previously included in income under the taxpayer's method of accounting must be included in income in such second tax year (Reg. § 1.451-5(c)).[68]

Certain manufacturers, wholesalers and retailers that receive advance payments for multi-year service warranty contracts may elect to recognize income from such advance payments as a series of equal payments over the life of the contracts. This election is permitted only if an eligible taxpayer purchases insurance to cover its obligations under a service warranty contract within 60 days after the sale of the contract (Rev. Proc. 97-38).[69]

Prepaid services and mixed prepayments. Taxpayers who receive advance payments for services and advance payments for the transfer of both goods and services are allowed a limited deferral beyond the tax year of receipt for certain advance payments (Rev. Proc. 2004-34). Generally, excludible payments include payments for services, the sale of goods (other than for the sale of goods for which the taxpayer uses a method of deferral for prepaid merchandise provided in Reg. § 1.451-5(b)(1)(ii)), the use (including by license or lease) of intellectual property, the occupancy or use of property if the occupancy or use is ancillary to the provision of services (for example, advance payments for the use of rooms or other quarters in a hotel, booth space at a trade show, campsite space at a mobile home park, and recreational or banquet facilities, or other uses of property, so long as the use is ancillary to the provision of services to the property user), the sale, lease, or license of computer software, guaranty or warranty contracts ancillary to an item or items described above, subscriptions (other than subscriptions for which an election under Code Sec. 455 is in effect), whether or not provided in a tangible or intangible format, memberships in an organization (other than memberships for which an election under Code Sec. 456 is in effect), or any combination of items.

The term "advance payment" does not include rent, insurance premiums, to the extent the recognition of those premiums is governed by Subchapter L, payments with respect to financial instruments (for example, debt instruments, deposits, letters of credit, notional principal contracts, options, forward contracts, futures contracts, foreign currency contracts, credit card agreements, financial derivatives, etc.), including pur-

---

Footnote references are to paragraphs of the 2008 Standard Federal Tax Reports.

[66] ¶ 21,005.027
[67] ¶ 21,016

[68] ¶ 21,016
[69] ¶ 20,620.20

ported prepayments of interest, payments with respect to service warranty contracts, payments with respect to warranty and guaranty contracts under which a third party is the primary obligor, and certain other payments.

Qualifying taxpayers generally may defer to the next succeeding tax year the inclusion in gross income for federal income tax purposes of advance payments to the extent the advance payments are not recognized in revenues for financial statement purposes (or, in certain cases, are not earned) in the tax year of receipt. Except in the case of certain short tax years, the IRS does not permit deferral to a tax year later than the next succeeding tax year. These rules neither restrict a taxpayer's ability to use the methods of deferral for the advance payment of merchandise (see *"Prepaid merchandise,"* above) nor limit the period of deferral available under that regulation.

Example 1: Advance payment for 48 dancing lessons under a one-year contract is received on November 1, 2007, by a calendar-year taxpayer. Eight lessons are given in 2007. The remaining lessons are provided in 2008. In its applicable financial statement, the dance studio recognizes $\frac{1}{6}$ of the payment in revenues for 2007 and $\frac{5}{6}$ of the payment in revenues for 2008. If the dance studio, an accrual-basis taxpayer, elects the above deferral method, $\frac{1}{6}$ of the payment is includible in 2007 income and $\frac{5}{6}$ of it is taxable as 2008 income, even if not all of the remaining 40 lessons are given in 2008.

Example 2: Assume the same facts as in the previous example, except that the advance payment is received for a 2-year contract under which up to 96 lessons are provided. The dance studio provides eight lessons in 2007, 48 lessons in 2008, and 40 lessons in 2009. In its applicable financial statement, the studio recognizes $\frac{1}{12}$ of the payment in revenues for 2007, $\frac{6}{12}$ of the payment in revenues for 2008, and $\frac{5}{12}$ of the payment in gross revenues for 2009. For federal income tax purposes, the studio must include $\frac{1}{12}$ of the payment in gross income for 2007 and the remaining $\frac{11}{12}$ of the payment in gross income for 2008.

Certain accrual-basis membership organizations and publishers can defer prepaid dues and subscription income (Code Secs. 455 and 456).[70]

Tax Benefit Rule. An amount that has been deducted from gross income in a prior year must be included in income in the year of recovery, but only to the extent that the deduction had reduced taxable income in the year of the deduction (Code Sec. 111(a)).[71]

Accrued Income. A number of Code provisions may require cash-basis taxpayers to report income that has not yet been received. The computation of such income often uses present value concepts. In addition, such Code provisions may require accrual-basis taxpayers to compute income for tax purposes in a manner that differs from generally accepted accounting methods. For a discussion of accruals of rental payments (Code Sec. 467), see ¶ 1541. For a discussion of original issue discount (Code Sec. 1272), see ¶ 1952. For a discussion of certain debt instruments issued for property (Code Sec. 1274), see ¶ 1954.

1539. Deferred and Accrued Expense. *Prepaid Expenses for Cash-Basis Taxpayers.* Cash-basis taxpayers may deduct certain prepaid *expenses* in the year paid under certain conditions. A distinction is made between expenditures that are more in the nature of expenses and those that are capital in nature. If the payment creates an asset having a useful life extending substantially beyond the end of the tax year in which paid, the expenditure may not be deductible, or may be deductible only in part, in that year. If payment is made for a capital asset or is capital in nature, a deferment and charge-off for depreciation, amortization or other comparable allowance are proper.[72] See ¶ 1201.

Thus, if a calendar-year taxpayer signs a three-year business property lease on December 1 of the tax year and agrees to pay an "additional rental" of $18,000 plus a monthly rental of $1,000 for 36 months, he can deduct only $1,500 for the tax year ($1,000 rent plus $\frac{1}{36}$ of $18,000). The $18,000 is an amount paid for securing the lease and must be amortized over the lease term.[73]

Footnote references are to paragraphs of the 2008 Standard Federal Tax Reports.

[70] ¶ 21,510, ¶ 21,520   [72] ¶ 21,817.038
[71] ¶ 7060   [73] ¶ 21,817.05, ¶ 21,817.635

Cash-basis farmers and ranchers can deduct prepaid feed costs in the year of payment if:

    (1) the advance feed expenditure is a payment and not a deposit;

    (2) the payment is for a business purpose; and

    (3) the deduction does not cause a material distortion of income.[74]

However, generally, no deduction is allowed to a cash-basis taxpayer (other than farming syndicates) in the year of prepayment for advance payments for feed, seed, fertilizer, or other supplies to the extent such prepayments exceed 50% of total deductible farming expenses (excluding prepaid supplies) (Code Sec. 464(f)).[75] (For rules applicable to farming syndicates, see ¶ 2032.) The limitation does not apply to a "farm-related taxpayer" if:

    (1) the aggregate prepaid farm supplies for the preceding three tax years are less than 50% of the aggregate deductible farming expenses (other than prepaid farm supplies) for that period or

    (2) the taxpayer has excess prepaid farm supplies for the tax year by reason of any change in business operation directly attributable to extraordinary circumstances.

A farm-related taxpayer is one whose principal residence is on a farm and who has a principal occupation of farming. Family members of such a taxpayer (as defined by Code Sec. 464(c)(2)(E)) also qualify for the exception.

In *S.A. Keller*,[76] the Eighth Circuit indicated that the three-pronged test for prepaid feed, described above, was appropriate in determining the deductibility of certain oil-drilling prepayments.

Estimated state income taxes paid in advance are deductible by a cash-basis taxpayer in the year paid (Rev. Rul. 56-124).[77]

See ¶ 1055 for a discussion of the allowance of deductions for prepaid interest payments. See also ¶ 2042 for a discussion of prepaid expenses of tax shelters.

Accrued Expenses for Accrual-Basis Taxpayers. Under the "all-events" test, an accrual-basis taxpayer is generally entitled to deduct the face amount of an accrued expense in the tax year in which (1) all of the events have occurred that determine the fact of liability and (2) the amount of the liability can be determined with reasonable accuracy. All of the events that establish liability for an amount, for the purpose of determining whether such amount has been incurred regarding any item, are treated as not occurring any earlier than the time that economic performance occurs (Code Sec. 461(h)).[78]

For a liability of a taxpayer that requires a payment for property or services, economic performance is deemed to occur as the property or services are provided to the taxpayer. If the liability arises out of the taxpayer's use of property, economic performance occurs as the taxpayer uses the property.

    Example 1: A partnership on the accrual basis contractually obligates itself in October 2007 to pay Techno Inc. $10,000 for research and development to be performed in 2008. No amount is deductible before performance is rendered in 2008.

However, taxpayers are permitted to accrue payments before services are rendered or property is received if the taxpayer can reasonably expect the services or property to be provided within 3½ months after payment (Reg. § 1.461-4(d)(6)(ii)).[79]

    Example 2: An accrual-method, calendar-year taxpayer makes payment on December 1, 2007, for goods it expects to receive by March 12, 2008. It may deduct the payment or otherwise take it into account for its 2007 tax year.

If the liability of the taxpayer requires him to provide services or property, then economic performance occurs as the taxpayer incurs costs (Reg. § 1.461-4(d)).[80]

Footnote references are to paragraphs of the 2008 Standard Federal Tax Reports.

[74] ¶ 21,817.205
[75] ¶ 21,840
[76] ¶ 21,817.209

[77] ¶ 21,817.1875
[78] ¶ 21,802
[79] ¶ 21,810

[80] ¶ 21,810

Example 3: Zop Corp., a calendar-year, accrual-method taxpayer, sells lawn mowers under a three-year warranty that obligates Zop to make reasonable repairs to each mower it sells. In 2007, Zop repairs, at a cost of $2,500, 12 mowers sold in 2006. Economic performance with respect to Zop's liability to perform services under the warranty occurs as Zop incurs costs in connection with the liability. Consequently, the $2,500 expense incurred by Zop is a deduction for the 2007 tax year.

However, certain manufacturers, wholesalers and retailers that make advance payments to purchase insurance policies that cover their obligations under multi-year service warranty contracts must capitalize the cost of the policies and deduct such cost ratably over the life of the policies. This rule applies regardless of whether the taxpayer uses the cash or accrual method (Rev. Proc. 97-38).[81]

Under an exception to the above general rules for economic performance, payment is considered to be economic performance for the following:

(1) liabilities to another person arising out of any workers' compensation, tort, or breach of contract claims against the taxpayer or any violation of law by the taxpayer;

(2) rebates and refunds;

(3) awards, prizes, and jackpots;

(4) insurance, warranty and service contracts; and

(5) taxes other than creditable foreign taxes.

The IRS may specify additional "payment liabilities" in the future (Reg. § 1.461-4(g)).[82]

Under certain limited circumstances, an irrevocable payment to a court-ordered settlement fund that completely extinguishes specified tort liabilities will constitute economic performance (Code Sec. 468B; Reg. § 1.461-2).[83]

Certain recurring items are treated as incurred in advance of economic performance by taxpayers other than tax shelters. Under this exception, an item is treated as incurred during a tax year if:

(1) the all-events test, without regard to economic performance, is satisfied during that year,

(2) the economic performance test is met within the shorter of 8½ months or a reasonable time after the close of the year,

(3) the item is recurring in nature and the taxpayer consistently treats similar items as incurred in the tax year in which the all-events test is met, and

(4) either the item is not material or accrual of the item in the year that the all-events test is met results in a better matching against the income to which it relates than accrual of the item in the tax year of economic performance.

In determining whether an item is material or whether a more proper matching against income results from deduction of an expense prior to economic performance, the treatment of the expense on financial statements is to be taken into account but will not necessarily govern the tax treatment of the expense (Code Sec. 461(h)(3)).[84]

A taxpayer may adopt the recurring item exception as part of its method of accounting for any type of expense for the first tax year in which that type of expense is incurred. Generally, the rules of Code Sec. 446(e) and Reg. § 1.446-1(e) apply to changes to or from the recurring item exception as a method of accounting (Reg. § 1.461-5(d)).[85]

An item is recurring if it can generally be expected to be incurred from one tax year to the next (Reg. § 1.461-5(b)(3)).[86] However, a taxpayer may treat a liability as recurring even if it is not incurred in each tax year. Also, a liability that has never previously been incurred may be treated as recurring if it is reasonable to expect that it will be incurred on a recurring basis in the future.

Footnote references are to paragraphs of the 2008 Standard Federal Tax Reports.

[81] ¶ 20,620.20, ¶ 21,817.027 [83] ¶ 21,950 [85] ¶ 21,811
[82] ¶ 21,810 [84] ¶ 21,802 [86] ¶ 21,811

1541. Deferred Payments Under Rental Agreements. Lessors and lessees of certain leaseback and long-term rental agreements under Code Sec. 467 and Reg. § 1.467-1 that involve the use of property must report income and expenses arising out of such agreements by applying statutory accrual-basis and present-value principles (Code Sec. 467).[87] Such treatment, in effect, is an extension of the principles embodied in the rules on taxation of original issue discount. Although the rules under Code Sec. 467 apply to the use of property, the IRS is given authority to extend similar rules to agreements for services.

"Section 467 rental agreements" cover tangible property with respect to which either (1) at least one amount, allocable to the use of property in the calendar year, is to be paid after the close of the following calendar year (deferred payments) or (2) there are increases in the amount to be paid as rent under the agreement (stepped rents). A "section 467 rental agreement" does not encompass a rental agreement in which the sum of the amounts to be paid is $250,000 or less.

The lessor or lessee of any section 467 agreement must report for any tax year (regardless of the accounting method used) the sum of (1) the accrued rental payments and (2) any interest for the year (calculated at the rate of 110% of the applicable federal rate compounded semiannually) on unpaid rents (amounts that were attributed to a prior tax year but are still unpaid as of the current tax year).

The accrued rental payments—except in tax-avoidance transactions and agreements that do not allocate rents—are calculated by (1) allocating rents in accordance with the agreement and (2) including the present value of rents allocable to the period but paid after the close of the period. In tax-avoidance transactions and agreements that do not allocate rents, the rent that accrues during the tax year is equal to the allocable portion of the "constant rental amount." The "constant rental amount" is equal to the amount which, if paid as of the close of each lease period, would result in an aggregate present value equal to the present value of the aggregate payments required under the lease.

Claim-of-Right Repayments

1543. Claim-of-Right Doctrine. Under an established principle of tax law, payments must be included in gross income if the taxpayer receives them without restriction under a claim of right. This is true even though the taxpayer may discover in a later year that he had no right to the payments in the earlier year and is required to repay the same amount. Under this claim-of-right doctrine, the taxpayer may deduct the repayments in the year in which they are made.

When the repayments exceed income for the year of repayment or when the income (after subtraction of such repayments) is taxed at a rate lower than that at which the income in the year of inclusion was taxed, the deduction does not compensate the taxpayer adequately for the tax paid in the earlier year. The law eliminates this inequity if the amount repaid exceeds $3,000. In such case, the taxpayer is to reduce his tax for the year of repayment by the amount of tax for the previous year which was attributable to inclusion of this amount; any excess is to be claimed as a refund. However, if a smaller tax liability results from simply deducting the repaid amount in the year of repayment, the taxpayer is to claim the deduction instead (Code Sec. 1341; Reg. § 1.1341-1).[88]

In either case, the adjustment is made for the year of repayment. The return for the prior year, i.e., the year in which the item was received, is not reopened; in no case will there be an allowance for interest on the tax paid for the earlier year.

> **Example:** In 2006, a single taxpayer reported taxable income of $55,000 (adjusted gross income of $63,450 minus $3,300 personal exemption minus $5,150 standard deduction), consisting entirely of sales commissions, on which he paid a tax of $10,314. In 2007, it is determined that the commissions were erroneously computed for 2006. Accordingly, the taxpayer pays back $6,000 of the commissions. His taxable income for 2007, without regard to the $6,000 repayment, is $13,200.

Footnote references are to paragraphs of the 2008 Standard Federal Tax Reports.

[87] ¶ 21,910   [88] ¶ 31,880, ¶ 31,881

The tax for 2007 will be computed as follows:

(a) Tax on $7,200 ($13,200 less $6,000)		$723
(b) Tax on $13,200		$1,606
Less: Difference between—		
Tax paid for 2006 on $55,000	$10,314	
Tax payable in 2006 on $49,000		
($55,000 − $6,000)	$8,814	1,500
		$106

The tax for 2007 is the lesser of the amount computed under (a) or (b). In this case, the amount computed under (b) is less than the amount computed under (a). Thus, the tax for 2007 is $106, the amount computed under (b).

When the tax for the year of restoration under a claim of right is reduced by the amount of the tax already paid on the item in a previous year, the amount restored is not considered for any purpose. For example, taxpayers cannot use such amount in computing a net operating loss for the year of restoration (Reg. § 1.1341-1(b)(2)).[89] The reduction of tax in the year of repayment does not apply where the taxpayer did, in fact, have an unrestricted right to receive the amount in the prior year and the obligation to repay arose as the result of subsequent events.

Reserves of Income and Expense

1545. Dealer's Reserve. Dealers who discount customers' installment paper with financial institutions that withhold a small percentage of the price and credit it to a "Dealer's Reserve Account" as security for the dealer's guaranty of payment of the installment paper must accrue such credits as income in the year when the installment paper is transferred to the financial institution.[90]

This has been applied to accrual-basis home sellers who guarantee buyers' loans by requiring them to accrue as income in the year of sale the proceeds pledged as loan security to the lender.[91] As to a cash-basis taxpayer, however, the pledged amounts are taxable to him only as they become available for withdrawal (the pledged amount was in a restricted savings account and could be withdrawn in specified amounts only as the buyer reduced the loan principal by certain amounts).[92]

1547. Reserve for Estimated Expense. Although reserves for contingent liabilities are often set up in business practice, amounts credited to them are generally not deductible for income tax purposes because the fact of liability is not fixed.[93] For example, advance deductions have been denied for additions to a reserve for expected cash discounts on outstanding receivables,[94] amounts credited by a manufacturer to a reserve for possible future warranty service,[95] and additions to a reserve covering estimated liability of a carrier for tort claims.[96] However, to the extent that the Code specifically provides for a deduction for a reserve for estimated expenses, the economic performance rules of Code Sec. 461(h) do not apply (Code Sec. 461(h)(5)).[97]

1549. Accrual of Vacation and Sick Leave Pay. A vacation or sick leave pay deduction is generally limited to the amount of pay earned during the year to the extent (1) the amount is paid to employees during the year or (2) the amount is vested as of the last day of the tax year and is paid to employees within 2.5 months after the end of the year. If such vacation or sick leave pay is not paid until after the expiration of such period, the employer may deduct vacation pay when paid and sick leave pay in its tax year that includes the last day of the employee's tax year for which the payment is reported as income by the employee (Code Sec. 404(a)(5); Temporary Reg. § 1.404(b)-1T).[98] However, vacation and sick leave pay incurred with respect to the production of real and tangible personal property or with respect to property acquired for resale is considered a direct labor cost that must be capitalized by taxpayers subject to the uniform capitalization rules (Reg. § 1.263A-1(e)(2)(i)(B)).[99] See ¶ 991.

Footnote references are to paragraphs of the 2008 Standard Federal Tax Reports.

[89] ¶ 31,881
[90] ¶ 21,005.032
[91] ¶ 21,005.032
[92] ¶ 21,005.032

[93] ¶ 21,817.688
[94] ¶ 21,817.034
[95] ¶ 21,817.034
[96] ¶ 21,817.65

[97] ¶ 21,802
[98] ¶ 21,817.033
[99] ¶ 13,811

An employer may deduct FICA and FUTA taxes attributable to accrued vacation pay only in the tax year that payments are actually made to employees.[100]

Long-Term Contract

1551. Special Treatment. A long-term contract is a building, installation, construction or manufacturing contract that is not completed within the tax year in which it is entered into. However, a manufacturing contract will not be considered long term unless the contract involves the manufacture of (1) unique items not normally carried in the finished goods inventory or (2) items normally requiring more than 12 calendar months to complete (regardless of the duration of the actual contract). The income from long-term contracts may be reported in either of the following ways:

(1) *Percentage-of-Completion Method.* Gross income may be reported annually according to the percentage of the contract completed in that year. The completion percentage, in the case of long-term contracts entered into after February 28, 1986, must be determined by comparing costs allocated and incurred before the end of the tax year with the estimated total contract costs (cost-to-cost method). In the case of contracts entered into before March 1, 1986, the completion percentage can be determined under the cost-to-cost method or by comparing the work completed to date with the total estimate of work to be completed. All expenditures made during the tax year must be deducted, taking into account unused material and supplies on hand at the beginning and end of the taxable period (Code Sec. 460(b)(1)(A) and Reg. § 1.460-4(b)).[101]

(2) *Completed-Contract Method.* In limited circumstances, net profit on the entire job may be reported in the year in which the contract is completed and accepted (Reg. § 1.460-4(a)).[102]

Under the completed-contract method, expenses allocable to the contract (i.e., contract costs) are deductible in the year in which the contract is completed. Expenses that are not allocated to the contract (i.e., period costs) are deductible in the year in which they are paid or incurred, depending on the method of accounting employed.[103] Regulations direct the proper allocation of expenses between contract costs and period costs (Reg. § 1.460-1(d))[104] and clarify when (1) a contract is to be considered completed (Reg. § 1.460-1(c)), (2) separate contracts are to be considered as one contract, and (3) one contract is to be considered as several (Reg. § 1.460-1(e)).

A taxpayer may change his method of accounting to conform with either of these special methods only after he secures permission from the IRS (Reg. § 1.460-4(a)).[105] See ¶ 1529. Permission is also required for a change from percentage-of-completion to completed-contract basis, or vice versa.

Long-Term Contracts After February 28, 1986. Most long-term contracts entered into after July 10, 1989, must be fully accounted for under the percentage-of-completion method. For long-term contracts entered into after February 28, 1986, and before July 11, 1989, for which the percentage-of-completion method is not used, taxpayers are required to use the percentage-of-completion capitalized-cost method. Under this method, a percentage of the contract items are taken into account under the percentage-of-completion method and a percentage of the contract items are taken into account under the taxpayer's normal method of accounting (e.g., the completed contract method, an accrual shipment method, etc.). For long-term contracts entered into after June 20, 1988, and before July 11, 1989 (other than certain qualified ship contracts), 90% of the contract items are taken into account under the percentage-of-completion method and 10% of the contract items are taken into account under the taxpayer's normal method of accounting. (For contracts entered into after October 13, 1987, and before June 21, 1988, 70% of the contract items are accounted for under the percentage-of-completion method and 30% are accounted for under the taxpayer's normal method of accounting, and for contracts entered into after February 28, 1986, and before October 14, 1987, the respective percentages are 40% and 60%.)

For example, if there is a long-term contract executed on July 10, 1989, a taxpayer who normally uses the completed-contract method can defer recognition of only 10% of

[100] ¶ 21,817.033
[101] ¶ 21,550, ¶ 21,555

[102] ¶ 21,555
[103] ¶ 21,560.029

[104] ¶ 21,560.044
[105] ¶ 21,560.50

the gross contract income, along with a deduction of 10% of the contract costs, until completion of the contract. The remaining 90% of such income and costs is, respectively, recognized and deducted to the same extent that it would be under the percentage-of-completion method (Code Sec. 460(a)).[106]

Home and Residential Construction Contracts. Neither the percentage-of-completion method nor the percentage-of-completion capitalized-cost method of accounting applies to home construction contracts (in which at least 80% of the estimated total costs to be incurred under the contract is attributable to dwelling units in a building with four or fewer dwelling units) and certain other construction contracts of small contractors (see below) (Code Sec. 460(e)).[107] The uniform capitalization rules apply to home construction contracts other than contracts of small contractors (Code Sec. 460(e)(1)).[108]

The percentage-of-completion capitalized-cost method applies to residential construction contracts that do not qualify as home construction contracts, but it is applied according to the 70%-30% rule rather than the 90%-10% rule discussed above (Code Sec. 460(e)(5)).[109]

Look-Back Rule. To the extent that the percentage-of-completion method applies to a long-term contract, a taxpayer who errs in his estimate of the contract price or costs must recompute his tax liability on the basis of the actual contract price and costs for the years that such method was used. Thus, if 40%, 70%, 90% or 100% (whichever applies) of the contract income was reported using the percentage-of-completion method, under the rule described above, the look-back rule is applied to that portion upon completion of the contract. The taxpayer may elect not to apply or reapply the look-back method if, for each prior contract year, the cumulative taxable income or loss under the contract, as determined using estimated contract price or costs, is within 10 percent of the cumulative taxable income or loss as determined using actual contract price and costs. A taxpayer will either pay or receive interest (at the rate for overpayment of tax provided by Code Sec. 6621, compounded daily) on the amount by which the recomputed tax liability for a year exceeds or is less than the previously reported tax liability (Code Sec. 460(b)(2)).[110] Only one rate of interest will apply for each "accrual period," the period which begins on the date after the original return due date for the tax year and which ends on the original return due date for the following tax year. The applicable "adjusted overpayment rate" of interest is the overpayment rate in effect for the calendar quarter in which the accrual period begins.

The look-back method does not apply to certain long-term contracts that are completed within two years of the contract commencement date and have a small gross contract price (Code Sec. 460(b) and Code Sec. 460(e)(1)(B)).[111]

Pass-through entities (partnerships, S corporations, and trusts) that are not closely held must use a simplified look-back method if substantially all of the income under a long-term contract is from sources in the United States (Code Sec. 460(b)(4)).[112] A closely held entity is an entity where 50% or more of the value of the beneficial interests are owned by five or fewer persons. The amount of taxes deemed overpaid or underpaid under a contract in any year is determined at the entity level and is the product of the amount of contract income overreported or underreported for the year times the top marginal tax rate applicable for the year (the top corporate tax rate, or the top individual tax rate if more than 50% of the beneficial interests in the entity are held by individuals).

Allocation and Capitalization of Costs. In general, all costs (including research and experimental costs) that directly benefit or are incurred because of a long-term contract are to be allocated to the contract under Code Sec. 451 and the regulations thereunder that apply to extended period long-term contracts. However, independent research and development costs, expenses incurred in making unsuccessful bids and proposals, and marketing, selling and advertising costs may be expensed. For a cost-plus or federal long-term contract, costs that are not allocated to the contract under the extended period long-term contract rules must be capitalized if identified by the taxpayer (or a related

---

Footnote references are to paragraphs of the 2008 Standard Federal Tax Reports.

[106] ¶ 21,550	[109] ¶ 21,560.027	[112] ¶ 21,550
[107] ¶ 21,560.04	[110] ¶ 21,560.033	
[108] ¶ 21,550	[111] ¶ 21,550	

¶1551

person) as attributable or allocable to the contract. Such an attribution or allocation can be created by the terms of the contract or by federal, state, or local laws and regulations. Allocation of production period interest is governed by rules (Code Sec. 263A(f)) (see ¶ 1561) that apply to property not produced under a long-term contract (Code Sec. 460(c)).

Pension expense (including previously deducted pension expense that represents past service costs) is subject to the uniform capitalization rules (Code Sec. 263A) and the long-term contract cost allocation rules (Code Sec. 460). Thus, an allocable portion of all otherwise deductible pension costs, whether they relate to current or past services, is included in the basis of property that is produced or held for resale or is allocated to long-term contracts that are subject to the cost allocation rules.

Small Construction Contracts Exception. Small construction contracts are generally not subject to the 40%, 70%, 90% or 100% (whichever is applicable) current recognition requirement, the look-back rules or the cost allocation rules (except for the production period interest rules). A small construction contract is one that is (1) expected to be completed within the two-year period beginning on the commencement date of the contract and (2) performed by a taxpayer whose average annual gross receipts for the three tax years preceding the tax year in which the contract is entered into do not exceed $10 million (Code Sec. 460(e)).

Inventories

1553. Need for Inventories. The use of inventories at the beginning and end of each year is required in most every case where the production, purchase or sale of merchandise is an income-producing factor. Inventories must also be used wherever necessary to clearly reflect income, in the opinion of the IRS (Code Sec. 471(a); Reg. § 1.471-1).[113] A taxpayer whose average annual gross receipts do not exceed $1,000,000 and certain taxpayers whose average annual gross receipts do not exceed $10,000,000 (Rev. Proc. 2002-28) are generally not required to use inventories or the accrual method of accounting (Rev. Proc. 2001-10). However, such a taxpayer who does not otherwise use inventories must treat merchandise inventory in the same manner as a material or supply that is not incidental (see Reg. § 1.162-3); the uniform capitalization rules (Code Sec. 263A) will not apply to such merchandise inventory.

A farmer may use the cash method of accounting for purchases and sales if he desires, (See the accrual method requirement for certain farming corporations at ¶ 2028.) However, any taxpayer, including a farmer, who uses inventories must use the accrual method of accounting for purchases and sales.

1555. Inventories Explained. Gross profit from business operations is calculated by subtracting from receipts the cost of goods sold. See ¶ 759. The cost of goods sold is calculated by adding the inventory at the beginning of the year to the cost of goods purchased or produced during the year and subtracting from this total the inventory at the end of the year. Use of the accrual basis and inventories more clearly reflects the income of a single accounting period through recognition of unsold goods on hand at the beginning and end of each tax year.

1557. Items Included in Inventory. An inventory is an itemized list, with valuations, of goods held for sale or consumption in a manufacturing or merchandising business. Taxpayers must usually verify the amount of items in inventory by a physical count of the items as of the last day of the tax year. Taxpayers may use estimates of inventory shrinkage that are confirmed by a physical count after year-end if the taxpayer normally does a physical inventory count at each location on a regular and consistent basis and the taxpayer makes proper adjustments to such inventories and to its estimating methods to the extent such estimates are greater than or less than the actual shrinkage.

Inventory should include all finished or partly finished goods and only those raw materials and supplies which have been acquired for sale or which will physically become a part of merchandise intended for sale. Merchandise should be included in

---

Footnote references are to paragraphs of the 2008 Standard Federal Tax Reports.

[113] ¶ 22,202, ¶ 22,203

inventory only if title to it is vested in the taxpayer. A seller should include in inventory goods under contract for sale but not yet segregated and applied to the contract and goods out on consignment. The seller should not include goods sold (including containers) where title has passed to the buyer. A buyer should include in inventory merchandise purchased (including containers) where title has passed to him, even where the merchandise is in transit or has not been physically received (Reg. § 1.471-1).[114]

Permission to include real estate held for sale by a real estate dealer in inventory has been denied.[115] Likewise, capital assets, equipment, accounts, notes, investments, cash, or similar assets may not be included in inventories.

For inventories of farmers and dealers in securities, see ¶ 1569 and ¶ 1903.

1559. Valuation of Inventory. An inventory must conform to the best accounting practice in the particular trade or business and it must clearly reflect income. An inventory that, under the best accounting practice, can be used in a balance sheet showing the financial position of the taxpayer will generally be regarded as clearly reflecting income. In determining whether income is clearly reflected, great weight is given to consistency in inventory practice (Reg. § 1.471-2),[116] but a legitimate accounting system will be disallowed where it distorts income.[117]

It is necessary to identify the particular goods in inventory so that proper costs can be applied to the quantities. Identification of inventories is ordinarily accomplished by the first-in, first-out (FIFO) rule, unless the items are specifically identified. This rule is discussed at ¶ 1564. A taxpayer can also elect to identify inventory items by use of the last-in, first-out (LIFO) rule discussed at ¶ 1565.

Either of two common methods for valuing inventories may be adopted: (1) cost or (2) lower of cost or market (Reg. § 1.471-2).[118] Opening and closing inventories must be valued by the same method.[119] If the "lower of cost or market" method is used, it must be consistently applied to each item in the inventory. Cost and market value are determined as to each item, and the lower amount is included in the inventory valuation. A taxpayer is not permitted to inventory the entire stock at cost and also at market and use the lower of the two results (Reg. § 1.471-4).[120] Deviations are permitted, however, as to goods inventoried under the LIFO method (¶ 1565) and as to animals inventoried under the "unit-livestock-price" method (¶ 1569).

Special rules apply to a dealer in securities. See ¶ 1903.

Whether the "cost" or the "lower of cost or market" method is used, inventoried goods that are unsalable, or unusable in normal transactions because of wear and tear, obsolescence or broken lots, should be valued at bona fide selling price, less cost of selling; that is, at the actual offering of goods during a period ending not later than 30 days after inventory date. Adjustment of the valuation on a reasonable basis, not less than scrap value, is permitted in the case of unsalable or unusable raw material or partly finished goods (Reg. § 1.471-2(c)).[121]

See ¶ 1561 for discussion of the costs included in the cost of inventory and ¶ 1563 for discussion of the "lower of cost or market" method.

1561. Inventory at Cost: Uniform Capitalization Rules. Uniform capitalization rules govern the inclusion in inventory or capital accounts of all allocable costs that are incurred with respect to real and tangible personal property that is produced by the taxpayer or acquired for resale and would otherwise be considered in computing taxable income (Code Sec. 263A(a) and (b)).[122] For this purpose, tangible personal property includes a film, sound recording, videotape, book, or similar property. Except for the interest capitalization rules, the uniform capitalization rules also apply to costs incurred with respect to real or personal (whether tangible or intangible) property that is acquired for resale. Certain small businesses with average annual gross receipts not

---

Footnote references are to paragraphs of the 2008 Standard Federal Tax Reports.

[114] ¶ 22,204.04	[117] ¶ 22,206.01	[120] ¶ 22,209
[115] ¶ 22,204.36	[118] ¶ 22,206.01	[121] ¶ 22,206.01
[116] ¶ 22,206.01	[119] ¶ 22,206.12	[122] ¶ 13,800

exceeding $10 million for the three previous years that acquire personal property for resale are exempt from these rules (Code Sec. 263A(b)(2)(B)).[123]

Costs attributable to inventory must be added to costs of producing or acquiring the inventory, and costs attributable to producing other property must be capitalized. Direct costs (direct material costs and direct labor costs) and the portion of indirect costs (described in Reg. § 1.263A-1(e)(3)(ii)) allocable to such property are subject to these rules.

The uniform capitalization rules replace the inventory cost rules of Code Sec. 471 in the case of property to which they apply. The rules do not apply to inventories valued at market under either the market method or the lower of cost or market method if the market valuation used by the taxpayer generally equals the property's fair market value (i.e., price of sale to customers less direct disposition costs). However, the uniform capitalization rules do apply in determining the market value of any inventory for which market is determined with reference to replacement cost or reproduction cost (Reg. § 1.263A-1(a)(3)).[124]

Costs incurred with respect to property produced for personal use, timber (including certain ornamental trees), or property produced under long-term contracts, or costs deductible as Code Sec. 174 research and experimental expenditures or as certain oil, gas, and other mineral property, foreign drilling, amortizable or developmental expenditures, and costs (other than circulation expenditures) subject to the ten-year amortization rule for tax preferences are excluded from such rules (Code Sec. 263A(c)).[125]

Certain costs incurred by an individual (or personal service corporation, ¶ 219) engaged in the business of being a writer, photographer, or artist (¶ 990A) that are otherwise deductible are also exempt from such rules (Code Sec. 263A(h)).[126]

In addition, the following costs may be currently deducted under Reg. § 1.263A-1(e)(4): marketing and selling expenses and general and administration expenses that do not directly benefit production or the acquisition of inventory.[127]

Interest Capitalization Rules. Interest costs paid or incurred during the production period to finance the construction, building, installation, manufacture, development, or improvement of real or tangible personal property that is produced by the taxpayer must be capitalized (Code Sec. 263A(f); Reg. § 1.263A-8).[128] Property subject to the interest capitalization requirement includes property that is produced by the taxpayer for use in its trade or business or in an activity for profit and that has (1) a long useful life (real property or any other property with a class life of 20 years or more), (2) an estimated production period exceeding two years, or (3) an estimated production period exceeding one year and a cost exceeding $1 million. The production period begins on the date on which production of the property starts and ends on the date on which the property is ready to be placed in service or is ready to be held for sale.

The interest capitalization rules also apply to property that is produced for a taxpayer under a contract (Code Sec. 263A(g)(2)).[129] Thus, the portion of the taxpayer-customer's interest expense allocable to costs required to be capitalized (including progress payments, advances to the contractor, and an allocable portion of the general and administrative expenses of the taxpayer) must be capitalized.

Capitalization of interest is not required for property acquired for resale (inventory held by a dealer) (Code Sec. 263A(f)(1)(B)).[130] Interest that constitutes qualified residence interest under Code Sec. 163(h) is also excluded from the capitalization rules (Code Sec. 263A(f)(2)(B)).[131]

The determination of whether interest expense is allocable to the production of property is made under the following rules. Interest on a debt that financed production or construction costs of a particular asset is first allocated and capitalized as part of the cost of the item. If the production or construction costs for an asset exceed the amount of this direct debt, interest on other loans is also subject to capitalization under an avoided-cost rule to the extent of the excess. An assumed interest rate based on the

---

Footnote references are to paragraphs of the 2008 Standard Federal Tax Reports.

[123] ¶ 13,800
[124] ¶ 13,811
[125] ¶ 13,800
[126] ¶ 13,800
[127] ¶ 13,811
[128] ¶ 13,800, ¶ 13,852
[129] ¶ 13,800
[130] ¶ 13,800
[131] ¶ 13,800

average interest rates on the taxpayer's outstanding debt, excluding debt specifically traceable to production or construction, may be used for this purpose. For purposes of the interest allocation rule, production or construction expenditures include cumulative production costs (including previously capitalized interest) required to be capitalized (Reg. § 1.263A-9 and Reg. § 1.263A-11).[132]

Interest relating to property used to produce property subject to the interest capitalization rules is also subject to capitalization to the extent such interest is allocable to the produced property as determined under the above rules (Code Sec. 263A(f)(3)).[133]

For flow-through entities (partnerships, S corporations, estates and trusts), the interest capitalization rules are applied first at the entity level and then at the beneficiary level (Code Sec. 263A(f)(2)(C)).[134]

Farming Businesses. For the uniform capitalization rules pertaining to farm businesses, see ¶ 999.

Inventory at Cost: Code Sec. 471 Rules. The rules below are to be used to value inventory at cost where the uniform capitalization rules do not apply. For merchandise on hand at the beginning of the year, "cost" is the amount at which it was included in the closing inventory of the preceding period. For merchandise *bought* after the beginning of the year, "cost" means the invoice price less trade or other discounts, except cash discounts approximating a fair interest rate, which may be deducted from cost, or reported as income, at the option of the taxpayer. Cost also includes transportation or other acquisition charges. For merchandise *produced* by the taxpayer, the costs attributed to inventoried goods must be determined under the uniform capitalization rules (see above).

1563. Inventory at "Cost or Market". If a "cost or market" inventory is used, the market value of each item is compared with the cost of the item, and the lower of the two values must be used for that item (¶ 1559).

> **Example:** A lumber dealer has three grades of lumber at the end of his tax year. They are valued as follows:

Grade	Cost	Market	Lower of Two
A	$45,000	$60,000	$45,000
B	20,000	15,000	15,000
C	5,000	5,000	5,000
	$70,000	$80,000	$65,000

If the lumber dealer is using the cost method, his ending inventory is valued at $70,000. If he is using the lower of cost or market method, his ending inventory is valued at $65,000.

Under normal conditions, market value is the prevailing current bid price at the inventory date in the volume in which the items are usually purchased by the taxpayer. If a current bid price is unobtainable, the best available evidence of fair market value must be used. Specific purchases or sales by the taxpayer or others, or compensation paid for cancellation of contracts for purchase commitments, may be used (Reg. § 1.471-4).[135]

The market value of goods in process and finished goods, for a manufacturer or processor, is reproduction cost. This is the total that materials, labor and factory burden or overhead would cost at current prices to bring the article to a comparable state of completion (Reg. § 1.471-4).[136]

The market price basis does not apply to goods on hand or in the process of manufacture for delivery under firm sale contracts at fixed prices entered into before the inventory date where the taxpayer is protected against actual loss. Such goods must be inventoried at cost (Reg. § 1.471-4).[137]

Footnote references are to paragraphs of the 2008 Standard Federal Tax Reports.

[132] ¶ 13,856, ¶ 13,864
[133] ¶ 13,800
[134] ¶ 13,800
[135] ¶ 22,209
[136] ¶ 22,209
[137] ¶ 22,209

A merchant may also use the "retail method" to approximate the lower of cost or market (Reg. § 1.471-8).[138]

If inventories are valued at cost under the lower of cost or market method, such valuation is subject to the uniform capitalization rules at ¶ 1561.

1564. "First-In, First-Out" (FIFO) Rule. The "first-in, first-out" (FIFO) method assumes that items purchased or produced first are the first items sold, consumed or otherwise disposed of. Accordingly, items in inventory at the end of the year are matched with the costs of similar items that were most recently purchased or produced. The FIFO method of valuation is utilized for items taken in inventory that have been so commingled that they cannot be identified with specific invoices; thus, they are considered to be the items most recently purchased or produced. The cost is the actual cost of the items purchased and produced during the period in which the quantity of items in inventory was acquired.

In the absence of an election to use the "last-in, first-out" method, inventory is identified under the FIFO method (Code Sec. 471).[139]

1565. "Last-In, First-Out" (LIFO) Rule. The "last-in, first-out" (LIFO) method is a means of identifying items in inventory and is based on cost values (Code Sec. 472).[140] Under the LIFO method, inventory is taken at cost, but the items contained in the inventory are treated as being, first, those contained in opening inventory, to the extent of the opening inventory (whether or not they are physically on hand), and, second, those acquired during the tax year. The items treated as still in the opening inventory are taken in order of acquisition, except for the first year in which the method is used. For that year, the items in the opening inventory are taken at the average cost of those items. The closing inventory of the preceding year must also be adjusted and an amended return filed to reflect the changes. In the case of a retailer or certain manufacturers, items deemed to have been purchased during the year, that is, inventory increases, may be taken, at the taxpayer's election, on the basis of the most recent purchases, or at average cost for the year, or in order of acquisition.

A taxpayer need not obtain advance permission from the IRS to elect to use the LIFO method but must adopt it on the return for the year in which the method is first used. In addition, the taxpayer must file a Form 851, Application to Use LIFO Inventory Method, with the return and accept any modifications or adjustments required by the IRS. The election applies only to the class or classes of goods specified in the application. Although the election to adopt LIFO must generally cover the entire inventory of a business, manufacturers or processors may elect to have the method apply to raw materials only, including those in finished goods and work-in-process (Reg. § 1.472-1(h)).[141] Furthermore, if LIFO is used for tax purposes, it generally must also be used in preparing annual financial statements for credit purposes or for the purpose of reports to stockholders, partners, or proprietors. For purposes of this "report rule," all members of the same group of financially related corporations are treated as one taxpayer.

Taxpayers using the LIFO method of accounting who acquire inventory items in a bulk bargain purchase at a substantial discount cannot use the cost of the inventory items as the base-year cost for substantially similar inventory items that are subsequently produced or acquired.[142] Taxpayers that voluntarily choose to change their method of accounting to conform to this rule must file Form 3115, Application for Change in Accounting Method.

1567. Dollar-Value LIFO Method. Instead of determining quantity increases of each item in the inventory and then pricing them, as is required under regular LIFO, the "dollar-value" LIFO method may be used (Reg. § 1.472-8).[143] The increase in LIFO value is determined by comparing the total dollar value of the beginning and ending inventories at base year (first LIFO year) prices and then converting any dollar-value increase to current prices by means of an index. Taxpayers are allowed, under the dollar-value LIFO

Footnote references are to paragraphs of the 2008 Standard Federal Tax Reports.

[138] ¶ 22,217	[140] ¶ 22,230	[142] ¶ 22,277
[139] ¶ 22,202	[141] ¶ 22,231	[143] ¶ 22,240.01

method, to determine base year dollars through the use of government indexes (Code Sec. 472(f)).[144]

Simplified Dollar-Value LIFO Method. Small businesses (those with average gross receipts for the three preceding years of $5 million or less) may elect to use a simplified dollar-value LIFO method to account for their inventories (Code Sec. 474(a) and (c)).[145] The election applies to all succeeding years unless the taxpayer obtains IRS permission to change to another method or becomes ineligible to use such method. If elected, it must be used to value all LIFO inventories.

The simplified dollar-value LIFO method replaces the single LIFO inventory pool method used by taxpayers with average annual gross receipts of $2 million or less. The single LIFO pool election may be revoked without the consent of the IRS or it may still be used by any taxpayer who continues to meet its requirements. However, the simplified dollar-value LIFO method may not be used for any year in which the single LIFO inventory pool method is used.

1569. Special Accounting Methods for Farmers. In addition to the standard cost and the lower of cost or market methods, a farmer on the accrual basis has a choice of two other systems. The "farm-price" method provides for the valuation of inventories at market price less the direct cost of disposition. If this method is used, it must be applied to the entire inventory except livestock which the taxpayer has elected to inventory under the "unit-livestock-price" method (Reg. § 1.471-6(d)).[146]

The "unit-livestock-price" method—adoptable when the farmer raises his own livestock or purchases young animals and raises them to maturity—provides for the valuation *of different classes* of animals at a standard unit price for each animal within a class. This method, once elected, must be applied to all livestock raised to maturity or purchased before maturity and raised to maturity, whether held for sale or for breeding, draft or dairy purposes.[147] This includes unweaned calves, according to the Tax Court.[148] Unit prices assigned to classes must account for normal cost of production. For purchased livestock, the cost should be increased in accordance with unit prices only for animals acquired in the first six months of the tax year (Reg. § 1.471-6(g)).[149]

The "crop" basis of accounting may be used with IRS consent for crops which have not been gathered and disposed of during the tax year in which they are planted (Reg. § 1.61-4(c)).[150] The entire cost of producing the crop must be deducted no earlier than in the year in which the crop income is realized.

1571. Change in Basis of Inventory. A change of inventory basis can be made only when authorized by the IRS. A change from a cash method to an inventory method is, in effect, a change to the accrual method of accounting for purchases and sales (Reg. § 1.446-1(c)(2) and Rev. Proc. 2002-9, modified by Rev. Proc. 2002-54). Permission to make such a change must generally be requested within the tax year that the change is to be effective (¶ 1529), with the exception of an election to change to the LIFO method. An election to use this method may be made by a statement on Form 970 attached to the first tax return in which it is used; however, adjustments will be required to prevent duplications and omissions of income and expenses (Reg. § 1.472-3 and Reg. § 1.472-4).[151]

Allocation and Reconstruction of Income

1573. Allocation by IRS. When two or more organizations, trades, or businesses are owned or controlled by the same interests, the IRS may allocate gross income, deductions or credits between them if it determines such action is necessary to prevent evasion of taxes or to clearly reflect income (Code Sec. 482).[152] Moreover, the IRS is specifically authorized by statute to allocate any income, deduction, credit, exclusion or other allowance between certain personal service corporations and their employee-owners when the principal purpose of forming or using such a corporation is to avoid or evade income tax. See ¶ 1575.

Footnote references are to paragraphs of the 2008 Standard Federal Tax Reports.

[144] ¶ 22,230
[145] ¶ 22,260
[146] ¶ 22,213

[147] ¶ 22,214.026
[148] ¶ 22,214.50
[149] ¶ 22,213

[150] ¶ 5601
[151] ¶ 22,234, ¶ 22,235
[152] ¶ 22,280

1575. Acquisitions to Avoid Tax. If a taxpayer acquires control of a corporation, directly or indirectly, to evade or avoid income tax by securing the benefit of a deduction, credit, or other allowance that would not otherwise be enjoyed, then such deduction, credit or other allowance will not be permitted. The same rules of disallowance apply to a corporation that acquires property of another corporation that was not controlled by the acquiring corporation or its stockholders and that acquires a basis determined by reference to the basis in the hands of the transferor corporation (Code Sec. 269(a)).[153] Code Sec. 269(b)[154] explicitly authorizes the IRS to deny an acquiring corporation the carryover and other tax benefits of a subsidiary corporation, acquired in a qualified stock purchase for which an election of asset acquisition treatment is not made, if the subsidiary corporation is liquidated under a plan adopted within two years of the acquisition date and the principal purpose of the liquidation is tax avoidance or evasion.

If (1) substantially all of the services of a personal service corporation (PSC) are performed for, or on behalf of, one other corporation, partnership, or other entity and (2) the principal purpose for forming or using the PSC is the avoidance or evasion of income tax by reducing the income of or securing the benefit of any expense, deduction, credit, exclusion or other allowance for any employee-owner that would not otherwise be available, then the IRS can allocate all income, credits, exclusions, or other allowances between the PSC and its employee-owners in order to prevent tax evasion or avoidance or to clearly reflect the income of both (Code Sec. 269A).[155] A PSC is a corporation the principal activity of which is the performance of personal services that are substantially performed by the employee-owners. The term "employee-owner" is defined as any employee who owns, on any day during the tax year, more than 10% of the PSC's outstanding stock.

1577. Income Reconstruction. When a taxpayer has kept either inadequate or no books or records, the IRS has authority to compute income in order to clearly reflect the taxpayer's income (Code Sec. 446(b)).[156] The methods for reconstructing income vary depending on the facts and circumstances, and the records that are available. The IRS has developed several methods for reconstructing a taxpayer's income. The methods used most often are:

(1) *Bank deposits and expenditures method.* All bank deposits are assumed to represent income unless the taxpayer can establish otherwise. Although the taxpayer is given an opportunity to show that the deposits do not represent income, the IRS is not required to link the bank deposits with an identified income-producing activity (Reg. § 1.446-1).[157]

(2) *Net worth method.* An opening net worth or total value of assets at the beginning of a given year is established. The IRS then shows increases in the taxpayer's net worth for each subsequent year and calculates the difference between the adjusted net values of the assets at the beginning and end of each year under examination. Nondeductible expenses are added to the increases. If the resulting amount is greater than reported taxable income for that year, then the excess is treated as unreported taxable income.[158]

(3) *Percentage or unit mark-up method.* This method is used where inventories are a necessary income-producing factor but have not been kept or were incorrectly taken. Net income is determined by applying certain percentages, such as gross profits to sales, net income to gross income, or net income to sales, derived from other taxpayers in similar types of businesses.[159]

Footnote references are to paragraphs of the 2008 Standard Federal Tax Reports.

[153] ¶ 14,250	[156] ¶ 20,606	[159] ¶ 20,620.047
[154] ¶ 14,250	[157] ¶ 20,620.046	
[155] ¶ 14,300	[158] ¶ 20,620.0462	

Chapter 16

BASIS FOR GAIN OR LOSS

Computing Gain or Loss

1601. Basis. The basis for computing gain or loss or depreciation on property acquired in most common transactions is outlined below, with references to the paragraphs where additional details appear. This basis, after adjustments described at ¶ 1611—¶ 1617, is subtracted from the amount realized to determine the amount of gain or loss from a sale or exchange (Code Sec. 1001).[1] Except where other rules are prescribed, the basis for gain or loss is determined under the law in effect when the property is sold.

Type of acquisition	Basis for gain or loss
Bargain purchases	
arm's-length	Cost (¶ 789)
corporation's, from nonstockholder	Cost (¶ 1660)
corporation's, from stockholder	Cost, unless saving is paid-in surplus (¶ 1660)
employee's	Cost plus amount taxable as compensation for services (¶ 789)
relative or friend	Cost, unless saving is a gift (¶ 1630)
stockholder's	Cost plus amount taxable as a dividend (¶ 789)
Bequests	For property acquired from a decedent, basis generally is fair market value at the date of the decedent's death (¶ 1633—¶ 1642)
property acquired in lieu of specific amount of bequest	Value assigned in settlement (¶ 1633)
Cash purchases	Cost (¶ 1604)
mortgage also assumed, or property taken subject to the mortgage	Full price, including mortgage amount (¶ 1725)
purchase money mortgage also given	Full purchase price (¶ 1725)
purchase notes also given	Full purchase price (¶ 1725)
redeemable ground rent assumed, or property taken subject to ground rent	Full purchase price (¶ 1725)
Community property	
survivor (death of spouse)	See "Bequests," above
Corporate property	
acquired for stock by controlled corporation	Transferor's basis (¶ 1663)
acquired for stock in taxable exchange	Fair market value of stock at time of exchange (¶ 1648)
contributions by nonstockholders	Zero (¶ 1660)
paid-in surplus	Transferor's basis (¶ 1660)
Dividend property	
corporate, stockholder of domestic corporation	Fair market value (¶ 735)
corporate, stockholder of foreign corporation	Fair market value (¶ 735)
noncorporate, stockholder	Fair market value (¶ 735)

Footnote references are to paragraphs of the 2008 Standard Federal Tax Reports.

[1] ¶ 29,220

Type of acquisition	Basis for gain or loss
Divorce or separation agreement	See ¶ 1734
Gift property	Donor's basis, increased by gift tax in some cases; basis for loss *limited* to lesser of donor's basis or fair market value at time of gift (¶ 1630)
Inventory goods	Last inventory value (¶ 1561)
Joint tenancy	
after death of one tenant	Basis depends on amount contributed by each joint tenant toward the original purchase price (¶ 1634, ¶ 1636)
Lessor's acquisitions of lessee's improvements	Zero, if excluded from income (¶ 764)
Life estate	Zero, if disposed of after October 9, 1969 (¶ 1633)
Livestock	
inventoried	Last inventory value (¶ 767)
purchased	Cost (¶ 767)
raised by accrual-basis farmer	Cost of raising (¶ 767)
raised by cash-basis farmer	Zero, if costs were charged to expense (¶ 767)
Mortgaged property (or property subject to redeemable ground rent)	Basis includes mortgage (or ground rent) (¶ 1725)
Partners' property	
partnership interest in exchange for contribution	Partners' adjusted basis of property contributed (¶ 443)
partnership interest purchased	Cost (¶ 434)
received in distribution other than liquidation	Partnership's adjusted basis at time of distribution (limited to partner's basis of his interest) (¶ 456)
received in partnership liquidation	Adjusted basis of partnership interest less cash received (¶ 456)
Partnership property	
after transfer of partnership interest or distributions to partners	Unaffected, unless election is made to adjust values (¶ 459, ¶ 467)
capital contribution	Partner's adjusted basis (¶ 443)
Purchase for more than value	Cost (¶ 1604), but excess may be a gift (¶ 1657)
Rehabilitated buildings, other than certified historic structures, for which investment credit on qualified expenditures available	Basis is reduced by allowable investment credit (¶ 1360); recaptured credit is added to basis (¶ 1364)
Repossessed property after installment sale	
personal property	Fair market value (¶ 1838)
real property reacquired in satisfaction of purchaser's indebtedness secured by property	Adjusted basis of indebtedness plus gain resulting from reacquisition and reacquisition costs (¶ 1843)
Spousal transfers	See ¶ 1734
Stock	
acquired in wash sale	Basis of stock sold, adjusted for difference between selling price of sold stock and purchase price of acquired stock (¶ 1939)
bonus stock	Allocable portion of basis of old stock (¶ 1620, ¶ 1907)
nontaxable stock dividend	Allocable share of basis of stock on which declared (¶ 1620, ¶ 1907)
qualified small business stock rollover	See ¶ 2397
purchased	See ¶ 1975, ¶ 1977
received for services	Amount reported as income, plus cash paid (¶ 1681)
S corporation	See ¶ 317
specialized small business investment company stock rollover	See ¶ 2397
taxable stock dividend	Fair market value when issued (¶ 738)

Type of acquisition	Basis for gain or loss
Stock rights	
nontaxable	Allocable share of basis of stock unless rights value is less than 15% of stock value (¶ 738, ¶ 1907)
taxable	Fair market value when issued (¶ 738)
Transfer in trust	Grantor's basis, plus gain or minus loss, upon transfer (¶ 1678)

1604. Adjusted Basis of Property. To determine the gain or loss from a sale or other disposition of property, the amount realized must be compared with the basis of the property to the taxpayer—generally measured by the original capital investment, adjusted to the date of sale (¶ 1611—¶ 1617) (Code Sec. 1011; Reg. § 1.1011-1).[2]

In most situations, the basis of property is its cost to the taxpayer (Code Sec. 1012).[3] When property is acquired in a fully taxable exchange, the cost of the property acquired is the fair market value (¶ 1695) of the property given up.[4] Since, in an arm's-length transaction, both are presumed to be equal in value, the basis of the acquired property can be expressed as its fair market value.

1607. "Substituted" Basis. A "substituted" basis is one that is continued or carried through from one taxpayer to another, or from one piece of property to another. The taxpayer has a substituted basis in property received as a gift (¶ 1630), in a transfer in trust (¶ 1678), or in a tax-free exchange (¶ 1651—¶ 1666). The taxpayer also has a substituted basis in a personal residence purchased before May 7, 1997 if the recognition of gain realized on the sale of a prior residence was deferred under former Code Sec. 1034.[5]

Property Acquired by Purchase

1611. Additions to Basis of Property. In computing gain or loss on the sale of business or investment property, or gain on the sale of personal property, the cost or other basis must be *adjusted* for any expenditure, receipt, loss, or other item that is a capital expenditure (Code Sec. 1016(a)(1); Reg. §§ 1.1016-1—1.1016-10).[6] This necessitates an addition for improvements made to the property since its acquisition.[7] For example, the cost of capital improvements such as an addition, new roof, newly installed central air conditioning, or electrical rewiring is added to the owner's basis. Other components that add to the cost basis of property include: brokers' commissions and lawyers' fees incurred in buying real estate; expenditures incurred in defending or perfecting title to property;[8] zoning costs;[9] the capitalized value of a redeemable ground rent (Code Sec. 1055); and sales tax, freight, installation and testing costs, excise taxes, and revenue stamps.[10]

Settlement Fees and Other Costs. The basis of real property includes settlement fees and closing costs such as abstract fees, charges for installing utility services, legal fees (including title search and preparation of the sales contract and deed), recording fees, surveys, transfer taxes, owner's title insurance, and amounts owed by the seller but paid by the buyer, such as back taxes or interest, recording or mortgage fees, charges for improvements or repairs, and sales commissions (Code Sec. 1012; Reg. § 1.1012-1(b); Rev. Rul. 68-528).[11] Amounts placed in escrow for future payments of items such as insurance and taxes do not increase basis. The creation of a mortgage does not diminish the owner's basis in a property. When a buyer assumes an existing mortgage and pays cash or other consideration, the buyer's basis of the property includes the outstanding portion of the mortgage and the value of the other consideration, and the seller realizes a benefit in the amount of the mortgage and the additional consideration (*B.B. Crane*, SCt, 47-1 USTC ¶ 9217).[12] Fees and costs related to getting a loan to purchase the property are not included in the basis of the property.

Footnote references are to paragraphs of the 2008 Standard Federal Tax Reports.

[2] ¶ 29,310, ¶ 29,311	[6] ¶ 29,410—¶ 29,426	[10] ¶ 29,335.021, ¶ 29,335.967,
[3] ¶ 29,330	[7] ¶ 29,412.84	¶ 29,335.577
[4] ¶ 29,335.01	[8] ¶ 29,412.844	[11] ¶ 29,330, ¶ 29,331
[5] ¶ 29,426.01	[9] ¶ 13,709.659	[12] ¶ 29,313.60

¶1604

Assessments. Assessments for improvements or other items that increase the value of a property are added to the basis of the property and not deducted as a tax. Such improvements may include streets, sidewalks, water mains, sewers, and public parking facilities. The amount of such an assessment may be a depreciable asset. For example, the cost of a mall enclosure paid for by a business taxpayer through an assessment is depreciable. Assessments for maintenance or for meeting interest charges on the improvements are currently deductible as a real property tax, although the burden is on the taxpayer to show the allocation of the amounts assessed to the different purposes (Code Sec. 164(c)(1); Reg. § 1.164-4).[13]

Legal fees for obtaining a decrease in an assessment levied against property to pay for local improvements are added to the basis of the property (Rev. Rul. 70-62).

Taxes. Any tax paid in connection with the acquisition of a property is treated as part of the cost of the property. A tax paid in connection with the disposition of a property reduces the amount realized on the disposition (Code Sec. 164(a)).[14]

In computing the cost of real property, the buyer cannot take into account any amount paid to the seller as reimbursement for real property taxes which are treated under Code Sec. 164(d) as imposed upon the purchaser (see ¶ 1032). This rule applies whether or not the sales contract calls for the buyer to reimburse the seller for real estate taxes paid or to be paid by the seller. However, where the buyer pays or assumes liability for real estate taxes imposed upon the seller, the taxes are considered part of the cost of the property. It is immaterial whether or not the sales contract specifies that the sale price has been reduced by, or is in any way intended to reflect, real estate taxes allocable to the seller (Reg. § 1.1012-1(b)).[15]

Checklist. See the checklist at ¶ 57 to determine whether an expense is deductible or must be capitalized and added to basis.

1614. Additions to Basis for Carrying Charges. A taxpayer may elect to treat taxes or other carrying charges (such as interest) on some property as capital charges rather than as an expense of the tax year (Code Sec. 266). The items chargeable to the capital account are:[16]

    (1) in the case of unimproved and unproductive real property: annual taxes, interest on a mortgage, and other carrying charges;

    (2) in the case of real property, whether improved or unimproved and whether productive or unproductive: interest on a loan, taxes of the owner of such property measured by compensation paid to the owner's employees, taxes of the owner on the purchase of materials or on the storage, use or other consumption of materials, and other necessary expenditures; these are items that are paid or incurred for the development or improvement of the property up to the time the development or construction work has been completed;

    (3) in the case of personal property: taxes of an employer measured by compensation for services rendered in transporting machinery or other fixed assets to the plant or installing them, interest on a loan to buy such property or to pay for transporting or installing it, and taxes of the owner imposed on the purchase of such property or on the storage, use or other consumption, paid or incurred up to the date of installation or the date when the property is first put to use by the taxpayer, whichever is later; and

    (4) any other taxes and carrying charges, otherwise deductible, which are chargeable to the capital account under sound accounting principles.

The election in (1) above is effective only for the year in which it is made. The election in (2) is effective until the development or construction work has been completed. The election in (3) is effective until the property is installed or first put to use, whichever date is later. The IRS determines whether the election in (4) is effective (Code Sec. 266; Reg. § 1.266-1).[17]

Footnote references are to paragraphs of the 2008 Standard Federal Tax Reports.

[13] ¶ 9500, ¶ 9508
[14] ¶ 9500
[15] ¶ 29,331
[16] ¶ 14,100, ¶ 14,101
[17] ¶ 14,100, ¶ 14,101

1617. Reductions in Basis. In order to determine the amount of gain or loss on the sale or other disposition of property, or the basis of property acquired in an exchange, and the basis for depreciation or depletion, the unadjusted basis (usually its cost, but in some cases the transferor's basis) of the property must be decreased by any items that represent a return of capital for the period during which the property has been held. These include:

(1) the Code Sec. 179 expense deduction for certain depreciable business assets (¶ 1208);

(2) the investment credit (but 50% of the energy credits and 50% of the reforestation credits for expenditures paid or incurred before October 23, 2004) (¶ 1360);

(3) tax-free dividends (¶ 738);

(4) recognized losses on involuntary exchanges (¶ 1687);

(5) casualty losses (¶ 1139);

(6) deductions previously allowed or allowable for amortization, depreciation, obsolescence or depletion (¶ 1201 and following); and

(7) unrecognized gains on tax-free exchanges (¶ 1719 and following).[18]

Depreciation. The basis of property is reduced by the amount of depreciation claimed, or if greater, the depreciation which should have been claimed under the method chosen (Code Sec. 1016(a)(2); Reg. § 1.1016-3).[19] If no depreciation or insufficient depreciation was claimed, the basis is nonetheless reduced by the full amount of depreciation that should have been claimed. In order to mitigate the effect of this rule, the IRS has issued procedures that allow the taxpayer to change to a proper method of accounting for depreciation and claim a downward adjustment to income that reflects the additional amount of depreciation that should have been claimed (Rev. Proc. 2007-16).

If excess depreciation was claimed on an asset, the basis of the asset is reduced by the amount of depreciation that should have been claimed plus the part of the excess depreciation deducted that actually reduced the taxpayer's tax liability.[20]

Motor Vehicles. The basis of an automobile must be reduced by the amount of any gas guzzler tax imposed by Code Sec. 4064 when use of vehicle begins not more than one year after the first retail sale (Code Sec. 1016(d)).[21] The basis of a vehicle for which the deduction for clean-fuel vehicles is claimed (¶ 1286) is reduced by the amount of the deduction, for vehicles placed in service before 2006 (Code Secs. 179A(e)(6) and 1016(a)(24)). The basis of a qualified electric vehicle for which a tax credit is allowable (¶ 1321) is reduced by the lesser of $4,000 or 10 percent of the vehicle's cost (Code Secs. 30(d) and 1016(a)(25)). A variety of alternative motor vehicle credits exist (see ¶ 1315 and following) which, if allowed, reduce the basis of qualifying vehicles placed in service after 2005 (Code Secs. 30B(h)(4) and 1016(a)(36)).

The basis of alternative fuel (clean-fuel) vehicle property used in a trade or business, or installed at the taxpayer's residence, and placed in service after 2005 is reduced by the credit (¶ 1316) allowed for such property, if the taxpayer elects to claim the credit (Code Secs. 30C(e)(1) and 1016(a)(37)).

Percentage Depletion. Even though a percentage depletion allowance is in excess of cost or other basis, it is not necessary to use a negative basis (less than zero) in computing gain on the sale of mineral property.[22] See ¶ 1294–¶ 1298.

Easements. Generally, the amount received for granting an easement for a limited use or for a limited period reduces the basis of the affected part of the property (Rev. Rul. 68-291). Gain is recognized to the extent that the amount received exceeds the basis of the affected part. The granting of a perpetual easement that denies the grantor any

---

Footnote references are to paragraphs of the 2008 Standard Federal Tax Reports.

[18] ¶ 29,410
[19] ¶ 29,410, ¶ 29,414
[20] ¶ 29,414, ¶ 29,416
[21] ¶ 29,410
[22] ¶ 29,412.675

beneficial use of the property may be considered a sale of property even though the grantor retains legal title.[23]

Energy Efficiency and Conservation—Residential. The basis of a dwelling unit for which an excludable energy conservation subsidy was provided by a public utility (¶ 884) must be reduced by the amount of the subsidy (Code Sec. 136(b)).[24]

The increase in basis of a personal residence that would result from certain expenditures that improve energy efficiency is reduced by credits allowed for those expenditures. An individual taxpayer's basis in nonbusiness energy property (i.e., the taxpayer's residence) must be reduced by the home improvement energy credit (¶ 1313) allowed for qualified energy efficiency improvements and residential energy property placed in service in 2006 and 2007 (Code Secs. 25C(f) and 1016(a)(34)). Similarly, the basis of an individual taxpayer's personal residence is reduced by the residential energy efficient property credit (¶ 1314) allowed for amounts spent on alternative energy equipment (such as solar or fuel cell equipment) placed in service during 2006, 2007 or 2008 (Code Sec. 25D(f) and (g), as amended by the Tax Relief and Health Care Act of 2006 (P.L. 109-432), and Code Sec. 1016(a)(35)). The basis of a qualified new energy-efficient home that a person acquires during 2006 or 2007, for use as a residence, from a contractor eligible for a general business credit for building the home (¶ 1344H) is reduced by the credit allowed (Code Secs. 45L(e) and 1016(a)(33)).

Energy Efficiency and Conservation—Business. The basis of an energy-efficient commercial building must be reduced by the deduction (¶ 1286A) allowed for the costs of placing such property into service during 2006, 2007 or 2008 (Code Sec. 179D(e) and (h), as amended by the Tax Relief and Health Care Act of 2006 (P.L. 109-432), and Code Sec. 1016(a)(32)). Small business refiners must reduce the basis of property on which a deduction (¶ 1285) is allowed for qualified capital costs paid or incurred to comply with Environmental Protection Agency sulfur regulations (Code Secs. 179B(c) and 1016(a)(30)). Additionally, the basis of a small business refiner's property must be reduced if the low sulfur diesel fuel production credit (¶ 1344E) is allowed with respect to such property (Code Secs. 45H(d) and 1016(a)(31)).

Homes Purchased Before May 7, 1997. The basis of a home purchased before May 7, 1997 must be reduced to reflect any gain realized on the sale of the prior home but deferred under former Code Sec. 1034.

Adoption Credit. The basis of a residence must be reduced by the amount of the adoption tax credit that was claimed with respect to improvements that increased that basis of the home (Code Sec. 23(g)).[25]

Canceled Debt. See ¶ 791.

Railroad Track. Eligible small- and mid-sized railroad companies must reduce the basis of track on which they have been allowed a railroad track maintenance credit (Code Secs. 45G(e)(3) and 1016(a)(29)). See ¶ 1344D.

Substituted Basis. Where the basis of the property is a substituted basis, the same adjustments must be made for the period the property was held by the transferor, donor, or grantor, or during the period the property was held by the person for whom the basis is to be determined (Code Sec. 1016(b)).[26]

1620. Apportionment of Cost or Other Basis. When a sale is made of parts of property purchased as a unit, as in a subdivision of real estate, allocation of the total basis is required.[27] Other instances where allocation of the cost or other basis is necessary include stock of different classes received as a dividend or pursuant to a reorganization, a split-up, split-off, or spin-off; stock received as a bonus with the purchase of stock of a different character; stock purchase warrants attached to debenture bonds; and depreciable and nondepreciable property purchased for a lump sum.

Trade or Business Purchased. The applicable asset acquisition rules of Code Sec. 1060 require the allocation of the purchase price of a trade or business acquired after

---

Footnote references are to paragraphs of the 2008 Standard Federal Tax Reports.

[23] ¶ 29,412.813, ¶ 30,422.148	[25] ¶ 29,412.0253	[27] ¶ 5605, ¶ 29,313.10
[24] ¶ 7560	[26] ¶ 29,410, ¶ 29,426.01	

March 15, 2001 among the assets in proportion to their fair market values in the following order (Reg. §§ 1.1060-1; 1.338-6):[28]

(1) Certificates of deposit, U.S. government securities, foreign currency, and actively traded personal property, including stock and securities.

(2) Assets marked to market at least annually and debt instruments, including accounts receivable.

(3) Stock in trade, inventory, and property held primarily for sale to customers.

(4) All other assets except section 197 intangibles, goodwill, and going concern value.

(5) Section 197 intangibles except goodwill and going concern value.

(6) Goodwill and going concern value whether or not they qualify as section 197 intangibles.

Before making the above allocation, the purchase price is first reduced by any cash and general deposit accounts (savings and checking) which the acquired business holds as assets. The allocation order for businesses acquired before March 16, 2001 is substantially similar.[29]

The buyer and seller of the assets of a trade or business are bound by any written agreements allocating consideration to the transferred assets. However, any allocation that is not found to be fair market value will be disregarded (Code Sec. 1060).[30]

The buyer and seller must attach Form 8594, Asset Acquisition Statement, to their income tax returns for the year of sale to report the allocation.

Land and Buildings. When a building and land are purchased for a lump sum, the purchase price must be allocated between the land and building on the basis of their fair market values. If the fair market values are uncertain, the allocation may be based on their assessed values for real estate tax purposes (Reg. §§ 1.61-6(a); 1.167(a)-5).

Subdivided Lots. The basis of each lot of a subdivided property is equal to the purchase price of the entire property multiplied by a fraction, the numerator of which is the fair market value of the lot and the denominator of which is the fair market value of the entire property. The cost of common improvements is also allocated among the individual lots. A developer who sells subdivided lots before development work is completed may include, with IRS consent, an allocation of the estimated future cost for common improvements in the basis of the lots sold (Rev. Proc. 92-29).[31]

See ¶ 1762 for a special rule relating to the recognition of capital gain on the sale of subdivided lots.

1623. Allocation of Basis—Bargain Sale to Charity. If a charitable deduction is available, the basis of property sold to charity for less than its fair market value must be allocated between the portion of the property "sold" and the portion "given" to charity, based on the fair market value of each portion. Thus, the seller-donor realizes some taxable gain even if the selling price did not exceed the seller-donor's cost or other basis for the entire property (Code Sec. 1011(b); Reg. § 1.1011-2).[32] The adjusted basis of the portion of property sold to a charity is computed as:

$$\frac{\text{Amount realized on sale to charity}}{\text{Fair market value of entire property}} \times \frac{\text{Adjusted basis of entire property}}{}$$

1626. Basis of Residential or Converted Property. Where property has been occupied by the taxpayer as a residence continually since its acquisition, no adjustment of the basis is made for depreciation since none is allowable. The cost of permanent

---

Footnote references are to paragraphs of the 2008 Standard Federal Tax Reports.

[28] ¶ 30,061, ¶ 16,281
[29] ¶ 30,063.024, ¶ 30,063.027, ¶ 30,063.031
[30] ¶ 30,060
[31] ¶ 29,313.576
[32] ¶ 29,310, ¶ 29,313.16

improvements to the property is added to the basis, as are special assessments paid for local benefits that improve the property.[33] Recoveries against a builder for defective construction reduce the basis.[34]

If residential property is converted to rental property, an adjustment should be made for depreciation from the date of the conversion. Thus, the basis for gain in the case of rented residential property is the taxpayer's cost or other statutory basis, less depreciation allowable while the property was rented or held for rental.

The basis for loss may not exceed the value at the time the residence was converted to rental use, taking into account subsequent basis adjustments, including reduction for allowable depreciation. This is only a limitation; if a smaller loss results from the use of the adjusted cost basis, it must be used (Reg. § 1.165-9(b)).[35] The value of the property upon conversion to rental use has no effect on the basis for gain. If converted property is sold for a price that is greater than the basis for loss but less than the basis for gain, there is no gain or loss.

If rental property is converted to a personal residence, adjustments to basis for depreciation end on the date of the conversion. Any gain on the sale of the property will be recognized (subject to the exclusion rules at ¶ 1705) and may be subject to depreciation recapture (¶ 1779). Loss will not be recognized.

Property Acquired by Gift, Bequest

1630. Property Acquired by Gift. If property was acquired by gift after 1920, the basis to the donee is the same as it would be in the hands of the donor or the last preceding owner by whom it was not acquired by gift (Code Sec. 1015(a); Reg. § 1.1015-1).[36] The basis for loss is the basis so determined (adjusted for the period prior to the date of the gift, as provided in ¶ 1611—¶ 1617) or the fair market value of the property at the time of the gift, whichever is lower.

In some cases, there is neither gain nor loss on the sale of property received by gift because the selling price is less than the basis for gain and more than the basis for loss.

If a gift tax was payable on a gift made after September 1, 1958, and before 1977, the basis of the property is increased by the amount of the gift tax, but not above the fair market value of the property at the time of the gift. As to gifts made before September 2, 1958, and held by the donee on that date, the basis is also increased by the amount of the gift tax, but not by more than any excess of the fair market value of the property at the time of the gift over the basis of the property in the hands of the donor at the time of the gift (Code Sec. 1015(d); Reg. § 1.1015-1).[37]

In the case of a gift made after 1976 on which the gift tax is paid, the basis of the property is increased by the amount of gift tax attributable to the net appreciation in value of the gift. The net appreciation for this purpose is the amount by which the fair market value of the gift exceeds the donor's adjusted basis immediately before the gift (Code Sec. 1015(d)(6)).[38]

For the basis of a life estate acquired by gift, see ¶ 1633.

1633. Property Acquired from a Decedent. Except as indicated at ¶ 1636 and ¶ 1639, the basis of any property, real or personal, acquired from a decedent is its fair market value on the date of the decedent's death or on the alternate valuation date described at ¶ 1642. Principally, this "stepped-up" basis rule applies to property acquired by bequest, devise or inheritance. It also applies to property required to be included in the decedent's gross estate for federal estate tax purposes even though it was the subject of a lifetime transfer, unless the transferee sold or otherwise disposed of the property before the decedent died. Property acquired by the decedent's estate, as well as property acquired directly from the decedent without passing through the estate, qualifies for a "stepped-up" basis (Code Sec. 1014; Reg. § § 1.1014-1— 1.1014-8).[39]

Footnote references are to paragraphs of the 2008 Standard Federal Tax Reports.

[33] ¶ 9508, ¶ 29,410, ¶ 29,412.84, ¶ 29,412.988
[34] ¶ 29,412.9968
[35] ¶ 10,102
[36] ¶ 29,390, ¶ 29,391
[37] ¶ 29,390, ¶ 29,391
[38] ¶ 29,390
[39] ¶ 29,370—¶ 29,378

Since, in community property states, each spouse has an undivided half interest in community property, an heir, devisee or legatee acquires the decedent's half interest from the deceased spouse and is entitled to a stepped-up basis under the foregoing general rule. Under Code Sec. 1014(b)(6), the surviving spouse is also entitled to a stepped-up basis for his or her half interest if at least half of the community property in question is includible in the decedent's gross estate for estate tax purposes.[40]

In most instances, a zero basis is assigned to a life estate that was acquired by gift or bequest and sold or disposed of after October 9, 1969. Interests covered by this exception to the usual rules are: (1) life interests in property; (2) interests for a term of years in property; and (3) income interests in trusts. The zero basis requirement does not apply where the life tenant and remainderman sell their interests simultaneously so that the entire ownership of the property is transferred to another person or group of persons (Code Sec. 1001(e); Reg. § 1.1001-1).[41]

Effective for property acquired from a decedent dying after December 31, 2009, the stepped-up basis at death rules will be repealed (Code Sec. 1014(f)) and replaced with modified carryover basis at death rules. More specifically, the recipient of the property will receive a basis equal to the lesser of the adjusted basis of the property in the hands of the decedent or the fair market value of the property on the date of the decedent's death. As a partial replacement for the repealed basis step-up, executors will be able to increase the basis of estate property by up to $1,300,000, or $3,000,000 in the case of property passing to a surviving spouse (Code Sec. 1022).[42]

1634. Joint Tenancy. When property is held in joint tenancy with right of survivorship (other than with a spouse), the basis of the property in the hands of the survivor will depend upon the amount contributed by each joint tenant toward the original purchase price and, in the case of depreciable property, the manner in which income is divided under local (state) law (Reg. § 20.2040-1(a)).

> **Example 1:** Tom Smith and Susan Jones (unmarried) purchased a townhouse for $100,000, which they held as joint tenants with right of survivorship. Tom contributed $30,000 and Susan $70,000. Susan died when the property was worth $200,000. 70% of the fair market value ($140,000) is included in Susan's estate. Tom's basis in the property is $170,000 ($30,000 + $140,000).

> **Example 2:** Assume that Tom and Susan held the townhouse as a rental property and that $25,000 of depreciation was allowed prior to Susan's death. If Tom and Susan are entitled to one-half of the income from the property under local law, Tom's basis would be reduced by $12,500 to $157,500 ($170,000 − $12,500).

Qualified Joint Interests. A qualified joint interest is an interest in property held by a husband and wife as tenants by the entirety or as joint tenants with the right of survivorship if the husband and wife are the only joint tenants. One-half of the fair market value of a qualified joint interest acquired after 1976 is included in the deceased spouse's estate regardless of the amount contributed by the surviving spouse (Code Sec. 2040(b)). The surviving spouse's basis in the remaining portion of the qualified joint interest is one-half of the original cost (regardless of the amount that the survivor actually contributed) reduced by any depreciation deductions allocable to the surviving spouse (IRS Pub. 559, Survivors, Executors, and Administrators).[43]

> **Example 3:** Assume the same facts as in **Example 1**, except that Tom and Susan are married. Tom's basis in the property is $150,000 ($50,000 (one-half of original cost) + $100,000 (one-half of fair market value included in Susan's estate).

1636. Carryover Basis Elections. Executors and administrators of estates of decedents dying after 1976 and before November 7, 1978, could elect to determine the basis under the otherwise repealed carryover basis rules.[44] The time for elections expired July

---

Footnote references are to paragraphs of the 2008 Standard Federal Tax Reports.

[40] ¶ 29,370

[41] ¶ 29,220, ¶ 29,221

[42] ¶ 29,370, ¶ 29,496

[43] ¶ 29,380.29, ¶ 29,380.33, ¶ 29,380.76

[44] ¶ 29,500.01

31, 1980, but valid elections will continue to affect computation of gain on dispositions of property to which such elections apply.

1639. Property Reacquired by Donor from Decedent. If a decedent who died after December 31, 1981, acquired appreciated property as a gift within one year of death and such property passed to, or was acquired by, the original donor or the original donor's spouse, then the basis of such property to the donor or the donor's spouse is the adjusted basis of such property to the decedent immediately prior to the decedent's death (Code Sec. 1014(e)).[45]

1642. Estate Tax Value. In determining the basis of property acquired from a decedent, the fair market value of the property at the time of the death of the decedent is usually the property's value as appraised for estate tax purposes. If there is no estate tax liability, the value is its appraised value as of the date of the decedent's death for the purpose of state inheritance or transmission taxes (Reg. § 1.1014-3(a)).[46] The Tax Court, however, has accepted a proven higher value.[47]

If the executor elects to value the decedent's estate for federal estate tax purposes by using the alternative valuation method prescribed by Code Sec. 2032, the value used to determine the basis of the property is not the value at the date of the decedent's death. It is, rather, the value at the date six months after death if the property is not sold, distributed, or otherwise disposed of within six months after the decedent's death. If the property is sold, distributed, or disposed of within six months of death, the value that is used in determining basis is the value of the property at the date of sale, distribution, or disposition.[48]

Property Acquired by Exchange

1648. Property Transferred to a Corporation in a Taxable Exchange for Its Stock. When a corporation acquires property for its stock in an exchange taxable to the transferor, its basis for the property is the fair market value of the stock on the date of the exchange. If the stock has no established market value at that time, it may be considered to be the equivalent of the fair market value of the property received.[49]

1651. Tax-Free Exchange Generally. If property is acquired in an exchange on which no gain or loss is recognized, the basis of the property is the same as that for the property exchanged (Code Sec. 1031(d); Reg. § 1.1031(d)-1).[50] This basis is known as a "substituted basis" (see ¶ 1607). It applies to:

 (1) exchanges of property held for productive use or investment solely for property of like kind (¶ 1721);

 (2) some exchanges of stock for stock of the same corporation (¶ 1728);

 (3) exchanges of property solely for stock or securities of a "controlled" corporation (¶ 1731); and

 (4) exchanges of stock or securities solely for stock or securities in a reorganization (¶ 2229).

1654. Equipment Partly Paid for by a Trade-In. No gain or loss is recognized when old business equipment is traded in as part payment on new equipment (¶ 1721). Since this is a "like-kind" exchange, the basis of the new equipment, for gain or loss or depreciation, is ordinarily the total of the adjusted basis of the trade-in plus whatever additional cash is needed (Reg. § 1.1031(d)-1).[51] In effect, the basis of the new property is its purchase price, increased or decreased according to whether the trade-in value of the old equipment is greater or less than its depreciated cost. See ¶ 1250 for special depreciation rules that apply to like-kind exchanges.

1657. Exchange Tax Free in Part. In an exchange, money or other property, which is not permitted to be received without the recognition of gain or loss (see ¶ 1723), may

---

Footnote references are to paragraphs of the 2008 Standard Federal Tax Reports.

[45] ¶ 29,370
[46] ¶ 29,373, ¶ 29,380.38
[47] ¶ 29,380.38

[48] ¶ 29,373, ¶ 29,380.762
[49] ¶ 29,225.272
[50] ¶ 29,602, ¶ 29,612

[51] ¶ 29,612

be received together with securities or property that is permitted to be received without the recognition of gain or loss. In such exchanges, the cost or other applicable basis of the property acquired is the same as that of the property exchanged, decreased by the amount of any money received by the taxpayer in the transaction and increased by the amount of gain or decreased by the amount of loss recognized in the exchange. If such "other property" is received in an exchange that is tax free in part, the cost or other basis of the property disposed of must be allocated between the property received tax free and such "other property," assigning to the "other property" an amount equivalent to its fair market value (Code Sec. 1031(d)).[52]

1660. Transfer to Corporation. If property was acquired by a corporation from a shareholder as paid-in surplus or as a contribution to capital, the basis of the property to the corporation is the same as it was in the hands of the transferor, increased by the amount of gain recognized by the transferor on the transfer (Code Sec. 362(a)(2)).[53]

As to property acquired for stock, the basis of the property is the fair market value of the stock at the time the property is acquired (¶ 1648), unless the transferors of the property "control" the property after the transfer (whether or not there is a reorganization). In such cases, the rules described at ¶ 1663 and ¶ 1666 govern.

As to property acquired subject to a built-in loss, see ¶ 1667. As to property acquired upon liquidation of a subsidiary, see ¶ 2261.

Property contributed to a corporation by nonstockholders on or after June 22, 1954, has a zero basis. Money contributed by an outsider on or after that date reduces the basis of corporate property acquired with it within 12 months after the contribution is received. To the extent that the contribution is not used to acquire property within this 12-month period, it reduces, as of the last day of the period, the basis of any other property held by the company (Code Sec. 362(c)).[54]

1663. Property Acquired in Exchange by "Controlled" Corporation. A corporation's basis in property acquired in an exchange with the corporation's owner (see ¶ 1731) is generally the same as the basis in the hands of the transferor, increased by any gain that is recognized by the transferor on the exchange (Code Sec. 362(a)(1); Reg. § 1.362-1).[55] As to property acquired subject to a built-in loss, see ¶ 1667.

1666. Reorganization Transfer to Corporation. If property is acquired in a reorganization, the basis of the transferor (increased by any recognized gain) follows through to the transferee corporation (Code Sec. 362(b); Reg. § 1.362-1).[56] As to property acquired subject to a built-in loss, see ¶ 1667.

1667. Limitations on Built-In Losses. If a corporation receives property in an exchange with an owner who is *not* subject to U.S. tax, and that property's fair market value is less than the transferee's adjusted basis (i.e., there is a built-in loss), the corporate transferee's basis in the property received is its fair market value immediately after the transfer (Code Sec. 362(e)(1)).[57] Thus, the foreign loss is not recognized for U.S. tax purposes. This treatment applies to property acquired as paid-in surplus or a contribution to capital (¶ 1660), in exchange for stock of a "controlled" corporation (i.e., a "351 exchange") (¶ 1663; see ¶ 1731), or in a reorganization (¶ 1666).

Similarly, if a corporation acquires property in a 351 exchange with an owner who *is* subject to U.S. tax, and the transferred property's adjusted basis exceeds its FMV, the corporate transferee's basis in the property is generally limited to its FMV immediately after the transaction. Any required basis reduction is allocated among the transferred properties in proportion to their built-in losses immediately before the transaction (Code Sec. 362(e)(2)). For this type of exchange, the transferor owner and transferee controlled corporation can make an irrevocable election to limit the owner's basis in the stock received—rather than the corporation's basis in the property—to the aggregate FMV of the transferred property (Code Sec. 362(e)(2)(C)). The IRS has provided guidance on the requirements of a valid election (Notice 2005-70).

Footnote references are to paragraphs of the 2008 Standard Federal Tax Reports.

[52] ¶ 29,602   [54] ¶ 16,610   [56] ¶ 16,610, ¶ 16,611
[53] ¶ 16,610   [55] ¶ 16,610, ¶ 16,611   [57] ¶ 16,610

1669. Assumption of Liabilities. Under certain facts in connection with a reorganization or transfer to a controlled corporation, the assumption of liabilities is not treated as the equivalent of cash (see ¶ 2233). In a determination of basis after such transfers, the corporation whose liabilities were assumed (or whose property was taken subject to the liabilities) will treat the assumption or acquisition as money received, to the extent of the liabilities (Code Secs. 358(d) and 1031(d)).[58]

This rule applies only to the corporation whose liabilities are assumed. It has no effect on the corporation that assumes the debts.

1672. Discharge of Debt. Under some conditions, a taxpayer realizes no income from a discharge of debt (¶ 791 and ¶ 885). Any amount so excluded from gross income reduces the basis of the property securing the debt (Code Sec. 1017).[59] Regulations prescribe the sequence of allocation where the debt is, or must be treated as, a general liability (Reg. §§ 1.108-4 and 1.1017-1).[60]

Other Acquired Property

1678. Transfer in Trust. If property is acquired by a transfer in trust, other than by a transfer in trust by gift, bequest or devise (for example, sale to the trust by the grantor), after December 31, 1920, its basis is the same as it would be in the hands of the trust's grantor, increased by the gain, or decreased by the loss, recognized to the grantor under the law in effect as of the date of such transfer (Code Sec. 1015(b)).[61]

1681. Stock or Other Property Received for Services. If stock or other property is given as compensation for services instead of cash, the fair market value of the property is income unless the property is subject to a substantial risk of forfeiture. The fair market value of the property included in income becomes its basis to the employee (Code Sec. 83).[62] If the property is sold to the employee for less than its market value, the difference between the amount paid and the value of the property is also income; in this case, the employee's basis for the property is the cash cost plus the amount reported as income (Reg. § 1.83-4(b)).[63]

If the stock or other property is subject to a substantial risk of forfeiture, no amount is included in income until the year that the property becomes substantially vested as the result of the removal of the risk of forfeiture (Code Sec. 83(a)). However, any income (such as a dividend) from the property, or right to use the property, that is subject to a substantial risk of forfeiture is included in income as compensation when received (Rev. Proc. 80-11; Rev. Proc. 83-38). The fair market value of the property (less any amount paid for it) is included in income when the property becomes substantially vested (Code Sec. 83(a); Reg. § 1.83-1(a)(1); Reg. § 1.61-1(a)).[64] Property is considered substantially vested when (1) it is either transferable to another person who is not required to give up the property or its value if the substantial risk of forfeiture occurs or (2) it is no longer subject to a substantial risk of forfeiture (Reg. § 1.83-3(b), (d)). A substantial risk of forfeiture exists if the right to the property depends on the future performance (or refraining from performance) of substantial services by any person or the occurrence of a condition related to the transfer (Code Sec. 83(c)(1); Reg. § 1.83-3(c)(1)).[65]

If property that is not substantially vested is sold or disposed of in an arm's-length transaction, the amount realized less any amount paid by the taxpayer for the property is included in the taxpayer's income as compensation in the year of the disposition (Code Sec. 83(a); Reg. § 1.83-1(b)(1)).[66]

A taxpayer who receives property subject to a substantial risk of forfeiture may elect to include the fair market value of the property (less any amount paid for the property) in income in the year that the property is received (Code Sec. 83(b)).[67] Once the value of

---

Footnote references are to paragraphs of the 2008 Standard Federal Tax Reports.

[58] ¶ 16,550, ¶ 29,602	[62] ¶ 6380	[66] ¶ 6390.60
[59] ¶ 29,430	[63] ¶ 6384	[67] ¶ 6390.77
[60] ¶ 7003E, ¶ 29,431	[64] ¶ 6390.03	
[61] ¶ 29,390	[65] ¶ 6390.465	

the property is included in income, any subsequent appreciation is taxed as capital gain when the property is disposed of, rather than as ordinary income.

The basis for determining gain or loss when the property is sold is the amount included in income in the election year plus any amount paid for the property. If the property is forfeited after the election is made and before the property is substantially vested, there is a loss equal to the amount paid for the property minus the amount realized from the forfeiture (Reg. § 1.83-2(a)). The Code Sec. 83(b) election is made by filing a written statement with the IRS center where the tax return is filed no later than 30 days after the date the property was transferred. This statement must also be attached to the taxpayer's return for the election year and provided to the employer (Reg. § 1.83-2(b), (c) and (d)). The election is revocable only with IRS consent (Reg. § 1.83-2(f)), which will generally be given only if the employee made the election because of a mistake of fact (not law). Consent will be granted only if the transferee applies for revocation within 60 days after discovering the mistake of fact (Rev. Proc. 2006-31).[68]

> **Example:** ABC corporation transfers 100 shares of its stock to an employee for $50 a share when the property has a fair market value of $150 per share. The employee must resell the stock to the corporation for $50 a share (regardless of its value) if the employee quits his job at any time within two years after receiving the stock. In this case, the right to the stock is subject to a substantial risk of forfeiture and no amount is included in income at the time of the transfer unless an election is made under Code Sec. 83(b). If the election is made, $10,000 (100 shares × ($150 FMV – $50 paid per share)) is included in income in the tax year of the transfer as compensation. The taxpayer's basis is $150 per share ($50 paid per share + $100 gain recognized per share).

For stock acquired under stock options, see ¶ 1922–¶ 1933.

For purposes of determining an individual's basis in property transferred in connection with the performance of services, rules similar to the annuity basis rules under Code Sec. 72(w) apply (Code Sec. 83(c)(4)).

1684. Equipment for Which Medical Deduction Claimed. The basis of equipment whose cost qualifies as a medical expense (see ¶ 1016) does not include that portion of its cost that has been claimed as an itemized deduction since such amounts are not properly capitalized. However, the equipment's basis includes that portion of the cost that is nondeductible because of the 7.5-percent floor (see ¶ 1015). To determine this portion, the total amount of the limitation (7.5% of the taxpayer's adjusted gross income) is multiplied by a fraction whose numerator is the cost of the equipment and whose denominator is the total amount of the taxpayer's medical expenses. Similarly, if a taxpayer's total allowable itemized deductions exceed the taxpayer's adjusted gross income, or are limited by the overall limitation on itemized deductions of high-income taxpayers (see ¶ 1014), that portion of the equipment's cost attributable to the nondeductible expenses may also be included in the equipment's basis.[69]

1687. Involuntary Conversion. The basis of property purchased as the result of an involuntary conversion (see ¶ 1713) on which gain is not recognized is the cost of the replacement property less the amount of gain not recognized on the conversion. If qualifying replacement property is received as the result of an involuntary conversion, the replacement property's basis is the same as the basis of the involuntarily converted property decreased by any loss recognized on the conversion and any money received and not spent on qualifying replacement property. The basis is increased by any gain recognized on the conversion and any cost of acquiring the replacement property (Code Sec. 1033(b)).[70] See ¶ 1250 for special depreciation rules.

1693. Property Transferred Between Spouses or Incident to Divorce. No gain or loss is recognized on a transfer of property from an individual to, or in trust for the benefit of, a spouse or a former spouse if the transfer to the former spouse is incident to the divorce of the parties (Code Sec. 1041) (see ¶ 1734). In such case, the basis of the

---

Footnote references are to paragraphs of the 2008 Standard Federal Tax Reports.

[68] ¶ 6390.77   [69] ¶ 29,412.9963, ¶ 29,413   [70] ¶ 29,640, ¶ 29,644

¶1684

transferred property in the hands of the transferee is the transferor's adjusted basis in the property. This nontaxable carryover basis provision does not apply to a spouse (or former spouse) who is a nonresident alien (Code Sec. 1041(d)).

Nonrecognition of gain is not permitted with respect to the transfer of property in trust to the extent that the sum of the amount of any liabilities assumed, plus the amount of any liabilities to which the property is subject, exceeds the total of the adjusted basis of the property transferred (Code Sec. 1041(e)).[71] The transferee's basis is adjusted to take into account any gain recognized.

Valuation Rules

1695. Fair Market Value. Fair market value is the standard for valuing property acquired by a corporation for its stock and for valuing a decedent's property at date of death. It is also used in determining whether and to what extent property received in an exchange is the equivalent of cash. The IRS has recognized a judicial definition of fair market value as being the price that property will bring when offered for sale by a willing seller to a willing buyer, neither being obliged to buy or sell.[72] Only in rare and extraordinary cases does property have no determinable fair market value (Reg. § 1.1001-1).[73]

If the fair market value of an asset received in an exchange (such as a contract to receive royalties) cannot be determined with fair certainty, gain is not realized on the exchange until after the total payments received under the contract exceed the cost (or other basis) of the property surrendered in exchange.[74] The Tax Court has applied the *Cohan* rule (estimated or approximate value) to estimate the value of patents, patent applications, and stock rights, where the taxpayer could not prove their exact value.[75]

Nonrecourse Indebtedness. In determining the amount of gain or loss (or deemed gain or loss) with respect to any property, the fair market value of such property is deemed not less than the amount of any nonrecourse indebtedness to which the property is subject (Code Sec. 7701(g)).[76]

1697. Valuation of Securities and Real Estate. The fair market value of securities traded on the open market, or on a recognized exchange, is ordinarily the average of the high and low quoted prices on the valuation date. If only a minimal number of shares are traded on the valuation date, or if other abnormal market conditions exist, an alternative valuation method may be necessary.[77]

When corporate stock is not sold on the open market, its fair market value depends upon many factors, including the nature and history of the business, economic outlook and condition of the industry, book value of stock and financial condition of the business, earning capacity of the company, dividend-paying capacity, goodwill, prior sales, size of the block to be valued, and market price of similar but listed stock.[78] Isolated sales of small portions of the stock or forced sales are not considered evidence of fair market value.[79]

Restrictive sales agreements must be considered in the valuation of stock. If the stock is subject to a repurchase option, its value may not exceed the amount for which it may be repurchased. If there are restrictions making sale of stock impossible, and its value is highly speculative, it does not have a fair market value.[80]

Accepted evidence of the fair market value of real estate includes sales of like property in the same locality,[81] testimony of real estate experts,[82] and offers to purchase.[83] Appraisal affidavits of a retrospective nature, standing alone, are generally not accorded great weight.[84]

Footnote references are to paragraphs of the 2008 Standard Federal Tax Reports.

[71] ¶ 29,800
[72] ¶ 29,225.1071
[73] ¶ 29,221
[74] ¶ 29,225.153
[75] ¶ 8520.586, ¶ 16,612.175

[76] ¶ 43,080
[77] ¶ 29,225.187, ¶ 29,225.242
[78] ¶ 29,225.228
[79] ¶ 29,225.234
[80] ¶ 29,225.2557, ¶ 29,225.2563

[81] ¶ 29,225.518
[82] ¶ 29,225.481
[83] ¶ 29,225.511
[84] ¶ 29,225.1055

Chapter 17

SALES AND EXCHANGES

CAPITAL GAINS

Sales and Exchanges of Property

1701. Gain or Loss from Sale or Exchange of Property. A taxpayer's realized gain from the sale or exchange of property must generally be recognized for income tax purposes (Code Sec. 1001(c)).[1] Gain is the amount the taxpayer "realized" from the sale minus the taxpayer's "adjusted basis" in the property (Code Sec. 1001(a)).[2] See ¶ 1703 for more information concerning how to determine the amount "realized" in a sale or exchange. A taxpayer's "adjusted basis" in the property is generally the property's original cost to the taxpayer plus the cost of any capital improvements, minus any depreciation or depletion (Code Secs. 1011, 1012 and 1016).[3] See ¶ 1604 and following for more information on adjusted basis. Some exchanges of property may be partially or totally tax free (see ¶ 1719 and following). A taxpayer has a loss when the adjusted basis of the property is more than the amount realized (Code Sec. 1001(a)). Not all losses are recognized for tax purposes. See ¶ 1101 for information on the deductibility of losses.

Basis in Property. See ¶ 1601 for a chart prepared by CCH that may be used to determine a taxpayer's basis in property.

Determining Tax Consequences. In order to determine the tax consequences of a sale or exchange, the following questions must be answered:

    (1) What is the *amount realized* on the sale? See ¶ 1703.

    (2) Is the gain or loss on the transaction *recognized*? See ¶ 1719.

    (3) What is the *amount* of gain or loss? See ¶ 1604.

    (4) Will the *capital gain and loss* provisions apply? See ¶ 1735.

    (5) Is any part of the gain attributable to depreciation recapture that must be treated as ordinary income? See ¶ 1779.

Recognized gain or loss on a sale or exchange is the portion of the realized gain or loss that is taken into account in calculating gross income.

Footnote references are to paragraphs of the 2008 Standard Federal Tax Reports.

[1] ¶ 29,220   [2] ¶ 29,220   [3] ¶ 29,310, ¶ 29,330, ¶ 29,410

¶1701

Installment Payments. When real or personal property is sold by a nondealer and part or all of the selling price is to be paid after the year of sale, the *recognized gain* from the sale must be reported on the installment method unless the taxpayer elects *not* to apply the installment method (Code Sec. 453(d)). See ¶ 1801 for information concerning the installment method.

Rollover into Specialized Small Business Investment Company Stock. Individuals and C corporations may elect to defer the recognition of capital gain from the sale of publicly traded securities if the sale proceeds are invested in the stock or a partnership interest of a "specialized small business investment company" (SSBIC) (Code Sec. 1044).[4] See ¶ 2394 for information.

Exclusion for Small Business Stock. A noncorporate taxpayer may exclude up to 50% of the gain from the sale of qualified small business stock issued after August 10, 1993 and held for more than five years (Code Sec. 1202(a)).[5] See ¶ 2396 for information. In addition, a noncorporate taxpayer may elect to roll over the realized gain from the sale of qualified small business stock held for more than six months if other small business stock is purchased during the 60-day period beginning on the date of sale (Code Sec. 1045). See ¶ 2397.

Demutualization of Life Insurance Company. A mutual insurance company can be converted into a stock company. As a result of this "demutualization" or conversion process, policyholders receive cash and/or shares of stock in exchange for their ownership interest in the former mutual company. According to the IRS, if the conversion from mutual company to stock company qualifies as a tax-free reorganization, any stock and/or cash received by the policyholder has a zero basis. As a result, when the stock is sold, the taxpayer is generally required to recognize capital gain to the extent of the net sales price. If cash is received, the capital gain is recognized in the year it is received. The taxpayer's holding period for the stock and the cash includes the time during which the taxpayer had an equity interest in the mutual insurance company. If the conversion did not qualify as a tax-free reorganization, capital gain must be recognized in the year the stock and/or cash is received. The taxpayer's holding period in the stock begins the day after it was received (IRS Pub. 550).

1703. Amount Realized. The amount realized on a sale or exchange is the total of all money received plus the fair market value of all other property or services received (Code Sec. 1001(b)).[6] If the property received in an exchange has no readily determinable fair market value, it is generally treated as being equal in value to the property it was exchanged for (*Philadelphia Park Amusement Co.*, CtCls, 54-2 USTC ¶ 9697).[7] Generally, the amount realized includes any liabilities from which the seller is relieved as a result of the sale or exchange (Reg. § 1.1001-2).[8]

The amount realized on the receipt of an annuity in exchange for property is the fair market value of the annuity contract at the time of the exchange. The entire amount of the gain or the loss is recognized at the time of the exchange, regardless of the taxpayer's method of accounting, and the consideration paid for the annuity contract is its fair market value. Some exchanges of property for an annuity before April 19, 2007, are not subject to these rules (Proposed Reg. § 1.1001-1(j)).[9]

A taxpayer who makes a gift of property on condition that the donee pay the resulting gift taxes realizes, and must recognize, a gain to the extent that the gift taxes paid by the donee exceed the donor's basis in the property (*V.P. Diedrich*, SCt, 82-1 USTC ¶ 9419).[10]

Gain or Loss from Sale of Residence

1705. Exclusion of Gain. An individual may exclude from income up to $250,000 of gain ($500,000 on a joint return in most situations) realized on the sale or exchange of a principal residence (Code Sec. 121(b)). Ownership and use tests must be met (see *"Ownership and Use,"* below). The exclusion may not be used more frequently than once every two years (Code Sec. 121(b)(3)).[11]

Footnote references are to paragraphs of the 2008 Standard Federal Tax Reports.

[4] ¶ 29,845	[7] ¶ 29,225.1523	[10] ¶ 29,226.3062
[5] ¶ 30,372	[8] ¶ 29,223	[11] ¶ 7260
[6] ¶ 29,220	[9] ¶ 29,221D	

Ownership and Use. As a general rule, gain may be excluded only if, during the five-year period that ends on the date of the sale or exchange, the individual owned and used the property as a principal residence for periods aggregating two years or more (i.e., a total of 730 days (365 × 2)). Short temporary absences for vacations or seasonal absences are counted as periods of use, even if the individual rents out the property during these periods of absence. However, an absence of an entire year is not considered a short temporary absence. The ownership and use tests may be met during nonconcurrent periods, provided that both tests are met during the five-year period that ends on the date of sale (Reg. § 1.121-1(c)).[12] If the residence was acquired in a like-kind exchange, the exclusion will not apply if the individual (or any person whose basis in the property is derived from the exchanging individual's basis) sells or exchanges the residence during the five-year period that begins on the date the residence was acquired (Code Sec. 121(d)(10)).

> **Example 1:** Wallace obtained a single family home in a like-kind exchange on September 1, 2002. After renting it out for 18 months he decided to move in and used it as his principal residence, beginning March 1, 2004. If Wallace sold the home before September 1, 2007, the exclusion is not available.

Relief for Military, Foreign Service, and Intelligence Personnel. A special exception to the two-out-of-five year rule exists for uniformed services, foreign service, and intelligence personnel called to active duty away from home. These individuals may elect to suspend the five-year test period (Code Sec. 121(d)(9)). The election is made by not reporting the gain from the sale of the residence on the tax return filed for the year of the sale (Reg. § 1.121-5(b)). The suspension period cannot last more than 10 years and the election may only be made with respect to one property (Reg. § 1.121-5(a)). When the election is made, it is effective during the period within which the individual, or his or her spouse, is on qualified official extended duty. The individual may revoke the election at anytime. The term "qualified official extended duty" is defined to mean, for uniformed services and foreign service personnel, any extended duty while serving at a duty station that is at least 50 miles from the individual's principal residence or while residing in government quarters under government orders (Code Sec. 121(d)(9)(C)(i)). For intelligence personnel, the duty station must be located outside the United States. The term "extended duty" is any period of active duty due to a call or order to such duty for a period in excess of 90 days or for an indefinite time (Code Sec. 121(d)(9)(C)(v)). This relief provision is retroactive to sales made after May 6, 1997 by members of the uniformed services and the foreign service. For employees of the intelligence community, the suspension of the test period is available for sales made after December 20, 2006 and before January 1, 2011.

Portion Not Used as Principal Residence. An individual cannot claim the exclusion for any portion of the gain that is allocable to the portion of the property that is *separate* from the actual residence (i.e., the "dwelling unit") and not used as a residence (Reg. § 1.121-1(e)(1)). See *"Reporting Requirements,"* below, for information concerning the IRS forms that may need to be filed.

> **Example 2:** Mary owned property that consisted of a residence, a stable and 35 acres. She used the stable and 28 acres for business purposes for more than 3 years during the 5-year period preceding the sale. However, the entire house and the remaining 7 acres were used as her principal residence for at least 2 years during the 5-year period preceding the sale. Mary sold the entire property and realized a gain of $24,000. Because the stable and the 28 acres used in the business were separate from her residence, she must allocate her basis and the amount realized between the residence and business portions. The portion of the gain allocable to the business portion of the property is not eligible for the exclusion. However, the gain allocable to the home and 7 acres is eligible for the exclusion (Reg. § 1.121-1(e)(4), Example 1).

The IRS has provided a number of examples that illustrate the allocation rules that are to be used in situations involving: (1) the nonresidential use of property not within the home, (2) the rental of the entire property not within the home, (3) the nonresidential use of a separate home, (4) the conversion of a separate home into the individual's

---

Footnote references are to paragraphs of the 2008 Standard Federal Tax Reports.

[12] ¶ 7261

home, (5) the depreciation of a portion of the individual's home, and (6) the nondepreciation of a portion of the individual's home (Reg. § 1.121-1(e)(4), Examples 1-6).

The disposition of property that has been used concurrently or consecutively as a home and for business purposes may be eligible for both the exclusion under Code Sec. 121 and the deferral of gain on like-kind exchanges (see ¶ 1721 for discussion of like-kind exchanges) (Rev. Proc. 2005-14).[13]

Married Individuals. The amount of excludable gain is $500,000 for married individuals filing jointly if:

> (1) either spouse meets the ownership test;

> (2) both spouses meet the use test; and

> (3) neither spouse is ineligible for exclusion by virtue of a sale or exchange of a residence within the prior two years (Code Sec. 121(b)(2)).[14]

The exclusion is determined on an individual basis. Thus, if a single individual who is otherwise eligible for an exclusion marries someone who has used the exclusion within the two years prior to the sale, the newly married individual is entitled to a maximum exclusion of $250,000. Once both spouses satisfy the eligibility rules and two years have passed since the exclusion was allowed to either of them, they may exclude up to $500,000 of gain on their joint return (Reg. § 1.121-2).

Deceased Spouse. When a spouse dies before the date of sale, the surviving spouse is considered as owning and living in the home for the same period as the deceased spouse. However, in order for this rule to apply, the surviving spouse must not have remarried before the date of sale (Reg. § 1.121-4(a)).

> **Example 3:** Erik owned and lived in his home since 1986. On July 10, 2006, he marries Helen and they both live in Erik's home. Erik dies on March 3, 2007 and Helen inherits the home. Helen does not remarry and on June 1, 2007, she sells the home. Helen satisfies the ownership and use tests because she is able to include the time that Erik owned and used the home.

Divorced Individuals. When a residence is transferred to an individual incident to a divorce, the time during which the individual's spouse or former spouse owned the residence is added to the individual's period of ownership. An individual who owns a residence is deemed to use it as a principal residence during the time the individual's spouse or former spouse has use of the home under a divorce or separation agreement (Code Sec. 121(d)(3)).[15]

Partial Exclusion. An individual who fails to meet the ownership and use requirements or the minimum two-year time period for claiming the full exclusion may nevertheless be eligible for a partial exclusion if the sale of the home is due to: (1) a change in place of employment, (2) health reasons, or (3) unforeseen circumstances (Code Sec. 121(c)(2)).[16] According to the IRS, in order for an individual to be eligible for the partial exclusion, the individual's *primary reason* for the sale must be related to one of these three reasons (Reg. § 1.121-3(b)). If the individual is able to satisfy one of the safe harbor tests that are discussed below, then the primary reason for the sale will be treated as having been due to employment, health, or unforeseen circumstances.

Change of Employment: Safe Harbor. The primary reason test will be satisfied if the individual's new place of employment is at least 50 miles farther from the residence sold or exchanged than was the former place of employment. If there was no former place of employment, the distance between the individual's new place of employment and the residence sold or exchanged must be at least 50 miles (Reg. § 1.121-3(c)).

Health Reasons: Safe Harbor. The primary reason test will be satisfied if the reason for the sale is to obtain, provide, or facilitate the diagnosis, cure, mitigation, or treatment of disease, illness, or injury (Reg. § 1.121-3(d)). Obtaining or providing medical or personal care for a "qualified individual" suffering from a disease, illness, or injury, will also qualify. The term "qualified individual" is very broad and includes the owner's spouse, as well as children, siblings, parents and others (Reg. § 1.121-3(f)). A physician's

---

Footnote references are to paragraphs of the 2008 Standard Federal Tax Reports.

[13] ¶ 7266.023   [15] ¶ 7260
[14] ¶ 7260   [16] ¶ 7260

recommendation for a change of homes for health reasons also qualifies. However, a sale or exchange that is merely beneficial to the general health of the individual is not a sale for health reasons (Reg. § 1.121-3(d)(1)).

Unforeseen Circumstances: Safe Harbor. Examples of situations that will be recognized by the IRS as unforeseen circumstances include (Reg. § 1.121-3(e)):

    (1) involuntary conversion of the home,

    (2) damage to the home from natural or man-made disasters or acts of terrorism, or

    (3) in the case of the taxpayer, taxpayer's spouse, a co-owner of the residence, or another member of the taxpayer's household:

        (a) death,

        (b) loss of employment entitling the individual to unemployment compensation,

        (c) change in employment status resulting in the taxpayer's inability to pay housing costs and living expenses,

        (d) divorce or legal separation, or

        (e) multiple births resulting from a single pregnancy.

A sale of a residence due to the individual's change in preference or improvement in financial position is *not* due to an unforeseen circumstance.

Other Tests. If the individual does not satisfy one of the safe harbor tests listed above, then the IRS will consider all the facts and circumstances when determining the principal reason for the sale. Factors that will be considered include: (1) the circumstances giving rise to the sale, (2) the individual's financial ability to maintain the property, and (3) material changes that would impact the suitability of the property as the individual's residence (Reg. § 1.121-3(b)).

Computing the Reduced Exclusion. The reduced exclusion is computed by multiplying the maximum allowable exclusion (i.e., $250,000 or $500,000) by a fraction (Reg. § 1.121-3(g)).

The numerator of the fraction is the shortest of (a) the period of time that the individual owned the property as a principal residence during the five-year period ending on the date of sale or exchange; (b) the period of time that the individual used the property as a principal residence during the five-year period ending on the date of sale or exchange; or (c) the period between the date of the most recent prior sale or exchange to which the exclusion applied and the date of the current sale or exchange. The numerator may be expressed in days or months.

The denominator of the fraction is either 730 days or 24 months (depending on the measure of time used in the numerator) (Reg. § 1.121-3(g)).

    Example 4: Al Jackson is an unmarried taxpayer who owned and used a principal residence for 12 months and then sold it in 2007 and moved in with his sister. He sold the home because he was unable to care for himself after sustaining injuries in an accident. Jackson had not excluded gain from the sale of a residence within the prior two years. He may exclude up to $125,000 of any gain that he realizes from the sale ($250,000 maximum exclusion × 12/24 = $125,000).

    Example 5: On September 1, 2006, Bill and Ruth Green purchase a townhouse in Boston for $450,000. A few months later, Ruth receives an offer of employment in Atlanta, and on July 1, 2007, the Greens sell their townhouse and move to Atlanta. Because they owned and resided in the townhouse for 10 months, they may exclude up to $208,333 of their realized gain ($500,000 maximum exclusion × 10/24 = $208,333).

Incapacity. If an individual becomes physically or mentally incapable of self-care, the individual is deemed to use a residence as a principal residence during the time in which the individual owns the residence and resides in a licensed care facility (e.g., a nursing home). In order for this rule to apply, the individual must have owned and used the

¶1705

residence as a principal residence for an aggregate period of at least one year during the five years preceding the sale or exchange (Code Sec. 121 (d) (7) (B)).[17]

Reporting Requirements. An individual who is qualified to exclude all of the realized gain from the sale of a home is not required to report the sale on the tax return for the year of sale. However, if there is a portion of the realized gain that must be recognized, the taxpayer generally reports the entire gain in Part I (Short-Term) or Part II (Long-Term) of Schedule D, Form 1040. Then, directly below the line where realized gain is reported, the amount of the prorated exclusion is entered and identified as "Section 121 exclusion." The exclusion is shown as a loss in Column (f). If the home was sold under the installment method and gain is recognized, Form 6252, Installment Sale Income, has to be filed.

If *part of the home* was used for business (e.g., home office), or to produce rental income, the individual does not need to allocate the basis of the property and the amount realized between the business portion of the home and the residential portion. However, gain must be recognized to the extent of claimed depreciation (see below). The rule is different when a *separate part of the property* was used for business purposes or rental income. For example, this situation would occur if the individual owned an apartment building and lived in one unit and rented out the other units. Generally, if the separate part of the property is used for business or rental purposes in the year of sale, the individual must treat the sale of the property as the sale of two properties (i.e., a residence and business or rental property). The sale of the business or rental portion of the property is reported on Form 4797, Sales of Business Property (IRS Pub. 523).

Gain Recognized to Extent of Depreciation. The exclusion does not apply, and gain is recognized, to the extent of any depreciation allowable with respect to the rental or business use of a principal residence after May 6, 1997 (Code Sec. 121 (d) (6) and Reg. § 1.121-1 (d) (1)). Note, however, that if the amount of depreciation allowed is less than the depreciation allowable, the taxpayer may limit the amount of gain recognized to the amount of depreciation allowed if the taxpayer can establish the amount claimed by adequate records or other sufficient evidence (Code Sec. 1250 (b) (3)).

> **Example 6:** Bob Blaine sold his main home in 2007 at a $30,000 gain. He meets the ownership and use tests to exclude the gain from his income. However, he used part of the home as a business office in 2006 and claimed $500 depreciation. Because the business office was part of his home (not separate from it), he does not have to allocate the basis and amount realized between the business part of the property and the part used as a home. In addition, he does not have to report any part of the gain on Form 4797. Bob reports his gain, exclusion, and taxable gain of $500 on Schedule D (Form 1040) (IRS Pub. 523).

Remainder Interests. The exclusion applies to gain on the sale or exchange of a remainder interest in a principal residence, provided the buyer is not a member of the taxpayer's family or other related entity as defined by Code Sec. 267 (b) or 707 (b) (Code Sec. 121 (d) (8)).[18]

Expatriates. The exclusion is not available to nonresident alien individuals who are subject to Code Sec. 877 (a) (1) because they gave up their U.S. citizenship for the principal purpose of tax avoidance (Code Sec. 121 (e); see ¶ 2457).[19]

Involuntary Conversions. For purposes of determining the allowable exclusion, the destruction, theft, seizure, requisition, or condemnation of property is treated as a sale or exchange of the residence. In addition, the ownership and use of property acquired in an involuntary conversion generally includes the ownership and use of the property treated as sold or exchanged. For purposes of the rules governing involuntary conversions (i.e., Code Sec. 1033), the amount realized from the sale or exchange of property is equal to the amount of realized gain, reduced by the amount of gain that is permitted to be excluded from income under the $250,000/$500,000 exclusion (Code Sec. 121 (d) (5)).[20]

Co-ops. The ownership of stock in a cooperative housing corporation is the equivalent of ownership of a residence if the seller, during the five-year period ending on

---

Footnote references are to paragraphs of the 2008 Standard Federal Tax Reports.

[17] ¶ 7260
[18] ¶ 7260

[19] ¶ 7260
[20] ¶ 7260

the date of sale, owned the stock for at least two years and lived in the house or apartment as a principal residence for at least two years (Code Sec. 121(d)(4)).[21]

Important Terms. In order to determine the gain or loss on the sale of a home, the individual must be able to determine the "selling price," "amount realized," and "adjusted basis" of the home. The "selling price" of a home is the total amount received. This includes cash, notes, debts assumed by the buyer, and the fair market value of services or property received. The "amount realized" is the selling price less selling expenses (e.g., commissions, legal fees, and advertising). "Adjusted basis" refers to the individual's original basis in the home, usually cost, plus capital improvements, minus depreciation claimed after May 6, 1997. The "amount realized" minus "adjusted basis" results in the individual's realized gain or loss. A loss on the individual's principal residence cannot be deducted because it is considered a personal expense.

Involuntary Conversion

1713. Gain or Loss from Involuntary Conversion. An involuntary conversion occurs when property is destroyed, stolen, condemned, or disposed of under the threat of condemnation and the taxpayer receives other property or money in payment (e.g., insurance proceeds or a condemnation award).

There are two specific sets of circumstances under which gain from compulsory or involuntary conversion of property is not recognized for tax purposes (Code Sec. 1033; Reg. § 1.1033(a)-1):[22]

(1) When property is converted involuntarily or by compulsion into other property that is similar or related in service or use, no gain is currently recognized. The basis of the old property is simply transferred to the new property. This nonrecognition rule is mandatory.

(2) When property is involuntarily converted into money (e.g., insurance proceeds after fire destroys a building), or into property that is not similar or related in service or use, the owner may elect to postpone gain recognition by buying replacement property within a specified replacement period. (See ¶ 1715 for information concerning replacement property.) When the involuntary conversion results in a gain, the taxpayer may make an election to recognize gain only to the extent that the amount realized from the converted property exceeds the cost of the replacement property. The election to defer all or part of the gain realized in the involuntary conversion is made by excluding the gain from gross income on the tax return for the year in which it is realized (Code Sec. 1033(a)(2)(A)). A taxpayer who has realized gain from an involuntary conversion must provide details of the involuntary conversion on the tax return for the tax year in which the gain is realized (see *"Required Statement,"* below).

Loss. Loss from an involuntary conversion is deductible only if the converted property was used in a business or for the production of income. However, casualty or theft losses on personal property may be deductible (¶ 1124 and ¶ 1748).

Residence. When an individual's principal residence has been involuntarily converted, the individual may exclude the realized gain as if the home had been sold, up to the $250,000/$500,000 maximum (see ¶ 1705) (Code Sec. 121(d)(5)).[23] If the total realized gain is more than the maximum allowable exclusion, the individual may defer recognizing the excess if replacement property is purchased (Code Sec. 121(d)(5)(B)). The sale of land within a reasonable period of time following the destruction of a principal residence can qualify as part of the involuntary conversion of the residence (Rev. Rul. 96-32).[24]

Livestock. The destruction of livestock by disease, or the sale or exchange of livestock because of disease, is treated as an involuntary conversion (Code Sec. 1033(d); Reg. § 1.1033(d)-1).[25] Sales or exchanges of livestock (except poultry) in excess of the number that would normally be sold, made solely on account of drought, flood, or other weather-related conditions, may also be entitled to involuntary conversion treatment (Code Sec. 1033(e); Reg. § 1.1033(e)-1).[26] The generally applicable two-year period for

---

Footnote references are to paragraphs of the 2008 Standard Federal Tax Reports.

[21] ¶ 7260

[22] ¶ 29,640, ¶ 29,641

[23] ¶ 7260

[24] ¶ 29,650.508

[25] ¶ 29,640, ¶ 29,646

[26] ¶ 29,640, ¶ 29,647

purchasing replacement property is extended to four years when the weather-related condition (e.g., drought) results in the area being eligible for assistance from the federal government (Code Sec. 1033(e)(2)). The IRS will generally extend the replacement period due to persistent drought in the taxpayer's region until the end of the taxpayer's first tax year ending after the region's first drought-free year (Notice 2006-82). The IRS will publish a list each year of the counties that suffered droughts sufficient to extend the replacement period (Notice 2007-80).

If, because of drought, flood, or other weather-related conditions, or soil or other environmental contamination, it is not feasible for a farmer to reinvest the proceeds from involuntarily converted livestock in property similar or related in service or use, the proceeds may be invested in other property, including real property, used for farming. The replacement property will then be treated as property similar or related in service or use to the converted livestock (Code Sec. 1033(f)).[27] However, real property will qualify as replacement property only if the conversion was due to soil or other environmental contamination (Code Sec. 1033(f)).

For treatment of certain gains and losses from involuntary conversions as capital gains and losses, see ¶ 1748.

Reporting Requirements. Form 4797, Sales of Business Property, is used to report the gain or loss from an involuntary conversion (other than from casualty or theft) of (a) business property, (b) capital assets used in a business, or (c) capital assets used in connection with a transaction entered into for profit. Form 4684, Casualties and Thefts, is used to report involuntary conversions from casualties and thefts. Schedule D (Form 1040) (Capital Gains and Losses) is used to report gains from involuntary conversions (other than from casualty of theft) of capital assets not held for business or profit.

Required Statement. A taxpayer is required to attach a statement to the tax return for the year in which gain is realized (e.g., the year in which insurance proceeds are received) (Reg. § 1.1033(a)-2(c)(2)). The statement should include such information as the date and details of the involuntary conversion and the insurance or other reimbursement received. If replacement property was acquired before the tax return is filed, the statement is to include a description of the replacement property, the date of acquisition and the cost of the replacement property. If replacement is to be made after the year in which the gain is realized, the statement should also state that the taxpayer intends to replace the property within the required replacement period.

1715. Replacement Property. A taxpayer does not recognize gain after an involuntary conversion (e.g., destruction, theft, or condemnation) to the extent that the converted property is replaced with property that is similar to, or related in use to, the property that was lost or taken. Generally, when money or dissimilar property is received, gain is recognized. However, if the taxpayer buys qualifying replacement property within the replacement period, the taxpayer can elect to postpone the recognition of gain. Even under this rule, gain must still be recognized to the extent that the net proceeds from the involuntary conversion are not invested in replacement property (Code Sec. 1033(a)(2)(A)).[28]

Replacement Property. "Replacement property" can be (a) other property *similar or related in service or use* to the property converted or (b) 80% control of a corporation owning such other property. An actual purchase must take place (e.g., title must have passed); an enforceable contract to purchase is not sufficient.[29] However, in a situation involving *real property* used in the taxpayer's trade or business (other than inventory or property held primarily for sale) or held for investment, the replacement property does not need to be *similar or related in service or use* to the converted property. Instead, the replacement property only needs to be of a "like-kind" to the converted property (¶ 1721) if the replacement property is held either for productive use in trade or business or for investment (Code Sec. 1033(g)).[30] However, this "like-kind" test, which is more liberal than the "similar use" standard that is generally applied, is not applicable to acquisitions of 80% control of a corporation owning such property or to involuntary

---

Footnote references are to paragraphs of the 2008 Standard Federal Tax Reports.

[27] ¶ 29,640   [29] ¶ 29,650.204
[28] ¶ 29,640   [30] ¶ 29,640

conversions by fire, storm, or other casualty (Code Sec. 1033(g)(2)).[31] For a discussion of what constitutes like-kind real property, see ¶ 1721.

A taxpayer may elect to treat an outdoor advertising display as real property except when the election to expense the property under Code Sec. 179 (¶ 1208) has been made (Code Sec. 1033(g)(3)).[32]

Basis of Replacement Property. See ¶ 1687 for a discussion of this topic.

Presidentially Declared Disasters. Business or investment property that is compulsorily or involuntarily converted as a result of a presidentially declared disaster need not be replaced with similar or related property. The replacement property will be deemed to be similar or related in service or use provided it is tangible property held for productive use in a trade or business. The replacement property must generally be acquired within two years (see *"Replacement Period,"* below) (Code Sec. 1033(h)(2)).[33]

Property Acquired from Related Persons. For a C corporation, a partnership in which one or more C corporations own more than a 50% interest, and any other taxpayer who realizes gain of more than $100,000 during the year on involuntary conversions, property acquired from a related person does not qualify as replacement property unless the related person obtained the property from an unrelated person during the replacement period (see *"Replacement Period,"* below). For partnerships or S corporations, the $100,000 limitation applies to both the partnership and each partner and to both the S corporation and each shareholder (Code Sec. 1033(i)).[34]

Replacement Period. Purchase of the replacement property, or of 80% control of a corporation that owns such property, must be completed within a period of time that begins on the actual date of the destruction, condemnation, etc., or the date on which the threat or imminence of condemnation or requisition begins, whichever is earlier. Generally, the replacement period ends two years after the close of the first tax year in which any part of the gain on the conversion is realized (Code Sec. 1033(a)(2)(B)(i)). The replacement period for business or investment real property can be as long as three years (see *"Real Property,"* below). For a principal residence in a declared disaster area, the replacement period is four years (see *"Residence: Special Rules,"* below). For property located in the Hurricane Katrina disaster area, the replacement period is five years, if substantially all of the use of the replacement property is in the disaster area (Act Sec. 405 of the Katrina Emergency Tax Relief Act of 2005 (P.L. 109-73)). For special rules that apply to livestock, see ¶ 1713. Taxpayers may apply for an extension of the applicable time period (see *"Application for Extension,"* below) (Code Sec. 1033(a)(2)(B)(ii)).[35]

> **Example:** Laura has a basis in a commercial building, excluding the underlying land, of $100,000. The building is destroyed by fire, and Laura receives a $120,000 settlement from her insurance company, thus realizing a gain of $20,000. If she acquires a new building for the same use for $120,000 (or more) within the prescribed replacement period, she may elect not to recognize any gain on the involuntary conversion. If the replacement building costs only $110,000, Laura must recognize $10,000 of gain if she elects nonrecognition treatment. Without her election, she must recognize the entire $20,000 gain.

Real Property. If business or investment *real* property (other than inventory) is condemned, the replacement period ends *three years,* rather than two years, after the close of the first tax year in which only part of the gain is realized (Code Sec. 1033(g)(4)).[36] The three-year period does not apply to property involuntarily converted through destruction (e.g., casualty) or theft.

Application for Extension. The replacement period may be extended by the IRS (Code Sec. 1033(a)(2)(B)).[37] The taxpayer applies for an extension with the IRS director for the area where the return was filed. The IRS does not provide a form that may be used to apply for the extension. The application should explain in detail the reasons for the extension request. An extension may be granted if the replacement property is being built and the replacement cannot be made within the replacement period. An extension

---

Footnote references are to paragraphs of the 2008 Standard Federal Tax Reports.

[31] ¶ 29,640	[34] ¶ 29,640	[37] ¶ 29,640
[32] ¶ 29,640	[35] ¶ 29,640	
[33] ¶ 29,640	[36] ¶ 29,640	

¶1715

will not be granted based on the scarcity or high price of replacement property (IRS Pub. 544).[38] The application should be filed before the statutory replacement period expires. However, a late request is considered if it is made within a reasonable period of time after the replacement period expires and there is reasonable cause for the untimely filing (Reg. § 1.1033(a)-2(c)(3)).[39]

Residence: Special Rules. Special rules apply to a principal residence or the contents of a principal residence that are involuntarily converted as the result of a disaster for which a presidential declaration is made (Code Sec. 1033(h)(4)).[40] No gain is recognized by reason of the receipt of insurance proceeds for *unscheduled* personal property that was part of the contents of the residence (Code Sec. 1033(h)(1)(A)). This is true regardless of the use to which the taxpayer puts the insurance money (Rev. Rul. 95-22). All other insurance proceeds (i.e., insurance reimbursement for *scheduled* items) for the residence or its contents are treated as a common pool of funds received for the conversion of a single item of property. Funds received for scheduled property must be used to purchase property that is similar or related in service or use to the converted residence (or its contents) in order for the taxpayer to avoid recognition of gain. Gain is recognized only to the extent that the amount of the pool of funds exceeds the cost of any property similar or related in service or use to the converted residence or its contents (Rev. Rul. 95-22). The replacement period is *four years* after the close of the first tax year in which any part of the gain upon the conversion is realized (Code Sec. 1033(h)(1)(B)). These rules also apply to the conversion of property in a rented residence if the rented residence served as the taxpayer's principal residence (Code Sec. 1033(h)(4)).[41]

1716. Condemnation Award. If only a portion of a tract of land is appropriated, the condemnation award may have two components: (1) compensation for the converted portion and (2) severance damages for the retained portion. The entire award is considered compensation for the condemned property unless both parties stipulate that a specific amount was paid for damage to the retained property (Rev. Rul. 59-173).[42]

Severance damages may be paid, for example, when access to the owner's land has been impaired, or because the owner must replace fences and plant trees to restore the retained property to its former use. The owner's net severance damages (i.e., gross severance damages minus legal expenses and other costs) reduce the basis of the retained property. Any excess of the severance damages over the owner's basis is gain (Rev. Rul. 68-37).[43] However, the owner may elect not to recognize the gain if it purchases replacement property (Rev. Rul. 83-49). See ¶ 1715 for the rules governing replacement property.

Transactions Between Related Persons

1717. Losses Not Allowed. Generally, a loss from the sale or exchange of property is not recognized when the parties to the transaction are related persons (Code Sec. 267(b); Reg. § 1.267(b)-1).[44] However, the buyer may be able to recognize the loss when he sells or exchanges the property at a gain (see *"Previously Disallowed Loss,"* below).

Related Persons. The term "related persons" includes:

(1) Members of a family (brother, sister, spouse, ancestor, or lineal descendant);

(2) An individual and a corporation if the individual owns (directly or indirectly) more than 50% in value of the outstanding stock;

(3) Two corporations that are members of a controlled group (at least 50% owned) of corporations;

(4) A grantor and a fiduciary of any trust;

(5) A fiduciary of one trust and a fiduciary of another trust, if the same person is grantor of both trusts;

(6) A fiduciary of a trust and any beneficiary of such trust;

Footnote references are to paragraphs of the 2008 Standard Federal Tax Reports.

[38] ¶ 29,650.135
[39] ¶ 29,642
[40] ¶ 29,640
[41] ¶ 29,640
[42] ¶ 29,650.504
[43] ¶ 29,650.504
[44] ¶ 14,150, ¶ 14,153

(7) A fiduciary of a trust and a beneficiary of another trust, if the same person is a grantor of both trusts;

(8) A fiduciary of a trust and a corporation more than 50% in value of the outstanding stock of which is directly or indirectly owned by or for the trust or a grantor of the trust;

(9) A person and an exempt charitable or educational organization controlled by the person or, if the "person" is an individual, by the individual or his family;

(10) A corporation and a partnership if the same persons own (a) more than 50% in value of the outstanding stock of the corporation and (b) more than 50% of the capital interest or profits interest in the partnership;

(11) An S corporation and another S corporation if the same persons own more than 50% in value of the outstanding stock of each corporation;

(12) An S corporation and a C corporation if the same persons own more than 50% in value of the outstanding stock of each corporation; or

(13) An executor and a beneficiary of an estate, except when the sale or exchange is made in satisfaction of a pecuniary bequest.

Stock Ownership. In determining stock ownership: (a) stock held by a corporation, partnership, estate, or trust is considered owned proportionately by its shareholders, partners, or beneficiaries; (b) individuals are considered to own stock owned by their families, as defined above; and (c) stock owned by an individual's partner is considered owned by the individual if the individual also owns stock in the corporation (Code Sec. 267(c)).[45]

Previously Disallowed Loss. When the "related person" rule results in a denial of a loss deduction to the transferor of the property, the original transferee will be able to use the loss when he sells or exchanges the property. However, the loss can only be recognized to the extent of the gain realized by the transferee (Reg. § 1.267(d)-1).[46]

> **Example:** A father sells business property with a $15,000 basis to his son for $5,000. The father's $10,000 realized loss is not deductible because he sold the property to a related person. Later, the son sells the property for $18,000 to an unrelated person. The son's realized gain is $13,000 (i.e., $18,000 minus $5,000). However, only $3,000 of this gain is recognized (i.e., $13,000 realized gain minus the father's $10,000 unrecognized loss).

Tax-Free Exchanges

1719. Exchange of Property. Gains from exchanges of property are generally recognized for tax purposes (Code Sec. 1001(c)).[47] However, some types of exchanges do not result in recognized gain or deductible loss. These types of tax-free exchanges are described in ¶ 1721–¶ 1734.

1721. Like-Kind Exchanges. No gain or loss is recognized upon the exchange of property held for productive use in a trade or business or for investment if the property received is of a like kind and is held either for productive use in a business or for investment. This nonrecognition rule does *not* apply to stock in trade or other property held primarily for sale, stocks, bonds, notes, certificates of trust, beneficial interests, partnership interests, securities or evidences of indebtedness or interest (Code Sec. 1031(a)(2); Reg. § 1.1031(a)-1).[48] Also, the like-kind exchange rules do not apply to exchanges of property the taxpayer uses for personal purposes (e.g., home or family car) (IRS Pub. 544). For treatment of "trade-in" allowances, see ¶ 1654. The disposition of a property used as a home and then converted to use as business property may be both a like-kind exchange and a sale of a principal residence qualifying for an exclusion of gain (Rev. Proc. 2005-14). See ¶ 1705 for discussion of the exclusion for gain from the sale of a principal residence.

Related Persons. If property received in a like-kind exchange between certain controlled partnerships (see ¶ 432) or related persons (see ¶ 1717) is disposed of within two years after the date of the last transfer that was part of the like-kind exchange, the

---

Footnote references are to paragraphs of the 2008 Standard Federal Tax Reports.

[45] ¶ 14,150   [47] ¶ 29,220
[46] ¶ 14,155   [48] ¶ 29,602, ¶ 29,603

original exchange will not qualify for nonrecognition treatment (Code Sec. 1031(f)).[49] Any gain or loss that was not recognized by the taxpayer on the original exchange must be recognized as of the date that the like-kind property is disposed of by either the taxpayer or the related party. The use of a qualified intermediary does not prevent a like-kind exchange from being treated as a related party transaction (*Teruya Bros., Ltd.*, 124 TC 45, Dec. 55,924). The running of the two-year period may be suspended when the holder of the exchanged property has substantially diminished the risk of loss by the use of a put, short sale, holding by another person of a right to acquire such property, or any other transaction (Code Sec. 1031(g)).[50] A disposition that would otherwise require recognition on the original exchange is not covered by the related-person rule if (1) neither the original exchange nor the disposition had as one of its principal purposes the avoidance of federal income tax, (2) the disposition was due to the death of either related party, or (3) the disposition was due to the compulsory or involuntary conversion of the property (see ¶ 1713) (Code Sec. 1031(f)(2)).

Basis. For the basis of property received in a like-kind exchange, see ¶ 1651.

Reporting. Form 8824, Like-Kind Exchanges, is used to report the like-kind exchange.

Like-Kind Property Defined. Property is of like kind if it is of the same nature or character. Most exchanges of real properties qualify as like-kind exchanges (Reg. § 1.1031(a)-1(b) and (c)).[51] However, real property located in the U.S. and real property located outside the U.S. are not like-kind property (Code Sec. 1031(h)(1)).[52]

Personal properties are like kind if they are of a like kind or class. Depreciable tangible personal properties are of a like class if they fall within the same general asset class or the same product class. For depreciable tangible personal property, asset classes follow those used for depreciation purposes and that are set forth in Rev. Proc. 87-56. Product classes are determined by reference to the six-digit product codes of the North American Industrial Classification System (Reg. § 1.1031(a)-2(b)).[53]

Personal property predominantly used in the U.S. and personal property predominantly used outside of the U.S. are not like-kind property (Code Sec. 1031(h)(2)).[54]

Exchanges involving intangible personal property or nondepreciable tangible personal property may qualify for like-kind exchange treatment only if the properties are like kind. For example, an exchange of a copyright on a novel for a copyright on another novel would generally be a like-kind exchange. However, an exchange of a copyright on a novel for a copyright on a song would not be a like-kind exchange. An exchange of goodwill or going concern value of one business for the goodwill or going concern value of another business is *not* a like-kind exchange (Reg. § 1.1031(a)-2(c)).[55]

1722. Deferred Like-Kind Exchanges. An exchange may qualify for like-kind treatment even if the replacement property is received after the relinquished property has been transferred by the taxpayer, provided that specific identification and receipt requirements are satisfied. This type of transaction is known as a Starker exchange (*B. Starker*, CA-9, 79-2 USTC ¶ 9541).[56] After transferring the relinquished property, the taxpayer must identify replacement property within 45 days and must receive the replacement property within 180 days (or, if earlier, by the due date (including extensions) of the transferor's return for the tax year in which the relinquished property was transferred) (Code Sec. 1031(a)(3); Reg. § 1.1031(k)-1).[57] The deadlines may be extended where the parties are affected by a presidentially declared disaster (Rev. Proc. 2005-27). Real property still under construction may qualify as like-kind exchange property (Reg. § 1.1031(k)-1(e)).[58] A taxpayer may identify: (1) up to three replacement properties or (2) any number of replacement properties provided their aggregate value does not exceed 200% of the aggregate value of all relinquished properties (Reg. § 1.1031(k)-1(c)(4)).[59]

Identifying Replacement Property. Replacement property must be identified before the end of the "identification period" that begins on the date that the relinquished

---

Footnote references are to paragraphs of the 2008 Standard Federal Tax Reports.

[49] ¶ 29,602, ¶ 29,608.2493
[50] ¶ 29,602
[51] ¶ 29,603
[52] ¶ 29,602

[53] ¶ 29,606
[54] ¶ 29,602
[55] ¶ 29,606
[56] ¶ 29,621.30

[57] ¶ 29,619
[58] ¶ 29,619
[59] ¶ 29,619

property is transferred and ends at midnight on the 45th day thereafter (Reg. § 1.1031(k)-1(b)(2)).[60] Replacement property is treated as identified only if it is designated as replacement property in either: (1) a written agreement covering the exchange that is signed by all parties before the end of the identification period or (2) a written document signed by the taxpayer and hand delivered, mailed, telecopied, or otherwise sent before the end of the identification period to a person involved in the exchange (such as an intermediary, escrow agent or title company) other than the taxpayer or a related party (Reg. § 1.1031(k)-1(c)).[61] In either situation, the replacement property must be unambiguously described. For example, for transactions involving real property, a street address or legal description is generally an adequate identification of the property.

Safe Harbors. The taxpayer may not actually or constructively receive cash and then use the proceeds to buy the replacement property. The following four safe harbors protect nonrecognition treatment in a deferred like-kind exchange in which a property or security interest is received by the transferor. The transferor is not considered in receipt of money or other property if the transaction involves:

    (1) qualifying security or guarantee arrangements,

    (2) qualified escrow accounts or trusts,

    (3) a qualified intermediary, or

    (4) payment of interest or a growth factor (Reg. § 1.1031(k)-1(g)).[62]

"Parking Transactions." An additional safe harbor is provided in situations involving what is termed a "reverse-Starker exchange" (i.e., an exchange in which replacement property is acquired before the relinquished property is transferred) (Rev. Proc. 2000-37).[63] The safe harbor rules provided by Rev. Proc. 2000-37 are aimed primarily at what are termed "parking transactions." In a parking transaction, the taxpayer "parks" the desired replacement property with a third party (i.e., the accommodation party) until the taxpayer arranges for the transfer of the relinquished property to the ultimate transferee in a simultaneous or deferred exchange. If the rules for this safe harbor are complied with, the IRS will not challenge the qualification of property as either "replacement property" or "relinquished property" or the treatment of the exchange accommodation titleholder as the beneficial owner of the property. In order for this safe harbor to come into play, the property must be held in a "qualified exchange accommodation arrangement" (QEAA). A QEAA must meet a number of requirements, including the following: (1) title of the property must be held by a person other than the taxpayer or a disqualified person and (2) the combined time period that the properties are held in a QEAA must not exceed 180 days. The safe harbor is not available when the replacement property held in a QEAA is property that was owned by the taxpayer within the 180-day period ending on the date that title or other indication of ownership of the property is transferred to the exchange accommodation titleholder (Rev. Proc. 2004-51).

Direct Deeding of Property. In an exchange of real property involving three parties (i.e., (1) the taxpayer, (2) the transferee (a qualified intermediary), and (3) a third party that supplies the replacement property), the exchange may qualify as like kind even if the third party deeds the replacement property directly to the taxpayer. Therefore, it is not necessary for the transferee to take title to the replacement property and then transfer title to the taxpayer (Rev. Rul. 90-34).[64]

1723. Exchange for Property of Like-Kind Plus Cash or Other Property. If unlike property or money is received in addition to the like-kind property, the taxpayer must recognize gain. However, the recognized gain is limited to the amount of the cash and the fair market value of the other property received (Code Sec. 1031(b); Reg. § 1.1031(b)-1).[65] A *loss* from a similar exchange may not be deducted (Code Sec. 1031(c); Reg. § 1.1031(c)-1).[66]

    Example: Bill exchanged real estate, with a basis of $10,000, for real estate with a fair market value of $12,000 and $4,000 in cash. His *realized* gain of $6,000 (i.e., $16,000 value received minus $10,000 basis) is *recognized* only to the extent of

---

Footnote references are to paragraphs of the 2008 Standard Federal Tax Reports.

[60] ¶ 29,619
[61] ¶ 29,619
[62] ¶ 29,621.85

[63] ¶ 29,620.01
[64] ¶ 29,621.30
[65] ¶ 29,602, ¶ 29,611

[66] ¶ 29,602, ¶ 29,612

¶1723

the $4,000 cash he received. His basis for the real estate he received is $10,000 (i.e., $10,000 basis in old property, minus $4,000 cash received, plus $4,000 *recognized* gain).

See ¶ 1728 and ¶ 1731 for situations involving stock exchanged for stock in the same corporation and the tax-free transfer of property to a controlled corporation.

1724. Exchange of Contracts. No gain or loss results from an exchange of:

    (1) life insurance contracts,

    (2) a life insurance contract for an endowment or an annuity contract,

    (3) two annuity contracts,

    (4) an endowment insurance contract for an annuity contract; or

    (5) two endowment insurance contracts if the new contract provides for regular payments beginning on a date not later than the date payments would have begun under the contract that was exchanged (Code Sec. 1035(a); Reg. § 1.1035-1).[67]

Gain or loss may be recognized if the exchange has the effect of transferring property to any person other than a United States person (Code Sec. 1035(c)).

Policyholders who surrender life insurance or annuity contracts of a financially troubled insurance company may qualify for nonrecognition of gain if, within 60 days, all cash received is reinvested in another policy or contract issued by another insurance company or in a single custodial account (Rev. Proc. 92-44).[68]

1725. "Like-Kind" Exchange of Mortgaged Real Estate. When taxpayers exchange mortgaged real estate for other real estate in an otherwise tax-free "like-kind" exchange, the amount of the mortgage from which they are relieved is treated as other property or money. If mortgaged property is exchanged for mortgaged property, the net reduction of the mortgage indebtedness is treated as other property or money (Reg. § 1.1031(d)-2).[69]

> **Example:** Kathy owned real property, which had a fair market value of $100,000 and an adjusted basis of $75,000 and was subject to a $70,000 mortgage. She exchanged the property for like-kind property, which had a fair market value of $60,000 and was subject to a $30,000 mortgage. Her entire realized gain must be recognized:

Fair market value of property received	$60,000
Less mortgage on that property	30,000
	$30,000
Mortgage on property transferred by Kathy	70,000
Total consideration received	$100,000
Less basis of property transferred	75,000
Gain realized	$25,000

The total realized gain is recognized because it is less than the $40,000 net mortgage reduction.

It is immaterial whether a mortgage is assumed by the purchaser or whether the property is acquired subject to a mortgage (Reg. § 1.1031(d)-2).[70]

1726. Exchange of Government Obligations. When regulations provide for it, obligations issued by the United States may be exchanged tax free for other such obligations (except to the extent that money is received in the exchange) (Code Sec. 1037; Reg. § 1.1037-1).[71] Municipal or state bonds may be exchanged pursuant to a refunding agreement without recognition of gain or loss, provided that there are no material differences in the terms of the exchanged bonds (Rev. Rul. 81-169).[72]

1728. Stock Exchanged for Stock of the Same Corporation. An exchange of common stock for common stock of the same corporation, or of preferred stock for preferred stock of the same corporation, does not result in recognized gain or deductible

---

Footnote references are to paragraphs of the 2008 Standard Federal Tax Reports.

[67] ¶ 29,680, ¶ 29,681   [69] ¶ 29,613, ¶ 29,615.035   [71] ¶ 29,720, ¶ 29,721

[68] ¶ 29,682.10   [70] ¶ 29,614   [72] ¶ 29,226.1117

loss (Code Sec. 1036(a); Reg. § 1.1036-1).[73] However, if money or other property is received in addition to the stock, gain (but not loss) may be recognized, but only to the extent of the money or fair market value of the other property received (¶ 1723) (Code Sec. 1031(b) and (c)).[74] Nonqualified preferred stock is not treated as stock for these purposes (Code Sec. 1036(b)).[75]

1729. Stock Exchanged for Property. No gain or loss is recognized to a corporation upon the receipt of money or other property in exchange for its stock (including treasury stock). Also, no gain or loss is recognized by a corporation upon the lapse or acquisition of an option, or with respect to a securities futures contract to buy or sell its stock (or treasury stock) (Code Sec. 1032(a)).[76]

1731. Tax-Free Transfer of Property to Controlled Corporation. No gain or loss is recognized if one or more persons (individuals, trusts or estates, partnerships or corporations) transfer property to a corporation solely in exchange for its stock and, immediately after the transfer, are in "control" of the transferee corporation. "Control" means the ownership of at least 80% of the voting stock and at least 80% of all other stock of the corporation. Stock rights or warrants are not considered to be stock (Code Sec. 351(a); Reg. § 1.351-1).[77] Nonqualified preferred stock is also not treated as stock (Code Sec. 351(g)). Stock is not considered issued in exchange for property if it is issued for services or unsecured debts of the transferee or for interest accrued to the transferor on debts owed by the transferee.[78]

If the transferor-stockholder receives other property (including securities) or cash in addition to the stock, any gain from the transfer (but not any loss) is recognized, but only up to the cash or the fair market value of the other property received (Code Sec. 351(b); Reg. § 1.351-2).[79] See ¶ 1723 for related rules. See ¶ 1663 for the basis of the property transferred to the controlled corporation.

1732. Property Exchanged to Avoid Conflicts of Interest. If an officer or employee of the executive branch or a judicial officer of the federal government sells, pursuant to a certificate of divestiture issued by the President or the Director of the Office of Government Ethics (to an executive branch officer or employee) or the Judicial Conference of the United States (to a judicial officer), any property in order to comply with conflict-of-interest requirements, the individual may elect to defer a portion of the gain from the sale (Code Sec. 1043).[80] The portion of the gain that must be recognized immediately is the excess of (a) the amount realized on the sale over (b) the cost (reduced by any basis adjustment attributable to a prior sale) of any U.S. obligation or diversified investment fund approved by the Office of Government Ethics and purchased by the individual during the 60-day period beginning on the date of the sale. Any nonrecognized gain is applied to reduce (in the order acquired) the basis of any qualified property that is purchased by the individual during the 60-day period.

The deferral option is also available to any spouse, minor or dependent child whose ownership of any property is attributable to a federal officer or employee under any applicable conflict-of-interest law (Code Sec. 1043(b)(1)(B)). Also subject to these rules are sales made by a trustee if any person subject to the rules has a beneficial interest in the principal or income of the trust. Part IV of Form 8824 (Like-Kind Exchanges) is used to report conflict-of-interest sales.

The deferral option is available to judicial officers only for sales after December 20, 2006.

1733. Tax-Free Sale of Stock to ESOP. If taxpayers (other than C corporations) make the proper election, they may sell qualified securities to an employee stock ownership plan (ESOP) or worker-owned cooperative and replace the securities with other securities without recognition of gain (Code Sec. 1042).[81]

1734. Transfers of Property Between Spouses or Former Spouses. No gain or loss is recognized for transfers of property from an individual to a spouse or to a former spouse incident to a divorce. The transferor's basis for the transferred property is

---

Footnote references are to paragraphs of the 2008 Standard Federal Tax Reports.

[73] ¶ 29,700, ¶ 29,701	[76] ¶ 29,622	[79] ¶ 16,402, ¶ 16,404B
[74] ¶ 29,602	[77] ¶ 16,402, ¶ 16,403	[80] ¶ 29,840
[75] ¶ 29,700	[78] ¶ 16,405.046	[81] ¶ 29,820

carried over to the transferee. In the case of a transfer to a former spouse, the transfer must occur within one year after the date on which the marriage ceased or must be related to the cessation of the marriage. This nonrecognition treatment is not available for transfers to spouses or former spouses who are nonresident aliens (Code Sec. 1041).[82]

Treatment of Capital Gain or Loss

1735. Characterization of Gain or Loss. A taxpayer must make a determination whether gain or loss from a transaction is *ordinary* or *capital* in nature. If the gain or loss is properly characterized as *capital*, the taxpayer's next step is to determine whether it is long-term or short-term. This two-step characterization process is necessary in order to compute the taxpayer's correct tax liability. See ¶ 1741 for the rules governing the definition of a capital asset.

Holding Period for Capital Assets. Gain or loss from the sale or exchange of a capital asset is characterized as either short-term or long-term depending on how long the asset was held by the taxpayer. See ¶ 1736 and ¶ 1777 for information concerning the determination of a taxpayer's holding period. If a taxpayer has both long-term and short-term transactions during the year, each type is reported separately and gains and losses from each type are netted separately. The net long-term capital gain or loss for the year is then combined with the net short-term capital gain or loss for the year to arrive at an overall (net) capital gain or loss. When capital gains exceed capital losses, the overall gain is included with the taxpayer's other income. However, net long-term capital gain is generally subject to a maximum tax rate of 15% for individuals and 35% for corporations. See ¶ 1736 for more information on the tax rates applied to long-term capital gains. When capital losses exceed capital gains, the taxpayer's deductible loss may be limited. See ¶ 1752 and ¶ 1757 for information on capital loss limits.

Reporting. In most situations, individuals use Schedule D (Capital Gains and Losses) of Form 1040 to report the sale or exchange of a capital asset.

1736. Tax on Capital Gains—Individual, Estate, Trust. Generally, gain from the sale of long-term capital assets is subject to a maximum capital gains tax rate of 15% (5% for individuals in the 10% or 15% tax bracket) (Code Sec. 1(h)(1)).[83] A 0% rate will replace the 5% rate for tax years beginning after December 31, 2007. Capital gains on collectibles are subject to a maximum rate of 28%, and unrecaptured Section 1250 gain is subject to a maximum rate of 25%.

Application of Capital Gains Rates. These capital gains rates apply to individuals, estates and trusts. In addition, the rates apply when a taxpayer is computing the income tax under the alternative minimum tax (AMT). See ¶ 1401 for information on AMT.

Installment Payments. Installment payments are subject to the capital gains rates in force at the time they are received, not those in force at the time of the original transaction.[84]

Dividend Income. Qualified dividend income is taxed at the same rate used to calculate an individual's capital gains tax (i.e., 15% maximum, or 5% for those in the 10% or 15% tax brackets). For more information concerning "qualified dividend income," see ¶ 733.

Investment Interest. When a taxpayer elects to treat any amount of net capital gain as investment interest under Code Sec. 163(d)(4)(B)(iii), that amount is subtracted from the total net capital gain in order to determine the amount subject to the maximum capital gains rate. See ¶ 1094 regarding investment interest.

Holding Period. A capital asset must be held "more than 12 months" in order for realized gain to be classified as long-term capital gain.

> **Example 1:** On November 2, 2006, John Aubrey purchased 100 shares of Gizmo Inc. for $5,000. On May 8, 2007, Aubrey sold the 100 shares for $20,000. Aubrey will compute his tax on his $15,000 capital gain by using his ordinary income tax rate (e.g., 10%, 15%, 25%, 28%, 33%, or 35%). The ordinary income rates apply because he did not hold the stock more than 12 months.

Footnote references are to paragraphs of the 2008 Standard Federal Tax Reports.

[82] ¶ 29,800   [83] ¶ 3260   [84] ¶ 3260.033

Example 2: Assume the same facts as in Example 1, except that Aubrey sold the shares on December 1, 2007. In this situation, he is entitled to use the long-term rate of 15% (or 5% if he is in the 10% or 15% tax bracket) because he held the stock more than 12 months.

Determining Holding Period. In determining how long an asset was held, the taxpayer begins counting on the date after the day the property was acquired. The same date of each following month is the beginning of a new month regardless of the number of days in the preceding month. For example, if property was acquired on March 1, 2007, the taxpayer's holding period began on March 2, 2007. The date the asset is disposed of is part of the holding period. See ¶ 1777 for additional information concerning the determination of a taxpayer's holding period.

Depreciable Real Estate. A maximum 25% rate is imposed on long-term capital gain attributable to certain prior depreciation that had been claimed on real property. This depreciation is referred to as "unrecaptured Section 1250 gain." Unrecaptured Section 1250 gain is defined as the excess of (Code Sec. 1(h)(6)(A)):[85]

(1) the amount of long-term capital gain (not otherwise treated as ordinary income) that would be treated as ordinary income if Code Sec. 1250(b)(1) included all depreciation and the applicable percentage that applied under Code Sec. 1250(a) was 100% over

(2) the excess of 28%-rate loss over 28%-rate gain.

Even under these capital gains rules, Code Sec. 1250 will continue to treat some prior claimed depreciation (i.e., usually the amount claimed in excess of the amount allowable under the straight-line method) as ordinary income.

Example 3: On December 1, 2007, William Drake sold a building for $1,000,000. The building had originally cost $700,000 and, over the years, Drake had claimed $300,000 in depreciation. Upon the sale of the building, Drake recognizes a total gain of $600,000. Of the $300,000 in claimed depreciation, $100,000 was in excess of that allowed under the straight-line method. Under the capital gains rules (Code Sec. 1(h)(7)(A)), $200,000 of the total claimed depreciation is classified as unrecaptured Section 1250 gain. This is because if Section 1250 had applied to all depreciation, and not only additional depreciation, $300,000 of Drake's long-term capital gain would have been treated as ordinary income. Based on these facts, the $100,000 in excess depreciation would be taxed as ordinary income, the $200,000 in unrecaptured Section 1250 gain would be subject to a maximum capital gains rate of 25%, and the remaining $300,000 of gain would be subject to a maximum capital gains rate of 15%.

MACRS Depreciation. Under MACRS, all depreciation on real property must be computed under the straight-line method. As a result, any gain on the sale of MACRS real property that was held more than 12 months and that is due to claimed deprecation will be classified as "unrecaptured Section 1250 gain" and subject to a maximum capital gains rate of 25%.

Pass-Through Entities. A pass-through entity (e.g., mutual funds, S corporations, partnerships, estates and trusts) allocates capital gains to its shareholders or beneficiaries (Code Sec. 1(h)(10)).[86] Capital gain distributions from a mutual fund are taxed as long-term capital gains regardless of how long the shareholder has owned the fund shares (Code Sec. 852(b)(3)(B)). If capital gain distributions are automatically reinvested in the fund, the reinvested amount is the basis of the additional shares (IRS Fact Sheet FS-2007-19).[87]

Collectibles. Generally, collectibles (e.g., stamps, antiques, gems, and most coins) are taxed at the maximum capital gain rate of 28% even if held more than 12 months (Code Sec. 1(h)(4)(A)(i)).[88]

Small Business Stock. When a taxpayer sells or exchanges certain small business stock (i.e., Sec. 1202 stock) that the taxpayer has held for more than five years, 50% of the gain may be excluded from the taxpayer's gross income. If the small business stock qualifies for this 50% exclusion, any recognized gain from the sale or exchange of the

---

Footnote references are to paragraphs of the 2008 Standard Federal Tax Reports.

[85] ¶ 3260   [87] ¶ 26,420

[86] ¶ 3260   [88] ¶ 3260

¶1736

stock is subject to a maximum capital gains rate of 28% (Code Sec. 1(h)(4)(A)(ii)).[89] See ¶ 2396 for more information concerning small business stock. The exclusion of gain from the sale or exchange of qualified small business stock is increased to 60% in the case of the sale or exchange of stock of an enterprise zone business (as defined in Code Sec. 1397C(a)) that operates within an empowerment zone and that was acquired after December 21, 2000 (Code Sec. 1202(a)(2)). See ¶ 999B for more information concerning empowerment zones and enterprise zone businesses.

1738. Corporate Capital Gains. A corporation is taxed on net capital gain at the regular tax rates, including the additional phase-out rates for high-income corporations (¶ 219). However, the corporate tax rate on *net capital gain* is limited to 35% for those tax years in which the regular corporate tax exceeds 35%, excluding the additional phase-out rates (Code Sec. 1201(a)).[90] The alternative tax rate of 35% is applied to the lesser of the corporation's net capital gain or its taxable income (Code Sec. 1201(a)).[91] However, because the alternative tax rate only applies when a corporation's ordinary income tax rate *exceeds* 35%, and the top corporate tax rate is currently 35%, this rule generally has no immediate impact on corporations.

See ¶ 1752 and ¶ 1756 for treatment of corporate capital losses.

1739. Netting of Gains and Losses. Noncorporate taxpayers have to follow specific netting procedures in calculating their recognized capital gain or loss for the tax year (Code Sec. 1(h)(1)).[92]

The basic netting procedures provide that within each tax rate group (e.g., 15% group), gains and losses are netted in order to arrive at a net gain or loss for the group. After this basic process has been completed, the following netting and ordering rules must be applied (Notice 97-59):[93]

(1) *Short-term capital gains and losses.* Short-term capital losses (including short-term loss carryovers from a prior year) are applied first to reduce short-term capital gains, if any, that would otherwise be taxable at ordinary income tax rates. A net short-term loss is used first to reduce any net long-term capital gain from the 28% group (Code Sec. 1(h)(5)).[94] Any remaining short-term loss is then used to reduce gain from the 25% group and then groups taxed at the lower capital gains rates (e.g., 15%) (Notice 97-59).[95]

(2) *Long-term capital gains and losses.* A net loss from the 28% group (including long-term capital loss carryovers) is used first to reduce gain from the 25% group, then to reduce net gain from the 15% group. A net loss from the 15% group is used first to reduce net gain from the 28% group, and then to reduce gain from the 25% group.

1740. Conversion Transactions. Capital gain from the disposition or termination of a position that is part of a "conversion transaction" is subject to recharacterization as ordinary income (Code Sec. 1258).[96] In general, the amount of capital gain treated as ordinary income is equal to the interest that would have accrued on the taxpayer's net investment at a yield equal to 120% of the applicable federal rate compounded semiannually, or, if the term of the conversion transaction is indefinite, 120% of the federal short-term rates in effect under Code Sec. 6621(b) compounded daily. See ¶ 83 for applicable federal interest rates.

A conversion transaction is generally one designed to convert ordinary income into capital gains. A transaction is a conversion transaction only if substantially all of the taxpayer's expected return is attributable to the time value of the taxpayer's net investment in the transaction (i.e., the taxpayer is in the economic position of a lender) (Code Sec. 1258(c)). In addition, the transaction must be:

(1) a transaction in which the taxpayer acquires property and on a substantially contemporaneous basis enters into a contract to sell the property (or substantially identical property) at a predetermined price;

(2) a straddle;

Footnote references are to paragraphs of the 2008 Standard Federal Tax Reports.

[89] ¶ 3260	[92] ¶ 3260	[95] ¶ 3285.55
[90] ¶ 30,352	[93] ¶ 3285.55	[96] ¶ 31,125
[91] ¶ 30,352	[94] ¶ 3260	

(3) marketed or sold as producing capital gains from a transaction in which the taxpayer's return is substantially from the time value of the net investment; or

(4) specified by the IRS in regulations.

Example: Sam Jones purchases stock on January 2, 2005, for $100 and agrees on the same day to sell it to Wendell Johnson on January 2, 2007, for $115. A portion of the $15 gain from the sale of the stock on January 2, 2007, equal to 120% of the applicable federal rate compounded semiannually for two years and applied to the $100 investment, is recharacterized as ordinary income.

Transactions of options dealers and commodities traders in the normal course of their trade or business of dealing in options or trading Section 1256 contracts are *not* conversion transactions (Code Sec. 1258(d)(5)(A)).[97] However, this exception does not apply to certain gains allocated to limited partners and limited entrepreneurs as defined in Code Sec. 464(e)(2) (Code Sec. 1258(d)(5)(C)).

Constructive Ownership Transactions. The amount of long-term capital gains that a taxpayer may recognize from certain constructive ownership transactions that arise from specified financial assets may be limited (Code Sec. 1260).[98] These "financial assets" include any equity interest in a pass-through entity (e.g., a partnership or REIT) (Code Sec. 1260(c)). The long-term gain is limited to the amount of gain that the taxpayer would have recognized if the financial asset had been held directly by the taxpayer during the term of the derivative contract. Any additional gain is recognized as ordinary income. Interest is imposed on the amount of ordinary income (Code Sec. 1260(b)).

1741. Capital Asset. A capital gain or loss arises from the sale or exchange of a *capital asset.* Generally, the term "capital asset" means any property (whether or not connected with a trade or business) *except the following* (Code Sec. 1221; Reg. § 1.1221-1):[99]

(1) an inventoriable asset;

(2) property held primarily for sale to customers in the ordinary course of the taxpayer's trade or business ("primarily" means "of first importance" or "principally," and not merely "substantially");[100]

(3) a note or account receivable acquired in the ordinary course of trade or business for services rendered or from the sale of stock in trade or property held for sale in the ordinary course of business;

(4) depreciable business property;

(5) real property used in the taxpayer's trade or business;

(6) a copyright, a literary, musical or artistic composition, a letter or memorandum, or similar property (but not a patent or invention) held by the taxpayer who created it, or by one whose basis in the property is determined by reference to the basis of the one who created it, or in the case of a letter, memorandum or similar property, a taxpayer for whom such property was prepared or produced; and

(7) a U.S. government publication (including the *Congressional Record*) held by a taxpayer who received it (or by another taxpayer in whose hands the publication would have a basis determined in whole or in part by reference to the original recipient's basis) other than by purchase at the price at which the publication is offered to the public.

Although creative works are generally not capital assets in the hands of their creators, a special rule allows taxpayers to treat the sale or exchange of a musical composition or a copyright in a musical work created by the taxpayer's personal efforts (or having a basis determined by the reference to the creator's basis) as the sale or exchange of a capital asset. This rules applies to sales or exchanges made in a tax year beginning after May 17, 2006 (Code Sec. 1221(b)(3)).

Additional Noncapital Assets. The following types of assets or transactions are also treated as "noncapital" assets: (1) commodities derivative financial instruments held by

Footnote references are to paragraphs of the 2008 Standard Federal Tax Reports.

[97] ¶ 31,125
[98] ¶ 31,140
[99] ¶ 30,420, ¶ 30,421
[100] ¶ 30,422.022, ¶ 30,575.021

commodities derivatives dealers (Code Sec. 1221(a)(6));[101] (2) hedging transactions entered into in the normal course of the taxpayer's business (Code Sec. 1221(a)(7));[102] and (3) supplies of a type regularly used or consumed by the taxpayer in the ordinary course of business (Code Sec. 1221(a)(8)).[103]

Gain from the sale of an individual's household furnishings, personal residence or automobile is generally taxed under the capital gains rates. However, loss from the sale is not recognized unless the property was held for the production of income. For example, if an individual sells a residence that had been partially used as rental property, the individual has to allocate the original cost of the building, the selling price, depreciation (applicable to the rental portion only), and selling expenses between the personal and rental portions of the building as if there were two separate transactions (Reg. § 1.121-1(e)(1)). Although gain on either portion would generally be recognized for income tax purposes, loss would be recognized only on the rental portion. (For additional information concerning the sale of a personal residence, see ¶ 1107, ¶ 1626, and ¶ 1705.) Stock and securities generally are considered to be held for production of income so that a loss on their sale is a capital loss.

The sale or exchange of property results in ordinary income or loss if the property is classified as a "noncapital asset." The Supreme Court has ruled that the definition of a capital asset must be broadly interpreted and that an asset must come within one of the statutory categories of "noncapital" assets listed above in order for the property to be excluded from capital asset treatment (*Arkansas Best Corp.*, SCt, 88-1 USTC ¶ 9210).[104] In its decision, the Court rejected the contention that ordinary income and loss treatment should apply to an asset that is otherwise capital simply because it is acquired for business purposes. Therefore, bank stock that was acquired by a holding company in order to prevent damage to the holding company's business reputation was held to be a capital asset even though it was acquired for a business purpose, because the stock did not fall within any of the exclusion categories. In an earlier decision, the Supreme Court ruled that hedging transactions that were an integral part of a business's inventory-purchase system were a noncapital asset because they were inventory (*Corn Products Refining*, SCt, 55-2 USTC ¶ 9746).[105] Gains and losses from most business hedges entered into in order to reduce risk of price changes or currency fluctuations are treated as ordinary gains and losses. The hedge must relate to ordinary income property held or to be held by the taxpayer who enters into the hedge. A taxpayer must make a same-day identification in its books and records of the hedges entered into (Reg. § 1.1221-2(e)(1)).[106] Gain or loss from the sale, exchange or termination of a "securities futures contract" as defined by Code Sec. 1234B(c) may be eligible for capital gain treatment (Code Sec. 1234B).

Special Rules. Special rules apply when the sale involves: (1) Code Sec. 1231 assets (see ¶ 1747); (2) a patent (see ¶ 1767); (3) depreciable property (see ¶ 1779); (4) farm property (see ¶ 1797); and (5) a partnership interest (see ¶ 434).

1742. Sale or Exchange Required. The capital gain and loss provisions apply to the *sale or exchange* of a capital asset (Code Sec. 1222; Reg. § 1.1222-1).[107] In the case of real estate, a sale or exchange occurs on the earlier of the date of conveyance or the date when the burden and benefits of ownership pass to the purchaser.[108] A sale or exchange is considered to have occurred when there is a corporate liquidation (¶ 2253), when securities become worthless (¶ 1764), and upon any failure to exercise a privilege or option on property that would have been a capital asset if acquired (¶ 1919).

When bonds with past-due interest are purchased "flat" (i.e., the bonds were in default of interest payments), aggregate interest payments that are for the prepurchase period and that are in excess of the purchase price but less than the face value of the bonds are properly characterized as capital gains because they are considered to be amounts received on retirement of the bonds (Rev. Rul. 60-284).[109]

Footnote references are to paragraphs of the 2008 Standard Federal Tax Reports.

[101] ¶ 30,420
[102] ¶ 30,420
[103] ¶ 30,420
[104] ¶ 30,422.6865
[105] ¶ 30,426.15
[106] ¶ 30,424
[107] ¶ 30,440, ¶ 30,441
[108] ¶ 21,005.04
[109] ¶ 5704.3075

The sale of an endowment insurance policy before its maturity or of a paid-up annuity contract before the annuity starting date results in ordinary income (*E.J. Arnfeld*, CtCls, 58-2 USTC ¶ 9692).[110]

1743. Sale of a Trade or Business. When a business is sold, generally each asset of the business is treated as being sold separately in determining the seller's income, gain or loss and the buyer's basis in each of the assets acquired (Rev. Rul. 55-79).[111] The *seller* must allocate the purchase price among the assets in order to determine the amount and character of any recognized gain or loss. The *buyer* must allocate the purchase price among the business assets to determine any allowable depreciation or amortization (Code Sec. 1060(a); Reg. § 1.1060-1(a)).[112] See ¶ 1620 for related information.

Residual Method. Under the residual method, the purchase price is first allocated to Class I assets (cash and cash equivalents). The remaining amount is then allocated in the following order:

(1) Class II assets (certificates of deposit, U.S. government securities, readily marketable stock or securities, and foreign currency);

(2) Class III assets (mark-to-market assets and certain debt instruments);

(3) Class IV assets (stock in trade and inventory);

(4) Class V (all assets other than Class I, II, III, IV, VI and VII assets);

(5) Class VI assets (Section 197 intangibles, except goodwill or going concern value (Section 197 intangibles include workforce in place, copyrights, and covenants not to compete)); and

(6) Class VII (goodwill and going concern value) (Reg. § 1.1060-1(c) and Reg. § 1.338-6).[113]

The buyer and seller may agree in writing to allocations of part or all of the consideration involved in the transaction and of the fair market value of any assets transferred. This allocation generally is binding on both parties, unless the IRS determines that the allocation is inappropriate (Code Sec. 1060(a)).[114]

Reporting. Generally, the purchaser and the seller must both file Form 8594, Asset Acquisition Statement, to report the sale of assets used in a trade or business when the purchaser's basis in the assets is determined wholly by the amount paid. The forms are attached to the tax returns for the year in which the sale took place.

Goodwill, Covenants Not to Compete, and Other Acquired Intangibles. See ¶ 1288 for information concerning the amortization of the cost of goodwill and other intangibles.

1744. Sale of Depreciable Assets Between Related Taxpayers. Capital gain treatment is denied when depreciable property (including patent applications) is sold or exchanged between related taxpayers (Code Sec. 1239(a)). This rule applies to sales or exchanges between:

(1) a person and all entities that are controlled by such person;

(2) a taxpayer and any trust in which the taxpayer or his spouse is a beneficiary unless such beneficiary interest is a remote contingent interest; and

(3) an executor of an estate and a beneficiary of the estate, unless the sale or exchange is in satisfaction of a pecuniary bequest (Code Sec. 1239(b)).[115]

For purposes of this rule, entities that are controlled by a taxpayer include:

(1) a corporation if the taxpayer owns (directly or indirectly) more than 50% of the value of its stock;

(2) a partnership if the taxpayer owns (directly or indirectly) more than 50% of the capital or profits interest; and

(3) certain entities that are related persons with respect to the taxpayer, including two corporations that are members of the same controlled group, a corporation and a partnership if the same persons own more than 50% of each, and two S corporations, or an S corporation and a C corporation, if the same persons own more than 50% of the stock of each (Code Sec. 1239(c); Reg. § 1.1239-1).[116]

Footnote references are to paragraphs of the 2008 Standard Federal Tax Reports.

110 ¶ 30,422.58
111 ¶ 30,422.125
112 ¶ 30,060, ¶ 30,061
113 ¶ 30,061
114 ¶ 30,060
115 ¶ 30,730
116 ¶ 30,730, ¶ 30,731

¶1743

Section 1231

1747. Property Used in Trade or Business. Business real estate or any depreciable business property is generally excluded from the definition of "capital assets" (¶ 1741). However, if the business property qualifies as Code Sec. 1231 property and gains from this property exceed any losses, then each gain or loss is treated as though it were from the sale of a long-term capital asset (Code Sec. 1231(a)(1)).[117] However, if the losses exceed the gains, all gains and losses are classified as ordinary gains and losses (Code Sec. 1231(a)(2)).

Reporting. Taxpayers use Form 4797, Sales of Business Property, to report Code Sec. 1231 transactions.

Section 1231 Property. Code Sec. 1231 property includes (Code Sec. 1231(b); Reg. § 1.1231-1 and Reg. § 1.1231-2):[118]

(1) Property used in the trade or business, subject to depreciation and held more than one year (but excluding property includible in inventory; property held primarily for sale to customers; a copyright; a literary, musical or artistic composition; a letter, memorandum or similar property (see item (6) at ¶ 1741); and government publications (see item (7) at ¶ 1741)).

(2) Real property used in the trade or business and held for more than one year (but excluding property includible in inventory or held primarily for sale to customers).

(3) Trade or business property (items (1) and (2), above) held for more than one year and involuntarily converted.

(4) Capital assets held for more than one year (for rules, see ¶ 1748).

(5) A crop sold with the land when the land has been held for more than one year.

(6) Livestock, as explained at ¶ 1750.

(7) Timber, domestic iron ore, or coal under conditions described at ¶ 1772.

When Code Sec. 1231 property is subject to depreciation recapture, the amount of the Code Sec. 1231 gain is the amount by which the total gain exceeds the amounts recaptured and taxed at ordinary income rates. The depreciation recapture rules are discussed at ¶ 1779 and following. Also, the recapture of certain farmland expenses may cause a reduction in Code Sec. 1231 gain (see ¶ 1797).

A loss that is disallowed by other provisions of the law (e.g., a sale between family members) is not taken into account in comparing Code Sec. 1231 gains and losses (Code Sec. 1231(a)(3)(B)).

Recapture of Net Section 1231 Losses. A taxpayer who has a net Section 1231 gain (i.e., excess of Section 1231 gains over Section 1231 losses) for the tax year must review the five preceding tax years for possible recapture of net Section 1231 losses for the prior years. If there were any net Section 1231 losses during the period, the taxpayer must treat the current year's net Section 1231 gain as ordinary income to the extent of the amount of unrecaptured net Section 1231 losses for that past period (Code Sec. 1231(c)).[119] The losses are to be recaptured on a first-in, first-out basis.

Example: Mary has a net Section 1231 gain of $23,000 for 2007. She had a net Section 1231 loss of $12,000 in 2005 and a net Section 1231 loss of $15,000 in 2006. For 2007, under the recapture rules, Mary must include her $23,000 net Section 1231 gain as ordinary income (i.e., she recaptures the $12,000 loss from 2005 and $11,000 of the $15,000 loss from 2006). The $4,000 balance of the loss from 2006 remains outstanding, and available for recapture if Mary realizes any net Section 1231 gain during 2008-2011.

1748. Involuntary Conversions. Gains and losses from the involuntary conversion of depreciable business property, or capital assets held for more than one year that were either used in a trade or business or in a transaction entered into for profit, are covered by the general rules of Code Sec. 1231 unless the nonrecognition rules for involuntary conversions apply (Reg. § 1.1231-1(e)).[120] Involuntary conversions are discussed at ¶ 1713. Recognized gains and losses resulting from theft or seizure or an exercise of

---

Footnote references are to paragraphs of the 2008 Standard Federal Tax Reports.

[117] ¶ 30,572

[118] ¶ 30,572, ¶ 30,573, ¶ 30,574

[119] ¶ 30,572

[120] ¶ 30,573, ¶ 30,575.027

power of requisition or condemnation are treated as Sec. 1231 gains or losses (Code Sec. 1231(a)(3)(A)(ii)).

When casualty or theft gains and losses result in a *net loss,* the transactions are not grouped with other Code Sec. 1231 transactions. Instead, the net loss is treated as an ordinary loss (Reg. § 1.1231-1(e)(3)).[121]

Personal Assets—Casualty and Theft Losses. Casualty and theft losses on personal assets (i.e., those not held in a trade or business or for investment) are excluded from the operation of Code Sec. 1231. Instead, gains and losses (in excess of the $100 floor per loss) from personal casualties and thefts are grouped separately. Any resulting net loss may be claimed as an itemized deduction to the extent it exceeds 10% of the taxpayer's adjusted gross income (AGI) (Code Sec. 165(h)).[122] See ¶ 1124 for information concerning casualty losses. If there is a net gain, it is classified as a capital gain. The period of time that the taxpayer owned the property determines whether the gain is long-term or short-term.

1750. Sale of Livestock. Capital gain treatment under Code Sec. 1231 applies to a sale or involuntary conversion of livestock (not including poultry) held for draft, breeding, dairy or sporting purposes. To qualify for this treatment, horses and cattle must be held for at least 24 months and all other livestock must be held for at least 12 months.[123] The holding period begins on the date of acquisition rather than on the date the animal is actually placed in one of the above uses (Code Sec. 1231(b)(3); Reg. § 1.1231-2).[124] Livestock includes fur-bearing animals such as chinchillas, mink and foxes.[125] For treatment of involuntary conversions of livestock due to disease or weather conditions, see ¶ 1713. For treatment of forced sales due to weather conditions (e.g., flood or drought), see ¶ 767.

1751. Lease or Distributor's Agreement Canceled. An amount received by a lessee for cancellation of a lease is treated as received in exchange for the lease. This rule applies also to amounts received by a distributor of goods for the cancellation of a distributor's agreement if the taxpayer has a substantial capital investment in the distributorship (Code Sec. 1241; Reg. § 1.1241-1).[126] If the lease or agreement is a Code Sec. 1231 asset, there will be a Code Sec. 1231 gain or loss (Rev. Rul. 2007-37).

Capital Loss Limitation, Carryover, Carryback

1752. Limitation on Capital Loss. To determine the deductibility of capital losses, all capital gains and losses (without distinction between long-term and short-term) incurred during the year must be totaled. Any capital losses are deductible only to the extent of any capital gains plus, in the case of noncorporate taxpayers, ordinary income of up to $3,000 (Code Sec. 1211).[127] Thus, both net long-term capital losses and net short-term capital losses may be used to offset up to $3,000 of an individual's ordinary income. Special rules for married persons, whether filing joint or separate returns, are at ¶ 1757. Unused losses are carried forward (see ¶ 1754).

> **Example:** During a tax year Janet Green, a single individual, had $30,000 of ordinary income, a net short-term capital loss of $3,500 and a net long-term capital loss of $300. Green's capital loss deduction is limited to $3,000 for the current tax year. The remaining $800 is carried forward.

Corporations. A corporation may use capital losses to offset only capital gains and not ordinary income (Code Sec. 1211(a)).[128] However, its capital losses may be carried back or carried forward (see ¶ 1756 for details).

1754. Individual's Net Capital Loss Carryover. Individuals and other noncorporate taxpayers may carry over a net capital loss to future tax years until the loss is used. A capital loss that is carried over to a later tax year retains its long-term or short-term character for the year to which it is carried. In determining the amount of the capital loss that can be carried over, short-term capital gain is increased by the lesser of:

Footnote references are to paragraphs of the 2008 Standard Federal Tax Reports.

[121] ¶ 30,573	[124] ¶ 30,572, ¶ 30,574	[127] ¶ 30,390
[122] ¶ 9802	[125] ¶ 30,575.154	[128] ¶ 30,390
[123] ¶ 30,575.037	[126] ¶ 30,750, ¶ 30,751	

¶1750

(1) the ordinary income offset (whether $3,000 or the amount of the overall net loss) or

(2) taxable income increased by that offset and the deduction for personal exemptions (any excess of allowable deductions over gross income for the loss year is treated as negative taxable income for this purpose) (Code Sec. 1212(b)).[129]

A short-term capital loss carryover first offsets short-term gain in the carryover year. If a net short-term capital loss results, this loss first offsets net long-term capital gain, and then up to $3,000 of ordinary income (¶1752). A long-term capital loss carryover first reduces long-term capital gain in the carryover year, then net short-term capital gain, and finally up to $3,000 of ordinary income.

> **Example:** Jack Crowe had taxable income of $30,000 for the current tax year and filed a joint return. In computing taxable income, he reported a net short-term capital loss of $1,000 and a net long-term capital loss of $6,000. Crowe would use his $1,000 net short-term loss to offset $1,000 of ordinary income; he would then use $2,000 of his net long-term capital loss to offset $2,000 of ordinary income. The remaining $4,000 of his net long-term capital loss would be carried over to the following tax year ($4,000 is carried over because it is less than his taxable income of $30,000 increased by the ordinary income offset of $3,000 and the deduction for personal exemptions).

Code Sec. 1256 Contract Loss. An individual (but not an estate, trust, or corporation) who has a net Code Sec. 1256 contracts loss (i.e., net loss from futures contracts, foreign currency contracts, nonequity options, dealer options, or dealer securities futures contracts) in a given tax year may elect to carry the loss back to the three prior tax years (Code Sec. 1212(c)).[130]

1756. Corporate Capital Loss Carryover and Carryback. A corporation may carry back a capital loss to each of the three tax years preceding the loss year. Any excess may be carried forward for five years following the loss year. However, the amount that can be carried back is limited to an amount that does not cause or increase a net operating loss in the carryback year (Code Sec. 1212(a)(1)).[131]

Any carryback or carryover is treated as short-term capital loss for the year to which it is carried. As such, it is grouped with any other capital losses for the year to which carried and is used to offset any capital gains. Any undeducted loss remaining after the three-year carryback and the five-year carryover is not deductible.

Foreign expropriation losses that can be carried over for 10 years are ineligible for three-year carryback. A foreign expropriation capital loss is the sum of the capital losses sustained (either directly or on securities that become worthless) by reason of the expropriation, intervention, seizure, or similar taking of property by the government of any foreign country, any political subdivision, or any agency or instrumentality of such a governmental unit (Code Sec. 1212(a); Reg. § 1.1212-1).[132]

A regulated investment company's capital loss can be carried over for eight years (Code Sec. 1212(a)(1)(C)(i)).[133]

A quick refund procedure is available for corporate net operating loss carrybacks for capital loss carrybacks (see ¶2773).

1757. Capital Gain or Loss of Husband and Wife. All the capital gains and losses of a husband and wife are computed on a joint return as if they were the gains and losses of one person (*W.C. Janney*, SCt, 40-2 USTC ¶9827).[134] If a husband and wife file separate returns, the capital loss deduction for each is limited to $1,500 (one-half of the limit for a joint return). If separate returns are filed the year after a net capital loss was reported on a joint return, any carryover is allocated on the basis of the individual net capital loss of the spouses for the prior year's tax year (Reg. § 1.1211-1(b)(7)).[135]

Footnote references are to paragraphs of the 2008 Standard Federal Tax Reports.

[129] ¶30,400	[132] ¶30,400, ¶30,401	[135] ¶30,391
[130] ¶30,400	[133] ¶30,400	
[131] ¶30,400	[134] ¶30,392.125	

1758. Partnership or S Corporation Capital Gain or Loss. The capital gains and losses of a partnership or S corporation are generally segregated from its ordinary net income and carried separately into the income of the individual partners or shareholders. Partners or shareholders treat their distributive share of the capital gain or loss as if it were their own capital gain or loss (see ¶ 431). The same rule applies for Code Sec. 1231 transactions (see ¶ 1747) (Code Secs. 702(a) and 1366(a)).[136] S corporations may be taxed on capital gains in very limited situations (see ¶ 337).

1760. Investors, Dealers and Traders. In order to determine whether a taxpayer's gains or losses are ordinary or capital in nature, it must be determined if the taxpayer entered into the transaction as an investor, dealer or trader. The following is an overview of how these terms are defined.

Investors. An investor is a taxpayer whose activities are limited to occasional transactions for his own account. The level of activity is less than that associated with a trade or business. Gains and losses of an investor are subject to the capital gains and loss rules.

Dealers. A dealer regularly purchases securities from, and sells securities to, customers in the ordinary course of a trade or business. Because they are in the business of buying and selling, the gains and losses of dealers are classified as ordinary gain or loss unless the securities are held primarily for personal investment (Code Sec. 1236). Securities that are held by a dealer for personal investment purposes must be clearly identified in the dealer's records before the close of the day on which they were acquired and must never be held primarily for sale to the dealer's customers (Code Sec. 1236(a)). Similarly, capital gain and loss treatment does not apply to real estate sales by a dealer in realty unless the property was held as an investment (*Suburban Realty Co.*, 80-1 USTC ¶ 9351).[137]

Traders. A securities trader (including a "day trader") buys and sells securities for the trader's own account. A trader's expectation of making a profit depends upon such circumstances as a rise in value or an advantageous purchase to enable him to sell at a price in excess of cost. The taxpayer's trading activity must be substantial, frequent, regular and continuous (*N. Boatner*, Dec. 52,211(M)).[138] Due to the fact that the securities that traders buy and sell are not held primarily for sale to customers, their gains and losses are generally treated as capital in nature and are reported on Schedule D (Form 1040) (Code Sec. 1221(a)(1)).[139] (Traders may make a "mark-to-market" election that allows them to treat gains and losses as ordinary (see ¶ 1901).) Traders claim their business expenses on Schedule C (Form 1040), Profit or Loss From Business, because they are in the business of trading. For the rules concerning the commissions paid by traders when buying and selling securities, see ¶ 1983.

Subdivision of Real Estate

1762. Subdivision and Sale of Real Estate. Noncorporate taxpayers and S corporations will not be treated as real estate dealers solely because they have subdivided a tract of land for sale (Code Sec. 1237(a)).[140] At least part of the gain on the sale of a lot is treated as capital gain when:

(1) the taxpayer has not previously held the tract or any lot or parcel thereof for sale in the ordinary course of business, and, in the same tax year as the sale occurs, does not hold any other real estate for sale in the ordinary course of business (this rule automatically disqualifies a real estate dealer);

(2) no "substantial" improvements are made while the tract is held by the taxpayer or pursuant to a contract of sale between the taxpayer and the buyer; and

(3) the taxpayer has held the particular lot sold for at least five years, unless it was acquired by inheritance or devise, in which case there is no minimum holding period requirement (Code Sec. 1237(a)(3)).[141]

There is an exception to the substantial-improvement rule noted at (2), above. Certain improvements, such as water, sewage, drainage, or road installation, are not considered substantial improvements if the property (including inherited property) is

---

Footnote references are to paragraphs of the 2008 Standard Federal Tax Reports.

[136] ¶ 25,080, ¶ 32,080　　　[138] ¶ 9900.129　　　[140] ¶ 30,690
[137] ¶ 30,575.244　　　[139] ¶ 30,420　　　[141] ¶ 30,690

held for at least 10 years and would not have been marketable at the prevailing local price for similar building sites without such improvements. The taxpayer must also elect *not* to adjust the basis of the property (or other property) or deduct the costs as expenses. The election is reported with the tax return for the year in which the lots covered by the election were sold. The election must include certain information including a plat of the subdivision and a list of all the improvements (Code Sec. 1237(b)(3); Reg. § 1.1237-1(c)(5)(iii)).[142]

The profits realized on the sales of the first five lots or parcels from the same tract are classified as capital gains. However, in the year in which the sixth sale or exchange is made, and, thereafter, gain on each sale is taxed as ordinary income to the extent of 5% of the selling price (Reg. § 1.1237-1(e)(2)(ii)). Selling expenses are deducted first from the 5% that would otherwise be considered ordinary income and then are used to reduce the capital gain on the sale or exchange. The selling expenses cannot be deducted from other income as ordinary business expenses (Code Sec. 1237(b)(2); Reg. § 1.1237-1).[143]

> **Example 1:** During the current tax year, Mark subdivides a tract of land that he bought approximately 10 years ago and sells three lots for $50,000 each. The adjusted basis for each lot is $30,000. Mark has a long-term capital gain of $20,000 from the sale of each lot.

> **Example 2:** Assume the same facts as in Example 1. Assume further that in the current tax year, Mark sells three additional lots, each having a basis of $30,000. The selling price of each lot is $50,000. Because he sold more than five lots, 5% of $50,000, or $2,500, of the gain on the sale of each of the six lots is ordinary income. The balance of the gain on each lot (i.e., $17,500) is treated as long-term capital gain.

If a taxpayer sells or exchanges any lots or parcels from a tract, and then does not sell or exchange any others for a period of five years from the last sale or exchange, the taxpayer can sell another five lots without having a portion of the gain taxed as ordinary income (Reg. § 1.1237-1(g)(2)).[144]

If a tract of land is bought with the purpose that it is to be subdivided and sold as separate lots or parcels, the seller must measure gain or loss on every lot or parcel sold on the basis of an equitable (not ratable) apportionment (such as their relative assessed valuations for real estate tax purposes) of the cost of the subdivision to each separate part (Reg. § 1.61-6(a)).[145]

Worthless Security

1764. Worthless Security. Loss from a security that becomes worthless is treated as a capital loss if the security is a capital asset. Generally, the loss is treated as occurring on the last day of the tax year in which the security becomes worthless (Code Sec. 165(g)).[146] This rule determines whether the capital loss is recognized as short-term or long-term as illustrated in the following example. Deduction for *partial* worthlessness is not allowed.[147]

> **Example:** On December 10, 2006, Judy Green purchased shares of Xetco Corporation for $5,000. On May 1, 2007, she received formal notification that the shares of Xetco were worthless. In claiming a capital loss for the worthless shares on her 2007 tax return, Judy must treat the shares as becoming worthless on December 31, 2007. As a result, her $5,000 capital loss is recognized as *long-term* even though she did not own the shares for more than 12 months before they became worthless.

Special rules apply to stock issued by a small business investment company (see ¶ 2392) and Code Sec. 1244 stock (see ¶ 2395). A bank may claim a bad debt deduction on the worthlessness (in whole or in part) of certain securities (Code Sec. 582(a)).[148] A bank's net loss from a sale or exchange of a bond is deductible in full as an ordinary loss (Code Sec. 582(c)).[149]

Footnote references are to paragraphs of the 2008 Standard Federal Tax Reports.

[142] ¶ 30,690, ¶ 30,691
[143] ¶ 30,690, ¶ 30,691
[144] ¶ 30,691

[145] ¶ 5605
[146] ¶ 9802
[147] ¶ 9905, ¶ 10,000

[148] ¶ 23,608
[149] ¶ 23,608

Patents and Royalties

1767. Patents. The transfer of a patent will be treated as the sale of a capital asset held for more than 12 months if certain requirements are met (Code Sec. 1235(a)). This treatment does *not* apply if the transfer was by gift or inheritance (Reg. § 1235-1(a)). The capital gains rule extends to the original inventor and another individual who acquired the patent from the original inventor (Code Sec. 1235(b)). However, the non-inventor must have acquired the patent before the invention was tested successfully under operating conditions (Reg. § 1.1235-2(d)(1)). The inventor's employer and certain related persons are not eligible for long-term capital gain treatment if they acquire the patent from the inventor (Code Sec. 1235(d)).[150]

Payment. The payment must be for all the substantial rights to the patent or for an undivided interest in such rights (Reg. § 1.1235-2(b)). The payment may be made in a lump-sum, periodically, or contingent upon the productivity or use of the property transferred (Reg. § 1.1235-1(a)).

1772. Timber, Coal or Iron Ore. A taxpayer may elect to treat the cutting of timber (for sale or for use in a trade or business) *as a sale or exchange* of timber cut during the year. The taxpayer must have owned the timber or held the contract right to cut the timber for more than one year (Code Sec. 631; Reg. §§ 1.631-1—1.631-2).[151] Under Code Sec. 1231, this timber is considered to be "property used in the trade or business" so that gain may be treated as long-term capital gain under certain conditions. See ¶ 1747 for information on Code Sec. 1231 property.

Making the Election. In order to make the election, a taxpayer must generally file Form T (Timber) (Forest Activities Schedule) with the tax return for the year in which the election is to be effective.

Timber, coal or domestic iron ore royalties are generally subject to Code Sec. 1231 (¶ 1747) treatment when the owner or a holder of an economic interest (including a lessee) disposes of it under a contract with a retained economic interest. An outright sale of timber will also qualify (Code Sec. 631(b)). This treatment generally is not available in the case of coal or iron ore mined outside the United States or when the coal or iron ore property is owned and operated by the same parties (Code Secs. 272 and 631(b) and (c)).[152]

Franchise Grant and Sale

1774. Ordinary Income from Franchise Grant. Amounts received from the transfer of a franchise, trademark, or tradename are generally treated as ordinary income by the transferor when the transferor retains any significant power, right, or continuing interest over the franchise, trademark, or tradename (Code Sec. 1253(a)).[153] Ordinary income treatment also applies to amounts received from the transfer, sale, or other disposition of a franchise, trademark, or tradename which are contingent on the transferred asset's productivity, use, or disposition (Code Sec. 1253(c)).[154]

1775. Rules for Payments by Transferee. Amounts paid or incurred on account of the transfer of a franchise, trademark, or tradename are amortized over 15 years under Code Sec. 197. See ¶ 1288 for details. Amortization is claimed on Form 4562, Depreciation and Amortization.

Contingent Serial Payments. A business deduction may be claimed for certain contingent serial payments paid or incurred on account of a transfer, sale, or other disposition of a trademark, tradename, or franchise. The deduction is allowed for payments that are contingent on the asset's productivity, use, or disposition if (1) the contingent amounts are paid as part of a series of payments that are payable at least annually throughout the term of the transfer agreement and (2) the payments are substantially equal in amount or payable under a fixed formula (Code Sec. 1253(d)(1)).[155]

Footnote references are to paragraphs of the 2008 Standard Federal Tax Reports.

[150] ¶ 30,650
[151] ¶ 24,150, ¶ 24,151, ¶ 24,153
[152] ¶ 14,309, ¶ 24,150, ¶ 24,110
[153] ¶ 31,040
[154] ¶ 31,040
[155] ¶ 31,040

Holding Period of Capital Asset

1777. Rules on Determination of Holding Period. The holding period for a capital asset is the length of time that the taxpayer owned the property before disposing of it through sale or exchange. Classifying the taxpayer's holding period as "short-term" or "long-term" determines the tax treatment of any recognized gain or loss (Code Secs. 1222 and 1223).[156] The lowest long-term capital gain tax rate is generally available when a capital asset has been held more than 12 months (Code Sec. 1(h)). See ¶ 1736 for the details concerning capital gains taxation.

Calculating the Holding Period. In most situations when determining how long an asset was held, the taxpayer begins counting on the date after the day the property was acquired. The same date of each following month is the beginning of a new month regardless of the number of days in the preceding month (Rev. Rul. 66-7).[157] The date the asset is disposed of is part of the holding period. However, there are special rules that must be applied when determining the holding period of assets acquired by gift, inheritance, exchange, etc. See "*Special Holding Periods,*" below.

> **Example 1:** If an asset is acquired on March 24, 2006, the first day on which it may be considered to have been held for more than one year is March 25, 2007.

If an asset is acquired on the last day of a month, the first day on which it may be considered to have been held for more than one year is *the first day of the thirteenth calendar month following the calendar month of acquisition.*[158]

> **Example 2:** An asset acquired on March 31, 2006, must be held until April 1, 2007, in order to be considered held for more than one year.

Special Holding Periods. The general rule is that a taxpayer's holding period begins the day after the asset was acquired. However, in some situations a taxpayer's holding period is considered to have begun at an earlier date. For example, the current owner is allowed to "tack on" a prior holding period when a tax-free exchange of property is involved. The following material presents an overview of the holding period rules as they apply to a variety of situations (e.g., tax-free exchanges, gifts and inheritance).

Tax-Free Exchange. When property is received in a tax-free exchange (see ¶ 1721— ¶ 1734), the holding period of the property given up by the taxpayer is added to ("tacked on") the holding period of the property that the taxpayer received in the exchange (Code Sec. 1223).[159]

Gift. In most situations, the holding period of property acquired by gift or transfer in trust includes the time the property was held by both the donor and the donee. This rule applies when the donee is required to use the donor's basis as his basis (Code Sec. 1223(2)).[160] However, when the fair market value at the time of the gift is used as the donee's basis, the holding period starts the day after the gift was made (IRS Pub. 544). See ¶ 1630 for information concerning what basis the donee is required to use.

Inherited. For property acquired from a decedent, if certain requirements are met, the long-term holding period test is generally considered to be met (Code Sec. 1223(9)).[161]

Converted. The holding period of property acquired in an involuntary conversion includes the holding period of the property converted if the basis of the new property is determined by reference to the basis of the old (Code Sec. 1223(1)(A)).[162]

Stock. The holding period for stock purchased on an exchange begins on the day following the day of purchase (i.e., the trade date), and ends on, and includes, the date of sale (rather than the day when payment is received and delivery is made (i.e., the settlement date)) (Rev. Rul. 93-84).[163] The holding period for stock received in a nontaxable stock distribution or in a "spin-off" includes the holding period of the related stock on which the distribution is made (Code Sec. 1223(1) and (5)).[164]

Options. When assets are acquired by the exercise of a purchase option, the holding period starts the day after the option is exercised.[165]

Footnote references are to paragraphs of the 2008 Standard Federal Tax Reports.

[156] ¶ 30,440, ¶ 30,460
[157] ¶ 30,463.3997
[158] ¶ 30,463.023, ¶ 30,463.4099
[159] ¶ 30,460

[160] ¶ 30,460
[161] ¶ 30,460
[162] ¶ 30,460
[163] ¶ 30,463.4383

[164] ¶ 30,460
[165] ¶ 30,463.4013

Partnership Property. The holding period for property distributed to a partner includes the period for which the partnership held the property (Code Sec. 735(b)).[166]

Treasury Obligations. In determining the holding period of U.S. Treasury Notes and Bonds sold at auction on the basis of yield, the acquisition date is the date the Secretary of Treasury, through news releases, gives notification of the successful bidders. The acquisition date of U.S. Treasury Notes sold through an offering on a subscription basis at a specified yield is the date the subscription is submitted (Rev. Rul. 78-5).[167]

Disposition of Depreciable Property

1779. Depreciation Recapture Rules. *Code Sec. 1245 Property.* A gain on the sale or other disposition of Code Sec. 1245 property (¶ 1785) is taxed as ordinary income to the extent of all depreciation or amortization deductions previously claimed on the property. Amounts expensed under Code Sec. 179 (¶ 1208), Code Sec. 179A (¶ 1286), Code Sec. 179B (¶ 1285), Code Sec. 179C (¶ 1285A), Code Sec. 179D (¶ 1286A), Code Sec. 179E (¶ 989A), Code Sec. 181 (¶ 977B), Code Sec. 190 (¶ 1287), Code Sec. 193 (for tertiary injectant costs), and Code Sec. 194 (¶ 1287), are considered amortization deductions (Code Sec. 1245(a)).[168]

The amount treated as ordinary income is the excess of the lower of (1) the property's recomputed basis or (2) the amount realized or fair market value, over the adjusted basis of the Code Sec. 1245 property. The recomputed basis is the property's adjusted basis plus previously allowed or allowable depreciation or amortization reflected in the adjusted basis.

A disposition of Code Sec. 1245 property includes a sale in a sale-and-leaseback transaction and a transfer upon the foreclosure of a security interest, but does not include a mere transfer of title to a creditor upon creation of a security interest or to a debtor upon termination of a security interest (Reg. § 1.1245-1).[169]

Code Sec. 1250 Property. Depreciable real property, other than that included within the definition of Code Sec. 1245 property, is subject to depreciation recapture under Code Sec. 1250. (Code Sec. 1250 property is defined at ¶ 1786.) Gain on the sale or other disposition of Code Sec. 1250 property is treated as ordinary income, rather than capital gain, to the extent of the excess of post-1969 depreciation allowances over the depreciation that would have been available under the straight-line method. See ¶ 1780. However, if Code Sec. 1250 property is held for one year or less, all depreciation (and not just the excess over straight-line depreciation) is recaptured (Code Sec. 1250(b)(1)).[170] See ¶ 1736 for capital gains treatment of "unrecaptured Section 1250 gain."

Special recapture rules phase out the recapture by reducing it by 1% for each full month the Code Sec. 1250 property is held over a specified period in the case of (1) residential rental property, (2) certain types of subsidized housing, and (3) Code Sec. 1250 property for which rapid depreciation of rehabilitation expenditures was claimed (Code Sec. 1250(a)(1)(B) and (2)(B)).[171]

The recapture rules apply notwithstanding any other provision of the Code. In the case of a sale to a related party (see ¶ 1717), gain that is not recaptured may still be treated as ordinary income under Code Sec. 1239.[172]

Code Sec. 1250 property may be made up of two or more "elements" with separate holding periods. When this occurs, the recapture must be determined separately for each element (Code Sec. 1250(f)(3)).[173]

Installment Sale. In the case of disposal of recapture property in an installment sale, any recapture income (i.e., ordinary income under Code Sec. 1245 or Code Sec. 1250) is to be recognized in the year of the disposition, and any gain in excess of the recapture income is to be reported under the installment method (Code Sec. 453(i)).[174] See ¶ 1823 for more information concerning this rule.

Footnote references are to paragraphs of the 2008 Standard Federal Tax Reports.

[166] ¶ 25,400	[169] ¶ 30,903	[172] ¶ 30,730
[167] ¶ 30,463.67	[170] ¶ 31,000	[173] ¶ 31,000
[168] ¶ 30,902	[171] ¶ 31,000	[174] ¶ 21,402

¶1779

Additional Recapture for Corporations. For corporations, the amount treated as ordinary income on the sale or other disposition of Code Sec. 1250 property is increased by 20% of the additional amount that would be treated as ordinary income if the property were subject to recapture under the rules for Code Sec. 1245 property (Code Sec. 291(a)(1)).[175]

Reporting Recapture. Form 4797, Sales of Business Property, is used to calculate and report the amount of recaptured depreciation.

1780. Depreciation Subject to Recapture. In general, depreciation on tangible property placed in service after 1986 is determined under the Modified Accelerated Cost Recovery System (MACRS). Property placed in service after 1980 and before 1987 is covered under the Accelerated Cost Recovery System (ACRS). See ¶ 1216 and following for information concerning the methods of computing allowable depreciation deductions.

MACRS. Gain on the disposition of tangible personal property is treated as ordinary income to the extent of previously allowed MACRS deductions. If property from a general asset account is disposed of, the full amount of proceeds realized on the disposition is treated as ordinary income to the extent the unadjusted depreciable basis of the account (increased by amounts allowed as deductions under Code Secs. 179 and 190 for assets in the account) exceeds previously recognized ordinary income from prior dispositions (Reg. § 1.168(i)-1(e)).[176]

Residential rental property and nonresidential real property that is placed in service after 1986 and is subject to the MACRS rules must be depreciated under the straight-line MACRS method. Therefore, recapture of depreciation on such property is not required because no depreciation in excess of straight-line depreciation could have been taken.

ACRS. Gain on the disposition of personal recovery property and nonresidential real recovery property is treated as ordinary income to the extent of previously allowed ACRS deductions.[177] Gain on the disposition of residential rental real recovery property is treated as ordinary income to the extent that ACRS deductions exceed straight-line ACRS depreciation over the recovery period applicable to such property. Consequently, there would be no recapture if the straight-line ACRS method was elected for real property.

On the disposition of assets from mass asset accounts, taxpayers recognize the amount of the proceeds realized as ordinary income to the extent of the unadjusted basis in the account less any amounts previously included in income. Any excess proceeds realized are treated as capital gain, unless a nonrecognition provision applies. As far as the recovery of depreciation is concerned, the mass asset account is treated as though there was no disposition of the asset, and the unadjusted basis of the property is left in the capital account until fully recovered in future years (Code Sec. 168(d)(2), prior to amendment by P.L. 97-34).

Amounts Excluded from Depreciation Adjustments. In determining the amount of additional depreciation taken before the disposition of Code Sec. 1250 property, a taxpayer's depreciation adjustments do *not* include amortization of emergency facilities, pollution control facilities, railroad grading and tunnel bores, child care facilities, expenditures to remove architectural and transportation barriers to the handicapped and elderly, or tertiary injectant expenses (Code Sec. 1250(b)(3)).[178]

1783. Recapture of Investment Credit Basis Reductions. In determining the amount of gain that is recaptured as ordinary income on a sale or disposition of depreciable personal property (Code Sec. 1245) or depreciable realty (Code Sec. 1250), the amount of an investment credit downward basis adjustment is subject to recapture (Code Sec. 50(a)). See ¶ 1360.

Footnote references are to paragraphs of the 2008 Standard Federal Tax Reports.

[175] ¶ 15,190
[176] ¶ 11,275B

[177] ¶ 30,909.023
[178] ¶ 31,000

1785. Code Sec. 1245 Property. Code Sec. 1245 property is property that is or has been depreciable (or subject to amortization under Code Sec. 197) and that is either:

(1) personal property (tangible and intangible) or

(2) other tangible property (not including a building or its structural components) used as an integral part of:

(a) manufacturing,

(b) production,

(c) extraction, or

(d) the furnishing of transportation, communications, electrical energy, gas, water, or sewage disposal services (Reg. § 1.1245-3).[179]

The term "other tangible property" includes research facilities or facilities for the bulk storage of fungible commodities used in connection with the activities in (a)-(d). A leasehold of Code Sec. 1245 property is also treated as Code Sec. 1245 property (Reg. § 1.1245-3).[180]

Livestock is considered Code Sec. 1245 property, and depreciation on purchased draft, breeding, dairy and sporting livestock is recaptured as ordinary income when sold. Raised livestock generally has no basis for depreciation, but to the extent that it does have a basis and is depreciated, it would be subject to recapture.[181]

Code Sec. 1245 property also includes so much of any real property (except "other property" described at (2) above) that has an adjusted basis reflecting adjustments for special amortization of pollution control facilities, clean-fuel vehicles and refueling property, refinery property, energy efficient commercial buildings, mine safety equipment, child care facilities, or railroad grading and tunnel bores; expenditures for removal of architectural and transportation barriers to the handicapped and elderly, reforestation, or tertiary injectants; and amounts expensed under Code Sec. 179. Code Sec. 1245 property also includes single purpose agricultural and horticultural structures and storage facilities used in connection with the distribution of petroleum products (Code Sec. 1245(a)(3)).[182]

1786. Code Sec. 1250 Property. Code Sec. 1250 property is any real property that is or has been depreciable under Code Sec. 167 but is not subject to recapture under Code Sec. 1245. This includes all intangible real property (such as leases of land or Code Sec. 1250 property), buildings and their structural components, and all tangible real property except Code Sec. 1245 property (Code Sec. 1250(c)).[183] For real property covered by Code Sec. 1245 rather than Code Sec. 1250, see ¶ 1785.

1788. Gift of Code Sec. 1245 or 1250 Property. The recapture rules at ¶ 1779 do not apply in the case of disposition by gift or to transfers at death (except a taxable transfer of Code Sec. 1245 or 1250 property in satisfaction of a specific bequest of money) (Reg. § 1.1245-4).[184] Upon a later sale, however, the donee will realize the same amount of ordinary income that the donor would have realized if the donor had retained the property and sold it (except in the case of a tax-exempt donee). Also, if the taxpayer contributes Code Sec. 1245 or 1250 property to a charitable organization, the allowable charitable contribution deduction is reduced by the amount that would have been treated as ordinary income if the taxpayer had sold the asset at its fair market value (Code Sec. 170(e)).[185] See ¶ 1062 concerning charitable gifts of appreciated property.

1789. Disposal in Tax-Free Transaction. When Code Sec. 1245 or Code Sec. 1250 property is disposed of in certain tax-free transactions (i.e., Code Secs. 332, 351, 361, 721, or 731), the transferor takes into account Code Sec. 1245 or Code Sec. 1250 gain only to the extent that gain is recognized under those sections (Code Secs. 1245(b)(3) and 1250(d)(3)).[186] However, when there is an otherwise tax-free transfer under one of those sections to a tax-exempt organization (other than a cooperative described in Code

---

Footnote references are to paragraphs of the 2008 Standard Federal Tax Reports.

[179] ¶ 30,905
[180] ¶ 30,905
[181] ¶ 30,909.021

[182] ¶ 30,902
[183] ¶ 31,000
[184] ¶ 30,906

[185] ¶ 11,600
[186] ¶ 30,902, ¶ 31,000

Sec. 521), Code Sec. 1245 or Code Sec. 1250 gain is recognized in full to the transferor. On a later sale of Code Sec. 1245 or Code Sec. 1250 property received in one of the above tax-free transactions, the transferee realizes Code Sec. 1245 or Code Sec. 1250 gain to the extent of the transferor's unrecognized Code Sec. 1245 or Code Sec. 1250 gain plus depreciation deducted by the transferee (not to exceed the actual gain).

1790. Exchange or Conversion. If Code Sec. 1245 or Code Sec. 1250 property is exchanged for like-kind property (¶ 1721) or is involuntarily converted (¶ 1713), Code Sec. 1245 or Code Sec. 1250 gain is recognized to the extent of any gain recognized on the exchange (if money or other property is received) or on the conversion (when the conversion proceeds are not all spent on replacement property), plus the fair market value of any property received in the exchange or acquired as replacement property that is not Code Sec. 1245 or Code Sec. 1250 property (Reg. § § 1.1245-4(d) and 1.1250-3(d)).[187]

1792. Partnership Distribution. No Code Sec. 1245 or Code Sec. 1250 gain is recognized on a distribution by a partnership to a partner when no gain is recognized under Code Sec. 731. However, under Code Sec. 751(c) and for the purposes of Code Secs. 731 and 741, the term "unrealized receivables" includes Code Sec. 1245 and Code Sec. 1250 gains (computed as if the partnership sold the property at its fair market value when distributed) (Code Sec. 751(c)).[188] Thus, ordinary income is realized to the extent of potential Code Sec. 1245 and Code Sec. 1250 gains in the sale of a partnership interest and in distributions to a partner (Reg. § § 1.1245-4(f) and 1.1250-3(f)).[189]

1793. Corporate Distribution. When a corporation distributes Code Sec. 1245 or Code Sec. 1250 property as a dividend or in partial or complete liquidation and no gain is otherwise recognized to the corporation under Code Secs. 311 or 336, Code Sec. 1245 or Code Sec. 1250 gain has to be recognized by the corporation to the same degree that it would have been had the corporation sold the property at its fair market value on the date of distribution (Reg. § § 1.1245-1(c) and 1.1250-1(c)).[190]

1795. Adjustments to Basis. When Code Sec. 1245 or Code Sec. 1250 gain is recognized in an exchange of like-kind property under Code Sec. 1031 or an involuntary conversion under Code Sec. 1033 (¶ 1790), the basis of the acquired property is to be determined under those Code sections (Reg. § 1.1245-5).[191]

> **Example:** Greg exchanges Code Sec. 1245 property with an adjusted basis of $10,000 for like-kind Code Sec. 1245 property with a fair market value of $9,000 and unlike property with a fair market value of $3,500. Gain of $2,500 is recognized because unlike property was received. The basis of the property acquired by Greg is $12,500 ($10,000 adjusted basis of the transferred property plus $2,500 recognized gain), of which $3,500 (fair market value) is allocated to the unlike property and the remaining $9,000 is allocated to the acquired like-kind property.

Farmers' Recaptures

1797. Recapture on Land Sale. If farm land is held for less than 10 years, a percentage of the total post-1969 deductions for soil and water conservation expenses will be recaptured as ordinary income on Form 4797, Sales of Business Property (Code Sec. 1252).[192] If the land is held for five years or less, the recapture percentage is 100%. The recapture percentage is 80% if disposal is within the sixth year after acquisition. For the seventh, eighth and ninth years, the recapture percentages are 60%, 40%, and 20%, respectively. There is no recapture after the ninth year (Code Sec. 1252(a)(3)).[193] See ¶ 982 concerning deductions for conservation expenses.

Exempt Transfers. Exceptions to this recapture rule exist for transfers by gift, transfers at death, and transfers in certain tax-free transactions (Reg. § 1.1252-2).[194] These exceptions are similar to those provided for in Code Sec. 1245(b). See related discussions at ¶ 1788 and ¶ 1789.

Footnote references are to paragraphs of the 2008 Standard Federal Tax Reports.

[187] ¶ 30,906, ¶ 31,003   [190] ¶ 30,903, ¶ 31,001   [193] ¶ 31,020
[188] ¶ 25,500   [191] ¶ 30,907   [194] ¶ 31,022
[189] ¶ 30,906, ¶ 31,003   [192] ¶ 31,020

Chapter 18

INSTALLMENT SALES

DEFERRED PAYMENTS

Reporting of Gain

1801. Use of Installment Method. The installment method is a special way of reporting gains (not losses) from sales of property when at least one payment is received in a tax year after the year of sale (deferred payments). Under the installment method, gain from the sale is prorated and recognized over the years in which payments are received. As a result, each payment received usually consists of interest, return of basis, and gain on the sale. If a sale qualifies for the installment method of reporting gain, the seller must use it or else affirmatively elect *not* to use it (see ¶ 1803). This rule applies to both cash and accrual basis taxpayers.

Prohibition for Dealer Dispositions. The installment method may only be used for reporting gain from nondealer sales of property other than inventory. Dealer dispositions of property (see ¶ 1808) may not be reported under the installment method (Code Sec. 453(b)(2)(A)).[1] Thus, all such payments are treated as if they were received in the year of disposition, even though a dealer expects to receive some payments in future years.

Gain Calculation. The amount of gain from an installment sale that is taxable in a given year is calculated by multiplying the payments received in that year by the gross profit ratio for the sale (Code Sec. 453(c)).[2] The gross profit ratio is equal to the anticipated gross profit divided by the total contract price (see ¶ 1813). However, gain from installment sales of depreciable property subject to recapture under Code Sec. 1245 or Code Sec. 1250 is determined under a special rule (see ¶ 1823).

> **Example:** On December 1, 2007, Bob Smith sells vacant land that he has held for investment purposes for a number of years. His basis in the land is $12,000. The total contract price is $15,000. Bob receives a $5,000 down payment, with the $10,000 balance due in monthly installments of $500 each, plus interest at the applicable federal rate, beginning on January 1, 2008. His anticipated gross profit from the sale is $3,000. His gross profit percentage is 20% ($3,000 gross profit ÷ $15,000 contract price). Under the installment method, Bob must report $1,000

Footnote references are to paragraphs of the 2008 Standard Federal Tax Reports.

[1] ¶ 21,402   [2] ¶ 21,402

¶1801

($5,000 × 20%) as long-term capital gain in 2007, $1,200 ($6,000 × 20%) in 2008, and $800 ($4,000 × 20%) in 2009. The interest is reported as ordinary income.

Reporting Requirements for Gain. Gain from an installment sale is reported on Form 6252, Installment Sale Income. This form must be filed with the tax return in the year of sale and in each year payments are received.

1802. Character of Gain on Installment Sale. Although use of the installment method determines when gain from an installment sale is reported, it does not affect the characterization of the gain as capital gain or ordinary income. The proper characterization depends on the nature of the asset sold (see ¶ 1735 and ¶ 1741).

1803. Election Not to Use Installment Method. If a taxpayer elects not to use the installment method, the entire gain is reported in the year of the sale, even though all of the sale proceeds are not received in that year (Code Sec. 453(d)).[3] The election is made by reporting the gain on Schedule D (Form 1040) or Form 4797, Sales of Business Property, whichever applies, instead of reporting the sale on Form 6252. The election must be made by the due date, including extensions, of the tax return for the year in which the installment sale is made (Temp. Reg. § 15A.453-1(d)(3)). In rare circumstances, the IRS will permit a late election if the taxpayer can show good cause for not making the election by the due date. Valid elections can be revoked only with IRS consent (Temp. Reg. § 15A.453-1(d)(4)).[4]

1805. Publicly Traded Property and Revolving Credit Plans. The installment method may *not* be used for: (1) sales of personal property under a revolving credit plan, (2) sales of stock or securities that are traded on an established securities market, or (3) to the extent provided by regulations, sales of other kinds of property that are regularly traded on an established market. All payments to be received from such sales are treated as received in the year of disposition (Code Sec. 453(k)).[5]

Dealer Sales

1808. Dealers May Not Use Installment Method. Dealers in real or personal property may not use the installment method to report the gain from "dealer dispositions." A "dealer disposition" includes (1) any disposition of personal property by a person who regularly sells or otherwise disposes of such property on an installment plan and (2) any disposition of real property that is held by the taxpayer for sale to customers in the ordinary course of the taxpayer's trade or business (Code Sec. 453(l)(1)).[6] However, there are some exceptions to these general rules for dispositions of farm property, residential lots and timeshares (Code Sec. 453(l)(2))[7] (see ¶ 1811).

1811. Exceptions to "Dealer Disposition" Rule. Certain types of transactions have been excluded from the term "dealer disposition." As a result, the installment method may be used to report gain from the following types of transactions (Code Sec. 453(l)(2)):

(1) the disposition of any property used or produced in the trade or business of farming,

(2) the disposition of any residential lot, provided that the dealer or any related person is not obligated to make any improvements to the lot, and

(3) the disposition of timeshare rights to use or own residential real property for not more than six weeks per year, or a right to use specified campgrounds for recreational purposes.

Payment of Interest. In order to use the installment method for the sale of residential lots and timeshares, the taxpayer must pay interest on the amount of tax attributable to the installment payments received during the year. The interest is calculated for the period beginning on the date of sale and ending on the date the payment is received

Footnote references are to paragraphs of the 2008 Standard Federal Tax Reports.

[3] ¶ 21,402   [5] ¶ 21,402   [7] ¶ 21,402
[4] ¶ 21,404   [6] ¶ 21,402

(Code Sec. 453(l)(3)).[8] The amount of interest is based upon the applicable federal rate in effect at the time of sale, compounded semiannually (see ¶ 1875).

Nondealer Sales

1813. Nondealer Dispositions of Property. For nondealer dispositions that are not subject to the Code Sec. 1245 or Code Sec. 1250 recapture provisions, the amount of income reported from an installment sale in any tax year (including the year of sale) is equal to the payments received during that year multiplied by the gross profit ratio for the sale. (For a discussion of the various forms of payment, see ¶ 1819.)

The gross profit ratio is the gross profit on the sale divided by the total contract price. The gross profit is the selling price of the property minus its adjusted basis. The selling price of the property is not reduced by any existing mortgage or encumbrance, or by any selling expenses, but is reduced by interest that is imputed under Code Secs. 483 or 1274 (see ¶ 1863 and following).

The total contract price (denominator of gross profit ratio) is the selling price minus that portion of qualifying indebtedness (see ¶ 1815) which the buyer assumes or takes the property subject to that does not exceed the seller's basis in the property (adjusted to reflect commissions and other selling expenses) (Temp. Reg. § 15A.453-1(b)(2)).[9] In the case of an installment sale that is a partially nontaxable like-kind exchange (see ¶ 1723), the gross profit is reduced by that portion of the gain that is not recognized, and the total contract price is reduced by the value of the like-kind property received (Code Sec. 453(f)(6)).[10]

For certain nondealer sales of property over $150,000, a special interest charge may apply (see ¶ 1825).

1815. Qualifying Indebtedness. For the purpose of determining the total contract price, qualifying indebtedness includes (1) any mortgage or other indebtedness encumbering the property and (2) any indebtedness not secured by the property but incurred or assumed by the purchaser incident to the acquisition, holding or operation of the property in the ordinary course of business or investment (Temp. Reg. § 15A.453-1(b)(2)(iv)).[11]

Qualifying indebtedness does not include an obligation of the seller incurred incident to the *disposition* of the property, nor does it include an obligation functionally unrelated to the acquisition, holding or operation of the property. Any obligation incurred or assumed in contemplation of disposition of the property is not qualifying indebtedness if recovery of the seller's basis is accelerated (Temp. Reg. § 15A.453-1(b)(2)(iv)).

1817. Wrap-Around Mortgage. When property encumbered by an outstanding mortgage is sold in exchange for an installment obligation equal to the mortgage, the installment obligation is said to "wrap around" the mortgage. The seller generally uses the payments received from the installment obligation to pay the "wrapped" mortgage. In this situation, the IRS will follow the Tax Court's position and will not treat the buyer as having taken the property subject to, or as having assumed, the seller's mortgage (*Professional Equities, Inc.*).[12] As a result, the seller does not have to reduce the total contract price by the amount of the wrapped mortgage.

1819. Installment Payments. When determining the amount of reportable income under the installment method, cash and the following debt instruments are treated as payments received:

(1) evidence of indebtedness of a person other than the buyer;

(2) evidence of indebtedness of the buyer that is payable on demand, readily tradable, or issued with coupons or in registered form;

Footnote references are to paragraphs of the 2008 Standard Federal Tax Reports.

[8] ¶ 21,402
[9] ¶ 21,404
[10] ¶ 21,402
[11] ¶ 21,404
[12] ¶ 21,412.80

¶1813

(3) a bank certificate or treasury note;

(4) qualifying indebtedness assumed, or taken subject to, by the buyer, to the extent it exceeds the seller's basis for the sold property as adjusted for selling expenses;

(5) seller's indebtedness to the buyer that is canceled; and

(6) indebtedness on the sold property (for which the seller is not personally liable) when the buyer is the obligee of the indebtedness (Temp. Reg. § 15A.453-1(b)(3)).[13]

Debt instruments in registered form that the seller can establish are not readily tradable are not considered payments. In addition, like-kind property received in a partially tax-free exchange (see ¶ 1723) that is part of an installment sale transaction is not treated as a payment for purposes of determining the amount of income to be reported under the installment method (Code Sec. 453(f)(6)).[14]

1821. Contingent Payment Sales. A contingent payment sale (i.e., one in which the total selling price is not determinable by the close of the tax year in which the sale occurs) must be reported on the installment method unless the seller elects not to use the installment method (Temp. Reg. § 15A.453-1(c)(1)).[15]

In a contingent payment sale, the basis of the property sold (including selling expenses) is allocated to payments received in each tax year and recovered as follows:

(1) for sales with a stated maximum selling price, basis is recovered according to a profit ratio based on the stated maximum selling price;

(2) for sales with a fixed payment period, basis is recovered ratably over the fixed period; and

(3) for sales with neither a maximum selling price nor a fixed payment period, basis is recovered ratably over a 15-year period (Temp. Reg. § 15A.453-1(c)(2)–(4)).[16]

However, alternate methods of basis recovery may be required when the normal method would substantially accelerate or inappropriately defer the recovery of basis (Temp. Reg. § 15A.453-1(c)(7)).[17]

The term "contingent payment sale" does not include transactions with respect to which the installment obligation represents, under applicable principles of tax law:

(1) a retained interest in the property which is the subject of the transaction;

(2) an interest in a joint venture or partnership;

(3) an equity interest in a corporation; or

(4) similar transactions, regardless of the existence of a stated maximum selling price or a fixed payment term (Temporary Reg. § 15A.453-1(c)(1)).

1823. Dispositions of Property Subject to Recapture Provisions. For installment sales of real or personal property to which Code Sec. 1245 or 1250 applies, any recapture income must be reported in the year of disposition, whether or not an installment payment is received in that year (Code Sec. 453(i)).[18] The ordinary income amount reported in the year of sale is added to the property's basis, and this adjusted basis is used in determining the remaining profit on the disposition.[19] The remaining profit amount is used to compute the gross profit percentage to be applied to each installment payment.

> **Example:** On December 1, 2007, Bob sells a rental building for a total contract price of $100,000, plus interest at the applicable federal rate. He receives a note due in yearly installments of $20,000, plus interest, beginning January 1, 2008. Bob's

---

Footnote references are to paragraphs of the 2008 Standard Federal Tax Reports.

[13] ¶ 21,404
[14] ¶ 21,402
[15] ¶ 21,404

[16] ¶ 21,404
[17] ¶ 21,404
[18] ¶ 21,402

[19] ¶ 21,402.049

adjusted basis in the building is $20,000. Assume that $10,000 of the total $80,000 gain is attributable to depreciation that must be recaptured as ordinary income under Code Sec. 1250 (see ¶ 1780). The $10,000 must be included in Bob's ordinary income for 2007 (the year of sale). The $10,000 is added to his $20,000 adjusted basis for purposes of determining the gross profit on the remaining gain. Therefore, gross profit is, $70,000 ($100,000 – $30,000). Of each $20,000 payment received in the following years, $14,000 is includible in income ($20,000 × ($70,000 ÷ $100,000)).

If a portion of the capital gain from an installment sale of depreciable real property consists of 25% gain, and another portion consists of 15% and/or 5% gain, the taxpayer is required to take the 25% gain into account before the 15% and/or 5% gain as payments are received (Reg. § 1.453-12).[20] The term "25% gain" refers to unrecaptured Code Sec. 1250 gain (see ¶ 1736), while 15% and/or 5% gain is the portion of the gain that is taxed at these lower capital gains rates.

1825. Special Interest Rule for Nondealers of Property. A special interest charge may apply to nondealer dispositions of real or personal property having a sales price over $150,000 (Code Sec. 453A).[21] The interest charge does not apply to nondealer dispositions of (1) property used in the business of farming or (2) personal use property. For this purpose, "personal use property" refers to property that is not substantially used in connection with the taxpayer's trade or business or in an investment activity (Code Sec. 1275(b)(3)). Also, the interest charge does not apply to dispositions of timeshares and residential lots (but the interest payment rule described in ¶ 1811 does apply) (Code Sec. 453A(b)(4)).

Generally, the interest charge is imposed on the tax deferred under the installment method with respect to outstanding installment obligations. However, the interest charge will not apply unless the face amount of all obligations held by the taxpayer that arose during and remain outstanding at the close of the tax year exceeds $5,000,000 (Code Sec. 453A(b)(2)(B)).[22]

If any indebtedness is secured by a nondealer installment obligation that arises from the disposition of any real or personal property having a sales price over $150,000, the net proceeds of the secured indebtedness will be treated as a payment received on the installment obligation on the later of the date that the indebtedness is secured or the date that the net proceeds are received (Code Sec. 453A(d)(1)).

Related-Party Sales

1833. Resale After Installment Sale to Related Persons. When a person makes an installment sale of property to a related person who sells the property before the installment payments are made in full, the amount realized by the related person from the second sale is treated as being received by the initial seller at the time of the second sale (Code Sec. 453(e)(1)).[23] A related person for this purpose includes the seller's spouse, child, grandchild, parent, grandparent, brother, sister, controlled corporation, partnership, trust, or estate (Code Sec. 453(f)(1)).[24] However, the resale rule does not generally apply when the second sale takes place more than two years after the first sale (Code Sec. 453(e)(2)).[25]

In applying the resale rule, the amount treated as received by the initial seller is limited to the *lesser* of (1) the total amount realized from the second disposition before the close of the tax year of disposition or (2) the total contract price for the first disposition, reduced by the sum of (a) the total amount received from the first disposition before the close of the year of the second disposition and (b) the total amount treated as received for prior years under the resale rule (Code Sec. 453(e)(3)).[26]

Footnote references are to paragraphs of the 2008 Standard Federal Tax Reports.

[20] ¶ 21,425
[21] ¶ 21,450
[22] ¶ 21,450
[23] ¶ 21,402
[24] ¶ 21,402
[25] ¶ 21,402
[26] ¶ 21,402

An exception applies for certain dispositions (Code Sec. 453(e)(6)):

(1) any sale or exchange of stock to the issuing corporation is not treated as a first disposition;

(2) a compulsory or involuntary conversion, and any transfer thereafter, is not treated as a second disposition if the first disposition occurred before the threat or imminence of the conversion; and

(3) any transfer after the earlier of the death of the person making the first disposition or the death of the person acquiring the property in the first disposition, and any transfer thereafter, is not treated as a second disposition.

1835. Depreciable Property Sales. Generally, the installment method cannot be used for installment sales of depreciable property between related persons. As a result, all payments are deemed received in the year of sale. However, the installment method may be used if the IRS is satisfied that tax avoidance was not one of the principal purposes of the sale (Code Sec. 453(g)).[27] For this purpose, the term "related person" is defined in Code Sec. 1239(b) (¶ 1744) and includes corporations and partnerships that are more than 50% owned, either directly or indirectly, by the same person.

Repossessions of Property

1838. Repossession of Personal Property. When personal property that was sold in an installment sale is repossessed, the repossession is treated as a disposition of the installment obligation. Gain or loss is measured by the difference between the seller's basis in the obligation and the fair market value of the property on the date of repossession. The seller's basis in the obligation is equal to the face value of the obligation minus the deferred gross profit on the sale at the time of repossession (IRS Pub. 537).[28] The character of the gain or loss, if any, on the repossession is the same as on the original sale.

If the installment obligation is not completely satisfied by repossession of the property, and the seller is unable to collect the balance of the debt, the seller may be able to claim a bad debt deduction for the portion of the obligation that is not satisfied through repossession (¶ 1145 and ¶ 1169).

1841. Repossession of Real Estate. When real property is sold on the installment method and the seller accepts an installment debt secured by the property, the seller will recognize only a limited amount of gain and no loss upon repossession of the property. Gain on the repossession is limited to the lesser of (Code Sec. 1038; Reg. § 1.1038-1):[29]

(1) the amount by which the amount of money and the fair market value of other property (other than obligations of the purchaser) received, prior to such reacquisition, with respect to the sale of such property, exceeds the amount of the gain on the sale of such property returned as income for periods prior to such reacquisition; or

(2) the amount by which the price at which the real property was sold exceeded its adjusted basis, reduced by the sum of (a) the amount of the gain on the sale of such property returned as income for periods prior to the reacquisition of such property, and (b) the amount of money and the fair market value of other property (other than obligations of the purchaser received with respect to the sale of such property) paid or transferred by the seller in connection with the reacquisition of such property.

The same rules apply when an estate or beneficiary repossesses real property that had been sold by a decedent on the installment method (Code Sec. 1038(g)).[30]

Repossession of Principal Residence. Special rules apply if a seller repossesses a principal residence that was sold under the installment method and realized gain from the sale was excluded under Code Sec. 121 (see ¶ 1705). If the seller resells the

---

Footnote references are to paragraphs of the 2008 Standard Federal Tax Reports.

[27] ¶ 21,402
[28] ¶ 21,406.048

[29] ¶ 29,740, ¶ 29,744
[30] ¶ 29,740

residence within one year of repossession, the original sale and the resale are treated as one transaction and realized gain is determined on the combined sale and resale (Code Sec. 1038(e)).[31] If the resale does not take place within one year, the general rules for repossessions of real property apply.

1843. Basis After Repossession of Real Estate. Generally, the seller's basis in repossessed real property is the adjusted basis of the debt secured by the property (determined at the time of the repossession), increased by any gain recognized at the time of the repossession and by the seller's repossession costs (Code Sec. 1038(c)).[32] If the debt to the seller is not discharged as a result of the repossession, the basis of the debt is zero. If, before repossession, the seller has treated the secured debt as having become worthless or partially worthless, then, upon repossession, the seller is considered to have received an amount equal to the amount that was treated as worthless. However, the seller's adjusted basis in the debt is increased by the same amount (Code Sec. 1038(d)).[33]

Dispositions of Installment Obligations

1846. Recognition of Gain or Loss. Gain or loss is generally recognized when installment obligations are sold, disposed of, or satisfied other than at face value (Code Sec. 453B(a)).[34] The amount of gain or loss is the difference between the basis of the obligation and either (1) the amount realized, if the obligation is satisfied other than at face value or is sold or exchanged; or (2) the fair market value of the obligation, if the obligation is distributed or disposed of other than by sale or exchange. For this purpose, the basis of the obligation to the transferor is the excess of the face value of the obligation over an amount equal to the income that would have been returnable had the obligation been satisfied in full (Code Sec. 453B(b)).[35]

The cancellation or lapse of an installment obligation is treated as a disposition other than a sale or exchange (Code Sec. 453B(f)).[36] This includes a self-canceling installment note that is extinguished at the death of the holder (*R.E. Frane Est.*).[37] Therefore, gain or loss is computed based on the fair market value of the obligation.

The character of any resulting gain or loss on the disposition of an installment obligation is determined by the character of the original asset that was sold (i.e., a capital or noncapital asset) (Code Sec. 453B(a)).[38] For a discussion of what constitutes a capital asset, see ¶ 1741.

1849. Transfers Between Spouses. The transfer of an installment obligation between spouses or incident to divorce (other than a transfer in trust) will not trigger recognition of gain. Thus, the same tax treatment applies to the transferee spouse that would have applied to the transferor spouse (Code Sec. 453B(g)).[39]

1854. Effect of Death on Installment Obligations. Installment obligations acquired from a decedent are considered income in respect of a decedent (see ¶ 182) (Reg. § 1.453-9(e)).[40] The taxpayer who receives such installment payments (estate, beneficiary, etc.) must report as income the same portion of the payments that would have been taxable income to the decedent (Reg. § 1.691(a)-5(a)).[41] The amount considered to be an item of gross income in respect of the decedent is the excess of the face value of the obligation over its basis in the hands of the decedent (Code Sec. 691(a)(4)).

A decedent seller's estate is deemed to have made a taxable disposition of an installment obligation if the obligation is transferred by bequest, devise, or inheritance to the obligor or if the estate allows the obligation to become unenforceable. If the decedent and obligor-recipient of the obligation were related persons, the fair market value of the obligation may not be determined at less than its face amount (Code Secs. 453(f)(1) and 691(a)(5)).[42]

Footnote references are to paragraphs of the 2008 Standard Federal Tax Reports.

[31] ¶ 29,740
[32] ¶ 29,740
[33] ¶ 29,740
[34] ¶ 21,470
[35] ¶ 21,470
[36] ¶ 21,470
[37] ¶ 21,471.15
[38] ¶ 21,470
[39] ¶ 21,470
[40] ¶ 24,900
[41] ¶ 24,905
[42] ¶ 21,402, ¶ 24,900

¶1843

Corporate Liquidations

1856. Shareholders of Liquidating Corporations. Liquidating corporations (other than certain liquidating S corporations (see below)) that distribute installment obligations to shareholders in exchange for their stock must currently recognize gain or loss from the distribution. However, a shareholder that receives a qualifying installment obligation may treat the exchange as though it were an ordinary sale of stock for an installment obligation. Thus, the shareholder may be able to use the installment method to report the gain from the exchange (Reg. § 1.453-11(a)(1)). Note that if the liquidating corporation is traded on an established securities market, installment sale treatment is not available (Code Sec. 453(k)(2); Reg. § 1.453-11(a)(2)(i)). However, a shareholder *may* use the installment method if the stock of the liquidating corporation is not traded on an established market, even if the obligation arose from the sale by the liquidating corporation of securities that are traded on an established market (so that the liquidating corporation could not have used the installment method). In order for this rule to apply, the liquidating corporation must not have been formed or used to avoid the prohibition against using the installment method for publicly traded stock (Reg. § 1.453-11(c)(5)).[43]

Gain on the transfer of a qualifying installment obligation to a shareholder during a liquidation (see ¶ 2253) is not immediately taxed to the shareholder. Instead, the payments received under the installment obligation are treated as payments for the stock, and any gain is included in the shareholder's income as payments are received. This rule applies when (Code Sec. 453(h)(1)(A)):

> (1) stockholders exchange their stock in the corporation in a Code Sec. 331 liquidation;

> (2) the corporation, during the 12-month period beginning with the adoption of the plan of liquidation, had sold some or all of its assets in exchange for an installment note;

> (3) the corporation, within that 12-month period, distributes the installment notes acquired in connection with those sales to the shareholders in exchange for their stock; and

> (4) the liquidation is completed within that 12-month period.

This rule does not apply to obligations arising from a sale of inventory, stock in trade, or assets held for sale to customers in the ordinary course of business unless those assets are sold in a bulk sale (Code Sec. 453(h)(1)(B)).[44]

S Corporation Liquidations. If an installment obligation is distributed by an S corporation in a complete liquidation, and the receipt of the obligation is not treated as payment for stock under the 12-month rule stated above, then, as a general rule, the corporation does not recognize gain or loss on the distribution. This is true even for accrual-basis S corporations (Code Sec. 453B(h)).[45]

Subsidiary Liquidations. In a complete liquidation of a subsidiary, in which gain or loss on distributions of property is generally not recognized by the parent or the subsidiary (see ¶ 2261), the distribution of installment obligations will not cause recognition of gain or loss (Code Sec. 453B(d)).[46]

Unstated Interest on Deferred Payments

1859. Inadequate or Unpaid Interest on Nonpublic Debt Instruments. Generally, when a sale or exchange of property for more than $3,000 involves the issuance of a debt instrument, the instrument should provide for the payment of adequate interest (Code Sec. 483(a), (d)(2)). If the instrument does not provide for the payment of adequate stated interest, interest income must be imputed to the seller or holder of the debt under the original issue discount (OID) rules of Code Sec. 1274 or the unstated interest rules of Code Sec. 483. However, the rules under Code Sec. 483 will apply only if the transaction does not come within the scope of Code Sec. 1274 (Code Sec. 483(d)(1)).[47]

Footnote references are to paragraphs of the 2008 Standard Federal Tax Reports.

[43] ¶ 21,419
[44] ¶ 21,402

[45] ¶ 21,470, ¶ 21,471.041
[46] ¶ 21,470

[47] ¶ 22,290

If neither Code Sec. 483 nor 1274 apply, interest may be imputed under other Code sections (Reg. § 1.483-1(a) and (c)(3); Reg. § 1.1274-1(b)). For example, interest is imputed to certain obligations given in exchange for services or for the use of property under Code Secs. 404 and 467 (¶ 1541), respectively (Reg. § 1.1274-1(a)). Further, the interest imputation rules of Code Sec. 7872 will apply to certain below-market demand loans (Reg. § 1.1274-1(b)(3)).

In addition, the Code Secs. 483 and 1274 rules do not apply to transfers of property between spouses, or incident to divorce (Code Sec. 1041), to cash method debt instruments (Code Sec. 1274A(c)), and to the purchaser who gives debt when buying personal use property (Code Sec. 1275(b)).

The following steps should be taken with respect to deferred contracts:

    (1) determine whether the transaction is covered by either Code Sec. 483 or 1274;

    (2) test for unstated interest or OID;

    (3) compute the total unstated interest or OID under the contract; and

    (4) apportion the unstated interest or OID over the payments.

The amount of unstated interest determined under Code Sec. 483 is classified as interest for tax purposes (Reg. § 1.483-1(a)(2)). As a result, it will be income to the seller and may be a deduction to the buyer. Similarly, the holder of the debt instrument must include a portion of the OID in income each year, and an interest deduction is allowed to the issuer. However, see the exceptions discussed at ¶ 1887.

Unstated Interest or OID

1863. Scope of Code Sec. 1274. The original issue discount (OID) rules apply to a debt instrument given as consideration for the sale or exchange of property if: (1) the stated redemption price at maturity for the debt instrument exceeds either the stated principal amount (when there is adequate stated interest) or the imputed principal amount (in any other situation) *and* (2) some or all of the payments under the instrument are due more than six months after the date of the sale or exchange (Code Sec. 1274(c)(1)). The term "stated redemption price at maturity" means the sum of all payments due under the debt instrument other than certain qualified interest payments (Code Sec. 1273(a)(2); Reg. § 1.1273-1(b)).[48] The "imputed principal amount" is the sum of the present value of all payments due under the instrument, as determined by discounting the payments at 100% of the applicable federal rate in effect on the date of the sale, compounded semiannually (Code Sec. 1274(b))[49] (see ¶ 1875).

Exceptions. In some cases debt instruments given in consideration for the sale or exchange of property are covered by the unstated interest rules of Code Sec. 483 (see ¶ 1868), rather than the OID rules. The unstated interest rules apply to instruments given for the sale or exchange of (Code Sec. 1274(c)(3); Reg. § 1.1274-1(b)):[50]

    (1) a farm for $1,000,000 or less by an individual, an estate, a testamentary trust, a small business corporation, or a partnership that meets requirements similar to those of a small business corporation;

    (2) a taxpayer's principal residence;

    (3) property for $250,000 or less;

    (4) publicly traded debt instruments or debt instruments issued for publicly traded property;

    (5) patents, to the extent that the amounts are contingent on the productivity, use, or disposition of the property transferred; and

    (6) land for $500,000 or less between related persons.

1868. Scope of Code Sec. 483. The unstated interest rules apply to any payments on the sale or exchange of property that are due more than six months after the sale or

---

Footnote references are to paragraphs of the 2008 Standard Federal Tax Reports.

[48] ¶ 31,280, ¶ 31,281   [49] ¶ 31,300   [50] ¶ 31,300, ¶ 31,301

exchange if any payments are due more than one year after the sale or exchange (Code Sec. 483).[51]

Exceptions. The rules under Code Sec. 483 do not apply in the following situations (Code Sec. 483(d); Reg. § 1.483-1(c)):

(1) debt instruments for which an issue price is determined under Code Sec. 1273(b)(1), (2) or (3), or Code Sec. 1274;

(2) sales for $3,000 or less;

(3) with respect to the buyer, any purchase of personal property or educational services (under Code Sec. 163(b)) on an installment basis if the interest charge cannot be ascertained and is treated as six percent; and

(4) sales or exchanges of patents to the extent of any payments that are contingent on the productivity, use or disposition of the property transferred.

1872. Testing for and Imputing OID or Unstated Interest. For purposes of the OID rules, there is adequate interest if the stated principal amount is less than or equal to the imputed principal amount (see ¶ 1863) (Code Sec. 1274(c)(2)).[52] Code Sec. 483 applies when there is "unstated interest." For this purpose, unstated interest is the excess of the total payments (excluding any interest payments) due more than six months after the date of sale over the total of their present values (including the present values of any interest payments). Generally, present value is determined by using a discount rate equal to the applicable federal rate determined under Code Sec. 1274(d) (Code Sec. 483(b); Reg. § 1.483-3).[53] Different discount rates apply to certain transactions (see ¶ 1879).

1875. Applicable Federal Rates. The IRS determines the federal short-term, mid-term and long-term rates for every calendar month based on the average market yields of specified maturities. For a sale or exchange, the applicable federal rate (AFR) is the lowest rate in effect for any month in the three-calendar-month period ending with the first calendar month in which there is a binding written contract (Reg. §§ 1.483-3(a); 1.1274-4(a)). The AFR is determined by reference to the term of the debt instrument, including renewal and extension options, as shown in the following table (Code Sec. 1274(d)).[54]

Term of Debt Instrument:	Applicable Federal Rate:
Not over 3 years	Federal short-term rate
Over 3 years but not over 9 years .	Federal mid-term rate
Over 9 years	Federal long-term rate

For the applicable federal rates, see ¶ 83.

1879. Special Rates in Certain Situations. In computing the imputed principal amount for the OID rules or the present value of the total payments for the unstated interest rules, the 100-percent AFR discount rate does *not* apply in the following situations.

Sales and Leasebacks. A discount rate of 110 percent of the federal rate, compounded semiannually, applies to sale and leaseback transactions (Code Sec. 1274(e); Reg. § 1.1274-4(a)(2)).[55]

Qualified Debt Instruments. A discount rate not in excess of nine percent (if less than the AFR), compounded semiannually, applies to most debt instruments given in consideration for the sale or exchange of property if the stated principal amount does not exceed $2,800,000, as adjusted for inflation (Code Sec. 1274A(a), (b) and (d); Reg. § 1.1274A-1(a)).[56] The 2007 inflation-adjusted amount is $4,800,800 for qualified debt instruments and $3,429,100 for cash-method debt instruments (Rev. Rul. 2007-4).[57]

Transfers of Land Between Family Members. The discount rate will not exceed six percent, compounded semiannually, in the case of transfers of land between family

---

Footnote references are to paragraphs of the 2008 Standard Federal Tax Reports.

[51] ¶ 22,290
[52] ¶ 31,300
[53] ¶ 22,290, ¶ 22,294

[54] ¶ 31,300
[55] ¶ 31,300, ¶ 31,304
[56] ¶ 31,320, ¶ 31,321

[57] ¶ 31,322.30

¶1879

members. This rule only applies if the aggregate sales price of all prior land sales between the family members during the calendar year does not exceed $500,000. However, this limit on the discount rate does not apply if any party to the sale is a nonresident alien (Code Sec. 483(e); Reg. § 1.483-3(b)).[58]

1881. Assumptions of Debt. If any person in connection with the sale or exchange of property assumes any debt instrument or acquires any property subject to any debt instrument, in determining whether the unstated interest or OID rules apply, the assumption or acquisition is not generally taken into account. However, when the instrument's terms and conditions are modified in a manner that would constitute an exchange, the unstated interest or OID rules may be applied (Code Sec. 1274(c)(4); Reg. §§ 1.483-1(d) and 1.1274-5(b)).[59]

1883. Including the Imputed Interest. The amount of OID to be included in the income of the holder of the instrument is the total of the daily portions of OID for each day of the tax year that the instrument is held (Code Sec. 1272(a)(1)). The daily portion is determined by allocating to each day in the accrual period the ratable portion of the increase in the adjusted issue price of the debt instrument. The increase in the issue price is computed by multiplying the adjusted issue price at the beginning of the accrual period by the yield to maturity (determined by compounding at the close of each accrual period) and subtracting from the result the sum of the interest payable under the instrument during such accrual period (Code Sec. 1272(a)(3); Reg. § 1.1272-1(b)).[60]

REMIC Rules. A special rule for determining OID applies to any regular interest in a real estate mortgage investment conduit (REMIC) (see ¶ 2358) or qualified mortgage held by a REMIC, and to debt instruments that have a maturity that is initially fixed but is accelerated based on prepayments (or other events) made on other debt obligations securing the debt instrument (Code Sec. 1272(a)(6)).[61] These special rules also apply to certain pooled debt instruments (Code Sec. 1272(a)(6)(C)).

Reporting Requirements. The reporting of OID and unstated interest depends upon whether the seller is on the cash or accrual basis. Cash basis sellers include OID in income as accrued and unstated interest as interest income in the year payments are received. Sellers on the accrual basis include both OID and unstated interest in income in the year payments are due (Reg. § 1.446-2(a) and Reg. § 1.1272-1(a)).[62]

Treatment of Interest by Borrowers

1887. Special Rules. Generally, the OID and unstated interest rules do not apply to a debt instrument given in consideration for the sale or exchange of personal use property. Thus, OID or unstated interest is not deductible by the issuer but must be accrued by the holder. Personal use property means any property substantially all the use of which by the taxpayer is not in connection with the taxpayer's trade or business or the for-profit and other activities described in Code Sec. 212 (Code Sec. 1275(b)(1), (3)).[63]

If a cash-basis borrower incurs debt in connection with the acquisition or carrying of personal use property, any OID or unstated interest is deductible only when paid (Code Sec. 1275(b)(2)).[64]

Generally, if a debt instrument is held by a related foreign person, any OID is not deductible by the issuer until paid. However, this rule does not apply if the OID is effectively connected with the related foreign person's conduct of a trade or business in the United States (Code Sec. 163(e)(3)(A)).[65]

Footnote references are to paragraphs of the 2008 Standard Federal Tax Reports.

[58] ¶ 22,290, ¶ 22,294
[59] ¶ 22,291, ¶ 31,300, ¶ 31,305
[60] ¶ 31,260, ¶ 31,261
[61] ¶ 31,260
[62] ¶ 20,610, ¶ 31,261
[63] ¶ 31,340
[64] ¶ 31,340
[65] ¶ 9102

¶1881

Chapter 19

SECURITIES TRANSACTIONS

Treatment of Securities Transactions

1901. Securities Transactions. Calculating the recognized gain or loss from the sale or exchange of securities generally follows the same rules that apply to other types of property (see ¶ 1701). However, in some situations there are special rules that must be applied. This chapter explains when these special rules must be used and how they are applied.

1903. Dealer in Securities. Securities held for sale by dealers to their customers in the ordinary course of business are not capital assets. For information regarding when a taxpayer is classified as a dealer, trader or investor, see ¶ 1760.

Mark-to-Market Requirements. The following mark-to-market rules apply to certain securities held by a dealer (Code Sec. 475(a)).[1]

(1) Any security that is classified as inventory in the hands of the dealer must be included in inventory at its fair market value.

(2) Any security that is not classified as inventory in the hands of the dealer and that is held at the close of the tax year is treated as if it were sold at its fair market value on the last business day of the year. The dealer must recognize any gain or loss that results from this deemed sale. Any gain or loss recognized under this rule is taken into account when calculating the dealer's gain or loss when he actually sells or exchanges the security (Code Sec. 475(a)(2)).

Exempt Securities. The following types of securities held by a dealer are exempt from the mark-to-market rules:

(1) securities held for investment;

(2) notes and bonds acquired for the dealer's business but not held for sale; and

(3) securities held for certain hedging purposes (Code Sec. 475(b)(1)).

In order for a security to be exempt from the mark-to-market requirements, it must be clearly identified in the dealer's records before the close of the day on which it was acquired, originated or entered into (Code Sec. 475(b)(2)).

Dealers in securities may hold and trade other securities for investment purposes. They are not required to inventory any securities that are held solely for investment purposes (Reg. § 1.471-5).[2]

The IRS has provided guidance on the mark-to-market requirement that addresses the definition of a securities dealer, exempt securities, and transitional issues (Rev. Rul. 97-39).

Fair Market Value. Under a safe harbor provision, securities dealers (and commodities dealers electing mark-to-market treatment) may use the fair market value of

Footnote references are to paragraphs of the 2008 Standard Federal Tax Reports.

[1] ¶ 22,265   [2] ¶ 22,211

securities as reported on the dealer's financial statements as their fair market value for purposes of mark-to-market accounting (Reg. § 1.475(a)-4).[3]

Commodity Dealers. Commodity dealers may make an election to have the mark-to-market requirements apply to them (Code Sec. 475(e)). See *"Making the Election,"* below.

Traders in Securities or Commodities. Traders in securities or commodities may make a mark-to-market election that allows them to treat their gains and losses as ordinary and not capital (Code Sec. 475(f)). See *"Making the Election,"* below. Traders are defined as taxpayers who are in the business of buying and selling securities and/or commodities for their own accounts. Traders differ from investors in that traders seek to profit from daily market movements, their buying and selling activity is substantial, and they carry on the activity with continuity and regularity. Traders differ from dealers in that traders do not deal with customers. (See ¶ 1760 for more information concerning the difference in tax treatment between investors, traders and dealers.) Although traders are allowed to deduct expenses that are related to their trading activities as business expenses, gains and losses from their trading are generally treated as capital in nature. This is because noncapital asset treatment only covers securities that are held primarily for sale to customers (Code Sec. 1221(a)(1)).

Making the Election. Dealers in commodities and traders in securities or commodities may make an election to use the mark-to-market method. The election is made by attaching a statement to the tax return for the year prior to the year in which the election is to take effect (e.g., the tax return for 2007 for the election to be effective for 2008). The statement must include:

(1) the Code provision that the election is being made under (e.g., Code Sec. 475(f));

(2) the tax year for which the election is to be effective; and

(3) the activity for which the election is being made (e.g., security trading) (Rev. Proc. 99-17).

When a mark-to-market election is made, the same mark-to-market rules that apply to dealers generally apply to the commodities dealer or the trader (Code Sec. 475(e)(1) and Code Sec. 475(f)(1)(D)).

Income Items

1905. Taxation of Stock Dividends and Stock Rights. Normally, a shareholder is not taxed on the value of a stock dividend or a stock right declared by a corporation on its own shares (Code Sec. 305(a)).[4] However, the distribution is taxed if it is:

(1) in lieu of money;

(2) a disproportionate distribution;

(3) a distribution of convertible preferred stock;

(4) a distribution of common and preferred stock;

(5) a dividend on preferred stock; or

(6) a transaction that increases the shareholder's proportionate interest (Code Sec. 305(b) and Code Sec. 305(c)).

See ¶ 738 for more information.

A corporation may give "stock rights" (i.e., the right to purchase a certain amount of stock at a specified price) to some or all of its shareholders. Usually, the distribution of these rights is not a taxable event at the time of distribution. When "nontaxable" rights are granted, tax consequences occur when the rights are exercised or transferred (see ¶ 1907). In contrast, when "taxable" rights are received, their fair market value is includible in income at the time of receipt (Code Sec. 305(b)). See ¶ 738 for more information.

1907. Nontaxable Stock Distributions. If the fair market value of a nontaxable distribution of stock or stock rights is 15% or more of the value of the stock, the stockholder's basis in the stock is allocated between the stock and the rights (Code Sec.

Footnote references are to paragraphs of the 2008 Standard Federal Tax Reports.

[3] ¶ 22,265E, ¶ 22,268.042   [4] ¶ 15,400

¶1905

307(b)). The allocation between the old stock and the new stock or the rights is made in proportion to their fair market values on the date of the distribution. The date of the distribution of the rights is the date on which the rights are distributed to the stockholder and *not* the record date (Reg. § 1.307-1).[5]

A taxpayer may *elect* to allocate basis in this way even if the nontaxable new stock or stock rights have a market value that is less than 15% of the value of the stock on which the distribution was made. If the election is not made, the basis of the rights is zero and the basis of the stock on which the rights are issued remains unchanged (Reg. § 1.307-2).[6] (This is also the rule if the rights are allowed to lapse, regardless of their value.) The election to allocate basis to rights must be made in a statement attached to the shareholder's return for the year in which the rights are received. The election is irrevocable with respect to the rights for which it is made. Also, the election must be made for all the rights received in a particular distribution by the shareholder on stock of the same class received by the shareholder at the time of the distribution (Reg. § 1.307-2).

> **Example:** Bob bought 100 shares of Yeta Company common stock at $125 per share and later received 100 rights entitling him to purchase 20 shares of new common stock in Yeta Company at $100 per share. When the rights were distributed, the old shares had a fair market value of $120 per share, and the rights had a fair market value of $3 each. Three weeks later, Bob sold his rights for $4 each. He elects to apportion basis.

Cost of old stock on which rights were distributed	$12,500.00
Market value of old stock at date of distribution of rights	12,000.00
Market value of rights at date of distribution	300.00
Cost apportioned to old stock after distribution of rights (12,000/12,300 of $12,500)	12,195.12
Cost apportioned to rights (300/12,300 of $12,500)	304.88
Selling price of rights	400.00
Gain ($400 – $304.88)	$95.12

In determining gain or loss from any later sale of the stock on which the rights were distributed, the adjusted cost of the old stock is $12,195.12, or $121.95 a share.

The holding period of nontaxable stock rights includes the holding period of the stock on which the rights are distributed. The holding period of the stock acquired by the exercise of the rights begins on the date that the rights are exercised (Reg. § 1.1223-1(e)).[7]

1909. Basis After Exercise of Nontaxable Rights. The basis for gain or loss on a sale of stock acquired by exercise of nontaxable rights is computed by adding the portion of the cost or other basis of the old stock allocated to the rights (determined as explained at ¶ 1907) to the subscription price of the new shares and dividing the sum by the number of shares obtained (Reg. § 1.307-1).[8]

1911. Corporation Dealing in Its Stock or Bonds. No gain or loss is recognized by a corporation when it receives money or other property in exchange for its own stock, including treasury stock, regardless of the nature of the transaction (Reg. § 1.1032-1(a)).[9] It does not matter if the stock was sold at a premium or a discount.

The nonrecognition rule also applies to the acquisition by a corporation of shares of its own stock in exchange for shares of its own stock (including treasury stock). Ordinarily, a corporation does not recognize gain or loss on the nonliquidating distribution of its stock (or rights) or on the distribution of property (e.g., a dividend) to shareholders. See ¶ 736 for information on nonliquidating distributions. However, a corporation generally must recognize gain (but not loss) on the distribution to its shareholders of appreciated property. Gain is recognized to the extent that the property's fair market value exceeds its adjusted basis (Code Sec. 311(b)(1)).[10] A corporation does not recognize gain or loss on bonds it issues at face value. If, however, it buys its bonds for less than their issue price or face value, the corporation will realize income

---

Footnote references are to paragraphs of the 2008 Standard Federal Tax Reports.

[5] ¶ 15,401	[7] ¶ 30,461	[9] ¶ 29,623
[6] ¶ 15,501B	[8] ¶ 15,401	[10] ¶ 15,550

(Reg. §1.61-12(c)).[11] When bonds are issued at a premium, the corporation must generally offset its interest expense with the premium it received (Reg. §1.163-13(a)).[12] Any amount allocable to a bond's conversion feature is not part of the bond premium (Code Sec. 171(b)(1)).[13] See ¶1967 for the tax treatment of a premium paid by the buyer of a bond.

Loss Items

1913. Surrender of Stock. A shareholder's surrender of a portion of his shares to the corporation will not result in a deductible loss. Instead, the basis of the stock surrendered is reallocated to the shareholder's basis in the remaining shares (Rev. Rul. 70-291).[14]

1915. Loss from Worthless Stock. A taxpayer may generally claim a capital loss in the year stock becomes *completely worthless* (Code Sec. 165(g); Reg. §1.165-5).[15] See ¶1764 for the rules that determine whether the capital loss is classified as short term or long term. A deduction may not be claimed for partially worthless stock. Limits on capital loss deductions are discussed at ¶1752. Loss on stock in a small business investment company is treated as an ordinary loss (see ¶2392), as is loss on stock in an affiliated corporation. A loss deduction for a worthless security may not be claimed by a securities dealer that is required to maintain an inventory of securities used in the dealer's business (Reg. §1.165-5(g)).[16]

1917. Bond as Bad Debt. Banks, financial institutions described in Code Sec. 591, and small business investment companies operating under the Small Business Investment Act of 1958 are the only taxpayers that may claim an ordinary loss for wholly or partially worthless corporate bonds (Code Sec. 582).[17] A dealer in securities takes such losses into account by making adjustments to inventory. For other taxpayers, a loss from bonds and other types of debt (e.g., debentures, or notes) is deductible only when the debt instrument is completely worthless (Code Sec. 165(g); Reg. §§1.165-4 and 1.165-5).[18] See ¶1752 for information concerning annual limits on capital losses (Code Sec. 1211).[19] For the rules used in determining if the loss is short term or long term, see ¶1764.

Options

1919. Option to Buy or Sell. An option is a right to buy (a "call" option) or sell (a "put" option) property at a stipulated price on or before a specified date. The buyer of an option is called the "holder." The seller of an option is called the "writer" (Rev. Rul. 78-182).[20]

A taxpayer has a capital gain or loss from the sale or exchange of an option or a capital loss on the failure to exercise it only if the property covered by the option would be a capital asset in the hands of the taxpayer. When a taxpayer fails to exercise an option, the option is deemed sold or exchanged on the day it expired (Code Sec. 1234(a)).[21]

In the case of an option on stock, securities, commodities or commodity futures, any gain of a nondealer grantor on the lapse of options is short-term capital gain. Also, any gain or loss of a nondealer grantor from a closing transaction is short-term capital gain or loss (Code Sec. 1234(b)(1)). The capital gain and loss provisions do not apply to options granted in the normal course of the taxpayer's business of granting options (Code Sec. 1234(b)(3)).[22]

Gain or loss is recognized on the exercise of an option on Code Sec. 1256 contracts (i.e., regulated futures contracts, foreign currency contracts, nonequity options and dealer equity options) (Code Sec. 1234(c)).[23]

1921. Stock Options. The cost of purchasing a put or call option on stock is a nondeductible capital expenditure (Rev. Rul. 71-521).[24]

Footnote references are to paragraphs of the 2008 Standard Federal Tax Reports.

[11] ¶5801, ¶5804.47
[12] ¶9302D
[13] ¶11,850
[14] ¶29,412.992
[15] ¶9802, ¶10,000
[16] ¶10,000
[17] ¶23,608
[18] ¶9802, ¶9905, ¶10,000
[19] ¶30,390
[20] ¶30,614.14
[21] ¶30,610
[22] ¶30,610
[23] ¶30,610
[24] ¶30,592.70

Holders of Stock Options. If the holder *sells* a stock option without exercising it, the difference between its cost and the amount he receives for it is either a long-term or short-term capital gain or loss, depending on how long he held it. If the option *expires*, its cost is either a long-term or short-term capital loss, depending on the taxpayer's holding period, which ends on the expiration date. If the holder *exercises a call*, its cost is added to the basis of the stock purchased. If the holder *exercises a put*, the amount realized on the sale of the underlying stock is reduced by the cost of the put when computing gain or loss on the sale of the stock. That gain or loss is long term or short term depending on the taxpayer's holding period for the underlying stock (Rev. Rul. 78-182).

Writers of Stock Options. If a taxpayer *writes* a call or a put, the amount received is not included in income at the time of receipt. Instead it is carried in a deferred account until: (1) the obligation expires, (2) the writer sells, in the case of a call, or buys, in the case of a put, the underlying stock when the option is exercised, or (3) the writer engages in a closing transaction. If the option expires, the amount received for writing the call or put is short-term capital gain. If a call is exercised and the writer sells the underlying stock, he increases the amount realized on the sale of the stock by the amount he received for the call when computing gain or loss on the stock sale. That gain or loss is long term or short term depending on the writer's holding period of the stock. If a put is exercised and the writer buys the underlying stock, he decreases his basis in the stock by the amount received for the put. His holding period for the stock begins on the date of the stock purchase, not on the date he wrote the put (Rev. Rul. 78-182).

Example 1: *Expiration.* Ten call options were issued on April 8, 2007, for $4,000. These equity options expired in December 2007 without being exercised. The holder (buyer) of the options recognizes a short-term capital loss of $4,000. The writer of the options recognizes a short-term capital gain of $4,000.

Example 2: *Closing transaction.* Assume the same facts as in Example 1, except that on May 10, 2007, the options were sold for $6,000. The holder (buyer) of the options who sold them recognizes a short-term capital gain of $2,000. If the writer of the options bought them back, he would recognize a short-term capital loss of $2,000.

Example 3: *Exercise.* Assume the facts as in Example 1, except that the options were exercised on May 27, 2007. The holder (buyer) adds the cost of the options to the basis of the stock bought through the exercise of the options. The writer adds the amount received from writing the options to the amount realized from selling the stock.

1922. Qualified vs. Nonqualified Employee Stock Options. Corporations may grant their employees the option to purchase stock in the corporation. Stock options may be given or sold to employees.

There are two kinds of employee stock options:

    (1) statutory or qualified options (i.e., the tax treatment of the options is governed by specific Code sections) and

    (2) nonstatutory or nonqualified options (i.e., the tax treatment of the options is governed under the more general Code principles of compensation and the recognition of income).

Basically, an employee stock option is an agreement under which the employee who holds the option has the right, but not the obligation, to purchase corporate shares at a fixed price on a fixed date or within a range of dates (Reg. § 1.421-7(a)(1)).[25]

1923. Nonqualified Stock Options. A nonqualified stock option is one that does not meet the requirements of, and so is not governed by, the rules of Code Secs. 421 through 424 (Reg. § 1.83-7(a)).[26]

Taxation Upon Grant. A nonqualified stock option is taxed when it is granted if the option has a " readily ascertainable fair market value" at that time (Reg. § § 1.83-1(a) and 1.83-7(a)).[27]

Footnote references are to paragraphs of the 2008 Standard Federal Tax Reports.

[25] ¶ 19,607   [26] ¶ 6388   [27] ¶ 6381, ¶ 6388

An option that is not actively traded on an established market has a readily ascertainable fair market value only if *all* of the following requirements are met (Reg. § 1.83-7(b)(2)):[28]

    (1) the option must be transferable;

    (2) the option must be exercisable immediately and in full when it is granted;

    (3) there can be no condition or restriction on the option that would have a significant effect on its fair market value; and

    (4) the fair market value of the *option privilege* (under Reg. § 1.83-7(b)(3))[29] must be readily ascertainable.

Because these requirements are seldom satisfied, most nonqualified options that are not traded on an established market do not have a readily ascertainable fair market value.

1924. Nonqualified Options Without Readily Ascertainable Fair Market Value. If a nonqualified option does not have a readily ascertainable fair market value, the exercise of the option, and not the grant, is the taxable event (Reg. § 1.83-7(a)).[30] When the employee exercises the option, the employee recognizes ordinary income in the amount of the fair market value of the stock purchased minus any amount paid for the stock or the option. Later, when the employee sells the stock, any gain or loss recognized is treated as capital gain or loss. The employee's holding period of the stock begins the day after the option was exercised. See ¶ 1681 for information concerning the tax consequences to the employee when stock or other property is received in payment for the employee's services.

1925. Nonqualified Options With Readily Ascertainable Fair Market Value. If a nonqualified option has a readily ascertainable fair market value, the employee must recognize ordinary income in the amount of that fair market value in the year the option is granted (Reg. § 1.83-1(a)).[31] If the employee paid for the option, he recognizes the value of the option minus its cost. The employee is not taxed again when he exercises the option and buys corporate stock. However, the employee is taxed when he sells the stock. The employee's basis in the stock is the fair market value of the option on which he paid taxes plus the amount he paid for the stock. Capital gain or loss is recognized when the stock is sold. The employee's holding period for the stock begins the day after the option was exercised.

1926. Lapse of Options. When an employee allows an option with a readily ascertainable fair market value to lapse, the employee's capital loss is determined by the employee's basis in the option (i.e., the value of the option that was taxed) (Code Sec. 1234(a)(2)).[32] The option is treated as if it were sold or exchanged on the date that it lapsed (Reg. § 1.1234-1(b)).

1927. Determining the Holding Period. In determining whether a capital gain or loss on stock is long term or short term, the taxpayer's holding period begins on the date after the option is exercised. See ¶ 1777 for rules used to determine holding period of various types of capital assets.

1928. Tax Treatment of Employer. An employer may deduct the value of a nonqualified stock option as a business expense for the tax year in which the option is included in the gross income of the employee. When the option has a readily ascertainable value, the employer is allowed the deduction for the year in which the option is granted (Reg. § 1.83-7(a)). When the option does not have a readily ascertainable value, the employer is allowed the deduction for the year in which the option is exercised (Reg. § 1.83-7(a)). The employer's deduction equals the amount of income recognized by the employee (Code Sec. 83(h)).[33]

When the employer and the employee have different tax years, the employer claims the deduction in the tax year in which or with which the employee's tax year ends (Code Sec. 83(h)).

Footnote references are to paragraphs of the 2008 Standard Federal Tax Reports.

[28] ¶ 6388   [30] ¶ 6388   [32] ¶ 30,610
[29] ¶ 6388   [31] ¶ 6381   [33] ¶ 6380

¶1924

Reporting Requirements. In most situations, when an employee exercises a nonstatutory stock option, employers are required to report the excess of the fair market value of the stock received over the amount that the employee paid for that stock (i.e., "the spread") on Form W-2 in boxes 1, 3 (up to the social security wage base), and 5. The employer must also show this amount in box 12, using Code V.

1929. Qualified Options. There are two kinds of statutory ("qualified") options (Reg. § 1.421-7(b)):[34] (1) incentive stock options, which are subject to the rules of Code Sec. 422,[35] and (2) options granted under employee stock purchase plans, which are subject to the rules of Code Sec. 423.[36]

In order to be recognized as a statutory option, the option must be exercisable only by the individual to whom it is granted unless the right to exercise passes by will or law at the grantee's death (Reg. § 1.421-1(b)(2)). The determination of whether an option qualifies as a statutory option is made when the option is granted, not when it is exercised or the stock is sold (Reg. § 1.421-1(b)(3)(i)).[37]

1930. Incentive Stock Options. An employee who receives incentive stock options (ISOs) recognizes income derived from them only upon the sale of the stock and not upon the grant or exercise of the options (Code Sec. 421(a)).[38] If certain holding period requirements are satisfied, the gain or loss on the sale of shares that were acquired by exercising the ISO are taxed at capital gains rates when the employee *sells* the stock. If the holding period requirements are not met, any gain is ordinary income up to the amount by which the stock's fair market value at the time of exercise exceeded the option price. Any excess gain is capital gain, and any loss is a capital loss (IRS Pub. 525). See ¶ 1931 for ISO requirements. See ¶ 1736 for the capital gains tax rates. Options that would otherwise be ISOs are treated as nonqualified stock options to the extent that the aggregate fair market value of the stock a taxpayer may acquire pursuant to ISOs that are exercisable for the first time during any tax year exceeds $100,000 (Code Sec. 422(d)).

1931. Requirements for ISOs. An ISO may allow the employee to purchase shares of the employer corporation or a parent or subsidiary corporation (Code Sec. 422(a)). ISOs must be granted under a plan adopted by the granting corporation and approved by its shareholders that sets out the total number of shares that may be issued under options and the employees who may receive the options (Reg. § 1.422-2(b)).

The options must be granted within 10 years from the date the plan is adopted or approved, whichever is earlier. Further, the options must be exercisable within 10 years from the date of the grant. The option price may not be less than the fair market value of the stock at the time the option is granted, and the option may not be transferable other than at the grantee's death. The option may be exercised only by the employee. Finally, the employee, *at the time the option is granted*, may not own stock with more than 10% of the total combined voting power of all classes of stock of the employer corporation or its parent or any subsidiary (Code Sec. 422(b)).[39]

The employee must remain an employee of the corporation from the time the option is granted until three months before the option is exercised (Reg. § 1.422-1(a)(1)(i)(B)). The three-month period is extended to one year if the employee ceased employment because of permanent and total disability (Reg. § 1.422-1(a)(3)). In order to receive ISO treatment, the employee must not dispose of the stock for at least two years from the date on which the option was granted and the stock must be held for at least one year after the option was exercised (Reg. § 1.422-1(a)(1)(i)(A)). However, these holding period requirements are waived in the event of the employee's death (Reg. § 1.421-1(b)(2)).

If the employee sells the shares before the required period ends (i.e., in a disqualifying disposition), gain on the sale is treated as compensation. Generally, the amount of compensation is the fair market value of the stock when the option was exercised less the exercise price (Reg. § 1.421-2(b)and Code Sec. 83(a)). The gain is recognized for the

---

Footnote references are to paragraphs of the 2008 Standard Federal Tax Reports.

[34] ¶ 19,607	[36] ¶ 19,900	[38] ¶ 19,602
[35] ¶ 19,800	[37] ¶ 19,607	[39] ¶ 19,800

tax year in which the sale occurs (Code Sec. 421(b)).[40] If the stock was acquired under options exercised after October 22, 2004, a disqualifying distribution is excluded from the definition of wages and so does not require income or employment tax withholding (Code Secs. 421(b) and 3121(a)).

Alternative Minimum Tax. The *excess*, if any, of the (1) fair market value of the stock received upon the exercise of the option over (2) the amount paid for the stock, plus any amount paid for the ISO, must generally be recognized as an AMT adjustment (Code Sec. 56(b)(3)).[41] See ¶ 1435 for information concerning the required AMT computations.

1932. Death of ISO Holder. In the event the holder of an ISO dies, the deceased's representative may exercise the option. The executor, administrator, or representative need not exercise the option within three months after the death of the employee (as would be the case if the employee left the service of the employer while living) (Reg. § 1.421-2(c)).

1933. Basis of ISO. An employee's basis in an ISO is the amount that the employee paid for the option. If the employee did not pay for the option and the option lapses, the employee does not have a deductible loss because he does not have a basis.

An employee's basis in *stock* purchased through an ISO is the amount he paid for the stock when the option was exercised (plus any amount he paid for the option).

1934. Employee Stock Purchase Plans. Employee stock purchase plans (ESPPs) are written, shareholder-approved plans under which employees are granted options to purchase shares of their employer's stock or the stock of a parent or subsidiary corporation for not less than 85 percent of their fair market value (Code Sec. 423(b)(1) and (2)).[42]

If the option price is less than the fair market value of the stock at the time the option is granted, the employee recognizes ordinary income in the amount of the *lesser* of: (1) the difference between the fair market value of the shares when sold (or the fair market value of the shares at the employee's death while owning the shares) and the option price for the shares or (2) the difference between the option price and the fair market value of the shares when the option was granted. The balance of any gain is treated as capital gain (Code Sec. 423(c)).[43] Withholding is not required with respect to amounts taxable under these rules (Code Sec. 423(c)).

An ESPP (employee stock purchase plan) should not be confused with an ESOP (employee stock ownership plan). While both plans involve company stock ending up in the hands of a corporation's employees, an ESOP is a retirement plan that holds employer stock for the benefit of participating employees. For information on ESOPs, see ¶ 2109.

1934A. Employee Stock Purchase Plan Special Rules. An employee stock purchase plan (ESPP) may grant employees the option to purchase stock in their employer or the employer's parent or subsidiary. To qualify for statutory treatment, the stock purchased under the option may not be sold within two years from the grant of the option and one year after the shares are transferred (Code Sec. 423(a)).[44]

The employee must remain employed by the corporation from the date the option is granted until three months before the option is exercised (Code Sec. 423(a)(2)).[45] An ESPP cannot grant options to any employee who has more than 5% of the voting power or value of the employer's stock, or that of any parent or subsidiary of the employer (Code Sec. 423(b)(3)).[46]

All full-time employees must be included in the plan, except those with less than two years of employment, highly compensated employees (as defined in Code Sec. 414(q)), part-time employees, and seasonal workers (Code Sec. 423(b)(4)).[47] The plan must be nondiscriminatory, though it may limit the amount of stock any employee can buy, and the amount of stock that each employee may become entitled to buy may be tied to compensation (Code Sec. 423(b)(5)).

Footnote references are to paragraphs of the 2008 Standard Federal Tax Reports.

[40] ¶ 19,602
[41] ¶ 5200
[42] ¶ 19,900
[43] ¶ 19,900
[44] ¶ 19,900
[45] ¶ 19,900
[46] ¶ 19,900
[47] ¶ 19,900

¶1932

The option price may not be less than the *lesser* of: (1) the fair market value of the stock at the time the option is granted or (2) the fair market value of the stock at the time the option is exercised (Code Sec. 423(b)(6)).[48] The option cannot be exercised later than 27 months from the date the option is granted (or five years from the date the option is granted, if the option price is based on the fair market value of the stock at the time the option is exercised) (Code Sec. 423(b)(7)).[49]

No employee can acquire the right to buy more than $25,000 of stock per year (valued at the time the option is granted) (Code Sec. 423(b)(8)).[50]

Wash Sales

1935. Wash Sale Losses Denied. Under the wash sale rules, a taxpayer who realizes a loss upon a sale or other disposition of stock or securities may not take a deduction for the loss. The wash sale rules apply if, within a period beginning 30 days before the date of the sale or disposition and ending 30 days after that date, the taxpayer has acquired, or has entered into a contract or option to acquire, substantially identical stock or securities (Code Sec. 1091(a); Reg. § 1.1091-1).[51] Similarly, a loss realized on the closing of a short sale of stock or securities is disallowed if within 30 days before or after the closing substantially identical stock or securities are sold or another short sale of substantially identical stock or securities is entered into (Code Sec. 1091(e)).[52] The wash sale rules also apply to a loss realized on the sale, exchange, or termination of a securities futures contract *to sell* stock or securities (Code Sec. 1091(e)). However, the wash sale rules do *not* apply to any loss attributable to a Section 1256 contract (Code Sec. 1256(f)(5)).

An acquisition by gift, bequest, inheritance, or tax-free exchange that is made within the 61-day period does not bring the wash sale rules into play. However, the wash sale rules cannot be avoided by arranging for delivery of the sold stock on a date that is beyond the 61-day period (Rev. Rul. 59-418).[53]

The wash sale rules apply to all taxpayers, including corporations. However, the rules do not apply to stock or securities dealers for losses sustained in a transaction in the course of their business.

When shares of the same corporation are purchased in separate lots, sold at the same time, and then reacquired within the prohibited time period, a loss on one lot may not be claimed to reduce the gain from the other shares.[54] Under the "related persons rule," the U.S. Supreme Court disallowed a loss deduction when identical securities were purchased by a taxpayer's spouse (*J. P. McWilliams*).[55] See ¶ 1717 for more information concerning losses between related persons.

For application of the wash sale rules to commodity futures contracts involving tax straddle positions, see ¶ 1948.

1937. "Substantially Identical" Securities. In determining whether stock or securities are substantially identical, all the facts and circumstances must be considered. Ordinarily, stocks or securities of one corporation are not considered substantially identical to stocks or securities of another corporation. However, they may be substantially identical in some cases. For example, in a reorganization, the stocks and securities of the predecessor and successor corporations may be substantially identical (IRS Pub. 550).

Bonds or preferred stock of a corporation are not ordinarily considered substantially identical to the common stock of the same corporation. However, when the bonds or preferred stock are convertible into common stock of the same corporation, the relative values, price changes, and other circumstances may make these bonds or preferred stock and the common stock substantially identical (Rev. Rul. 77-201).

1939. Basis After Wash Sale. When a loss is disallowed because of the wash sale rules, the disallowed loss is added to the cost of the new stock or securities. The result is the taxpayer's basis in the new stock or securities. This adjustment postpones the loss

---

Footnote references are to paragraphs of the 2008 Standard Federal Tax Reports.

[48] ¶ 19,900
[49] ¶ 19,900
[50] ¶ 19,900
[51] ¶ 30,180, ¶ 30,181
[52] ¶ 30,180
[53] ¶ 30,183.104
[54] ¶ 30,183.11
[55] ¶ 30,183.109

deduction until the disposition of the new stock or securities (Code Sec. 1091(d); Reg. § 1.1091-2).[56]

> **Example:** Betty buys 100 shares of Rapid Corporation stock for $1,000. She sells these shares for $750 and within 30 days from the sale Betty buys another 100 shares of Rapid Corporation for $800. Because Betty purchased substantially identical stock, she cannot deduct the $250 loss that she realized on the sale. However, Betty adds the disallowed loss of $250 to the cost of her new shares. As a result, her basis in the new shares is $1,050 ($800 cost, plus the $250 loss she could not claim under the wash sale rules).

1941. Holding Period. When there has been a wash sale, the holding period of the new securities includes the period that the taxpayer held the securities on which the loss was not deductible (Code Sec. 1223(4); Reg. § 1.1223-1).[57] For more information concerning the determination of a taxpayer's holding period, see ¶ 1777.

Short Sales

1944. Short Sales. A short sale occurs when a taxpayer enters into an agreement to sell property that he does not own (or owns but does not want to sell). The seller enters into the transaction because he expects to profit from the future decline in the price of the property. A short sale involves the following two steps: (1) the taxpayer sells short by borrowing property (e.g., shares of stock) and delivering this property to the buyer, and (2) at a later date, the seller purchases similar property and "covers" the transaction by delivering this property to the original lender. This last step is called "closing the sale."[58] Generally, the seller does not recognize gain or loss on the transaction until he delivers the property to the lender and the short sale is closed.

A short sale results in a capital gain or loss if the property used to close the sale is a capital asset (Code Sec. 1233(a)). However, hedging transactions generally result in ordinary income or loss (Reg. § 1.1233-2).[59] See ¶ 1949 for information on hedging.

Holding Period. Generally, short sellers determine whether they have a short-term or long-term capital gain or loss by determining the amount of time they held the property that they deliver to the lender.

> **Example:** On January 2, 2006, Mary Edwards enters into an agreement to sell 100 shares of Niftexo Corporation for $10 a share to Susan Croft. Mary does not own any Niftexo shares, so she borrows the 100 shares from her broker and delivers these shares to Susan. On May 1, 2007, Mary purchases 100 shares of Niftexo at a price of $15 a share. The same day she delivers these shares to her broker in order to replace the shares she had borrowed (i.e., she closes out her short sale). Her recognized loss of $500 is short term because her holding period of the Niftexo shares is determined by the amount of time she held the shares (i.e., less than one day).

Special Holding Period Rules. Special rules may have to be used to determine whether gain or loss is short term or long term when the seller owned or acquired substantially identical property to that sold short. One special rule stipulates that when the seller has held substantially identical property for one year or less on the date of the short sale, or if the seller acquired substantially identical property after the short sale and by the date the sale is closed, then *gain* is recognized as short term when the short sale is closed, and the holding period of the substantially identical property begins on the closing of the short sale, or on the date the property is sold, whichever happens first (Code Sec. 1233(b)).[60]

Another special rule applies when the seller held substantially identical property for more than one year and the seller has a *loss*. In this situation, the loss is classified as long term (Code Sec. 1233(d)). The loss is long term even when the property used to close the short sale is held by the seller for one year or less. Special holding period rules apply to brokers' arbitrage transactions (Code Sec. 1233(f); Reg. § 1.1233-1).[61]

Footnote references are to paragraphs of the 2008 Standard Federal Tax Reports.

[56] ¶ 30,180, ¶ 30,182	[58] ¶ 30,592.355	[60] ¶ 30,590
[57] ¶ 30,460, ¶ 30,461	[59] ¶ 30,590, ¶ 30,591C	[61] ¶ 30,590, ¶ 30,591

Timing of Gain or Loss. If a short seller has a gain on the transaction when the replacement property is purchased, the gain is recognized at that time. A loss is not recognized until the replacement property is delivered to the lender (Rev. Rul. 2002-44).

Constructive Sale Treatment. In the past, certain hedging strategies such as short sales against the box, forward contracts, and notional principal contracts could be used to lock in gains on appreciated financial positions without immediate recognition of income. However, the rules under Code Sec. 1259 limit these strategies by treating certain hedging transactions as "constructive sales" (Code Sec. 1259(a)).[62]

If there is a constructive sale of an appreciated financial position, the taxpayer must recognize gain as if the position were sold, assigned, or otherwise terminated at its fair market value *as of the date of the constructive sale* and immediately repurchased. Any gain or loss subsequently realized on the position is adjusted to reflect gain recognized on the constructive sale. The taxpayer's holding period begins as if the taxpayer had first acquired the position on the date of the constructive sale (Code Sec. 1259(a)(2)).

"Appreciated financial position" generally means any position with respect to any stock, debt instrument, or partnership interest if there would be gain if the position were sold, assigned, or otherwise terminated at its fair market value (Code Sec. 1259(b)(1)). However, there are some exceptions to this general definition. One exception is made for any position that is marked to market. A second exception is made for any position with respect to debt instruments if three conditions are satisfied (Code Sec. 1259(b)(2)):

(1) the debt unconditionally entitles the holder to receive a specified principal amount;

(2) interest payments are payable based on a fixed rate or, to the extent provided in regulations, at a variable rate; and

(3) the debt is not convertible into stock of the issuer or any related person.

A taxpayer is treated as making a constructive sale of an appreciated position if the taxpayer enters into certain types of transactions or attempts to avoid Code Sec. 1259 by having a related person enter into one of these transactions. A constructive sale is deemed to occur when a taxpayer does any of the following (Code Sec. 1259(c)(1)):

(1) enters into a short sale of the same or substantially identical property;

(2) enters into an offsetting notional principal contract with respect to the same or substantially identical property;

(3) enters into a futures or forward contract to deliver the same or substantially identical property;

(4) has entered into a short sale, an offsetting notional principal contract, or a forward or futures contract and acquires a long position in the same or substantially identical property; or

(5) to the extent prescribed in regulations, enters into other transactions having substantially the same effect as the four types of transactions listed above.

Exclusion. Contracts for the sale of appreciated financial assets that are not publicly traded are excluded from the definition of a constructive sale if the contract settles within one year after the date it was entered into (Code Sec. 1259(c)(2)).

Safe Harbor for Short-Term Hedges. Code Sec. 1259 provides a safe harbor for certain short-term hedges that would otherwise be treated as constructive sales (Code Sec. 1259(c)(3)).[63] Under this exception for certain "closed transactions," a transaction that would otherwise be treated as a constructive sale is disregarded if three conditions are satisfied:

(1) the transaction is closed on or before the end of the 30th day after the end of the tax year in which the transaction was entered into;

(2) the taxpayer holds the appreciated financial position throughout the 60-day period beginning on the date the transaction is closed; and

(3) at no time during that 60-day period is the taxpayer's risk of loss with respect to the position reduced by a circumstance that would be described in Code Sec. 246(c)(4) if references to stock included references to such position.

Footnote references are to paragraphs of the 2008 Standard Federal Tax Reports.

[62] ¶ 31,130   [63] ¶ 31,130

The circumstances referred to in Code Sec. 246(c)(4) are as follows:

(1) the taxpayer has an option to sell, is under a contractual obligation to sell, or has made (but not closed) a short sale of substantially identical stock or securities;

(2) the taxpayer is the grantor of an option to buy substantially identical stock or securities; or

(3) under IRS regulations, the taxpayer has diminished his or her risk of loss by holding one or more other positions with respect to substantially similar or related property.

The "closed transaction" exception also applies to certain reestablished positions (Code Sec. 1259(c)(3)(B)).

1946. Dividends and Payments in Lieu of Dividends. An amount equal to the dividend paid by a short seller to one who lends him stock to sell short may be deductible as investment interest expense (as an itemized deduction). See ¶ 1094 for information on investment interest. The borrower may not deduct the payments unless the short sale is held open for at least 45 days. The 45-day period is extended to one year if extraordinary dividends are involved. If the short sale is closed by the 45th day after the date of the short sale (one year or less in the case of an extraordinary dividend), the short seller must instead increase the basis of the stock used to close the short sale by the amount of the payment (Code Sec. 263(h)(1)).[64]

These 45-day and one-year periods are suspended for any period in which the borrower holds options to buy substantially identical property or holds one or more positions in such property (Code Sec. 263(h)(4)).[65]

Tax Straddles

1948. Straddle Transactions. Taxpayers who are investors are prevented from using various tax-motivated straddle transactions (positions in a transaction that balance or offset each other) to defer income or to convert short-term capital gain into long-term capital gain. Losses incurred on sales of actively traded personal property, including most stock, are deferred to the extent that the taxpayer had gains in offsetting positions that were not closed out by year-end (Code Sec. 1092(a)).[66]

If a straddle is "identified" on the taxpayer's books, a loss realized on any position in the straddle is reflected by increasing the basis of offsetting positions that have unrealized gain (Code Sec. 1092(a)(2)(A)). These rules are generally effective for positions established on or after October 22, 2004.

Generally, positions in regulated futures contracts, foreign currency contracts, nonequity options, dealer equity options, and dealer securities futures contracts (known collectively as "Section 1256 contracts") are treated as if they were sold on the last day of the year. Any capital gains or losses arising under this rule are treated as if they were 60% long-term and 40% short-term without regard to the actual holding period (Code Sec. 1256(a)).[67]

Hedging transactions generally are exempt from the straddle rules. However, special rules apply to restrict limited partners' and limited entrepreneurs' deductions for hedging losses (Code Secs. 1092(e) and 1256(e)–(f)).[68] See ¶ 1949 for discussion of hedging transactions. Special rules also apply to grantors of qualified covered call options (Code Sec. 1092(c)(4)) and options market-makers and commodities traders (Code Sec. 1256(f)).

Taxpayers are also prohibited from converting ordinary income into capital gains through the use of straddle transactions if substantially all the taxpayer's expected return is attributable to the time value of his net investment. These rules generally do not apply to the normal trade of options dealers (Code Sec. 1258(d)(5)).[69]

1949. Hedging Transactions. A hedging transaction is one a taxpayer enters into in the normal course of business primarily to reduce the risk of interest rate or price

---

Footnote references are to paragraphs of the 2008 Standard Federal Tax Reports.

[64] ¶ 13,700	[66] ¶ 30,200	[68] ¶ 30,200, ¶ 31,100
[65] ¶ 13,700	[67] ¶ 31,100	[69] ¶ 31,128.03

¶1946

changes or currency fluctuations (Code Sec. 1221(a)(7); Reg. § 1.1221-2).[70] Generally, the property involved in a hedging transaction is not classified as a capital asset. As a result, gain or loss on most hedging transactions is classified as ordinary income or loss. This rule also applies when a short sale or option is part of a hedging transaction (Reg. § 1.1221-2(a)(2)).[71]

In order to be classified as a hedging transaction, the transaction must be entered into in the normal course of the taxpayer's business in order to manage risk. For example, the risk that the taxpayer seeks to manage may involve such events as price changes, interest rate changes, or currency fluctuations (Reg. § 1.1221-2(b)).[72] The determination of whether a transaction was entered into in order to manage the taxpayer's business risk is based upon all the facts and circumstances (Reg. § 1.1221-2(c)(3)). A transaction that is not a hedging transaction may be a straddle. See ¶ 1948 for discussion of straddles.

Identification. The hedging transaction must be identified before the close of the day on which the taxpayer entered into the transaction (Reg. § 1.1221-2(f)(1)).[73] The taxpayer must identify the property that is being hedged within 35 days after the transaction is entered into (Reg. § 1.1221-2(f)(2)). The taxpayer's identification of the hedged property must be unambiguous and become part of the taxpayer's books and records (Reg. § 1.1221-2(f)(4)).

Corporate Bonds and Other Debt Instruments

1950. Discounts, Premiums, and Issue Expenses. A bond is issued at a *discount* when the issue price is less than the face value of the bond. A bond is issued at a *premium* when the issue price is more than the amount payable at maturity. The amount received as a premium must generally be amortized by the issuer and used as an offset against its allowable interest deduction (Reg. § 1.163-13(a)). Any expenses related to issuing the bond (that is, printing, advertising, legal fees) are amortized over the life of the bond and deducted as business expenses.[74]

1952. Original Issue Discount. "Original issue discount" (OID) is the difference between the issue price (as defined in Code Sec. 1273(b))[75] of a debt instrument and its stated redemption price at maturity. If the difference is less than ¼ of 1% per year on the redemption price from the date of issue to the date of maturity, the OID is "zero" (Code Sec. 1273(a)(3)).[76]

Income Inclusion. Holders of bonds and debt instruments having a more-than-one-year maturity and originally issued after July 1, 1982, must include in income the sum of the daily portion of original issue discount determined for each day during the tax year the instrument is held (Code Sec. 1272(a)(1)). However, this rule does not apply to certain debt obligations (e.g., certain loans between natural persons, tax-exempt obligations, or U.S. savings bonds) (Code Sec. 1272(a)(2)).[77]

A holder's basis in a bond is increased by the amount of OID that has been required to be included in the holder's gross income (Code Sec. 1272(d)(2)).[78]

Interest Deduction. In the case of any debt instrument issued after July 1, 1982, the portion of OID allowable as a deduction to the issuer for any tax year is equal to the aggregate daily portions of the OID for days during that tax year (Code Sec. 163(e)).[79] The daily portions of OID for any day are to be determined under the formula contained in Code Sec. 1272(a)(3).[80]

Information Statement for Recipients. Any issuer with any bond outstanding or any other evidence of indebtedness in registered form issued at a discount must generally furnish the holder and the IRS with an information statement (Form 1099-OID) for the calendar year if there is OID of at least $10 (Code Sec. 6049(c)).[81]

Stripped Bonds and Stripped Coupons. Special rules govern stripped bonds and stripped coupons purchased or sold after July 1, 1982 (Code Sec. 1286(a)).[82] Under this type of arrangement, one taxpayer strips an interest coupon from a bond and sells either the bond or the coupon. The bond and the coupon are treated as separate debt

---

Footnote references are to paragraphs of the 2008 Standard Federal Tax Reports.

[70] ¶ 30,420, ¶ 30,424
[71] ¶ 30,424
[72] ¶ 30,424
[73] ¶ 30,424
[74] ¶ 5804.01, ¶ 5804.22

[75] ¶ 31,280
[76] ¶ 31,280
[77] ¶ 31,260, ¶ 31,262
[78] ¶ 31,260
[79] ¶ 9102

[80] ¶ 31,260, ¶ 31,262.04
[81] ¶ 36,020
[82] ¶ 31,480, ¶ 31,481

instruments issued with an OID. The buyer of a stripped bond treats as OID the bond's value at maturity minus the price paid by the buyer. The buyer of a stripped coupon treats as OID the interest to be paid on the due date of the coupon minus the price paid by the buyer (Code Sec. 1286(a)). The seller of the stripped coupon or stripped bond must include in income the interest that accrued before the date of sale and that was not previously included in income. Market discount must also be included in the seller's income. Both of these included items increase the seller's basis in the bond and coupons. The seller then allocates this adjusted basis between the item kept (e.g., the bond) and the item sold (e.g., the coupon) based on the fair market value of the items. The difference between the sales price of the item and its adjusted basis is the seller's gain or loss (Code Sec. 1286(b)).[83]

Stripped Stock. Preferred stock purchased after April 30, 1993, that has been stripped of some or all of its dividend rights is treated in the same manner as stripped bonds. OID is equal to the stated redemption price minus the amount paid for the stock (Code Sec. 305(e)).[84]

Tax-Exempt and Stripped Tax-Exempt Bonds. OID on a tax-exempt bond is generally treated as tax-exempt interest. However, when a tax-exempt bond is stripped, only a portion of the OID is treated as coming from a tax-exempt obligation. The balance is treated as OID on a taxable obligation. The Code contains the rules for determining the tax-exempt portion of the OID (Code Sec. 1286(d)).[85] See ¶ 1956 for related information.

1954. Certain Debt Instruments Issued for Property. Generally, whenever a sale of property involves the issuance of a debt instrument with deferred payments, Code Sec. 1274 operates to ensure that adequate interest is charged and paid on the obligation (Code Sec. 1274(a)).[86] Code Sec. 1274 applies to an instrument if:

    (1) some or all of the payments under the instrument are due more than six months after the sale and

    (2) the stated redemption price at maturity of the instrument exceeds:

        (a) the instrument's stated principal amount, if there is adequate stated interest; or

        (b) its imputed principal amount, if there is not adequate stated interest.

Exemptions. Exemptions from Code Sec. 1274 coverage are provided for debt instruments arising from (Code Sec. 1274(c)(3)):

    (1) sales for $250,000 or less;

    (2) sales of principal residences covered by Code Sec. 121;

    (3) sales of farms by individuals, estates, testamentary trusts, or small business corporations or partnerships for $1 million or less;

    (4) land transfers between related parties that are covered by Code Sec. 483(e);

    (5) sales of patents for amounts that are contingent on the productivity, use, or disposition of the property transferred; or

    (6) in the case of the borrower, sales or exchanges of personal use property (Code Sec. 1275(b)).[87]

If a debt-for-property transaction is not covered by the Code Sec. 1274 rules, the transaction may be subject to the imputed interest rules of Code Sec. 483 (see ¶ 1859).

    Certain annuity contracts governed by Code Sec. 72 are excluded from the definition of "debt instrument" (Code Sec. 1275(a)(1)(B)).[88]

Adequate Interest. Interest is adequate if an instrument's stated principal amount is less than or equal to its imputed principal amount. The imputed principal amount is determined by totaling the present values of all payments due on the instrument discounted at the applicable federal rate (AFR). For transactions in which a debt instrument is given in consideration for the sale or exchange of property (other than new Code Sec. 38 property) and the stated principal amount of the instrument does not exceed an inflation-adjusted amount (e.g., $4,800,800 for 2007) (Rev. Rul. 2007-4), a 9%

Footnote references are to paragraphs of the 2008 Standard Federal Tax Reports.

[83] ¶ 31,480
[84] ¶ 15,303
[85] ¶ 31,480.23
[86] ¶ 31,300
[87] ¶ 31,340
[88] ¶ 31,340

¶1954

rate may be substituted for the AFR (Code Sec. 1274A).[89] For a sale-leaseback transaction, a rate equal to 110% of the AFR applies (Code Sec. 1274(e)).

Joint Election. For sales or exchanges of property (other than new Code Sec. 38 property), the lender and borrower may jointly elect out of the Code Sec. 1274 rules and take the interest on the debt instrument into account under the cash method of accounting. The election can be made only if:

> (1) the stated principal amount of the instrument does not exceed an inflation adjusted amount (e.g., $3,429,100 for 2007) (Rev. Rul. 2007-4);

> (2) the lender is on the cash-basis method of accounting and is not a dealer with respect to the property sold or exchanged; and

> (3) the Code Sec. 1274 rules would otherwise have applied to the transaction (Code Sec. 1274A(c)).[90]

Applicable Federal Rate. The applicable federal rate, which is determined monthly, will depend upon the maturity of the debt instrument. See ¶ 83.

1956. OID on Tax-Exempt Bonds. Although OID on tax-exempt obligations is exempt from federal income tax, OID must be accrued for purposes of increasing the holder's tax basis in determining gain or loss if the bond is sold prior to maturity (Code Sec. 1288).[91] The holder is to accrue OID for various "accrual periods" using the constant-interest method, under which OID is allocated over the life of a bond by making adjustments to the issue price of the bond for each accrual period. The amount of OID allocated over an accrual period is determined by (1) multiplying the adjusted issue price of the bond by its yield to maturity and then (2) subtracting the interest payable as "qualified periodic interest" from the product. In determining OID on tax-exempt obligations, tax-exempt interest must be excluded. The tables at ¶ 84 present applicable federal interest rates that have been adjusted to account for tax-exempt interest (Code Sec. 1272(a)).[92] A portion of OID on a stripped tax-exempt obligation may be subject to tax. See ¶ 1952 for information.

1958. Market Discount Bonds. Gain from the sale of a market discount bond purchased after April 30, 1993, is treated as ordinary income to the extent of accrued market discount on the bond (Code Sec. 1276). A market discount bond is a bond that was purchased at a discount from face value.

If the bond was originally issued at a discount, then the bond's revised issue price, or original issue price plus accrued OID, is substituted for the purchase price to determine if the bond is a market discount bond. Market discount bonds do not include obligations that mature within one year of issuance, U.S. savings bonds, installment bonds, and tax-exempt bonds purchased before May 1, 1993. The accrued market discount on a bond may be figured under either the ratable accrual method (Code Sec. 1276(b)(1)) or, upon the irrevocable election of the taxpayer with respect to a particular bond, the constant interest method (Code Sec. 1276(b)(2)).[93] Instead of recognizing interest income upon the disposition of a market discount bond, a taxpayer may elect to include market discount in income currently using either the ratable accrual method or the constant interest method (Code Sec. 1278(b)(1)(B)).[94] This election, which is revocable only with the consent of the IRS, applies to all market discount bonds acquired during and after the tax year of the election. The election is made by filing a statement with the taxpayer's timely filed tax return that states that the market discount has been included in income under the provisions of Code Sec. 1276(b). The statement should also indicate how the amount included in income was calculated (Rev. Proc. 92-67).

Any partial payment of principal on a market discount bond is ordinary income to the extent of accrued market discount on the bond for obligations acquired after October 22, 1986 (Code Sec. 1276(a)(3)).[95] The payment that is included in gross income will reduce the amount of accrued market discount.

Net direct interest expenses on debt incurred to purchase or continue a market discount bond acquired after July 18, 1984, may be deducted currently only to the extent

---

Footnote references are to paragraphs of the 2008 Standard Federal Tax Reports.

[89] ¶ 31,320
[90] ¶ 31,320
[91] ¶ 31,520, ¶ 31,521

[92] ¶ 31,260
[93] ¶ 31,360
[94] ¶ 31,400

[95] ¶ 31,360

that the expenses exceed the market discount allocable to the number of days the bond is held by the taxpayer (Code Sec. 1277).[96] The taxpayer may elect to take any deferred interest deduction in a subsequent year to the extent of net interest income from the market discount bond. Any deferred interest expense that remains (whether or not the election is made) is deducted in the year of disposition.

1961. Discount on Short-Term Obligations. For short-term governmental obligations that have a fixed maturity date that is not more than one year from the date of issuance, certain taxpayers are required to accrue the acquisition discount in income along with any interest payable on the obligation. An obligation for this purpose includes a bond, debenture, note, certificate, or other evidence of debt, but not a tax-exempt obligation (Code Sec. 1283(a)(1)). Accrual of acquisition discount is required on short-term obligations:

(1) held by accrual method taxpayers;

(2) held by banks;

(3) held primarily for sale to customers in the ordinary course of trade or business;

(4) held by regulated investment companies or common trust funds;

(5) that have been identified by the taxpayer as part of a hedging transaction under Code Sec. 1256(e)(2);[97] and

(6) that are stripped bonds or coupons while held by the person who stripped them or someone else whose basis in them is determined by reference to the basis in his hands (Code Sec. 1281(b)).[98]

In the case of short-term obligations other than government obligations, current inclusion under the OID rules applies unless the holder elects to use the acquisition discount rules (Code Sec. 1283(c)).[99]

Net direct interest expense is deductible only to the extent that it exceeds the sum of (1) the acquisition discount (excess of stated redemption price over basis) for each day during the year that the bond is held by the taxpayer and (2) the amount of any interest payable on the obligation that accrues during the year but is not included in gross income for that year because of the taxpayer's accounting method. The daily portion of the acquisition discount is equal to the total discount divided by the number of days from the acquisition date to the maturity date (Code Secs. 1282(a) and 1283(b)(1)).[100]

1963. Unregistered Obligations. Most corporate and government obligations are required to be in registered form if the payor is to deduct interest (Code Sec. 163(f)(1)).[101] An excise tax is imposed on issues of registration-required obligations (other than tax-exempt bonds) that are not in registered form (Code Sec. 4701).[102] The excise tax is equal to one percent of the principal amount of the obligation multiplied by the number of calendar years (or portions thereof) during the term of the obligation (Code Sec. 4701(a)). This is the period beginning on the date of issuance of the obligation and ending on the date of maturity.

If a registration-required obligation is not in registered form, any gain realized on its sale or other disposition is taxed as ordinary income (Code Sec. 1287)[103] and loss deductions will be denied (Code Sec. 165(j))[104] unless the issuance of the obligation was subject to the excise tax under Code Sec. 4701 or certain other specified exceptions under Code Sec. 165(j)(3) apply. Issuers of registration-required obligations face the loss of deductions for interest (including OID) on the bonds (Code Sec. 163(f))[105] and cannot reduce earnings and profits by the amount of any interest on the obligation (Code Sec. 312(m)).[106]

1965. Discounted U.S. Bonds Received in Tax-Free Exchange. Some types of U.S. savings bonds may be exchanged tax free for other types of U.S. savings bonds (see

Footnote references are to paragraphs of the 2008 Standard Federal Tax Reports.

[96] ¶31,380
[97] ¶31,100
[98] ¶31,420
[99] ¶31,460
[100] ¶31,440, ¶31,460
[101] ¶9102
[102] ¶33,941
[103] ¶31,500
[104] ¶9802
[105] ¶9102
[106] ¶15,600

¶ 730) (Code Sec. 1037).[107] When the original bond was issued at a discount, an amount equal to what would have been ordinary income from OID if the exchange had been taxable is ordinary income when the bond received in exchange is disposed of or redeemed at a gain.

1967. Bond Premium Amortization by Bondholder. When a bond owner has paid a premium over the face amount of a taxable bond, he has the option of (1) amortizing the premium until bond maturity and reducing his basis in the bond by the amortized amount or (2) not amortizing and treating the premium as part of his bond basis (Code Sec. 171(a)(1)).[108] The amortization method must be elected (Reg. § 1.171-4).[109] The taxpayer makes the election by reporting the amortization on the tax return for the first year the election is to apply and attaching a statement to the tax return that the amortization election is being made under Code Sec. 171. For a dealer in municipal bonds, see ¶ 1970.

No amortization is allowed for tax-exempt bonds. However, reduction in the basis of the bond by the amount of the bond premium is required (Code Sec. 1016(a)(5)).[110] Generally for taxable bonds, the amount of bond premium that can be amortized for a tax year (and deducted currently) is calculated under a constant yield method (Code Sec. 171(b)).[111]

If a bond is received in an exchange and the basis of the bond is determined at least in part from the basis of the property given up in the exchange, the basis of the bond cannot exceed its fair market value immediately after the exchange for purposes of determining bond premium. This rule generally does not apply to an exchange of securities in a reorganization (Code Sec. 171(b)(4)).[112]

Premium on Convertible Bond. Amortization is not allowed for any part of a premium that is paid for the conversion feature in a convertible bond (Code Sec. 171(b)(1); Reg. § 1.171-2).[113] A corporation's deduction for the premium it is called upon to pay to repurchase its own convertible indebtedness is generally limited to the amount of the normal call premium (Code Sec. 249(a)).[114]

1970. Dealer in Tax-Exempt Bonds. A dealer in tax-exempt obligations must amortize any premiums just as if the interest on the bonds had been taxable. A dealer who does not inventory his securities or who inventories them at cost must reduce the adjusted basis of any municipal bonds he sells during the year by the total amortization for the period they were held. A dealer who values his inventories at other than cost (for example, market value) must annually reduce the "cost of securities sold" by amortization on municipal bonds held during the year (Code Sec. 75(a)).

When a tax-exempt obligation is purchased and is sold or otherwise disposed of within 30 days after acquisition, or matures or is callable more than five years after it is acquired, an amortization adjustment must be made unless the bond is sold or disposed of at a gain. Thus, a dealer who inventories at other than cost and holds at the end of the year a bond maturing or callable more than five years after acquisition does not have to reflect amortization on it in his "cost of securities sold." If it is sold at a gain, no amortization adjustment is to be made. If it is not sold at a gain, his "cost of securities sold" is then reduced by the amortization for the entire period it was held (Code Sec. 75(b)(1); Reg. § 1.75-1).[115]

Accounting Issues

1973. Time of Sale. Taxpayers who sell stock or securities traded on an established securities market must recognize gains and losses on the *trade date* and not on the settlement date. This rule holds true even if the taxpayer uses the accrual method of accounting. The installment rules do not apply to these sales (Code Sec. 453(k)).[116] See ¶ 1777 for the rules used to determine whether the taxpayer's holding period was short term or long term.

Footnote references are to paragraphs of the 2008 Standard Federal Tax Reports.

[107] ¶ 29,720, ¶ 29,723	[111] ¶ 11,850	[115] ¶ 6250, ¶ 6251
[108] ¶ 11,850	[112] ¶ 11,850	[116] ¶ 21,402
[109] ¶ 11,854	[113] ¶ 11,850, ¶ 11,852	
[110] ¶ 29,410	[114] ¶ 13,400	

1975. Identification of Stock. When a taxpayer can identify the shares of stock or bonds sold, his basis is the cost or other basis of the particular shares of stock or bonds. However, if a taxpayer buys and sells securities at various times in varying quantities and cannot adequately identify the shares that are sold, the basis of the securities sold is the basis of the securities acquired first (Reg. § 1.1012-1(c)).[117] See " *First-In, First-Out'* Rule," below. Except for mutual fund shares, a taxpayer may *not* use the average price per share to figure gain or loss on the sale of the shares.

Mutual Fund Shares. An owner of mutual fund shares may choose to use the average basis of shares owned in the fund if the shares were acquired at various times and prices and if they were left on deposit in an account kept by a custodian or agent for receiving or redeeming the shares (Reg. § 1.1012-1(e)).[118] The average basis is determined by using either the double-category method or the single-category method. Under the double-category method, all shares in an account at the time of each sale of shares are divided into two categories: those held for the long-term capital gain holding period and those held for the short-term capital gain holding period. The cost or other basis of each share in a category is the cost or other basis of all shares in that category at the time of the sale divided by the total number of shares in the category. Under the single-category method, all shares in an account are combined.[119]

"First-In, First-Out" Rule. If stock is sold from lots purchased on different dates and at different prices and the identity of the lots cannot be determined, the stock sold must ordinarily be charged first against the earliest purchases (Reg. § 1.1012-1(c)).[120] Most courts hold, however, that after a nontaxable reorganization in which the taxpayer receives shares of stock in another corporation in exchange for the original shares, the "first-in, first-out" rule is not applicable.[121]

1977. Allocation of Cost of Shares. When securities of different classes are purchased as a unit, as when one share of preferred and two of common stock are bought for a lump sum, their cost should be apportioned between the different classes according to their respective fair market values when acquired. If this is impracticable, no gain or loss is realized from any sale until after the proceeds exceed the aggregate cost of the entire unit.[122]

1980. Margin Trading Account. A margin trading account is not a unitary investment, and a taxpayer cannot merely report net gains or losses.[123] The records and tax return must account for each transaction.

1983. Commissions. Commissions paid on the *purchase* of securities are not deductible, either as business or nonbusiness expenses. Instead, these fees must be added to the taxpayer's cost of the securities. Commissions paid on the *sale* of securities are deductible as business expenses only by dealers in securities (Reg. § 1.263(a)-2(e)).[124] Traders and investors must treat selling commissions as an offset against the selling price.[125] See ¶ 1760 for information concerning the proper classification of a taxpayer as a trader, dealer or investor.

A "wrap fee" on a brokerage account, paid by an investor in lieu of commissions on individual trades, is a currently deductible investment expense and is claimed as a miscellaneous itemized deduction on the individual's Schedule A (IRS Chief Counsel Advice 200721015).

Footnote references are to paragraphs of the 2008 Standard Federal Tax Reports.

[117] ¶ 29,331
[118] ¶ 29,331
[119] ¶ 29,335.03

[120] ¶ 29,331, ¶ 29,336
[121] ¶ 29,336.451
[122] ¶ 29,313.005

[123] ¶ 9805.912
[124] ¶ 13,703
[125] ¶ 8521.1484

Chapter 20

TAX SHELTERS ☐ AT-RISK
RULES ☐ PASSIVE LOSSES

Administrative Provisions

2001. Tax Shelter Defined. Prior to October 23, 2004, the term "tax shelter" was defined as any investment that met certain criteria with respect to the "tax shelter ratio," and that had to be registered under relevant federal securities law (or was a substantial investment, or was sold under an exception to the registration requirements that required the filing of a notice with a governmental agency) (Temporary Reg. § 301.6111-1T, Q&A 4). Other entities, plans, arrangements or transactions could also be considered tax shelters if they had as a significant purpose the avoidance or evasion of federal income tax for a corporate participant (Code Sec. 6111(d), prior to amendment by the American Jobs Creation Act of 2004 (P.L. 108-357); Reg. § 301.6111-2(a)). However, effective on that date, the IRS now investigates "reportable transactions," rather than tax shelters.

> **Comment:** Although the regulation defining tax shelters has not been withdrawn, it does not reflect the statutory changes that took effect in 2004.

> See ¶ 2005 for the definition and discussion of reportable transactions, material advisors, and other currently applicable terms.

2004. Registration of Tax Shelters. An organizer of a tax shelter, including a confidential corporate tax shelter, was required to register the shelter with the IRS on Form 8264 (Code Sec. 6111(a), prior to amendment by the American Jobs Creation Act of 2004 (P.L. 108-357)).[1] If the principal organizer did not do so, the duty fell upon any other participant in the organization of the shelter or any person participating in its sale or management. These rules with respect to registration of tax shelters have been repealed. Instead, each material advisor with respect to any reportable transaction (including any listed transaction) is required to timely file an information return with the IRS (in whatever form and manner the IRS may prescribe) (Code Sec. 6111). The return must be filed on whatever date is specified by the IRS.

The repeal of the tax shelter rules and replacement with the rules requiring disclosure of reportable transactions by material advisors applies to transactions with

---

Footnote references are to paragraphs of the 2008 Standard Federal Tax Reports.

[1] ¶ 37,000, ¶ 37,002

respect to which material aid, assistance or advice is provided after October 22, 2004. The penalty for failure to furnish information regarding reportable transactions applies to returns the due date of which is after October 22, 2004 (Act Sec. 816(c) of the American Jobs Creation Act of 2004 (P.L. 108-357)). For further information about the rules requiring disclosure of reportable transactions by material advisors and the penalties that apply to failure to follow those rules, see ¶ 2005.

2005. Reportable Transactions. Each material advisor is required to timely file an information return with the IRS for any reportable transaction, including any listed transaction (Code Sec. 6111(a)).[2] The return must be filed with the IRS in the form and manner and on the date that the IRS prescribes.

The material advisor's information return will include: (1) information identifying and describing the transaction; (2) information describing any potential tax benefits expected to result from the transaction; and (3) such other information as the IRS may prescribe. It is expected that the IRS may seek from the material advisor the same type of information that the IRS may request from a taxpayer in connection with a reportable transaction.

A material advisor means any person: (1) who provides material aid, assistance, or advice with respect to organizing, promoting, selling, implementing, or carrying out any reportable transaction and (2) who directly or indirectly derives gross income in excess of $250,000 ($50,000 in the case of a reportable transaction substantially all of the tax benefits from which are provided to natural persons) for such aid, assistance, or advice (Code Sec. 6111(b)).

The IRS may prescribe regulations which provide: (1) that only one material advisor has to file an information return in cases in which two or more material advisors would otherwise be required to file information returns with respect to a particular reportable transaction; (2) exemptions from the requirements of this section; and (3) other rules as may be necessary or appropriate to carry out the purposes of this section (including, for example, rules regarding the aggregation of fees in appropriate circumstances) (Code Sec. 6111(c)).

The term "reportable transaction" means any transaction with respect to which information is required to be included with a return or statement because, as determined under regulations prescribed under the general requirements for returns, statements or lists (Code Sec. 6011), that transaction is of a type which the IRS determines as having a potential for tax avoidance or evasion (Code Sec. 6707A(c)(1)). The IRS had issued regulations that define reportable transactions (Reg. § 1.6011-4, as amended by T.D. 9350) (see ¶ 2006).

There are five categories of reportable transactions specified in the regulation: listed transactions, confidential transactions, transactions with contractual protection, loss transactions, and transactions of interest (Reg. § 1.6011-4(b), as amended by T.D. 9350). The last category, transactions of interest, is a new category that encompasses transactions that are the same as, or similar to, transactions identified by the IRS by notice, regulation, or other published guidance. A transaction will not be considered a reportable transaction, or will be excluded from any individual category of reportable transaction, if the IRS makes a determination by published guidance that the transaction is not subject to these reporting requirements. The IRS may make a determination by individual letter. Special rules apply for regulated investment companies (RICs) or lease transactions (Reg. § 1.6011-4(b)(8), as amended by T.D. 9350). The IRS has issued guidance which provides that certain losses (Rev. Proc. 2004-66) or certain book-tax differences (Rev. Proc. 2004-67) are not taken into account in determining whether a transaction is a reportable transaction.

Penalties. A penalty is imposed on any material advisor who fails to file an information return, or who files a false or incomplete information return regarding a reportable transaction (including a listed transaction) for returns (Code Sec. 6707(a)). These penalty provisions are intended to be clearer and more meaningful than the former tax shelter registration penalties that they replace. Under this new penalty regime, a $50,000

Footnote references are to paragraphs of the 2008 Standard Federal Tax Reports.

[2] ¶ 37,002.021

penalty is generally assessed for failure to furnish required information with respect to a reportable transaction (Code Sec. 6707(a)). A much stiffer penalty applies to the failure to file a return regarding listed transactions. In such cases, the penalty assessed will be the greater of: (1) $200,000 or (2) 50 percent of the gross income derived by the person required to file the return with respect to aid, assistance, or advice that is provided with respect to the listed transaction. The 50-percent limit in (2), above, is raised to 75 percent in cases involving an intentional failure or act (Code Sec. 6707(b)).

A new, independent penalty is imposed on taxpayers who fail to disclose a reportable transaction (Code Sec. 6707A(a); Notice 2005-11). In the case of natural persons, the amount of the penalty for reportable transactions is $10,000 and $100,000 in the care of listed transactions. The amount of the penalty for all other persons in the case of reportable transactions is $50,000, while it is $200,000 for listed transactions (Code Sec. 6707A(b)).

This information return penalty cannot be waived with respect to a listed transaction (Code Secs. 6707(c) and 6707A(d)). As to reportable transactions other than listed transactions, the penalty can be rescinded (or abated) only in exceptional circumstances (i.e. abatement of the penalty would promote compliance with the tax laws and effective tax administration). The authority to rescind a penalty can only be exercised by the IRS Commissioner personally or the head of the Office of Tax Shelter Analysis; this authority to rescind cannot otherwise be delegated by the Commissioner. Thus, a revenue agent, an Appeals officer, or other IRS personnel cannot rescind the penalty. The decision to rescind a penalty must be accompanied by a record describing the facts and reasons for the action and the amount rescinded. There is no right to appeal a refusal to rescind a penalty (Notice 2005-11).

The IRS has now provided procedures for making a rescission request with respect to penalties under Code Secs. 6707(c) and 6707A(d). Any person seeking rescission of a penalty under these statutes must make a written request within 30 days after the date that the IRS sends notice and demand for payment of the penalty. If the penalty is paid (not including interest) prior to date that notice and demand is sent, the written request must be made within 30 days from the date of payment. In order to request rescission, the person must have either exhausted the administrative remedies available within the IRS Office of Appeals or agreed in writing to the assessment of the penalty and not to file or prosecute a claim for refund or credit of the penalty. The IRS guidance sets forth information items required with the request, as well as factors considered in granting or denying the request. Collection efforts of the IRS will not be suspended because a rescission request has been made (Rev. Proc. 2007-21).

The accuracy-related penalty applicable to tax shelters has been replaced with a new accuracy-related penalty that applies to listed transactions and reportable transactions with a significant tax avoidance purpose (Code Secs. 6662 and 6662A). The penalty rate and defenses available to avoid the penalty vary depending on whether the transaction was adequately disclosed. See ¶ 2854 for discussion of the accuracy-related penalty.

2006. Disclosure Statement. Every taxpayer that has participated directly or indirectly in a reportable transaction and who is required to file a tax return must attach a disclosure statement to its return (Reg. § 1.6011-4(a)).[3] The fact that a transaction is a reportable transaction will not affect the legal determination of whether the taxpayer's treatment of the transaction is proper.

IRS Form 8886, Reportable Transaction Disclosure Statement, must be used as the reportable transaction disclosure statement. The disclosure statement for a reportable transaction must be attached to the taxpayer's tax return for each tax year for which a taxpayer participates in a reportable transaction. In addition, a copy of the disclosure statement must be sent to the Office of Tax Shelter Analysis (OTSA) at the same time that any disclosure statement is first filed with the taxpayer's tax return (Reg. § 1.6011-4(d) and (e), as amended by T.D. 9350). If a reportable transaction results in a loss that is carried back to a prior year, the disclosure statement for the reportable transaction must be attached to the taxpayer's application for tentative refund or

---

Footnote references are to paragraphs of the 2008 Standard Federal Tax Reports.

[3] ¶ 37,001B

amended tax return for that prior year. In the case of a taxpayer that is a partnership, an S corporation, or a beneficiary of a trust, the disclosure statement for a reportable transaction must be attached to the partnership's, S corporation's, or trust's tax return for each tax year in which the partnership, S corporation, or trust participates in the transaction (Reg. § 1.6011-4(e), as amended by T.D. 9350).

Special reporting rules apply to listed transactions and loss transactions. Also, in some cases, taxpayers must make multiple disclosures of a reportable transaction (Reg. § § 1.6011-4(d) and (e), as amended by T.D. 9350). Furthermore, in the case of most transactions with a significant book-tax difference, the taxpayer will be treated as having satisfied the obligation to disclose the transaction if the taxpayer discloses on a Schedule M-3 each item of income, gain, loss, deduction, or credit for which the difference between the amount included in the taxpayer's financial statement net income (loss) for the tax year and the amount included in taxable income for the tax year ("difference") is greater than $10 million (Rev. Proc. 2004-45).

A taxpayer may submit a request to the IRS for a ruling as to whether a transaction is subject to the disclosure requirements. If a taxpayer requests a ruling on the merits of a specific transaction on or before the date that disclosure would otherwise be required and receives a favorable ruling, the disclosure rules will be deemed to have been satisfied. However, such ruling request must fully disclose all relevant facts relating to the transaction. If a taxpayer is uncertain whether a transaction must be disclosed, the taxpayer may make a protective disclosure. The taxpayer must disclose the transaction and indicate on the disclosure statement that the taxpayer is uncertain whether the transaction is required to be disclosed and that the disclosure statement is being filed on a protective basis. In accordance with the instructions to Form 8886, the taxpayer must retain a copy of all documents and other records related to a transaction subject to disclosure. The retained documents and records are those that are material to an understanding of the tax treatment or tax structure of the transaction (Reg. § § 1.6011-4(f) and (g), as amended by T.D. 9350).

2008. Advisee Lists. Each material advisor (as defined in Code Sec. 6111(b)(1)(A); see ¶ 2005) with respect to any reportable transaction (as defined in Code Sec. 6707A(c)) is required to maintain a list identifying each person with respect to whom that advisor acted as a material advisor with respect to the transaction, and containing any other information required by the IRS (Code Sec. 6112(a)). The IRS has set forth, by regulation, the requirements for the preparation and maintenance of advisee lists, including persons required to be included on lists, contents of the list, definitions, and requirements for retention and furnishing of the lists (Reg. § 301.6112-1, as amended by T.D. 9352). Any person required to maintain advisee lists with respect to reportable transactions who receives a written request from the IRS, but who fails to make the lists available within 20 business days, may be assessed a $10,000 penalty for each day of failure after the 20th business day (Code Sec. 6708(a)(1)). The penalty will be applied to persons required to maintain lists who fail to maintain required lists, maintain incomplete lists, or maintain complete lists but do not make them available to the IRS after receiving a written request (Conference Committee Report to the American Jobs Creation Act of 2004 (H.R. Conf. Rep. No. 108-755)). All information that is required to be included in the advisee lists must be retained for seven years (Code Sec. 6112(b)(1)(B)).

Prior Law. Prior to October 23, 2004, a person who organized or sold an interest in a tax shelter subject to the former registration rule (see ¶ 2004) or in any other potentially abusive plan or arrangement was required to maintain a list of the investors (Code Sec. 6112(a), prior to amendment by the American Jobs Creation Act of 2004 (P.L. 108-357); Reg. § 301.6112-1, prior to amendment by T.D. 9352).[4] A $50 penalty could be assessed for each name omitted from the investor list, and the maximum penalty per year was $100,000 (Code Sec. 6708(a), prior to amendment by the American Jobs Creation Act of 2004 (P.L. 108-357)).[5]

2009. Tax Advisor Rules. The IRS has the authority to regulate the practice of persons representing taxpayers before that agency. The rules on practice before the IRS

Footnote references are to paragraphs of the 2008 Standard Federal Tax Reports.

[4] ¶ 37,020   [5] ¶ 40,095, ¶ 40,100.01

are found in Circular 230, which contains specific rules relating to tax shelters. In particular, Circular 230 regulates persons who provide "covered opinions" (as well as other written advice), setting forth best practices and compliance procedures for practitioners (Rules Governing Authority to Practice (Circular 230), § 10.35).[6]

A covered opinion is written advice (including e-mail) that is issued by a practitioner, and that deals with a federal tax issue that arises from a listed transaction, or from a transaction designed with the avoidance or evasion of taxation as a principal or significant purpose of that transaction. A covered opinion must identify and consider all relevant facts and may not be based on unreasonable factual or legal assumptions, representations, statements for findings that the practitioner knows or should know are incorrect or incomplete. Such an opinion must also meet other requirements, such as relating the law to the relevant facts, and not including internally inconsistent legal analyses or conclusions.

Certain types of advice are excluded from the covered opinion requirements, including advice from in-house tax professionals to their employers, advice provided after the client has filed his or her tax return, and negative advice, in which an advisor tells a client that a transaction will not provide the purported tax benefit (Circular 230, § 10.35(b)(2)(ii)).

All covered opinions must disclose compensation arrangements, along with any referral agreements between the practitioner and the person promoting the tax shelter.

2011. Abusive Tax Shelters Penalty. A penalty is imposed against the promoters of abusive tax shelters (Code Sec. 6700(a)).[7] The penalty is 50 percent of the gross income derived, or to be derived, from the abusive plan or arrangement activities engaged in, other than promotion activities involving gross valuation overstatements (Code Sec. 6700(a)). The penalty for promotion of activities involving gross valuation overstatements is an amount equal to the lesser of $1,000 or 100% of the gross income derived, or to be derived, by the promoter from the activity. In applying the penalty, promotion of each entity or activity is a separate activity and each sale of an interest in the shelter is a separate activity. According to the U.S. Court of Appeals for the Fifth Circuit, assessment of the penalty is not barred by any statute of limitations.[8]

2012. Injunctions. An injunction may be obtained with respect to the following acts: (1) promoting an abusive tax shelter (Code Sec. 6700; see ¶ 2011); (2) aiding someone in understating a tax liability in a return or other document (Code Sec. 6701; see ¶ 2518); (3) failing to furnish information about a reportable transaction (Code Sec. 6707; see ¶ 2005); or (4) failing to maintain a list of advisees (also known as an "investor list") (Code Sec. 6708; see ¶ 2008) (Code Sec. 7408).[9] Once a court has enjoined a person from engaging in one or more of the above activities, the court may expand the injunction to include any other activity that is subject to a penalty under tax law (Code Sec. 7408(b)).

2014. Accounting Method. Tax shelters are generally required to use the accrual method of accounting (see ¶ 1515).

Oil, Gas, and Geothermal Wells

2020. Characteristics of Oil and Gas Shelters. There are a number of tax shelters that involve the oil and gas industries. Characteristics of these shelters include: (1) special rules for deducting expenses associated with drilling, in the case of wells outside the United States (see ¶ 989 and ¶ 1425); (2) exemption from the rules limiting the deductibility of passive losses (see ¶ 2053 and following); (3) limitation of deductions under the at-risk rules to the amount that the investor could actually lose in the enterprise (see ¶ 2045); (4) deductibility for depletion of natural resources (although this deduction is not available in computation of the alternative minimum tax; see ¶ 1440); and (5) application of certain special accounting rules.[10]

2025. Recapture of Intangible Drilling Costs. For property placed in service after 1986, when oil, gas, geothermal, or other mineral properties are disposed of, certain

---

Footnote references are to paragraphs of the 2008 Standard Federal Tax Reports.

[6] ¶ 43,808.051, ¶ 43,808.65   [8] ¶ 38,963.42   [10] ¶ 21,817.023, ¶ 39,651G.88
[7] ¶ 40,025, ¶ 40,030   [9] ¶ 41,670, ¶ 41,673.01

expensed costs are recaptured as ordinary income. Exploration and intangible drilling and development costs are recaptured to the extent that they would have been included in the adjusted basis of the property if they had not been deducted. Depletion is subject to recapture to the extent that it reduced the adjusted basis of such property. These recapture rules do not apply to property originally acquired under a binding written contract entered into before September 26, 1985.

For property placed into service before 1987, the amount recaptured is the lower of (1) the amounts deducted for intangible drilling expenses on a productive well that exceed the amounts which would have been allowed had the intangible drilling expenses been charged to a capital account instead of being deducted or (2) the excess of the gain realized from a sale, exchange, or involuntary conversion over the adjusted basis of the property or, in the case of any other disposition, the excess of fair market value over the adjusted basis of the property (Code Sec. 1254).[11]

Recapture is computed on Form 4797, Sale of Business Property.

Farming Operations

2028. Accrual Accounting for Farm Corporations. Certain corporations and partnerships having a corporation as a partner that are engaged in the business of farming must use the accrual method of accounting (Code Sec. 447(a)).[12] In addition, these taxpayers are required to capitalize their preproductive period expenses (see ¶ 999) (Code Sec. 263A).[13]

All farming corporations are subject to the accrual accounting rule except:

(1) S corporations,

(2) corporations or partnerships engaged in the trade or business of operating a nursery or sod farm, or raising or harvesting trees (other than fruit and nut trees), and

(3) corporations having annual gross receipts of $1 million or less for each prior tax year beginning after 1975 (including the receipts of predecessor corporations and members of a controlled group).

A family corporation meets the gross-receipts test if its gross receipts do not exceed $25 million for each prior tax year beginning after 1985. A family corporation is defined as:

(1) any corporation in which at least 50% of the total combined voting power of all classes of voting stock and at least 50% of all other classes of the corporation's stock are owned by members of the same family and

(2) any of the closely held corporations described in Code Sec. 447(h) (Code Sec. 447(d)(2)(c)).[14]

If a corporation or qualified partnership (each of the partners of which is a corporation) has, for a 10-year period ending with its first taxable year after 1975, and for all subsequent years, used an annual accrual method of accounting with respect to its trade or business of farming, and the entity raises crops which are harvested a year or more after planting, it may continue to use this method (Code Sec. 447(g)).[15]

2032. Expenses of Farming Syndicates. A farming syndicate is a tax shelter (Code Sec. 461(i)(4))[16] and must use the accrual method of accounting (see ¶ 1515).

A farming syndicate is any farming partnership or enterprise (other than a corporation that is not an S corporation) if at any time (1) interests in the enterprise or partnership have been offered for sale in an offering required to be registered with any federal or state agency having authority to regulate such offering or (2) more than 35% of the losses during any period are allocable to limited partners or limited entrepreneurs (Code Sec. 464(c)(1)(B)).

A limited entrepreneur is one who has an interest (other than a limited partnership interest) in an enterprise and who does not actively participate in the enterprise's management (Code Sec. 464(e)(2)(A)). An individual will not be treated as a limited

---

Footnote references are to paragraphs of the 2008 Standard Federal Tax Reports.

[11] ¶ 31,066
[12] ¶ 20,700, ¶ 20,701
[13] ¶ 13,800, ¶ 13,833.01
[14] ¶ 20,700, ¶ 20,701.025
[15] ¶ 20,700
[16] ¶ 21,802

partner or limited entrepreneur in a farming enterprise (other than one with respect to which securities have been registered) if the individual:

(1) has his principal residence on the farm on which the farming enterprise is being carried on;

(2) has an interest attributable to active participation in management of the farming enterprise for a period of not less than five years;

(3) as his principal business activity, actively participates in the management of a farming enterprise, regardless of whether he actively participates in the management of the enterprise in question; or

(4) actively participates in the management of another farming enterprise involving the raising of livestock (or is so treated under either (1) or (2)) and owns an interest in an enterprise involving the further processing of the livestock raised in the enterprise.

If an individual meets any of these conditions, any member of his family who owns an interest in a farming enterprise that is attributable to the individual's active participation will not be treated as a limited partner or limited entrepreneur (Code Sec. 464(c)(2)).[17]

Cash-method farmers who purchase feed, seed and similar supplies for use in a later tax year are limited in their ability to claim current deductions for these prepaid expenses. To the extent that prepaid farm expenses (including prepaid poultry expenses) exceed 50% of total deductible farming expenses, these expenses may be deducted only when used or consumed.

If the farmer qualifies for one of two possible exceptions, he may deduct the cost of the prepaid expenses (Code Sec. 464(f)).[18] The first exception applies if a farm-related taxpayer satisfies the 50% test on the basis of the three preceding years. The second exception applies if a farm-related taxpayer fails to satisfy the 50% test due to a change in business operations directly attributable to extraordinary circumstances.

Economic Performance

2042. Prepaid Expenses. Under Code Sec. 461(i),[19] a tax shelter is prohibited from using the recurring-item exception to the economic performance rule (see ¶ 1539). However, economic performance with respect to the drilling of an oil or gas well will be considered to have occurred within a tax year if drilling commences within 90 days of the close of the tax year. For purposes of these rules, a tax shelter is:

(1) any enterprise (other than a C corporation) that is required to register its offering with a state or federal agency,

(2) any partnership, entity, plan, or arrangement, the significant purpose of which is tax evasion or avoidance, and

(3) any partnership or entity (other than a C corporation) if more than 35% of its losses are allocable to limited partners or limited entrepreneurs.

Limitations on Loss Deductions

2045. Limit of Losses to Amount at Risk. Code Sec. 465 generally limits a taxpayer's deductible loss to the amount that the taxpayer has at risk with respect to an activity.[20] The rules, which apply to individuals and certain closely held corporations, are designed to prevent taxpayers from offsetting trade, business, or professional income by losses from investments in activities that are largely financed by nonrecourse loans for which they are not personally liable. Even if it has been determined that the loss is deductible under the at-risk rules, the loss may still be limited by the passive activity loss rules (see ¶ 2053).

Under the at-risk rules, loss deductions are limited to the amount of the taxpayer's cash contribution and the adjusted basis of other property which he contributes to the activity, plus any amounts borrowed for use in the activity if the taxpayer has personal liability for the borrowed amounts or has pledged assets not used in the activity as

---

Footnote references are to paragraphs of the 2008 Standard Federal Tax Reports.

[17] ¶ 21,840, ¶ 21,843
[18] ¶ 21,840, ¶ 21,843
[19] ¶ 21,802, ¶ 21,817
[20] ¶ 21,850, ¶ 21,893

security for the borrowed amounts. The taxpayer will not be considered at risk with respect to amounts protected against loss through nonrecourse financing, guarantees, stop-loss agreements, or similar arrangements (Code Sec. 465(b)).[21] Also, amounts are not at risk if they are borrowed from (1) a creditor who has an interest other than as a creditor (which has been defined as a capital or net profits interest) or (2) a person related to a person with such an interest (Code Sec. 465(b)(3); Reg. §§ 1.465-8 and 1.465-20).[22]

Personal liability of the taxpayer for borrowed amounts generally hinges on whether the taxpayer is the ultimate obligor of the liability with no recourse against any other party.[23]

Generally, the at-risk rules apply to all activities engaged in as a trade or business or for the production of income (Code Sec. 465(c)),[24] which specifically includes:

    (1) holding, producing, or distributing motion pictures or video tapes,

    (2) farming,

    (3) leasing of Sec. 1245 property (see ¶ 1785),

    (4) exploring for, or exploiting, oil and gas resources, and

    (5) exploring for, or exploiting, geothermal deposits.

For investment tax credit at-risk rules, see ¶ 1356.

The two activities not subject to the at-risk rules are: (1) the holding of real estate (other than mineral property) placed in service before January 1, 1987, and (2) the leasing of equipment by closely held corporations (i.e., those with five or fewer individuals owning more than 50% of the stock) (Code Sec. 465(c)(4)).

In the case of the five specifically identified activities above, each film or tape, each piece of Sec. 1245 property, each farm and each oil, gas, or geothermal property is treated as a separate activity. However, for a partnership or an S corporation, all leased Sec. 1245 properties that are placed in service in the same tax year are treated as a single activity (Code Sec. 465(c)).[25] Trade or business activities subject to the at-risk rules are to be aggregated and treated as a single activity if the taxpayer actively participates in the management of the trade or business or, where the trade or business is carried on by a partnership or S corporation, if 65% or more of the losses for the tax year are allocable to persons who actively participate in the management (Code Sec. 465(c)(3)(B)).

Form 6198 is used to compute the deductible loss, if any, under the at-risk rules.

Limitations on Losses and Credits

2053. General Rules. Generally, losses from passive activities may not be deducted from nonpassive income (for example, wages, interest, or dividends) (Code Sec. 469).[26] Similarly, tax credits from passive activities are generally limited to the tax allocable to those activities. In determining a taxpayer's allowable loss, the at-risk rules discussed at ¶ 2045 are applied before the passive activity loss rules.

Generally, to the extent that the total deductions from passive activities exceed the total income from these activities for the tax year, the excess (the passive activity loss) is not allowed as a deduction for that year. A disallowed loss is suspended and carried forward as a deduction from the passive activity in the next succeeding tax year (Reg. § 1.469-1(f)(4)).[27] Any unused suspended losses are allowed in full when the taxpayer disposes of his entire interest in the activity in a fully taxable transaction (Code Sec. 469(g)) (see ¶ 2076).[28]

Special rules apply to rental real estate activities in which a taxpayer actively participates (see ¶ 2063). Losses and credits that are attributable to limited partnership interests are generally treated as arising from a passive activity (Code Sec. 469(h)(2)).[29] See ¶ 2059. Losses from a working interest in oil and gas property are not subject to the passive activity limitations if the working interest is held directly or through an entity

---

Footnote references are to paragraphs of the 2008 Standard Federal Tax Reports.

[21] ¶ 21,850, ¶ 21,893.05	[24] ¶ 21,850, ¶ 21,893.025	[27] ¶ 21,961B
[22] ¶ 21,850, ¶ 21,893.05	[25] ¶ 21,850, ¶ 21,893.027	[28] ¶ 21,960
[23] ¶ 21,893.35	[26] ¶ 21,960, ¶ 21,966	[29] ¶ 21,960

that does not limit liability, such as an interest as a general partner (Code Sec. 469(c)(3); Temp. Reg. § 1.469-1T(e)(4)(ii)).[30]

Forms. Most taxpayers use Forms 8582 and 8582-CR to calculate their allowable passive losses and credits. Form 8810 is used by personal service corporations and closely held C corporations. Form 8825 is used by partnerships and S corporations to report income and deductible expenses from rental real estate activities.

2054. Publicly Traded Partnerships. Special rules apply to losses from publicly traded partnerships (PTPs). A PTP is a partnership whose interests are traded on an established securities market or are readily tradable on a secondary market (or its substantial equivalent) (Code Sec. 469(k)(2)).[31] A taxpayer's net income from a PTP may not be used to offset net losses from other PTPs or net losses from other passive activities.[32] A disallowed loss from a PTP is carried forward and allowed as a deduction in a tax year when the PTP has net income or when the taxpayer disposes of his entire interest in the PTP (Code Sec. 469(k)).[33]

Mutual funds, which are taxed under the regulated investment company (RIC) rules (see ¶ 403, ¶ 2301, and ¶ 2054), may invest in PTPs while retaining their RIC status. The income from the PTP is treated as passive activity income to the investing fund, and losses from the PTP are passive losses which cannot be used to offset any income other than from the same PTP (Code Sec. 469(k)(4)).[34]

2056. Taxpayers Covered. The passive activity rules apply to individuals, estates, trusts (other than grantor trusts), and personal service corporations (Code Sec. 469(a)(2)).[35] Although the passive activity rules do not apply to grantor trusts, partnerships, and S corporations directly, the owners of these entities are subject to the rules. See ¶ 2054 for discussion of special rules applicable to publicly traded partnerships.

Closely Held C Corporations. A rule preventing the offset of passive activity losses against portfolio income, but not against net active income, applies to closely held C corporations (other than personal service corporations). A closely held C corporation's net active income is equal to its taxable income figured without any income or loss from a passive activity or any portfolio income or loss (Code Sec. 469(e)(2)(A)).[36]

2058. Activity Defined. In order to correctly apply the passive loss rules, taxpayers must determine which of their operations constitute an "activity." For tax years ending after May 10, 1992, an activity is defined under Reg. § 1.469-4.[37]

One or more trade or business activities are treated as a single activity if they constitute an appropriate economic unit for the measurement of gain or loss for PAL purposes (Reg. § 1.469-4(c)).[38] Five factors listed in the regulations are given the greatest weight in determining whether an activity or group of activities constitutes an appropriate economic unit:

    (1) similarities or differences in types of business,

    (2) extent of common control,

    (3) extent of common ownership,

    (4) geographical location, and

    (5) business interdependencies among the activities.[39]

Once activities are grouped together or kept separate, they may not be regrouped by the taxpayer in future years unless the original grouping was clearly inappropriate or became inappropriate due to a material change in facts and circumstances (Reg. § 1.469-4(e)).[40] The IRS may disallow and regroup a taxpayer's grouping of activities that does not reflect an appropriate economic unit and has circumvention of the passive activity loss rules as a primary purpose (Reg. § 1.469-4(f)(1)).[41]

Footnote references are to paragraphs of the 2008 Standard Federal Tax Reports.

[30] ¶ 21,960	[34] ¶ 21,966.001, ¶ 21,966.059	[38] ¶ 21,964B
[31] ¶ 21,960	[35] ¶ 21,960, ¶ 21,966.02	[39] ¶ 21,966.031
[32] ¶ 21,966.059	[36] ¶ 21,960, ¶ 21,966.0205,	[40] ¶ 21,964B, ¶ 21,966.031
[33] ¶ 21,960	¶ 21,966.0545, ¶ 21,966.0285	[41] ¶ 21,964B
	[37] ¶ 21,964B, ¶ 21,966.021	

Activities Held Through Partnerships or S Corporations. Activities are first grouped by partnerships or S corporations at the entity level (Reg. § 1.469-4(d)(5)).[42] If appropriate, a partner or shareholder should further combine these activities with other activities outside the entity.

Rental Activities. Rental activities are grouped according to the "appropriate economic unit" standard stated above (Reg. § 1.469-4(c)). However, a rental real estate activity may not be combined with an activity involving the rental of personal property (Reg. § 1.469-4(d)(2)).[43]

Combining Trade or Business and Rental Activities. A rental activity may not be grouped with a trade or business activity unless either the rental activity is insubstantial in relation to the trade or business activity or the trade or business activity is insubstantial in relation to the rental activity (Reg. § 1.469-4(d)(1)(i)).[44] The regulations add a third alternative—that each owner of the trade or business have the same proportionate ownership interest in the rental activity, in which case the portion of the rental activity that involves the rental of items of property to a trade or business activity may be grouped with the trade or business activity (Reg. § 1.469-4(d)(1)(i)(C)).

> **Example:** The Getaway Partnership owns a 10-story building in which it operates a travel agency on three floors and rents seven floors to tenants. The partnership is divided into two activities: a travel agency activity and a rental real estate activity. Deductions and credits attributable to the building are allocable to the travel agency activity only to the extent that they relate to the space occupied by the travel agency during the tax year.

Partial Disposition of Activity. If the taxpayer disposes of *substantially all* of an activity, he may treat the interest disposed of as a separate activity, provided that he can establish the amount of gross income, deductions and credits allocable to that part of the activity for the tax year (Reg. § 1.469-4(g)).[45] This provision is designed to allow taxpayers to claim suspended passive losses even though they have not disposed of their entire interest in an activity (see ¶ 2076).

2059. Passive Activity Defined. A passive activity is one that involves the conduct of any trade or business in which the taxpayer does not materially participate (Code Sec. 469(c)).[46] Any rental activity is a passive activity whether or not the taxpayer materially participates. However, there are special rules for real estate rental activities (see ¶ 2063) and real estate professionals (see ¶ 2064).[47]

Trading personal property that is actively traded, such as stocks and bonds, for the account of owners of interests in the activity is not a passive activity. For example, the activity of a partnership that trades stock using money contributed by the partners is not a passive activity (Temp. Reg. § 1.469-1T(e)(6)).

Generally, to be considered as materially participating in an activity during a tax year, an individual must satisfy any one of the following tests:

(1) the individual participates more than 500 hours;

(2) the individual's participation constitutes substantially all of the participation in the activity;

(3) the individual participates for more than 100 hours and this participation is not less than the participation of any other individual;

(4) the activity is a "significant participation activity" (see below) and the individual's participation in all significant participation activities exceeds 500 hours;

(5) the individual materially participated in the activity for any five years of the 10 years that preceded the year in question;

(6) the activity is a "personal service activity" (see below) and the individual materially participated in the activity for any three years preceding the tax year in question; or

Footnote references are to paragraphs of the 2008 Standard Federal Tax Reports.

[42] ¶ 21,964B, ¶ 21,966.0315 [44] ¶ 21,964B, ¶ 21,966.0325 [46] ¶ 21,960
[43] ¶ 21,964B, ¶ 21,966.032 [45] ¶ 21,964B, ¶ 21,966.033 [47] ¶ 21,962B, ¶ 21,966.021

(7) the individual satisfies a facts and circumstances test that requires the individual to show participation on a regular, continuous, and substantial basis for more than 100 hours during the tax year.

With respect to test (7), an individual's participation in managing the activity does not count toward the 100-hour requirement if any other person received compensation for managing the activity or any other person spent more time managing the activity (Temp. Reg. § 1.469-5T(a)).[48]

Limited Partners. Losses and credits attributable to limited partnership interests are treated as arising from a passive activity unless the limited partner participated for more than 500 hours (test (1)), the limited partner materially participated in five of the 10 preceding tax years (test (5)), or the activity is a personal service activity in which the limited partner materially participated for any three preceding tax years (test (6)). A general partner who also holds a limited partnership interest is not treated as a limited partner (Code Sec. 469(h)(2); Temp. Reg. § 1.469-5T(e)).

Special rules are also provided for determining the material participation of limited partners (Temp. Reg. § 1.469-5T(e)(2)),[49] certain retired or disabled farmers (Temp. Reg. § 1.469-5T(h)(2)),[50] and personal service and closely held corporations (Temp. Reg. § 1.469-1T(g)(2) and (g)(3)(i)).[51]

Significant Participation Activity. A significant participation activity is one in which the taxpayer participates more than 100 hours during the tax year but does not materially participate under any of the other six tests set forth above (Temp. Reg. § 1.469-5T(c)).[52]

Personal Service Activity. A personal service activity involves the performance of personal service in (1) the fields of health (including veterinary services), law, engineering, architecture, accounting, actuarial services, the performing arts, or consulting or (2) any other trade or business in which capital is not a material income-producing factor (Temp. Reg. § 1.469-5T(d)).[53]

Definition of Participation. Generally, any work done by an individual with respect to an activity that the individual owns an interest in is treated as participation (Reg. § 1.469-5(f)(1)). However, participation does not include work that is not customarily done by an owner if one of the principal purposes for performing the work is to avoid the passive activity limitations (Temp. Reg. § 1.469-5T(f)(2)(i)).

Spouse's Participation. In applying the material participation tests, an individual's participation includes his spouse's participation even if the spouse does not own an interest in the activity and separate returns are filed (Temp. Reg. § 1.469-5T(f)(3)).

Participation as an Investor. Work done in an individual's capacity as an investor in an activity, such as studying and reviewing the activity's financial statements and operational reports, preparing summaries or analyses of the activity's finances or operations for personal use, and monitoring the finances or operations of the activity in a nonmanagerial capacity, is not counted as participation (Temp. Reg. § 1.469-5T(f)(2)(ii)).

Proving Participation. Participation may be established by any reasonable means. It is not necessary to maintain contemporaneous daily records of participation. An approximate number of hours of participation may be based on appointment books, calendars, or narrative summaries (Temp. Reg. § 1.469-5T(f)(4)).

Rental Activities

2062. Special Rules for Rental Activities. In general, a rental activity is treated as a passive activity (Code Sec. 469(c)(2)).[54] An activity is a "rental activity" if (1) during the tax year, tangible property held in connection with the activity is used by customers or is held for use by customers, and (2) the gross income of the activity represents amounts paid mainly for the use of the tangible property (Temp. Reg. § 1.469-1T(e)(3)(i)).[55] However, if any one of the following tests is met, the activity is not considered to be a rental activity for purposes of the passive loss rules:

Footnote references are to paragraphs of the 2008 Standard Federal Tax Reports.

[48] ¶ 21,965, ¶ 21,966.026   [51] ¶ 21,962   [54] ¶ 21,960
[49] ¶ 21,965   [52] ¶ 21,965, ¶ 21,966.026   [55] ¶ 21,962
[50] ¶ 21,965   [53] ¶ 21,965, ¶ 21,966.026

(1) the average period of customer use of the property is seven days or less;

(2) the average period of customer use is 30 days or less and significant personal services are provided by or on behalf of the owner;

(3) without regard to the period of customer use, extraordinary personal services are provided by or on behalf of the owner;

(4) the rental of the property is incidental to a nonrental activity;

(5) the property is customarily made available during defined business hours for the nonexclusive use of customers; or

(6) the taxpayer provides property for use in an activity that is conducted by a partnership, S corporation, or joint venture in which the taxpayer owns an interest and the activity is not a rental activity (Temp. Reg. § 1.469-1T(e)(3)(ii)).[56]

2063. Active Participation in Rental Real Estate Activity. There is a limited exception to the passive loss rules in the case of losses from rental real estate in which the taxpayer or the taxpayer's spouse actively participates (Code Sec. 469(i)).[57] The exception is available only to individual taxpayers or their estates for tax years ending less than two years after the date of death. The estate qualifies during this period if the decedent actively participated before his death (Code Sec. 469(i)(4)(A)).

The active participation standard is less stringent than the material participation standard. An individual may meet the active participation requirement if he participates in the making of management decisions (for example, approving new tenants, deciding on rental terms, approving expenditures) or arranges for others to provide services (for example, repairs) in a significant and bona fide sense.[58] The requirement for active participation applies in the year in which the loss arose as well as the year in which the loss is allowed under the $25,000 allowance rule. However, real estate professionals may be able to treat rental property activities as nonpassive activities (¶ 2064).

Under this exception, up to $25,000 of passive losses and the deduction equivalent of tax credits that are attributable to rental real estate may be used as an offset against income from nonpassive sources (for example, dividends and wages) each year. To be eligible for this exception, the individual must own at least a 10% interest of all interests in the activity throughout the year. The interest of an individual's spouse is taken into account in determining 10% ownership (Code Sec. 469(i)(6)).[59] This $25,000 maximum amount is reduced, but not below zero, by 50% of the amount by which adjusted gross income exceeds $100,000.

"Adjusted gross income" is computed for purposes of this exception by disregarding: taxable social security and railroad retirement benefits, the exclusion for qualified U.S. savings bonds used to pay higher education expenses, the exclusion for employer adoption assistance payments, passive activity income or loss included on Form 8582, any overall loss from a publicly traded partnership, rental real estate losses allowed to real estate professionals, deductions attributable to domestic production activities, deductions for contributions to IRAs and pension plans, and the deductions for one-half of self-employment tax, interest on student loans, and higher education expenses (Code Sec. 469(i)(3)(E)).[60] The $25,000 is completely phased out when modified adjusted gross income reaches $150,000 (Code Sec. 469(i)(3)).[61]

Separate Returns. For married taxpayers who file separate returns and live apart, up to $12,500 of passive losses may be used to offset income. This amount is reduced by 50% of the amount by which the taxpayer's modified adjusted gross income exceeds $50,000. The special allowance is completely phased out when modified adjusted gross income reaches $75,000. Married taxpayers who file separately and live together at any time during the tax year are not eligible for the special allowance (Code Sec. 469(i)(5)).[62]

Rehabilitation and Low-Income Housing Tax Credits and Commercial Revitalization Deduction. For the rehabilitation tax credit (see ¶ 1347) and low-income housing credits

---

Footnote references are to paragraphs of the 2008 Standard Federal Tax Reports.

[56] ¶ 21,962, ¶ 21,966.022   [59] ¶ 21,960   [62] ¶ 21,960
[57] ¶ 21,960, ¶ 21,966.035   [60] ¶ 21,960
[58] ¶ 21,966.0353   [61] ¶ 21,960

¶2063

on property placed in service before 1990, the phaseout range for offsetting tax on up to $25,000 of nonpassive income is between $200,000 and $250,000 of adjusted gross income ($100,000 and $125,000 for a married taxpayer filing separately and living apart). No AGI limitation applies to the low-income housing credits for property placed in service after 1989 (¶ 1334) (Code Sec. 469(i)(3)(B) and (C)).[63] The individual need not actively participate in the activity to which the credits relate (Code Sec. 469(i)(6)(B)).[64] The AGI limitation and active participation requirement also do not apply to the commercial revitalization deduction for buildings placed in service in renewal communities (Code Sec. 469(i)(3)(C) and (i)(6)(B)(iii) (see ¶ 999C).

2064. Real Estate Professionals. Certain real estate professionals may be able to treat rental real estate activities as nonpassive (Code Sec. 469(c)(7)).[65] To qualify, (1) more than one-half of the personal services performed in trades or businesses by the taxpayer during the tax year must involve real property trades or businesses in which the taxpayer (or the taxpayer's spouse) materially participates, and (2) the taxpayer must perform more than 750 hours of service during the tax year in real property trades or businesses in which the taxpayer (or the taxpayer's spouse) materially participates. These two requirements must be satisfied by one spouse if a joint return is filed. Assuming that the requirements for the exception are satisfied, the passive activity loss rules are not applied.

Personal services performed as an employee are not taken into account for purposes of (1) and (2) unless the employee owns more than a 5-percent interest in the employer.

A real property trade or business is a business with respect to which real property is developed or redeveloped, constructed or reconstructed, acquired, converted, rented or leased, operated or managed, or brokered (Code Sec. 469(c)(7)(C)).

The exception for real estate professionals is applied as if each interest of the taxpayer in rental real estate is a separate activity. However, a taxpayer may elect to treat all interests in rental real estate as a single activity for purposes of satisfying the material participation requirements.

A closely held corporation qualifies as a real estate professional if more than 50 percent of its annual gross receipts for the tax year are from real property trades or businesses in which it materially participates.

Portfolio Income

2066. Separate Accounting Required. Portfolio income is not treated as income from a passive activity; it must be accounted for separately, and passive losses and credits generally may not be applied against it. The term "portfolio income" includes interest, dividends, annuities and royalties, as well as gain or loss from the disposition of income-producing or investment property that is not derived in the ordinary course of a trade or business (Code Sec. 469(e)(1)).[66] No exception is provided for the treatment of portfolio income arising from working capital (amounts set aside for the reasonable needs of the business) (Code Sec. 469(e)(1)(B)).[67]

In the case of a lending transaction between a taxpayer and a pass-through entity in which the taxpayer owns a direct or indirect interest, a self-charged interest rule treats certain interest income as passive activity gross income and certain interest expense as passive activity deductions (Reg. § 1.469-7). These rules also apply to lending transactions between identically owned pass-through entities.[68]

Tax Treatment of Current Losses and Credits

2070. Current Losses. Generally, a loss arising from a passive activity is deductible against the net income of another passive activity. Losses that are not deductible for a particular tax year because there is insufficient passive activity income to offset them (suspended losses) are carried forward indefinitely and are allowed as deductions against passive income in subsequent years (Code Sec. 469(b)).[69] Unused suspended

Footnote references are to paragraphs of the 2008 Standard Federal Tax Reports.

[63] ¶ 21,960
[64] ¶ 21,960
[65] ¶ 21,960, ¶ 21,966.024

[66] ¶ 21,960, ¶ 21,966.041, ¶ 21,966.042
[67] ¶ 21,960

[68] ¶ 21,966.042
[69] ¶ 21,960, ¶ 21,966.0552

losses are allowed in full on a fully taxable disposition of the taxpayer's entire interest in the activity (see ¶ 2076).

2073. Current Credits. Credits arising with respect to passive activities are generally treated in the same manner as losses, except that suspended credits are not allowed on disposition of the activity.[70] Thus, credits may be used to offset the tax attributable to net passive income (the difference between the tax that the taxpayer would have to pay (1) on all income and (2) on taxable income other than net passive income). In both cases, the effect of credits is disregarded.

In general, unused credits can be carried forward indefinitely. However, the character of a credit relating to a passive activity changes, in effect, when the credit becomes allowable under the passive loss rules (either there is sufficient passive income to allow its use, or it is within the scope of the $25,000 benefit for real estate activities). At this time, the credit is aggregated with credits relating to nonpassive activities of the taxpayer to determine whether all such credits are allowable considering the other limitations that apply to the use of credits (see ¶ 1323).[71]

Tax Treatment of Suspended Losses and Credits

2076. Carryforward of Suspended Losses and Credits. When a taxpayer disposes of his entire interest in a passive activity in a taxable transaction, his suspended passive losses (see ¶ 2070) may be applied against his active income (Code Sec. 469(g)).[72] However, these losses must first be applied against the taxpayer's net income or gain from passive activities (Code Sec. 469(g)(1)(A)).[73] Suspended credits are not allowed upon the disposition of a passive activity.

Entire Interest. A disposition of a taxpayer's entire interest involves a disposition of the interest in all entities that are engaged in the activity and, to the extent the activity is held in the form of a sole proprietorship, of all of the assets used or created in the activity. If a partnership or S corporation conducts two or more separate activities and the entity disposes of all the assets used or created in one activity, the disposition constitutes a disposition of the entire interest. The same rule applies to grantor trusts.[74]

In some instances, a taxpayer may claim a deduction for suspended losses even though he disposes of less than his entire interest (see ¶ 2058).

Taxable Transactions. To qualify as a fully taxable disposition, the disposition generally must be a sale of the interest to a third party in an arm's-length transaction and must not be a sham, a wash sale, or a transfer of repurchase rights.[75]

If a taxpayer disposes of an interest in a passive activity in a taxable transaction with a related party as defined by Code Sec. 267(b)[76] or with a controlled partnership as defined by Code Sec. 707(b)(1),[77] the suspended losses will not be triggered (Code Sec. 469(g)(1)(B)).[78] In these circumstances the taxpayer will be able to claim the loss only when the related person or controlled partnership disposes of the activity in a taxable transaction with an unrelated person. Abandonment is a fully taxable disposition.

Installment Sales. An installment sale of a taxpayer's interest triggers the allowance of suspended losses. Losses are allowed in the ratio that the gain recognized in each year bears to the total gain. Gain from a pre-1987 installment sale that is recognized in post-1986 tax years may be treated as passive activity income if the activity would have been treated as a passive activity.[79]

Death. A transfer by reason of the taxpayer's death causes suspended losses to be allowed in the year of death to the extent that they exceed the amount by which the basis of the interest is increased under Code Sec. 1014.[80]

Gifts. Disposition of a passive activity by gift does *not* trigger the suspended losses. Instead, the basis of the transferred interest is increased by the amount of such losses (Code Sec. 469(j)(6)).[81]

Footnote references are to paragraphs of the 2008 Standard Federal Tax Reports.

[70] ¶ 21,966.057	[74] ¶ 21,966.0552	[78] ¶ 21,960
[71] ¶ 21,966.0575	[75] ¶ 21,966.0552	[79] ¶ 21,966.0541
[72] ¶ 21,960	[76] ¶ 14,150	[80] ¶ 21,960
[73] ¶ 21,960	[77] ¶ 25,480	[81] ¶ 21,960

Exchanges. An exchange of a taxpayer's interest in a passive activity in a nonrecognition transaction (e.g., a Code Sec. 1031 like-kind exchange—see ¶ 1721) does not trigger suspended losses. However, to the extent that the taxpayer recognizes gain on the transaction (for example, to the extent of boot received), the gain is treated as passive activity income against which passive losses may be deducted.[82]

Casualty or Theft. A casualty or theft loss involving property used in a passive activity does not constitute a complete disposition of the taxpayer's interest in the activity unless loss of all property used or created in the activity results.[83]

Activity No Longer Passive. In the tax year that an activity ceases to be a passive activity, previously suspended losses from that activity are permitted to be claimed as deductions against the activity's net income. Similarly, prior year suspended passive activity credits may offset the current year's tax liability that is allocable to the current year's net income from the former passive activity. Tax liability for this purpose is figured on the net income as reduced by the prior year suspended losses (Code Sec. 469(f)(1)).[84]

Cessation of Closely Held C Corporation or PSC Status. If a closely held C corporation or a personal service corporation (PSC) changes its status, suspended losses from prior years will continue to be subject to the limitations that were imposed before the status changed (see ¶ 2056). Losses arising in years after the year in which the corporation's status changes are not subject to the passive loss rules (Code Sec. 469(f)(2)).

Treatment of Loss on Disposition. When a taxpayer disposes of a passive activity in a taxable transaction, any net passive loss from the activity must first be applied against income or gain from the taxpayer's other passive activities. Any remaining loss from the activity is then classified as nonpassive and may be used to offset income from nonpassive activities (for example, wages and interest income) (Code Sec. 469(g)(1)(A)).[85]

Tax-Exempt Use Property

2080. Limits on Tax-Exempt Use Losses. A taxpayer leasing property to a government or other tax-exempt entity (i.e., sale-in, lease-out (SILO) arrangement) is not allowed to claim deductions that are related to the property (known as tax-exempt use property) to the extent that they exceed the taxpayer's income from the lease payments (a tax-exempt use loss), subject to certain exceptions (Code Sec. 470).[86] Tax-exempt use property is generally defined in Code Sec. 168(h). It includes property owned by a partnership (or other pass-through entity) that has at least one tax-exempt partner and the allocations of partnership items attempt to inappropriately transfer the deductions from the tax-exempt partner to the taxable partners.

Tax-exempt losses disallowed may be carried over to the next tax year and can be deducted to the extent of the taxpayer's net income from the property for that year. If property ceases to be tax-exempt use property during the lease term, the carried over loss cannot be used to offset income from other property. If the property is disposed of, any disallowed loss is available under rules similar to passive activity losses (see ¶ 2076). However, the limitation on tax-exempt use property losses is applied before the passive activity rules.

Footnote references are to paragraphs of the 2008 Standard Federal Tax Reports.

[82] ¶ 21,966.0553
[83] ¶ 21,966.0553
[84] ¶ 21,960
[85] ¶ 21,960
[86] ¶ 21,970

Chapter 21
RETIREMENT PLANS

Types of Plans

2101. Introduction. An employer who wants to provide retirement benefits for employees will customarily establish a pension, profit-sharing or stock bonus plan that qualifies for certain tax benefits (Code Sec. 401).[1] Among the tax benefits offered by a qualified retirement plan are: a tax exemption for the fund that is established to provide benefits (Code Sec. 501(a); Reg. § 1.401(f)-1(c)(1));[2] deductions by the employer for contributions made to the fund (Code Sec. 404);[3] and tax deferral for the employee on the employer's contributions and earnings on the retirement fund (Code Secs. 402(a) and 403(a)(1)).[4]

Tax Credit for Employers. Employers with 100 or fewer employees can claim a tax credit based on 50 percent of the cost of establishing and/or maintaining a new retirement plan. The credit can be taken for three tax years. The maximum credit for any tax year is $500 (see ¶ 1344B).

Tax Credit for Individuals. Individuals that meet specific requirements are able to claim a nonrefundable tax credit based upon their qualified retirement savings contributions (see ¶ 1307).

2103. Qualified Retirement Plans. There are two broad categories of qualified retirement plans: defined benefit plans and defined contribution plans. *Defined benefit plans* include pension and annuity plans that offer a specific retirement benefit to employees (Code Sec. 414(j)).[5] The benefit is usually in the form of a monthly retirement pension that is based on the employee's wages and years of service with the employer. An employer's annual contributions to the plan are based on actuarial assumptions and are not allocated to individual accounts maintained for the employees (Reg. § 1.401-1(b)(1)(i))[6]. *Defined contribution plans* include profit-sharing, stock bonus, and money purchase plans. A separate account is provided for each employee covered by the plan and the employee's retirement benefit is based solely on the contributions to the account and any investment gains and earnings (Code Sec. 414(i)).[7]

Cash Balance Plans. A "cash balance plan" is a defined benefit pension plan that provides benefits for each employee participant by reference to the amount of the participant's hypothetical account balance. Each participant's hypothetical account balance is credited with hypothetical allocations and earnings determined under a formula

---

Footnote references are to paragraphs of the 2008 Standard Federal Tax Reports.

[1] ¶ 17,502	[4] ¶ 18,202, ¶ 18,270	[7] ¶ 19,150
[2] ¶ 18,100, ¶ 22,602	[5] ¶ 19,150	
[3] ¶ 18,330	[6] ¶ 17,504	

¶2101

selected by the employer that is stated in the plan document. The hypothetical allocations and earnings are designed to mimic the allocations of actual contributions under a defined contribution plan (e.g., a money purchase pension plan). However, the main difference between a money purchase plan and a cash balance plan is that interest is credited to each participant's account at a specified rate (i.e., the participants' accounts do not vary with actual investment performance) (Notice 96-8).[8] Within the past few years, cash balance plans have been challenged on the ground that older employees may be discriminated against when an employer converts a defined benefit plan into a cash balance plan. At this point, the controversy has not been resolved. However, the Pension Protection Act of 2006 provided some protection for conversions after June 29, 2005 (Code Sec. 411(b)(5), as added by the Pension Protection Act of 2006 (P.L. 109-280)).[9]

2105. Profit-Sharing Plans. Profit-sharing plans are a type of defined contribution plan (¶ 2103). The employer is not required to contribute every year or any particular percentage of profits or other particular amount, but contributions must be substantial and recurring. A profit-sharing plan must have a definite written formula for allocating contributions among the participants (Reg. § 1.401-1(b)(1)(ii)).[10] The term "profit-sharing plan" is a misnomer because a plan may qualify as such even if contributions exceed current and accumulated profits of the employer. In addition, a profit-sharing plan may be maintained by a not-for-profit organization (Code Sec. 401(a)(27)).[11]

2106. Money Purchase Plans. A money purchase plan is a type of defined contribution plan (¶ 2103). However, unlike a profit-sharing plan, an employer's annual contributions are fixed in the terms of the plan (Reg. § 1.401-1(b)(1)(i)).[12] For example, under a money purchase plan, the plan may require that the employer contribute five percent of each participating employee's wages, regardless of whether the employer shows a profit for the year.

2107. Annuity Plans. An annuity plan is a defined benefit plan (¶ 2103) funded through the direct purchase by the employer of an annuity contract or contracts (Code Secs. 403(a)(1)[13] and 404(a)(2)).[14]

2109. Stock Bonus Plans and ESOPs. A stock bonus plan is a defined contribution plan (¶ 2103) that must generally follow the same rules as a profit-sharing plan except that distributed benefits usually are in the form of employer's stock (Reg. § 1.401-1(b)(1)(iii)).[15] An employee stock ownership plan (ESOP) is a special type of stock bonus plan that, if certain requirements are met, provides special tax advantages including the following (Code Secs. 409 and 4975(e)(7)):[16]

(1) An ESOP will qualify for an exemption from certain of the prohibited transaction rules that apply in the case of loans made by disqualified persons to qualified plans (Code Sec. 4975(d)(3)).[17]

(2) Under some circumstances a shareholder, other than a C corporation, may elect not to recognize gain on the sale of qualified securities to an ESOP (Code Sec. 1042).[18] Nonrecognition depends upon the shareholder purchasing qualified replacement property within a specific period of time.

(3) A C corporation is entitled to a deduction for dividends on its stock held by an ESOP that are: (a) paid in cash directly to participants in the ESOP; (b) paid to the ESOP and subsequently distributed to the participants in cash no later than 90 days after the end of the plan year in which the dividends are paid to the ESOP; or (c) used to repay an ESOP loan (Code Sec. 404(k)).[19] In addition, C corporations may deduct dividends that are, at the election of plan participants or their beneficiaries, paid to an ESOP and reinvested in qualified employer securities.

Footnote references are to paragraphs of the 2008 Standard Federal Tax Reports.

[8] ¶ 17,508.127	[12] ¶ 17,504	[16] ¶ 18,950, ¶ 34,400
[9] ¶ 19,076.0345	[13] ¶ 18,270	[17] ¶ 34,400
[10] ¶ 17,504	[14] ¶ 18,330	[18] ¶ 29,820
[11] ¶ 17,502	[15] ¶ 17,504	[19] ¶ 18,330

(4) Contributions to an ESOP that are used to pay the principal on loans that were incurred to purchase employer securities may be deducted to the extent that they do not exceed 25 percent of the compensation paid to participants (Code Sec. 404(a)(9)).[20] This contribution rule does not apply to S corporations.

2110. SIMPLE Retirement Plans. A Savings Incentive Match Plan for Employees (SIMPLE plan) may be maintained in any year by an employer who has 100 or fewer employees who received at least $5,000 of compensation from the employer for the preceding year (Code Secs. 401(k)(11) and 408(p)(2)(C)).[21] The employer must not maintain any other retirement plan, except for its collectively bargained employees. An eligible employer who establishes and maintains a SIMPLE plan for at least one year, but subsequently fails to qualify as an eligible employer, will continue to be treated as an eligible employer for the two years following the last year in which it did qualify.

Domestic Workers. Compensation paid to certain domestic workers qualifies for SIMPLE plan contributions, even though the compensation may not be subject to income tax withholding (Code Sec. 408(p)(6)(A)(i)).

Types of SIMPLE Plans. There are two types of SIMPLE plans: (1) SIMPLE IRAs (see ¶ 2185) and (2) SIMPLE 401(k) plans (see ¶ 2112).

2111. 401(k) Plans. Under a 401(k) plan, each participating employee has the option of taking an amount of compensation in cash or having it paid to the plan (an "elective contribution"). If the plan meets certain requirements the normal constructive receipt rule is preempted and the employees do not have to recognize the deferred amounts immediately (Code Secs. 401(k) and 402(e)(3); Reg. §§ 1.401(k)-1 and 1.402(a)-1(d)).[22] 401(k) plans are sometimes called "cash or deferred arrangements" (CODAs).

There are two sets of comprehensive regulations governing 401(k) plans. The 2004 regulations generally apply for plan years beginning on or after January 1, 2006, though plan sponsors may elect to apply them to plan years ending after December 29, 2004. The 1991 regulations apply until the 2004 regulations become applicable to a plan. The 2004 regulations make minor changes with regard to the subjects covered in the 1991 regulations, and add provisions governing several additional subjects, including the actual deferral percentage test, the safe harbor nondiscrimination requirements, and the SIMPLE 401(k) requirements (¶ 2112). The discussions below refer to the 2004 regulations (except where noted).

Qualification requirements. A 401(k) plan must generally be part of a profit-sharing (¶ 2105) or stock bonus plan (¶ 2109) that, in addition to meeting the requirements of a qualified plan (¶ 2117 and following), meets the following special requirements (Code Sec. 401(k)(2) and (4)):[23]

• participants have the option of having the employer contribute amounts to the plan on their behalf or receiving those amounts in cash;

• the plan is prohibited from distributing amounts attributable to elective contributions *earlier* than one of the following events:

(a) severance from employment, death or disability,

(b) termination of the plan without establishment or maintenance of another defined contribution plan (Code Sec. 401(k)(10)),

(c) attainment of age 59½, or

(d) employee hardship (see below); however, distributions at age 59½ or for hardship are not permitted in the case of a money purchase pension plan;

• the plan must not provide for distributions merely by reason of a stated period of participation or the lapse of a fixed number of years;

• the plan must provide that the participant's right to the value of the account that is attributable to elective contributions be fully vested at all times;

Footnote references are to paragraphs of the 2008 Standard Federal Tax Reports.

[20] ¶ 18,330
[21] ¶ 17,502, ¶ 18,902
[22] ¶ 17,502, ¶ 18,110, ¶ 18,202, ¶ 18,203
[23] ¶ 17,502

- the plan must not require as a condition of participation that an employee complete more than one year of service with the employer; and

- the plan must not condition any other employee benefit (apart from matching contributions) upon an employee's election to make contributions to the 401(k) plan.

A partnership may maintain a 401(k) plan, and individual partners may make elective contributions to the plan based on their compensation for the services they provide to the partnership (Reg. § 1.401(k)-1(a)(6)(i)).[24] In addition, under the 2004 regulations a sole proprietor is permitted to maintain a 401(k) plan. In fact, most self-employed individuals will find that their tax deductible contributions to a 401(k) plan will be greater than that allowed to other types of self-employed retirement plans (see ¶ 2152). The Federal Thrift Savings Plan, which is often called the "Thrift Savings Plan," provides federal employees with the same savings and tax benefits that private employers offer their employees with 401(k) plans (Code Sec. 7701(j)).[25]

Annual Limit on Elective Deferrals. An employee's aggregate elective deferrals to 401(k) plans, SEP plans, and 403(b) plans (but not Code Sec. 457 plans, see ¶ 2197B) are subject to an annual limit (Code Sec. 402(g)).[26] The limit does not just apply to each plan to which the employee makes elective deferrals but instead applies to the aggregate amount of all the elective deferrals made by the employee for the year to all plans. The limit is $15,500 for 2007 and 2008 (Notice 2006-98; IRS News Release IR-2007-171).

> **Example 1:** Tony, age 45, works for two employers. Each of the employers offers a 401(k) plan and Tony participates in both plans. During 2007, Tony defers $10,000 of his wages into the 401(k) plan of Employer A and $6,000 of his wages into the 401(k) plan of Employer B. For 2007, Tony has made an excess deferral of $500 ($16,000 in aggregate deferrals – $15,500 maximum deferral allowable).

401(k) Catch-Up Contributions. Individuals who will be at least age 50 by the end of the tax year may make an additional "catch-up" contribution to most types of retirement plans (e.g., 401(k), IRA, 403(b) and 457 plans). The maximum amount of the annual catch-up contribution depends upon the type of plan involved as well as the tax year for which the contribution is being made (Code Sec. 414(v)).[27] The maximum "catch-up" contribution to a 401(k) plan is $5,000 for 2007 and 2008. Catch-up contributions may only be made if the plan permits this type of contribution.

Excess Contributions. Elective deferrals that exceed the annual limit are included in the employee's income and subject to a 10 percent penalty (Code Secs. 402(g)(1), (g)(2)(A)(i) and 4979).[28] The employee may withdraw the excess contribution from the plan before April 15 of the following tax year along with any attributable income. If the employee has made elective deferrals to more than one plan, then the employee can designate the amount of the excess that is to be withdrawn from each plan. If the excess contribution remains in the plan past the April 15 distribution date, it will be taxed a second time when distributed (Reg. § 1.402(g)-1(e)(8)(iii)).[29] The 10 percent penalty will not apply if the excess is distributed within 2½ months following the plan year in which the excess contribution was made.

Matching Contributions. As a general rule, matching contributions made to a 401(k) plan by the employer are not treated as an employee's elective contributions and are, therefore, not subject to the annual limit on deferrals. In addition, matching contributions made by a self-employed person to a 401(k) plan are not treated as part of the individual's elective contributions (Code Sec. 402(g)(8)).[30]

Hardship Distributions. A 401(k) plan may allow hardship distributions up to the amount of the participant's elective deferrals. A hardship distribution is one that: (1) is made because of the employee's immediate and heavy financial need and (2) does not exceed the amount necessary to satisfy that need (Reg. § 1.401(k)-1(d)(3)).[31] Types of expenses that satisfy the requirement of immediate and heavy financial need include:

Footnote references are to paragraphs of the 2008 Standard Federal Tax Reports.

[24] ¶ 18,110B
[25] ¶ 43,080
[26] ¶ 18,202

[27] ¶ 19,150
[28] ¶ 18,202, ¶ 34,520
[29] ¶ 18,220, ¶ 34,520

[30] ¶ 18,202
[31] ¶ 18,110

(a) medical expenses of the employee, spouse and dependents;

(b) expenditures (excluding mortgage payments) to purchase a principal residence for the employee;

(c) post-secondary tuition for the employee, spouse, children or dependents;

(d) expenditures to stave off eviction or foreclosure with respect to the employee's principal residence;

(e) burial or funeral expenses for the employee's deceased parent, spouse, children or dependents; and

(f) expenses for the repair of casualty damage to the employee's principal residence.

An immediate and heavy financial need also includes any amounts necessary to pay any income taxes or penalties reasonably anticipated to result from the distribution. To the extent allowed under the plan, if medical, tuition, or funeral expenses incurred on behalf of the employee's spouse or dependent are deemed to be an immediate and heavy financial need, the incurring of the same expenses with regard to the employee's beneficiary under the plan can also be considered an immediate and heavy financial need (Notice 2007-7).

A distribution will be treated as necessary to satisfy the employee's immediate and heavy financial need if the following requirements are met:

(1) the distribution is not in excess of the amount needed to satisfy the financial need;

(2) the employee has obtained all distributions and nontaxable loans available under all plans of the employer; and

(3) the distribution triggers the suspension of elective contributions on behalf of the employee and other employee contributions to any deferred compensation plan of the employer for at least six months (Reg. § 1.401(k)-1(d)(3)(iii)).[32]

Example 2: Bill takes a hardship distribution from his 401(k) plan on April 1, 2007. In order to satisfy one of the safe harbor requirements, Bill will not be able to make any elective deferrals or after-tax contributions to the plan until October 1, 2007 (i.e., six-month suspension of contributions).

A hardship distribution is included in the employee's income and is subject to the 10 percent penalty on early distributions unless an exception applies (see ¶ 2157). A hardship distribution generally may *not* be rolled over into an IRA or other type of retirement plan (Code Sec. 402(c)(4)(C)).[33] However, hardship distributions that are qualified hurricane distributions can be recontributed and the recontribution will be treated as a rollover (Code Sec. 1400Q(a)(3), (b)). For discussion of qualified hurricane distributions, see ¶ 2155.

A hardship distribution that was a qualified reservist distribution may be recontributed to an IRA. Qualified reservist distributions are included in income but not subject to the 10 percent penalty on early distributions. See ¶ 2173.

Discrimination Testing. A 401(k) plan must meet a special "actual deferral percentage" (ADP) test, which is designed to limit the extent to which elective contributions of "highly compensated employees" may exceed elective contributions of rank and file employees (Code Sec. 401(k)(3); Reg. § 1.401(k)-2).[34] The first step in the test is to determine the actual deferral ratio (ADR) (expressed as a percentage) of each highly compensated employee's elective contribution for the year being tested to that employee's compensation for the same year. The next step is to determine the average of those individual ratios (expressed as a percentage). The average ADR for highly compensated individuals is then compared against the *preceding plan year* average ADR for rank and file employees. The average ratio (referred to as the actual deferral percentage (ADP)) of the highly compensated group may not exceed:

(1) 125 percent of the ADP of the rank and file group if the ADP of that group is eight percent or more;

Footnote references are to paragraphs of the 2008 Standard Federal Tax Reports.

[32] ¶ 18,112.35 [33] ¶ 18,202 [34] ¶ 17,502, ¶ 18,110

¶2111

(2) 200 percent of the ADP of the rank and file group if the ADP of that group is two percent or less; or

(3) the ADP of the rank and file group plus two percentage points if the ADP of that group is between two and eight percent.

The employer may elect to calculate the ADP for rank and file employees with reference to data for the current year. This election may not be revoked without permission of the IRS. If the test year is the first year of the plan, other than a successor plan, the ADP of rank and file employees for the preceding plan year is deemed to be three percent or, if the employer elects, the ADP calculated on the basis of rank and file employees for the first plan year.

Safe Harbor Discrimination Rules. The ADP test will be deemed satisfied if the plan satisfies *either* one of the following alternatives:

(1) The employer must make matching contributions on behalf of each rank and file employee in an amount equal to: (a) 100 percent of the employee's elective contributions not exceeding three percent of the employee's compensation and (b) 50 percent of the employee's elective contributions in excess of three percent but not in excess of five percent of the employee's compensation (Code Sec. 401(k)(12)).[35] Also, at any rate of elective contribution, the matching rate for any highly compensated employee must not be greater than the matching rate for any rank and file employee. Even if the rate of matching contributions with respect to any rate of elective contributions is not equal to the *percentage* required by the 100/50 match rule, the plan will be treated as having satisfied that rule if (a) the rate of the employer's matching contributions does not increase as an employee's rate of elective contributions increases and (b) the aggregate *amount* of matching contributions at the rate of elective contributions is at least equal to the aggregate amount of matching contributions that would have been made if matching contributions satisfied the 100/50 match rule.

(2) The employer must contribute to a defined contribution plan at least three percent of compensation on behalf of each rank and file employee eligible to participate in the plan. The contribution must be made whether or not the employee makes an elective contribution or an after-tax contribution.

The ADP safe harbor will only be satisfied, however, if all participating employees are given written notice, within a reasonable period before each year, of their rights and obligations under the plan. The notice must be accurate and comprehensive and written in a manner calculated to be understood by the average employee eligible to participate.

Highly Compensated Employees. For purposes of the ADP test, a highly compensated employee is any employee who was:

(1) a five percent or more owner of the employer during the plan year or the preceding year or

(2) an employee who had compensation for the preceding year in excess of $100,000 for 2007 ($105,000 for 2008) (Notice 2006-98; IRS News Release IR-2007-171) and, if the employer elects, was among the top 20 percent of employees by compensation for the preceding year (Code Sec. 414(q)(1)).[36]

2112. SIMPLE 401(k) Plans. An eligible employer (see ¶ 2185) may adopt a "Savings Incentive Match Plan for Employees" (SIMPLE plan) as part of a 401(k) plan (Code Sec. 401(k)(11)).[37] Generally, a SIMPLE 401(k) must meet the same requirements that apply to other 401(k) plans. However, in lieu of satisfying the ADP test (¶ 2111), a SIMPLE 401(k) plan established by an employer may qualify by satisfying the following requirements (for a discussion of SIMPLE IRAs, see ¶ 2185 and following).

Employee Contributions. Each employee eligible to participate in the SIMPLE 401(k) plan must have the right to make annual elective contributions, expressed as a percentage of compensation but not exceeding $10,500 for 2007 and for 2008. An employee age 50 or over may make an additional catch-up contribution of $2,500 for 2007 and for 2008

Footnote references are to paragraphs of the 2008 Standard Federal Tax Reports.

[35] ¶ 17,502   [36] ¶ 19,150   [37] ¶ 17,502

(Code Sec. 414(v)(2)(B)(ii)).[38] Nondeductible employee contributions and rollover contributions may not be made to a SIMPLE 401(k). Matching contributions made by the employer are not treated as elective contributions and are, therefore, not included in the annual limit on elective contributions (Code Sec. 408(p)(9)).[39]

Employer Contributions. Generally, the employer must match the annual elective contribution of each employee to a SIMPLE 401(k) in an amount not exceeding three percent of the employee's compensation (Code Sec. 401(k)(11)(B)).[40] However, instead of making matching contributions, an employer may elect to make nonelective contributions of two percent of compensation for each employee who is eligible to participate in the arrangement and who has at least $5,000 of compensation. Employees must be notified that the employer has chosen to make the two percent contribution within a reasonable period of time before the 60th day before the beginning of the calendar year. The amount of compensation that can be taken into account in calculating the employee and employer contributions is subject to limitation (see ¶ 2128).

Top-Heavy Rules. The strict rules that apply to "top-heavy plans" (see ¶ 2139) do not apply to SIMPLE 401(k) plans (Code Sec. 401(k)(11)(D)(ii)).[41]

Employer's Deduction. An employer's deduction for contributions to a defined contribution plan is generally limited to the *greater* of: (1) 25 percent of the compensation paid or accrued during the tax year to beneficiaries under a stock bonus or profit-sharing plan or (2) the amount that the employer is required to contribute to a SIMPLE 401(k) plan for the year (Code Sec. 404(a)(3)(A)(i)(I) and (II)).[42] Thus, an employer's deductions for its contributions to a SIMPLE 401(k) may be greater than the general limit of 25 percent of compensation paid.

Vesting. All contributions to a SIMPLE 401(k) must be fully vested when made, and the plan cannot impose any restrictions on withdrawals (Code Sec. 401(k)(11)).[43]

Establishing a SIMPLE 401(k). The IRS has issued a model amendment that may be used by employers that want to adopt a plan that contains a SIMPLE 401(k) plan (Rev. Proc. 97-9).[44] The model amendment sets forth the requirements concerning such matters as employee contributions, employer options concerning its contributions and notification to employees.

2113. Plans Covering Self-Employed Persons. No distinction is generally made between pension, profit-sharing and other retirement plans (e.g., a 401(k) plan or SEP IRA) established by corporations and those established by individual proprietors and partnerships. In the past, the terms "Keogh Plan" or "H.R. 10 Plan" were used to distinguish a retirement plan established by a self-employed individual from a plan established by a corporation or other entity. However, self-employed retirement plans are now generally referred to by the name that is used for the particular type of plan (e.g., SEP IRA, SIMPLE 401(k), or self-employed 401(k)).

Even though there is general parity between retirement plans established by a self-employed individual and plans established by other business entities, special rules have to be considered. For example, the term "employee" generally includes a participant in a plan of an unincorporated enterprise who is a partner or a sole proprietor (Code Sec. 401(c)).[45] References to "compensation," in the case of a proprietor or partner, are to the "earned income" of that person from the business for which the plan is established. Basically, "earned income" is the individual's net earnings from self-employment for purposes of the tax on self-employment income (see ¶ 2670) minus: (1) the allowable deductions for contributions to the retirement plan on behalf of that individual and (2) the individual's deduction from gross income for 50 percent of the self-employment tax (see ¶ 923). When references are made to the "employer," a sole proprietor is treated as his or her own employer. However, a partnership is considered to be the employer of each partner. As a result, sole proprietors may establish their own retirement plans. Only a partnership may establish a retirement plan for its partners.

Footnote references are to paragraphs of the 2008 Standard Federal Tax Reports.

[38] ¶ 19,150	[41] ¶ 17,502	[44] ¶ 18,112.80
[39] ¶ 18,902	[42] ¶ 18,330	[45] ¶ 17,502
[40] ¶ 17,502	[43] ¶ 17,502	

For more information on self-employed retirement plans, including special computations that are required when determining the owner's deductible contributions, see ¶ 2152.

2115. Retirement Plans of S Corporations. A retirement plan established by an S corporation is generally governed by the same rules that apply to plans established by other corporations. As a result, S corporation shareholders are not entitled to claim retirement plan deductions based on their pro rata share of pass-through income from the S corporation. A court has ruled that this income could not be treated as earnings from self-employment for retirement plan purposes (*A.R. Durando*, CA-9, 95-2 USTC ¶ 50,615).

Qualification and Other Plan Requirements

2117. Introduction. A retirement plan must be recognized by the IRS as "qualified" in order for its sponsoring employer and participating employees to be eligible for the tax benefits that are usually associated with retirement plans (e.g., current tax deductions and tax deferred earnings). A plan becomes "qualified" by satisfying the requirements of Code Sec. 401.[46]

The fundamental requirement is that the plan not discriminate in employee coverage (see ¶ 2119) or in the amount or availability of contributions or benefits in favor of highly compensated employees (see ¶ 2111). Plans that primarily benefit an employer's key employees (i.e., "top-heavy plans") are subject to additional requirements (see ¶ 2139).[47]

2119. Participation and Coverage. Two of the basic requirements of most qualified plans are that they meet minimum participation standards and coverage requirements.

Participation. Generally, a qualified plan may not condition an employee's participation in the plan on the completion of more than one year of service or the attainment of more than 21 years of age, whichever occurs later. Once these conditions are met an employee must be eligible to participate within six months or, if earlier, by the first day of the plan's next accounting year. However, participation may be conditioned on completion of two years of service if, after no more than two years of service, each participant has a vested right to their entire accrued benefit under the plan (Code Sec. 410(a)(1)).[48]

Minimum Coverage Requirement. Generally, a plan may meet the minimum coverage requirement in one of two ways:

(1) By satisfying a "ratio percentage test." Under this test, the percentage of rank and file employees who benefit from the plan is divided by the percentage of highly compensated employees (see ¶ 2111) who benefit. The test is satisfied if the ratio is at least 70 percent (Code Sec. 410(b)(1); Reg. § 1.410(b)-2(b)(2)).[49]

(2) By satisfying an "average benefit test." This test is satisfied if: (a) the plan benefits such employees as qualify under a classification set up by the employer and found by the IRS not to discriminate in favor of highly compensated employees and (b) the average benefit percentage for nonhighly compensated employees is at least 70 percent of the average benefit percentage for highly compensated employees. An employee's "benefit percentage" comprises the employer-provided contributions (including forfeitures) or benefits under all qualified plans of the employer, expressed as a percentage of the employee's compensation (see ¶ 2128) (Code Sec. 410(b)(2); Reg. §§ 1.410(b)-2, 1.410(b)-4 and 1.410(b)-5).[50]

Additional Rule for Defined Benefit Plans. A defined benefit plan must also benefit at least the lesser of: (1) 50 employees or (2) the greater of (a) 40 percent of all employees or (b) two employees (one employee if there is only one employee) (Code Sec. 401(a)(26)).[51]

Footnote references are to paragraphs of the 2008 Standard Federal Tax Reports.

[46] ¶ 17,507

[47] ¶ 19,250

[48] ¶ 18,970

[49] ¶ 18,970, ¶ 18,988

[50] ¶ 18,970, ¶ 18,988, ¶ 18,990, ¶ 18,991

[51] ¶ 17,502

2121. Vesting. A qualified plan must satisfy minimum vesting requirements (Code Sec. 411(a)).[52] Employee contributions must be vested (i.e., nonforfeitable) at all times. With regard to employer contributions, vesting may usually be accomplished under either of the following methods.

Graded Vesting. Under this method, 20 percent of an employee's accrued benefit from employer contributions must vest after three years of service and an additional 20 percent must vest after each additional year of service.[53] After seven years of service, the employee will be 100 percent vested.

Cliff Vesting. Under this method, an employee has no vested interest in the accrued benefit from employer contributions until the employee has completed five years of service but then must be 100 percent vested.[54]

Vesting of Employer's Matching Contributions. A qualified plan must provide for faster vesting of an employer's matching contributions. The plan must either provide for "cliff vesting" of such contributions after three years of service or a "graded vesting" schedule that provides for 20 percent vesting after two years of service and an additional 20 percent each year until 100 percent vesting is achieved after six years of service (Code Sec. 411(a)(12)).

Pension Protection Act of 2006. For contributions made in plan years beginning after 2006, all employer contributions to most defined contribution plans are required to vest on the accelerated schedule that applies to matching contributions. Plans may maintain separate vesting schedules for those contributions made before 2007 and those made after 2006 (Code Sec. 411(a)(2), as amended by the Pension Protection Act of 2006 (P.L. 109-280); Notice 2007-7).

2125. Nondiscrimination Testing of Employee and Matching Contributions. A special nondiscrimination test applies to contributions by plan participants and matching contributions by employers to a qualified plan (Code Sec. 401(m); Reg. § 1.401(m)-1).[55] Matching contributions are those made by the employer on account of a contribution by a participant or because of an elective contribution by a participant under a 401(k) plan. The actual contribution percentage (ACP) test is essentially the same as the ADP test imposed on 401(k) plans (see ¶ 2111), except that it is applied to employee contributions and matching contributions rather than the elective contributions. There are two sets of comprehensive regulations governing matching contributions. The 2004 regulations generally apply for plan years beginning on or after January 1, 2006, though plan sponsors may elect to apply them to plan years ending after December 29, 2004. The 1991 regulations apply until the 2004 regulations become applicable to a plan.

The ACP test need not be satisfied if either of two alternative safe harbors is satisfied (Code Sec. 401(m)(11)).[56] These alternatives are the same as the ADP requirements discussed at ¶ 2111. Failure to satisfy the ACP test will not result in disqualification of the plan if the excess contributions (and the income allocable to them) are distributed within 12 months following the plan year in which they arose (Code Sec. 401(m)(6)(A)).[57] However, the employer is subject to a 10 percent tax based on the amount of the excess contributions unless the contributions (and the income allocable to them) are distributed to the highly compensated participants within 2½ months after the plan year in which they arose (Code Sec. 4979(f)(1)).[58] The amount of a corrective distribution (other than the portion representing the employee's contributions) is included in the employee's gross income. However, the 10 percent penalty on early distributions (see ¶ 2157) does not apply (Code Sec. 401(m)(7)).[59]

2127. Limits on Contributions and Benefits. A qualified plan must limit the benefits or contributions that may be provided for an individual participant (Code Sec. 415).[60] See ¶ 2151 for the limits imposed on annual *deductions*.

Defined Benefit Plan Limits. The maximum annual retirement benefit for any participant may not exceed the *lesser* of $180,000 (for 2007 or 100 percent of the

---

Footnote references are to paragraphs of the 2008 Standard Federal Tax Reports.

[52] ¶ 19,050, ¶ 19,076	[55] ¶ 17,502, ¶ 18,121	[58] ¶ 34,520, ¶ 34,523
[53] ¶ 19,050, ¶ 19,076	[56] ¶ 17,502	[59] ¶ 17,502, ¶ 18,123.044
[54] ¶ 19,050, ¶ 19,076	[57] ¶ 17,502, ¶ 18,123.044	[60] ¶ 19,200

participant's average compensation (not exceeding $225,000 for 2007) for the participant's three consecutive calendar years of highest compensation (Code Secs. 401(a)(17) and 415(b)(1)(A); Notice 2006-98;). For 2008, the dollar limit on annual benefits is $185,000, and the limit on considered compensation is $230,000 (IRS News Release IR-2007-171).[61]

The maximum annual benefit is actuarially reduced when retirement benefits are paid before age 62 (Code Sec. 415(b)(2)(C)) and increased when benefits are not paid until after age 65 (Code Sec. 415(b)(2)(D)). If certain requirements are met, an annual benefit of up to $10,000 may be provided by the plan even if that exceeds the 100 percent of compensation limit (Code Sec. 415(b)(4)). The benefit limit and the compensation limit are reduced in the case of individuals with less than 10 years of service with the employer (Code Sec. 415(b)(5)).[62]

Defined Contribution Plan Limits. For 2007, the annual addition to a participant's account may not exceed the *lesser* of: (1) 100 percent of the participant's compensation (not exceeding $225,000) or (2) $45,000. For 2008, the limit on considered compensation is $230,000 and the dollar limit is $46,000 (Code Secs. 401(a)(17) and 415(c)(1)(A); Reg. § 1.401(a)(17)-1; Notice 2006-98; IRS News Release IR-2007-171). The term "annual addition" includes employer and employee contributions and forfeitures (Code Sec. 415(c)(2)).

Catch-Up Contributions. Individuals who will be at least 50 years of age by the end of the tax year are permitted, if the plan allows it, to make "catch-up" contributions to a variety of employer-sponsored defined contribution plans (e.g., 401(k), SARSEPs, SIMPLE, 403(b) and 457 plans). Catch-up contributions to IRAs (traditional or Roth) are also permitted. The maximum amount of the catch-up contribution depends upon the type of plan involved. For example, the maximum catch-up contribution to a 401(k), 403(b), SARSEP, or 457 plan is $5,000 for 2007 and for 2008. The maximum catch-up contribution to a SIMPLE 401(k) or SIMPLE IRA is $2,500 for 2007 and for 2008 (Code Sec. 414(v)(2)(B)). For traditional and Roth IRAs, the maximum catch-up contribution is $1,000 for 2007 and for 2008 (Code Sec. 219(b)(5)(B)).

2128. Compensation Limits. A plan will not qualify unless the annual compensation of each employee taken into account under the plan for any year does not exceed a specific dollar amount (Code Sec. 401(a)(17)).[63] The maximum amount of compensation that may be considered is $225,000 for 2007 ($230,000 for 2008) (Notice 2006-98; IRS News Release IR-2007-171).[64] The compensation limit must be considered: (1) when determining an employee's maximum benefit or contribution and (2) when applying the nondiscrimination rules (Reg. § 1.401(a)(17)-1(a)).[65] An employee's "compensation" includes wages, as well as amounts received under some employee benefit plans that may be excluded from an employee's gross income (e.g., cafeteria plans and transportation fringe benefits) (Code Sec. 415(c)(3)(D)).[66]

2131. Requirement of Joint and Survivor and Pre-Retirement Survivor Annuities. A qualified plan that pays benefits in the form of an annuity must generally provide for their payment in the form of a joint and survivor annuity for the participant and the surviving spouse (Code Secs. 401(a)(11)(A)(i) and 417).[67] The annuity must be the actuarial equivalent of an annuity for the single life of the employee, and the survivor portion may not be less than 50 percent of the annuity paid during the joint lives of the employee and spouse (Code Sec. 417(b)).[68] A pre-retirement survivor annuity must be provided for the surviving spouse of a vested participant who dies prior to the earliest retirement age (Code Sec. 417(c)).[69]

An employee may "elect out" of either the joint and survivor or pre-retirement survivor annuity. However, the election may only be made with the written consent of the spouse and the consent must be witnessed by a notary public or plan representative

---

Footnote references are to paragraphs of the 2008 Standard Federal Tax Reports.

[61] ¶ 17,502, ¶ 19,150, ¶ 19,200
[62] ¶ 19,200
[63] ¶ 17,502

[64] ¶ 19,150
[65] ¶ 17,902
[66] ¶ 19,200

[67] ¶ 17,502, ¶ 19,260
[68] ¶ 19,260
[69] ¶ 17,729, ¶ 19,260

(Code Sec. 417(a)(2)).[70] The spouse's consent cannot be given in a prenuptial agreement (Reg. § 1.401(a)-20, Q&A-28).[71]

2133. Payment of Benefits. A plan will not qualify unless it provides that the payment of benefits will begin (unless the participant elects otherwise) no later than the 60th day after the *latest* of the close of the plan year in which:

> (1) the participant attains the earlier of age 65 or the normal retirement age specified in the plan;

> (2) the participant marks the 10th anniversary of enrollment in the plan; or

> (3) the participant terminates service with the employer (Code Sec. 401(a)(14)).[72]

Mandatory Cash-Outs. A qualified plan may pay out the balance of a participant's account without the participant's consent if the present value of the benefit does not exceed $5,000 (Code Sec. 411(a)(11)(A)).[73] If the present value of the benefit exceeds $1,000, and the participant does not elect otherwise, a mandatory distribution must be transferred directly to an IRA established by the plan for the benefit of the participant (Code Sec. 401(a)(31)(B), Notice 2005-5).

Phased Retirement Arrangements. The status under the current law of arrangements that allow workers to begin to receive distributions before full retirement is not clear. However, for years beginning after 2006, a plan will not fail to be a qualified retirement plan merely because it allows distributions to plan participants who are still working but have attained age 62 (i.e., working retirement) (Code Sec. 401(a)(36), as added by the Pension Protection Act of 2006 (P.L. 109-280)).

2135. Required Minimum Distributions (RMDs). A qualified plan must satisfy a minimum distribution requirement (Code Sec. 401(a)(9)).[74] Under this requirement, distribution of the employee's interest in the plan must begin by the "required beginning date." A participant's required beginning date (except in the case of a five percent owner) is April 1 of the calendar year following *the later of:*

> (1) the calendar year in which the participant attains age 70½ or

> (2) the calendar year in which the employee retires.

For a five percent owner (see ¶ 2139), the required beginning date is April 1 of the year following the year in which the individual reached age 70½.

If the employee's entire interest is not distributed by the required beginning date, then the employee's interest must generally be paid out over a period that does not exceed the life or life expectancy of the participant or the combined lives or life expectancies of the participant and his or her designated beneficiary (Code Sec. 401(a)(9)(A)).[75] IRS regulations provide the details concerning required minimum distributions (RMDs). These regulations apply to RMDs from qualified plans, 403(b) plans, 457 plans and IRAs (Reg. § 1.401(a)(9)-1). Distributions made to a participant or the beneficiary of a participant must satisfy the RMD rules in each calendar year. The RMD for a year is generally equal to the participant's accrued benefit or account balance as of the end of the prior year, divided by the appropriate distribution period (Reg. §§ 1.401(a)(9)-5, Q & A-1, 1.401(a)(9)-6, Q & A-1).

If RMDs begin while the participant is alive, the distribution period is derived from one of two tables. The *Uniform Lifetime Table* is used to determine the distribution period for lifetime distributions to an unmarried individual or to a married individual if the individual's spouse is either: (1) not the sole designated beneficiary or (2) is the sole designated beneficiary and is not more than 10 years younger than the individual (Reg. § 1.401(a)(9)-9, Q & A-2). The *Joint and Last Survivor Table* is used to determine the distribution period for lifetime distributions to a married individual whose spouse is the sole beneficiary and is more than 10 years younger than the individual (Reg. § 1.401(a)(9)-9, Q & A-3). The *Uniform Lifetime Table* is reproduced below.

Footnote references are to paragraphs of the 2008 Standard Federal Tax Reports.

[70] ¶ 17,729, ¶ 19,260	[72] ¶ 17,502	[74] ¶ 17,502
[71] ¶ 17,729, ¶ 17,730.0435	[73] ¶ 19,050	[75] ¶ 17,502

Required Distributions After Participant's Death. If required distributions have been made to the participant before his or her death, then any remaining benefit payable to a beneficiary may be payable over the longer of the life expectancy of the beneficiary or of the participant (Code Sec. 401(a)(9)(B)(i); Reg. § 1.401(a)(9)-5, Q & A-5(a)).[76]

If required distributions have not been made to the participant before his or her death, then the participant's entire interest is to be distributed to the beneficiary within five years after the death (Code Sec. 401(a)(9)(B)(ii)).[77] However, most beneficiaries will be able to take advantage of one of two exceptions to the five-year distribution rule (Reg. § 1.401(a)(9)-5, Q & A-5(b)).

First, the five-year rule does not apply when:

(1) any portion of the participant's interest is payable to (or for the benefit of) a designated beneficiary;

(2) the portion of the participant's interest to which the beneficiary is entitled will be distributed over the life of the beneficiary or over a period not extending beyond the life expectancy of the beneficiary (for this purpose, the *Single Life Table* provided in the regulations and reproduced below is used to determine an individual beneficiary's life expectancy (Reg. § 1.401(a)(9)-9, Q & A-1)); and

(3) the distributions commence no later than one year after the date of the participant's death (Code Sec. 401(a)(9)(B)(iii)).[78]

Second, the five-year rule does not apply if:

(1) the designated beneficiary is the participant's surviving spouse;

(2) the portion of the participant's interest to which the surviving spouse is entitled will be distributed over the life of that spouse (or over a period not exceeding his or her life expectancy); and

(3) the distributions commence no later than the date on which the participant would have attained age 70½ (Code Sec. 401(a)(9)(B)(iv)).[79]

If the surviving spouse dies before payments are required to begin, the five-year rule is to be applied as if the surviving spouse were the participant. Payments to a surviving spouse under a qualified joint and survivor annuity (¶ 2131) will satisfy this second exception.

Final Determination of Beneficiary. A beneficiary must be designated as of the date of the employee's death. However, the final determination of who is a beneficiary is not made until September 30 of the year following the calendar year of death (Reg. § 1.401(a)(9)-4, Q&A-4(a)). As a result, if an individual does not remain a beneficiary on the September 30 deadline, the individual is not taken into consideration when determining the RMDs that must be made from the retirement account. For example, individuals who are named beneficiaries as of the time of the participant's death may not be beneficiaries by the September 30 deadline because they have disclaimed their right to any portion of the retirement account.

Penalty for Failure to Receive RMDs. An excise tax is imposed on an employee or beneficiary who does not take an RMD. The tax is 50 percent of the amount by which the RMD exceeds the distribution actually made (Code Sec. 4974(a)).[80] The tax may be waived if the RMD shortfall is due to reasonable error and if steps are taken to correct it. The penalty is reported on Form 5329, Additional Taxes on Qualified Plans (Including IRAs) and Other Tax Favored Accounts. If the individual believes that the tax should not apply due to reasonable error, the tax should be paid and a letter of explanation attached to Form 5329. If the IRS waives the tax, it will issue a refund.

Footnote references are to paragraphs of the 2008 Standard Federal Tax Reports.

[76] ¶ 17,502
[77] ¶ 17,502
[78] ¶ 17,502
[79] ¶ 17,502
[80] ¶ 34,380

Uniform Lifetime Table

Age of employee	Distribution period	Age of employee	Distribution period
70	27.4	92	10.2
71	26.5	93	9.6
72	25.6	94	9.1
73	24.7	95	8.6
74	23.8	96	8.1
75	22.9	97	7.6
76	22.0	98	7.1
77	21.2	99	6.7
78	20.3	100	6.3
79	19.5	101	5.9
80	18.7	102	5.5
81	17.9	103	5.2
82	17.1	104	4.9
83	16.3	105	4.5
84	15.5	106	4.2
85	14.8	107	3.9
86	14.1	108	3.7
87	13.4	109	3.4
88	12.7	110	3.1
89	12.0	111	2.9
90	11.4	112	2.6
91	10.8	113	2.4
		114	2.1
		115+	1.9

Single Life Table (for use by beneficiaries)

Age	Life Expectancy	Age	Life Expectancy	Age	Life Expectancy	Age	Life Expectancy
0	82.4	27	56.2	55	29.6	83	8.6
1	81.6	28	55.3	56	28.7	84	8.1
2	80.6	29	54.3	57	27.9	85	7.6
3	79.7	30	53.3	58	27.0	86	7.1
4	78.7	31	52.4	59	26.1	87	6.7
5	77.7	32	51.4	60	25.2	88	6.3
6	76.7	33	50.4	61	24.4	89	5.9
7	75.8	34	49.4	62	23.5	90	5.5
8	74.8	35	48.5	63	22.7	91	5.2
9	73.8	36	47.5	64	21.8	92	4.9
10	72.8	37	46.5	65	21.0	93	4.6
11	71.8	38	45.6	66	20.2	94	4.3
12	70.8	39	44.6	67	19.4	95	4.1
13	69.9	40	43.6	68	18.6	96	3.8
14	68.9	41	42.7	69	17.8	97	3.6
15	67.9	42	41.7	70	17.0	98	3.4
16	66.9	43	40.7	71	16.3	99	3.1
17	66.0	44	39.8	72	15.5	100	2.9
18	65.0	45	38.8	73	14.8	101	2.7
19	64.0	46	37.9	74	14.1	102	2.5
20	63.0	47	37.0	75	13.4	103	2.3
21	62.1	48	36.0	76	12.7	104	2.1
22	61.1	49	35.1	77	12.1	105	1.9
23	60.1	50	34.2	78	11.4	106	1.7
24	59.1	51	33.3	79	10.8	107	1.5
25	58.2	52	32.3	80	10.2	108	1.4
26	57.2	53	31.4	81	9.7	109	1.2
		54	30.5	82	9.1	110	1.1
						111+	1.0

2137. Anti-Assignment Provision. A qualified plan must provide that benefits under the plan may not be assigned or otherwise transferred (Code Secs. 401(a)(13) and 414(p)).[81] An exception is made for assignments ordered by a "qualified domestic relations order" (QDRO) issued under a state's domestic relations law (see ¶ 2166) (Code Secs. 401(a)(13)(B) and 414(p)). In addition, a participant's benefits may be reduced when the individual has committed a breach of fiduciary duty or committed a criminal act against the plan.

2139. Top-Heavy Plans. More stringent qualification requirements must be met for qualified plans or tax-sheltered annuity arrangements that primarily benefit an employer's key employees. These plans are referred to in the Code as "top-heavy plans" (Code Sec. 416(a)).[82] Most qualified plans must include language stating that they will comply with the top-heavy rules if they become top-heavy. However, the top-heavy requirements do not apply to SIMPLE 401(k) (¶ 2112) or SIMPLE IRA (¶ 2185) plans. A plan is top heavy if the accrued benefits or account balances of key employees are more than 60 percent of the total benefits or balances under the plan.

Accelerated Vesting. For any plan year in which a plan is top heavy, the benefits of each employee for that year must *either* be: (1) 100 percent vested if the employee has at least three years of service or (2) 20 percent vested after two years of service with a 20 percent increase for each later year of service (Code Sec. 416(b)).[83] See ¶ 2121 for the general vesting requirements.

Minimum Benefits and Contributions for Non-Key Employees. In any plan year in which a *defined benefit plan* is top heavy, each participating non-key employee must be provided with a retirement benefit that is not less than two percent of average annual compensation (see ¶ 2128), for the employee's five consecutive years of highest compensation, multiplied by years of service (up to a maximum of ten years of service) (Code Sec. 416(c)(1)).[84]

In any plan year in which a *defined contribution plan* is top heavy, each participating non-key employee must be provided with a contribution that is not less than three percent of such employee's compensation for that year. Employer matching contributions are taken into account when determining if this contribution requirement has been met. If the contribution rate for the key employee receiving the largest contribution is less than three percent, then the contribution rate for such key employee is used to determine the minimum contribution for non-key employees (Code Sec. 416(c)(2)).[85]

Key Employee Defined. A key employee is defined as an employee who, at any time during the plan year, is:

    (1) an officer with compensation in excess of $145,000 for 2007 ($150,000 for 2008) (Notice 2006-98; IRS News Release IR-2007-171);[86]

    (2) a more-than-five-percent owner; or

    (3) a more-than-one-percent owner who received more than $150,000 (not subject to an inflation adjustment) in compensation (Code Sec. 416(i)(1)(A)).[87]

In the case of a corporate employer, an employee is a five-percent owner when the employee owns more than five percent of the employer's outstanding stock or stock possessing more than five percent of the total combined voting power of all of the employer's stock. When the employer is not a corporation, a five-percent owner is any employee who owns more than five percent of the capital or profits interest in the employer. An employee is also treated as owning stock owned by certain members of the employee's family or, in the case of any employer which is not a corporation, by partnerships, estates, trusts or corporations in which the employee has an interest (Code Sec. 416(i)(1)(B)). The same rules apply to determine whether an individual owner is a one-percent owner.

Footnote references are to paragraphs of the 2008 Standard Federal Tax Reports.

[81] ¶ 17,502, ¶ 19,150
[82] ¶ 19,250, ¶ 19,253
[83] ¶ 19,250

[84] ¶ 19,250
[85] ¶ 19,250
[86] ¶ 19,150

[87] ¶ 19,250

2141. Minimum Funding Standards. In order to ensure that defined benefit pension plans are adequately funded, minimum and full-funding limits are imposed. Annual contributions to a defined benefit pension plan by the employer must meet a minimum funding standard which includes amortization of past service liability (liability arising from a participant's service before the plan was established) as well as current plan costs (Code Sec. 412(b)(1)).[88] Traditionally, the interest rate of the 30-year Treasury bond has been used by employers to calculate their funding obligations to their defined benefit plans (Code Sec. 412(b)(5)(B)(ii)(I)). However, for plan years beginning in calendar years 2004 through 2007, the Treasury bond rate has been replaced with a rate based on long-term corporate bonds (Code Sec. 412(b)(5)(B)(ii)(II), as amended by the Pension Protection Act of 2006 (P.L. 109-280)).

In order to prevent employers from claiming tax deductions for contributions to a plan in excess of the amount necessary to fund plan benefits, plans are subject to a "full-funding limitation". For plan years beginning in 2006 and 2007, the full-funding limit is the excess, if any, of 150 percent of the current liability under the plan, including normal cost, over the value of the plan's assets (Code Sec. 404(a)(1)(A) and (D), as amended by the Pension Protection Act of 2006 (P.L. 109-280)). As applied to a money purchase pension plan, the funding requirements are satisfied if the promised contributions are made in each year (Prop. Reg. § 1.412(b)-1(a)). The funding requirements do not apply to profit-sharing, stock bonus, government or church plans (Code Sec. 412(h)). Failure to meet minimum funding requirements or correct shortfalls will generally subject the employer to an excise tax, though the IRS may temporarily waive the requirement for a particular year in the event of business hardship (Code Sec. 4971).[89]

Pension Protection Act of 2006. The Pension Protection Act of 2006 made major changes in the funding rules that will take effect for plan years beginning after 2007. Employers maintaining single-employer defined benefit plans will be required to make minimum contributions each year. Full funding of plans will be required, with existing shortfalls required to be eliminated over seven years (Code Secs. 412, 430 and 436, as amended and added by the Pension Protection Act of 2006 (P.L. 109-280)). The funding requirements applicable to multiemployer plans have also been revised for years after 2007 (Code Secs. 431 and 432, as added by the Pension Protection Act of 2006 (P.L. 109-280)).

2143. Prohibited Transactions. Certain transactions between a qualified employees' trust and a plan fiduciary or other "disqualified person" are prohibited (Code Sec. 4975(c)).[90] The "disqualified person" who engages in the prohibited transaction is liable for excise taxes based upon the amount of the prohibited transaction. The basic excise tax rate is 15 percent. If the prohibited transaction is not corrected before the IRS assesses the tax or mails a notice of deficiency regarding it, the excise tax rate increases to 100 percent (Code Sec. 4975(b)).[91]

Plan Loans. Loans of plan assets to owners of the employer, including owner-employees, are generally prohibited transactions. Loans of IRA assets to the account owner are always prohibited, but a loan from an employer plan may qualify for an exception to the rule (Code Sec. 4975(f)(6)(B)(iii)). Loans from employer plans to disqualified persons are not prohibited if certain requirements are met, including the following (Code Sec. 4975(d)(1)):

  (1) loans have to be available to all participants on a reasonably equivalent basis;

  (2) the plan must explicitly provide for such loans;

  (3) the loan must have a reasonable rate of interest; and

  (4) the loan must be adequately secured.

For this purpose, the term "owner-employee" is defined as: (1) a self-employed person who owns the entire interest in an unincorporated trade or business (e.g., a sole proprietor) or (2) an individual who owns more than a 10 percent capital or profits interest in a partnership (Code Sec. 401(c)(3)).

Footnote references are to paragraphs of the 2008 Standard Federal Tax Reports.

[88] ¶ 19,100   [90] ¶ 34,400
[89] ¶ 34,320   [91] ¶ 34,400

¶2141

2145. Returns. Generally, a qualified retirement plan (¶ 2117) must file Form 5500 each year (Code Sec. 6058).[92] Form 5500 and accompanying schedules are used to report detailed information concerning various aspects of employee benefit plans (e.g., accountant's report, information concerning the fiduciary and financial information). However, some plans may be able to file a simpler Form 5500-EZ. This form may be filed if a plan's only participants are an individual and spouse who together own the business (whether or not incorporated) for which the plan is established. Form 5500-EZ may also be used by the plan of a partnership if the only participants are partners and their spouses. Form 5500 or 5500-EZ need not be filed if certain conditions are met (e.g., the plan, and any other plan of the employer, had total assets of $100,000 or less at the end of every plan year beginning on or after January 1, 1994). Welfare benefit plans are generally not required to file annual reports (Notice 2002-24).

Plan Years Beginning After 2006. The Pension Protection Act of 2006 requires that, for plan years beginning after 2006, simplified reporting requirements be imposed for plans with fewer than 25 participants, and that the exclusion from filing for plans with total assets of $100,000 or less be extended to one-participant plans with total assets of $250,000 or less at the end of a plan year (Sec. 1103 of the Pension Protection Act of 2006 (P.L. 109-280)). Specific guidance regarding this simplified reporting option will be included in the instructions to the 2007 Form 5500.

Due Date. If a Form 5500 or Form 5500-EZ has to be filed, as a general rule, the form and its required schedules have to be filed no later than the last day of the seventh month after the plan year ends (e.g., July 31 for calendar year plans). A one-time extension of 2½ months may be obtained by filing Form 5558, Application for Extension of Time to File Certain Employee Plan Returns. An automatic extension for filing Form 5500 or Form 5500-EZ will be granted if certain conditions are met (e.g., the plan year and the employer's tax year are the same and the employer has been granted an extension to file its tax return). Penalties may be imposed for failure to file the required annual information return or, in the case of defined benefit plans, the actuarial report (Schedule B of Form 5500) (Code Sec. 6652).[93]

Contributions Deduction

2147. Contributions by Employers and Employees. Contributions by an employer to a *defined contribution plan* (e.g., 401(k) plan) or a *defined benefit plan* are deductible, subject to the annual limits discussed at ¶ 2151. Employee contributions, with the notable exception of contributions made to traditional IRAs (see ¶ 2170), are generally not deductible. However, an employee's elective deferrals to retirement plans such as qualified 401(k) plans, SEP IRAs, and SIMPLE plans are excluded from the employee's gross income.

The annual limits on deductions (see ¶ 2151) are related to the contributions allowed to qualified plans (see ¶ 2127). In the case of a defined contribution plan, contributions that are in excess of the maximum allowed amount may not be deducted (Code Sec. 404(j)(1)(B)).[94] In the case of a defined benefit plan, contributions that are in excess of the amount that is actuarially necessary to provide the maximum allowed benefit are not deductible (Code Sec. 404(j)(1)(A)).[95]

2149. General Rules for Deduction for Contributions. Employers are allowed to deduct their contributions to a qualified plan whether or not the rights of the employees to the contributions are forfeitable. Generally, contributions are deductible only for the tax year when paid regardless of whether the taxpayer uses the cash or accrual method of accounting. (However, excess contributions may be carried over to later years (see ¶ 2151).) A deductible contribution is deemed made on the last day of the tax year if it is paid no later than the due date (including extensions) of the taxpayer's return (Code Sec. 404(a)(6)).[96] However, in the case of most defined benefit plans, the deadline for making the required contribution to the funding standard account is 8½ months after the close of the plan year (Code Sec. 412(c)(10)). As a result, the required funding date

---

Footnote references are to paragraphs of the 2008 Standard Federal Tax Reports.

[92] ¶ 36,500
[93] ¶ 39,480, ¶ 39,490.025
[94] ¶ 18,330
[95] ¶ 18,330
[96] ¶ 18,330

may actually come before the last day for making deductible contributions. Interest may be charged if the contribution to the standard account is not made by the due date (Code Sec. 412(m)).

Elective and matching contributions under a 401(k) plan (see ¶ 2111), and other types of defined contribution plans (see ¶ 2103) are not deductible by the employer for a tax year if they are attributable to compensation earned by participants after the end of that year (Rev. Rul. 90-105 and Rev. Rul. 2002-46).[97]

2151. Limits on Deductions for Contributions. There are limits on the annual deductions that may be claimed for an employer's contributions to a qualified plan. In applying these limits, the amount of an employee's compensation that may be taken into account may not exceed $225,000 for 2007 ($230,000 for 2008) (Code Sec. 404(l); Notice 2006-98; IRS News Release IR-2007-171).[98]

Defined Benefit Pension Plans. Defined benefit plans are limited in the amount of annual benefits that they may pay (Code Sec. 415(b)(1)) and the contributions that may be deducted to fund such benefits (Code Sec. 404(a)). An employer may use either one of the following methods for determining the annual limit on the deduction that may be claimed for contributions to a defined benefit plan (Code Sec. 404(a)(1)(A)):[99]

> (1) *Level Funding Method.* An amount necessary to provide, for all participants under the plan, the remaining unfunded cost of their past and current service credits distributed as a level amount or level percentage of compensation over the remaining service of each participant. Under this method, the past service liability for each participant is deducted ratably over the employee's projected years of service until retirement (Code Sec. 404(a)(1)(A)(ii)).

> (2) *Normal Cost Method.* An amount equal to the normal ("current") cost of the plan plus, if past service or other supplementary credits are provided, an amount not in excess of that necessary to amortize these credits in equal payments over 10 years (Code Sec. 404(a)(1)(A)(iii)). However, all defined benefit plans may deduct 100 percent of their unfunded current liability (Code Sec. 404(a)(1)(D)(i)).[100]

Profit-Sharing and Stock Bonus Plans. For profit-sharing or stock bonus plans, the maximum deduction for contributions is 25 percent of the compensation of all the participants in the plan (Code Sec. 404(a)(3)(A)(i)(I)).[101] For the deduction limits that apply to SIMPLE plans, see ¶ 2185C.

> **Example:** In 2007, Titanic Corporation paid $1,250,000 in compensation to its employees who participated in its profit-sharing plan. As a result of 25 percent limit, Titanic will be able to contribute and deduct a maximum of $312,500 ($1,250,000 × 25 percent) to the profit-sharing plan.

Money Purchase Pension Plans. Defined contribution plans that are subject to the funding standards of Code Sec. 412(c) (e.g., money purchase plans) are subject to the same limits as profit-sharing or stock bonus plans when determining the maximum deduction (i.e., 25 percent of compensation) (Code Sec. 404(a)(3)(A)(v)).[102]

Employer Maintaining More Than One Type of Plan. If an employer makes contributions to a defined contribution plan and also to a defined benefit plan, there is an overall limit on the deduction of these contributions. The deduction is limited to the *greater* of: (1) 25 percent of the compensation paid or accrued for that year to the participants in all such plans or (2) the amount necessary to satisfy the minimum funding standards of Code Sec. 412. The overall limitation does not apply when no individual is a participant in more than one plan maintained by the employer (Code Sec. 404(a)(7)(A) and (C)).[103] Also, the overall deduction limit does not apply when only "elective contributions" (e.g., contributions made under 401(k) plans or SEP plans) are made to any of the employer's defined contribution plans during the tax year (Code Sec. 404(a)(7)(C)(ii)).

Footnote references are to paragraphs of the 2008 Standard Federal Tax Reports.

[97] ¶ 18,347.27	[100] ¶ 18,330	[103] ¶ 18,330
[98] ¶ 18,330	[101] ¶ 18,330	
[99] ¶ 18,330	[102] ¶ 18,330	

Elective Deferrals. Elective deferrals made by employees are not taken into account when determining deduction limits for stock bonus and profit-sharing plans, combination defined benefit and defined contribution plans, and ESOPs (Code Sec. 404(n)). The term "elective deferrals" includes amounts contributed to 401(k) plans, SEPs, SIMPLEs, and 403(b) plans (Code Sec. 402(g)(3)).

Compensation. "Compensation," for purposes of the deduction limits for stock bonus and profit-sharing plans, combination defined benefit and defined contribution plans, self-employed plans and ESOPs, includes certain amounts that are generally excluded from gross income (e.g., certain disability benefits and elective deferrals) (Code Sec. 404(a)(12)).

Carryovers. When an employer's contribution exceeds the maximum deductible amount for the year, the excess amount may be carried over and deducted in later tax years. However, the total of the carryovers and the regular contributions in the carry-over year may not exceed the deductible limit for that year (Code Sec. 404(a)(1)(E) and (3)(A)(ii)).[104] Similarly, if the 25 percent overall limit for contributions to different types of plans is exceeded, the excess may be carried over. However, the combination of carryovers and regular deductions for any succeeding year may not exceed 25 percent of the compensation paid to participants in that year (Code Sec. 404(a)(7)(B)).[105]

2152. Plan Covering Self-Employed Participants. Contributions and deductions for a self-employed participant covered by a qualified plan are subject to the same basic rules that apply to participants who are common law employees. The deduction limits are based in part on the compensation paid to eligible employees participating in the plan. For this purpose, a self-employed individual's compensation is his or her earned income, defined as the net earnings from self-employment reduced by (Code Sec. 401(c)(2)(A)):[106]

(1) the deduction allowed for contributions made on behalf of the self-employed participant (Code Sec. 401(c)(2)(A)(v)).[107] When the entire contribution is deductible, the equivalent of this reduction is achieved by limiting the contribution to a percentage of earned income (calculated without regard to the deduction) determined by dividing the nominal rate by the integer one plus that rate. See *"Percentage Equivalents,"* below, for more information.

Example 1: If the plan calls for a contribution equal to 10 percent of each participant's compensation, the contribution on behalf of a self-employed participant is determined by dividing 10 percent by 1.10. The result, 9.0909 percent, is the contribution rate for the self-employed individual.

(2) the deduction from gross income that is allowed for 50 percent of the self-employment tax paid by the self-employed participant (Code Sec. 401(c)(2)(A)(vi)).[108] See ¶ 2670 for information concerning the computation of the self-employment tax and the related deduction for a portion of that tax.

Calculating the Deduction for the Self-Employed. In IRS Publication 560 (Retirement Plans for Small Business), the IRS provides the procedure for calculating deductible contributions to a plan that defines contributions as a percentage of compensation (e.g., a SEP-IRA). The procedure is as follows:

(1) The self-employed participant's net earnings from self-employment are reduced by 50 percent of the self-employment tax.

(2) The net earnings as reduced in (1) are multiplied by the reduced contribution rate applicable to self-employed participants (see Example 1, above).

Percentage Equivalents. In IRS Publication 560 (Retirement Plans for Small Business), the IRS provides a rate table that may be used to determine the reduced contribution rate that applies to a self-employed individual's contributions to a SEP or other type of defined contribution plan. For example, under the rate table, if the maximum plan contribution rate is 15 percent, the maximum deduction percentage for contributions to the self-employed individual's own plan is 13.0435 percent. The 15

Footnote references are to paragraphs of the 2008 Standard Federal Tax Reports.

| [104] ¶ 18,330 | [106] ¶ 17,502 | [108] ¶ 17,502 |
| [105] ¶ 18,330 | [107] ¶ 17,502 | |

percent rate applies to employees. Under the rate table, if the plan's maximum contribution rate is 25 percent, a 20 percent rate applies to the self-employed individual, and the 25 percent rate applies to employees.[109]

> **Example 2:** Mary Van is self-employed and has one employee, Bob Halin. Mary has adopted a SEP-IRA for her business and for 2007 has decided to contribute the maximum percentage (i.e., 25 percent) to the retirement plan. For 2007, Bob's salary was $30,000. Therefore, Mary may contribute a maximum of $7,500 ($30,000 x 25 percent) to his SEP-IRA. She will claim the $7,500 contribution as a business expense on Line 19 (Pension and profit-sharing plans) of her 2007 Schedule C.

> **Example 3:** Assume the same facts as in Example 2. Mary's net profit for 2007 as shown on Line 31 of Schedule C is $70,000. In determining her earnings for the purpose of computing the maximum deductible contribution that she may make to her own SEP-IRA, Mary must deduct 50 percent of her self-employment tax from the net earnings shown on Schedule C. As a result, her self-employment earnings for computing her SEP-IRA contribution are $65,054 ($70,000 (net earnings on Schedule C) – $4,946 (50 percent of self-employment tax)). Under the "percentage equivalent adjustment," Mary applies a 20 percent contribution rate and not the 25 percent rate she used for her employee. Therefore, Mary's maximum contribution to her own SEP-IRA is $13,011 ($65,054 x 20 percent). Mary claims the deduction on Line 28 (Self-employed SEP, SIMPLE, and qualified plans), page 1, of her 2007 Form 1040.

401(k) Plan for the Self-Employed. In general, the same rules that apply to 401(k) plans established by other types of entities apply to the 401(k) plans of self-employed taxpayers (see ¶ 2111) (Reg. § 1.401(k)-1(a)(6)(i)). This makes a 401(k) plan more advantageous than other types of self-employment plans (e.g., SEPs), because the taxpayer may make both employer contributions and elective employee contributions (subject to the general limit for additions to defined contributions plans, see "*Defined Contribution Plan Limits,*" above). Self-employed 401(k) plans may also offer the possibility of being able to make loans to participating employees (see ¶ 2143).

Retirement Contribution for Partner. A partnership's deduction for retirement contributions on behalf of a partner must be allocated solely to that partner (Reg. § 1.404(e)-1A(f)).[110] It cannot be allocated among all of the partners pursuant to the partnership agreement (see ¶ 428 concerning allocations made under a partnership agreement).

Contribution Is Not a Business Expense. A contribution to a qualified plan for the benefit of a self-employed individual is not a business expense of that individual (*D.L. Gale,* 91-2 USTC ¶ 50,356).[111] Thus, it is not deductible on Schedule C of Form 1040 or page 1 of Form 1065 and is not deductible in calculating self-employment tax. For a sole proprietorship, the contribution is claimed as an adjustment to gross income on page 1 of Form 1040. For a partnership, the contribution is shown on Schedule K-1 of Form 1065 (Partner's Share of Income, Credits, Deductions, etc.) and deducted from gross income on page 1 of the partner's Form 1040 (see ¶ 431 concerning the separate reporting of partnership items).

SEP-IRA Rules. The rules governing SEP-IRAs are discussed in detail at ¶ 2184.

Taxation of Benefits

2153. Treatment of Lump-Sum Distribution. Employees born before January 2, 1936 may elect to have their lump-sum distributions from qualified retirement plans taxed under favorable rates. All other distributions are taxed under the annuity rules (¶ 2155). A lump-sum distribution is a distribution of a participant's entire interest in a qualified plan. The amount distributed (or, in the case of multiple distributees, a distributee's portion of it) must be received within a single tax year of the distributee. In the case of a participant other than a self-employed person, the distribution must be made:

Footnote references are to paragraphs of the 2008 Standard Federal Tax Reports.

[109] ¶ 17,933.036   [110] ¶ 18,359   [111] ¶ 18,347.17

¶2153

(1) because of the participant's death;

(2) due to separation from the service of the employer; or

(3) after the individual has attained age 59½.

In the case of a self-employed person, the distribution must be made because of the individual's death or it must be made after age 59½, unless the individual was previously disabled (Code Sec. 402(e)(4)(D)(i)).[112]

The rules applicable to lump-sum distributions are applied without regard to community property laws (Code Sec. 402(e)(4)(D)(iii)). As a result, a lump-sum distribution is considered to belong entirely to the participant, rather than half to the participant and half to his or her spouse (*R.L. Karem*, TC, Dec. 49,091).[113] However, a spouse may acquire an interest in retirement plan assets by means of a qualified domestic relations order (see ¶ 2166).

Determining Taxable Amount. The entire amount of the lump-sum distribution is not always subject to taxation. To determine the taxable portion of the lump-sum distribution, subtract from the total amount of the distribution the following:

(1) nondeductible amounts contributed to the plan by the participant (less any previous distributions the participant received that were not includible in gross income);

(2) any premiums paid by the plan to furnish a participant with life insurance protection that were included in gross income (see ¶ 2156);

(3) any repayments of loans from the plan that were included in gross income (¶ 2164);

(4) the current actuarial value of any annuity contract that was included in the lump-sum distribution; and

(5) net unrealized appreciation in any employer securities that were distributed as part of the lump-sum distribution (unless the taxpayer elects to be taxed on this appreciation).

If the net unrealized appreciation is excluded from gross income upon distribution of the securities, tax is deferred until the securities are sold or exchanged. The cost or other basis of the employer securities is included in the taxable portion of the distribution (Code Sec. 402(e)(4)(B)).[114]

Born Before January 2, 1936. In order to be able to use the favorable tax treatment discussed below, the employee must have been born before January 2, 1936. However, a beneficiary of an employee born before January 2, 1936 may also qualify. A spouse or former spouse who was named as an alternate payee under a qualified domestic relations order (see ¶ 2166) will also qualify if the employee was born before January 2, 1936. The recipient (employee, beneficiary, or alternate payee) must elect to use this special tax treatment for all such amounts received during the tax year (Code Sec. 402(d)(4)(B), before amendment by P.L. 104-188). Also, this special treatment is *not* available if any portion of the lump-sum distribution is rolled over into another plan (Code Sec. 402(d)(4)(K), before amendment by P.L. 104-188).[115]

Taxation of Lump-Sum Distributions. If the participant was born before January 2, 1936, the distributee may choose among the options listed below for computing the tax on a lump-sum distribution of the participant's benefit. However, choices (2) and (3) may be selected only if the participant was a participant during at least five tax years preceding the year of distribution (Code Sec. 402(d)(4)(F), before amendment by P.L. 104-188).[116]

(1) A distributee may include the entire taxable amount in gross income. If this is done, it will be combined with all other gross income and, after deductions, taxed at the normal rates applying to income received in the tax year.

Footnote references are to paragraphs of the 2008 Standard Federal Tax Reports.

[112] ¶ 18,217A.01
[113] ¶ 18,207.11

[114] ¶ 18,202
[115] ¶ 18,217A.01

[116] ¶ 18,217A.01

(2) A distributee may calculate a separate tax on the entire taxable amount by employing a 10-year averaging method (Sec. 1122(h)(5) of the Tax Reform Act of 1986).[117]

(3) A distributee may: (a) pay a separate 20 percent tax on the pre-1974 portion of the taxable amount and (b) calculate a separate tax under the 10-year averaging method for the post-1973 portion of the taxable amount (Sec. 1122(h)(3) of the Tax Reform Act of 1986).[118] If the 20 percent flat tax is elected, the 20 percent rate is applied to the entire pre-1974 amount and not to that amount after it has been reduced by capital losses.

Making the Election. The distributee must make an election to use the averaging method (Code Sec. 402(d)(4)(B)(ii), before amendment by P.L. 104-188).[119] An election must also be made in order to use the flat 20 percent tax for the pre-1974 portion of a lump-sum distribution (Sec. 1122(h)(3) and (4) of the Tax Reform Act of 1986). There are no special procedures for making an election. Form 4972, Tax on Lump-Sum Distributions, is used to compute the tax under the options that are available to the individual. In the event that a lump-sum distribution is shared by two or more distributees, the tax for each distributee is figured by using the method that is stipulated in the instructions to Form 4972.

An election to use 10-year averaging may be made only once for each plan participant (Code Sec. 402(d)(4)(B), before amendment by P.L. 104-188; Sec. 1122(h)(5) of the Tax Reform Act of 1986). Therefore, a person is permitted to make an averaging election for a lump-sum distribution received from his own plan and another election for a lump-sum distribution received as a beneficiary of another plan.

An election to apply a flat 20 percent tax to the pre-1974 portion of such a distribution can be made only once with respect to the same participant. The election is treated as an election to use averaging, thus precluding any averaging for a subsequent lump-sum distribution with respect to the same participant (Sec. 1122(h) of the Tax Reform Act of 1986).

10-Year Averaging Computation. Under 10-year averaging, the tax is computed (using the tax rates in the table below) on ¹/₁₀ of the excess of the portion of the distribution subject to averaging over the minimum distribution allowance. The result is then multiplied by 10. The minimum distribution allowance is: (1) the lesser of $10,000 or one-half of the portion subject to averaging, (2) reduced, but not below zero, by 20 percent of the amount by which the portion subject to averaging exceeds $20,000. If the amount subject to averaging is $70,000 or more, the minimum distribution is zero.

Ten-Year Averaging Rate Table

Over—	But Not Over—	The Tax Is	of the Amount Over—
$ –0–	$1,190	11%	$–0–
1,190	2,270	$130.90 + 12%	1,190
2,270	4,530	260.50 + 14%	2,270
4,530	6,690	576.90 + 15%	4,530
6,690	9,170	900.90 + 16%	6,690
9,170	11,440	1,297.70 + 18%	9,170
11,440	13,710	1,706.30 + 20%	11,440
13,710	17,160	2,160.30 + 23%	13,710
17,160	22,880	2,953.80 + 26%	17,160
22,880	28,600	4,441.00 + 30%	22,880
28,600	34,320	6,157.00 + 34%	28,600
34,320	42,300	8,101.80 + 38%	34,320
42,300	57,190	11,134.20 + 42%	42,300
57,190	85,790	17,388.00 + 48%	57,190
85,790	. . . .	31,116.00 + 50%	85,790

Footnote references are to paragraphs of the 2008 Standard Federal Tax Reports.

[117] ¶ 18,217A.021   [118] ¶ 18,217A.021   [119] ¶ 18,217A.021

When calculating the tax under 10-year averaging on a distribution inherited from a decedent, the beneficiary may take a deduction for the federal estate tax (see ¶ 191) allocable to the lump-sum distribution (Code Sec. 691(c)(1)).[120]

Annuity Contract Distributed. A lump-sum distribution may include an annuity contract. If so, the contract is not taxed as a part of the lump-sum distribution. Rather, annuity payments are taxed under the annuity rules (see ¶ 817 and following). However, the contract has an impact on the calculation of tax under 10-year averaging. Essentially, the actuarial value of the contract is included in the amount subject to averaging and the tax calculated on that amount. Then a separate tax is calculated on the actuarial value of the annuity alone. The latter is subtracted from the former, and the difference is the final tax (Code Sec. 402(d)(2), before amendment by P.L. 104-188).[121]

2155. Taxation of Distributions. The tax treatment of a distribution other than a lump-sum distribution to an individual born before January 2, 1936 (¶ 2153) depends on the form of the distribution. If the plan distribution takes the form of an annuity (i.e., periodic pension payment), it is taxable under the annuity rules (see ¶ 817 and following) (Code Secs. 402(a) and 403(a)(1)). For this purpose, the benefits derived from the employee's contributions to a defined contribution plan and the earnings on them may be treated as a separate contract from benefits derived from the employer's contributions (Code Sec. 72(d)(2)).[122] A participant's separate account in a defined benefit plan is treated as a defined contribution plan if the plan provides a benefit derived from employer contributions that is based partly on the balance of the separate account (Code Sec. 414(k)(2)).[123]

If a plan distribution is not in the form of an annuity, the following rules apply (Code Sec. 72(e); Reg. § 1.72-11):[124]

(1) If a distribution is made *before* the annuity starting date, it is treated in much the same way as an annuity distribution; that is, there is excluded from income that portion of the distribution that bears the same ratio to the distribution as the investment in the contract bears to the value of the contract (Code Sec. 72(e)(2)(B)). The total amount excluded cannot exceed the employee's investment in the contract.

(2) A nonannuity distribution made *on or after* the annuity starting date is generally included in full in gross income unless it reduces the dollar amount of subsequent annuity payments (Code Sec. 72(e)(2)(A)).

U.S. Civil Service Retirement Benefits. Retired federal employees generally receive annuity payments under the Civil Service Retirement System (CSRS) or the Federal Employee Retirement System (FERS). The portion of the payment that represents the employee's after-tax contributions to the retirement plan is not taxed. Form CSA 1099R will generally show the non-taxable portion of the CSRS or FERS payment as calculated under the simplified method (see ¶ 839) (IRS Pub. 721).

Death In Line of Duty. The amount paid as a survivor annuity to the spouse, former spouse or child of a "public safety officer" killed in the line of duty is generally excludable from the recipient's gross income when the annuity is provided under a governmental retirement plan (Code Sec. 101(h)). The term "public safety officer" includes law enforcement officers, firefighters, and members of an ambulance crew, or public rescue squad (Omnibus Crime Control and Safe Streets Act of 1968, Section 1204). A chaplain killed in the line of duty may also be classified as a public safety office for purpose of this exclusion.

Victims of Terrorism. If certain requirements are met, death benefits paid by an employer due to the death of an employee who was a victim of a terrorist act may be excluded from income (Code Sec. 101(i)). For this purpose, a self-employed individual may be considered an employee (Code Sec. 101(i)(3)).

Qualified Hurricane Distributions. Certain special rules apply for victims of 2005's major hurricanes. The first $100,000 of distributions received from eligible retirement

---

Footnote references are to paragraphs of the 2008 Standard Federal Tax Reports.

[120] ¶ 25,300
[121] ¶ 18,217A.0565
[122] ¶ 6102
[123] ¶ 17,507.0295, ¶ 19,150
[124] ¶ 6102, ¶ 6113

plans, which include IRAs and employer plans, by a qualified individual, on or after a specified date and before January 1, 2007, are "qualified hurricane distributions." A qualified individual is an individual whose principal place of abode on a specified date was in a hurricane disaster area and who sustained an economic loss as a result of the storm. For residents of the Hurricane Katrina disaster area, the distribution must have been made on or after August 25, 2005, and their principal place of abode must have been in the Hurricane Katrina disaster area on August 28, 2005. For residents of the Hurricane Rita disaster area, the distribution must have been made on or after September 23, 2005, and their principal place of abode must have been in the Hurricane Rita disaster area on September 23, 2005. For residents of the Hurricane Wilma disaster area, the distribution must have been made on or after October 23, 2005, and their principal place of abode must have been in the Hurricane Wilma disaster area on October 23, 2005 (Code Sec. 1400Q(a)(4)(A)).

Unless the recipient elects otherwise, qualified hurricane distributions are included in income ratably over three years, beginning with the year the distribution is received. If the distributee dies during the first or second year, the amount that has not been taxed is included in income in the year of the distributee's death (Code Sec. 1400Q(a)(5)). An individual who received any qualified hurricane distributions may recontribute the amount of those distributions to an eligible retirement plan at any time during the three-year period beginning on the day after the distribution was received. To the extent that such a recontribution is made, the original distribution will be nontaxable (Code Sec. 1400Q(a)(3)). The individual can file an amended return or returns to claim a refund of the tax attributable to the amount recontributed.

Employer Securities. Distributions of an employer's securities under circumstances not involving a lump-sum distribution (e.g., distributions spread over more than one tax year) are subject to the above rules except for unrealized appreciation attributable to shares that were purchased with the employee's own contributions (Code Sec. 402(e)(4)(A)).[125] That appreciation is not taxed until the securities are sold.

Loss. An employee may claim a loss on his return if he receives, entirely in cash or worthless securities, a distribution of his entire benefit from a qualified plan and the distribution is less than the employee's remaining basis in the plan (Rev. Rul. 72-305). The deductible loss is claimed on Schedule A (Form 1040) as a miscellaneous itemized deduction that is subject to the 2 percent floor.

2156. Cost of Insurance Protection. Some retirement plans provide incidental life insurance protection for participants. Even though a plan is qualified, the cost of current life insurance protection provided by the plan to employees is included in the participating employees' gross income. The amount of current life insurance protection for a year is equal to the excess of the amount payable upon death over the cash value of the policy at the end of the year (Reg. § 1.72-16(b)(3)). The cost of this protection is determined by tables issued by the IRS (see ¶ 721) (Code Sec. 72(m)(3)(B)).[126]

Retired Public Safety Officers. For tax years beginning after 2006, retired public safety officers can exclude from income up to $3,000 per year of distributions from a governmental retirement plan. The exclusion applies only for amounts that are deducted from the retiree's distributions and paid directly to an insurer for health or long-term care insurance (Code Sec. 402(l), as added by the Pension Protection Act of 2006 (P.L. 109-280)).

2157. Penalty on Early Distributions. Generally, taxable distributions from a qualified retirement plan or IRA are subject to an additional 10 percent penalty tax if they are made before the participant reaches age 59½ (Code Sec. 72(t)(1)). The 10 percent penalty tax will *not* apply to the portion of the early distribution that was timely and properly rolled over into an IRA or other qualified plan (see ¶ 2188).

Exceptions to Penalty Tax. Even if the distribution is not rolled over, the 10 percent penalty tax does *not* apply to (Code Sec. 72(t)):

Footnote references are to paragraphs of the 2008 Standard Federal Tax Reports.

[125] ¶ 18,202   [126] ¶ 6126, ¶ 6140.0255

¶2156

(1) distributions upon death or disability of the participant;

(2) distributions after separation from service that are part of a series of substantially equal periodic payments over the life of the participant or the joint lives of the participant and the beneficiary;

(3) distributions after the participant's separation from service, provided the participant reached age 55 before separating from service (Notice 87-13, Q&A-20) (age 50, in the case of distributions made after August 17, 2006, from a government plan to a retired police officer, firefighter, or emergency medical services provider (Code Sec. 72(t)(10), as added by the Pension Protection Act of 2006 (P.L. 109-280)));[127]

(4) distributions to a nonparticipant under a qualified domestic relations order (see ¶ 2166);

(5) distributions not exceeding deductible medical expenses (determined without regard to whether deductions are itemized) (Code Sec. 72(t)(2)(B));[128]

(6) certain distributions by ESOPs of dividends on employer securities (Code Sec. 72(t)(2)(A));[129]

(7) distributions made on account of the IRS's levy against the participant's account;

(8) qualified hurricane distributions (see ¶ 2155) (Code Sec. 1400Q(a)(1));[130] and

(9) qualified reservist distributions (see ¶ 2173).

Penalty Tax on IRA Distributions. The exceptions to the 10 percent penalty described above generally apply to IRA distributions. However, the exception for distributions after a separation from service after age 55 does not apply to IRA distributions. Also, though the transfer of an IRA interest under a divorce or separation agreement is not a taxable event, subsequent distributions from a transferred IRA are not excluded from the penalty. Some additional exceptions to the penalty apply for IRA distributions only (see ¶ 2179).

SIMPLE Plan Penalty. For employees who withdraw any amount from a SIMPLE plan during the first two years of participation, the 10 percent penalty is increased to 25 percent (Code Sec. 72(t)(6)).

Reporting the Penalty. As a general rule, individuals have to file Form 5329, Additional Taxes on Qualified Plans (Including IRAs) and Other Tax-Favored Accounts, to report the penalty that they owe on an early distribution. However, Form 5329 need *not* be filed if Distribution Code 1 (i.e., early distribution) is correctly shown on in Box 7 of the Form 1099-R received by the individual. In this situation, the penalty is reported directly on the individual's Form 1040, page 2, Line 60. Form 5329 should also be filed by individuals who believe that the Form 1099-R that they received incorrectly indicates that they are liable for a penalty.

2164. Loans from Qualified Plans. Unless certain requirements are met, a loan to a participant from a qualified plan, including 403(b) and 457 plans, is treated as a distribution and included in the participant's gross income (Code Sec. 72(p)(1)(A)). A pledge or assignment of any part of a participant's interest in a plan is treated as a loan for this purpose (Code Sec. 72(p)(1)(B); Reg. § 1.72(p)-1).[131]

Allowable loans. Subject to specific dollar limits, a loan will not be treated as a distribution if the loan must be repaid within five years or the loan proceeds must be used (within a reasonable time after the date of the loan) to acquire a dwelling unit that is to be used as the principal residence of the participant. When determining if a plan loan is allowable, all plans of the employer are treated as a single plan (Code Sec 72(p)(2)(D)(ii)).[132] The exceptions do not apply unless substantially level amortization of the loan is required, with payments not less frequent than quarterly (Code Sec. 72(p)(2)(C); Reg. § 1.72(p)-1, Q&A-4, -9, and -10).[133]

Footnote references are to paragraphs of the 2008 Standard Federal Tax Reports.

[127] ¶ 6140.775

[128] ¶ 6102

[129] ¶ 6102

[130] ¶ 6140.0682

[131] ¶ 6102, ¶ 6133

[132] ¶ 6102

[133] ¶ 6140.0374

As a general rule, the *refinancing* of a home loan does not qualify under the exception that applies to loan proceeds used to acquire a principal residence (Reg. § 1.72(p)-1, Q&A-8(a)). However, the repayment of a loan from a third party that was used to acquire the principal residence may qualify under the exception.

> **Example 1:** On July 1, 2007, Betty purchases a home that she will use as a principal residence. She pays a portion of the purchase price with a $50,000 loan from Global Bank. On August 1, 2007, Betty borrows $50,000 from her 401(k) plan. A few days later, Betty uses the money from the plan loan to pay the $50,000 she owes Global Bank. Based on these facts, the plan loan would be treated as having been used to acquire Betty's principal residence (Reg. § 1.72(p)-1, Q&A-8(b)). As a result, Betty's plan loan would *not* be treated as a taxable distribution.

Loan Limits. A loan from a qualified plan will be treated as a distribution only to the extent that, when added to the balances of all other loans to the participant (whenever made), the proceeds exceed the *lesser* of $50,000 or half the present value (but not less than $10,000) of the plan participant's vested benefits under the plan. The $50,000 amount must be reduced by the excess (if any) of: (1) the highest outstanding balance of loans from the plan during the one-year period ending on the day preceding the date of the loan over (2) the outstanding balance of those loans on the date of the loan (Code Sec. 72(p)(2)).[134]

> **Example 2:** Jane Smith is a participant in her employer's qualified profit-sharing plan. She wishes to borrow the maximum amount subject to the five-year repayment rule on July 1, 2007. On that date, the value of her vested interest in the plan is $120,000. Her highest loan balance during the period July 1, 2006, through June 30, 2007, was $40,000, and her balance on July 1, 2007 is $35,000. The maximum amount that Jane may borrow on July 1, 2007, is $10,000. This is the amount that, when added to her $35,000 loan balance, does not exceed $45,000. The $45,000 amount is determined by reducing the $50,000 loan limit by the excess of her highest loan balance for the past year ($40,000) over the loan balance at the time of the new loan ($35,000). This amount is less than half the value of her vested interest in the plan ($60,000).

Hurricane Relief. The $50,000 and one-half of present value of vested benefits limits are increased to $100,000 and the full present value of vested benefits for loans to certain "qualified individuals" affected by 2005's major hurricanes (Code Sec. 1400Q(c)(1)). Qualified individuals are those whose principal place of abode was in a hurricane disaster area on a specified date and who sustained an economic loss as a result of the storm. The increased limits apply to loans made:

> (1) on or after September 24, 2005 and before January 1, 2007, to individuals whose principal place of abode was in the Hurricane Katrina disaster area on August 28, 2005;

> (2) on or after December 21, 2005 and before January 1, 2007, to individuals whose principal place of abode was in the Hurricane Rita disaster area on September 23, 2005; or

> (3) on or after December 21, 2005 and before January 1, 2007, to individuals whose principal place of abode was in the Hurricane Wilma disaster area on October 23, 2005.

In addition to the increased limits, the loan repayment requirements are suspended for one year for qualified individuals (Code Sec. 1400Q(c)(2)). For qualified individuals, all payments due on or after the "qualified beginning date" and before January 1, 2007 are suspended for one year. Subsequent due dates are also extended, and the suspension period is not taken into account in determining the term of the loan or whether it is amortized on a substantially level basis. Loans may accrue additional interest during the suspension period, depending on the terms of the plan and the loan documents. For qualified individuals residing in the Hurricane Katrina disaster area, the qualified beginning date is August 25, 2005; for those residing in the Hurricane Rita disaster are,

---

Footnote references are to paragraphs of the 2008 Standard Federal Tax Reports.

[134] ¶ 6102

¶2164

the qualified beginning date is September 23, 2005; and for those residing in the Hurricane Wilma disaster area, the qualified beginning date is October 23, 2005.

Example 3: Paul Boucher lives in New Orleans, suffered an economic loss as a result of Hurricane Katrina, and is a participant in his employer's qualified profit-sharing plan. Paul had an outstanding loan from the plan at the time of the storm, with payments due on the first of each month and the final payment due December 1, 2007. The payment originally due on September 1, 2005, is not due until September 1, 2006, and the final payment is due December 1, 2008.

Example 4: Bess Browder lives in the Hurricane Rita disaster area and suffered an economic loss as a result of the storm. She is a participant in her employer's qualified profit-sharing plan. Under the terms of the plan, loans are available but must be repaid over five years by payroll deduction, beginning with the first paycheck after the distribution of the loan funds. If Bess obtains a loan in December of 2006, the beginning of her repayments is suspended until the following December. If she obtains a loan in January of 2007, her repayments will begin immediately.

2166. Distribution to a Nonparticipant Incident to Divorce or Separation. A distribution made by a qualified plan to an "alternate payee" (e.g., spouse, ex-spouse, child or other dependent of the participant) under the terms of a qualified domestic relations order (QDRO) is taxable to the alternate payee and not to the participant (Code Sec. 402(e)(1)(A)).[135] The QDRO rules apply to distributions made by a number of types of plans (e.g., 401(k), 403(b) plans and 457 plans) (Code Sec. 414(p)(10) and Code Sec. 414(p)(12)). See ¶ 2167 for information on 403(b) plans and ¶ 2197B for information on 457 plans.

QDRO Defined. A qualified domestic relations order (QDRO) is a judgment, decree or order (including approval of a property settlement agreement) made under a state's domestic relations or community property law. The QDRO must relate to the provision of child support, alimony or marital property rights to a spouse, former spouse, child or other dependent of a plan participant. In order to be "qualified," the order must meet specified requirements as to content and generally may not require the plan to pay benefits that are not otherwise payable under the terms of the plan (Code Sec. 414(p)).[136]

Payment of the entire amount due the spouse or ex-spouse under a QDRO is eligible for special tax averaging treatment (see ¶ 2153) if it would be eligible had it been paid to the participant (i.e., lump-sum treatment). Distributions made under the terms of a QDRO may qualify for rollover into an IRA or other type of plan (see ¶ 2191 for rollover options).

The participant's "investment in the contract" (see ¶ 2155) is allocated between the participant and the spouse or ex-spouse, pro rata, on the basis of the present value of all benefits awarded to the spouse or ex-spouse and the present value of all benefits reserved to the participant (Code Sec. 72(m)(10)).[137]

Transfers of IRAs. Transfer of an individual's interest in an IRA by the terms of a divorce or separation agreement that meets the qualifications of Code Sec. 71(b)(2) is not considered to be a taxable transfer. The transferred interest becomes the property of the spouse or ex-spouse and may be rolled over (see ¶ 2191) (Code Sec. 408(d)(6)).

Tax-Sheltered Annuity Arrangements (403(b) Plans)

2167. Deferred Compensation Plans of Exempt Organizations and Public Schools. A public school system or tax-exempt educational, charitable, or religious organization may provide retirement benefits for its employees through the purchase of annuities or by contributing to a custodial account invested in mutual funds (Code Sec. 403(b)(1)(A)).[138] This type of retirement plan is commonly referred to as a "403(b) plan" or "tax-sheltered annuity plan" (TSA). Generally, the employee's rights in the annuity or account must be nonforfeitable (Code Sec. 403(b)(1) and (7)).[139]

Footnote references are to paragraphs of the 2008 Standard Federal Tax Reports.

[135] ¶ 18,202   [137] ¶ 6102   [139] ¶ 18,270
[136] ¶ 19,150   [138] ¶ 18,270

Limit on Annual Addition. There is a limit imposed on the total amount of the "annual addition" that may be made to an employee's 403(b) account. This annual limit is sometimes called the "maximum amount contributable" (MAC). The annual addition or MAC is made up of the following three types of contributions:

(1) elective contributions made by the employee;

(2) nonelective contributions made by the employer; and

(3) after-tax contributions made by the employee (Code Sec. 403(b)(1)).[140]

Generally, for 2007, the annual addition can not be more than the *lesser* of $45,000 or 100 percent of the employee's compensation (Code Sec. 415(c)(1)). For 2008 the dollar limit is $46,000 (IRS News Release IR-2007-171). There are also limits on the amount of elective deferrals that an employee may make to a 403(b) plan. Employees who will be at least age 50 by the end of the year may make "catch-up contributions" to a 403(b) plan. The maximum catch-up contribution to a 403(b) plan is $5,000 for 2007 and for 2008 (Code Sec. 414(v)). Qualified employees of certain organizations (e.g., schools, hospitals, churches, and home health service organizations) who are covered by an annuity contract under a 403(b) plan may defer additional amounts of their compensation (Code Sec. 402(g)(7)(A)). For this purpose, a "qualified employee" is one who has completed 15 years of service with the organization (Code Sec. 402(g)(7)(C)).

The annual limit on an employee's elective deferrals (i.e., $15,500 for 2007 and for 2008) generally applies to all of an employee's deferrals under any 403(b), SEP, SIMPLE or 401(k) plan (Code Sec. 402(g)(3); Notice 2006-98; IRS News Release IR-2007-171). However, employees are not required to coordinate their maximum deferral under a 457 plan with their contributions made to 403(b) plans (Code Sec. 457(c), before amendment by P.L. 107-16). See ¶ 2197B for information on 457 plans.

> **Example:** Tom Aubrey, age 45, is employed by a corporation that offers a 401(k) plan for its employees. He also works for a hospital that offers a 403(b) plan. For 2007, Tom's total contributions to the 401(k) plan and the 403(b) plan may not exceed $15,500.

Distributions from 403(b) Plans. Payments to an employee from a 403(b) plan are taxed under the annuity rules explained at ¶ 817 and following. However, any employee contributions that were excluded from wages are not treated as part of the employee's investment in the contract. Distributions may generally be made because of the employee's death, disability, severance from employment, attainment of age 59½, or financial hardship (Code Sec. 403(b)(7)(A)(ii) and (b)(11)). Distributions that do not meet these requirements are subject to the 10 percent tax on early distributions (¶ 2157). The required minimum distribution (RMD) rules also apply (see ¶ 2135) (Reg. § 1.403(b)-3).

Distributions from a 403(b) plan may be rolled over into an IRA or another 403(b) plan, as well as to other types of employer plans (e.g., a 401(k) plan or 457 plan) (Code Sec. 403(b)(8)(A)). Although the employee has the right to make the rollover, the other plans (e.g., 403(b), 457, or 401(k)) are not required to accept the rollover. The spousal rollover rules that apply to other types of employer sponsored plans and the written explanation requirements also apply to a beneficiary under a qualified annuity plan (Code Sec. 403(a)(4)(B)).

Ministers. Contributions to a church plan on behalf of a self-employed minister are excludable from the minister's income to the extent that the contribution would be excludable if the minister was an employee of the church (Code Sec. 414(e)(5)(E)).[141] In addition, if a minister is employed by an organization other than a church and the organization is not otherwise participating in a church plan, then the minister does not have to be included as an employee under the retirement plan of the organization for purposes of the nondiscrimination rules (Code Sec. 414(e)(5)(C)).[142] Alternative contribution limits apply in some situations to clergy, lay employees and foreign missionaries (Code Sec. 415(c)(7)).

Footnote references are to paragraphs of the 2008 Standard Federal Tax Reports.

[140] ¶ 18,270   [141] ¶ 19,150   [142] ¶ 19,150

¶2167

Traditional IRAs

2168. Individual Retirement Accounts (IRAs). Individuals who receive compensation, including alimony, that is includible in gross income and who are under age 70½ during the tax year are entitled to make contributions to traditional individual retirement accounts (IRAs) (Code Sec. 219(f)). Amounts earned in a traditional IRA are not taxed until distributions are made (Code Sec. 408(e)(1)).[143] Generally, contributions to a traditional IRA may be deducted. However, when the individual, or the individual's spouse, is an active participant in an employer-maintained retirement plan, the deduction may be reduced or eliminated (see ¶ 2170) (Code Sec. 219(g)).[144] Nondeductible contributions may be made to a traditional IRA and/or Roth IRA (Code Sec. 408(o)).[145] Roth IRAs are discussed at ¶ 2180 and following.

IRA Contributions. For tax years 2005 through 2007, the maximum combined contribution by an individual to his or her traditional and Roth IRAs is $4,000. For 2008, it will be $5,000. Starting in 2009, the maximum contribution will be subject to an annual inflation adjustment (Code Sec. 219(b)(5)(A)). An individual who will be at least age 50 by the end of the tax year is allowed to make additional contributions to a traditional or Roth IRA. For tax years beginning after 2005, the maximum catch-up contribution is $1,000 (Code Sec. 219(b)(5)(B)). For tax years 2007 through 2009, certain individuals who participated in a bankrupt employer's 401(k) plan will be able to make additional catch-up contributions (Code Sec. 219(b)(5)(C), as amended by the Pension Protection Act of 2006 (P.L. 109-280)).

> **Example 1:** Bob will be 50 years old on December 28, 2007. Assuming he meets the income requirements, his maximum contribution to his traditional IRA and/or Roth IRA for 2007 is $5,000 ($4,000 in regular contributions and $1,000 in catch-up contributions).

> **Example 2:** Assume the same facts as in Example 1, except that Bob will not reach age 50 until December 28, 2008. In this situation, his maximum contribution to his traditional IRA and/or Roth IRA for 2007 is $4,000. For 2008, his maximum contribution is $6,000 ($5,000 in regular contributions and $1,000 in catch-up contributions).

Individuals have until the due date of their tax returns to make contributions to their IRAs for the return year (e.g., April 15). Filing extensions are *not* taken into account. If the contribution is made by the due date, it will be treated as having been made on the last day of the tax year for which the return is filed (Code Sec. 219(f)(3)).[146] A deduction may be claimed for a contribution even though the contribution had not yet been made when the return is filed. However, the contribution must be made by the due date of the tax return (Rev. Rul. 84-18).[147]

If a contribution to a traditional IRA is *less* than the allowable maximum for that year, the individual cannot contribute more in a later year to make up the difference. If a contribution is *more* than the allowable maximum, the excess contribution may be withdrawn on or before April 15 or carried over and deducted in later years to the extent that the actual contributions in those later years are less then the allowable maximum (Code Sec. 219(f)(6)).[148] However, the excess contribution is subject to a six percent tax each year until it is corrected (Code Sec. 4973(a)).[149] The individual reports the six percent tax on Form 5329, Additional Taxes on Qualified Plans (Including IRAs) and Other Tax-Favored Accounts.

Compensation. For purposes of determining an individual's eligibility to make contributions to an IRA, the term "compensation" includes earned income and alimony. The term does *not* include pensions, annuities or other forms of deferred compensation. However, under a safe-harbor rule, the IRS will accept as compensation the amount properly shown in box 1 on the individual's Form W-2 as wages, tips, and other compensation, less any amount properly shown for nonqualified plans (e.g., box 11 of

---

Footnote references are to paragraphs of the 2008 Standard Federal Tax Reports.

[143] ¶ 18,902	[146] ¶ 18,922.0227	[149] ¶ 34,360
[144] ¶ 12,650	[147] ¶ 18,922.87	
[145] ¶ 18,902	[148] ¶ 18,922.0228	

the 2007 Form W-2) (Rev. Proc. 91-18).[150] The compensation of a self-employed person is the individual's "earned income," as defined at ¶ 2113 (Code Sec. 219(f)(1)).[151] Effective for tax years beginning after 2003, combat pay earned by a member of the Armed Forces and excluded from gross income under Code Sec. 112 will be treated as compensation for purposes of the limit on IRA contributions. Since the rule applies retroactively, individuals who received excluded combat pay during 2004 or 2005 may make IRA contributions (and file an amended return claiming the deduction) for those years at any time before May 29, 2009 (Code Sec. 219(f)(7), as added by the Heroes Earned Retirement Opportunities Act (P.L. 109-227)).

Tax Refunds. Beginning in 2007, a taxpayer may choose to have a refund of federal income taxes directly deposited into his or her IRA. The IRA must be established before the request for the direct deposit is made. The deposit counts against the taxpayer's annual contribution limit. Thus, the taxpayer should inform the IRA trustee which year the direct deposit contribution is for. The taxpayer must also verify that the direct deposit is made to the IRA by the due date or his or her return for that year (without regard to extensions). To request a direct deposit of an entire refund into an IRA, the taxpayer should complete Line 74 of Form 1040. However, if a taxpayer chooses to have a refund split and deposited in up to three different accounts (e.g., savings, checking, and IRA), then Form 8888, Direct Deposit of Refund to More Than One Account, must be used.

Allowable Investments. Although IRAs may hold almost any investment, they are generally prohibited from investing in "collectibles" (e.g., antiques and stamps). However, certain U.S. gold and silver bullion coins minted since October 1986 may be held by an IRA. An IRA may also hold certain platinum and state-issued coins, as well as gold, silver, platinum, and palladium bullion (Code Sec. 408(m)(3)).[152]

Deemed IRAs. Qualified plans may allow employees to make voluntary contributions to a separate account that will be deemed to be a traditional IRA or Roth IRA if the account meets all the requirements of the particular type of IRA (Code Sec. 408(q)). An employee's contributions to this account count against the annual limit on IRA contributions (Reg. § 1.408(q)-1(a)).

2170. IRA Deduction Limits in General. The maximum deduction that an individual may take for contributions to an IRA may be reduced when the individual (or spouse) is an active participant in a retirement plan maintained by an employer (including qualified plans, simplified employee pensions (SEPs), SIMPLE accounts, and governmental retirement plans) (Code Sec. 219(g)).[153] When an individual is an active participant in an employer's plan, the amount of the deductible IRA contribution depends upon the individual's adjusted gross income and filing status. For details of the phaseout ranges for married individuals filing jointly, see ¶ 2172. For single individuals and married individuals filing separate returns, see ¶ 2171.

Active Participant Defined. In the case of a defined benefit pension plan, an individual is considered to be an active participant if she is eligible to participate for any part of the plan year ending with or within the tax year, even though the individual may elect not to do so. In the case of a money-purchase pension plan, an individual is an active participant if any employer contribution or any forfeiture is required to be allocated to his account for the plan year ending with or within the tax year. In the case of a profit-sharing or stock bonus plan, an individual is an active participant if any employer contribution (including an elective contribution under a 401(k) plan) or any forfeiture is allocated to the individual's account during the tax year. Finally, an individual is an active participant for any tax year in which the individual makes a voluntary or mandatory employee contribution (Notice 87-16).[154] Social Security and Railroad Retirement (Tier I or Tier II) are not retirement arrangements for purposes of determining active participation. An individual is *not* considered an active participant in an employer-sponsored plan merely because the individual's spouse is an active participant (Code Sec. 219(g)(7)).[155]

Footnote references are to paragraphs of the 2008 Standard Federal Tax Reports.

[150] ¶ 18,922.0232
[151] ¶ 12,650
[152] ¶ 18,902
[153] ¶ 18,922.023, ¶ 18,922.0231
[154] ¶ 18,922.865
[155] ¶ 12,650

Social Security Recipients. An employed individual (either the taxpayer or spouse) who: (1) is covered by a retirement plan; (2) is currently receiving social security benefits; and (3) wants to determine the allowable deduction for contributions to a traditional IRA must compute taxable social security benefits twice. The first computation is for the purpose of determining the tentative amount of social security benefits that must be included in gross income if the individual did not make any IRA contribution. This computation determines the amount of hypothetical adjusted gross income for purposes of the IRA phaseout provision. The second computation determines the actual amount of taxable social security benefits by taking into account the deductible IRA contribution that was determined under the first computation. The necessary worksheets for these computations are contained in IRS Publication 590 (Individual Retirement Arrangements (IRAs)). See also ¶ 716.

2171. Deduction Limit for Single Persons and Married Persons Filing Separate Returns. For a single individual, head of household, or a married individual who files a separate return, contributions to traditional IRAs are generally deductible to the extent that they do not exceed the lesser of: (1) the "deductible amount" (for 2007, $4,000 or $5,000 if catch-up contributions are allowable, for 2008, $5,000 or $6,000) or (2) the individual's compensation for that year that is includible in gross income ("includible compensation") (Code Sec. 219(b)(1)).[156] However, the maximum allowable deduction may be reduced when the individual is an active participant in an employer-maintained retirement plan (Code Sec. 219(g)).[157] For information regarding the IRA deduction limits for married persons filing joint returns, see ¶ 2172.

Single Individuals or Head of Household. For 2007, when a single individual or head of household is an active participant in an employer's retirement plan, the IRA deduction will begin to phase-out when modified adjusted gross income (AGI) reaches $52,000. The deduction is completely phased-out when modified AGI reaches $62,000 (Code Sec. 219(g)(3)(B)(ii); Rev. Proc. 2006-53). For 2008, the phaseout range will be from $53,000 to $63,000 (Code Sec. 219(g)(8), as added by the Pension Protection Act of 2006 (P.L. 109-280); IRS News Release IR-2007-171).

Married Filing Separately. When an individual files as "married filing separately" and the individual, or the spouse, is an active participant in an employer's retirement plan, the IRA deduction begins to phase-out when the individual's modified AGI exceeds $0. The deduction is completely phased-out when modified AGI is $10,000 or more (Code Sec. 219(g)(3)(B)(iii)). This phaseout range is not adjusted for inflation. When determining if an individual is married or single for the purpose of determining which IRA deduction limit applies, spouses who file separate returns and live apart at all times during a tax year are *not* considered to be married during that tax year (Code Sec. 219(g)(4)).[158]

Modified Adjusted Gross Income. When determining the taxpayer's AGI for deduction limit rules, the taxpayer's AGI is modified by taking into account Code Sec. 86 (the inclusion in income of Social Security and Railroad Retirement benefits) and Code Sec. 469 (the disallowance of passive activity losses) and by not taking into account Code Sec. 135 (exclusion of interest on educational U.S. Savings Bonds), Code Sec. 137 (exclusion of employer-paid adoption assistance), Code Sec. 221 (deduction for student loan interest), Code Sec. 222 (deduction for qualified tuition and related expenses), Code Sec. 911 (foreign earned income and housing exclusion), and the deduction for contributions to IRAs (Code Sec. 219(g)(3)(A)).[159]

2172. Deduction Limit for Married Persons Filing Joint Returns. When a married couple files a joint return, usually each spouse may make contributions to his or her IRA up to the annual dollar limit (for 2007, $4,000 or $5,000 if a catch-up contribution is allowable; for 2008, $5,000 or $6,000). If one spouse has little or no compensation, that spouse may "borrow" his or her spouse's compensation for purposes of enabling the maximum contribution (Code Sec. 219(c)).[160]

Footnote references are to paragraphs of the 2008 Standard Federal Tax Reports.

[156] ¶ 18,922.023
[157] ¶ 18,922.023
[158] ¶ 18,922.023
[159] ¶ 12,650
[160] ¶ 18,922.0231

For 2007, the IRAs of the spouse with the greater amount of compensation ("higher-paid spouse") may receive deductible contributions of up to the lesser of: (a) $4,000 or $5,000 if catch-up contributions are allowable (as reduced for active participation) or (b) his or her compensation. The IRAs of the spouse with the lesser amount of compensation ("lower-paid spouse") may receive deductible contributions equal to the lesser of:

(1) $4,000, or $5,000 if catch-up contributions are allowable (as reduced for active participation), or

(2) the sum of:

(a) the compensation of the lower-paid spouse and

(b) the compensation of the higher-paid spouse, reduced by: (i) the deduction allowed to the higher-paid spouse for IRA contributions, (ii) the amount of any designated nondeductible IRA contribution on behalf of the higher-paid spouse, and (iii) the amount of any contribution on behalf of the higher-paid spouse to a Roth IRA (Code Sec. 219(c)(1)(B)).

AGI Limits for Married Individuals. If both individuals are active participants in an employer's qualified retirement plan, their ability to claim a deduction for contributions made to traditional IRAs depends upon the amount of their modified AGI (see ¶ 2170). For 2007, the allowable IRA deduction will be reduced when modified AGI is between $83,000 and $103,000 (Code Sec. 219(g)(2)(A)(ii); Rev. Proc. 2006-53). For 2008, the deduction will be reduced when modified AGI is between $85,000 and $105,000 (Code Sec. 219(g)(8), as added by the Pension Protection Act of 2006 (P.L. 109-280); IRS News Release IR-2007-171).[161]

Example 1: Ralph and Alice file a joint return for 2007. They are both employed and both are covered by their employers' qualified plans. Their AGI for 2007 is $110,000. Because they are both active participants in qualified plans sponsored by their employers and their AGI exceeds the high end of the phaseout range for 2007 (i.e., $103,000), they are not allowed to make deductible IRA contributions for 2007. They may make nondeductible contributions to traditional IRAs. As an alternative, they should consider the tax advantages of making their contributions to Roth IRAs (see ¶ 2180).

An individual will *not* be considered an active participant in an employer-sponsored plan merely because the individual's spouse is treated as an active participant (Code Sec. 219(g)(7)).[162] However, the maximum deductible IRA contribution for an individual who is not an active participant, but whose spouse is, will be phased out in 2007 at an AGI between $156,000 and $166,000 (jointly computed). For 2008, this phaseout range will be $159,000 to $169,000 (IRS News Release IR-2007-171; Rev. Proc. 2006-53).

Example 2: Bob is covered by a 401(k) plan sponsored by his employer. His wife, Betty, is not employed. The couple files a joint income tax return for 2007, reporting adjusted gross income of $120,000. Betty may make a deductible contribution to a traditional IRA for the year because she is not an active participant in an employer-sponsored retirement plan and their combined AGI is below $156,000. However, Bob may not make a deductible IRA contribution because their combined AGI is above the phaseout range for active participants who are married and filing jointly ($83,000 to $103,000 for 2007).

Example 3: Assume the same facts as in Example 1, except that the couple's AGI was $200,000 for 2007. Neither Bob nor Betty would be able to make a deductible contribution to a traditional IRA.

2173. Nondeductible Contributions to Traditional IRAs. An individual may make nondeductible contributions to a traditional IRA. These contributions may not exceed the *excess* of: (1) the maximum allowable contribution for the year (e.g., $4,000 or $5,000 if catch-up contributions are allowable, for 2007; $5,000 or $6,000 for 2008) over (2) the amount actually allowed as a deduction for the year (Code Sec. 408(o)(2)(B)(i)).[163] In applying this rule, an individual may elect to treat otherwise deductible contributions as nondeductible contributions (Code Sec. 408(o)(2)(B)(ii)). However, the tax advantages

---

Footnote references are to paragraphs of the 2008 Standard Federal Tax Reports.

[161] ¶ 12,650   [162] ¶ 12,650   [163] ¶ 18,902, ¶ 18,922.0238

of funding a Roth IRA should be considered before making nondeductible contributions to a traditional IRA (see ¶ 2180).

> **Example:** In 2007, Bill Webb, age 48 and single, had earned income of $52,000 and a modified AGI of $57,000. He is an active participant in his employer's 401(k) plan. Because his modified AGI exceeds $52,000, a maximum contribution to a traditional IRA would not be fully deductible. Bill determines that his maximum deductible contribution for 2007 would be $2,000. As a result, he could make an additional $2,000 nondeductible IRA contribution. As alternatives to making the nondeductible contribution to a traditional IRA, Bill should consider the long-range tax advantages of contributing the nondeductible $2,000 to a Roth IRA, or contributing all of the $4,000 to a Roth IRA (see ¶ 2180).

Nondeductible contributions may be made up to and including the due date of the return for the tax year. A filing extension does *not* extend the due date for making the contribution (Code Sec. 219(f)(3)). This same deadline applies to deductible IRA contributions and Roth IRA contributions. Nondeductible contributions to a traditional IRA must be reported on Form 8606, Nondeductible IRAs, which is attached to Form 1040 or Form 1040A.

Reservist Contributions. Certain "qualified reservist distributions" are not subject to the tax on early distributions and may be recontributed to an IRA as a nondeductible contribution without counting against the dollar limits applicable to IRA contributions (Code Sec. 72(t)(2)(G), as added by the Pension Protection Act of 2006 (P.L. 109-280)). A qualified reservist distribution is a distribution that is made: (1) from an IRA or from an individual's elective deferrals under an employer plan; (2) to an individual who is a reservist who was called to active duty for a period of more than 179 days (or an indefinite period); and (3) during the period beginning on the date the reservist was called to active duty and ending on the date the active duty ended. The call-up date must have been after September 11, 2001 and before December 31, 2007. A recontribution may be made no later than two years after the end of the active duty period, or if later, August 17, 2008. A reservist who took a distribution after being called up and paid the early distribution penalty may file a claim for refund of the penalty.

2174. Excess Contributions. Annual contributions to a traditional IRA and/or Roth IRA in excess of the allowable amount (e.g., $4,000 or $5,000 if catch-up contributions are allowable, for 2007; $5,000 or $6,000, for 2008) are subject to a cumulative six percent tax, which is reported on Form 5329, Additional Taxes on Qualified Plans (Code Sec. 4973).[164] See ¶ 2168 and ¶ 2178 for methods to avoid this tax.

2175. Tax Credit for Retirement Contributions. Individuals with low to moderate incomes may be able to claim a nonrefundable credit based upon their contributions to IRAs (traditional and/or Roth) as well other types of qualified retirement plans (see ¶ 1307).

2177. Distribution Requirements. Distributions to the owner of a traditional IRA must begin no later than April 1 following the calendar year in which the owner reaches age 70½ (Reg. § 1.408-8, Q & A-3).

> **Example:** Dave reached age 70½ on August 20, 2006. Thus, Dave must receive a required minimum distribution (RMD) for 2006 by April 1, 2007. For 2007, the first year after he reached 70½, the RMD must be received by December 31, 2007. In subsequent years, he must receive the RMD by December 31 of each year.

The period over which distributions from a traditional IRA must be made to an owner (or to a beneficiary following the death of an owner) are generally governed by rules similar to those for RMDs from qualified employer-sponsored plans (see ¶ 2135) (Code Sec. 408(a)(6) and (b)(3)).[165] A few special rules affecting RMDs from IRAs are discussed below.

Inherited Traditional IRA: Spouse. A surviving spouse may elect to treat an inherited traditional IRA as his or her own. One way to make the election is to have the account

---

Footnote references are to paragraphs of the 2008 Standard Federal Tax Reports.

[164] ¶ 34,360   [165] ¶ 18,902

redesignated as an account belonging to the surviving spouse as owner rather than beneficiary. Alternatively, the surviving spouse will be treated as having made this election if: (1) any amounts in the IRA are not distributed within the time period that applied to the decedent or (2) the surviving spouse makes contributions (including rollover contributions) to the inherited IRA. In order to make the election, the surviving spouse must be the sole beneficiary of the IRA and have an unlimited right to withdraw amounts from it (Reg. § 1.408-8, Q&A-5).[166] When a trust is named as the beneficiary of the IRA, this requirement has not been satisfied even if the spouse is the sole beneficiary of the trust. When the surviving spouse makes the election, he or she is treated as the owner of the IRA for all purposes. If the election is not made, then the RMDs are determined as though the spouse was the beneficiary of the IRA (see ¶ 2135).

Inherited Traditional IRA: Nonspouse. A nonspouse beneficiary who inherits an IRA cannot treat it as his or her own account, but must take RMDs determined under the rules applicable to beneficiaries receiving distributions from a qualified plan (see ¶ 2135). When an individual other than the decedent's spouse receives a lump sum distribution from an IRA, the individual may not roll over that distribution into another IRA and the distribution, minus the aggregate amount of the owner's nondeductible IRA contributions, is taxed as ordinary income in the year the distribution is received (Rev. Rul. 92-47).[167]

Trust Named as Beneficiary. When a trust is named as the beneficiary of the IRA, the beneficiaries of the trust will be treated as the deceased individual's beneficiaries if certain requirements are met (Reg. § 1.401(a)(9)-4, Q&A-5). The requirements include: (1) validity of the trust; (2) identification of the trust's beneficiaries; and (3) the delivery of proper documentation to the plan administrator (Reg. § 1.401(a)(9)-4, Q&A-6).

More Than One IRA. If an individual is required to receive an RMD from more than one traditional IRA in a calendar year, the amount of the minimum distribution from each IRA must be calculated separately and the separate amounts totalled. However, the total may be withdrawn from one or more of the IRAs in whatever amounts the individual chooses (Reg. § 1.408-8, Q&A-9).[168]

2178. Taxation of Distributions. If an individual never made nondeductible contributions to a traditional IRA, then any distributions from the IRA are fully taxable to the owner or beneficiary as ordinary income. However, if nondeductible contributions were made, the owner has a *cost basis* in the IRA. An individual's cost basis in distributions made from a traditional IRA is the sum of the nondeductible contributions made to the IRA minus any prior withdrawals or distributions of nondeductible contributions (Notice 87-16). The recovery of this basis is not recognized as taxable income. As a result, the individual must determine how much of the IRA distribution is nontaxable. The taxable and nontaxable portions of the distribution are generally determined under the same rules that apply to annuity payments (see ¶ 817 and following) (Code Sec. 72 and Code Sec. 408(d)(1)). When applying these rules (Code Sec. 408(d)(1), (2)):[169]

> (1) all traditional IRAs of an individual (including SEPs described at ¶ 2184 and SIMPLE accounts described at ¶ 2185) are treated as a single contract;

> (2) all distributions during the individual's tax year are treated as one distribution;

> (3) the value of the contract, the income on the contract, and the investment in the contract are calculated (after adding back distributions made during the year) as of the close of the calendar year in which the tax year of the distribution begins; and

> (4) total withdrawals excludable from income in all tax years cannot exceed the taxpayer's investment in the contract in all tax years.

Charitable Distributions. For tax years beginning in 2007, an individual may have up to $100,000 per year of their IRA balance distributed to a charitable organization without recognizing income on the distribution (Code Sec. 408(d)(8), as added by the Pension

---

Footnote references are to paragraphs of the 2008 Standard Federal Tax Reports.

[166] ¶ 18,917A   [168] ¶ 18,917A
[167] ¶ 18,922.26   [169] ¶ 18,902

Protection Act of 2006 (P.L. 109-280)). The exclusion from income only applies to a distribution that is otherwise includible in income and is made directly to a charitable organization on or after the date the account owner reaches age 70½. The account owner is not allowed a deduction for the contribution.

HSA Funding Distributions. In tax years beginning after 2006, an otherwise taxable IRA distribution that is transferred directly to the IRA owner's health savings account (HSA) may be excluded from income if the individual so elects (Code Sec. 408(d)(9), as added by the Tax Relief and Health Care Act of 2006 (P.L. 109-432)). Each individual can make such an election only for one year. The dollar amount excluded cannot exceed the annual limitation on the individual's HSA contribution for the year (see ¶ 1020A). The exclusion is lost if the individual ceases to be eligible to contribute to an HSA during the twelve months after the contribution. In such a case, the distribution is subject to tax and a 10-percent penalty is imposed.

Reporting Requirements. Form 8606, Nondeductible IRAs, is used to report the taxable portion of an IRA distribution if the individual ever made nondeductible contributions.

> **Example:** Jane Albright owns two traditional IRAs. During the past few years, Jane made a deductible contribution of $1,000 to IRA #1 and a nondeductible contribution of $500 to IRA #2. During 2007, Jane withdrew $1,500 from IRA #1 and made a $2,000 nondeductible contribution to IRA #2. At the end of 2007, Jane's cost basis in the IRAs was $2,500 (i.e., the total of her nondeductible contributions to both IRAs). On December 31, 2007, the account balance of IRA #1 is $8,500, and the account balance of IRA #2 is $6,000. The nontaxable portion of her $1,500 withdrawal is $234 ($2,500 (cost basis) ÷ $16,000 (account balance + withdrawal) × $1,500 (withdrawal)). The balance of the distribution ($1,266) is included in Jane's gross income for 2007.

Estate Tax. If the distributee is the beneficiary of the IRA owner and the value of the IRA is included in the owner's estate for federal estate tax purposes, the distributee is entitled to deduct the estate tax allocable to the IRA (see ¶ 191) (Rev. Rul. 92-47).[170]

Return of Contributions. A distribution from a traditional IRA that represents the return of a contribution made for a particular tax year will not be included in the individual's income if (Code Sec. 408(d)(4)):[171]

> (1) the distribution is made before the due date (including extensions) of the individual's tax return for that year;

> (2) no deduction is allowed with respect to the contribution; and

> (3) the distribution includes any net income earned by the contribution.

The net income earned by the contribution is included in income for the tax year in which the contribution was made even if the distribution is received in the following year.

Recognizing Loss on IRA. An IRA owner can recognize a loss on traditional IRA investments, but only when all amounts from all of the owner's traditional IRA accounts have been distributed and the total distributions are less than any unrecovered basis in the accounts. The recognized loss is claimed on Schedule A as a miscellaneous itemized deduction, subject to the two-percent floor (IRS Pub. 590 (Individual Retirement Arrangements)). If the individual never made nondeductible contributions to any of the traditional IRAs, the realized loss can not be deducted because the individual has no tax basis in the IRAs.

2179. Early Distributions. Generally, if the individual is under age 59½, a distribution from a traditional IRA is subject to the 10 percent penalty tax on early distributions. However, many of the exceptions to the early distribution penalty that apply to distributions from qualified plans also apply to early distributions from a traditional IRA (see ¶ 2157). The early retirement exception applicable to distributions from qualified plans does *not* apply to a distribution from a traditional IRA (Code Sec. 72(t)(3)(A)).[172]

Footnote references are to paragraphs of the 2008 Standard Federal Tax Reports.

[170] ¶ 18,922.26   [171] ¶ 18,902   [172] ¶ 6102

In addition to the exceptions discussed at ¶ 2157, the following exceptions apply to early distributions from an IRA:

(1) *Medical Insurance Premiums of Unemployed Individuals.* To the extent that they do not exceed qualifying medical insurance premiums, distributions from an IRA (including a SEP or SIMPLE account) to certain unemployed individuals are not subject to the 10 percent penalty tax (Code Sec. 72(t)(2)(D)).[173] Eligible unemployed individuals are those who have received federal or state unemployment compensation for 12 consecutive weeks. A self-employed individual will be treated as having received unemployment compensation if, under federal or state law, the individual would have received unemployment compensation but for being self-employed. Qualifying premiums are deductible premiums for the medical care of the unemployed individual, spouse and dependents. The distributions must be received in the tax year during which unemployment compensation is received or in the following year. In determining whether the premiums are deductible, the 7.5 percent medical expense floor (see ¶ 1015) is ignored. This exception to the 10 percent penalty ceases to apply after the individual has been reemployed for 60 days (not necessarily consecutive) after initial unemployment.

(2) *Education Expenses.* The 10 percent penalty does not apply if the individual uses the IRA distribution to pay for "qualified higher education expenses" for the individual, the individual's spouse or child, or a grandchild of the individual or the individual's spouse. Qualified expenses included tuition at a post-secondary educational institution, books, fees, supplies and equipment (Code Sec. 72(t)(2)(E)).[174]

(3) *First-Time Homebuyer Expenses.* The 10 percent penalty tax does not apply if the individual uses the IRA distribution for certain expenses of a first-time homebuyer. Only $10,000 during the individual's lifetime may be withdrawn without a penalty for this purpose. Qualified expenses include acquisition costs, settlement charges and closing costs. The principal residence may be for the individual or the individual's spouse, child or grandchild, or an ancestor of the individual or the individual's spouse. In order to be considered a "first-time homebuyer," the person buying the residence (and spouse, if married) must not have had an ownership interest in a principal residence during the two-year period ending on the date that the new home is acquired (Code Sec. 72(t)(2)(F)).[175]

(4) *Return of Nondeductible Contributions.* The 10 percent penalty does not apply to the portion of the distribution that represents a return of nondeductible IRA contributions (i.e., the individual's cost basis in the IRA) (see ¶ 2178).

The 10 percent early distribution penalty is generally reported on Part I of Form 5329, Additional Taxes on Qualified Plans. If an exception to the penalty exists (e.g., early distribution due to total and permanent disability), the individual provides this information to the IRS on Line 2 of Part I of Form 5329. However, if no exception exists and "Code 1" (i.e., early distribution, no known exception) is correctly shown in Box 7 of Form 1099-R, Form 5329 does not have to be filed. Instead, the amount of the penalty is reported directly on the taxpayer's Form 1040.

Roth IRAs

2180. Roth IRAs. In general, a Roth IRA is subject to the same rules that apply to a traditional IRA (see ¶ 2168). However, contributions to a Roth IRA are never deductible (Code Sec. 408A(c)(1)).[176] In addition, the buildup within a Roth IRA (e.g., interest, dividends and/or price appreciation) may be free from federal income tax when the individual withdraws money from the account. The following material highlights additional rules that apply to Roth IRAs.

Contribution Limits. For 2007, the maximum annual contribution that may generally be made to Roth IRAs and traditional IRAs is $4,000. For 2008, the maximum will be $5,000. The maximum annual contribution is the amount that may be contributed to *both*

Footnote references are to paragraphs of the 2008 Standard Federal Tax Reports.

[173] ¶ 6102
[174] ¶ 6102
[175] ¶ 6102
[176] ¶ 18,925

types of IRAs combined, not the amount that may be contributed to each type. However, rollover contributions into a Roth IRA are not counted against the annual maximum (Reg. § 1.408A-3, Q&A-3(c)).[177] In addition, unlike traditional IRAs, individuals may make contributions to a Roth IRA after reaching age 70½ (Code Sec. 408A(c)(4)).[178] An individual who will be at least age 50 by the end of the tax year is permitted to make an additional contribution to a Roth or traditional IRA. The maximum annual amount of the catch-up contribution is $1,000 for 2007 and for 2008 (Code Sec. 219(b)(5)(B)). For tax years 2007 through 2009, certain individuals who participated in a bankrupt employer's 401(k) plan will be able to make additional catch-up contributions to their IRAs (Code Sec. 219(b)(5)(C), as amended by the Pension Protection Act of 2006 (P.L. 109-280)).

Income Limits. The ability of an individual to make a contribution to a Roth IRA depends upon the amount of the individual's modified AGI. For 2007, the maximum yearly contribution that can be made to a Roth IRA is phased out for a single individual with modified AGI between $99,000 and $114,000, for joint filers with modified AGI between $156,000 and $166,000, and for individuals who are married filing separately with modified AGI between $0 and $10,000 (Reg. § 1.408A-3, Q&A-3(b)).[179] For 2008, the phaseout ranges for single individuals and joint filers will run from $101,000 to $116,000 (for singles) and $159,000 to $169,000 (for joint filers) (Code Sec. 408A(c)(3)(C), as amended by the Pension Protection Act of 2006 (P.L. 109-280); Rev. Proc. 2006-53; IRS News Release IR-2007-171). Modified AGI is generally calculated as it is for traditional IRAs (see ¶ 2171). However, for Roth IRA purposes, modified AGI does not include the income reported from the conversion of a traditional IRA into a Roth IRA (Code Sec. 408A(c)(3)(C)(i)).

2180A. Taxation of Roth Distributions. "Qualified distributions" from a Roth IRA are not included in the recipient's gross income and are not subject to the additional 10 percent penalty for early withdrawals. To be treated as a "qualified distribution," the distribution must satisfy a five-year holding period and meet one of four requirements discussed below (Code Sec. 408A(d)(2)).

To satisfy the five-year holding period, the Roth IRA distribution (including distributions allocable to rollover contributions) may not be made before the end of the five-year period beginning with the first tax year for which the individual made a contribution to the Roth IRA (Reg. § 1.408A-6, Q&A-2).[180] The five-year holding period ends on the last day of the individual's fifth consecutive tax year after the holding period started (Reg. § 1.408A-6, Q&A-5(b)). Generally, each Roth IRA owner has only one five-year period for all of the Roth IRAs that the individual owns (however, see ¶ 2180B).

> **Example 1:** Jack Matrin made his first contribution to a Roth IRA on September 15, 1999. The contribution was for the 1999 tax year. On December 27, 2000, Jack made another contribution to a Roth IRA. This contribution was for the 2000 tax year. On December 30, 2001, he made another contribution to a Roth IRA. This contribution was for the 2001 tax year. The five-year holding period for all of Jack's Roth IRAs is considered to have started on January 1, 1999. Distributions made after December 31, 2003, will have satisfied the five-year holding period.

> **Example 2:** Mary Smith made her first contribution to a Roth IRA on April 15, 2006. The contribution was for 2005. The five-year holding period for this Roth IRA and all of her subsequent Roth IRA contributions will be considered to have started on January 1, 2005.

In addition to satisfying the five-year holding period, a distribution will constitute a "qualified distribution" only if it is: (Code Sec. 408A(d)(2)):[181]

(1) made on or after the date on which the individual attains age 59½;

(2) made to a beneficiary (or the individual's estate) on or after the individual's death;

(3) attributable to the individual's being disabled; or

(4) a distribution to pay for "qualified first-time homebuyer expenses" (see ¶ 2179).

Footnote references are to paragraphs of the 2008 Standard Federal Tax Reports.

[177] ¶ 18,927	[179] ¶ 18,927	[181] ¶ 18,925
[178] ¶ 18,925	[180] ¶ 18,928	

Distribution Ordering Rules. When an individual receives a "nonqualified distribution" from a Roth IRA, a portion of the distribution may be included in gross income. In order to determine the amount that is includible in gross income, specific ordering rules are applied (Code Sec. 408A(d)(4)(B)). Under these rules, regular Roth contributions are deemed to be withdrawn first, then amounts transferred from traditional IRAs (starting with amounts first transferred). Withdrawals of transferred amounts are treated as coming first from amounts that were included in income. Earnings are treated as withdrawn after contributions (Reg. § 1.408A-6, Q&A-8). Thus, no amount is included in gross income until all the after-tax contributions have been distributed.

If an individual receives a nonqualified distribution from a Roth IRA, a 10 percent penalty tax will generally apply to any portion of the distribution that is included in gross income. However, the 10 percent early withdrawal penalty may not apply if the distribution satisfies one of several exceptions (e.g., qualified higher education expenses and, under limited circumstances, medical insurance and payments). These are the same exceptions that apply to early distributions from traditional IRAs (see ¶ 2179) (Reg. § 1.408A-6, Q&A-5).[182] These exceptions are sometimes referred to as the "72(t) exceptions" because they are authorized by Code Sec. 72(t)(2).

Loss on Roth IRA. When an individual has a loss on a Roth IRA account, the loss can be recognized on the individual's income tax return but only when all the amounts in all the Roth IRA accounts have been distributed and the total distributions are less than the individual's unrecovered basis, if any. The basis is the total amount of the nondeductible contributions in the Roth IRAs. The loss is claimed as a miscellaneous itemized deduction, subject to the two-percent floor that applies to certain miscellaneous itemized deductions on Schedule A, Form 1040 (IRS Pub. 590 (Individual Retirement Arrangements)). A similar rule applies to traditional IRAs (see ¶ 2178) (Notice 89-25, Q&A-7). The loss rule applies separately to each kind of IRA. Thus, to report a loss on a Roth IRA, all the Roth IRAs (but not traditional IRAs) owned by the individual have to be liquidated, and to report a loss on a traditional IRA, all the traditional IRAs (but not Roth IRAs) owned by the individual have to be liquidated (IRS Pub. 590 (Individual Retirement Arrangements)).

> **Example 3:** On January 5, 2007, Bill King made his first nondeductible contribution of $2,000 to a Roth IRA which invested the funds in a mutual fund. This was the only Roth IRA owned by Bill. On December 10, 2007, Bill sold all the mutual shares in the Roth IRA and received $1,500. He did not roll the money over into another Roth IRA. Because the $1,500 distribution is less than his $2,000 basis and he liquidated his only Roth IRA, Bill may claim the $500 loss as a miscellaneous itemized deduction, subject to the two-percent floor, on his Schedule A. The $1,500 distribution is not subject to the 10 percent penalty generally imposed on early distributions because it is a nontaxable return of Bill's Roth contribution (Reg. § 1.408A-6, Q&A-5). However, he would have to report the withdrawal on Form 8606, Nondeductible IRAs, even though it is not taxable.

Reporting Roth IRA Distributions. Distributions from Roth IRAs are reported on Part III of Form 8606. If the 10 percent early distribution tax applies, it is reported on Form 5329, Additional Taxes on Qualified Plans (Including IRAs) and Other Tax-Favored Accounts.

2180B. Rollovers and Conversions. Distributions from one Roth IRA can be rolled over or converted tax free to another Roth IRA. Amounts in a traditional IRA can be rolled over or converted into a Roth IRA but only if: (1) the taxpayer's adjusted gross income for the tax year does not exceed $100,000 and (2) the taxpayer is not married filing separately (Code Sec. 408A(c)(3)(B)). Generally, amounts transferred or converted from a traditional IRA into a Roth IRA must be included in gross income but are not considered when determining the $100,000 AGI limit (Code Sec. 408A(c)(3)(C)(i)). For tax years beginning after 2009, the adjusted gross income limit will be eliminated, allowing higher income taxpayers to convert traditional IRAs to Roth accounts (Code Sec. 408A(c)(3)).

Footnote references are to paragraphs of the 2008 Standard Federal Tax Reports.

[182] ¶ 18,928

¶2180B

Distributions of Conversion Contributions. If within the five-year period starting with the year in which an individual made a conversion contribution of an amount from a traditional IRA to a Roth IRA, the individual takes a distribution from a Roth IRA of an amount that is attributable to the portion of the conversion contribution that was included in income, then generally the individual will be liable for the 10 percent penalty on early distributions (Reg. § 1.408A-6, Q&A-5(c)). However, there are a number of exceptions to the penalty (see ¶ 2179). The five-year period is separately determined for each conversion contribution made to a Roth IRA.

2180C. Recharacterization. An individual who has made contributions to a Roth or traditional IRA may later decide that a contribution to an IRA of the other type is more advantageous. If certain requirements are met, the contribution can be recharacterized and treated as having been originally made to the desired type of IRA (Code Sec. 408A(d)(6)). Recharacterizing an IRA contribution requires transferring amounts previously contributed to a traditional or Roth IRA (plus any resulting net income or minus any resulting net loss) to a new IRA of the opposite type and electing to have the amounts treated as having been transferred to the second IRA at the time they actually were contributed to the first IRA (Reg. § 1.408A-5, Q&A-1). The transfer must be from trustee to trustee. Generally, taxpayers have until the due date (including extensions) of the tax return for the year in which the contribution was made to make the recharacterization (Reg. § 1.408A-5, Q&A-1(b)). A recharacterization must be reported on the taxpayer's tax return. In some situations Form 8606, Nondeductible IRAs, must be filed, along with a statement explaining the nature of the recharacterization (IRS Pub. 590 (Individual Retirement Arrangements)).

> **Example:** On June 1, 2007, Judy properly and timely converted her traditional IRAs to a Roth IRA. At the time, she and her husband, Joe, expected to have modified AGI of less than $100,000 for 2007. On December 5, 2007, Judy received an unexpected bonus that increased their modified AGI to more than $100,000. On December 15, 2007, in order to reverse the now forbidden conversion, Judy set up a traditional IRA with the same trustee. She then instructed the trustee of the Roth IRA to make a trustee-to-trustee transfer of the conversion contribution made to the Roth IRA (including net income allocable to it since the date of the conversion) to the new traditional IRA. She also notified the trustee that she was electing to recharacterize the contribution to the Roth IRA and treat it as if it had been contributed to the new traditional IRA. Because of the recharacterization, Judy and Joe have no taxable income to report from the conversion on their 2007 tax return. Because the entire amount was recharacterized, Judy is not required to report the recharacterization on Form 8606. However, she must file a statement with her Form 1040 explaining the recharacterization (Form 8606 Instructions).

2180D. Reconversions. A "reconversion" is a conversion from a traditional IRA to a Roth IRA of an amount that had previously been recharacterized as a contribution to the traditional IRA after having been earlier converted to a Roth IRA (Notice 2000-30). An IRA owner who converts an amount from a traditional IRA to a Roth IRA during any tax year and then transfers that amount back to a traditional IRA by means of a recharacterization may not reconvert that amount from the traditional IRA to a Roth IRA before the *later* of: (1) the beginning of the tax year following the tax year in which the amount was converted to a Roth IRA or (2) the end of the 30-day period beginning on the day on which the IRA owner transfers the amount from the Roth IRA back to a traditional IRA by means of a recharacterization (regardless of whether the recharacterization occurs during the tax year in which the amount was converted to a Roth IRA or the following tax year) (Reg. § 1.408A-5, Q&A-9(a)(1)).

2180E. Distribution Rules. The *pre-death* required minimum distribution (RMD) requirements (see ¶ 2135) that apply to qualified plans and traditional IRAs do *not* apply to Roth IRAs (Code Sec. 408A(c)(5)). Thus, owners of Roth IRAs are not required to take distributions by April 1 of the year following the calendar year in which they attain age 70½.

As a general rule, the *post-death* RMD rules do apply to Roth IRAs (Reg. § 1.408A-6, Q&A-14(a)). If the sole beneficiary is the decedent's spouse, the spouse may delay distributions until the decedent would have attained age 70½ or may treat the Roth IRA as his or her own (Reg. § 1.408A-6, Q&A-14(b)).

2180F. Deemed Roth IRAs. Qualified plans may allow employees to make voluntary contributions to an account that will be deemed to be a Roth IRA if the account meets all the requirements of a Roth IRA (Code Sec. 408(q)). An employee's contribution to this account counts towards the maximum annual contribution that may be made to a Roth IRA ($4,000 or $5,000 if catch-up contributions are allowable, for 2007; $5,000 or $6,000 for 2008).

2180G. Roth Contributions to Qualified Plans. Plans that allow employees to make pre-tax elective deferrals (401(k) and 403(b) plans) may also allow participating employees to designate all or part of their elective deferrals to the plan to be treated as after-tax Roth contributions (Code Sec. 402A).[183] From the plan administrator's perspective these designated Roth contributions are generally treated the same as pre-tax deferrals under the plan, except that the plan must account for them separately (see ¶ 2111 for discussion of 401(k) plans). They are subject to the same restrictions on distributions and the same nonforfeitability provisions as other elective deferrals under the arrangement and are treated as elective deferrals for purposes of the actual deferral percentage test.

As with regular Roth IRAs, earnings generated by these elective contributions are not currently taxed and, if certain qualifications are met, distributions are not taxed either. However, unlike a Roth IRA, amounts held in a Roth 401(k) account are subject to the required minimum distribution rules (see ¶ 2135).

Simplified Employee Pensions (SEPs)

2184. Simplified Employee Pensions (SEPs). A simplified employee pension (SEP) is a type of retirement plan under which an employer makes contributions to IRAs of employees (Code Sec. 408(k)).[184] For 2007, annual contributions by an employer to a SEP are excluded from the employee's gross income to the extent that the contributions do not exceed the *lesser* of: (1) 25 percent of the participant's compensation ($225,000 maximum for 2007, $230,000 maximum for 2008) or (2) $45,000 ($46,000 for 2008) (Code Sec. 402(h); Notice 2006-98; IRS News Release IR-2007-171).[185] If the employer exceeds the annual limit on contributions, the employee is generally taxed on the amount of the excess contribution (see ¶ 2174) (Code Sec. 4973(a)).[186] In the case of a SEP established by an unincorporated employer, the "compensation" of a self-employed participant (partner or proprietor) is "earned income" (see also ¶ 2152) (Code Sec. 408(k)(7)(A), (B)).[187]

In order to deduct its SEP contributions for a particular year, the employer must make the contributions by the due date (including extensions) of its tax return for that tax year (Code Sec. 404(h)).[188] The contributions are made to the SEP-IRAs that have been established by, or for, each eligible employee.

> **Example:** J. B. Books, Inc. is a calendar year corporation. A few years ago, the corporation established a SEP plan for its eligible employees. Its contributions to the separate SEP-IRAs for 2007 must generally be made by the due date of its tax return (i.e., March 17, 2008). However, if it has requested a six-month filing extension, the contributions may be made up to September 15, 2008.

Although the employer's deduction cannot exceed 25 percent of the employee's compensation (not in excess of $225,000 for 2007 and $230,000 for 2008 (Notice 2006-98; IRS News Release IR-2007-171)), any excess can be carried over and deducted (subject to the percentage limitation for the carryover year) in later years. In addition, when an employer maintains another type of defined contribution plan, the contributions to a SEP

Footnote references are to paragraphs of the 2008 Standard Federal Tax Reports.

[183] ¶ 18,230
[184] ¶ 18,902

[185] ¶ 18,202
[186] ¶ 34,360

[187] ¶ 18,902
[188] ¶ 18,330

must be taken into account when determining compliance with the annual limit imposed on deductible contributions to the plans (see ¶ 2151) (Code Sec. 404(h)(2)).[189]

Nondiscriminatory employer contributions under a SEP must be made for each employee who: (1) has reached age 21; (2) has performed services for the employer during at least three of the immediately preceding five years; and (3) received at least a specific dollar amount of compensation from the employer for the year ($500 for 2007 and 2008) (Code Sec. 408(k)(2)).[190]

Employee Contributions. Employees may make contributions to their SEP-IRA that are independent of their employer's contributions. However, the employee's total contributions to a SEP-IRA, a traditional IRA, and/or a Roth IRA are subject to a yearly maximum ($4,000 for 2007 or $5,000 if catch-up contributions are allowable; $5,000 and $6,000 for 2008) (Code Sec. 219(b)(5)). As with traditional IRAs, the employee's gross income, filing status, and employer plan participation determine whether the employee's contribution to the SEP-IRA is deductible (see ¶ 2170).

Establishing a SEP-IRA. Most employers are able to establish a SEP plan by completing a Form 5305-SEP, Simplified Employee Pension—Individual Retirement Accounts Contribution Agreement. The form is *not* filed with the IRS. Instead, it is retained by the employer as evidence that a SEP plan has been established. All eligible employees must be given a copy of the Form 5305-SEP. Certain employers should not use Form 5305-SEP (e.g., employers that are currently maintaining another qualified plan, or use the services of leased employees). An employer may establish a SEP-IRA for a particular year as late as the due date, including extensions, for the income tax return for that year.

Distributions. Distributions from a SEP are taxed under the rules that apply to distributions from an IRA (Code Secs. 402(h)(3) and 408(d)).[191] See ¶ 2178 for a discussion of these rules.

Salary Reduction SEPs (SARSEPs). In plan years beginning before 1997, an employer could establish a salary reduction (cash or deferred) arrangement as part of a SEP.[192] Such an arrangement—commonly known as a SARSEP—may not be established in plan years beginning after 1996. However, SARSEPs established before 1997 may continue to operate, subject to the same conditions and requirements that have always applied (Sec. 1421(c) of P.L. 104-188).[193]

Top-Heavy SEP. If a SEP is top heavy (see ¶ 2139), each participant who is not a key employee must be provided with a contribution that is not less than three percent of his compensation. If the rate for the key employee receiving the largest contribution is less than three percent, the contribution rate for that employee is used to determine the minimum contribution for non-key employees (Code Sec. 408(k)(1)(B)).[194]

SIMPLE Plans

2185. SIMPLE IRAs. An eligible employer (see ¶ 2185A) may adopt a "Savings Incentive Match Plan for Employees" (SIMPLE) IRA plan (see ¶ 2112 for a discussion of SIMPLE 401(k) plans). Generally, a SIMPLE IRA must meet the requirements that apply to traditional IRAs. However, contributions to an employee's SIMPLE IRA are limited to: (1) employee contributions made under a salary reduction agreement (see ¶ 2185B) and (2) employer contributions that are made as either "matching contributions" or "nonelective contributions" (see ¶ 2185C).

The IRS has issued two model forms that may be used by employers that want to establish a SIMPLE IRA for their employees. Form 5304-SIMPLE is used when the employer permits each employee to choose the financial institution that will receive the SIMPLE contributions. Form 5305-SIMPLE is used when the employer makes the determination which financial institution will receive the contributions. Both forms also contain information that can be used to notify employees of the existence of the plan. Although the completed forms do not have to be filed with the IRS, they must be kept in order to show that the plan was adopted by the employer.

Footnote references are to paragraphs of the 2008 Standard Federal Tax Reports.

[189] ¶ 18,330
[190] ¶ 18,902

[191] ¶ 18,202
[192] ¶ 18,902

[193] ¶ 18,902
[194] ¶ 18,902

Top-Heavy Rules. The special rules for top-heavy plans (see ¶ 2139) do not apply to SIMPLE plans (Code Sec. 416(g)(4)(G)).[195]

2185A. Eligible Employers and Employees. A SIMPLE 401(k) (¶ 2112) or IRA (¶ 2185) plan may only be established by any employer that has 100 or fewer employees who received at least $5,000 in compensation during the preceding tax year (Code Sec. 408(p)(2)(C)(i)). As a general rule, the employer may not make contributions to any other qualified plan starting with the year the SIMPLE plan goes into effect.[196] However, employers may adopt a SIMPLE plan for noncollectively bargained employees and at the same time maintain a qualified plan for collectively bargained employees (Code Sec. 408(p)(2)(D)).[197]

Eligible employees. If the employer has established a SIMPLE plan, an employee must be eligible to participate in any calendar year if he or she received at least $5,000 of compensation from the employer during each of the *two* preceding calendar years and is reasonably expected to receive at least $5,000 in compensation during the current calendar year (Code Sec. 408(p)(4)(A)).[198] Nonresident alien employees and employees covered by a collective bargaining agreement may be excluded from participation (Code Sec. 408(p)(4)(B)).[199]

A self-employed individual is treated as an employee and may participate in a SIMPLE plan if the minimum compensation requirement is met (Code Sec. 408(p)(6)(B)).[200] For this purpose, compensation means earned income (see ¶ 2113) (Code Sec. 408(p)(6)(A)(ii)).[201] Self-employed persons who have elected out of the self-employment tax (SECA) on religious grounds under Code Sec. 1402(g) may base their retirement plan contributions, including contributions to SIMPLE IRAs, on their self-employment income that is exempt from SECA (Code Sec. 408(p)(6)(A)).

2185B. Employee Salary Reduction Contributions. A SIMPLE IRA must permit each eligible employee (¶ 2185A) to elect to have the employer make payments either: (1) directly to the employee in cash or (2) as a contribution (expressed as a percentage of compensation) to the employee's SIMPLE account (Code Sec. 408(p)(2)(A)(ii)).[202] No contributions other than the employee's salary reduction contributions and employer contributions (see ¶ 2185C) may be made to a SIMPLE account (Code Sec. 408(p)(2)(A)(iv)).[203] However, a rollover from another SIMPLE account may be received (Code Sec. 408(d)(3)(G)).[204] The employer must deposit the employee's elective contributions into the SIMPLE IRA within 30 days after the end of the month in which the amounts would have been paid to the employee. Elective contributions by an employee are fully vested when made (Code Sec. 408(p)(3)).[205]

Dollar Limit on Employee Contributions. An employee's elective contributions to a SIMPLE IRA for 2007 and 2008 are limited to $10,500 for each year (Code Sec. 408(p)(2)(A)(ii) and (E); Notice 2006-98; IRS News Release IR-2007-171).[206] In addition, employees who will be at least age 50 by the end of the year, are allowed to make additional catch-up contributions of $2,500 for 2007 and for 2008 (Code Sec. 414(v)(2)(B)(ii)). The maximum dollar limit (e.g., $10,500 for 2007) is the only limit on employee contributions. An employer may not place a limit on the percentage of salary an employee may elect to defer in the plan (except in order to comply with the annual dollar limit).

> **Example:** Dan's employer offers a SIMPLE IRA to its employees. During 2007, Dan, who is 60 years old, will earn $15,000. His maximum allowable contribution to his SIMPLE IRA would be $13,000 ($10,500 in regular contributions and $2,500 in catch-up contributions) (Notice 98-4, Q&A D-2).

Under a SIMPLE plan, each eligible employee must have the right to elect, during the 60-day period preceding the beginning of any calendar year (and the 60-day period preceding the employee's first day of eligibility), to participate in the plan for that

---

Footnote references are to paragraphs of the 2008 Standard Federal Tax Reports.

[195] ¶ 19,250	[199] ¶ 18,902	[203] ¶ 18,902
[196] ¶ 18,902	[200] ¶ 18,902	[204] ¶ 18,902
[197] ¶ 18,902	[201] ¶ 18,902	[205] ¶ 18,902
[198] ¶ 18,902	[202] ¶ 18,902	[206] ¶ 18,902

calendar year or to modify the amount of his or her contributions to the plan for that calendar year (Code Sec. 408(p)(5)(C)).[207] In addition, an employee may terminate participation in the SIMPLE plan at any time during a calendar year. However, the plan may prohibit reentry until the beginning of the following calendar year (Code Sec. 408(p)(5)(B)).[208]

2185C. Employer's Matching or Nonelective Contributions. An employer is required to make contributions to its employees' SIMPLE IRAs under one of two methods: (1) matching contributions on employee contributions of up to three percent of compensation (Code Sec. 408(p)(2)(A)(iii)) or (2) nonelective contributions (Code Sec. 408(p)(2)(B)). An employer may elect to limit its matching contribution, for a particular year, to a smaller percentage of compensation (not less than one percent). The election may not be made by an employer in more than two out of every five years. If the SIMPLE account did not exist during the full five-year period, the election may still be made in up to two of the years in which it did exist (Code Sec. 408(p)(2)(C)(ii)).[209] Employees must be notified of the employer's election to contribute less than three percent a reasonable time before the beginning of the 60-day period at the end of each calendar year during which employees designate the amount of their election contributions for the following calendar year. Matching contributions to SIMPLE IRAs that are made on behalf of self-employed individuals are not treated as elective contributions made by the individuals (Code Sec. 408(p)(9)).

> **Example 1:** Ralph, age 52, participates in his employer's SIMPLE IRA plan and for 2007 his salary will be $50,000. He elects to defer the maximum amount into the plan (i.e., $13,000 ($10,500 in regular contributions and $2,500 in catch-up contributions)). Under the plan, the employer makes a maximum matching contribution for each participating employee, up to the three percent limit. Therefore, the employer will make a $1,500 ($50,000 × three percent) matching contribution to Ralph's SIMPLE IRA.

Nonelective Contributions. The matching contribution requirement is considered to be satisfied if the employer elects to make nonelective contributions of two percent of compensation for each employee who is eligible to participate in the plan and who has at least $5,000 of compensation from the employer for the calendar year. The compensation that may be taken into account in determining the two percent nonelective contribution may not exceed an annual limit (e.g., $225,000 for 2007 and $230,000 for 2008) (Code Sec. 408(p)(2)(B)(ii)).[210]

> **Example 2:** Assume the same facts as in Example 1, above, except that Ralph's employer decided to base its contributions on the nonelective contributions option. In this situation, Ralph would still be allowed to contribute $13,000 to his SIMPLE IRA. However, the employer's contribution would be $1,000 ($50,000 × two percent).

Vesting. The employee's right to both matching contributions and nonelective contributions of the employer (and the earnings on these contributions) in a SIMPLE IRA must be fully vested at all times (Code Sec. 408(p)(3)).[211]

Employer's Deduction. An employer can deduct SIMPLE IRA contributions in the tax year with or within which the calendar year for which the contributions were made ends. Contributions for a particular tax year may be deducted if they are made for that tax year and are made by the due date, including extensions of the employer's tax return for that year (Code Sec. 404(m)).[212]

2185D. Distributions from SIMPLE IRAs. Distributions from a SIMPLE IRA are taxable to the employee (or the beneficiary or estate of the employee) under the rules that govern distributions from traditional IRAs (see ¶ 2178) (Code Sec. 408(p)(1)(A)).[213]

Rollovers. If the employee has participated in the SIMPLE IRA for at least two years, a distribution may be rolled over into other types of retirement plans (e.g., employer

---

Footnote references are to paragraphs of the 2008 Standard Federal Tax Reports.

[207] ¶ 18,902
[208] ¶ 18,902
[209] ¶ 18,902
[210] ¶ 18,902
[211] ¶ 18,902
[212] ¶ 18,922.0272
[213] ¶ 18,902

qualified plans, 403(b) plans and 457 plans) (Code Sec. 408(d)(3)(A)). If the employee has not participated in the SIMPLE plan for two years, the distribution may only be rolled over into another SIMPLE plan (Code Sec. 408(d)(3)(G)).

Penalty on Early Distributions. The 10 percent penalty that applies to early distributions from IRAs also applies to distributions from SIMPLE IRAs. See ¶ 2179 for information on this penalty and its exceptions. However, the 10 percent penalty is increased to 25 percent when the employee takes an early distribution within two years after the employee's first participation in a SIMPLE arrangement (Code Sec. 72(t)(6)).[214]

Rollovers

2186. Tax-Free Rollovers of Distributions from Traditional IRAs. An individual may withdraw all or part of the assets of one traditional IRA and exclude the withdrawal from income if the individual transfers it to another traditional IRA or returns it to the same IRA. However, the transfer or return must generally be accomplished within 60 days after the withdrawal. It is not necessary that the entire amount withdrawn be transferred, but only the amount that is in fact transferred during the 60-day period will not be taxed. Any portion of the withdrawal that is not rolled over within the 60-day period will be taxed as ordinary income and may be subject to a 10 percent penalty (see ¶ 2179). The IRS has the authority to grant a waiver of the 60-day rule in situations involving equity, good conscience, or situations beyond the control of the individual (Code Sec. 408(d)(3)(I); Rev. Proc. 2003-16).

Waiting Period. Once an individual has made a tax-free rollover, he or she must wait at least one year from the date of receipt of the amount withdrawn before becoming eligible to engage in another rollover (Code Sec. 408(d)(3)(B)).[215] According to the IRS, the one-year limitation applies separately to each IRA owned by the taxpayer (IRS Pub. 590). Thus, a distribution received from one IRA of the taxpayer may be rolled over even though a distribution from another IRA of the taxpayer was received less than a year before and was also rolled over. A mere change of trustee or custodian for an IRA is not considered a rollover (although it is also tax free) and, therefore, the one-year limitation does not apply.[216]

Required Distributions. Rollover from one traditional IRA to another is *not* available for a required minimum distribution (see ¶ 2177) (Code Sec. 408(d)(3)(E)).[217] See ¶ 2180 regarding a rollover from a traditional IRA into a Roth IRA. Rollovers from SIMPLE plans are discussed at ¶ 2185D.

Rollovers from IRAs to Employer Plans. Generally, an eligible rollover distribution from an IRA may be rolled over into a qualified plan, 403(b) plan or 457 plan (Code Sec. 408(d)(3)(A)). A rollover of after-tax contributions can be made from one IRA to another IRA. However, after-tax contributions in the IRA cannot be rolled over into an employer's qualified plan (Code Sec. 408(d)(3)(A)(ii)).

2188. Tax-Free Rollovers Between Qualified Plans or To Traditional IRAs. In many situations, a distribution from a qualified plan may be rolled over and thus excluded from current income (Code Sec. 402(c)).[218] Any part of the taxable portion of a distribution from a qualified plan may be rolled over to a traditional IRA or to another qualified plan, unless the distribution is one of a series of substantially equal payments made: (1) over the life (or life expectancy) of the participant or the joint lives (or joint life expectancies) of the participant and his or her beneficiary or (2) over a specified period of 10 years or more (Code Sec. 402(c)(4)).[219] In addition, a distribution may not be rolled over if it is required to be made under the required minimum distribution (RMD) rules discussed at ¶ 2135 (Code Sec. 402(c)(4)(B)).[220] Generally, the rollover must be made within 60 days. The IRS has the authority to grant a waiver of the 60-day rule in situations involving equity, good conscience, or situations beyond the control of the individual (Code Sec. 408(d)(3)(I)).

Footnote references are to paragraphs of the 2008 Standard Federal Tax Reports.

[214] ¶ 6102
[215] ¶ 18,902
[216] ¶ 18,922.75

[217] ¶ 18,902
[218] ¶ 18,202
[219] ¶ 18,202

[220] ¶ 18,202

¶2186

Ten-year averaging and the special 20 percent tax (see ¶ 2153) are not available if any part of a lump-sum distribution is rolled over (Code Sec. 402(d)(4)(K), before amendment by P.L. 104-188).[221] Also, if a distribution that is not a lump-sum distribution is rolled over, averaging is not available as to a subsequent lump-sum distribution (Code Sec. 402(c)(10), before amendment by P.L. 104-188).[222]

Direct Transfers. All qualified plans must permit a participant (or a spouse or ex-spouse of a participant who is an alternate payee under a QDRO) to elect to have any distribution that is eligible for rollover treatment transferred directly to an eligible transferee plan specified by the participant (Code Sec. 401(a)(31)(A)).[223] In the case of a qualified plan funded by a trust (instead of an annuity contract or contracts), the recipient plan must be a defined contribution plan the terms of which permit the acceptance of rollover distributions. The defined contribution plan that accepts the transfer must agree to separately account for the pre-tax and after-tax portions of the amount that is transferred (Code Sec. 401(a)(31)(C)(i)).

Eligible Retirement Plans. The term "eligible retirement plan" for purposes of rollover distributions includes IRAs, qualified plans, 403(b) plans and 457 plans (Code Sec. 402(c)(8)(B)). Rollovers of after-tax amounts may be rolled over into a defined contribution plan if the new plan agrees to separately account for these amounts (Code Sec. 401(a)(31)(C)). Effective for tax years after 2006, after-tax contributions can be rolled over into any qualified plan or 403(b) plan that provides for separate accounting (Code Sec. 402(c)(2)(A), as amended by the Pension Protection Act of 2006 (P.L. 109-280)). The amount transferred is considered to come from pre-tax amounts first and then from post-tax amounts (Code Sec. 402(c)(2)).

Mandatory Rollovers. A qualified plan must provide for a direct rollover (i.e., a trustee to trustee transfer) from the plan into an IRA when the plan makes a mandatory distribution of the participant's benefit (an involuntary cash-out) (Code Sec. 401(a)(31)). The rule applies when a mandatory distribution from a qualified plan exceeds $1,000 and the plan specifies that nonforfeitable benefits that do not exceed $5,000 must be distributed immediately. However, the employee must have the right to elect to receive the distribution or have it rolled over into another IRA or qualified plan (Notice 2005-5).

Withholding. If a distributee does not elect a direct transfer, and receives the distribution and then transfers the funds to an eligible plan within 60 days, the payor of the distribution must withhold 20 percent of the distribution (Code Sec. 3405(c)).[224] If the distributee does elect a direct transfer, there is no withholding.

Written Explanation. The plan administrator must provide a written explanation to a recipient of the distribution options (including the direct trustee-to-trustee transfer option) within a reasonable period of time before making an eligible rollover distribution (Code Sec. 402(f)).[225]

Tax-Sheltered Annuities. Rules similar to those discussed above also apply in the case of 403(b) plans (Code Sec. 403(a)(4)(B)).[226]

2190. Rollover by Successor After Death of Participant. When a distribution from a qualified plan that would be eligible for rollover treatment if made to the employee is received by the participant's surviving spouse, the spouse may roll that distribution into an account maintained in the survivor's name under the same terms and conditions that would have applied to the employee (see ¶ 2188) (Code Sec. 402(c)(9)).[227] Successors other than a surviving spouse who receive a distribution from a qualified plan are not entitled to roll over that distribution to an IRA or to another qualified plan account in their own name (Code Sec. 402(c)(9)).[228] Effective for distributions after 2006, a non-spouse beneficiary can roll a qualified plan distribution into an IRA established in the name of the decedent. The IRA is treated as an inherited IRA. This allows the beneficiary to take distributions from the IRA in accordance with the RMD rules, instead of taking

---

Footnote references are to paragraphs of the 2008 Standard Federal Tax Reports.

[221] ¶ 18,202	[224] ¶ 33,620	[227] ¶ 18,202
[222] ¶ 18,202	[225] ¶ 18,202	[228] ¶ 18,202
[223] ¶ 17,502	[226] ¶ 18,270	

the entire distribution into income in the year of the plan distribution (Code Sec. 402(c)(11), as added by the Pension Protection Act of 2006 (P.L. 109-280)). The surviving spouse of the owner of an IRA is also eligible to roll over any amount received from that IRA to another IRA or qualified plan (see ¶ 2186) (Code Sec. 408(d)(3)(C)(ii)(II)).[229] This cannot be done by any other successor to the IRA (Code Sec. 408(d)(3)(C)).[230]

2191. Rollovers Incident to Divorce. When a participant's spouse or former spouse is awarded all or part of the participant's interest in a qualified plan or 403(b) plan by a qualified domestic relations order (QDRO) (see ¶ 2166), the distribution of any part of that interest to the spouse or former spouse may be rolled over on the same terms that would apply if the distribution were made to the participant (Code Sec. 414(p)(10)).[231] The QDRO provisions also apply to 457 plans (i.e., eligible deferred compensation plans of state and local governments and tax-exempt organizations, see ¶ 2197B).

The transfer of all or a portion of an IRA to a spouse or former spouse under a divorce or separation instrument that meets the definition established by Code Sec. 71(b)(2) is a nontaxable transaction as to both parties, and the IRA is thereafter treated as that of the spouse or former spouse (Code Sec. 408(d)(6)).[232] Accordingly, the spouse or former spouse may roll over to another IRA or IRAs all or any part of the interest transferred to him or her (see ¶ 2186).

2192. IRA as Conduit for Transfers Between Qualified Plans. For distributions made prior to January 1, 2002, an amount rolled over to a traditional IRA from a qualified plan could only be rolled over to another qualified plan if the "conduit" IRA at no time held assets other than those rolled over from the qualified plan, assets attributable to reinvestment of those assets, and earnings of those assets. As a general matter, this "conduit" rule is no longer needed because of the expansion of rollover options (Code Sec. 408(d)(3)(A)(ii)).[233] See ¶ 2186 for rollovers between IRAs. See ¶ 2188 for rollovers between qualified plans and IRAs.

2193. Rollovers of 403(b) and 457 Plan Assets. See ¶ 2167 for the rollover of assets from a 403(b) plan. See ¶ 2197B for the rollover of 457 plan assets. Rollovers between various types of qualified plans are discussed at ¶ 2188.

Nonqualified Plans

2194. Nonqualified Plans. An employer may maintain a retirement or other deferred compensation plan that is not a qualified plan (see ¶ 2117). If such a plan is *funded* (i.e., the employer makes contributions to a trust or purchases an annuity contract or contracts), the participants realize income and the employer is entitled to deductions under the rules set forth below. As to *unfunded* deferred compensation plans, see ¶ 723 and ¶ 906. However, nonqualified deferred compensation plans are subject to strict requirements after December 31, 2004 (Code Sec. 409A). These requirements are discussed at ¶ 2197A.

2195. Income of the Plan. In the case of a nonqualified plan funded through a trust, the trust is not exempt (i.e., the plan's earnings are generally taxable to the trust) (Code Sec. 641).[234] The grantor trust rules (see ¶ 573 and following) ordinarily do not apply to a nonqualified plan. Therefore, the participant is not usually treated as the owner of his share of the trust's assets and is not subject to tax on the trust's income. However, if a participant's contributions as of any date exceed the employer's contributions on behalf of the participant, the participant is treated as the owner of the portion of the trust attributable to his contributions and is subject to tax on the income from that portion (Reg. § 1.402(b)-1(b)(6)).[235]

Footnote references are to paragraphs of the 2008 Standard Federal Tax Reports.

[229] ¶ 18,902	[232] ¶ 18,902	[235] ¶ 18,208
[230] ¶ 18,902	[233] ¶ 18,902	
[231] ¶ 19,150	[234] ¶ 24,260	

2196. Income of a Participant. Contributions of (or premiums paid by) the employer in the case of a nonqualified plan are taxable to the participant when made if they are substantially vested at that time. If contributions are made to a nonqualified plan at a time when the participant's interest in the plan is not substantially vested and the interest subsequently becomes substantially vested, the value of the participant's interest that is attributable to the employer's contributions is generally includible in the employee's income at the time of vesting. If only a portion of a participant's interest becomes substantially vested, the amount included in income is the amount that would have been included if the entire interest had vested multiplied by the percentage that did become substantially vested.

Rank-and-file employees are not taxable on amounts contributed to, or earned by, a trust that is not exempt solely because of the plan's failure to satisfy the nondiscriminatory coverage requirements described at ¶ 2119. However, each highly compensated employee (¶ 2111) is subject to tax on the value of the vested accrued benefit attributable to employer contributions as of the close of the employer's tax year that ends with or within the tax year in which the trust loses its exemption. If the trust continues to be nonexempt for failure to satisfy the coverage requirements, a highly compensated employee is subject to tax on the excess of the current value of his or her vested accrued benefit attributable to employer contributions over the value of the previously taxed portion of that benefit (Code Sec. 402(b)(4)).[236]

The participant's investment (basis) in a nonqualified plan is increased by any amounts included in his or her income under the above rules. Actual distributions from a nonqualified plan are taxed under the rules described at ¶ 817 and following if they take the form of an annuity. Otherwise, they are considered to be derived first from plan earnings and asset appreciation (taxable gain) rather than from the employee's investment (basis) in the plan (Code Secs. 402(b) and 403(c)).[237]

2197. Employer's Deduction. The employer is entitled to a deduction for contributions to, or premiums paid under, a nonqualified plan on behalf of an employee in the tax year of the employer in which an amount attributable to the contribution is includible in the gross income of the employee under the rules discussed at ¶ 2196 (Code Sec. 404(a)(5)).[238] If more than one employee participates, this rule applies only if separate accounts are maintained for each employee.

2197A. Nonqualified Deferred Compensation Plans (after 12/31/04). Unless certain plan design and funding requirements are met, amounts deferred under a nonqualified deferred compensation plan are included in income to the extent they are not subject to a substantial risk of forfeiture. (Code Sec. 409A).[239] The plan design rules apply to amounts deferred after December 31, 2004. The funding rules, relating to assets held in offshore or creditor-protected trusts, apply as of January 1, 2005 to both newly and previously deferred compensation (Act Sec. 403(hh)(3)(A) of the Gulf Opportunity Zone Act of 2005 (P.L. 109-135)). The IRS was authorized to issue regulations that spell out the details of these requirements, and regulations have been issued (Code Sec. 409A(e)). The proposed regulations can be relied upon for years beginning before January 1, 2008; the final regulations must be satisfied for years beginning on or after January 1, 2008, and can be relied upon for earlier years.

Definition of "Nonqualified Deferred Compensation Plan." A nonqualified deferred compensation plan is generally defined as any plan that provides for the deferral of compensation, other than a qualified employer plan, certain foreign plans, and certain types of employer-provided welfare benefit plans (e.g., vacation plans, death benefit plans, or disability plans). Eligible 457(b) plans are not nonqualified deferred compensation plans; ineligible 457(f) plans may be (Code Sec. 409A(d)(1); Proposed Reg. § 1.409A-1(a)(2), (4); Reg. § 1.409A-1(a)).

Footnote references are to paragraphs of the 2008 Standard Federal Tax Reports.

[236] ¶ 18,202

[237] ¶ 18,202, ¶ 18,270

[238] ¶ 18,330

[239] ¶ 18,952

General Rule. If certain operational and design requirements are *not* met, all amounts deferred under a nonqualified deferred compensation plan, for all tax years, are currently includible in gross income to the extent they are not subject to a substantial risk of forfeiture (Code Sec. 409A(a)(1)(A)). In addition, for the year that the deferred compensation is included in income, any tax due must be increased by an interest charge, as well as by 20 percent of the included deferred compensation (Code Sec. 409A(a)(1)(B)(i)).

Distribution Rules. Distributions from nonqualified deferred compensation plans may be made upon the employee's separation from service, disability, or death, or at a specified time. Distributions may also be made upon a change in the effective ownership or control of the employer, or in the event of an unforeseeable emergency (Code Sec. 409A(a)(2)(A)). Distributions to key employees resulting from a separation from service must not be made until six months after the separation, unless the former employee dies in the interim (Code Sec. 409A(a)(2)(B)). A nonqualified deferred compensation plan generally cannot allow the acceleration of the time or schedule of any payment under the plan, though the regulations permit some exceptions (Code Sec. 409A(a)(3); Proposed Reg. § 1.409A-3(h); Reg. § 1.409A-3(j)).

Election Rules. A nonqualified deferred compensation plan must meet certain requirements regarding the participants' elections to defer compensation and to receive distributions (Code Sec. 409A(a)(4)). Compensation for services performed during a tax year can be deferred only if the participant's election to defer is made before the close of the preceding tax year. In the case of the first year in which a participant becomes eligible to participate in the plan, the election may be made within 30 days after the date the participant becomes eligible to participate. That election is effective only for compensation with respect to services performed after the election is made. A plan may allow subsequent elections to delay or change the form of payments under the plan under limited circumstances.

Funding. Generally, if the nonqualified deferred compensation plan uses an offshore trust, or places assets outside the United States, the plan will not defer the compensation (Code Sec. 409A(b)(1)). Also, if the plan provides that its assets will become restricted to the payment of benefits under the plan if there is a change in the employer's financial health, or if the assets actually become so restricted, the plan will not defer compensation (Code Sec. 409A(b)(2)). These rules apply to all deferred compensation, regardless of when it was deferred. The IRS has issued guidance providing that a plan will be treated as satisfying the funding requirements if it comes into conformity with the rules on or before December 31, 2007 (Notice 2006-33).

A nonqualified plan will also not defer compensation to the extent of contributions made on behalf of or restricted to benefits for certain employees at a time when the employer or its defined benefit plan are experiencing financial difficulties. This provision applies if the plan is in at-risk status (under Code Sec. 430(i), as added by the Pension Protection Act of 2006); if the plan sponsor is in bankruptcy; and during the 12-month period beginning six months before the plan terminates, if the plan is underfunded (Code Sec. 409A(b)(3), as amended by the Pension Protection Act of 2006 (P.L. 109-280)).

Form W-2 Reporting. The total amount of deferrals under a nonqualified deferred compensation plan are required to be shown on the employee's Form W-2 (Code Sec. 6051(a)(13)). If the individual is not an employee, the amount must be shown on Form 1099-MISC (Code Sec. 6041(g)). These rules apply even if the amount of deferred compensation is not currently taxable. The IRS has the authority to establish minimum amounts that do not have to be shown. If income is recognized because the plan does not satisfy the rules, it is reported with Code Z in Box 12 of Form W-2. For non-employees, the income to be recognized is reported in Boxes 7 and 15b of Form 1099-MISC.

2197B. Deferred Compensation Plans of Exempt Employers ("Sec. 457 Plans"). Special rules apply to certain deferred compensation plans sponsored by state and local governments and private tax-exempt organizations (commonly referred to as Sec. 457

plans). Under a state or local government plan, compensation deferred under the plan is only included in income when it is paid to the employee. However, for plans of tax-exempt organizations, deferred compensation is includible when paid or made available (Code Sec. 457(a)(1)). As with other types of retirement plans, special requirements have to be met by Sec. 457 plans.

Availability of Benefits. Compensation is deferred for any calendar month under a Sec. 457 plan only if an agreement providing for deferral is entered into before the beginning of that month (Code Sec. 457(b)(4)). Benefits are not considered to be made available under the plan if the participant or beneficiary may elect, before any benefits become payable, to defer payment of some or all of them to a fixed or determinable future time. In addition, amounts deferred under an eligible plan are not considered to be made available to the participant solely because the individual may choose among various investment options under the plan, whether before or after benefit payments have commenced (Reg. § 1.457-8(b)(2)).[240] After benefits have become payable but before they have commenced, the participant or beneficiary may elect to defer them to a date later than that originally elected. Only one such election may be made (Code Sec. 457(e)(9)(B)).[241]

Limitation on Deferral. The maximum amount that can be deferred is the *lesser* of: (1) 100 percent of the participant's includible compensation or (2) $15,500, for 2007 and for 2008 (Code Sec. 457(b)(2); Notice 2006-98; IRS News Release IR-2007-171).[242] The dollar amount is indexed for inflation (Code Sec. 457(e)(15)).[243] The maximum deferral to a Sec. 457 plan does not have to be coordinated with contributions made to other types of retirement plans (Code Sec. 457(c), before amendment by P.L. 107-16). Participants in a Sec. 457 plan are permitted to make additional deferrals of income for one or more of the last three tax years that end before normal retirement age (Code Sec. 457(b)(3)). The allowable deferral for such participants is increased, up to a limit of twice the standard dollar amount for the year, by the amount of allowable deferrals not made in previous plan years.

Catch-Up Contributions. Employees covered by a Code Sec. 457 state or governmental plan who will be at least 50 years of age by the end of the year are able to make special catch-up contributions to the plan (Code Sec. 414(v)). The maximum catch-up contribution is $5,000 for tax years beginning in 2007 or 2008. However, during the last three years of employment that end before attaining normal retirement age, a special formula is used to determine the maximum contribution (Code Sec. 457(e)(18)).

Other Requirements. A Sec. 457 plan must satisfy the required minimum distribution (RMD) rules that are generally imposed on qualified plans (see ¶ 2135) (Code Sec. 457(d)(2)). Distributions of deferred amounts must not be made available before the calendar year in which the participant attains age 70½, is severed from employment, or is faced with an unforeseen emergency (Code Sec. 457(d)(1)).[244] An unforeseeable emergency must be defined in the plan as a severe financial hardship to the participant that results from a sudden unexpected illness or accident of the participant or a dependent of the participant or a loss of the participant's property due to casualty or other similar extraordinary and unforeseeable circumstances beyond the control of the participant. Hardship withdrawals may not be made to the extent that the financial hardship can be relieved by insurance, liquidation of the participant's assets (if liquidation would not cause financial hardship), or by stopping deferrals under the plan. In addition, withdrawals of amounts for unforeseeable emergencies is permitted only to the extent reasonably needed to satisfy the emergency. The need for funds to purchase a new home or to meet the college expenses of the participant's children is *not* an unforeseeable emergency (Reg. § 1.457-6(c)(2)(i)). The Pension Protection Act of 2006 requires the IRS to amend the rules to provide that, to the extent allowed under the plan, if the occurrence of an event with regard to the employee's spouse or dependent would

---

Footnote references are to paragraphs of the 2008 Standard Federal Tax Reports.

[240] ¶ 21,532	[242] ¶ 21,531	[244] ¶ 21,531
[241] ¶ 21,531	[243] ¶ 21,531	

be a hardship, the occurrence of the same event with regard to the employee's beneficiary under the plan would also be a hardship (Notice 2007-7, Q&A-5).

Rollovers. An employee participating in a governmental Sec. 457 plan may roll over distributions into a variety of retirement plans (e.g., IRAs, 401(k) plans and 403(b) plans) (Code Sec. 457(e)(16)). Similarly, in some circumstances, assets from these plans may be rolled over into a Sec. 457 plan (see ¶ 2186 and ¶ 2188).

Ineligible Plans. Compensation deferred under a nonqualified plan of a state or local government or other tax-exempt organization that is not an eligible Sec. 457 plan is includible in the income of a participant or beneficiary for the first tax year in which there is no substantial risk of forfeiture (Code Sec. 457(f)(1)(A) and (2)(E)).[245]

Welfare Benefits

2198. Unfunded Welfare Benefits. Welfare benefits provided directly by an employer to an employee are deductible by the employer only in its tax year that includes the end of the tax year in which the employee includes the benefits in gross income (or would include such benefits in gross income if they were taxable to the employee) (Code Sec. 404(b)(2)(A)).[246] An employer may not accrue and deduct unpaid welfare benefits. This rule applies to any benefit which—if it were classified as compensation— would be deferred compensation. See ¶ 906 for information regarding the determination of compensation.

· **2199. Funded Welfare Benefits.** Special rules govern deductions for employer contributions to funded welfare benefit plans (Code Sec. 419).[247] The rules also govern contributions to welfare benefit plans on behalf of independent contractors.

Essentially, an employer is prohibited from deducting contributions to a welfare benefit plan in excess of the benefits actually paid by the plan during the tax year. However, under some circumstances, for plans providing disability, medical, supplemental unemployment and severance, or life insurance benefits, deductions may also be taken for additions to a reserve (referred to as a "qualified asset account") (Code Sec. 419A(a)).[248] Specifically, the employer may deduct contributions paid or accrued to a welfare benefit fund to the extent that the contributions do not exceed the "qualified cost" of the fund for its tax year ending with or within the tax year of the employer, reduced by the "after-tax income" of the fund for that tax year.

Qualified Cost. The qualified cost of the fund consists of two elements: (1) the qualified direct cost and (2) the allowable addition, if any, to a qualified asset account (Code Sec. 419(c)(1)).[249] A qualified asset account is one maintained by a welfare benefit fund for the payment of such costs as medical, SUB, severance pay and life insurance benefits (including associated administrative costs) (Code Sec. 419A(a)).[250] Generally, the allowable addition for a tax year is the amount that will bring the account to a level (the "account limit") that is reasonably and actuarially necessary to fund the payment of incurred but unpaid benefits and, in the case of post-retirement medical and life insurance benefits, to fund the payment of such benefits on a level basis over the working lives of the covered employees (based on current medical costs). For employers who do not support higher additions to a qualified asset account by actuarial certifications, there are safe harbor additions for the various benefits. Limits are placed on the level of disability and SUB or severance pay benefits that may be considered in establishing the account limit for such benefits.

After-Tax Income. The after-tax income of a welfare benefit plan is its gross income reduced by the sum of: (a) the deductions allowed by the Code that are directly connected with the production of that income and (b) the federal income tax imposed on the fund (Code Secs. 419 and 419A; Temp. Reg. §§ 1.419-1T, 1.419A-1T and 1.419A-2T).[251]

Footnote references are to paragraphs of the 2008 Standard Federal Tax Reports.

[245] ¶ 21,531
[246] ¶ 18,330
[247] ¶ 19,295

[248] ¶ 19,298
[249] ¶ 19,295
[250] ¶ 19,298

[251] ¶ 19,295, ¶ 19,296, ¶ 19,298, ¶ 19,299, ¶ 19,300

Chapter 22

CORPORATE ACQUISITIONS
REORGANIZATIONS
LIQUIDATIONS

Corporate Division

2201. "Spin-Off," "Split-Off," and "Split-Up" Exchanges. Nonrecognition-of-gain benefits apply to receipt of stock in connection with corporate exchanges in distributions known as "spin-offs," "split-offs," or "split-ups."

Spin-Off. A "spin-off" occurs when a corporation distributes stock or securities in another corporation controlled by it (through at least 80 percent stock ownership) without requiring shareholders to surrender any shares. The distribution is pro rata. The recipients do not surrender any of their stock in the controlling corporation (Code Sec. 355; Reg. § 1.355-1).[1] A new or existing corporation may be used for the spin-off (Reg. § 1.355-1(b)).[2]

Split-Off. A "split-off" is a type of corporate separation in which a parent corporation distributes to some or all of its shareholders stock in a newly formed or pre-existing controlled corporation, under the same conditions as in a "spin-off," except that the shareholders surrender a part of their stock in the parent corporation for the stock in the controlled corporation. The distribution may be pro rata but usually is not.

Split-Up. In a "split-up," the distributing corporation's shareholders surrender all shares held in the distributing corporation and in return receive new shares in two or more controlled subsidiaries the distributing corporation controlled immediately before the distribution. The subsidiaries may be pre-existing or newly formed.

To attain nonrecognition treatment, the transaction must have a valid corporate business purpose and it cannot be primarily a tax-avoidance device (Reg. § 1.355-2).[3] Also immediately after the transaction, the distributing and controlled corporation must be engaged in the active conduct of a trade or business. This requirement does not apply to the distributing corporation if immediately before the distribution, it had no assets other than stock in the controlled corporation. The trade or business must have been actively conducted throughout the five-year period immediately preceding the date of the distribution (Code Sec. 355(b); Reg. § 1.355-3).[4] Other limitations relate to continuity of interest on the part of the owners (Reg. § 1.355-2(c)),[5] the amount of securities distributed, taxable acquisitions within five years, and receipt of other property or "boot" (Code Sec. 355(a)(3)).[6]

Footnote references are to paragraphs of the 2008 Standard Federal Tax Reports.

[1] ¶ 16,460, ¶ 16,462
[2] ¶ 16,461
[3] ¶ 16,463
[4] ¶ 16,460, ¶ 16,464
[5] ¶ 16,463
[6] ¶ 16,460

Basis Rules. With an exchange of stock and/or securities, the basis of the old stock or securities becomes the basis of the new stock or securities ("substituted basis"). If the exchange is partially taxable, the basis of the old stock or securities is decreased by the sum of the money and fair market value of "other property" received and increased by the amount of gain recognized and the amount treated as a dividend. If any loss is recognized, the basis of the property received is decreased by that amount. If some old stock is retained, allocation is made as though the stock were first surrendered and then received in exchange (Code Sec. 358).[7]

Morris Trust Rules. Restrictions have been imposed on certain spin-offs that follow the fact pattern of *Morris Trust* (66-2 USTC ¶ 9718) (Code Sec. 355(e)).[8] If either the controlled or distributing corporation is acquired pursuant to a plan or arrangement in existence on the date of distribution, gain is generally recognized by the distributing corporation as of the date of the distribution. Recognition can be avoided if more than 50 percent of the historical shareholders retain ownership in the distributing and acquiring corporations. Acquisitions occurring within the four-year period beginning two years before the date of distribution are presumed to have occurred pursuant to a plan or arrangement.

Corporate Reorganization

2205. Tax-Free Exchange in Reorganization. A corporation recognizes no gain or loss on the exchange of property solely for stock or securities of another corporation when the exchange is made pursuant to a plan of reorganization (Code Secs. 351 and 368).[9] Both sides of the transaction are eligible for nonrecognition. However, to achieve such a favorable tax outcome, transactions must satisfy strict statutory and nonstatutory requirements.

Although no gain or loss is generally recognized by a transferor on the transfer of property pursuant to a plan of reorganization, gain is recognized on any "boot" (property that does not qualify for nonrecognition treatment) as if it were sold to the distributee at its fair market value. In addition, no gain or loss is recognized by a corporation on the disposition, pursuant to a plan of reorganization, of stock or securities that were received under the plan and are the stock or securities of another corporation that is a party to the reorganization (Code Sec. 361).[10] There cannot be a tax-free "reorganization" unless there is an "exchange" of properties as distinguished from a "sale" (Code Sec. 368; Reg. § 1.368-2).[11] For exchanges of depreciable property, see ¶ 1779. See also ¶ 2465 regarding corporate inversion transactions that may be a part of a reorganization.

Basis Rules. Generally, the basis of stock and securities received by a corporation in a reorganization is the same as the basis of the property transferred to the acquiring corporation, adjusted for any gain or loss recognized on the exchange and the value of any money or other property ("boot") received (Code Sec. 358(a)).[12] Boot received from the acquiring corporation generally takes a basis equal to its fair market value at the time of the transaction (Code Sec. 362(b)).[13]

2209. "Reorganization" Defined. A qualified "reorganization" must fall within one of seven categories (each referred to by a letter corresponding to the statutory provisions of Code Sec. 368):[14]

Type (A) reorganization: a statutory merger or consolidation (that is, a merger or consolidation under the corporation laws of the United States, a state, or the District of Columbia);

Type (B) reorganization: the acquisition by one corporation of the stock of another corporation, in exchange solely for all or a part of its own or its parent's voting stock, if the acquiring corporation has control (see below) of the other corporation immediately after the acquisition, whether or not it had control before the acquisition;

Footnote references are to paragraphs of the 2008 Standard Federal Tax Reports.

[7] ¶ 16,550	[10] ¶ 16,580	[13] ¶ 16,610
[8] ¶ 16,460, ¶ 16,466.0497	[11] ¶ 16,750, ¶ 16,752	[14] ¶ 16,750
[9] ¶ 16,402, ¶ 16,750	[12] ¶ 16,550	

Type (C) reorganization: the acquisition by one corporation of substantially all of the properties of another corporation, in exchange solely for all or a part of its own or its controlling parent's voting stock, followed (unless waived by the IRS) by the acquired corporation's distribution of all its property pursuant to the plan of reorganization;

Type (D) reorganization: a transfer by a corporation of all or a part of its assets to another corporation if, immediately after the transfer, the transferor or one or more of its shareholders is in control of the corporation to which the assets are transferred. The term "shareholders" includes those who were shareholders immediately before the transfer, but only if the stock or securities of the corporation to which the assets are transferred are distributed under the plan of reorganization in a transaction described at ¶ 2201 or ¶ 2205;

Type (E) reorganization: a recapitalization (¶ 2225);

Type (F) reorganization: a mere change in the identity, form, or place of organization of one corporation; or

Type (G) reorganization: a transfer by a corporation in bankruptcy of all or part of its assets to another corporation, but only if stocks or securities of the transferee corporation are distributed to the shareholders tax free or partially tax free.

"Control" Defined. The term "control" means the ownership of stock possessing at least 80 percent of the combined voting power of all classes of stock entitled to vote and at least 80 percent of the total number of shares of all other classes of stock of the corporation (Code Sec. 368(c)).[15] The 80-percent figures are changed to 50 percent in the case of nondivisive (D) reorganizations (Code Secs. 368(a)(2)(H)(i) and 304(c)).[16]

2211. Solely for Voting Stock. Under a (B) reorganization, "solely for voting stock" means that the acquiring corporation cannot use cash or nonvoting stock in the exchange or the reorganization becomes taxable (Reg. § 1.368-2(c)).[17] The "solely" requirement is relaxed for a (C) reorganization in that "substantially all the assets" must be acquired solely for voting stock (¶ 2217).[18]

2213. "Securities" Defined. Ordinarily, the term "securities" would include corporate bonds and debentures and any other corporate obligations in the nature of registered certificates, numbered serially, maturing after a relatively long period, bearing interest coupons, and secured by property of the corporation. The U.S. Supreme Court (*Pinellas Ice & Cold Storage Co.*, 3 USTC ¶ 1023) has held that ordinary promissory notes are not "securities."[19]

2217. Substantially All. What constitutes "substantially all" of the properties of a corporation for purposes of a C reorganization (Code Sec. 368(a)(1)(C))[20] is not spelled out in the Code. It has been held that a transfer of about two-thirds in value of the assets, or 68 percent or even 75 percent of all the corporate property, is not "substantially all." One court held, however, that 85.2 percent, which included all property except cash, was "substantially all" (*Western Industries Co.*, 36-1 USTC ¶ 9083).[21] Other cases held substantially all the voting stock was transferred when over 90 percent of the stock changed hands (*B.R. Britt*, 40-2 USTC ¶ 9644, and *Cortland Specialty Co.*, 3 USTC 980).[22]

The IRS interprets the "substantially all" requirement, for the purpose of issuing ruling letters, as requiring a transfer of assets representing at least 90 percent of the fair market value of the net assets and at least 70 percent of the fair market value of the corporation's gross assets held immediately before the transfer (Rev. Proc. 77-37).[23]

2221. Party to a Reorganization—Plan of Reorganization. Code Sec. 368(b)[24] contains a limited definition of "a party to a reorganization" (see ¶ 2205), including a corporation resulting from a reorganization and both corporations in a reorganization resulting from the acquisition by one corporation of stock or properties of another. In an (A), (B), (C) or (G) reorganization (¶ 2209), a party to a reorganization includes a

---

Footnote references are to paragraphs of the 2008 Standard Federal Tax Reports.

[15] ¶ 16,750
[16] ¶ 16,750, ¶ 15,375
[17] ¶ 16,752
[18] ¶ 16,750, ¶ 16,753.0231

[19] ¶ 16,433.61
[20] ¶ 16,750
[21] ¶ 16,753.709
[22] ¶ 16,753.709

[23] ¶ 16,753.53
[24] ¶ 16,750

controlling corporation if its stock is exchanged and likewise includes a controlled subsidiary that receives any of the assets or stock exchanged.

A plan of reorganization is required in connection with a tax-free exchange (Reg. § 1.368-2).[25] The plan does not need to be a formal written document; however, the safest practice would be to incorporate the plan into the corporate records. The plan may be amended as circumstances change so long as the reorganization remains in compliance with Code Sec. 368(a) (¶ 2209).

2225. Recapitalization. The Code does not define the term "recapitalization," but the U.S. Supreme Court (*Southwest Consolidated Corporation*, 42-1 USTC ¶ 9248)[26] has stated that the term contemplates "reshuffling of a capital structure within the framework of an existing corporation." Thus, an (E) reorganization (¶ 2209) takes place, for example, when a corporation discharges outstanding bond indebtedness by issuing preferred stock to the shareholders in exchange for the bonds instead of paying them off in cash; when 25 percent of a corporation's preferred stock is surrendered for cancellation and no-par-value common stock is issued; or when previously authorized but unissued preferred stock is issued in exchange for outstanding common stock (Reg. § 1.368-2(e)).[27]

2229. Exchange of Securities or Property for Securities. An exchange of securities in a reorganization is tax free only to the extent that the principal amount received does not exceed the principal amount surrendered (Code Sec. 354(a)(2))[28] (¶ 2201 and ¶ 2205). No gain or loss is recognized if a party to a reorganization (¶ 2221) exchanges property pursuant to the plan of reorganization (¶ 2221) solely for stock or securities (¶ 2213) in another corporation that is a party to the reorganization (Code Sec. 361).[29] Unlike the exchange of securities, the party exchanging property must be a corporation and the principal amount is not subject to a percentage test. However, securities received in a Code Sec. 351 exchange are treated as boot (¶ 1731). Nonqualified preferred stock is treated as boot (Code Sec. 351(g)).[30]

2233. Assumption of Liabilities. A release from liabilities assumed by a transferee or a disposition of property subject to liabilities in:

(1) an exchange in reorganization under Code Sec. 361 (¶ 2229),

(2) a transfer to a controlled corporation under Code Sec. 351 (¶ 1731), or

(3) certain bankruptcy reorganizations or foreclosures (¶ 2247)

is not "other property or money" received by the taxpayer and does not prevent the transaction from being tax free (Code Sec. 357).[31] But if it appears that the principal purpose of the assumption of liabilities is to avoid income tax, or the purpose is not a bona fide business purpose, the liability assumed is treated as other property or money (unless the taxpayer can prove to the contrary) (Code Sec. 357(b)(1)).[32]

In a Code Sec. 351 exchange in which liabilities are assumed, if a cash-basis transferor's payment of such liabilities would have given rise to a deduction, the amount of liability assumed for purposes of Code Sec. 357(c)[33] does not include such liability. This rule does not apply to the extent incurring the liability results in the creation of, or an increase in, the basis of any property (Code Sec. 357(c)(3)).[34]

If the liabilities assumed, or to which the property is subject, exceed the total basis of all the properties transferred in a Code Sec. 351 exchange or a (D) reorganization (¶ 2209), the excess is treated as gain from a sale or exchange of a capital asset or a noncapital asset, depending on the nature of the encumbered asset transferred (Code Sec. 357(c)(1) and (c)(2)).[35] As to the basis of property after an assumption of liabilities, see ¶ 1669.

Footnote references are to paragraphs of the 2008 Standard Federal Tax Reports.

[25] ¶ 16,752	[29] ¶ 16,580	[33] ¶ 16,520
[26] ¶ 16,753.476	[30] ¶ 16,402	[34] ¶ 16,520
[27] ¶ 16,752	[31] ¶ 16,520	[35] ¶ 16,520
[28] ¶ 16,431	[32] ¶ 16,520	

2237. Dividend Distribution in Reorganization. A distribution of money or other property to a stockholder as part of a plan of reorganization may be taxed as a dividend if it has the effect of a taxable dividend, even if the money or other property is received in an exchange which is, in part, tax free (Code Sec. 356; Reg. § 1.356-1).[36] The constructive ownership rules discussed at ¶ 743 are applied in determining dividend equivalency. A distribution within this provision is taxable as a dividend, not to exceed the recognized gain, to the extent the distributing company has, on hand, earnings or profits sufficient to cover the distribution.

2241. Liquidation as Part of Reorganization. Under a plan of reorganization, a corporation often acquires, for all or part of its stock, all of the stock in another corporation from the stockholders of the latter. As the final step in the reorganization, the acquiring corporation may liquidate the latter company, acquiring those assets by surrendering its own stock. This last step in the reorganization may be accomplished tax free under Code Sec. 332, relating to property received by one corporation on complete liquidation of another (¶ 2261).

Enforced Reorganization

2247. Federal Order or Bankruptcy Act. In general, no gain is recognized to a corporation transferring property to another corporation which is a member of the same "system group" if the transfer is ordered by the Securities and Exchange Commission (Code Sec. 1081).[37] Special provisions cover the nonrecognition of gain or loss with respect to certain bankruptcy, foreclosure and similar proceedings (Code Sec. 368(a)(1)(G)).[38]

Corporate Liquidation

2253. Gain or Loss to Shareholders. Amounts distributed in complete liquidation of a corporation are usually treated as full payment in exchange for the stock (Code Sec. 331; Reg. § 1.331-1).[39] The shareholder's gain or loss from a distribution is determined by comparing the amount distributed (including the fair market value of any property received) to the cost or other basis of the stock. The resulting gain or loss is capital.

If property received in a complete liquidation is subject to a liability, the distributee's recognition of gain or loss is adjusted to reflect this assumption. Thus, if a shareholder receives property for which he otherwise would recognize a gain of $8,000, but which is subject to a liability of $3,000, the gain recognized would be $5,000 (*B.B. Crane*, 47-1 USTC ¶ 9217).[40]

A distribution that is one of a series of distributions in redemption of all of a corporation's stock pursuant to a plan is treated as a complete liquidation (Code Sec. 346(a)).[41] If a liquidation distribution is made as one of a series of distributions intended eventually to result in complete liquidation of the corporation, no gain is realized by the shareholder until the entire cost of the stock is recovered. If complete liquidation covers two or more consecutive tax years, the distribution first offsets the shareholder's basis for the stock and the excess is gain in the year received. The gain is not allocable to all of the years in which distributions were received (Rev. Rul. 85-48).[42]

Partial Liquidation. A distribution of corporate assets to a *noncorporate* shareholder is treated as being in exchange for stock (whether or not stock is actually surrendered) if the distribution is in partial liquidation of the corporation. Such a distribution must not be essentially equivalent to a dividend (determined by reference to the effect on the corporation rather than the effect on the shareholders) but rather must be made pursuant to a plan and must occur within the tax year in which the plan is adopted or within the succeeding tax year. The Code does not provide a definition of "partial liquidation"—it is generally understood that the phrase refers to a contraction of the business of the corporation—but does provide a "safe harbor," under which a distribu-

---

Footnote references are to paragraphs of the 2008 Standard Federal Tax Reports.

[36] ¶ 16,490, ¶ 16,491   [39] ¶ 16,002, ¶ 16,003   [42] ¶ 16,004.163
[37] ¶ 30,120   [40] ¶ 29,225.042
[38] ¶ 16,750   [41] ¶ 16,351

tion will qualify as a partial liquidation if it is attributable to the corporation's ceasing to conduct a trade or business that it actively conducted for at least five years ending with the date of the distribution and if the corporation continues to conduct at least one other trade or business immediately after the distribution (Code Sec. 302(b)(4) and (e)(3)).[43]

2257. Recognition of Gain or Loss. Generally, property distributed in a complete liquidation of a corporation is deemed to have been sold by the corporation at its fair market value and any gain or loss will be recognized by the liquidating corporation (Code Sec. 336).[44] If the distributed property is subject to a liability or if the distributee assumes a liability upon the distribution, the fair market value of the property is deemed to be no less, for purposes of determining gain or loss, than the amount of the liability. The following exceptions to this general recognition rule apply:

(1) No gain or loss is recognized upon any exchange or distribution that is tax free under the corporate organization and reorganization provisions (Code Secs. 351–368;[45] see ¶ 1731 and ¶ 2201–¶ 2241).

(2) No gain or loss is generally recognized in connection with the complete liquidation of a controlled subsidiary into its parent corporation (see ¶ 2261).

(3) No loss is recognized with respect to a distribution of property to a related person within the meaning of Code Sec. 267[46] (see ¶ 905), unless the property (a) is distributed to all shareholders on a pro rata basis and (b) was not acquired by the liquidating corporation in a Code Sec. 351[47] transaction or as a contribution to capital during the five years preceding the distribution (Code Sec. 336(d)(1)).[48]

(4) Recognition of loss may be limited if the distributed property was initially acquired by the liquidating corporation, either by tax-free transfer to a controlled corporation or as a contribution to capital, as part of a plan whose principal purpose was the recognition of loss on the property in connection with the liquidation. In these circumstances, the basis of the property for purposes of determining loss is reduced, but not below zero, by the excess of the adjusted basis of the property on the date of contribution over its fair market value. There is a presumption of tax-avoidance purpose with respect to any such transfer within the two-year period prior to the adoption of the plan of liquidation (Code Sec. 336(d)(2)).[49]

(5) No gain or loss is recognized if a corporation owning 80 percent of the voting power and value of another corporation elects to treat any disposition (sale, exchange or distribution) of the subsidiary's stock as a disposition of all of the subsidiary's assets (Code Sec. 336(e)).[50]

2261. Liquidation of Subsidiary. If distributions in complete liquidation are made by a subsidiary to a parent corporation (owning at least 80 percent by value and voting power of the subsidiary), then no gain or loss on the distributions is recognized by either the parent corporation or the liquidating subsidiary (Code Secs. 332 and 337).[51] For this purpose, the 80-percent control requirement must be met by direct ownership and not by reason of the aggregation rules. In addition, property distributed to a controlling domestic corporation in satisfaction of a debt owed by the liquidating subsidiary will be treated as a distribution in liquidation for these purposes (Code Sec. 337(b)(1)).[52] However, the distribution of earnings by a U.S. holding company to a foreign corporation in a complete liquidation will be treated as a taxable dividend if the U.S. holding company was in existence for less than five years (Code Sec. 332(d)).

If a minority shareholder receives property in such a liquidation, the distribution is treated as a nonliquidating redemption. Thus, gain (but not loss) is recognized by the liquidating corporation (Code Sec. 336).[53] Gain or loss also is recognized on distributions to 80-percent distributees that are foreign corporations (Code Sec. 367(e))[54] and

---

Footnote references are to paragraphs of the 2008 Standard Federal Tax Reports.

[43] ¶ 15,325
[44] ¶ 16,200
[45] ¶ 16,402–¶ 16,750
[46] ¶ 14,150

[47] ¶ 16,402
[48] ¶ 16,200
[49] ¶ 16,200
[50] ¶ 16,200

[51] ¶ 16,050, ¶ 16,225
[52] ¶ 16,225
[53] ¶ 16,200
[54] ¶ 16,640

¶2257

tax-exempt organizations, unless the property is used by that organization in a trade or business unrelated to its tax-exempt purpose (Code Sec. 337(b)(2)).[55]

Basis. After a complete liquidation of a subsidiary, a parent company usually holds the distributed assets with the same basis that the assets formerly had in the hands of the subsidiary. However, the basis of the assets in the hands of the parent corporation will be the fair market value at the time of the distribution if: (1) the subsidiary recognizes gain or loss in the liquidation or (2) the parent's aggregate adjusted basis in such property exceeds its fair market value immediately after the liquidation (Code Sec. 334(b)).[56]

2265. Acquisition of Stock Treated as Acquisition of Assets. If a parent corporation acquires, by purchase, 80-percent control of a second corporation (the subsidiary) within a 12-month period, the parent may irrevocably elect to have the subsidiary treated as if it had sold and purchased its own assets (Code Sec. 338; Reg. § 1.338-3).[57] If the election is made, the subsidiary is treated as a new corporation after the date of acquisition of 80-percent control. The hypothetical sale is deemed to have occurred on the date of acquisition of control. The subsidiary's tax year as the "selling corporation" ends on that date, its carryovers and other tax attributes disappear, and, as the "purchasing corporation," it becomes a member of the affiliated group including the parent on the day following that date. Gain or loss will be recognized by the subsidiary as though it had sold all of its assets at fair market value in a single transaction on the acquisition date. Recapture items will typically be taken into account on the final return of the "selling corporation." The election is to be made no later than the 15th day of the 9th month, beginning after the month in which 80-percent control is acquired. The parent is not required to liquidate the subsidiary, but, if it does, it will succeed to the basis of the subsidiary as increased by the hypothetical purchase.

There are detailed rules to ensure consistency of treatment for acquisitions of stock or assets by and from members of an affiliated group of corporations (Reg. § 1.338-4(h)).[58] A corporate seller may treat a sale of its 80-percent-controlled subsidiary as a sale of the subsidiary's underlying assets. The assets receive a stepped-up basis to fair market value, and the selling consolidated group recognizes gain or loss attributable to the assets, but there is no separate tax on the seller's gain attributable to the stock. This treatment also applies in situations when the selling corporation owns 80 percent of the subsidiary's stock by value and voting power but does not file a consolidated return (Code Sec. 338(h)(10)(B)).[59]

Collapsible Corporation

2273. "Collapsible" Corporation. Despite the general rule relating to complete liquidation outlined at ¶ 2253, a shareholder owning more than five percent of the stock in a "collapsible" corporation is denied capital gain treatment on a distribution of the corporation's assets or a sale of the stock. This rule applies regardless of the holding period of the stock.

> **Note:** The collapsible corporation rules are repealed for tax years beginning after December 31, 2002 (Act Sec. 302(e)(4) of P.L. 108-27). However, the repeal is only temporary. Without future Congressional action, the collapsible corporation rules will apply to tax years beginning after December 31, 2008.

A "collapsible" corporation is formed principally to manufacture, construct, produce or purchase certain property—or to hold stock in another corporation formed for the same purpose—with a view to distributing the property or selling or exchanging the corporation's stock before the corporation realizes two-thirds of the taxable income to be derived from the property. In this way, the shareholders could realize capital gains for the bulk of the assets rather than ordinary income (Code Sec. 341).[60] Property held in a collapsible corporation is called "Sec. 341 assets."

Footnote references are to paragraphs of the 2008 Standard Federal Tax Reports.

[55] ¶ 16,225
[56] ¶ 16,150

[57] ¶ 16,275, ¶ 16,278
[58] ¶ 16,279

[59] ¶ 16,275
[60] ¶ 16,300

The presumption that a corporation is collapsible arises if the fair market value of its Sec. 341 assets is (1) 50 percent or more of the fair market value of its total assets (not including cash, stock in other corporations, or bonds, debentures, investment notes, etc., that are capital assets, or any U.S., state or local bonds) and (2) 120 percent or more of the adjusted basis of its Sec. 341 assets (Reg. § 1.341-3).[61] This presumption may be overcome by evidence.

The collapsible corporation provisions do not apply if, at the time of the sale or exchange or distribution, the net unrealized appreciation in "subsection (e)" assets of the corporation does not exceed 15 percent of its net worth (Reg. § 1.341-6).[62] "Subsection (e)" assets are, in general, property of the corporation which would result in ordinary income if they were sold for a gain (Code Sec. 341(e)).[63] The collapsible corporation provisions do not apply to a sale of stock in a corporation which consents to recognize gain on the disposition of corporate assets (Code Sec. 341(f)).[64]

Carryforwards

2277. Carryforwards Permitted for Many Types of Transactions. The law allows a successor corporation to use carryovers of a predecessor to a limited extent. This privilege is available to the following corporations:

(1) a parent after complete liquidation of a subsidiary (¶ 2261); and

(2) the transferee in a nontaxable corporate acquisition of property in a type (A), (C), (D), (F) or (G) reorganization (¶ 2209). In a (D) or (G) reorganization, however, substantially all the assets must be acquired and the transferor must distribute all its assets (Code Sec. 381; Reg. § 1.381(a)-1).[65]

These carryover provisions are mandatory, even though in some cases they will work to the disadvantage of the successor. They do not apply after a split-up, split-off, or spin-off type of reorganization (¶ 2201), or other divisive reorganization. The carryforward items are listed in Code Sec. 381(c).[66] Note that in the complete liquidation of a subsidiary, if the election described in ¶ 2265 is made, there is no carryforward of attributes of the subsidiary for the periods prior to the parent's acquisition.

Carrybacks. Carrybacks of net operating losses (¶ 1176) and net capital losses are permitted from one corporate entity to another only in the case of an (F) reorganization—i.e., a mere change in identity, form, or place of organization.

2281. Limitations on Use of Carryforwards. After a reorganization or other change in corporate ownership, the use of certain carryforwards may be limited or prohibited. The carryforwards involved concern:

(1) net operating losses (NOLs),

(2) unused general business credit,

(3) corporate minimum tax credit,

(4) foreign tax credit, and

(5) capital loss carryovers (Code Secs. 382 and 383).[67]

After an ownership change (see below), the amount of *income* that a corporation may offset each year by preacquisition NOL carryforwards is generally limited to an amount determined by multiplying the value of the equity of the corporation just prior to the ownership change by the federal long-term tax-exempt rate (see ¶ 85) in effect on the date of the change (Code Sec. 382(b)(1)).[68] Any unused limitation may be carried forward and added to the next year's limitation. In addition, NOL carryforwards are eliminated completely unless the business continuity requirements for reorganizations (Reg. § 1.368-1(d))[69] are satisfied for the two-year period following the ownership change. The annual income limitation is reduced by the recognition of any built-in losses (the amount by which a corporation's adjusted basis in its assets exceeds their fair

---

Footnote references are to paragraphs of the 2008 Standard Federal Tax Reports.

[61] ¶ 16,305
[62] ¶ 16,310
[63] ¶ 16,300

[64] ¶ 16,300
[65] ¶ 17,002, ¶ 17,003
[66] ¶ 17,002, ¶ 17,031.01

[67] ¶ 17,101, ¶ 17,200
[68] ¶ 17,101
[69] ¶ 16,751

market value on the date of the ownership change) and increased by the recognition of built-in gains. An exception to the limitations on NOL carryforwards is provided in bankruptcy situations, with certain restrictions (Code Sec. 382(l)(5); Reg. § 1.382-9).[70]

Two kinds of ownership changes can trigger the income limitation: (1) a change involving a five-percent shareholder and (2) any tax-free reorganization (other than divisive and (F) reorganizations). In either case, one or more of the five-percent shareholders must have increased their percentage of ownership in the corporation by more than 50 percent over their lowest pre-change ownership percentage (generally within three years of the ownership change) (Code Sec. 382; Temp. Reg. § 1.382-2T).[71]

Similar rules apply to the other carryforwards, including those for net capital losses, unused general business credit and foreign taxes (Code Sec. 383; Reg. § 1.383-1).[72]

Pre- and Post-change Allocation. A loss corporation must allocate net operating loss or taxable income and net capital loss or gain for the change year between the pre-change period and the post-change period either by (1) ratably allocating an equal portion to each day in the change year or (2) electing to treat its books as closed on the date of the change (Reg. § 1.382-6).[73] If a "closing of the books" election is made, the amounts allocated to either period may not exceed the NOL or taxable income and net capital loss or gain for the change year.

Worthless Stock. In order to prevent a double tax benefit, the NOLs of a corporation may not be carried forward after an ownership change if a shareholder with 50 percent or more control (prior to the ownership change) claims, within three years, a worthless stock deduction with respect to the stock (Code Sec. 382(g)(4)(D)).[74]

Tax Avoidance Purpose. NOLs and other carryforwards may be disallowed if an acquisition is made with a tax avoidance purpose (see ¶ 1575).

2285. Limitation on Preacquisition Losses. A corporation (or any member of its affiliated group) may not use its preacquisition losses (NOLs, net built-in losses, net capital losses, and credit carryforwards) against the built-in gains of a company (1) whose assets are acquired in an (A), (C) or (D) reorganization (¶ 2209) or (2) that becomes directly or indirectly controlled (80-percent ownership of its stock by vote and value) by the acquiring corporation. The restriction generally applies to built-in gains recognized within five years of the acquisition date, unless 50 percent or more of the gain company has been owned by the loss corporation (or a member of its group) for five years prior to the acquisition (Code Sec. 384).[75]

The unrealized built-in gains of either the acquired or acquiring corporation are subject to the restriction. It applies to any successor corporation to the same extent as to its predecessor, and all members of the same affiliated group before the acquisition are treated as one corporation.

Footnote references are to paragraphs of the 2008 Standard Federal Tax Reports.

[70] ¶ 17,101, ¶ 17,111F
[71] ¶ 17,101, ¶ 17,107D
[72] ¶ 17,200, ¶ 17,204
[73] ¶ 17,111
[74] ¶ 17,101
[75] ¶ 17,300

Chapter 23

SPECIAL CORPORATE STATUS

Mutual Funds

2301. Qualification as a Mutual Fund. Mutual funds (regulated investment companies) are domestic corporations that act as investment agents for their shareholders, typically investing in corporate and government securities and distributing income earned from the investments as dividends. Mutual funds may escape corporate taxation because, unlike ordinary corporations, they are entitled to claim a deduction for dividends paid to shareholders against their ordinary income and net capital gain. A corporation qualifies as a mutual fund if it makes an irrevocable election to be treated as such by filing a tax return on Form 1120-RIC and it meets the following requirements (Code Sec. 851):[1]

- the corporation must be registered under the Investment Company Act of 1940 as a management company, unit investment trust, business development company, or as a type of common trust fund;

- at least 90 percent of its gross income is derived from dividends, interest, payments with respect to certain securities loans, gains from the sale or disposition of stock or securities, other income derived from the business of investing including the net investment income derived from qualified publicly traded partnerships;

- at the close of each quarter of the tax year, at least 50 percent of its total assets are invested in cash, government securities, securities of other mutual funds, and the securities of other issuers (so long as the securities of any given issuer do not exceed five percent of the value of the mutual fund's assets or 10 percent of the issuer's outstanding voting securities);

- at the close of each quarter of the tax year, no more than 25 percent of the total value of its assets are invested in the securities of any one issuer (other than government securities or securities of other mutual funds), the securities of two or more issuers controlled by the mutual fund and engaged in a related trade or business, or the securities of one or more qualified publicly traded partnership; and

- it distributes at least 90 percent of its annual investment company taxable income (¶ 2303) and its net tax-exempt interest income (¶ 2307) to its shareholders (there is no threshold for net capital gains) (Code Sec. 852(a)).[2]

2303. Taxation of Mutual Funds. A mutual fund (regulated investment company) is subject to taxation at regular corporate income tax rates on its "investment company taxable income" (Code Sec. 852(b); Reg. § 1.852-3).[3] Investment company taxable income is computed on Form 1120-RIC in the same manner as the taxable income of an ordinary corporation with the following adjustments:

Footnote references are to paragraphs of the 2008 Standard Federal Tax Reports.

[1] ¶ 26,400   [2] ¶ 26,420   [3] ¶ 26,420, ¶ 26,424

- gross income is the fund's ordinary income (net capital gains are not included);
- a deduction is allowed for any ordinary dividends paid (however, no deduction is allowed for dividends of capital gains or tax-exempt interest);
- no deduction is allowed for dividends received;
- no deduction is allowed for net operating losses (NOLs);
- taxable income of a short tax year is not annualized; and
- if the fund so elects, taxable income is computed by disregarding the short-term discount obligation rules of Code Sec. 454(b).

For purposes of the dividend paid deduction, dividends declared and payable by a mutual fund in October, November or December in a calendar year will be treated as paid on December 31 of that year even if they are actually paid in January of the following calendar year (Code Sec. 852(b)(7)). On the other hand, a mutual fund may generally not claim a deduction for dividend distributions if it singles out a one class of shareholders, or one or more members of a class of shareholders, for special dividend treatment unless such treatment was originally intended when the dividend rights were created (Code Sec. 562(c); Rev. Rul. 89-81).[4] The IRS has issued guidance describing the conditions under which distributions to mutual fund shareholders may vary and nevertheless be deductible as dividends, including the treatment of distributions to shareholders that differ as a result of the allocation and payment of fees and expenses (Rev. Proc. 99-40).[5]

Excise Taxes. A nondeductible excise tax is generally imposed on a mutual fund that does satisfy minimum distribution requirements (Code Sec. 4982).[6] The tax is four percent of the excess of any "required distribution" for the calendar year over the amount actually distributed for the calendar year. For this purpose, the required distribution is the sum of 98 percent of the fund's ordinary income for the year, plus 98 percent of its net capital gain income for the one-year period ending October 31 of the calendar year. Special rules apply in how a mutual fund treats post-October 31 capital gains and foreign currency losses.

2305. Capital Gains of Mutual Funds. A mutual fund (regulation investment company) may avoid corporate level tax on its net capital gains by distributing such gains to shareholders. However, if it elects to retain some of its net capital gains, then it will be subject to taxation at regular corporate capital gains rates on the excess of its net capital gains for the tax year over the amount of any capital gains dividends paid during the year (Code Sec. 852(b)(3)).[7] Form 2438 is used to figure and report the fund's capital gains. Although, the fund is taxed on its undistributed net capital gains, it may elect to pass-through the net capital gains and tax paid to shareholders. Form 2439 is used to inform each shareholder at the end of the tax year of his portion of the undistributed capital gains and tax paid for that year (¶ 2309 and ¶ 2311).

2307. Tax-Exempt Interest of Mutual Funds. A mutual fund (regulated investment company) may pass on tax-exempt interest earned on state or local bonds to its shareholders in the form of exempt-interest dividends, but only if the bonds represent at least 50 percent of the value of the fund's assets at the close of each quarter of its tax year (Code Sec. 852(b)(5)).[8]

2309. Designation of Mutual Fund Distributions. Within 60 days after the close of its tax year, a mutual fund (regulated investment company) is required to notify its shareholders of the portion of distributions made during the tax year which are capital gains dividends (¶ 2305), exempt-interest dividends (¶ 2307), and ordinary dividends eligible for the reduced tax rate for qualifying dividends (¶ 2311) and which may be deducted by corporate shareholders (Code Sec. 854(b)).[9] Capital gains and exempt interest dividends received from a mutual fund are not eligible for the dividends-received deduction. For this purpose, the aggregate amount of dividends designated as qualified dividends by the mutual fund is limited to the aggregate amount of dividends it

---

Footnote references are to paragraphs of the 2008 Standard Federal Tax Reports.

[4] ¶ 23,470, ¶ 26,433.50   [6] ¶ 34,640   [8] ¶ 26,420
[5] ¶ 26,433.28   [7] ¶ 26,420   [9] ¶ 26,460

received during the tax year. The aggregate amount of dividends which may be designated as exempt interest is limited to the fund's tax-exempt interest income for the year reduced by any expenses incurred in earning such income (Code Sec. 852(b)(5)(A)).[10]

2311. Taxation of Mutual Fund Distributions. The tax treatment of a distribution received from a mutual fund (regulated investment company) will depend on how the distribution is designated (¶ 2309). Distributions designated as ordinary dividends are generally taxed to the shareholder as ordinary income. However, they may be eligible to be taxed at a lower rate (¶ 733) if the aggregate amount of dividends received by the fund during the year is less than 95 percent of its gross income (Code Sec. 854(b)(1)(B)).[11] Distributions designated as tax-exempt interest may generally be excluded from the shareholder's gross income (Code Sec. 852(b)(5)(B)).[12] However, exempt-interest dividends derived from private activity bonds constitute a tax preference item for alternative minimum tax purposes (¶ 1425).

Distributions designated as capital gains may be treated as long-term capital gains by the shareholder for income and alternative minimum tax purposes, regardless of how long they held their mutual fund stock (Code Sec. 852(b)(3)(B)).[13] This includes any undistributed capital gains passed-through by the mutual fund (¶ 2305). The shareholder is entitled to a credit or refund for their portion of any capital gain taxes paid by the mutual fund on the undistributed capital gains (Code Sec. 852(b)(3)(D)). In addition, the shareholder may increase their basis of their mutual fund shares by the difference between the undistributed capital gains and their deemed portion of taxes paid.

A distribution that is not out of a mutual fund's earnings and profits is a return of the shareholder's investment. Return-of-capital distributions are generally not subject to tax and reduce the shareholder's basis in their mutual fund shares. On the other hand, mutual fund distributions which are automatically reinvested by the shareholder into more shares of the fund must be taxed as if they had actually been received by shareholder in cash. Thus, reinvested ordinary dividends and reinvested capital gain distributions are generally taxed as income, reinvested exempt-interest dividends are not reported as income, and reinvested return-of-capital distributions are reported as a return of capital (IRS Publications 564).

2313. Sale of Mutual Fund Stock. The sale, exchange, or redemption of shares in a mutual fund (regulated investment company) is treated as the sale of capital assets. However, if the shareholder sells or exchanges their mutual fund shares at a loss within six months after being purchased, then the loss must generally be treated as a long-term capital loss (rather than a short-term capital loss) to the extent of any capital gains allocated to the stock (whether distributed or not) (Code Sec. 852(b)(4)).[14] In addition, the amount of loss that may be claimed must also be reduced by the amount of any exempt-interest dividend received on the shares. A mutual fund shareholder may also not claim any loss from the sale or exchange of mutual fund if the wash sale rules apply (¶ 1935).

2317. Deficiency Dividends of Mutual Funds. A corporation may avoid being disqualified as a mutual fund (regulated investment company) if there is a "determination" (¶ 2337) that results in an adjustment which could preclude compliance with the normal income distribution requirements. In this case, the corporation may qualify as a mutual fund if it makes a deficiency distribution to its shareholders equal to the portion of accumulated earnings and profits attributable to the non-fund year, over any interest charges. The distribution must be made within 90 days of the determination and it must be designated as being taken into account for the non-fund year (Code Sec. 852(e)).[15] This option is not available if the company was disqualified for fraudulent tax evasion.

2318. Basis in Mutual Fund Shares. A shareholder's basis in his shares of a mutual fund (regulated investment company) is usually the cost to purchase the shares, including any fees or load charges incurred to acquire or redeem them. However, fees or load charges will not be added to shareholder's original basis if the shareholder

---

Footnote references are to paragraphs of the 2008 Standard Federal Tax Reports.

[10] ¶ 26,420   [12] ¶ 26,420   [14] ¶ 26,420
[11] ¶ 26,460   [13] ¶ 26,420   [15] ¶ 26,420

acquires a reinvestment right, disposes of the shares within 90 days of being purchased, and acquires new shares in the same (or another) mutual fund, for which the fee or load charge is reduced or waived because of the reinvestment right (Code Sec. 852(f)).[16] In such cases, the omission of the load charge from basis applies to the extent the charge does not exceed the reduction in the load charge for the new investment. To the extent that a load charge is not taken into account in determining the purchaser's gain or loss, it is treated as incurred in connection with the acquisition of the second-acquired shares.

The original basis of mutual fund shares acquired by reinvesting distributions (even exempt-interest dividends) is the amount of the distributions used to buy each full or fractional share. A shareholder's original basis in shares acquired by gift is generally the donor's adjusted basis. However, if the fair market value of the shares was more than the donor's adjusted basis, then the shareholder's basis is the donor's adjusted basis at the time of the gift, plus all or part of any gift tax paid on the gift. A shareholder's basis in mutual fund shares that are inherited is generally the fair market value of the shares at the decedent's death (or the alternate valuation date if the estate chooses). However a shareholder's original basis is determined, it must be adjusted for such post-acquisition occurrences as reinvestment of distributions and return of capital distributions (¶ 2311).

2320. Foreign Tax Credit of Mutual Funds. A mutual fund (regulated investment company) may elect to have its foreign tax credit taken by its shareholders on their tax returns instead of its own. However, the election can only be made if more than 50 percent of the value of the fund's total assets at the close of the tax year consists of stock or securities in foreign corporations and it has distributed at least 90 percent of its investment company taxable income (¶ 2303) and net tax-exempt interest for the year (Code Sec. 853).[17]

2323. Mutual Fund Distributions After Tax Year Ends. A mutual fund (regulated investment company) may elect to throw back to the prior tax year all or part of a dividend (including a capital gain dividend) that is declared after the year is closed but before the due date for the filing of its return (including any extensions) *if* the entire declared dividend is paid: (1) within the 12-month period following the close of the tax year and (2) no later than the date of the first regular dividend payment after the declaration (Code Sec. 855).[18] The shareholder must generally treat the dividend as received in the tax year in which the distribution is made (¶ 2303).

Real Estate Investment Trusts

2326. Qualification as a REIT. A real estate investment trust (REIT) is any corporation, trust or association that acts as an investment agent specializing in real estate and real estate mortgages (Code Sec. 856).[19] REITs may escape corporation taxation because, unlike ordinary corporations, they are entitled to claim a deduction for dividends paid to shareholders against their ordinary income and net capital gains. An entity qualifies as a REIT if it makes an election to be treated as such by filing a tax return on Form 1120-REIT and it meets certain requirements as to ownership and organization, source of income, investment of assets, and distribution of income to shareholders. The REIT election may be revoked voluntarily, but the organization will be prohibited from making a new REIT election for the four tax years after the revocation. An organization may elect REIT status even if it fails the ownership test in the first year.

Ownership and Organization Requirements. To be eligible for REIT status, an entity must be taxable as a domestic corporation. Foreign corporations, trusts and associations, as well as financial institutions such as banks and insurance companies, are not eligible. An eligible entity must be managed by one or more trustees or directors during the entire tax year. It must also adopt an annual accounting period of a calendar year. An entity making a REIT election may change its accounting period without consent accordingly (Code Sec. 859).[20]

Footnote references are to paragraphs of the 2008 Standard Federal Tax Reports.

[16] ¶ 26,420
[17] ¶ 26,440
[18] ¶ 26,480
[19] ¶ 26,500
[20] ¶ 26,560

Beneficial ownership in a REIT must be evidenced by transferable shares or certificates of interest. The REIT must have at least 100 beneficial owners for 335 days of a 12-month tax year. For this purpose, ownership cannot be closely held as determined under the personal holding company rules (¶ 285) (Code Sec. 856(h)).[21] However, attribution to another partner in a partnership is ignored. In addition, a pension trust will generally not be treated as a single owner but any REIT shares or certificates of interest held by the trust will be treated as directly held by its beneficiaries. This look-through rule does not apply if persons disqualified from dealings with the pension trust own five percent or more of the value of the REIT and the REIT has accumulated earning and profits attributable to a year it did not qualify as a REIT (¶ 2337).

Income Requirements. An entity must satisfy the following income tests each tax year in order to qualify as a REIT (Code Sec. 856(c)(2) and (c)(3)):[22]

- at least 95 percent of the entity's gross income (excluding gross income from prohibited transactions) must be from real-property sources (rents from real property, gain from the disposition of real property) and from investments (dividends, interest, gains from dispositions of securities); and

- at least 75 percent of the entity's gross income (excluding gross income from prohibited transactions) must be from real-property sources (rents from real property, gain from the disposition of real property or mortgage interests, income and gain from foreclosure property, qualified temporary investment income).

For this purpose, rents from real property includes rents from interests in real property, charges for services customarily provided in connection with the rental of real property (utilities, maintenance), and rent attributable to personal property incidental to rental of real property (less than 15 percent of fair market value). Rents from real property does *not* include amounts received from any person in which the REIT owns 10 percent or greater interest (unless received from a taxable REIT subsidiary (¶ 2340) and at least 90 percent of the leased spaced is rented to third parties), amounts based on income or profits of a tenant or debtor (unless certain conditions are met), and amounts received from tenants for noncustomary services unless provided through an independent contractor or a *de minimis* amount is received (Code Sec. 856(d)).

An entity that fails to meet either of the income tests for any tax year may still qualify as a REIT if it identifies the failure on a separate schedule prescribed by the IRS, the failure is due to reasonable cause and not willful neglect, and the REIT pays a tax (Code Secs. 856(c)(6)). The tax is equal to the greater of the amount by which the entity fails to meet either the 95-percent or 75-percent income test, multiplied by the fraction of the REIT's taxable income over its gross income for the tax year (857(b)(5)).[23]

Asset Requirements. A REIT must meet the following requirements regarding its assets at the close of each quarter of the tax year:

- at least 75 percent of the value of its total assets must consist of real estate assets (including interests in a REMIC), cash items (including receivables), and government securities;

- no more than 25 percent of the value of its total assets can be invested in securities other than those representing real estate assets or government securities;

- no more than 20 percent of the value of total assets are invested in securities of taxable REIT subsidiaries (¶ 2340); and

- except for government securities and securities of taxable REIT subsidiaries (¶ 2340), no more than five percent of the value of its total assets can be invested in the securities of any one issuer and investment in the securities of any one issuer cannot exceed 10 percent of the total value or voting power of the outstanding securities of that issuer (Code Sec. 856(c)(4)).[24]

For purposes of the limitation that a REIT may not hold more than 10 percent of the value of the outstanding securities of a single issuer, certain obligations will not be

---

Footnote references are to paragraphs of the 2008 Standard Federal Tax Reports.

[21] ¶ 26,500
[22] ¶ 26,500
[23] ¶ 26,520
[24] ¶ 26,500

¶2326

considered a security of the issuer including "straight debt" securities, loans to an individual or estate, section 467 rental agreements (¶ 1541), or any obligation to pay rents from real property (Code Sec. 856(m)). A straight debt security is debt payable on demand or at a date certain where the interest rate and interest payments are not contingent on profits, the borrower's discretion, or similar factors, and there is no convertibility (directly or indirectly) into stock (Code Sec. 1361(c)(5)(B)). However, special rules are provided permitting certain contingencies of straight debt.

An entity that fails to meet any of the asset requirements for a particular tax quarter may still qualify as a REIT if: (1) it identifies the failure on a separate schedule prescribed by the IRS; (2) failure is due to reasonable cause and not willful neglect; (3) the assets causing the failure are disposed of within six months of the last day of the quarter the failure occurred; and (4) the REIT pays a tax (Code Sec. 856(c)(7)). The tax is the greater of $50,000 or the tax on the net income generated by the assets during the period of failure at the highest corporate rate. A REIT will also not lose its exempt status for a *de minimis* failure to meet the five or 10 percent asset requirements if the failure is due to ownership of assets the total value of which does not exceed the lesser of one percent of the total value of the REIT's assets at the end of a tax quarter or $10 million.

Distribution of Income. To qualify as a REIT, an entity generally must distribute to its shareholders during the tax year the sum of 90 percent of its ordinary taxable income (determined without the deduction for dividends paid) (¶ 2329) and 90 percent of its net income from foreclosure property, over its excess noncash income (Code Sec. 857(a)).[25] The IRS has the authority to waive this requirement if failure to meet it is due to distributions necessary to avoid imposition of certain excise taxes.

Other Failures. If an entity fails to satisfy one or more requirements of REIT qualification other than the income tests or asset requirements, then the entity may still retain REIT qualification if the failure is due to reasonable cause and not willful neglect. However, the REIT must pay a penalty of $50,000 for each failure (Code Sec. 856(g)(5)).

2329. Taxation of REITs. An entity that qualifies as a real estate investment trust (REIT) (¶ 2326) will be subject to regular corporate income tax rates on its taxable income (Code Sec. 857(b)).[26] A REIT's taxable income is computed on Form 1120-REIT in the same manner as an ordinary corporation with the following adjustments:

- a deduction is allowed for dividends paid (but calculated without regard to dividends attributable to the net income from foreclosure property);

- net income from foreclosure property or a prohibited transaction is disregarded;

- the dividends received deductions (¶ 235 and following) are not allowed;

- net operating losses (NOLs) in a tax year an entity is a REIT may only be carried forward, while NOLs in tax year an entity is not a REIT may not be carried back to any year the entity was a REIT (Code Sec. 172(b)(1)(B));[27]

- any taxes or penalties imposed because of failure of the REIT to comply with the income or asset tests (¶ 2326) is disregarded, as well as any excise tax imposed on improper allocations between a REIT and its taxable subsidiaries (¶ 2340); and

- taxable income is not annualized in the case of a change in accounting periods.

For purposes of the dividends-paid deduction, dividends declared and payable in October, November or December of a calendar year will be treated as paid on December 31 of that year even if they are actually paid in January of the following calendar year (Code Sec. 857(b)(9)).[28] Special rules also apply in determining the tax on net income from foreclosure property and any net built-in gains of C corporation assets that become REIT assets through a conversion transaction.

Capital Gains. If a REIT has any net capital gains in the tax year, the tax imposed on REIT taxable income is the lesser of: (1) the regular corporate tax on REIT taxable

---

Footnote references are to paragraphs of the 2008 Standard Federal Tax Reports.

[25] ¶ 26,520
[26] ¶ 26,520

[27] ¶ 12,002
[28] ¶ 26,520

income, or (2) the regular corporate tax on REIT taxable income, determined by excluding net capital gains and by computing the deduction for dividends paid without capital gain dividends, plus 35 percent of the net capital gain reduced by any capital gain dividends paid (Code Sec. 857(b)(3)). Form 2438 is used to figure and report the REIT's capital gains.

A REIT may avoid the tax on its net capital gains by distributing such gains to shareholders (¶ 2331). The REIT must designate any distributions as capital gain dividends in a written notice to shareholders or beneficiaries with its annual report or within 30 days of the end of the tax year. For purposes of determining the maximum amount of capital gain dividends that a REIT may pay for a tax year, the REIT may not offset its net capital gains with the amount of any NOL. In addition, the REIT must increase the amount of any NOL carryover to the extent it pays capital gains dividends in excess of its net income. If the REIT does retain any net capital gains it may elect to pass-through those undistributed amounts and the tax it paid to its shareholders. Form 2439 must be used to inform each shareholder and beneficiary of their portion of any undistributed capital gains and any tax paid. The form must be provided within 60 days of the close of the REIT's tax year.

Other Taxes. A REIT may be subject to the following taxes in addition to the above:

• a tax at the highest corporate rate on net income from foreclosure property (Code Sec. 857(b)(4));

• a 100 percent tax on the net income derived from a prohibited transaction (disposition of property other than foreclosure property that is held for sale to customers in the ordinary course of business) (Code Sec. 857(b)(6));

• a four percent excise tax on the amount of any taxable income which is undistributed at the end of the tax year (Code Sec. 4981);[29] and

• a 100 percent tax on the excess portion of rents, deductions and interest when a REIT and taxable REIT subsidiary (¶ 2340) fail to engage in an arms-length transaction (Code Sec. 857(b)(7)).

2331. Taxation of REIT Distributions. The tax treatment of a distribution received from a real estate investment trust (REIT) will depend on how the distribution is designated. Distributions designated as ordinary dividends are generally taxed to the shareholder as ordinary income. However, they may be eligible to be taxed at a lower rate (¶ 733) if the aggregate amount of dividends received by the fund during the year is less than 95 percent of its gross income (Code Sec. 857(c)).[30] Distributions designated as tax-exempt interest may generally be excluded from the shareholder's gross income. However, exempt-interest dividends derived from private activity bonds constitute a tax preference item for alternative minimum tax purposes (¶ 1425).

Distributions designated as capital gains may be treated as long-term capital gains by the shareholder for income and alternative minimum tax purposes, regardless of how long they held their interest in the REIT (Code Sec. 857(b)(3)). This includes any undistributed capital gains passed-through by the mutual fund (¶ 2329). The shareholder is entitled to a credit or refund for their portion of any capital gain taxes paid by the mutual fund on the undistributed capital gains. In addition, the shareholder may increase their basis of their mutual fund shares by the difference between the undistributed capital gains and their deemed portion of taxes paid.

A distribution that is not out of a REIT's earnings and profits is a return of the shareholder's investment. Return-of-capital distributions are generally not subject to tax and reduce the shareholder's basis. On the other hand, distributions which are automatically reinvested by the shareholder into more shares of the fund must be taxed as if they had actually been received by the shareholder in cash. Thus, reinvested ordinary dividends and reinvested capital gain distributions are generally taxed as income, reinvested exempt-interest dividends are not reported as income, and reinvested return-of-capital distributions are reported as a return of capital (IRS Publications 564).

Footnote references are to paragraphs of the 2008 Standard Federal Tax Reports.

[29] ¶ 34,620   [30] ¶ 26,520

¶2331

2334. Sale of REIT Stock. The sale or exchange of stock or beneficial interest in a real estate investment trust (REIT) is treated as the sale of a capital asset. However, if the shareholder or beneficiary sells or exchanges their interest at a loss within six months after it was purchased, the loss must generally be treated as a long-term capital loss (rather than a short-term loss) to the extent of any capital gains allocated to their interest (whether distributed or not) (Code Sec. 857(b)(8)).[31] This rule does not apply to losses incurred on the disposition of REIT stock or beneficial interest pursuant to a plan that provides for the periodic liquidation of such shares or interests. For purposes of determining whether a taxpayer has held REIT stock or beneficial interest for six months, rules similar to those for the dividends-received deduction are applied (¶ 237).

2337. Deficiency Dividends of REITs. An entity may avoid being disqualified as a real estate investment trust (REIT) if there is a "determination" that results in an adjustment which could preclude compliance with the normal income distribution requirements. In this case, the entity may qualify as a REIT if it makes a deficiency distribution to its shareholders equal to the portion of accumulated earnings and profits attributable to the non-REIT year (less any interest charges) (Code Sec. 860).[32] The distribution must be made within 90 days of the determination and it must be designated as being taken into account for the non-REIT year. The REIT is allowed a deduction in the tax year the deficiency dividend is made if a claim for the deduction is filed within 120 days of the determination. No deduction is allowed in the case of fraud. For this purpose, a "determination" includes a decision of the Tax Court, a closing agreement, or an agreement signed by the IRS, as well as the unilateral identification by the REIT of a failure to pay out enough accumulated earnings and profits from non-REIT years.

2339. REIT Distributions After Tax Year Ends. A real estate investment trust (REIT) may elect to throw back to the prior tax year all or part of a dividend (including a capital gain dividend) that is declared after the year is closed but before the due date for filing its return (including extensions) if the entire declared dividend is paid: (1) within the 12-month period following the close of the tax year and (2) no later than the date of the first regular dividend payment after the declaration (Code Sec. 858).[33] The shareholder must generally treat the dividend as received in the tax year in which the distribution is made (¶ 2331).

2340. REIT Subsidiaries. A real estate investment trust (REIT) may own a "qualified REIT subsidiary" and treat all of the subsidiary's assets, liabilities, and items of income, deduction, and credit as its own (Code Sec. 856(i)).[34] A qualified subsidiary is any corporation other than a "taxable REIT subsidiary," all of the stock of which is held by the REIT. A taxable REIT subsidiary is any corporation which is owned, in whole or in part, by the REIT and which both entities elect using Form 8875 to treat as a taxable REIT subsidiary (Code Sec. 856(l)). A taxable REIT subsidiary can be used by the REIT to provide noncustomary services to its tenants or to manage and operate properties without causing the amounts received or accrued to be disqualified as rents from real property (¶ 2326). The election to be treated as a taxable REIT subsidiary can only be revoked with the consent of both the REIT and the subsidiary.

Real Estate Mortgage Investment Conduits

2343. Qualification as a REMIC. A real estate mortgage investment conduit (REMIC) is an entity that holds a fixed pool of mortgages and issues multiple classes of interests in itself to investors (Code Sec. 860D).[35] A REMIC is treated like a partnership for federal tax purposes with its income passed through to its interest holders (¶ 2344). Thus, a REMIC is not subject to taxation on its income, though it is subject to taxes on prohibited transactions (¶ 2355), income from foreclosure property (¶ 2356), and on certain contributions received after its startup day (¶ 2357). It also may be required to withhold taxes on amounts paid to foreign holders of regular or residual interests (¶ 2367). An entity qualifies as REMIC if it makes an irrevocable election to be treated as such by filing a tax return on Form 1066 during its first tax year of existence and if it meets certain requirements as to its investors (¶ 2344) and assets (¶ 2345). If an entity

---

Footnote references are to paragraphs of the 2008 Standard Federal Tax Reports.

[31] ¶ 26,520
[32] ¶ 26,580
[33] ¶ 26,540
[34] ¶ 26,500
[35] ¶ 26,660

ceases to qualify as a REMIC at any time during the tax year, it will not be treated as a REMIC for that or any later tax year. A REMIC is required to file an information return with the IRS on Form 8811 within 30 days of its startup day (and 30 days from any change of information provided in a previously filed Form 8811) identifying its representative for reporting tax information (Reg. § 1.6049-7).[36]

2344. Investors' Interests. In order to qualify as a real estate mortgage investment conduit (REMIC), all of the interests in the entity must be either "regular interests" or a single class of "residual interests." However, a de minimis interest that is neither a regular nor a residual interest can be created to facilitate the REMIC creation. A regular interest is any interest that is issued on the startup day of the REMIC with fixed terms and that is designated as a regular interest. A regular interest may be issued in the form of debt, stock, interest in a partnership or trust, or any other form permitted by state law so long as it unconditionally entitles the holder to receive a specific principal amount and interest based on a fixed rate (or permitted variable rate) (Code Sec. 860G(a)(1)).[37] An interest-only regular interest may also be issued which entitles the holder to receive interest payments determined by reference to the interest payable and which cannot vary on qualified mortgages.

A regular interest will not fail to meet these requirements merely because the timing of principal payments are contingent or can be reduced as a result of the nonoccurrence of a contingent payment. In addition, an interest will not fail to be considered a regular interest if the principal amount may be reduced as a result of a nonoccurrence of a contingent payment with respect to a reverse mortgage loan held by the REMIC. The REMIC must file information returns on Form 1099-INT for each regular interest holder that has been paid $10 or more interest, including original issue discount (OID), during the tax year.

A residual interest is an interest issued on the REMIC's startup day that is not a regular interest and that is designated as a residual interest. There may be only one class of residual interests and any distribution with respect to such interests must be pro rata (Code Sec. 860G(a)(2)).[38] Furthermore, a REMIC must have reasonable arrangements to ensure that residual interests are not held by certain disqualified organizations (governments, exempt organizations, cooperatives). For each quarter of its tax year, a REMIC must send a Schedule Q of Form 1066 to residual interest holders reporting their share of the REMIC's income or loss (Reg. § 1.860F-4(e)).[39]

2345. Qualified Mortgages and Permitted Investments of REMICs. In order to qualify as a real estate mortgage investment conduit (REMIC), substantially all of an entity's assets must consist of "qualified mortgages" and "permitted investments" at the close of the third month beginning after the startup day and all times thereafter (Code Sec. 860D(a)(4)).[40] A qualified mortgage is any obligation principally secured by an interest in real property that: (1) is transferred to the REMIC on the startup day in exchange for regular or residual interests; (2) is purchased by the REMIC within three months after the startup day pursuant to a fixed price contract in effect on the startup day; or (3) represents an increase in the principal under the original terms of the obligation attributable to an advance made to the obligor under the terms of a reverse mortgage or other obligation after the start-up day and which is purchased by the REMIC pursuant to a fixed price contract in effect on the start-up day (Code Sec. 860G(a)(3)).[41] A qualified mortgage may also include any qualified replacement mortgage and a regular interest in another REMIC transferred on the startup day in exchange for a regular or residual interest. Permitted investments include amounts received under qualified mortgages for a temporary period, intangible property held for payment of expenses as part of a qualified reserve fund, and foreclosure property acquired in connection with the default of a qualified mortgage (Code Sec. 860G(a)(5)).[42]

Footnote references are to paragraphs of the 2008 Standard Federal Tax Reports.

[36] ¶ 36,036	[39] ¶ 26,701	[42] ¶ 26,720
[37] ¶ 26,720	[40] ¶ 26,660	
[38] ¶ 26,720	[41] ¶ 26,720	

¶2344

2349. Transfer of Property to REMICs. No gain or loss is recognized when property is transferred to a real estate mortgage investment conduit (REMIC) in exchange for a regular or residual interest (Code Sec. 860F(b); Reg. § 1.860F-2(b)).[43] The basis of a regular or residual interest received in the exchange is equal to the total adjusted basis of the property transferred, plus any expenses. If the transferor receives more than one interest in the REMIC (both a regular and residual interest), then the basis must be allocated among the interests in accordance with their respective fair market values. The basis of the property received by the REMIC in exchange for a regular or residual interest is its fair market value immediately after the transfer.

The issue price of a regular or residual interest is generally determined under the same rules as for determining the issue price for the original issue discount of debt instruments (¶ 1952) (Code Sec. 860G(a)(10)).[44] If the issue price of a regular interest in a REMIC exceeds its adjusted basis, then the excess is included in the transferor's gross income as if it were a market discount bond (¶ 1958). If the issue price of a residual interest exceeds its adjusted basis, then the excess is included in the transferor's gross income ratably over the anticipated weighted average life of the REMIC. If the adjusted basis of a regular interest exceeds the issue price, then the excess is allowable as a deduction to the transferor under the rules similar to those governing amortizable bond premiums (¶ 1967). If the adjusted basis of a residual interest exceeds the issue price, then the excess is allowed as a deduction to the transferor over the anticipated weighted average life of the REMIC.

2352. Taxable Income of REMICs. While a real estate mortgage investment conduit (REMIC) is not generally taxed on its income, its taxable income must still be determined (¶ 2361) in the same manner as an individual, except that it must use the accrual method of accounting and make the following adjustments:

- regular interests in the REMIC are treated as debt;

- market discount on any bond is included in gross income as the discount accrues;

- no item of income, gain, loss or deduction from a prohibited transaction is taken into account (¶ 2355);

- the deductions for personal exemptions, foreign taxes, charitable contributions, net operating losses (NOLs), itemized deductions (except those paid or incurred for the production of income) and depletion are not allowed;

- the amount of any net income from foreclosure property is reduced by the amount of tax imposed on that income;

- gain or loss from the disposition of assets, including qualified mortgages and permitted investments, is treated as ordinary gain or loss rather than gain or loss from a capital asset;

- interest expenses (other than the portion allocable to tax-exempt interest) may be deducted without regards to the investment interest limitation;

- debts owed to the REMIC are treated as nonbusiness debts for purposes of the bad debt deduction; and

- the REMIC is not treated as carrying on a trade or business and ordinary and necessary operating expenses may only be deducted as expenses incurred for the production of income (without regard to the two-percent floor on itemized deductions) (Code Sec. 860C(b); Reg. § 1.860C-2).[45]

2355. Prohibited Transactions of REMICs. A real estate mortgage investment conduit (REMIC) is required to pay a 100-percent tax on its *net income* from a prohibited transaction (losses are not taken into account for this purpose) (Code Sec. 860F(a)).[46] The disposition of any qualified mortgage is considered a prohibited transaction unless

---

Footnote references are to paragraphs of the 2008 Standard Federal Tax Reports.

[43] ¶ 26,700, ¶ 26,700B
[44] ¶ 26,720
[45] ¶ 26,640, ¶ 26,640B
[46] ¶ 26,700

it is a qualified disposition. For this purpose, a qualified disposition is: (1) the substitution of a qualified replacement mortgage for a qualified mortgage (or the repurchase in lieu of substitution of a defective obligation); (2) the bankruptcy or insolvency of the REMIC; (3) a disposition incident to foreclosure or default of a mortgage; or (4) a qualified liquidation.

Prohibited transactions of a REMIC also include: the receipt of any income from an asset that is neither a qualified mortgage or permitted investment (¶ 2345); the receipt of any amount that represents a fee or compensation for services; and the receipt of gain from the disposition of any cash flow investment unless the disposition is made pursuant to a qualified liquidation. A disposition required to prevent default on a regular interest where the threatened default results from a default on one or more qualified mortgages is not deemed a prohibited transaction.

2356. Foreclosure Property. A real estate mortgage investment conduit (REMIC) is subject to tax at the highest corporate income tax rate on its *net income* from foreclosure property for the tax year (Code Sec. 860G(c)).[47] For this purpose, net income from foreclosure property is the excess of gain from the sale or other disposition of stock in trade or property held by the REMIC for sale to customers in the ordinary course of a trade or business, plus the gross income derived from foreclosure property during the tax year, over deductions derived from the production of such income (Code Sec. 857(b)(4)(B)).[48] Foreclosure property is any interest in real property and personal property incident to real property acquired by a REMIC as a result of default of a qualified mortgage held by it. A REMIC must treat property as foreclosure property before the due date (including extensions) of its annual return for the year in which the property was acquired. Property ceases to be foreclosure property three years after it is acquired, unless extensions are granted (Code Sec. 856(e)).[49]

2357. Post-startup Contributions to REMICs. A real estate mortgage investment conduit (REMIC) that receives contributions of property after its startup day is subject to a tax equal to the full value of the contribution (Code Sec. 860G(d)).[50] Exceptions to the tax are provided for cash contributions: to facilitate a clean-up call or a qualified liquidation; in the nature of a guarantee; made during the three-month period that begins on the startup day; made by a holder of a residual interest in the REMIC to a qualified reserve fund; or permitted under regulations.

2358. Taxation of Regular Interests. Holders of regular interests in a real estate mortgage investment conduit (REMIC) are taxed as if their interests were debt instruments, except that income derived from their interests must be computed under the accrual method of accounting (Code Sec. 860B).[51] Gain on the disposition of a regular interest is treated as ordinary income to the extent of unaccrued original issue discount, computed at 110 percent of the applicable federal rate effective at the time the interest was acquired. The REMIC must file report interest payments of $10 or more to regular interest holders and the IRS (Form 1099-INT).

2361. Taxation of Residual Interests. Each holder of a residual interest of a real estate mortgage investment conduit (REMIC) is required to take into account their daily portion of the taxable income or net loss of the REMIC (¶ 2352) for each day during the tax year on which they hold their interest (Code Sec. 860C).[52] The daily portion is determined on the basis of quarterly computations of the REMIC's taxable income or net loss with such amounts being allocated among all residual interests in proportion to their respective holdings on that day (reported on Schedule Q of Form 1066). The holder treats his portion of taxable income and net loss as ordinary income or loss. However, the amount of loss that the holder may take into account in any calendar quarter cannot exceed his adjusted basis in the residual interest (as determined without regard to any required basis decreases). Any allocated loss which is disallowed may be carried forward to succeeding calendar quarters indefinitely.

Footnote references are to paragraphs of the 2008 Standard Federal Tax Reports.

[47] ¶ 26,720
[48] ¶ 26,520
[49] ¶ 26,500
[50] ¶ 26,720
[51] ¶ 26,620
[52] ¶ 26,640

Distributions made by the REMIC to holders of residual interests are received tax free to the extent that they do not exceed each holder's adjusted basis in his or her interest. Any excess is treated as gain from the sale or exchange of the interest. The basis of a holder's residual interest is increased by the daily portion of REMIC taxable income allocated to the residual interest holder. The holder's basis is decreased, but not below zero, by the amount of any distribution received and the daily portion of the REMIC net loss allocated to the interest holder. When a residual interest in a REMIC is disposed of, these adjustments are treated as occurring immediately before the disposition.

Income in Excess of Daily Accruals. A holder of a residual interest may not reduce its taxable income (or alternative minimum taxable income) for the tax year below his "excess inclusion" for the year (Code Sec. 860E).[53] A holder's excess inclusion is equal to the excess of the net income passed through to the holder each calendar quarter over a deemed interest component that is referred to as the "daily accrual." The effect is to prevent a holder from offsetting its excess inclusion with any net operating losses or in calculating alternative minimum tax. Excess inclusions are also treated as unrelated business income for tax-exempt holders (¶ 655). Where a residual interest is held by a mutual fund, real estate investment trust (REIT), common trust fund, or cooperative, a portion of the dividends paid by such organizations to their shareholders are treated as excess inclusions.

Application of Wash Sale Rules. Except as provided in the regulations, the wash sale rules (¶ 1935) apply to dispositions of residual interests where a seller of the interest acquires any residual interest in any REMIC (or any interest in a taxable mortgage pool (¶ 2368) that is comparable to a residual interest) within a period beginning six months before the date of sale or disposition and ending six months after that date (Code Sec. 860F(d)).[54]

Transfers to Disqualified Organizations. If a disqualified organization (government, exempt organization, cooperative) holds a residual interest in a REMIC at any time during the tax year, then an excise tax is imposed against the person or entity that has transferred the interest to the organization (Code Sec. 860E(e)).[55] The tax is the highest corporate income tax rate on the present value of the total excess inclusion that is anticipated for the interest after the transfer takes place. A disqualified organization may not get around this tax by holding the interest in a pass-through entity.

2364. REMIC Interests as Real Estate Interests. Regular and residual interests in a real estate mortgage investment conduit (REMIC) are treated as real estate assets for purposes of determining whether an organization qualifies as a real estate investment trust (REIT) (¶ 2326). However, if in any calendar quarter less than 95 percent of the REMIC's assets are real estate assets, the REIT is treated as holding directly its proportionate share of the assets and income of the REMIC (Code Sec. 856(c)(5)(E)).[56] Any regular or residual interest in a REMIC can also qualify as an "asset" for purposes of determining whether an organization is a domestic building and loan association (Code Sec. 7701(a)(19)).[57] If 95 percent or more of REMIC assets qualify as an "asset" for this purpose, then the entire interest in the REMIC can qualify as an asset. If one REMIC owns interests in a another REMIC, then the character of the second REMIC's assets flow through for purposes of making this determination.

2367. Foreign Holders of REMIC Interests. If the holder of a residual interest in a real estate mortgage investment conduit (REMIC) is a nonresident alien or a foreign corporation, then for withholding and income tax purposes (¶ 2425): (1) amounts includible in the holder's gross income are taken into account when paid or distributed, or when the interest is disposed of, and (2) no exemption from the 30-percent tax imposed on U.S.-source income not effectively connected with a U.S. business applies to any excess inclusion (¶ 2431) (Code Sec. 860G(b)).[58]

Footnote references are to paragraphs of the 2008 Standard Federal Tax Reports.

[53] ¶ 26,680
[54] ¶ 26,700
[55] ¶ 26,680
[56] ¶ 26,500
[57] ¶ 43,080
[58] ¶ 26,720

2368. Taxable Mortgage Pools. If a mortgage pool does not elect or qualify as a real estate mortgage investment conduit (REMIC) (or as a financial asset securitization investment trust (FASIT) prior to January 1, 2005, ¶ 2369), it may qualify as a taxable mortgage pool (TMP). An entity is a taxable mortgage pool if: (1) substantially all the assets of which consist of debt obligations (or interests therein) and more than 50 percent of the obligations (or interests) consist of real estate mortgages; (2) the entity is the obligor under debt obligations with two or more maturities; and (3) the terms for payment under the entity's obligations are tied to payments being made on the obligations held by the entity (Code Sec. 7701(i)).[59] A taxable mortgage pool is taxed as a separate corporation and may not join with any other corporation in filing a consolidated return. Any portion of an entity that meets the requirements above is treated as a taxable mortgage pool. However, no domestic savings and loan association can qualify to be a taxable mortgage pool.

Financial Asset Securitization Investment Trusts

2369. FASITs Defined. For tax years prior to January 1, 2005, a qualified entity could elect to be treated as a financial asset securitization investment trust (FASIT) (Code Secs. 860H—860L, prior to repeal by the American Jobs Creation Act of 2004 (P.L. 108-357)).[60] A FASIT is a pass-through entity used to secure debt obligations such as credit card receivables, home equity loans and auto loans. A FASIT must be entirely owned by a taxable C corporation. Any residual income of the FASIT is passed through and taxed to the owner. The advantage offered by a FASIT is that asset-backed securities issued by a FASIT are treated as debt for federal tax purposes. Thus, interest paid to investors is deductible.

Insurance Companies

2370. Taxation of Life Insurance Companies. A life insurance company is generally taxed on its taxable income and net capital gain at regular corporate tax rates (Code Sec. 801).[61] Taxable income for this purpose is the life insurance company's gross income less deductions for the following: claims, benefits, and losses accrued; net increases in various reserves (¶ 2372); policyholder dividends (¶ 2373); dividends received (subject to limitations); operational losses (¶ 2377); consideration received for assumption of the company's liabilities; and dividend reimbursements paid to another insurance company (Code Sec. 805).[62]

All other deductions allowed to a corporation are also permitted, subject to some modifications (for example, no deduction for net operating losses (NOLs) is allowed). Small life insurance companies (gross assets of less than $500 million) may claim an additional deduction based on their tentative taxable income (Code Sec. 806).[63] A life insurance company uses Form 1120-L to figure and report its taxable income.

A business entity qualifies as a life insurance company if: (1) more than half of its business activities consist of issuing life insurance or annuity contracts or reinsuring risks underwritten by other insurance companies, and (2) more than half of its total reserves for paying off insurance obligations are made up of life insurance reserves, unearned premiums, and unpaid losses on noncancellable life, accident, or health policies that are not included in life insurance (Code Sec. 816).[64]

2372. Net Change in Reserves. Life insurance companies may deduct the net increase in certain reserves or include the net decrease in such reserves that have occurred during the tax year. The deduction for an increase in reserves takes into account increases due to both premiums and interest credited to the reserves. In general, the net increase or decrease is computed by comparing the closing balance for reserves, reduced by the policyholders' share of tax-exempt interest, to the opening balance of the reserves (Code Sec. 807).[65]

Footnote references are to paragraphs of the 2008 Standard Federal Tax Reports.

[59] ¶ 43,080	[62] ¶ 25,770	[65] ¶ 25,810
[60] ¶ 26,730	[63] ¶ 25,790	
[61] ¶ 25,710	[64] ¶ 25,990	

¶2368

In determining net changes in reserves, property and casualty companies (as well as life insurance companies subject to reserve requirements) must discount their reserves to account for the time value of money. The deduction for unpaid losses is limited to the amount of discounted unpaid losses. Any net decrease in loss reserves results in income inclusion, but the inclusion is computed on a discounted basis (Code Sec. 846).[66] Insurance companies that are required to discount unpaid losses may claim an additional deduction up to the excess of undiscounted unpaid losses over related discounted unpaid losses (Code Sec. 847).[67]

2373. Policyholder Dividends. Life insurance companies may claim a deduction for dividends or similar distributions paid or accrued to policyholders during the tax year. A policyholder dividend includes excess interest, premium adjustments, experience related refunds, and any amount paid or credited to policyholders not based on a fixed amount in the contract but dependent on the experience rate of the company or the discretion of management. (Code Sec. 808).[68] For tax years prior to 2005, a mutual life insurance company must reduce the amount of its deduction for dividends by a "differential earnings amount" (Code Sec. 809, prior to repeal by the American Jobs Creation Act of 2004 (P.L. 108-357)).[69]

2377. Operations Loss Deduction. A life insurance company may claim an "operations loss deduction," which is the excess of its life insurance deductions over its life insurance gross income (subject to limitations). An operational loss may be carried back three years and carried forward 15 years. The company, however, may elect to forgo the entire carryback period for an operational loss for any tax year. In addition, if the company qualifies as a new life insurance company, the operational loss for any tax year may be carried forward 18 years (Code Sec. 810).[70]

2378. Taxation of Other Insurance Companies. Insurance companies that do not meet the definition of a "life insurance company" (¶ 2370) are subject to taxation at regular corporate income tax rates on their taxable income (Code Secs. 831(a) and 832).[71] Insurance companies (other than life insurance companies) are exempt from taxation if gross receipts for the tax year do not exceed $600,000 and no more than 50 percent of such receipts consist of premiums ($150,000 and 35 percent, respectively, for mutual life insurance companies) (Code Sec. 501(c)(15)).[72] An insurance company, with net written premiums of no more than $1.2 million for the tax year, may elect to be taxed only on its taxable investment income, such as gross investment income less deductions for tax-free interest, investment expenses, real estate expenses, depreciation, paid or accrued interest, capital losses, trade or business deductions and certain corporate deductions (Code Secs. 831(b) and 834).[73]

2380. Foreign Insurance Companies. A foreign company carrying on an insurance business within the United States that would otherwise qualify as an insurance company if it were a domestic company is taxable as an insurance company on its U.S.-source income effectively connected with the conduct of any U.S. trade or business (¶ 2429) (Code Sec. 842).[74]

Bank and Trust Companies

2383. Taxation of Banks. Banks and other financial institutions are generally subject to the same tax rules as corporations. However, unlike other taxpayers, banks are not subject to capital loss limitations with respect to the worthlessness of debt securities. Instead, banks may treat these losses as bad debt losses. In addition, the capital loss limitations generally do apply to banks with respect to worthless stocks and stock rights (Code Sec. 582).[75]

Footnote references are to paragraphs of the 2008 Standard Federal Tax Reports.

[66] ¶ 26,330
[67] ¶ 26,350
[68] ¶ 25,830
[69] ¶ 25,850

[70] ¶ 25,870
[71] ¶ 26,130, ¶ 26,150
[72] ¶ 22,602
[73] ¶ 26,130, ¶ 26,190

[74] ¶ 26,250
[75] ¶ 23,608

The method that is used to deduct bad debts of a bank depends on the type and size of the institution in question (Code Sec. 585).[76] A small bank (average adjusted basis of all assets of $500 million or less) may add to its bad debt reserves an amount based on its actual experience as shown by losses for the current and preceding five tax years. A thrift institution that would be treated as a small bank may utilize this method as well. Large banks, on the other hand, are required to use either a specific charge-off method, in which the bank's debt reserves are recaptured over a four-year period, or the cut-off method, in which recoveries and losses are reflected as adjustments to the bank's reserve account.

Definition of a Bank. For this purpose, a bank is defined as a corporation with a substantial part of its business consisting of either receiving deposits and making loans, or exercising fiduciary powers similar to those permitted to national banks. This includes commercial banks and trust companies, mutual savings banks, building and loan associations, cooperative banks, and federal savings and loan associations (Code Sec. 581).[77] These latter "banks," however, are allowed a deduction for dividends paid or credited to depositors (Code Sec. 591).[78]

Sale or Exchange of Securities. In the case of certain financial institutions, the sale or exchange of a bond, debenture, note, certificate, or other evidence of indebtedness is not considered a sale or exchange of a capital asset (Code Sec. 582(c)).[79] Instead, net gains and losses from such transactions are treated as ordinary income and losses. A financial institution for this purpose includes commercial banks, mutual savings banks, domestic building and loan associations, cooperative banks, business development corporations, and small business investment companies.

2389. Common Trust Funds. A common trust fund is an investment vehicle established by a bank in the form of a state-law trust to handle the investment and reinvestment of money contributed to it in its capacity as a trustee, executor, administrator or guardian. For tax purposes, a common trust fund is treated in a manner similar to that of a partnership (Code Sec. 584).[80] Instead of the trust being subject to tax, each participant that invests in the trust fund must include his proportionate share of the trust fund's income or loss on his own return. This includes a participant's share of dividends received by the fund which are eligible for the reduced tax rate on qualified dividends (¶ 733). The admission and withdrawal of a participant, however, does not result in a gain or loss to the common trust fund.

Small Business Investment Companies

2392. Taxation of Small Business Investment Companies. A small business investment company (SBIC) is a private corporation that operates under the Small Business Investment Act of 1958 to provide capital to small business concerns through the purchase of convertible debentures. An SBIC is generally treated as a corporation for federal tax purposes with a few exceptions. First, an SBIC may treat as ordinary loss any loss on the sale or exchange of stock of a small business concern if the stock was received under the conversion privilege of a debenture acquired under section 304 of the Small Business Investment Act of 1958 (Code Sec. 1243).[81] Second, an SBIC may deduct 100 percent (rather than 70 percent) of the dividends it receives from taxable domestic corporations (Code Sec. 243(a)(2)).[82]

Any taxpayer whose sustains a loss on the sale of SBIC stock (or if the stock becomes worthless) is entitled to treat the loss as an ordinary loss (Code Sec. 1242).[83] The SBIC, however, must be actually operating at the time the loss is sustained by the taxpayer. In addition, the loss is not subject to the limitations on the allowance of nonbusiness deductions in computing net operating losses (NOLs) (Reg. § 1.1242-1(b)).[84]

2394. Rollover into Small Business Investment Companies. Individuals and C corporations may elect to defer recognition of capital gain realized upon the sale of

---

Footnote references are to paragraphs of the 2008 Standard Federal Tax Reports.

[76] ¶ 23,650	[79] ¶ 23,608	[82] ¶ 13,051
[77] ¶ 23,602	[80] ¶ 23,630	[83] ¶ 30,753
[78] ¶ 23,690	[81] ¶ 30,770	[84] ¶ 30,754

publicly traded securities if the taxpayers use the sale proceeds within 60 days to purchase common stock or partnership interest in a specialized small business investment company (SSBIC) (Code Sec. 1044).[85] To the extent that the sale proceeds exceed the cost of the SSBIC common stock or partnership interest, gain must be recognized. For this purpose, an SSBIC is a partnership or corporation licensed under section 301(d) of the Small Business Investment Act of 1958 to finance small business concerns owned by disadvantaged persons.

An individual taxpayer (as well as married taxpayers filing a joint return) can roll over no more than $50,000 of gain in any given tax year or $500,000 during his or her lifetime ($25,000 or $250,000 for a married person filing separately). For a C corporation, the annual and cumulative limits are $250,000 or $1 million. All corporations that are members of the same controlled group are treated as one taxpayer for this purpose, and any gain excluded by the predecessor of a C corporation is treated as gain excluded by the successor corporation. The deferred gain is reflected as a basis reduction. However, basis is not reduced when calculating gain eligible for the 50-percent exclusion for qualified small business stock (¶ 2396).

The election to rollover gain into an SSBIC (which is revocable with IRS consent) must be made by the due date (including extensions) for the taxpayer's return for the year in which the publicly traded securities are sold. For individuals, the election is made by reporting the entire gain from the sale on Schedule D of Form 1040. A separate statement must also be attached showing: how the nonrecognized gain was calculated; the SSBIC in which the sale proceeds were invested; the date the SSBIC stock or partnership interest was purchased; and the basis of the SSBIC interest (Reg. § 1.1044(a)-1(b)).[86]

Small Business Corporations

2395. Code Sec. 1244 Stock. An individual may take an ordinary loss deduction for a loss sustained on the sale, exchange, or worthlessness of small business stock (referred to as Code Sec. 1244 stock), even if the stock is a capital asset in the taxpayer's hands.[87] The maximum amount deductible as an ordinary loss in any tax year is $50,000 ($100,000 on a joint return). A loss that is disallowed because of these dollar limitations can be carried back or carried over as a net operating loss (NOL). For stock to qualify as Code Sec. 1244 stock, it must be stock of a domestic corporation (including preferred stock) issued after November 6, 1978, and which meets the following requirements:

- the stock must have been issued to an individual stockholder or a partner in a partnership in exchange for money or property other than stock or securities (while the stock may be issued to a partnership, only individuals who are partners at the time the stock is acquired may take an ordinary loss);[88]

- the issuing corporation must be a small business corporation, meaning that at the time the stock was issued the aggregate amount of money and other property (taken into account at its adjusted basis) received by the corporation as a contribution to capital and as a paid-in surplus (not only for the stock in question but any previously issued stock) does not exceed $1 million (qualification as a small business corporation under the S corporation rules does not automatically qualify a corporation's stock for Code Sec. 1244 purposes); and

- during the corporation's five most recent tax years ending before the date the stock is sold by the taxpayer, more than 50 percent of its gross receipts must have been derived from sources other than royalties, rents, dividends, interest, annuities, and gains from the sales of securities (the corporation must be largely an operating company, meaning that ordinary loss treatment under Code Sec. 1244 is not available to corporations with little or no gross receipts) (Reg. § 1.1244(c)-1(e)(2)).[89]

Additional requirements must be met for stock issued after June 30, 1958, and before November 7, 1978 (Reg. § 1.1244(c)-1(f)).

Footnote references are to paragraphs of the 2008 Standard Federal Tax Reports.

[85] ¶ 29,845
[86] ¶ 29,845B
[87] ¶ 30,790
[88] ¶ 30,800.59
[89] ¶ 30,793, ¶ 30,800.545

Small Business Stock

2396. Exclusion of Capital Gain from Small Business Stock. A noncorporate taxpayer can exclude from gross income 50 percent of any gain from the sale or exchange of qualified small business stock held for more than five years (Code Sec. 1202(a)).[90] The exclusion is 60 percent if the qualified small business stock issued by a corporation in an empowerment zone. Eligible gain from any single issuer is subject to a cumulative limit for any given tax year to the greater of: (1) $10 million reduced by the aggregate amount of eligible gain taken in prior years ($5 million for married taxpayers filing separately), or (2) 10 times the taxpayer's adjusted basis of all qualified stock of the issuer disposed of during the tax year. For alternative minimum tax purposes, seven percent of the excluded gain is a preference item (¶ 1425) (Code Sec. 57(a)(7)).[91]

To be eligible as qualified small business stock, the stock must be issued after August 10, 1993, and acquired by the taxpayer at its original issue (directly or through an underwriter) in exchange for money, property, or as compensation for services provided to the corporation (Code Secs. 1202(c) and (d)).[92] Stock acquired through the conversion of stock (such as preferred stock) that was qualified stock in the taxpayer's hands is also qualified stock in the taxpayer's hands. However, small business stock does not include stock that has been the subject of certain redemptions that are more than de minimis. A taxpayer who acquires qualified stock by gift or inheritance is treated as having acquired such stock in the same manner as the transferor and adds the transferor's holding period to his or her own. A partnership may distribute qualified stock to its partners as long as the partner held his partnership interest when the stock was acquired, and only to the extent that his share of the partnership has not increased since then. Qualified stock acquired by exercising options or warrants, or converting debt, is deemed acquired at original issue.

The issuing corporation must be a domestic C corporation (*other* than a mutual fund (regulated investment company), cooperative, or other similar "pass-though" corporation). The corporation must have aggregate gross assets that do not exceed $50 million as of the date of issuance. All corporations that are members of the same parent-subsidiary controlled group are treated as one corporation in determining whether the qualified small business requirements have been met. In addition, at least 80 percent of the value of the corporation's assets must be used in the active conduct of one or more qualified trades or businesses. For this purpose, the performance of services in the fields of health, law, engineering, architecture, etc., is not a qualified trade or business, nor are the hospitality, farming, insurance, financing or mineral extraction industries. However, a specialized small business investment company, licensed under section 301(d) of the Small Business Investment Act of 1958, will meet the active business test (¶ 2392).

2397. Rollover of Small Business Stock. A noncorporate taxpayer may elect to roll over capital gain from the sale of qualified small business stock (¶ 2396) held for more than six months if other qualified small business stock is purchased during the 60-day period beginning on the date of sale (Code Sec. 1045).[93] The replacement stock must meet the active business requirement for the six-month period following its purchase. Except for purposes of determining whether the active business test six-month holding period is met, the holding period of the stock purchased includes the holding period of the stock sold. Gain will only be recognized to the extent that the amount realized on the sale exceeds the cost of the replacement stock. The basis of the newly purchased stock must be reduced by the amount of gain rolled over.

Footnote references are to paragraphs of the 2008 Standard Federal Tax Reports.

[90] ¶ 30,372
[91] ¶ 5300

[92] ¶ 30,372
[93] ¶ 29,850

¶2396

Chapter 24

U.S. TAXATION OF FOREIGN ACTIVITIES AND FOREIGN TAXPAYERS

Overview

2401. Taxation of Worldwide Income. The United States taxes the worldwide income of U.S. citizens, resident aliens and domestic corporations, without regard to whether the income arose from a transaction or activity originating outside its geographic borders (¶ 2402). To prevent income from being subject to double taxation, once in the United States and once in a foreign country, U.S. taxpayers may be entitled to a credit for foreign taxes paid or accrued (¶ 2475). Nonresident aliens and foreign corporations are generally taxed in the same manner as U.S. citizens and domestic corporations on income that is "effectively connected" with a trade or business conducted within the United States (¶ 2425). Income not effectively connected with a U.S. trade or business, such as "fixed and determinable, annual, or periodic income," will generally be taxed at a 30-percent rate. Special rules apply with regard to U.S. shareholders of foreign controlled corporations and the taxation of U.S. manufacturers' who export their products overseas.

U.S. Citizens and Residents Living Abroad

2402. Foreign Earned Income Exclusion. A qualifying individual (¶ 2404) who works abroad may elect (¶ 2408) to exclude from gross income a certain amount of foreign earned income attributable to his or her residence in a foreign country during the tax year (Code Sec. 911(a)(1) and (b)(2)).[1] For calendar year 2007, the maximum amount of foreign earned income that may be excluded is $85,700 (the maximum amount for calendar year 2008 is $87,600). The exclusion is computed on a daily basis. Therefore, the maximum limit must be reduced ratably for each day during the calendar year that the taxpayer does not qualify for the exclusion. The exclusion is also limited to the excess of the individual's foreign earned income for the year over his or her foreign housing exclusion (¶ 2403).

> **Example 1:** Andy is a U.S. citizen who qualified as a bona fide resident of Peru for all of 2006 and who received $78,000 in salary for work he did in Peru. Assuming he claimed no foreign housing exclusion, Andy was able to exclude all of the salary from his gross income for 2006. Andy continues to work in Peru until October 31, 2007, when his employer permanently reassigns him to the United States. During this time, Andy received a salary of $90,000 for his work in Peru in 2007. Assuming he claimed no foreign housing exclusion, the maximum amount of foreign earned income he can exclude from his gross income in 2007 is $71,378

Footnote references are to paragraphs of the 2008 Standard Federal Tax Reports.

[1] ¶ 28,040

($85,700 multiplied by ratio of the number of days he was a bona fide resident of Peru ($^{304}/_{365}$)).

Effective for tax years beginning after 2005, the amount of foreign earned income (and foreign housing costs) excluded from an individual's gross income will be used for purposes of determining the rate of income and alternative minimum tax that applies to his or her nonexcluded income (Code Sec. 911(f)).[2] An individual's tentative tax will be the excess of the tax that would be imposed on their income (determined without regard to the exclusions), and the tax that would be imposed on the excluded amount(s). For this purpose, the amount(s) excluded from gross will be reduced by the aggregate amount of any deductions or other exclusions otherwise disallowed.

> **Example 2:** Toby, a single individual, elects to exclude $75,700 of his foreign earned income and $10,000 of his foreign housing expenses from his gross income in 2007. After the exclusions, Toby has $100,000 in other taxable income. As a result, his tentative tax for 2007 is $29,235.75. This is the excess of the tax that would be imposed on his total income without regard to the excluded amounts ($185,700) ($47,349.25), over the tax that would be imposed on the $85,700 excluded from gross income ($18,114).

Foreign earned income includes wages, salaries, professional fees and other amounts received as compensation for personal services actually rendered when the taxpayer's tax home was located in a foreign country and the taxpayer met either the bona fide residence or physical presence test (Code Sec. 911(b)(1) and (d)(2); Reg. §1.911-3).[3] If the taxpayer engages in a trade or business where both personal services and capital are material income-producing factors, no more than 30 percent of the taxpayer's share of the net profits can be treated as earned income.

Foreign earned income does not include amounts paid by the United States or its agencies to its employees, received after the close of the tax year following the tax year in which the services were performed, and received as pensions, annuities or social security payments. It also does not include amounts included in the taxpayer's gross income as allowances for meal or lodging furnished for the convenience of an employer (see ¶ 873 and ¶ 2406), recaptured moving expenses, or because of an employer's contributions to a nonexempt trust or nonqualified annuity. Income earned in a country in which the United States imposes travel restrictions is also not considered foreign earned income.

A taxpayer that elects to claim the exclusion for foreign earned income (or the foreign housing exclusion) is prohibited from claiming any deduction, exclusion or tax credit (including the foreign tax credit) that is properly allocable to the excluded amounts (Code Sec. 911(d)(6); Reg. §1.911-6(a)).[4] For example, a taxpayer may not deduct unreimbursed employee business expenses against wages that are excluded as foreign earned income.

2403. Foreign Housing Exclusion. In addition to the election to exclude foreign earned income (¶ 2402), a qualified individual (¶ 2404) may elect (¶ 2408) to exclude from gross income a certain amount of foreign housing expenses provided by his or her employer (Code Sec. 911(a)(2) and (c)).[5] For this purpose, foreign housing is provided by an employer if any amount is paid or incurred by the employer on the taxpayer's behalf and included in the taxpayer's foreign earned income (for example, housing allowance or reimbursement).

The maximum amount of an individual's foreign housing expenses that may be excluded from gross income is the excess of: (1) his or her reasonable "foreign housing expenses" for the tax year, over (2) a "base housing amount" equal to 16 percent of the maximum foreign earned income exclusion amount for the calendar year ($85,700 for 2007), multiplied by the number of days of foreign residence or presence by the individual for the year (16 percent of $85,700 is $13,712 or $37.57 per day). However, foreign housing expenses may be excluded only to the extent of the lesser of the

---

Footnote references are to paragraphs of the 2008 Standard Federal Tax Reports.

[2] ¶ 28,040
[3] ¶ 28,040, ¶ 28,043
[4] ¶ 28,040, ¶ 28,046
[5] ¶ 28,040

expenses attributable to employer-provided amounts or the individual's foreign earned income for the taxable year.

> **Caution Note:** Effective for tax years beginning after 2005, the amount of foreign housing expenses (and foreign earned income) excluded from an individual's gross income will be used for purposes of determining the rate of income and alternative minimum tax (AMT) that applies to his or her nonexcluded income (see ¶ 2402).

Housing expenses. A taxpayer's "foreign housing expenses" are the reasonable costs paid or incurred during the tax year for providing housing for the taxpayer and his family (if they reside with the taxpayer) (Reg. § 1.911-4).[6] Eligible expenses include rent or the fair rental value of housing provided in kind by an employer, utilities (other than telephone charges), real or personal property insurance, household repairs, rental of furniture and accessories, and residential parking. They do not include expenses that are otherwise deductible (depreciation, interest, taxes) or that are extravagant. They also do not include the cost of buying property (including mortgage payments), capital improvements to property, purchased furniture or accessories, or the cost of domestic labor. On the other hand, housing expenses may include any expenses related to a second foreign household for the taxpayer's family if they do not reside with the taxpayer because of adverse conditions. If a husband and wife are both qualified individuals with foreign earned income, special rules apply which may allow them both to claim the foreign housing exclusion or deduction (Reg. § 1.911-5).[7]

Effective for tax years beginning after 2005, the "reasonable" amount of foreign housing expenses of an individual that may be used in calculating a taxpayer's foreign housing exclusion is limited to 30 percent of the maximum foreign earned income exclusion amount for the year, computed on a daily basis and multiplied by the number of days of foreign residence or presence by the taxpayer for the year (Code Sec. 911(c)(2)).[8] Thus, the maximum amount of foreign housing expenses that may generally be used in calculating the foreign housing exclusion for 2007 is limited to $25,710 (30 percent of $85,700) or $70.44 per day. The IRS may adjust this limitation for specific geographic locations that have higher housing costs relative to the United States (Notice 2007-77).[9] However, the taxpayer must actually reside within the geographic limits of the high-cost location identified by the IRS to claim the adjusted limit (the taxpayer cannot reside in a suburb of the location to claim the adjusted limit).

> **Example:** Fisher is a U.S. citizen who has made his tax home in Sydney and been a bona fide resident of Australia for the past few years. However, on September 1, 2007, Fisher flies back to the United States on permanent assignment for his employer. Thus, he was a foreign resident or present in a foreign country for 243 days of the 2007 tax year. During this time, Fisher had $150,000 of foreign earned income in 2007, including $30,000 provided by his employer for foreign housing expenses.
>
> Sydney is not a location identified by the IRS as having higher housing costs relative to the United States. Thus, in calculating his foreign housing exclusion, Fisher's reasonable foreign housing expenses are limited to the standard amount of $70.44 per day. As a result, his exclusion is $7,987. This is the difference between his reasonable housing expenses of $17,117 ($70.44 x 243 days), less his base housing amount of $9,130 ($37.57 x 243 days). On the other hand, if Fisher's tax home while he was a bona fide resident of Australia was in Perth, then the limit on his reasonable foreign housing expenses would be $109.59 per day. As a result, his exclusion would be $17,500. This is the difference between his reasonable housing expenses of $26,630 ($109.59 x 243 days), less his base housing amount of $9,130 ($37.57 x 243 days).

Self-Employment. A self-employed taxpayer is entitled to deduct from gross income a certain amount of foreign housing expenses in lieu of the exclusion (Code Sec. 911(c)(4); Reg. § 1.911-4(e)).[10] The deduction is limited to the amount by which the taxpayer's foreign earned income for the tax year exceeds his foreign earned income

---

Footnote references are to paragraphs of the 2008 Standard Federal Tax Reports.

[6] ¶ 28,044	[8] ¶ 28,040	[10] ¶ 28,040, ¶ 28,044
[7] ¶ 28,045	[9] ¶ 28,049.225	

exclusion. Any amount that exceeds the deduction limit can be carried forward one tax year. If the taxpayer has foreign earned income that consists of both employer provided amounts and self-employment amounts, then the taxpayer may elect to exclude that part of their housing expenses that are provided by their employer and also claim a deduction for any remaining housing expenses attributed to self-employment income.

2404. Eligibility for Exclusions. In order to qualify for the foreign earned income exclusion (¶ 2402) and the foreign housing exclusion (¶ 2403), an individual's tax home must be in a foreign country and he or she must satisfy either the bona fide residence test or the physical presence test (Code Sec. 911(d)(1); Reg. § 1.911-2).[11] A foreign country is any territory, including airspace and territorial waters, under the sovereignty of a government other than the United States. The exclusions, however, will be denied if the taxpayer is present in a foreign country in which travel is generally restricted (Code Sec. 911(d)(8)).

Tax Home. "Tax home" for this purpose has the same meaning as it does for determining the deductibility of traveling expenses away from home (¶ 950). An individual's tax home is where his principal place of business is located, regardless of where he maintains a family home (Code Sec. 911(d)(3)). The location of a taxpayer's tax home often depends on whether a work assignment is temporary or indefinite. However, an individual is not considered to have a tax home in a foreign country for any period during which his abode is in the United States. Temporary presence or maintenance of a dwelling in the United States does not necessarily mean that an abode is in the United States during that time.

Bona Fide Residence. A U.S. citizen may qualify for the foreign income or housing exclusions if he or she is a bona fide resident of a foreign country for an uninterrupted period that includes a full tax year (Code Sec. 911(d)(1)(A) and (d)(5)). This determination is based on all of the facts and circumstances including the taxpayer's intentions regarding the length and nature of their stay. It is not determined by the taxpayer's status under the laws of the foreign country. Nor does a taxpayer automatically acquire bona fide residence status by merely living in a foreign country for a year. The taxpayer does not have to be a bona fide resident of the same foreign country for the entire period and the foreign country in which the taxpayer is a bona fide resident does not have to be the primary place of employment. Once the bona fide residence requirement is met, the taxpayer is permitted the exclusions for any tax year in which the period of residence began or ended.

> **Example 1:** Barney is a calendar-year taxpayer whose salary is $100,000 per year. On January 1, 2006, he establishes bona fide residence in Canada. If his residence lasts until March 31, 2007, he qualifies for an exclusion of $82,400 of his foreign earned income in 2006 under the bona fide residence test since residence was established for a full tax year in a foreign country. He also qualifies for the exclusion of $21,132 of his foreign earned income ($85,700 × $^{90}/_{365}$) for the portion of the 2007 tax year he was a resident in Canada.

Physical Presence. A U.S. citizen or resident alien may qualify for the foreign income or housing exclusions if he is present in a foreign country (or countries) for 330 days out of any consecutive 12-month period (Code Sec. 911(d)(1)(B)). The taxpayer does not have to be present in the foreign country solely for business purposes to meet this test and the 330 days do not have to be consecutive. In addition, the taxpayer can select any 12-month period in which he meets the physical presence test.

> **Example 2:** Betty is a U.S. citizen who leaves San Francisco on February 3, 2007, and arrives in Spain at 11 p.m. on that same day. During December, 2007, Betty vacations in France for ten days. She leaves Spain to move back to the United States at 7 a.m. on January 10, 2008. Betty will meet the 330-day test during either the twelve-month period beginning at midnight of January 10, 2007, or the twelve-month period beginning at midnight of February 4, 2007. The first qualifying day of presence for either period is February 4, 2007.

Footnote references are to paragraphs of the 2008 Standard Federal Tax Reports.

[11] ¶ 28,040, ¶ 28,042

Waiver of Time Requirements. Relief from either the bona fide residence or the physical presence test is provided to an individual if he or she was forced to flee a foreign country because of civil unrest, war, or other adverse conditions (Code Sec. 911(d)(4)). To qualify for the relief, the individual must have been bona fide resident of, or present in, the foreign country on or prior to the date the IRS determines that adverse conditions exist in the foreign country and individuals are required to leave. In addition, the taxpayer must establish that he could reasonably be expected to have satisfied the residency requirement had the adverse conditions not arisen. The IRS publishes the names of countries for which this waiver is available annually.

2406. Camps Located in a Foreign Country. In addition to the exclusion of foreign earned income (¶ 2402) and foreign housing expenses (¶ 2403), an individual may be able to exclude the value of meals and lodging provided by his or her employer in a camp located in a foreign country if three requirements are met (Code Sec. 119(c)).[12] First, the lodging must be provided for the convenience of the employer because the place where the employee's services are performed is in a remote area where satisfactory housing is unavailable. Second, the location of the camp must be as near as practicable to the place where the employee's services are performed. Third, the lodging must be provided in a common area, not open to the public, that normally accommodates 10 or more employees.

2408. Electing the Exclusions. A qualified individual (¶ 2404) must make a separate election with respect to the foreign earned income exclusion (¶ 2402) and the foreign housing exclusion (¶ 2403). The elections are made by filing Form 2555 (or Form 2555-EZ) with the taxpayer's timely-filed income tax return (including extensions), amended return, or a late-filed return if filed within one year after the due date of the return (not including extensions) (Code Sec. 911(e); Reg. § 1.911-7).[13] Once made, the election will remain in effect for the current tax year and all subsequent years unless revoked with approval from the IRS. A taxpayer that revokes the election without IRS approval will be prohibited from making a new election for at least the next five tax years. A self-employed taxpayer does not have to make an election in order to claim the foreign housing deduction. If both a husband and wife qualify for the foreign earned income exclusion or the foreign housing exclusion or deduction, each must file a separate Form 2555 regardless of whether they file a joint return or separate returns.

An individual that claims either the foreign earned income or foreign housing exclusion may not claim the foreign tax credit (¶ 2475) for any income excluded. Similarly, a taxpayer eligible for the earned income tax credit (¶ 1375) may not claim both the credit and either of the exclusions. Claiming the foreign tax credit or earned income credit in these circumstances may result in the revocation of the elections to exclude foreign earned income or foreign housing expenses.

2409. Resident Aliens. A resident alien is generally taxed in the same manner as a U.S. citizen. For this purpose, residency is determined under the lawful permanent residence test or the substantial presence test (Code Sec. 7701(b)(1)).[14] An alien who does not qualify under either of these tests will be treated as a nonresident alien for federal income, employment and excise tax purposes (unless treated as a resident under a tax treaty). Some individuals may also be eligible to elect resident status. For additional rules regarding the change of resident status during a tax year, see ¶ 2451.

Lawful Permanent Resident Test. An alien who is a lawful permanent resident of the United States under U.S. immigration laws (receives a "green card") will be considered a resident alien for federal income tax purposes (Reg. § 301.7701(b)-1(b)).[15] Resident status begins in the first calendar year in which the alien is a lawful resident and is physically present in the United States for at least one day. Resident status continues until permanent resident status is terminated.

Substantial Presence Test. An alien will be considered a resident if the individual is present in the United States for at least 31 days during the calendar year and 183 days

---

Footnote references are to paragraphs of the 2008 Standard Federal Tax Reports.

[12] ¶ 7220
[13] ¶ 28,040, ¶ 28,047
[14] ¶ 43,080
[15] ¶ 43,117

for the current and two preceding calendar years. For purposes of the 183-day require-ment, each day present in the United States during the current calendar year counts as a full day, each day in the first preceding year as ⅓ of a day, and each day in the second preceding year as ⅙ of a day (Code Sec. 7701(b)(3); Reg. §301.7701(b)-1(c)).[16] A number of exceptions exist as to what days an alien is considered to be present in the United States (for example, commuters, exempt individuals, medical conditions prevent-ing departure, individuals in transit). Presence in U.S. territories or possessions does not count as presence in the United States for this purpose.

Elective Resident Status. An individual is permitted to elect resident status in a calendar year if the individual does not otherwise qualify under the substantial presence test (Code Sec. 7701(b)(4); Reg. §301.7701(b)-4(c)(3)).[17] To qualify for the election, the alien must:

- not be a resident alien in the election year or the prior calendar year;

- meet the substantial presence test in the next calendar year;

- be present in the United States for at least 31 consecutive days in the election year; and

- be present in the United States for at least 75 percent of the days during the period from the first day of the 31-day presence period through the end of the election year.

If these requirements are met, the individual's election to be treated as a resident alien of the United States will be effective for that portion of the year beginning with the first day that both the 31-day and 75 percent requirements are met.

An alien may also elect resident status (and thereby file a joint return) if the individual is married to a U.S. citizen or resident at the end of the tax year (Code Sec. 6013(g) and (h)).[18] The taxpayer may be either a nonresident or resident alien at the end of the tax year for the election to be made. However, both spouses must join in the election and it is effective for the entire tax year and all subsequent tax years for federal income tax and withholding purposes unless neither spouse is a U.S. citizen or resident at any time during a tax year. The election may also be jointly revoked by the couple or terminated by reason of death, separation, divorce, or by the IRS for failure to keep adequate records. Once terminated, the election may not be made again by the couple.

2410. Resident of U.S. Possessions. Generally, an individual who is a bona fide resident of a U.S. possession during the entire tax year may exclude from gross income for U.S. tax purposes any possession-source income (Code Sec. 931).[19] The exclusion, however, does not apply to income that is received for services performed as an employee of the United States. The individual may also not claim a tax credit or deduction that is attributable to the amount of excluded income. For this purpose, a U.S. possession includes American Samoa, Guam, the Northern Mariana Islands, Puerto Rico and the U.S. Virgin Islands. However, special rules apply to residents of Puerto Rico (¶ 2415) and the Virgin Islands (¶ 2416). Different filing requirements apply depending on the possession involved.

An individual will be considered a bona fide resident of a U.S. possession if the person: (1) is present in the possession for at least 183 days during the tax year and (2) does not have a tax home outside the possession and a closer connection to the United States or a foreign country during the tax year (Code Sec. 937).[20] An individual who does not satisfy the 183-day rule may nevertheless be considered a bona fide resident of a U.S. possession if the individual: (1) spends no more than 90 days in the United States during the tax year; (2) had no more than $3,000 of earned income in the United States and was present for more days in the possession than in the United States; or (3) the individual has no permanent connection to the United States (Reg. §1.937-1).[21] An individual with worldwide gross income of more than $75,000 must file Form 8898 for the tax year in which the individual becomes or ceases to be a bona fide resident of a U.S. possession. A spouse's income is not included when calculating an individual's

---

Footnote references are to paragraphs of the 2008 Standard Federal Tax Reports.

[16] ¶ 43,080, ¶ 43,117	[18] ¶ 35,160	[20] ¶ 28,395
[17] ¶ 43,080, ¶ 43,120	[19] ¶ 28,240	[21] ¶ 28,396

worldwide gross income for this purpose. In addition, if married taxpayers are each required to file Form 8898, then a separate Form 8898 must be filed for each spouse regardless of whether a joint return is filed.

2415. Resident of Puerto Rico. A U.S. citizen or resident alien who is a bona fide resident of Puerto Rico (see ¶ 2410) during the entire tax year may exclude from gross income for U.S. tax purposes, any income derived from sources within Puerto Rico (Code Sec. 933).[22] If the taxpayer gives up Puerto Rican residence after having been a bona fide resident for at least two years, then the taxpayer may claim a partial exclusion for the tax year of the residence change. In either case, the exclusion does not apply to income received for services performed as an employee of the United States or agency thereof. The taxpayer may also not claim any tax credit or deduction (except the deduction for personal exemptions) which is attributable to the amount of excluded income.

A U.S. citizen who has income from Puerto Rican sources will be liable for the payment of taxes to Puerto Rico and may have to file a tax return with the United States. Generally, a U.S. citizen who is a resident of Puerto Rico for the entire tax year must pay taxes to Puerto Rico on income from worldwide sources. However, if U.S.-source income is also reported on an individual's Puerto Rican tax return, a credit may be claimed against the Puerto Rican tax in an amount up to the amount allowable for income taxes paid to the United States.

2416. Resident of Virgin Islands. A U.S. citizen or resident (other than a bona fide resident of the U.S. Virgin Islands, see ¶ 2410) who has income from sources within the U.S. Virgin Islands or effectively connected with a trade or business in the Virgin Islands is required to file an income tax return with both the United States and the U.S. Virgin Islands (Code Sec. 932).[23] The tax owed to the Virgin Islands is determined on Form 8689 by multiplying the total tax owed on the United States return (after certain adjustments) by the ratio of adjusted gross income from the Virgin Islands to worldwide adjusted gross income. The Virgin Islands' tax liability (if paid) is credited against the individual's total U.S. tax liability. An individual who qualifies as a bona fide resident of the U.S. Virgin Islands (or who files a joint U.S. return with a U.S. citizen or resident with Virgin Islands income) will generally have no U.S. tax liability so long as the taxpayer reports all income from all sources on the return filed with the Virgin Islands.

2419. Puerto Rico and Possession Tax Credits. A domestic corporation with a substantial portion of business in a U.S. possession may elect to claim a tax credit for taxes paid on business income derived from the possession and qualified investment income earned in the possession (Code Sec. 936).[24] The credit is generally unavailable to new claimants for tax years beginning after 1995. However, grandfather rules permit existing claimants to claim the credit for tax years prior to 2006. An existing credit claimant is a corporation that was actively conducting a trade or business in a possession on October 13, 1995, and which an election is in effect for the tax year including October 13, 1995. A corporation also qualifies as an existing claimant if it acquires all of the trade or business of an existing claimant. The addition of a substantial new line of business after October 13, 1995, will cause an existing claimant to cease to be eligible for the credit. Form 5712 must be used by a domestic corporation for the election. Form 5735 is used to figure the possession corporate tax credit. The credit is generally allowed against federal income taxes and is figured separately for each possession. For purposes of the credit, a "U.S. possession" includes Puerto Rico, Guam, American Samoa, the Northern Mariana Islands, and the U.S. Virgin Islands. However, an existing claimant with respect to Puerto Rico may figure its credit separately using an economic activity limitation (Code Sec. 30A).[25] Special rules also apply for existing claimants from all possessions except the Virgin Islands.

Footnote references are to paragraphs of the 2008 Standard Federal Tax Reports.

[22] ¶ 28,300   [24] ¶ 28,380
[23] ¶ 28,280   [25] ¶ 4058

Nonresident Aliens and Foreign Corporations

2425. Method of Taxation. A nonresident alien (¶ 2409) and foreign corporation are generally taxed in the same manner as a U.S. citizen or domestic corporation on all income that is "effectively connected" with the conduct of a trade or business in the United States (¶ 2429). For this purpose, a nonresident alien who is married to a U.S. citizen or resident must use the tax rate schedule for married individuals filing separately unless the election to be treated as a resident is elected. Nonresident aliens who are unmarried must use the tax rate schedule for single individuals. The head of household tax rate schedule may not be used (Reg. § 1.2-2(b)(6)).[26] If any U.S.-source income received by a nonresident alien or foreign corporation is not effectively connected with a U.S. trade or business, then it will be taxed at a flat 30-percent rate. This may include fixed or determinable periodic income (¶ 2431) or capital gains (¶ 2435). A flat 30-percent tax rate will also apply to the profits (and certain interest amounts) of a U.S. branch of a foreign corporation that are remitted to the foreign corporation during the tax year (¶ 2433).

A nonresident alien or foreign corporation who engages in trade or business in the United States at any time during the tax year or who has taxable income must generally file an income tax return (Code Secs. 6012 and 6072(c)).[27] For a nonresident alien, Form 1040NR is used for this purpose. For a foreign corporation, Form 1120F is used for this purpose. The returns are due on or before the 15th day of the 6th month following the close of the tax year (June 15 for calendar year taxpayers). Nonresident aliens and foreign corporations who do not engage in a U.S. trade or business at any time during the tax year do not have to file a return for U.S.-source income if their tax liability for that year is fully satisfied by the withholding of the tax (¶ 2447).

2427. Source of Income Rules. The U.S. taxation of nonresident aliens and foreign corporations (¶ 2425), as well as the application of the limitations of the foreign tax credit to U.S. citizens and domestic corporations (¶ 2475), is dependent on the determination of the source of a taxpayer's income. Generally, income is either derived from U.S. sources or foreign sources in the following manner (Code Secs. 861, 862, and 865):[28]

- interest income is sourced to the residence or country of incorporation of the obligor (the method and place of payment are irrelevant);

- dividend income, scholarships, grants, prizes, and awards are sourced to the residence of the payor;

- compensation for personal services is sourced to the place where the services are rendered (the location of the payor's residence, where the services are contracted for, and place of payment are irrelevant);

- rents and royalties are sourced to the location of the property;

- gain on the sale of real property is sourced to the location of the property (see ¶ 2442);

- gain on the sale of inventory is sourced to where the sale occurs (where title to the inventory passes);

- gain on the sale of personal property that is not inventory is sourced to the residence of the seller (except for depreciable personal property, intangible property, or stock of an affiliate).

Other items of income are allocated or apportioned to sources within or without the United States as provided in regulations or other IRS rulings (for example, mixed-source income) (Code Sec. 863).[29] Where allocation of an item of income is not provided, then it must be construed.

U.S. taxpayers are allowed deductions directly related to U.S.-source or foreign-source income to determine taxable income. Generally, deductions are first allocated to the activity or property from which the class of income is derived. If any expense or loss

---

Footnote references are to paragraphs of the 2008 Standard Federal Tax Reports.

[26] ¶ 3325
[27] ¶ 35,142, ¶ 36,720

[28] ¶ 27,120, ¶ 27,151, ¶ 27,200
[29] ¶ 27,160

¶2425

is not directly related to any specific item of income, then it must be apportioned ratably between certain statutory and residual groupings. However, special apportionment rules are provided for items such as interest expenses, research and development expenditures, losses from the disposition of property, income taxes, legal and accounting fees and stewardship fees (Code Sec. 864(e) and (f); Reg. § 1.861-8).[30]

2429. Effectively Connected Income. A nonresident alien (¶ 2409) and foreign corporation are taxed in the same manner as a U.S. citizen or domestic corporation on all income that is "effectively connected" with the conduct of a trade or business in the United States (Code Secs. 871(b) and 882(a)).[31] For this purpose, all income, gain, or loss from sources within the United States is generally treated as effectively connected with the conduct of a U.S. trade or business (see also ¶ 2442) (Code Sec. 864(c)).[32] There are two exceptions.

First, fixed or determinable annual or periodical income (¶ 2431) from U.S. sources, as well as capital gains from U.S. sources (¶ 2435) will only be treated as "effectively connected" income if: (1) the income, gain or loss is derived from assets used or held for use in the conduct of a U.S. trade or business, or (2) the activities of a U.S. trade or business are a material factor in the realization of the income, gain or loss. In applying these factors, consideration is given to whether or not the asset or income involved was separately accounted for by the trade or business. In addition, a nonresident alien who is a member of a partnership (or the beneficiary of an estate or trust) which at any time within the tax year is engaged in a trade or business within the United States is considered to be engaged in a U.S. trade or business (Code Sec. 875).[33]

Second, income, gain or loss from *foreign sources* will not be treated as "effectively connected" with the conduct of a U.S. trade or business unless the nonresident alien or foreign corporation maintains an office or other fixed place of business in the United States at any time during the tax year to which the income, gain or loss is attributable (Code Sec. 864(c)).[34] Under these circumstances, the following foreign-source income (or the economic equivalent of such income) will be treated as "effectively connected" with a U.S. trade or business:

- rents and royalties derived from the use of intangible property;
- dividends or interest derived from the active conduct of a banking, financial or similar business through securities or debt obligations; or
- income from the disposition of inventory or personal property held for the sale in the normal course of business through a U.S. office.

Trade or Business. Whether a nonresident alien or foreign corporation is conducting a trade or business within the United States is a facts and circumstances test determined on a yearly basis.[35] However, the conduct of a U.S. trade or business denotes a considerable, continuous and regular course of activity by the taxpayer or through an agent, partnership, estate or trust. Thus, the taxpayer need not be present in the United States to be engaged in a U.S. trade or business. For this purpose, a trade or business includes the performance of personal services at any time during the tax year unless the services are performed by a nonresident alien who is temporarily present in the United States for a period of 90 days or less, compensation received for the services is less than $3,000, and the services are performed for another nonresident alien, foreign corporation or foreign partnership (Code Sec. 864(b)).[36] A trade or business also does not generally include the trading of stocks or securities through a resident broker, commission agent, custodian, or other independent agent unless the individual or foreign corporation is a dealer.

2431. Fixed or Determinable Periodic Income. Fixed or determinable periodic income of a nonresident alien or foreign corporation received from U.S. sources is generally taxed at a flat 30 percent (or lower treaty) rate if such income is not effectively connected with the conduct of a U.S. trade or business (¶ 2429). Generally, the meaning

---

Footnote references are to paragraphs of the 2008 Standard Federal Tax Reports.

[30] ¶ 27,138, ¶ 27,180   [33] ¶ 27,380   [36] ¶ 27,180
[31] ¶ 27,320, ¶ 27,500   [34] ¶ 27,180
[32] ¶ 27,180   [35] ¶ 27,189.20

of the term "fixed or determinable periodical income" includes interest, dividends, rents, salaries, wages, premiums, annuities, compensation, remunerations, emoluments and any other item of annual or periodical gain, profit or income (Code Secs. 871(a) and 881(a)).[37] This includes royalties for timber, coal and iron ore, as well as for the use of patents, copyrights, secret processes formulas and other like property.

Social Security Benefits. For purposes of computing a nonresident alien's fixed or determinable periodic income subject to the flat 30-percent tax (as well as for withholding purposes (¶ 2447)), 85 percent of any Social Security benefits received must be included (Code Sec. 871(a)(3)).[38]

Original Issue Discount. For a sale or exchange of an original issue discount (OID) obligation, the amount of the OID accruing while the obligation was held by a nonresident alien or foreign corporation is subject to the 30-percent tax. A payment on an OID obligation is also subject to the tax to the extent that the payment reflects OID accruing while the obligation was held by the nonresident or foreign corporation (Code Secs. 871(a)(1)(C) and 881(a)(3)).[39] For this purpose, an OID obligation includes any bond or other evidence of indebtedness having OID (Code Sec. 871(g)). It does not include any obligation payable 183 days or less from its date of original issue or any tax-exempt obligation. For a discussion of OID, see ¶ 1952.

Portfolio Interest. U.S.-source portfolio interest is generally not considered fixed or determinable periodic income subject to the flat 30-percent tax. Exempt portfolio interest includes any interest and OID accrued on an obligation in either bearer or registered form held by the nonresident alien or foreign corporation (Code Sec. 871(h) and Code Sec. 881(c)).[40] A bearer obligation is any obligation that is not in registered form that: (1) has arrangements that are reasonably designed to ensure that it will be sold or resold only to non-U.S. persons; (2) the interest is payable only outside of the United States; and (3) on the face of the obligation, there is a statement that any U.S. person who holds it will be subject to limitations under U.S. tax law. A registered obligation is an obligation with respect to which the U.S. person who would otherwise be required to withhold tax from interest paid on it has received a statement stating that the beneficial owner is not a U.S. person (Form W-8BEN).

Portfolio interest does not include contingent interest or interest received by a nonresident alien or foreign corporation that is a 10-percent shareholder. Interest is generally contingent if it is determined by reference to any receipts, income or change in value of property of the debtor or a related person (Code Sec. 871(h)(4)). Other types of contingent interest may be identified by the IRS to prevent tax avoidance. For this purpose, a 10-percent shareholder is any person who owns 10 percent or more of the total combined voting power of all classes of stock in a corporation or 10 percent or more of a capital or profits interest in a partnership (Code Sec. 871(h)(3)). Additional exceptions apply as to the types of interest received by a foreign corporation that will not be considered portfolio interest, including interest received by a foreign corporation that is a bank or a controlled foreign corporation (CFC).

Other Interest and Dividend Income. Nonresident aliens and foreign corporations are not subject to U.S. taxes on interest from bank deposits that are not effectively connected with a U.S. trade or business. The exemption also applies to a percentage of any dividend paid by a domestic corporation in which at least 80 percent of its gross income for the three preceding years is income from a foreign business (Code Secs. 871(i) and 881(d)).

U.S. Possession Corporations. A corporation created or organized in, or under, the laws of Guam, American Samoa, the Northern Mariana Islands, or the U.S. Virgin Islands is not considered a "foreign" corporation and thus is not subject to the 30-percent tax on fixed or determinable income if certain requirements are met. However, U.S.-source dividends paid to a Puerto Rico corporation are subject to U.S. taxation and withholding at a 10-percent rate (Code Sec. 881(b)).[41]

Footnote references are to paragraphs of the 2008 Standard Federal Tax Reports.

[37] ¶ 27,320, ¶ 27,480   [39] ¶ 27,320, ¶ 27,480   [41] ¶ 27,480
[38] ¶ 27,320   [40] ¶ 27,320, ¶ 27,480

¶2431

Mutual Fund Distributions. For tax years beginning after December 31, 2004, "interest-related" dividends and short-term capital gains dividends received by a nonresident alien or foreign corporation from a mutual fund (regulated investment company) are exempt from U.S. taxation under certain circumstances (Code Secs. 871(k) and 881(e)).

2433. Branch Profits Tax. Foreign corporations that operate businesses in the United States may be required to pay a branch profits tax and a branch-level interest tax in addition to the tax on income effectively connected with the conduct of a U.S. trade or business (¶ 2429) (Code Sec. 884).[42] The branch profits tax is 30 percent (or lower by treaty) of the foreign corporation's dividend equivalent amount. This is the amount of the foreign corporation's effectively connected after-tax earnings that is not reinvested in a U.S. trade or business by the close of the tax year or that is disinvested in a later tax year. The branch interest tax is 30 percent (or lower by treaty) of the amount of interest paid by a U.S. branch of a foreign corporation with respect to a liability and notional excess interest amounts. If there is a conflict between the branch profits tax or branch-level interest tax with any U.S. income tax treaty, special rules are provided to determine the extent to which the treaty takes priority.

2435. Capital Gains of Foreign Persons. The net capital gains of nonresident aliens and foreign corporations which are effectively connected with the conduct of a U.S. trade or business are taxed in the same manner as the capital gains of a U.S. citizen, resident alien, or domestic corporation (¶ 2429). Net capital gains which are not effectively connected with the conduct of a U.S. trade or business and which are not fixed or determinable periodic income (¶ 2431) are completely exempt from taxation (Code Secs. 871(a)(2) and 881(a)).[43] However, in the case of a nonresident alien, the exemption only applies if the individual is not present in the United States for at least 183 days during the tax year. If the 183-day period is met, then the net capital gains of the nonresident alien not effectively connected to a conduct of a U.S. trade or business are subject to the flat 30-percent tax rate that applies to fixed and determinable income (¶ 2431).

2438. Community Income. If a nonresident alien is married to a U.S. citizen or resident and does not elect to be treated as a resident (¶ 2409), then any community income is to be treated as follows:

- earned income (other than from a trade or business, or partnership income) is treated as income of the spouse who earned it;

- trade or business income (other than from a partnership) is treated as the separate income of the spouse carrying on the trade or business (unless carried on jointly);

- partnership income is treated as the income of the spouse who is the partner with no portion attributed to the other spouse; and

- all other community income from separate property of one spouse is treated as the income of that spouse (Code Sec. 879).[44]

2442. Disposition of U.S. Real Property Interest. Nonresident aliens and foreign corporations are taxed on the net gains from the disposition of U.S. real property interests as if such gains or losses were effectively connected with the conduct of a U.S. trade or business (¶ 2429) (Code Sec. 897(a)).[45] Thus, in the case of a nonresident alien, the net gains may be subject to both regular federal income and alternative minimum tax. A foreign corporation may be subject to both regular federal income tax and the branch-level taxes (¶ 2433). A foreign corporation that holds a U.S. real property interest may elect to be treated as a domestic corporation for this purpose if, under any treaty obligation of the United States, the foreign corporation is entitled to non-discriminatory treatment for its U.S. real property interests (Code Sec. 897(i)).[46]

Footnote references are to paragraphs of the 2008 Standard Federal Tax Reports.

[42] ¶ 27,540
[43] ¶ 27,320, ¶ 27,480
[44] ¶ 27,460
[45] ¶ 27,700
[46] ¶ 27,700

Real Property Interests. A U.S. real property interest means an interest in real property (including a mine, well, or other natural deposit) located in the United States or the U.S. Virgin Islands. Real property includes land and improvements, personal property associated with the use of the real property, and unsevered timber, crops, and minerals. The foreign person's interest can be a direct ownership, fee-ownership, or co-ownership of the property, as well as any leasehold or option to acquire the property. An interest in U.S. real property does not include an interest in U.S. real property held solely as a creditor.

An interest in U.S. real property also includes any indirect ownership interest through a U.S. real property holding corporation (USRPHC). A corporation is a USRPHC if the fair market value of its U.S. real property interests is at least 50 percent of the fair market value of all of its real property interests and any other property used in its business. For this purpose, a corporation is considered to own a proportionate share of the assets held through a partnership, trust or estate, as well as a domestic or foreign corporation in which it holds a controlling interest. Whether a corporation is a USRPHC is generally determined the last day of the corporation's tax year, the date on which the corporation acquires a U.S. real property interest, *and* the date on which the corporation disposes of a real property interest located outside the United States or disposes of other assets used in a trade or business during the calendar year (Code Sec. 897(c); Reg. § 1.897-2).[47]

A U.S. real property interest does not include any interest in a corporation if as of the date of disposition, the corporation has already disposed of all of its U.S. real property interests in a transaction in which it recognized gain (the cleansing rule). In addition, if a corporation has a class of stock that is regularly traded on an established securities market, then such stock will be treated as a U.S. real property interest only in the hands of a taxpayer who owns more than five percent of the total fair market value of that class of stock

Dispositions Other Than by Sale. If a foreign corporation distributes a U.S. real property interest with respect to its stock, then the corporation will recognize gain (but not loss) to the extent that the fair market value of the property at the time of distribution exceeds its adjusted basis (Code Sec. 897(d); Temporary Reg. § 1.897-5T(c)).[48] However, a foreign corporation may avoid recognizing gain if, at the time of the distribution, the distributee would be subject to U.S. taxation on a subsequent disposition of the property and if the distributed property in the hands of the distributee is no greater than its carryover basis increased by any amount of gain recognized by the distributing corporation. The foreign corporation is required to file a U.S. income tax return to report the distribution, even if it has no tax liability. A foreign corporation may also avoid or at least limit the amount of gain recognized with regard to distributions in certain parent-subsidiary liquidations and reorganizations (Code Sec. 897(e)).

Investment Entities. Generally, any distribution by a qualified investment entity to a nonresident alien, foreign corporation, or other qualified investment entity will, to the extent attributable to gain from the sale or exchange of a U.S. real property interest, be treated as gain from the sale or exchange of a U.S. real property interest (Code Sec. 897(h)).[49] For purposes of this look-through rule, a qualified investment entity includes any real estate investment trust (REIT) (¶ 2326) and any mutual fund (regulated investment company, ¶ 2301) that is a USRPHC. However, in determining whether a mutual fund is a USRPHC, the regularly traded stock exception in defining a USRPHC (see above) will not apply. In addition, the mutual fund must include its interest in any other domestically controlled REIT or mutual fund that is a USRPHC.

The look-through rule will not apply to any distribution from the qualified investment entity with respect to a class of stock that is regularly traded on an established securities market in the United States if the foreign distributee did not own more than five percent of the class of stock at any time within one year of the distribution. To the

---

Footnote references are to paragraphs of the 2008 Standard Federal Tax Reports.

[47] ¶ 27,700, ¶ 27,702   [48] ¶ 27,700, ¶ 27,706   [49] ¶ 27,700

¶2442

extent this exception applies, the distribution from the qualified investment entity will be treated as a dividend, and not as effectively connected income.

Similarly, an interest in a domestically controlled qualified investment entity will not be treated as a U.S. real property interest and any gain from the sale of that interest by a qualified investment entity will not be passed through to a nonresident alien or foreign corporation. However, the gain will be passed through if a wash sale transaction is involved. For this purpose, a wash sale transaction is one in which: (1) the interest in a domestically controlled qualified investment entity is disposed of within 30 days prior to a distribution by the qualified entity that would be treated as gain from the sale or exchange of a U.S. real property interest; and (2) a substantially identical interest is reacquired within 61 days of the distribution.

Withholding. In order to ensure that foreign investors in U.S. real property interests will pay taxes on gain realized upon disposition, a withholding tax is imposed (Code Sec. 1445; Reg. § 1.1445-1).[50] Generally, the transferee of any U.S. real property interest is required to withhold and deduct a tax equal to 10 percent of the amount realized by the foreign person-transferor. The withholding rate may be as high as 35 percent in the case of a distribution made by a qualified investment entity with respect to gain from the disposition of a U.S. real property interest. In either case, if the transferee fails to withhold the required tax, the transferor may be held liable for the tax. The tax must be reported on Form 8288 or 8288-A and must be transmitted to the IRS within 20 days of the transfer of the property.

2444. Deductions and Tax Credits. Nonresident aliens and foreign corporations are generally permitted allowable deductions and tax credits to the extent to which gross income is effectively connected with the conduct of a U.S. trade or business (Code Secs. 873, 874 and 882(c)).[51] This includes the credit (¶ 2475) for foreign taxes paid or accrued on income effectively connected with the conduct with a U.S. trade or business. In addition, the limits that apply to the foreign tax credit for U.S. citizens, resident aliens and corporations also apply to nonresident aliens and foreign corporations (¶ 2479) (Code Sec. 906).[52] Both nonresident aliens and foreign corporations are permitted to deduct charitable contributions, regardless of whether income is effectively connected with a U.S. trade or business. In addition, nonresident aliens may also deduct one personal exemption (with certain exceptions) and casualty or theft losses (so long as the property is located in the United States).

As a prerequisite to claiming allowable deductions and credits, a nonresident alien or foreign corporation must file an accurate and timely return of the taxpayer's effectively connected income (Code Secs. 874(a) and 882(c)(2)).[53] Any deduction or credit claimed may not be used to offset other U.S.-source income. In addition, expenses relating to both U.S. and foreign-source income must be apportioned. If a return is not filed, then the IRS may prepare one for the taxpayer but no deductions and credits will be allowed other than the credit for withheld taxes or for federal excise taxes on gasoline and special fuels.

2447. Withholding on Payments to Foreign Taxpayers. Foreign taxpayers are generally subject to a flat 30-percent tax on U.S.-source income that is *not* effectively connected with the conduct of a U.S. trade or business (¶ 2425). However, to ensure collection and payment of the tax, a withholding agent must withhold 30 percent of the gross amount paid to a foreign taxpayer which is subject to tax (Code Secs. 1441 and 1442).[54] A lower withholding rate may apply to scholarship or fellowship grants, gross investment income, and dispositions of U.S. real property interests. A tax treaty may also reduce the rate of withholding (¶ 2462).

Persons Subject to Withholding. Only income of a foreign taxpayer is subject to these withholding rules. A foreign taxpayer includes any nonresident alien, including a bona fide resident of Puerto Rico or an alien resident of Guam, the Northern Mariana Islands, the U.S. Virgin Islands and American Samoa (Reg. § 1.1441-1(c)).[55] A nonresident alien

---

Footnote references are to paragraphs of the 2008 Standard Federal Tax Reports.

[50] ¶ 32,780, ¶ 32,781	[52] ¶ 27,920	[54] ¶ 32,702, ¶ 32,720
[51] ¶ 27,360, ¶ 27,363, ¶ 27,500	[53] ¶ 27,363, ¶ 27,500	[55] ¶ 32,703

who elects resident status for income tax purposes (¶ 2409) will still be considered a foreign taxpayer for withholding purposes. A foreign taxpayer will include foreign corporations, partnerships, estates, trusts and the foreign branch of U.S. financial institutions in certain circumstances.

Income Subject to Withholding. Income is subject to the withholding requirement if it is from sources within the United States and is fixed or determinable periodic income (¶ 2431). If the source of the income cannot be determined at the time of payment (¶ 2427), it will be treated as being from sources within the United States (Reg. § 1.1441-2(a)).[56] In addition, income payable for personal services performed in the United States will be treated as from sources within the United States, regardless of where the location of the contract, place of payment or residence of payer. Income effectively connected with the conduct of a U.S. trade or business is not subject to the withholding requirement, including income received as wages (¶ 2429). Instead, such income is generally subject to the tax and withholding rules as if the foreign taxpayer were a U.S. citizen, resident or domestic entity (see ¶ 2601 and following). However, special rules apply to the effectively connected income of a partnership (foreign or domestic) that is allocable to its foreign partners (Code Sec. 1446).[57]

Withholding Agent. The withholding agent is the person or entity required to deduct, withhold and pay any tax on income paid to a foreign taxpayer (Reg. § 1.1441-7).[58] This duty is imposed on all persons (acting in whatever capacity) that have the control, receipt, custody, disposal or payment of any items of income which are subject to withholding. Thus, the withholding agent may be any individual, corporation, partnership, trust, or other entity (including a foreign intermediary or partnership). A withholding agent may designate an authorized agent on its behalf. However, the withholding agent is personally liable for any tax required to be withheld except in the case of certain conduit financing arrangements (Code Sec. 1461).[59] This liability is independent of the tax liability of the foreign taxpayer for whom any income is paid. Even if the foreign taxpayer pays the tax, the withholding agent may still be liable for any interest, penalties or additions for failure to withhold (Code Sec. 1463).[60] A refund or credit of any overpayment is made to the withholding agent unless the tax was actually withheld (Code Sec. 1464).[61] The withholding agent is indemnified against any person claiming any tax properly withheld.

A withholding agent will not be required to withhold any amount if the payee is a U.S. person or a person that may be treated as the beneficial owner of the payment (Reg. § 1.1441-1).[62] Absent actual knowledge (or reason to know), the withholding agent must obtain valid documentation from the payee that it is either a U.S. payee or beneficial owner. Generally, a U.S. payee is any person required to furnish Form W-9. While such persons are not subject to withholding as a foreign taxpayer, they may be subject to Form 1099 reporting and withholding requirements. A beneficial owner is any person or entity that is required to furnish Form W-8BEN, Form W-8ECI or Form W-8EXP. Payment to an intermediary (whether qualified or not), flow-through entity or U.S. branch of a foreign entity may be treated as a U.S. payee for these purposes so long as valid documentation is provided on Form W-8IMY. In all cases in which valid documentation cannot be provided, the withholding agent may presume a person to be a U.S. payee or beneficial owner only under specified rules.

Returns. Every withholding agent must file an annual information return on Form 1042-S to report income paid to a foreign taxpayer during the tax year that is subject to withholding (unless an exception applies) (Reg. § § 1.1461-1 and 1.6302-2).[63] A separate Form 1042-S must be filed for each recipient, as well as for each type of income that is paid to the same recipient. Form 1042 is used by the withholding agent to report and pay the withholding taxes. Both forms must be filed regardless of whether or not taxes were required to be withheld. The forms must generally be filed by March 15 of the year following the year in which the income was paid. The amount of tax required to be

---

Footnote references are to paragraphs of the 2008 Standard Federal Tax Reports.

[56] ¶ 32,704	[59] ¶ 32,820	[62] ¶ 32,703
[57] ¶ 32,800	[60] ¶ 32,860	[63] ¶ 32,821, ¶ 38,062
[58] ¶ 32,714	[61] ¶ 32,880	

¶2447

withheld will determine whether the withholding agent must deposit the taxes prior to the due date for filing the returns and how frequently such amounts must be deposited. Penalties may be imposed for failure to file, to provide complete and correct information, as well as for failure to pay any taxes.

2451. Entry, Departure or Change of Residence During Tax Year. An alien who establishes or abandons U.S. residence during the tax year is taxable for that year as if it comprised two separate periods—one as a resident alien and one as a nonresident alien. For the period of nonresidence, the alien need not include any income from sources outside the United States unless that income is effectively connected with a U.S. trade or business (¶ 2429). Income not effectively connected with a U.S. trade or business is subject to the flat 30 percent rate (or lower treaty rate).

For the period of residence, an alien is subject to all taxes in the same manner as a U.S. citizen (Reg. § 1.871-13).[64] This includes one personal exemption and any additional exemptions to the extent that the amount claimed for the exemptions does not exceed the taxable income of the individual for the period of residency. Residency status for a tax year begins on the earlier date of when the lawful permanent residence test or substantial presence test is satisfied (¶ 2409) (Reg. § 301.7701(b)-4).[65] If the individual was a resident alien in the previous tax year, then residency begins on the first day of the current tax year. Residency status may terminate before the end of the tax year under either the lawful permanent residence test or substantial presence test, but only if the alien is not a U.S. resident at any time during the following tax year.

Generally, no alien (whether resident or nonresident) is permitted to depart the United States or any of its possessions without first obtaining a certificate of compliance from the IRS (sailing or departure permit). The certificate is proof that the individual has discharged all of his or her U.S. income tax liability (Code Sec. 6851(d); Reg. § 1.6851-2).[66] The certificate must be obtained at least two weeks before the individual leaves the United States. Resident aliens (whether they have taxable income or not for the tax year) and nonresident aliens having no taxable income for the tax year must file Form 2063 to obtain the certificate of compliance. Nonresident aliens with taxable income for the tax year must file Form 1040C to obtain the certificate of compliance. The forms do not constitute an individual's final tax return and Form 1040 or Form 1040NR must still be filed after the individual's tax year ends. Payment of any tax is not required prior to departure if it is determined that tax collection will not be jeopardized by the alien's departure. Individuals, who abandon U.S. citizenship or long-term residency for tax avoidance purposes are subject to special rules (¶ 2457).

2453. Foreign Student or Exchange Visitor. A nonresident alien individual who is not otherwise engaged in a U.S. trade or business but who is temporarily present in the United States under immigration laws as a visiting student, teacher, trainee, or specialist will be considered to be engaged in a U.S. business (Code Sec. 871(c)).[67] This means that any portion of a scholarship or fellowship grant from U.S. sources (including incidental expenses) that is not excludable from gross income (¶ 879) will be considered as income effectively connected with the conduct of a U.S. trade or business (¶ 2429). Such income will also be subject to a special withholding rate of 14 percent (Code Sec. 1441(b); Reg. § 1.1441-4(c)).[68] Compensation paid by a foreign employer to a person in the United States as an exchange student or visitor described above are exempt from tax (Code Sec. 872(b)(3)).[69]

2455. Foreign Ship or Aircraft. U.S.-source earnings of a foreign ship or aircraft are exempt from U.S. taxation if that exemption is available to foreign persons who reside in a country that grants a U.S. citizen or corporation an equivalent exemption (Code Sec. 872(b)).[70]

2457. Expatriation to Avoid Income Tax. An individual who gives up U.S. citizenship or long-term residence within the preceding 10 years will be subject to U.S. income

---

Footnote references are to paragraphs of the 2008 Standard Federal Tax Reports.

[64] ¶ 27,341
[65] ¶ 43,120
[66] ¶ 40,402, ¶ 40,405

[67] ¶ 27,320
[68] ¶ 32,702, ¶ 32,708
[69] ¶ 27,344

[70] ¶ 27,344

and alternative minimum taxation in the current tax year as if they are a U.S. citizen or resident alien (Code Sec. 877).[71] The taxes, however, will only be imposed if the amount of liability is greater than the amount of U.S. taxes imposed under the rules for nonresident aliens (¶ 2425). If the taxes are imposed, gross income includes any U.S.-source income and income, despite its source, that is effectively connected with the conduct of a U.S. trade or business. For this purpose, special source rules may apply that would recharacterize foreign-source income as U.S.-source income (¶ 2427). Deductions are allowed to the extent that they are allocable to the gross income subject to tax, with an exception that allows for casualty losses for property located in the United States, charitable contributions and one personal exemption. Although a capital loss carryover is not available, losses are allowed if income from the transaction would be included when determining tax liability.

For an individual who expatriates after June 3, 2004, the expatriation tax will not apply (and the individual will be taxed as a nonresident alien) if the individual: (1) for the calendar year 2007, had average annual net income tax liability in excess of $136,000 for the five-year period preceding the date of loss of citizenship ($139,000 for calendar year 2008); (2) had a net worth of $2 million or more on the date of loss of citizenship; or (3) fails to certify under penalties of perjury that he has complied with all U.S. tax obligations for the preceding five tax years (Code Sec. 877(a) and (c); Rev. Proc. 2006-53). Dual citizens or minors may be excepted from these requirements.

An individual will continue to be taxed as a U.S. citizen or resident alien (rather than taxed as an expatriate) if he or she is present in the United States for more than 30 days in any calendar year during the 10-year period following termination of citizenship or residency (Code Sec. 877(g)).[72] For this purpose, an individual is treated as present in the United States on any day that he or she is physically present in the United States at any time during that day. However, a day of physical presence is disregarded if the individual is performing services in the United States for an unrelated employer, has certain ties to countries other than the United States, is unable to leave the United States because of a medical condition that arose while present in the United States, or because the person was an exempt individual (teachers, trainees, students, and certain professional athletes).

Expatriation Act. An individual who would otherwise cease to be treated as a U.S. citizen or long-term resident under these rules will nonetheless continue to be taxed as a U.S. citizen or long-term resident until he or she gives notice of an expatriating act (with the requisite intent to relinquish citizenship or residency) (Code Secs. 6039G and 7701(n)).[73] The notice must be provided to the U.S. Secretary of State in the case of a U.S. citizen, and to the U.S. Secretary of Homeland Security in the case of a long-term resident. In addition to the notice, the expatriate must file an information return on Form 8854 in each tax year that the expatriation rules apply to the individual.

Expatriation Before June 4, 2004. For individuals who expatriate on or before June 4, 2004, the alternative expatriate tax regime will apply only if the primary purpose of giving up U.S. citizenship or long-term residency was the avoidance of U.S. taxation. A tax avoidance purpose is presumed if: (1) the individual's annual net income tax for the five years preceding the date of loss of citizenship exceeds $124,000 (for 2004) or (2) the individual's net worth on the date of loss of citizenship was at least $622,000 (for 2004). Individuals may rebut this presumption (and the tax will not apply) only if they submit a complete ruling request in good faith.

2462. Tax Treaties. The United States has negotiated a network of tax treaties with other countries to avoid the double taxation of taxpayers on the same income and to prevent taxpayers from evading taxation. In addition, the United States has enacted strict anti-abuse rules to prevent individual's from treaty shopping and incorporated exchange of information clauses in many tax treaties to facilitate the enforcement of these rules. These anti-abuse rules deny treaty benefits to nonresidents of either the United States or its treaty partner that funnel income through the treaty country only to take advantage of reduced tax rates.

Footnote references are to paragraphs of the 2008 Standard Federal Tax Reports.

[71] ¶ 27,420   [72] ¶ 27,420   [73] ¶ 35,692, ¶ 43,080

Generally, the Code is to be applied to a taxpayer with "due regard" to treaty obligations of the United States (Code Sec. 894).[74] However, in instances where a U.S. taxpayer takes the position that a treaty overrules or modifies the Code or regulations, disclosure of the position must generally be made with the taxpayer's tax return on Form 8833 (Code Sec. 6114; Reg. § 301.6114-1).[75] If a return is not otherwise required to be filed, a return must nevertheless be filed for purposes of making the required disclosure. The determination whether a treaty-based return position is required to be reported is made by comparing the taxpayer's tax liability under current law to that same tax liability as it would exist if the relevant treaty positions did not exist. Any difference must be reported. Failure to disclose the difference may result in a penalty (Code Sec. 6712).[76]

Tax treaties between the United States and foreign countries generally reduce the tax rate for income paid. Some countries will allow the withholding of tax at the treaty-reduced rate. Other countries, however, withhold tax at their statutory tax rate and refund any difference with the treaty-reduced rate upon receiving proof of residency. To apply for certification of U.S. residency to receive the benefits under a tax treaty, a taxpayer must file Form 8802 at least 30 days before the certificate is needed. If the application is approved, the IRS will provide the residency certification to the taxpayer on Form 6166. A nonresident alien or foreign corporation is not entitled under any U.S. income tax treaty to any reduced rate of withholding tax on an item of income derived through an entity treated as a partnership (or other fiscally transparent entity) if:

- the income is not treated by the treaty partner as an item of income of such foreign person;

- the foreign country does not impose tax on a distribution of the item by the U.S. entity to the foreign person; and

- the treaty does not contain a provision addressing its applicability in the case of an item of income derived through a partnership (Code Sec. 894(c)).[77]

2465. Corporate Inversions. Effective for tax years ending after March 4, 2003, special rules apply for the tax treatment of corporate inversion transactions. Generally, an inversion transaction is where a U.S. corporation reincorporates in a foreign jurisdiction and thereby replaces the U.S. parent corporation of a multinational corporate group with a foreign parent corporation. Inversion transactions may take many different forms, including stock inversions, asset inversions, and various combinations. In any case, if former shareholders of a U.S. corporation hold 80 percent or more (by vote or value) of the stock of a foreign corporation after the transaction, the foreign corporation will be treated as a domestic corporation for U.S. tax purposes (Code Sec. 7874).[78] If the former shareholders hold at least 60 percent but less than 80 percent of the stock of the foreign corporation after the transaction, then the taxable income of the expatriated entity during the applicable period cannot be less than the inversion gain.

Taxation of U.S. Export Companies

2468. Domestic International Sales Corporations. Prior to 1985, a company which generated income from the sale of exports was permitted to defer the taxation of income through the use of a domestic international sale corporation (DISC). DISCs were basically domestic subsidiaries that would sell products manufactured in the United States to customers in foreign countries. The income generated by the DISC would not be taxed until paid back to the parent company in the form of dividends. The DISC rules were replaced with the foreign sales corporation (FSC) rules (¶ 2470). However, a DISC geared toward small businesses may still exist if the income deferred by shareholders is limited and any interest charge is paid on such deferred amounts (Code Sec. 995).[79] The election to be treated as an interest-charge DISC is made on Form 4876A.

2470. Foreign Sales Corporations. The foreign sales corporation (FSC) rules were enacted in 1985 to gradually replace domestic international sales corporations (DISCs)

Footnote references are to paragraphs of the 2008 Standard Federal Tax Reports.

[74] ¶ 27,640	[76] ¶ 40,135	[78] ¶ 43,969
[75] ¶ 37,060, ¶ 37,061	[77] ¶ 27,640	[79] ¶ 29,020

(¶ 2468). Like DISCs, the FSC rules were designed to promote the export of U.S.-manufactured products by allowing a percentage of an FSC's income earned from the sale of qualified export property to be exempt from U.S. tax (Code Secs. 921 through 927, prior to repeal by P.L. 106-519).[80] Further, corporate FSC shareholders were entitled to a 100-percent dividends received deduction on dividends attributable to exempt and after-tax nonexempt FSC income. The FSC rules, however, were repealed and no corporation may elect to be an FSC after September 30, 2000 (see, however, ¶ 2471). Transactions occurring in the ordinary course of trade or business before January 1, 2002, or after December 31, 2001, that were engaged in pursuant to a binding contract between a taxpayer and an unrelated party which was itself in effect on September 30, 2000, are not eligible for transitional relief from the repeal of the FSC rules (Act Sec. 513(a) of the Tax Increase Prevention and Reconciliation Act of 2005 (P.L. 109-222)).

2471. Extraterritorial Income Exclusion. Effective for transactions that arise after September 30, 2000, a U.S. taxpayer may exclude from gross income extraterritorial income to the extent that is "qualifying foreign trade income" (Code Sec. 114, prior to repeal by the American Jobs Creation Act of 2004 (P.L. 108-357)).[81] The exclusion is generally repealed for tax years beginning after 2004. However, a gradual phaseout will occur for tax years prior to 2007. For transactions occurring in 2005, taxpayers may exclude 80 percent of their extraterritorial income from their gross income. For transactions occurring in 2006, taxpayers may exclude 60 percent of their ETI from their gross income. Furthermore, in tax years after 2004 and beginning before May 18, 2006, the ETI exclusion remains in effect for transactions that occur in the ordinary course of a trade or business pursuant to a binding contract between the taxpayer and an unrelated person that was in effect on September 17, 2003.

Generally, qualifying foreign trade income is defined as the amount of gross income which, if excluded, would reduce the taxpayer's taxable income by the greater of: 30 percent of foreign sale and lease income; 1.2 percent of foreign trading gross receipts; or 15 percent of foreign trade income (Code Sec. 941(a), prior to repeal by the American Jobs Creation Act of 2004 (P.L. 108-357)).[82] Expenses attributable to excluded ETI are not allowed as deductions, thus taxpayers must allocate expenses between excluded and nonexcluded foreign trade income. In addition, no foreign tax credit will be allowed for any foreign income taxes paid or accrued with respect to excluded ETI. All taxpayers that claim the extraterritorial income exclusion must attach Form 8873 to their income tax return to determine the amount to be excluded from gross income.

Foreign Tax Credit or Deduction

2475. Foreign Tax Credit or Deduction. Subject to certain limitations (¶ 2479), a U.S. taxpayer is allowed a credit or deduction against U.S. income and alternative minimum tax liability for certain taxes imposed by foreign countries and possessions of the United States (Code Sec. 901; Reg. § 1.901-1).[83] The credit or deduction is intended to relieve U.S. taxpayers of double taxation on foreign-source income. The credit or deduction must be claimed for all creditable foreign taxes paid or accrued during the tax year for which a U.S. return is required (¶ 2477). Partial credits and deductions are not permitted except in limited circumstances (Code Sec. 275(a)(4)).[84] For example, foreign taxes that are otherwise deductible (foreign real property taxes) may still be deducted even if the credit is claimed. A taxpayer on the cash method of accounting may elect to claim a credit for foreign taxes in the year they accrue. Once made, however, the election is irrevocable for the current and all later tax years.

Generally, it is more advantageous to take the credit because it is taken against a taxpayer's U.S. liability on a dollar-for-dollar basis. In contrast, a deduction for foreign taxes merely reduces a taxpayer's income subject to tax. In addition, an individual who deducts foreign taxes must claim the taxes as an itemized deduction. A taxpayer claims the foreign tax credit by filing Form 1116 (for individuals) or Form 1118 (for corpora-

---

Footnote references are to paragraphs of the 2008 Standard Federal Tax Reports.

[80] ¶ 28,080
[81] ¶ 7105
[82] ¶ 28,400
[83] ¶ 27,820, ¶ 27,821
[84] ¶ 14,500

¶2471

tions) with the taxpayer's income tax return. An election to take the credit or deduction on a joint return applies to the qualifying foreign taxes paid or accrued by both spouses. If married taxpayers file separate returns, either may take the credit or deduction without regard to the other.

Individuals may elect to claim the foreign tax credit without filing Form 1116 but instead by entering the credit directly on their tax return. To be eligible to make this election: (1) all of the taxpayer's foreign source income must be passive income; (2) all of the income and any foreign taxes paid on it was reported on a qualified payee statement (Form 1099); and (3) the total creditable foreign taxes are less than $300 ($600 for joint filers). If a taxpayer makes an election to report their foreign tax credit this way, then the foreign tax credit limitations will not apply (¶ 2479). However, the taxpayer cannot carryover any credit to another tax year. This election is not available to corporations, estates or trusts.

The election to claim the credit or deduction for creditable foreign taxes must be made each tax year. It may be exercised or changed at any time while the statute of limitations to claim any refund or credit remains open for the year in question (Code Sec. 6511(d)(3); Reg. § 1.901-1(d) and (e)).[85] Generally, this is three years from the time the return was filed or two years from the time the tax was paid, whichever is later. However, in the case of an overpayment resulting from a credit for foreign taxes, a claim for credit or refund may be filed within 10 years from the time the return is filed or two years from the time the tax is paid, whichever is later. For a partnership, the election is made by the individual partners. An election made on a joint return generally applies to the foreign taxes of both spouses.

Taxpayers entitled to claim the foreign tax credit include: U.S. citizens, domestic corporations, resident aliens (including bona fide residents of Puerto Rico for the entire tax year (¶ 2415)), and nonresident aliens and foreign corporations with respect to foreign taxes paid or accrued on foreign-source income effectively connected with the conduct of a U.S. trade or business (¶ 2429). A taxpayer who is a partner in a partnership, shareholder in an S corporation, or beneficiary of an estate or trust may claim the credit or deduction with respect to the taxpayer's proportionate share of creditable foreign taxes paid or accrued by the entity (Code Secs. 901(b) and (c)).[86] Similarly, a shareholder of a mutual fund may be able to claim the credit or deduction based on the shareholder's share of creditable foreign taxes paid by the fund that it chooses to pass through.

2477. Creditable Foreign Taxes. A U.S. taxpayer is allowed a credit or deduction (¶ 2475) against U.S. income and alternative minimum tax liability for any income, war profits, and excess profits taxes paid or accrued during the tax year (as well as taxes paid or accrued in lieu of these taxes) to any foreign country or U.S. possession (Code Secs. 901 and 903; Reg. § 1.901-2).[87] To be creditable, a foreign tax must be a levy the predominant character of which is that of a compulsory income tax according to U.S. tax principles. Penalties, fines, interest, customs duties and similar obligations are not taxes for this purpose. A payment to a foreign government in exchange for a specific economic benefit is also not considered a creditable tax. A economic benefit is any good, service, fee, right or discharge of an obligation that is not available on substantially the same terms to all persons subject to income taxes in the foreign country. A foreign tax paid for retirement, unemployment, or disability benefits is generally not a payment for a specific economic benefit. However, no credit or deduction is allowed for social security taxes paid or accrued to a foreign country with which the United States has a social security agreement.

The foreign tax credit or deduction is not available for the withholding of creditable foreign taxes unless certain minimum holding period requirements are met. In order to claim the credit for foreign withholding taxes paid with respect to a dividend or any other item of gain or income (other than a dividend) from property, the taxpayer must hold the underlying stock or property for: (1) 16 days within the 31-day period beginning 15 days before the ex-dividend date (the date the right to receive payment arises), or (2)

Footnote references are to paragraphs of the 2008 Standard Federal Tax Reports.

[85] ¶ 39,060, ¶ 27,821   [86] ¶ 27,820   [87] ¶ 27,820, ¶ 27,822, ¶ 27,860

to the extent that the recipient is under an obligation to make related payments with respect to positions in substantially similar or related property (Code Sec. 901(k) and 901(l)). In the case of preferred stock with dividends attributable to periods aggregating more than 366 days, the holding period is 46 days within the 91-day period beginning 45 days before the ex-dividend date. These holding period requirements do not apply for any property held in a foreign country in the active conduct of a business of the taxpayer as a dealer in such property.

A U.S. taxpayer may not claim the foreign tax credit or deduction for any foreign taxes paid or accrued on income excluded from U.S. gross income. This includes income excluded under the foreign earned income or foreign housing exclusions (¶ 2402), extraterritorial income (¶ 2471), or income from a U.S. possession (¶ 2410 and ¶ 2415). The taxpayer may also not claim a credit or deduction for taxes paid or accrued to the extent that: the taxpayer is certain to receive a refund or credit or the tax is used as a subsidy; the liability is dependent on the availability of a foreign tax credit in another jurisdiction; the taxes are paid or accrued to a country with which the United States does not conduct diplomatic relations or which is designated as supporting acts of international terrorism; or the taxes are attributable to boycott income (¶ 2496). Special rules also apply to taxes on certain oil and mineral income.

2479. Foreign Tax Credit Limitations. In determining the amount of the foreign tax credit to claim, a taxpayer is subject to an overall limitation that prevents using the credit to reduce U.S. income tax liability on U.S.-source income. The total amount of a taxpayer's foreign tax credit may not exceed the taxpayer's entire U.S. income tax liability (determined without regard to the credit) multiplied by a fraction equal to the taxpayer's foreign-source taxable income over taxable income from all sources (Code Sec. 904(a)).[88] The limitation, however, must be calculated separately for certain categories of foreign source income (¶ 2481). Accordingly, taxable income from each category of foreign source income must be determined. Special rules also apply if the taxpayer has an overall foreign loss (¶ 2483).

Taxable income is the taxpayer's gross income less any applicable deductions that relate to the particular source of income. In the case of an individual, estate or trust, the deduction for personal exemptions is not allowed in computing taxable income (Code Sec. 904(b)). In addition, the individual's U.S. tax liability must be reduced by the sum of the nonrefundable personal credits (see ¶ 1301 and following) prior to application of the foreign tax credit. However, for tax years beginning 2000 through 2006, the foreign tax credit may be applied against the taxpayer's U.S. tax liability before application of the nonrefundable personal credits (Code Sec. 904(i)). In the case of a corporation, taxable income does not include any portion of income taken into account for purposes of the possession tax credit (¶ 2419).

De minimis Exemption. An individual with $300 or less of creditable foreign taxes ($600 if married filing jointly) will be exempt from the foreign tax credit limitation, provided they have no foreign-source income other than qualified passive income (Code Sec. 904(k)). The exemption is not automatic. To qualify, an individual must elect to take the exemption for the tax year directly on Form 1040 (see also ¶ 2475).

U.S.-Owned Foreign Corporations. Certain amounts derived from U.S.-owned foreign corporations may be treated as U.S.-source income for purposes of the foreign tax credit limitation including interest, dividends, subpart F inclusions (¶ 2487), and amounts currently taxed under the qualified electing fund rules (Code Sec. 904(h); Reg. § 1.904-5).[89] Generally, interest and subpart F inclusions are treated as U.S.-source income to the extent such amounts are attributable to the U.S.-source income of the U.S.-owned foreign corporation. Dividends are generally treated as U.S.-source income in proportion to the U.S.-source earnings and profits of the U.S.-owned foreign corporation. These rules will not apply if less than 10 percent of the corporation's earnings and profits for the tax year are earnings and profits attributable to sources within the United States. For this purpose, a "U.S.-owned foreign corporation" is any foreign corporation if 50 percent or more of the total combined voting power of all classes of stock in the

---

Footnote references are to paragraphs of the 2008 Standard Federal Tax Reports.

[88] ¶ 27,880   [89] ¶ 27,880, ¶ 27,886

corporation entitled to vote, or the total value of the stock of the corporation, is held by U.S. persons. The IRS has been authorized to issue regulations that would require taxpayers to source the income of any member of an affiliated group of corporations, or to modify the consolidated return regulations, to the extent necessary to prevent avoidance of the foreign tax credit limitation rules (Code Sec. 904(j)).[90]

Carryover. When the amount of creditable foreign taxes paid or accrued by a taxpayer during the tax year exceeds the limitation for that year, the excess may generally be carried back one year and then carried forward ten years. (Code Sec. 904(c); Reg. § 1.904-2(d)).[91] The one-year carryback period applies to excess foreign tax credits arising in tax years beginning after October 22, 2004. The 10-year carryforward period applies to excess credits carried to any tax year ending after October 22, 2004. A two-year carryback period applies to excess foreign tax credits arising in tax years beginning on or before October 22, 2004. A five-year carryforward period applies to excess credits carried to any tax year ending on or before October 22, 2004. The amount that may be carried back and forward is limited to the amount by which the credit limitation in the carryback or forward year exceeds the amount of foreign taxes paid or accrued in that year. In addition, any excess credits must be carried back and forward to their own separate basket of income (¶ 2481). A foreign tax credit in one income category can only be carried back and forward to that same category in another tax year. It cannot offset other taxes imposed on income in another basket.

A carryback to a year in which foreign taxes were deducted rather than credited may reduce the remaining carryover without resulting in a refund. A taxpayer may belatedly elect to claim a foreign tax credit for that carryback year in order to avoid this problem. For this purpose, the 10-year statute of limitations for filing a credit or refund is determined from the date for filing the taxpayer's return in which the foreign taxes were paid or accrued. In any event, the taxpayer must pay interest on any deficiency that is eliminated by a carryback (Code Sec. 6601(d)).[92] An individual electing the *de minimis* exemption may not carryback or carryforward any excess foreign taxes to an election year.

2481. Separate Limitations for Various Categories of Income. For tax years beginning after 2006, a taxpayer is required to compute the foreign tax credit limitation (¶ 2479) separately for two categories of income: passive income and general income. These categories are generally referred to as baskets (Code Sec. 904(d); Reg. § 1.904-4).[93] To determine taxable income in each basket, the taxpayer must allocate the expenses, losses, and other deductions that are definitely related to the income allocated to each basket. Similarly, the amount of foreign taxes paid or accrued that are related to one of the baskets may include only those taxes that are related to income in that basket. If a tax is related to both baskets, the taxpayer must apportion the tax. However, if creditable foreign taxes were imposed on amounts that do not constitute income under U.S. tax law ("base difference items"), then they will be treated as imposed on general category income.

Generally, any income that is not included in the passive income basket is considered part of the general income basket. Passive income for this purpose includes investment income such as dividends, interest, rents and royalties, as well as income from a qualified electing fund (¶ 2490). However, it does not include any rents or royalties that are derived in the active conduct of a trade or business, regardless of whether such rents or royalties are received from a related or an unrelated person. In addition, passive income does not include certain export financing interest and highly taxed income.

Look-through rules apply to U.S. shareholders of controlled foreign corporations (CFC) (¶ 2487) requiring that the shareholder's earnings be treated in the same manner in which the earnings would have been treated if they were held in their original form by the CFC (Code Sec. 904(d)(3); Reg. § 1.904-5). Earnings of a CFC to which this rule applies includes interest, Subpart F inclusions, rents or royalties, and dividends received

---

Footnote references are to paragraphs of the 2008 Standard Federal Tax Reports.

[90] ¶ 27,880
[91] ¶ 27,883

[92] ¶ 39,410
[93] ¶ 27,880, ¶ 27,885

or accrued. A *de minimis* exception to the look-through rules exists for income that is excluded from subpart F income. The exception applies if a CFC's base company income (without regard for allocable deductions), together with its gross insurance income, constitutes less than five percent of the corporation's gross income or $1 million. Under this exception, all of the foreign corporation's base company income and gross insurance income (other than income that would be financial services income) is treated as general limitation income.

Effective for tax years prior to 2007, a taxpayer was required to compute the foreign tax credit limitation separately for nine baskets of income. The baskets included: passive income; high-withholding tax interest; financial services income; shipping income; dividends received by a corporation from noncontrolled Code Sec. 902 corporations ("10/50 corporations"); certain dividends from domestic international sales corporations (DISC) (¶ 2468); foreign trade income (¶ 2471); certain distributions from foreign sales corporations (FSC) or former FSC (¶ 2470); and all other income not included in the above categories (general limitation income).

2483. Recapture of Foreign Losses. An overall foreign loss sustained in a tax year and used to offset U.S.-source income is subject to recapture in later tax years by recharacterizing some foreign-source income as U.S.-source income (Code Sec. 904(f)).[94] For this purpose, an overall foreign loss is the amount by which gross income from foreign sources is exceeded by the sum of expenses, losses and other deductions properly allocable to such income. Any net operating loss (NOL) deduction, foreign expropriation losses and uncompensated casualty or theft losses are not taken into account. The overall foreign loss must be determined for each separate foreign tax credit category or basket (¶ 2481). Thus, a taxpayer can have an overall foreign loss, a passive income foreign loss, or a general income foreign loss, in any given tax year. However, a taxpayer must allocate a foreign loss in one foreign tax credit basket to foreign taxable income in the other basket before allocating the loss to U.S.-source income and creating an overall foreign loss.

Generally, the amount of foreign-source income that must be recaptured and recharacterized as U.S.-source income is limited to the lesser of the taxpayer's overall foreign loss (to the extent not used in prior tax years) or 50 percent of the taxpayer's foreign-source taxable income for the tax year. However, if a taxpayer disposes of assets used in its trade or business predominantly outside the United States in a taxable disposition, or disposes of stock in a controlled foreign corporation (CFC) (¶ 2487) in which it owns more than 50 percent, then 100 percent of the gain must be recaptured. Fifty percent of the recognized gain is recaptured under the general rule above and the remainder recaptured to the extent of the taxpayer's overall foreign loss balance. Special recapture rules also apply if the disposition is nontaxable. For these purposes, property is considered used predominantly outside the United States if, during a three-year period ending on the date of disposition, the property was located outside the United States more than 50 percent of the time.

2485. Deemed Paid Credit. The foreign tax credit is available to a U.S. corporate shareholder that owns 10 percent or more of the voting stock in a foreign corporation from which it receives a dividend (or deemed to receive a dividend through an affiliated group or a partnership) (Code Sec. 902).[95] The amount of the "deemed paid" or "indirect credit" is determined by reference to the portion of the foreign corporation's post-1986 foreign income taxes that the dividend received by the domestic corporation bears to the foreign corporation's post-1986 undistributed earnings. A corporation electing to take the indirect credit must increase ("gross up") its tax base by including not only the dividend but the tax deemed paid by the foreign corporation (Code Sec. 78).[96] Additionally, the indirect credit is subject to the foreign tax credit limitation (¶ 2479).

The indirect credit is allowed to a domestic shareholder for foreign taxes paid by a lower-tier foreign corporation if the foreign corporation is a member of a qualified group and the foreign corporation owns 10 percent or more of the voting stock of the member of the qualified group from which it receives a dividend (Code Sec. 902(b)). A qualified

---

Footnote references are to paragraphs of the 2008 Standard Federal Tax Reports.

[94] ¶ 27,880   [95] ¶ 27,840   [96] ¶ 6350

¶2483

group includes any foreign corporation in a chain that includes the first-tier corporation and foreign corporations through the sixth-tier. However, a corporation below the third-tier will not be included in the qualified group unless it is a controlled foreign corporation (CFC) (¶ 2487) and the domestic corporation is a U.S. shareholder. Whether the ownership requirements are met is determined at the time dividends are received. However, a qualified group cannot aggregate their shares in a foreign corporation to meet the ownership requirements.

Shareholders of Foreign Corporations

2487. Controlled Foreign Corporation. A U.S. shareholder of a foreign corporation that is a "controlled foreign corporation" (CFC) for an uninterrupted period of 30 days or more during the tax year must include in gross income its proportionate share of the CFC's "Subpart F income" (whether distributed or not) (Code Sec. 951).[97] A foreign corporation is a CFC if more than 50 percent of its total voting power or value is owned by U.S. shareholders (Code Sec. 957).[98] A "U.S. shareholder" is any U.S. person (citizen, resident, domestic corporation, partnership, estate or trust) that owns 10 percent or more of the total combined voting power of the foreign corporation. Ownership may be direct, indirect, or constructive (¶ 743) with certain exceptions (Code Sec. 958).[99]

A U.S. taxpayer includes Subpart F income in gross income only if it is a shareholder on the last day of the CFC's tax year. However, the U.S. shareholder includes the Subpart F income from that portion of the year that the corporation qualifies as a CFC. The shareholder includes Subpart F income in gross income as a dividend (see ¶ 733). Actual distributions are excluded from gross income to the extent they have already been accounted for by the shareholder (Code Sec. 959).[100] To prevent double taxation, the earnings and profits of the corporation and the basis of the shareholder's shares must be adjusted accordingly. Thus, any Subpart F income includible in the shareholder's gross income is generally treated as a contribution to capital increasing the shareholder's basis (Code Sec. 961).[101] Similarly, the shareholder's basis is reduced if he receives a distribution that is excluded from gross income. Similar adjustments must be made in basis of stock of a lower-tiered CFC (or the basis of any other CFC stock) which the U.S. shareholder is considered owning.

A domestic corporation is allowed a foreign tax credit for any taxes paid by the CFC for income that is attributed or distributed to it as a U.S. shareholder (Code Sec. 960).[102] An individual U.S. shareholder may make a special election to be taxed as a domestic corporation for this purpose and thus be eligible for the foreign tax credit (Code Sec. 962).[103]

Includible Income. CFC income which is includible in a U.S. shareholder's gross income includes the shareholder's pro rata share of the corporation's Subpart F income and earnings deemed invested in U.S. property during the tax year (see also ¶ 2496A) (Code Secs. 951 and 956).[104] Subpart F income includes the sum of the corporation's insurance income, foreign base company income, as well as boycott income, illegal payments (¶ 2496A) and income from countries not diplomatically recognized by the U.S. government (Code Sec. 952).[105] A CFC's Subpart F income is limited for any tax year to its total earnings and profits for that year. Income will be included in gross income as subpart F income if either the foreign personal holding company rules (¶ 2488) or the passive foreign investment company (¶ 2490) rules apply. In addition, a U.S. person who is a qualified shareholder of an foreign investment company (¶ 2489) is not required to apply the subpart F inclusion rules to any income in which the company elected to distribute.

For the above purposes, subpart F insurance income is generally any income that is attributable to the issuance or reissuance of any insurance or annuity contract in connection with property in a country other than the one in which the CFC is created or organized, as well insurance life or health insurance of residents in any other country.

Footnote references are to paragraphs of the 2008 Standard Federal Tax Reports.

[97] ¶ 28,470	[100] ¶ 28,630	[103] ¶ 28,690
[98] ¶ 28,590	[101] ¶ 28,670	[104] ¶ 28,470, ¶ 28,570
[99] ¶ 28,610	[102] ¶ 28,650	[105] ¶ 28,490

¶2487

Effective for tax years before January 1, 2009, it generally does not include any insurance income from the insuring or reinsuring risks in the CFC's home country (Code Sec. 953(e)).[106]

Foreign base company income is made up of several categories of income including foreign personal holding company income (FPHCI). Generally, FPHCI is passive income such as dividends, interest, rent and royalty income. However, FPHCI does not include rents and royalties derived from a trade or business and received from a person other than a related person. Also, effective for tax years of a CFC beginning before January 1, 2009, FPHCI does not include certain income derived in the active conduct of a banking, financing or similar business, or in the conduct of an insurance business (i.e., active financing income) (Code Sec. 954(h) and (i)).[107] However, effective for tax years of CFCs beginning after December 31, 2005, and before January 1, 2009, dividends, rents and royalties received by one CFC from a related CFC will *not* be treated as FPHCI provided the payments are attributable and allocable to neither subpart F income nor income that is effectively connected to a U.S. trade or business (Code Sec. 954(c)).[108]

Sale or Exchange of CFC Stock. If a U.S. shareholder sells, exchanges or redeems stock in a CFC, any gain recognized will be included in the gross income of the taxpayer as an ordinary dividend to the extent of the foreign corporation's earnings and profits allocable to the stock (Code Sec. 1248).[109] Any gain exceeding such earnings and profits is treated as capital gain. The shareholder may claim a foreign tax credit for the taxes paid by the CFC on the income. However, the credit may be less than the indirect credit (¶ 2485) because it will not apply to as many tiers of foreign corporations.

Temporary Dividend Deduction. A corporation that is a U.S. shareholder of a CFC may elect to deduct from gross income an amount equal to 85 percent of the cash dividends received from a CFC during the tax year for which the election is in effect (Code Sec. 965(a)).[110] The election is valid only for taxpayer's last tax year that begins before October 22, 2004, or the first tax year that begins during the one-year period beginning on October 22, 2004. Numerous limitations apply to the deduction, and special rules apply for dividends paid indirectly from CFCs.

Returns. A U.S. citizen or resident who is an officer, director or 10-percent shareholder of a CFC is required to file with his income tax return an information return on Form 5471 (Code Sec. 6038).[111] Failure to timely file the required information may result in penalties and a reduced foreign tax credit. U.S. shareholders are also required to report acquisitions, reorganizations and dispositions of ownership interests in a CFC during the tax year (Code Sec. 6046).[112] U.S. shareholders of controlled foreign partnerships are also subject to these reporting requirements (Form 8865).

2488. Foreign Personal Holding Companies. The foreign personal holding company (FPHC) rules have been repealed for tax years of foreign corporations beginning after December 31, 2004, and tax years of U.S. shareholders whose tax year ends with or within which such tax years of foreign corporations end. Prior to repeal, a U.S. shareholder of a foreign corporation that was a FPHC had to include in gross income their proportionate share of undistributed FPHC income as an ordinary dividend (Code Sec. 551, prior to repeal by the American Jobs Creation Act of 2004 (P.L. 108-357)).[113] The earnings and profits of the company and the shareholder's basis was adjusted accordingly. A foreign corporation was a FPHC if at least 60 percent of its gross income generally consisted of passive income, including gains in stocks and other securities and more than 50 percent of its outstanding stock was owned by five or fewer U.S. citizens or residents. A U.S. citizen or resident who was an officer, director or 10-percent shareholder of a FPHC was required to file with his or her income tax return an information return on Form 5471 (Code Sec. 6035).[114] Failure to file the return, or filing an incomplete return, resulted in penalties (Code Sec. 6679).[115]

Footnote references are to paragraphs of the 2008 Standard Federal Tax Reports.

[106] ¶ 28,510
[107] ¶ 28,530
[108] ¶ 28,530
[109] ¶ 30,960
[110] ¶ 29,725
[111] ¶ 35,540
[112] ¶ 35,940
[113] ¶ 23,310
[114] ¶ 35,480
[115] ¶ 39,835

¶2488

2489. Foreign Investment Company. The rules relating to foreign investment companies have been repealed for tax years of foreign corporations beginning after December 31, 2004, and tax years of U.S. shareholders whose tax year ends with or within which such tax years of foreign corporation's end. Prior to repeal, any gain realized by a U.S. shareholder on the sale or exchange of stock held for at least one year in a foreign investment company was treated as ordinary income to the extent of the taxpayer's share of the company's earnings and profits accumulated in tax years beginning after 1962 (Code Sec. 1246, prior to repeal by the American Jobs Creation Act of 2004 (P.L. 108-357)).[116] A foreign investment company was any foreign corporation that was: (1) registered with the Securities and Exchange Commission as a management company or unit investment trust or (2) engaged (or holding itself out as being engaged) primarily in the business of investing, reinvesting or trading in securities, commodities or any interest at a time when 50 percent or more of its voting stock or total value was held by U.S. persons.

2490. Passive Foreign Investment Company. Generally, a U.S. shareholder of a passive foreign investment company (PFIC) who receives an "excess distribution" with respect to its stock or disposes of its PFIC stock during the tax year must allocate such income or gain ratably to each day they held the stock (Code Sec. 1291).[117] The amount allocated to current tax year or any prior tax year in which the corporation was not a PFIC is taxed as ordinary income. The amount allocated to any other year is taxed at the highest rate applicable for that year, plus interest from the due date for the taxpayer's return for that year. For this purpose, an excess distribution is any part of a distribution received from the PFIC which is greater than 125 percent of the average distribution received by the shareholder during the three preceding tax years. A PFIC is defined as any foreign corporation that derives at least 75 percent of its gross income for the tax year from passive investments or at least 50 percent of its average total assets held for the year produce passive income or are held for the production of passive income (Code Sec. 1297).[118]

Instead of paying the additional tax on deferrals, a U.S. shareholder of a PFIC may elect to treat the corporation as a "qualified electing fund" (QEF). Under such circumstances, the shareholder must include in gross income each year as ordinary income its pro rata share of earnings of the corporation, and as long-term capital gain, its pro rata share of the net capital gain of the corporation (Code Secs. 1293 and 1295).[119] The inclusions are made for the shareholder's tax year in which or with which the QEF's tax year ends. Once made, the QEF election is revocable only with the IRS's consent and is effective for the current tax year and all subsequent tax years. Under certain circumstances, the U.S. shareholder can elect to defer payment of the tax on any undistributed earnings (Code Sec. 1294).[120]

Another option that a U.S. shareholder of a PFIC may make to avoid the additional tax on the deferral of income is to make a mark-to-market election with respect to its PFIC stock that is marketable (Code Sec. 1296).[121] Under this election, the shareholder annually includes in gross income as ordinary income an amount equal to the excess of the fair market value of the PFIC stock as of the close of the tax year over its adjusted basis. If the stock has declined in value, an ordinary loss deduction is allowed limited to the net amount of gain previously included in income.

2491. Sale or Exchange of Patent, Etc. to Foreign Corporations. A U.S. person who controls a foreign corporation (at least 50 percent of voting power of all stock) directly or indirectly must recognize gain from the sale or exchange of a patent, invention, model, design, copyright, secret formula or process, or any other similar property right to the foreign corporation as ordinary income rather than capital gain (Code Sec. 1249).[122]

Footnote references are to paragraphs of the 2008 Standard Federal Tax Reports.

[116] ¶ 30,920
[117] ¶ 31,540
[118] ¶ 31,620

[119] ¶ 31,560, ¶ 31,600
[120] ¶ 31,580
[121] ¶ 31,610

[122] ¶ 30,980

2492. Reorganization Involving Foreign Corporations. Generally, the transfer of appreciated property to a corporation may not be taxable under the organization, reorganization and liquidation rules (¶ 2201 and following). However, to prevent a U.S. person from avoiding taxes by transferring property from the United States to a foreign corporation, a taxpayer will be required to recognize gain in what would otherwise be a tax-free transaction (Code Sec. 367).[123] Exceptions exist for assets which are to be used in an active trade or business, qualifying transfers of stock and securities, and tangible assets. Inventory and other noncapital assets denominated in foreign currency do not qualify for the exception. Additionally, a taxpayer who transfers intangible property will be deemed to receive royalty payments for the property. The payments create a super-royalty that is re-evaluated on an annual basis.

2493. Transfers to Foreign Trusts. When a U.S. person transfers property to a foreign trust with a U.S. beneficiary (determined on an annual basis), the U.S. person will be treated as the owner of the portion of the trust attributable to the property (Code Sec. 679; Reg. § 1.679-1).[124] If the transferor and another person would be treated as owner of the same portion of the trust, then the U.S. transferor will be treated as the owner. Thus, any income received by the trust with respect to the property is taxable to the transferor under the grantor trust rules (¶ 571 and following). This rule applies without regard to whether the transferor retains any power or interest in the property. It also applies regardless whether the transfer is direct or indirect. Exceptions exist for foreign trusts established by a will and transfers made by reason of death of a U.S. person. Additionally, the rule does not apply if the property is transferred to the foreign trust in exchange for consideration equal to its fair market value.

2494. Information Reporting on Foreign Partnerships. A number of reporting requirements apply with respect to foreign partnerships. A foreign partnership must file a return if it has gross income that is either U.S.-source income (¶ 2427) or income effectively connected with a U.S. trade or business (¶ 2429) (Code Sec. 6031(e)).[125] Also, a U.S. partner that controls a foreign partnership is required to file an annual information return on Form 5471 (¶ 2487). A U.S. person that is 10-percent partner in a foreign partnership must report the acquisition or disposition of an interest in the partnership or a change in his proportional interest in the partnership (Code Sec. 6046A).[126] Failure to file an information return for this purpose will result in a $10,000 penalty per occurrence (Code Sec. 6679).[127] Finally, U.S. persons must report the contribution of property to a foreign partnership (Code Sec. 6038B).[128]

International Boycotts, Illegal Payments, Records

2496. International Boycotts. Participation by a taxpayer in, or cooperation with, an international boycott may result in the reduction or denial of: available foreign tax credits (¶ 2475); the deferral of tax allowed to foreign subsidiaries (¶ 2485); the deferral of tax allowed to domestic international sales corporation (DISC) shareholders (¶ 2468); and the extraterritorial income exclusion for qualifying trade income (¶ 2471) (Code Sec. 999; Temporary Reg. § 7.999-1).[129] The amount of the benefits to be denied is determined from the ratio of the value of the sales or purchases of goods and services (or other transactions) arising from the boycott activity to the total value of the foreign sales or purchases of goods and services (or other transactions).

Participation in, or cooperation with, an international boycott occurs when a person, in order to do business in a certain country, agrees not to do business with a specified second country or with other countries doing business in specified countries. An agreement not to hire employees of, or to do business with, other companies whose employees are of a specified nationality, race or religion is also boycott activity. The following countries may require participation in, or cooperation with, an international boycott: Kuwait, Lebanon, Libya, Qatar, Saudi Arabia, Syria, United Arab Emirates and the Republic of Yemen.[130] The reduction of foreign tax credit extends to the credit that

---

Footnote references are to paragraphs of the 2008 Standard Federal Tax Reports.

[123] ¶ 16,640	[126] ¶ 35,960	[129] ¶ 29,080, ¶ 29,081
[124] ¶ 24,820, ¶ 24,820B	[127] ¶ 39,835	[130] ¶ 29,083.15
[125] ¶ 35,381	[128] ¶ 35,580	

¶2492

the taxpayer is entitled to as a shareholder as well as to the credit for foreign taxes he paid himself (Code Sec. 908).[131] Taxpayers who participate in or cooperate with a boycott and derive income from such activities must report such information to the IRS by filing Form 5713 when their income tax is due (including extensions).

2496A. Illegal Payments. If an illegal bribe, kickback, or other payment is made by, or on behalf of, a controlled foreign corporation (CFC) (¶ 2487) or a domestic international sales corporation (DISC) (¶ 2468), either directly or indirectly to an official, employee, or agent-in-fact of a foreign government, the amount of the bribe, kickback or other payment will affect shareholders. In the case of a CFC, the amount is included as Subpart F income for the year and thus is included in the shareholder's income (Code Sec. 952(a)(4)).[132] In the case of a DISC, the amount is considered a constructive dividend and must be included in the shareholders' income (Code Sec. 995(b)(1)(F)(iii)).[133] However, such payments may be deductible in certain circumstances, despite their possible illegality (¶ 972).

2496B. Information from Foreign Sources. The IRS may make a formal document request for foreign records if the normal summons procedure fails to produce the requested documentation (Code Sec. 982).[134] The request for formal documentation supplements the administrative summons procedure and does not prevent the use of any other Code provisions to obtain documents.

Foreign Currency Transactions

2497. Functional Currency. All federal income tax determinations must be made in the taxpayer's functional currency (Code Sec. 985).[135] Generally, the functional currency of a U.S. taxpayer will be the U.S. dollar. However, in the case of a qualified business unit (QBU), the functional currency is the currency in which it conducts a significant part of its activities and which is used in keeping its books and records. For this purpose, a QBU is any separate and clearly identified unit of a trade or business of the taxpayer which maintains its own books and records (for example, foreign subsidiary of a U.S. corporation or a foreign corporation) (Code Sec. 989).[136] Special rules apply in determining when foreign income taxes and foreign earnings and profits must be translated into U.S. dollars (Code Secs. 986 and 987).[137]

2498. Nonfunctional Currency Transactions. Foreign currency gain or loss attributable to a nonfunctional currency transaction is treated separately from the underlying transaction. Generally, it is treated as ordinary gain or loss but is not treated as interest income or expenses (Code Sec. 988).[138] However, gain of an individual from the disposition of foreign currency in a personal transaction is not taxable, provided that the gain realized does not exceed $200. A "personal transaction" is any transaction other than one with respect to which properly allocable expenses are deductible as trade or business expenses under Code Sec. 162 or expenses incurred in the production of income under Code Sec. 212. It also refers to an individual's currency exchange transactions that are entered into in connection with business travel but does not affect tax treatment of capital losses.

Footnote references are to paragraphs of the 2008 Standard Federal Tax Reports.

[131] ¶ 27,964	[134] ¶ 28,820	[137] ¶ 28,860, ¶ 28,880
[132] ¶ 28,490	[135] ¶ 28,840	[138] ¶ 28,900
[133] ¶ 29,020	[136] ¶ 28,920	

Chapter 25

RETURNS ☐ PAYMENT OF TAX

Filing

2501. Income Tax Returns—Types of Returns. Individuals who must file income tax returns use Form 1040EZ, 1040A, or 1040, along with any appropriate schedules; fiduciaries of estates and trusts who must file income tax returns use Form 1041; corporations must file income tax returns on Form 1120 or 1120-A; and partnerships must file information returns on Form 1065.

The following specialized income tax return forms for individuals also exist: Form 1040-C for a departing alien; Form 1040NR for a nonresident alien; Form 1040-SS (self-employment) for a resident of the Virgin Islands, Guam, American Samoa or the Northern Mariana Islands; and Form 1040-PR or 1040SS (self-employment) for a resident of Puerto Rico.

Specialized forms for certain types of corporations also exist:

(1) Schedule PH, attached to Form 1120, for a U.S. personal holding company;

(2) Form 1120-IC-DISC for an interest charge domestic international sales corporation;

(3) Form 1120F for a foreign corporation;

(4) Form 1120-FSC for a foreign sales corporation;

(5) Form 1120L for a life insurance company;

(6) Form 1120-PC for a property and casualty insurance company;

(7) Form 1120-POL for a political organization;

(8) Form 1120-REIT for a real estate investment trust;

(9) Form 1120-RIC for a regulated investment company; and

(10) Form 1120S for an S corporation.

Rules for determining which individuals must file an income tax return are set out at ¶ 109; rules for determining who must pay estimated tax are covered at ¶ 2682. Rules for corporation returns appear at ¶ 211. For rules applicable to partners and partnerships, see ¶ 406.

Employers who withhold income tax, social security tax, or both from their employees' wages must file quarterly returns on Form 941 to report the amount of tax withheld and their share of social security tax.[1] Applicable to tax years beginning on or after January 1, 2006, "small employers," i.e., those with an estimated employment tax liability of $1,000 or less, may instead file an annual return on Form 944 (rather than a quarterly return on Form 941) (see ¶ 2650). Individuals who pay annual cash wages of $1,500 or more for domestic service in their private homes must file Schedule H (Form 1040) to report and pay employer and employee social security taxes and any income tax withheld at the employee's request (IRS Publication 926). Employers who pay wages for agricultural labor (including household employees in a private home on a farm operated

---

Footnote references are to paragraphs of the 2008 Standard Federal Tax Reports.

[1] ¶ 33,662.01

¶2501

for profit) must file Form 943 annually to report and pay social security taxes and voluntary income tax withholding. In addition, employers must file Form 940 annually to report and pay federal unemployment taxes.

2503. Electronic Filing. Electronic filing allows qualified filers to transmit tax return information directly to an IRS Service Center, usually over the internet. Taxpayers may e-file their tax returns through a paid preparer (or an electronic return originator), by using a personal computer, access to the internet, and commercial tax preparation software, or by qualifying for and enrolling in the Free File program. Individual taxpayers who e-file their returns can authorize direct debit payment from their checking or savings account on a specified date. Taxpayers may also charge their taxes by credit card or pay their taxes electronically through the Electronic Federal Tax Payment System (EFTPS) (IRS Fact Sheet FS-2007-11).

The Treasury Department has launched Free File as a public-private sector initiative with commercial software providers to provide free tax return preparation and electronic filing service for middle- and low-income taxpayers with an adjusted gross income of $52,000 or less (Internal Revenue News Release IR-2007-11). Free File is available at the IRS website at www.irs.gov (Internal Revenue News Release IR-2007-10).

At one time, electronic filers were required to submit their signatures on paper, using Form 8453. However, taxpayers may now file electronically without submitting any additional paperwork by substituting their signature with a Self-Select Personal Identification Number (PIN), or if using a paid preparer, that preparer's Practitioner PIN (IRS Fact Sheet FS-2007-8).

Corporations, S corporations and exempt organizations may also elect to electronically file, respectively, Forms 1120, 1120S and 990. However, effective for tax years ending on or after December 31, 2005, the IRS now requires certain organizations to submit those returns on magnetic media. Corporations/S corporations with assets of $50 million or more must file Forms 1120/ 1120S for tax years ending on or after December 31, 2005 on magnetic media (Temporary Reg. § 301.6011-5T; Temporary Reg. § 301.6037-2T). For tax years ending on or after December 31, 2006, corporations/S corporations with assets of $10 million or more must also file Forms 1120/ 1120S on magnetic media. In addition, exempt organizations with assets of $100 million or more must file Form 990 for tax years ending on or after December 31, 2005 on magnetic media (Temporary Reg. § 301.6033-4T). For tax years ending on or after December 31, 2006, the magnetic media filing requirement is expanded to include Forms 990 filed by exempt organizations with assets of $10 million or more and Forms 990-PF filed by private foundations or Code Sec. 4947(a)(1) trusts. The term "magnetic media" includes electronic filing, as well as filing on magnetic tape cartridge. Although electronic filing is not required for any corporation, S corporation or exempt organization filing less than 250 returns during the calendar year, the IRS encourages such organizations to do so.

2505. Income Tax Returns—When to File. Subject to an exception for deadlines falling on a Saturday, Sunday or holiday (see ¶ 2549), the due dates for income tax returns are as follows:

Individual, trust, estate, and partnership income tax returns are due on or before the 15th day of the 4th month following the close of the tax year, typically April 15 in the case of a calendar-year taxpayer (Code Sec. 6072; Reg. § 1.6072-1(a)).[2] The final income tax return of a decedent for a fractional part of a year is due on the same date as would apply had the taxpayer lived the entire year (i.e., the 15th day of the 4th month following the close of the 12-month period that began on the first day of the fractional year) (Reg. § 1.6072-1(b)).[3]

A domestic corporation or foreign corporation having a U.S. office must file its corporate income tax return on or before the 15th day of the 3rd month after the close of the tax year (for 2008, that would be March 17 for a calendar-year corporation, because March 15 falls on a Saturday). A foreign sales corporation must file its U.S. income tax return by the 15th day of the 3rd month after the end of its tax year (Instructions for Form 1120-FSC). The return of an interest charge domestic international sales corpora-

---

Footnote references are to paragraphs of the 2008 Standard Federal Tax Reports.

[2] ¶ 36,720, ¶ 36,721   [3] ¶ 36,721

tion (IC-DISC), an exempt farmers' cooperative, or other cooperative organization is due on or before the 15th day of the 9th month following the close of the tax year (September 15 for a calendar-year taxpayer) (Reg. § 1.6072-2).[4]

The due date for income tax returns of organizations exempt from tax under Code Sec. 501(a) (other than employees' trusts under Code Sec. 401(a)) is the 15th day of the 5th month following the close of the tax year (Reg. § 1.6072-2(c)).[5]

A taxpayer filing as a nonresident alien who is not subject to the wage withholding described at ¶ 2601 and a foreign corporation not having an office or place of business in the U.S. may file a return as late as the 15th day of the 6th month after the close of the tax year (Reg. § 1.6072-1(c) and Reg. § 1.6072-2(b)).[6] However, a nonresident alien who has wages subject to withholding is required to file a return on or before the 15th day of the 4th month following the close of the tax year.

A taxpayer may correct an error in a return, without incurring interest or penalties, by filing an amended return (Form 1040X) and paying any additional tax due on or before the last day prescribed for filing the original return.[7]

2509. Extension of Time. An individual is granted an automatic extension of six months for filing a return (but *not* for payment of tax) by properly filing Form 4868 before the normal due date of the return (Temporary Reg. § 1.6081-4T).[8] Form 4868 may be filed electronically or by mail. Filing extensions can be obtained without making tax payments, so long as taxpayers properly estimate their tax liability on the form. If the requesting taxpayers do not properly estimate their tax liability, the extension request will be denied, and the IRS will charge interest and a penalty for late payment. If the amount of tax included with the extension request is less than sufficient to cover the taxpayer's liability, the taxpayer will be charged interest on the overdue amount. However, no late-payment penalty will be imposed if the tax paid through withholding, estimated tax payments, or any payment accompanying Form 4868 is at least 90% of the total tax due with Form 1040 and if the remaining unpaid balance is paid with the return within the extension period (Temporary Reg. § 1.6081-4T; Reg. § 301.6651-1).[9] An automatic extension should not be requested if the taxpayer has asked the IRS to compute the tax or if the taxpayer is under a court order to file the return by the original due date.

Individuals Residing Outside the United States. U.S. citizens or residents living outside the U.S. and Puerto Rico (including military personnel) are granted an automatic extension up to and including the 15th day of the sixth month following the close of their tax year for filing a return if they attach a statement to their return showing that they are entitled to such an extension (Reg. § 1.6081-5; Temporary Reg. § 1.6081-5T).[10] In addition, the time for payment of tax is also extended for two months unless the IRS specifies otherwise. However, interest will be assessed on any unpaid tax from the due date of the return (without regard to the automatic extension) until the tax is paid (IRS Publication 54). The automatic filing extension runs concurrently with the automatic six-month extension allowed to all individuals. Thus, the maximum automatic extension is only six months from the regular due date. However, the application for the automatic six-month extension is timely if it is filed by the due date established by the two-month extension. If an individual outside the U.S. needs more than the automatic extension in order to meet either the bona fide residence or the physical presence test for the foreign earned income or housing exclusion, Form 2350 should be filed. Such filing will entitle the individual to additional time for filing the return but not for paying the tax.

Corporations. A corporation or an S corporation is entitled to an automatic extension of six months for filing its return, provided that it timely and properly files Form 7004 and deposits the full amount of the tax due with Form 8109. However, the IRS may terminate this extension at any time by mailing to the taxpayer, or to the person requesting the extension, notice of such termination at least 10 days prior to the termination date fixed in the notice (Reg. § 1.6081-3 and Temporary Reg. § 1.6081-3T).[11]

Footnote references are to paragraphs of the 2008 Standard Federal Tax Reports.

[4] ¶ 36,724	[7] ¶ 35,141.045	[10] ¶ 36,795, ¶ 36,795A
[5] ¶ 36,724	[8] ¶ 36,793	[11] ¶ 36,790, ¶ 36,790A
[6] ¶ 36,721, ¶ 36,724	[9] ¶ 36,794.01	

¶2509

Other Entities. An automatic extension of time (through the 15th day of the 6th month following the close of the tax year) is also granted to a partnership that keeps its books and records outside the U.S. and Puerto Rico, a domestic corporation that transacts its business and keeps its books and records outside the U.S. and Puerto Rico, a foreign corporation that maintains an office or place of business within the U.S., and a domestic corporation whose principal income is from sources within U.S. possessions (Reg. § 1.6081-5(a); Temporary Reg. § 1.6081-5T).[12] The automatic filing extension runs concurrently with the automatic six-month filing extension allowed for most businesses.

The following entities must use Form 8868 to apply for extensions of time for filing returns: various trusts filing Forms 1041-A, 5227, and 6069; certain exempt organizations filing Forms 990, 990-PF, 990-BL, 990-T, and 4720; and certain charitable organizations filing Form 8870. Partnerships filing Form 1065, real estate mortgage investment conduits filing Form 1066, and estates and trusts filing Form 1041 should use Form 7004 to apply for an automatic six-month filing extension.

2513. Place for Filing Returns. An individual, estate, or trust must file returns with the Service Center indicated at ¶ 3, except for certain charitable and split-interest trusts and pooled-income funds (see Instructions for Form 1041).

A corporation, S corporation or partnership must file its return with the Service Center indicated in the instructions to the entity's return (Form 1120, Form 1120S or Form 1065).

2517. Return Preparers. In addition to the prohibition against disclosure of return information (see ¶ 2894), a person who prepares any tax returns (or refund claims) for compensation is subject to the following rules:

(1) The preparer must include an identifying number (either social security number or alternative preparer identification number) on the taxpayer's return (Reg. § 1.6109-2). The preparer must sign the return after its completion but before its presentation to the taxpayer for signature. For paper returns, the preparer must manually sign the return or use any of three alternative methods that include either a facsimile of the tax preparer's signature or the individual preparer's printed name: (1) rubber stamp, (2) mechanical device, or (3) computer software program (Notice 2004-54). For electronically filed individual income tax returns submitted by tax practitioners, the preparer must sign the return using a Self-Select Personal Identification Number (PIN) or a Practitioner PIN (Internal Revenue News Release IR-2007-130). If the preparer is employed by another return preparer, the employer must furnish the identifying numbers of both the employer and the employee-preparer (Code Sec. 6109(a) and Code Sec. 7701(a)(36), as amended by the Small Business and Work Opportunity Tax Act of 2007 (P.L. 110-28); Reg. § 1.6695-1(b)).[13]

(2) The preparer must provide the taxpayer with a completed copy of the prepared return (in either paper or electronic form) no later than the time the original return is presented for signing. The preparer must also keep, for three years following the close of the return period, a copy of the return (in either paper or electronic form) or a list of the names, identification numbers, and tax years of taxpayers for whom returns were prepared (Code Sec. 6107; Reg. § 1.6107-1; Reg. § 1.6107-2).[14] The preparer need not sign the taxpayer's copy of the return.

(3) The preparer must keep a record, for three years following the close of the return period to which the record relates, of the name, taxpayer identification number (TIN), and principal place of work of each tax return preparer employed or engaged by the preparer at any time during the return period (Reg. § 1.6060-1).[15] The "return period" is defined as the 12-month period beginning on July 1 of each year.

Small Business Tax Act. Applicable to returns prepared after May 25, 2007, under the Small Business and Work Opportunity Tax Act of 2007 (P.L. 110-28), the rules discussed above pertain to preparers of *any* returns (Code Secs. 6060, 6107, 6109(a),

---

Footnote references are to paragraphs of the 2008 Standard Federal Tax Reports.

[12] ¶ 36,795, ¶ 36,795A   [13] ¶ 36,960, ¶ 39,961C,   [14] ¶ 36,920, ¶ 36,921
                                       ¶ 43,114.01   [15] ¶ 36,561

6695 and 7701(a)(36), as amended by the Small Business and Work Opportunity Tax Act of 2007 (P.L. 110-28)). Thus, these rules pertain to not only preparers of income tax returns, but also to preparers of estate and gift tax, employment tax, excise tax and exempt organization returns.

2518. Return Preparer Penalties. Several penalties may be assessed against tax return preparers.

Failure to Follow Procedures. A tax return preparer who fails to meet the requirements in (1)-(3) as described in ¶ 2517 may be assessed the following penalties, unless the failure is due to reasonable cause and not to willful neglect:

    (1) $50 for each failure to sign a return, to furnish an identifying number, or to furnish the taxpayer with a copy of the prepared return;

    (2) $50 for each failure to retain a copy of prepared returns or a list of taxpayers for whom returns were prepared; and

    (3) $50 for each failure to retain and make available a record of preparers employed, plus $50 for each failure to include an item required in such record.

The penalty for failure to sign a return will not be imposed against preparers of Form 1041 who use a facsimile signature and meet certain other requirements. A $500 penalty is assessable against a preparer who endorses or negotiates another's refund check (other than a bank preparer who negotiates customers' refund checks for bank account deposits) (Code Sec. 6695; Reg. § 1.6695-1).[16]

Understatement of Taxpayer's Liability. Applicable to returns prepared prior to May 26, 2007, a $250 penalty may be imposed against a return preparer for each tax return or claim for refund that understates the taxpayer's liability due to an unrealistic position (Code Sec. 6694(a), prior to amendment by the Small Business and Work Opportunity Tax Act of 2007 (P.L. 110-28)).[17] The penalty is increased to $1,000 per return or refund claim if the understatement is willful or reckless (Code Sec. 6694(b), prior to amendment by the Small Business and Work Opportunity Tax Act).[18]

Undisclosed positions on a tax return or refund claim prepared before May 26, 2007 that result in an understatement of liability must have a "realistic possibility" (i.e., a one-in-three chance) of being sustained on the merits to avoid penalty, or must be disclosed and have a reasonable and nonfrivolous basis (Reg. § 1.6694-2(b)(1)).[19] Disclosures generally must be made on Form 8275 or 8275-R, as appropriate, except that the disclosure may be made on a return pursuant to an annual revenue procedure (Reg. § 1.6662-4(f) and Reg. § 1.6694-2(c)(3)).[20] The penalty may be excused if there is a reasonable cause for the understatement and the return preparer acted in good faith.

Applicable to returns prepared after May 25, 2007, the penalty for understatement of a tax liability is increased from $250 to the greater of (a) $1,000 or (b) 50 percent of the income derived (or to be derived) by the preparer with respect to the return or refund claim (Code Sec. 6694(a), as amended by the Small Business and Work Opportunity Tax Act of 2007 (P.L. 110-28)). Furthermore, the standard for undisclosed positions has changed from a "realistic possibility" standard to a "reasonable belief" standard, which requires that: (1) the preparer knew, or reasonably should have known, of the position; (2) there was not a reasonable belief that the tax treatment of the position would more likely than not be the proper treatment; and (3) the position was not disclosed or there was not a reasonable basis for the position. As before, the penalty will not be imposed if the preparer shows that there was reasonable cause for the understatement and the preparer acted in good faith. The penalty increases to the greater of (a) $5,000 or (b) 50 percent of the income derived (or to be derived) by the preparer with respect to the return or refund claim if the understatement is willful or reckless (Code Sec. 6694(b), as amended by the Small Business and Work Opportunity Tax Act).

To assist tax return preparers in the transition to the new penalty provisions, the IRS will temporarily allow the previous "realistic possibility" standard to apply to all income tax returns, amended returns, and refund claims due on or before December 31,

---

Footnote references are to paragraphs of the 2008 Standard Federal Tax Reports.

[16] ¶ 39,965, ¶ 39,966   [18] ¶ 39,955   [20] ¶ 39,651H, ¶ 39,957
[17] ¶ 39,955, ¶ 39,956A.01   [19] ¶ 39,957

2007 (including extensions). For estate, gift and generation-skipping tax returns due on or before December 31, 2007, and employment and excise tax returns due on or before January 31, 2008, the reasonable basis standard under the accuracy-related and fraud penalty provisions (Code Sec. 6662) will be applied in determining whether the return preparer penalty will be imposed. This transitional relief also applies to estimated tax returns due on or before January 15, 2008 (Notice 2007-54).

Failure To Be Diligent in Claiming Earned Income Credit. Tax preparers must comply with due diligence requirements for returns or refund claims asserting eligibility for the earned income credit (Code Sec. 6695(g); Reg. § 1.6695-2).[21] Each failure to observe the requirements regarding the amount of, or eligibility for, the credit will result in a penalty of $100, in addition to any other penalty imposed.

Aiding or Abetting in Tax Liability Understatement. A penalty of $1,000 may also be imposed on persons for aiding or abetting in an understatement of tax liability on a return, claim or other document ($10,000 in the case of a corporation) (Code Sec. 6701).[22] Only one penalty may be imposed per taxpayer per period; however, the tax period may not necessarily be a tax year. For instance, understatements on quarterly employment tax returns may give rise to four separate penalties for a calendar year (Code Sec. 6701(b)(3)).[23] According to the Sixth Circuit, no statute of limitations applies to bar the penalty.[24] Generally, this penalty may be imposed in addition to other penalties. However, this penalty will not be imposed if either the return preparer penalty for understatements due to unreasonable positions or the penalty for promoting abusive tax shelters has been applied with respect to the same tax return or refund claim (Code Sec. 6701(f)).[25]

2521. Protest Returns. A civil penalty of $5,000 will be imposed upon any person (including an individual, a trust, estate, partnership, association, company or corporation) who files a purported tax return (income or otherwise) if (1) the purported return fails to contain sufficient information from which the substantial correctness of the amount of tax liability can be judged or contains information that on its face indicates that the amount of tax shown is substantially incorrect and (2) such conduct arises from a frivolous position or from a desire to delay or impede administration of the tax laws. This penalty is imposed in addition to any other penalties imposed on the taxpayer (Code Sec. 6702, as amended by the Tax Relief and Health Care Act of 2006 (P.L. 109-432)).[26] The penalties may be reduced at the discretion of the Secretary of the Treasury in order to promote compliance with, and administration of, the federal tax laws. If a person withdraws a submission within 30 days after receiving notice that the return is a specified frivolous submission, the penalty will not be imposed.

A $5,000 civil penalty may also be imposed on any person who files a "specified frivolous submission." A "specified frivolous submission" is a specified submission that either (1) is based on a position that has been identified as frivolous in a prescribed frivolous positions list; or (2) reflects a desire to delay or impede the administration of federal tax laws. A "specified submission" is:

> (1) a request for a hearing after the IRS files a notice of lien under Code Sec. 6320 or the taxpayer receives a pre-levy collection due process hearing notice under Code Sec. 6330; and

> (2) an application relating to (a) an agreement for payment of tax liability in installments under Code Sec. 6159, (b) an offer-in-compromise under Code Sec. 7122, or (c) a taxpayer assistance order under Code Sec. 7811.

A list of frivolous positions may be found in Notice 2007-30. The list is not conclusive, and will be periodically revised. Returns or submissions that contain positions not prescribed in the Notice, but which on their face have no basis for validity in existing law, or which have been deemed frivolous in a published opinion by the U.S. Tax Court or other court of competent jurisdiction may also be subject to the $5,000 penalty.

Footnote references are to paragraphs of the 2008 Standard Federal Tax Reports.

[21] ¶ 39,965, ¶ 39,968 [23] ¶ 40,033, ¶ 40,035.10 [25] ¶ 40,033
[22] ¶ 40,033 [24] ¶ 40,035.10 [26] ¶ 40,040

Also, up to $25,000 may be assessed by the Tax Court against a taxpayer who institutes or maintains proceedings primarily for delay or on frivolous grounds or who unreasonably fails to pursue available administrative remedies. Other courts may require a taxpayer to pay a penalty of up to $10,000 if the taxpayer's action against the IRS for unauthorized collection activities appears to be a frivolous or groundless proceeding (Code Sec. 6673).[27] The Tax Court has held that a penalty for instituting proceedings primarily for delay is properly assessed against the tax matters person of an S corporation, rather than against the entity or its other shareholders.[28]

2523. Books and Records. Taxpayers are required to keep accurate, permanent books and records so as to be able to determine the various types of income, gains, losses, costs, expenses and other amounts that affect their income tax liability for the year (Reg. § 1.6001-1(a)). The records must be retained for as long as they may be, or may become, "material" for any federal tax purpose. Generally, records that support an item of income or a deduction on a tax return should be kept at least for the period of limitation for that return. See ¶ 2726, ¶ 2732, ¶ 2734, ¶ 2738 and ¶ 2517 (regarding return preparers) regarding applicable limitation periods.

Payment of Tax

2525. Place of Payment. The tax shown on the tax return is to be paid to the internal revenue officer with whom the return is filed unless, as in the case of corporations, the tax is required to be deposited with an authorized depository (Code Sec. 6151(a)). See ¶ 2513.

The IRS requests that individuals use a payment voucher, Form 1040-V, for any balance due on any Forms 1040.

2529. Time of Payment. In general, the tax shown on an income tax return is to be paid, without assessment or notice and demand, at the time fixed for filing the return, determined without regard to any extension of time for filing the return. See ¶ 2505. However, exceptions apply when:

(1) a taxpayer shows that payment on the return due date will result in undue hardship (see ¶ 2537, below);

(2) a taxpayer is residing outside the United States on the return due date (see ¶ 2509); or

(3) a taxpayer elects to have the IRS compute the tax (¶ 124), in which case payment is due within 30 days after the IRS mails a notice and demand (Code Sec. 6151(b)(1)).[29]

The IRS also has the authority to enter into a written agreement with the taxpayer, allowing for the full or, in most situations, partial payment of any tax in installments, if such an agreement will facilitate the collection of a tax liability (Code Sec. 6159).[30] The fee for entering into an installment agreement is $105 ($52 for direct debit installment agreements, where the payments are deducted directly from the taxpayer's bank account). For low income taxpayers, the fee is $43, regardless of the method of payment.[31]

2533. Taxes of Member of Armed Forces upon Death. When a member of the Armed Forces dies while serving in a combat zone or as a result of wounds, disease, or injury incurred while so serving, the final income tax liability for that individual's year of death and any prior year ending on or after the first day served in a combat zone will not be assessed. Any unpaid taxes of such individual that relate to tax years prior to service in a combat zone may also be abated. A similar tax forgiveness rule applies to U.S. military and civilian employees who die as the result of wounds or injury occurring outside the United States in a terroristic or military action against the United States or any of its allies (Code Sec. 692).[32] Tax forgiveness has also been extended with respect to astronauts who die in the line of duty (Code Sec. 692(d)(5)).

2537. Extension of Time for Payment of Tax. As noted at ¶ 2509, an extension of time for filing the return ordinarily does not postpone the time for payment. The IRS,

---

Footnote references are to paragraphs of the 2008 Standard Federal Tax Reports.

[27] ¶ 39,785	[29] ¶ 37,080	[31] ¶ 37,180C
[28] ¶ 39,790.47	[30] ¶ 37,180	[32] ¶ 24,920

¶2523

however, may extend the time of payment of the tax shown on the return for up to six months (or longer if the taxpayer is abroad) upon a showing of undue hardship. A taxpayer applying for an extension of the time to pay tax must file Form 1127 on or before the original due date for payment of the tax. The application must be accompanied by evidence showing the undue hardship that would result if the extension were refused, a statement of the assets and liabilities of the taxpayer, and a statement of the receipts and disbursements of the taxpayer for the three months preceding the original due date for payment of tax (Code Sec. 6161(a); Reg. § 1.6161-1).[33]

As a condition to the granting of an extension, the taxpayer may be required to furnish a bond (Code Sec. 6165; Reg. § 1.6165-1).[34] If an extension of time for payment of tax is granted, interest on the tax liability will accrue (see ¶ 2838) from the original due date until the date on which the balance is fully paid (Reg. § 1.6161-1(d)).[35]

Military and Government Personnel. Armed Forces members and civilians serving in support of the Armed Forces who serve in a designated combat zone (see ¶ 895) or in a contingency operation or are hospitalized outside the United States as a result of an injury received while serving in a combat zone/contingency operation qualify for an extension for filing returns and paying tax for the period of combat/contingency operation service or hospitalization plus 180 days (Code Sec. 7508(a)).[36] This extension is also available to such a taxpayer's spouse who wishes to file a joint return (Code Sec. 7508(c)).[37]

Disaster Areas. The IRS is authorized to postpone deadlines for filing returns and paying taxes for up to one year for taxpayers affected by a presidentially declared disaster (Code Sec. 7508A).[38]

2541. Extension of Time for Payment of Deficiency in Tax. An extension of time for payment of a deficiency of tax may be granted for a period of not more than 18 months where timely payment of the deficiency would result in undue hardship. Such an extension may be applied for according to the procedure for an extension of time for payment of tax outlined in ¶ 2537. An additional period of not more than 12 months may be granted in an exceptional case. A request for an extension will be refused if the deficiency was due to negligence, intentional disregard of income tax rules and regulations, or fraud (Code Sec. 6161(b); Reg. § 1.6161-1(a)(2) and (c)).[39]

2545. Forms of Payment. Payment of taxes must be made by a commercially acceptable means deemed appropriate by the IRS. Such means of payment include personal or cashier's check, money order, credit, debit or charge cards, or electronic funds withdrawal (Code Sec. 6311; Reg. § 301.6311-2).[40] Credit card payments may be charged to VISA, MasterCard, American Express and Discover cards, although the private companies that process such payments may charge a convenience fee (FS 2007-11). Electronic funds withdrawal is free and allows taxpayers to schedule payments to be withdrawn directly from their bank accounts, but is available only to those taxpayers who e-file. Additionally, taxpayers may use the Electronic Federal Tax Payment System (EFTPS), a free tax payment system provided by the Treasury that allows taxpayers to pay online or via telephone (IRS Publication 966).

Weekend and Holiday Deadlines

2549. "Deadlines" Falling on a Weekend or Holiday. If the last day for performing any act (such as filing a return, paying tax, or filing a claim for credit or refund) falls on Saturday, Sunday, or a legal holiday, the act is timely if it is performed on the next day that is not a Saturday, Sunday, or a legal holiday (Reg. § 301.7503-1).[41] The term "legal holiday" means a legal holiday in the District of Columbia. In the case of a return, statement, or other document required to be filed with an IRS office, the term "legal holiday" also includes a statewide legal holiday in the state in which the office is located (such as Patriots' Day in Massachusetts) (Code Sec. 7503).[42]

Footnote references are to paragraphs of the 2008 Standard Federal Tax Reports.

[33] ¶ 37,200, ¶ 37,201
[34] ¶ 37,260, ¶ 37,261
[35] ¶ 37,201
[36] ¶ 42,686

[37] ¶ 42,686
[38] ¶ 42,687A
[39] ¶ 37,200, ¶ 37,201
[40] ¶ 38,085

[41] ¶ 42,631
[42] ¶ 42,630

2553. Timely Mailing as Timely Filing and Paying. Any return, claim, statement, or document that must be filed with the IRS or the Tax Court, or any payment required to be made on or before a particular date, is regarded as having been timely filed or paid if it is actually delivered by mail or the date of the U.S. postmark falls on or before the due date (Code Sec. 7502(a)).[43] Federal tax returns (including claims, statements, or other documents) mailed from outside the U.S. are timely if they bear the official timely dated postmark of the foreign country.

Returns, claims, statements or other documents properly sent by registered mail are considered to have been filed on time if the date of registration falls on or before the due date of the document. Such documents properly sent by certified mail are timely filed if the certified mail sender's receipt is postmarked on or before the due date of the document. Delivery by properly registered or certified mail is presumed to have occurred if the envelope or package was correctly addressed to the office for filing (Reg. § 301.7502-1(c)(2) and (d)).[44]

The IRS has expanded the timely-mailed-is-timely-filed rule to designated private delivery services (Code Sec. 7502(f)).[45] See ¶ 3 for a listing of the available delivery services.

The timely-mailed-is-timely-filed rule has also been expanded to cover returns filed electronically (Reg. § 301.7502-1). The date of an electronic postmark given by an authorized electronic return transmitter will be deemed to be the filing date if the date of the electronic postmark is on or before the filing due date.

A tax deposit received by an authorized depository (no longer including Federal Reserve Banks) after the due date for the deposit is timely if it has been properly mailed at least two days before the prescribed due date. However, if any person is required to deposit tax more than once a month and the deposit amounts to $20,000 or more, the deposit must be received on or before the prescribed due date in order to be timely (Code Sec. 7502(e), Reg. § 301.7502-2).[46]

Signature

2557. Signatures on Returns. Forms 1040, 1040A, and 1040EZ must be signed by the individual taxpayer (Reg. § 1.6061-1).[47] The return contains a declaration that it is made under the penalties of perjury (Code Sec. 6065).[48] In the case of a joint return, both the husband and the wife must sign. If the taxpayer did not prepare the return, the return must be signed by the taxpayer and the tax return preparer (see ¶ 2517). If a decedent's return is filed by a representative, the representative should sign the return on the line indicated for the taxpayer and attach a written power of attorney.

For a discussion of the signing requirements applicable to electronically filed returns, see ¶ 2503.

Fiscal-Year Taxpayers

2561. Proration. When the effective date of a tax rate change occurs within a tax year, a taxpayer must compute the tax for the entire tax year by using both the old and the new rates (Code Sec. 15).[49] The final tax is the sum of (1) the tax calculated at the old rates that is proportionate to the portion of the tax year before the effective date of the new tax and (2) the tax calculated at the new rates that is proportionate to the portion of the tax year beginning with the effective date.

When the tax rate change involves the highest rate of income tax, the taxpayer must compute the tax for the year by using a weighted average of the highest rates before and after the change determined on the basis of the respective portions of the tax year before the date of change and on or after the date of change.

Information Returns and Payment at Source

2565. Payments Made in Course of Trade or Business. Every person engaged in a trade or business, including a partnership and a nonprofit organization, must file information returns for each calendar year for certain payments made during such year

---

Footnote references are to paragraphs of the 2008 Standard Federal Tax Reports.

[43] ¶ 42,620
[44] ¶ 42,621
[45] ¶ 42,620

[46] ¶ 42,620, ¶ 42623
[47] ¶ 36,603
[48] ¶ 36,680

[49] ¶ 3385

in the course of the payor's trade or business (Code Sec. 6041—Code Sec. 6050V).[50] In many cases the information contained on such returns must be reported to the IRS by means of magnetic media such as tape cartridges or electronic filing (Rev. Proc. 2007-51). Recipients must be furnished a copy of the information return or a comparable statement. While payee statements are generally required to be in written form, persons required to furnish recipients copies of forms in the Form 1099 series and any other information return issued under Code Sec. 6041—Code Sec. 6050V may furnish electronic payee statements (Sec. 401 of the Job Creation and Worker Assistance Act of 2002 (P.L. 107-147)). Payee statements for Form W-2 may also be filed electronically (Reg. § 31.6051-1). The following information returns are among those currently being filed:

Form 1098. Persons file this form if they receive $600 or more in mortgage interest from an individual in the course of a trade or business. Points paid directly by a borrower (including seller-paid points) for the purchase of a principal residence must be reported on Form 1098.[51] Refunds and reimbursements of overpaid mortgage interest, and mortgage insurance premiums of $600 or more must also be reported on Form 1098 (Reg. § 1.6050H-2).[52]

Form 1098-E. Financial institutions, governmental units or educational institutions must file this form when, in the course of a trade or business, they receive interest of $600 or more in a calendar year on a student loan that is used solely to pay for qualified higher education expenses.

Form 1098-T. An educational institution that receives qualified tuition and related expenses on behalf of a student or by any other entity must file this form when, in the course of a trade or business, it reimburses or refunds qualified tuition and related expenses under an insurance arrangement.

Form 1099-A. Persons who lend money in connection with their trade or business and, in full or partial satisfaction of the debt, acquire an interest in property that is security for the debt must file this form. The form must also be filed if the person has reason to know that the property securing the debt has been abandoned.

Form 1099-B. Brokers are to use this form to report sales (including short sales) of stock, bonds, commodities, regulated futures contracts, foreign currency contracts, forward contracts, and debt instruments. Barter exchanges are to use the form to report exchanges of property or services through the exchange (Code Sec. 6045).[53] Also, trustees and middlemen of widely held fixed investment trusts (WHFITs) must report the non *pro rata* partial principal payments, trust sales proceeds, redemption asset proceeds, redemption proceeds, sales asset proceeds and the sales proceeds that are attributable to a trust interest holder (TIH) for the calendar year on this form. Filing is not required for transactions involving property or services with a fair market value of less than $1 (Notice 2000-6).

Form 1099-C. Financial institutions, credit unions and federal agencies must file this form for each debtor for whom a debt of $600 or more was cancelled. Multiple discharges of debt of less than $600 during a year need not be aggregated unless the separate discharges occurred with the purpose of evading the reporting requirements. The returns must be filed regardless of whether the debtor is subject to tax on the discharged debt. For example, debts discharged in bankruptcy must be reported (Code Sec. 6050P).[54]

Form 1099-DIV. Corporate payors file this form for each person:

    (1) to whom payments of $10 or more in distributions, such as dividends, capital gains, or nontaxable distributions, were made on stock;

    (2) for whom any foreign tax was withheld and paid on dividends and on other distributions on stock if the recipient can claim a credit for the tax;

    (3) for whom any federal income tax was withheld under the backup withholding rules; or

    (4) to whom payments of $600 or more were made as part of a liquidation.

Footnote references are to paragraphs of the 2008 Standard Federal Tax Reports.

[50] ¶ 35,820 et seq.
[51] ¶ 36,186.035
[52] ¶ 36,184
[53] ¶ 35,920
[54] ¶ 36,310

S corporations use this form only to report distributions made during the calendar year out of accumulated earnings and profits.

Form 1099-G. Government units use this form to report payments of $10 or more for unemployment benefits and state and local tax refunds, credits, or offsets, and payments of $600 or more in taxable grants.

Form 1099-H. Health insurance providers are required to file this return to report any advance payments of the credit for health insurance costs they are entitled to receive on behalf of individuals under Code Sec. 7527 (Code Sec. 6050T).

Form 1099-INT. Payors file this form for each person to whom payments of $10 or more in interest were paid, including interest on bearer certificates of deposit and interest on U.S. Savings Bonds, Treasury bills, Treasury notes, and Treasury bonds. Interest paid in the course of a trade or business is reportable when the amount totals $600 or more for any person. Form 1099-INT must also be filed to report interest of $10 or more (other than original issue discount) accrued to a REMIC regular interest holder during the year or paid to the holder of a collateralized debt obligation. Additionally, trustees and middlemen of WHFITs must report the gross amount of interest exceeding $10 that is attributable to a TIH for the calendar year on this form.

Form 1099-MISC. This form is filed by payors for each person to whom at least $10 in gross royalty payments, or $600 for rents or services in the course of a trade or business, was paid. Some of the items reported on this form are:

(1) payments for real estate, machine and pasture rentals;

(2) royalties paid to authors;

(3) prizes and awards that were not paid for services rendered;

(4) amounts withheld as backup withholding;

(5) payments by medical and health care insurers to each physician or health care provider under health, accident and sickness insurance programs;

(6) compensation such as fees, commissions and awards, and golden parachute payments paid to a nonemployee for services, including payments to attorneys for legal services (Code Sec. 6045(f));

(7) notification of the occurrence of sales of $5,000 or more of consumer products to a person on a buy-sell or commission basis for resale anywhere other than in a permanent retail establishment;

(8) fishing boat proceeds;

(9) fish purchases of $600 or more paid in cash for resale (Code Sec. 6050R);

(10) crop insurance proceeds of $600 or more; and

(11) any deferrals for the year under a nonqualified deferred compensation plan (Code Sec. 6041(g)).

Form 1099-OID. Issuers of bonds or certificates of deposit, and trustees and middlemen of widely held fixed investment trusts (WHFITs) use this form to report original issue discount of $10 or more (Reg. § 1.671-5).

Form 1099-PATR. Cooperatives use this form to report distributions of $10 or more to patrons.

Form 1099-R. Payors file this form to report any distributions of $10 or more from retirement or profit-sharing plans, individual retirement arrangements (IRAs), simplified employee pensions (SEPs), annuities or insurance contracts.

Form 1099-S. This form is used to report the sale or exchange of real estate and the real property taxes imposed on the purchaser as a result of the sale or exchange. Included are sales or exchanges of residences, land, commercial buildings, condominium units, and stock in cooperative housing corporations.[55] The form must be filed by the person responsible for closing the real estate transaction or, if no such person exists, by the mortgage lender, the transferor's broker, the transferee's broker or the transferee, in that order. Payments of timber royalties under a "pay-as-cut" contract are also reported on the form.

Footnote references are to paragraphs of the 2008 Standard Federal Tax Reports.

[55] ¶ 35,929

¶2565

Form 5498. This form is filed by the account trustee for each person for whom an IRA or a SEP was maintained. Contributions made during the year to the IRA (including rollover contributions and contributions under a SEP plan) and the fair market value of the IRA or SEP account on December 31 must be reported here. Form 5498 is due by May 31 of the year following the year of contribution.

Form 8027. Each employer that runs a "large food or beverage establishment" (see ¶ 2601) must file an annual return of the receipts from food or beverage operations and tips reported by employees. In addition, in certain circumstances, the employer is required to allocate amounts as tips to employees.

Form 8300. Each person engaged in a trade or business who, in the course of such trade or business, receives more than $10,000 in cash in one transaction (or two or more related transactions) must file this form. The form is to be filed with the IRS by the 15th day after the transaction, and a similar statement is to be provided to the payor on or before January 31 of the calendar year following the year of receipt.

Form W-2. This form is to be furnished to both the Social Security Administration and the recipient. Employers use the form to report wages, tips, other compensation, withheld income and FICA taxes, and advance earned income credit (EIC) payments. Bonuses, vacation allowances, severance pay, moving expense payments, some kinds of travel allowances and third-party payments of sick pay are included.

Due Dates. Unless otherwise specified, the above information returns for 2007 are to be provided to the IRS by February 28, 2008, and to recipients by January 31, 2008. Form W-2 is to be provided to the Social Security Administration by February 29, 2008, and to recipients by January 31, 2008. The due date for filing information returns with the IRS is extended to March 31, 2008 for returns filed electronically (Code Sec. 6071(b); Reg. § 31.6071(a)-1(a)(3)(i)). Form 8809 is used to request an automatic 30-day extension of time to file Forms 1098, 1099, W-2G, 1042-S, 5498 and 8027 with the IRS or Form W-2 with the Social Security Administration. A further 30-day extension may also be obtained by filing Form 8809, but reasonable cause must be shown. Form 8809 cannot be used to request an extension of time to furnish required statements to recipients.

Other Information Returns. Other information returns are required with respect to:

(1) a U.S. person's acquisition of, or change of interest in, a foreign partnership (Code Sec. 6046A);

(2) cases of liquidation or dissolution of a corporation, including an exempt organization (Code Sec. 6043);

(3) corporate recapitalizations (Code Sec. 6043);

(4) corporate mergers and acquisitions (Code Sec. 6043A);

(5) organizations or reorganizations of foreign corporations (Code Sec. 6046);

(6) creation of, or transfers to, foreign trusts or the death of a U.S. citizen or resident who had been treated as the owner of, or whose estate included any portion of, a foreign trust (Code Sec. 6048);

(7) U.S. persons who own interests in foreign partnerships or corporations (Code Sec. 6038);

(8) U.S. persons who transfer property to foreign partnerships or corporations (Code Sec. 6038B);

(9) payors of long-term care benefits (Code Sec. 6050Q);

(10) U.S. persons (other than tax-exempt organizations) that receive foreign gifts during the tax year totaling more than $10,000 ($13,258 in 2007) (Code Sec. 6039F);

(11) individuals who lose citizenship, and long-term residents who terminate residency in the United States (Code Sec. 6039G);

(12) Alaska Native Settlement Trusts (Code Sec. 6039H);

(13) dispositions by charitable donees within two years (within three years, for returns filed after September 1, 2006) of donated property with a value in excess of $5,000, and, also, charitable donees of intellectual property (Code Sec. 6050L, as amended by the Pension Protection Act of 2006 (P.L. 109-280));

¶2565

(14) applicable to life insurance contracts issued after August 17, 2006, employer-owned life insurance contracts (Code Sec. 6039I, as added by P.L. 109-280);

(15) applicable to charges made after December 31, 2009, charges or payments for qualified long-term insurance contracts under combined arrangements (Code Sec. 6050U, as added by P.L. 109-280);

(16) applicable to acquisitions of contracts after August 17, 2006, and before August 18, 2008, acquisitions of interests in insurance contracts by exempt organizations (Code Sec. 6050V, as added by P.L. 109-280); and

(17) applicable to calendar years beginning after December 20, 2006, transfers of corporate stock to an employee in connection with the exercise of stock options acquired by the employee through an employee stock purchase plan or through an incentive stock option (Code Sec. 6039, as amended by the Tax Relief and Health Care Act of 2006 (P.L. 109-432)).

In addition, the head of each federal executive agency generally must file Forms 8596 and 8596-A on a quarterly basis stating the name, address, and taxpayer identification number (TIN) of each person to whom the agency makes payments of remuneration of $600 or more (Code Sec. 6041A).[56]

2570. Interest in Foreign Bank. A U.S. person who has a financial interest in or signature authority over any bank, securities, or other financial account in a foreign country that exceeded $10,000 in aggregate value at any time during the calendar year must report that relationship by filing Form TD F 90-22.1 with the Treasury Department before July 1 of the following year.[57]

2579. Taxpayer Identification Number. Persons filing returns and other documents must record on such items a taxpayer identification number (TIN). Individuals use their social security number on Forms 1040, 1040A, and 1040EZ. Executors of individuals' estates who must file Form 706 are to use both their social security number and the decedent's social security number. For corporations, partnerships, estates and trusts, and similar nonindividual taxpayers, the identifying number is the employer identification number.

A prospective adoptive parent can apply for an adoptive taxpayer identification number (ATIN) for a child who is in the process of being adopted (Reg. § 301.6109-3). Application for an ATIN must be made on Form W-7A.

Persons who file information returns (see ¶ 2565) may request the recipient of any payments to furnish his TIN on Form W-9.

Nonresident aliens who cannot obtain a TIN may use an IRS-issued individual number (ITIN) (Notice 2004-1). Form W-7 is used to obtain an ITIN. The Form W-7 must be accompanied by an original, completed income tax return.

A penalty of $50 per failure applies to a taxpayer who omits his own TIN from a required return, statement, or document. Failure to furnish one's TIN to another person when so required or to include another person's TIN in any document for information reporting purposes will also give rise to a $50 penalty. The maximum penalty per calendar year for failure to include TINs is $100,000 (Code Secs. 6723 and 6724(d)(3)).[58]

Footnote references are to paragraphs of the 2008 Standard Federal Tax Reports.

[56] ¶ 35,840   [57] ¶ 35,141.48   [58] ¶ 40,250, ¶ 40,275

¶2570

Chapter 26
WITHHOLDING □ ESTIMATED TAX

Withholding on Wages

2601. Withholding of Income Tax on Wages. Withholding of income tax by an employer is required on each of an employee's wage payments. Generally, the term "wages" includes all remuneration (other than fees paid to a public official) for services performed by an employee for an employer, including the cash value of all remuneration (including benefits) paid in any medium other than cash (Code Sec. 3401(a)).[1] Salaries, fees, bonuses, commissions on sales or on insurance premiums, taxable fringe benefits, pensions and retirement pay (unless taxed as an annuity) are, if paid as compensation for services, subject to withholding (Reg. § 31.3401(a)-1(a)(2)).[2]

The term "employer" includes not only individuals and organizations engaged in trade or business, but also organizations exempt from income, social security and unemployment taxes (Reg. § 31.3401(d)-1).[3] Withholding also applies to wages and salaries of employees, corporate officers, or elected officials of federal, state, and local government units (Code Sec. 3401(c)).[4]

The term "employee" must be distinguished from an "independent contractor" for purposes of employment tax obligations. An employer does not generally have to withhold taxes on payments to independent contractors. In addition to the common law definition that focuses on the control that is exercised over what work is done and how it is done, the IRS will use a 20-factor test to assist in making this determination. The factors are:

(1) employee compliance with instructions required,

(2) training,

(3) integration of worker's services into the business,

(4) services are rendered personally,

(5) ability to hire, supervise and pay assistants,

(6) a continuing relationship,

(7) set hours of work are established,

Footnote references are to paragraphs of the 2008 Standard Federal Tax Reports.

[1] ¶ 33,502
[2] ¶ 33,503
[3] ¶ 33,537
[4] ¶ 33,502

  (8) full time is required,

  (9) work performed on business's premises,

  (10) services performed in a set order or sequence,

  (11) oral or written reports required,

  (12) payment by hour, week or month,

  (13) payment of business and/or travel expenses,

  (14) tools and materials furnished,

  (15) worker invests in facilities,

  (16) worker can realize a profit or loss,

  (17) worker performs services for more than one business at a time,

  (18) worker makes services available to the general public,

  (19) business has the right to discharge worker, and

  (20) worker has the right to terminate the relationship (Rev. Rul. 87-41).[5]

Tips. Cash tips paid directly to an employee by a customer and tips paid over to the employee for charge customers must be accounted for by the employee in a written statement furnished to the employer on or before the 10th day of the month following the month when they are received (see IRS Pub. 531). The employee reports the tips on Form 4070, Employee's Report of Tips to Employer, or on a similar statement. An exception exists if the tips received by the employee in the course of his employment by a single employer amount to less than $20 in a calendar month (Code Secs. 3401(a)(16) and 6053(a)).[6] These tips are not subject to withholding (Code Sec. 3401(a)(16)(B)).[7] However, the only tips that an employer must report on Form W-2 are those that are actually reported to him by the employee (Code Sec. 6051(a)).[8]

A large food and beverage establishment (one which normally has more than 10 employees on a typical business day and in which tipping is customary) must file annual information returns (Form 8027; see ¶ 2565). These returns must report gross food and beverage sales receipts, employee-reported tip income, total charge receipts, and total charge tips (Code Sec. 6053(c); Reg. § 31.6053-3).[9] Such employers must allocate among their employees who customarily receive tip income an amount equal to the excess of eight percent of gross receipts over reported tips. This allocation is not required if the employees voluntarily report total tips equal to at least eight percent of gross sales. If it can be shown that average tips are not eight percent of gross sales, the employer or a majority of its employees may apply to the IRS to have the allocation reduced from eight percent, but not to below two percent (Code Sec. 6053(c)).[10]

Compensation. Retroactive wages and overtime payments under the Fair Labor Standards Act are subject to withholding, although payments under the Act for liquidated damages are not.[11] Settlement awards of back pay are also subject to withholding.[12]

The basis used in determining compensation, whether piecework, percentage of profits, hourly rate, or fixed salary, is immaterial. Overtime, vacation allowances[13] and dismissal payments[14] are wages subject to withholding, as are Christmas gift merchandise certificates given to employees (although the value of turkeys, hams or other merchandise of nominal value distributed at Christmas or on other holidays to promote goodwill is *not* subject to withholding)[15] and payments by employers made directly to employees for health insurance.[16]

Withholding is based on *gross* wage payments before deductions such as those under the federal or state unemployment insurance laws, those for pension funds (except deductible contributions to IRAs, (see ¶ 2609)), insurance, etc., or those for liabilities of the employee paid by the employer.[17]

Footnote references are to paragraphs of the 2008 Standard Federal Tax Reports.

[5] ¶ 33,538.66
[6] ¶ 33,502, ¶ 36,460
[7] ¶ 33,502
[8] ¶ 36,420
[9] ¶ 36,460, ¶ 36,463
[10] ¶ 36,460
[11] ¶ 33,506.1866
[12] ¶ 33,506.1813
[13] ¶ 33,506.397, ¶ 33,562.01
[14] ¶ 33,506.1853
[15] ¶ 33,506.1825
[16] ¶ 33,506.1871
[17] ¶ 33,506.023

¶2601

Employers required to withhold tax with respect to non-cash fringe benefits may deem those benefits paid at any time on or after the date on which they are provided but no later than the last day of the calendar quarter in which they are provided (Temp. Reg. § 31.3501(a)-1T).[18] Withholding on payments, other than wages, to nonresident aliens is governed by special rules covered at ¶ 2447.

Wages subject to withholding include amounts received under a nonqualified deferred compensation plan that are includible in an employee's gross income under Code Sec. 409A for the year of inclusion (see ¶ 2197A) (Code Sec. 3401(a)).

2604. Included and Excluded Wages. If an employee works on two jobs for the same employer, and only a part of the remuneration is "wages" (e.g., a construction worker who also works on his employer's farm (exempt employment)), all of the remuneration is treated alike—either (1) all is subject to withholding if more than half of the time is spent performing services for which wages are received or (2) all is excluded if more than half of the time spent is in exempt services—provided the payroll period is not longer than 31 consecutive days (Reg. § 31.3402(e)-1).[19]

An employer is required to withhold income tax from "wages" paid for "employment" regardless of the circumstances under which the employee is employed or the frequency or size of amounts of the individual wage payments.[20] Tax must be withheld from the wages paid for *each* payroll period.[21] However, see ¶ 2634 as to an employee's possible exemption from withholding.

When a retail commission salesperson is occasionally paid other than in cash, the employer is not required to withhold income tax for the noncash payments (Reg. § 31.3402(j)-1).[22] However, the fair market value of the noncash payments, such as prizes, must be included on the Form W-2 furnished to the employee as part of the total pay earned by the employee during the calendar year.[23]

Withholding is also available, if the payee so requests, for wage continuation payments (i.e., sick pay) received from a third party pursuant to a health or accident plan in which the employer participates (Code Sec. 3402(o); Reg. § 31.3402(o)-3).[24] Payments of sick pay made directly by employers to their employees are automatically subject to withholding.[25] Employers who are third-party payors of sick pay are not required to withhold income taxes from payments unless the employee has requested withholding on Form W-4S.[26]

2607. Certain Gambling Winnings. Certain gambling winnings are subject to withholding. An amount equal to the product of the third lowest rate of tax applicable to single filers is required to be withheld. For 2007 and 2008, the applicable tax rate is 25 percent (Code Sec. 3402(q))[27] (see IRS Pub. 505). This withholding requirement is imposed on winnings of more than $5,000 from sweepstakes, wagering pools, and lotteries. Withholding is generally imposed on other types of gambling winnings (including pari-mutual pools with respect to horse races, dog races and jai alai) only if the winnings exceed $5,000 and at least 300 times the wager. In addition, the payor of gambling winnings from these activities must report winnings of more than $600 by filing Form W-2G (Certain Gambling Winnings). Backup withholding (see ¶ 2645) is required if the winner of reportable amounts does not furnish his TIN to the payor. No withholding is required on winnings from bingo, keno, or slot machines. However, for winnings of $1,200 or more from a bingo game or slot machine and for winnings of $1,500 or more from a keno game, the payor must file Form W-2G (Code Secs. 3402(q) and 6041; Reg. § 1.6041-1).[28] Withholding is imposed on proceeds from wagering transactions other than bingo, keno or slot machines at the rate stated above if such proceeds exceed $5,000, regardless of the odds of the wager.

2609. Exempt Remuneration of Employees. Some types of salaries or wages are *specifically* excluded by law from the definition of "wages" for income tax *withholding* purposes (Code Sec. 3401(a)). Specifically excluded are amounts paid for the services of:

Footnote references are to paragraphs of the 2008 Standard Federal Tax Reports.

[18] ¶ 33,661, ¶ 33,662.058
[19] ¶ 33,551
[20] ¶ 33,593.165
[21] ¶ 33,544.20

[22] ¶ 33,574
[23] ¶ 33,575.01, ¶ 33,575.20
[24] ¶ 33,542, ¶ 33,584
[25] ¶ 33,542, ¶ 33,585.021

[26] ¶ 33,584, ¶ 33,585.021
[27] ¶ 33,542
[28] ¶ 33,542, ¶ 35,820, ¶ 35,821, ¶ 35,835

- newspaper carriers under age 18 delivering to customers;
- newspaper and magazine vendors buying at fixed prices and retaining excess from sales to customers;
- agricultural workers who are not subject to FICA withholding;
- domestic workers;
- cash or noncash tips of less than $20 per month;
- moving expenses;
- certain employer contributions to IRAs and deferred compensation plans;
- individuals not working in the course of the employer's business (less than $50 paid and less than 24 days worked during the current or preceding quarter);
- employees of foreign governments and international organizations;
- armed forces personnel serving in a combat zone;
- foreign earned income if excludable from gross income; and
- members of a religious order performing services for the order or associated institution.

The employer's cost of group-term life insurance, including any amount in excess of $50,000 coverage, which is taxable to the employee as compensation, is exempt from withholding (Code Secs. 79(a)(1) and 3401(a)(14); Reg. § 31.3401(a)(14)-1).[29] However, the employer must report the cost of the insurance coverage includible in the employee's gross income on Form W-2 (Reg. § 1.6052-1).[30] An employer's reimbursement of an employee's moving expenses is also exempt if it is reasonable to believe a moving expense deduction will be allowable to the employee under Code Sec. 217 (Code Sec. 3401(a)(15)).[31] In addition, the value of any meals or lodging excludable by the employee from gross income under Code Sec. 119 (see ¶ 873) is exempt from withholding (Reg. § 31.3401(a)-1(b)(9)).[32]

Benefits provided by an employer to an employee in the form of certain educational assistance (see ¶ 871),[33] dependent care assistance, fellowship or scholarship grants, National Health Service Corps loan repayments or nontaxable fringe benefits (such as working condition fringe benefits (see ¶ 863)) are not subject to withholding if it is reasonable to believe that the employee is entitled to exclude the payment from income (Code Sec. 3401(a)). Benefits provided by the employer in the form of medical care reimbursement made to or for the benefit of an employee under a self-insured medical reimbursement plan are excluded from wages for withholding purposes (Code Sec. 3401(a)(20)).[34] Amounts paid to, or on behalf of, an employee or his beneficiary to an individual retirement plan pursuant to a simplified employee pension are not wages subject to withholding if it is reasonable to believe that the employee will be entitled to an exclusion for such payments (Code Sec. 3401(a)(12)) (see IRS Pub. 15-B).[35]

Effective for stock acquired pursuant to an option exercised after October 22, 2004, withholding is not required on a disqualifying disposition of stock acquired through exercise of either an incentive stock option or through an employee stock purchase plan (ESPP) (Act Sec. 251(b) and (c) of the American Jobs Creation Act of 2004 (P.L. 108-357)). Neither is withholding required when compensation is recognized in connection with an ESPP discount under Code Sec. 423(c).

In many cases, however, employee and employer may enter into a mutual agreement to withhold from the employee's remuneration (Code Sec. 3402(p)).[36] To effectuate this agreement, the employee must submit Form W-4 to the employer, and the employer must begin withholding.

Certain Federal Payments. Taxpayers may request voluntary withholding from certain federal payments. The payments include social security benefits, crop disaster payments, Commodity Credit Corporation loans, and any other payment to be specified in regulations by the IRS (Code Sec. 3402(p)(1)).[37]

Footnote references are to paragraphs of the 2008 Standard Federal Tax Reports.

[29] ¶ 6360, ¶ 33,502, ¶ 33,527
[30] ¶ 36,441
[31] ¶ 33,502, ¶ 33,506.207
[32] ¶ 33,503, ¶ 33,506.1880
[33] ¶ 7353.01
[34] ¶ 33,502
[35] ¶ 33,502
[36] ¶ 33,542
[37] ¶ 33,542

¶2609

Unemployment Benefits. Similarly, states are required to permit voluntary withholding on unemployment compensation at a rate of 10 percent (Code Sec. 3402(p)(2)).[38]

2611. Other Payments *Not* Subject to Withholding. Generally, withholding does not apply to payments made to physicians, lawyers, dentists, veterinarians, contractors, public stenographers, auctioneers, and others pursuing an independent trade, business or profession in which their services are offered to the public because they are not considered employees (Reg. § 31.3401(c)-1(c)).[39]

Payments of supplemental unemployment compensation are treated as wages, but withholding applies only to the extent that such benefits are includable in the employee's gross income (Code Sec. 3402(o)).[40] Guaranteed annual wage payments made during periods of unemployment pursuant to a collective bargaining agreement are "wages" subject to withholding.[41] However, strike benefits (other than hourly wages received for strike-related duties) paid by a union to its members are not subject to withholding.[42]

Death benefit payments to beneficiaries or to the estates of deceased employees and payments to such persons of compensation due but unpaid at the time of the decedent's death are not subject to withholding.[43]

Benefits paid under workers' compensation laws (other than nonoccupational disability benefits) are not taxable compensation for services performed and are not subject to withholding[44] nor are amounts received by employees as reimbursements for medical care or as payments for permanent injury or for loss of bodily function (Code Sec. 3401(a)(20)).[45] Also, employer-provided health insurance coverage paid for by salary reduction does not constitute wages for withholding purposes.[46]

For more information concerning amounts paid to employees as advances or reimbursements for traveling, meals, etc., see ¶ 2662 and ¶ 2663.

2612. Computation of Income Tax Withholding. To calculate an employee's income tax withholding, an employer should follow a few basic steps:

(1) calculate the employee's wages for the applicable payroll period;

(2) determine the payroll period, such as weekly, biweekly or monthly;

(3) determine the number of the employee's allowances from the filled-out Form W-4, Employee's Withholding Allowance Certificate; and

(4) choose the withholding method, generally the percentage or wage-bracket method (Code Sec. 3402(a)).

Other factors to consider in the calculation include whether the employee is a recent hire or only works part-time, whether the employee has more than one employer, and whether the employee receives any supplemental wage payments.

Methods of Withholding

2614. Major Methods of Withholding. The law provides two methods of computing the tax to be withheld: (1) the "percentage" method (see ¶ 2616) and (2) the "wage bracket" method (see ¶ 2619) (Code Secs. 3402(b), (c) and (h)).[47] For other permissible methods of withholding, see ¶ 2627.

Regardless of which method is used, the amount of withholding will depend upon the amount of wages paid, the number of exemptions claimed by the employee on the withholding exemption certificate (see ¶ 2634), the employee's marital status, and the payroll period of the employee (see ¶ 2621) (Code Secs. 3402(a), (f) and (g)).[48]

See Employer's Tax Guide (Circular E), IRS Publication 15, for additional information.

2616. Percentage Method. If the employer selects the percentage method of withholding, the employer must:

Footnote references are to paragraphs of the 2008 Standard Federal Tax Reports.

[38] ¶ 33,542
[39] ¶ 33,536
[40] ¶ 33,542
[41] ¶ 33,506.3683
[42] ¶ 33,506.3678
[43] ¶ 33,506.1856
[44] ¶ 33,506.035
[45] ¶ 33,502
[46] ¶ 33,506.1871
[47] ¶ 33,542
[48] ¶ 33,542

(1) multiply the amount of one withholding exemption for the payroll period by the number of exemptions claimed on the employee's Form W-4;

(2) subtract the amount determined in (1) from the employee's wages; and

(3) apply the appropriate percentage rate table to the resulting figure to determine the amount of withholding (Code Sec. 3402(a)).[49]

Each withholding exemption is equal to one personal exemption as provided in Code Sec. 151(b) prorated to the payroll period (Code Sec. 3402(a)(2)). Thus, if the payroll period is monthly and the personal exemption is $3,400 in 2007 (to increase to $3,500 in 2008), then the amount of one withholding exemption is $3,400 divided by 12 or $283.

Percentage method withholding tables for both single (including heads of household) and married employees for each of the payroll periods are provided for use in determining the amount of tax to be withheld (Code Sec. 3402(a)).[50] The IRS has approved and issued alternative formula tables for percentage method withholding that were devised for computing withheld tax under different payroll systems and equipment.[51]

2619. Wage Bracket Method. The wage bracket tables provided by the IRS for graduated withholding cover weekly, biweekly, semimonthly and monthly payroll periods.[52] Separate tables for each period are provided for single persons (including heads of household) and married persons. The proper columns to be used by the employer are determined by the total number of exemptions claimed on the employee's withholding exemption certificate. These tables produce about the same result as the percentage method tables and are designed to accommodate different payroll systems and equipment (see IRS Pub. 15).

If the wage bracket method is used, wages in excess of the highest wage bracket in the tables may, at the election of the employer, be rounded off to the nearest dollar (Reg. § 31.3402(c)-1(e)).[53]

2621. Payroll Period. The employee's correct "payroll period" (the period of service for which a payment of wages is ordinarily made to an employee) will determine the exemption amount (see ¶ 2616 and ¶ 2619) to be used if the employer uses the percentage method or the correct table to be used if the employer uses the wage bracket method. Daily, weekly, biweekly, semimonthly, monthly, quarterly, semiannual and annual payroll periods have separate tables for the percentage computation. Any other payroll period is a miscellaneous payroll period. Wages may also be paid for periods that are not payroll periods (see ¶ 2624).

2624. Computation of Withholding Allowance. If an employee has an established payroll period, the amount of the withholding allowance (for the percentage method) is determined by the payroll period, without regard to the time the employee is actually engaged in performing services during such period.

If the payment is for a period that is not a payroll period, such as when wages are paid upon completion of a particular project, the exemption (or the amount withheld, if the wage bracket method is used) is computed based on a miscellaneous payroll period containing a number of days (including Sundays and holidays) equal to those in the period covered by the payment (Code Sec. 3402(b); Reg. § 31.3402(c)-1(c)(2)).[54]

If the wages are paid without regard to any period, the tax to be withheld is the same as for a miscellaneous payroll period containing the number of days equal to the days (including Sundays and holidays) which have elapsed since (1) the date of the last payment of wages by the employer during the calendar year, (2) the date of commencement of employment with the employer during such year, or (3) January 1 of such year, whichever is later (Code Sec. 3402(b); Reg. § 31.3402(c)-1(c)(3)).[55]

2627. Alternative Methods of Withholding. An employer may withhold on the basis of average wages by using estimated quarterly wages, annualized wages, cumula-

---

Footnote references are to paragraphs of the 2008 Standard Federal Tax Reports.

[49] ¶ 33,542
[50] ¶ 151—¶ 152, ¶ 33,542
[51] ¶ 153
[52] ¶ 154
[53] ¶ 33,547
[54] ¶ 33,542, ¶ 33,547
[55] ¶ 33,542, ¶ 33,547

tive wages, or any method which produces substantially the same amount of withholding as the percentage or wage bracket method (Code Sec. 3402(h); Reg. §§31.3402(h)(1)-1—31.3402(h)(4)-1).[56]

2629. Employee Requests to Increase Withholding. An employee may request on Form W-4 that the employer withhold additional amounts (Code Sec. 3402(i); Reg. §§31.3402(i)-1 and 31.3402(i)-2).[57]

In addition, amounts may be voluntarily withheld from certain types of income that are not subject to mandatory withholding (see¶ 2609). Thus, for example, magazine vendors, domestic workers, etc., may enter into an agreement with their employer to have income tax withheld (Code Sec. 3402(p); Reg. §31.3401(a)-3).[58]

Withholding Exemptions

2632. Claiming Withholding Exemptions. Every employee is entitled to his or her own withholding exemption and one for each dependent. A married employee may claim a withholding exemption for his or her spouse if the latter does not claim one. An employee who can be claimed as a dependent on another person's tax return, such as a parent's return, may not claim a withholding exemption (Code Sec. 3402(f)(1)).[59] No withholding exemption is allowed for unborn children even though the birth is expected to occur within the tax year. Employees with more than one job may not claim an exemption that is currently in effect with another employer (Code Sec. 3402(f)(7)).[60]

In order to avoid excess withholding, a standard deduction allowance may be claimed by an employee, provided that the employee does not have a spouse who is receiving wages subject to withholding and does not have withholding certificates in effect with more than one employer. The standard deduction allowance is equivalent to one withholding exemption (or more than one if regulations so prescribe) (Code Sec. 3402(f)(1)(E)).[61]

Additional withholding allowances are available to an employee who can show that he or she will have large itemized deductions, deductible alimony payments, moving expenses, employee business expenses, retirement contributions, net losses from Schedules C, D, E, and F of Form 1040, or tax credits. An eligible employee should file Form W-4 with the employer (Code Sec. 3402(m); Reg. §31.3402(m)-1).[62]

2634. Withholding Exemption Certificate. Before an employee is allowed any withholding exemptions, he must file a withholding exemption certificate, Form W-4, with his employer showing the number of exemptions to which he is entitled (Code Sec. 3402(f)(2); Reg. §31.3402(f)(2)-1).[63] Otherwise, withholding must be computed as if the employee were single and claiming no other exemptions. A widow or widower may claim "married" status for purposes of withholding if she or he qualifies as a surviving spouse (Code Sec. 3402(l)(3)).[64] See ¶ 175.

An employee who certifies to his employer that he had no income tax liability for his preceding tax year and anticipates none for the current tax year may be exempt from the withholding provisions (Code Sec. 3402(n); Reg. §31.3402(n)-1).[65] Form W-4 should be used, and should be renewed annually, by any employee claiming this exemption.

Most Forms W-4 are retained by the employer. Employers need only submit withholding certificates to the IRS if directed to do so by the Service. Further, the IRS may issue a notice to the employer that specifies the maximum number of withholding exemptions the employee may claim. Generally, the employer is bound by this determination until otherwise advised by the IRS (Reg. §31.3402(f)(2)-1(g)).[66] A $500 civil penalty may be assessed against any individual who decreases his rate of withholding by claiming excess withholding allowances on Form W-4 (Code Sec. 6682).[67] In addition, a criminal penalty may be imposed against any individual who willfully supplies false withholding information or fails to supply withholding information (Code Sec. 7205).[68]

Footnote references are to paragraphs of the 2008 Standard Federal Tax Reports.

[56] ¶ 33,542, ¶ 33,566— ¶ 33,569
[57] ¶ 33,542, ¶ 33,571, ¶ 33,572
[58] ¶ 33,508, ¶ 33,542
[59] ¶ 33,542
[60] ¶ 33,542
[61] ¶ 33,542
[62] ¶ 33,542, ¶ 33,579
[63] ¶ 33,542, ¶ 33,554
[64] ¶ 33,542
[65] ¶ 33,542, ¶ 33,580
[66] ¶ 33,554
[67] ¶ 39,845
[68] ¶ 41,325

2637. Change in Status. When any change occurs that affects the number of withholding exemptions to which an employee is entitled, the employee may file a new exemption certificate if the number of exemptions increases. However, the employee must file a new certificate within 10 days if the number of exemptions decreases after the occurrence of any of the following events (Code Sec. 3402(f)(2)(B); Reg. § 31.3402(f)(2)-1(b)):[69]

(1) The spouse for whom the employee has been claiming an exemption is divorced or legally separated from the employee or claims his or her own exemption on a separate certificate.

(2) The support of a claimed dependent is taken over by someone else, and the employee no longer expects to claim that person as a dependent.

(3) The employee discovers that a dependent (other than a qualifying child) for whom an exemption was claimed will receive sufficient income of his own for the calendar year to disqualify him as a dependent (see ¶ 137).

(4) Circumstances have changed so that the employee is no longer entitled to claim an exemption based on one of the deduction or credit items listed at ¶ 2632.

An employee who claimed "no liability" (see ¶ 2634) must file a new Form W-4 within 10 days from the time he anticipates that he will incur liability for the year or before December 1 if he anticipates liability for the next year (Reg. § 31.3402(f)(2)-1(c)).[70]

The death of a spouse or dependent does not affect the withholding exemption for that year (Reg. § 31.3402(f)(2)-1(b)(1)(ii)) unless the employee's tax year is not a calendar year and the death occurs in that part of the calendar year preceding the employee's tax year.[71]

An employee may file an amended withholding exemption certificate, increasing the number of exemptions, at any time that he becomes eligible for an additional dependency or an extra exemption based on one of the deduction or credit items listed at ¶ 2632.

A withholding exemption certificate furnished to the employer that replaces an existing certificate can be effective for the first payment after the certificate is received if so elected by the employer. However, the replacing certificate must be effective for the first payroll period that ends on or after the 30th day after the day on which the new certificate is furnished (Code Sec. 3402(f)(3)(B)).[72]

Supplemental Wages

2639. Supplemental Payments and Tips. Special rules apply when the employee is paid supplemental wages (bonus, overtime pay, commissions, etc.).

If supplemental wages are paid at the same time as regular wages, the two are added together and the withholding tax is computed on the total as a single wage payment. If the supplemental wages are not paid at the same time as the regular wages, the supplemental wages may be added either to the regular wages for the preceding payroll period or for the current payroll period within the same calendar year. Under an alternative method, the employer may treat the supplemental wages as wholly separate from regular wages and withhold at a flat rate on the supplemental wage payment without any allowance for exemptions and without reference to any regular payment of wages. The flat rate cannot be less than the third lowest rate of tax applicable to single filers (25 percent for tax years beginning in 2007 and 2008). Once the total of supplemental wage payments made to an employee, within a calendar year, exceeds $1,000,000, the excess will be subject to withholding at the highest income tax rate (35 percent for tax years beginning in 2007 and 2008). This rule applies regardless of the method otherwise used to withhold supplemental wages paid to the employee. (Reg. § 31.3402(g)-1;[73] Act Sec. 904(b) of the American Jobs Creation Act of 2004 (P.L. 108-357) (see IRS Pub. 15 and IRS Pub. 505).

Footnote references are to paragraphs of the 2008 Standard Federal Tax Reports.

[69] ¶ 33,542, ¶ 33,554, ¶ 33,560.03   [70] ¶ 33,554   [72] ¶ 33,542
[71] ¶ 33,554   [73] ¶ 33,561

A vacation allowance is subject to withholding as if it were a regular wage payment for the vacation period. If the vacation allowance is paid in addition to the regular wage, it is a "supplemental payment" (Reg. § 31.3402(g)-1(c)).[74]

An employer must collect both income tax and employee social security or railroad retirement tax on tips reported by an employee from wages due the employee or other funds that the employee makes available. Tips may be treated as if they were supplemental wages subject to the flat withholding rate (25 percent for 2007 and 2008) without allowance for exemptions, provided that income tax has been withheld on the employee's regular wages. Otherwise, the tips must be treated as part of the current or preceding wage payment of the same calendar year and are subject to the regular graduated withholding rates.[75]

Withholding on Certain Government Payments

2641. Government Payments. Applicable to payments made after December 31, 2010, the federal government, every state and local government and their political subdivisions and instrumentalities (including multi-state agencies) are required to withhold tax at the rate of three percent on certain payments to persons providing any property or services (Code Sec. 3402(t)). Any payment made in connection with a government voucher or certificate program that acts as a payment for services or property is subject to the withholding requirement. Withholding is required even if the government entity making the payment is not the recipient of the property or services. The withholding requirement does not apply to payments determined by a needs or income test, such as food stamps or welfare payments.

Withholding on Pensions, Interest and Dividends

2643. Pensions, Annuities and Certain Deferred Income. In the case of taxable payments from an employer-sponsored pension, annuity, profit-sharing, stock bonus or other deferred compensation plan, withholding is required unless the recipient elects not to have tax withheld (Code Sec. 3405).[76] The same rule applies to an IRA or an annuity, endowment, or life insurance contract issued by a life insurance company. The recipient's election not to have withholding apply remains in effect until revoked. The payor must notify the recipient that an election may be made and of the right to revoke such election. The election is generally not available with respect to foreign-delivered payments to persons subject to U.S. tax on their world-wide income. "Foreign-delivered," for this purpose, means outside the U.S. or its possessions.[77]

Amount Withheld. The amount withheld depends on whether the distributions are periodic payments or nonperiodic payments.

For periodic payments (annuity and similar periodic payments), withholding is made as though the payment was a payment of wages for the appropriate payroll period and, if the recipient does not have a withholding exemption certificate (Form W-4P) in effect, he is treated as a married individual claiming three exemptions. However, these exemptions are not available to a payee failing to file a certificate if the payee fails to furnish a taxpayer identification number (TIN) to a payor or if the IRS notifies the payor that the payee's TIN is incorrect (Code Sec. 3405(a) and (e)(12)). Under the general rule, the withholding rate on nonperiodic distributions is 10 percent (Code Sec. 3405(b)).[78] Special withholding rules apply to distributions that were eligible for rollover but not directly transferred from the distributing plan to an eligible transferee plan. The withholding rate on such distributions is 20 percent instead of 10 percent. The withholding requirement is mandatory and distributees cannot elect to forego withholding on rollover eligible distributions (Code Sec. 3405(c)).[79]

Qualified Hurricane Katrina Distributions. Qualified Hurricane Katrina, Rita, and Wilma distributions are treated as received in an eligible rollover distribution for some purposes but are not subject to 20-percent withholding (Code Sec. 1400Q(a)(6)(A)). See the discussion of the definition and taxation of qualified Hurricane Katrina distributions at ¶ 2155.

Footnote references are to paragraphs of the 2008 Standard Federal Tax Reports.

[74] ¶ 33,561
[75] ¶ 33,506.056
[76] ¶ 33,620
[77] ¶ 33,620.75
[78] ¶ 33,620
[79] ¶ 33,620

2645. Backup Withholding. A backup withholding system requires a payor to deduct and withhold income tax from reportable payments, such as interest or dividends, if:

(1) the payee fails to furnish his TIN to the payor in the manner required;[80]

(2) the IRS notifies the payor that the TIN furnished by the payee is incorrect;[81]

(3) there has been a notified payee underreporting, described in Code Sec. 3406(c),[82] of interest, dividend, patronage dividend income, or other reportable payments; or

(4) there has been a payee certification failure described in Code Sec. 3406(d) with respect to interest, dividend, patronage dividend payments, or other reportable payments.[83]

The payor is required to withhold an amount equal to the product of the fourth lowest rate of tax applicable to single filers. This rate is 28 percent for tax years beginning in 2007 and 2008 (Code Sec. 3406(a)) (see IRS Pub. 15-T and IRS Pub. 505).

FICA Tax

2648. FICA Tax Rates. Under the Federal Insurance Contributions Act, an employer is required to withhold social security taxes (including hospital insurance tax) from wages paid to an employee during the year and must also match the tax withheld from the employee's wages. For 2007, the combined tax rate is 7.65 percent, which consists of a 6.2 percent component for old-age, survivors, and disability insurance (OASDI) and a 1.45 percent component for hospital insurance (Medicare). The OASDI rate applies only to wages paid within an OASDI wage base ($97,500 in 2007 and $102,000 in 2008). There is no cap on wages subject to the Medicare tax (Code Secs. 3101, 3111 and 3121(a)).[84]

If an employee works for more than one employer, each employer must withhold and pay FICA taxes on the wages paid. In such instance, the employee's FICA tax withheld for the year might exceed the maximum employee tax for the year. If this happens, the employee must take the excess as a credit against his income tax (see ¶ 1372 as to limitation) (Reg. § 1.31-2)[85] or, if he is not required to file an income tax return, he may file a special refund claim (Reg. § 31.6413(c)-1).[86] The same rule applies to taxes withheld under the Railroad Retirement Tax Act.

If an individual is concurrently employed by two or more related corporations and all remuneration is disbursed to the individual through a common paymaster for the group, the common paymaster is responsible for the reporting and payment of FICA and FUTA taxes. However, the other related corporations remain jointly and severally liable for their appropriate share of the taxes (Reg. § 31.3121(s)-1).

In the case of persons performing domestic services in a private home of the employer and persons performing agricultural labor, if the employer pays the employee's liability for FICA taxes or state unemployment taxes without deduction from the employee's wages, those payments are not wages for FICA purposes (Code Sec. 3121(a)(6)).

Return and Payment by Employer

2650. Employer Return and Deposit of Taxes. An employer subject to either income tax withholding or social security taxes, or both, must file a quarterly return or, if eligible, an annual return. Form 941 is the quarterly return form, which combines the reporting of income and FICA taxes withheld from wages, tips, supplemental unemployment compensation benefits, and third-party payments of sick pay (see ¶ 2604). Form 944 is the annual return, which, under the Form 944 Program (see below, under *Form 944 Program*), is generally filed by "small employers," i.e., employers with an estimated annual employment tax liability of $1,000 or less. Taxes on wages for agricultural

---

Footnote references are to paragraphs of the 2008 Standard Federal Tax Reports.

[80] ¶ 33,654.034	[83] ¶ 33,640, ¶ 33,654.032	[86] ¶ 38,754
[81] ¶ 33,654.30	[84] ¶ 114	
[82] ¶ 33,640, ¶ 33,654.026	[85] ¶ 4063	

¶2645

employees, including domestic services on a farm operated for profit, are reported annually on Form 943. Nonpayroll items are separately deposited and annually reported on Form 945.

Form 941 is due on or before the last day of the month following the quarter involved. However, an extension of time for filing is automatically granted to the 10th day of the second month following the close of the calendar quarter if the return is accompanied by depositary receipts showing timely deposits in full payment of taxes due for the period (Reg. § 31.6071(a)-1).[87]

Forms W-2, 1099-R, and Transmittal Form W-3 must be filed with the Social Security Administration (SSA) by the last day of February of the year following the year included in the return. The SSA transmits the income tax information on the return to the IRS.

Domestic Workers/Nanny Tax. Employers must withhold and pay FICA taxes on the wages of their household workers if cash wages paid in calendar year 2007 total $1,500 or more ($1,600 in 2008) (Code Sec. 3121(a)(7)(B) and (x)).

Employers must report and pay required employment taxes for domestic employees on Schedule H of their own Form 1040 or 1040A. While withheld amounts no longer have to be deposited on a monthly basis, employers do need an employer identification number (EIN) to include on Form W-2 (see ¶ 2655) and Schedule H. To obtain an EIN, employers should complete Form SS-4 (Application for Employer Identification Number).

Employers must increase either their quarterly estimated tax payments or the income tax withholding on their own wages in order to satisfy employment tax obligations with respect to domestic workers. Failure to withhold for domestic workers results in liability for the penalty for underpayment of estimated tax (see ¶ 2682).

Deposit Rules. Generally, an employer must deposit the income tax withheld and the FICA taxes with an authorized commercial bank depositary.

Depositors are classified as either monthly or semiweekly depositors. An employer's status for a given calendar year is determined annually, based on the employer's employment tax reporting history during a 12-month lookback period ending on June 30 of the preceding year (Reg. § 31.6302-1(b)(1)).

An employer generally must deposit employment taxes on a monthly basis during 2008, if, during the lookback period from July 1, 2006, through June 30, 2007, the amount of the aggregate employment taxes reported was $50,000 or less. Monthly depositors are required to deposit each month's taxes on or before the 15th day of the following month. If the 15th day is not a banking day, the employer has until the next banking day thereafter to make the deposit

An employer that reported more than $50,000 in aggregate employment taxes during the 2006-2007 lookback period will be a semiweekly depositor in 2008. Semiweekly depositors generally are required to deposit their taxes by the Wednesday after payday, if payday falls on a Wednesday, Thursday or Friday. For all other paydays, the deposit is due by the Friday following payday. Semiweekly depositors will always have at least three banking days after the payday to make the deposit.

For new employers, during the first calendar year of business, the tax liability for each quarter of the lookback period is considered to be zero. Therefore, the employer is a monthly depositor for the first calendar year of business.

Notwithstanding these general rules, employers with $100,000 or more of accumulated liability during a monthly or semiweekly period are required to deposit the funds by the first banking day after the $100,000 threshold is reached. Also, employers accumulating deposits of less than $2,500 in 2008 during the quarter may skip the deposits entirely and send full payment with their quarterly employment tax returns (*de minimus* rule). As a result, employers with employment tax liabilities of less than $2,500 per return period in 2008 are no longer required to make monthly deposits but may instead pay in full with a timely filed return (see IRS Pub. 15).

Footnote references are to paragraphs of the 2008 Standard Federal Tax Reports.

[87] ¶ 36,702

The deposit rules apply to employment taxes that are reported on a quarterly or annual basis, such as Form 941, Employer's Quarterly Federal Tax Return, and Form 943, Employer's Annual Tax Return for Agricultural Workers. Special deposit rules apply to "small employers" eligible to participate in the Form 944 Program (see below, under *Form 944 Program*).

As a safe harbor, employers that fail to deposit the full amount of taxes will not be penalized if the shortfall does not exceed the greater of $100 or two percent of the amount of employment taxes required to be deposited, provided that the shortfall is deposited on or before a prescribed makeup date.

Penalties will also be abated if an employer shows that a failure to deposit the full amount of the employment taxes was due to reasonable cause, as provided in Code Sec. 6656 (Reg. § 31.6302-1).[88]

Amounts withheld under the Code Sec. 3406 backup withholding requirements are treated as employment taxes subject to these deposit rules. However, employers are permitted to treat the backup withholding amounts separately from other employment taxes for purposes of the deposit rules (Reg. § 31.6302-3).[89]

Different monthly and semimonthly deposit requirements apply to taxes withheld from nonresident aliens and foreign corporations (Reg. § 1.6302-2).[90]

Only an original Form 8109, Federal Tax Deposit Coupons, may be used to make a deposit. Under the IRS's AUTOGEN program, taxpayers automatically receive new FTD coupon books as they are needed.[91]

Form 944 Program. The IRS has established an Employers' Annual Federal Tax Program (Form 944) called the Form 944 Program (Temporary Reg. §§ 31.6011(a)-1T, 31.6011(a)-4T and 31.6302-1T).[92] The Form 944 Program requires certain "small employers" to file an annual Form 944 rather than a quarterly Form 941. Generally, Form 944 is due January 31 of the year following the year for which the return is filed.

Eligibility for the Form 944 Program is generally limited to employers with an annual estimated employment tax liability of $1,000 or less. The IRS provides written notice to employers it believes are qualified for the program. A notified employer that does not wish to participate in the Form 944 Program must notify the IRS that it prefers to electronically file quarterly Forms 941, or that it anticipates that its annual employment tax liability will exceed $1,000. An employer that does not receive notice from the IRS may ask to participate in the program if it believes its annual employment tax liability will not exceed $1,000.

Most participating employers can pay their employment taxes annually with their Form 944, rather than making monthly or semi-weekly deposits. A participating employer, however, may not discover that its actual annual employment tax liability exceeded the $1,000 threshold until it files its Form 944 on the following January 31. These employers can avoid the penalty for failing to make a timely monthly deposit of their January taxes, so long as they fully pay their January employment taxes by March 15.

A modified lookback period applies for determining whether a participating employer that eventually discovers that it is not eligible for the Form 944 Program is a monthly or semi-weekly depositor. For those employers, the lookback period is the second calendar year preceding the current calendar year. For instance, the lookback period for 2008 is calendar year 2006.

A participating employer whose actual total employment tax liability exceeds $2,500 but whose employment tax liability for a quarter of the year is less than $2,500 is eligible for the *de minimus* rule applicable to quarterly Form 941 filers (see above). Such an employer is allowed to apply the quarterly *de minimus* rule if it deposits the employment taxes that accumulated during a quarter by the last day of the month following the close of the quarter. If an employer's tax liability for a quarter does not qualify for *de minimus* treatment, the employer must make deposits either monthly or semi-weekly, whichever is appropriate, in order to avoid the failure-to-deposit penalty.

Footnote references are to paragraphs of the 2008 Standard Federal Tax Reports.

[88] ¶ 38,055B
[89] ¶ 38,055D
[90] ¶ 38,062
[91] ¶ 38,070.075, ¶ 38,070.107
[92] ¶ 35,131C, ¶ 38,055BB

Electronic Fund Transfer. The IRS has issued final regulations that change which taxpayers must make deposits using the Electronic Federal Tax Payment System (EFTPS) (Reg. § 31.6302-1(h)).[93] Taxpayers that exceed threshold aggregate amounts of employment and other taxes during a determination period (12-month period) must deposit by EFTPS (Reg. § 31.6302-1(h)(2)).[94] A taxpayer is required to make deposits using EFTPS in 2008 if (1) the total deposits of all depositary taxes (such as employment tax, excise tax and corporate income tax) in 2006 was more than $200,000 or (2) the taxpayer was required to use EFTPS in 2007. The date on which taxpayers must begin using EFTPS depends on when the threshold level of $200,000 is met. A chart showing the threshold amounts, including the determination period for these amounts, and the date when deposits by EFTPS must begin, follows:

Threshold Amount	Determination Period	Effective Date
$ 50,000	1/1/1995—12/31/1995	July 1, 1997
50,000	1/1/1996—12/31/1996	January 1, 1998
50,000	1/1/1997—12/31/1997	January 1, 1999
200,000	1/1/1998—12/31/1998	January 1, 2000
200,000	1/1/1999—12/31/1999	January 1, 2001
200,000	1/1/2000—12/31/2000	January 1, 2002
200,000	1/1/2001—12/31/2001	January 1, 2003
200,000	1/1/2002—12/31/2002	January 1, 2004
200,000	1/1/2003—12/31/2003	January 1, 2005
200,000	1/1/2004—12/31/2004	January 1, 2006
200,000	1/1/2005—12/31/2005	January 1, 2007
200,000	1/1/2006—12/31/2006	January 1, 2008
200,000	1/1/2007—12/31/2007	January 1, 2009

Once a taxpayer is required to make EFTPS deposits applying the new threshold, all future deposits must be made by EFTPS, regardless of whether the amount is reached in each calendar year thereafter. If a taxpayer is required to use EFTPS and fails to do so, a 10-percent penalty may be imposed. Also, taxpayers that are not required to use EFTPS may participate in the payment system voluntarily (Reg. § 31.6302-1(h)(2)).[95]

Timeliness of Deposits. The timeliness of deposits is determined by the date they are received by an authorized depositary. However, a deposit received by the depositary after the due date is considered timely if the employer establishes that it was mailed on or before the second day before the prescribed due date (Code Sec. 7502(e)). In determining banking days for deposit purposes, Saturdays, Sundays and legal holidays are excluded, but the mailing date (on or before the second day before the prescribed due date) is not extended under such circumstances. However, the above timely mailing exception does not apply to a large depositor (i.e., with respect to any deposit of $20,000 or more by any person who is required to deposit the tax more than once a month). This type of deposit must be made by the due date, regardless of the method of delivery (Code Sec. 7502(e)(3)).[96]

2652. Disregarded Entities. Final regulations require that a disregarded entity be treated as a separate entity responsible for employment tax liabilities (Reg. § 301.7701-2(c)).[97] The rule applies to such disregarded entities as a qualified subchapter S subsidiary (QSub) and a limited liability company (LLC). A disregarded entity continues to be disregarded for other federal tax purposes.

The regulations do not take effect until January 1, 2009. For wages paid prior to January 1, 2009, disregarded entities and their owners may continue to use procedures permitted by Notice 99-6. Under Notice 99-6, the owner of a disregarded entity can handle employment taxes under the owner's name and taxpayer identification number (TIN). Alternatively, a disregarded entity that was an entity under state law can handle employment taxes under its own name and TIN.

2653. Advance Payment of Earned Income Credit. Although advance payments of the earned income credit (see ¶ 1375) are not compensation for withholding purposes,

---

Footnote references are to paragraphs of the 2008 Standard Federal Tax Reports.

[93] ¶ 38,055B   [95] ¶ 38,055B   [97] ¶ 43,082
[94] ¶ 38,055B   [96] ¶ 42,620

the payments must be separately reported on Form W-2. Failure to make advance payments when required is considered a failure to deduct and withhold taxes (Code Sec. 3507).[98]

An employer may reduce its deposit of employment taxes due with respect to each payroll period for all employees by the sum of any credits advanced during the same period.[99]

2655. Statements to Employees. On or before January 31, every employer is required to furnish every employee with copies of Form W-2 for taxes withheld during the preceding calendar year. Employers may elect, with the consent of the employee, to furnish electronic, rather than written, payee statement of Form W-2 (Reg. § 31.6051-1(j)).[100] When employment terminates before the end of the calendar year, there is no reasonable expectation of reemployment, and the employee submits a written request for the information, Form W-2 must be furnished within 30 days of the written request, if the 30-day period ends before January 31 (Code Sec. 6051(a)).[101]

Form W-2 is a multiple-part wage statement with several copies; Copy A is sent to the SSA, Copy 1 is sent to the state, Copy B is kept by the employee and attached to his or her federal tax return, Copy C is retained for the employee's records, Copy 2 is attached to the employee's state, city, or local tax return, and Copy D is kept in the employer's records. Employers must file electronically rather than paper returns if 250 or more Forms W-2 are to be filed with the SSA. Hardship waivers may be requested.[102]

If the social security tax imposed on tips reported by the employee exceeds the tax that has been collected by the employer, the employer is required to furnish the employee with a statement showing the amount of the excess (Code Sec. 6053(b)).[103]

2658. Employer Penalties. Every employer required to withhold tax on wages is liable for payment of the tax whether or not it is collected. The employer's liability is relieved, however, after showing that the employee's related income tax liability has been paid (Reg. § 31.3402(d)-1).[104]

Any responsible person—typically a corporate officer or employee—who willfully fails to withhold, account for, or pay over withholding tax to the government is subject to a penalty equal to 100 percent of such tax (Code Sec. 6672).[105] The penalty is a collection device, usually assessed only when the tax cannot be collected from the employer, and results in a personal liability not dischargeable by bankruptcy.[106]

Civil and criminal penalties can be imposed under Code Secs. 6674 and 7204 if an employer willfully fails to furnish or furnishes a false or fraudulent Form W-2 statement (see ¶ 2655) to an employee.[107]

Failure to Make Timely Deposits. A four-tier graduated penalty applies to failures to make timely deposits of tax, unless the failure is due to reasonable cause and not willful neglect. The penalty amount varies with the length of time within which the taxpayer corrects the failure to make the required deposit. The penalty is assessed as follows:

(1) two percent of the amount of the underpayment if the failure is for no more than five days;

(2) five percent of the amount of the underpayment if the failure is for more than five days but for no more than 15 days; and

(3) 10 percent of the amount of the underpayment if the failure is for more than 15 days.

However, the penalty will be imposed at the rate of 15 percent of the amount of the underpayment if a required tax deposit is not made on or before the day that is 10 days after the date of the first delinquency notice to the taxpayer, or, if earlier, on or before the day on which notice and demand for immediate payment of tax is given in cases of jeopardy (Code Sec. 6656(a) and (b)).[108]

Footnote references are to paragraphs of the 2008 Standard Federal Tax Reports.

[98] ¶ 33,780
[99] ¶ 33,781, ¶ 33,783
[100] ¶ 36,421
[101] ¶ 36,420

[102] ¶ 33,594.03
[103] ¶ 36,460
[104] ¶ 33,549
[105] ¶ 39,775

[106] ¶ 39,780.39
[107] ¶ 39,795, ¶ 41,320
[108] ¶ 39,580

Deposits generally are applied to the most recent tax liability within the quarter (Rev. Proc. 2001-58).[109] Any depositor to whom the IRS mails a penalty notice may, within 90 days of the date of the notice, designate how the payment is to be applied in order to minimize the amount of the penalty.

FUTA Tax

2661. FUTA Tax Rate. The Federal Unemployment Tax Act imposes a tax on employers who employed one or more persons in covered employment on at least one day in each of 20 weeks during the current or preceding calendar year or who paid wages (in covered employment) of at least $1,500 ($20,000 for agricultural labor or $1,000 for household employees) in a calendar quarter in the current or preceding calendar year. The tax is based on the first $7,000 of certain wages paid during the calendar year to each employee. The full rate of tax is 6.2 percent through 2007, but the employer is allowed a partial credit against this tax based on its state unemployment insurance tax liability (Code Secs. 3301 and 3302) (see IRS Pub. 15).

In the case of persons performing domestic services in a private home of the employer and persons performing agricultural labor, if the employer pays the employee's liability for FICA taxes or state unemployment taxes without deducting those taxes from the employee's wages, the amounts paid by the employer are not wages for FUTA purposes (Code Sec. 3306(b)(6)), but they are wages for income tax withholding purposes (see ¶ 2601).[110] The temporary surtax rate of 0.2 percent expired after December 31, 2007 (Code Sec. 3301). Therefore, for 2008 and thereafter, the full FUTA tax rate is 6 percent.

Withholding on Expense Allowances

2662. Accountable Plans v. Nonaccountable Plans. An employer's withholding obligations with respect to amounts paid to employees under an expense allowance or reimbursement arrangement depend upon whether the amounts are paid under an accountable or a nonaccountable plan (see ¶ 943). Amounts paid under an accountable plan, to the extent of an employee's substantiated expenses, may be excluded from an employee's gross income, are not required to be reported on the employee's Form W-2, and are exempt from withholding of income and employment taxes (FICA, FUTA, railroad retirement, and railroad unemployment taxes) (Reg. §§ 1.62-2(c)(4), 1.62-2(h)(1) and 31.3401(a)-4(a)).[111] Amounts paid under a nonaccountable plan are included in the employee's gross income, reported on Form W-2 and subject to withholding (Reg. § 1.62-2(c)(5)).[112] If expenses are reimbursed under an accountable plan, but either the expenses are not substantiated within a reasonable period of time or amounts in excess of substantiated expenses are not returned within a reasonable period of time, the excess or unsubstantiated amounts paid are treated as paid under a nonaccountable plan and are subject to withholding no later than the first payroll period following the end of the reasonable period of time (Reg. §§ 1.62-2(h)(2)(i)(A) and 31.3401(a)-4(b)(1)).[113]

Withholding Rate. Expense reimbursements that are subject to withholding may be added to the employee's regular wages for the appropriate payroll period, and withheld taxes may be computed on the total. Alternatively, the employer may withhold at the flat rate applicable to supplemental wages (see ¶ 2639) if the expense reimbursement or allowance is paid separately or is separately identified (Reg. § 31.3401(a)-4(c), Act Sec. 13273 of P.L. 103-66 and Act Sec. 101(c)(11) of P.L. 107-16).[114]

2663. Per Diem Allowances for Automobile, Meal, and Lodging Expenses. If the amount of an employee's expenses is substantiated through the use of an IRS-approved per diem allowance, any amounts paid to the employee exceeding the amounts deemed substantiated are subject to income and employment tax withholding (Reg. §§ 1.62-2(h)(2)(i)(B) and 31.3401(a)-4(b)(1)(ii)).[115] (See ¶ 947 for standard mileage rate

---

Footnote references are to paragraphs of the 2008 Standard Federal Tax Reports.

[109] ¶ 39,585.235
[110] ¶ 114, ¶ 33,506.021
[111] ¶ 6004, ¶ 33,508A

[112] ¶ 6004
[113] ¶ 6004, ¶ 33,508A
[114] ¶ 33,508A

[115] ¶ 6004, ¶ 33,508A

and FAVR allowances for automobile expenses; see ¶ 954 et seq. for per diem methods relating to meal and lodging expenses.)

For per diem or mileage allowances paid in advance, withholding on any excess must occur no later than the first payroll period following the payroll period in which the expenses for which the advance was paid (i.e., the days or miles of travel) are substantiated by the employee. For a per diem or mileage allowance paid as a reimbursement, the excess amounts reimbursed are subject to withholding when paid.

Self-Employment Tax

2664. Rate and Payment. The combined rate of tax on self-employment income (see ¶ 2670) is 15.3 percent.[116] The rate consists of a 12.4 percent component for old-age, survivors, and disability insurance (OASDI) and a 2.9 percent component for hospital insurance (Medicare) (see IRS Pub. 334).

The self-employment tax, which is computed on Schedule SE of Form 1040, is treated as part of the income tax and must also be taken into account for purposes of the estimated tax (Code Sec. 6654(f)).[117] A married couple filing a joint return must file separate Schedules SE where each spouse is self-employed.

2667. Persons Subject to Tax. An individual who is self-employed is subject to the self-employment tax, the purpose of which is to provide social security and Medicare benefits to such individuals. This tax is assessed on the individual's self-employment income (see ¶ 2670). However, members of religious orders who have taken vows of poverty are not subject to the tax when they perform duties connected with their religious order (Code Sec. 1402(c)).[118]

A duly ordained, commissioned, or licensed minister of a church, a member of a religious order (who has not taken a vow of poverty), or a Christian Science practitioner may elect not to be covered by social security by filing an exemption certificate, Form 4361, which contains a statement indicating that he is opposed by conscience or religious principle to the acceptance of any public insurance. The statement must include a declaration that he has informed the ordaining, commissioning, or licensing body of the church of his opposition to such insurance (Code Sec. 1402(e)(1)).[119]

An individual who has conscientious objections to insurance by reason of an adherence to established tenets or teachings of a religious sect of which he is a member may also be exempt (Code Sec. 1402(g)).[120] A qualified individual must apply for an exemption on or before the due date of the income tax return for the second tax year for which he had earnings from self-employment of $400 or more from his religious activities (Reg. § 1.1402(e)-3A).[121]

Services performed by employees for a church or church-controlled organization may be excluded from social security coverage if the church or organization makes a valid election under Code Sec. 3121(w). However, such employees will be liable for self-employment tax on remuneration paid for such services unless the remuneration is less than $100 per year (Code Secs. 1402(a)(14) and (j)).[122]

A U.S. citizen who works for an employer that is exempt from the social security tax because it is either a foreign government or instrumentality or an international organization is treated as self-employed and wages are subject to the self-employment tax (Code Sec. 1402(c)(2)).[123] Also, a resident of Puerto Rico, the Virgin Islands, Guam or American Samoa who is not a citizen of the United States is subject to the self-employment tax (Code Sec. 1402(b)).[124]

2670. Self-Employment Income. The self-employment tax is 15.3 percent and consists of two taxes—an OASDI (i.e., social security) tax of 12.4 percent and a Medicare tax of 2.9 percent. The tax is based on "self-employment income," which is defined as "net earnings from self-employment." For 2007, the OASDI base is $97,500 ($102,000 for 2008). There is no cap for the Medicare component. However, if wages subject to social security or railroad retirement tax are received during the tax year, the

---

Footnote references are to paragraphs of the 2008 Standard Federal Tax Reports.

[116] ¶ 32,541, ¶ 32,543.07	[119] ¶ 32,560	[122] ¶ 32,560
[117] ¶ 39,550	[120] ¶ 32,560	[123] ¶ 32,560
[118] ¶ 32,560	[121] ¶ 32,593	[124] ¶ 32,560

maximum is reduced by the amount of wages on which these taxes were paid (Code Sec. 1402(b)).[125] If net earnings from self-employment are less than $400, no self-employment tax is payable.

"Net earnings from self-employment" consist of: (1) the gross income derived from any trade or business, less allowable deductions attributable to the trade or business, and (2) the taxpayer's distributive share of the ordinary income or loss of a partnership engaged in a trade or business (Reg. § 1.1402(a)-1).[126] The term "trade or business" does not include services performed as an employee other than services relating to certain: (1) newspaper and magazine sales, (2) sharing of crops, (3) foreign organizations, and (4) sharing of fishing catches (Code Sec. 1402(c)(2)).[127]

There are special rules for computing net earnings from self-employment (including a special optional method of computing net earnings from nonfarm self-employment) (Code Sec. 1402(a)).[128] Rents from real estate and from personal property leased with the real estate, and the attributable deductions, are excluded unless received by the individual in the course of his business as a real estate dealer.

Dividends and interest from any bond, debenture, note, certificate or other evidence of indebtedness issued with interest coupons or in registered form by any corporation are excluded from net earnings from self-employment income unless received by a dealer in stocks and securities in the course of his business. Other interest received in the course of any trade or business is not excluded. Gain or loss from the sale or exchange of property that is not stock in trade or held primarily for sale is excluded, as is gain or loss from the sale or exchange of a capital asset.

Termination payments received by former insurance salespersons are excludable from net earnings from self-employment under certain circumstances (Code Sec. 1402(k)). The exclusion applies if:

(1) the amount is received after the termination of the individual's agreement to perform services for the company,

(2) the individual performs no services for the company after the termination . and before the close of the tax year,

(3) the payment is conditioned upon the salesperson agreeing not to compete with the company for at least one year following termination, and

(4) the payment amount depends primarily on policies sold by or credited to the individual during the last year of the agreement and/or the extent to which the policies remain in force for some period after the termination and does not depend on the length of service or overall earnings from services performed for the company.

Eligibility for the payment may be based on length of service.[129]

Even though the rental value of a parsonage (or a parsonage rental allowance) and the value of meals and lodging furnished for the convenience of the employer are not included in a minister's gross income for income tax purposes (see ¶ 873 and ¶ 875), they are taken into account in calculating net earnings from self-employment (Code Sec. 1402(a)(8)).[130] The same is true of amounts excluded from gross income as foreign earned income (see ¶ 2401). However, self-employment income does not include a minister's retirement benefits received from a church plan or the rental value of a parsonage allowance as long as each was furnished after the date of retirement.[131]

One business deduction that cannot be taken in calculating net earnings from self-employment for the tax year is the deduction allowed for 50 percent of the self-employment tax for the same tax year (see ¶ 923). However, the law provides a substitute for that deduction. This is an amount determined by multiplying net earnings from self-employment (calculated without regard to the substitute deduction) by one-half of the self-employment tax rate for the year (Code Sec. 1402(a)(12)).[132] For 2007, this is 7.65 percent of the net earnings from self-employment.

Footnote references are to paragraphs of the 2008 Standard Federal Tax Reports.

[125] ¶ 32,560
[126] ¶ 32,561
[127] ¶ 32,560

[128] ¶ 32,560
[129] ¶ 32,560, ¶ 32,578.053
[130] ¶ 32,560

[131] ¶ 32,599.58
[132] ¶ 32,560, ¶ 32,543.07

Example: Aileen Smith, a self-employed individual, has $40,000 of net earnings from self-employment in 2007 (determined without regard to the substitute deduction). Her self-employment tax for 2007 would be computed as follows:

Self-employment net earnings	$40,000
Less: $40,000 × 7.65%	3,060
Reduced self-employment net earnings	$36,940
Tax rate on self-employment income	×15.3%
Self-employment tax for 2007	$ 5,652

2673. Optional Method for Nonfarm Self-Employment. A taxpayer may be able to use an optional method to compute net earnings from self-employment if the net earnings from nonfarm self-employment are: (a) less than $1,600 and (b) less than two-thirds of gross nonfarm income. In addition, this optional method may only be used if the taxpayer had net earnings from self-employment of $400 or more in at least two of the three years immediately preceding the year in which the nonfarm optional method is elected (see IRS Pub. 334).

If the taxpayer is eligible to use this optional method, he may elect to report two-thirds of his gross nonfarm income, up to $1,600, as his net earnings from self-employment. The purpose of this optional method is to permit taxpayers to pay into the social security system and thus obtain or increase their benefits, even though they are not otherwise eligible because their net self-employment income is under $400. This optional method may not be used more than five times by any individual.[133] Note that the $1,600 amount refers to net earnings after reduction by the 7.65 percent deduction amount.

2676. Farmer's Self-Employment Income. A special method for determining self-employment net earnings is provided for farm operators whether they own the land they farm, rent on a fixed rental basis, or rent under a share-farming arrangement. Rentals received by the owner or tenant of the land under a share-farming arrangement—the farm is operated by a third party (share-farmer who may be a subtenant)—are treated as self-employment income if the owner or tenant participates materially with the share-farmer working the land in the production or management of the production of an agricultural or horticultural commodity. (There is no material participation if the owner or tenant does not participate in operations and has turned over management of the land to an agent, such as a professional farm management company.) The share-farmer is also considered a self-employed person (Code Sec. 1402(a)(1)).[134]

A self-employed farmer has to pay the self-employment tax if his net earnings from self-employment are $400 or more (Code Sec. 1402(b)).[135] However, an optional method for reporting income from farming, providing for greater credit toward benefits under old-age and survivors insurance, is available to a farmer. If his gross income for the tax year is not more than $2,400, he can report two-thirds of his gross income as net earnings from self-employment (Code Sec. 1402(a)).[136]

Example: In 2007, Breanna Jones had $2,200 of gross income from her farm operations. Although her actual net earnings amounted to $1,300, she reported $1,466.67 (⅔ of $2,200) as net earnings from self-employment subject to self-employment tax. In electing to pay the tax on the larger amount, she receives a greater credit toward social security benefits.

If a farmer has more than $2,400 of gross income from farm operations, he may report either his actual net earnings or, if his net earnings are less than $1,600, $1,600 as net earnings (Code Sec. 1402(a)).[137] As in the case of the nonfarm optional method, the $1,600 amount refers to net earnings after reduction by the 7.65 percent deduction. There is no limit on the number of times a taxpayer may use this optional method.

Payment of Estimated Taxes

2679. Purpose. To provide for current payment of income taxes not collected through withholding, the law requires individuals in some instances to pay a portion of

---

Footnote references are to paragraphs of the 2008 Standard Federal Tax Reports.

[133] ¶ 32,578.034
[134] ¶ 32,560
[135] ¶ 32,560
[136] ¶ 32,560
[137] ¶ 32,560

their tax currently. The general rule is that at least 90 percent of an individual's final income tax is to be paid through either withholding or estimated tax payments.

For the payment of estimated taxes, an individual is to use the appropriate payment voucher attached to Form 1040-ES. Estimated tax installments required of an individual are based on the penalty exception provisions of Code Sec. 6654.[138]

In general, the estimated tax is the amount of income and self-employment tax (as well as other taxes reported on Form 1040) that an individual estimates will have to be paid for the tax year after subtracting any estimated credits against tax. For rules on payment of corporate estimated tax, see ¶ 225–¶ 231. For a discussion of the estimated tax rules for trusts and estates, see ¶ 518.

2682. Who Should Estimate for 2008. No penalty for failure to pay estimated tax will apply to an individual whose tax liability for the year, after credit for withheld taxes, is less than $1,000. Also, a U.S. citizen or resident need not pay estimated tax if he or she had no tax liability for the preceding tax year, provided such year was a 12-month period. Under circumstances of hardship or following an individual's retirement or disability, the penalty may be waived (Code Sec. 6654(e)).[139]

Individuals who do not qualify for any of these exceptions may generally avoid the penalty for failure to pay estimated tax by:

(1) paying at least 90 percent of the tax shown on the current year's return,

(2) paying 100 percent of the tax shown on the prior year's return, or

(3) paying installments on a current basis under an annualized income installment method.

However, an individual may not use the 100-percent-of-prior-year's-tax safe harbor if the prior year was not a 12-month period.

The required payments may be made either through withholding or payment of annual installments. The annualization method is suitable for taxpayers whose income is received or accrued more heavily in one part of the year (Code Sec. 6654(d)).

An individual with adjusted gross income in excess of $150,000 ($75,000 for a married individual filing separately) in 2007 or thereafter can avoid the estimated tax penalty by paying 110 percent of the amount of tax shown on the prior year's tax return, providing the prior year was a full year (Code Sec. 6654(d)(1)(C)).[140]

Married taxpayers may make a joint estimated tax payment, even if they are living separate and apart (Reg. § 1.6654-2(e)(5)). Joint estimated payment are not allowed if:

(1) there is a decree of separate maintenance or divorce;

(2) the married taxpayers have different tax years; or

(3) the taxpayer's spouse is a nonresident alien (including a bona fide resident of Puerto Rico or U.S. possession to which Code Sec. 931 applies for the entire tax year), unless an election has been made under Code Sec. 6013 to treat the spouse as a resident alien or the spouse becomes a resident alien during the tax year.

Joint estimated payments are based on the aggregate taxable income. In the event that estimated self-employment taxes are required, the amount of estimated self-employment tax is based on the separate income of that individual.

Employers of domestic workers who fail to satisfy their obligations for FICA and FUTA withholding, through regular estimated tax payments or increased tax withholding from their own wages, may be liable for estimated tax penalties (see ¶ 2650).

Payment Requirements

2685. Estimated Tax Payment Due Dates. For estimated tax purposes, the year is broken down into four payment periods,[141] and a 2008 calendar-year individual is required to pay his estimated tax in four installments as follows:

Footnote references are to paragraphs of the 2008 Standard Federal Tax Reports.

[138] ¶ 39,550
[139] ¶ 39,550
[140] ¶ 39,550
[141] ¶ 39,560.0215

Installment	Due date
First	April 15, 2008
Second	June 16, 2008
Third	September 15, 2008
Fourth	January 15, 2009

For fiscal-year individuals, the due dates for the four estimated tax payments are:

(1) the 15th day of the fourth month of the fiscal year,

(2) the 15th day of the sixth month of the fiscal year,

(3) the 15th day of the ninth month of the fiscal year, and

(4) the 15th day of the first month after the end of the fiscal year.

If the due date for making an estimated tax payment falls on a Saturday, Sunday or legal holiday, the payment will be timely if made on the next day that is not a Saturday, Sunday or legal holiday.[142]

If an individual is not liable for estimated tax on March 31, 2008, but his tax situation changes so that he becomes liable for estimated tax at some point after March 31, then he must make estimated tax payments as follows:

(1) if he becomes required to pay estimated tax after March 31 and before June 1, then he should pay 50 percent of his estimated tax on or before June 16, 2008, 25 percent on September 15, 2008, and 25 percent on January 15, 2009;

(2) if he becomes required to pay estimated tax after May 31 and before September 1, then he should pay 75 percent of his estimated tax on or before September 15, 2008, and 25 percent on January 15, 2009; or

(3) if he becomes required to pay estimated tax after August 31, then he should pay 100 percent of his estimated tax by January 15, 2009 (1040-ES).

Nonresident Alien Individuals. Nonresident alien individuals (except those whose wages are subject to withholding) must pay estimated taxes in three installments (June 16 and September 15 in 2008 and January 15 in 2009). Fifty percent of the annual payment must be made on the first installment due date and 25 percent on each of the remaining two installment due dates (Code Sec. 6654(j)).[143]

2688. Return as Substitute for Last Installment of 2007 Estimated Tax. The fourth (last) tax installment for a tax year need not be made if the taxpayer files a Form 1040 tax return and pays the balance of the tax on or before January 31, 2008, or, for a fiscal year, on or before the last day of the month following the close of the fiscal year. Filing a final 2007 return by January 31, 2008, with payment of any tax due will not avoid an addition to tax for underpayment of any of the first three installments that were due for the year, but it will terminate the period of underpayment (and, therefore, the accrual of further additions) as of January 15, 2008 (Code Sec. 6654(h)).[144]

2691. Farmer or Fisherman. A farmer or fisherman who expects to receive at least two-thirds of his gross income for the tax year from farming or fishing, or who received at least two-thirds of his gross income for the previous tax year from farming or fishing, may pay estimated tax for the year in one installment. Thus, a qualifying farmer or fisherman may wait until January 15, 2008, to make his 2007 estimated tax payment. The entire amount of 2007 estimated tax must be paid at that time. However, this January 15 payment date may be ignored if the farmer or fisherman files his income tax return for 2007 and pays the entire tax due by March 3, 2008. The penalty for underpayment of estimated tax (see ¶ 2875) does not apply unless a farmer or fisherman underpays his tax by more than one-third (Code Sec. 6654(i)).[145] If a joint return is filed, a farmer or fisherman must consider his or her spouse's gross income in determining whether at least two-thirds of gross income is from farming or fishing.

Footnote references are to paragraphs of the 2008 Standard Federal Tax Reports.

[142] ¶ 42,635.01   [144] ¶ 39,550
[143] ¶ 39,550   [145] ¶ 39,550

Chapter 27

EXAMINATION OF RETURNS
COLLECTION OF TAX

Organization of IRS

2701. Organization and Functions. The Internal Revenue Service (IRS) is the Treasury Department unit that has responsibility for determining, assessing, and collecting internal revenue taxes and enforcing the internal revenue laws. The IRS consists of an Associate Office in Washington, D.C., and a field organization. The Associate Office is the Office of the Commissioner of Internal Revenue, who heads the IRS. Among the principal offices of the IRS are: the Office of the Deputy Commissioner (Operations); the Office of the Associate Commissioner (Policy and Management); the Office of the Associate Commissioner (Computer Services); the Office of the Assistant Commissioner (Taxpayer Service and Returns Processing); and the Office of the Chief Counsel. The Office of Inspector General of the Treasury Department has oversight responsibility for the internal investigations performed by the Office of Assistant Commissioner (Inspection) of the IRS.

At one time, IRS field offices were divided into four geographic regions, each headed by a Regional Commissioner. However, pursuant to the IRS Restructuring and Reform Act of 1998, the IRS has reorganized itself by doing away with the four regional divisions and organizing itself into four units serving groups of taxpayers with similar needs. As of October 1, 2000, the IRS has put into operation the following operating divisions:

(1) Wage and Investment, serving individual taxpayers with wage and investment income;

(2) Small Business/Self-Employed, serving self-employed individuals and small businesses (C corporations, S corporations and partnerships) with assets of less than $10 million;

(3) Large and Mid-Size Business, serving corporations with assets of at least $10 million; and

(4) Tax-Exempt and Government Entities, serving employee plans, exempt organizations, and government entities.

IRS field offices also include 10 IRS service centers, with mailing addresses in the following cities: Austin, Texas; Kansas City, Missouri; Andover, Massachusetts; Ogden, Utah; Atlanta, Georgia; Philadelphia, Pennsylvania; Memphis, Tennessee; Holtsville, New York; Cincinnati, Ohio; and Fresno, California. The service centers currently receive and process tax and information returns, manage accounts, and conduct simple audits through correspondence based on a taxpayer's geographic location. However, these activities are in the process of being assigned to service centers based on whether a taxpayer's return relates to an individual or a business, the taxpayer's geographical

location, and the operating division to which the center, as part of the IRS reorganization, will eventually report.

The IRS also maintains a national computer center located near Martinsburg, West Virginia.

In addition, a nine-member IRS Oversight Board has been created to ensure that the IRS is organized and operated to carry out its new mission to place a greater emphasis on serving the public and meeting taxpayers' needs (Code Sec. 7802).[1]

2703. Office of Chief Counsel. The legal work of the IRS is performed by the Office of the Chief Counsel.[2] The Chief Counsel is a member of the Commissioner's executive staff and acts as counsel and legal adviser to the Commissioner in all matters pertaining to the administration and enforcement of the Internal Revenue laws. There are also Division Counsels, subject to the general supervision of the Chief Counsel, in each of the new IRS operating divisions (see ¶ 2701).

2705. Appeals Procedure. If a tax return is examined by the IRS and the taxpayer does not agree with the results of the examination, further appeal within the IRS is permitted.[3] Once the IRS has issued a preliminary 30-day letter, the taxpayer has the right to appeal to a local Appeals Office by filing a written request for appellate consideration. This is the only level of appeal within the IRS (disregarding the functions of the National Taxpayer Advocate) (¶ 2707). Appeals conferences are conducted in an informal manner. A taxpayer who requests a conference may also need to file a formal written protest. However, if the protested amount is not more than $25,000, a small case request may be made instead of a formal written protest (IRS Publication 556). Taxpayers who wish to forego the right to submit a protest to the Appeals Office after receiving a 30-day letter can file a petition in the Tax Court within 90 days after the receipt of a statutory notice of deficiency.

The IRS is required to develop certain appeals dispute resolution procedures (Code Sec. 7123).[4] Accordingly, the IRS has established procedures under which any taxpayer may request early referral of issues from the examination or collection division to the Office of Appeals (Rev. Proc. 99-28). Additionally, procedures have been developed under which either a taxpayer or the Office of Appeals may request nonbinding mediation of any unresolved issue at the conclusion of the appeals procedure or an unsuccessful attempt to enter into a closing agreement or an offer in compromise (Rev. Proc. 2002-44). Also, an appeals arbitration process under which the Office of Appeals and the taxpayer may jointly request binding arbitration has been established (Rev. Proc. 2006-44).

Small business and self-employed taxpayers can resolve their tax disputes through fast-track mediation (IR-2002-80). Disputes will be resolved through this expedited process within 40 days, compared to several months using the regular appeals process.

Large- and mid-size businesses can resolve their tax disputes through a fast-track settlement program (Rev. Proc. 2003-40). The goal for this program is to reach settlement within 120 days. A similar fast-track settlement program for small businesses and self-employed taxpayers is being tested by the IRS (Announcement 2006-61).

2707. Taxpayer Assistance Orders. The National Taxpayer Advocate assists taxpayers in resolving problems with the IRS and has the authority to issue a taxpayer assistance order where the taxpayer is suffering, or is about to suffer, significant hardship as a result of the IRS's actions (Code Sec. 7803(c); Code Sec. 7811).[5] "Significant hardship" means any serious privation caused to the taxpayer as the result of the IRS's administration of revenue laws. Mere economic or personal inconvenience to the taxpayer does not constitute significant hardship (Reg. § 301.7811-1(a)(4)).[6] The following four specific factors, among other things, must be considered by the Advocate when determining whether there is a significant hardship:

    (1) whether there is an immediate threat of adverse action;

    (2) whether there has been a delay of more than 30 days in resolving the taxpayer's account problems;

Footnote references are to paragraphs of the 2008 Standard Federal Tax Reports.

[1] ¶ 43,254
[2] ¶ 43,258

[3] ¶ 43,336, ¶ 43,352.033
[4] ¶ 41,132

[5] ¶ 43,304, ¶ 43,312
[6] ¶ 43,308

(3) whether the taxpayer will have to pay significant costs (including fees for professional representation) if relief is not granted; or

(4) whether the taxpayer will suffer irreparable injury, or a long-term adverse impact, if relief is not granted (Code Sec. 7811(a)).[7]

An application for a taxpayer assistance order may be filed by the taxpayer or a duly authorized representative who may request remedial action, such as the release of the taxpayer's property from IRS levy or the immediate reissuance of a lost refund check. Form 911 is to be used for this purpose. Any relevant limitations period is suspended from the date on which the application is filed until the Advocate makes a decision on the application, unless the order provides for the continuation of the suspension beyond the date of the order. Such orders are binding on the IRS unless modified or rescinded by the Advocate, IRS Commissioner or Deputy Commissioner. The Advocate can take independent action and issue an assistance order without an application by the taxpayer. The statute of limitations, however, is not suspended when the Advocate issues an order independently.[8]

Orders issued, or actions taken, by the Advocate are to be applied to private debt collection agencies (PDCs) that are used by the IRS to recover federal debts (see ¶ 2735) (Code Sec. 7811(g)). Such orders and actions apply to PDCs to the same extent and in the same manner as they would apply to the IRS.

Examination

2708. Examination of Return. The IRS examines a taxpayer's books and records either at the place of business where the books and records are maintained (a field examination) or at an IRS office.[9] The type of examination affects the internal appeals procedure (see ¶ 2705).

The Taxpayer Bill of Rights requires the IRS to provide a written statement detailing the taxpayer's rights and the IRS's obligations during the audit, appeals, refund and collection process. The IRS must also explain the audit and collection (Code Sec. 7521(b)).[10]

The taxpayer has the right to make an audio recording of any in-person interview conducted by the IRS upon ten days' advance notice (Code Sec. 7521(a)).[11] Moreover, a taxpayer is guaranteed the right to be represented by any individual currently permitted to practice before the IRS, unless the IRS notifies the taxpayer that the representative is responsible for unreasonable delay or hindrance (Code Sec. 7521(c)).[12] Any interview must be suspended when the taxpayer clearly requests the right to consult with a representative.[13] Further, unless it issues an administrative summons, the IRS cannot require the taxpayer to accompany the representative to the interview.[14]

The IRS has granted administrative relief to taxpayers in hostage situations or in a combat zone, or who are continuously hospitalized as a result of injuries received in a combat zone, or who are affected by a presidentially declared disaster area, by suspending tax examination and collection actions during their detention. Examination and collection actions that can be precluded or suspended include tax return audits, mailings of notices and other actions involving the collection of overdue taxes.[15]

2709. Third-Party Summonses. The IRS may issue summonses to third-party recordkeepers (attorneys, enrolled agents, banks, brokers, accountants, etc.) and other third parties for the production of records concerning the business transactions or affairs of a taxpayer. The taxpayer is to be notified of the summons within three days of service of the summons (but in no case later than the 23rd day before the day fixed in the summons for production of records). However, notice is not required with respect to any summons:

Footnote references are to paragraphs of the 2008 Standard Federal Tax Reports.

[7] ¶ 43,304
[8] ¶ 43,304, ¶ 43,308, ¶ 43,312.01
[9] ¶ 43,332, ¶ 43,352.021

[10] ¶ 42,790, ¶ 42,791.01
[11] ¶ 42,790, ¶ 42,791.021
[12] ¶ 42,790, ¶ 42,791.035

[13] ¶ 42,790, ¶ 42,791.03
[14] ¶ 42,960, ¶ 42,791.035
[15] ¶ 42,686

(1) served on the person with respect to whose liability the summons is issued, or any officer or employee of the person;

(2) issued to determine whether or not records of the business transactions or affairs of an identified person have been made or kept; and

(3) issued in certain criminal investigations.

Any taxpayer who is entitled to notice may intervene in any proceeding for the enforcement of the summons in question. The taxpayer also has the right to begin a proceeding to quash the summons if, within 20 days after the day the notice of summons was served on or mailed to him, he files a petition to quash the summons in a district court having jurisdiction and notifies the IRS and the third party by mailing a copy of the petition by certified or registered mail to each one. Although notice is not required for a "John Doe" summons (i.e., issued to determine the identity of a person having a numbered bank account or similar arrangement), such a summons may be issued only after the IRS has shown adequate grounds for serving the summons, and an ex parte court proceeding is held to determine its validity (Code Sec. 7609).[16]

If a taxpayer intervenes in a dispute between the IRS and a third party and the dispute is not resolved within six months, the statute of limitations period will be suspended beginning on the date that is six months after the summons is served and continuing until the dispute is resolved. This provision also applies with respect to "John Doe" summonses (Code Sec. 7609(e)).[17]

The IRS is required to provide reasonable notice in advance to a taxpayer before contacting third parties with respect to examination or collection activities regarding the taxpayer (Code Sec. 7602(c); Reg. § 301.7602-2).[18] However, notice is not required: (1) with respect to any contact authorized by the taxpayer; (2) if the IRS determines that the notice would jeopardize collection of any tax; or (3) with respect to any pending criminal investigation.

Assessment and Collection of Tax

2711. Assessment of Deficiency. A "deficiency" is the excess of the correct tax liability over the tax shown on the return (if any), plus amounts previously assessed (or collected without assessment) as a deficiency, and minus any rebates made to the taxpayer (Code Sec. 6211).[19] For this purpose, the tax shown on the return is the amount of tax before credits for estimated tax paid, withheld tax, or amounts collected under a termination assessment (Code Sec. 6211(b)).[20]

The IRS is authorized to assess taxes (Reg. § 301.6201-1).[21] The collection process begins when a notice of deficiency is sent to the taxpayer's last known address by registered or certified mail (Code Sec. 6212).[22] In each deficiency notice, the IRS must provide a description of the basis for the assessment, an identification of the amount of tax, interest and penalties assessed (Code Sec. 7522),[23] and the date determined to be the last day on which the taxpayer may file a petition with the Tax Court (Code Sec. 6213(a)).[24] However, the failure by the IRS to specify the last day on which to file a petition will not invalidate an otherwise valid deficiency notice if the taxpayer was not prejudiced by the omission.[25]

Within 90 days after notice of the deficiency is mailed (or within 150 days after mailing if the notice is addressed to a person outside the U.S.), the taxpayer may file a petition with the Tax Court for a redetermination of the deficiency (Code Sec. 6213).[26] Payment of the assessed amount after the deficiency notice is mailed does not deprive the Tax Court of jurisdiction over the deficiency (Reg. § 301.6213-1(b)(3)).[27]

If the taxpayer does not file a Tax Court petition within the 90-day time period, the tax may be collected (see ¶ 2735). A taxpayer's property may be seized to enforce collection if there is a failure to pay an assessed tax within 30 days after notice of levy (Code Sec. 6331(d)(2)).[28] However, the notice and waiting period does not apply if the

---

Footnote references are to paragraphs of the 2008 Standard Federal Tax Reports.

[16] ¶ 42,890	[21] ¶ 37,503	[26] ¶ 37,545
[17] ¶ 42,890, ¶ 42,897.021	[22] ¶ 37,540	[27] ¶ 37,546
[18] ¶ 42,820, ¶ 42,897.021	[23] ¶ 42,800	[28] ¶ 38,185
[19] ¶ 37,535	[24] ¶ 37,545	
[20] ¶ 37,535	[25] ¶ 37,544.25	

IRS finds that the collection of tax is in jeopardy (see ¶ 2713). Notices of levy must provide a description of the levy process in simple and nontechnical terms (Code Sec. 6331).[29]

Mathematical or Clerical Errors. A notice of tax due because of mathematical or clerical errors is not a deficiency notice, and the taxpayer has no right to file a petition with the Tax Court for redetermining the deficiency. A taxpayer who receives notice of additional tax due to mathematical or clerical error has 60 days after the notice is sent in which to file a request for abatement of any part of the assessment. Any reassessment must be made under the regular notice-of-deficiency procedures. During the 60-day period, the IRS cannot proceed to collect upon the summary assessment (Code Sec. 6213(b)(1) and (f)).

2712. Waiver of Deficiency Restrictions. The taxpayer has the right to waive the restrictions on assessment and collection of all or part of a deficiency at any time, whether or not a notice of deficiency has been issued (Code Sec. 6213(d)).[30] This is done by executing Form 870. Execution of a waiver of the restrictions on assessment and collection of the entire deficiency in advance of the statutory ("90-day") notice relieves the IRS of sending such a notice and precludes appeal to the Tax Court.[31] However, an appeal to the Tax Court is not precluded if the waiver covers only part of the deficiency or is executed after receipt of the 90-day deficiency notice. Payment of an amount as tax before issuance of the statutory notice has the effect of a waiver,[32] and, if the amount paid equals or exceeds the amount of a subsequently determined deficiency, it deprives the Tax Court of jurisdiction (Reg. § 301.6213-1(b)(3)).[33]

2713. Jeopardy and Termination Assessments. The IRS can immediately assess a deficiency if the assessment and collection of tax would be jeopardized by delay or if the collection of tax would be otherwise jeopardized, as, for example, when a taxpayer is leaving the country or seeking to hide assets (Code Sec. 6851;[34] Code Sec. 6861[35]). If a jeopardy assessment is made prior to the mailing of the notice of deficiency, the notice must be mailed to the taxpayer within 60 days after the assessment (Code Sec. 6861(b)).[36] If a termination assessment is made, the assessment ends the taxpayer's tax year only for purposes of computing the amount of tax that becomes immediately due and payable. It does not end the tax year for any other purpose. In the case of a termination assessment, the IRS must issue the taxpayer a notice of deficiency within 60 days of the later of (1) the due date (including extensions) of the taxpayer's return for the full tax year or (2) the day on which the taxpayer files the return (Code Sec. 6851(b)).[37]

The IRS may presume that the collection of tax is in jeopardy if an individual in physical possession of more than $10,000 in cash or its equivalent does not claim either ownership of the cash or that it belongs to another person whose identity the IRS can readily ascertain and who acknowledges ownership of the cash. In this case, the IRS may treat the entire amount as gross income taxable at the highest rate specified in Code Sec. 1. The possessor of the cash is entitled to notice of, and the right to challenge, the assessment. However, should the true owner appear, he will be substituted for the possessor and all rights will vest in him (Code Sec. 6867).[38]

2719. Injunction to Restrain Collection. The Code prohibits a suit to restrain the assessment or collection of any tax (Code Sec. 7421(a))[39] or to restrain the enforcement of liability against a transferee or fiduciary (Code Sec. 7421(b)).[40] Nevertheless, injunctive relief may be available in rare cases if irreparable harm[41] will be done to the taxpayer and the taxpayer shows, at the outset of the suit, that the government could not collect the tax under any circumstances.[42] However, injunctive relief may be obtained for assessment or collection actions (other than jeopardy or termination assessments) if a notice of deficiency has not been mailed to the taxpayer, the period for filing a Tax Court petition has not expired, or a Tax Court proceeding with respect to the tax is pending (Code Sec. 6213(a)).[43]

Footnote references are to paragraphs of the 2008 Standard Federal Tax Reports.

[29] ¶ 38,185
[30] ¶ 37,545
[31] ¶ 37,549.9612
[32] ¶ 37,549.032
[33] ¶ 37,546

[34] ¶ 40,402
[35] ¶ 40,460
[36] ¶ 40,460
[37] ¶ 40,402
[38] ¶ 40,580

[39] ¶ 41,680
[40] ¶ 41,680
[41] ¶ 41,683.70
[42] ¶ 41,683.69
[43] ¶ 37,545

¶2719

2721. Closing Agreement. The IRS is authorized to enter into a written agreement with a taxpayer in order to determine conclusively the tax liability for a tax period that ended prior to the date of the agreement (Form 866) or to determine one or more separate items affecting the tax liability for any tax period (Form 906). A closing agreement may also be entered for tax periods that end subsequent to the date of the agreement. Closing agreements may be entered into in order to finally resolve questions of tax liability (Code Sec. 7121; Reg. § 301.7121-1).[44] For example, a fiduciary may desire a final determination before an estate is closed or trust assets distributed. Closing agreements are final, conclusive, and binding upon both parties. They cannot be reopened or modified except upon a showing of fraud or malfeasance or the misrepresentation of a material fact.[45] Generally, the IRS is not precluded from later determining additions to tax absent terms in the agreement that specifically address the issue of additions to tax.[46]

2723. Compromise of Tax and Penalty. The IRS may compromise the tax liability in most civil or criminal cases before referral to the Department of Justice for prosecution or defense. The Attorney General or a delegate may compromise any case after the referral. However, the IRS may not compromise certain criminal liabilities arising under internal revenue laws relating to narcotics, opium, or marijuana. Interest and penalties, as well as tax, may be compromised (Code Sec. 7122; Reg. § 301.7122-1).[47] Offers-in-compromise are submitted on Form 656 accompanied by a financial statement on Form 433-A for an individual or Form 433-B for businesses (if based on inability to pay) (Reg. § 601.203(b)).[48] A taxpayer who faces severe or unusual economic hardship may also apply for an offer-in-compromise by submitting Form 656. If the IRS accepts an offer-in-compromise, the payment is allocated among tax, penalties, and interest as stated in the collateral agreement with the IRS. If no allocation is specified in the agreement and the amounts paid exceed the total tax and penalties owed, the payments will be applied to tax, penalties, and interest in that order, beginning with the earliest year. If the IRS agrees to an amount that does not exceed the combined tax and penalties, and there is no agreement regarding allocation of the payment, no amount will be allocated to interest.[49]

A $150 user fee is required for many offers-in-compromise (Reg. § 300.3). Taxpayers must normally pay the user fee at the time a request to compromise is submitted. No user fee is imposed with respect to offers (1) that are based solely on doubt as to liability or (2) that are made by low-income taxpayers (i.e., taxpayers whose total monthly income falls at or below income levels based on the U.S. Department of Health and Human Services poverty guidelines). If an offer is accepted to promote effective tax administration or is accepted based on doubt as to collectibility and a determination that collecting more than the amount offered would create economic hardship, the fee will be applied to the amount of the offer or, upon the taxpayer's request, refunded to the taxpayer. The fee will not be refunded if an offer is withdrawn, rejected or returned as nonprocessible. The IRS treats offers received by taxpayers in bankruptcy as nonprocessible, even though two district courts have held that the IRS must consider such offers (*R.H. Macher*, DC Va., 2004-1 USTC ¶ 50,114 (Nonacq.); *W.K. Holmes*, DC Ga., 2005-1 USTC ¶ 50,230). However, two bankruptcy courts have held in favor of the IRS on this issue (*1900 M Restaurant Associates, Inc.*, BC-DC D.C., 2005-1 USTC ¶ 50,313; *W. Uzialko*, BC-DC Pa., 2006-1 USTC ¶ 50,297).

Detailed IRS procedures for the submission and processing of offers-in-compromise are reflected in Rev. Proc. 2003-71.

Partial payment requirement. Taxpayers are required to make nonrefundable partial payments with the submission of any offer-in-compromise (Code Sec. 7122(c)). Taxpayers who submit a lump-sum offer (any offer that will be paid in five or fewer installments) must include a payment of 20 percent of the amount offered. Taxpayers who submit a periodic payment offer must include payment of the first proposed installment with the offer and continue making payments under the terms proposed while the offer is being

---

Footnote references are to paragraphs of the 2008 Standard Federal Tax Reports.

[44] ¶ 41,080, ¶ 41,081, ¶ 41,090, ¶ 43,364
[45] ¶ 41,080, ¶ 41,081, ¶ 41,090.279, ¶ 43,364
[46] ¶ 41,090.279
[47] ¶ 41,110, ¶ 41,111
[48] ¶ 43,372
[49] ¶ 9104.63

evaluated. Offers that are submitted to the IRS without the required partial payments will be returned to the taxpayer as nonprocessible. However, the IRS is authorized to issue regulations waiving the payment requirement for offers based solely on doubt as to liability or filed by low income taxpayers. Pending the issuance of regulations, the IRS has announced that it will waive the payment requirement for such offers (Notice 2006-68).

The required partial payments are applied to the taxpayer's unpaid liability and are not refundable. However, taxpayers may specify the liability to which they want their payments applied. Additionally, the user fee (see above) is applied to the taxpayer's outstanding tax liability. Any offer that is not rejected within 24 months of the date it is submitted is deemed to be accepted. However, any period during which the tax liability to be compromised is in dispute in any judicial proceeding is not taken into account in determining the expiration of the 24-month period (Code Sec. 7122(f)).

2724. Partial Payments. Allocations for partial payments of assessed federal income taxes, penalties and interest made by a taxpayer will be respected (Code Sec. 6501(c)(4)). A partial payment on deficiencies received without instructions for its application will be applied to tax, penalties, and interest in that order, in the order (time) that best serves the government's interest.

Limitation Period for Assessment and Collection

2726. General Three-Year Period. Generally, all income taxes must be assessed within three years after the original return is filed (the last day prescribed by law for filing if the return was filed before the last day).[50] In the case of pass-through entities, the three-year rule begins to run at the time the pass-through entity's shareholder or other beneficial owner files an individual income tax return. A return filed prior to its due date is deemed to have been filed on the due date. A proceeding in court without assessment for collection of the tax must commence within the same period (Code Sec. 6501; Reg. § 301.6501(a)-1).[51] The period can be extended by a written agreement between the taxpayer and the IRS (Code Sec. 6501(c)(4); Reg. § 301.6501(c)-1(d)).[52] Interest on any tax may be assessed and collected at any time during the period within which the tax itself may be collected (but only up to the date on which payment of the tax is received) (Reg. § 301.6601-1(f)).[53]

If, within the 60-day period ending on the last day of the assessment period, the IRS receives an amended return or written document from the taxpayer showing that additional tax is due for the year in question, the period in which to assess such additional tax is extended for 60 days after the day on which the IRS receives the amended return or written document (Code Sec. 6501(c)(7)).[54]

If unused foreign tax credits have been carried back, the statute of limitations on assessment and collection for the year to which the carryback is made will not close until one year after the expiration of the period within which a deficiency may be assessed for the year from which the carryback was made (Code Sec. 6501(i); Reg. § 301.6501(i)-1).[55]

Deficiencies attributable to carryback of a net operating loss, a capital loss or the general business credit and research credit may be assessed within the period that applies to the loss or credit year. Deficiencies attributable to the carrying back of one of those credits as a result of the carryback of a net operating loss, capital loss or other credit may be assessed within the period that applies to the loss or other credit year (Code Sec. 6501(h) and (j)).[56]

2728. Request for Prompt Assessment. A corporation that is contemplating dissolution, is in the process of dissolving, or has actually dissolved, or a decedent or an estate of a decedent (for taxes other than the estate tax imposed by chapter 11), may request a prompt assessment (Code Sec. 6501(d)).[57] If such a request is made, an assessment or a proceeding in court without assessment for the collection of any tax

---

Footnote references are to paragraphs of the 2008 Standard Federal Tax Reports.

[50] ¶ 38,960, ¶ 38,963
[51] ¶ 38,960, ¶ 38,961
[52] ¶ 38,960, ¶ 38,966, ¶ 38,967.025
[53] ¶ 39,412
[54] ¶ 38,960
[55] ¶ 38,960, ¶ 38,977
[56] ¶ 38,960, ¶ 39,080.034
[57] ¶ 38,960

must then be begun within 18 months after the receipt of a written request for a prompt assessment. In the case of a corporation, however, the 18-month period will not apply unless the corporation has completed or will eventually complete its dissolution at or before the end of the 18-month period. This provision does not apply in the cases described at ¶ 2732 and ¶ 2734. It also does not apply for personal holding company taxes in certain instances or where a waiver filed by the taxpayer extends the assessment period beyond the 18-month period (Reg. § 301.6501(d)-1).[58]

2730. Return Executed by IRS Official. A return executed by an IRS official or employee in which the taxpayer has not filed a return will not start the running of the statute of limitations on assessment and collection (Code Secs. 6020 and 6501(b)(3); Reg. § 301.6501(b)-1(c)).[59]

2732. False Return or No Return. Tax may be assessed or a court proceeding to collect tax may be commenced at any time if:

> (1) the return is false or fraudulent,
>
> (2) there is a willful attempt to evade tax, or
>
> (3) no return is filed (Reg. § 301.6501(c)-1).[60]

In addition, in the case of a fraudulent return, the government may impose additional taxes at any time, without regard to statutes of limitations, although the burden of proof falls on the government to prove fraud by the taxpayer.[61]

2733. Listed Transactions. If a taxpayer fails to include any information required by Code Sec. 6011 (¶ 2006) on a tax return or statement relating to a listed transaction, the statute of limitations with respect to that transaction will not expire before one year after the earlier of: (1) the date on which the information is furnished to the IRS, or (2) the date that a material advisor satisfies the list maintenance requirements of Code Sec. 6112 (¶ 2008) with respect to the IRS's request relating to the taxpayer's transaction (Code Sec. 6501(c)(10)).

2734. Omission of Over 25% of Income. If the taxpayer omits from gross income (total receipts, without reduction for cost) an amount in excess of 25% of the amount of gross income stated in the return, a six-year limitation period on assessment applies. An item will not be considered as omitted from gross income if information sufficient to apprise the IRS of the nature and amount of such item is disclosed in the return or in any schedule or statement attached to the return (Code Sec. 6501(e); Reg. § 301.6501(e)-1(a)).[62]

2735. Collection After Assessment. After assessment of tax made within the statutory period of limitation (¶ 2726), the tax may be collected by levy or a proceeding in court commenced within 10 years after the assessment or within any period for collection agreed upon in writing between the IRS and the taxpayer before the expiration of the 10-year period. The period agreed upon by the parties may be extended by later written agreements so long as they are made prior to the expiration of the period previously agreed upon. The IRS has to notify taxpayers of their right to refuse an extension each time one is requested (Code Sec. 6501(c)(4)). If a timely court proceeding has commenced for the collection of the tax, then the period during which the tax may be collected is extended until the liability for tax (or a judgment against the taxpayer) is satisfied or becomes unenforceable.

Generally effective after 1999, the 10-year limitations period on collections may not be extended if there has not been a levy on any of the taxpayer's property. If the taxpayer entered into an installment agreement with the IRS, however, the 10-year limitations period may be extended for the period that the limitations period was extended under the original terms of the installment agreement plus 90 days. If, in any request made on or before December 31, 1999, a taxpayer agreed to extend the 10-year period of limitations on collections, the extension will expire on the latest of:

Footnote references are to paragraphs of the 2008 Standard Federal Tax Reports.

[58] ¶ 38,960, ¶ 38,968, ¶ 38,969.01

[59] ¶ 35,240, ¶ 35,241, ¶ 38,960, ¶ 38,963.65, ¶ 38,964

[60] ¶ 38,960, ¶ 38,966, ¶ 38,967.021

[61] ¶ 38,967.04

[62] ¶ 38,960, ¶ 38,970, ¶ 38,971.021

(1) the last day of the original 10-year limitations period,

(2) December 31, 2002, or

(3) in the case of an extension in connection with an installment agreement, the 90th day after the extension.

Interest accrues on a deficiency from the date the tax was due (determined without regard to extensions) until the date payment is received at the rate specified at ¶ 2838 (Reg. § 301.6601-1(a)(1)).[63] Interest may be assessed and collected during the period in which the related tax may be collected (Code Sec. 6601(g)).[64]

Private Debt Collection Agencies. The IRS is authorized to use private debt collection agencies (PDCs) to recover federal debts (Code Sec. 6306). PDCs may be used to locate and contact taxpayers owing outstanding tax liabilities of any type and to arrange payment of those taxes. PDCs are authorized to offer taxpayers who cannot pay in full an installment agreement (see ¶ 2529) providing for full payment of the taxes over a five-year period. If the taxpayer is unable to pay the outstanding tax liability in full over a five-year period, the PDC would obtain specific financial information from the taxpayer and provide that information to the IRS for further processing.

The IRS is absolved from liability for damages for any unauthorized collection activities of persons performing services under a qualified tax collection contract. However, the PDCs will be liable for unauthorized collection activities in the same manner and to the same extent as the IRS and its employees. Rules similar to those under Code Sec. 7433, regarding suits for damages in connection with the collection of tax (see ¶ 2798), apply (Code Sec. 7433A). PDCs are required to inform every taxpayer contacted of the availability of assistance from the Taxpayer Advocate (see ¶ 2707). A taxpayer may request in writing to work with the IRS instead of the PDC to resolve the outstanding tax debt (Announcement 2006-63).

2736. Suspension of Assessment Period. When an income, estate or gift tax deficiency notice is mailed, the running of the period of limitations on assessment and collection of any deficiency is suspended for 90 days (150 days for a deficiency notice mailed to persons outside the United States) (not counting Saturday, Sunday, or a legal holiday in the District of Columbia as the 90th or 150th day), plus an additional 60 days thereafter in either case (Code Sec. 6503(a)(1)).[65] If a petition is filed with the Tax Court, the running of the period of limitations is suspended until the Tax Court's decision becomes final and for an additional 60 days thereafter (Code Sec. 6503(a)(1); Reg. § 301.6503(a)-1).[66]

The 10-year statute of limitations for collection after assessment is also suspended from the date the IRS wrongfully seizes or receives a third party's property to 30 days after the earlier of (1) the date the IRS returns the property or (2) the date on which a judgment secured in a wrongful levy action becomes final. Similarly, with respect to wrongful liens, the 10-year limitations period is suspended from the time the third-party owner is entitled to a certificate of discharge of lien until 30 days after the earlier of (1) the date that the IRS no longer holds any amount as a deposit or bond that was used to satisfy the unpaid liability or that was refunded or released or (2) the date that the judgment in a civil action becomes final (see ¶ 2755) (Code Sec. 6503(f)).[67]

For Chapter 11 bankruptcy cases, the running of the period of limitations is suspended during the period of the automatic stay on collection of taxes and for an additional period ending 60 days after the day the stay is lifted for assessments and for six months thereafter for collection (Code Sec. 6503(h)).[68] In receivership and other bankruptcy cases (such as Chapter 13) where a fiduciary is required to give written notice to the IRS of an appointment or authorization to act, the assessment period is suspended from the date the proceedings are instituted and ending 30 days after the day of notice to the IRS of such appointment. The extension period cannot exceed two years (Code Sec. 6872).[69]

If the taxpayer and the IRS agree to the rescission of a deficiency notice, the statute of limitations again begins to run as of the date of the rescission and continues to run for the period of time that remains on the date the notice was issued (Code Sec. 6212(d)).[70]

Footnote references are to paragraphs of the 2008 Standard Federal Tax Reports.

[63] ¶ 39,412	[66] ¶ 39,030, ¶ 39,031	[69] ¶ 40,640
[64] ¶ 39,410	[67] ¶ 39,030	[70] ¶ 37,540
[65] ¶ 39,030	[68] ¶ 39,030	

2738. Suit for Recovery of Erroneous Refund. The government may sue to recover an erroneous refund (including, but not limited to, one made after the applicable refund period described in ¶ 2763) within two years after such refund was paid (Code Sec. 6532(b)).[71] However, a suit may be commenced within five years if any part of the refund was induced by fraud or misrepresentation of a material fact (Code Sec. 6532(b); Reg. § 301.6532-2).[72]

2740. Criminal Prosecution. A criminal prosecution must generally be started within three years after the offense is committed (Code Sec. 6531).[73] However, a six-year period applies in a case where there is:

(1) fraud or an attempt to defraud the United States or an agency thereof, by conspiracy or otherwise;

(2) a willful attempt to evade or defeat any tax or payment;

(3) willful aiding or assisting in the preparation of a false return or other document;

(4) willful failure to pay any tax or make any return (except certain information returns) at the time required by law;

(5) a false statement verified under penalties of perjury or a false or fraudulent return, statement or other document;

(6) intimidation of a U.S. officer or employee;

(7) an offense committed by a U.S. officer or employee in connection with a revenue law; or

(8) a conspiracy to defeat tax or payment (Code Sec. 6531).[74]

Claim Against Transferee or Fiduciary

2743. Collection from Transferee of Property. The liability of a transferee of property is generally assessed and collected in the same manner as is any other deficiency imposed by the IRS (Reg. § 301.6901-1(a)).[75] The term "transferee" includes an heir, legatee, devisee, distributee of an estate of a deceased person, the shareholder of a dissolved corporation, the assignee or donee of an insolvent person, the successor of a corporation, a party to a Code Sec. 368(a) reorganization, and all other classes of distributees. Such term also includes, with respect to the gift tax, a donee (without regard to the solvency of the donor) and, with respect to the estate tax, any person who, under Code Sec. 6324(a)(2), is personally liable for any part of such tax (Reg. § 301.6901-1(b)).[76]

2745. Transferee Assessment and Collection Period. Unless a taxpayer has filed a false return with intent to evade tax (¶ 2732), an assessment against a transferee or fiduciary must be made within the following periods:

(1) in the case of an initial transferee, within one year after the expiration of the period of limitation for assessment against the taxpayer;

(2) in the case of a transferee of a transferee, within one year after the expiration of the period of limitation for assessment against the preceding transferee or three years after the expiration of the period of limitation for assessment against the taxpayer, whichever of these two periods expires first;

(3) if a timely court proceeding has been brought against the taxpayer or last preceding transferee, within one year after the return of execution in such proceeding; or

(4) in the case of a fiduciary, within one year after the liability arises or within the limitations period for collection of the tax (¶ 2726), whichever is the later (Code Sec. 6901; Reg. § 301.6901-1(c)).[77]

2747. Collection from Fiduciary. In order to receive advance notice from the IRS with respect to assessments, every fiduciary must give written notice to the IRS of his fiduciary capacity. If this notice (Form 56) is not filed, the IRS may proceed against the

---

Footnote references are to paragraphs of the 2008 Standard Federal Tax Reports.

[71] ¶ 39,270, ¶ 39,272, ¶ 39,280.01
[72] ¶ 39,270, ¶ 39,280.01
[73] ¶ 39,240
[74] ¶ 39,240
[75] ¶ 40,701, ¶ 40,720.01
[76] ¶ 40,701
[77] ¶ 40,700

¶2738

property in the hands of the fiduciary after mailing notice of the deficiency or other liability to the taxpayer's last known address, even if the taxpayer is then deceased or is under legal disability. The fiduciary may be relieved of any further liability by filing with the IRS written notice and evidence of the termination (Reg. § 301.6903-1).[78]

Bankruptcy or Receivership of Taxpayer

2750. Tax Collection Procedure. When a taxpayer's assets are taken over by a receiver appointed by the court, the IRS may immediately assess the tax if it has not already been lawfully assessed. The IRS may also assess the tax on (1) the debtor's estate under U.S. Code Title 11 bankruptcy proceedings or (2) the debtor, if the tax liability has become *res judicata* pursuant to a Title 11 bankruptcy determination (Code Sec. 6871(a) and (b)).[79] Tax claims may be presented to the court before which the receivership (or a Title 11 bankruptcy) is pending, despite the pendency of proceedings in the Tax Court. However, in the case of a receivership proceeding, no petition shall be filed with the Tax Court after the appointment of the receiver (Code Sec. 6871(c)).[80] The trustee of the debtor's estate in a Title 11 bankruptcy proceeding may intervene on behalf of the debtor's estate in any Tax Court proceeding to which the debtor is a party (Code Sec. 7464).[81]

Liens and Levies

2751. Property Subject to Liens. If a taxpayer fails to pay an assessed tax for which payment has been demanded, the amount due (including interest and penalties) constitutes a lien in favor of the United States upon all the taxpayer's property (real, personal, tangible, and intangible), including after-acquired property and rights to property (Reg. § 301.6321-1).[82] Whether the taxpayer owns or has an interest in property is determined under the appropriate state law.[83] Once the taxpayer's rights in the property are established, federal law determines priorities among competing creditors (Code Sec. 6323)[84] and controls whether specific property is exempt from levy (see ¶ 2753). Once a tax lien arises, it continues until the tax liability is paid or the lien becomes unenforceable due to a lapse of time (Code Sec. 6322).[85] Time has lapsed if 10 years have passed from the date of assessment (or longer, if the taxpayer waives restrictions on collection) during which the IRS has not attempted to collect the tax either by suit or distraint (Code Sec. 6502(a)).[86]

2753. Property Subject to Levy. Although a tax lien attaches to all the debtor's property, some property is exempt from levy. The following are among the items that are exempt from levy to some extent:

(1) wearing apparel and school books;

(2) fuel, provisions, furniture, and personal effects (up to $7,720 for 2007 and $7,900 for 2008);

(3) unemployment benefits;

(4) books and tools of a trade, business, or profession (up to $3,860 for 2007 and $3,950 for 2008);

(5) undelivered mail;

(6) certain annuity and pension payments;

(7) workers' compensation;

(8) judgments for support of minor children;

(9) certain AFDC, social security, state and local welfare payments and Job Training Partnership Act payments;

(10) certain amounts of wages, salary, and other income; and

(11) certain service-connected disability payments (Code Sec. 6334(a)).[87]

Footnote references are to paragraphs of the 2008 Standard Federal Tax Reports.

[78] ¶ 40,730, ¶ 40,811
[79] ¶ 40,610
[80] ¶ 40,610, ¶ 40,630.01
[81] ¶ 42,120

[82] ¶ 38,135A, ¶ 38,136
[83] ¶ 38,136.01
[84] ¶ 38,145
[85] ¶ 38,140

[86] ¶ 39,020.021
[87] ¶ 38,210, ¶ 38,225.01

¶2753

Certain specified payments are not exempt from levy if the Secretary of the Treasury approves the levy. Among the items so covered are certain wage replacement payments as specified at Code Sec. 6334(f).[88]

The IRS may not seize any real property used as a residence by the taxpayer or any real property of the taxpayer (other than rental property) that is used as a residence by another person in order to satisfy a liability of $5,000 or less (including tax, penalties and interest). In the case of the taxpayer's principal residence, the IRS may not seize the residence without written approval of a federal district court judge or magistrate (Code Sec. 6334(a)(13); Code Sec. 6334(e)).[89] Unless collection of tax is in jeopardy, tangible personal property or real property (other than rented real property) used in the taxpayer's trade or business may not be seized without written approval of an IRS district or assistant director. Such approval may not be given unless it is determined that the taxpayer's other assets subject to collection are not sufficient to pay the amount due and the expenses of the proceedings. Where a levy is made on tangible personal property essential to the taxpayer's trade or business, the IRS must provide an accelerated appeals process to determine whether the property should be released from levy (Code Sec. 6343(a)(2)).[90] See ¶ 2755.

Levies are prohibited if the estimated expenses of the levy and sale exceed the fair market value of the property (Code Sec. 6331(f)).[91] Also, unless the collection of tax is in jeopardy, a levy cannot be made on any day on which the taxpayer is required to respond to an IRS summons (Code Sec. 6331(g)).[92] Further, financial institutions are required to hold amounts garnished by the IRS for 21 days after receiving notice of the levy to provide the taxpayer time to notify the IRS of any errors (Code Sec. 6332(c)).[93]

2754. Recording and Priority of Tax Liens. Until notice of a tax lien has been properly recorded, it is not valid against any bona fide purchaser for value, mechanic's lienor, judgment lien creditor or holder of a security interest (such as a mortgagee or pledgee, for example) (Code Sec. 6323(a)).[94] Also, even a properly recorded tax lien may not be valid against so-called superpriorities, which include purchases of securities and automobiles, retail purchases, casual sales of less than $1,290 in 2007 ($1,320 in 2008), certain possessory liens securing payment for repairs to personal property, real property taxes and special assessment liens, mechanic's liens for repairs and improvements to certain residential property, attorneys' liens, certain insurance contracts and deposit secured loans (previously referred to as passbook loans) (Code Sec. 6323(b)).[95] In addition, security interests arising from commercial financing agreements may be accorded superpriority status (Code Sec. 6323(c)).[96]

Notice of a federal tax lien must be filed in the one office designated by the state in which the property is situated (Code Sec. 6323(f)).[97] Generally, personal property is situated in the state where the taxpayer resides (rather than where domiciled); for real property, the situs is its physical location. If, in the case of either real or personal property, the state designates more than one office or does not designate an office where notice must be filed, notice of the lien must be filed with the Clerk of the U.S. District Court for the district in which the property is situated. If state law provides that a notice of lien affecting personal property must be filed in the county clerk's office located in the taxpayer's county of residence and also adopts a federal law that requires a notice of lien to be filed in another location in order to attach to a specific type of property, the state is deemed to have designated only one office for the filing of the notice. Thus, to protect its lien, the IRS need only file its notice in the county clerk's office located in the taxpayer's home county. Notice regarding property located in the District of Columbia is filed with the Recorder of Deeds of the District of Columbia. Special rules apply in a state that requires public indexing for priority liens against realty.

A forfeiture under local law of property seized by any law enforcement agency or other local governmental branch relates back to the time the property was first seized,

---

Footnote references are to paragraphs of the 2008 Standard Federal Tax Reports.

[88] ¶ 38,210
[89] ¶ 38,210, ¶ 38,225.01
[90] ¶ 38,270, ¶ 38,274.01
[91] ¶ 38,185

[92] ¶ 38,185
[93] ¶ 38,185
[94] ¶ 38,145
[95] ¶ 38,145

[96] ¶ 38,145
[97] ¶ 38,145

unless, under local law, a claim holder would have priority over the interest of the government in the property (Code Sec. 6323(i)(3)).[98]

The IRS may not levy against property while a taxpayer has a pending offer in compromise or installment agreement (Code Sec. 6331(k)).[99] If the offer in compromise or installment agreement is ultimately rejected, the levy prohibition remains in effect for 30 days after the rejection and during the pendency of any appeal of the rejection, providing the appeal is filed within 30 days of the rejection. No levy may be made while the installment agreement is in effect. If the installment agreement is terminated by the IRS, no levy may be made for 30 days after the termination and during the pendency of any appeal.

2754A. Notice and Opportunity for Hearing. The IRS must notify any person subject to a lien of the existence of the lien within five days of the lien being filed (Code Sec. 6320; Reg. § 301.6320-1). Among other requirements, the notice must address the person's right to request a hearing during the 30-day period beginning on the sixth day after the lien is filed. Similarly, at least 30 days prior to the IRS filing a notice of levy on any person's property or right to property, the IRS must provide notice of the right to a hearing (Code Sec. 6330; Reg. § 301.6320-1). Whether in connection with the notice of lien or notice of intent to levy, the hearing is to be held by the IRS Office of Appeals. At the hearing, the taxpayer may raise any issue relevant to the appropriateness of the proposed collection activity if such issue was not raised at a previous hearing. The taxpayer has 30 days after the hearing determination to appeal the determination to the Tax Court, which has exclusive jurisdiction over appeals of hearing determinations.

Applicable to levies served on or after November 23, 2007, a taxpayer subject to a levy for the collection of employment taxes cannot request a hearing if the taxpayer already requested a hearing regarding unpaid employment taxes arising in the two-year period before the beginning of the taxable period at issue (Code Sec. 6330(h), as added by the Small Business and Work Opportunity Tax Act of 2007 (P.L. 100-28)).

2755. Release of Tax Liens and Levies. Taxpayers may appeal the filing of a notice of lien in the public record and petition for release. If filed in error, the IRS must release the lien and state that the lien was erroneous (Code Sec. 6326(b)). The request for relief must be based on one of the following grounds: (1) the tax liability had been satisfied before the lien was filed; (2) the assessing of the tax liability violated either the notice of deficiency procedures or the Bankruptcy Code; or (3) the limitations period for collecting the liability had expired prior to the filing of the lien (Code Sec. 6326; Reg. § 301.6326-1).[100]

Further, the IRS may withdraw a public notice of tax lien before payment in full if:

(1) the filing of the notice was premature or not in accord with administrative procedures;

(2) the taxpayer has entered into an installment agreement to satisfy the tax liability;

(3) withdrawal of the notice would facilitate the collection of the tax liability; or

(4) the withdrawal of the notice would be in the best interest of the taxpayer and the government, as determined by the National Taxpayer Advocate (Code Sec. 6323(j)).[101]

The withdrawal of a notice of tax lien does not affect the underlying tax lien; rather, the withdrawal simply relinquishes any lien priority the IRS had obtained when the notice was filed.

The IRS is required to release a levy if:

(1) the underlying liability is satisfied or becomes unenforceable due to lapse of time;

(2) the IRS determines that the release of the levy will facilitate the collection of tax;

Footnote references are to paragraphs of the 2008 Standard Federal Tax Reports.

[98] ¶ 38,145
[99] ¶ 38,185
[100] ¶ 38,175, ¶ 38,176
[101] ¶ 38,160.0756

(3) an installment payment agreement has been executed by the taxpayer with respect to the liability;

(4) the IRS determines that the levy is creating a financial hardship; or

(5) the fair market value of the property exceeds the liability, and the partial release of the levy would not hinder the collection of tax (Code Sec. 6343(a)).[102]

In addition, a taxpayer may request that the IRS sell the levied property (Code Sec. 6335(f); Reg. § 301.6335-1(d)).[103]

The IRS has been given authority to return property that has been levied upon if:

(1) the levy was premature or not in accordance with administrative procedure;

(2) the taxpayer has entered into an installment agreement to satisfy the tax liability, unless the agreement provides otherwise;

(3) the return of the property will facilitate collection of the tax liability; or

(4) with the consent of the taxpayer or the Taxpayer Advocate, the return of the property would be in the best interests of the taxpayer and the government (Code Sec. 6343(d)).[104]

Property is returned in the same manner as if the property had been wrongfully levied upon, except that the taxpayer is not entitled to interest.

A taxpayer may bring a suit in federal district court if an IRS employee knowingly or negligently fails to release a tax lien on the taxpayer's property after receiving written notice from the taxpayer of the IRS's failure to release the lien (Code Sec. 7432).[105] The taxpayer may recover actual economic damages plus the costs of the action. Injuries such as inconvenience, emotional distress, and loss of reputation are not compensable damages unless they result in actual economic harm. Costs of the action that may be recovered are limited generally to certain court costs and do not include administrative costs or attorney's fees, although attorney's fees may be recoverable under Code Sec. 7430 (see ¶ 2796) (Reg. § 301.7432-1(c)).[106] A two-year statute of limitations, measured from the date on which the cause of action accrued, applies (Code Sec. 7432(d)(3)).[107]

Third-Party Owners. A third-party owner of property against which a federal tax lien has been filed may obtain a certificate of discharge with respect to the lien on such property (Code Sec. 6325(b)(4)).[108] The certificate is issued if (1) the third-party owner deposits with the IRS an amount of money equal to the value of the government's interest in the property as determined by the IRS or (2) the third-party owner posts a bond covering the government's interest in the property in a form acceptable by the IRS.

If the IRS determines that (1) the liability to which the lien relates can be satisfied from other sources or (2) the value of the government's interest in the property is less than the IRS's prior determination of the government's interest in the property, then the IRS will refund (with interest) the amount deposited and release the bond applicable to such property. Within 120 days after a certificate of discharge is issued, the third-party owner may file a civil action against the United States in a federal district court for a determination of whether the government's interest in the property (if any) has less value than that determined by the IRS (Code Sec. 7426(a)(4) and (b)(5)).[109]

Mitigation of Effect of Statute of Limitations

2756. Correction of Errors in Certain Cases. The Code provides rules in Code Sec. 1311—Code Sec. 1314 (Reg. § 1.1311(a)-1— Reg. § 1.1314(c)-1)[110] for relief from some of the inequities caused by the statute of limitations and other provisions that would otherwise prevent equitable adjustment of various income tax hardships. Adjustments are permitted, even though the limitation period for assessment or refund for the year at issue may have otherwise expired, when a determination under the income tax laws:

Footnote references are to paragraphs of the 2008 Standard Federal Tax Reports.

[102] ¶ 38,270, ¶ 38,274.01
[103] ¶ 38,230, ¶ 38,231, ¶ 38,234.025
[104] ¶ 38,274.023
[105] ¶ 41,760, ¶ 41,768.01
[106] ¶ 41,761
[107] ¶ 41,760
[108] ¶ 38,165
[109] ¶ 41,710
[110] ¶ 31,800—¶ 31,865

(1) requires the inclusion in gross income of an item that was erroneously included in the income of the taxpayer for another tax year or in the gross income of a "related taxpayer";

(2) allows a deduction or credit that was erroneously allowed to the taxpayer for another tax year or to a "related taxpayer";

(3) requires the exclusion from gross income of an item included in a return filed by the taxpayer or with respect to which tax was paid and which was erroneously excluded or omitted from the gross income of the taxpayer for another tax year or from the gross income of a "related taxpayer" for the same or another tax year;

(4) requires the correction of income or deduction items of estates or trusts or beneficiaries of either as between such "related taxpayers";

(5) establishes the basis of property by making adjustments to such basis for items that should have been added to, or deducted from, income of preceding years;

(6) requires the allowance or disallowance of a deduction or credit to a corporation where a correlative deduction or credit should have been allowed (or disallowed) to a related taxpayer that is a member of an affiliated group of corporations (where there is an 80% common ownership);

(7) requires the exclusion from gross income of an item not included in a return filed by the taxpayer and with respect to which the tax was not paid but which is includible in the gross income of the taxpayer for another tax year or in the gross income of a related taxpayer; or

(8) disallows a deduction or credit that should have been allowed, but was not allowed, to the taxpayer for another tax year or to a related taxpayer for the same or another tax year.[111]

Refunds and Credits

2759. Claim for Refund or Credit. A claim for refund for an overpayment of income taxes is generally made on the appropriate income tax return. However, once the return has been filed and the taxpayer believes the tax is incorrect, the claim for refund by an individual who filed Form 1040, 1040A, or 1040EZ is made on Form 1040X. The refund claim is made on Form 1120X by a corporation that filed Form 1120.[112] A claim for refund or credit for an overpayment of income taxes for which a form other than Form 1040, 1040A, 1040EZ, 1120, or 990T was filed is made on the appropriate amended tax return (Reg. § 301.6402-3).[113]

2760. Amendment of Refund Claim. A timely claim for refund based upon one or more specific grounds may not be amended to include other and different grounds after the statute of limitations has expired (Reg. § 301.6402-2(b)).

2761. Refund or Credit After Appeal to Tax Court. Where the taxpayer has been mailed a notice of deficiency and has filed a petition with the Tax Court (see ¶ 2778), no credit or refund is allowable, and the taxpayer may not sue in any other court for any part of the tax for the tax year in question (Code Sec. 6512).[114] A credit or refund may be allowed or a suit may be instituted, however, to recover:

(1) an overpayment determined by a decision of the Tax Court that has become final;

(2) any amount collected in excess of an amount computed in accordance with a final decision of the Tax Court;

(3) any amount collected after the expiration of the period of limitation upon the beginning of levy or a proceeding in court for collection;

(4) overpayments attributable to partnership items;

Footnote references are to paragraphs of the 2008 Standard Federal Tax Reports.

[111] ¶ 31,820, ¶ 31,829.021
[112] ¶ 38,518, ¶ 38,519.01, ¶ 38,519.075
[113] ¶ 38,518, ¶ 38,519.12, ¶ 38,519.26
[114] ¶ 39,090, ¶ 39,100.01

(5) any amount that was collected within the period following the mailing of a notice of deficiency during which the IRS is prohibited from collecting by levy or through a court proceeding; and

(6) any amount that is not contested on an appeal from a Tax Court decision.

The Tax Court can order the refund of a tax overpayment plus interest if the IRS has not made a refund to the taxpayer within 120 days after the decision fixing the amount of the refund has become final (Code Sec. 6512(b)).[115]

The Tax Court is empowered to resolve disputes regarding the amount of interest to be charged on a tax deficiency redetermined pursuant to a Tax Court order. The action must be brought within one year from the date on which the decision ordering the redetermination of taxes became final. Further, the taxpayer must pay the entire redetermined deficiency, plus the entire amount of interest, before the Tax Court can hear the case (Code Sec. 7481(c)).[116]

2763. Limitations on Credit or Refund. Generally, a taxpayer may file a claim for refund within three years from the time the return was filed or within two years from the time the tax was paid, whichever is later. If no return was filed by the taxpayer, the claim must be filed within two years from the time the tax was paid (Code Sec. 6511(a)).[117] For this purpose, a return filed before the due date is treated as filed on the due date (Code Sec. 6513(a)).[118] Taxpayers who fail to file a return as of the date the IRS mails a deficiency notice may recover in the Tax Court taxes paid during the three years preceding the IRS mailing date (Code Sec. 6512(b)(3)).[119]

If the claim relates to the deductibility of bad debts or worthless securities, the period is seven years; if it relates to the credit for foreign taxes, the period is 10 years. If the refund claim relates to a net operating loss or a capital loss carryback, the period is that period which ends three years after the time prescribed by law for filing the return (including extensions thereof) for the tax year of the NOL or capital loss carryback. To the extent that an overpayment is due to unused credit carrybacks that arise as the result of the carryback of an NOL or capital loss, the claim may be filed during the period that ends three years after the time prescribed by law for filing the return (including extensions thereof) for the tax year of the unused credit that results in such carryback (Code Sec. 6511(d); Reg. § 301.6511(d)-2).[120]

The statute of limitations on refund claims is suspended during any period that an individual is "financially disabled," i.e., under a medically determinable mental or physical impairment that: (1) can be expected to result in death or that has lasted or can be expected to last for a continuous period of not less than one year and (2) renders the person unable to manage his or her financial affairs (Code Sec. 6511(h)).[121] The suspension of the limitations period does not apply for any period during which the taxpayer's spouse or another person is authorized to act on behalf of the individual in financial matters.

2764. Refund Reduction for Past-Due, Legally Enforceable Debts. The Treasury Department's Financial Management Service (FMS) will reduce the amount of any tax refund payable to a taxpayer by the amount of any past-due, legally enforceable nontax debt that is owed to any federal agency. Debts that are less than $25 and those that have been delinquent for more than 10 years are exempt. In most cases, the creditor federal agencies must have first attempted to collect the debt by using salary offset and administrative procedures. The federal agency is also required to notify the taxpayer that a debt will be referred to the FMS for refund offset if the debt remains unpaid after 60 days or if there is insufficient evidence that the debt is either not past due or not legally enforceable (31 CFR § 285.2).

The FMS has also promulgated rules governing the offset of tax refunds against past-due child and spousal support (31 CFR § 285.3) and against state income tax debts reduced to judgment (31 CFR § 285.8).

Footnote references are to paragraphs of the 2008 Standard Federal Tax Reports.

[115] ¶ 39,090, ¶ 39,100.021   [118] ¶ 39,120   [121] ¶ 39,060
[116] ¶ 42,420   [119] ¶ 39,090
[117] ¶ 39,060   [120] ¶ 39,060, ¶ 39,067

¶2763

2765. Interest on Refund. When a return has been properly filed in processible form, interest is allowed on a refund from the date of overpayment to a date preceding the date of the refund check by not more than 30 days (Code Sec. 6611(b)(2)).[122] If a return is filed late, no interest is allowed for any day before the date on which it is filed (Code Sec. 6611(b)(3)).[123] No interest is payable on a refund arising from an original tax return if the refund is issued by the 45th day after the later of the due date for the return (determined without regard to any extensions) or the date the return is filed (Code Sec. 6611(e)).[124] Similarly, if a refund claimed on an amended return or claim for refund is issued within 45 days after the date the amended document was filed, interest is not payable for that period, although interest is payable from the due date of the original return to the date the amended document was filed. If a refund is not issued within the 45-day grace period, interest is payable for the period from the due date of the original return to the date the refund is paid.

The interest rate the IRS must pay for overpayment of taxes by corporate taxpayers is the short-term federal rate plus two percentage points (Code Sec. 6621(a)(1)).[125] The rate of interest on overpayments for noncorporate taxpayers is equal to the federal short-term rate plus three percentage points (which is equal to the interest rate on underpayments of tax). For large corporate overpayments (any portion that exceeds $10,000), the rate is reduced to the sum of the short-term federal rate plus one-half of one percentage point. These rates are adjusted quarterly, with each successive rate becoming effective two months after the date of each quarterly adjustment. The rates for the first through fourth quarters of 2007 were 8% for noncorporate taxpayers and 7% for corporate taxpayers (5.5% for large corporate overpayments).[126]

Overlapping Overpayments and Underpayments. The interest rates for overpayments and underpayments have been equalized (sometimes referred to as "global interest netting") for any period of mutual indebtedness between taxpayers and the IRS (Code Sec. 6621(d)). No interest is imposed to the extent that underpayment and overpayment interest run simultaneously on equal amounts. The net zero interest rate applies regardless of whether an underpayment otherwise would be subject to the increased interest rate imposed on large corporate underpayments or an overpayment otherwise would be subject to a reduced interest rate because it was a corporate overpayment in excess of $10,000. Although global interest netting is available to both corporate and noncorporate taxpayers, its effect on noncorporate taxpayers is mitigated due to the equalization of the underpayment and overpayment interest rates for such taxpayers.

2773. Quick Carryback Refund and Postponement of Tax Payment. A corporation (other than an S corporation) that has an overpayment of tax as a result of a net operating loss, capital loss, business and research credits, or a claim-of-right adjustment can file an application on Form 1139 for a tentative adjustment or refund of taxes for a year affected by the carryback of such loss or credits or by such adjustment. A noncorporate taxpayer can apply for similar adjustments on Form 1045.[127] For provisions on the quick refund of a capital loss carryback, see ¶ 1188.

The application itself is not a formal refund claim and its rejection in whole or in part cannot be made the basis of a refund suit. However, the taxpayer can file a regular claim for refund within the limitation period (see ¶ 2763), and this claim can be made the basis for a suit. For losses and credits, the IRS must allow or disallow the refund or credit within 90 days from the later of (1) the date the application is filed or (2) the last day of the month in which the return for the loss or unused credit year is due (giving effect to extensions of time). For claim-of-right adjustments, the IRS must allow or disallow the refund or credit within 90 days from the later of (1) the date the application is filed or (2) the date of the overpayment (Code Sec. 6411(b) and (d)).[128]

If a corporation (but no other taxpayer) expects a net operating loss carryback from the current (unfinished) tax year, it can, subject to certain limitations, extend the time for payment of all or a part of the tax still payable for the immediately preceding year by filing a statement on Form 1138 (Reg. § 1.6164-1).[129]

Footnote references are to paragraphs of the 2008 Standard Federal Tax Reports.

[122] ¶ 39,430	[125] ¶ 39,450	[128] ¶ 38,720
[123] ¶ 39,430	[126] ¶ 39,455.01	[129] ¶ 37,241
[124] ¶ 39,430	[127] ¶ 38,726	

The Courts

2776. Organization of Tax Court. The primary function of the U.S. Tax Court is to review deficiencies asserted by the IRS for additional income, estate, gift, or self-employment taxes (Code Sec. 7442)[130] or special excise taxes imposed on taxpayers under Chapters 41-44 of the Code (Code Sec. 6512).[131] The Tax Court is the only judicial body from which relief may be obtained without the payment of tax. The Tax Court also may issue declaratory judgments on the initial or continuing qualification of a retirement plan under Code Sec. 401, a tax-exempt organization under Code Sec. 501(c)(3) or Code Sec. 170(c)(2), a private foundation under Code Sec. 509(a), a private operating foundation under Code Sec. 4942(j)(3), or a tax-exempt farmers' cooperative under Code Sec. 521. However, a revocation of tax-exempt status for failure to file an annual information return or notice is not subject to an action for declaratory judgment relief. The Tax Court also may rule on the tax-exempt interest status of a government bond issue (Code Sec. 7428, Code Sec. 7476 and Code Sec. 7478; Tax Court Rule 210).[132] Declaratory judgment powers are also provided for (1) estate tax installments, (2) gift tax revaluations, and (3) employment status determinations.

The Tax Court's offices and trial rooms are located in Washington, D.C., but trials are also conducted in principal cities throughout the country. At the time of filing a petition, the taxpayer should file a request indicating where he prefers the trial to be held. The court imposes a filing fee of $60 (Code Sec. 7451).[133]

In any Tax Court case, other than small tax cases (see ¶ 2784), the findings of fact and opinion must generally be reported in writing. However, in appropriate cases, a Tax Court judge may state orally, and record in the transcript of the proceedings, the findings of fact or opinion in the case (Code Sec. 7459).[134] In such cases, the court must provide to all parties in the case either a copy of the transcript pages, which record the findings or opinion, or a written summary of such findings or opinion (Tax Court Rule 152).[135]

2778. Appeal to the Tax Court. Before the IRS can assess a deficiency, it generally must mail a deficiency notice to the taxpayer. The taxpayer then has an opportunity to appeal, within 90 days after the notice is mailed, to the Tax Court, if it has jurisdiction (see ¶ 2711). A notice based solely upon a mathematical or clerical error is not considered a notice of deficiency (Code Sec. 6213).[136] If the notice is mailed to a person outside the United States, the period is 150 days instead of 90 days (Code Sec. 6213).[137] The period is counted from midnight of the day on which the notice is mailed.[138] Saturday, Sunday, or a legal holiday in the District of Columbia is not counted as the 90th or 150th day (Reg. § 301.6213-1(a)).[139]

When a petition to the Tax Court is properly addressed and mailed within the prescribed time for filing, with the postage prepaid, the date of the U.S. postmark stamped on the cover in which the petition is mailed is the date of filing. For a petition that is mailed from a foreign country, this rule applies only if the petition is given to a designated international delivery service (Rev. Rul. 2002-23). If a petition is sent by registered or certified mail, the date of registration or certification is the date of mailing and is prima facie evidence that the petition was delivered to the Tax Court (Reg. § 301.7502-1).[140]

If a taxpayer has filed a Tax Court petition before a jeopardy assessment or levy is made, the Tax Court is given concurrent jurisdiction with the federal district courts with respect to the taxpayer's challenge of the jeopardy assessment or levy (Code Sec. 7429(b)(2)).[141] Similarly, if there is a premature assessment of tax made while a proceeding with respect to that tax is pending in the Tax Court, the Tax Court has concurrent jurisdiction with the federal district court to restrain the assessment and collection of tax (Code Sec. 6213).[142]

Footnote references are to paragraphs of the 2008 Standard Federal Tax Reports.

[130] ¶ 42,058.01
[131] ¶ 39,090
[132] ¶ 41,720, ¶ 42,134, ¶ 42,154, ¶ 42,370
[133] ¶ 42,072

[134] ¶ 42,110
[135] ¶ 42,312
[136] ¶ 37,545
[137] ¶ 37,545
[138] ¶ 37,549.34

[139] ¶ 37,546
[140] ¶ 42,621
[141] ¶ 41,725, ¶ 41,736.025
[142] ¶ 37,545

¶2776

2782. Burden of Proof. The IRS has the burden of proof in the Tax Court with respect to a factual issue that is relevant to determining a taxpayer's tax liability if the taxpayer presents credible evidence with respect to that issue *and* satisfies three applicable conditions discussed below (Code Sec. 7491):

(1) The taxpayer must comply with the substantiation and recordkeeping requirements of the Internal Revenue Code and regulations.

(2) The taxpayer must cooperate with reasonable requests by the IRS for witnesses, information, documents, meetings and interviews.

(3) Taxpayers *other than individuals* must meet the net worth limitations that apply for awarding attorneys' fees under Code Sec. 7430. Thus, corporations, trusts, and partnerships whose tax worth exceeds $7 million cannot benefit from this provision.

Further, in any court proceeding where the IRS solely uses statistical information from unrelated taxpayers to reconstruct an item of an *individual* taxpayer's income, such as the average income for taxpayers in the area in which the taxpayer lives, the burden of proof is on the IRS with respect to that item of income. Also with respect to individuals only, the IRS must initially come forward with evidence that it is appropriate to apply a penalty, addition to tax, or additional amount before the court can impose the penalty.

In cases in which the burden of proof does not shift to the IRS, in general, the taxpayer has the burden of proof in the Tax Court. However, a taxpayer must only establish that the IRS is in error and not whether any tax is owed (Tax Court Rule 142).[143] The IRS bears the burden of proof with respect to any new matter, increase in deficiency, or affirmative defenses raised in its answer. Further, the burden of proving fraud and liability as a transferee is upon the IRS (Code Sec. 6902 and Code Sec. 7454).[144] The IRS also has the burden of proof in certain proceedings involving foundation managers, e.g., where a manager knowingly participated in self-dealing.[145]

2784. Small Tax Cases. The Tax Court maintains relatively informal procedures for the filing and handling of cases where neither the tax deficiency in dispute (including additions to tax and penalties) nor the amount of claimed overpayment exceeds $50,000. Usually taxpayers represent themselves, although they may be represented by anyone admitted to practice before the Tax Court. Each decision is final and cannot be appealed by either the taxpayer or the government (Code Sec. 7463).[146] The filing fee is $60.[147]

2786. Appeal from Tax Court Decision. A taxpayer who loses in the Tax Court may appeal the case (unless the case was tried as a small tax case, ¶ 2784) to the proper U.S. Court of Appeals[148] by filing a notice of appeal with the clerk of the Tax Court. The notice must be filed within 90 days after the Tax Court decision is entered. However, if one party to the proceeding files a timely notice of appeal, any other party to the proceeding may take an appeal by filing a notice of appeal within 120 days after the decision of the Tax Court is entered (Code Sec. 7483).[149]

A taxpayer who wants the assessment postponed pending the outcome of the appeal must file an appeal bond with the Tax Court guaranteeing payment of the deficiency as finally determined (Code Sec. 7485).[150]

2788. Acquiescence and Nonacquiescence by Commissioner. The IRS announces in the Internal Revenue Bulletin if it has decided to acquiesce or not acquiesce in a regular decision of the Tax Court. Any acquiescence or nonacquiescence may be withdrawn, modified or reversed at any time and any such action may be given retrospective, as well as prospective, effect.[151]

An acquiescence or nonacquiescence relates only to the issue or issues decided adversely to the government. Acquiescence means the IRS accepts the conclusion reached and does not necessarily mean acceptance and approval of any or all of the reasons assigned by the court for its conclusions. Acquiescences are to be relied on by

---

Footnote references are to paragraphs of the 2008 Standard Federal Tax Reports.

[143] ¶ 42,302, ¶ 42,302.615
[144] ¶ 40,780, ¶ 42,081,
¶ 42,302
[145] ¶ 42,081, ¶ 42,302

[146] ¶ 42,118
[147] ¶ 42,072, ¶ 42,180
[148] ¶ 42,440

[149] ¶ 42,477
[150] ¶ 42,500
[151] ¶ 43,282.01

IRS officers and others concerned as conclusions of the IRS only with respect to the application of the law to the facts in the particular case.

2790. Suits for Refund of Tax Overpayments. After the IRS rejects a refund claim for an alleged tax overpayment, suit can be maintained in the Court of Federal Claims or a District Court. A suit may be brought in the Court of Federal Claims against the United States to recover any overpayment of tax, regardless of amount (Judicial Code Sec. 1491).[152] Final decisions of the Court of Federal Claims are appealable to the Court of Appeals for the Federal Circuit.[153] All civil actions against the United States for the recovery of any internal revenue tax (regardless of amount) alleged to have been erroneously or illegally assessed or collected may be brought against the United States as defendant in a U.S. District Court with right of trial by jury in any action if either party makes a specific request for a jury trial.[154] Filing a proper claim for refund or credit (see ¶ 2759) is a condition precedent to a suit for recovery of overpaid taxes (Code Sec. 7422(a)).[155]

If, prior to the hearing on a taxpayer's refund suit in a District Court or the Court of Federal Claims, a notice of deficiency is issued on the subject matter of the taxpayer's suit, then the District Court or Court of Federal Claims proceedings are stayed during the period of time in which the taxpayer can file a petition with the Tax Court and for 60 days thereafter. If the taxpayer files a petition with the Tax Court, then the District Court or the Court of Federal Claims loses jurisdiction as to any issues over which the Tax Court acquires jurisdiction. If the taxpayer does not appeal to the Tax Court, the United States may then counterclaim in the taxpayer's suit within the period of the stay of proceedings even though the time for such pleading may otherwise have expired (Code Sec. 7422(e)).[156]

2792. Time to Bring Suit. A suit or proceeding based upon a refund claim must be brought within two years from the date the IRS mails, by registered or certified mail, notice of disallowance of the part of the claim to which such suit or proceeding relates or within two years from the date the taxpayer waives notification of disallowance of his claim. The two-year period of limitation for filing suit may be extended by written agreement between the taxpayer and the IRS (Code Sec. 6532(a)).[157]

Unless a bankruptcy proceeding has begun, no action can be brought before the expiration of six months from the date of filing the refund claim unless the IRS renders a decision on the claim before the six months are up. In bankruptcy proceedings, the six-month period is reduced to 120 days (Code Sec. 6532(a)).[158]

2794. Supreme Court. Either party may seek a review of a Court of Appeals decision by the Supreme Court (Code Sec. 7482(a))[159] through a petition for a writ of certiorari.

2796. Attorneys' Fees and Court Costs. A "prevailing party"—any party (other than the United States or a creditor of the taxpayer) who has substantially prevailed with respect to the amount in controversy or the most significant issue or issues—may be awarded litigation costs in most civil tax litigation, including declaratory judgment proceedings (Code Sec. 7430).[160] In addition, a prevailing party can recover reasonable administrative costs incurred after the earlier of:

> (1) the date the taxpayer received the decision notice from the IRS Office of Appeals,

> (2) the date of the deficiency notice, or

> (3) the date on which the first letter of proposed deficiency is sent that allows the taxpayer an opportunity for administrative review in the IRS Office of Appeals.

These awards may be made if the taxpayer meets certain net worth limitations and the IRS fails to prove that its position was substantially justified. When litigation costs are involved, the IRS's position is the government's position taken in the litigation proceeding or administratively by the IRS District Counsel. In the case of administrative costs, the IRS's position is the position taken as of the earlier of (1) the date the taxpayer

---

Footnote references are to paragraphs of the 2008 Standard Federal Tax Reports.

[152] ¶ 41,571, ¶ 41,605.01	[155] ¶ 41,685	[158] ¶ 39,270
[153] ¶ 41,605.045	[156] ¶ 41,685	[159] ¶ 41,583, ¶ 42,440
[154] ¶ 41,605.01	[157] ¶ 39,270	[160] ¶ 41,740

received a decision notice from the IRS Office of Appeals or (2) the date of the deficiency notice. Litigation costs include:

(1) expenses of expert witnesses,

(2) costs of any study, analysis, engineering report, test, or project, which was found by the court to be necessary for the preparation of its case,

(3) fees of an individual authorized to practice before the court or the IRS, whether or not an attorney (generally not in excess of $170 per hour for 2007 and 2008), unless an affidavit is presented that establishes a special factor for a higher rate, such as the unavailability of qualified representatives at the customary rate, and

(4) court costs.

Other litigation costs may include, as held by the Tax Court, mileage and parking fees incurred by a *pro se* or represented taxpayer to attend a Tax Court hearing, as well as (as conceded by the IRS) postage and shipping costs (*J.M. Dunaway*, 124 TC 80, CCH Dec. 55,593). Reasonable attorneys' fees may also be awarded to specified persons who represent, on a *pro bono* basis or for a nominal fee, taxpayers who are prevailing parties (Code Sec. 7430).[161]

A taxpayer is considered to have substantially prevailed if the liability determined by the court is equal to or less than the amount for which the taxpayer would have been prepared to settle the case (excluding interest) (Code Sec. 7430(c)(4)(E) and (g); Reg. § 1.7430-7).[162] The written qualified settlement offer must be made at any time during the time from the issuance of the 30-day letter to a date 30 days before the date the case is first set for trial.

However, no costs will be awarded where the prevailing party failed to exhaust all of the administrative remedies within the IRS (Code Sec. 7430(b); Reg. § 301.7430-1).[163] The tender of a qualified settlement offer (see preceding paragraph) does not satisfy the requirement to exhaust all administrative remedies (*Haas & Associates Accounting Corporation*, 117 TC 48, CCH Dec. 54,447). Further, costs will be denied for any portion of the proceeding where the prevailing party caused unreasonable delay (Code Sec. 7430(b)(4)).[164] A taxpayer who prevails in an IRS proceeding must apply to the IRS for administrative costs before the 91st day after the date the final IRS determination of tax, interest or penalty was mailed to the taxpayer. If the IRS denies the application for costs, the taxpayer must petition the Tax Court within 90 days of the IRS mailing of the denial.

An order granting or denying an award for litigation costs becomes part of the decision or judgment in the case and is subject to appeal in the same manner as the decision or judgment (Code Sec. 7430).[165]

2798. Suit for Damages in Connection with Collection of Tax. A taxpayer may bring a suit in federal district court for damages sustained in connection with the collection of any federal tax because an IRS employee recklessly or intentionally disregarded any provision of the Internal Revenue Code, any IRS regulations or certain provisions of the Bankruptcy Code (Code Sec. 7433).[166] A suit may also be brought for negligent disregard of the Internal Revenue Code or any IRS regulations. Except as provided in Code Sec. 7432 relating to damage awards for failure to release liens (see ¶ 2755), this action is the taxpayer's exclusive remedy for recovering damages caused by reckless, intentional or negligent disregard of such provisions and regulations by IRS employees. The suit must be brought within two years after the right of action accrues.

The award is limited to the costs of the action plus any actual direct economic damages sustained by the taxpayer, up to a maximum award of $1 million for reckless or intentional actions and $100,000 for acts of negligence (Reg. § 301.7433-1(b)).[167] The IRS must comply with certain provisions of the Fair Debt Collection Practices Act so that the treatment of tax debtors by the IRS is at least equal to that required of private sector debt collectors (Code Sec. 6304). Taxpayers may bring a damages action under Code Sec. 7433 against the IRS for violations of these provisions.

Footnote references are to paragraphs of the 2008 Standard Federal Tax Reports.

[161] ¶ 41,740
[162] ¶ 41,740
[163] ¶ 41,740, ¶ 41,742

[164] ¶ 41,740
[165] ¶ 41,740
[166] ¶ 41,770, ¶ 41,778

[167] ¶ 41,771

Chapter 28

PENALTIES ☐ INTEREST

Failure to File Returns or Pay Tax

2801. Failure to File Returns. A failure to file any tax return within the time prescribed by the Code may result in an addition to tax. This penalty is 5% for each month (or fraction thereof) during which there is a failure to file any return, up to 25%. If the tax return is not filed within 60 days of the prescribed due date (including extensions), the penalty will not be less than the lesser of $100 or 100% of the tax due on the return (Code Sec. 6651(a)).[1] The late-filing addition runs for the period up to the date the IRS actually receives the late return (Rev. Rul. 73-133).[2] The penalty is computed only on the net amount of tax due, if any, on the return after credit has been given for amounts paid through withholding, estimated tax and any other credits claimed on the return (Code Sec. 6651(b); Reg. § 301.6651-1(a), (b) and (d)).[3]

The fraud and accuracy-related penalties will not apply in the case of a fraudulent failure to file a return. Instead, the failure-to-file penalty is increased to 15% for each month, up to 75% (Code Sec. 6651(f)).[4]

The failure-to-file penalty is not imposed when the taxpayer can show that the failure to file was due to reasonable cause and not to willful neglect. Mere absence of willful neglect is not "reasonable cause."[5] "Reasonable cause" did not exist when: (1) the taxpayer relied upon the advice of an agent; (2) the taxpayer relied on the accountant to perform the purely ministerial function of filing;[6] or (3) an officer of the corporate taxpayer misjudged the extension date.[7] However, failure to file a return upon a lawyer's or certified public accountant's advice that there was no income to report, or that the taxpayer was not liable for tax, has been held to be reasonable cause when the taxpayer supplied complete information to the tax professional.[8]

2805. Failure to Pay Tax. A penalty is imposed for failure to pay, when due, those taxes (other than estimated taxes) shown by a taxpayer on his return, unless the failure is due to reasonable cause (Code Sec. 6651(a)(2)).[9] The same penalty is imposed on additional taxes determined to be due on audit for which the IRS has made a demand for payment, but this penalty runs only for the period of nonpayment beginning after the 21st *calendar* day (10th *business* day if the amount demanded is at least $100,000) following the demand (Code Sec. 6651(a)(3)).[10] The addition to tax is one-half of 1% of the tax not paid, for each month (or part of a month) it remains unpaid, up to a maximum of 25%. The penalty increases to 1% per month beginning with either the 10th day after notice of levy is given or the day on which notice and demand is made in the case of a jeopardy assessment. For taxpayers who enter into installment agreements

---

Footnote references are to paragraphs of the 2008 Standard Federal Tax Reports.

[1] ¶ 39,470	[5] ¶ 39,475.028, ¶ 39,475.34	[9] ¶ 39,470
[2] ¶ 39,475.021, ¶ 39,475.33	[6] ¶ 39,475.42, ¶ 39,475.72	[10] ¶ 39,470, ¶ 39,475.022
[3] ¶ 39,470, ¶ 39,472	[7] ¶ 39,475.705	
[4] ¶ 39,470, ¶ 39,475.022	[8] ¶ 39,475.41, ¶ 39,475.68	

¶2801

with the IRS, the penalty for failure to timely pay taxes is reduced to one-quarter of 1% of the tax not paid (Code Sec. 6651(h); Reg. § 301.6651-1(a)(4)). If a taxpayer files a late return that is subject to both the failure-to-file and failure-to-pay penalties, the former may be reduced by the latter. However, if no return is filed or if a late-filed return understates the amount required to be shown on the return, the failure-to-pay penalty attributable to additional tax demanded by the IRS may not be used to offset any portion of the failure-to-file penalty. If the penalty for failure to file beyond 60 days applies, the penalty may not be reduced by a failure-to-pay penalty that is also imposed below the lesser of $100 or 100% of the tax due (Code Sec. 6651(a), (c) and (d)).[11]

2809. Automatic Extension of Time for Filing. An automatic extension of time to file a tax return (¶ 2509) is not an extension of time to pay the tax due under the return (Reg. § 1.6081-3(c) and Reg. § 1.6081-4(b)).[12] However, an individual taxpayer can avoid a failure-to-pay penalty by making an estimate of the tax due and paying that estimate (reduced by any amounts already paid in through withholding or estimated tax payments over the course of the tax year) with the request for extension of time to file. If the balance of tax due is remitted when the income tax return is filed, no penalty for failure to pay will apply unless the unpaid amount is more than 10% of the total tax liability. Similar rules apply for corporations (Reg. § 301.6651-1(c)(3) and (4)).[13]

2811. Frivolous Return Penalty. In addition to other penalties that may be imposed, there is a $5,000 penalty for filing a frivolous return. A frivolous return is one that omits information necessary to determine the taxpayer's tax liability, shows a substantially incorrect tax, is based upon a frivolous position (e.g., that wages are not income) or is based upon the taxpayer's desire to impede the collection of tax. A return based on the taxpayer's altering or striking out the "penalty of perjury" language above the signature line also constitutes a frivolous return (Code Sec. 6702).[14]

2813. Abatement of Penalties and/or Interest. The IRS shall abate certain penalties that result from reliance on incorrect IRS advice if (1) the advice was furnished in writing in response to a specific written request from the taxpayer and (2) the taxpayer reasonably relied upon the advice (Code Sec. 6404(f)).[15] However, penalties will be abated only if the taxpayer furnished adequate and accurate information in making the request. Taxpayers entitled to abatement should file Form 843, Claim for Refund and Request for Abatement, with copies of the relevant written documents attached (Reg. § 301.6404-3(d)).[16]

If the IRS extends the due date for filing income tax returns and for paying any tax due for taxpayers located in a presidentially declared disaster area, the IRS will abate the interest that would otherwise accrue for the extension period (Code Sec. 6404(h)).[17]

The accrual of interest and penalties will be suspended after 18 months (36 months for notices sent after November 25, 2007) unless the IRS sends the taxpayer a notice within 18/36 months following the later of: (1) the original due date of the return (without regard to extensions) or (2) the date on which a timely return is filed (Code Sec. 6404(g), as amended by the Small Business and Work Opportunity Tax Act of 2007 (P.L. 110-28)).[18] The suspension of interest and penalties is available only for individuals and only for income taxes. Although the suspension pertains only to tax related to timely filed returns (i.e., returns filed by the original due date or by the extended due date), the IRS has expanded this rule to cover additional tax voluntarily reported by a taxpayer, after a timely original return has been filed, on an amended return or in correspondence with the IRS (Rev. Rul. 2005-4). The suspension begins on the day after the end of the 18-month/36-month period and ends on the day that is 21 days after the date on which the notice is made. The suspension does not stop the accrual of:

(1) the failure to pay and failure to file penalties;

(2) any interest, penalty or other addition to tax in a case involving fraud;

(3) any interest, penalty, addition to tax, or additional amount with respect to any tax liability shown on the return;

Footnote references are to paragraphs of the 2008 Standard Federal Tax Reports.

[11] ¶ 39,470

[12] ¶ 36,790, ¶ 36,793

[13] ¶ 39,472

[14] ¶ 40,040, ¶ 40,043.01, ¶ 40,043.60, ¶ 40,043.70

[15] ¶ 38,570

[16] ¶ 38,576

[17] ¶ 38,570

[18] ¶ 38,570

(4) any interest, penalty or other addition to tax with respect to any gross misstatement;

(5) any interest, penalty or other addition to tax with respect to any reportable avoidance transaction or listed transaction (pertaining to tax shelters); or

(6) any criminal penalty.

Document and Information Return Penalties

2814. Information Reporting Penalties. Three distinct categories of penalties apply to failures to file required information returns and payee statements:

(1) failure to file an information return or to include correct information on an information return (Code Sec. 6721);[19]

(2) failure to file a payee statement or to include correct information on a payee statement (Code Sec. 6722);[20] and

(3) failure to comply with other information reporting requirements, which includes all reporting failures not covered by the other two categories (Code Sec. 6723).[21]

2816. Failure to File Correct Information Returns. A time-sensitive three-tier penalty structure is imposed for (1) any failure (other than a failure due to reasonable cause and not to willful neglect) to file correct information returns (see ¶ 2565) with the IRS on or before the required filing date, (2) any failure to include all the information required to be shown on a return, or (3) the inclusion of incorrect information (Code Sec. 6721(a)).[22] The penalty applies also to any failure to file, when required, electronically or by means of magnetic media, but is imposed only on the number of returns exceeding 250 (Code Sec. 6724(c)).[23] The penalty amounts for each of the prescribed time periods are as follows:

(1) For any reporting failure corrected within 30 days after the return's filing date, the amount of the penalty is $15 per return, up to a maximum of $75,000 for a calendar year (Code Sec. 6721(b)(1)).[24] The calendar-year maximum is $25,000 for small businesses (i.e., firms having average annual gross receipts of less than $5 million for the three most recent tax years (fiscal or calendar) ending before the calendar year for which the return was filed) (Code Sec. 6721(d)(1)(B)).[25]

(2) For any reporting failure corrected within the period beginning 31 days after the return's filing date up to August 1 of the calendar year in which the return had to be filed, the penalty is $30 per return, up to a maximum of $150,000 ($50,000 for small businesses) for a calendar year (Code Sec. 6721(b)(2) and (d)(1)(C)).[26]

(3) For any reporting failure corrected after August 1, the penalty is $50 per return, up to a maximum of $250,000 ($100,000 for small businesses) for a calendar year (Code Sec. 6721(a)(1) and (d)(1)(A)).[27]

A certain *de minimis* number of returns timely filed with incorrect or omitted information that are corrected on or before August 1 of the calendar year in which the returns are due will be treated as having been filed correctly, and no penalty will be imposed on them. This exception is limited to the greater of (1) 10 returns or (2) one-half of 1% of the total number of information returns required to be filed during the calendar year. The *de minimis* exception does not apply to a failure to file an information return (Code Sec. 6721(c)).[28]

If the failure to file an information return or to include all the required correct information is due to intentional disregard of the filing requirements, neither the three-tier penalty nor the *de minimis* exception will apply. Instead, the penalty for each failure is the greater of:

(1) $100 or

(2) 10% of the aggregate amount of the items required to be reported correctly in the case of a return other than a return required under:

Footnote references are to paragraphs of the 2008 Standard Federal Tax Reports.

[19] ¶ 40,210
[20] ¶ 40,230
[21] ¶ 40,250
[22] ¶ 40,210, ¶ 40,220.023

[23] ¶ 40,275, ¶ 40,285.021
[24] ¶ 40,210
[25] ¶ 40,210, ¶ 40,220.027
[26] ¶ 40,210, ¶ 40,220.027

[27] ¶ 40,210, ¶ 40,220.027
[28] ¶ 40,210, ¶ 40,220.025

(a) Code Sec. 6045(a) (brokers' transactions with customers),

(b) Code Sec. 6041A(b) (payments of remuneration for direct sales),

(c) Code Sec. 6050H (information on mortgage interest received in a trade or business from individuals),

(d) Code Sec. 6050I (information on cash receipts from a trade or business),

(e) Code Sec. 6050J (information on foreclosures and abandonments of security),

(f) Code Sec. 6050K (information on exchanges of certain partnership interests), or

(g) Code Sec. 6050L (information on certain dispositions of donated property).

The penalty equals the greater of $100 or 5% for returns required under Code Sec. 6045(a), Code Sec. 6050K, or Code Sec. 6050L. In the case of a return required under Code Sec. 6050I(a) (cash receipts of more than $10,000 in a trade or business), the penalty equals the greater of $25,000 or the amount of cash received in the transaction, up to a maximum of $100,000. Applicable to acquisitions of contracts after August 17, 2006, and before August 18, 2008, in the case of any return required under Code Sec. 6050V (acquisitions of interests in insurance contracts by exempt organizations), the penalty equals the greater of $100 or 10% of the value of any benefit of any contract with respect to which information is required to be included on the return. In addition, the intentional disregard penalties are not considered in figuring the yearly maximum penalty of $250,000 for failures not attributable to intentional disregard (Code Sec. 6721(e)).[29]

No penalty is imposed for inconsequential omissions and inaccuracies that do not prevent or hinder the IRS from adequately processing the return. Errors and omissions that relate to a taxpayer identification number, to the surname of a person required to receive a copy of the information provided, or to any monetary amounts are never considered inconsequential (Reg. § 301.6721-1(c)).[30]

2823. Failure to Furnish Correct Payee Statement. A penalty of $50 per statement (up to a maximum of $100,000 per payor per calendar year) may be imposed for (1) any failure (other than a failure due to reasonable cause and not to willful neglect) to furnish a payee statement on or before the required filing date, (2) any failure to include all the information required to be shown on a payee statement, or (3) the inclusion of incorrect information with respect to a payee statement. Payee statements include the following:

(1) information-at-source payments under Code Sec. 6041(d);

(2) payments in connection with services and direct sales under Code Sec. 6041A(e);

(3) taxable mergers and acquisitions under Code Sec. 6043A;

(4) brokers under Code Sec. 6045(b) or (d);

(5) certain stock options under Code Sec. 6039(a);

(6) group-term life insurance under Code Sec. 6052(b);

(7) catch shares of certain fishing boat crews under Code Sec. 6050A(b);

(8) income tax withheld from employees' wages under Code Sec. 6051;

(9) tip income reportable by employers under Code Sec. 6053(b) or (c);

(10) mortgage interest payments under Code Sec. 6050H(d);

(11) cash payments in excess of $10,000 under Code Sec. 6050I(e), (g)(4) or (g)(5);

(12) foreclosures and abandonments under Code Sec. 6050J(e);

(13) exchanges of certain partnership interests under Code Sec. 6050K(b);

(14) certain dispositions of donated property under Code Sec. 6050L(c);

Footnote references are to paragraphs of the 2008 Standard Federal Tax Reports.

[29] ¶ 40,210, ¶ 40,220.029   [30] ¶ 40,213

(15) pass-through income, deductions, etc., to partners under Code Sec. 6031(b) or (c) to beneficiaries of estates and trusts under Code Sec. 6034A, and to S corporation shareholders under Code Sec. 6037(b);

(16) payments of royalties under Code Sec. 6050N(b);

(17) statements relating to returns regarding payments of dividends and corporate earnings and profits under Code Sec. 6042(c);

(18) statements regarding payments of patronage dividends under Code Sec. 6044(e);

(19) statements regarding interest payments under Code Sec. 6049(c);

(20) statements relating to the cancellation of indebtedness by certain financial entities under Code Sec. 6050P(d);

(21) payments for certain purchases of fish for resale under Code Sec. 6050R;

(22) distributions from individual retirement accounts under Code Sec. 408(i) and from employee benefit plans under Code Sec. 6047(d);

(23) payments relating to qualified tuition and related expenses under Code Sec. 6050S;

(24) returns relating to certain company-owned life insurance held by a natural person where a trade or business is directly or indirectly the beneficiary under the policy under Code Sec. 264(f)(5)(A)(iv);[31] and

(25) applicable to charges made after December 31, 2009, charges or payments for qualified long-term insurance contracts under combined arrangements (Code Sec. 6050U).

In the case of intentional disregard of the requirements with respect to payee statements, the penalty imposed is identical to that for failures to file an information return or to include correct information. See ¶ 2816. Similarly, the intentional disregard penalty is not considered in applying the yearly maximum penalty of $100,000 for failures not attributable to intentional disregard (Code Sec. 6722(c)).[32] In addition, the regulatory exception from the imposition of the penalty (Reg. § 301.6721-1(c))[33] in the case of inconsequential omissions and inaccuracies on a payee statement continues to apply. See ¶ 2816.

2833. Failure to Comply with Other Information Reporting Requirements. A penalty of $50, up to a maximum of $100,000 for a calendar year, is imposed for each failure to comply with any specified information reporting requirement on or before the prescribed time (Code Sec. 6723).[34] The penalty will not be imposed if it can be shown that the failure was due to reasonable cause and not to willful neglect.

The specified information reporting requirements that are subject to the penalty include:

(1) the requirement that a transferor of an interest in a partnership promptly give notice to the partnership concerning the transfer;

(2) the requirement that a person include his taxpayer identification number (TIN) on any return, statement, or other document (other than an information return or payee statement), furnish his TIN to another person, or include the TIN of another person on any return, statement, or other document made with respect to that person;

(3) the requirement on returns reporting alimony payments that the TIN of the payee be furnished to the payor or that the payee's TIN be included on the payor's return;

(4) the requirement that a person include the TIN of any dependent on his return; and

(5) the requirement that a person who deducts qualified residence interest under Code Sec. 163 on any seller-provided financing include the name, address and TIN of the person to whom such interest is paid or accrued (Code Sec. 6724(d)(3)).[35]

Footnote references are to paragraphs of the 2008 Standard Federal Tax Reports.

[31] ¶ 40,230, ¶ 40,275
[32] ¶ 40,230, ¶ 40,240.023
[33] ¶ 40,213
[34] ¶ 40,250, ¶ 40,265.01
[35] ¶ 40,275

Underpayments of Tax—Interest

2838. Interest on Underpayment of Tax. Interest on underpayments of tax is imposed at the federal short-term rate plus three percentage points (Code Sec. 6621(a)(2)). The interest rates, which are adjusted quarterly, are determined during the first month of a calendar quarter and become effective for the following quarter.

Interest accrues from the date the payment was due (determined without regard to any extensions of time) until it is received by the IRS. Interest is to be compounded daily, except for additions to tax for underpayment of estimated tax by individuals and corporations (Code Sec. 6601).[36] The interest rate on underpayments for the first through fourth quarters of 2007 was 8%.[37]

If a carryback of a net operating loss, investment credit, work incentive program credit, jobs credit, or a net capital loss eliminates or reduces a deficiency otherwise due for such earlier year, the taxpayer remains liable for interest on unpaid income taxes (including deficiencies later assessed by the IRS) for the carryback year. The entire amount of the deficiency will be subject to interest from the last date prescribed for payment of the income tax of the carryback year up to the due date (excluding extensions) for filing the return for the tax year in which the loss or credit occurred (Code Sec. 6601(d); Reg. § 301.6601-1(e)).[38]

Large Corporate Tax Underpayments. Interest on large underpayments of tax by corporations is imposed at the federal short-term rate plus five percentage points (Code Sec. 6621(c)(1); Reg. § 301.6621-3).[39] A large corporate underpayment is any tax underpayment by a C corporation that exceeds $100,000 for any tax period. For purposes of determining the $100,000 threshold, underpayments of different types of taxes (for example, income and employment taxes) as well as underpayments relating to different tax periods are not added together. The tax period is the tax year in the case of income tax or, in the case of any other tax, the period to which the underpayment relates (Code Sec. 6621(c)(3)).[40]

The interest rate applies to time periods after the 30th day after the earlier of (1) the date the IRS sends the first letter of proposed deficiency that allows the taxpayer an opportunity for administrative review in the IRS Office of Appeals (a 30-day letter) or (2) the date the IRS sends a deficiency notice under Code Sec. 6212 (a 90-day letter) (see ¶ 2778). The 30-day period does not begin unless the underpayment shown in the letter or notice exceeds $100,000 (Code Sec. 6621(c)(2)(B)(iii)). An IRS notice that is later withdrawn because it was issued in error will not trigger the higher rate of interest on large corporate underpayments (Code Sec. 6621(c)(2)(A)).[41] If the underpayment is not subject to deficiency payments, the 30-day period begins to run following the sending of any letter or notice by the IRS that notifies the taxpayer of the assessment or proposed assessment of the tax. A letter or notice is disregarded if the full amount shown as due is paid during the 30-day period (Code Sec. 6621(c)(2)(B)).[42] The interest rate on large corporate underpayments for the first through fourth quarters of 2007 was 10%.[43]

Overlapping Overpayments and Underpayments. The interest rates for overpayments and underpayments have been equalized (sometimes referred to as "global interest netting") for any period of mutual indebtedness between taxpayers and the IRS. See ¶ 2765.

Abatement of Interest. The IRS has the authority to abate interest in cases where the additional interest was caused by IRS errors or delays (Code Sec. 6404(e)). However, the IRS may act only if there was an error or delay in performing either a ministerial act or a managerial act (including loss of records by the IRS, transfers of IRS personnel, extended illness, extended personnel training or extended leave) and only if the abatement relates to a tax of the type for which a notice of deficiency is required. Such taxes would be those relating to income, generation-skipping transfers, estate, gift and certain excise taxes, but not abatement of interest for employment taxes or other excise taxes.

Footnote references are to paragraphs of the 2008 Standard Federal Tax Reports.

[36] ¶ 39,410, ¶ 39,412, ¶ 39,415.01, ¶ 39,450, ¶ 39,455.01, ¶ 39,460, ¶ 39,560.01

[37] ¶ 39,455.021
[38] ¶ 39,410, ¶ 39,415.026
[39] ¶ 39,450, ¶ 39,453, ¶ 39,455.03

[40] ¶ 39,450
[41] ¶ 39,450, ¶ 39,455.03
[42] ¶ 39,450, ¶ 39,455.03
[43] ¶ 39,455.021

Taxpayers requesting an abatement of interest generally must file a separate Form 843 for each tax period for each type of tax with the IRS Service Center where their tax return was filed or, if unknown, with the Service Center where their most recent tax return was filed.

Suspension of Interest. In order to avoid the accrual of underpayment interest, a taxpayer may make a cash deposit with the IRS for future application against an underpayment of income, gift, estate, generation-skipping or certain excise taxes that have not been assessed at the time of the deposit (Code Sec. 6603). To the extent that a deposit is used by the IRS to pay a tax liability, the tax is treated as paid when the deposit is made and no interest underpayment is imposed. Furthermore, if the dispute is resolved in favor of the taxpayer or the taxpayer withdraws the deposited money before resolution of the dispute, interest is payable on the deposit at the federal short-term rate.

2845. Interest on Additions and Penalties. Interest on penalties and additions to tax for failure to file, for failure to pay the stamp tax, and for the accuracy-related and fraud penalties (see ¶ 2854 and ¶ 2866) will be imposed for the period beginning on the due date of the return (including extensions) and ending on the date of payment. However, if payment is made within 21 calendar days after notice and demand is made (10 *business* days if the amount demanded is at least $100,000), then interest will stop running after the date of notice and demand (Code Sec. 6601(e)(3)). For all other penalties, interest will be imposed only if the addition to tax or penalty is not paid within the 21-or 10-day period after notice and demand is made and then only for the period from the date of notice and demand to the date of payment (Code Sec. 6601(e)(2)).[44] For rules governing the allocation of interest on tax liabilities paid pursuant to a compromise or partial payment, see ¶ 2723 and ¶ 2724, respectively.

Underpayments of Tax—Penalties

2854. Accuracy-Related Penalty. The two penalties primarily applicable to underpayments of tax are the accuracy-related penalty (Code Sec. 6662)[45] and the fraud penalty (Code Sec. 6663).[46] See ¶ 2866.

The accuracy-related penalty consolidates all of the penalties relating to the accuracy of tax returns. It is equal to 20% of the portion of the underpayment that is attributable to one or more of the following: (1) negligence or disregard of rules or regulations (¶ 2856), (2) substantial understatement of income tax (¶ 2858), (3) substantial valuation misstatement (¶ 2860), and (4) substantial overstatements of pension liabilities (¶ 2862) (Code Sec. 6662(a) and (b)).[47]

The accuracy-related penalty is entirely separate from the failure to file penalty (¶ 2801) and will not be imposed if no return, other than a return prepared by the IRS when a person fails to make a required return, is filed (Code Sec. 6664(b)).[48] In addition, the accuracy-related penalty will not apply to any portion of a tax underpayment on which the fraud penalty is imposed. Also, no penalty is imposed with respect to any portion of any underpayment if the taxpayer shows that there was reasonable cause for the underpayment and that the taxpayer acted in good faith (Code Sec. 6664(c)).[49]

2856. Negligence or Disregard of Rules and Regulations. If any part of an underpayment of tax is due to negligence or careless, reckless or intentional disregard of rules and regulations, the 20% accuracy-related penalty will be imposed on that portion of the underpayment attributable to the negligence or intentional disregard of rules and regulations (Code Sec. 6662(a) and (c)).[50] Negligence includes the failure to reasonably comply with tax laws, to exercise reasonable care in preparing a tax return, to keep adequate books and records, or to substantiate items properly (Reg. § 1.6662-3(b)(1)).[51] Taxpayers may not avoid the negligence penalty merely by adequately disclosing a return position which is "not frivolous" on Form 8275, Disclosure Statement, or Form

---

Footnote references are to paragraphs of the 2008 Standard Federal Tax Reports.

[44] ¶ 39,410
[45] ¶ 39,651
[46] ¶ 39,656
[47] ¶ 39,651
[48] ¶ 39,660, ¶ 39,661.03
[49] ¶ 39,660, ¶ 39,661.022
[50] ¶ 39,651, ¶ 39,651G.01
[51] ¶ 39,651D, ¶ 39,651G.01

8275-R, Regulation Disclosure Statement (Conference Committee Report to P.L. 103-66).[52]

2858. Substantial Understatement of Income Tax. The IRS may impose the 20% accuracy-related penalty when there is a substantial understatement of income tax. A substantial understatement exists when the understatement for the year exceeds the greater of (1) 10% of the tax required to be shown on the return (including self-employment tax) or (2) $5,000. In the case of corporations (other than S corporations or personal holding companies), a substantial understatement exists when the understatement exceeds the lesser of (1) 10% of the tax required to be shown on the return (or, if greater, $10,000) or (2) $10,000,000 (Code Sec. 6662(d).[53]

Taxpayers generally may avoid all or part of the penalty by showing:

(a) that they acted in good faith and there was reasonable cause for the understatement,

(b) that the understatement was based on substantial authority, or

(c) if there was a reasonable basis for the tax treatment of an item, the relevant facts affecting the item's tax treatment were adequately disclosed on Form 8275 (Form 8275-R for return positions contrary to regulations) (Code Sec. 6662(d)(2) and Code Sec. 6664(c); Reg. § 1.6662-4(d)—Reg. § 1.6662-4(f)).[54]

Substantial authority generally means that the likelihood that a taxpayer's position is correct is somewhere between 50% and the more lenient reasonable basis standard used in applying the negligence penalty. The disclosure exception does not apply to tax shelter items. Further, a corporation does not have a reasonable basis for its tax treatment of an item attributable to a multi-party financing transaction if the treatment does not clearly reflect the income of the corporation. Some items may be disclosed on the taxpayer's return, instead of on Form 8275, pursuant to an IRS Revenue Procedure relating to the tax year.

Only the following are authority for purposes of determining whether a position is supported by substantial authority:

(1) the Internal Revenue Code and other statutory provisions,

(2) proposed, temporary and final regulations construing the statutes,

(3) revenue rulings and procedures,

(4) tax treaties and the regulations thereunder, and Treasury Department and other official explanations of such treaties,

(5) court cases,

(6) congressional intent as reflected in committee reports, joint explanatory statements of managers included in conference committee reports, and floor statements made prior to enactment by one of a bill's managers,

(7) General Explanations of tax legislation prepared by the Joint Committee on Taxation (the Blue Book),

(8) private letter rulings and technical advice memoranda issued after October 31, 1976,

(9) actions on decisions and general counsel memoranda issued after March 12, 1981 (as well as general counsel memoranda published in pre-1955 volumes of the Cumulative Bulletin),

(10) Internal Revenue Service information and press releases, and

(11) notices, announcements and other administrative pronouncements published by the IRS in the Internal Revenue Bulletin (Reg. § 1.6662-4(d)(3)(iii)).[55]

2860. Substantial Valuation Misstatement. The 20% accuracy-related penalty is imposed on any portion of an underpayment resulting from any substantial income tax valuation misstatement. There is a substantial valuation misstatement if (1) the value of any property, or adjusted basis of any property, claimed on a tax return is 150% or more of the amount determined to be the correct amount of the valuation or the adjusted

---

Footnote references are to paragraphs of the 2008 Standard Federal Tax Reports.

[52] ¶ 39,651.45
[53] ¶ 39,651

[54] ¶ 39,651, ¶ 39,660, ¶ 39,651H, ¶ 39,652.022

[55] ¶ 39,651H

basis, (2) the price for any property, or use of property, or services in connection with any transaction between persons described in Code Sec. 482 is 200% or more, or 50% or less, of the correct Code Sec. 482 valuation, or (3) the net Code Sec. 482 transfer price adjustment exceeds the lesser of $5 million or 10% of the taxpayer's gross receipts (Code Sec. 6662(e)).

The penalty is doubled to 40% in cases of "gross valuation misstatements" where claimed value or adjusted basis exceeds the correct value or adjusted basis by 200% or more (Code Sec. 6662(h)). A gross valuation misstatement with respect to a controlled taxpayer transaction (Code Sec. 482) occurs if the price claimed exceeds 400% or more, or 25% or less, of the amount determined to be the correct price or the net Code Sec. 482 transfer price adjustment for the year exceeds the lesser of $20 million or 20% of the taxpayer's gross receipts.

No penalty is imposed unless the portion of the underpayment attributable to the substantial valuation misstatement exceeds $5,000, or $10,000 in the case of corporations other than S corporations or personal holding companies (Code Sec. 6662(e)(2)).[56] The penalty will not be imposed if it is shown that there was reasonable cause for an underpayment and the taxpayer acted in good faith; however, the reasonable cause exception for underpayments due to gross valuation misstatements on charitable deduction property has been eliminated, although the exception still exists for substantial valuation misstatements on charitable deduction property and for gross valuation misstatements on property for which a charitable deduction is not being claimed (Code Sec. 6664(c)).[57]

2862. Substantial Overstatement of Pension Liabilities. The 20% accuracy-related penalty is imposed on any portion of any underpayment resulting from a substantial overstatement of pension liabilities. A substantial overstatement occurs if the actuarial determination of pension liabilities is 200% or more of the amount determined to be correct. The penalty is doubled to 40% of the underpayment if a portion of the substantial overstatement to which the penalty applies is attributable to a gross valuation misstatement of 400% or more. The penalty applies only if the portion of the underpayment attributable to the overstatement exceeds $1,000 (Code Sec. 6662(a), (f), and (h)).[58] The penalty will not be imposed if it is shown that there was a reasonable cause for an underpayment and the taxpayer acted in good faith (Code Sec. 6664(c)).[59]

2866. Fraud. The fraud penalty is imposed at the rate of 75% on the portion of any underpayment that is attributable to fraud (Code Sec. 6663).[60] The fraud penalty will not apply, however, if no return is filed other than a return prepared by the IRS when a person fails to make a required return (Code Sec. 6664(b)).[61] Although the failure to file penalty is entirely separate from the fraud penalty, in cases of a fraudulent failure to file, the failure to file penalty will be imposed at a higher rate. See ¶ 2801. If any portion is attributable to fraud, it is presumed that the entire underpayment is attributable to fraud, unless the taxpayer establishes otherwise by a preponderance of the evidence with respect to any item. The accuracy-related penalty will not apply to any portion of an underpayment on which the fraud penalty is imposed. The IRS must meet its burden of proof in establishing fraud by clear and convincing evidence (Code Sec. 6663(b)).[62]

2870 Tax Shelters. An accuracy-related penalty is provided for understatements resulting from listed and reportable transactions (Code Sec. 6662A). The penalty applies to understatements attributable to (1) any listed transaction and (2) any reportable transaction with a significant tax avoidance purpose. "Listed transaction" and "reportable transaction" are defined by reference to new Code Sec. 6707A (see ¶ 2005), which, in turn, defines those terms by reference to applicable regulations under Code Sec. 6011. A reasonable cause exception is provided under Code Sec. 6664(d).

Underpayments of Estimated Tax

2875. Addition to Tax for Underpayment of Estimated Tax by Individuals. An underpayment of estimated tax by an individual and most trusts and estates will result in

---

Footnote references are to paragraphs of the 2008 Standard Federal Tax Reports.

[56] ¶ 39,651, ¶ 39,654.02, ¶ 39,654.03, ¶ 39,654.04

[57] ¶ 39,660, ¶ 39,661.022

[58] ¶ 39,651, ¶ 39,654A.01

[59] ¶ 39,660, ¶ 39,661.022

[60] ¶ 39,656, ¶ 39,658.01

[61] ¶ 39,660, ¶ 39,661.03

[62] ¶ 39,656, ¶ 39,658.022

imposition of an addition to tax equal to the interest that would accrue on the underpayment for the period of the underpayment (Code Sec. 6654(a)).[63] For the applicable rate of interest, see ¶ 2838. In determining the addition to tax for an underpayment of individual estimated tax, the federal short-term rate that applies during the third month following the tax year of the underpayment will also apply during the first 15 days of the fourth month following such tax year (Code Sec. 6621(b)(2)(B)).[64] Changes in the interest rate apply to amounts of underpayments outstanding on the date of change or arising thereafter.[65] An individual can avoid any penalty for underpayment of estimated tax by making payments as set forth in ¶ 2679 et seq. See ¶ 518 for the rules regarding trusts and estates.

2881. Waiver of Underpayment Penalty. The IRS is authorized to waive the penalty for underpayment of estimated tax if the underpayment is either due to casualty, disaster, or other unusual circumstances and the imposition of the penalty would be against equity and good conscience. The penalty may also be waived for an individual who retired after having attained age 62, or who became disabled, in the tax year for which the estimated payment was due or in the preceding tax year and the underpayment was due to reasonable cause and not to willful neglect (Code Sec. 6654(e)(3)).[66] Otherwise, the addition to tax is mandatory where there is an underpayment.[67]

2889. "Underpayment" Form 2210. When insufficient estimated tax was paid during the year, the taxpayer should complete and attach Form 2210 (Form 2210F for Farmers and Fishermen) to explain which test (¶ 2682) was met to avoid the addition to tax or, if no tests were met, how the amount of the addition to tax due was computed.

2890. Underpayment of Estimated Tax by Corporations. If estimated taxes are underpaid by a corporation (including an S corporation), a penalty is imposed in the amount of the interest that accrues on the underpayment for the period of the underpayment (Code Sec. 6655). The rate of interest is the rate charged on underpayment of taxes determined under Code Sec. 6621 (¶ 2838). The additions are calculated for quarterly periods ending with the installment due dates. Generally, additions to tax apply to the difference between payments made by the due date of the installment and the lesser of an installment based on (1) 100% of the tax shown on the current year's tax return or (2) 100% of the tax shown on the preceding year's return (prior-year safe harbor) (for a 12-month tax year). However, use of the prior-year safe harbor is not available to "large" corporations, i.e., corporations that have taxable income of $1 million or more for any of the three immediately preceding tax years. No additions to tax will be assessed if the corporation's tax liability is less than $500 for the tax year.[68]

Erroneous Tax Refund Claims

2891. Erroneous Refund or Credit Claims. Applicable to claims filed or submitted after May 25, 2007, erroneous income tax refund or credit claims made for an "excessive amount" are subject to a penalty equal to 20 percent of the excessive amount (Code Sec. 6676, as added by the Small Business and Work Opportunity Tax Act of 2007 (P.L. 110-28)). The penalty does not apply to claims for refunds or credits relating to the earned income credit (¶ 1375), which has a separate set of rules.

An "excessive amount" is the amount by which the refund or credit claim exceeds the amount allowable under the Code for the tax year. However, if it can be shown that the claim for the excessive amount has a reasonable basis, the penalty will not apply. In addition, the penalty does not apply to any portion of the excessive amount of a refund claim or credit that is subject to an accuracy-related penalty (¶ 2854 and ¶ 2870), or the fraud penalty (¶ 2866).

Unauthorized Disclosures

2892. Confidentiality of Returns. Returns and tax return information are confidential and may not be disclosed to federal or state agencies or employees except as provided in Code Sec. 6103.[69] A return is defined as any tax return, information return, declaration of estimated tax, or claim for refund filed under the Internal Revenue Code.

Footnote references are to paragraphs of the 2008 Standard Federal Tax Reports.

[63] ¶ 39,550
[64] ¶ 39,450
[65] ¶ 39,451

[66] ¶ 39,550, ¶ 39,560.01,
¶ 39,560.03
[67] ¶ 39,560.21

[68] ¶ 39,565, ¶ 39,575.023
[69] ¶ 36,880, ¶ 36,894

Return information includes the taxpayer's identity, the nature, source or amount of income, payments, receipts, deductions, net worth, tax liability, deficiencies, closing (and similar) agreements, and information regarding the actual or possible investigation of a return. The prohibition on disclosure applies to all officers and employees of the United States, of any state, and of any local child support enforcement agency. It also applies to most other persons who have had access to returns or return information by virtue of permitted disclosures of such returns or information under Code Sec. 6103.[70]

Agreements and information received under a tax convention with a foreign government (including a U.S. possession) are confidential and generally cannot be disclosed (Code Sec. 6105).

2893. Remedies for Unauthorized Disclosures. Taxpayers whose privacy has been invaded by an unlawful disclosure of returns or return information under Code Secs. 6103 or 6104 (pertaining to tax-exempt organizations) may bring a civil suit for damages. Upon a finding of liability, the taxpayer may recover the greater of $1,000 for each unauthorized disclosure or the amount of the actual damages sustained as a result of the disclosure. Punitive damages, as well as litigation costs, may be recovered if the disclosure was willful or grossly negligent (Code Sec. 7431).[71] Felony charges can also be brought against individuals who have made unauthorized and willful disclosures of any return information (Code Sec. 7213).[72]

2894. Disclosure of Return Information. A return preparer who uses return information for any purpose other than to prepare a return, or who makes an unauthorized disclosure of return information, is subject to a $250 penalty for each disclosure, up to a maximum of $10,000. If the action is undertaken knowingly or recklessly, the preparer may be subject to criminal penalties or a fine of up to $1,000, or up to a year in jail, or both, together with the cost of prosecution (Code Sec. 6713 and Code Sec. 7216).[73] A taxpayer may bring a civil action for damages against the U.S. government if an IRS employee offers the taxpayer's representative favorable tax treatment in exchange for information about the taxpayer (Code Sec. 7435).[74]

Unauthorized Return Inspections

2896. Penalties for Unauthorized Inspections. A taxpayer may bring a civil action against the United States if a government employee knowingly or negligently inspects, without authorization, any return or return information under Code Secs. 6103 or 6104 (pertaining to tax-exempt organizations) of that taxpayer. The same action may also be taken against any other person who browses through returns or return information without proper authorization (Code Sec. 7431).[75] Criminal penalties for willful unauthorized return inspection can also be imposed against any federal employee or IRS contractor. In addition, penalties may be imposed against any state employee or other person who acquires the return or return information under Code Secs. 6103 or 6104 (pertaining to tax-exempt organizations), which permits the use of federal return information for other government purposes, such as state tax and child support collection, law enforcement, social welfare program administration, and statistical use (Code Sec. 7213A).[76]

Criminal Penalties

2898. Crimes. Criminal penalties may be incurred when the taxpayer (a) willfully fails to make a return, keep records, supply required information, or pay any tax or estimated tax, (b) willfully attempts in any manner to evade or defeat the tax, or (c) willfully fails to collect and pay over the tax. In addition to the felony charges listed in the preceding sentence, misdemeanor charges can be brought for (1) making fraudulent statements to employees, (2) filing a fraudulent withholding certificate, or (3) failing to obey a summons. The criminal penalties are in addition to the civil penalties (Code Sec. 7201—Code Sec. 7212). A good faith misunderstanding of the law or a good faith belief that one is not violating the law negates the willfulness element of a tax evasion charge.[77]

Footnote references are to paragraphs of the 2008 Standard Federal Tax Reports.

[70] ¶ 36,894.026
[71] ¶ 41,750
[72] ¶ 41,350, ¶ 41,353.01
[73] ¶ 40,155, ¶ 41,365, ¶ 41,370
[74] ¶ 41,785
[75] ¶ 41,750
[76] ¶ 41,354
[77] ¶ 41,318.034

Chapter 29

ESTATE, GIFT AND GENERATION-SKIPPING TRANSFER TAX

Transfer Tax System

2901. Estate, Gift, and Generation-Skipping Transfer Tax System. The estate, gift, and generation-skipping transfer (GST) taxes were designed to form a unified transfer tax system on the transfer of property at death (estate tax), during life (gift tax), and on transfers that skip a generation (GST tax). However, in 2001, the Economic Growth and Tax Relief Reconciliation Act of 2001 (P.L. 107-16) (EGTRRA) prospectively repealed the estate and GST taxes for estates of decedents dying after December 31, 2009 (Code Sec. 2210(a), as amended by EGTRRA) while retaining the gift tax, although in a modified form.[1]

As of 2004, the estate and gift taxes no longer share a single applicable credit amount (formerly the unified credit). The gift tax applicable credit amount was raised to $345,800 (sheltering the first $1 million of a donor's lifetime gifts) in 2002 and remains at this amount through repeal in 2010 without adjustment for inflation (Code Sec. 2505(a)(1), as amended by EGTRRA). In 2004, the estate tax applicable credit amount increased to $555,800 and sheltered the first $1.5 million of a decedent's estate (the applicable exclusion amount) (Code Sec. 2010(c), as amended by EGTRRA). The applicable credit amount remained at this amount for 2005, but it increased again for 2006 to $780,800 and shelters the first $2 million. The applicable exclusion amount in effect for the years leading up to repeal of the estate and GST taxes in 2010 remains at $2 million in 2007 and 2008 and increases to $3.5 million in 2009 (Code Sec. 2010(c), as amended by EGTRRA). Also starting in 2004 and continuing through 2009, the lifetime GST tax exemption amount is the same as the estate tax applicable exclusion amount ($2 million in 2007) and is no longer adjusted for inflation.[2]

This increase in the amount of the exemptions for the estate and GST taxes is accompanied by a gradual decrease in the top marginal tax rate applicable to the estate, gift and GST taxes, as follows:

48% in 2004;

47% in 2005;

46% in 2006; and

45% in 2007, 2008 and 2009 (Code Sec. 2001(c)(2), as amended by EGTRRA).[3]

In 2010, when the estate and GST taxes have been repealed, the highest gift tax rate will be 35 percent.

All of these changes, however, are scheduled to expire (or "sunset") for estates of decedents dying, gifts made, or generation-skipping transfers after December 31, 2010. Thus, after the one-year repeal of the estate and GST taxes in 2010, the Code provisions

Footnote references are to paragraphs of the Federal Estate and Gift Tax Reports.

[1] ¶ 8990   [2] ¶ 1401, ¶ 10,403, ¶ 12,585   [3] ¶ 1201

governing the estate, gift, and GST taxes in effect prior to EGTRRA's 2001 changes will spring back to life in 2011 unless Congress takes further action.

Gift Tax

2903. Transfers Subject to Gift Tax. The gift tax applies to the transfer of property by gift, whether the gift is direct or indirect, and whether the transfer is in trust or otherwise. However, transfers to qualifying political organizations are not considered gifts (Code Sec. 2501(a)(5)).[4] The property transferred may be real, personal, tangible, or intangible (Code Sec. 2511; Reg. § 25.2511-1(a)).[5] The donor makes a gift to the extent that the value of the property transferred exceeds the consideration (that is, any property or services received in return for the transfer (Code Sec. 2512(b)). The transferred property or evidence of it must be delivered to the donee and the donor must relinquish all control over the property for the gift to be completed.

Indirect gifts, such as transfers in trust and the cancellation of indebtedness, are subject to the gift tax (Code Sec. 2511). Other examples of indirect gifts include certain assignments of benefits, permission to withdraw funds deposited by a donor from a joint account, and below-market interest rate loans (Reg. § 25.2511-1(c), (h)). However, a spouse's waiver of the right to a joint and survivor annuity in a qualified plan is not a gift.[6]

A gratuitous transfer of property by a corporation is considered to be a gift by the shareholders to the donee while a gift to a corporation is considered to be a gift to its shareholders (Reg. § 25.2511-1(h)). In addition, creating a family limited partnership and transferring control of a closely held company often involves a gift. Transfer of stock and securities is a gift even if the securities are exempt from tax. The transfer of an option is a gift. Also, gratuitous transfers made by guardians or conservators under court orders are gifts. Conversely, a transfer pursuant to a will contest settlement entered into at arm's length is generally not a gift.

Valuation. Generally, the value of the property for gift tax purposes is its fair market value. That is, the price at which the property would change hands between a willing buyer and a willing seller, both knowing all of the relevant facts. Special valuation rules apply for determining the amount of a gift if a transferor retains (1) an equity interest in a corporation or partnership transferred to a family member or (2) an interest in a trust to or for the benefit of a family member (Code Secs. 2701, 2702 and 2704).[7]

Qualified Disclaimers. The donee of a gift may make a qualified disclaimer of the entire interest or a portion of it without making a taxable gift. A qualified disclaimer (1) must be in writing, (2) must be received by the transferor (or the transferor's representative) within nine months of the date of the transfer, (3) the beneficiary may not accept any of the benefits from the transferred property, and (4) the property being disclaimed must pass to someone other than, and without direction from, the disclaiming beneficiary (Code Sec. 2518).[8]

Nonresident Alien Donors. A donor who is neither a U.S. citizen nor a U.S. resident (in other words, a nonresident alien)[9] is subject to gift tax on transfers of real and tangible property situated in the United States (Code Sec. 2101(a), Code Sec. 2501(a)). Transfers of intangible property by a nonresident alien generally are not subject to gift tax (Code Sec. 2501(a)(2)). Taxable gifts are taxed at the same rates that apply to U.S. citizens (Code Sec. 2501(a)(1)).[10]

2905. Gift Tax Annual Exclusion. In 2007 and 2008, the first $12,000 of gifts of a present interest made by a donor during the calendar year to each donee are not included in the total amount of the donor's taxable gifts during that year (Code Sec. 2503(b)). Therefore, these amounts are neither taxed nor do they use up any of the donor's lifetime gift tax applicable credit amount. Also, spouses who consent to split

---

Footnote references are to paragraphs of the Federal Estate and Gift Tax Reports.

[4] ¶ 9245
[5] ¶ 10,514
[6] ¶ 9649, ¶ 10,181.05

[7] ¶ 13,551, ¶ 14,001, ¶ 14,651
[8] ¶ 11,339
[9] ¶ 7525, ¶ 7550

[10] ¶ 9245

¶2903

their gifts may transfer a total of $24,000 per donee in 2007 and 2008 free of gift and GST tax (Code Sec. 2513(a)).[11]

If the donor's spouse is not a U.S. citizen, an annual exclusion of $125,000 for 2007 (Rev. Proc. 2006-53) and $128,000 for 2008 (Rev. Proc. 2007-66) is allowed for present interest gifts to the spouse that would qualify for the marital deduction if the spouse were a U.S. citizen (Code Sec. 2523(i)(2)).[12] The annual exclusion is available to all donors, including nonresident citizens.

The annual exclusion is allowed for gifts of present interests but not for gifts of future interests in property. Present interests include any interests, whether vested or contingent, that are available for the donee's immediate use, possession or enjoyment (Reg. § 25.2503-3(b)). A transfer of property for the benefit of a minor pursuant to the Uniform Transfers to Minors Act (UTMA), the Uniform Gifts to Minors Act (UGMA), or the Gifts of Securities to Minors Act (GSMA) is considered to be a completed gift of the full fair market value of the property.[13]

Transfers in Trust. The number of annual exclusions available for a gift in trust is determined by the number of trust beneficiaries who have a present interest in the gifted property. A transfer to a trust that allows a beneficiary the unrestricted right to the immediate use, possession, or enjoyment of the transferred property or the income from the property, such as a life estate or term certain, is a present interest gift that qualifies for the annual exclusion (Reg. § 25.2503-3(b)). However, such unrestricted gifts through a trust are rarely made. Normally, limits are placed on the beneficiary's right to use, possess, or enjoy the trust property. However, a gift of the right to demand a portion of a trust corpus is a gift of a present interest, so long as the donee-beneficiary is aware of his or her right to make the demand. Typically, the beneficiary of such a trust (known as a *Crummey* trust) is given the right to demand an amount of corpus equal to the annual gift tax exclusion for a limited period of time, such as 60 days. If the persons who have a right of withdrawal do not have a present income interest in the trust or a vested remainder interest, however, the IRS may question the claimed annual exclusion.[14]

Gifts to Minors. Gifts to minors may qualify for the annual exclusion if they meet the requirements of Code Sec. 2503(c).[15] The property and income from it must be expended by or for the benefit of the minor, and any income and principal not expended must be paid to the minor at age 21, or to his or her estate if the minor dies before age 21 (Code Sec. 2503(c); Reg. § 25.2503-4(a)).[16] However, if a transfer of property is made under a parent's legal obligation to support a minor, the transfer is not a gift.[17]

2907. Exclusion for Educational or Medical Payment. In addition to the annual exclusion, an unlimited gift tax exclusion is allowed for amounts paid on behalf of a donee *directly* to an educational organization, provided such amounts constitute tuition payments. Amounts paid for books, dormitory fees, or board on behalf of the donee are not eligible for the exclusion. Amounts paid *directly* to health care providers for medical services on behalf of a donee also qualify for the unlimited gift tax exclusion. Medical expense payments are excludable without regard to the percentage limitations imposed for income tax purposes. Both the medical and tuition exclusions are available without regard to the relationship between the donor and donee (Code Sec. 2503(e)).[18]

2908. Gifts to Spouse. In computing the taxable gifts of a married donor, a marital deduction is allowed for property that passes to the donor's spouse. As a result, an unlimited amount of property (other than certain terminable interests) can be transferred between spouses. The gift tax marital deduction is not available, however, if the spouse is not a U.S. citizen at the time of the gift (Code Sec. 2523).[19] Instead, gifts to a noncitizen spouse are eligible for a gift tax annual exclusion of up to $125,000 in 2007 and $128,000 in 2008, as adjusted for inflation (Code Sec. 2523(i)). In addition, a gift tax marital deduction is not allowed for transfers of terminable interests in property. A terminable interest in property is an interest that will terminate or fail on the lapse of

---

Footnote references are to paragraphs of the Federal Estate and Gift Tax Reports.

[11] ¶ 10,960	[14] ¶ 9649, ¶ 9891, ¶ 9950.07	[17] ¶ 9649
[12] ¶ 9649, ¶ 11,662, ¶ 11,850	[15] ¶ 9649, ¶ 9891, ¶ 9950.07	[18] ¶ 9649, ¶ 10,095
[13] ¶ 9649, ¶ 10,041.05	[16] ¶ 9996	[19] ¶ 11,662

time or on the occurrence or failure to occur of some contingency. For example, terminable interests include life estates, terms for years, and annuities. However, a gift tax marital deduction will be allowed if the donee spouse is given a life estate with a general power of appointment of qualified terminable interest property (QTIP), or if the donor and spouse are named as the only non-charitable beneficiaries of a qualified charitable remainder trust (see ¶ 2926).[20]

2909. Gifts to Charity. In determining a donor's taxable gifts, a gift tax charitable deduction is available for transfers to charitable organizations (federal, state and local governmental entities, charitable organizations, fraternal societies (if the property is used for charitable purposes), or veterans' organizations). The charitable deduction is not limited to gifts for use within the United States, unless the donor is a nonresident alien at the time of the gift (Code Sec. 2522).[21] A deduction may also be allowed for the value of the charitable interest in a split-interest transfer (in which there are both charitable and noncharitable beneficiaries) provided the charitable interest is in a qualified form (i.e., charitable remainder annuity trust, charitable remainder unitrust, charitable lead annuity trust, charitable lead unitrust, or a pooled income fund) (see ¶ 2932).

2910. Computing the Gift Tax Liability. The gift tax is calculated by first determining the total value of the donor's gifts for the current calendar year. That amount is reduced by any exclusions (annual, educational and medical[22]) and deductions (marital and charitable). The sum of all taxable gifts made by the donor in all prior years is then added to the current year's taxable gifts to arrive at the applicable tax rate. The donor's gift tax liability for 2007 is then determined by (1) calculating a tentative tax on the sum of all taxable gifts made in 2007 and in preceding calendar years, (2) calculating a tentative tax on only the taxable gifts in preceding calendar years, and (3) then subtracting the tentative tax determined in step (2) from the tentative tax determined in step (1) (Code Sec. 2502). The resulting tax due is then reduced by the donor's available lifetime gift tax applicable credit amount. The result of calculating the gift tax in this manner is that prior gifts push the current year's gifts into higher tax brackets. The value of a gift is its fair market value on the date of the gift.[23]

If a gift is adequately disclosed on the gift tax return and the gift tax statute of limitations has expired, the IRS may not revalue the donor's lifetime gifts when computing the estate tax liability upon the donor's death if the value of the gift has been finally determined for gift tax purposes (Code Sec. 2001(f)). There is a three-year statute of limitations for gift tax returns (Code Sec. 2504(c)).

The gift tax applicable credit amount in 2007 is $345,800, which effectively shields the first $1 million of a donor's lifetime gifts from gift tax (Code Sec. 2505(a)(1)).[24] Note that the million and first dollar (that is, the first dollar that becomes taxable) is taxed at the rate that would apply to gifts in the amount of $1,000,001 (41 percent in 2007) rather than the rate that would apply to a gift of $1 (18 percent).

2911. Donor Is Primarily Liable to File Return and Pay Gift Tax. Gift tax returns must be filed by individual donors for gifts of more than $12,000 in 2007 that do not qualify for an exclusion (Code Sec. 6019). Gift tax returns must be filed on Form 709, U.S. Gift (and Generation-Skipping Transfer) Tax Return. The donor is primarily liable for the payment of the gift tax (Code Sec. 6019).[25]

Estate Tax

2912. Gross Estate. The federal estate tax is imposed on the transfer of a person's property at the time of that person's death. The amount of the tax is determined by applying the relevant tax rates to the taxable estate, that is the gross estate reduced by any deductions. The gross estate of a U.S. citizen or resident decedent includes the value of all property described in Code Sec. 2033 through Code Sec. 2044, whether real or personal, tangible or intangible, wherever situated. Effectively executed disclaimers

---

Footnote references are to paragraphs of the Federal Estate and Gift Tax Reports.

[20] ¶ 11,662	[22] ¶ 9649	[24] ¶ 10,403
[21] ¶ 11,486	[23] ¶ 10,622	[25] ¶ 9245, ¶ 20,125, ¶ 20,301

¶2909

prevent the property subject to the disclaimer from being included in the gross estate (Code Sec. 2046 and Code Sec. 2518).[26]

Qualified terminable interest property (QTIP) for which an election was made to qualify it for the marital deduction in the estate of the first spouse to die, or on the gift tax return of the donor spouse, is included in the gross estate of the surviving or donee spouse (Code Sec. 2044(a)).[27]

2913. Transferred Property in Which Decedent Retained an Interest. When a decedent retains some control over gifts of property made during life, the property may be added back to the decedent's gross estate. The transfers subject to this rule include:

(1) gifts in which the decedent retains a life estate or the right to the income, possession, or enjoyment of the property[28] or the right to designate who will enjoy the property,[29] including gifts of stock in which voting rights are retained (Code Sec. 2036);[30]

(2) gifts in which the decedent retains a right to a reversionary interest that exceeds five percent of the value of the transferred property and possession or enjoyment of the property can be obtained only by surviving the decedent (Code Sec. 2037(a));[31] and

(3) gifts in which the decedent holds a power to alter, amend, revoke, or terminate the gift (Code Sec. 2038(a)(1); Reg. § 20.2038-1(a)).[32]

If income from transferred property is used to discharge a legal obligation of the decedent, such as the decedent's obligation to support his or her dependents, the decedent is considered to have a right to income from the property and the property is includible in his or her gross estate (Reg. § 20.2036-1(b)(2)).[33]

An estate valuation freeze is a technique used to limit the value of closely held business interests owned by an individual by transferring the future appreciation in value of the business to the next generation of the owner's family while retaining certain interests in the business. This technique has been severely limited by the special valuation rules (Code Secs. 2701– 2704) which treat transfers of family business interests unfavorably for gift tax purposes by valuing certain types of interests retained by the donor in such exchanges at zero.[34]

If a lifetime transfer is a sale for adequate and full consideration, the property that is transferred is not included in the transferor's gross estate (Code Sec. 2036(a)). However, if the transfer is not for adequate and full consideration, the amount included in the decedent's estate is the full value of the property subject to the decedent's retained interest. If the interest or right is reserved over only part of the property transferred, only the reserved portion is included in the gross estate (Reg. § 20.2036-1(a)).[35]

2914. Gifts Made Within Three Years of Death. Gifts made within three years of the donor's death ordinarily are not includible in the donor's gross estate. However, gifts made within three years of death are included in the donor's gross estate if the gift consists of interests in property that would otherwise be included in the gross estate because of the donor's retained powers, such as the power to alter, amend, revoke, or terminate the gift (Code Sec. 2035(a); see also ¶ 2913). Similarly, a gift of life insurance that would have been includible in the decedent's gross estate because of his retention of incidents of ownership in the policy is includible if the policy was transferred within three years of the decedent's date of death (Code Sec. 2035(a)). Gifts made from a decedent's revocable trust within three years of death, however, are not included in the decedent's gross estate, rather they are treated as if made directly by the decedent (Code Sec. 2035(e); see also Code Sec. 2038). Gift tax paid on all transfers made within three years of death is included in the gross estate (Code Sec. 2035(b)).[36]

Footnote references are to paragraphs of the Federal Estate and Gift Tax Reports.

[26] ¶ 5980, ¶ 11,339	[30] ¶ 4901	[34] ¶ 13,551, ¶ 14,001, ¶ 14,501, ¶ 14,651
[27] ¶ 5901	[31] ¶ 5001	
[28] ¶ 4901	[32] ¶ 5101	[35] ¶ 4901
[29] ¶ 4901	[33] ¶ 4925	[36] ¶ 4801

2915. Life Insurance. Proceeds of insurance on a decedent's life payable to or for the benefit of his or her estate, and insurance payable to other beneficiaries in which the decedent retained incidents of ownership, are included in the decedent's gross estate (Code Sec. 2042(1) and (2); Reg. § 20.2042-1(b)(1)). Insurance that is paid to a named beneficiary but that must be used to meet expenses of the decedent's estate, such as debts and taxes, is included in the decedent's gross estate.[37]

Incidents of Ownership. If proceeds of insurance on the life of a decedent are payable to a beneficiary other than the decedent's estate, they are included in the decedent's gross estate if the decedent has retained an incident of ownership in the life insurance policy on the date of death (Code Sec. 2042(2); Reg. § 20.2042-1(c)). The term "incidents of ownership" is not limited in its meaning to ownership of the policy in the technical legal sense. The term refers to the right of the insured or his estate to the economic benefits of the policy. Some incidents of ownership include the power to change the beneficiary, the ability to pledge the policy as security for a loan, the ability to borrow against the policy, or a reversionary interest by which the insured or the insured's estate may regain one of the previously stated rights under certain circumstances. If the decedent transfers a life insurance policy or an incident of ownership in the policy within three years of his death, the proceeds are included in his gross estate (Code Sec. 2035(a)).[38] However, generally only one-half of the proceeds of life insurance purchased with community property is included in the estate of the insured spouse, even if the decedent possessed an incident of ownership (Reg. § 20.2042-1(b)(2)).[39]

A person insured under a key-employee insurance arrangement usually has no interest in the insurance. None of its proceeds will be included in the insured's gross estate. However, the arrangement will be accounted for in determining a value for any stock that the insured may have owned in the company.[40]

In the case of split-dollar life insurance, death proceeds from the employee's portion of the policy are included in the employee's estate if:

   (1) the proceeds are payable to, or for the benefit of, the employee's estate, or

   (2) the employee holds an incident of ownership in the policy at death or transfers an incident of ownership to a third party less than three years before death.

Gift tax liability for employer-paid premiums may arise if a co-owner of the policy is neither the employer nor the employee.[41]

2917. Annuities and Retirement Benefits. In general, the value of an annuity or other payment receivable by any beneficiary by reason of surviving the decedent is included in a decedent's gross estate. The annuity or other payment is not taxable under the rules unless it is payable under a contract by agreement and the following factors exist:

   (1) the contract or agreement was entered into after March 31, 1931;

   (2) the contract or agreement is not a policy of insurance on the decedent's life;

   (3) the decedent possessed the right to receive the payments during his or her lifetime; and

   (4) payments under the contract are determined based on the decedent's life or life expectancy (Code Sec. 2039(a)).[42]

The value of an annuity or other payment included in a decedent's gross estate is the portion of its value attributable to the portion of the purchase price contributed by the decedent. Any contribution made by a decedent's employer or former employer by reason of his or her employment is considered to be made by the decedent (Code Sec. 2039(b)).[43]

Footnote references are to paragraphs of the Federal Estate and Gift Tax Reports.

[37] ¶ 5651, ¶ 5715

[38] ¶ 4801, ¶ 5651

[39] ¶ 5670, ¶ 5715

[40] ¶ 5670, ¶ 5760

[41] ¶ 5780.183

[42] ¶ 5201

[43] ¶ 5201

With respect to estate tax valuation of a qualified account, such as an IRA, the value of the account is the fair market value of the assets in the account without any discount for the income tax liability that would be triggered if the estate or beneficiary were to take a distribution of the assets in order to sell them.[44]

2918. Powers of Appointment. Property subject to a general power of appointment is included in the gross estate of the holder if the power exists at death (Code Sec. 2041(a)(2)). The exercise or release of a general power during the life of the holder is a transfer subject to gift tax (Code Sec. 2514(b)).[45] A power of appointment is a right given to someone other than the donor of property to dispose of the property. The holder of the power of appointment has a general power if the holder may exercise it in favor of himself or herself, the holder's creditors, the holder's estate, or the creditors of the holder's estate (Code Sec. 2041(b), Code Sec. 2514(c)). Powers that expressly cannot be exercised in favor of any of these are special or limited powers (Reg. § 20.2041-1(c)(1)). A power is not general if its exercise is limited by an ascertainable standard (Code Sec. 2041(b)(1)(A), Code Sec. 2514(c)(1)). A power is not general if the creator of the power must join in its exercise or if a co-holder of the power has a substantial adverse interest (Code Sec. 2041(b)(1)(C), Code Sec. 2514(c)(3)(A)). The incompetence of the holder of the power to exercise the power does not affect whether the power is taxable to the power holder.[46]

2919. Jointly Held Property. The entire value of jointly held property with the right of survivorship, including joint bank accounts and U.S. savings bonds registered in two names, is included in a decedent's gross estate except for the portion of the property for which the surviving joint tenant furnished consideration. If the joint property was received by the decedent and the other joint tenants as a gift or bequest, the decedent's fractional share of the property is included in the decedent's gross estate (Code Sec. 2040(a)).[47] If the joint tenants are spouses, it generally does not matter who furnished the consideration for the property; one-half of the value of a "qualified joint interest" is included in the gross estate of the first spouse to die (Code Sec. 2040(b)).[48]

The creation of a joint interest in property results in a taxable gift by the person supplying the consideration to the noncontributing joint tenant. Creation of a joint bank account or joint brokerage account is not a taxable gift until a joint owner withdraws funds (Reg. § 25.2511-1(h)). If a donor purchased property and conveyed title to himself and another as joint tenants with rights of survivorship but which rights may be defeated by either owner severing his interest, the donor made a gift to the other joint owner in the amount of one-half of the property's value. A transfer of joint property to a third party is a gift of the value of each joint owner's share.[49]

2921. Community Property. Community property is all property acquired by means other than gift, devise, bequest, and inheritance by spouses domiciled in community property jurisdictions. Separate property is property other than community property.[50] One-half of the value of all community property owned by a married couple is includible in the gross estate of the first of the spouses to die (Code Sec. 2033). This rule of inclusion applies even though the surviving spouse elects to allow his or her share of the community property to pass according to the will of the decedent spouse.[51]

2922. Valuation of Gross Estate. The value of property that is included in the gross estate is its fair market value on the date of the decedent's death (Code Sec. 2031; Reg. § 20.2031-1(b)). The fair market value of property includible in the gross estate is the price at which it would change hands between a willing buyer and a willing seller, both having reasonable knowledge of relevant facts.[52]

Alternate Valuation. Instead of valuing property includible in the gross estate as of the date of death, the executor may elect to value the gross estate at the fair market value of the property on the alternate valuation date, which is the date six months after the date of the decedent's death. To use the alternate valuation, the election must

---

Footnote references are to paragraphs of the Federal Estate and Gift Tax Reports.

[44] ¶ 3011	[47] ¶ 5401	[50] ¶ 4675
[45] ¶ 5501, ¶ 11,054	[48] ¶ 5401	[51] ¶ 4675
[46] ¶ 5501, ¶ 11,054	[49] ¶ 10,528	[52] ¶ 3011

decrease the value of the gross estate and the amount of estate and GST taxes imposed on the property included in the gross estate. The alternate valuation election is irrevocable (Code Sec. 2032). The election is made on Form 706, U.S. Estate (and Generation-Skipping Transfer) Tax Return. The amount of any marital or charitable deduction is adjusted based on the alternate value of assets passing to charity or a surviving spouse (Code Sec. 2032(b); Reg. § 20.2032-1(g)).[53] When the alternate valuation election is made, all property included in the gross estate is valued at the alternate valuation date (Reg. § 20.2032-1(d)).[54] However, if property is sold, exchanged, distributed, or otherwise disposed of during the six-month period, it is valued on the date of disposition rather than the alternate valuation date (Code Sec. 2032(a)(1)).[55]

Special Use Valuation. If a farm or real property used in a closely held business is included in the gross estate, the executor may elect to value the property at its "current use" rather than at its "highest and best use." Special use valuation is obtained pursuant to an irrevocable election by an executor to value real property used in a farm, trade, or business (Code Sec. 2032A).[56] The limitation on the reduction in value resulting from special use valuation is $940,000 in 2007 and $960,000 in 2008.

Special use value is elected on the estate tax return by, among other things, completing the notice of election and submitting a recapture agreement.[57] If the qualified heir ceases to use the farm property for farming or sells the property to a nonfamily member within 10 years of the decedent's date of death, an additional estate tax, the recapture tax, is due (Code Sec. 2032A(c))[58] and Form 706-A, U.S. Additional Estate Tax Return, must be filed.

2925. Deductions from Gross Estate—In General. A deduction from the gross estate is allowed for funeral expenses, administration expenses, claims against the estate, certain taxes, and unpaid mortgages or other indebtedness allowable under the local law governing the administration of the decedent's estate (Code Sec. 2053(a)). For expenses that are not paid before filing the estate tax return, an estimated amount may be deducted if it is ascertainable with reasonable certainty (Reg. § 20.2053-1(b)(3)). Estate administration expenses may generally be deducted on either the decedent's estate tax return or the estate's income tax return, but not on both (Code Sec. 642(g); Reg. § 1.642(g)-1).[59]

Expenses incurred in connection with the decedent's funeral, including reasonable expenses for a tombstone, mausoleum, or burial lot, are deductible (Code Sec. 2053(a)(1)).[60] Administration expenses are deductible if actually and necessarily incurred in the administration of the estate. Administration expenses include fees paid to surrogates, appraisers, and accountants. Paid attorney's fees or fees reasonably expected to be paid are also deductible (Code Sec. 2053(a)(2); Reg. § 20.2053-3(a)).[61] Claims that are a personal obligation of the decedent, existing and enforceable against him at the time of his death, and allowable under local law, are deductible. Liabilities imposed by law or arising out of torts committed by the decedent are also deductible (Reg. § 20.2053-4).[62] The full value of any unpaid mortgage or other indebtedness charged against property for which the decedent is personally liable, plus interest accrued on the debt to the date of death, is deductible if the property's entire value undiminished by the mortgage or indebtedness is included in the gross estate (Code Sec. 2053(a)(4)).[63] Federal and state estate, succession, legacy, or inheritance taxes are generally not deductible, but unpaid gift taxes on gifts made before death are deductible. Unpaid income taxes are deductible if they are on income properly includible in an income tax return of a decedent for a period before his death (Reg. § 20.2053-6).[64] A deduction is allowed for losses arising from fires, storms, shipwrecks, or other casualties or thefts that are incurred during estate administration and not compensated for by insurance (Code Sec. 2054).[65]

Footnote references are to paragraphs of the Federal Estate and Gift Tax Reports.

[53] ¶ 3801, ¶ 3830
[54] ¶ 3830
[55] ¶ 3801
[56] ¶ 4001
[57] ¶ 4001
[58] ¶ 4001
[59] ¶ 16,675, ¶ 16,825
[60] ¶ 6040
[61] ¶ 6040, ¶ 6090
[62] ¶ 6170
[63] ¶ 6040
[64] ¶ 6210
[65] ¶ 6320

2926. Estate Tax Marital Deduction. In determining a married decedent's taxable estate, an unlimited deduction is allowable for property that passes to the decedent's surviving spouse (Code Sec. 2056). In order to qualify for the deduction, the decedent must be married and survived by his or her spouse, the spouse must be a U.S. citizen, the property must be included in the decedent's gross estate and pass to the surviving spouse, and the property must not be a nondeductible terminable interest. The estate tax marital deduction is not available if the decedent's surviving spouse is not a U.S. citizen unless the spouse becomes a citizen before the estate tax return is filed or the property passes to a qualified domestic trust (QDOT) (Code Sec. 2056(d) and Code Sec. 2056A).[66]

Passing Requirement. Property must pass from the decedent to a surviving spouse for a transfer to be deductible (Code Sec. 2056(a)). Bequests and inheritances, dower and curtesy interests, joint property, property received under antenuptial agreements, annuities, and life insurance may pass from the decedent to the surviving spouse. Property received by a spouse under a state law right of election against the will satisfies the passing requirement (Code Sec. 2056(c); Reg. § 20.2056(c)-2(c)). Property passing to the spouse as a result of another person's qualified disclaimer is considered to pass from the decedent (Reg. § 20.2056(d)-2(b)).[67]

Terminable Interest Rule. The terminable interest rule bars deduction for any nondeductible terminable interest. A terminable interest in property is an interest that terminates or fails because of the lapse of time or the occurrence of an event (Code Sec. 2056(b)(1)). A nondeductible terminable interest is an interest in which a person, other than the surviving spouse, receives an interest in property from the decedent and, upon the termination of the spouse's interest in the same property, the other person may possess or enjoy the property. Property interests passing to a spouse that are conditioned on the spouse's survival of a period of six months or less, or on the spouse's survival in a common disaster, are not subject to the terminable interest rule (Code Sec. 2056(b)(3)).[68]

Qualified Terminable Interest Property. Qualified terminable interest property (QTIP) is excluded from the terminable interest rule. To qualify as QTIP, the surviving spouse must have the right to all the income from the property for life, payable no less frequently than annually (Code Sec. 2056(b)(7); Reg. § 20.2056(b)-7(a)). A surviving spouse's income interest may be contingent upon the executor's QTIP election and still be considered a "qualifying income interest for life" (Reg. § 20.2056(b)-7).[69] In addition, no person may have a power to appoint any of the property to any person other than the surviving spouse during the surviving spouse's life. An election on Form 706, U.S. Estate (and Generation-Skipping Transfer) Tax Return, is necessary to designate property as QTIP (Code Sec. 2056(b)(7)(B)(v)). Once the QTIP election is made, the surviving spouse must include the property remaining at death in his or her gross estate even though the surviving spouse has no control over its disposition (Code Sec. 2044). However, the estate tax that is attributable to the QTIP included in the spouse's estate may be recovered from the QTIP (Code Sec. 2207A).[70]

Life Estate with Power of Appointment. A life estate with a power of appointment qualifies for the marital deduction if:

(1) the surviving spouse is entitled to all the income from the entire interest or a specific portion of the interest for life;

(2) the income is payable at least annually;

(3) the spouse has the power to appoint the property (or the specific portion) to himself or herself or to his or her estate;

(4) the power is exercisable by the spouse alone and in all events; and

(5) no other person has the power to appoint property to anyone but the surviving spouse (Code Sec. 2056(b)(5)).

Footnote references are to paragraphs of the Federal Estate and Gift Tax Reports.

[66] ¶ 6501, ¶ 7001, ¶ 7045   [68] ¶ 6501   [70] ¶ 5901, ¶ 6501, ¶ 8800
[67] ¶ 6501, ¶ 6975   [69] ¶ 6850.07

There is a similar exception to the terminable interest rule for life insurance proceeds held by an insurer in which the spouse has a right to all payments and a power of appointment (Code Sec. 2056(b)(6); Reg. § 20.2056(b)-6(c)).[71]

Amount of the Marital Deduction. The marital deduction is limited to the net value of property passing to the spouse. Death taxes, debts, and administration expenses payable from the marital bequest, mortgages on property passing to the spouse, and insufficient estate assets to fund the marital bequest all reduce the amount of the deduction (Code Sec. 2056(b)(4); Reg. § 20.2056(b)-4(a)).[72] However, administration expenses allocable to an estate's income do not necessarily reduce the amount of the marital deduction (*O. Hubert Est.*, SCt, 97-1 USTC ¶ 60,261).[73]

2932. Estate Tax Charitable Deduction. An unlimited estate tax charitable deduction is available for transfers to federal, state, and local governmental entities; charitable organizations; fraternal societies (if the property is used for charitable purposes); veterans' organizations; or an employee stock ownership plan if the transfer qualifies as a qualified gratuitous transfer. The bequest must have a public rather than a private purpose (Code Secs. 2055(a)).[74]

Transfers of Partial Interests. If an interest in property passes from a transferor to a charity and an interest in the same property passes to a noncharitable recipient, the transfer must take one of the following forms:

(1) charitable remainder annuity trust, which provides for a fixed-dollar amount to be paid to the noncharitable income beneficiary annually, or charitable remainder unitrust, which provides for a fixed percentage of trust assets, valued annually, to be paid to the noncharitable income beneficiary annually (Code Sec. 2055(e)(2) and Code Sec. 2522(c)(2));[75]

(2) charitable lead trust with guaranteed annuity or unitrust amount paid to charity (Code Sec. 170(f)(2), Code Sec. 2055(e)(2), and Code Sec. 2522(c)(2));[76]

(3) remainder interest in a farm or personal residence (Code Sec. 2055(e)(2) and Code Sec. 2522(c)(2));[77]

(4) copyrightable work of art separate from its copyright (Code Sec. 2055(e)(4) and Code Sec. 2522(c)(3));[78] or

(5) qualified conservation contribution (Code Sec. 170(f)(3), Code Sec. 2055(e)(2), Code Sec. 2522(c)(2)).[79]

The amount of the estate tax charitable deduction must be reduced by the administration expenses and death taxes paid from the property transferred to charity (Code Sec. 2055(c); Reg. § 20.2055-3(a)).[80] However, administration expenses allocable to an estate's income do not necessarily reduce the amount of the charitable deduction (*O. Hubert Est.*, SCt, 97-1 USTC ¶ 60,261).[81]

2933. Family-Owned Business Deduction. Certain estates of decedents dying after December 31, 1997, and before January 1, 2004, could elect to deduct up to $675,000 of a qualified family-owned business interest (QFOBI) from the decedent's gross estate (Code Sec. 2057).[82] A qualified family-owned business is any interest in a trade or business regardless of form with a principal place of business in the U.S., the ownership of which is held at least (1) 50 percent by one family, (2) 70 percent by two families, or (3) 90 percent by three families. One of the requirements for a decedent's interest to qualify as a QFOBI was that the decedent, or a member of the decedent's family, had to have owned and materially participated in the business for at least five of the eight years preceding the decedent's death. Further, a qualified heir will continue to be subject to a recapture tax after the decedent's death if the heir, or a member of the heir's family, does not materially participate in the business for at least five years of any eight-year period within 10 years following the decedent's death. The principal factors to

---

Footnote references are to paragraphs of the Federal Estate and Gift Tax Reports.

[71] ¶ 6501, ¶ 6801
[72] ¶ 6501, ¶ 6745
[73] ¶ 6755.674
[74] ¶ 6360

[75] ¶ 6360, ¶ 11,486, ¶ 16,901
[76] ¶ 6360, ¶ 11,486, ¶ 16,901
[77] ¶ 6360
[78] ¶ 6360

[79] ¶ 6360, ¶ 11,486
[80] ¶ 6360, ¶ 6430
[81] ¶ 6380.18
[82] ¶ 7391

be considered regarding "material participation" include physical work and participation in management decisions. To report a taxable event for recapture tax purposes, the heir must file Form 706-D, U.S. Additional Estate Tax Return Under Code Sec. 2057. Another requirement for the QFOBI deduction is that the decedent must have been a U.S. citizen or resident at the time of death. In addition, the aggregate value of the decedent's QFOBIs passing to qualified heirs must exceed 50 percent of the decedent's adjusted gross estate.

Recapture Tax After Repeal. Pursuant to EGTRRA, the QFOBI deduction is repealed for the estates of decedents dying after December 31, 2003 (Code Sec. 2057). However, the legislative history of EGTRRA indicates that the recapture provision is retained after the repeal of the QFOBI deduction. Note that the recapture tax provisions also may continue to apply after the repeal of the estate tax (in 2010).

2934. Credits Against the Estate Tax. A number of credits are available to offset a decedent's federal estate tax liability. The most important credit is the applicable credit amount (formerly the unified credit) (see ¶ 2901). For 2007, the credit is $780,800 and can be used to offset an estate tax liability on a taxable estate of $2 million.

State Death Tax Credit (Repealed). Prior to 2005, the estate tax was offset by state death taxes actually paid to a state or the District of Columbia. This credit for state death taxes was limited by a graduated rate table that used the adjusted taxable estate as a base (the taxable estate reduced by $60,000 (Code Sec. 2011)).[83] (see ¶ 43). Pursuant to EGTRRA, the state death tax credit was reduced annually in 25-percent increments, starting in 2002, until it was completely repealed in 2005. For estates of decedents dying in 2004, the state death tax credit was reduced by 75 percent (Code Sec. 2011(b), as amended by EGTRRA). In 2005, the credit was replaced by a *deduction* that will continue until the phaseout of the federal estate tax (in 2010). In addition, the state death tax deduction is subject to a limitations period, which generally requires the deduction to be claimed within four years after the estate tax return is filed.

Federal Estate Tax Paid on Prior Transfers. A credit is available for federal estate tax paid on prior transfers to the decedent from a person who died within 10 years before or two years after the decedent. The credit is limited to the lesser of the estate tax attributable to the transferred property in the transferor's estate or the estate tax attributable to the transferred property in the decedent's estate (Code Sec. 2013). If the transferor predeceased the decedent by more than two years, the credit allowed is a reduced percentage of the maximum amount allowable.[84]

Foreign Death Taxes. A credit against estate tax is available for foreign death taxes paid on property located in a foreign country but included in the gross estate of a U.S. citizen or resident. The credit is limited to the lesser of the foreign or the U.S. tax attributable to the property. If a treaty exists with the foreign country, the credit provided for under the treaty or Code Sec. 2014 may be used, whichever results in the lower amount of estate tax (Code Sec. 2014).[85] The estate must file Form 706-CE, Certificate of Payment of Foreign Death Tax, to claim the credit.

Gift Tax Paid on Gifts Included in Gross Estate. For gifts made before 1977, the gift tax paid on gifts included in the gross estate is a credit to the estate tax. The credit is limited to the lesser of the gift tax paid or the estate tax attributable to inclusion of the gift in the gross estate (Code Sec. 2012).[86]

2937. Computing the Estate Tax Liability. The estate tax computation begins with a calculation of the gross estate. The gross estate is valued at the fair market value on the decedent's date of death or, if elected, on the alternate valuation date, which is six months after the date of death (Code Secs. 2031 and 2032). Deductions for state death taxes, charitable and marital bequests, and estate administration expenses as well as other allowable deductions are subtracted to find the taxable estate (Code Sec. 2051). The amount of adjusted taxable gifts made after 1976 is added to the taxable estate. A tentative tax is computed by applying the applicable tax rates from the unified rate

---

Footnote references are to paragraphs of the Federal Estate and Gift Tax Reports.

[83] ¶ 1551
[84] ¶ 2001

[85] ¶ 2301
[86] ¶ 1901

schedule (see ¶ 42) to the sum of the amount of the taxable estate and the adjusted taxable gifts. The tentative tax is then reduced by the amount of gift tax payable on the post-1976 gifts. The resulting amount is the gross estate tax which is reduced by any credits, including the applicable credit amount (Code Sec. 2010(c)), credits for foreign death taxes paid (Code Sec. 2014), the credit for tax on prior transfers (Code Sec. 2013), and the credit for gift tax paid on pre-1977 gifts included in the gross estate (Code Sec. 2012).[87] An estate tax reduction is available for the estates of U.S. citizens or residents who are active members of the Armed Forces and who are killed in action while serving in a combat zone (Code Sec. 2201). This special treatment has been extended to include a "specified terrorist victim," as defined by Code Sec. 692(d)(4) (see ¶ 2533) and any astronaut whose death occurs in the line of duty.

2938. Filing Estate Tax Return and Liability for Payment. Form 706, U.S. Estate (and Generation-Skipping Transfer) Tax Return, must be filed for every U.S. citizen or resident decedent whose gross estate exceeds $2 million in 2007 (Code Sec. 6018(a)). In the years before the repeal of the estate tax (¶ 2901), the filing threshold will remain the same in 2008 and increase to $3.5 million in 2009 (Code Sec. 2010(c), as amended by EGTRRA). In 2007, 2008, and 2009, the top estate tax rate is 45%. The estate tax table is at ¶ 42.

Filing the Return. The return must be filed by the executor, administrator, or person in possession of the estate's assets (Code Sec. 2203, Code Sec. 6018(a)). The return is due within nine months of a decedent's date of death, but a six-month extension of time to file is available (Code Sec. 6075(a); Reg. § 20.6075-1).[88] The six-month extension is automatically available if (1) Form 4768, Application for Extension of Time to File a Return and/or Pay U.S. Estate (and Generation-Skipping Transfer) Taxes is filed before the due date; (2) the application is filed with the IRS office designated in the application's instructions; and (3) an estimate of the amount of estate and GST tax liability is included.

Paying the Tax. The estate tax must be paid within nine months after the decedent's death (Code Sec. 6075(a), Code Sec. 6151(a)) by the executor or person in possession of the estate's property (Code Sec. 2002; Reg. § 20.2002-1). The tax may be paid with a check, money order,[89] draft, credit card, or debit card (Code Sec. 6311(a)).[90] The time for payment of the estate tax may be extended for a period of one year past the due date (Code Sec. 6161(a)(1)). For reasonable cause, the time for payment may be extended for up to 10 years (Code Sec. 6161(a)(2)).[91]

2939. Election to Pay Estate Tax in Installments. If an estate includes a farm or closely held business whose value exceeds 35 percent of the adjusted gross estate, the executor may elect to pay the estate and generation-skipping transfer taxes in as many as 10 annual installments following a deferral period of as many as five years (Code Sec. 6166(a)(1)). The amount of tax that may be deferred is limited to the tax attributable to the business interest (Code Sec. 6166(a)(2)). A *two-percent* interest rate applies to that portion of the estate tax deferred on the first $1 million (indexed annually for inflation) in *taxable* value of the closely held business, computed as follows: the tentative tax on the sum of $1 million plus the applicable exclusion amount ($2 million in 2007) which sum is then reduced by the applicable credit amount ($780,800 in 2007). The $1 million amount is indexed for inflation (Code Sec. 6601(j)). The inflation-adjusted figure for 2007 is $1.25 million. In 2007, the two-percent portion is $562,500 (a tentative tax of $1,343,300 is computed on the sum of $1,250,000 plus the applicable exclusion amount of $2,000,000, which sum is then reduced by the applicable credit amount of $780,800). A closely held corporation may redeem stock from the estate of a decedent or from the beneficiaries of the estate to pay estate taxes and administrative expenses if the stock comprises 35 percent of the gross estate. This redemption of stock is generally not treated as a disqualifying disposition for purposes of the installment payment of the estate tax (Code Sec. 6166(g)(1)(B)).[92]

Footnote references are to paragraphs of the Federal Estate and Gift Tax Reports.

[87] ¶ 1201, ¶ 1401, ¶ 1551, ¶ 1901, ¶ 2001, ¶ 2301, ¶ 3011, ¶ 6010

[88] ¶ 20,301

[89] ¶ 20,501

[90] ¶ 20,510, ¶ 20,845

[91] ¶ 20,301, ¶ 20,501, ¶ 20,575, ¶ 20,635

[92] ¶ 20,650, ¶ 21,620

2940. Estate Taxation of Nonresident Aliens. A decedent who is neither a U.S. citizen nor a U.S. resident (in other words, a nonresident alien)[93] is subject to estate tax on real, tangible, and intangible property situated in the United States (Code Sec. 2103). Intangible property situated in the United States includes stock in domestic corporations, bonds, and debt obligations of U.S. obligors, U.S. partnership assets, and U.S. property owned by a trust in which the nonresident alien has an interest. The value of such property in a nonresident alien's gross estate is not reduced by indebtedness secured by the property if the decedent was personally liable for the debt, even though the personal debt deduction allowed a nonresident alien may fall short of the amount actually owed (*H.H. Fung Est.,* CA-9 (unpublished opinion), 2003-1 USTC ¶ 60,460, aff'g, 117 TC 247, Dec. 54,560 (2001)).[94]

The estate of a nonresident alien is taxed at the same estate tax rates that apply to U.S. citizens' estates (Code Sec. 2101(b); Reg. § 20.2101-1). Except where provided by treaty, the unified credit is $13,000 (Code Sec. 2102(c)(1)). The estate may claim deductions for a pro rata share of expenses, debts, and losses, a marital deduction if the surviving spouse is a U.S. citizen, and a charitable deduction (Code Sec. 2106(a)(1); Reg. § 20.2106-2(a)(2)). An estate tax return must be filed if a nonresident alien's gross estate situated in the United States exceeds $60,000 (Code Sec. 6018(a)(2)).[95] The estate must file Form 706-NA, U.S. Estate (and Generation-Skipping Transfer) Tax Return for Nonresident Noncitizens. If a former citizen or long-term resident who is subject to the alternative tax regime of Code Sec. 877(b) dies within 10 years of relinquishment of citizenship or residency, an estate tax is imposed on the transfer of U.S.-situs property, including the decedent's pro rata share of the U.S. property held by a foreign corporation. The estate tax is computed on the taxable estate using the same estate tax rate schedule used for the estate of a U.S. citizen or resident (Code Sec. 2107(a), Code Sec. 2501(a)(3)(B); Reg. § § 20.2107-1(a) and 25.2511-1(b)). The expatriate is also subject to gift tax on transfers of property situated in the United States (Code Sec. 2501(a)(3)).[96] An individual is subject to the alternative tax regime if the individual: (1) has average annual net income for the five years preceding the loss of citizenship greater than $136,000 for 2007; (2) has net worth on the date of loss of citizenship of $2 million or more; or (3) fails to certify compliance with all federal tax obligations for the five-year period unless he or she is a dual citizen or minor without substantial contact with the U.S. (Code Sec. 877(a)(2), Code Sec. 2107(a)(2)(A), and Code Sec. 2501(a)(3)(B)).[97] The estate and gift tax Code provisions may be affected by provisions contained in foreign tax treaties (Code Sec. 7852(d)).[98]

Generation-Skipping Transfer Tax

2942. Transfers Subject to Tax. Every generation-skipping transfer (GST) is subject to the GST tax (Code Sec. 2601). However, the GST tax will not apply to transfers made after December 31, 2009, as the GST tax is scheduled to be repealed along with the estate tax in 2010 (Code Sec. 2664, as added by EGTRRA). Note, however, that the GST tax repeal is scheduled to expire (or "sunset") for generation-skipping transfers after December 31, 2010. The GST rate gradually deceases in the years leading to the repeal. For 2007, 2008, and 2009, the top tax rate is 45 percent.

A GST takes one of three forms. A direct skip is a transfer to a skip person that is also subject to estate or gift tax. A skip person is two generations or more younger than the transferor (Code Sec. 2612(c)(1); Reg. § 26.2612-1(a)(1)). However, if the parent of the grandchild is dead, a gift to the grandchild is not a direct skip (Code Sec. 2612(c)(2)). A taxable termination occurs when an interest in property held in trust terminates and trust property is held for or distributed to a skip person (Code Sec. 2652(c)). Finally, a taxable distribution is any distribution from a trust that is not a taxable termination or direct skip (Code Sec. 2612(b)). Transfers that are not subject to gift tax because of the gift tax annual exclusion and unlimited exclusion for direct

---

Footnote references are to paragraphs of the Federal Estate and Gift Tax Reports.

[93] ¶ 7550
[94] ¶ 7725, ¶ 7825

[95] ¶ 7525, ¶ 7550, ¶ 7625, ¶ 8025, ¶ 8055, ¶ 20,075
[96] ¶ 8125, ¶ 8150, ¶ 9245, ¶ 10,528

[97] ¶ 8125, ¶ 9245
[98] ¶ 22,870

payment of medical and tuition expenses are not subject to GST tax (Code Sec. 2642(c)(1)).[99]

2943. Lifetime Exemption. Individual taxpayers are allocated a lifetime exemption that shields $2 million (in 2007) in GSTs from the tax (Code Sec. 2631). In 2003, the GST tax exemption was an inflation-adjusted $1.12 million. In 2004, the exemption was no longer adjusted for inflation; instead it became tied to the estate tax exemption. Married couples may treat transfers as if made one-half by each spouse under Code Sec. 2513. A married couple may transfer assets valued at $4 million exempt from GST tax (each individual's GST exemption is $2 million in 2007) (Code Sec. 2652(a)(2)). Prior to the repeal of the GST tax in 2010, the amount of the GST tax exemption is scheduled to remain at $2 million in 2008 and increase to $3.5 million in 2009 (Code Sec. 2631(c), as amended by EGTRRA).

The tax is computed by multiplying the taxable amount of the transfer by the applicable rate (Code Sec. 2602). The applicable rate is a flat rate equal to the product of the maximum estate tax rate and the inclusion ratio with respect to the transfer (Code Sec. 2641(a); Reg. § 26.2641-1). The inclusion ratio for any property transferred in a GST is the excess (if any) of one over the "applicable fraction" determined for the trust from which a GST is made or, in the case of a direct skip, the applicable fraction determined for such a skip. The applicable fraction is determined as follows: the numerator is the amount of the GST exemption allocated to the trust or the property transferred to the direct skip. Its denominator is the value of the property transferred to the trust (or involved in the direct skip) reduced by the sum of any federal estate or state death tax attributable to the property that was recovered from the trust and any estate or gift tax charitable deductions allowed (Code Sec. 2642(a)(2); Reg. § 26.2642-1).[100]

2944. Filing the Return and Paying the GST Tax. The executor must file the return (Form 706, Schedules R and R-1) and pay the tax for direct skips occurring at death. The transferor is responsible for filing the return (Form 709, U.S. Gift (and Generation-Skipping Transfer) Tax Return) and paying the tax on lifetime direct skips (Code Sec. 2603(a)(3); Reg. § 26.2662-1(c)(1)). The trustee is responsible for filing the return (Form 706-GS(T) , Generation-Skipping Transfer Tax Return for Terminations) and paying the tax on taxable terminations (Code Sec. 2603(a)(2)). The transferee is responsible for filing the return (Form 706-GS(D) , Generation-Skipping Transfer Tax Return for Distributions) and paying the tax on taxable distributions (Code Sec. 2603(a)(1); Reg. § 26.2662-1(c)(1)).[101]

Footnote references are to paragraphs of the Federal Estate and Gift Tax Reports.

[99] ¶ 12,025, ¶ 12,225, ¶ 12,315   [100] ¶ 12,585, ¶ 12,625, ¶ 12,170, ¶ 12,790   [101] ¶ 13,160, ¶ 13,200, ¶ 13,225, ¶ 21,045, ¶ 21,070, ¶ 21,090

Topical Index

References are to paragraph (¶) numbers

802

Topical Index
References are to paragraph (¶) numbers

ACC

BEN

CAL

COM

DED

DEF

DIR

DIS

EDU

FOR

GAM

GRO

INC

OWN

REC

858

STO

TAX

WIT

The CCH
U.S. Master™ Guide Series

.CCH
a Wolters Kluwer business

Convenient, inexpensive and indispensable desktop resources designed to provide fast and accurate answers.

The *U.S. Master Guide™* Series of quick-reference handbooks is designed to provide you with fast answers to your clients' or your business' questions — questions that might normally be very time-consuming to research. Created in the tradition of the *U.S. Master Tax Guide®*, the best-selling tax guide in the industry for more than 90 years, these convenient, desktop resources are loaded with facts, practical examples, checklists, rate tables and other useful tools that help you find the information you need quickly and easily.